ALL · IN · ONE

CISSP®

EXAM GUIDE

Fifth Edition

Shon Harris

New York • Chicago • San Francisco • Lisbon
London • Madrid • Mexico City • Milan • New Delhi
San Juan • Seoul • Singapore • Sydney • Toronto

The *McGraw-Hill* Companies

Cataloging-in-Publication Data is on file with the Library of Congress

McGraw-Hill books are available at special quantity discounts to use as premiums and sales promotions, or for use in corporate training programs. To contact a representative, please e-mail us at bulksales@mcgraw-hill.com.

CISSP® All-in-One Exam Guide, Fifth Edition

234567890 DOC DOC 109876543210

ISBN: Book p/n 978-0-07-160219-8 and CD p/n 978-0-07-160220-4
of set 978-0-07-160217-4
MHID: Book p/n 0-07-160219-4 and CD p/n 0-07-160220-8
of set 0-07-160217-8

Sponsoring Editor
Timothy Green

Editorial Supervisor
Jody McKenzie

Project Editor
Emilia Thiuri

Acquisitions Coordinator
Meghan Riley

Technical Editor
Jerry Cochran

Copy Editors
Jan Jue and Bart Reed

Proofreader
Linda Medoff

Indexer
Jack Lewis

Production Supervisor
James Kussow

Composition
Apollo Publishing Services

Illustration
Lyssa Wald

Art Director, Cover
Jeff Weeks

Cover Designer
Pattie Lee

I lost my greatest hero two years ago, George Fairbairn, my Grandpa. He has taught me many things about life that cannot be taught in books, but only by example: integrity, unconditional love, humility, and the importance of internal strength and courage.

I dedicate this book to my Grandpa and my wonderful and supportive family. I am truly lucky because most of my best friends are also my family members, especially my mother, Kathy Conlon, and my husband, David Harris.

ABOUT THE AUTHOR

Shon Harris, CISSP , is the president of Logical Security, a security consultant, a former engineer in the Air Force's Information Warfare unit, an instructor, and an author. She has authored two best-selling CISSP books, was a contributing author to *Hacker's Challenge: Test Your Incident Response Skills Using 20 Scenarios,* and a contributing author to *Gray Hat Hacking: The Ethical Hacker's Handbook* (both published by McGraw-Hill). Shon has taught computer and information security to a wide range of clients, some of which have included RSA, Department of Defense, Department of Energy, National Security Agency (NSA), Bank of America, Defense Information Systems Agency (DISA), BMC, West Point, and many more.

Shon was recognized as one of the top 25 women in the information security field by *Information Security Magazine.*

About the Technical Editor

Jerry Cochran has worked in the information technology industry for the last 22 years for leaders such as Microsoft and Hewlett-Packard. Directly involved in information security for the last 11 years, Jerry currently works for Microsoft Corporation as a principal security strategist in the Trustworthy Computing Group, where he leads the Global Security Strategy team. At Microsoft, he is focused on cybersecurity technology and policy issues and manages engagement with governments around the world on cybersecurity and critical infrastructure protection.

In his other life, Jerry is a military reservist and holds the rank of chief master sergeant in the U.S. Air Force, where he is the senior enlisted manager of the 262nd Network Warfare Squadron that is part of the 24th Air Force and the Air National Guard. Jerry is a contributing editor, technical editor, and author of over 200 articles for printed publications and two information technology–related books from Digital Press. He holds a B.S. in engineering and technology management, an A.S. in electronics technology, and an A.S. in information systems technology. Jerry has held numerous industry certifications over the course of his career and currently holds the Certified Information Systems Security Professional (CISSP) and Certified Information Security Manager (CISM) certifications.

About the Contributing Editors

Michael J. Lester holds a master's degree in information systems security from Boston University (an NSA "Center of Excellence") and around 20 industry certifications, including CISSP, CISA, CCE #876, Security+, MCSE:Security, CCSE+, and ITIL. He was an author for *Gray Hat Hacking: The Ethical Hacker's Handbook,* First Edition (McGraw-Hill), a book on advanced penetration testing techniques, and many other articles and presentations.

He has written courseware and lectured on Microsoft security, penetration testing, Linux/Unix security, and infrastructure security. He is the chief instructor for Shon Harris's Logical Security, LLC, and he teaches and develops courses on CISSP, hacking/pen-testing, digital forensics/eDiscovery, CISA, and others. Microsoft employed Michael as a subject matter expert (SME) to create and tech edit the exams for the Windows Server 2008 (Longhorn) Microsoft Certified IT Professional (MCITP) certifications.

In his consulting work he has worked for household name organizations, including Bridgestone/Firestone, Warner Bros., the Department of Defense, Northrop Grumman, Novo Nordisk, and the U.S. House of Representatives. For these clients he has stood up entire security programs, regulatory compliance programs (OCC, SOX, HIPAA, GLBA), and Payment Card Industry Data Security Standards (PCI DSS) compliance programs, and he has worked on similar projects. He has performed vulnerability assessments and penetration tests, and is sought after for his document writing work (diagrams, policies, standards, procedures) and presentations. He also has experience implementing the ITIL, CoBIT, and ISO 17799 frameworks.

Michael is currently authoring a book on digital forensics as well as teaching and consulting. His resume can be found at www.ParadigmShiftConsulting.com.

Bobby E. Rogers is a principal information security analyst with Dynetics, Inc., a national technology firm specializing in the certification and accreditation process for the U.S. government. He also serves as a penetration testing team lead for various government and commercial engagements. Bobby recently retired from the U.S. Air Force after almost 21 years, where he served as a computer networking and security specialist and designed and managed networks all over the world. His IT security experience includes several years working as an information assurance manager and a regular consultant to U.S. Air Force military units on various cybersecurity/computer abuse cases. He has held several positions of responsibility for network security in both the Department of Defense and private company networks. His duties have included perimeter security, client-side security, security policy development, security training, and computer crime investigations. As a trainer, he has taught a wide variety of IT-related subjects in makeshift classrooms in desert tents as well as in formal training centers. Bobby is also an accomplished author, having written numerous IT articles in various publications and training materials for the U.S. Air Force. In addition, he has authored numerous security training videos.

CONTENTS AT A GLANCE

CONTENTS

FOREWORDS

It is a scary world out there—for individuals and for businesses. According to a November 2009 web site survey by Netcraft, the Internet is approaching a quarter of a billion web sites. And in March 2009, Google reported that the Internet contains over 25.2 billion web pages. That is a lot of risky turf with a lot of opportunity for the bad guys. In the most recent annual report from the FBI's Internet Crime Complaint Center (IC3), IC3 received over 275,000 reports of crime, a 33% increase over the previous year. The attacks are more frequent, more targeted, and more successful.

Identity theft affected nearly 10 million people in the U.S. in 2008, up 22% from 2007, according to a 2009 report from Javelin Strategy and Research. There are many reasons to pursue increased knowledge and awareness in the realm of information systems security.

If you are currently in, or are looking for, a position in information technology, you should have, or should be actively pursuing, your CISSP certification. Many companies and government departments now require CISSP certification before considering you for a position in their IT departments. As of November 2009, Monster lists over 800 jobs that request or require the CISSP certification, and Indeed.com lists over 3,000 CISSP-related job opportunities. Get your CISSP to increase your "hire-ability" and to increase your retention factor on the job.

According to PayScale, a salary survey web site, it is not at all uncommon for the salary of a CISSP to range between $75,000 and $120,000 annually, with the average compensation settling in at around $90,000 U.S. Indeed.com shows CISSP job opportunities with compensation ranging from $60,000 to over $140,000 U.S. Get your CISSP to increase your income.

As you realize the value of your personal and corporate information assets, you may begin to realize just how vulnerable and exploitable they really are. The body of knowledge that makes up the CISSP provides details on how the bad guys gain access to your systems, and how you can and should be protecting yourself and those valuable information assets. Get your CISSP to improve your vision and understanding of prudent security, and how to identify and protect your own valuable information assets.

Because you have applied effort and have achieved a heightened level of knowledge and understanding of the topic, sign up for, take, and pass the CISSP certification exam. You've worked for it. Now add the credential to your resume.

Increasing your knowledge of the security of information systems and valuable information assets will only improve your world. You should be using this book, Shon Harris's *CISSP All-In-One Exam Guide*, which is the golden bible on CISSP certification and one of the first and best CISSP resources for developing your knowledge of information systems security.

Shon Harris has been researching and writing this CISSP study guide (this edition and previous editions) for as long as I've known her. Shon is the consummate researcher, forever probing, studying, expanding, and refining her details. With a strong focus in the field of IT security, she balances that academic understanding with real-word experience through consulting companies with security and compliance issues. She is a worthy professional associate, as well as a close, trusted, and valued friend. A better soul is difficult to find.

Her CISSP study guide is second to none, and continues to be a best seller for good reason. This book is well written, comprehensive, and well targeted, helping thousands of students and professionals prepare for and achieve the CISSP certification. It covers a seemingly diverse array of topics that coalesce into the well-rounded skill set required of a security professional. This book is the best starting point to begin your approach to CISSP certification. It is also the best finishing point for putting the final polish on the massive volume of information you'll need as your exam date draws near. Congratulations, reader, on your professional choices and successes so far, and on your upcoming CISSP certification.

David R. Miller
Security and Compliance Consultant, Author, Instructor
MicroLink Corporation

I remember my first exposure to a computer, during my senior year in high school. I was working in the evenings cleaning office buildings. One of those buildings was the First Bank of Evergreen Park, Illinois, and as I swept the floors in the basement, the single employee working was feeding a stack of cards to this behemoth of a machine. He sat at a machine that fed check after check, and he typed card after card and then fed the machine the card deck. That was 1969, and I couldn't comprehend the value.

In 1980, after a ten-year stint in the Army, I went back to college and was "forced" to take two computer courses as part of the core curriculum—I became hooked. While I was taking an Introduction to Computer Science class in Europe, and consulting for the European Organization for Nuclear Research (known as CERN), Tim Berners-Lee wrote a program that allowed links to be made between nodes. He returned to CERN in 1984, and worked on the problem of needing to share data without the same machine or operating system. He wrote a proposal in 1989 for "a large hypertext database with typed links," but few took notice. Little did he know that he had laid the foundation for what was to become known as the Internet.

Now, some 20 years later, the Internet plays a prominent role in our everyday life. When I'm on the road, it's not unusual for me to log in and tell my digital video recorder to record a program so I can watch it later. I take my Blackberry everywhere I go, and it's typical for me to answer an e-mail or two between shots on the golf course. The capabilities we have to socialize, shop, and bank without leaving our living room are phenomenal.

Unfortunately, all of these capabilities have also afforded the seedier side of the world an opportunity to exploit all elements of today's society. Corporate and government data, banking records, and our very identities are all potentially at risk. This combination has led to an unprecedented need for professionals who are knowledgeable and able to counter these risks.

Enter the International Information Systems Security Certification Consortium (ISC)² in 1988 and the Certified Information Systems Security Professional standard in 1994, with ten domains that form the profession's common body of knowledge. To attain this certification one has to possess the knowledge to survive a grueling six-hour-long, 250-question examination whose questions are often confusing and will weed out those who don't know the material.

I took the CISSP examination in 2002 after reading Shon Harris's *All-In-One CISSP Study Guide for the CISSP Exam* and attending a workshop that Shon taught. Even though I have been an information security professional since 1987, I was thrilled to receive the e-mail that told me I had passed.

The CISSP certification is recognized worldwide as the premier information security credential. Many employers encourage their information security staffs to attain this credential, and the U. S. Department of Defense recognizes the CISSP credential as one of those at the highest level.

Since 2002, I've gotten to know Shon Harris. She is a passionate professional who loves to help people learn. She knows the material contained within the Common Body of Knowledge backward and forward. She constantly revises her work to make sure her readers have every opportunity to fully understand the material within the context that (ISC)² has defined.

It's my great honor to write a Foreword for the latest edition of Shon's *All-in-One Exam Guide*. I am especially grateful for this opportunity to encourage everyone involved with the information security business to take the time to obtain the knowledge and experience necessary to sit for and successfully obtain the CISSP credential. Through her books, Shon Harris can help that goal become reality.

Thomas P. Madden, CISSP, CISM

ACKNOWLEDGMENTS

I would like to thank Sam Tomaino for attempting to explain to me many, many years ago how computers work; Dan Ferguson for never complaining about the bombardment of questions I continually fling his way and for fostering my never-ceasing curiosity and quest for knowledge; and my Dad (Tom Conlon), who had the courage to renew and deepen our relationship. Each one of these people has helped me write this book in more ways than they will ever know.

For my fifth edition, I would also like to thank the following individuals for taking the time to help me with some new topics:

- Dr. Dorothy Denning, professor in the Department of Defense Analysis at the Naval Postgraduate School, for always graciously answering my questions whenever I've hit a wall.

- David Miller, whose work ethic, loyalty, and friendship have inspired me. I am truly grateful to have David as part of my life. I never would have known the secret world of tequila without him.

- Allen Harper, whose knowledge, impeccable character, and honesty have made him a role model to many in this world—including myself. He is an officer in the Marines who voluntarily went to war (Baghdad, Iraq) in 2007; we are all thankful for your dedication and sacrifices for all of us, Allen.

- Clement Dupuis, who, with his deep passion for sharing and helping others, has proven a wonderful and irreplaceable mentor and friend.

- Mike Lester, who is probably the smartest and funniest guy I have ever known, and really comes through when I need him the most. Thanks a lot, Sparky. We will work on getting you to understand the months of the year and where static electricity comes from.

- Faiz Ahmad Shuja, who has helped me get more projects done than anyone. I could not have gotten this book and others done and out the door without him.

- Kumar Polisetty, who always comes through when my team needs him the most. Thanks for always going the extra mile for the Logical Security team!

- The Logical Security team: Mark Bedell, Wayne Deutsch, Susan Lauson, Bill Griffin, and Christine Collings. I never express my deep appreciation for each one of you enough.

- Tom and Kathy Conlon, my parents. Without their love and support, my life would be a whole lot different today.

Most especially, I would like to thank my husband, David Harris, for his continual support and love. Without his steadfast confidence in me, I would not have been able to accomplish half the things I have taken on in my life.

INTRODUCTION

Computer, information, and physical security are becoming more important at an exponential rate since the continual increase in computer crimes. Over the last few years, the necessity for computer and information security has grown rapidly as web sites have been defaced, Denial-of-Service attacks have increased, credit card information has been stolen, publicly available hacking tools have become more sophisticated, and today's viruses and worms cause more damage than ever before.

Companies have had to spend millions of dollars to clean up the effects of these issues and millions of dollars more to secure their perimeter and internal networks with equipment, software, consultants, and education. But after September 11, 2001, the necessity and urgency for this type of security has taken on a new paradigm. It is slowly becoming apparent that governments, nations, and societies are vulnerable to many different types of attacks that can happen over the network wire and airwaves. Societies depend heavily on all types of computing power and functionality, mostly provided by the public and private sectors. This means that although governments are responsible for protecting their citizens, it is becoming apparent that the citizens and their businesses must become more secure to protect the nation as a whole.

This type of protection can really only *begin* through proper education and understanding, and must continue with the dedicated execution of this knowledge. This book is written to provide a foundation of the many different areas that make up effective security. We need to understand *all* of the threats and dangers we are vulnerable to and the steps that must be taken to mitigate these vulnerabilities.

Becoming a CISSP

This chapter presents the following:
- The definition of a CISSP
- Reasons to become a CISSP
- What the CISSP exam entails
- The Common Body of Knowledge and what it contains
- The history of (ISC)² and the CISSP exam
- An assessment test to gauge your current knowledge of security

This book is intended not only to provide you with the necessary information to help you gain a CISSP certification, but also to welcome you into the exciting and challenging world of security.

The Certified Information Systems Security Professional (CISSP) exam covers ten different subjects, more commonly referred to as *domains.* The subject matter of each domain can easily be seen as its own area of study, and in many cases individuals work exclusively in these fields as experts. For many of these subjects, you can consult and reference extensive resources to become an expert in that area. Because of this, a common misconception is that the only way to succeed at the CISSP exam is to immerse yourself in a massive stack of texts and study materials. Fortunately, an easier approach exists. By using this fifth edition of the *CISSP All-in-One Exam Guide,* you can successfully complete and pass the CISSP exam and achieve your CISSP certification. The goal of this book is to combine into a single resource all the information you need to pass the CISSP exam. This book should also serve as a useful reference tool long after you've achieved your CISSP certification.

Why Become a CISSP?

As our world changes, the need for improvements in security and technology continues to grow. Security was once a hot issue only in the field of technology, but now it is becoming more and more a part of our everyday lives. Security is a concern of every organization, government agency, corporation, and military unit. Ten years ago *computer and information security* was an obscure field that only concerned a few people. Because the risks were essentially low, few were interested in security expertise. Ethical hacking and vulnerability assessments required great talent and knowledge and thus were not a common practice.

Things have changed, however, and today corporations and other organizations are desperate to recruit talented and experienced security professionals to help protect the resources they depend on to run their businesses and to remain competitive. With a CISSP certification, you will be seen as a security professional of proven ability who has successfully met a predefined standard of knowledge and experience that is well understood and respected throughout the industry. By keeping this certification current, you will demonstrate your dedication to staying abreast of security developments.

Consider the reasons for attaining a CISSP certification:

- To meet the growing demand and to thrive in an ever-expanding field
- To broaden your current knowledge of security concepts and practices
- To bring security expertise to your current occupation
- To become more marketable in a competitive workforce
- To show a dedication to the security discipline
- To increase your salary and be eligible for more employment opportunities

The CISSP certification helps companies identify which individuals have the ability, knowledge, and experience necessary to implement solid security practices, perform risk analysis, identify necessary countermeasures, and to help the organization as a whole to protect its facility, network, systems, and information. The CISSP certification also shows potential employers you have achieved a level of proficiency and expertise in skill sets and knowledge required by the security industry. The increasing importance placed on security in corporate success will only continue in the future, leading to even greater demands for highly skilled security professionals. CISSP certification shows that a respected third-party organization has recognized an individual's technical and theoretical knowledge and expertise, and distinguishes that individual from those who lack this level of knowledge.

Understanding and implementing security practices is an essential part of being a good network administrator, programmer, or engineer. Job descriptions that do not specifically target security professionals still often require that a potential candidate have a good understanding of security concepts as well as how to implement them. Due to staff size and budget restraints, many organizations can't afford separate network and security staffs. But they still believe security is vital to their organization. Thus, they often try to combine knowledge of technology and security into a single role. With a CISSP designation, you can put yourself head and shoulders above other individuals in this regard.

The CISSP Exam

Because the CISSP exam covers the ten domains making up the CISSP Common Body of Knowledge (CBK), it is often described as being "an inch deep and a mile wide," a reference to the fact that many questions on the exam are not very detailed and do not require you to be an expert in every subject. However, the questions do require you to be familiar with many different security subjects.

The CISSP exam comprises 250 multiple-choice questions, and you have six hours to complete it. The questions are pulled from a much larger question bank to ensure the exam is as unique as possible for each entrant. In addition, the test bank constantly changes and evolves to more accurately reflect the real world of security. The exam questions are continually rotated and replaced in the bank as necessary. Each question has four answer choices, only one of which is correct. Only 225 questions are graded, while 25 are used for research purposes. The 25 research questions are integrated into the exam, so you won't know which go toward your final grade. To pass the exam, you need a minimum raw score of 700 points out of 1,000. Questions are weighted based on their difficulty; not all questions are worth the same number of points. The exam is not product- or vendor-oriented, meaning no questions will be specific to certain products or vendors (for instance, Windows 2000, Unix, or Cisco). Instead, you will be tested on the security models and methodologies used by these types of systems.

(ISC)², which stands for International Information Systems Security Certification Consortium, has also added scenario-based questions to the CISSP exam. These questions present a short scenario to the test taker rather than asking the test taker to identify terms and/or concepts. A scenario-based question would be worded something like "John returned from lunch and found that the company's IDS indicated that a critical server has had continuous ICMP traffic sent to it for over 45 minutes, which is taking up 85 percent of the server's CPU resource. What does John need to do at this point?"

The goal of the scenario-based questions is to ensure that test takers not only know and understand the concepts within the CBK, but also can apply this knowledge to real-life situations. This is more practical because in the real world, you won't be challenged by having someone asking you "What is the definition of collusion?" You need to know how to detect and prevent collusion from taking place, in addition to knowing the definition of the term.

 NOTE Hundreds of scenario-based questions have been added to the CD-ROM in the back of this book to help you prepare for this exam.

The (ISC)² requires candidates for any of the (ISC)² credentials to obtain an endorsement of their candidature exclusively from an (ISC)²-certified professional in good standing. The professional endorsing the candidate can hold any (ISC)² certification, such as the CISSP, SSCP (Systems Security Certified Professional), or CAP (Certification and Accreditation Professional). This sponsor will vouch for your years of experience.

After passing the exam, you will be asked to supply documentation, supported by a sponsor, proving that you indeed have this type of experience. The sponsor must sign a document vouching for the security experience you are submitting. So, make sure you have this sponsor lined up prior to registering for the exam and providing payment. You don't want to pay for and pass the exam, only to find you can't find a sponsor for the final step needed to achieve your certification.

The reason behind the sponsorship requirement is to ensure that those who achieve the certification have real-world experience to offer companies. Book knowledge is extremely important for understanding theory, concepts, standards, and regulations, but it can never replace hands-on experience. Proving your practical experience supports the relevance of the certification.

A small sample group of individuals selected at random will be audited after passing the exam. The audit consists mainly of individuals from (ISC)² calling on the candidates' sponsors and contacts to verify the test taker's related experience.

What makes this exam challenging is that most candidates, although they work in the security field, are not necessarily familiar with all ten CBK domains. If a security professional is considered an expert in vulnerability testing or application security, for example, she may not be familiar with physical security, cryptography, or security practices. Thus, studying for this exam will broaden your knowledge of the security field.

The exam questions address the ten CBK security domains, which are described in Table 1-1.

(ISC)² attempts to keep up with changes in technology and methodologies in the security field by adding numerous new questions to the test question bank each year. These questions are based on current technologies, practices, approaches, and standards. For example, the CISSP exam given in 1998 did not have questions pertaining to wireless security, but present and future exams will.

Other examples of material not on past exams include security governance, instant messaging, phishing, botnets, VoIP, and spam. Though these subjects weren't issues in the past, they are now.

The test is based on internationally accepted information security standards and practices. If you look at the (ISC)² web site for test dates and locations, you may find, for example, that the same test is offered this Tuesday in California and next Wednesday in Saudi Arabia.

If you do not pass the exam, you have the option of retaking it as soon as you like. (ISC)² used to subject individuals to a waiting period before they could retake the exam, but this rule has been removed. (ISC)² keeps track of which exam version you were given on your first attempt and ensures you receive a different version for any retakes. (ISC)² also provides a report to a CISSP candidate who did not pass the exam, detailing the areas where the candidate was weakest. Though you could retake the exam soon afterward, it's wise to devote additional time to these weak areas to improve your score on the retest.

Domain	Description
Access Control	This domain examines mechanisms and methods used to enable administrators and managers to control what subjects can access, the extent of their capabilities after authorization and authentication, and the auditing and monitoring of these activities. Some of the topics covered include: • Access control security models • Identification and authentication technologies and techniques • Access control administration • Single sign-on technologies • Attack methods
Telecommunications and Network Security	This domain examines internal, external, public, and private communication systems; networking structures; devices; protocols; and remote access and administration. Some of the topics covered include: • OSI model and layers • Local area network (LAN), metropolitan area network (MAN), and wide area network (WAN) technologies • Internet, intranet, and extranet issues • Virtual private networks (VPNs), firewalls, routers, bridges, and repeaters • Network topologies and cabling • Attack methods
Information Security and Risk Management	This domain examines the identification of company assets, the proper way to determine the necessary level of protection required, and what type of budget to develop for security implementations, with the goal of reducing threats and monetary loss. Some of the topics covered include: • Data classification • Policies, procedures, standards, and guidelines • Risk assessment and management • Personnel security, training, and awareness
Application Security	This domain examines the security components within operating systems and applications and how to best develop and measure their effectiveness. It looks at software life cycles, change control, and application security. Some of the topics covered include: • Data warehousing and data mining • Various development practices and their risks • Software components and vulnerabilities • Malicious code

Table 1-1   Security Domains That Make Up the CISSP CBK

Domain	Description
Cryptography	This domain examines methods and techniques for disguising data for protection purposes. This involves cryptography techniques, approaches, and technologies. Some of the topics covered include: • Symmetric versus asymmetric algorithms and uses • Public key infrastructure (PKI) and hashing functions • Encryption protocols and implementation • Attack methods
Security Architecture and Design	This domain examines concepts, principles, and standards for designing and implementing secure applications, operating systems, and systems. This covers international security measurement standards and their meaning for different types of platforms. Some of the topics covered include: • Operating states, kernel functions, and memory mapping • Enterprise architecture • Security models, architectures, and evaluations • Evaluation criteria: Trusted Computer Security Evaluation Criteria (TCSEC), Information Technology Security Evaluation Criteria (ITSEC), and Common Criteria • Common flaws in applications and systems • Certification and accreditation
Operations Security	This domain examines controls over personnel, hardware, systems, and auditing and monitoring techniques. It also covers possible abuse channels and how to recognize and address them. Some of the topics covered include: • Administrative responsibilities pertaining to personnel and job functions • Maintenance concepts of antivirus, training, auditing, and resource protection activities • Preventive, detective, corrective, and recovery controls • Standards, compliance, and due care concepts • Security and fault tolerance technologies
Business Continuity Planning (BCP) and Disaster Recovery Planning (DRP)	This domain examines the preservation of business activities when faced with disruptions or disasters. It involves the identification of real risks, proper risk assessment, and countermeasure implementation. Some of the topics covered include: • Business resource identification and value assignment • Business impact analysis and prediction of possible losses • Unit priorities and crisis management • Plan development, implementation, and maintenance

Table 1-1 Security Domains That Make Up the CISSP CBK *(continued)*

Domain	Description
Legal Regulations, Compliance, and Investigation	This domain examines computer crimes, laws, and regulations. It includes techniques for investigating a crime, gathering evidence, and handling procedures. It also covers how to develop and implement an incident-handling program. Some of the topics covered include: • Types of laws, regulations, and crimes • Licensing and software piracy • Export and import laws and issues • Evidence types and admissibility into court • Incident handling
Physical (Environmental) Security	This domain examines threats, risks, and countermeasures to protect facilities, hardware, data, media, and personnel. This involves facility selection, authorized entry methods, and environmental and safety procedures. Some of the topics covered include: • Restricted areas, authorization methods, and controls • Motion detectors, sensors, and alarms • Intrusion detection • Fire detection, prevention, and suppression • Fencing, security guards, and security badge types

Table 1-1 Security Domains That Make Up the CISSP CBK *(continued)*

CISSP: A Brief History

Historically, the field of computer and information security has not been a structured and disciplined profession; rather, the field has lacked many well-defined professional objectives and thus has often been misperceived.

In the mid-1980s, members of the computer security profession recognized they needed a certification program that would give their profession structure and provide ways for computer security professionals to demonstrate competence and to present evidence of their qualifications. Establishing such a program would help the credibility of the computer and information security profession as a whole and the individuals who make up the profession.

In November 1988, the Special Interest Group for Computer Security (SIG-CS) of the Data Processing Management Association (DPMA) brought together several organizations interested in forming a security certification program. They included the Information Systems Security Association (ISSA), the Canadian Information Processing Society (CIPS), the Computer Security Institute (CSI), Idaho State University, and several U.S. and Canadian government agencies. As a voluntary joint effort, these organizations developed the necessary components to offer a full-fledged security certification for interested professionals. (ISC)² was formed in mid-1989 as a nonprofit corporation to develop a security certification program for information systems security practitioners.

The certification was designed to measure professional competence and to help companies in their selection of security professionals and personnel. (ISC)² was established in North America, but quickly gained international acceptance and now offers testing capabilities all over the world.

Because security is such a broad and diversified field in the technology and business world, the original consortium decided on an information systems security CBK composed of ten domains that pertain to every part of computer, network, business, and information security. In addition, because technology continues to rapidly evolve, staying up-to-date on security trends, technology, and business developments is required to maintain the CISSP certification. The group also developed a Code of Ethics, test specifications, a draft study guide, and the exam itself.

How Do You Become a CISSP?

To become a CISSP, start at www.isc2.org, where you will find an exam registration form you must fill out and send to (ISC)². You will be asked to provide your security work history, as well as documents for the necessary educational requirements. Graduating with a master's degree from one of the listed National Centers of Excellence and having two years of experience will also qualify you. These National Centers of Excellence are listed at www.nsa.gov/ia/academia/CAE.pdf, and the list of colleges and universities is growing. You will also be asked to read the (ISC)² Code of Ethics and to sign a form indicating that you understand these requirements and promise to abide by them. You then provide payment along with the completed registration form, where you indicate your preference as to the exam location. The numerous testing sites and dates can be found at www.isc2.org.

Although (ISC)² used to count cumulative years of job experience toward the requirements to take the CISSP exam, it has tightened its criteria; test takers must carry out full-time employment in two or more domains. People often think they do not have the necessary experience required to take this exam when they actually do, so it's always a good idea to contact (ISC)² directly to find out if you are indeed qualified before throwing away this chance.

What Does This Book Cover?

This book covers everything you need to know to become an (ISC)²-certified CISSP. It teaches you the hows and whys behind corporations' development and implementation of policies, procedures, guidelines, and standards. It covers network, application, and system vulnerabilities, what exploits them, and how to counter these threats. The book explains physical security, operational security, and why systems implement the security mechanisms they do. It also reviews the U.S. and international security criteria and evaluations performed on systems for assurance ratings, what these criteria mean, and why they are used. This book also explains the legal and liability issues that surround computer systems and the data they hold, including such subjects as computer crimes, forensics, and what should be done to properly prepare computer evidence associated with these topics for court.

While this book is mainly intended to be used as a study guide for the CISSP exam, it is also a handy reference guide for use after your certification.

Tips for Taking the CISSP Exam

The test is 250 questions, and you are given up to six hours to take it. The exams are monitored by CISSP proctors. Depending on the facility that hosts the test, you may or may not be allowed to bring in food or drink, so plan ahead and eat a good breakfast full of protein and fructose for brainpower. Proctors who allow food and beverages typically require they be in a closable container and generally do not allow you to place them on the desk or table where you could spill anything on your exam paper. Some proctors let you keep your goodies in a bag next to you on the floor, or at the front or back of the room. Proctors may inspect the contents of any and all articles entering the test room. Restroom breaks are usually limited to allowing only one person to leave at a time, so drinking 15 cups of coffee right before the exam might not be the best idea.

The exam questions are not long, which is good because the test has so many questions, but this also means you get less information about what the questions are really asking for. Make sure to read the question and its answers thoroughly instead of reading a few words and immediately assuming you know what the question is asking. Some of the answer choices may have only subtle differences, so be patient and devote time to reading through the question more than once.

As with most tests, it is best to go through the questions and answer those you know immediately; then go back to the ones causing you difficulty. The CISSP exam is not computerized, so you will receive a piece of paper with bubbles to fill in, and one of several colored exam booklets containing the questions. If you scribble outside the lines on the answer sheet, the machine that reads your answers may count a correct answer as wrong. I suggest you go through each question and mark the right answer in the booklet with the questions. Repeat this process until you have completed your selections. Then go through the questions again and fill in the bubbles. This approach leads to less erasing and fewer potential problems with the scoring machine. You are allowed to write and scribble on your question exam booklet any way you choose. You will turn it in at the end of your exam with your answer sheet, but only answers on the answer sheet will be counted, so make sure you transfer all your answers to the answer sheet.

Other certification exams may be taking place simultaneously in the same room, such as exams for certification as an SSCP (Systems Security Certified Professional), IS-SAP or ISSMP (Architecture and Management concentrations, respectively), or ISSEP (Engineering concentration), which is the (ISC)²/NSA government certification. These other exams vary in length and duration, so don't feel rushed if you see others leaving the room early; they may be taking a shorter exam.

Another certification offered by (ISC)² is the Certification and Accreditation Professional (CAP). This was developed by (ISC)² along with the U.S. Department of State's Office of Information Assurance to create what they consider the gold standard in the field of global information security. This CAP credential is intended to be an objective gauge of the level of knowledge, abilities, and skills personnel will be required to have to participate in the certification and accreditation process. This deals directly with those professionals tasked with the creation and assessment of a formalized process to be used in determining risk and establishing security requirements. They will also be tasked with ensuring that information systems possess the security necessary to counter potential risks. This is another certification that, depending upon your field, can benefit not only your career but also the organization you work for.

When finished, don't immediately turn in your exam. You have six hours, so don't squander it just because you might be tired or anxious. Use the time wisely. Take an extra couple of minutes to make sure you answered every question, and that you did not accidentally fill in two bubbles for the same question.

Unfortunately, exam results take some time to be returned. (ISC)² states it can take up to six weeks to get your results to you, but on average it takes from four days to two weeks to receive your results through e-mail and/or the mail.

If you passed the exam, the results sent to you will not contain your score—you will only know that you passed. Candidates who do not pass the test are *always* provided with a score, however. Thus, they know exactly which areas to focus more attention on for the next exam. The domains are listed on this notification with a ranking of weakest to strongest. If you do not pass the exam, remember that many smart and talented security professionals didn't pass on their first try either, chiefly because the test covers such a broad range of topics.

One of the most commonly heard complaints is about the exam itself. The questions are not longwinded, like many Microsoft tests, but at times it is difficult to distinguish between two answers that seem to say the same thing. Although (ISC)² has been removing the use of negatives, such as "not," "except for," and so on, they do still appear on the exam. This is slowly being remedied and should become less and less of an issue over time.

Note that (ISC)² is currently introducing scenario-based questions, which will be long and will expect you to understand concepts in more than one domain to properly answer the question.

Another complaint heard about the test is that some questions seem a bit subjective. For example, whereas it might be easy to answer a technical question that asks for the exact mechanism used in Secure Sockets Layer (SSL) that protects against man-in-the-middle attacks, it's not quite as easy to answer a question that asks whether an eight-foot perimeter fence provides low, medium, or high security. This complaint is mentioned here not to criticize (ISC)² and the test writers, but to help you better prepare for the test.

This book covers all the necessary material for the test and contains many questions and self-practice tests. Most of the questions are formatted in such a way as to better prepare you for what you will encounter on the actual test. So, make sure to read all the material in the book, and pay close attention to the questions and their formats. Even if you know the subject well, you may still get some answers wrong—it is just part of learning how to take tests.

Familiarize yourself with industry standards and expand your technical knowledge and methodology outside the boundaries of what you use today. I cannot stress enough that just because you are the top dog in your particular field, it doesn't mean you are properly prepared for every domain the exam covers. Take the assessment test in this chapter to gauge where you stand, and be ready to read a lot of material new to you.

How to Use This Book

Much effort has gone into putting all the necessary information into this book. Now it's up to you to study and understand the material and its various concepts. To best benefit from this book, you might want to use the following study method:

1. Study each chapter carefully and make sure you understand each concept presented. Many concepts must be fully understood, and glossing over a couple here and there could be detrimental to you. The CISSP CBK contains over 300 individual topics, so take the time needed to understand them all.

2. Make sure to study and answer all of the questions at the end of the chapter, as well as those on the CD-ROM included with the book. If any questions confuse you, go back and study those sections again. Remember, some of the questions on the actual exam are a bit confusing because they do not seem straightforward. I have attempted to draft several questions in the same manner to prepare you for the exam. So do not ignore the confusing questions, thinking they're not well-worded. Instead, pay even closer attention to them because they are there for a reason.

3. If you are not familiar with specific topics, such as firewalls, laws, physical security, or protocol functionality, use other sources of information (books, articles, and so on) to attain a more in-depth understanding of those subjects. Don't just rely on what you think you need to know to pass the CISSP exam.

4. After reading this book, study the questions and answers, and take the practice tests. Then review the (ISC)² study guide and make sure you are comfortable with each bullet item presented. If you are not comfortable with some items, revisit those chapters.

5. If you have taken other certification exams—such as Cisco, Novell, or Microsoft—you might be used to having to memorize details and configuration parameters. But remember, the CISSP test is "an inch deep and a mile wide," so make sure you understand the concepts of each subject *before* trying to memorize the small, specific details.

Questions

To get a better feel for your level of expertise and your current level of readiness for the CISSP exam, run through the following questions:

1. What is derived from a passphrase?

   A. A personal password

   B. A virtual password

   C. A user ID

   D. A valid password

2. Which access control method is user-directed?

   A. Nondiscretionary

   B. Mandatory

   C. Identity-based

   D. Discretionary

3. Which item is not part of a Kerberos authentication implementation?

   A. A message authentication code

   B. A ticket-granting ticket

   C. Authentication service

   D. Users, programs, and services

4. If a company has a high turnover rate, which access control structure is best?

   A. Role-based

   B. Decentralized

   C. Rule-based

   D. Discretionary

5. In discretionary access control, who/what has delegation authority to grant access to data?

   A. A user

   B. A security officer

   C. A security policy

   D. An owner

6. Remote access security using a token one-time password generation is an example of which of the following?

   A. Something you have

   B. Something you know

   C. Something you are

   D. Two-factor authentication

7. What is a crossover error rate (CER)?

   A. A rating used as a performance metric for a biometric system

   B. The number of Type I errors

   C. The number of Type II errors

   D. The number reached when Type I errors exceed the number of Type II errors

8. What does a retina scan biometric system do?

   A. Examines the pattern, color, and shading of the area around the cornea

   B. Examines the patterns and records the similarities between an individual's eyes

   C. Examines the pattern of blood vessels at the back of the eye

   D. Examines the geometry of the eyeball

9. If you are using a synchronous token device, what does this mean?

   A. The device synchronizes with the authentication service by using internal time or events.

   B. The device synchronizes with the user's workstation to ensure the credentials it sends to the authentication service are correct.

   C. The device synchronizes with the token to ensure the timestamp is valid and correct.

   D. The device synchronizes by using a challenge-response method with the authentication service.

10. What is a clipping level?

   A. The threshold for an activity

   B. The size of a control zone

   C. Explicit rules of authorization

   D. A physical security mechanism

11. Which intrusion detection system would monitor user and network behavior?

   A. Statistical/anomaly-based

   B. Signature-based

   C. Static

   D. Host-based

12. When should a Class C fire extinguisher be used instead of a Class A?

   A. When electrical equipment is on fire

   B. When wood and paper are on fire

   C. When a combustible liquid is on fire

   D. When the fire is in an open area

13. How does halon suppress fires?

   A. It reduces the fire's fuel intake.

   B. It reduces the temperature of the area.

   C. It disrupts the chemical reactions of a fire.

   D. It reduces the oxygen in the area.

14. What is the problem with high humidity in a data processing environment?

  A. Corrosion

  B. Fault tolerance

  C. Static electricity

  D. Contaminants

15. What is the definition of a power fault?

  A. Prolonged loss of power

  B. Momentary low voltage

  C. Prolonged high voltage

  D. Momentary power outage

16. Who has the primary responsibility of determining the classification level for information?

  A. The functional manager

  B. Middle management

  C. The owner

  D. The user

17. Which best describes the purpose of the ALE calculation?

  A. It quantifies the security level of the environment.

  B. It estimates the loss potential from a threat.

  C. It quantifies the cost/benefit result.

  D. It estimates the loss potential from a threat in a one-year time span.

18. How do you calculate residual risk?

  A. Threats × risks × asset value

  B. (Threats × asset value × vulnerability) × risks

  C. SLE × frequency = ALE

  D. (Threats × vulnerability × asset value) × control gap

19. What is the Delphi method?

  A. A way of calculating the cost/benefit ratio for safeguards

  B. A way of allowing individuals to express their opinions anonymously

  C. A way of allowing groups to discuss and collaborate on the best security approaches

  D. A way of performing a quantitative risk analysis

20. What are the necessary components of a smurf attack?

  A. Web server, attacker, and fragment offset

  B. Fragment offset, amplifying network, and victim

   C. Victim, amplifying network, and attacker

   D. DNS server, attacker, and web server

21. What do the reference monitor and security kernel do in an operating system?

   A. Intercept and mediate a subject attempting to access objects

   B. Point virtual memory addresses to real memory addresses

   C. House and protect the security kernel

   D. Monitor privileged memory usage by applications

Answers

1. B
2. D
3. A
4. A
5. D
6. A
7. A
8. C
9. A
10. A
11. A
12. A
13. C
14. A
15. D
16. C
17. D
18. D
19. B
20. C
21. A

Security Trends

This chapter presents the following:
- Evolution of computing and how it relates to security
- Different areas that fall under the security umbrella
- Politics that affect security
- Introduction of information warfare
- Examples of security exploits
- A layered approach to security

Security is a fascinating topic because it covers so many different areas (physical, network, platform, application, and so on), each with its own risks, threats, and solutions. When information security is discussed, the theme is usually hackers and software vulnerabilities. Although these are big security concerns, they are only two components within the larger field of security issues. Hacking is foremost in people's minds with regard to security because it is considered flashy and newsworthy, whereas not much coverage is given to what is going on behind the scenes with corporations' global security issues and with the Internet as a whole.

How Security Became an Issue

Various computer books usually have a history section that sets the stage for where society is today pertaining to computing and data processing. Unlike histories that tell of times long past, the history of computing typically begins in the 1960s. A lot has happened in a short period, and computer security is just starting to attract the limelight.

Roughly 25 years ago, the only computers were mainframes. They were few and far between and were used for specialized tasks, usually running large batch jobs, one at a time, and carrying out complex computations. If users were connected to the mainframes, it was through "dumb" terminals that had limited functionality and were totally dependent on the mainframe for their operations and processing environment. This was a *closed environment*, with little threat of security breaches or vulnerabilities being exploited. This does not mean things were perfect, that security vulnerabilities did not exist, and people lived in a computing utopia. Instead, it meant that a handful of people working in a "glass house" knew how to operate the mainframe. They decided who could access the mainframe and when. This provided a much more secure environment, because of its simplicity, than what we see in today's distributed and interconnected world.

In the days of mainframes, web sites describing how to break into a specific application or operating system did not exist. Relatively few people understood network stacks and protocols compared with the vast number of individuals who understand stacks and protocols today. Point-and-click utilities that can overwhelm buffers or interrogate ports did not exist. This was a truly closed environment that only a select few understood.

If networks were connected, it was done in a crude fashion for specific tasks, and corporations did not totally depend on data processing as they do today. The operating systems of that time had problems, software bugs, and vulnerabilities, but not many people were interested in taking advantage of them. Mainframe operators were at the command line, and if they encountered a software problem, they usually just went in and manually changed the programming code. All this was not that long ago, considering where we are today.

As companies became more dependent on the computing power of mainframes, the functionality of the systems grew, and various applications were developed. It was clear that giving employees only small time-slices of access to the mainframes was not as productive as it could be. Processing and computing power was brought closer to the employees, enabling them to run small jobs on their desktop computers, while the big jobs still took place within the glass house. This trend continued and individual computers became more independent and autonomous, only needing to access the mainframe for specific functionality.

As individual personal computers became more efficient, they continually took on more tasks and responsibilities. People discovered that several users accessing a mainframe was an inefficient model; some major components needed to be more readily available so users could perform their tasks in an efficient and effective way. This thinking led to the birth of the client/server model. Although many individual personal computers had the processing power to compute their own calculations and perform their own logic operations, it did not make sense that each computer held information needed by all other computers. Thus, programs and data were centralized on servers, with individual computers accessing them when necessary and accessing the mainframes less frequently, as shown in Figure 2-1.

With the increasing exposure to computing and processing, individuals who used computers learned more about using the technology and getting the most out of it. However, the good things in life often have a darker side. Taking technology down from the pedestal of the mainframe and putting it into so many individuals' hands led to many issues never dealt with in the mainframe days. Now thousands of inexperienced users had much more access to important data and processes. Barriers and protection mechanisms were not in place to protect employees and systems from mistakes, so important data got corrupted accidentally, and individual mistakes affected many other systems instead of just one.

Because so many more people were using systems, the software had to be made more "idiot-proof" so that a larger group could use the same platform. Computer operators in the mainframe days understood what the systems expected, how to format

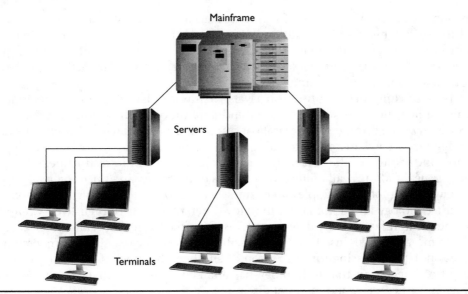

Mainframe

Servers

Terminals

Figure 2-1 The relationship between a mainframe, servers, and terminals

input, and how to properly read output. When this power was put into individuals' desktops, every imaginable (and unimaginable) input was used, which corrupted information and mangled operating systems.

Companies soon realized that employees had to be protected from themselves and that data had to be protected from mishaps and mistakes. The employees needed layers of software between them and the operating system components and the data they could potentially destroy. Implementing these layers not only enhanced security—by separating users from the core of the operating systems and files—but also increased productivity, as functionality continued to be added to make computers more useful to businesses and individuals.

As the computing world evolved, symbiotic relationships grew among the technological advances of hardware, circuitry, processing power, and software. Once a breakthrough was made that enabled a computer to contain more memory and hard drive space, new software was right on its heels to use it and demand more. When software hit a wall because it was not supplied with the necessary registers and control units, the hardware industry was Johnny-on-the-spot to develop and engineer the missing pieces to the equations. As the hardware end grew to provide a stable and rich platform for software, programmers developed software that provided functionality and possibilities not even conceived of a few years earlier. It has been a wonderful game of leapfrog that does not seem to have any end in sight.

Lovely story, but what does it mean to security?

In the beginning, the issues associated with bringing computing closer to individuals brought along many mistakes, technological hurdles, and operational issues not encountered in the workforce before. Computers are tools. Just as a knife can be a useful tool to cut meat and vegetables, it can also be a dangerous tool in the hands of someone with malicious intent. The vast capabilities and functionality that computers have brought to society have also brought complex and troubling methods of destruction, fraud, abuse, and insecurity.

Because computers are built on layers (hardware platform, chips, operating systems, kernels, network stacks, services, and applications), these complex issues have been interwoven throughout the strata of computing environments. Plugging the holes, writing better software, and providing better perimeter security are often easier said than done because of the density of functionality within an infrastructure, interoperability issues, and the availability requirements of the necessary functionality.

Over a short period, people and businesses have come to depend greatly upon computer technology and automation in many different aspects of their lives. Computers run public utilities, military defense systems, financial institutions, and medical equipment, and are heavily used in every possible business sector. Almost every company relies on data processing for one reason or another. This level of dependence and the extent of integration that technology has attained in our lives have made security a much more necessary and essential discipline.

Computer security is a marathon to be run at a consistent and continual pace. It is not a short sprint, and it is not for those who lack dedication or discipline.

Areas of Security

Security has a wide base that touches on several different areas. The developers of the CISSP exam had the vision to understand this and to demand that an individual who claims to be a security expert and wants to achieve this certification must also show that his expertise does not just lie in one area of security. Many areas of security affect each other. Physical security is interrelated with information security, database security lies on top of operating system security, operations security affects how computer systems are used, disaster recovery deals with systems in emergency situations, and almost every instance has some type of legal or liability issue tied to it. Technology, hardware, people, and procedures are woven together as a security fabric, as illustrated in Figure 2-2. When it is time to identify and resolve a specific problem, several strands of the security fabric may need to be unraveled and scrutinized so the best and most effective solution can be provided.

This chapter addresses some specific security issues regarding computers, information, and organizations. This is not an attempt to cover all relevant subjects, but rather to show specific instances to give you an idea of the vast area that security encompasses. The information in these sections is provided to set the stage for the deeper levels of coverage that will be addressed in the following chapters.

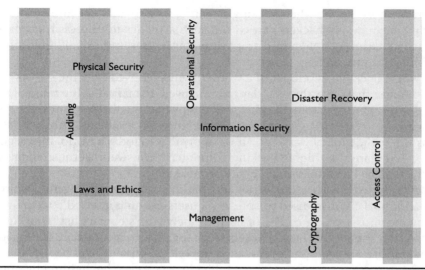

Figure 2-2 Technology, hardware, people, and procedures are woven together as a security fabric.

Benign to Scary

Computers and networks touch every facet of modern life. We are increasingly dependent on computer/network technology for communication, funds transfers, utility management, government services, military action, and maintaining confidential information. We use technology to provide energy, water supplies, emergency services, defense systems, electronic banking, and public health services. At the same time, this technology is being abused to perform illegal or malicious activities, such as to steal credit card numbers, use telephone systems fraudulently, illegally transmit trade secrets and intellectual property, deface web sites for political reasons, disrupt communications, reveal critical national secrets and strategies, and even to commit extortion.

The term "information warfare" covers many different activities that pertain to individuals, organizations, and nations. *Information warfare* can be defined as any action to deny, exploit, corrupt, or destroy the enemy's information and its function, while at the same time protecting oneself against those same actions. Governments have used information warfare techniques to gather tactical information for years. Organizations have stolen competitors' trade secrets and plans for new products. Individuals have also used computers to steal money, access personal financial information, steal individual identification information, deface web sites, and to cause destruction to draw attention to a particular cause.

There once was a time when hacking activities, viruses, and malware incidents were relatively benign. Many hackers carried out such activities to impress their peers and show they were clever enough to disrupt some businesses, but overall their intent was not to inflict massive damages to an entity.

But where once the developer of a worm or virus received only the self-satisfaction of overcoming a challenge, things today have changed dramatically. The trend of hacking for "fun" is disappearing, to be quickly replaced by hacking with profit-driven motives. There is an old saying that goes, "Why did the thief rob the bank?" Answer: "Because that was where the money was kept." If we apply that to today's world, it may go more like this: "Why are the thieves hacking computers?" Answer: "Because today that is where the financial information and critical data are kept."

Today, security breaches, malware, and hacking often target specific victims and have specific goals. Viruses used to spread via users opening infected attachments, followed by the virus sending copies of itself to the victim's contact list. Thus, it simply replicated itself—big deal. Now, hackers work together to steal data used for identity theft, raid funds from online accounts, and carry out extortion when holes are discovered in a company's security program. Some individuals are even being hired by organized crime rings for just such objectives.

In short, hacking is constantly evolving. In an industry driven by continual technological innovation, hackers remain abreast of these changes and often are a step ahead of the good guys who are trying to protect company assets. The level of sophistication has increased as well because the stakes are now that much higher. It is not unheard of for organizations to secretly employ hackers to perpetrate all kinds of maliciousness against their competitors. Everything from business contracts, customer lists, industrial secrets, product blueprints, and financial data can be culled from an organization's computer systems by those with the necessary technological skills if aided by security weaknesses at the target organization. Routinely, news stories arise about international crime rings targeting banks and credit card companies through cyberattacks, the results of which are the loss of millions of dollars, through identity fraud and outright theft of funds. In many cases, the greatest damage done to these companies is to their reputations and the confidence consumers have in the organizations.

Evidence of the Evolution of Hacking

Several incidents indicate that not only is hacking activity on the rise, but the sophistication of the attacks is also advancing rapidly. Alarmingly, a majority of attacks are using methods that have been understood for quite some time and for which fixes have been readily available. This proves that not enough network maintainers have kept up-to-date on security changes and have installed the necessary patches or configurations.

It is an unfortunate but common occurrence to see hackers exploiting the various computer vulnerabilities in order to steal millions of credit card and account numbers from systems associated with e-commerce, online banking, or the retail sector. Some hackers will extort the organization with the threat of releasing the sensitive data to others. The hackers will offer a "security service" to fix the systems they have attacked for a fee, and if the institutions do not agree to pay, the attackers will threaten to do even more damage by posting the customers' credit card numbers on web sites available to the public. Some organizations call the hacker's bluff and refuse to pay, while some organizations pay the "hush money" and get the FBI involved.

The public is often very much in the dark about the kinds of damage worms, viruses, and hacks have inflicted on companies. Unless these events make the news, the attacked organization usually only notifies their customers when absolutely necessary, or just sends them new cards and account numbers without any real explanation as to why they are being issued. It is usually only when more and more people are affected by attacks that they make the news and the general public becomes aware of them. Because of this common secrecy regarding security breaches, a majority of the states in America have privacy laws that require customers to be told of those issues that could directly affect them.

Organizations have their own motivation behind keeping the news about these kinds of attacks as quiet as possible. First, they don't want to lose their customers due to a lack of confidence and thereby lose their revenue. Second, they don't want to announce to the world that they have holes in their enterprises that lead right to the company jewels. Public knowledge of these vulnerabilities can bring about a storm of new attackers. It is similar to being attacked by a shark in the ocean only to have more sharks appear for their afternoon snack. It is not pretty.

You can visit www.cybercrime.gov to see convictions that have taken place. Following are some items that never hit the headlines:

- On July 15, 2009, a former director of information technology for an organ and tissue donation center was sentenced to two years in prison for hacking into her former company's network. She was charged with a criminal indictment for unauthorized computer access. She also had to pay $94,222 to her former employer for the damages she inflicted.

- A man was convicted for hacking into financial institutions and credit card processing centers to obtain credit card information. He purchased merchandise and then sold the rest of the credit card numbers on his web site named CardersMarket. CardersMarket had about 4,500 members around the world.

- On July 19, 2009, an engineer in California was convicted for economic espionage and working for the People's Republic of China. He stole Boeing trade secrets, as in information about the Space Shuttle program.

- On June 26, 2009, it was discovered that a man downloaded his employer's trade secrets on a thumb drive before he quit and went to work for his former employer's competitor.

- A mutual fund management company had their former network administrator attempt to extort better severance benefits, including extended medical coverage and stellar references from the company, by threatening to damage the computer systems and company data. The network administrator also threatened to contact the *Wall Street Journal*, *Newsweek*, and the New York *Daily News* to publicize the damage that would take place.

Sadly, the examples at www.cybercrime.gov represent only a small percentage of the hacking activity going on. These attacks were identified and reported. Most are not. Many organizations do not report hacking activity because they are afraid of damaging their reputation, losing the faith of their customer base, and adversely affecting their shareholders and stock prices. Other attacks go unnoticed or unidentified, and thus are not reported, while international attacks against military and government systems typically go unreported to the public. So, even though computers and networks remain great tools and have brought society much advancement, like many other tools, they are often used for sinister purposes.

Let's look at some of the attacks that have made *some* of the headlines:

- In July 2009 one of the gadgets that most of us are addicted to, the BlackBerry, was compromised. Hackers sent a piece of code that BlackBerry owners thought was a safe update for the Java code that runs on this device, but instead it was a piece of spyware that allowed the hackers to intercept e-mail and text messages. The "update software" was labeled: "Etisalat network upgrade for BlackBerry service. Please download to ensure continuous service quality." This sounds convincing enough. It is probable that many BlackBerry devices have been infected by this malicious code, and it is just laying dormant without the owners knowing about it.

- It was also discovered in 2009 that over 166,000 computers that were infected with botnet software resided in 74 different countries and pointed to several U.S. web sites. The goal of most botnets is to carry out denial of service (DoS) attacks and to render their victim systems unusable. Botnet software connects to control servers that give the infected systems instructions on which victim to attack and how. So all of these systems connected to one of the eight controllers every three minutes and carried out DoS attacks on web sites all over the nation. Was one of the infected computers yours? How can you be sure?

- Many of us have Facebook, MySpace, and Twitter accounts, and they could be a venue to allow our systems to be infected and to infect our friends and loved ones. A worm called Koobface can be installed on a computer, and when a user logs into one of these social networking sites, it sends a bogus tweet (or message) that has a link to what seems like a video. The link actually goes to a server that installs the worm on the new system. So if you log into your Twitter account, a message that you do not create or send can go from your account to others, trick them into clicking on a link, and then infecting their system. This is not a way to make new friends.

- Another loved gadget is the iPhone. In April 2009 a bug in the software was discovered that allows someone to crash the iPhone software, disconnect from the network that the iPhones use, and potentially execute code remotely on it. The remote code could allow someone to turn on the microphone of the phone and allow it to become a bugging device. As of this writing, this vulnerability is still being studied, but it is a good indicator of what is going on in the world.

There was a time when people could understand most if not all of the software that was running on computers, the hardware, and could work on their own cars. Now our TVs, microwaves, cars, and telephones are small and complex computers running software that is full of vulnerabilities yet to be uncovered. Soon the computers will unite and turn on humans and take over the world. Right now you don't need to worry about that, just concentrate on passing your CISSP exam.

How Are Nations Affected?

The art of war requires soldiers to outmaneuver the enemy and strike them down if necessary. In traditional warfare, the enemy was usually easily detectable. They were driving a tank, bombing from an airplane, attacking from a submarine, or shooting missiles. Today, the enemy may be harder to find, some attacks are harder to track, and the objectives of the attacker are at times more nebulous. Many governments' military intelligence agencies have had to develop new methods of collecting information on potential foreign enemy movement, conducting surveillance, and proving guilt in criminal activities.

Although militaries still train most soldiers how to shoot, fight in combat, and practice evasive maneuvers, a new type of training is being incorporated. Because a majority of the military vehicles, weapons systems, and communication systems are controlled by technology, new soldiers must know how to use these technological tools to achieve the same goal of the soldier of the past—to win in war. Today's soldiers need to know not only how to operate the new technology-driven weapons systems, but also how to defend these systems from attacks and possibly use them to attack the enemy's defense systems.

Disrupting communication has always been an important tactic in war because it impedes proper planning and warnings of imminent attacks. Knocking out communication lines is one of the first steps in the recipe of a successful attack. Today, most military communication is handled through computer-based systems, and the tools to disrupt communication of the enemy have changed. For example, the CIA reported to a U.S. congressional committee that foreign nations include information warfare in their military arsenal and provide defensive and offensive attack methods. These nations are devising documentation, strategic plans, and tools to carry out information warfare on other nations.

During the Persian Gulf War in 1991, it was reported that hackers from the Netherlands penetrated 34 American military sites that supported Operation Desert Storm activities. They extracted information about the exact location of military troops, weapon details, and movement of American warships. It could have been a different war if Saddam Hussein had actually bought this information when it was offered to him, but he did not—he thought it was a trick.

In another example, it was reported that the Irish Republican Army stole telephone bills to determine the addresses of potential targets in their political attacks. Authorities seized a batch of computer disks in Belfast and were able to decrypt the information after months of effort. This information was most likely gained by successfully hacking into the telephone company's database.

A report declassified in May 1995 stated that prior to the August 1991 coup attempt in the Soviet Union, the KGB had been writing and developing viruses to disrupt computer systems during times of war. Another report, by the U.S. Defense Intelligence Agency, indicated that Cuba had developed viruses to infect and damage U.S. civilian computers. There is no proof these viruses were released and actually caused damage, but there is no proof they *weren't* released either. It has also been reported that during the 1999 Kosovo Air Campaign, fake messages were injected into Yugoslavia's computer-integrated air defense systems to point the weapons at false targets. Examples like these make it clear that military use of computer-based tools and attacks is growing in sophistication and utilization.

Critical to the function of the Internet are the 13 root DNS servers that participate in managing Internet traffic. If some of these go down, some web sites may become unreachable, and some e-mail may not delivered. If they all came down, the Internet would basically stop functioning. On February 6, 2007, another cyberattack occurred that targeted the 13 root DNS servers. Three computers used in this capacity were overwhelmed, but to the great relief of many, the attack went largely unnoticed by most computer users around the globe. Computer scientists involved claim this is due to the increased resiliency of the Internet and the sharing of duties that has taken place since the last major attack upon these computers in 2002.

Today, reports indicate that many terrorist groups are now using propaganda on the Internet to find prospective recruits. Luckily, these tactics have also spawned their cyber opposites, such as the cyber-antiterrorist group, Internet Haganah, founded by Aaron Weisburd. Weisburd, and others like him, now track down terrorist-related web sites and pose as individuals sympathetic to the web sites' creators. They then gather as much information as they can and pass it along to various law enforcement agencies in order to shut down the web sites and, when possible, prosecute those responsible.

In another aspect of cyberterrorism, the U.S. Department of Defense believes at least 20 countries have now established cyber war organizations in an effort to create and develop the tools and techniques needed to attack other national militaries and civilian targets via the Internet. Possible cyber wars like this are already a reality. The number of attacks and intrusion attempts on the Department of Defense (DoD) has continued to rise in recent years. In some cases, the DoD has endured more than 500 cyberattacks a day. Fortunately, the number of successful attempts has declined due to a strategic effort to train personnel and to implement the best security measures available.

Almost every task in an individual's day interrelates with a technology that is controlled or monitored by a computer-based system. Turning on the lights, paying a gas bill, flying on a plane, talking on the telephone, and receiving medical treatment are all events that depend on large computer systems monitoring and providing a flow of service. Even sophisticated military defense systems rely on commercial power, communication, transportation, and monitoring capabilities that are computer based. A country's strength depends on its privately owned critical infrastructures and industries. These private-sector infrastructures have already been victimized by computer attacks, and a concerted attack on any of these key economic sectors or governmental services could have widespread ramifications. Most governments have recognized this vulnerability and have started taking the necessary defense steps because it is very likely that in future wars a country's entire infrastructure could be targeted via these new methods—computer-generated attacks.

 NOTE   The examples here are U.S.-centric, but the CISSP exam is not. It has evolved over the years to have a greater international focus.

The world's war strategies have moved from large organized groups fighting each other to smaller, noncentralized terrorist groups attacking each other and countries directly. Because of this, sometimes information warfare is more successful and crucial than conventional weapons.

If country A is attacking country B, the leaders and top decision-makers are usually apparent, and who they are is not secret. In terrorist groups, many times it is hard to identify the leaders, their goals, tribal affiliations, and the social and political structure of the groups themselves. It is hard to penetrate these terrorist groups, so intelligence that is gathered through information warfare means is commonly the only thing countries have to work with.

The amazing feats of information warfare tactics reach from implanting malware on enemies' systems, building products that could be used to spy and relay data back to the developers, infecting combat devices to allow for remote control, and other intriguing approaches. One item that may not be thought of as "information warfare" is affecting how terrorist groups and countries are carrying out their internal or external political fights—social networking.

At one time many countries had tighter, more defined and controlled boundaries. Physical control and the control of conventional news media allowed leaders to dictate who came in and out of their areas and how their activities were viewed by the world. Today people in different countries can take pictures or videos with their cell phones and upload them to YouTube for the world to see. Individuals can post real-time information on Twitter and other social networks, which took place during the presidential election of the Iran president in 2009. Social networks have flattened the world of social media and control of information.

After the Iran presidential election, protesters in great numbers stated their opinions on a medium that did not exist during their last presidential election. People around the world could get more up-to-date information through Twitter, YouTube, and reading blogs than from the conventional news stations. Many news stations also tuned to these networks to get their information.

The use of technology is making the world smaller, making almost all information accessible and real-time data available to thousands and millions within seconds. This is not only changing our social interaction, but also world events.

How Are Companies Affected?

Many companies fail to understand how security implementations help their bottom line. After all, businesses are created to turn a profit, and if there is no direct correlation for an item—tying it in neatly to the linear concept of cost and profit—that item is often given low priority. Thankfully, more companies today are discovering how security affects their bottom line in ways they never expected.

If a company suffers a security breach, it must deal with a wide range of issues it likely wasn't prepared for. Several companies recently had their databases attacked and their customers' information compromised. Once customers find out that a company is not protecting their confidential and financial information properly, they will often take their business elsewhere. If the number of customers affected is in the range witnessed over the last year (10,000 to 1.4 million credit cards stolen at a time), and if the company loses a similar number of customers at one time, the company could go out of business. Of course, these events also affect the reputation of the company, its shareholders, and its stock price. In addition, the customers can sue the company, which could result in punitive damages and court fees. This would definitely impact the bottom line.

 NOTE Companies have added detailed security questions to requests from business partners. Many requests for proposal (RFPs) now include questions regarding security practices, infrastructure, and how data will be protected.

Organizations have had trade secrets and intellectual property stolen by employees who left to work for a competitor. In such instances, unless the original company has taken the proper steps to protect this data and informed its employees that this action is wrong, the company has no legal recourse. The company must practice due care both inside and outside its walls to protect its intellectual property from competitors. (For more information on legal issues, see Chapter 10.)

The industry is seeing more and more cases of employees being fired for improper use of computer systems. Many large companies have instituted policies of zero tolerance with respect to unauthorized or improper computer and Internet usage. However, if companies do not take the proper steps by having a comprehensive security policy in place and providing security awareness to the employees, they are often successfully sued for unfairly ending employment.

Companies and organizations are increasingly finding themselves responsible for compliance with more and more regulations pertaining to how they handle their data and personal information. The following is a short list of different privacy and confidentiality regulations:

- Electronic Communications Policy (ECP)
- Health Insurance Portability and Accountability Act (HIPAA)
- Public Records Act (PRA)
- Information Practices Act (IPA)
- Family Educational Rights and Privacy Act (FERPA)
- Children's Online Privacy Protection Act (COPPA)
- Fair Credit Reporting Act (FCRA)

- Gramm-Leach-Bliley Act
- Sarbanes-Oxley Act of 2002

Each year this list expands.

Many other regulations that companies need to comply with in conducting their business are imposed at the state and federal levels. It is important to know that many of these regulations go much further than to just dictate the levels of protection a company must provide for the data they are responsible for. It is becoming more common to see these newer regulations requiring that CEOs and CFOs of organizations be held personally responsible, and perhaps criminally negligent, if anything untoward occurs in regard to the data they have been entrusted with. Long gone are the days where upper management can claim they didn't realize what was going on at lower levels of their organization. These regulations and laws can hold them directly accountable, and require them to sign off on regular reports and audits pertaining to the financial health and security of their organizations.

Another way a company can lose money and time is by being ill-prepared to react to a situation. If a network does not have properly configured security mechanisms, the company's IT staff usually spends unnecessary time and resources putting out fires. In addition, when they are racing in a chaotic manner to find a solution, they may be creating more open doors into the network without realizing it. Without proper security planning, a lot of money, staff productivity, and time are wasted that could be used for other tasks. As discussed in subsequent chapters in this book, companies that have a solid incident response plan or disaster recovery plan in place will know what to do in the event of a physical intrusion or cyberattack.

Many companies are covered by insurance in case of a natural disaster or a major security breach. However, to get a good insurance rate, companies must prove they have a solid security program and that they are doing all they can to protect their own investments. In some cases, insurance providers refuse to pay for a company's loss because the company failed to have the correct security measures in place. A recent legal case involved a company that did not have a security policy, proper security mechanisms, and an updated disaster recovery plan in place. When disaster struck, the insurance company refused to pay. The case went to court and the insurance company won; however, the greater loss to the company was not the court case.

Every business market is full of competition. If a company endures a security compromise that makes the press—which has been happening almost every month—it will have an even harder time attracting new business. A company wants to be in a position where all the customers come to it when *another* company suffers a security compromise, not the other way around.

The U.S. Government's Actions

One of the U.S. government's responsibilities is to protect American resources, people, and their way of life. A complex task the government has been faced with recently is protecting several critical infrastructures from computer-based attacks. Because computer technology is relatively young and changing rapidly, and because security has only come into real focus over the last few years, all these core infrastructures contain their own vulnerabilities. If attackers disrupt these infrastructures, the ramifications may be far reaching. For example, if attackers were able to take down electrical grids, thus forcing the government to concentrate on that crisis, they could then launch military strikes on other fronts. This might sound like a John Grisham novel, but the U.S. government must consider such scenarios and devise defensive plans to respond. One of the biggest threats the United States faces is that terrorists or a hostile nation will attempt to inflict economic damage, disrupt business or productivity, and degrade our defense response by attacking the critical infrastructures.

On July 15, 1996, President Clinton approved the establishment of the President's Commission on Critical Infrastructure Protection (PCCIP). The responsibility of this commission was to investigate the types of attacks that were happening, extrapolate how attacks could evolve in the future, determine how they could affect the nation's computer infrastructures, and assess how vulnerable these structures were to such attacks at that time.

The PCCIP published its sobering report, "Critical Foundations: Protecting America's Infrastructures," in 1997. The report outlined the current vulnerability level of critical U.S. infrastructures pertaining to criminal activity, natural disasters, international terrorists, hackers, foreign national intelligence, and information warfare. Longstanding security weaknesses, placing federal operations at serious risk, were identified and reported. In response to this report, President Clinton signed two orders, Presidential Decision Directives (PDDs) 62 and 63, to improve the nation's defenses against terrorism, other computer-based attacks, and information warfare activities. The focus of these directives was to address cyberattacks at a national level.

The report recognized that many of the nation's critical infrastructures were privately owned and operated. It was obvious the government and the private sector had to work together to properly and successfully defend against cyberattacks. In fact, it was recognized that these government departments could *not* provide this level of protection without the help and sharing of information with the public sector. The position of national coordinator was created within the Executive Office of the President to facilitate a partnership between the government and the private sector. The goal was for the government and the private sector to work together to strengthen the nation's defenses against cyberterrorism, theft, fraud, and other criminal activity. Out of this came the Critical Infrastructure Assurance Office (CIAO) under the Department of Commerce, Information Sharing and Analysis Centers (ISACs), and the National Infrastructure Protection Center (NIPC) under the sponsorship of the FBI. Recently, the NIPC was fully integrated into the Information Analysis and Infrastructure Protection Directorate of the Department of Homeland Security (DHS). Thus, the former NIPC's responsibilities of physical and cybercritical infrastructure assessment are now being addressed by two new divisions.

ISACs provide a mechanism that enables information sharing among members of a particular industry sector. The information comes from public-sector organizations and government agencies, and is shared by both. Sources of information can be authenticated or anonymous, and the information can pertain to vulnerabilities, incidents, threats, and solutions. Submitted information is directed to the appropriate team members, who then investigate each submittal, quantify the seriousness of the vulnerability, and perform a trend analysis to identify steps that might thwart this type of attack. The intent is to enhance the security of individual organizations, as well as the entire nation, one industry sector at a time.

In 2002, President Bush created the Department of Homeland Security in response to the attack on the United States on September 11, 2001. Divisions of information technology and cybersecurity were included, and specific committees and roles were developed to protect against attacks that could negatively affect the nation's infrastructure. The bill was signed November 25, 2002, and allocated $2.12 billion for technology and cybersecurity.

As with the position of drug czar in the war on drugs, in many countries in recent years there has also been a call for the appointment of a cyber czar—that is, a government official responsible for keeping the critical infrastructure of a country's cyberworld secure and protected. In the United States, it has proved to be a revolving-door post at the White House, with no real momentum. The position has been a part of the Department of Homeland Security and actually oversees two other divisions: the National Communications System division and the National Cyber Security division. Many experts in the security industry feel that ever since President Bush issued his national strategy to secure cyberspace in February 2003, not enough has been done, and that those policies that have been created have been, for the most part, nonstarters. Since 2001, more than four people have held the position of cyber czar, and in one instance (Howard Schmitt), for only two months. Many of the cyber czars have quit due to a lack of support or a feeling that the position and its division weren't being taken seriously by other government agencies. Late into 2006, the position remained open, with the Bush administration claiming they were whittling down the list of possible candidates. Finally, in 2007, Greg Garcia was named as DHS's first assistant secretary for communications and cyber security.

In 2008, President Bush's administration developed the Comprehensive National Cybersecurity Initiative (CNCI). This is the National Security Presidential Directive 54 (aka Homeland Security Presidential Directive 23), and its overall goal is how to improve the protection of the U.S. federal systems and the sensitive information on them from nefarious hackers. It has been reported that Bush requested $40 billion for this initiative to be used over several years to shore up the necessary levels of protection for government networks and security processes.

So, what is in this CNCI and how does it apply? Its main goals are to bring together the very fragmented approach that the U.S. government has used to carry out its cybersecurity initiatives, to expand and improve upon the existing programs and processes, and to reduce the increasing risks that threaten the nation.

There are several components to the CNCI, and many are still classified and have not been released. Some of the items that have been released are improving intrusion-detection and intrusion-prevention processes with the government monitoring systems; reducing the number of external connections to government systems; research; counter-intelligence; training; public-private collaboration; and increasing the security of supply chains that can directly affect the United States' interests and protection.

The crux is basically like everything in security—identify and reduce vulnerabilities, increase threat awareness, and lock things down. The difference between "regular security" issues and issues of security in the government is the government. Many of you work in organizations and corporations that have their fair share of politics, turf wars, and personal agendas—just think if you needed to get huge government agencies, the presidential administration, and Congress to agree upon something.

In 2009, President Obama ordered a review of federal cybersecurity activities. Some of the main goals were to identify how to better protect transportation, power grids, financial markets, chemical sectors, and more. (Security professionals have only been talking about this for over ten years…sigh.) The nation's cyber infrastructure is recognized as a strategic asset, but the big stumbling block is still, who is in charge and how do we herd these cats to actually make some progress.

As of this writing, the Obama team cannot find anyone who will take on the job of cyber czar. The concerns are that the position will have a lot of responsibilities, but no power or funding. Also, anyone who fills this position would struggle with the turf wars among the DHS, NSA, and other government agencies. While the Obama administration is working to coordinate how military systems are used to develop cyber weapons, civil liberty advocates are concerned at how this type of "Big Brother" move will affect American citizens. No wonder the cyber czar position is currently still open!

Critics and industry insiders claim it is tough to fill this position for several reasons. The first is the strong perception that the job holds no real power or influence in government circles. Critics say the presidential administrations talk a big game, but in reality do very little—if anything—to fight cyberterrorism. (The trend now is changing.) The second reason is the need to find people who are properly qualified to hold the position. This is difficult due to the specific requirements of the job, such as having a strong understanding, not only of the nature of current threats and the technology involved, but also in having the foresight to implement strategies that will protect the nation's computer infrastructure in the future as well. Such undertakings require both active and proactive planning, and a forceful implementation of policies. The third reason for the difficulties in hiring is that the private sector at this time pays more, and offers more, to those individuals best suited for the position. The candidates must also understand how the nation's politics work and be able to work within, and be successful in, these types of roles.

Government leadership also often claims that the private sector isn't doing enough to secure the nation's infrastructure. To this, though, the private sector usually responds that the government still must do more, and take their own initiatives, and claims that the government is doing little, if anything, in these areas. Many criticisms of this type focus on the lack of leadership and cohesive policies coming from the Department of Homeland Security. Audits of both the DHS and the Department of Defense's security procedures have given failing scores in recent evaluations, leaving the private sector questioning the government's leadership abilities. The government, in turn, criticizes the evaluation process they've undergone. At the end of the day, however, both the private and government sectors must work together and grow stronger in these areas because the threats to the nation's cyber infrastructure are becoming more dangerous all the time.

Politics and Laws

Governments all over the world have started to look at computing and the security issues that surround it more seriously over the last few years. There is continual dialogue about transborder issues pertaining to cryptography—what can be encrypted, at what strength, and by whom. Broader issues are also injected when an attack comes from another country that does not regulate such activity or that does not consider it to be illegal behavior. Different countries' legal systems are meeting many unprecedented challenges with regard to computer security.

As the Internet brings the world closer together, governments are beginning to reach agreements upon matters pertaining to computers, security, boundaries, and acceptable behavior. One sign of countries attempting to get in step with each other is the acceptance of the *Common Criteria* (discussed at length in Chapter 5). Until the acceptance of the Common Criteria, most countries had their own way of evaluating and testing the security and assurance of a system or device. For instance, the United States has used the Trusted Computer System Evaluation Criteria (TCSEC), which is referred to as the Orange Book. The Canadians have the Canadian Trusted Computer Product Evaluation Criteria (CTCPEC), the Europeans have the Information Technology Security Evaluation Criteria (ITSEC), and other countries have developed their own criteria on how to determine the level of trust to place in the security of particular products and systems. The Common Criteria is an attempt to take the best of all of these methods and provide the world with one way of determining a product's security features and protection level. In other words, it is an attempt to harmonize and standardize by using one common tool to measure trust in products and systems.

Other than different countries viewing computer security differently, another barrier to proper security is how investigators deal with computer crimes. The courts have been continually playing catch-up. The legal system cannot keep ahead of (or even in step with) technology, which it must do to regulate it effectively and to determine who is guilty or innocent. It is hard for a judge or jury to declare who is guilty or innocent in a computer crime because they are not educated on these types of crimes. Investigators have a hard time collecting usable evidence to present in court, and lawyers have few cases to cite as precedent because not many cases exist yet. But more convictions are taking place every year.

In addition, these difficulties start with law enforcement, which lacks personnel skilled in computer technology and computer forensics. If a person is accused of a cybercrime, law officers must search for evidence. But what do they search for? Law enforcement personnel do not necessarily know how to dump data from memory into a file or how to find remnants of data after the criminal has formatted the drive, nor do they necessarily understand how computer crimes take place so that they can look for the right clues. Law enforcement must know how to remove evidence from computer systems and drives in a way that does not corrupt the data and that preserves its integrity so it is admissible in court. They must gain much more computer knowledge and skills to be able to deal with computer crimes.

NOTE Law enforcement has greatly increased their skills in identifying and fighting computer crime, but such tech knowledge is not yet pervasive in all departments. For the latest information on these developments, visit www .hightechcrimecops.org.

Computers are used in many types of crimes and provide many types of barriers that law enforcement and the courts are not used to dealing with. Data and communication may be encrypted, and there can be jurisdiction issues if a crime took place, for example, in Europe but originated in North America. Also, much of the communication is spoofed, so law enforcement must know how to track down criminals through binary, hexadecimal, and packet header means.

These barriers and issues help criminals who are computer savvy. If they do get caught, many are not prosecuted to the extent they would be if they had committed a crime that the courts were used to dealing with.

Even though law enforcement has been lagging behind cybercrime, initiatives exist at many levels to try and deal with the problem. Many international organizations such as the G8, the United Nations, and the European Union are trying to promote cooperation and harmonization in dealing with global computer crime.

The Organisation for Economic Co-operation and Development (OECD) is an international group made up of 30 member countries and is actively involved with 70 other countries. This international organization is made up of, and serves, developed countries that accept the principles of a free market and representative democracy. Its purpose is to promote trade and economic growth for member and nonmember nations, to provide intergovernmental discussions on sundry economic and social issues, to collect and publish information, and to provide short-term economic forecasts.

The group covers a wide range of topics (education, trade, science and innovation, and so on) that would be more successful if all the countries followed the same standards. OECD is not a governing body that cranks out standards that must be followed, but they do provide guidelines, documentation, advice, and statistics to help the different countries work together for mutual benefit. Many governments use this information to shape their laws and regulations so their nations can prosper nationally and internationally.

While the OECD deals with many different issues, the *OECD Principles* address financial stability through proper corporate governance. Unfortunately, there's not much meat to them, given that they are just guidelines, not laws or regulations. The theme of the Principles is proper corporate governance, transparency, adequate accounting, external independent audits, internal company controls, the eradication of conflicts of interest, and so on.

The OECD defines the purpose of these principles in the following manner:

The OECD Principles of Corporate Governance were endorsed by OECD Ministers in 1999 and have since become an international benchmark for policy makers, investors, corporations and other stakeholders worldwide. They have advanced the corporate governance agenda and provided specific guidance for legislative and regulatory initiatives in both OECD and non-OECD countries. The Financial Stability Forum has designated the Principles as one of the 12 key standards for sound financial systems. The Principles also provide the basis for an extensive programme of cooperation between OECD and non-OECD countries and underpin the corporate governance component of World Bank/ IMF Reports on the Observance of Standards and Codes (ROSC).

Think of the OECD Principles as the granddaddy of all corporate governance rules for the world. Different governments have built upon these principles to devise laws and regulations that made sense to their environments, including the United States, which used them to develop SOX (Sarbanes-Oxley Act of 2002).

NOTE The Sarbanes-Oxley Act of 2002 (SOX) is legislation enacted in response to the high-profile Enron, WorldCom, and other financial scandals, to protect shareholders and the general public from accounting misdeeds and fraudulent practices in publicly owned companies.

Although SOX deals specifically with financial reporting, the OECD Principles have a farther reach because proper corporate governance provides more than just correct financial books. Corporate governance affects the volatility in retirement savings, facilitating access to capital, public savings, investment, market confidence, and so on. SOX focuses on truthful financial statements, whereas the OECD Principles focus on the processes of corporate governance itself. The central goal of the Principles is to help encourage economic stability and growth.

CAUTION You are expected to know about the OECD Principles for the CISSP exam. We will cover them in a later chapter also, but this information is not just "interesting"; it is a "need-to-know."

Tough issues face local police forces, Interpol, international judicial systems, the FBI, the CIA, and other organizations. However, with change comes growth. Governments are developing laws and procedures to effectively deal with computer crimes. Crime-fighting agencies are increasing personnel to include people with technology skills and are requiring computer security in many parts of these organizations.

So What Does This Mean to Us?

Evidence and trend analyses show that people, businesses, and countries are becoming increasingly dependent on computer/network technology for communication, funds transfers, utility management, government services, and military action. If any of these were to experience a major disruption, millions of people could be affected. As our dependence grows, so should our protective measures.

The reality of the world today is that the majority of computer attacks, hacks, and cracks are no longer done for kicks and thrills. Greed and financial gain are the greatest motivators for most attacks these days. The perpetrators are no longer just individuals trying to make a name for themselves; instead, more organized crime and financial motivation are behind these attacks. The gamut runs from botnets to spammers to identity theft. The lure of fast money through anonymous means brings all kinds of malicious elements out of the woodwork to take a crack at hacking and cybercrime. The fact that many organizations don't want to report these kinds of crimes and have the public know about these attacks only sweetens the lure for criminals to steal and extort every possible dime out of their victims.

Militaries are quietly growing their information warfare units. This growth is a response to the computer-related military actions that have already occurred and reflects an awareness of the need to plan for the future. Computer networks, communication systems, and other resources not only are prime targets to reconfigure or destroy in a war or crisis, but they are also good tools to use to watch other nations' movements and to evaluate their intentions during peacetime.

The antes are being raised, security issues are becoming more serious, and the effects are more detrimental. Take the necessary steps to protect yourself, your company, and your country.

Hacking and Attacking

There has been a distinct evolution of hacking, cracking, and attacking. At one time, it was a compliment to be called a hacker because it meant you took the time to learn things about computers that others did not know and had the discipline and desire to find out what makes a computer tick. These people did not perform malicious acts, but rather were the ones called upon when really tough problems left everyone else scratching their heads.

As computers became more widespread as tools, this definition started to change. The new hackers took on a profile of geeky young men who would rather spend their time pinging computers all over the Internet than looking for dates. Even this profile has evolved. Girls and women have joined this once all-male club and are just as knowledgeable and dangerous as the guys. Hacking is on the rise, and the profile of an attacker is changing. However, the real change in the profile is that the serious attackers indulge themselves for specific reasons and have certain types of damage or fraud in mind.

The dangerous attacker is the one who is willing to do his homework. He will build a profile about the victim, find all the necessary information, and uncover many possible ways of getting into an environment before actually attempting it. The more an attacker knows about the environment, the more access points he has at his disposal. Attackers are usually groups of determined and knowledgeable individuals that are hard to stop.

Another dangerous evolutionary pattern is that the tools available to hackers these days are easy to use. It used to take a certain skill set to be able to enter a computer through a port, reconfigure system files, find the hidden data, and get out without being noticed. Today, there are many tools with graphical user interface (GUI) front-ends that only require a person to enter an IP address or range, and then click the Start button. Some of these tools provide a quiet mode, which means the interrogations and exploit attempts will use methods and protocols that may not show up on intrusion detection systems (IDSs) or cause the user of that computer to recognize something is going on. These tools enable people to carry out sophisticated attacks even if they do not understand the tool or the attack itself.

The proliferation of tools on the Internet, the ease of use of these tools, and the availability of web sites and books describing exactly how to exploit vulnerabilities have greatly increased the hacker population. So, some attack tools whose creation may have required in-depth knowledge of protocol behaviors or expert programming skills are now available to a wide range of people who have not necessarily heard of Transmission Control Protocol/Internet Protocol (TCP/IP).

As more vulnerabilities are uncovered every week, many more people are interested in trying out the exploits. Some just want to satisfy their curiosity, some want bragging rights over other hackers, and some have distinct destructive goals to accomplish (most have financial gain in mind).

There is another aspect to hacking and attacking, though. It is natural to focus on the evil aspects, but hacking can also be looked at as a continuous challenge to the computing society to come up with better products, practices, and procedures. If hackers were not continually trying to break products, the products would not necessarily continue to evolve in the way they have. Sure, products would continue to grow in functionality, but not necessarily in security.

So maybe instead of looking at hackers as selfish individuals out to cause harm and destruction, they can be looked at as the thorn in the side of the computing society that keeps it on its toes and ensures that the next product will provide greater functionality, but in a secure manner.

Management

Security is a complex matter for many companies. Management usually feels the IT department is responsible for choosing the correct technologies, installing and maintaining them, and keeping the environment secure. In general, management has never really been pulled inside the realm of computers and the issues that surround them. This distance and mentality hurts many companies when it comes to dealing with security effectively.

Historically, management has been responsible only for hitting its numbers—whether it be profit margins, sales goals, or productivity marks—and for managing people and projects. It has not had to think much about firewalls, hackers, and security breaches. However, this mindset is fading, and the new trend demands that management be much more involved in security and aware of how it affects the company as a whole.

It is management's responsibility to set the tone for what role security will play in the organization. Management must decide which data is valuable and needs to be protected, who is responsible for protecting the data, to what extent employees may access and use the data, and what the consequences are for noncompliance. However, as of this writing, few corporations see these issues in this light and instead bounce the responsibility for security back to the IT staff. The reason, usually, is not that management is trying to avoid blame for security lapses or to shirk its responsibility, but rather that it lacks understanding of what information and enterprise security entails. Many organizations incorrectly assume that information security is a technical issue. It is not. Information security is a management issue that may require technical solutions. This is why information security professionals are so important. They must understand not only the goals and objectives of the organization, but also the technical issues involved in securing those assets that are most important.

Good security does not begin and end with erecting a firewall and installing antivirus software. Good security is planned, designed, implemented, and maintained, and is capable of evolving. For security to be a good fit for a company, it must be in line with the company's business goals and objectives. Management needs to understand security issues and how security affects the company and its customers so that proper resources, time, and funding can be provided. In other words, information security should be applied in a top-down approach. Unfortunately, many times security is kept within the IT department, which can be overwhelmed with daily tasks and dealing with weekly disasters. In these cases, security is done in a reactive, bottom-up approach, which drastically reduces its effectiveness. In addition, when the IT department requests funds for security purposes, their entreaty often falls on deaf ears.

It is too much responsibility to put the full brunt of the security of a whole company on the IT department. Security must be understood, supported, and funded from the top down. Management does not need to know the security mechanisms used, the protocols in place, or the configurations of components, but it does need to set the stage for everyone else to follow. Management should provide the framework, as well as the delegate who will fill in the rest.

In February 2004, Wells Fargo Bank suffered its second theft of a laptop computer that contained confidential information from its customer database. The first laptop that was stolen, in November 2003, contained a database of 200,000 customer records. In the February 2004 incident, two Wells Fargo employees were in a St. Louis, Missouri, gas station/convenience store, with their rental car parked outside. When they returned to their car, all the contents of the vehicle, including the laptop in the trunk, were gone. Wells Fargo waited more than a month before it notified the affected customers.

In early December 2006, the laptop of an employee of Boeing in Seattle, Washington, was stolen from his car. The computer contained files with the names, salary information, Social Security numbers, home addresses, phone numbers, and dates of birth of both former and current employees. In all, the information of more than 382,000 individuals was lost. The day after the event was reported, Boeing fired the employee who lost the laptop. Over a month later, the laptop was recovered, but the extent of the damage could never be fully determined.

On November 23, 2006, two computers (a desktop and a laptop) were stolen from Electronic Registry Systems, a contractor that provides cancer patient registry data processing services. The files on these computers contained the personal information of cancer patients from hospitals in Tennessee, Ohio, Georgia, and Pennsylvania dating back to 1977 at some of the facilities. The theft affected more than 63,000 patients.

Thefts like this can occur at any time and to anyone within an organization. In another incident, on December 6, 2006, a report containing the names and account numbers of 1,800 customers was stolen from the car of the vice president of Premier Bank. Luckily, no Social Security numbers were involved.

In August 2008, around 130 employees from UCLA Medical Center were accused of prying into medical records of celebrities and other individuals. One person sold Farrah

Fawcett's personal information on her cancer treatment. It is reported that George Cloo-ney's medical information was breached after he was involved in a motorcycle accident.

In 2009, the Department of Veterans Affairs (VA) agreed to pay $20 million to mil-itary and nonmilitary personnel who initiated a class action lawsuit. In 2006, a laptop and external hard drive were stolen, which contained the names, dates of birth, and Social Security numbers of about 26.5 million active duty troops and veterans.

The FBI reported in January 2009 that laptop thefts have increased around 48 percent over the last two years. They also reported that mobile phone robberies have increased by 33 percent. Since 2006, MP3 player thefts have risen by 91 percent. Today the information we keep on mobile phones and digital players ranges from personal e-mails to sensitive company data.

The Computer Security Institute's 2008 Computer Crime & Security Survey stated that theft costs a majority of the large corporations an average of 640 laptops, 1,985 USB memory sticks, 1,075 smart phones, and 1,324 other data devices per year. The institute estimates that each year up to 800,000 memory devices (laptops, smart phones, memory sticks) are lost or stolen.

When a company is hacked and thousands of customers' credit cards are stolen, in-tellectual property is taken, confidential information is leaked, or the organization's reputation is damaged, the management will be held accountable and expected to ex-plain why due diligence and due care were not practiced in protecting the company and its resources. These explanations may be given to corporate offices, shareholders, judges, and customers. So it should be management who truly understand how security works within the organization and who should be calling the shots from the beginning.

A Layered Approach

Networks have advanced in functionality and complexity. Because vulnerabilities can take place at different layers of an infrastructure, it has been necessary for vendors, de-velopers, administrators, and security professionals to understand these layers and how each should be protected.

Often, you hear about a "layered approach" (or defense-in-depth approach) to security. You are supposed to implement different layers of protection to protect networks from different types of attacks. But what does a layered approach really mean? How do you know if you are applying a layered approach?

These are excellent questions that should be explored in depth if you are serious about protecting your interior and exterior networks from all possible security compro-mises and breaches. To protect an environment, you must truly understand the environ-ment, the fixes to be applied, the differences among the numerous vendor applications and hardware variations, and how attacks are actually performed. The road to a secure environment is a winding one, with some bumps, sharp turns, and attacks that lunge out from the dark. However, the most important thing when navigating this road to security is to understand the facets of the adventure and that the road never ends.

The description of a layered approach to security can be an abstract and nebulous topic because theory must be represented and implemented in reality. Many times, a layered approach means implementing solutions at different spectrums of the network.

The spectrums can range from the programming code, the protocols that are being used, the operating system, and the application configurations, through to user activity and the security program that is supposed to govern all of these issues. A layered approach presents layers of barriers that an attacker must go through and compromise to get to the sought-after resource. Running antivirus software only on workstations is not a layered approach in battling viruses. Running antivirus software on each workstation, file server, and mail server and applying content filtering via a proxy server is considered a layered approach toward combating viruses. This is just one example of what must take place.

How is file access protection provided in a layered approach? If an administrator puts all users in specific groups and dictates what those groups can and cannot do with the company's files, this is only one layer in the approach. To properly protect file access, the administrator must do the following:

- Configure application, file, and Registry access control lists (ACLs) to provide more granularity to users' and groups' file permissions.
- Configure the system default user rights (in a Windows environment) to give certain types of users certain types of rights.
- Consider the physical security of the environment and the computers, and apply restraints where required.
- Place users into groups that have implicit permissions necessary to perform their duties—and no more.
- Draft and enforce a strict logon credential policy so that not all users are logging on as the same user.
- Implement monitoring and auditing of file access and actions to identify any suspicious activity.

Sound like overkill? It really isn't. If an administrator makes all users log in using different accounts, applies file and Registry ACLs, configures groups, and monitors audit logs but does not consider physical security, a user could use a USB drive with a simple program to get around all other security barriers. All of these components must work in a synergistic manner to provide a blanket of security that individual security mechanisms could not fulfill on their own.

An Architectural View

Once we look at different types of vulnerabilities, attacks, and threats, we find they exist at different layers within a network. We dig into more of the technology of an environment and the complexity of each of these technologies at each layer. This applies to the various protocols, applications, hardware, and security mechanisms that work at one or more of the seven layers of the OSI model. (The OSI model is fully described in Chapter 7.) IP spoofing is an attack at the network layer, ARP attacks happen at the data link layer, traffic sniffing occurs at several layers, and viruses enter through the application layer. If an organization just employs strict password rules and a firewall, it leaves many layers vulnerable to other types of attacks.

Organizations often put too much faith in their shiny new firewalls, IDSs, and antivirus software. Once one or more of these solutions are implemented, a false sense of security may lull the IT staff and travel up to management. It is more important to look at the flow of data in and out of a network and how the applications and devices work together. This is an architectural view, versus a device or application view.

Taking an architectural view, you must look at the data flow in and out of the environment, how this data is being accessed, modified, and monitored at different points, and how all the security solutions relate to each other in different situations. The firewall, for instance, is only part of the overall architecture. It is the architecture itself that needs to have an adequate level of security, not just the firewall. A network could either perform as a well-tuned orchestra or as several pieces that play wonderfully by themselves but that give you a headache when they are all brought into the same room. Each individual security component could be doing its job by protecting its piece of the network, but the security function may be lost when it is time to interrelate or communicate with another security component.

Each environment is dissimilar because of the many variations in installed hardware, software, technologies, and configurations. However, the main differences between environments are the goals each is trying to achieve. A local area network (LAN) provides authentication, resources to its users, and an overall controlled inner atmosphere. A wide area network (WAN) provides connections between users at remote sites through protocol tunneling and access control. An e-commerce arrangement provides a web interface to Internet users, connection to data held on back-end servers, access control, and a different type of authentication from what LANs and WANs use. These diverse goals require different architectures, but can use the same basic security concepts.

A Layer Missed

Many environments do not contain all the devices and components in the previous list of security vulnerabilities and solutions. The following example shows how employing several security mechanisms can seemingly provide a fully secured environment yet leave a small doorway of opportunity available that the clever attacker can take advantage of.

A network that has a firewall with packet filtering, a proxy server with content filtering, its public and private DNS records clearly separated, SSL for Internet users, IPSec for VPN connections, and public key infrastructure (PKI), as well as restricted service and port configuration, may seem like a fortified environment, and a network administrator most likely implemented these mechanisms with the best intentions. However, one problem is that it is fortified only for a moment in time. Without a scanning device that probes the environment on a scheduled basis or an IDS that looks out for suspicious activity, the environment could be vulnerable even after the company has spent thousands of dollars to protect it. Technology and business drivers continually change, and so do networks and environments. When you configure a new application, apply a patch, or install a device, the change to the environment could have unpredictable consequences (not to mention the new ways hackers have found to circumvent the original security mechanisms).

Bringing the Layers Together

It is not always necessary to purchase the newest security solutions on the market or to pay top dollar for the hardware solution instead of buying the cheaper software solution. It *is* necessary to be aware of where threats can develop and to take steps to make sure all your bases are covered. That's what is meant by a layered approach.

In the computer and network world, the complexity of the levels can be a bit overwhelming at times. The most important first step is to understand the environment that needs to be protected. Many times, new IT members enter an environment that was established years ago by another group of people. The environment is continually added on to; it is never stagnant. Usually, there is no up-to-date network diagram because IT's daily tasks are time-consuming, there is a lack of useful documentation, and no one person understands how the entire network works. This means that when something goes wrong, 80 percent of the effort and time is spent in a chaotic scramble for a solution. It does not need to work this way, and there would be fewer security compromises if this scene were not so common.

Instead of looking at updating that old network diagram (or creating a first one) as a boring task, you could approach it as a fact-finding mission for crucial information. Instead of putting down the IT staff after a successful hacker attack, you could change your attitude and think of what new practices need to be employed. New software, patches, and devices should be tested prior to implementation for any unforeseen events. An IDS should be established in potentially vulnerable segments of the network, if not in all segments. Security scans to seek out new vulnerabilities should take place regularly, not just when an audit is around the corner. In addition, every security administrator should stay up-to-date on the recent security compromises, be aware of how changes to the network could open a door to clever attackers, and keep those intrusion detection and antivirus signatures current.

Keeping current on network, software, configurations, and education can be overwhelming, but most of us in this line of work love to learn. Being effective in managing security means we will never stop learning.

Education

Generally, if a person is considered a security specialist, she must have the interest and discipline to teach herself security issues, go to seminars and conferences all over the world, read stacks of books, and have a wide range of experience in different environments. There has been no uniform, standardized way of teaching security in vocational schools or universities in the past. Some educational institutions offer security classes in their CIS or MIS programs, and some offer master's degrees or doctorates in computer security. However, such programs are few and far between.

Networking, programming, and engineering are widely taught. Security may be sprinkled in as an elective or not even offered because there has not been a high demand or need for this type of knowledge in the job market. However, computer and information security is gaining in importance, need, and demand. This has caused several schools to offer security classes and programs, and others will probably become available as the job market demands more individuals with this skill set.

NOTE To find out about colleges offering security programs that have met the NSA's Center of Excellence criteria, visit www.nsa.gov/ia/academia/caeiae.cfm.

Not only do more security courses and programs need to be offered, but business, networking, programming, and engineering classes also must integrate security education into them. Security should not be looked upon as an extra component or an option to be added later. It should be interwoven into the code as a program is being developed, and interwoven into the education of our new professionals. It should be an important piece of architecture and engineering, and it should be understood and practiced when networks are being built, added to, and maintained.

Most governments have recognized that education is an important part of protecting their country's critical infrastructure. Countries have set up criteria for schools to follow, with government grants and subsidies awarded as incentives for schools who meet the criteria. If countries want to protect themselves and their resources from computer attacks and cyberattacks, they must provide their citizens with the necessary education.

Summary

This chapter has touched on only a few of the exciting things that are happening within the field of computer and information security and has presented the types of damage that can occur if security is not taken seriously. It has been recognized for quite some time that computers, data processing capabilities, and the Internet are extremely important tools for a vast array of reasons, but it has only recently been recognized that securing these items is an important task.

This chapter is intended to prepare you for the chapters that follow. Some chapters, or sections within chapters, might seem more interesting than others, but the CISSP certification was developed to ensure that you broaden your horizon when looking at, and dealing with, security issues. Information security would not be as effective if it were not provided with strong physical security. Thus, it is important to know how each part works, and how they overlap and integrate. No part of security would be totally effective if it were not enforced by regulations, laws, and liability responsibilities. The courts and law enforcement agencies are becoming more involved in many issues of computer security, and understanding these issues can help you determine what is acceptable and what is illegal, and how to deal with the issues that fall in between.

Each chapter hereafter ends with a section called "Quick Tips." This section provides a clear-cut bulleted list of items that outlines what is important in the chapter for the CISSP exam. The same is true for the questions at the end of the chapter and on the accompanying CD-ROM; they help you zero-in on some of the most critical concepts in the chapter. As stated before, these questions are presented in such a way as to prepare you for the exam. Each type of exam has its own way of asking questions. Novell and Microsoft may give simulations and longwinded, scenario-based questions. Cisco gives short questions that get right to the point. (ISC)² asks short, cognitive questions and added scenario-based questions to the exam as of 2007. Knowing how the exam is structured will help you achieve the CISSP certification.

Information Security and Risk Management

This chapter presents the following:
- Security management responsibilities
- Difference between administrative, technical, and physical controls
- Three main security principles
- Risk management and risk analysis
- Security policies
- Information classification
- Security-awareness training

We hear about viruses causing millions of dollars in damages, hackers from other countries capturing credit card information from financial institutions, web sites of large corporations and governments being defaced for political reasons, and hackers being caught and sent to jail. These are the more exciting aspects of computer security, but realistically these activities are not what the average corporation or security professional must usually deal with when it comes to daily or monthly security tasks. Although viruses and hacking get all the headlines, security management is the core of a company's business and information security structure.

Security Management

Security management includes risk management, information security policies, procedures, standards, guidelines, baselines, information classification, security organization, and security education. These core components serve as the foundation of a corporation's security program. The objective of security, and a security program, is to protect the company and its assets. A risk analysis identifies these assets, discovers the threats that put them at risk, and estimates the possible damage and potential loss a company could endure if any of these threats were to become real. The risk analysis helps management construct a budget with the necessary funds to protect the recognized assets from their identified threats and develop applicable security policies that provide direction for security activities. Security education and awareness takes this information to each and every employee within the company so everyone is properly informed and can more easily work toward the same security goals.

The process of security management is a continuous one that begins with the assessment of risks and the determination of needs, followed by the monitoring and evaluation of the systems and practices involved. This is then followed by the promoting of awareness, which would involve making all the necessary elements of the organization understand the issues that need to be addressed. The last step is the implementation of policies and controls intended to address the risks and needs first defined. Then the cycle starts all over again. In this way, the process continually evaluates and monitors the security environment of an organization and allows it to adapt and grow to meet its security needs.

Security management has changed over the years because networked environments, computers, and the applications that hold information have changed. Information used to be held in a mainframe, which is a more centralized network structure. The mainframe and management consoles used to access and configure the mainframe were placed in a centralized area instead of having the distributed networks we see today. Only certain people were allowed access, and only a small set of people knew how the mainframe worked, which drastically reduced security risks. Users were able to access information on the mainframe through "dumb" terminals (they were called this because they had little or no logic built into them). There was not much need for strict security controls to be put into place. However, the computing society did not stay in this type of architecture. Now, most networks are filled with personal computers that have advanced logic and processing power; users know enough about the systems to be dangerous; and the information is not centralized within one "glass house." Instead, the information lives on servers, workstations, and other networks. Information passes over wires and airways at a rate not even conceived of 10 to 15 years ago.

The Internet, extranets (business partner networks), and intranets not only make security much more complex, but they also make security even more critical. The core network architecture has changed from being a localized, stand-alone computing environment to a distributed computing environment that has increased exponentially with complexity. Although connecting a network to the Internet adds more functionality and services for the users and expands the company's visibility to the Internet world, it opens the floodgates to potential security risks.

Today, a majority of organizations could not function if they were to lose their computers and computing capabilities. Computers have been integrated into the business and individual daily fabric, and their sudden unavailability would cause great pain and disruption. Many of the larger corporations already realize that their *data* is as much an asset to be protected as their physical buildings, factory equipment, and other physical assets. As networks and environments have changed, so has the need for security. Security is more than just a firewall and a router with an access list; these systems must be managed, and a big part of security is managing the actions of users and the procedures they follow. This brings us to security management practices, which focus on the continuous protection of company assets.

Security Management Responsibilities

Okay, who is in charge and why?

In the world of security, management's functions involve determining objectives, scope, policies, priorities, and strategies. Management needs to define a clear scope and, before 100 people run off in different directions trying to secure the environment, to determine actual goals expected to be accomplished from a security program. Management also needs to evaluate business objectives, security risks, user productivity, and functionality requirements and objectives. Finally, management must define steps to ensure that all of these issues are accounted for and properly addressed.

Many companies look at the business and productivity elements of the equation only and figure that information and computer security fall within the IT administrator's responsibilities. In these situations, management is not taking computer and information security seriously, the consequence of which is that security will most likely remain underdeveloped, unsupported, underfunded, and unsuccessful. Security needs to be addressed at the highest levels of management. The IT administrator can consult with management on the subject, but the security of a company should not be delegated entirely to the IT or security administrator.

Security management relies on properly identifying and valuing a company's assets, and then implementing security policies, procedures, standards, and guidelines to provide integrity, confidentiality, and availability for those assets. Various management tools are used to classify data and perform risk analysis and assessments. These tools identify vulnerabilities and exposure rates and rank the severity of identified vulnerabilities so that effective countermeasures can be implemented to mitigate risk in a cost-effective manner. Management's responsibility is to provide protection for the resources it is responsible for and the company overall. These resources come in human, capital, hardware, and informational forms. Management must concern itself with ensuring that a security program is set up that recognizes the threats that can affect these resources and be assured that the necessary protective measures are put into effect.

The necessary resources and funding need to be available, and strategic representatives must be ready to participate in the security program. Management must assign responsibility and identify the roles necessary to get the security program off the ground and to keep it thriving and evolving as the environment changes. Management must also integrate the program into the current business environment and monitor its accomplishments. Management's support is one of the most important pieces of a security program. A simple nod and a wink will not provide the amount of support required.

The Top-Down Approach to Security

I will be making the rules around here.
Response: You are nowhere near the top—thank goodness!

When a house is built, the workers start with a blueprint of the structure, then pour the foundation, and then erect the frame. As the building of the house continues, the workers know what the end result is supposed to be, so they add the right materials, insert doors and windows as specified in the blueprints, erect support beams, provide sturdy ceilings and floors, and add the plaster and carpet and smaller details until the house is complete. Then inspectors come in to ensure that the structure of the house and the components used to make it are acceptable. If this process did not start with a blueprint and a realized goal, the house could end up with an unstable foundation and doors and windows that don't shut properly. As a result, the house would not pass inspection—meaning much time and money would have been wasted.

Building a security program is analogous to building a house. When designing and implementing a security program, the security professionals must determine the functionality and realize the end result expected. Many times, companies just start locking down computers and installing firewalls without taking the time to understand the overall security requirements, goals, and assurance levels they expect from security as a whole within their environment. The team involved in the process should start from the top with very broad ideas and terms and work its way down to detailed configuration settings and system parameters. At each step, the team should keep in mind the overall security goals so each piece it adds will provide more granularity to the intended goal. This helps the team avoid splintering the main objectives by running in 15 different directions at once.

The next step is to develop and implement procedures, standards, and guidelines that support the security policy and to identify the security countermeasures and methods to be put into place. Once these items are developed, the security program increases in granularity by developing baselines and configurations for the chosen security controls and methods.

If security starts with a solid foundation and develops over time with understood goals and objectives, a company does not need to make drastic changes midstream. The process can be methodical, requiring less time, funds, and resources, and provide a proper balance between functionality and protection. This is not the norm, but with your insight, maybe you can help your company approach security in a more controlled manner. You could provide the necessary vision and understanding of how security should be properly planned and implemented, and how it should evolve in an organized manner, thereby helping the company avoid a result that is essentially a giant heap of disjointed, flawed security products.

A security program should use a *top-down approach*, meaning that the initiation, support, and direction come from top management, work their way through middle management, and then reach staff members. In contrast, a *bottom-up approach* refers to a situation in which the IT department tries to develop a security program without getting proper management support and direction. A bottom-up approach is usually less effective, not broad enough, and doomed to fail. A top-down approach makes sure the people actually responsible for protecting the company's assets (senior management) are driving the program.

Security Administration and Supporting Controls

We have this ladder, some rubber bands, and this Band-Aid.
Response: Okay, we have supporting controls covered then.

If no security officer role currently exists, one should be established by management. The security officer role is directly responsible for monitoring a majority of the facets of a security program. Depending on the organization, security needs, and size of the environment, the security administration may consist of one person or a group of individuals who work in a central or decentralized manner. Whatever its size, the security administration requires a clear reporting structure, an understanding of responsibilities, and testing and monitoring capabilities to make sure compromises do not slip in because of a lack of communication or comprehension.

Information owners should dictate which users can access their resources and what those users can do with those resources after they access them. The security administration's job is to make sure these objectives are implemented. The following controls should be utilized to achieve management's security directives:

- **Administrative controls** These include the developing and publishing of policies, standards, procedures, and guidelines; risk management; the screening of personnel; conducting security-awareness training; and implementing change control procedures.

- **Technical controls (also called logical controls)** These consist of implementing and maintaining access control mechanisms, password and resource management, identification and authentication methods, security devices, and the configuration of the infrastructure.

- **Physical controls** These entail controlling individual access into the facility and different departments, locking systems and removing unnecessary floppy or CD-ROM drives, protecting the perimeter of the facility, monitoring for intrusion, and environmental controls.

Figure 3-1 illustrates how the administrative, technical, and physical controls work together to provide the necessary level of protection.

The *information owner* (also called the data owner) is usually a senior executive within the management group of the company, or the head of a specific department. The information owner has the corporate responsibility for data protection and would be the one held liable for any negligence when it comes to protecting the company's information assets. The person who holds this role is responsible for assigning classifications to information and for dictating how the data should be protected. If the information owner does not lay out the foundation of data protection and ensure the directives are being enforced, she would be violating the due care concept.

 NOTE *Due care* is a legal term and concept used to help determine liability in a court of law. If someone is practicing due care, they are acting responsibly and will have a lower probability of being found negligent and liable if something bad takes place.

By having a security administration group, a company ensures it does not lose focus on security and that it has a hierarchical structure of responsibility in place. The security officer's job is to ensure that management's security directives are fulfilled, not to construct those directives in the first place. There should be a clear communication path between the security administration group and senior management to make certain the security program receives the proper support and to ensure management makes

Figure 3-1 Administrative, technical, and physical controls should work in a synergistic manner to protect a company's assets.

the decisions. Too often, senior management is extremely disconnected from security issues, despite the fact that when a serious security breach takes place, senior management must explain the reasons to business partners, shareholders, and the public. After this humbling experience, the opposite problem tends to arise—senior management becomes too involved. A healthy relationship between the security administration

An Example of Security Management

Anyone who has been involved with a security initiative understands it involves a balancing act between securing an environment and still allowing the necessary level of functionality so that productivity is not affected. A common scenario that occurs at the start of many security projects is that the individuals in charge of the project know the end result they want to achieve and have lofty ideas of how quick and efficient their security rollout will be, but they fail to consult the users regarding what restrictions will be placed upon them. The users, upon hearing of the restrictions, then inform the project managers that they will not be able to fulfill certain parts of their job if the security rollout actually takes place as planned. This usually causes the project to screech to a halt. The project managers then must initialize the proper assessments, evaluations, and planning to see how the environment can be slowly secured and how to ease users and tasks delicately into new restrictions or ways of doing business. Failing to consult users or to fully understand business processes during the planning phase causes many headaches and wastes time and money. Individuals who are responsible for security management activities must realize they need to understand the environment and plan properly before kicking off the implementation phase of a security program.

group and senior management should be developed from the beginning, and communication should easily flow in both directions.

Inadequate management can undermine the entire security effort in a company. Among the possible reasons for inadequate management are that management does not fully understand the necessity of security; security is in competition with other management goals; management views security as expensive and unnecessary; or management applies lip service instead of real support to security. Powerful and useful technologies, devices, software packages, procedures, and methodologies are available to provide the exact level of security required, but without proper security management and management support, none of this really matters.

Fundamental Principles of Security

Now, what are we trying to accomplish again?

Security programs have several small and large objectives, but the three main principles in all programs are availability, integrity, and confidentiality. These are referred to as the *AIC triad*. The level of security required to accomplish these principles differs with each company, because each has its own unique combination of business and security goals and requirements. All security controls, mechanisms, and safeguards are implemented to provide one or more of these principles, and all risks, threats, and vulnerabilities are measured for their potential capability to compromise one or all of the AIC principles. Figure 3-2 illustrates the AIC triad. Some documentation on this topic may reverse the acronym order, calling it the *CIA triad*, but it still refers to the concepts shown in Figure 3-2.

Availability

Emergency! I can't get to my data!
Response: Turn the computer on!

The systems and networks should provide adequate capacity to perform in a predictable manner with an acceptable level of performance. They should be able to recover from disruptions in a secure and quick manner so productivity is not negatively affected. Single points of failure should be avoided, backup measures should be taken, redundancy mechanisms should be in place when necessary, and the negative effects from environmental components should be prevented. Necessary protection mechanisms must be in place to protect against inside and outside threats that could affect the availability and productivity of the network, systems, and information. *Availability* ensures reliability and timely access to data and resources to authorized individuals.

System availability can be affected by device or software failure. Backup devices should be used and be available to quickly replace critical systems, and employees should be skilled and on hand to make the necessary adjustments to bring the system back online. Environmental issues like heat, cold, humidity, static electricity, and contaminants can also affect system availability. These issues are addressed in detail in Chapter 6. Systems should be protected from these elements, properly grounded electrically, and closely monitored.

Figure 3-2
The AIC triad

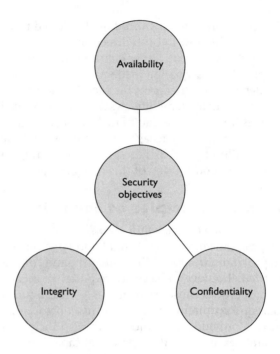

Integrity

Integrity is upheld when the assurance of the accuracy and reliability of the information and systems is provided, and any unauthorized modification is prevented. Hardware, software, and communication mechanisms must work in concert to maintain and process data correctly and to move data to intended destinations without unexpected alteration. The systems and network should be protected from outside interference and contamination.

Environments that enforce and provide this attribute of security ensure that attackers, or mistakes by users, do not compromise the integrity of systems or data. When an attacker inserts a virus, logic bomb, or back door into a system, the system's integrity is compromised. This can, in turn, harm the integrity of information held on the system by way of corruption, malicious modification, or the replacement of data with incorrect data. Strict access controls, intrusion detection, and hashing can combat these threats.

Users usually affect a system or its data's integrity by mistake (although internal users may also commit malicious deeds). For example, users with a full hard drive may unwittingly delete configuration files under the mistaken assumption that deleting a boot.ini file must be okay because they don't remember ever using it. Or, for example, a user may insert incorrect values into a data processing application that ends up charging a customer $3 million instead of $300. Incorrectly modifying data kept in databases is another common way users may accidentally corrupt data—a mistake that can have lasting effects.

Security should streamline users' capabilities and give them only certain choices and functionality, so errors become less common and less devastating. System-critical files should be restricted from viewing and access by users. Applications should provide mechanisms that check for valid and reasonable input values. Databases should let only authorized individuals modify data, and data in transit should be protected by encryption or other mechanisms.

Confidentiality

Confidentiality ensures that the necessary level of secrecy is enforced at each junction of data processing and prevents unauthorized disclosure. This level of confidentiality should prevail while data resides on systems and devices within the network, as it is transmitted, and once it reaches its destination.

Attackers can thwart confidentiality mechanisms by network monitoring, shoulder surfing, stealing password files, and social engineering. These topics will be addressed in more depth in later chapters, but briefly, *shoulder surfing* is when a person looks over another person's shoulder and watches their keystrokes or views data as it appears on a computer screen. *Social engineering* is when one person tricks another person into sharing confidential information, for example, by posing as someone authorized to have access to that information. Social engineering can take many other forms. Indeed, any one-to-one communication medium can be used to perform social engineering attacks.

Users can intentionally or accidentally disclose sensitive information by not encrypting it before sending it to another person, by falling prey to a social engineering attack, by sharing a company's trade secrets, or by not using extra care to protect confidential information when processing it.

Confidentiality can be provided by encrypting data as it is stored and transmitted; by using network traffic padding, strict access control, and data classification; and by training personnel on the proper procedures.

Availability, integrity, and confidentiality are critical principles of security. You should understand their meaning, how they are provided by different mechanisms, and how their absence can negatively affect an environment, all of which help you best identify problems and provide proper solutions.

Every solution, whether it be a firewall, consultant, or security program, must be evaluated by its functional requirements and its assurance requirements. *Functional requirements* evaluation means, "Does this solution carry out the required tasks?" *Assurance requirements* evaluation means, "How sure are we of the level of protection this solution provides?" Assurance requirements encompass the integrity, availability, and confidentially aspects of the solution.

Security Definitions

I am vulnerable and see you as a threat.
Response: Good.

The words "vulnerability," "threat," "risk," and "exposure" often are used to represent the same thing, even though they have different meanings and relationships to each other. It is important to understand each word's definition, but it is more important to understand each concept's relationship to the other concepts.

A *vulnerability* is a software, hardware, procedural, or human weakness that may provide an attacker the open door he is looking for to enter a computer or network and have unauthorized access to resources within the environment. A vulnerability characterizes the absence or weakness of a safeguard that could be exploited. This vulnerability may be a service running on a server, unpatched applications or operating system software, unrestricted modem dial-in access, an open port on a firewall, lax physical security that allows anyone to enter a server room, or unenforced password management on servers and workstations.

A *threat* is any potential danger to information or systems. The threat is that someone, or something, will identify a specific vulnerability and use it against the company or individual. The entity that takes advantage of a vulnerability is referred to as a *threat agent*. A threat agent could be an intruder accessing the network through a port on the firewall, a process accessing data in a way that violates the security policy, a tornado wiping out a facility, or an employee making an unintentional mistake that could expose confidential information or destroy a file's integrity.

A *risk* is the likelihood of a threat agent taking advantage of a vulnerability and the corresponding business impact. If a firewall has several ports open, there is a higher likelihood that an intruder will use one to access the network in an unauthorized method. If users are not educated on processes and procedures, there is a higher likelihood that an employee will make an intentional or unintentional mistake that may destroy data. If an intrusion detection system (IDS) is not implemented on a network, there is a higher likelihood an attack will go unnoticed until it is too late. Risk ties the vulnerability, threat, and likelihood of exploitation to the resulting business impact.

An *exposure* is an instance of being exposed to losses from a threat agent. A vulnerability exposes an organization to possible damages. If password management is lax and password rules are not enforced, the company is exposed to the possibility of having users' passwords captured and used in an unauthorized manner. If a company does not have its wiring inspected and does not put proactive fire prevention steps into place, it exposes itself to potentially devastating fires.

A *countermeasure*, or *safeguard*, is put into place to mitigate the potential risk. A countermeasure may be a software configuration, a hardware device, or a procedure that eliminates a vulnerability or that reduces the likelihood a threat agent will be able to exploit a vulnerability. Examples of countermeasures include strong password management, a security guard, access control mechanisms within an operating system, the implementation of basic input/output system (BIOS) passwords, and security-awareness training.

If a company has antivirus software but does not keep the virus signatures up-to-date, this is a vulnerability. The company is vulnerable to virus attacks. The threat is that a virus will show up in the environment and disrupt productivity. The likelihood of a virus showing up in the environment and causing damage is the risk. If a virus infiltrates the company's environment, then a vulnerability has been exploited and the company is exposed to loss. The countermeasures in this situation are to update the signatures and install the antivirus software on all computers. The relationships among risks, vulnerabilities, threats, and countermeasures are shown in Figure 3-3.

Applying the right countermeasure can eliminate the vulnerability and exposure, and thus reduce the risk. The company cannot eliminate the threat agent, but it can protect itself and prevent this threat agent from exploiting vulnerabilities within the environment.

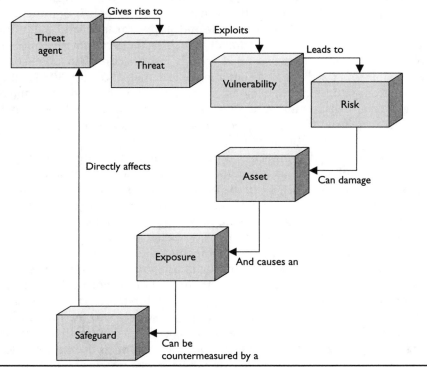

Figure 3-3   The relationships among the different security components

> ## Order of Concepts
>
> The proper order in which to evaluate these concepts as they apply to your own network is threat, exposure, vulnerability, countermeasures, and, lastly, risk. This is because there can be a threat (new SQL attack) but unless your company has the corresponding vulnerability (SQL server with the necessary configuration), the company is not exposed and it is not a vulnerability. If the vulnerability does reside in the environment, then a countermeasure is applied to reduce the risk.

Security Through Obscurity

We write all of the sensitive data backwards and upside down to fool the bad guys.

An improper understanding about the risks and requirements can lead to all kinds of problems for an organization. Typically, this results in bad security practices. Things such as security through obscurity become common practices that usually have damaging results. The root of the issue here is the lack of understanding about what the Information Age is really like, what kinds of tools malevolent forces have at their disposal, and the resourcefulness of attackers. This lack of understanding typically leads defenders to the most devastating mistake they can make: believing their opponent is less intelligent than they are. This leads to simple and sloppy mistakes and the proliferation of a false sense of security. Included are ideas such as: flaws cannot be exploited if they are not common knowledge; compiled code is more secure than open-source code because people can't see the code; moving HTTP traffic to port 8088 will provide enough protection; developing personal encryption algorithms will stop the crackers; and if we all wear Elvis costumes, no one can pick us out to conduct social engineering attacks. These are just a few of the kinds of potentially damaging ideas that can result from taking a security-by-obscurity approach.

This is a controversial approach and yet is principal in the areas of computer security and cryptography. Reliance on confusion to provide security can be dangerous. Though everyone wants to believe in the innate goodness of their fellow man, no security professional would have a job if this were actually true. In security, a good practice is illustrated by the old saying, "There are only two people in the world I trust: you and me . . . and I'm not so sure about you." This is a better attitude to take, because security really can be compromised by anyone, at any time.

A layperson's example of security through obscurity is the old practice of putting a spare key under a doormat in case you are locked out of the house. You assume that no one knows about the spare key, and as long as they don't, it can be considered secure. The vulnerability here is that anyone could gain easy access to the house if they have access to that hidden spare key, and the experienced attacker (in this example, a burglar) knows that these kinds of vulnerabilities exist and takes the appropriate steps to seek them out. This is the same thing with other security systems and practices. Setting up confusing or "tricky" countermeasures does not provide the assurance level that a solid, defense-in-depth, security program can.

In the world of cryptography, the Kerckhoffs' principle embodies the ideas against security through obscurity. Back in the 1880s, Mr. Kerckhoffs stated that no algorithm should be kept secret; only the key should be the secret component. His message is to

---

If Not Obscurity, Then What?

Throughout this book, best practices, open standards, and implementing and maintaining security controls in an effective manner will be discussed. The development of a security program with layers of protection may take more time in the beginning, but in the long run it provides a better chance of keeping your organization out of both the frying pan and the fire.

---

assume that the attacker can figure out your algorithm and its logic, so ensure that the key is properly protected—which the attacker would need to make the algorithm decode sensitive data.

Organizational Security Model

My security model is shaped like a pile of oatmeal.
Response: Lovely.

An organizational security model is a framework made up of many entities, protection mechanisms, logical, administrative, and physical components, procedures, business processes, and configurations that all work together to provide a security level for an environment. Each model is different, but all models work in layers: one layer provides support for the layer above it, and protection for the layer below it. Because a security model is a framework, companies are free to plug in different types of technologies, methods, and procedures to accomplish the necessary protection level for their environment. Figure 3-4 illustrates the pieces that can make up a security model.

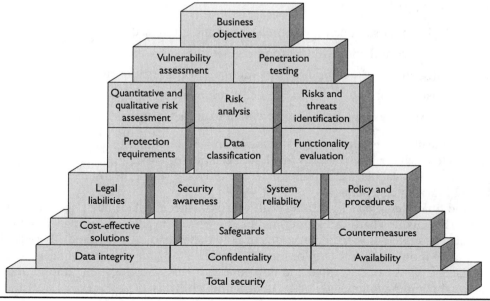

Figure 3-4 A comprehensive and effective security model has many integrated pieces.

Effective security requires a balanced approach and application of all security components and procedures. Some security components are technical (access control lists and encryption) and some are nontechnical (physical and administrative, such as developing a security policy and enforcing compliance), but each has an important place within the framework, and if one is missing or incomplete, the whole framework may be affected.

A security model has various layers, but it also has different types of goals to accomplish in different timeframes. You might have a goal for yourself today to brush your teeth, run three miles, finish the project you have been working on, and spend time with your kids. These are daily goals, or *operational goals*. You might have midterm goals: to complete your master's degree, write a book, and get promoted. These take more time and effort and are referred to as *tactical goals*. Your long-term goals may be to retire at age 55, save enough money to live comfortably, and live on a houseboat. These goals are *strategic goals* because they look farther into the future.

The same thing happens in security planning. Daily goals, or operational goals, focus on productivity and task-oriented activities to ensure that the company functions in a smooth and predictable manner. A midterm goal, or tactical goal, could be to integrate all workstations and resources into one domain so that more central control can be achieved. Long-term goals, or strategic goals, could be to move all the branches from dedicated communication lines to frame relay, implement IPSec virtual private networks (VPNs) for all remote users, and to integrate wireless technology with the necessary security measures into the environment.

Security planning can be broken down into three different areas: strategic, tactical, and operational. *Strategic* planning is the plans that fall in line with the business and information technology goals. The goals of strategic planning have a longer or broader horizon and can extend out as far as five years. Strategic planning may include some of the following goals:

- Make sure risks are properly understood and addressed.
- Ensure compliance with laws and regulations.
- Integrate security responsibilities throughout the organization.
- Create a maturity model to allow for continual improvement.
- Use security as a business achievement to attract more customers.

Tactical planning refers to the initiatives and other support that must be implemented to reach the broader goals that have been put forth by the strategic planning. In general, the tactical plans are shorter in length or have a shorter planning horizon than those of the strategic plans.

And finally, *operational* planning deals with very specific plans, their deadlines, and goals. This involves hard dates and timelines by which the goals of the plan should be completed, as well as specific directions in how they are to be completed. These goals tend to be more of a short-term or interim nature to mitigate risks until larger tactical or strategic plans can be created and implemented. The following are examples of operational planning to help you better understand what it is:

- Perform security risk assessment.
- Do not allow security changes to decrease productivity.
- Maintain and implement controls.
- Continually scan for vulnerabilities and roll out patches.
- Track compliance with policies.

This approach to planning is called the *planning horizon*. A company usually cannot implement all changes at once, and some changes are larger than others. Many times, certain changes cannot happen until other changes take place. If a company wants to implement its own certificate authority and implement a full public key infrastructure (PKI) enterprisewide, this cannot happen in a week if the company currently works in decentralized workgroups with no domain structure. So, its operational goals would be to keep production running smoothly and to make small steps toward readying the environment for a domain structure. Its tactical goal would be to put all workstations and resources into a domain structure, and to centralize access control and authentication. Its strategic goal would be to have all workstations, servers, and devices within the enterprise use the PKI to provide authentication, encryption, and more secure communication channels.

Security works best if the company's operational, tactical, and strategic goals are defined and work to support each other, which can be much harder than it sounds.

Security Program Components

I have a security policy, so I must have a security program.
Response: You have just begun, my friend.

Today, organizations, corporations, government agencies, and individuals are more involved in information security than ever before. With more regulations being promulgated by governments, continuing increases in both the number of attacks and the cost of fighting hackers and malware, and increasing dependence upon computing technology, concerns about information security are expanding from IT departments to the boardrooms.

Most security professionals welcome this shift because it means the decision makers are finally involved and more progress can be made enterprisewide. Experienced security professionals have always known that technology is just a small portion of overall organizational security. Businesspeople, who are now becoming more responsible and liable for security, are not so thrilled about this shift, however.

The common scenario in businesses and organizations is as follows: A CEO and board members eventually are forced to look at information security because of new regulations, because the costs of viruses and attacks have reached a threshold, or because a civil suit has been filed regarding a security breach. The company typically hires a consultant, who tells the CEO and board that they need a security policy and a network assessment. The company usually pays for both to be done and, with that accomplished, believes the company is secure. However, this is a false sense of security, because the company still has no security program.

The company then hires a security officer, typically called either a corporate security officer (CSO) or a chief information security officer (CISO). Senior management hires this person so they can delegate him or her all security activities and responsibilities, but fails to give this person any real authority or budget. Then, when security compromises take place, the CSO becomes the sacrificial lamb—because someone always needs to be blamed.

Now, as security professionals, we have three choices for dealing with this common scenario:

- Stick our heads in the sand, and hope all of this just goes away.
- Continue to be frustrated and confused, develop ulcers, and shake our fists at the unfriendly security gods in the sky.
- Understand that we, as a society, are in the first basic steps of our evolution in information security and therefore must be committed to learn and practice the industry's best practices.

The CISOs are responsible for having a strong understanding of the business processes and objectives for the organization, and then with that information they must be able to communicate to senior management about the risks that are threatening the organization, and what regulations and requirements the government has imposed that they will need to adhere to and comply with. This information will need to be reported to management through meetings and documentation. They will need to develop and provide security-awareness programs, and understand the business objectives of the organization. The CISOs will also need to develop the budget for any of the activities that are related to information security. Other tasks that will fall to the CISOs are the development of policies, procedures, baselines, standards, and guidelines. By having access to and understanding of this material, they can maintain awareness of emerging threats to and vulnerabilities of the organization. Staying abreast of emerging technologies will also provide them valuable information and tools they can implement or consider. Evaluation of responses to security incidents also falls to the CISO, as well as the task of developing a security compliance program and establishing security metrics. Auditors may be used during the evaluation processes, and they can be used from both internal and external sources. By fulfilling all of these job responsibilities and requirements, the CISO will be more effective in making sure the security of the organization is working properly and that it addresses the risks that the business environment may create for it.

It is important that the security elements of the organization report as high as possible in the chain of management. This is because with new government regulations and direct business impacts, it is vital that there is a limitation on any possible kinds of miscommunication that can potentially occur during the reporting process. It is also important that at whatever level the security elements are reporting to they maintain a strong working relationship that reinforces the credibility and reliability of the security elements. The last thing you want is the credibility of the CISO to come under question when they are reporting on the security of the organization. This is an individual who will be relied upon to properly report about the security status of the organization. This means when the CISO is reporting to the chief executive officer, it will not only reduce any miscommunications, but also ensure that the correct information is being provided to the proper individuals.

The CISO will also need to be reporting information to the information technology (IT) department as well as reporting to other elements of the organization such as security, the administrative services department, the insurance and risk management department, the legal department, the business unit, and the internal audit department. Effective and clear communications between the security elements and the other departments of the organization will go a long way toward enforcing security and mitigating risks.

Security Frameworks

The *Control Objectives for Information and related Technology (CobiT)* is a framework and set of best practices developed by the Information Systems Audit and Control Association (ISACA) and the IT Governance Institute (ITGI). It defines goals for the controls that should be used to properly manage IT and to ensure that IT maps to business needs. CobiT is broken down into four domains: Plan and Organize, Acquire and Implement, Deliver and Support, and Monitor and Evaluate. Each category drills down into subcategories. For example, the Acquire and Implement category contains the following subcategories:

- Acquire and Maintain Application Software
- Acquire and Maintain Technology Infrastructure
- Develop and Maintain Procedures
- Install and Accredit Systems
- Manage Changes

So this CobiT domain provides goals and guidance to companies when they purchase, install, test, certify, and accredit IT products. This is very powerful because most companies use an ad hoc and informal approach when making purchases and carrying out procedures.

CobiT lays out executive summaries, management guidelines, frameworks, control objectives, an implementation toolset, and audit guidelines. A majority of regulation compliance and audits are built on the CobiT framework. So if you want to make your auditors happy, you should learn, practice, and implement the control objects, which are considered industry best practices.

People who are new to CobiT quickly get overwhelmed by it, because it is massive and basically impossible to implement fully even in a 24-month period. Under each of these domains CobiT provides control objectives, control practices, goal indicators, performance indicators, success factors, and maturity models. It lays out a complete roadmap that can be followed to accomplish each of the 34 control objectives this model deals with.

Figure 3-5 illustrates how the framework connects business requirements, IT resources, and IT processes. Many IS auditors use this framework as their criteria when determining the efficiency of the implemented controls. This means that if you want to pass an assurance audit, it is a good idea to know and fulfill control objectives in your company as it makes sense.

CobiT was derived from the COSO framework, developed by the Committee of Sponsoring Organizations (COSO) of the Treadway Commission in 1985 to deal with fraudulent financial activities and reporting. The COSO framework is made up of the following components:

- **Control environment**
  - Management's philosophy and operating style
  - Company culture as it pertains to ethics and fraud
- **Risk assessment**
  - Establishment of risk objectives
  - Ability to manage internal and external change
- **Control activities**
  - Policies, procedures, and practices put in place to mitigate risk
- **Information and communication**
  - Structure that ensures that the right people get the right information at the right time
- **Monitoring**
  - Detecting and responding to control deficiencies

Figure 3-5
CobiT components

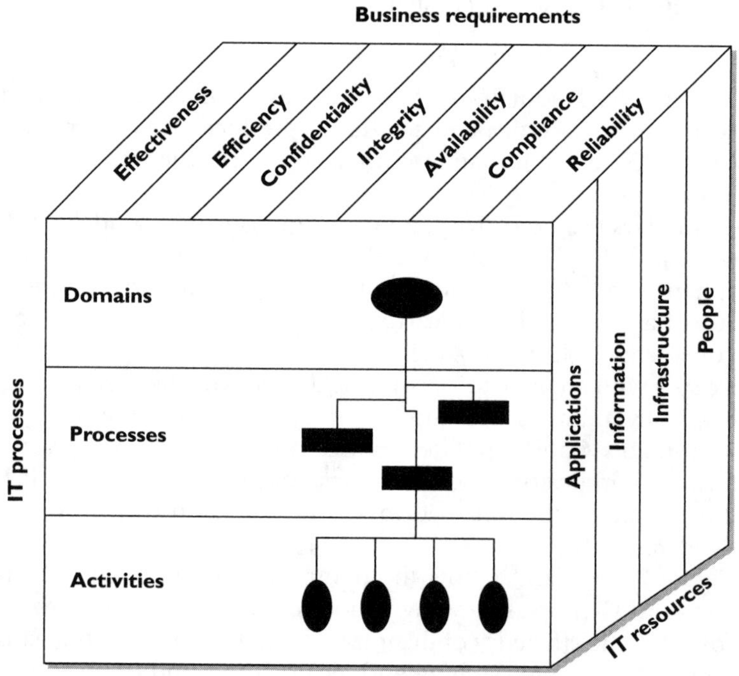

COSO is a model for corporate governance and CobiT is a model for IT governance. COSO deals more at the strategic level, while CobiT focuses more at the operational level. You can think of CobiT as a way to meet many of the COSO objectives, but only from the IT perspective. COSO deals with non-IT items also, as in company culture, financial accounting principles, board of director responsibility, and internal communication structures. COSO was formed to provide sponsorship for the National Commission on Fraudulent Financial Reporting, an organization that studies deceptive financial reports and what elements lead to them.

Developing and rolling out a security program is not as difficult as many organizations make it out to be, but it is new to them, and new things are usually scary and confusing. This is why they should turn to standards and industry best practices, which provide the guidance and recipe for how to set up and implement a full security program.

The most common standard used to be ISO 17799, which was derived from the de facto standard: British Standard 7799 (BS7799). It is an internationally recognized Information Security Management (ISM) Standard that provides high-level conceptual recommendations on enterprise security. The British Standard actually has two parts: BS7799 Part 1, which outlines control objectives and a range of controls that can be used to meet those objectives; and BS7799 Part 2, which outlines how a security program can be set up and maintained. BS7799 Part 2 also served as a baseline that organizations could be certified against. An organization would choose to be certified against the ISO 17799 standard to provide confidence to their customer base and partners and to be used as a marketing tool. To become certified, an authorized third party would evaluate the organization against the requirements in ISO 17799 Part 2. The organization could be certified against all or just a portion of ISO 17799 Part 2.

Confusion and Security

Today, many business-oriented people who are not security professionals are responsible for rolling out security programs and solutions. Without proper education and training on these matters, companies end up wasting much time and money.

"Implement port authentication, an IPSec VPN, a trusted front end, and intrusion prevention."

"To prevent a trusted front end we need to use IPSec to protect against port authentication."

While there has been plenty of controversy regarding the benefits and drawbacks of ISO 17799, it has been the agreed upon mechanism to describe security processes and was the benchmark we use to indicate a "correct infrastructure." It is made up of ten domains, which are very close to the CISSP Common Body of Knowledge (CBK).

We have moved from the more ambiguous ISO 17799 standard to a whole list of ISO standards that will either help you understand and compartmentalize these best practices, or confuse you and make you very angry. Sometimes the effort to simplify can cause more confusion. So here we go . . .

ISO likes things neat and tidy. It uses different series numbers to represent specific types of standards. For example, the ISO 9000 series comprises many standards that deal with quality control for business processes. A new series, ISO/IEC 27000, is used for assurance and security standards. ISO has overhauled the 17799 standards to correspond with their current numbering format. Following are the ISO/IEC series that are used as blueprints for organizations to follow when developing their security program:

- **ISO/IEC 27001** Based on British Standard BS7799 Part 2, which is establishment, implementation, control, and improvement of the Information Security Management System

- **ISO/IEC 27002** Code of practice providing good practice advice on ISMS (previously known as ISO 17799), itself based on British Standard BS 7799 Part 1

- **ISO/IEC 27004** A standard for information security management measurements

- **ISO/IEC 27005** Designed to assist the satisfactory implementation of information security based on a risk management approach

- **ISO/IEC 27006** A guide to the certification/registration process

- **ISO/IEC 27799** A guide to illustrate how to protect personal health information

NOTE The remaining standards can be found at www.27000.org.

I have found it easier to understand the older de facto standard, ISO 17799, before trying to decipher all of the ISO security best practice standards. These are laid out next. The ISO/IEC 27002 (formerly ISO 17799) domains are as follows:

- **Information security policy for the organization** Map of business objectives to security, management's support, security goals, and responsibilities.

- **Creation of information security infrastructure** Create and maintain an organizational security structure through the use of a security forum, a security officer, defining security responsibilities, authorization processes, outsourcing, and independent reviews.

- **Asset classification and control**   Develop a security infrastructure to protect organizational assets through accountability and inventory, classification, and handling procedures.

- **Personnel security**   Reduce risks that are inherent in human interaction by screening employees, defining roles and responsibilities, training employees properly, and documenting the ramifications of not meeting expectations.

- **Physical and environmental security**   Protect the organization's assets by properly choosing a facility location, erecting and maintaining a security perimeter, implementing access control, and protecting equipment.

- **Communications and operations management**   Carry out operations security through operational procedures, proper change control, incident handling, separation of duties, capacity planning, network management, and media handling.

- **Access control**   Control access to assets based on business requirements, user management, authentication methods, and monitoring.

- **System development and maintenance**   Implement security in all phases of a system's lifetime through development of security requirements, cryptography, integrity, and software development procedures.

- **Business continuity management**   Counter disruptions of normal operations by using continuity planning and testing.

- **Compliance**   Comply with regulatory, contractual, and statutory requirements by using technical controls, system audits, and legal awareness.

NOTE   The CISSP exam can be a bit antiquated, and many times it is hard to keep up-to-date with all of the security industry changes. It is important for you to understand the BS7799, ISO 17799, and the new ISO/IEC 27000 series. You should understand the overall purpose of each generation of security best practices, and pay close attention to the ISO/IEC 27000 series since it is the newest generation.

CobiT and COSO provide the "what is to be achieved," but not the "how to achieve it." This is where ITIL and the ISO/IEC 27000 series come in. The Information Technology Infrastructure Library (ITIL) is the de facto standard of best practices for IT service management. ITIL was created because of the increased dependence on information technology to meet business needs. Unfortunately, a natural divide exists between businesspeople and IT people in every organization because they use different terminology and have different focuses within the organization. The lack of a common language and understanding of each other's domain (business versus IT) has caused many companies to ineffectively blend their business objectives and IT functions. This improper blending usually generates confusion, miscommunication, missed deadlines, missed opportunities, increased cost in time and labor, and frustration on both the business and technical sides of the house. ITIL is a customizable framework that is provided in a set of books or in an online format. It provides the goals, the general activities necessary to achieve these goals, and the input and output values for each process required to meet these determined goals. Where CobiT defines IT goals, ITIL provides the steps at the process level on how to achieve those goals. Although ITIL has a component that deals with security, its focus is more toward internal service level agreements between the IT department and the "customers" it serves. The customers are usually internal departments.

NOTE   The technically correct names for the ISO standards listed earlier are ISO/IEC with a following number (ISO/IEC 17799:2005, ISO/IEC 27001:2005, and so on). IEC is the International Electrotechnical Commission, which jointly works with ISO to create global standards. In the industry, and on the exam, you could see the standards presented with or without "IEC," but they are still referring to the same standards. Just using "ISO" is an abbreviation.

Security Governance

We have security governance because I said so and it is written in our charter. Now, what is security governance again?

   Security governance is very similar to corporate and IT governance because functionality and goals overlap among the three. All three work within an organizational structure of a company and have the same goals of helping to ensure the company will survive and thrive—each just has a different focus. As requirements in corporate governance have increased due to regulations and legislation, the need for security governance has increased as well. And as the global marketplace increases, so does the need to comply with the laws and practices of the countries where you are conducting business. Just as the boards of directors of organizations are being held more and more accountable for the business practices and performance of their organizations, the need for information security governance has become more and more important in ensuring that the proper mechanisms are in place to provide the board of directors, as well as management, with proper oversight so as to manage the risks to the organization and to limit potential damages.

   Many professional- and adult-sounding definitions of security governance can be found, such as the following issued by the IT Governance Institute in its *Board Briefing on IT Governance,* 2nd edition:

> *Governance is the set of responsibilities and practices exercised by the board and executive management with the goal of providing strategic direction, ensuring that objectives are achieved, ascertaining that risks are managed appropriately, and verifying that the enterprise's resources are used responsibly.*

   This definition is absolutely correct, but remains at a high level that is difficult for many of us mere mortals to fully understand or know how to actually carry out. This is more like a strategic policy statement, while the real skill is to properly interpret and transform it into meaningful tactical and operational functions and practices.

Security governance is all of the tools, personnel, and business processes necessary to ensure that the security implemented meets the organization's specific needs. It requires organizational structure, roles and responsibilities, performance measurement, defined tasks, and oversight mechanisms. This definition is not much better than the preceding definition, is it?

Let's compare two companies. Company A has an effective security governance program in place and Company B does not. Now, to the untrained eye it would seem as though Companies A and B are equal in their security practices because they both have security policies, procedures, standards, the same security technology controls (firewalls, IDSs, identity management, and so on), and a security team run by a security officer. You may think, "Man, these two companies are on the ball and quite evolved in their security programs." But if you look closer, you will see some critical differences (listed in Table 3-1).

Does the organization you work for look like Company A or Company B? Most organizations today have many of the pieces and parts to a security program (policies, standards, firewalls, security team, IDS, and so on), but the management is not truly involved, and security has not permeated throughout the organization. Instead, organizations have all of these pieces and parts and have a small security team that is responsible for making sure security is properly carried out throughout the whole company—which is close to impossible. If security were just a technology issue, then this security team could properly install, configure, and maintain the products, and the company would get a gold star and pass the audit with flying colors. But that is not how the world of information security works today. It is much more than just technological solutions. Security professionals need to understand that security must be utilized throughout the organization, and having several points of responsibility and accountability is critical. Security governance is a coherent system of integrated security components (products, personnel, training, processes, policies, and so on) that exist to ensure the organization survives and, hopefully, thrives.

 NOTE It is easier to purchase a security solution than to attempt to change the culture of an organization. Even if the company has the most up-to-date and advanced products on the market, the company cannot achieve the necessary degree of security if the products are being used by untrained, apathetic, and careless employees. Evaluating the culture of an organization is very important when assessing an organization's security posture.

For there to be security governance, there must be something to govern. The collection of the controls that an organization must have in place is collectively referred to as a security program.

Company A	Company B
Board members understand that information security is critical to the company and demand to be updated quarterly on security performance and breaches.	Board members do not understand that information security is in their realm of responsibility and focus solely on corporate governance and profits.
CEO, CFO, CIO, and business unit managers participate in a risk management committee that meets each month, and information security is always one topic on the agenda to review.	CEO, CFO, and business unit managers feel as though information security is the responsibility of the CIO, CISO, and IT department and do not get involved.
Executive management sets an acceptable risk level that is the basis for the company's security policies and all security activities.	CISO took some boilerplate security policies and inserted his company's name and had the CEO sign them.
Executive management holds business unit managers responsible for carrying out risk management activities for their specific business units.	All security activity takes place within the security department, thus security works within a silo and is not integrated throughout the organization.
Critical business processes are documented along with the risks that are inherent at the different steps within the business processes.	Business processes are not documented and not analyzed for potential risks that can affect operations, productivity, and profitability.
Employees are held accountable for any security breaches they participate in, either maliciously or accidentally.	Policies and standards are developed, but no enforcement or accountability practices have been envisioned or deployed.
Security products, managed services, and consultants are purchased and deployed in an informed manner. They are also constantly reviewed to ensure they are cost-effective.	Security products, managed services, and consultants are purchased and deployed without any real research or performance metrics to determine the return on investment or effectiveness.
The organization is continuing to review its processes, including security, with the goal of continued improvement.	The organization does not analyze its performance for improvement, but continually marches forward and makes similar mistakes over and over again.

Table 3-1   Comparison of Company A and Company B

Security Program Development

It is important to understand that a security program has a life cycle that is always continuing, because it should be constantly evaluated and improved upon. The life cycle of any process can be described in different ways. We will use the following steps:

1. Plan and organize.
2. Implement.
3. Operate and maintain.
4. Monitor and evaluate.

Many organizations do not follow a life cycle approach in developing, implementing, and maintaining their security management program. This is because they do not know how, or they feel as though this approach is cumbersome and a waste of time. The result of not following a life cycle structure usually results in the following:

- Written policies and procedures that are not mapped to and supported by security activities
- Severe disconnect and confusion between different individuals throughout the organization who are attempting to protect company assets
- No way of assessing progress and the return on investment of spending and resource allocation
- No way of fully understanding the security program deficiencies and of having a standardized way of improving upon the deficiencies
- No assurance of compliance to regulations, laws, or policies
- Relying fully on technology for all security solutions
- A patchwork of point solutions and no holistic enterprise solution
- A "fire alarm" approach to any breaches instead of a calm proactive and detective approach
- A false sense of security with an undercurrent of confusion

Without setting up a life cycle approach to a security program and the security management that maintains the program, an organization is doomed to treat security as merely another project. Anything treated as a project has a start and stop date, and at the stop date everyone disperses to other projects. Many organizations have had good intentions in their security program kickoffs, but did not implement the proper structure to ensure that security management was an ongoing and continually improving process. The result was a lot of starts and stops over the years and repetitive work that cost more than it should, with diminishing results.

The main components of each phase are provided in the following:

- Plan and Organize
  - Establish management commitment.
  - Establish oversight steering committee.
  - Assess business drivers.
  - Carry out a threat profile on the organization.
  - Carry out a risk assessment.
  - Develop security architectures at an organizational, application, network, and component level.
  - Identify solutions per architecture level.
  - Obtain management approval to move forward.
- Implement
  - Assign roles and responsibilities.

- Develop and implement security policies, procedures, standards, baselines, and guidelines.
- Identify sensitive data at rest and in transit.
- Implement the following *blueprints*:
    - Asset identification and management
    - Risk management
    - Vulnerability management
    - Compliance
    - Identity management and access control
    - Change control
    - Software development life cycle
    - Business continuity planning
    - Awareness and training
    - Physical security
    - Incident response
- Implement solutions (administrative, technical, physical) per blueprint.
- Develop auditing and monitoring solutions per blueprint.
- Establish goals, service level agreements (SLAs), and metrics per blueprint.
- Operate and Maintain
    - Follow procedures to ensure all baselines are met in each implemented blueprint.
    - Carry out internal and external audits.
    - Carry out tasks outlined per blueprint.
    - Manage service level agreements per blueprint.
- Monitor and Evaluate
    - Review logs, audit results, collected metric values, and SLAs per blueprint.
    - Assess goal accomplishments per blueprint.
    - Carry out quarterly meetings with steering committees.
    - Develop improvement steps and integrate into the Plan and Organize phase.

Many of the items mentioned in the previous list are covered throughout this book. This list was provided to show how all of these items can be rolled out in a sequential and controllable manner.

NOTE Various organizations, consulting companies, and security professionals may follow different approaches to setting up a security program, but overall they cover the same topics. Although every organization has different acceptable risk levels, implemented controls, threats, and business drivers, each of the security programs contains basically the same components. Some components are just emphasized more than others based on the company's business and security needs.

Although these models and frameworks are very helpful, they are also very high level. For example, if a framework simply states that an organization must secure its data, a great amount of work will be called for. This is where the security professional really rolls up her sleeves, by developing security blueprints. *Blueprints* are important tools to identify, develop, and design security requirements for specific business needs. These blueprints must be customized to fulfill the organization's security requirements, which are based on its regulatory obligations, business drivers, and legal obligations. For example, let's say Company Y has a privacy policy, and their security team has developed standards and procedures pertaining to the privacy strategy the company should follow. The blueprint will then get more granular and lay out the processes and components necessary to meet requirements outlined in the policy, standards, and requirements. This would include at least the following:

- A diagram of the company network
- Where the sensitive data resides within the network
- The network segments that the sensitive data transverses
- The different security solutions in place (VPN, SSL, PGP) that protect the sensitive data
- Third-party connections where sensitive data is shared
- Security measures in place for third-party connections
- And more . . .

The blueprints to be developed and followed depend upon the organization's business needs. If Company Y uses identity management, there must be a blueprint outlining roles, registration management, authoritative source, identity repositories, single sign-on solutions, and so on. If Company Y does not use identity management, there is no need to build a blueprint for this. Many of the blueprints most organizations need to develop are listed in the following:

- Security management
- Business continuity
- Logging and monitoring
- Identity management
- Application integrity
- Infrastructure
- Asset management
- Physical and environmental security
- And more . . .

So the blueprint will lay out the security solutions, processes, and components the organization uses to match its security and business needs. These blueprints must be applied to the different business units within the organization. For example, the identity management practiced in each of the different departments should follow the crafted blueprint. Following these blueprints throughout the organization allows for standardization, easier metric gathering, and governance. The blueprints should follow best practices and are commonly mapped to the ISO 17799 framework. Figure 3-6 illustrates where these blueprints come into play when developing a security program. We will dig deeper into blueprints and their components in Chapter 5.

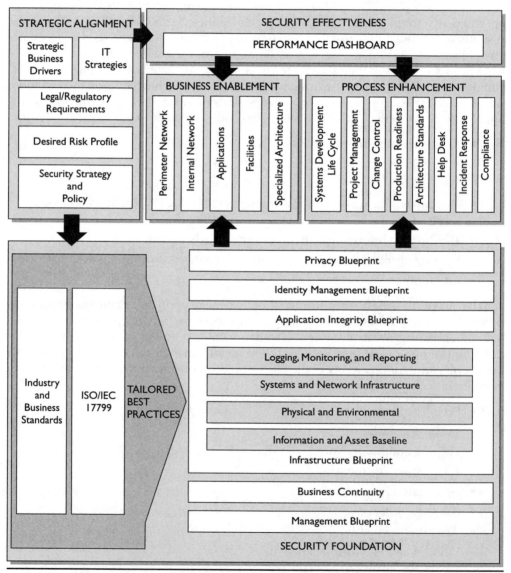

Figure 3-6 Blueprints must map the security and business requirements.

NOTE Remember to understand not only ISO 17799, but also the ISO/IEC 27000 security best practice series.

Information Risk Management

Life is full of risk.

Risk in the context of security is the possibility of damage happening, and the ramifications of such damage should it occur. *Information risk management (IRM)* is the *process* of identifying and assessing risk, reducing it to an acceptable level, and implementing the right mechanisms to maintain that level. There is no such thing as a 100-percent secure environment. Every environment has vulnerabilities and threats to a certain degree. The skill is in identifying these threats, assessing the probability of them actually occurring and the damage they could cause, and then taking the right steps to reduce the overall level of risk in the environment to what the organization identifies as acceptable.

Risks to a company come in different forms, and they are not all computer related. When a company purchases another company, it takes on a lot of risk in the hope that this move will increase its market base, productivity, and profitability. If a company increases its product line, this can add overhead, increase the need for personnel and storage facilities, require more funding for different materials, and maybe increase insurance premiums and the expense of marketing campaigns. The risk is that this added overhead might not be matched in sales; thus, profitability will be reduced or not accomplished.

When we look at information security, note that a corporation needs to be aware of several types of risk and address them properly. The following items touch on the major categories:

- **Physical damage** Fire, water, vandalism, power loss, and natural disasters
- **Human interaction** Accidental or intentional action or inaction that can disrupt productivity
- **Equipment malfunction** Failure of systems and peripheral devices
- **Inside and outside attacks** Hacking, cracking, and attacking
- **Misuse of data** Sharing trade secrets, fraud, espionage, and theft
- **Loss of data** Intentional or unintentional loss of information through destructive means
- **Application error** Computation errors, input errors, and buffer overflows

Threats must be identified, classified by category, and evaluated to calculate their damage potential to the company. Real risk is hard to measure, but prioritizing the potential risks in order of which ones must be addressed first is possible.

Who Really Understands Risk Management?

Unfortunately, the answer to this question is that not enough people inside or outside of the security profession really understand risk management. Even though information security is big business today, the focus is more on applications, devices, protocols, viruses, and hacking. Although these items all must be considered and weighed in risk management processes, they should be considered small pieces of the overall security puzzle, not the main focus of risk management.

Security is now a business issue, but businesses operate to make money, not to just be secure. A business is concerned with security only if potential risks threaten its bottom line, which they can in many ways, such as through the loss of reputation and their customer base after a database of credit card numbers is compromised; through the loss of thousands of dollars in operational expenses from a new computer worm; through the loss of proprietary information as a result of successful company espionage attempts; through the loss of confidential information from a successful social engineering attack; and so on. It is critical that security professionals understand these individual threats, but it is more important they understand how to calculate the risk of these threats and map them to business drivers.

Knowing the difference between the definitions of "vulnerability," "threat," and "risk" may seem trivial to you, but it is more critical than most people truly understand. A vulnerability scanner can identify dangerous services that are running, unnecessary accounts, and unpatched systems. That is the easy part. But if you have a security budget of only $120,000 and you have a long list of vulnerabilities that need attention, do you have the proper skill to know which ones should be dealt with first? Since you have a finite amount of money and an almost infinite number of vulnerabilities, how do you properly rank the most critical vulnerabilities to ensure that your company is addressing the most critical issues *and* providing the most return on investment of funds?

This is what risk management is all about, and to organizations, corporations, and businesses around the world, it is more important than IDS, ethical hacking, malware, and firewalls. But risk management is not as "sexy" and therefore does not get its necessary attention or implementation.

Information Risk Management Policy

How do I put all of these risk management pieces together?
Response: Let's check out the policy.

Proper risk management requires a strong commitment from senior management, a documented process that supports the organization's mission, an IRM policy, and a delegated IRM team.

The IRM policy should be a subset of the organization's overall risk management policy *(risks to a company include more than just information security issues)* and should be mapped to the organizational security policies. The IRM policy should address the following items:

- The objectives of the IRM team
- The level of risk the company will accept and what is considered an acceptable level of risk
- Formal processes of risk identification
- The connection between the IRM policy and the organization's strategic planning processes

- Responsibilities that fall under IRM and the roles to fulfill them
- The mapping of risk to internal controls
- The approach toward changing staff behaviors and resource allocation in response to risk analysis
- The mapping of risks to performance targets and budgets
- Key indicators to monitor the effectiveness of controls

The IRM policy provides the infrastructure for the organization's security risk management processes and procedures and should address all issues of information security, from personnel screening and the insider threat to physical security and firewalls. It should provide direction on how the IRM team relates information on company risks to senior management and how to properly execute management's decisions on risk mitigation tasks.

The Risk Management Team

Each organization is different in its size, security posture requirements, and security budget. One organization may have one individual responsible for IRM (poor soul) or a team that works in a coordinated manner. The overall goal of the team is to ensure the company is protected in the most cost-effective manner. This goal can be accomplished only if the following components are in place:

- An established risk acceptance level provided by senior management
- Documented risk assessment processes and procedures
- Procedures for identifying and mitigating risks
- Appropriate resource and fund allocation from senior management
- Contingency plans where assessments indicate they are necessary
- Security-awareness training for all staff members associated with information assets
- The ability to establish improvement (or risk mitigation) teams in specific areas when necessary
- The mapping of legal and regulation compliancy requirements to control and implement requirements
- The development of metrics and performance indicators so as to measure and manage various types of risks
- The ability to identify and assess new risks as the environment and company changes
- The integration of IRM and the organization's change control process to ensure that changes do not introduce new vulnerabilities

Obviously, this list is a lot more than just buying a new shiny firewall and calling the company safe.

The IRM team, in most cases, is not made up of employees with the dedicated task of risk management. It consists of people who already have a full-time job in the company and are now tasked with something else. Thus, senior management support is necessary so proper resource allocation can take place.

Of course, all teams need a leader, and IRM is no different. One individual should be singled out to run this rodeo and, in larger organizations, this person should be spending 50 to 70 percent of their time in this role. Management must dedicate funds to making sure this person receives the necessary training and risk analysis tools needed to ensure it is a successful endeavor.

Risk Analysis

I have determined that our greatest risk is this paperclip.
Response: Nice work.

   Risk analysis, which is really a tool for risk management, is a method of identifying vulnerabilities and threats and assessing the possible impacts to determine where to implement security safeguards. Risk analysis is used to ensure that security is cost-effective, relevant, timely, and responsive to threats. Security can be quite complex, even for well-versed security professionals, and it is easy to apply too much security, not enough security, or the wrong security components, and to spend too much money in the process without attaining the necessary objectives. Risk analysis helps companies prioritize their risks and shows management the amount of money that should be applied to protecting against those risks in a sensible manner.

A risk analysis has four main goals:

- Identify assets and their value to the organization.
- Identify vulnerabilities and threats.
- Quantify the probability and business impact of these potential threats.
- Provide an economic balance between the impact of the threat and the cost of the countermeasure.

Risk analysis provides a *cost/benefit comparison*, which compares the annualized cost of safeguards to the potential cost of loss. A safeguard, in most cases, should not be implemented unless the annualized cost of loss exceeds the annualized cost of the safeguard itself. This means that if a facility is worth $100,000, it does not make sense to spend $150,000 trying to protect it.

It is important to figure out what you are *supposed* to be doing before you dig right in and start working. Anyone who has worked on a project without a properly defined scope can attest to the truth of this statement. Before an assessment and analysis is started, the team must carry out **project sizing** to understand what assets and threats should be evaluated. Most assessments are focused on physical security, technology security, or personnel security. Trying to assess all of them at the same time can be quite an undertaking.

One of the team's tasks is to create a report that details the asset valuations. Senior management should review and accept the lists, and make them the scope of the IRM project. If management determines at this early stage that some assets are not important, the risk assessment team should not spend additional time or resources evaluating those assets. During discussions with management, everyone involved must have a firm understanding of the value of the security AIC triad—availability, integrity, and confidentiality—and how it directly relates to business needs.

Management should outline the scope, which most likely will be dictated by organizational governance, risk management, and compliance as well as budgetary constraints. Many projects have run out of funds, and consequently stopped, because proper project sizing was not conducted at the onset of the project. Don't let this happen to you.

A risk analysis helps integrate the security program objectives with the company's business objectives and requirements. The more the business and security objectives are in alignment, the more successful the two will be. The analysis also helps the company draft a proper budget for a security program and its constituent security components. Once a company knows how much its assets are worth and the possible threats they are exposed to, it can make intelligent decisions about how much money to spend protecting those assets.

A risk analysis must be supported and directed by senior management if it is to be successful. Management must define the purpose and scope of the analysis, appoint a team to carry out the assessment, and allocate the necessary time and funds to conduct the analysis. It is essential for senior management to review the outcome of the risk assessment and analysis and to act on its findings. After all, what good is it to go through all the trouble of a risk assessment and *not* react to its findings? Unfortunately, this does happen all too often.

The Risk Analysis Team

Each organization has different departments, and each department has its own functionality, resources, tasks, and quirks. For the most effective risk analysis, an organization must build a risk analysis team that includes individuals from many or all departments to ensure that all of the threats are identified and addressed. The team members may be part of management, application programmers, IT staff, systems integrators, and operational managers—indeed, any key personnel from key areas of the organization. This mix is necessary because if the risk analysis team comprises only individuals from the IT department, it may not understand, for example, the types of threats the accounting department faces with data integrity issues, or how the company as a whole would be affected if the accounting department's data files were wiped out by an accidental or intentional act. Or, as another example, the IT staff may not understand all the risks the employees in the warehouse would face if a natural disaster were to hit, or what it would mean to their productivity and how it would affect the organization overall. If the risk analysis team is unable to include members from various departments, it should, at the very least, make sure to interview people in each department so it fully understands and can quantify all threats.

The risk analysis team must also include people who understand the processes that are part of their individual departments, meaning individuals who are at the right levels of each department. This is a difficult task, since managers tend to delegate any sort of risk analysis task to lower levels within the department. However, the people who work at these lower levels may not have adequate knowledge and understanding of the processes that the risk analysis team may need to deal with.

When looking at risk, it's good to keep several questions in mind. Raising these questions helps ensure that the risk analysis team and senior management know what is important. Team members must ask the following: What event could occur (threat event)? What could be the potential impact (risk)? How often could it happen (frequency)? What level of confidence do we have in the answers to the first three questions (certainty)? A lot of this information is gathered through internal surveys, interviews, or workshops.

Viewing threats with these questions in mind helps the team focus on the tasks at hand and assists in making the decisions more accurate and relevant.

Risk Ownership

One of the more important questions that face people working within an organization is who owns the risk? The answer really isn't straightforward because it depends upon the situation and what kind of risk is being discussed. Senior management owns the risk present during the operation of the organization, but there may be times when senior management also relies upon data custodians or business units to conduct work, and it is during these times that these other elements of the organization also shoulder some of the responsibility of risk ownership. Granted, it always ultimately rests on senior management, but they also must be able to trust that the work they have delegated is being handled in a manner that understands, accepts the existence of, and works to minimize the risks the organization faces in the course of its regular operations.

The Value of Information and Assets

If information does not have any value, then who cares about protecting it?

The value placed on information is relative to the parties involved, what work was required to develop it, how much it costs to maintain, what damage would result if it were lost or destroyed, what enemies would pay for it, and what liability penalties could be endured. If a company does not know the value of the information and the other assets it is trying to protect, it does not know how much money and time it should spend on protecting them. If you were in charge of making sure Russia does not know the encryption algorithms used when transmitting information to and from U.S. spy satellites, you would use more extreme (and expensive) security measures than you would use to protect your peanut butter and banana sandwich recipe from your next-door neighbor. The value of the information supports security measure decisions.

The previous examples refer to assessing the value of *information* and protecting it, but this logic applies toward an organization's facilities, systems, and resources. The value of the company's facilities must be assessed, along with all printers, workstations, servers, peripheral devices, supplies, and employees. You do not know how much is in danger of being lost if you don't know what you have and what it is worth in the first place.

Costs That Make Up the Value

An asset can have both quantitative and qualitative measurements assigned to it, but these measurements need to be derived. The actual value of an asset is determined by the cost it takes to acquire, develop, and maintain it. The value is determined by the importance it has to the owners, authorized users, and unauthorized users. Some information is important enough to a company to go through the steps of making it a trade secret.

The value of an asset should reflect all identifiable costs that would arise if the asset were actually impaired. If a server cost $4,000 to purchase, this value should not be input as the value of the asset in a risk assessment. Rather, the cost of replacing or repairing it, the loss of productivity, and the value of any data that may be corrupted or lost must be accounted for to properly capture the amount the company would lose if the server were to fail for one reason or another.

The following issues should be considered when assigning values to assets:

- Cost to acquire or develop the asset
- Cost to maintain and protect the asset
- Value of the asset to owners and users
- Value of the asset to adversaries
- Value of intellectual property that went into developing the information
- Price others are willing to pay for the asset
- Cost to replace the asset if lost
- Operational and production activities affected if the asset is unavailable
- Liability issues if the asset is compromised
- Usefulness and role of the asset in the organization

Understanding the value of an asset is the first step to understanding what security mechanisms should be put in place and what funds should go toward protecting it. A very important question is how much it could cost the company to *not* protect the asset.

Determining the value of assets may be useful to a company for a variety of reasons, including the following:

- To perform effective cost/benefit analyses
- To select specific countermeasures and safeguards
- To determine the level of insurance coverage to purchase
- To understand what exactly is at risk
- To conform to due care and to comply with legal and regulatory requirements

Assets may be tangible (computers, facilities, supplies) or intangible (reputation, data, intellectual property). It is usually harder to quantify the values of intangible assets, which may change over time. How do you put a monetary value on a company's reputation? Sometimes that's harder to figure out than a Rubik's Cube.

Identifying Threats

Okay, what should we be afraid of?

Earlier, it was stated that the definition of a risk is the probability of a threat agent exploiting a vulnerability to cause harm to a computer, network, or company, and the resulting business impact. Many types of threat agents can take advantage of several types of vulnerabilities, resulting in a variety of specific threats, as outlined in Table 3-2, which represents only a sampling of the risks many organizations should address in their risk management programs.

Other types of threats can arise in a computerized environment that are much harder to identify than those listed in Table 3-2. These other threats have to do with application and user errors. If an application uses several complex equations to produce results, the threat can be difficult to discover and isolate if these equations are incorrect or if the application is using inputted data incorrectly. This can result in *illogical processing* and *cascading errors* as invalid results are passed on to another process. These types of problems can lie within applications' code and are very hard to identify.

User errors, intentional or accidental, are easier to identify by monitoring and auditing user activities. Audits and reviews must be conducted to discover if employees are inputting values incorrectly into programs, misusing technology, or modifying data in an inappropriate manner.

Once the vulnerabilities and associated threats are identified, the ramifications of these vulnerabilities being exploited must be investigated. Risks have *loss potential*,

Threat Agent	Can Exploit This Vulnerability	Resulting in This Threat
Malware	Lack of antivirus software	Virus infection
Hacker	Powerful services running on a server	Unauthorized access to confidential information
Users	Misconfigured parameter in the operating system	System malfunction
Fire	Lack of fire extinguishers	Facility and computer damage, and possibly loss of life
Employee	Lack of training or standards enforcement Lack of auditing	Sharing mission-critical information Altering data inputs and outputs from data processing applications
Contractor	Lax access control mechanisms	Stealing trade secrets
Attacker	Poorly written application Lack of stringent firewall settings	Conducting a buffer overflow Conducting a denial-of-service attack
Intruder	Lack of security guard	Breaking windows and stealing computers and devices

Table 3-2 Relationship of Threats and Vulnerabilities

meaning what the company would lose if a threat agent were actually to exploit a vulnerability. The loss may be corrupted data, destruction of systems and/or the facility, unauthorized disclosure of confidential information, a reduction in employee productivity, and so on. When performing a risk analysis, the team also must look at *delayed loss* when assessing the damages that can occur. Delayed loss has negative effects on a company after a vulnerability is initially exploited. The period can be anywhere from 15 minutes to years after the exploitation. Delayed loss may include reduced productivity over a period, damage to the company's reputation, reduced income to the company, accrued late penalties, extra expense to get the environment back to proper working conditions, the delayed collection of funds from customers, and so forth.

For example, if a company's web servers are attacked and taken offline, the immediate damage could be data corruption, the man-hours necessary to place the servers back online, and the replacement of any code or components required. The company could lose revenue if it usually accepts orders and payments via its web site. If it takes a full day to get the web servers fixed and back online, the company could lose a lot more sales and profits. If it takes a full week to get the web servers fixed and back online, the company could lose enough sales and profits to not be able to pay other bills and expenses. This would be a delayed loss. If the company's customers lose confidence in it because of this activity, it could lose business for months or years. This is a more extreme case of delayed loss.

These types of issues make more complex the process of properly quantifying losses that specific threats could cause, but they must be taken into consideration to ensure reality is represented in this type of analysis.

Methodologies for Risk Assessment

Risk assessment has several different methodologies. Let's take a look at a couple of them.

NIST SP 800-30 and *800-66* are methodologies that can be used by the general public, but the initial creation of 800-66 was designed to be implemented in the healthcare field and other regulated industries. While 800-66 was designed to be used by HIPAA clients, it can also be readily adopted and used by other regulated industries. 800-66, specifically, is an example of the kind of methodology that was intended for one regulated industry but that can be adopted and used by another.

The NIST approach is specific to IT threats and how they relate to information security risks. It lays out the following steps:

- System characterization
- Threat identification
- Vulnerability identification
- Control analysis
- Likelihood determination

- Impact analysis
- Risk determination
- Control recommendations
- Results documentation

The NIST SP 800=30 Risk Management methodology is commonly used by security consultants, security officers and internal IT departments, and focuses mainly on computer systems. An individual or small team collects data from network and security practice assessments, and from people within the organization. This data is used as input values to the risk analysis steps outlined in the 800-30 document.

A second type of risk assessment methodology is called *FRAP*, which stands for Facilitated Risk Analysis Process. It is designed to explore a qualitative risk assessment process in a manner that allows for tests to be conducted on different aspects and variations of the methodology. The intent of this methodology is to provide an organization with the means of deciding what course and actions must be taken in specific circumstances to deal with various issues. This will allow, through the use of a prescreening process, users to determine the areas that really demand and need risk analysis within an organization. FRAP is designed in such a manner that it claims anyone with good facilitation skills will be capable of operating it successfully.

Another methodology called *OCTAVE* (Operationally Critical Threat, Asset, and Vulnerability Evaluation) was created by Carnegie Mellon University's Software Engineering Institute. It is a methodology that is intended to be used in situations where people manage and direct the risk evaluation for information security within their company. This places the people that work inside the organization in the power positions as being able to make the decisions regarding what is the best approach for evaluating the security of their organization. This relies on the idea that the people working in these environments best understand what is needed and what kind of risks they are facing.

While both the NIST and OCTAVE methodologies focus on IT threats and information security risks, *AS/NZS 4360* takes a much broader approach to risk management. This methodology can be used to understand a company's financial, capital, human safety, and business decisions risks. Although it can be used to analyze security risks, it was not created specifically for this purpose.

 NOTE You can find information on the relationship between these various risk management approaches and how they should be used in an article by Shon Harris at http://searchsecurity.techtarget.com/generic/0,295582,sid14_gci1191926,00.html

Failure and Fault Analysis

We have a lot of potential failure vulnerabilities, but we would rather not look at them.

Failure Modes and Effect Analysis (FMEA) is a method for determining functions, identifying functional failures, and assessing the causes of failure and their failure effects through a structured process. The application of this process to a chronic failure enables the determination of where exactly the failure is most likely to occur. This is very helpful in pinpointing where a vulnerability exists, as well as in determining exactly what kind of scope the vulnerability entails—meaning, what would be the secondary ramifications of its exploitation? This in turn not only makes it easier to apply a corrective fix to the vulnerability, but it also allows for a much more effective application of resources to the issue. Think of it as being able to look into the future and locate areas that have the potential for failure, or to find vulnerabilities and then apply corrective measures to them before they do become actual liabilities.

By following a specific order of steps, the best results can be maximized for a Failure Mode Analysis:

1. Start with a block diagram of a system or control.

2. Consider what happens if each block of the diagram fails.

3. Draw up a table in which failures are paired with their effects and an evaluation of the effects.

4. Correct the design of the system, and adjust the table until the system is not known to have unacceptable problems.

5. Have several engineers review the failure modes and effects analysis.

Table 3-3 is an example of how an FMEA can be carried out and documented. Although most companies will not have the resources to do this level of detailed work for every system and control, it should be carried out on critical functions and systems that can drastically affect the company.

 NOTE Compliance auditors review the documentation of processes, controls, testing activities, and results. This type of documentation (as long as it is accurate) will illustrate to the auditors how well your organization knows its systems and how you plan to address failures that may take place.

FMEA was first developed for systems engineering. Its purpose is to examine the potential failures in products and the processes involved with them. This approach proved to be successful and has been more recently adapted for use in evaluating of risk management priorities and mitigating known threat vulnerabilities.

Prepared by:							
Approved by:							
Date:							
Revision:							
				Failure Effect on ...			
Item Identification	Function	Failure Mode	Failure Cause	Component or Functional Assembly	Next Higher Assembly	System	Failure Detection Method
IPS application content filter	Inline perimeter protection	Fails to close	Traffic overload	Single point of failure Denial of service	IPS blocks ingress traffic stream	IPS is brought down	Health check status sent to console and e-mail to security administrator
Central antivirus signature update engine	Push updated signatures to all servers and workstations	Fails to provide adequate, timely protection against malware	Central server goes down	Individual node's antivirus software is not updated	Network is infected with malware	Central server can be infected and/ or infect other systems	Heartbeat status check sent to central console, and page network administrator
Fire suppression water pipes	Suppress fire in building 1 in 5 zones	Fails to close	Water in pipes freezes	None	Building 1 has no suppression agent available	Fire suppression system pipes break	Suppression sensors tied directly into fire system central console
Etc.							

Table 3-3 How an FMEA Can Be Carried Out and Documented

FMEA is used in assurance risk management because of the level of detail, variables, and complexity that continues to rise as corporations understand risk at more granular levels. This methodical way of identifying potential pitfalls is coming into play more as the need for risk awareness—down to the tactical and operational levels—continues to expand.

While FMEA is most useful as a survey method to identify major failure modes in a given system, the method is not as useful in discovering complex failure modes that may be involved in multiple systems or subsystems. A *fault tree analysis* usually proves to be a more useful approach to identifying failures that can take place within more complex environments and systems.

Fault tree analysis follows this general process. First, an undesired effect is taken as the root or top event of a tree of logic. Then, each situation that has the potential to cause that effect is added to the tree as a series of logic expressions. Fault trees are then labeled with actual numbers pertaining to failure probabilities. This is typically done by using computer programs that can calculate the failure probabilities from a fault tree.

Figure 3-7 shows a simplistic fault tree and the different logic symbols used to represent what must take place for a specific fault event to occur.

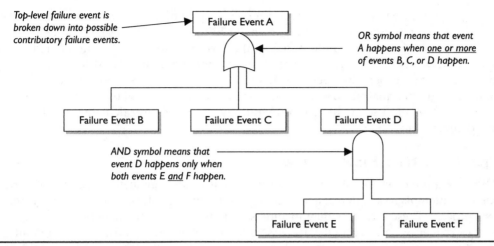

Figure 3-7   Fault tree and logic components

When setting up the tree, you must accurately list all the threats or faults that can occur with a system. The branches of the tree can be divided into general categories such as physical threats, networks threats, software threats, Internet threats, and component failure threats. Then, once all possible general categories are in place, you can trim them and effectively prune the branches from the tree that won't apply to the system in question. In general, if a system is not connected to the Internet by any means, remove that general branch from the tree.

Some of the most common software failure events that can be explored through a fault tree analysis are the following:

- False alarms
- Insufficient error handling
- Sequencing or order
- Incorrect timing outputs
- Valid but not expected outputs

Of course, because of the complexity of software and heterogeneous environments, this is a very small list.

NOTE   Six Sigma is a process improvement methodology. It is the "new and improved" Total Quality Management (TQM) that hit the business sector in the 1980s. Its goal is to improve process quality by using statistical methods of measuring operation efficiency and reducing variation, defects, and waste. Six Sigma is being used in the assurance industry in some instances to measure the success factors of different controls and procedures.

Up to now, we have secured management's support of the risk analysis, constructed our team so it represents different departments in the company, placed a value on each of the company's assets, and identified all the possible threats that could affect the assets. We have also taken into consideration all potential and delayed losses the company may endure per asset per threat. We have carried out a failure mode analysis and/or a fault tree analysis to understand the underlying causes of the identified threats. The next step is to use qualitative or quantitative methods to calculate the actual risk the company faces.

Quantitative Risk Analysis

The two approaches to risk analysis are quantitative and qualitative. *Quantitative risk analysis* attempts to assign real and meaningful numbers to all elements of the risk analysis process. These elements may include safeguard costs, asset value, business impact, threat frequency, safeguard effectiveness, exploit probabilities, and so on. When all of these are quantified, the process is said to be quantitative. Quantitative risk analysis also provides concrete probability percentages when determining the likelihood of threats. Each element within the analysis (asset value, threat frequency, severity of vulnerability, impact damage, safeguard costs, safeguard effectiveness, uncertainty, and probability items) is quantified and entered into equations to determine total and residual risks.

Purely quantitative risk analysis is not possible because the method attempts to quantify qualitative items, and there are always uncertainties in quantitative values. How do you know how often a vulnerability will be exploited? How do you know the exact monetary business impact that would arise?

Quantitative and qualitative approaches have their own pros and cons, and each applies more appropriately to some situations than others. Company management and the risk analysis team, and the tools they decide to use, will determine which approach is best.

NOTE Quantitative analysis uses risk calculations that attempt to predict the level of monetary losses and the probability for each type of threat. Qualitative analysis does not use calculations. Instead, it is more opinion- and scenario-based.

Automated Risk Analysis Methods

Collecting all the necessary data that needs to be plugged into risk analysis equations and properly interpreting the results can be overwhelming if done manually. Several automated risk analysis tools on the market can make this task much less painful and, hopefully, more accurate. The gathered data can be reused, greatly reducing the time required to perform subsequent analyses. The risk analysis team can also print reports and comprehensive graphs to present to the management.

NOTE Vulnerability assessment and risk analysis tools are available in freeware and commercial versions. Obtaining serious results often requires taking a serious approach to finding the tools that best serve the accuracy of the project.

The objective of these tools is to reduce the manual effort of these tasks, perform calculations quickly, estimate future expected losses, and determine the effectiveness and benefits of the security countermeasures chosen. Most automatic risk analysis products port information into a database and run several types of scenarios with different parameters to give a panoramic view of what the outcome will be if different threats come to bear. For example, after such a tool has all the necessary information inputted, it can be rerun several times with different parameters to compute the potential outcome if a large fire were to take place; the potential losses if a virus were to damage 40 percent of the data on the main file server; how much the company would lose if an attacker were to steal all the customer credit card information held in three databases; and so on. Running through the different risk possibilities gives a company a more detailed understanding of which risks are more critical than others, and thus which ones to address first. Figure 3-8 shows a simple output of this process.

Steps of a Risk Analysis

Many methods and equations can be used when performing a quantitative risk analysis, and many different variables can be inserted into the process. This section covers some of the main steps that should take place in every risk analysis.

Step 1: Assign Value to Assets For each asset, answer the following questions to determine its value:

- What is the value of this asset to the company?
- How much does it cost to maintain?
- How much does it make in profits for the company?
- How much would it be worth to the competition?
- How much would it cost to re-create or recover?
- How much did it cost to acquire or develop?
- How much liability do you face if the asset is compromised?

Figure 3-8
A simplistic example showing the severity of current threats versus the probability of them occurring

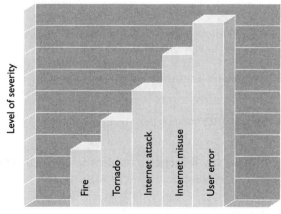

Step 2: Estimate Potential Loss per Threat   To estimate potential losses posed by threats, answer the following questions:

- What physical damage could the threat cause and how much would that cost?
- How much loss of productivity could the threat cause and how much would that cost?
- What is the value lost if confidential information is disclosed?
- What is the cost of recovering from this threat?
- What is the value lost if critical devices were to fail?
- What is the single loss expectancy (SLE) for each asset, and each threat?

This is just a small sample of questions that should be answered. The specific questions will depend upon the types of threats the team uncovers.

Step 3: Perform a Threat Analysis   Take the following steps to perform a threat analysis:

- Gather information about the likelihood of each threat taking place from people in each department. Examine past records and official security resources that provide this type of data.
- Calculate the annualized rate of occurrence (ARO), which is how many times the threat can take place in a 12-month period.

Step 4: Derive the Overall Annual Loss Potential per Threat   To derive the overall loss potential per threat, do the following:

- Combine potential loss and probability.
- Calculate the annualized loss expectancy (ALE) per threat by using the information calculated in the first three steps.
- Choose remedial measures to counteract each threat.
- Carry out cost/benefit analysis on the identified countermeasures.

Step 5: Reduce, Transfer, Avoid, or Accept the Risk   For each risk, you can choose whether to reduce, transfer, or accept the risk:

- **Risk reduction methods**
  - Install security controls and components.
  - Improve procedures.
  - Alter the environment.
  - Provide early detection methods to catch the threat as it's happening and reduce the possible damage it can cause.

- Produce a contingency plan of how business can continue if a specific threat takes place, to reduce further damages of the threat.

- Erect barriers to the threat.

- Carry out security-awareness training.

- **Risk transfer** For example, buy insurance to transfer some of the risk.

- **Risk acceptance** Live with the risks and spend no more money toward protection.

- **Risk avoidance** Discontinue the activity that is causing the risk.

Because we are stepping through a quantitative risk analysis, real numbers are used and calculations are necessary. *Single loss expectancy (SLE)* and *annualized loss expectancy (ALE)* were mentioned in the previous analysis steps. The SLE is a dollar amount that is assigned to a single event that represents the company's potential loss amount if a specific threat were to take place:

asset value × exposure factor (EF) = SLE

The *exposure factor (EF)* represents the percentage of loss a realized threat could have on a certain asset. So, for example, if a data warehouse has the asset value of $150,000, it might be estimated that if a fire were to occur, 25 percent of the warehouse would be damaged (and not more, because of a sprinkler system and other fire controls, proximity of a firehouse, and so on), in which case the SLE would be $37,500. This figure is derived to be inserted into the ALE equation:

SLE × annualized rate of occurrence (ARO) = ALE

The *annualized rate of occurrence (ARO)* is the value that represents the estimated frequency of a specific threat taking place within a one-year timeframe. The range can be from 0.0 (never) to 1.0 (once a year) to greater than one (several times a year) and anywhere in between. For example, if the probability of a flood taking place in Mesa, Arizona, is once in 1,000 years, the ARO value is 0.001.

So, if a fire taking place within a company's data warehouse facility can cause $37,500 in damages, and the frequency (or ARO) of a fire taking place has an ARO value of 0.1 (indicating once in ten years), then the ALE value is $3,750 ($37,500 × 0.1 = $3,750).

Accepting Risk

When a company decides to accept a risk, the decision should be based on cost (countermeasure costs more than potential loss) and an acceptable level of pain (company can live with the vulnerability and threat). But the company must also understand this is a visibility decision, insofar as accepting a specific risk may impact its industry reputation.

The ALE value tells the company that if it wants to put in controls or safeguards to protect the asset from this threat, it can sensibly spend $3,750 or less per year to provide the necessary level of protection. Knowing the real possibility of a threat and how much damage, in monetary terms, the threat can cause is important in determining how much should be spent to try and protect against that threat in the first place. It would not make good business sense for the company to spend more than $3,750 per year to protect itself from this threat.

Now that we have all these numbers, what do we do with them? Let's look at the example in Table 3-4, which shows the outcome of a risk analysis. With this data, the company can make intelligent decisions on what threats must be addressed first because of the severity of the threat, the likelihood of it happening, and how much could be lost if the threat were realized. The company now also knows how much money it should spend to protect against each threat. This will result in good business decisions, instead of just buying protection here and there without a clear understanding of the big picture. Because the company has a risk of losing up to $6,500 if data is corrupted by virus infiltration, up to this amount of funds can be earmarked toward providing antivirus software and methods to ensure that a virus attack will not happen.

We have just explored the ways of performing risk analysis through quantitative means. This method tries to measure the loss in monetary value and assign numeric sums to each component within the analysis. As stated previously, however, a pure quantitative analysis is difficult to achieve all the time, as well as all the resources required to gather all of the necessary information and values.

A quantitative analysis is also considered subjective, not objective, to many people. Although we can look at past events, do our best to assess the value of the assets, and contact agencies that provide frequency estimates of disasters happening in our area, we still cannot say for a fact that we have a 10 percent chance of a fire happening in a year and that it will cause exactly $230,000 in damage. In quantitative risk analysis, we can do our best to provide all the correct information, and by doing so we will come close to the risk values, but we cannot predict the future and how much the future will cost us or the company.

Asset	Threat	Single Loss Expectancy (SLE)	Annualized Rate of Occurrence (ARO)	Annualized Loss Expectancy (ALE)
Facility	Fire	$230,000	0.1	$23,000
Trade secret	Stolen	$40,000	0.01	$400
File server	Failed	$11,500	0.1	$1,150
Data	Virus	$6,500	1.0	$6,500
Customer credit card info	Stolen	$300,000	3.0	$900,000

Table 3-4 Breaking Down How SLE and ALE Values Are Used

Results of a Risk Analysis

The risk analysis team should have clearly defined goals. The following is a short list of what generally is expected from the results of a risk analysis:

- Monetary values assigned to assets
- Comprehensive list of all possible and significant threats
- Probability of the occurrence rate of each threat
- Loss potential the company can endure per threat in a 12-month time span
- Recommended safeguards, countermeasures, and actions

Although this list looks short, there is usually an incredible amount of detail under each bullet item. This report will be presented to senior management, which will be concerned with possible monetary losses and the necessary costs to mitigate these risks. Although the reports should be as detailed as possible, there should be executive abstracts so senior management can quickly understand the overall findings of the analysis.

 NOTE A risk analysis is considered fully quantitative if all elements of the process are quantified (asset value, business impact, frequency, countermeasure effectiveness, countermeasure costs, probability, and uncertainty).

Qualitative Risk Analysis

I think we are secure.
Response: Great! Let's all go home.

Another method of risk analysis is *qualitative*, which does not assign numbers and monetary values to components and losses. Instead, qualitative methods walk through different scenarios of risk possibilities and rank the seriousness of the threats and the validity of the different possible countermeasures based on opinions. (A wide sweeping analysis can include hundreds of scenarios.) Qualitative analysis techniques include judgment, best practices, intuition, and experience. Examples of qualitative techniques to gather data are Delphi, brainstorming, storyboarding, focus groups, surveys, questionnaires, checklists, one-on-one meetings, and interviews. The risk analysis team will determine the best technique for the threats that need to be assessed, as well as the culture of the company and individuals involved with the analysis.

The team that is performing the risk analysis gathers personnel who have experience and education on the threats being evaluated. When this group is presented with a scenario that describes threats and loss potential, each member responds with their gut feeling and experience on the likelihood of the threat and the extent of damage that may result.

> ## Uncertainty
>
> In risk analysis, *uncertainty* refers to the degree to which you lack confidence in an estimate. This is expressed as a percentage, from 0 to 100 percent. If you have a 30 percent confidence level in something, then it could be said you have a 70 percent uncertainty level. Capturing the degree of uncertainty when carrying out a risk analysis is important, because it indicates the level of confidence the team and management should have in the resulting figures.

A scenario approximately one page long is written for each major threat. The "expert," who is most familiar with this type of threat, should review the scenario to ensure it reflects how an actual threat would be carried out. Safeguards that would diminish the damage of this threat are then evaluated, and the scenario is played out for each safeguard. The exposure possibility and loss possibility can be ranked as high, medium, or low on a scale of 1 to 5 or 1 to 10. Once the selected personnel rank the possibility of a threat happening, the loss potential, and the advantages of each safeguard, this information is compiled into a report and presented to management to help it make better decisions on how best to implement safeguards into the environment. The benefits of this type of analysis are that communication must happen among team members to rank the risks, safeguard strengths, and identify weaknesses, and the people who know these subjects the best provide their opinions to management.

Let's look at a *simple* example of a qualitative risk analysis.

The risk analysis team writes a one-page scenario explaining the threat of a hacker accessing confidential information held on the five file servers within the company. The risk analysis team then distributes the one-page scenario to a team of five people (the IT manager, database administrator, application programmer, system operator, and operational manager), who are also given a sheet to rank the threat's severity, loss potential, and each safeguard's effectiveness, with a rating of 1 to 5, 1 being the least severe, effective, or probable. Table 3-5 shows the results.

This data is compiled and inserted into a report and presented to management. When management is presented with this information, it will see that its staff (or a chosen set of security professionals) feels that purchasing a firewall will protect the company from this threat more than purchasing an intrusion detection system, or setting up a honeypot system.

This is the result of looking at only one threat, and management will view the severity, probability, and loss potential of each threat so it knows which threats cause the greatest risk and should be addressed first.

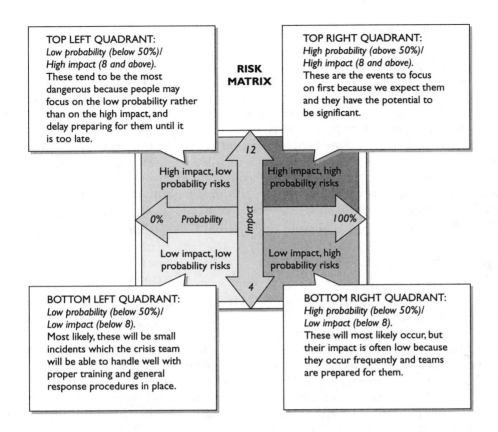

TOP LEFT QUADRANT:
Low probability (below 50%)/ High impact (8 and above).
These tend to be the most dangerous because people may focus on the low probability rather than on the high impact, and delay preparing for them until it is too late.

TOP RIGHT QUADRANT:
High probability (above 50%)/ High impact (8 and above).
These are the events to focus on first because we expect them and they have the potential to be significant.

RISK MATRIX

High impact, low probability risks

High impact, high probability risks

0%   Probability

100%

Low impact, low probability risks

Low impact, high probability risks

BOTTOM LEFT QUADRANT:
Low probability (below 50%)/ Low impact (below 8).
Most likely, these will be small incidents which the crisis team will be able to handle well with proper training and general response procedures in place.

BOTTOM RIGHT QUADRANT:
High probability (below 50%)/ Low impact (below 8).
These will most likely occur, but their impact is often low because they occur frequently and teams are prepared for them.

Threat = Hacker Accessing Confidential Information	Severity of Threat	Probability of Threat Taking Place	Potential Loss to the Company	Effectiveness of Firewall	Effectiveness of Intrusion Detection System	Effectiveness of Honeypot
IT manager	4	2	4	4	3	2
Database administrator	4	4	4	3	4	1
Application programmer	2	3	3	4	2	1
System operator	3	4	3	4	2	1
Operational manager	5	4	4	4	4	2
Results	3.6	3.4	3.6	3.8	3	1.4

Table 3-5   Example of a Qualitative Analysis

The Delphi Technique

The oracle Delphi told me that everyone agrees with me.
Response: Okay, let's do this again—anonymously.

The *Delphi technique* is a group decision method used to ensure that each member gives an honest opinion of what he or she thinks the result of a particular threat will be. This avoids a group of individuals feeling pressured to go along with others' thought processes and enables them to participate in an independent and anonymous way. Each member of the group provides his or her opinion of a certain threat and turns it in to the team that is performing the analysis. The results are compiled and distributed to the group members, who then write down their comments anonymously and return them to the analysis group. The comments are compiled and redistributed for more comments until a consensus is formed. This method is used to obtain an agreement on cost, loss values, and probabilities of occurrence without individuals having to agree verbally.

Quantitative vs. Qualitative

So which method should we use?

Each method has its advantages and disadvantages, some of which are outlined in Table 3-6 for purposes of comparison.

The risk analysis team, management, risk analysis tools, and culture of the company will dictate which approach—quantitative or qualitative—will be used. The goal of either method is to estimate a company's real risk and to rank the severity of the threats so the correct countermeasures can be put into place within a practical budget.

Table 3-6 refers to some of the positive aspects of the qualitative and quantitative approaches. However, not everything is always easy. In deciding to use either a qualitative or quantitative approach, the following points might need to be considered:

Qualitative Cons

- The assessments and results are basically subjective.
- Usually eliminates the opportunity to create a dollar value for cost/benefit discussions.
- Difficult to track risk management objectives with subjective measures.
- Standards are not available. Each vendor has its own way of interpreting the processes and their results.

Delphi Methods

In this text we are describing the consensus Delphi method, where experts help to identify the highest priority security issues and corresponding countermeasures. Another Delphi method, the Modified Delphi technique, is a silent form of brainstorming. Participants develop ideas individually and silently with no group interaction. The ideas are submitted to a group of decision makers for consideration and action.

Attribute	Quantitative	Qualitative
Requires no calculations		X
Requires more complex calculations	X	
Involves high degree of guesswork		X
Provides general areas and indications of risk		X
Is easier to automate and evaluate	X	
Used in risk management performance tracking	X	
Provides credible cost/benefit analysis	X	
Uses independently verifiable and objective metrics	X	
Provides the opinions of the individuals who know the processes best		X
Shows clear-cut losses that can be accrued within one year's time	X	

Table 3-6 Quantitative vs. Qualitative Characteristics

Quantitative Cons

- Calculations are more complex. Can management understand how these values were derived?
- Without automated tools, this process is extremely laborious.
- More preliminary work is needed to gather detailed information about environment.
- Standards are not available. Each vendor has its own way of interpreting the processes and their results.

Protection Mechanisms

Okay, so we know we are at risk, and we know the probability of it happening. Now, what do we do?
Response: Run.

The next step is to identify the current security mechanisms and to evaluate their effectiveness.

Because a company has such a wide range of threats (not just computer viruses and attackers), each threat type must be addressed and planned for individually. Access control mechanisms used as security safeguards are discussed in Chapter 4. Software applications and data malfunction considerations are covered in Chapters 5 and 11. Site location, fire protection, site construction, power loss, and equipment malfunctions are examined in detail in Chapter 6. Telecommunication and networking issues are analyzed and presented in Chapter 7. Business continuity and disaster recovery concepts are addressed in Chapter 9. All of these subjects have their own associated risks and planning requirements.

This section addresses identifying and choosing the right countermeasures for computer systems. It gives the best attributes to look for and the different cost scenarios to investigate when comparing different types of countermeasures. The end product of the analysis of choices should demonstrate why the selected control is the most advantageous to the company.

Countermeasure Selection

A security *countermeasure,* sometimes called a *safeguard,* must make good business sense, meaning it is cost-effective (its benefit outweighs its cost). This requires another type of analysis: a *cost/benefit analysis*. A commonly used cost/benefit calculation for a given safeguard is

(ALE before implementing safeguard) – (ALE after implementing safeguard) – (annual cost of safeguard) = value of safeguard to the company

For example, if the ALE of the threat of a hacker bringing down a web server is $12,000 prior to implementing the suggested safeguard, and the ALE is $3,000 after implementing the safeguard, while the annual cost of maintenance and operation of the safeguard is $650, then the value of this safeguard to the company is $8,350 each year.

The cost of a countermeasure is more than just the amount filled out on the purchase order. The following items should be considered and evaluated when deriving the full cost of a countermeasure:

- Product costs
- Design/planning costs
- Implementation costs
- Environment modifications
- Compatibility with other countermeasures
- Maintenance requirements
- Testing requirements
- Repair, replacement, or update costs
- Operating and support costs
- Effects on productivity
- Subscription costs
- Extra man- or woman-hours for monitoring and responding to alerts
- Beer for the headaches that this new tool will bring about

 WARNING As a consultant, I have repeatedly seen companies purchase new security products without understanding that they will need the staff to maintain those products. Although tools automate tasks, many companies were not even carrying out these tasks before, so they do not save on man-hours, but many times require more hours.

Consider an example. Company A decides that to protect many of its resources, purchasing an IDS is warranted. So, the company pays $5,500 for an IDS. Is that the total cost? Nope. This software should be tested in an environment that is segmented from the production environment to uncover any unexpected activity. After this testing is complete and the IT group feels it is safe to insert the IDS into its production environment, the IT group must install the monitoring management software, install the sensors, and properly direct the communication paths from the sensors to the management console. The IT group may also need to reconfigure the routers to redirect traffic flow, and it definitely needs to ensure that users cannot access the IDS management console. Finally, the IT group should configure a database to hold all attack signatures, and then run simulations.

Costs associated with an IDS alert response should most definitely be considered. Now that Company A has an IDS in place, security administrators may need additional alerting equipment such as pagers or BlackBerry devices. And then there are the time costs associated with a response to an IDS event.

Anyone who has worked in an IT group knows that some adverse reaction almost always takes place in this type of scenario. Network performance can take an unacceptable hit after installing a product, if it is an inline or proactive product. Users may no longer be able to access the Unix server for some mysterious reason. The IDS vendor may not have explained that two more service patches are necessary for the whole thing to work correctly. Staff time will need to be allocated for training, and to respond to all of the positive and false positive alerts the new IDS sends out.

So, for example, the cost of this countermeasure could be $5,500 for the product, $2,500 for training, $3,400 for the lab and testing time, $2,600 for the loss in user productivity once the product was introduced into production, and $4,000 in labor for router reconfiguration, product installation, troubleshooting, and installation of the two service patches. The real cost of this countermeasure is $18,000. If our total potential loss was calculated at $9,000, we went over budget by 100 percent when applying this countermeasure for the identified risk. Some of these costs may be hard or impossible to identify before they are incurred, but an experienced risk analyst would account for many of these possibilities.

Functionality and Effectiveness of Countermeasures

The countermeasure doesn't work, but it's pretty.
Response: Good enough.

The risk analysis team must evaluate the safeguard's functionality and effectiveness. When selecting a safeguard, some attributes are more favorable than others. Table 3-7 lists and describes attributes that should be considered *before* purchasing and committing to a security protection mechanism.

Safeguards can provide deterrence attributes if they are highly visible. This tells potential evildoers that adequate protection is in place and that they should move on to an easier target. Although the safeguard may be highly visible, attackers should not be able to discover the way it works, thus enabling them to attempt to modify the safeguard, or know how to get around the protection mechanism. If users know how to disable the antivirus program that is taking up CPU cycles or know how to bypass a proxy server to get to the Internet without restrictions, they will do so.

Characteristic	Description
Modular	It can be installed or removed from an environment without adversely affecting other mechanisms.
Provides uniform protection	A security level is applied to all mechanisms it is designed to protect in a standardized method.
Provides override functionality	An administrator can override the restriction if necessary.
Defaults to least privilege	When installed, it defaults to a lack of permissions and rights instead of installing with everyone having full control.
Independent of safeguards and the asset it is protecting	The safeguard can be used to protect different assets, and different assets can be protected by different safeguards.
Flexibility and security	The more security the safeguard provides, the better. This functionality should come with flexibility, which enables you to choose different functions instead of all or none.
User interaction	Does not panic users.
Clear distinction between user and administrator	A user should have fewer permissions when it comes to configuring or disabling the protection mechanism.
Minimum human intervention	When humans have to configure or modify controls, this opens the door to errors. The safeguard should require the least possible amount of input from humans.
Asset protection	Asset is still protected even if countermeasure needs to be reset.
Easily upgraded	Software continues to evolve, and updates should be able to happen painlessly.
Auditing functionality	There should be a mechanism that is part of the safeguard that provides minimum and/or verbose auditing.
Minimizes dependence on other components	The safeguard should be flexible and not have strict requirements about the environment into which it will be installed.
Easily usable, acceptable, and tolerated by personnel	If the safeguards provide barriers to productivity or add extra steps to simple tasks, users will not tolerate it.
Must produce output in usable and understandable format	Important information should be presented in a format easy for humans to understand and use for trend analysis.

Table 3-7 Characteristics to Seek When Obtaining Safeguards

Characteristic	Description
Must be able to reset safeguard	The mechanism should be able to be reset and returned to original configurations and settings without affecting the system or asset it is protecting.
Testable	The safeguard should be able to be tested in different environments under different situations.
Does not introduce other compromises	The safeguard should not provide any covert channels or backdoors.
System and user performance	System and user performance should not be greatly affected.
Universal application	The safeguard can be implemented across the environment and does not require many, if any, exceptions.
Proper alerting	Thresholds should be able to be set as to when to alert personnel of a security breach, and this type of alert should be acceptable.
Does not affect assets	The assets in the environment should not be adversely affected by the safeguard.

Table 3-7 Characteristics to Seek When Obtaining Safeguards *(continued)*

Putting It Together

To perform a risk analysis, a company first decides what assets must be protected and to what extent. It also indicates the amount of money that can go toward protecting specific assets. Next, it must evaluate the functionality of the available safeguards and determine which ones would be most beneficial for the environment. Finally, the company needs to appraise and compare the costs of the safeguards. These steps and the resulting information enable management to make the most intelligent and informed decisions about selecting and purchasing countermeasures. Figure 3-9 illustrates these steps.

We Are Never Done

Only by reassessing the risks on a periodic basis can a statement of safeguard performance be trusted. If the risk has not changed, and the safeguards implemented are functioning in good order, then it can be said that the risk is being properly mitigated. Regular IRM monitoring will support the information security risk ratings.

Vulnerability analysis and continued asset identification and valuation are also important tasks of risk management monitoring and performance. The cycle of continued risk analysis is a very important part of determining whether the safeguard controls that have been put in place are appropriate and necessary to safeguard the assets and environment.

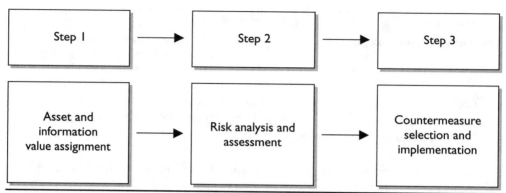

Figure 3-9   The main three steps in risk analysis

Total Risk vs. Residual Risk

The reason a company implements countermeasures is to reduce its overall risk to an acceptable level. As stated earlier, no system or environment is 100 percent secure, which means there is always some risk left over to deal with. This is called *residual risk*.

Residual risk is different from *total risk*, which is the risk a company faces if it chooses not to implement any type of safeguard. A company may choose to take on total risk if the cost/benefit analysis results indicate this is the best course of action. For example, if there is a small likelihood that a company's web servers can be compromised and the necessary safeguards to provide a higher level of protection cost more than the potential loss in the first place, the company will choose not to implement the safeguard, choosing to deal with the total risk.

There is an important difference between total risk and residual risk and which type of risk a company is willing to accept. The following are conceptual formulas:

threats × vulnerability × asset value = total risk
(threats × vulnerability × asset value) × controls gap = residual risk

You may also see these concepts illustrated as the following:

total risk
total risk – countermeasures = residual risk

NOTE   The previous formulas are not constructs you can actually plug numbers into. They are instead used to illustrate the relation of the different items that make up risk in a conceptual manner. This means no multiplication or mathematical functions actually take place. It is a means of understanding what items are involved when defining either total or residual risk.

During a risk assessment, the threats and vulnerabilities are identified. The possibility of a vulnerability being exploited is multiplied by the value of the assets being assessed, which results in the total risk. Once the controls gap (protection the control cannot provide) is factored in, the result is the residual risk. Implementing countermeasures is a way of mitigating risks. Because no company can remove all threats, there will always be some residual risk. The question is what level of risk the company is willing to accept.

Handling Risk

Now that we know about the risk, what do we do with it?
Response: Hide it behind that plant.

Once a company knows the amount of total and residual risk it is faced with, it must decide how to handle it. Risk can be dealt with in four basic ways: transfer it, reject it, reduce it, or accept it.

Many types of insurance are available to companies to protect their assets. If a company decides the total or residual risk is too high to gamble with, it can purchase insurance, which would *transfer the risk* to the insurance company.

If a company decides to terminate the activity that is introducing the risk, this is known as *risk avoidance*. For example, if a company allows employees to use instant messaging (IM), there are many risks surrounding this technology. The company could decide not to allow any IM activity by their users because there is not a strong enough business need for its continued use. Discontinuing this service is an example of risk avoidance.

Another approach is *risk mitigation*, where the risk is decreased to a level considered acceptable enough to continue conducting business. Examples of this kind of approach toward handling risk can be seen in many aspects of our lives. The implementation of firewalls, training, and intrusion/detection protection systems represent types of risk mitigation.

The last approach is to *accept the risk*, which means the company understands the level of risk it is faced with, as well as the potential cost of damage, and decides to just live with it and not implement the countermeasure. Many companies will accept risk when the cost/benefit ratio indicates that the cost of the countermeasure outweighs the potential loss value.

A crucial issue with risk acceptance is understanding *why* this is the best approach for a specific situation. Unfortunately, today many people in organizations are accepting risk and not understanding fully what they are accepting. This usually has to do with the relative newness of risk management in the security field and the lack of education and experience in those personnel who make risk decisions. When business managers are charged with the responsibility of dealing with risk in their department, most of the time they will accept whatever risk is put in front of them because their real goals pertain to getting a project finished and out the door. They don't want to be bogged down by this silly and irritating security stuff.

Risk acceptance should be based on several factors. For example, is the potential loss lower than the countermeasure? Can the organization deal with the "pain" that will come with accepting this risk? This second consideration is not purely a cost decision, but may entail noncost issues surrounding the decision. For example, if we accept this risk, we must add three more steps in our production process. Does that make sense for us? Or if we accept this risk, more security incidents may arise from it, and are we prepared to handle those?

The individual, or group, accepting risk must also understand the potential visibility of this decision. Let's say it has been determined that the company does not need to actually protect customers' first names, but it does have to protect other items like Social Security numbers, account numbers, and so on. So these current activities are in compliance with the regulations and laws, but what if your customers find out you are not properly protecting their names and they associate such things with identity fraud because of their lack of education on the matter? The company may not be able to handle this potential reputation hit; even if it is doing all it is supposed to be doing. Perceptions of a company's customer base are not always rooted in fact, but the possibility that customers will move their business to another company is a potential *fact* your company must comprehend.

Figure 3-10 shows how a risk management program can be set up, which ties together all the concepts covered in this section.

Policies, Standards, Baselines, Guidelines, and Procedures

The risk assessment is done. Let's call it a day.
Response: Nope, there's more to do.

Computers and the information processed on them usually have a direct relationship with a company's critical missions and objectives. Because of this level of importance, senior management should make protecting these items a high priority and

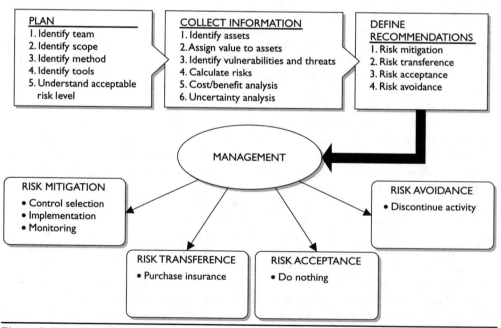

Figure 3-10 How a risk management program can be set up

provide the necessary support, funds, time, and resources to ensure that systems, networks, and information are protected in the most logical and cost-effective manner possible. A comprehensive management approach must be developed to accomplish these goals successfully. This is because everyone within an organization may have a different set of personal values and experiences they bring to the environment with regard to security, and it is important to make sure everyone is regarding the security of the organization at a level that meets the needs of the organization as determined by laws, regulations, requirements, and the goals and needs for the organization that have been determined by risk assessments of the environment of the organization.

For a company's security plan to be successful, it must start at the top level and be useful and functional at every single level within the organization. Senior management needs to define the scope of security and identify and decide what must be protected and to what extent. Management must understand the regulations, laws, and liability issues it is responsible for complying with regarding security and ensure that the company as a whole fulfills its obligations. Senior management also must determine what is expected from employees and what the consequences of noncompliance will be. These decisions should be made by the individuals who will be held ultimately responsible if something goes wrong. But it is a common practice to bring in the expertise of the security officers to collaborate in ensuring that sufficient policies and controls are being implemented to achieve the goals being set and determined by senior management.

A security program contains all the pieces necessary to provide overall protection to a corporation and lays out a long-term security strategy. A security program should have security policies, procedures, standards, guidelines, baselines, security-awareness training, an incident response plan, and a compliance program. The human resources and legal departments must be involved in the development and enforcement of some of these elements.

The language, level of detail, formality of the policy, and supporting mechanisms should be examined by the policy developers. Security policies, standards, guidelines, and procedures must be developed with a realistic view to be most effective. Highly structured organizations usually follow guidelines in a more uniform way. Less structured organizations may need more explanation and emphasis to promote compliance. The more detailed the rules are, the easier it is to know when one has been violated. However, overly detailed documentation and rules can prove to be more burdensome than helpful. On the other hand, many times, the more formal the rules, the easier they are to enforce. The business type, its culture, and its goals must be evaluated to make sure the proper language is used when writing security documentation.

Security Policy

Oh look, this paper tells us what we need to do. I am going to put smiley-face stickers all over it.

A *security policy* is an overall general statement produced by senior management (or a selected policy board or committee) that dictates what role security plays within the organization. A security policy can be an organizational policy, an issue-specific policy, or a system-specific policy. In an *organizational security policy*, management establishes how a security program will be set up, lays out the program's goals, assigns responsibilities, shows the strategic and tactical value of security, and outlines how enforcement should be carried out. This policy must address relative laws, regulations, and liability issues, and how they are to be satisfied. The organizational security policy provides scope and direction for all future security activities within the organization. It also describes the amount of risk senior management is willing to accept.

The organizational security policy has several important characteristics that must be understood and implemented:

- Business objectives should drive the policy's creation, implementation, and enforcement. The policy should not dictate business objectives.

- It should be an easily understood document that is used as a reference point for all employees and management.

- It should be developed and used to integrate security into all business functions and processes.

- It should be derived from and support all legislation and regulations applicable to the company.

- It should be reviewed and modified as a company changes, such as through adoption of a new business model, a merger with another company, or change of ownership.

- Each iteration of the policy should be dated and under version control.

- The units and individuals who are governed by the policy must have access to the applicable portions and not be expected to have to read all policy material to find direction and answers.

- It should be created with the intention of having the policies in place for several years at a time. This will help ensure policies are forward thinking enough to deal with potential changes in any near-future security environments that may arise.

- It should use language that is direct and commanding and avoid weaker tones and directives. Words like "should" or "may" need to be replaced with "shall" or "must."

- The level of professionalism in the presentation of the policies reinforces their importance as well as the need to adhere to them.

- It should not contain language that isn't readily understood by everyone. Use clear and declarative statements that are easy to understand and adopt.

- It should be reviewed on a regular basis and adapted to correct incidents that have occurred since the last review and revision of the policies.

A process for dealing with those that choose not to comply with the security policies must be developed and enforced so there is a structured method of response to noncompliance. This establishes a process that others can understand and thus recognize not only what is expected of them, but also what they can expect as a response to their noncompliance.

Why Have Policies in Place?

The following summarizes the importance of a security policy:

- Identifies assets the company considers valuable
- Provides authority to the security team and its activities
- Provides a reference to review when conflicts pertaining to security arise
- States the company's goal and objectives pertaining to security
- Outlines personal responsibility
- Helps to prevent unaccounted-for events (surprises)
- Defines the scope and functions of the security team
- Outlines incident response responsibilities
- Outlines the company's response to legal, regulatory, and standards of due care

It is through these policies that security programs can be set up with a strong foundation and an organized method of response to security issues, as well as expectations for personnel within the organization as to who is in charge during certain kinds of incidents.

Different types of security policies can be implemented in an organization. These policies can be adapted to fit the specific needs of their environment.

An *issue-specific policy*, also called a functional implementing policy, addresses specific security issues that management feels need more detailed explanation and attention to make sure a comprehensive structure is built and all employees understand how they are to comply with these security issues. For example, an organization may choose to have an e-mail security policy that outlines what management can and cannot do with employees' e-mail messages for monitoring purposes, that specifies which e-mail functionality employees can or cannot use, and that addresses specific privacy issues.

As a more specific example, an e-mail policy might state that management can read any employee's e-mail messages that reside on the mail server, but not when they reside on the user's workstation. The e-mail policy might also state that employees cannot use e-mail to share confidential information or pass inappropriate material, and that they may be subject to monitoring of these actions. Before they use their e-mail clients, employees should be asked to confirm that they have read and understand the e-mail policy, either by signing a confirmation document or clicking Yes in a confirmation dialog box. The policy provides direction and structure for the staff by indicating what they can and cannot do. It informs the users of the expectations of their actions, and it provides liability protection in case an employee cries "foul" for any reason dealing with e-mail use.

NOTE A policy needs to be technology- and solution-independent. It must outline the goals and missions, but not tie the organization to specific ways of accomplishing them.

A *system-specific policy* presents the management's decisions that are specific to the actual computers, networks, applications, and data. This type of policy may provide an approved software list, which contains a list of applications that may be installed on individual workstations. This policy may describe how databases are to be used and protected, how computers are to be locked down, and how firewalls, IDSs, and scanners are to be employed.

Policies are written in broad terms to cover many subjects in a general fashion. Much more granularity is needed to actually support the policy, and this happens with the use of procedures, standards, and guidelines. The policy provides the foundation. The procedures, standards, and guidelines provide the security framework. And the necessary security components, implementations, and mechanisms are used to fill in the framework to provide a full security program and secure infrastructure.

Standards

Some things you just gotta do.

Standards refer to mandatory activities, actions, or rules. Standards can give a policy its support and reinforcement in direction. Standards can be internal or can be externally mandated (government laws and regulations).

Types of Policies

Policies generally fall into one of the following categories:

- **Regulatory**   This type of policy ensures that the organization is following standards set by specific industry regulations. It is very detailed and specific to a type of industry. It is used in financial institutions, healthcare facilities, public utilities, and other government-regulated industries.

- **Advisory**   This type of policy strongly advises employees as to which types of behaviors and activities should and should not take place within the organization. It also outlines possible ramifications if employees do not comply with the established behaviors and activities. This policy type can be used, for example, to describe how to handle medical information or financial transactions, or how to process confidential information.

- **Informative**   This type of policy informs employees of certain topics. It is not an enforceable policy, but rather one that teaches individuals about specific issues relevant to the company. It could explain how the company interacts with partners, the company's goals and mission, and a general reporting structure in different situations.

Organizational security standards may specify how hardware and software products are to be used. They can also be used to indicate expected user behavior. They provide a means to ensure that specific technologies, applications, parameters, and procedures are implemented in a uniform manner across the organization. An organizational standard may require that all employees wear their company identification badges at all times, that they challenge unknown individuals about their identity and purpose for being in a specific area, or that they encrypt confidential information. These rules are usually compulsory within a company, and if they are going to be effective, they must be enforced.

As stated in an earlier section, tactical and strategic goals are different. A strategic goal can be viewed as the ultimate endpoint, while tactical goals are the steps necessary to achieve it. As shown in Figure 3-11, standards, guidelines, and procedures are the tactical tools used to achieve and support the directives in the security policy, which is considered the strategic goal.

Baselines

The term *baseline* has a couple of definitions. A baseline can refer to a point in time that is used as a comparison for future changes. Once risks have been mitigated, and security put in place, a baseline is formally reviewed and agreed upon, after which, all further comparisons and development are measured against it. A baseline results in a consistent reference point.

Let's say that your doctor has told you that you weigh 400 pounds due to your diet of donuts, pizza, and soda. (This is very frustrating to you because the TV commercial said you could eat whatever you wanted and just take their very expensive pills every day and lose weight.) The doctor tells you that you need to exercise each day and elevate your heart rate to double its normal rate for 30 minutes twice a day. How do you know when you are at double your heart rate? You find out your baseline (regular heart rate) by using one of those arm thingies with a little ball attached. So you start at your baseline and continue to exercise until you have doubled your heart rate or die, whichever comes first.

Baselines are also used to define the minimum level of protection required. In security, specific baselines can be defined per system type, which indicates the necessary settings and the level of protection being provided. For example, a company may stipulate that all accounting systems must meet an Evaluation Assurance Level (EAL) 4 baseline. This means that only systems that have gone through the Common Criteria process and achieved this rating can be used in this department evaluation. Once the systems are properly configured, this is the necessary baseline. When new software is installed, when patches or upgrades are applied to existing software, or when other changes to the system take place, there is a good chance the system may no longer be providing its necessary minimum level of protection (its baseline). Security personnel must assess the systems as changes take place and ensure that the baseline level of security is always being met. If a technician installs a patch on a system and does not ensure the baseline is still being met, there could be new vulnerabilities introduced into the system that will allow attackers easy access to the network.

Figure 3-11
Policy establishes the strategic plans, and the lower elements provide the tactical support.

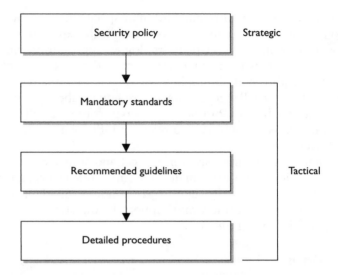

NOTE Baselines that are not technology-oriented should be created and enforced within organizations as well. For example, a company can mandate that while in the facility all employees must have a badge with a picture ID in view at all times. It can also state that visitors must sign in at a front desk and be escorted while in the facility. If these are followed, then this creates a baseline of protection.

CAUTION While the term "baseline" is interpreted differently in the industry, you should note that software and hardware configurations are commonly referred to as baselines. Specific configurations will provide the minimum amount of security required. This is the interpretation you will most likely run into on the exam.

Guidelines

Guidelines are recommended actions and operational guides to users, IT staff, operations staff, and others when a specific standard does not apply. Guidelines can deal with the methodologies of technology, personnel, or physical security. Life is full of gray areas, and guidelines can be used as a reference during those times. Whereas standards are specific mandatory rules, guidelines are general approaches that provide the necessary flexibility for unforeseen circumstances.

A policy might state that access to confidential data must be audited. A supporting guideline could further explain that audits should contain sufficient information to allow for reconciliation with prior reviews. Supporting procedures would outline the necessary steps to configure, implement, and maintain this type of auditing.

Procedures

Procedures are detailed step-by-step tasks that should be performed to achieve a certain goal. The steps can apply to users, IT staff, operations staff, security members, and others who may need to carry out specific tasks. Many organizations have written procedures on how to install operating systems, configure security mechanisms, implement access control lists, set up new user accounts, assign computer privileges, audit activities, destroy material, report incidents, and much more.

Procedures are considered the lowest level in the policy chain because they are closest to the computers and users (compared to policies) and provide detailed steps for configuration and installation issues.

Procedures spell out how the policy, standards, and guidelines will actually be implemented in an operating environment. If a policy states that all individuals who access confidential information must be properly authenticated, the supporting procedures will explain the steps for this to happen by defining the access criteria for authorization, how access control mechanisms are implemented and configured, and how access activities are audited. If a standard states that backups should be performed, then the procedures will define the detailed steps necessary to perform the backup, the timelines of backups, the storage of backup media, and so on. Procedures should be detailed enough to be both understandable and useful to a diverse group of individuals.

To tie these items together, let's walk through an example. A corporation's security policy indicates that confidential information should be properly protected. It states the issue in very broad and general terms. A supporting standard mandates that all customer information held in databases must be encrypted with the Advanced Encryption Standard (AES) algorithm while it is stored and that it cannot be transmitted over the Internet unless IPSec encryption technology is used. The standard indicates what type of protection is required and provides another level of granularity and explanation. The supporting procedures explain exactly how to implement the AES and IPSec technologies, and the guidelines cover how to handle cases when data is accidentally corrupted or compromised during transmission. All of these work together to provide a company with a security structure.

Implementation

Where are the policies that we spent $100,000 to develop?
Response: What is a policy again?

Unfortunately, security policies, standards, procedures, baselines, and guidelines often are written because an auditor instructed a company to document these items, but then they are placed on a file server and are not shared, explained, or used. To be

---

Modular Elements

Standards, guidelines, and baselines should not be in one large document. Each has a specific purpose and a different audience. A document describing how to be in compliance with a specific regulation may go to the management staff, whereas a detailed procedure on how to properly secure a specific operating system would be directed toward an IT member. Keeping standards, guidelines, and baselines separate and modular helps for proper distribution and updating when necessary.

useful, they must be put into action. No one is going to follow the rules if people don't know the rules exist. Security policies and the items that support them not only must be developed, but must also be implemented and enforced.

To be effective, employees need to know about security issues within these documents; therefore, the policies and their supporting counterparts need visibility. Awareness training, manuals, presentations, newsletters, and legal banners can achieve this visibility. It must be clear that the directives came from senior management and that the full management staff supports these policies. Employees must understand what is expected of them in their actions, behaviors, accountability, and performance.

Implementing security policies and the items that support them shows due care by the company and its management staff. Informing employees of what is expected of them and the consequences of noncompliance can come down to a liability issue. If a company fires an employee because he was downloading pornographic material to the company's computer, the employee may take the company to court and win if the employee can prove he was not properly informed of what was considered acceptable and unacceptable use of company property and what the consequences were. Security-awareness training is covered in later sections, but understand that companies that do not supply this to their employees are not practicing due care and can be held negligent and liable in the eyes of the law.

Due Care and Due Diligence

Due care and due diligence are terms used throughout this book. *Due diligence* is the act of investigating and understanding the risks the company faces. A company practices *due care* by developing and implementing security policies, procedures, and standards. Due care shows that a company has taken responsibility for the activities that take place within the corporation and has taken the necessary steps to help protect the company, its resources, and employees from possible threats. So, due diligence is understanding the current threats and risks, and due care is implementing countermeasures to provide protection from those threats. If a company does not practice due care and due diligence pertaining to the security of its assets, it can be legally charged with negligence and held accountable for any ramifications of that negligence.

The following are some tricks to remember the difference between these two concepts. Due Diligence = Do Detect. Due diligence maps with Do Detect. It is the steps you take to identify the risks using best practices, published standards, and other tools. Due Care = Do Correct. This is what you do to correct the threat identified or to minimize it to an acceptable level of risk.

Information Classification

My love letter to my dog is top secret.
Response: As it should be.

Earlier, this chapter touched upon the importance of recognizing what information is critical to a company and assigning a value to it. The rationale behind assigning values to different types of data is that it enables a company to gauge the amount of funds and resources that should go toward protecting each type of data, because not all data has the same value to a company. After identifying all important information, it should be properly classified. A company has a lot of information that is created and maintained. The reason to classify data is to organize it according to its sensitivity to loss, disclosure, or unavailability. Once data is segmented according to its sensitivity level, the company can decide what security controls are necessary to protect different types of data. This ensures that information assets receive the appropriate level of protection, and classifications indicate the priority of that security protection. The primary purpose of data classification is to indicate the level of confidentiality, integrity, and availability protection that is required for each type of data set.

Data classification helps ensure data is protected in the most cost-effective manner. Protecting and maintaining data costs money, but it is important to spend this money for the information that actually requires protection. Going back to our very sophisticated example of U.S. spy satellites and the peanut butter and banana sandwich recipe, a company in charge of encryption algorithms used to transmit data to and from U.S. spy satellites would classify this data as top secret and apply complex and highly technical security controls and procedures to ensure it is not accessed in an unauthorized method and disclosed. On the other hand, the sandwich recipe would have a lower classification, and your only means of protecting it might be to not talk about it.

Each classification should have separate handling requirements and procedures pertaining to how that data is accessed, used, and destroyed. For example, in a corporation, confidential information may be accessed only by senior management and a select few throughout the company. Accessing the information may require two or more people to enter their access codes. Auditing could be very detailed and its results monitored daily, and paper copies of the information may be kept in a vault. To properly erase this data from the media, degaussing or zeroization procedures may be required. Other information in this company may be classified as sensitive, allowing a slightly larger group of people to view it. Access control on the information classified as sensitive may require only one set of credentials. Auditing happens but is only reviewed weekly, paper copies are kept in locked file cabinets, and the data can be deleted using regular measures when it is time to do so. Then, the rest of the information is marked public. All employees can access it, and no special auditing or destruction methods are required.

Private Business vs. Military Classifications

Earlier, we touched on how organizations choose different security models, depending upon the type of organization, its goals, and its objectives. Military organizations are more concerned than most private-sector businesses about not disclosing confidential information. Private-sector businesses are usually more interested in the integrity and availability of data. These different perspectives affect data classification also.

To properly implement data classifications, a company must first decide upon the sensitivity scheme it is going to use. One company may choose to use only two layers of classifications, while another company may choose to use more. Table 3-8 explains the types of classifications available. Note that some classifications are used for commercial businesses, whereas others are military classifications.

Classification	Definition	Examples	Organizations That Would Use This
Public	• Disclosure is not welcome, but it would not cause an adverse impact to company or personnel.	• How many people are working on a specific project • Upcoming projects	Commercial business
Sensitive	• Requires special precautions to ensure the integrity and confidentiality of the data by protecting it from unauthorized modification or deletion. • Requires higher than normal assurance of accuracy and completeness.	• Financial information • Details of projects • Profit earnings and forecasts	Commercial business
Private	• Personal information for use within a company. • Unauthorized disclosure could adversely affect personnel or the company.	• Work history • Human resources information • Medical information	Commercial business

Table 3-8 Commercial Business and Military Data Classification

Classification	Definition	Examples	Organizations That Would Use This
Confidential	• For use within the company only. • Data exempt from disclosure under the Freedom of Information Act or other laws and regulations. • Unauthorized disclosure could seriously affect a company.	• Trade secrets • Healthcare information • Programming code • Information that keeps copany competitive	Commercial business Military
Unclassified	• Data is not sensitive or classified.	• Computer manual and warranty information • Recruiting information	Military
Sensitive but unclassified (SBU)	• Minor secret. • If disclosed, it may not cause serious damage.	• Medical data • Answers to test scores	Military
Secret	• If disclosed, it could cause serious damage to national security.	• Deployment plans for troops • Nuclear bomb placement	Military
Top secret	• If disclosed, it could cause grave damage to national security.	• Blueprints of new wartime weapons • Spy satellite information • Espionage data	Military

Table 3-8 Commercial Business and Military Data Classification *(continued)*

The following shows the levels of sensitivity from the highest to the lowest for commercial business:

- Confidential
- Private
- Sensitive
- Public

The following shows the levels of sensitivity from the highest to the lowest for the military:

- Top secret
- Secret

- Confidential
- Sensitive but unclassified
- Unclassified

A commonly used classification set employed in the commercial sector is described next:

- **For official use only**   Financially sensitive
- **Proprietary**   Protects competitive edge
- **Privileged**   Ensures conformance with business standards and laws
- **Private**   Contains records about individuals

It is important to not go overboard and come up with a long list of classifications, which will only cause confusion and frustration for the individuals who will use the system. The classifications should not be too restrictive and detailed-oriented either, because many types of data may need to be classified.

Each classification should be unique and separate from the others and not have any overlapping effects. The classification process should also outline how information and applications are controlled and handled through their life cycles (from creation to termination).

Once the scheme is decided upon, the company or government agency must develop the criteria it will use to decide what information goes into which classification. The following list shows some criteria parameters an organization may use to determine the sensitivity of data:

- The usefulness of data
- The value of data
- The age of data
- The level of damage that could be caused if the data were disclosed
- The level of damage that could be caused if the data were modified or corrupted
- Legal, regulatory, or contractual responsibility to protect the data
- Effects the data has on national security
- Who should be able to access the data
- Who should maintain the data
- Where the data should be kept
- Who should be able to reproduce the data
- Which data require labels and special marking
- Whether encryption is required for the data
- Whether separation of duties is required
- Lost opportunity costs that could be incurred if the data were not available or were corrupted

Data are not the only things that must be classified. Applications and sometimes whole systems must be classified. The applications that hold and process classified information should be evaluated for the level of protection they provide. You do not want a program filled with security vulnerabilities to process and "protect" your most sensitive information. The application classifications should be based on the assurance (confidence level) the company has in the software and the type of information it can store and process.

NOTE   An organization must make sure that whoever is backing up classified data—and whoever has access to backed-up data—has the necessary clearance level. A large security risk can be introduced if low-end technicians with no security clearance have access to this information during their tasks.

CAUTION   The classification rules must apply to data no matter what format it is in: digital, paper, video, fax, audio, and so on.

Now that we have chosen a sensitivity scheme, the next step is to specify how each classification should be dealt with. We must specify provisions for access control, identification, and labeling, along with how data in specific classifications are stored, maintained, transmitted, and destroyed. We also must iron out auditing, monitoring, and compliance issues. Each classification requires a different degree of security and, therefore, different requirements from each of the mentioned items.

Classification Controls

I marked our top secret stuff as "top secret."
Response: Great, now everyone is going to want to see it. Good job.

As mentioned earlier, which types of controls are implemented per classification depends upon the level of protection that management and the security team have determined is needed. The numerous types of controls available are discussed throughout this book. But some considerations pertaining to sensitive data and applications are common across most organizations:

- Strict and granular access control for all levels of sensitive data and programs (see Chapter 4 for coverage of access controls, along with file system permissions that should be understood)
- Encryption of data while stored and while in transmission (see Chapter 8 for coverage of all types of encryption technologies)
- Auditing and monitoring (determine what level of auditing is required and how long logs are to be retained)
- Separation of duties (determine whether two or more people must be involved in accessing sensitive information to protect against fraudulent activities; if so, define and document procedures)
- Periodic reviews (review classification levels, and the data and programs that adhere to them, to ensure they are still in alignment with business needs; data

or applications may also need to be reclassified or declassified, depending upon the situation)

- Backup and recovery procedures (define and document)
- Change control procedures (define and document)
- Physical security protection (define and document)
- Information flow channels
- Data dictionary review
- Proper disposal actions, such as shredding, degaussing, and so on (define and document)
- File and file system access permissions (define and document)
- Marking and labeling
  - The cover and inside documents should be labeled.
  - All media should be marked and labeled (magnetic, optical media).

Data Classification Procedures

The following outlines the necessary steps for a proper classification program:

1. Define classification levels.
2. Specify the criteria that will determine how data are classified.
3. Have the data owner indicate the classification of the data she is responsible for.
4. Identify the data custodian who will be responsible for maintaining data and its security level.
5. Indicate the security controls, or protection mechanisms, required for each classification level.
6. Document any exceptions to the previous classification issues.
7. Indicate the methods that can be used to transfer custody of the information to a different data owner.
8. Create a procedure to periodically review the classification and ownership. Communicate any changes to the data custodian.
9. Indicate procedures for declassifying the data.
10. Integrate these issues into the security-awareness program so all employees understand how to handle data at different classification levels.

It is important that once the organization has an understanding of the different levels of protection that must be provided, it can develop the necessary classification levels it will use. Keep some of the following ideas in mind as your organization develops its classification levels:

- Too many classification levels will be impractical and confusing.
- Too few classification levels will give the perception of how little value is placed on the process and how little it will be used.
- There should be no overlap in the criteria definitions between classification levels.
- Classification levels should be developed for both data and software.

Layers of Responsibility

Senior management and other levels of management understand the vision of the company, the business goals, and the objectives. The next layer down is the functional management, whose members understand how their individual departments work, what roles individuals play within the company, and how security affects their department directly. The next layers are operational managers and staff. These layers are closer to the actual operations of the company. They know detailed information about the technical and procedural requirements, the systems, and how the systems are used. The employees at these layers understand how security mechanisms integrate into systems, how to configure them, and how they affect daily productivity. Every layer offers different insight into what type of role security plays within an organization, and each should have input into the best security practices, procedures, and chosen controls to ensure the agreed upon security level provides the necessary amount of protection without negatively affecting the company's productivity.

Although each layer is important to the overall security of an organization, some specific roles must be clearly defined. Individuals who work in smaller environments (where everyone must wear several hats) may get overwhelmed with the number of roles presented next. Many commercial businesses do not have this level of structure in their security teams, but many government agencies and military units do. What you need to understand are the responsibilities that must be assigned, and whether they are assigned to just a few people or to a large security team. These roles are the data owner, data custodian, system owner, security administrator, security analyst, application owner, supervisor (user manager), change control analyst, data analyst, process owner, solution provider, user, product line manager, and the guy who gets everyone coffee.

Who's Involved?

I don't want to be involved. I have heard that it is a lot of work.
Response: Yes, indeed. It will require many in the organization to stretch their understanding and responsibilities.

Many companies, and security professionals, are struggling with what security programs and governance really are and how responsibilities should be assigned throughout the organization. Identifying roles and responsibilities should happen very quickly when developing a security program, so we will discuss common roles and entities in corporations and their responsibilities as they pertain to asset protection.

The Board of Directors

Hey, Enron was successful for many years. What's wrong with their approach?

The **board of directors** is a group of individuals who are elected by the shareholders of a corporation to oversee the fulfillment of the corporation's charter. The goal of the board is to ensure the shareholders' interests are being protected and that the corporation is being run properly. They are supposed to be unbiased and independent individuals who oversee the executive staff's performance in running the company.

For many years, too many people who held these positions either looked the other way regarding corporate fraud and mismanagement or depended too much on executive management's feedback instead of finding out the truth about their company's health themselves. We know this because of all of the corporate scandals uncovered in 2002 (Enron, WorldCom, Global Crossing, and so on). The boards of directors of these corporations were responsible for knowing about these types of fraudulent activities and putting a stop to them to protect shareholders. Many things caused the directors not to play the role they should have. Some were intentional, some not. These scandals forced the U.S. government and the Securities and Exchange Commission (SEC) to place more requirements, and potential penalties, on the boards of directors of publicly traded companies. This is why many companies today are having a harder time finding candidates to fulfill these roles—personal liability for a part-time job is a real downer.

Independence is important if the board members are going to truly work for the benefit of the shareholders. This means the board members should not have immediate family who are employees of the company, the board members should not receive financial benefits from the company that could cloud their judgment or create conflicts of interests, and no other activities should cause the board members to act other than as champions of the company's shareholders. This is especially true if the company must comply with the Sarbanes-Oxley Act (SOX). Under this Act, the board of directors can be held personally responsible if the corporation does not properly maintain an internal corporate governance framework, and/or if financials reported to the SEC are incorrect.

NOTE Other regulations also call out requirements of boards of directors, as in the Gramm-Leach-Bliley Act (GLBA). But SOX is a regulation that holds the members of the board personally responsible, thus they can each be fined or go to jail.

CAUTION The CISSP exam does not cover anything about specific regulations (SOX, HIPPA, GLBA, Basel II, SB 1386, and so on). So do not get wrapped up in studying these for the exam. However, it is critical that the security professional understand the regulations and laws of the country and region she is working within.

Principles of Federal Prosecution of Business Organizations

The Department of Justice provides the following guidelines for attorneys when attempting to prosecute corporate wrongdoings:

Do the corporation's directors exercise independent review over proposed corporate actions rather than unquestioningly ratifying officers' recommendations; are the directors provided with information sufficient to enable the exercise of independent judgment; are internal audit functions conducted at a level sufficient to ensure their independence and accuracy; and have the directors established an information and reporting system in the organization reasonably designed to provide management and the board of directors with timely and accurate information sufficient to allow them to reach an informed decision regarding the organization's compliance with the law.

More information can be found at www.usdoj.gov/dag/cftf/corporate_guide-lines.htm.

Executive Management

I am very important, but I am missing a "C."
Response: Then you are not so important.

This motley crew is made up of individuals whose titles start with a C. The *chief executive officer (CEO)* has the day-to-day management responsibilities of an organization. This person is often the chairperson of the board of directors and is the highest ranking officer in the company. This role is for the person who oversees the company's finances, strategic planning, and operations from a high level. The CEO is usually seen as the visionary for the company and is responsible for developing and modifying the company's business plan. They set budgets, form partnerships, decide on what markets to enter, what product lines to develop, how the company will differentiate itself, and so on. This role's overall responsibility is to ensure that the company grows and thrives.

NOTE The CEO can delegate tasks, but not necessarily responsibility. More and more regulations dealing with information security are holding this role's feet to the fire, which is why security departments across the land are receiving more funding. Personal liability for the decision makers and purse-string holders has loosened those purse strings, and companies are now able to spend more money on security than before.

The *chief financial officer (CFO)* is responsible for the corporation's account and financial activities, and the overall financial structure of the organization. This person is responsible for determining what the company's financial needs will be and how to finance those needs. The CFO must create and maintain the company's capital structure, which is the proper mix of equity, credit, cash, and debt financing. This person oversees forecasting and budgeting and the processes of submitting quarterly and annual financial statements to the SEC and stakeholders.

The CFO and CEO are responsible for informing stakeholders (creditors, analysts, employees, management, investors) of the firm's financial condition and health. After the corporate debacles uncovered in 2002, the U.S. government and the SEC started doling out stiff penalties to people who held these roles and abused them, as shown in the following:

- January 2004—Enron ex-Chief Financial Officer Andrew Fastow was given a 10-year prison sentence for his accounting scandals, which was a reduced term because he cooperated with prosecutors.

- June 2005—John Rigas, the CEO of Adelphia Communications Corp., was sentenced to 15 years in prison for his role in the looting and debt-hiding scandal that pummeled the company into bankruptcy. His son, who also held an executive position, was sentenced to 20 years.

- July 2005—WorldCom ex-Chief Executive Officer Bernard Ebbers was sentenced to 25 years in prison for his role in orchestrating the biggest corporate fraud in the nation's history.

- August 2005—Former WorldCom chief financial officer Scott Sullivan was sentenced to five years in prison for his role in engineering the $11 billion accounting fraud that led to the bankruptcy of the telecommunications powerhouse.

- December 2005—The former chief executive officer of HealthSouth Corp. was sentenced to five years in prison for his part in the $2.7 billion scandal.

These are only the big ones that made it into all the headlines. Other CEOs and CFOs have also received punishments for "creative accounting" and fraudulent activities.

 NOTE Although the preceding activities took place years ago, these were the events that motivated the U.S. government to create new laws and regulations to control different types of fraud.

Figure 3-12 shows how the board members are responsible for setting the organization's strategy and risk appetite (how much risk the company should take on). The board is also responsible for receiving information from executives, as well as for the assurance (auditing committee). With these inputs, the board is supposed to ensure that the company is running properly, thus protecting shareholders' interests. Also notice that the business unit owners are the risk owners, not the security department. Too many companies are not extending the responsibility of risk out to the business units, which is why the CISO position is commonly referred to as the sacrificial lamb.

The Chief Information Officer
On a lower rung of the food chain is the *chief information officer (CIO)*. This individual can report to the CEO or CFO, depending upon the corporate structure, and is responsible for the strategic use and management of information systems and technology within the organization. Over time, this position has become more strategic and less

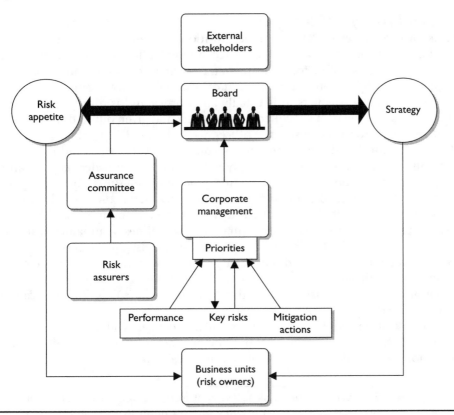

Figure 3-12 Risk must be understood at different departments and levels.

operational in many organizations. CIOs oversee and are responsible for the day-in-day-out technology operations of a company, but because organizations are so dependent upon technology, they are being asked to sit at the big boys' corporate table more and more.

CIO responsibilities have extended to working with the CEO (and other management) on business-process management, revenue generation, and how business strategy can be accomplished with the company's underlying technology. This person usually should have one foot in techno-land and one foot in business-land to be effective, because she is bridging two very different worlds.

The CEO sets the stage for the protection of company assets and is ultimately responsible for the success of the company security program. Direction should be coming down from the CEO, and there should be clear lines of communication between the board of directors, the C-level staff, and mid-management. In SOX, the CEO and CFO have outlined responsibilities and penalties they can be *personally* liable for if those responsibilities are not carried out. The SEC wanted to make sure these roles cannot just allow their companies to absorb fines if they misbehave. Under this law they can personally be fined millions of dollars and/or go to jail. Such things always make them perk up during meetings.

The Chief Privacy Officer

The *chief privacy officer (CPO)* is a newer position, created mainly because of the increasing demands on organizations to protect a long laundry list of different types of data. This role is responsible for ensuring that customer, company, and employee data are kept safe, which keeps the company out of criminal and civil courts and hopefully out of the headlines. This person is usually an attorney and is directly involved with setting policies on how data are collected, protected, and given out to third parties. The CPO often reports to the chief security officer.

It is important that the company understand the privacy, legal, and regulatory requirements the organization must comply with. With this knowledge, you can then develop the organization's policies, standards, procedures, controls, and contract agreements to see if privacy requirements are being properly met. Remember also that organizations are responsible for knowing how their suppliers, partners, and other third parties are protecting this sensitive information. Many times, companies will need to review these other parties (which have copies of data needing protection).

Some companies have carried out risk assessments without including the penalties and ramifications they would be forced to deal with if they did not properly protect the information they are responsible for. Without including these liabilities, risk cannot be properly assessed.

The organization should document how privacy data are collected, used, disclosed, archived, and destroyed. Employees should be held accountable for not following the organization's standards on how to handle this type of information.

 NOTE Carrying out a risk assessment from the perspective of the protection of sensitive data is called a *privacy impact analysis.* You can review "How to Do a Privacy Assessment" at www.actcda.com/resource/multiapp.pdf to understand the steps.

Since properly protecting sensitive data is so critical to organizations today, these requirements should be baked into many different business processes, such as purchasing and/or developing software that will house sensitive data, establishing IT communication mechanisms, and implementing and configuring security products. In each of these examples, the question "What type of data will be stored or transmitted through this?" should be asked to ensure that the right level of protection is being provided.

The Chief Security Officer

Hey, we need a sacrificial lamb in case things go bad.
Response: We already have one. He's called the chief security officer.

The *chief security officer (CSO)* is responsible for understanding the risks that the company faces and for mitigating these risks to an acceptable level. This role is responsible for understanding the organization's business drivers and for creating and maintaining a security program that facilitates these drivers, along with providing security,

International Requirements

If the organization is exchanging data with European entities, it may need to adhere to the *safe harbor* requirements. Europe has always had tighter control over protecting privacy information than the United States and other parts of the world. So in the past when U.S. and European companies needed to exchange data, there was confusion and interruption of business because the lawyers had to get involved to figure out how to work within the structures of the differing laws. To clear up this mess, a "safe harbor" framework was created, which outlines how any entity that is going to move privacy data to and from Europe must go about protecting it. U.S. companies that deal with European entities can become certified according to this rule base so that data transfer can happen more quickly and easily. More information can be found at www.export.gov/safeharbor/sh_overview.html.

Global organizations that move data across other country boundaries must also be aware of and follow the *Organisation for Economic Co-operation and Development (OECD) Guidelines* and *transborder information flow* rules. Almost every country has its own rules pertaining to what private data is and how it should be protected and dealt with. As the digital and information age came upon us, these different laws started to negatively affect business and international trade. The OECD is an international organization that helps different governments come together and tackle the economic, social, and governance challenges of a globalized economy. Thus, the OECD came up with guidelines for the various countries to follow so data are properly protected and everyone follows the same type of rules. More information can be found at www.oecd.org/document/18/0,2340,en_2649_34255_1815186_1_1_1_1,00.html.

Organizations that do not follow these types of rules and guidelines (whether knowingly or otherwise) can be fined, sued, and their business disrupted. Some companies have had to actually move their WAN connections because they were transferring privacy data through a country and breaking its law without knowing it.

compliance with a long list of regulations and laws, and any customer expectations or contractual obligations.

The creation of this role is a mark in the "win" column for the security industry because it means security is finally being seen as a business issue. Previously, security was stuck in the IT department and was viewed solely as a technology issue. As organizations saw the need to integrate security requirements and business needs, the need of creating a position for security in the executive management team became more of a necessity. The CSO's job is to ensure that business is not disrupted in any way due to security issues. This extends beyond IT and reaches into business processes, legal issues, operational issues, revenue generation, reputation protection, risk management—and all of this must be done in a cost-effective manner!

> ## CSO vs. CISO
>
> The CSO and chief information security officer (CISO) may have similar or very different responsibilities. How is that for clarification? It is up to the individual organization to define the responsibilities of these two roles and whether they will use both, either, or neither. By and large, the CSO role usually has a farther-reaching list of responsibilities compared to the CISO role. The CISO is usually focused more on technology and has an IT background. The CSO usually is required to understand a wider range of business risks, including physical security—not just technological risks.
>
> The CSO is usually more of a businessperson and typically is present in larger organizations. If a company has both roles, the CISO reports directly to the CSO.

The IS Security Steering Committee

Our steering committee just ran us into a wall.

A *security steering committee* is responsible for making decisions on tactical and strategic security issues within the enterprise as a whole and should not be tied to one or more business units. The group should be made up of people from all over the organization so they can view risks and the effects of security decisions on individual departments and the organization as a whole. The CEO should head this committee, and the CFO, CIO, department managers, and chief internal auditor should all be on it.

This committee should meet at least quarterly and have a well-defined agenda. Some of the group's responsibilities are listed next:

- Define the acceptable risk level for the organization.
- Develop security objectives and strategies.
- Determine priorities of security initiatives based on business needs.
- Review risk assessment and auditing reports.
- Monitor the business impact of security risks.
- Review major security breaches and incidents.
- Approve any major change to the security policy and program.

They should also have a clearly defined vision statement in place that is set up to work with and support the organizational intent of the business. The statement should be structured in a manner that provides support for the goals of confidentiality, integrity, and availability as they pertain to the business objectives of the organization. This in turn should be followed, or supported, by a mission statement that provides support and definition to the processes that will apply to the organization and allow it to reach its business goals.

The Audit Committee

The *audit committee* should be appointed by the board of directors to help it review and evaluate the company's internal operations, internal audit system, and the transparency and accuracy of financial reporting so the company's investors, customers, and creditors have continued confidence in the organization.

This committee is usually responsible for at least the following items:

- The integrity of the company's financial statements and other financial information provided to stockholders and others
- The company's system of internal controls
- The engagement and performance of the independent auditors
- The performance of the internal audit function
- Compliance with legal requirements and company policies regarding ethical conduct

The goal of this committee is to provide independent and open communications among the board of directors, the company's management, the internal auditors, and external auditors. Financial statement integrity and reliability is crucial to every organization, and many times pressure from shareholders, management, investors, and the public can directly affect the objectivity and correctness of these financial documents. In the wake of high-profile corporate scandals, the audit committee's role has shifted from just overseeing, monitoring, and advising company management to enforcing and ensuring accountability on the part of all individuals involved. This committee must take input from external and internal auditors and outside experts to help ensure the company's internal control processes and financial reporting are taking place properly.

The Data Owner

The *data owner* (information owner) is usually a member of management who is in charge of a specific business unit, and who is ultimately responsible for the protection and use of a specific subset of information. The data owner has due care responsibilities and thus will be held responsible for any negligent act that results in the corruption or disclosure of the data. The data owner decides upon the classification of the data she is responsible for and alters that classification if the business need arises. This person is also responsible for ensuring that the necessary security controls are in place, defining security requirements per classification and backup requirements, approving any disclosure activities, ensuring that proper access rights are being used, and defining user access criteria. The data owner approves access requests or may choose to delegate this function to business unit managers. And the data owner will deal with security violations pertaining to the data she is responsible for protecting. The data owner, who obviously has enough on her plate, delegates responsibility of the day-to-day maintenance of the data protection mechanisms to the data custodian.

The Data Custodian

Hey, custodian, clean up my mess!
Response: I'm not that type of custodian.

The *data custodian* (information custodian) is responsible for maintaining and protecting the data. This role is usually filled by the IT or security department, and the duties include performing regular backups of the data, periodically validating the integrity of the data, restoring data from backup media, retaining records of activity, and

> ## Data Owner Issues
>
> Each business unit should have a data owner who protects the unit's most critical information. The company's policies must give the data owners the necessary authority to carry out their tasks.
>
> This is not a technical role, but rather a business role that must understand the relationship between the unit's success and the protection of this critical asset. Not all businesspeople understand this role, so they should be given the necessary training.

fulfilling the requirements specified in the company's security policy, standards, and guidelines that pertain to information security and data protection.

The System Owner

I am god over this system!
Response: You are responsible for a printer? Your mother must be proud.

The system owner is responsible for one or more systems, each of which may hold and process data owned by different data owners. A system owner is responsible for integrating security considerations into application and system purchasing decisions and development projects. The system owner is responsible for ensuring that adequate security is being provided by the necessary controls, password management, remote access controls, operating system configurations, and so on. This role must ensure the systems are properly assessed for vulnerabilities and must report any to the incident response team and data owner.

The Security Administrator

Hey, I have administrator rights!
Response: Great, you're a security administrator. I quit.

Anyone who has a root account on Unix or Linux systems or an administrator account on Windows or Macintosh systems actually has security administrator rights. (Unfortunately, too many people have these accounts in most environments.) This means they can give and take away permissions, set security configurations, and mess everything up if they are having a bad day.

However, just because a person has a root or administrator account does not mean they are fulfilling the security administrator role. A security administrator's tasks are many, and include creating new system user accounts, implementing new security software, testing security patches and components, and issuing new passwords. (The security administrator should not actually approve new system user accounts. This is the responsibility of the supervisor.) The security administrator must make sure access rights given to users support the policies and data owner directives.

The Security Analyst

I have analyzed your security and you have it all wrong.
Response: What a surprise.

The security analyst role works at a higher, more strategic level than the previously described roles and helps develop policies, standards, and guidelines, as well as set various baselines. Whereas the previous roles are "in the weeds" and focus on pieces and parts of the security program, a security analyst helps define the security program elements and follows through to ensure the elements are being carried out and practiced properly. This person works more at a design level than at an implementation level.

The Application Owner

Some applications are specific to individual business units—for example, the accounting department has accounting software, R&D has software for testing and development, and quality assurance uses some type of automated system. The application owners, usually the business unit managers, are responsible for dictating who can and cannot access their applications (subject to staying in compliance with the company's security policies, of course).

Since each unit claims ownership of its specific applications, the application owner for each unit is responsible for the security of the unit's applications. This includes testing, patching, performing change control on the programs, and making sure the right controls are in place to provide the necessary level of protection.

The Supervisor

The supervisor role, also called user manager, is ultimately responsible for all user activity and any assets created and owned by these users. For example, suppose Kathy is the supervisor of ten employees. Her responsibilities would include ensuring that these employees understand their responsibilities with respect to security, distributing initial passwords, making sure the employees' account information is up-to-date, and informing the security administrator when an employee is fired, suspended, or transferred. Any change that pertains to an employee's role within the company usually affects what access rights they should and should not have, so the user manager must inform the security administrator of these changes immediately.

The Change Control Analyst

As someone wise once said, the only thing that is constant is change. So, when change does take place, someone must make sure it's safe. The change control analyst is responsible for approving or rejecting requests to make changes to the network, systems, or software. This role must make certain that the change will not introduce any vulnerabilities, that it has been properly tested, and that it is properly rolled out. The change control analyst needs to understand how various changes can affect security, interoperability, performance, and productivity. Or, a company can choose to just roll out the change and see what happens. . . .

The Data Analyst

Having proper data structures, definitions, and organization is very important to a company. The data analyst is responsible for ensuring that data is stored in a way that makes the most sense to the company and the individuals who need to access and work with it. For example, payroll information should not be mixed with inventory information, the purchasing department needs to have a lot of its values in monetary terms, and the inventory system must follow a standardized naming scheme. The data analyst may be responsible for architecting a new system that will hold company information or advise in the purchase of a product that will do so.

The data analyst works with the data owners to help ensure that the structures set up coincide with and support the company's business objectives.

The Process Owner

Ever heard the popular mantra, "Security is not a product, it's a process"? The statement is very true. Security should be considered and treated like any another business process—not as its own island, nor like a redheaded stepchild with cooties. (*The author is a redheaded stepchild, but currently has no cooties.*)

All organizations have many processes: how to take orders from customers; how to make widgets to fulfill these orders; how to ship the widgets to the customers; how to collect from customers when they don't pay their bills; and so on. An organization could not function properly without well-defined processes.

The process owner is responsible for properly defining, improving upon, and monitoring these processes. A process owner is not necessarily tied to one business unit or application. Complex processes involve many variables that can span different departments, technologies, and data types.

The Solution Provider

I came up with the solution to world peace, but then I forgot it.
Response: Write it down on this napkin next time.

Every vendor you talk to will tell you *they* are the right solution provider for whatever ails you. In truth, several different types of solution providers exist, because the world is full of different problems. This role is called upon when a business has a problem or requires a process to be improved upon. For example, if Company A needs a solution that supports digitally signed e-mails and an authentication framework for employees, it would turn to a public key infrastructure (PKI) solution provider. A solution provider works with the business unit managers, data owners, and senior management to develop and deploy a solution to reduce the company's pain points.

The User

The *user* is any individual who routinely uses the data for work-related tasks. The user must have the necessary level of access to the data to perform the duties within their position and is responsible for following operational security procedures to ensure the data's confidentiality, integrity, and availability to others.

The Product Line Manager

Who's responsible for explaining business requirements to vendors and wading through their rhetoric to see if the product is right for the company? Who is responsible for ensuring compliance to license agreements? Who translates business requirements into objectives and specifications for the developer of a product or solution? Who decides if the company *really* needs to upgrade their operating system version every time Microsoft wants to make more money? That would be the product line manager.

This role must understand business drivers, business processes, and the technology that is required to support them. The product line manager evaluates different products in the market, works with vendors, understands different options a company can take, and advises management and business units on the proper solutions needed to meet their goals.

The Auditor

The function of the auditor is to provide a method for ensuring independently that management and shareholders of an organization can rely upon the appropriateness of security objectives as well as the information they are being provided with regarding the status of the organization as a whole. The auditor is brought in to an organization to determine if the controls that have been implemented by the administration for either technical or physical attributes have reached, and comply with, the security objectives that are either required for the organization by legislation or that have been deemed necessary by the governance of the organization. Auditors can conduct either internal or external auditing of an organization, and a combination of both will usually provide the most comprehensive and objective evaluation of the organization. The biggest concern for auditors is the question of bias and objectivity. The use of a third party for reviews will typically alleviate that issue, and in some instances legal mandates and regulations prevent even third-party auditors from working for too many years in a row with a single organization in order to prevent them from becoming too close and thereby compromising their objectivity in evaluations and audits.

Why So Many Roles?

A decision maker is not the proper role for the data custodian or system administrator in protecting system resources. They may have the technical knowledge of how security mechanisms should be implemented and configured, but they should not be put into a position of deciding how the company approaches security and what security measures should be implemented. Too many times companies handle security at the administrator level. In these situations, security is not viewed in broad enough terms. Proper risk analysis is usually not performed. Senior management is not fully aware of the risks the company faces. Not enough funds are available for security, and when a security breach takes place, there is no efficient way of dealing with it. As stated previously, security should work in a top-down fashion to be ultimately successful.

A company's security is not tied only to the type of firewall installed and the timeliness of security patches being applied. A company is an environment filled with various resources, activities, people, and practices. The security of the environment must be approached in a holistic way, with each part of security addressed in a serious and responsible manner. Although most environments will not contain all of the roles outlined previously, all of these responsibilities still must be carried out.

Personnel

Many facets of the responsibilities of personnel fall under management's umbrella, and several facets have a direct correlation to the overall security of the environment.

Although society has evolved to be extremely dependent upon technology in the workplace, people are still the key ingredient to a successful company. But in security circles, people are often the weakest link. Either accidentally through mistakes or lack of training or intentionally through fraud and malicious intent, personnel cause more serious and hard-to-detect security issues than hacker attacks, outside espionage, or equipment failure. Although the future actions of individuals cannot be predicted, it is possible to minimize the risks by implementing preventive measures. These include hiring the most qualified individuals, performing background checks, using detailed job descriptions, providing necessary training, enforcing strict access controls, and terminating individuals in a way that protects all parties involved.

Structure

If a company wants to have effective employee safety, management must put in place a certain structure and actually follow it. This structure includes clear definitions of responsibilities, lines of authority, and acceptable reprimands for specific activities. A clear-cut structure takes the mystery out of who does what, and how things are handled in different situations.

Several items can be put into place to reduce the possibilities of fraud, sabotage, misuse of information, theft, and other security compromises. *Separation of duties* makes sure that one individual cannot complete a critical task by herself. In the movies, when a submarine captain needs to launch a nuclear torpedo to blow up the enemy and save civilization as we know it, the launch usually requires three codes to be entered into the launching mechanism by three different senior crewmembers. This is an example of separation of duties, and it ensures that the captain cannot complete such an important and terrifying task all by herself.

NOTE Separation of duties may also reduce errors. If one person makes a mistake, there is a high probability that another person will catch and correct it.

In an organization that practices separation of duties, collusion must take place for fraud to be committed. *Collusion* means that at least two people are working together to cause some type of destruction or fraud.

In a software development environment, there should be clear distinctions between programmers, testing environments, libraries, operations, and production. Programmers should be able to work on their code and test it as needed. Once the programmer is finished with her tasks, she turns the code over to quality assurance, who in turn run their own tests in another environment that mirrors the production environment. Once the code passes all the necessary tests, it should be stored in a software library.

When it is necessary for the code to go into production, it moves from the library to the production environment. Code should not go from the programmer directly to production without testing and checking it into the library. The test environment should be clearly differentiated from the production environment to ensure that untested code does not accidentally go into production. And the programmer should not tinker with the software once it is in production. These clear-cut methods make sure no steps are skipped in the phases of software development, and that changes are not made in unstructured and dangerous ways.

Hiring Practices

I like your hat. You're hired!

Depending on the position to be filled, a level of screening should be done by human resources to ensure the company hires the right individual for the right job. Skills should be tested and evaluated, and the caliber and character of the individual should be examined. Joe might be the best programmer in the state, but if someone looks into his past and finds out he served prison time because he continually flashes old ladies in parks, the hiring manager might not be so eager to bring Joe into the organization.

Nondisclosure agreements must be developed and signed by new employees to protect the company and its sensitive information. Any conflicts of interest must be addressed, and there should be different agreements and precautions taken with temporary and contract employees.

References should be checked, military records reviewed, education verified, and if necessary, a drug test should be administered. Many times, important personal behaviors can be concealed, and that is why hiring practices now include scenario questions, personality tests, and observations of the individual, instead of just looking at a person's work history. When a person is hired, he is bringing in his business skills and whatever other baggage he carries. A company can reduce its heartache pertaining to personnel by first conducting useful and careful hiring practices.

Also, when references are being checked, it may be a good idea to have a background check performed on the potential new employee. These can cover things not readily apparent or obvious during the course of a simple reference check. Many organizations do not feel they have the time or resources to conduct background checks on their potential employees because they need to fill positions as quickly as possible. This can lead to hiring a person for "right now" instead of the "right person." Employees represent an investment on the part of the organization, and by taking the time and hiring the right people for the jobs, the organization will be able to maximize their investment and achieve a better return.

A more detailed background check can reveal some interesting information. Things like unexplained gaps in employment history, the validity and actual status of professional certifications, criminal records, driving records, job titles that have been misrepresented, credit histories, unfriendly terminations, appearances on suspected terrorist watch lists, and even real reasons for having left previous jobs can all be determined through the use of background checks. This has real benefit to the employer and the organization because it serves as the first line of defense for the organization against being attacked from within. Any negative information that can be found in these areas could be indicators of potential problems that the potential employee could create for the company at a later date. Take the credit report for instance. On the surface, this may seem to be something the organization doesn't need to know about, but if the report indicates the potential employee has a poor credit standing and a history of financial problems, it could mean you don't want to place them in charge of the organization's accounting, or even the petty cash.

Ultimately, the goal here is to achieve several different things at the same time by using a background check. You're trying to mitigate risk, lower hiring costs, and also lower the turnover rate for employees. All this is being done at the same time you are trying to protect your existing customers and employees from someone gaining employment in your organization who could potentially conduct malicious and dishonest actions that could harm you, your employees, and your customers as well as the general public. In many cases, it is also harder to go back and conduct background checks after the individual has been hired and is working. This is because there will need to be a specific cause or reason for conducting this kind of investigation, and if any employee moves to a position of greater security sensitivity or potential risk, a follow-up investigation should be considered.

Possible background check criteria could include

- A Social Security number trace
- A county/state criminal check
- A federal criminal check
- A sexual offender registry check
- Employment verification
- Education verification
- Professional reference verification
- An immigration check

Additional verification checks for higher-level or sensitive positions could include

- Office of Foreign Asset Control (OFAC)—USA PATRIOT Act
- Professional license/certification verification
- Credit report
- Drug screening

 NOTE If a low-level background check was carried out for an employee who is now moving into a more sensitive position, a more in-depth background check may be required.

Employee Controls

A management structure must be in place to make sure everyone has someone to report to and that the responsibility for another person's actions is spread equally and intelligently. Consequences for noncompliance or unacceptable behavior must be communicated before an event takes place. Proper supervisory skills must be acquired and used to ensure that operations go smoothly and that any out-of-the-ordinary activities can be taken care of before they get out of control.

Rotation of duties (rotation of assignments) is an important control to keep each department a healthy and productive part of the company. No one person should stay in one position for a long time because they may end up having too much control over a segment of the business. Such total control could result in fraud, data modification, and misuse of resources. Employees in sensitive areas should be forced to take their vacations, which is known as a *mandatory vacation* policy. While they are on vacation, other individuals fill their positions and thus can usually detect any fraudulent errors or activities. Two of the many ways to detect fraud or inappropriate activities would be the discovery of activity on someone's user account while they're supposed to be away on vacation, or if a specific problem stopped while someone was away and not active on the network. These anomalies are worthy of investigation.

Two variations of separation of duties and control are *split knowledge* and *dual control*. In both cases, two or more individuals are authorized and required to perform a duty or task. In the case of split knowledge, no one person knows or has all the details to perform a task. For example, two managers might be required to open a bank vault, with each only knowing part of the combination. In the case of dual control, two individuals are again authorized to perform a task, but both must be available and active in their participation to complete the task or mission. For example, two officers must perform an identical key-turn in a nuclear missile submarine, each out of reach of the other, to launch a missile. The control here is that no one person has the capability of launching a missile, because they cannot reach to turn both keys at the same time.

Termination

Because terminations can happen for a variety of reasons, and terminated people have different reactions, companies should have a specific set of procedures to follow with every termination. For example:

- The employee must leave the facility immediately under the supervision of a manager or security guard.
- The employee must surrender any identification badges or keys, complete an exit interview, and return company supplies.
- That user's accounts and passwords should be disabled or changed immediately.

It seems harsh and cold when this actually takes place, but too many companies have been hurt by vengeful employees who have lashed out at the company when their positions were revoked for one reason or another. If an employee is disgruntled in any way, or the termination is unfriendly, that employee's accounts should be disabled right away, and all passwords on all systems changed.

Security-Awareness Training

Our CEO said our organization is secure.
Response: He needs more awareness training than anyone.

The management's directives pertaining to security are captured in the security policy, and the standards, procedures, and guidelines are developed to support these directives. However, these directives will not be effective if no one knows about them and how the company expects them to be implemented. For security to be successful and effective, everyone from senior management on down to the rest of the staff must be fully aware of the importance of enterprise and information security. All employees should understand the underlying significance of security and the specific security-related requirements expected of them.

The controls and procedures of a security program should reflect the nature of the data being processed. A company that sells baseball cards would not need the level of structured controls and security procedures required of a company that develops heat-seeking missiles. These different types of companies would also have very different cultures. For a security-awareness program to be effective, these considerations must be understood. The program should be developed in a way that makes sense for that environment.

For an organization to achieve the desired results of its security program, it must communicate the what, how, and why of security to its employees. Security-awareness training should be comprehensive, tailored for specific groups, and organizationwide. The goal is for each employee to understand the importance of security to the company as a whole and to each individual. Expected responsibilities and acceptable behaviors must be clarified, and noncompliance repercussions, which could range from a warning to dismissal, must be explained before being invoked. This can best be achieved though a formalized process of security-awareness training.

Because security is a topic that can span many different aspects of an organization, it can be difficult to communicate the correct information to the right individuals. By using a formalized process for security-awareness training, you can establish a method that will provide you with the best results for making sure security policies and procedures are presented to the right people in an organization. This way you can make sure everyone understands what a corporate security policy is, why having the security policy is important, and how it fits into the individual's role in the organization. Taking this approach will also allow you to address any individuals who may feel they do not have any security responsibilities in their current work role. It is also an ideal time to impress upon them the need to comply with the security policies as well as lay out what the penalties for noncompliance will be. Issues such as how the new policies and procedures will affect the organization and what types of things employees should be looking for can also be properly explained.

Like other training or planning, the higher levels may be more general and deal with broader concepts and goals, and as it moves down to specific jobs and tasks, the training will become more situation-specific as it directly applies to certain positions within the company.

Different Types of Security-Awareness Training

I want my training to have a lot of pictures and pop-up books.

A security-awareness program is typically created for at least three types of audiences: management, staff, and technical employees. Each type of awareness training must be geared toward the individual audience to ensure each group understands its particular responsibilities, liabilities, and expectations. If technical security training were given to senior management, their eyes would glaze over as soon as protocols and firewalls were mentioned. On the flip side, if legal ramifications, company liability issues pertaining to protecting data, and shareholders' expectations were discussed with the IT group, they would quickly start a game of hangman or tic-tac-toe with their neighbor.

Members of management would benefit the most from a short, focused security-awareness orientation that discusses corporate assets and financial gains and losses pertaining to security. They need to know how stock prices can be negatively affected by compromises, understand possible threats and their outcomes, and know why security must be integrated into the environment the same way as other business processes. Because members of management must lead the rest of the company in support of security, they must gain the right mindset about its importance.

Mid-management would benefit from a more detailed explanation of the policies, procedures, standards, and guidelines and how they map to the individual departments for which they are responsible. Middle managers should be taught why their support for their specific departments is critical and what their level of responsibility is for ensuring that employees practice safe computing activities. They should also be shown how the consequences of noncompliance by individuals who report to them can affect the company as a whole and how they, as managers, may have to answer for such indiscretions.

The technical departments must receive a different presentation that aligns more to their daily tasks. They should receive a more in-depth training to discuss technical configurations, incident handling, and recognizing different types of security compromises.

Each group needs to know to whom it should report suspicious activity and how to handle these situations. Employees should not try to combat an attacker or address fraudulent activities by themselves. Each employee should be told to report these issues to upper management, and then upper management should determine how to handle the situation.

The presentation given to staff members must demonstrate why security is important to the company and to them individually. The better they understand how insecure activities can negatively affect them, the more willing they will be to participate in preventing such activities. This presentation should have many examples of acceptable and unacceptable activities. Examples of these activities can include questioning an unknown individual in a restricted portion of the facility, appropriate usage of Internet and e-mail, not removing company-owned material, and intellectual property issues. It is usually best to have each employee sign a document indicating they have heard and understand all the security topics discussed, and that they also understand the ramifications of noncompliance. This reinforces the policies' importance to the employee and also provides evidence down the road if the employee claims they were never told of these expectations.

Security training should happen periodically and continually. We learn mostly by repetition, and this training should take place at least once a year. The goal is to get individuals to understand not only how security works in their environment, but also why it is important. The main reason to perform security-awareness training is to modify employees' behavior and attitude toward security.

Various methods should be employed to reinforce the concepts of security awareness. Things like banners, employee handbooks, and even posters can be used as ways to remind employees about their duties and the necessities of good security practices. Refresher courses should be performed annually to reemphasize the importance of the security policies and practices of their organization. This also provides an ideal situation to remind people about the policies, standards, baselines, and guidelines they should be adhering to, as well as practices for incident reporting, and how they can be affected by malware, social engineering, and other hazards.

Evaluating the Program

Security-awareness training is a type of control, and just like any other control, it should be monitored and evaluated for its effectiveness. There is no reason to spend money on something that is not working, and there is no reason not to improve something if it needs improvement. Therefore, after employees attend awareness training, a company may give them questionnaires and surveys to gauge their retention level and to get their feedback about the training, to evaluate the program's effectiveness. Unfortunately, some people will be resistant and negative because they feel as though they are being forced to do something they do not want to do, or are being talked down to. Just expect this attitude here and there, and use your wonderful wit, charm, and communication skills with them.

A good indication of the effectiveness of the program can be captured by comparing the number of reports of security incidents made before and after the training. If the reports increased after the training, this means people were listening and followed through on the information provided to them.

 NOTE For online training, capture individuals' names and what training modules have or have not been completed within a specific period. This can then be integrated into their job performance documentation.

Security-awareness training must repeat the most important messages in different formats; be kept up-to-date; be entertaining, positive, and humorous; be simple to un-

Degree or Certification

Awareness training and materials remind employees of their responsibilities pertaining to protecting company assets. Training provides skills needed to carry out specific tasks and functions. Education provides management skills and decision-making capabilities. Table 3-9 provides more information on the differences between awareness, training, and education.

derstand; and—most important—be supported by senior management. Management must allocate the resources for this activity and enforce its attendance within the organization.

Specialized Security Training

Companies today spend a lot of money on security devices and technologies, but they commonly overlook the fact that individuals must be trained to use these devices and technologies. Without such training, the money invested toward reducing threats is wasted, and the company is still insecure. Many individuals seem to agree that people are the weakest link in security, but not enough effort goes into educating them.

Different roles require different types of training (firewall administration, risk management, policy development, IDSs, and so on). A skilled staff is one of the most critical components to the security of a company, and not enough companies are spending the funds and energy necessary to give their staffs proper levels of security education.

	Awareness	Training	Education
Attribute	"What"	"How"	"Why"
Level	Information	Knowledge	Insight
Learning objective	Recognition and retention	Skill	Understanding
Example teaching method	*Media* • Videos • Newsletters • Posters	*Practical Instruction* • Lecture and/or demo • Case study • Hands-on practice	*Theoretical Instruction* • Seminar and discussion • Reading and study • Research
Test measure	True/False Multiple Choice (Identify learning)	Problem solving—i.e., recognition and resolution (apply learning)	Essay (interpret learning)
Impact timeframe	Short-term	Intermediate	Long-term

Table 3-9 Aspects of Awareness, Training, and Education

Summary

A security program should address issues from a strategic, tactical, and operational view, as shown in Figure 3-13. Security management embodies the administrative and procedural activities necessary to support and protect information and company assets throughout the enterprise. It includes development and enforcement of security policies and their supporting mechanisms: procedures, standards, baselines, and guidelines. It encompasses risk management, security-awareness training, and proper countermeasure selection and implementation. Personnel (hiring, terminating, training, and management structure) and operational (job rotation and separation of duties) activities must also be conducted properly to ensure a secure environment. Management must understand the legal and ethical responsibilities it is required to respect and uphold.

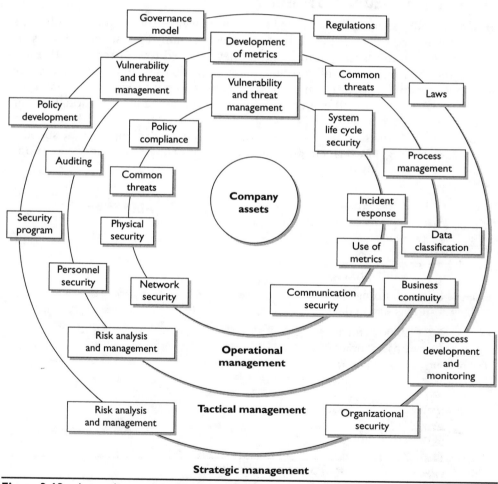

Figure 3-13   A complete security program contains many items.

Security is a business issue and should be treated as such. It must be properly integrated into the company's overall business goals and objectives because security issues can negatively affect the resources the company depends upon. More and more corporations are finding out the price paid when security is not given the proper attention, support, and funds. This is a wonderful world to live in, but bad things can happen. The ones who realize this notion not only survive, but also thrive.

Quick Tips

- A vulnerability is the absence of a safeguard (in other words, it is a weakness) that can be exploited.
- A threat is the possibility that someone or something would exploit a vulnerability, intentionally or accidentally, and cause harm to an asset.
- A risk is the probability of a threat agent exploiting a vulnerability and the loss potential from that action.
- Reducing vulnerabilities and/or threats reduces risk.
- An exposure is an instance of being exposed to losses from a threat.
- A countermeasure, also called a safeguard, mitigates the risk.
- A countermeasure can be an application, software configuration, hardware, or procedure.
- If someone is practicing due care, they are acting responsibly and will have a lower probability of being found negligent and liable if a security breach takes place.
- Security management has become more important over the years because networks have evolved from centralized environments to distributed environments.
- The objectives of security are to provide availability, integrity, and confidentiality protection to data and resources.
- Strategic planning is long term, tactical planning is midterm, and operational planning is day to day. These make up a planning horizon.
- ISO/IEC 27002 (formerly ISO 17799 Part 1) is a comprehensive set of controls comprising best practices in information security and provides guidelines on how to set up and maintain security programs.
- Security components can be technical (firewalls, encryption, and access control lists) or nontechnical (security policy, procedures, and compliance enforcement).
- Asset identification should include tangible assets (facilities and hardware) and intangible assets (corporate data and reputation).
- Project sizing, which means to understand and document the scope of the project, must be done before a risk analysis is performed.

- Assurance is a degree of confidence that a certain security level is being provided.
- CobiT is a framework that defines goals for the controls that should be used to properly manage IT and to ensure that IT maps to business needs.
- CobiT is broken down into four domains; Plan and Organize, Acquire and Implement, Deliver and Support, and Monitor and Evaluate.
- ISO/IEC 27001 is the standard for the establishment, implementation, control, and improvement of the Information Security Management System.
- Security management should work from the top down (from senior management down to the staff).
- Governance is the set of responsibilities and practices exercised by the board and executive management with the goal of providing strategic direction, ensuring that objectives are achieved, ascertaining that risks are managed appropriately, and verifying that the enterprise's resources are used responsibly.
- Which security model a company should choose depends on the type of business, its critical missions, and its objectives.
- The OECD is an international organization that helps different governments come together and tackle the economic, social, and governance challenges of a globalized economy.
- Risk can be transferred, avoided, reduced, or accepted.
- An example of risk transference is when a company buys insurance.
- Ways to reduce risk include improving security procedures and implementing safeguards.
- Threats × vulnerability × asset value = total risk
- (Threats × vulnerability × asset value) × controls gap = residual risk
- The main goals of risk analysis are the following: identify assets and assign values to them, identify vulnerabilities and threats, quantify the impact of potential threats, and provide an economic balance between the impact of the risk and the cost of the safeguards.
- Information risk management (IRM) is the *process* of identifying, assessing, and reducing risk to an acceptable level and implementing the right mechanisms to maintain that level of risk.
- Failure Modes and Effect Analysis (FMEA) is a method for determining functions, identifying functional failures, and assessing the causes of failure and their failure effects through a structured process.
- A fault tree analysis is a useful approach to detect failures that can take place within complex environments and systems.
- A quantitative risk analysis attempts to assign monetary values to components within the analysis.

- A purely quantitative risk analysis is not possible because qualitative items cannot be quantified with precision.

- Capturing the degree of uncertainty when carrying out a risk analysis is important, because it indicates the level of confidence the team and management should have in the resulting figures.

- When determining the value of information, the following issues must be considered: the cost to acquire and develop data; the cost to maintain and protect data; the value of the data to owners, users, and adversaries; the cost of replacement if the data is lost; the price others are willing to pay for the data; lost opportunities; and the usefulness of the data,

- Automated risk analysis tools reduce the amount of manual work involved in the analysis. They can be used to estimate future expected losses and calculate the benefits of different security measures.

- Single loss expectancy (SLE) is the amount that could be lost if a specific threat agent exploited a vulnerability.

- Single loss expectancy × frequency per year = annualized loss expectancy (SLE × ARO = ALE).

- Qualitative risk analysis uses judgment and intuition instead of numbers.

- Qualitative risk analysis involves people with the requisite experience and education evaluating threat scenarios and rating the probability, potential loss, and severity of each threat based on their personal experience.

- The Delphi technique is a group decision method where each group member can communicate anonymously.

- When choosing the right safeguard to reduce a specific risk, the cost, functionality, and effectiveness must be evaluated and a cost/benefit analysis performed.

- A security policy is a statement by management dictating the role security plays in the organization.

- Procedures are detailed step-by-step actions that should be followed to achieve a certain task.

- A standard specifies how hardware and software are to be used. Standards are compulsory.

- A baseline is a minimum level of security.

- Guidelines are recommendations and general approaches that provide advice and flexibility.

- Job rotation is a control to detect fraud.

- Mandatory vacations are a control type that can help detect fraudulent activities.

- Separation of duties ensures no single person has total control over an activity or task.

- Split knowledge and dual control are two aspects of separation of duties.
- Data is classified to assign priorities to data and ensure the appropriate level of protection is provided.
- Data owners specify the classification of data.
- Security has functional requirements, which define the expected behavior from a product or system, and assurance requirements, which establish confidence in the implemented products or systems overall.
- The security program should be integrated with current business objectives and goals.
- Management must define the scope and purpose of security management, provide support, appoint a security team, delegate responsibility, and review the team's findings.
- The risk management team should include individuals from different departments within the organization, not just technical personnel.
- A qualitative rating would be expressed in high, medium, or low, or on a scale of 1 to 5 or 1 to 10. A quantitative result would be expressed in dollar amounts and percentages.
- Safeguards should default to least privilege, and have fail-safe defaults and override capabilities.
- Safeguards should be imposed uniformly so everyone has the same restrictions and functionality.
- A key element during the initial security planning process is to define reporting relationships.
- The data custodian (information custodian) is responsible for maintaining and protecting data.
- A security analyst works at a strategic level and helps develop policies, standards, and guidelines, and also sets various baselines.
- Application owners are responsible for dictating who can and cannot access their applications, as well as the level of protection these applications provide for the data they process and for the company.

Questions

Please remember that these questions are formatted and asked in a certain way for a reason. You must remember that the CISSP exam is asking questions at a conceptual level. Questions may not always have the perfect answer, and the candidate is advised against always looking for the perfect answer. The candidate should look for the best answer in the list.

1. Who has the primary responsibility of determining the classification level for information?

    A. The functional manager

    B. Senior management

    C. The owner

    D. The user

2. Which group causes the most risk of fraud and computer compromises?

    A. Employees

    B. Hackers

    C. Attackers

    D. Contractors

3. If different user groups with different security access levels need to access the same information, which of the following actions should management take?

    A. Decrease the security level on the information to ensure accessibility and usability of the information.

    B. Require specific written approval each time an individual needs to access the information.

    C. Increase the security controls on the information.

    D. Decrease the classification label on the information.

4. What should management consider the most when classifying data?

    A. The type of employees, contractors, and customers who will be accessing the data

    B. Availability, integrity, and confidentiality

    C. Assessing the risk level and disabling countermeasures

    D. The access controls that will be protecting the data

5. Who is ultimately responsible for making sure data is classified and protected?

    A. Data owners

    B. Users

    C. Administrators

    D. Management

6. What is a procedure?

    A. Rules on how software and hardware must be used within the environment

    B. Step-by-step directions on how to accomplish a task

    C. Guidelines on how to approach security situations not covered by standards

    D. Compulsory actions

7. Which factor is the most important item when it comes to ensuring security is successful in an organization?

    A. Senior management support

    B. Effective controls and implementation methods

    C. Updated and relevant security policies and procedures

    D. Security awareness by all employees

8. When is it acceptable to not take action on an identified risk?

    A. Never. Good security addresses and reduces all risks.

    B. When political issues prevent this type of risk from being addressed.

    C. When the necessary countermeasure is complex.

    D. When the cost of the countermeasure outweighs the value of the asset and potential loss.

9. What are security policies?

    A. Step-by-step directions on how to accomplish security tasks

    B. General guidelines used to accomplish a specific security level

    C. Broad, high-level statements from the management

    D. Detailed documents explaining how security incidents should be handled

10. Which is the most valuable technique when determining if a specific security control should be implemented?

    A. Risk analysis

    B. Cost/benefit analysis

    C. ALE results

    D. Identifying the vulnerabilities and threats causing the risk

11. Which best describes the purpose of the ALE calculation?

    A. Quantifies the security level of the environment

    B. Estimates the loss possible for a countermeasure

    C. Quantifies the cost/benefit result

    D. Estimates the loss potential of a threat in a span of a year

12. Tactical planning is

    A. Midterm

    B. Long term

    C. Day-to-day

    D. Six months

13. What is the definition of a security exposure?

   A. An instance of being exposed to losses from a threat

   B. Any potential danger to information or systems

   C. An information security absence or weakness

   D. A loss potential of a threat

14. An effective security program requires a balanced application of

   A. Technical and nontechnical methods

   B. Countermeasures and safeguards

   C. Physical security and technical controls

   D. Procedural security and encryption

15. The security functionality defines the expected activities of a security mechanism, and assurance defines

   A. The controls the security mechanism will enforce

   B. The data classification after the security mechanism has been implemented

   C. The confidence of the security the mechanism is providing

   D. The cost/benefit relationship

16. Which statement is true when looking at security objectives in the private-business sector versus the military sector?

   A. Only the military has true security.

   B. Businesses usually care more about data integrity and availability, whereas the military is more concerned with confidentiality.

   C. The military requires higher levels of security because the risks are so much higher.

   D. The business sector usually cares most about data availability and confidentiality, whereas the military is most concerned with integrity.

17. How do you calculate residual risk?

   A. Threats × risks × asset value

   B. (Threats × asset value × vulnerability) × risks

   C. SLE × frequency = ALE

   D. (Threats × vulnerability × asset value) × controls gap

18. Which of the following is not a purpose of doing a risk analysis?

   A. Delegating responsibility

   B. Quantifying the impact of potential threats

   C. Identifying risks

   D. Defining the balance between the impact of a risk and the cost of the necessary countermeasure

19. Which of the following is not a management role in the process of implementing and maintaining security?

    A. Support

    B. Performing risk analysis

    C. Defining purpose and scope

    D. Delegating responsibility

20. Why should the team that will perform and review the risk analysis information be made up of people in different departments?

    A. To make sure the process is fair and that no one is left out.

    B. It shouldn't. It should be a small group brought in from outside the organization because otherwise the analysis is biased and unusable.

    C. Because people in different departments understand the risks of their department. Thus, it ensures the data going into the analysis is as close to reality as possible.

    D. Because the people in the different departments are the ones causing the risks, so they should be the ones held accountable.

21. Which best describes a quantitative risk analysis?

    A. A scenario-based analysis to research different security threats

    B. A method used to apply severity levels to potential loss, probability of loss, and risks

    C. A method that assigns monetary values to components in the risk assessment

    D. A method that is based on gut feelings and opinions

22. Why is a truly quantitative risk analysis not possible to achieve?

    A. It is possible, which is why it is used.

    B. It assigns severity levels. Thus, it is hard to translate into monetary values.

    C. It is dealing with purely quantitative elements.

    D. Quantitative measures must be applied to qualitative elements.

23. If there are automated tools for risk analysis, why does it take so much time to complete?

    A. A lot of data must be gathered and input into the automated tool.

    B. Management must approve it and then a team must be built.

    C. Risk analysis cannot be automated because of the nature of the assessment.

    D. Many people must agree on the same data.

24. Which of the following is a legal term that pertains to a company or individual taking reasonable actions and is used to determine liability?

    A. Standards

    B. Due process

    C. Due care

    D. Downstream liabilities

25. What is CobiT and where does it fit into the development of information security systems and security programs?

    A. Lists of standards, procedures, and policies for security program development

    B. Current version of ISO 17799

    C. A framework that was developed to deter organizational internal fraud

    D. Open standards for control objectives

26. What are the four domains that make up CobiT?

    A. Plan and Organize, Acquire and Implement, Deliver and Support, and Monitor and Evaluate

    B. Plan and Organize, Maintain and Implement, Deliver and Support, and Monitor and Evaluate

    C. Plan and Organize, Acquire and Implement, Support and Purchase, and Monitor and Evaluate

    D. Acquire and Implement, Deliver and Support, and Monitor and Evaluate

27. What is the ISO/IEC 27799 standard?

    A. A standard on how to protect personal health information

    B. The new version of BS 17799

    C. Definitions for the new ISO 27000 series

    D. The new version of NIST 800-60

28. CobiT was developed from the COSO framework. What are COSO's main objectives and purpose?

    A. COSO is a risk management approach that pertains to control objectives and IT business processes.

    B. COSO deals with the strategic level while CobiT focuses more at the operational level.

    C. COSO addresses corporate culture and policy development.

    D. COSO is a fault tolerance system.

29. OCTAVE, NIST 800-30, and AS/NZS 4360 are different approaches to carrying out risk management within companies and organizations. What are the differences between these methods?

    A. NIST and OCTAVE are corporate based.

    B. NIST and OCTAVE are IT based.

    C. AS/NZS is IT based.

    D. NIST and AS/NZS are corporate based.

30. Which of the following is a risk analysis method that attempts to determine where a failure is likely to occur?

    A. Spanning tree

    B. AS/NZS

    C. NIST

    D. Failure Modes and Effect Analysis

31. What has been developed to help countries and their governments draw up laws and regulations to protect private data in a similar manner?

    A. Safe OECD

    B. ISO\IEC

    C. Organisation for Economic Co-operation and Development

    D. CPTED

Answers

1. **C.** A company can have one specific data owner or different data owners who have been delegated the responsibility of protecting specific sets of data. One of the responsibilities that goes into protecting this information is properly classifying it.

2. **A.** It is commonly stated that internal threats comprise 70–80 percent of the overall threat to a company. This is because employees already have privileged access to a wide range of company assets. The outsider who wants to cause damage must obtain this level of access before she can carry out the type of damage internal personnel could dish out. A lot of the damages caused by internal employees are brought about by mistakes and system misconfigurations.

3. **C.** If data is going to be available to a wide range of people, more granular security should be implemented to ensure that only the necessary people access the data and that the operations they carry out are controlled. The security implemented can come in the form of authentication and authorization technologies, encryption, and specific access control mechanisms.

4. **B.** The best answer to this question is B, because to properly classify data, the data owner must evaluate the availability, integrity, and confidentiality requirements of the data. Once this evaluation is done, it will dictate which employees, contractors, and users can access the data, which is expressed in answer A. This assessment will also help determine the controls that should be put into place.

5. **D.** The key to this question is the use of the word "ultimately." Though management can delegate tasks to others, it is ultimately responsible for everything that takes place within a company. Therefore, it must continually ensure that data and resources are being properly protected.

6. **B.** Procedures are step-by-step instructions. Standards are rules that must be followed; thus, they are compulsory. Guidelines are recommendations.

7. **A.** Without senior management's support, a security program will not receive the necessary attention, funds, resources, and enforcement capabilities.

8. **D.** Companies may decide to live with specific risks they are faced with if the cost of trying to protect themselves would be greater than the potential loss if the threat were to become real. Countermeasures are usually complex to a degree, and there are almost always political issues surrounding different risks, but these are not reasons to not implement a countermeasure.

9. **C.** A security policy captures senior management's perspectives and directives on what role security should play within the company. Security policies are usually general and use broad terms so they can cover a wide range of items.

10. **B.** Although the other answers may seem correct, B is the best answer here. This is because a risk analysis is performed to identify risks and come up with suggested countermeasures. The ALE tells the company how much it could lose if a specific threat became real. The ALE value will go into the cost/benefit analysis, but the ALE does not address the cost of the countermeasure and the benefit of a countermeasure. All the data captured in answers A, C, and D are inserted into a cost/benefit analysis.

11. **D.** The ALE calculation estimates the potential loss that can affect one asset from a specific threat within a one-year time span. This value is used to figure out the amount of money that should be earmarked to protect this asset from this threat.

12. **A.** Three types of goals make up the planning horizon: operational, tactical, and strategic. Tactical goals are midterm goals that must be accomplished before the overall strategic goal is accomplished.

13. **A.** An exposure is an instance of being exposed to losses from a threat agent. A vulnerability can cause an organization to be exposed to possible damages. For example, if password management is lax and password rules are not enforced, the company can be exposed to the possibility of having users' passwords captured and used in an unauthorized manner.

14. **A.** Security is not defined by a firewall, an access control mechanism, a security policy, company procedures, employee conduct, or authentication technologies. It is defined by all of these and how they integrate together within an environment. Security is neither purely technical nor purely procedural, but rather a mix of the two.

15. **C.** The functionality describes how a mechanism will work and behave. This may have nothing to do with the actual protection it provides. Assurance is the level of confidence in the protection level a mechanism will provide. When systems and mechanisms are evaluated, their functionality and assurance should be examined and tested individually.

16. **B.** Although answer C may seem correct to you, it is a subjective answer. Businesses will see their threats and risks as being more important than another organization's threats and risks. The military has a rich history of having to keep its secrets secret. This is usually not as important in the commercial sector relative to the military.

17. **D.** The equation is more conceptual than practical. It is hard to assign a number to an individual vulnerability or threat. This equation enables you to look at the potential loss of a specific asset, as well as the controls gap (what the specific countermeasure cannot protect against). What remains is the residual risk, which is what is left over after a countermeasure is implemented.

18. **A.** The other three answers are the main reasons to carry out a risk analysis. An analysis is not carried out to delegate responsibilities. Management will take on this responsibility once the results of the analysis are reported to it and it understands what actually needs to be carried out.

19. **B.** The number one ingredient management must provide when it comes to security is support. Management should define the role and scope of security and allocate the funds and resources. Management also delegates who does what pertaining to security. It does not carry out the analysis, but rather is responsible for making sure one is done and that management acts on the results it provides.

20. **C.** An analysis is only as good as the data that goes into it. Data pertaining to risks the company faces should be extracted from the people who understand best the business functions and environment of the company. Each department understands its own threats and resources, and may have possible solutions to specific threats that affect its part of the company.

21. **C.** A quantitative risk analysis assigns monetary values and percentages to the different components within the assessment. A qualitative analysis uses opinions of individuals and a rating system to gauge the severity level of different threats and the benefits of specific countermeasures.

22. **D.** During a risk analysis, the team is trying to properly predict the future and all the risks that future may bring. It is somewhat of a subjective exercise and requires educated guessing. It is very hard to properly predict that a flood will

take place once in ten years and cost a company up to $40,000 in damages, but this is what a quantitative analysis tries to accomplish.

23. **A.** An analysis usually takes a long time to complete because of all the data that must be properly gathered. There are generally many different sources for this type of data, and properly extracting it is extremely time-consuming. In most situations, it involves setting up meetings with specific personnel and going through a question-and-answer process.

24. **C.** A company's or individual's actions can be judged by the Prudent Person Rule, which looks at how a prudent or reasonable person would react in similar situations. Due care means to take these necessary actions to protect the company and its assets, customers, and employees. Computer security has many aspects pertaining to practicing due care. If management does not ensure these things are in place, it can be found negligent.

25. **D.** The Control Objectives for Information and related Technology (CobiT) is a framework developed by the Information Systems Audit and Control Association (ISACA) and the IT Governance Institute (ITGI). It defines goals for the controls that should be used to properly manage IT and ensure IT maps to business needs.

26. **A.** CobiT has four domains: Plan and Organize, Acquire and Implement, Deliver and Support, and Monitor and Evaluate. Each category drills down into subcategories. For example, Acquire and Implement contains the following subcategories:

- Acquire and Maintain Application Software
- Acquire and Maintain Technology Infrastructure
- Develop and Maintain Procedures
- Install and Accredit Systems
- Manage Changes

27. **A.** It is referred to as the *health informatics,* and its purpose is to provide guidance to health organizations and other holders of personal health information on how to protect such information via implementation of ISO/IEC 27002.

28. **B.** COSO deals more at the strategic level while CobiT focuses more at the operational level. CobiT is a way to meet many of the COSO objectives, but only from the IT perspective. COSO deals with non-IT items also, as in company culture, financial accounting principles, board of director responsibility, and internal communication structures. Its main purpose is to help ensure fraudulent financial reporting cannot take place in an organization.

29. **B.** While both the NIST and OCTAVE methodologies focus on IT threats and information security risks, AS/NZS 4360 takes a much broader approach to

risk management. This methodology can be used to understand a company's financial, capital, human safety, and business decisions risks. Although it can be used to analyze security risks, it was not created specifically for this purpose.

30. **D.** Failure Modes and Effect Analysis (FMEA) is a method for determining functions, identifying functional failures, and assessing the causes of failure and their failure effects through a structured process. The application of this process to a chronic failure enables the determination of where exactly the failure is most likely to occur.

31. **C.** The Organisation for Economic Co-operation and Development (OECD) is an international organization that helps different governments come together and tackle the economic, social, and governance challenges of a globalized economy. Thus, the OECD came up with guidelines for the various countries to follow so data are properly protected and everyone follows the same type of rules.

Access Control

This chapter presents the following:
- Identification methods and technologies
- Authentication methods, models, and technologies
- Discretionary, mandatory, and nondiscretionary models
- Accountability, monitoring, and auditing practices
- Emanation security and technologies
- Intrusion detection systems
- Possible threats to access control practices and technologies

A cornerstone in the foundation of information security is controlling how resources are accessed so they can be protected from unauthorized modification or disclosure. The controls that enforce access control can be technical, physical, or administrative in nature.

Access Controls Overview

Access controls are security features that control how users and systems communicate and interact with other systems and resources. They protect the systems and resources from unauthorized access and can be components that participate in determining the level of authorization after an authentication procedure has successfully completed. Although we usually think of a user as the entity that requires access to a network resource or information, there are many other types of entities that require access to other network entities, and resources that are subject to access control. It is important to understand the definition of a subject and an object when working in the context of access control.

Access is the flow of information between a subject and an object. A *subject* is an active entity that requests access to an object or the data within an object. A subject can be a user, program, or process that accesses an object to accomplish a task. When a program accesses a file, the program is the subject and the file is the object. An *object* is a passive entity that contains information. An object can be a computer, database, file, computer program, directory, or field contained in a table within a database. When you look up information in a database, you are the active subject and the database is the passive object. Figure 4-1 illustrates subjects and objects.

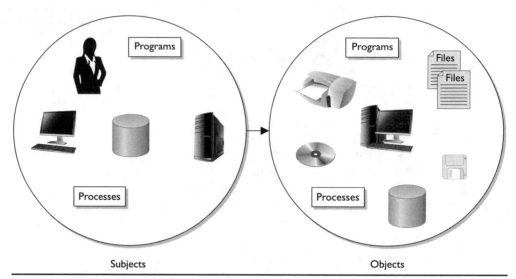

Figure 4-1   Subjects are active entries that access objects, while objects are passive entities.

Access control is a broad term that covers several different types of mechanisms that enforce access control features on computer systems, networks, and information. Access control is extremely important because it is one of the first lines of defense in battling unauthorized access to systems and network resources. When a user is prompted for a username and password to use a computer, this is access control. Once the user logs in and later attempts to access a file, that file may have a list of users and groups that have the right to access it. If the user is not on this list, the user is denied. This is another form of access control. The users' permissions and rights may be based on their identity, clearance, and/or group membership. Access controls give organizations the ability to control, restrict, monitor, and protect resource availability, integrity, and confidentiality.

Security Principles

The three main security principles for any type of security control are:

- Availability
- Integrity
- Confidentiality

These principles, which were touched upon in Chapter 3, will be a running theme throughout this book because each core subject of each chapter approaches these principles in a unique way. In Chapter 3, you read that security management procedures include identifying threats that can negatively affect the availability, integrity, and confidentiality of the company's assets and finding cost-effective countermeasures that will protect them. This chapter looks at the ways the three principles can be affected and protected through access control methodologies and technologies.

Every control that is used in computer and information security provides at least one of these security principles. It is critical that security professionals understand all of the possible ways these principles can be provided and circumvented.

Availability

Hey, I'm available.
Response: But no one wants you.

Information, systems, and resources must be available to users in a timely manner so productivity will not be affected. Most information must be accessible and available to users when requested so they can carry out tasks and fulfill their responsibilities. Accessing information does not seem that important until it is inaccessible. Administrators experience this when a file server goes offline or a highly used database is out of service for one reason or another. Fault tolerance and recovery mechanisms are put into place to ensure the continuity of the *availability* of resources. User productivity can be greatly affected if requested data is not readily available.

Information has various attributes, such as accuracy, relevance, timeliness, and privacy. It may be extremely important for a stockbroker to have information that is accurate and timely, so he can buy and sell stocks at the right times at the right prices. The stockbroker may not necessarily care about the privacy of this information, only that it is readily available. A soft drink company that depends on its soda pop recipe would care about the privacy of this trade secret, and the security mechanisms in place need to ensure this secrecy.

Integrity

Information must be accurate, complete, and protected from unauthorized modification. When a security mechanism provides *integrity*, it protects data, or a resource, from being altered in an unauthorized fashion. If any type of illegitimate modification does occur, the security mechanism must alert the user or administrator in some manner. One example is when a user sends a request to her online bank account to pay her $24.56 water utility bill. The bank needs to be sure the integrity of that transaction was not altered during transmission, so the user does not end up paying the utility company $240.56 instead. Integrity of data is very important. What if a confidential e-mail was sent from the secretary of state to the president of the United States and was intercepted and altered without a security mechanism in place that disallows this or alerts the president that this message has been altered? Instead of receiving a message reading, "We would love for you and your wife to stop by for drinks tonight," the message could be altered to say, "We have just bombed Libya." Big difference.

Confidentiality

This is my secret and you can't have it.
Response: I don't want it.

Confidentiality is the assurance that information is not disclosed to unauthorized individuals, programs, or processes. Some information is more sensitive than other information and requires a higher level of confidentiality. Control mechanisms need to be in place to dictate who can access data and what the subject can do with it once they have accessed it. These activities need to be controlled, audited, and monitored. Examples of information that could be considered confidential are health records, financial account information, criminal records, source code, trade secrets, and military tactical plans. Some security mechanisms that would provide confidentiality are encryption, logical and physical access controls, transmission protocols, database views, and controlled traffic flow.

It is important for a company to identify the data that must be classified so the company can ensure that the top priority of security protects this information and keeps it confidential. If this information is not singled out, too much time and money can be spent on implementing the same level of security for critical and mundane information alike. It may be necessary to configure virtual private networks (VPNs) between organizations and use the IPSec encryption protocol to encrypt all messages passed when communicating about trade secrets, sharing customer information, or making financial transactions. This takes a certain amount of hardware, labor, funds, and overhead. The same security precautions are not necessary when communicating that today's special in the cafeteria is liver and onions with a roll on the side. So, the first step in protecting data's confidentiality is to identify which information is sensitive and to what degree, and then implement security mechanisms to protect it properly.

Different security mechanisms can supply different degrees of availability, integrity, and confidentiality. The environment, the classification of the data that is to be protected, and the security goals must be evaluated to ensure the proper security mechanisms are bought and put into place. Many corporations have wasted a lot of time and money not following these steps and instead buying the new "gee whiz" product that recently hit the market.

Identification, Authentication, Authorization, and Accountability

I don't really care who you are, but come right in.

For a user to be able to access a resource, he first must prove he is who he claims to be, has the necessary credentials, and has been given the necessary rights or privileges to perform the actions he is requesting. Once these steps are completed successfully, the user can access and use network resources; however, it is necessary to track the user's activities and enforce accountability for his actions. *Identification* describes a method of ensuring that a subject (user, program, or process) is the entity it claims to be. Identification can be provided with the use of a username or account number. To be properly *authenticated*, the subject is usually required to provide a second piece to the credential set. This piece could be a password, passphrase, cryptographic key, personal identification number (PIN), anatomical attribute, or token. These two credential items are compared to information that has been previously stored for this subject. If these credentials match the stored information, the subject is authenticated. But we are not done yet.

Once the subject provides its credentials and is properly identified, the system it is trying to access needs to determine if this subject has been given the necessary rights and privileges to carry out the requested actions. The system will look at some type of access control matrix or compare security labels to verify that this subject may indeed access the requested resource and perform the actions it is attempting. If the system determines that the subject may access the resource, it *authorizes* the subject.

Race Condition

A *race condition* is when processes carry out their tasks on a shared resource in an incorrect order. A race condition is possible when two or more processes use a shared resource, as in data within a variable. It is important that the processes carry out their functionality in the correct sequence. If process 2 carried out its task on the data before process 1, the result will be much different than if process 1 carried out its tasks on the data before process 2.

In software, when the authentication and authorization steps are split into two functions, there is a possibility an attacker could use a race condition to force the authorization step to be completed *before* the authentication step. This would be a flaw in the software that the attacker has figured out how to exploit. A race condition occurs when two or more processes use the same resource and the sequences of steps within the software can be carried out in an improper order, something which can drastically affect the output. So, an attacker can force the authorization step to take place before the authentication step and gain unauthorized access to a resource.

Although identification, authentication, authorization, and accountability have close and complementary definitions, each has distinct functions that fulfill a specific requirement in the process of access control. A user may be properly identified and authenticated to the network, but he may not have the authorization to access the files on the file server. On the other hand, a user may be authorized to access the files on the file server, but until she is properly identified and authenticated, those resources are out of reach. Figure 4-2 illustrates the four steps that must happen for a subject to access an object.

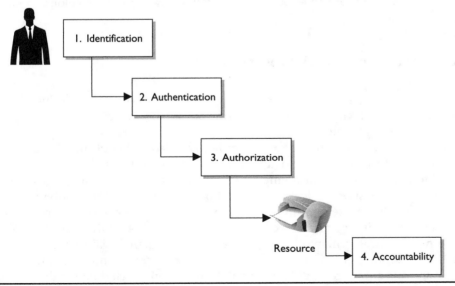

Figure 4-2 Four steps must happen for a subject to access an object: identification, authentication, authorization, and accountability.

The subject needs to be held accountable for the actions taken within a system or domain. The only way to ensure accountability is if the subject is uniquely identified and the subject's actions are recorded.

Logical access controls are tools used for identification, authentication, authorization, and accountability. They are software components that enforce access control measures for systems, programs, processes, and information. The logical access controls can be embedded within operating systems, applications, add-on security packages, or database and telecommunication management systems. It can be challenging to synchronize all access controls and ensure all vulnerabilities are covered without producing overlaps of functionality. However, if it were easy, security professionals would not be getting paid the big bucks!

 NOTE The words "logical" and "technical" can be used interchangeably in this context. It is conceivable that the CISSP exam would refer to logical and technical controls interchangeably.

An individual's identity must be verified during the authentication process. Authentication usually involves a two-step process: entering public information (a username, employee number, account number, or department ID), and then entering private information (a static password, smart token, cognitive password, one-time password, PIN, or digital signature). Entering public information is the identification step, while entering private information is the authentication step of the two-step process. Each technique used for identification and authentication has its pros and cons. Each should be properly evaluated to determine the right mechanism for the correct environment.

 NOTE A cognitive password is based on a user's opinion or life experience. The password could be a mother's maiden name, a favorite color, or a dog's name.

Identification and Authentication

Now, who are you again?

Once a person has been identified, through the user ID or a similar value, she must be authenticated, which means she must prove she is who she says she is. Three general factors can be used for authentication: *something a person knows, something a person has,* and *something a person is.* They are also commonly called authentication by knowledge, authentication by ownership, and authentication by characteristic.

Verification 1:1 is the measurement of an identity against a single claimed identity. The conceptual question is, "Is this person who he claims to be?" So if Bob provides his identity and credential set, this information is compared to the data kept in an authentication database. If they match, we know that it is really Bob. If the identification is 1: N (many), the measurement of a single identity is compared against multiple identities. The conceptual question is, "Who is this person?" An example is if fingerprints were found at a crime scene, the cops would run them through their database to identify the suspect.

Something a person knows (authentication by knowledge) can be, for example, a password, PIN, mother's maiden name, or the combination to a lock. Authenticating a person by something that she knows is usually the least expensive to implement. The downside to this method is that another person may acquire this knowledge and gain unauthorized access to a system or facility.

Something a person has (authentication by ownership) can be a key, swipe card, access card, or badge. This method is common for accessing facilities, but could also be used to access sensitive areas or to authenticate systems. A downside to this method is that the item can be lost or stolen, which could result in unauthorized access.

Something specific to a person (authentication by characteristic) becomes a bit more interesting. This is not based on whether the person is a Republican, a Martian, or a moron—it is based on a physical attribute. Authenticating a person's identity based on a unique physical attribute is referred to as biometrics. (For more information, see the upcoming section, "Biometrics.")

Strong authentication contains two out of these three methods: something a person knows, has, or is. Using a biometric system by itself does not provide strong authentication because it provides only one out of the three methods. Biometrics supplies what a person is, not what a person knows or has. For a strong authentication process to be in place, a biometric system needs to be coupled with a mechanism that checks for one of the other two methods. For example, many times the person has to type a PIN number into a keypad before the biometric scan is performed. This satisfies the "what the person knows" category. Conversely, the person could be required to swipe a magnetic card through a reader prior to the biometric scan. This would satisfy the "what the person has" category. Whatever identification system is used, for strong authentication to be in the process, it must include two out of the three categories. This is also referred to as *two-factor authentication*.

Identity is a complicated concept with many varied nuances, ranging from the philosophical to the practical. A person can have multiple digital identities. For example, a user can be JPublic in a Windows domain environment, JohnP on a Unix server, JohnPublic on the mainframe, JJP in instant messaging, JohnCPublic in the certification authority, and IWearPanties at myspace.com. If a company would want to centralize all of its access control, these various identity names for the same person may put the security administrator into a mental health institution.

Creating or issuing secure identities should include three key aspects: uniqueness, nondescriptive, and issuance. The first, uniqueness, refers to the identifiers that are specific to an individual, meaning every user must have a unique ID for accountability. Things like fingerprints and retina scans can be considered unique elements in determining identity. Nondescriptive means that neither piece of the credential set should indicate the purpose of that account. For example, a user ID should not be "administrator," "backup_operator," or "CEO." The third key aspect in determining identity is issuance. These elements are the ones that have been provided by another authority as a means of proving identity. ID cards are a kind of security element that would be considered an issuance form of identification.

> ## Identification Component Requirements
> When issuing identification values to users, the following should be in place:
>
> - Each value should be unique, for user accountability.
> - A standard naming scheme should be followed.
> - The value should be nondescriptive of the user's position or tasks.
> - The value should not be shared between users.

Identity Management

There are too many of you who want to access too much stuff. Everyone just go away!

Identity management is a broad and loaded term that encompasses the use of different products to identify, authenticate, and authorize users through automated means. To many people, the term also includes user account management, access control, password management, single sign-on functionality, managing rights and permissions for user accounts, and auditing and monitoring of all of these items. The reason that individuals, and companies, have different definitions and perspectives of identity management (IdM) is because it is so large and encompasses so many different technologies and processes. Remember the story of the four blind men who are trying to describe an elephant? One blind man feels the tail and announces, "It's a tail." Another blind man feels the trunk and announces, "It's a trunk." Another announces it's a leg, and another announces it's an ear. This is because each man cannot see or comprehend the whole of the large creature—just the piece he is familiar with and knows about. This analogy can be applied to IdM because it is large and contains many components and many people may not comprehend the whole—only the component they work with and understand.

> ## Access Control Review
> The following is a review of the basic concepts in access control:
>
> - Identification
>   - Subjects supplying identification information
>   - Username, user ID, account number
> - Authentication
>   - Verifying the identification information
>   - Passphrase, PIN value, biometric, one-time password, password
> - Authorization
>   - Using criteria to make a determination of operations that subjects can carry out on objects
>   - "I know who you are, now what am I going to allow you to do?"
> - Accountability
>   - Audit logs and monitoring to track subject activities with objects

It is important for security professionals to understand not only the whole of IdM, but understand the technologies that make up a full enterprise IdM solution. IdM requires management of uniquely identified entities, their attributes, credentials, and entitlements. IdM allows organizations to create and manage digital identities' life cycles (create, maintain, terminate) in a timely and automated fashion. The enterprise IdM must meet business needs and scale from internally facing systems to externally facing systems. In this section, we will be covering many of these technologies and how they work together.

Selling identity management products is now a flourishing market that focuses on reducing administrative costs, increasing security, meeting regulatory compliance, and improving upon service levels throughout enterprises. The continual increase in complexity and diversity of networked environments only increases the complexity of keeping track of who can access what and when. Organizations have different types of applications, network operating systems, databases, enterprise resource management (ERP) systems, customer relationship management (CRM) systems, directories, mainframes—all used for different business purposes. Then the organizations have partners, contractors, consultants, employees, and temporary employees. (Figure 4-3 actually provides the simplest view of most environments.) Users usually access several different types of systems throughout their daily tasks, which makes controlling access and providing the necessary level of protection on different data types difficult and full of obstacles. This complexity usually results in unforeseen and unidentified holes in asset protection, overlapping and contradictory controls, and policy and regulation noncompliance. It is the goal of identity management technologies to simplify the administration of these tasks and bring order to chaos.

The following are many of the common questions enterprises deal with today in controlling access to assets:

- What should each user have access to?
- Who approves and allows access?
- How do the access decisions map to policies?
- Do former employees still have access?
- How do we keep up with our dynamic and ever-changing environment?
- What is the process of revoking access?
- How is access controlled and monitored centrally?
- Why do employees have eight passwords to remember?
- We have five different operating platforms. How do we centralize access when each platform (and application) requires its own type of credential set?
- How do we control access for our employees, customers, and partners?
- How do we make sure we are compliant with the necessary regulations?
- Where do I send in my resignation? I quit.

The traditional identity management process has been manual, using directory services with permissions, access control lists (ACLs), and profiles. This approach has proven incapable of keeping up with complex demands and thus has been replaced

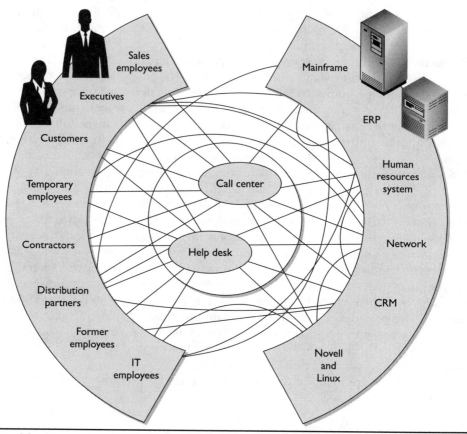

Figure 4-3 Most environments are chaotic in terms of access.

with automated applications rich in functionality that work together to create an identity management infrastructure. The main goals of identity management (IdM) technologies are to streamline the management of identity, authentication, authorization, and the auditing of subjects on multiple systems throughout the enterprise. The sheer diversity of a heterogeneous enterprise makes proper implementation of IdM a huge undertaking.

Many identity management solutions and products are available in the marketplace. For the CISSP exam, the following are the types of technologies you should be aware of:

- Directories
- Web access management
- Password management
- Legacy single sign-on
- Account management
- Profile update

Directories   Most enterprises have some type of directory that contains information pertaining to the company's network resources and users. Most directories follow a hierarchical database format, based on the X.500 standard, and a type of protocol, as in Lightweight Directory Access Protocol (LDAP), that allows subjects and applications to interact with the directory. Applications can request information about a particular user by making an LDAP request to the directory, and users can request information about a specific resource by using a similar request.

The objects within the directory are managed by a directory service. The *directory service* allows an administrator to configure and manage how identification, authentication, authorization, and access control take place within the network. The objects within the directory are labeled and identified with namespaces.

In a Windows environment when you log in, you are logging in to a domain controller (DC), which has a hierarchical directory in its database. The database is running a directory service (Active Directory), which organizes the network resources and carries out user access control functionality. So once you successfully authenticate to the DC, certain network resources will be available to you (the print service, file server, e-mail server, and so on) as dictated by the configuration of AD.

How does the directory service keep all of these entities organized? By using *namespaces*. Each directory service has a way of identifying and naming the objects they will manage. In databases based on the X.500 standard that are accessed by LDAP, the directory service assigns distinguished names (DNs) to each object. Each DN represents a collection of attributes about a specific object, and is stored in the directory as an entry. In the following example, the DN is made up of a common name (cn) and domain components (dc). Since this is a hierarchical directory, .com is the top, LogicalSecurity is one step down from .com, and Shon is at the bottom (where she belongs).

```
dn: cn=Shon Harris,dc=LogicalSecurity,dc=com
cn: Shon Harris
```

This is a very simplistic example. Companies usually have large trees (directories) containing many levels and objects to represent different departments, roles, users, and resources.

A directory service manages the entries and data in the directory and also enforces the configured security policy by carrying out access control and identity management functions. For example, when you log in to the DC, the directory service (AD) will determine what resources you can and cannot access on the network.

NOTE   We touch on directory services again in the "Single Sign-On" section of this chapter.

Organizing All of This Stuff

In a database directory based on the X.500 standard, the following rules are used for object organization:

- The directory has a tree structure to organize the entries using a parent-child configuration.
- Each entry has a unique name made up of attributes of a specific object.
- The attributes used in the directory are dictated by the defined schema.
- The unique identifiers are called distinguished names.

The schema describes the directory structure and what names can be used within the directory, among other things. (Schema and database components are covered more in-depth in Chapter 11.)

The following diagram shows how an object (Kathy Conlon) can have the attributes of ou=General ou=NCTSW ou=pentagon ou=locations ou=Navy ou=DoD ou=U.S. Government C=US.

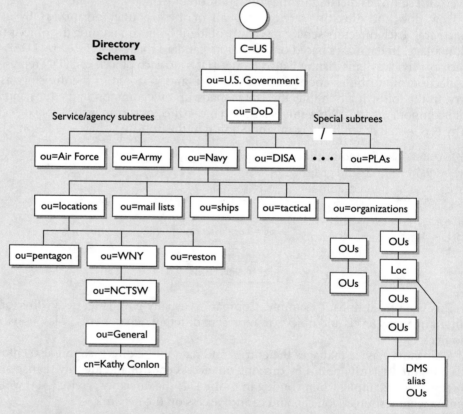

Note that OU stands for organizational unit. They are used as containers of other similar OUs, users, and resources. They provide the parent-child (sometimes called tree-leaf) organization structure.

So are there any problems with using a directory product for identity management and access control? Yes, there's always something. Many legacy devices and applications cannot be managed by the directory service because they were not built with the necessary client software. The legacy entities must be managed through their inherited management software. This means that most networks have subjects, services, and resources that can be listed in a directory and controlled centrally by an administrator through the use of a directory service. Then there are legacy applications and devices that the administrator must configure and manage individually.

The Directories' Role in Identity Management   A directory used for IdM is specialized database software that has been optimized for reading and searching operations. It is the main component of an identity management solution. This is because all resource information, users' attributes, authorization profiles, roles, potential access control policies, and more are stored in this one location. When other IdM software applications need to carry out their functions (authorization, access control, assigning permissions), they now have a centralized location for all of the information they need.

As an analogy, let's say I'm a store clerk and you enter my store to purchase alcohol. Instead of me having to find a picture of you somewhere to validate your identity, go to another place to find your birth certificate to obtain your true birth date, and find proof of which state you are registered in, I can look in one place—your driver's license. The directory works in the same way. Some IdM application may need to know a user's authorization rights, role, employee status, or clearance level, so instead of this application having to make requests to several databases and other applications, it makes its request to this one directory.

A lot of the information stored in an IdM directory is scattered throughout the enterprise. User attribute information (employee status, job description, department, and so on) is usually stored in the HR database, authentication information could be in a Kerberos server, role and group identification information might be in a SQL database, and resource-oriented authentication information is stored in Active Directory on a domain controller. These are commonly referred to as identity stores and are located in different places on the network. Something nifty that many identity management products do is create meta-directories or virtual directories. A *meta-directory* gathers the necessary information from multiple sources and stores them in one central directory. This provides a unified view of all users' digital identity information throughout the enterprise. The meta-directory synchronizes itself with all of the identity stores periodically to ensure the most up-to-date information is being used by all applications and IdM components within the enterprise.

A *virtual directory* plays the same role and can be used instead of a meta-directory. The difference between the two is that the meta-directory physically has the identity data in its directory, whereas a virtual directory does not and points to where the actual data resides. When an IdM component makes a call to a virtual directory to gather identity information on a user, the virtual directory will point to where the information actually lives.

Figure 4-4 illustrates a central LDAP directory that is used by the IdM services: access management, provisioning, and identity management. When one of these services accepts a request from a user or application, it pulls the necessary data from the directory to be able to fulfill the request. Since the data needed to properly fulfill these requests are stored in different locations, the metadata directory pulls the data from these other sources and updates the LDAP directory.

Web Access Management Web access management (WAM) software controls what users can access when using a web browser to interact with web-based enterprise assets. This type of technology is continually becoming more robust and experiencing increased deployment. This is because of the increased use of e-commerce, online banking, content providing, web services, and more. The Internet only continues to grow and its importance to businesses and individuals increases as more and more functionality is provided. We just can't seem to get enough of it.

Figure 4-5 shows the basic components and activities in a web access control management process.

1. User sends in credentials to web server.
2. Web server validates user's credentials.
3. User requests to access a resource (object).
4. Web server verifies with the security policy to determine if the user is allowed to carry out this operation.
5. Web server allows access to the requested resource.

This is a simple example. More complexity comes in with all the different ways a user can authenticate (password, digital certificate, token, and others), the resources and services that may be available to the user (transfer funds, purchase product, update profile, and so forth), and the necessary infrastructure components. The infrastructure

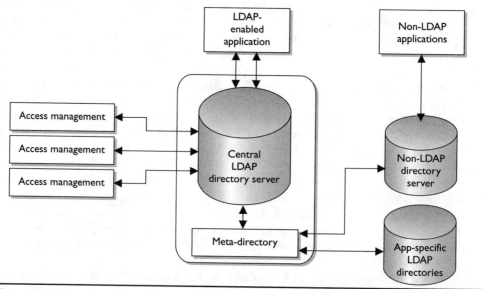

Figure 4-4 Meta-directories pull data from other sources to populate the IdM directory.

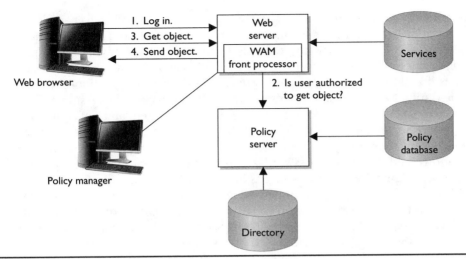

Figure 4-5 A basic example of web access control

is usually made up of a web server farm (many servers), a directory that contains the users' accounts and attributes, a database, a couple of firewalls, and some routers, all laid out in a tiered architecture. But let's keep it simple right now.

The WAM software is the main gate between users and the corporate web-based resources. It is commonly a plug-in for a web server, so it works as a front-end process. When a user makes a request for access, the web server software will query a directory (described in the last section), an authentication server, and potentially a back-end database before serving up the resource the user requested. The WAM console allows the administrator to configure access levels, authentication requirements, and account setup workflow steps, and to perform overall maintenance.

WAM tools usually also provide a single sign-on capability so that once a user is authenticated at a web site, she can access different web-based applications and resources without having to log in multiple times. When a product provides a single sign-on capability in a web environment, the product must keep track of the user's authentication state and security context as the user moves from one resource to the next.

For example, if Kathy logs on to her online bank web site, the communication is taking place over the HTTP protocol. This protocol itself is stateless, which means it will allow a web server to pass the user a web page and then the connection is closed and the user is forgotten about. Many web servers work in a stateless mode because they have so many requests to fulfill and they are just providing users with web pages. Keeping a constant connection with each and every user who is requesting to see a web page would exhaust the web server's resources. When a user has to log on to a web site is when "keeping the user's state" is required and a continuous connection is needed.

When Kathy first goes to her bank's web site, she is viewing publicly available data that do not require her to authenticate before viewing. A constant connection is not being kept by the web server, thus it is working in a stateless manner. Once she clicks Access My Account, the web server sets up a secure connection (SSL) with her browser and requests her credentials. After she is authenticated, the web server sends a cookie (small text file) that indicates she has authenticated properly and the type of access she should be allowed. When Kathy requests to move from her savings account to her checking account, the web server will assess the cookie on Kathy's web browser to see if she has the rights to access this new resource. The web server continues to check this cookie during Kathy's session to ensure no one has hijacked the session and that the web server is continually communicating with Kathy's system and not someone else's.

The web server continually asks Kathy's web browser to prove she has been authenticated, which the browser does by providing the cookie information. (The cookie information could include her password, account number, security level, browsing habits, and/or personalization information.) As long as Kathy is authenticated, the web server software will keep track of each of her requests, log her events, and make changes that she requests that can take place in her security context. Security context is the authorization level she is assigned based on her permissions, entitlements, and access rights.

Once Kathy ends the session, the cookie is usually erased from the web browser's memory and the web server no longer keeps this connection open or collects session state information on this user.

NOTE A cookie can be in the format of a text file stored on the user's hard drive (permanent) or it can be only held in memory (session). If the cookie contains any type of sensitive information, then it should only be held in memory and be erased once the session has completed.

As an analogy, let's say I am following you in a mall as you are shopping. I am marking down what you purchase, where you go, and the requests you make. I know everything about your actions; I document them in a log, and remember them as you continue. (I am keeping state information on you and your activities.) You can have access to all of these stores if every 15 minutes you show me a piece of paper that I gave you. If you fail to show me the piece of paper at the necessary interval, I will push a button and all stores will be locked—you no longer have access to the stores, I no longer collect information about you, and I leave and forget all about you. Since you are no longer able to access any sensitive objects (store merchandise), I don't need to keep track of you and what you are doing.

As long as the web browser serves up the cookie to the web browser, Kathy does not have to provide credentials as she asks for different resources. This is what single sign-on is. You only have to provide your credentials once and the continual validation that you have the necessary cookie will allow you to go from one resource to another. If you end your session with the web server and need to interact with it again, you must re-authenticate and a new cookie will be sent to your browser and it starts all over again.

NOTE We will cover specific single sign-on technologies later in this chapter along with their security issues.

So the WAM product allows an administrator to configure and control access to internal resources. This type of access control is commonly put in place to control external entities requesting access. The product may work on a single web server or a server farm.

Password Management

Wouldn't it be easier for everyone to just use the value "password" for their password?
Response: Yes! Let's do that, and then no password management will ever be needed.

We cover password requirements, security issues, and best practices later in this chapter. At this point, we need to understand how password management can work within an IdM environment.

Help-desk workers and administrators commonly complain about the amount of time they have to spend resetting passwords when users forget them. Another issue is the number of different passwords the users are required to remember for the different platforms within the network. When a password changes, an administrator must connect directly to that management software of the specific platform and change the password value. This may not seem like much of a hassle, but if an organization has 4000 users and seven different platforms, and 35 different applications, it could require a full-time person to continually make these password modifications. And who would really want *that* job?

Different types of password management technologies have been developed to get these pesky users off the backs of IT and the help desk by providing a more secure and automated password management system. The most common password management approaches are listed next.

- **Password Synchronization** Reduces the complexity of keeping up with different passwords for different systems.
- **Self-Service Password Reset** Reduces help-desk call volumes by allowing users to reset their own passwords.
- **Assisted Password Reset** Reduces the resolution process for password issues for the help desk. This may include authentication with other types of authentication mechanisms (biometrics, tokens).

Password Synchronization If users have too many passwords they need to keep track of, they will write the passwords down on a sticky note and cleverly hide this under their keyboard or just stick it on the side of their monitor. This is certainly easier for the user, but not so great for security.

Password synchronization technologies can allow a user to maintain just one password across multiple systems. The product will synchronize the password to other systems and applications, which happens transparently to the user.

The goal is to require the user to memorize only one password and have the ability to enforce more robust and secure password requirements. If a user only needs to remember one password, he is more likely to not have a problem with longer, more complex strings of values. This reduces help-desk call volume and allows the administrator to keep her sanity for just a little bit longer.

One criticism of this approach is that since only one password is used to access different resources, now the hacker only has to figure out one credential set to gain unauthorized access to all resources. But if the password requirements are more demanding (12 characters, no dictionary words, three symbols, upper and lower letters, and so on) and the password is changed out regularly, the balance between security and usability can be acceptable.

Self-Service Password Reset Some products are implemented to allow users to reset their own passwords. This does not mean that the users have any type of privileged permissions on the systems to allow them to change their own credentials. Instead, during the registration of a user account, the user can be asked to provide several personal questions (school graduated from, favorite teacher, favorite color, and so on) in a question and answer form. When the user forgets his password, he may be required to provide another authentication mechanism (smart card, token) and to answer these previously answered questions to prove his identity. If he does this properly, he is allowed to change his password. If he does not do this properly, he is fired because he is an idiot.

Products are available that allow users to change their passwords through other means. For example, if you forgot your password, you may be asked to answer some of the questions answered during the registration process of your account. If you do this correctly, an e-mail is sent to you with a link you must click. The password management product has your identity tied to the answers you gave to the questions during your account registration process and to your e-mail address. If the user does everything correctly, he is given a screen that allows him to reset his password.

CAUTION The product should not ask for information that is publicly available, as in your mother's maiden name, because anyone can find that out and attempt to identify himself as you.

Assisted Password Reset Some products are created for help-desk employees who need to work with individuals when they forget their password. The help-desk employee should not know or ask the individual for her password. This would be a security risk since only the owner of the password should know the value. The help-desk employee also should not just change a password for someone calling in without authenticating that person first. This can allow social engineering attacks where an attacker calls the help desk and indicates she is someone who she is not. If this took place, then an attacker would have a valid employee password and could gain unauthorized access to the company's jewels.

The products that provide assisted password reset functionality allow the help-desk individual to authenticate the caller before resetting the password. This authentication process is commonly performed through the question and answer process described in the previous section. The help-desk individual and the caller must be identified and authenticated through the password management tool before the password can be changed. Once the password is updated, the system that the user is authenticating to should require the user to change her password again. This would ensure that only she (and not she and the help-desk person) knows her password. The goal of an assisted password reset product is to reduce the cost of support calls and ensure all calls are processed in a uniform, consistent, and secure fashion.

Various password management products on the market provide one or all of these functionalities. Since IdM is about streamlining identification, authentication, and access control, one of these products is typically integrated into the enterprise IdM solution.

Legacy Single Sign-On We will cover specific single sign-on (SSO) technologies later in this chapter, but at this point we want to understand how SSO products are commonly used as an IdM solution, or part of a larger IdM enterprise-wide solution.

An SSO technology allows a user to authenticate one time and then access resources in the environment without needing to re-authenticate. This may sound the same as password synchronization, but it is not. With password synchronization, a product takes the user's password and updates each user account on each different system and application with that one password. If Tom's password is *iwearpanties*, then this is the value he must type into each and every application and system he must access. In an SSO situation, Tom would send his password to one authentication system. When Tom requests to access a network application, the application will send over a request for credentials, but the SSO software will respond to the application for Tom. So in SSO environments, the SSO software intercepts the login prompts from network systems and applications and fills in the necessary identification and authentication information (that is, the username and password) for the user.

Even though password synchronization and single sign-on are different technologies, they still have the same vulnerability. If an attacker uncovers a user's credential set, she can have access to all the resources that the legitimate user may have access to.

An SSO solution may also provide a bottleneck or single point of failure. If the SSO server goes down, users are unable to access network resources. This is why it's a good idea to have some type of redundancy or fail-over technology in place.

Most environments are not homogeneous in devices and applications, which makes it more difficult to have a true enterprise SSO solution. Legacy systems many times require a different type of authentication process than the SSO software can provide. So potentially 80 percent of the devices and applications may be able to interact with the SSO software and the other 20 percent will require users to authenticate to them directly. In many of these situations, the IT department may come up with their own homemade solutions, such as using login batch scripts for the legacy systems.

Are there any other downfalls with SSO we should be aware of? Well, it can be expensive to implement, especially in larger environments. Many times companies evaluate purchasing this type of solution and find out it is too cost prohibitive. The other issue is that it would mean all of the users' credentials for the company's resources are stored in one location. If an attacker was able to break in to this storehouse, she could access whatever she wanted, and *do* whatever she wanted, with the company's assets.

As always, security, functionality, and cost must be properly weighed to determine the best solution for the company.

Account Management Account management is often not performed efficiently and effectively in companies today. Account management deals with creating user accounts on all systems, modifying the account privileges when necessary, and decommissioning the accounts when they are no longer needed. Most environments have their IT department create accounts manually on the different systems, users are given excessive rights and permissions, and when an employee leaves the company, many or all of the accounts stay active. This is because a centralized account management technology has not been put into place.

Account management products attempt to attack these issues by allowing an administrator to manage user accounts across multiple systems. When there are multiple directories containing user profiles or access information, the account management software allows for replication between the directories to ensure each contains the same up-to-date information.

Now let's think about how accounts are set up. In many environments, when a new user needs an account, a network administrator will set up the account(s) and provide some type of privileges and permissions. But how would the network administrator know what resources this new user should have access to and what permissions should be assigned to the new account? In most situations, he doesn't—he just wings it. This is how users end up with too much access to too much stuff. What should take place instead is implementing a workflow process that allows for a request for a new user account. This request is approved, usually, by the employee's manager, and the accounts are automatically set up on the systems, or a ticket is generated for the technical staff to set up the account(s). If there is a request for a change to the permissions on the account or if an account needs to be decommissioned, it goes through the same process. The request goes to a manager (or whoever is delegated with this approval task), the manager approves it, and the changes to the various accounts take place.

The automated workflow component is common in account management products that provide IdM solutions. Not only does this reduce the potential errors that can take place in account management, each step (including account approval) is logged and tracked. This allows for accountability and provides documentation for use in backtracking if something goes wrong. It also helps ensure that only the necessary amount of access is provided to the account and that there are no "orphaned" accounts still active when employees leave the company. In addition, these types of processes are the kind your auditors will be looking for—and we always want to make the auditors happy!

NOTE   These types of account management products are commonly used to set up and maintain internal accounts. Web access control management is used mainly for external users.

As with SSO products, enterprise account management products are usually expensive and can take years to properly roll out across the enterprise. Regulatory requirements, however, are making more and more companies spend the money for these types of solutions—which the vendors love!

Provisioning   Let's review what we know, and then build upon these concepts.

Most IdM solutions pull user information from the HR database, because the data are already collected and held in one place and are constantly updated as employee or contractors' statuses change. So user information will be copied from the HR database (referred to as the *authoritative source*) into a directory, which we covered in an early section.

When a new employee is hired, the employee's information, along with his manager's name, is pulled from the HR database into the directory. The employee's manager is automatically sent an e-mail asking for approval of this new account. After the manager approves, the necessary accounts are set up on the required systems.

Over time, this new user will commonly have different identity attributes, which will be used for authentication purposes, stored in different systems in the network. When a user requests access to a resource, all of his identity data has already been copied from other identity stores and the HR database and held in this centralized directory (sometimes called the *identity repository*). This may be a meta-directory or a virtual directory. The access control component of the IdM system will compare the user's request to the IdM access control policy and ensure the user has the necessary identification and authentication pieces in place before allowing access to the resource.

When this employee is fired, this new information goes from the HR database to the directory. An e-mail is automatically generated and sent to the manager to allow this account to be decommissioned. Once this is approved, the account management software disables all of the accounts that had been set up for this user.

This example illustrates user account management and provisioning, which is the life-cycle management of identity components.

Why do we have to worry about all of this identification and authentication stuff? Because users always want something—they are very selfish. Okay, users actually need access to resources to carry out their jobs. But what do they need access to, and what level of access? This question is actually a very difficult one in our distributed, heterogeneous, and somewhat chaotic environments today. Too much access to resources opens the company up to potential fraud and other risks. Too little access means the user cannot do his job. So we are required to get it just right.

User provisioning refers to the creation, maintenance, and deactivation of user objects and attributes as they exist in one or more systems, directories, or applications, in response to business processes. User provisioning software may include one or more of the following components: change propagation, self-service workflow, consolidated user administration, delegated user administration, and federated change control. User objects may represent employees, contractors, vendors, partners, customers, or other recipients of a service. Services may include electronic mail, access to a database, access to a file server or mainframe, and so on.

Great. So we create, maintain, and deactivate accounts as required based on business needs. What else does this mean? The creation of the account also is the creation of the access rights to company assets. It is through provisioning that users are given access, or access is taken away. Throughout the life cycle of a user identity, access rights, permissions, and privileges should change as needed in a clearly understood, automated, and audited process.

By now, you should be able to connect how these different technologies work together to provide an organization with streamlined IdM. Directories are built to contain user and resource information. A metadata directory pulls identity information that resides in different places within the network to allow IdM processes to only have to get the needed data for their tasks from this one location. User management tools allow for automated control of user identities through their lifetimes and can provide provisioning. A password management tool is in place so that productivity is not slowed down by a forgotten password. A single sign-on technology requires internal users to only authenticate once for enterprise access. Web access management tools provide a

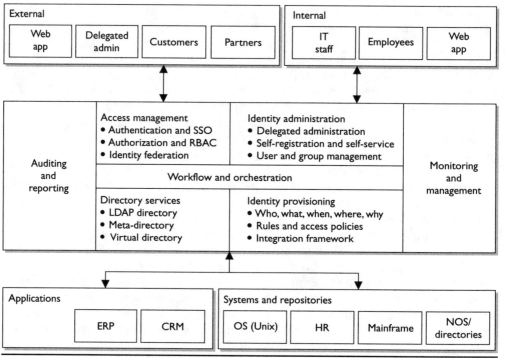

Figure 4-6 Enterprise identity management system components

single sign-on service to external users and controls access to web-based resources. Figure 4-6 provides a visual example of how many of these components work together.

Profile Update Most companies do not just contain the information "Bob Smith" for a user and make all access decisions based on this data. There can be a plethora of information on a user that is captured (e-mail address, home address, phone number, panty size, and so on). When this collection of data is associated with the identity of a user, we call it a profile.

The profile should be centrally located for easier management. IdM enterprise solutions have profile update technology that allows an administrator to create, make changes, or delete these profiles in an automated fashion when necessary. Many user profiles contain nonsensitive data that the user can update himself (called *self service*). So if George moved to a new house, there should be a profile update tool that allows him to go into his profile and change his address information. Now, his profile may also contain sensitive data that should not be available to George—for example, his access rights to resources or information that he is going to get laid off on Friday.

You have interacted with a profile update technology if you have requested to update your personal information on a web site, as in Orbitz, Amazon, or Expedia. These companies provide you with the capability to sign in and update the information they allow you to access. This could be your contact information, home address, purchasing preferences, or credit card data. This information is then used to update their customer relationship management (CRM) system so they know where to send you their junk mail advertisements or spam messages.

Digital Identity

An interesting little fact that not many people are aware of is that a *digital identity* is made up of attributes, entitlements, and traits. Many of us just think of identity as a user ID that is mapped to an individual. The truth is that it is usually more complicated than that.

A user's identity can be a collection of her attributes (department, role in company, shift time, clearance, and others), her entitlements (resources available to her, authoritative rights in the company, and so on), and her traits (biometric information, height, sex, and so forth).

So if a user requests access to a database that contains sensitive employee information, the IdM solution would need to pull together the necessary identity information and her supplied credentials before she is authorized access. If the user is a senior manager (attribute), with a Secret clearance (attribute), and has access to the database (entitlement)—she is granted the permissions Read and Write to certain records in the database Monday through Friday, 8 A.M. to 5 P.M. (attribute).

Another example is if a soldier requests to be assigned an M-16 firearm. She must be in the 34th division (attribute), have a Top Secret clearance (attribute), her supervisor must have approved this (entitlement), and her physical features (traits) must match the ID card she presents to the firearm depot clerk.

The directory (or meta-directory) of the IdM system has all of this identity information centralized, which is why it is so important.

Many people think that just logging in to a domain controller or a network access server is all that is involved in identity management. But if you peek under the covers, you can find an array of complex processes and technologies working together.

The CISSP exam is not currently getting into this level of detail (entitlement, attribute, traits) pertaining to IdM, but in the real world there are many facets to identification, authentication, authorization, and auditing that make it a complex beast.

Federation The world continually gets smaller as technology brings people and companies closer together. Many times, when we are interacting with just one web site, we are actually interacting with several different companies—we just don't know it. The reason we don't know it is because these companies are sharing our identity and authentication information behind the scenes. This is not done for nefarious purposes necessarily, but to make our lives easier and to allow merchants to sell their goods without much effort on our part.

For example, a person wants to book an airline flight and a hotel room. If the airline company and hotel company use a federated identity management system, this means they have set up a trust relationship between the two companies and will share customer identification and, potentially, authentication information. So when I book my flight on Southwest, the web site asks me if I want to also book a hotel room. If I click "Yes," I could then be brought to the Hilton web site, which provides me with information on the closest hotel to the airport I'm flying into. Now, to book a room I don't have to log in again. I logged in on the Southwest web site, and that web site sent my information over to the Hilton web site, all of which happened transparently to me.

A *federated identity* is a portable identity, and its associated entitlements, that can be used across business boundaries. It allows a user to be authenticated across multiple IT systems and enterprises. Identity federation is based upon linking a user's otherwise distinct identities at two or more locations without the need to synchronize or consolidate directory information. Federated identity offers businesses and consumers a more convenient way of accessing distributed resources and is a key component of e-commerce.

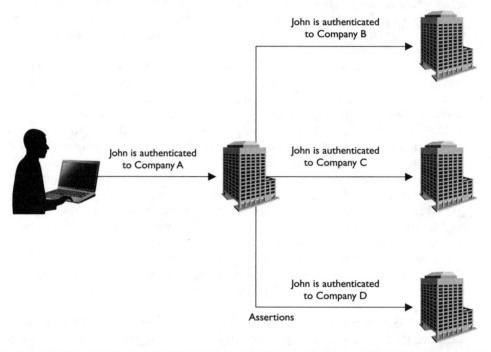

 NOTE Federation identity and all of the IdM technologies we have discussed so far are usually more complex than what has been presented in this text. This is just the "one-inch deep" overview that the CISSP exam expects of test takers. To get more in-depth information on IdM, visit the author's web site at www.logicalsecurity.com/IdentityManagement.

Who Needs Identity Management?
The following are good indications that an identity management solution might be right for your company:

- If users have more than six username and password combinations
- If it takes more than one day to set up and provision an account for new employees
- If it takes more than one day to revoke all access and disable the account of a terminated employee
- If access to critical resources cannot be restricted
- If access to critical resources cannot be audited or monitored

The following sections explain the various types of authentication methods commonly used and integrated in many identity management processes and products today.

Access Control and Markup Languages

You can only do what I want you to do when interacting with my web portal.

If you can remember when *HyperText Markup Language (HTML)* was *all* we had to make a static web page, you're old. Being old in the technology world is different than in the regular world; HTML came out in the early 1990s. HTML came from *Standard Generalized Markup Language (SGML)*, which came from the *Generalized Markup Language (GML)*. We still use HTML, so it is certainly not dead and gone; the industry has just improved upon the markup languages available to use.

A markup language is a way to structure text and how it will be viewed. When you adjust margins and other formatting capabilities in a word processor, you are marking up the text in the word processor's markup language. If you develop a web page, you are using some type of markup language. You can control how it looks and some of the actual functionality the page provides.

A more powerful markup language, *Extensible Markup Language (XML)*, was developed as a specification to create various markup languages. From this specification more specific XML standards were created to provide individual industries the functions they required. Individual industries have different needs in how they use markup languages, but there is an interoperability issue of the industries still needing to be able to communicate to each other.

NOTE XML is used for many more purposes than just building web pages and web sites.

Let's walk through this. An automobile company will need to work with data as in pricing, parts, paint color, model, and so on. Let's compare this to a company that creates automobile tires. This company will need to work with data elements as in production steps, inventory, synthetic rubber types, shipping steps to automobile companies, and such. Now these companies need to be able to communicate to each other's computers and applications. If an automobile company has a markup language tag of <model> that is defined as a car model and the tire company uses the same tag, <model>, but its definition is of tire models—then there is a communication, or interoperability issue. Since the automobile company needs to tell the tire company the type of tires it needs for its inventory, if the company uses the markup tag of <model>, the automobile company would be sending the word "Mustang" when it needs to send a model number that represents a tire type.

So for the automobile and tire company to be able to communicate, they need to speak the same language. This means that their applications need to both use and understand XML. But each company has different types of data that they need to work with, so each uses a derivate standard of XML that best fits their needs.

Very interesting, but what does this have to do with access control? There has been a markup language that is built on the XML framework that exchanges information on what users should get access to what resources and services. So let's say that the automobile company and tire company only allow inventory managers within the automobile company to order tires. If Bob logs into the automobile company's inventory software and orders 40 tires, how does the tire company know that this request is coming from an authorized vendor and user within the inventory managers group? The automobile company's software can pass user and group identity information to the tire company's software. The tire company uses this identity information to make an authorization decision that then allows Bob's request for 40 tires to be filled.

The markup language that can provide this type of functionality is the *Service Provisioning Markup Language (SPML)*. This language allows company interfaces to pass service requests, and the receiving company provisions (allows) access to these services. Since both the sending and receiving companies are following one standard (XML), this type of interoperability can take place.

What if the automobile and tire companies have a trust model set up and share identity, authorization, and authentication methods? This means if Bob is authenticated and authorized within the automobile's software application, this application can pass this information on to the tire company's application, and Bob does not need to be authenticated twice. So when Bob logs into the automobile inventory application, his identity is authenticated, and he is given authorization to order tires. Bob's authorization information is passed over to the tire application, and it just accepts that Bob can carry out the ordering function instead of authenticating and authorizing him for the second time. This means that the automobile and tire company have security domains that trust each other either mutually or one way. The company that is sending the authorization data is referred to as the *producer of assertions* and the receiver is called the *consumer of assertions*.

Companies should not be making authorization decisions willy-nilly. For example, an XML developer for the tire company should not just make the decision that the inventory managers can do a specific functionality, accounting managers can do another functionality, and that Sue can do whatever she wants. The company needs to have application-specific security policies indicating which roles and individuals can carry out specific functions. These decisions should not be up to the application developer. The automobile and tire companies need to follow the same security policies so when an inventory manager logs into the automobile application, both companies are in agreement on what this role can carry out. This is the purpose of the *eXtensible Access Control Markup Language (XACML)*. Application security policies can be shared with other applications to ensure that both are following the same security rules.

NOTE Who develops and keeps track of all of these standardized languages? The *Organization for the Advancement of Structured Information Standards (OASIS)*. This organization develops and maintains the standards for how various aspects of web-based communication are built and maintained.

Let's see what we learned here. Organizations need a way to control how their information is used internally within their applications. XML is the standard that provides the metadata structures to allow this expression of data. Organizations need to be able to communicate their information, and since XML is a global standard, as long as they both follow the XML rules, they can exchange data back and forth. Users on the sender's side need to be able to access services on the receiver's side, which the SPML provides. The receiving side needs to make sure the user who is making the request is properly authenticated by the sending company before allowing access to the requested service, which is provided by the SAML. To ensure that the sending and receiving companies follow the same security rules, they must follow the same security policies, which is the functionality that the XACML provides.

 NOTE XML is covered from an application view in Chapter 11.

To dig into these markup languages and their functions, visit the following web sites:

- www.oasis-open.org/home/index.php
- www.w3.org/XML
- http://saml.xml.org/
- http://identitymngr.sourceforge.net/

Biometrics

I would like to prove who I am. Please look at the blood vessels at the back of my eyeball.
Response: Gross.

Biometrics verifies an individual's identity by analyzing a unique personal attribute or behavior, which is one of the most effective and accurate methods of verifying identification. Biometrics is a very sophisticated technology; thus, it is much more expensive and complex than the other types of identity verification processes. A biometric system can make authentication decisions based on an individual's behavior, as in signature dynamics, but these can change over time and possibly be forged. Biometric systems that base authentication decisions on physical attributes (such as iris, retina, or fingerprint) provide more accuracy, because physical attributes typically don't change, absent some disfiguring injury, and are harder to impersonate.

Biometrics is typically broken up into two different categories. The first is the physiological. These are traits that are physical attributes unique to a specific individual. Fingerprints are a common example of a physiological trait used in biometric systems.

The second category of biometrics is known as behavioral. This is based on a characteristic of an individual to confirm his identity. An example is signature dynamics. Physiological is "what you are" and behavioral is "what you do."

A biometric system scans a person's physiological attribute or behavioral trait and compares it to a record created in an earlier enrollment process. Because this system inspects the grooves of a person's fingerprint, the pattern of someone's retina, or the pitches of someone's voice, it must be extremely sensitive. The system must perform accurate and repeatable measurements of anatomical or behavioral characteristics. This type of sensitivity can easily cause false positives or false negatives. The system must be calibrated so these false positives and false negatives occur infrequently and the results are as accurate as possible.

When a biometric system rejects an authorized individual, it is called a *Type I error* (false rejection rate). When the system accepts impostors who should be rejected, it is called a *Type II error* (false acceptance rate). The goal is to obtain low numbers for each type of error, but Type II errors are the most dangerous and thus the most important to avoid.

When comparing different biometric systems, many different variables are used, but one of the most important metrics is the *crossover error rate (CER)*. This rating is stated as a percentage and represents the point at which the false rejection rate equals the false acceptance rate. This rating is the most important measurement when determining the system's accuracy. A biometric system that delivers a CER of 3 will be more accurate than a system that delivers a CER of 4.

NOTE Crossover error rate (CER) is also called equal error rate (EER).

What is the purpose of this CER value anyway? Using the CER as an impartial judgment of a biometric system helps create standards by which products from different vendors can be fairly judged and evaluated. If you are going to buy a biometric system, you need a way to compare the accuracy between different systems. You can just go by the different vendors' marketing material (they all say they are the best), or you can compare the different CER values of the products to see which one really is more accurate than the others. It is also a way to keep the vendors honest. One vendor may tell you, "We have absolutely no Type II errors." This would mean that their product would not allow any imposters to be improperly authenticated. But what if you asked the vendor how many Type I errors their product had and she sheepishly replied, "We average around 90 percent of Type I errors." That would mean that 90 percent of the authentication attempts would be rejected, which would negatively affect your employees' productivity. So you can ask about their CER value, which represents when the Type I and Type II errors are equal, to give you a better understanding of the product's overall accuracy.

Individual environments have specific security level requirements, which will dictate how many Type I and Type II errors are acceptable. For example, a military institution that is very concerned about confidentiality would be prepared to accept a certain number of Type I errors, but would absolutely not accept any false accepts (Type II errors). Because all biometric systems can be calibrated, if you lower the Type II error rate by adjusting the system's sensitivity, it will result in an increase in Type I errors. The military institution would obviously calibrate the biometric system to lower the Type II errors to zero, but that would mean it would have to accept a higher rate of Type I errors.

Biometrics is the most expensive method of verifying a person's identity, and it faces other barriers to becoming widely accepted. These include user acceptance, enrollment timeframe, and throughput. Many times, people are reluctant to let a machine read the pattern of their retina or scan the geometry of their hand. This lack of enthusiasm has slowed down the widespread use of biometric systems within our society. The enrollment phase requires an action to be performed several times to capture a clear and distinctive reference record. People are not particularly fond of expending this time and energy when they are used to just picking a password and quickly typing it into their console. When a person attempts to be authenticated by a biometric system, sometimes the system will request an action to be completed several times. If the system was unable to get a clear reading of an iris scan or could not capture a full voice verification print, the individual may have to repeat the action. This causes low throughput, stretches the individual's patience, and reduces acceptability.

Processing Speed

When reviewing biometric devices for purchase, one component to take into consideration is the length of time it takes to actually authenticate users. From the time a user inserts data until she receives an accept or reject response should take five to ten seconds.

During enrollment, the user provides the biometric data (fingerprint, voice print) and the biometric reader converts this data into binary values. Depending on the system, the reader may create a hash value of the biometric data, or it may encrypt the data, or do both. The biometric data then goes from the reader to a back-end authentication database where her user account has been created. When the user needs to later authenticate to a system, she will provide the necessary biometric data (fingerprint, voice print) and the binary format of this information is compared to what is in the authentication database. If they match, then the user is authenticated.

In Figure 4-7, we see that biometric data can be stored on a smart card and used for authentication. Also, you might notice that the match is 95 percent instead of 100 percent. Obtaining a 100 percent match each and every time is very difficult because of the level of sensitivity of the biometric systems. A smudge on the reader, oil on the person's finger, and other small environmental issues can stand in the way of matching 100 percent. If your biometric system was calibrated so it required 100 percent matches, this would mean you would not allow any Type II errors and that users would commonly not be authenticated in a timely manner.

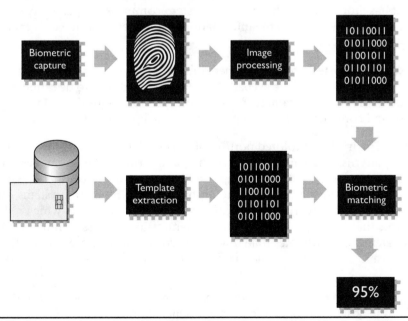

Figure 4-7 Biometric data is turned into binary data and compared for identity validation.

The following is an overview of the different types of biometric systems and the physiological or behavioral characteristics they examine.

Fingerprint   Fingerprints are made up of ridge endings and bifurcations exhibited by friction ridges and other detailed characteristics called minutiae. It is the distinctiveness of these minutiae that gives each individual a unique fingerprint. An individual places his finger on a device that reads the details of the fingerprint and compares this to a reference file. If the two match, the individual's identity has been verified.

NOTE   Fingerprint systems store the full fingerprint, which is actually a lot of information that takes up hard drive space and resources. The finger-scan technology extracts specific features from the fingerprint and stores just that information, which takes up less hard drive space and allows for quicker database lookups and comparisons.

Palm Scan   The palm holds a wealth of information and has many aspects that are used to identify an individual. The palm has creases, ridges, and grooves throughout that are unique to a specific person. The palm scan also includes the fingerprints of each finger. An individual places his hand on the biometric device, which scans and captures this information. This information is compared to a reference file and the identity is either verified or rejected.

Hand Geometry   The shape of a person's hand (the shape, length and width of the hand and fingers) defines hand geometry. This trait differs significantly between people and is used in some biometric systems to verify identity. A person places her hand on a device that has grooves for each finger. The system compares the geometry of each finger, and the hand as a whole, to the information in a reference file to verify that person's identity.

Retina Scan   A system that reads a person's retina scans the blood-vessel pattern of the retina on the backside of the eyeball. This pattern has shown to be extremely unique between different people. A camera is used to project a beam inside the eye and capture the pattern and compare it to a reference file recorded previously.

Iris Scan   The iris is the colored portion of the eye that surrounds the pupil. The iris has unique patterns, rifts, colors, rings, coronas, and furrows. The uniqueness of each of these characteristics within the iris is captured by a camera and compared with the information gathered during the enrollment phase. Of the biometric systems, iris scans are the most accurate. The iris remains constant through adulthood, which reduces the type of errors that can happen during the authentication process. Sampling the iris offers more reference coordinates than any other type of biometric. Mathematically, this means it has a higher accuracy potential than any other type of biometric.

NOTE   When using an iris pattern biometric system, the optical unit must be positioned so the sun does not shine into the aperture; thus, when implemented, it must have proper placement within the facility.

Signature Dynamics   When a person signs a signature, usually they do so in the same manner and speed each time. Signing a signature produces electrical signals that can be captured by a biometric system. The physical motions performed when someone is signing a document create these electrical signals. The signals provide unique characteristics that can be used to distinguish one individual from another. Signature dynamics provides more information than a static signature, so there are more variables to verify when confirming an individual's identity and more assurance that this person is who he claims to be.

Signature dynamics is different from a digitized signature. A digitized signature is just an electronic copy of someone's signature and is not a biometric system that captures the speed of signing, the way the person holds the pen, and the pressure the signer exerts to generate the signature.

Keystroke Dynamics   Whereas signature dynamics is a method that captures the electrical signals when a person signs a name, keystroke dynamics captures electrical signals when a person types a certain phrase. As a person types a specified phrase, the biometric system captures the speed and motions of this action. Each individual has a certain style and speed, which translate into unique signals. This type of authentication is more effective than typing in a password, because a password is easily obtainable. It is much harder to repeat a person's typing style than it is to acquire a password.

Voice Print   People's speech sounds and patterns have many subtle distinguishing differences. A biometric system that is programmed to capture a voice print and compare it to the information held in a reference file can differentiate one individual from another. During the enrollment process, an individual is asked to say several different words. Later, when this individual needs to be authenticated, the biometric system jumbles these words and presents them to the individual. The individual then repeats the sequence of words given. This technique is used so others cannot attempt to record the session and play it back in hopes of obtaining unauthorized access.

Facial Scan   A system that scans a person's face takes many attributes and characteristics into account. People have different bone structures, nose ridges, eye widths, forehead sizes, and chin shapes. These are all captured during a facial scan and compared to an earlier captured scan held within a reference record. If the information is a match, the person is positively identified.

Hand Topography   Whereas hand geometry looks at the size and width of an individual's hand and fingers, hand topology looks at the different peaks and valleys of the hand, along with its overall shape and curvature. When an individual wants to be authenticated, she places her hand on the system. Off to one side of the system, a camera snaps a side-view picture of the hand from a different view and angle than that of systems that target hand geometry, and thus captures different data. This attribute is not unique enough to authenticate individuals by itself and is commonly used in conjunction with hand geometry.

Biometrics are not without their own sets of issues and concerns. Because they depend upon the specific and unique traits of living things there can be problems that arise. Living things are notorious for not remaining the same, which means they won't present static biometric information for each and every login attempt. Voice recognition can be hampered by a user with a cold. Pregnancy can change the patterns of the retina. Someone could lose a finger. Or all three could happen. You just never know in this crazy world.

Some biometric systems actually check for the pulsation and/or heat of a body part to make sure it is alive. So if you are planning to cut someone's finger off or pluck out someone's eyeball so you can authenticate yourself as a legitimate user, it may not work. Although not specifically stated, I am pretty sure this type of activity falls outside the bounds of the CISSP ethics you will be responsible for upholding once you receive your certification.

Passwords

User identification coupled with a reusable password is the most common form of system identification and authorization mechanisms. A password is a protected string of characters that is used to authenticate an individual. As stated previously, authentication factors are based on what a person knows, has, or is. A password is something the user knows.

Passwords are one of the most often used authentication mechanisms employed today. It is important the passwords are strong and properly managed.

Password Management   Although passwords are the most commonly used authentication mechanisms, they are also considered one of the weakest security mechanisms available. Why? Users usually choose passwords that are easily guessed (a spouse's name, a user's birth date, or a dog's name), or tell others their passwords, and many times write the passwords down on a sticky note and cleverly hide it under the keyboard. To most users, security is usually not the most important or interesting part of using their computers—except when someone hacks into their computer and steals confidential information, that is. Then security is all the rage.

This is where password management steps in. If passwords are properly generated, updated, and kept secret, they can provide effective security. Password generators can be used to create passwords for users. This ensures that a user will not be using "Bob" or "Spot" for a password, but if the generator spits out "kdjasijew284802h," the user will surely scribble it down on a piece of paper and safely stick it to the monitor, which defeats the whole purpose. If a password generator is going to be used, the tools should create uncomplicated, pronounceable, nondictionary words to help users remember them so they aren't tempted to write them down.

If the users can choose their own passwords, the operating system should enforce certain password requirements. The operating system can require that a password contain a certain number of characters, unrelated to the user ID, include special characters, include upper- and lowercase letters, and not be easily guessable. The operating system can keep track of the passwords a specific user generates so as to ensure no passwords are reused. The users should also be forced to change their passwords periodically. All of these factors make it harder for an attacker to guess or obtain passwords within the environment.

If an attacker is after a password, she can try a few different techniques:

- **Electronic monitoring** Listening to network traffic to capture information, especially when a user is sending her password to an authentication server. The password can be copied and reused by the attacker at another time, which is called a *replay attack*.

- **Access the password file** Usually done on the authentication server. The password file contains many users' passwords and, if compromised, can be the source of a lot of damage. This file should be protected with access control mechanisms and encryption.

- **Brute force attacks** Performed with tools that cycle through many possible character, number, and symbol combinations to uncover a password.

- **Dictionary attacks** Files of thousands of words are compared to the user's password until a match is found.

- **Social engineering** An attacker falsely convinces an individual that she has the necessary authorization to access specific resources.

- **Rainbow table** An attacker uses a table that contains all possible passwords already in a hash format.

Certain techniques can be implemented to provide another layer of security for passwords and their use. After each successful logon, a message can be presented to a user indicating the date and time of the last successful logon, the location of this logon, and whether there were any unsuccessful logon attempts. This alerts the user to any suspicious activity, and whether anyone has attempted to log on using his credentials. An administrator can set operating parameters that allow a certain number of failed logon attempts to be accepted before a user is locked out; this is a type of *clipping level*. The user can be locked out for five minutes or a full day after the threshold (or clipping level) has been exceeded. It depends on how the administrator configures this mechanism. An audit trail can also be used to track password usage and both successful and unsuccessful logon attempts. This audit information should include the date, time, user ID, and workstation the user logged in from.

A password's lifetime should be short but practical. Forcing a user to change a password on a more frequent basis provides more assurance that the password will not be guessed by an intruder. If the lifetime is too short, however, it causes unnecessary management overhead, and users may forget which password is active. A balance between protection and practicality must be decided upon and enforced.

As with many things in life, education is the key. Password requirements, protection, and generation should be addressed in security-awareness programs so users understand what is expected of them, why they should protect their passwords, and how passwords can be stolen. Users should be an extension to a security team, not the opposition.

NOTE Rainbow tables contain passwords already in their hashed format. The attacker just compares a captured hashed password with one that is listed in the table to uncover the plaintext password. This takes much less time than carrying out a dictionary or brute force attack.

Password Checkers Several organizations test user-chosen passwords using tools that perform dictionary and/or brute force attacks to detect the weak passwords. This helps make the environment as a whole less susceptible to dictionary and exhaustive attacks used to discover users' passwords. Many times the same tools employed by an attacker to crack a password are used by a network administrator to make sure the password is strong enough. Most security tools have this dual nature. They are used by security professionals and IT staff to test for vulnerabilities within their environment in the hope of uncovering and fixing them before an attacker finds the vulnerabilities. An attacker uses the same tools to uncover vulnerabilities to exploit before the security professional can fix them. It is the never-ending cat-and-mouse game.

If a tool is called a *password checker*, it is a tool used by a security professional to test the strength of a password. If a tool is called a *password cracker*, it is usually used by a hacker; however, most of the time, these tools are one and the same.

You need to obtain management's approval before attempting to test (break) employees' passwords with the intent of identifying weak passwords. Explaining you are trying to help the situation, not hurt it, *after* you have uncovered the CEO's password is not a good situation to be in.

Password Hashing and Encryption In most situations, if an attacker sniffs your password from the network wire, she still has some work to do before she actually knows your password value, because most systems hash the password with a hashing algorithm, commonly MD4 or MD5, to ensure passwords are not sent in cleartext.

Although some people think the world is run by Microsoft, other types of operating systems are out there, such as Unix and Linux. These systems do not use registries and SAM databases, but contain their user passwords in a file cleverly called "shadow." Now, this shadow file does not contain passwords in cleartext; instead, your password is run through a hashing algorithm, and the resulting value is stored in this file. Unix-type systems zest things up by using salts in this process. *Salts* are random values added to the encryption process to add more complexity. The more randomness entered into the encryption process, the harder it is for the bad guy to decrypt and uncover your password. The use of a salt means that the same password can be encrypted into several thousand different formats. This makes it much more difficult for an attacker to uncover the *right* format for your system.

Password Aging Many systems enable administrators to set expiration dates for passwords, forcing users to change them at regular intervals. The system may also keep a list of the last five to ten passwords (password history) and not let the users revert back to previously used passwords.

Limit Logon Attempts A threshold can be set to allow only a certain number of unsuccessful logon attempts. After the threshold is met, the user's account can be locked for a period of time or indefinitely, which requires an administrator to manually unlock the account. This protects against dictionary and other exhaustive attacks that continually submit credentials until the right combination of username and password is discovered.

Cognitive Password

What is your mother's name?
Response: Shucks, I don't remember. I have it written down somewhere.

Cognitive passwords are fact- or opinion-based information used to verify an individual's identity. A user is enrolled by answering several questions based on her life experiences. Passwords can be hard for people to remember, but that same person will not likely forget her mother's maiden name, favorite color, dog's name, or the school she graduated from. After the enrollment process, the user can answer the questions asked of her to be authenticated, instead of having to remember a password. This authentication process is best for a service the user does not use on a daily basis because it takes longer than other authentication mechanisms. This can work well for help-desk services. The user can be authenticated via cognitive means. This way, the person at the help desk can be sure he is talking to the right person, and the user in need of help does not need to remember a password that may be used once every three months.

One-Time Password

How many times is my one-time password good for?
Response: You are fired.

A *one-time password (OTP)* is also called a dynamic password. It is used for authentication purposes and is only good once. After the password is used, it is no longer valid; thus, if a hacker obtained this password, it could not be reused. This type of authentication mechanism is used in environments that require a higher level of security than static passwords provide. One-time password generating tokens come in two general types: synchronous and asynchronous.

The token device is the most common implementation mechanism for OTP and generates the one-time password for the user to submit to an authentication server. The following sections explain these concepts.

The Token Device   The token device, or password generator, is usually a handheld device that has an LCD display and possibly a keypad. This hardware is separate from the computer the user is attempting to access. The token device and authentication service must be synchronized in some manner to be able to authenticate a user. The token device presents the user with a list of characters to be entered as a password when logging on to a computer. Only the token device and authentication service know the meaning of these characters. Because the two are synchronized, the token device will present the exact password the authentication service is expecting. This is a one-time password, also called a token, and is no longer valid after initial use.

Synchronous   A *synchronous token device* synchronizes with the authentication service by using time or a counter as the core piece of the authentication process. If the synchronization is time-based, the token device and the authentication service must hold the same time within their internal clocks. The time value on the token device and a secret key are used to create the one-time password, which is displayed to the user. The user enters this value and a user ID into the computer, which then passes them to

SecurID

SecurID, from RSA Security, Inc., is one of the most widely used time-based tokens. One version of the product generates the one-time password by using a mathematical function on the time, date, and ID of the token card. Another version of the product requires a PIN to be entered into the token device.

RSA SecurID Time-Synchronous Two-Factor Authentication

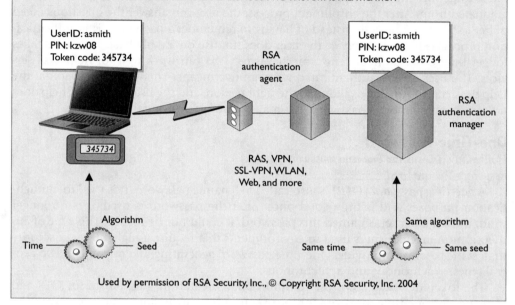

UserID: asmith
PIN: kzw08
Token code: 345734

RSA authentication agent

UserID: asmith
PIN: kzw08
Token code: 345734

RSA authentication manager

345734

RAS, VPN, SSL-VPN, WLAN, Web, and more

Algorithm
Time — Seed

Same algorithm
Same time — Same seed

Used by permission of RSA Security, Inc., © Copyright RSA Security, Inc. 2004

the server running the authentication service. The authentication service decrypts this value and compares it to the value it expected. If the two match, the user is authenticated and allowed to use the computer and resources.

If the token device and authentication service use *counter-synchronization*, the user will need to initiate the creation of the one-time password by pushing a button on the token device. This causes the token device and the authentication service to advance to the next authentication value. This value and a base secret are hashed and displayed to the user. The user enters this resulting value along with a user ID to be authenticated. In either time- or counter-based synchronization, the token device and authentication service must share the same secret base key used for encryption and decryption.

Asynchronous   A token device using an *asynchronous token*–generating method employs a challenge/response scheme to authenticate the user. In this situation, the authentication server sends the user a challenge, a random value also called a nonce. The user enters this random value into the token device, which encrypts it and returns a value the user uses as a one-time password. The user sends this value, along with a username, to the authentication server. If the authentication server can decrypt the value and it is the same challenge value sent earlier, the user is authenticated, as shown in Figure 4-8.

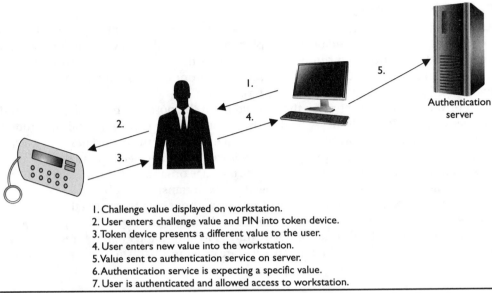

1. Challenge value displayed on workstation.
2. User enters challenge value and PIN into token device.
3. Token device presents a different value to the user.
4. User enters new value into the workstation.
5. Value sent to authentication service on server.
6. Authentication service is expecting a specific value.
7. User is authenticated and allowed access to workstation.

Figure 4-8 Authentication using an asynchronous token device includes a workstation, token device, and authentication service.

NOTE The actual implementation and process that these devices follow can differ between different vendors. What is important to know is that asynchronous is based on challenge/response mechanisms, while synchronous is based on time- or counter-driven mechanisms.

Both token systems can fall prey to masquerading if a user shares his identification information (ID or username) and the token device is shared or stolen. The token device can also have battery failure or other malfunctions that would stand in the way of a successful authentication. However, this type of system is not vulnerable to electronic eavesdropping, sniffing, or password guessing.

If the user has to enter a password or PIN into the token device before it provides a one-time password, then strong authentication is in effect because it is using two factors—something the user knows (PIN) and something the user has (the token device).

NOTE One-time passwords can also be generated in software, in which case a piece of hardware such as a token device is not required. These are referred to as *soft tokens* and require that the authentication service and application contain the same base secrets, which are used to generate the one-time passwords.

Cryptographic Keys

Another way to prove one's identity is to use a private key by generating a digital signature. A digital signature could be used in place of a password. Passwords are the weakest form of authentication and can be easily sniffed as they travel over a network. Digital signatures are forms of authentication used in environments that require higher security protection than what is provided by passwords.

A private key is a secret value that should be in the possession of one person, and one person only. It should never be disclosed to an outside party. A digital signature is a technology that uses a private key to encrypt a hash value (message digest). The act of encrypting this hash value with a private key is called *digitally signing* a message. A digital signature attached to a message proves the message originated from a specific source, and that the message itself was not changed while in transit.

A public key can be made available to anyone without compromising the associated private key; this is why it is called a public key. We explore private keys, public keys, digital signatures, and public key infrastructure (PKI) in Chapter 8, but for now, understand that a private key and digital signatures are other mechanisms that can be used to authenticate an individual.

Passphrase

A *passphrase* is a sequence of characters that is longer than a password (thus a "phrase") and, in some cases, takes the place of a password during an authentication process. The user enters this phrase into an application and the application transforms the value into a *virtual password*, making the passphrase the length and format that is required by the application. (For example, an application may require your virtual password to be 128 bits to be used as a key with the AES algorithm.) If a user wants to authenticate to an application, such as Pretty Good Privacy (PGP), he types in a passphrase, let's say StickWithMeKidAndYouWillWearDiamonds. The application converts this phrase into a virtual password that is used for the actual authentication. The user usually generates the passphrase in the same way a user creates a password the first time he logs on to a computer. A passphrase is more secure than a password because it is longer, and thus harder to obtain by an attacker. In many cases, the user is more likely to remember a passphrase than a password.

Memory Cards

The main difference between memory cards and smart cards is their capacity to process information. A *memory card* holds information but cannot process information. A *smart card* holds information and has the necessary hardware and software to actually process that information. A memory card can hold a user's authentication information so the user only needs to type in a user ID or PIN and present the memory card, and if the data that the user entered matches the data on the memory card, the user is successfully authenticated. If the user presents a PIN value, then this is an example of two-factor authentication—something the user knows, and something the user has. A memory card can also hold identification data that are pulled from the memory card by a reader. It travels with the PIN to a back-end authentication server. An example of a memory card is a swipe card that must be used for an individual to be able to enter a building. The user enters a PIN and swipes the memory card through a card reader. If this is the correct combination, the reader flashes green and the individual can open the door and enter the building. Another example is an ATM card. If Buffy wants to withdraw $40 from her checking account, she needs to enter the correct PIN and slide the ATM card (or memory card) through the reader.

Memory cards can be used with computers, but they require a reader to process the information. The reader adds cost to the process, especially when one is needed per computer, and card generation adds additional cost and effort to the whole authentication process. Using a memory card provides a more secure authentication method than using a password because the attacker would need to obtain the card and know the correct PIN. Administrators and management must weigh the costs and benefits of a memory token–based card implementation to determine if it is the right authentication mechanism for their environment.

Smart Card

My smart card is smarter than your memory card.

A smart card has the capability of processing information because it has a microprocessor and integrated circuits incorporated into the card itself. Memory cards do not have this type of hardware and lack this type of functionality. The only function they can perform is simple storage. A smart card, which adds the capability to process information stored on it, can also provide a two-factor authentication method because the user may have to enter a PIN to unlock the smart card. This means the user must provide something she knows (PIN) and something she has (smart card).

Two general categories of smart cards are the contact and the contactless types. The *contact* smart card has a gold seal on the face of the card. When this card is fully inserted into a card reader, electrical fingers wipe against the card in the exact position that the chip contacts are located. This will supply power and data I/O to the chip for authentication purposes. The *contactless* smart card has an antenna wire that surrounds the perimeter of the card. When this card comes within an electromagnetic field of the reader, the antenna within the card generates enough energy to power the internal chip. Now, the results of the smart card processing can be broadcast through the same antenna, and the conversation of authentication can take place. The authentication can be completed by using a one-time password, by employing a challenge/response value, or by providing the user's private key if it is used within a PKI environment.

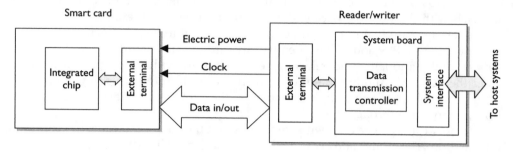

Contact type

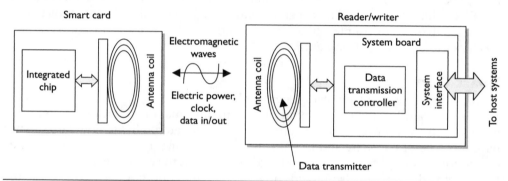

Contactless type

NOTE Two types of contactless smart cards are available: hybrid and combi. The hybrid card has two chips, with the capability of utilizing both the contact and contactless formats. A combi card has one microprocessor chip that can communicate to contact or contactless readers.

The information held within the memory of a smart card is not readable until the correct PIN is entered. This fact and the complexity of the smart token make these cards resistant to reverse-engineering and tampering methods. If George loses the smart card he uses to authenticate to the domain at work, the person who finds the card would need to know his PIN to do any real damage. The smart card can also be programmed to store information in an encrypted fashion, as well as detect any tampering with the card itself. In the event that tampering is detected, the information stored on the smart card can be automatically wiped.

The drawbacks to using a smart card are the extra cost of the readers and the overhead of card generation, as with memory cards, although this cost is decreasing. The smart cards themselves are more expensive than memory cards because of the extra integrated circuits and microprocessor. Essentially, a smart card is a kind of computer, and because of that it has many of the operational challenges and risks that can affect a computer.

Smart cards have several different capabilities, and as the technology develops and memory capacities increase for storage, they will gain even more. They can store personal information in a storage manner that is tamper resistant. This also allows them to have the ability to isolate security-critical computations within themselves. They can be used in encryption systems in order to store keys and have a high level of portability as well as security. The memory and integrated circuit also allow for the capacity to use encryption algorithms on the actual card and use them for secure authorization that can be utilized throughout an entire organization.

Smart Card Attacks   Smart cards are more tamperproof than memory cards, but where there is sensitive data there are individuals who are motivated to circumvent any countermeasure the industry throws at them.

Over the years, people have become very inventive in the development of various ways to attack smart cards. For example, individuals have introduced computational errors into smart cards with the goal of uncovering the encryption keys used and stored on the cards. These "errors" are introduced by manipulating some environmental component of the card (changing input voltage, clock rate, temperature fluctuations). The attacker reviews the result of an encryption function after introducing an error to the card, and also reviews the correct result, which the card performs when no errors are introduced. Analysis of these different results may allow an attacker to reverse-engineer the encryption process, with the hope of uncovering the encryption key. This type of attack is referred to as *fault generation*.

Side-channel attacks are nonintrusive and are used to uncover sensitive information about how a component works, without trying to compromise any type of flaw or weakness. As an analogy, suppose you want to figure out what your boss does each day at lunch time but you feel too uncomfortable to ask her. So you follow her, and you see she enters a building holding a small black bag and exits exactly 45 minutes later with the same bag and her hair not looking as great as when she went in. You keep doing this day after day and come to the conclusion that she must be working out. Now you could have simply read the sign on the building that said "Gym," but we will give you the benefit of the doubt here and just not call you for any further private investigator work.

So a noninvasive attack is one in which the attacker watches how something works and how it reacts in different situations instead of trying to "invade" it with more intrusive measures. Some examples of side-channel attacks that have been carried out on smart cards are *differential power analysis* (examining the power emissions released during processing), *electromagnetic analysis* (examining the frequencies emitted), and timing (how long a specific process takes to complete). These types of attacks are used to uncover sensitive information about how a component works without trying to compromise any type of flaw or weakness. They are commonly used for data collection. Attackers monitor and capture the analog characteristics of all supply and interface connections and any other electromagnetic radiation produced by the processor during normal operation. They can also collect the time it takes for the smart card to carry out its function. From the collected data, the attacker can deduce specific information she is after, which could be a private key, sensitive financial data, or an encryption key stored on the card.

Interoperability

An ISO/IEC standard, 14443, outlines the following items for smart card standardization:

- **ISO/IEC 14443-1** Physical characteristics
- **ISO/IEC 14443-3** Initialization and anticollision
- **ISO/IEC 14443-4** Transmission protocol

In the industry today, lack of interoperability is a big problem. Although vendors claim to be "compliant with ISO/IEC 14443," many have developed technologies and methods in a more proprietary fashion. The lack of true standardization has caused some large problems because smart cards are being used for so many different applications. In the United States, the DoD is rolling out smart cards across all of their agencies, and NIST is developing a framework and conformance testing programs specifically for interoperability issues.

Software attacks are also considered noninvasive attacks. A smart card has software just like any other device that does data processing, and anywhere there is software there is the possibility of software flaws that can be exploited. The main goal of this type of attack is to input instructions into the card that will allow the attacker to extract account information, which he can use to make fraudulent purchases. Many of these types of attacks can be disguised by using equipment that looks just like the legitimate reader.

If you would like to be more intrusive in your smart card attack, give *microprobing* a try. Microprobing uses needles and ultrasonic vibration to remove the outer protective material on the card's circuits. Once this is completed, data can be accessed and manipulated by directly tapping into the card's ROM chips.

Authorization

Now that I know who you are, let's see if I will let you do what you want.

Although authentication and authorization are quite different, together they compose a two-step process that determines whether an individual is allowed to access a particular resource. In the first step, authentication, the individual must prove to the system that he is who he claims to be—a permitted system user. After successful authentication, the system must establish whether the user is authorized to access the particular resource and what actions he is permitted to perform on that resource.

Authorization is a core component of every operating system, but applications, security add-on packages, and resources themselves can also provide this functionality. For example, suppose Marge has been authenticated through the authentication server and now wants to view a spreadsheet that resides on a file server. When she finds this spreadsheet and double-clicks the icon, she will see an hourglass instead of a mouse pointer. At this stage, the file server is seeing if Marge has the rights and permissions to view the requested spreadsheet. It also checks to see if Marge can modify, delete, move, or copy the file. Once the file server searches through an access matrix and finds that Marge does indeed have the necessary rights to view this file, the file opens up on Marge's desktop. The decision of whether or not to allow Marge to see this file was based on access criteria. Access criteria are the crux of authentication.

Access Criteria

You can perform that action only because we like you, and you wear a funny hat.

We have gone over the basics of access control. This subject can get very granular in its level of detail when it comes to dictating what a subject can or cannot do to an object or resource. This is a good thing for network administrators and security professionals, because they want to have as much control as possible over the resources they have been put in charge of protecting, and a fine level of detail enables them to give individuals just the precise level of access they need. It would be frustrating if access control permissions were based only on full control or no access. These choices are very limiting, and an administrator would end up giving everyone full control, which would provide no protection. Instead, different ways of limiting access to resources exist, and if they are understood and used properly, they can give just the right level of access desired.

Granting access rights to subjects should be based on the level of trust a company has in a subject and the subject's need to know. Just because a company completely trusts Joyce with its files and resources does not mean she fulfills the need-to-know criteria to access the company's tax returns and profit margins. If Maynard fulfills the need-to-know criteria to access employees' work histories, it does not mean the company trusts him to access all of the company's other files. These issues must be identified and integrated into the access criteria. The different access criteria can be enforced by roles, groups, location, time, and transaction types.

Using *roles* is an efficient way to assign rights to a type of user who performs a certain task. This role is based on a job assignment or function. If there is a position within a company for a person to audit transactions and audit logs, the role this person fills would only need a read function to those types of files. This role would not need full control, modify, or delete privileges.

Using *groups* is another effective way of assigning access control rights. If several users require the same type of access to information and resources, putting them into a group and then assigning rights and permissions to that group is easier to manage than assigning rights and permissions to each and every individual separately. If a specific printer is available only to the accounting group, when a user attempts to print to it, the group membership of the user will be checked to see if she is indeed in the accounting group. This is one way that access control is enforced through a logical access control mechanism.

Physical or logical location can also be used to restrict access to resources. Some files may be available only to users who can log on interactively to a computer. This means the user must be physically at the computer and enter the credentials locally versus logging on remotely from another computer. This restriction is implemented on several server configurations to restrict unauthorized individuals from being able to get in and reconfigure the server remotely.

Logical location restrictions are usually done through network address restrictions. If a network administrator wants to ensure that status requests of an intrusion detection management console are accepted only from certain computers on the network, the network administrator can configure this within the software.

Time of day, or temporal isolation, is another access control mechanism that can be used. If a security professional wants to ensure no one is accessing payroll files between the hours of 8:00 P.M. and 4:00 A.M., that configuration can be implemented to ensure access at these times is restricted. If the same security professional wants to ensure no bank account transactions happen during days on which the bank is not open, she can indicate in the logical access control mechanism this type of action is prohibited on Sundays.

Temporal access can also be based on the creation date of a resource. Let's say Russell started working for his company in March of 2007. There may be a business need to allow Russell to only access files that have been created after this date and not before.

Transaction-type restrictions can be used to control what data is accessed during certain types of functions and what commands can be carried out on the data. An online banking program may allow a customer to view his account balance, but may not allow the customer to transfer money until he has a certain security level or access right. A bank teller may be able to cash checks of up to $2,000, but would need a supervisor's access code to retrieve more funds for a customer. A database administrator may be able to build a database for the human resources department, but may not be able to read certain confidential files within that database. These are all examples of transaction-type restrictions to control the access to data and resources.

Default to No Access

If you're unsure, just say no.

Access control mechanisms should default to no access so as to provide the necessary level of security and ensure no security holes go unnoticed. A wide range of access levels is available to assign to individuals and groups, depending on the application and/or operating system. A user can have read, change, delete, full control, or no access permissions. The statement that security mechanisms should default to no access means that if nothing has been specifically configured for an individual or the group she belongs to, that user should not be able to access that resource. If access is not explicitly allowed, it should be implicitly denied. Security is all about being safe, and this is the safest approach to practice when dealing with access control methods and mechanisms. In other words, all access controls should be based on the concept of starting with zero access, and building on top of that. Instead of giving access to everything, and then taking away privileges based on need to know, the better approach is to start with nothing and add privileges based on need to know.

Most access control lists (ACLs) that work on routers and packet-filtering firewalls default to no access. Figure 4-9 shows that traffic from Subnet A is allowed to access Subnet B, traffic from Subnet D is not allowed to access Subnet A, and Subnet B is allowed to talk to Subnet A. All other traffic transmission paths not listed here are not allowed by default. Subnet D cannot talk to Subnet B because such access is not explicitly indicated in the router's ACL.

Need to Know

If you need to know, I will tell you. If you don't need to know, leave me alone.

The **need-to-know** principle is similar to the **least-privilege** principle. It is based on the concept that individuals should be given access only to the information they absolutely require in order to perform their job duties. Giving any more rights to a user just

Authorization Creep

I think Mike's a creep. Let's not give him any authorization to access company stuff.
Response: Sounds like a great criterion. All creeps—no access.

As employees work at a company over time and move from one department to another, they often are assigned more and more access rights and permissions. This is commonly referred to as authorization creep. It can be a large risk for a company, because too many users have too much privileged access to company assets. In the past, it has usually been easier for network administrators to give more access than less, because then the user would not come back and require more work to be done on her profile. It is also difficult to know the exact access levels different individuals require. This is why user management and user provisioning are becoming more prevalent in identity management products today and why companies are moving more toward role-based access control implementation. Enforcing least privilege on user accounts should be an ongoing job, which means each user's rights are permissions that should be reviewed to ensure the company is not putting itself at risk.

NOTE   Rights and permission reviews have been incorporated into many regulatory induced processes. As part of the SOX regulations, managers have to review their employees' permissions to data on an annual basis.

asks for headaches and the possibility of that user abusing the permissions assigned to him. An administrator wants to give a user the least amount of privileges she can, but just enough for that user to be productive when carrying out tasks. Management will decide what a user needs to know, or what access rights are necessary, and the administrator will configure the access control mechanisms to allow this user to have that level of access and no more, and thus the least privilege.

For example, if management has decided that Dan, the copy boy, needs to know where the files he needs to copy are located and needs to be able to print them, this fulfills Dan's need-to-know criteria. Now, an administrator could give Dan full control of all the files he needs to copy, but that would not be practicing the least-privilege principle. The administrator should restrict Dan's rights and permissions to only allow him to read and print the necessary files, and no more. Besides, if Dan accidentally deletes all the files on the whole file server, whom do you think management will hold ultimately responsible? Yep, the administrator.

It is important to understand that it is management's job to determine the security requirements of individuals and how access is authorized. The security administrator configures the security mechanisms to fulfill these requirements, but it is not her job to determine security requirements of users. Those should be left to the owners. If there is a security breach, management will ultimately be held responsible, so it should make these decisions in the first place.

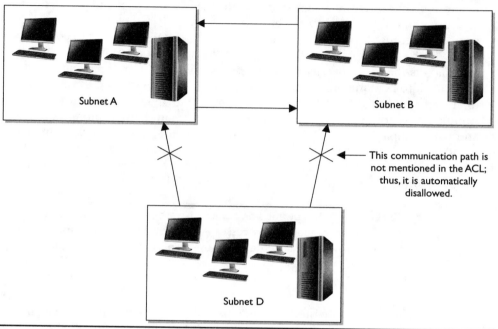

Access Control List

- Subnet A can access Subnet B.
- Subnet D cannot access Subnet A.
- Subnet B can access Subnet A.

This communication path is not mentioned in the ACL; thus, it is automatically disallowed.

Figure 4-9   What is not explicitly allowed should be implicitly denied.

Single Sign-On

I only want to have to remember one username and one password for everything in the world!

Many times employees need to access many different computers, servers, databases, and other resources in the course of a day to complete their tasks. This often requires the employees to remember multiple user IDs and passwords for these different computers. In a utopia, a user would need to enter only one user ID and one password to be able to access all resources in all the networks this user is working in. In the real world, this is hard to accomplish for all system types.

Because of the proliferation of client/server technologies, networks have migrated from centrally controlled networks to heterogeneous, distributed environments. The propagation of open systems and the increased diversity of applications, platforms, and operating systems have caused the end user to have to remember several user IDs and passwords just to be able to access and use the different resources within his own network. Although the different IDs and passwords are supposed to provide a greater level of security, they often end up compromising security (because users write them down) and causing more effort and overhead for the staff that manages and maintains the network.

As any network staff member or administrator can attest to, too much time is devoted to resetting passwords for users who have forgotten them. More than one employee's productivity is affected when forgotten passwords have to be reassigned. The network staff member who has to reset the password could be working on other tasks, and the user who forgot the password cannot complete his task until the network staff member is finished resetting the password. Many help-desk employees report that a majority of their time is spent on users forgetting their passwords. System administrators have to manage multiple user accounts on different platforms, which all need to be coordinated in a manner that maintains the integrity of the security policy. At times the complexity can be overwhelming, which results in poor access control management and the generation of many security vulnerabilities. A lot of time is spent on multiple passwords, and in the end they do not provide us with more security.

The increased cost of managing a diverse environment, security concerns, and user habits, coupled with the users' overwhelming desire to remember one set of credentials, has brought about the idea of *single sign-on (SSO)* capabilities. These capabilities would allow a user to enter credentials one time and be able to access all resources in primary and secondary network domains. This reduces the amount of time users spend authenticating to resources and enables the administrator to streamline user accounts and better control access rights. It improves security by reducing the probability that users will write down passwords and also reduces the administrator's time spent on adding and removing user accounts and modifying access permissions. If an administrator needs to disable or suspend a specific account, she can do it uniformly instead of having to alter configurations on each and every platform.

So that is our utopia: log on once and you are good to go. What bursts this bubble? Mainly interoperability issues. For SSO to actually work, every platform, application, and resource needs to accept the same type of credentials, in the same format, and interpret their meanings the same. When Steve logs on to his Windows XP workstation and gets authenticated by a mixed-mode Windows 2000 domain controller, it must authenticate him to the resources he needs to access on the Apple computer, the Unix server running NIS, the mainframe host server, the MICR print server, and the Windows

XP computer in the secondary domain that has the plotter connected to it. A nice idea, until reality hits.

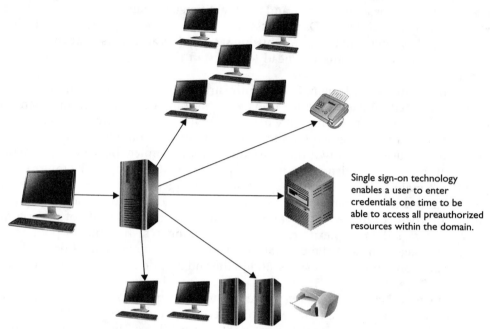

Single sign-on technology enables a user to enter credentials one time to be able to access all preauthorized resources within the domain.

There is also a security issue to consider in an SSO environment. Once an individual is in, he is in. If an attacker was able to uncover one credential set, he would have access to every resource within the environment that the compromised account has access to. This is certainly true, but one of the goals is that if a user only has to remember one password, and not ten, then a more robust password policy can be enforced. If the user has just one password to remember, then it can be more complicated and secure because he does not have nine other ones to remember also.

SSO technologies come in different types. Each has its own advantages and disadvantages, shortcomings, and quality features. It is rare to see a real SSO environment; rather, you will see a cluster of computers and resources that accept the same credentials. Other resources, however, still require more work by the administrator or user side to access the systems. The SSO technologies that may be addressed in the CISSP exam are described in the next sections.

Kerberos

Sam, there is a three-headed dog in front of the server!

Kerberos is the name of a three-headed dog that guards the entrance to the underworld in Greek mythology. This is a great name for a security technology that provides authentication functionality, with the purpose of protecting a company's assets. Kerberos is an authentication protocol and was designed in the mid-1980s as part of MIT's Project Athena. It works in a client/server model and is based on symmetric key cryptography. The protocol has been used for years in Unix systems and is currently the default authentication method for Windows 2000, 2003, and 2008 operating systems. In addition, Apple's Mac OS X, Sun's Solaris, and Red Hat Enterprise Linux 4 all use Kerberos authentication as well. Commercial products supporting Kerberos are becoming more frequent, so this one might be a keeper.

Kerberos is an example of a single sign-on system for distributed environments, and is a de facto standard for heterogeneous networks. Kerberos incorporates a wide range of security capabilities, which gives companies much more flexibility and scalability when they need to provide an encompassing security architecture. It has four elements necessary for enterprise access control: scalability, transparency, reliability, and security. However, this open architecture also invites interoperability issues. When vendors have a lot of freedom to customize a protocol, it usually means no two vendors will customize it in the same fashion. This creates interoperability and incompatibility issues.

Kerberos uses symmetric key cryptography and provides end-to-end security. Although it allows the use of passwords for authentication, it was designed specifically to eliminate the need to transmit passwords over the network. Most Kerberos implementations work with shared secret keys.

Main Components in Kerberos The Key Distribution Center (KDC) is the most important component within a Kerberos environment. The KDC holds all users' and services' secret keys. It provides an authentication service, as well as key distribution functionality. The clients and services trust the integrity of the KDC, and this trust is the foundation of Kerberos security.

The KDC provides security services to *principals*, which can be users, applications, or network services. The KDC must have an account for, and share a secret key with, each principal. For users, a password is transformed into a secret key value. The secret key is used to send sensitive data back and forth between the principal and the KDC, and is used for user authentication purposes.

A *ticket* is generated by the ticket granting service (TGS) on the KDC and given to a principal when that principal, let's say a user, needs to authenticate to another principal, let's say a print server. The ticket enables one principal to authenticate to another principal. If Emily needs to use the print server, she must prove to the print server she is who she claims to be and that she is authorized to use the printing service. So Emily requests a ticket from the TGS. The TGS gives Emily the ticket, and in turn, Emily passes this ticket on to the print server. If the print server approves this ticket, Emily is allowed to use the print service.

A KDC provides security services for a set of principals. This set is called a *realm* in Kerberos. The KDC is the trusted authentication server for all users, applications, and services within a realm. One KDC can be responsible for one realm or several realms. Realms are used to allow an administrator to logically group resources and users.

So far, we know that principals (users and services) require the KDC's services to authenticate to each other; that the KDC has a database filled with information about each and every principal within its realm; that the KDC holds and delivers cryptographic keys and tickets; and that tickets are used for principals to authenticate to each other. So how does this process work?

The Kerberos Authentication Process   The user and the KDC share a secret key, while the service and the KDC share a different secret key. The user and the requested service do not share a symmetric key in the beginning. The user trusts the KDC because they share a secret key. They can encrypt and decrypt data they pass between each other, and thus have a protected communication path. Once the user authenticates to the service, they too will share a symmetric key (session key) that will enable them to encrypt and decrypt the information they need to pass to each other. This is how Kerberos provides data transmission protection.

Here are the exact steps:

1. Emily comes in to work and enters her username and password into her workstation at 8 A.M.

    The Kerberos software on Emily's computer sends the username to the authentication service (AS) on the KDC, which in turn sends Emily a ticket granting ticket (TGT) that is encrypted with Emily's password (secret key).

2. If Emily has entered her correct password, then this TGT is decrypted and Emily gains access to her local workstation desktop.

3. When Emily needs to send a print job to the print server, her system sends the TGT to the ticket granting service (TGS), which runs on the KDC. (This allows Emily to prove she has been authenticated and allows her to request access to the print server.)

4. The TGS creates and sends a second ticket to Emily, which she will use to authenticate to the print server. This second ticket contains two instances of the same session key, one encrypted with Emily's secret key and the other encrypted with the print server's secret key. The second ticket also contains an *authenticator*, which contains identification information on Emily, her system's IP address, sequence number, and a timestamp.

5. Emily's system receives the second ticket, decrypts and extracts the session key, adds a second authenticator set of identification information to the ticket, and sends the ticket on to the print server.

    a. The print server receives the ticket, decrypts and extracts the session key, and decrypts and extracts the two authenticators in the ticket. If the printer server can decrypt and extract the session key, it knows the KDC created the ticket, because only the KDC has the secret key used to encrypt the session key. If the authenticator information that the KDC and the user put into the ticket matches, then the print server knows it received the ticket from the correct principal.

6. Once this is completed, it means Emily has been properly authenticated to the print server and the server prints her document.

This is an extremely simplistic overview of what is going on in any Kerberos exchange, but it gives you an idea of the dance taking place behind the scenes whenever you interact with any network service in an environment that uses Kerberos. Figure 4-10 provides a simplistic view of this process.

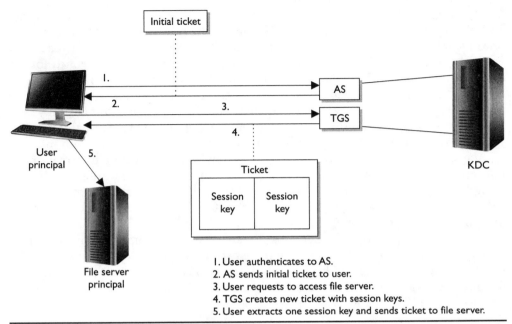

Figure 4-10 The user must receive a ticket from the KDC before being able to use the requested resource.

The authentication service is the part of the KDC that authenticates a principal, and the TGS is the part of the KDC that makes the tickets and hands them out to the principals. TGTs are used so the user does not have to enter his password each time he needs to communicate with another principal. After the user enters his password, it is temporarily stored on his system, and any time the user needs to communicate with another principal, he just reuses the TGT.

Be sure you understand that a session key is different from a secret key. A secret key is shared between the KDC and a principal and is static in nature. A session key is shared between two principals and is generated when needed and destroyed after the session is completed.

If a Kerberos implementation is configured to use an *authenticator*, the user sends to the printer server her identification information and a timestamp and sequence number encrypted with the session key they share. The printer server decrypts this information and compares it with the identification data the KDC sent to it about this requesting user. If the data is the same, the printer server allows the user to send print jobs. The timestamp is used to help fight against replay attacks. The printer server compares the sent timestamp with its own internal time, which helps determine if the ticket has been sniffed and copied by an attacker, and then submitted at a later time in hopes of impersonating the legitimate user and gaining unauthorized access. The printer server checks the sequence number to make sure that this ticket has not been submitted previously. This is another countermeasure to protect against replay attacks.

The primary reason to use Kerberos is that the principals do not trust each other enough to communicate directly. In our example, the print server will not print anyone's print job without that entity authenticating itself. So none of the principals trust each other directly; they only trust the KDC. The KDC creates tickets to vouch for the individual principals when they need to communicate. Suppose I need to communicate directly with you, but you do not trust me enough to listen and accept what I am saying. If I first give you a ticket from something you do trust (KDC), this basically says, "Look, the KDC says I am a trustworthy person. The KDC asked me to give this ticket to you to prove it." Once that happens, *then* you will communicate directly with me.

The same type of trust model is used in PKI environments. (More information on PKI is presented in Chapter 8.) In a PKI environment, users do not trust each other directly, but they all trust the certificate authority (CA). The CA vouches for the individuals' identities by using digital certificates, the same as the KDC vouches for the individuals' identities by using tickets.

So why are we talking about Kerberos? Because it is one example of a single sign-on technology. The user enters a user ID and password one time and one time only. The tickets have time limits on them that administrators can configure. Many times, the lifetime of a TGT is eight to ten hours, so when the user comes in the next day, he will have to present his credentials again.

 NOTE Walking through these steps for the first time can be confusing. You can review a free animated overview of Kerberos at www.logicalsecurity.com/kerberos.

Weaknesses of Kerberos The following are some of the potential weaknesses of Kerberos:

- The KDC can be a single point of failure. If the KDC goes down, no one can access needed resources. Redundancy is necessary for the KDC.
- The KDC must be able to handle the number of requests it receives in a timely manner. It must be scalable.
- Secret keys are temporarily stored on the users' workstations, which means it is possible for an intruder to obtain these cryptographic keys.
- Session keys are decrypted and reside on the users' workstations, either in a cache or in a key table. Again, an intruder can capture these keys.
- Kerberos is vulnerable to password guessing. The KDC does not know if a dictionary attack is taking place.
- Network traffic is not protected by Kerberos if encryption is not enabled.
- If the keys are too short, they can be vulnerable to brute force attacks.
- Kerberos needs all client and server clocks to be synchronized.

Kerberos must be transparent (work in the background without the user needing to understand it), scalable (work in large, heterogeneous environments), reliable (use dis-

Kerberos and Password-Guessing Attacks

Just because an environment uses Kerberos does not mean the systems are vulnerable to password-guessing attacks. The operating system itself will (should) provide the protection of tracking failed login attempts. The Kerberos protocol does not have this type of functionality, so another component must be in place to counter these types of attacks. No need to start ripping Kerberos out of your network environment after reading this section; your operating system provides the protection mechanism for this type of attack.

tributed server architecture to ensure there is no single point of failure), and secure (provide authentication and confidentiality).

SESAME

I said "open Sesame" and nothing happened.
Response: It is broken then.

The *Secure European System for Applications in a Multi-vendor Environment (SESAME)* project is a single sign-on technology developed to extend Kerberos functionality and improve upon its weaknesses. SESAME uses symmetric and asymmetric cryptographic techniques to authenticate subjects to network resources.

NOTE Kerberos is a strictly symmetric key–based technology, whereas SESAME is based on both asymmetric and symmetric key cryptography.

Kerberos uses tickets to authenticate subjects to objects, whereas SESAME uses Privileged Attribute Certificates (PACs), which contain the subject's identity, access capabilities for the object, access time period, and lifetime of the PAC. The PAC is digitally signed so the object can validate it came from the trusted authentication server, which is referred to as the Privileged Attribute Server (PAS). The PAS holds a similar role to that of the KDC within Kerberos. After a user successfully authenticates to the authentication service (AS), he is presented with a token to give to the PAS. The PAS then creates a PAC for the user to present to the resource he is trying to access. Figure 4-11 shows a basic overview of the SESAME process.

NOTE Kerberos and SESAME can be accessed through the Generic Security Services Application Programming Interface (GSS-API), which is a generic API for client-to-server authentication. Using standard APIs enables vendors to communicate with and use each other's functionality and security. Kerberos Version 5 and SESAME implementations allow any application to use their authentication functionality as long as the application knows how to communicate via GSS-API.

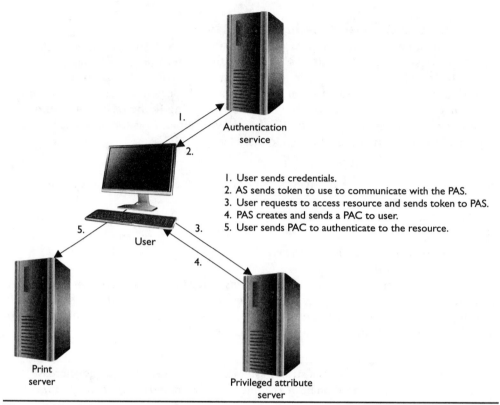

1. User sends credentials.
2. AS sends token to use to communicate with the PAS.
3. User requests to access resource and sends token to PAS.
4. PAS creates and sends a PAC to user.
5. User sends PAC to authenticate to the resource.

Figure 4-11 SESAME is very similar to Kerberos.

Security Domains

I am highly trusted and have access to many resources.
Response: So what.

The term "domain" has been around a lot longer than Microsoft, but when people hear this term, they often think of a set of computers and devices on a network segment being controlled by a server that runs Microsoft software, referred to as a domain controller. A domain is really just a set of resources available to a subject. Remember that a subject can be a user, process, or application. Within an operating system, a process has a domain, which is the set of system resources available to the process to carry out its tasks. These resources can be memory segments, hard drive space, operating system services, and other processes. In a network environment, a domain is a set of physical and logical resources that is available, which can include routers, file servers, FTP service, web servers, and so forth.

The term *security domain* just builds upon the definition of domain by adding the fact that resources within this logical structure (domain) are working under the same security policy and managed by the same group. So, a network administrator may put all of the accounting personnel, computers, and network resources in Domain 1 and all of the management personnel, computers, and network resources in Domain 2. These items fall into these individual containers because they not only carry out similar types of business functions, but also, and more importantly, have the same type of trust level. It is this common trust level that allows entities to be managed by one single security policy.

The different domains are separated by logical boundaries, such as firewalls with ACLs, directory services making access decisions, and objects that have their own ACLs indicating which individuals and groups can carry out operations on them. All of these security mechanisms are examples of components that enforce the security policy for each domain.

Domains can be architected in a hierarchical manner that dictates the relationship between the different domains and the ways in which subjects within the different domains can communicate. Subjects can access resources in domains of equal or lower trust levels. Figure 4-12 shows an example of hierarchical network domains. Their communication channels are controlled by security agents (firewalls, router ACLs, directory services), and the individual domains are isolated by using specific subnet mask addresses.

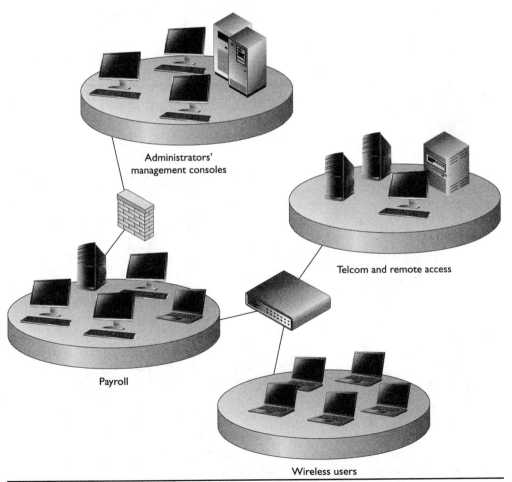

Administrators'
management consoles

Telcom and remote access

Payroll

Wireless users

Figure 4-12   Network domains are used to separate different network segments.

Remember that a domain does not necessarily pertain only to network devices and segmentations, but can also apply to users and processes. Figure 4-13 shows how users and processes can have more granular domains assigned to them individually based on their trust level. Group 1 has a high trust level and can access both a domain of its own trust level (Domain 1) and a domain of a lower trust level (Domain 2). User 1, who has a lower trust level, can access only the domain at his trust level and nothing higher. The system enforces these domains with access privileges and rights provided by the file system and operating system security kernel.

So why are domains in the "Single Sign-On" section? Because several different types of technologies available today are used to define and enforce these domains and security policies mapped to them: domain controllers in a Windows environment, enterprise resource management (ERM) products, Microsoft Passport (now Windows Live ID), and the various products that provide SSO functionality. The goal of each of them is to allow a user (subject) to sign in one time and be able to access the different domains available without having to reenter any other credentials.

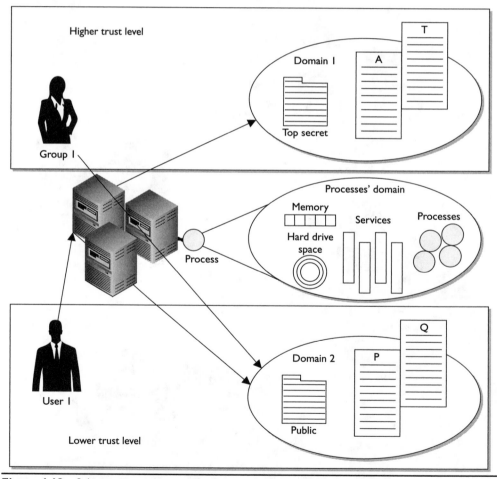

Figure 4-13 Subjects can access specific domains based on their trust levels.

Directory Services

A network service is a mechanism that identifies resources (printers, file servers, domain controllers, and peripheral devices) on a network. A network directory service contains information about these different resources, and the subjects that need to access them, and carries out access control activities. If the directory service is working in a database based on the X.500 standard, it works in a hierarchical schema that outlines the resources' attributes, such as name, logical and physical location, subjects that can access them, and the operations that can be carried out on them.

In a database based on the X.500 standard, access requests are made from users and other systems using the LDAP protocol. This type of database provides a hierarchical structure for the organization of objects (subjects and resources). The directory service develops unique distinguished names for each object and appends the corresponding attribute to each object as needed. The directory service enforces a security policy (configured by the administrator) to control how subjects and objects interact.

Network directory services provide users access to network resources transparently, meaning that users don't need to know the exact location of the resources or the steps required to access them. The network directory services handle these issues for the user in the background. Some examples of directory services are Lightweight Directory Access Protocol (LDAP), Novell NetWare Directory Service (NDS), and Microsoft Active Directory (AD). Note: Directory services were also covered in the "Identity Management" section, earlier in this chapter.

Thin Clients

Hey, where's my operating system?
Response: You don't deserve one.

Diskless computers, sometimes thin clients, cannot store much information because of their lack of onboard storage space and necessary resources. This type of client/server technology forces users to log on to a central server just to use the computer and access network resources. When the user starts the computer, it runs a short list of instructions and then points itself to a server that will actually download the operating system, or interactive operating software, to the terminal. This enforces a strict type of access control, because the computer cannot do anything on its own until it authenticates to a centralized server, and then the server gives the computer its operating system, profile, and functionality. Thin-client technology provides another type of SSO access for users because users authenticate only to the central server or mainframe, which then provides them access to all authorized and necessary resources.

In addition to providing an SSO solution, a thin-client technology offers several other advantages. A company can save money by purchasing thin clients instead of powerful and expensive PCs. The central server handles all application execution, processing, and data storage. The thin client displays the graphical representation and sends mouse clicks and keystroke inputs to the central server. Having all of the software in one location, instead of distributed throughout the environment, allows for easier administration, centralized access control, easier updates, and standardized configurations. It is also easier to control malware infestations and the theft of confidential data because the thin clients often do not have CD-ROM, DVD, or USB ports.

Examples of Single Sign-On Technologies

- **Kerberos** Authentication protocol that uses a KDC and tickets, and is based on symmetric key cryptography
- **SESAME** Authentication protocol that uses a PAS and PACs, and is based on symmetric and asymmetric cryptography
- **Security domains** Resources working under the same security policy and managed by the same group
- **Thin clients** Terminals that rely upon a central server for access control, processing, and storage

NOTE The technology industry came from a centralized model, with the use of mainframes and dumb terminals, and is in some ways moving back toward this model with the use of terminal services, Citrix, Service Oriented Architecture, and so on.

Access Control Models

An *access control model* is a framework that dictates how subjects access objects. It uses access control technologies and security mechanisms to enforce the rules and objectives of the model. There are three main types of access control models: discretionary, mandatory, and nondiscretionary (also called role based). Each model type uses different methods to control how subjects access objects, and each has its own merits and limitations. The business and security goals of an organization will help prescribe what access control model it should use, along with the culture of the company and the habits of conducting business. Some companies use one model exclusively, whereas others combine them to be able to provide the necessary level of protection.

These models are built into the core or the kernel of the different operating systems and possibly their supporting applications. Every operating system has a security kernel that enforces a reference monitor concept, which differs depending upon the type of access control model embedded into the system. For every access attempt, before a subject can communicate with an object, the security kernel reviews the rules of the access control model to determine whether the request is allowed.

The following sections explain these different models, their supporting technologies, and where they should be implemented.

Discretionary Access Control

Only I can let you access my files.
Response: Mother, may I?

If a user creates a file, he is the owner of that file. An identifier for this user is placed in the file header. Ownership might also be granted to a specific individual. For example, a manager for a certain department might be made the owner of the files and resources within her department. A system that uses *discretionary access control (DAC)* enables the owner of the resource to specify which subjects can access specific resources.

This model is called discretionary because the control of access is based on the discretion of the owner. Many times department managers, or business unit managers, are the owners of the data within their specific department. Being the owner, they can specify who should have access and who should not.

In a DAC model, access is restricted based on the authorization granted to the users. This means users are allowed to specify what type of access can occur to the objects they own. If an organization is using a DAC model, the network administrator can allow resource owners to control who has access to their files. The most common implementation of DAC is through ACLs, which are dictated and set by the owners and enforced by the operating system. This can make a user's ability to access information dynamic versus the more static role of mandatory access control (MAC).

Most of the operating systems you may be used to dealing with are based on DAC models, such as all Windows, Linux, and Macintosh systems, and most flavors of Unix. When you look at the properties of a file or directory and see the choices that allow you to control which users can have access to this resource and to what degree, you are witnessing an instance of ACLs enforcing a DAC model.

DACs can be applied to both the directory tree structure and the files it contains. The PC world has access permissions of No Access, Read (r), Write (w), Execute (x), Delete (d), Change (c), and Full Control. The Read attribute lets you read the file but not make changes. The Change attribute allows you to read, write, execute, and delete the file but does not let you change the ACLs or the owner of the files. Obviously, the attribute of Full Control lets you make any changes to the file and its permissions and ownership.

It is through the discretionary model that Sam can share his D: drive with David so David can copy all of Sam's MP3s. Sam can also block access to his D: drive from his manager so his manager does not know Sam is wasting valuable time and resources by downloading MP3s and sharing them with friends.

Mandatory Access Control

In a *mandatory access control (MAC)* model, users and data owners do not have as much freedom to determine who can access files. The operating system makes the final decision and can override the users' wishes. This model is much more structured and strict and is based on a security label system. Users are given a security clearance (secret, top secret, confidential, and so on), and data is classified in the same way. The clearance and classification data are stored in the security labels, which are bound to the specific subjects and objects. When the system makes a decision about fulfilling a request to access an object, it is based on the clearance of the subject, the classification of the object, and the security policy of the system. The rules for how subjects access objects are

---

Identity-Based Access Control

DAC systems grant or deny access based on the identity of the subject. The identity can be a user identity or a group membership. So, for example, a data owner can choose to allow Bob (user identity) and the Accounting group (group membership identity) to access his file.

made by the security officer, configured by the administrator, enforced by the operating system, and supported by security technologies.

Security labels are attached to all objects; thus, every file, directory, and device has its own security label with its classification information. A user may have a security clearance of secret, and the data he requests may have a security label with the classification of top secret. In this case, the user will be denied because his clearance is not equivalent or does not dominate (equal or higher than) the classification of the object.

 NOTE The terms "security labels" and "sensitivity labels" can be used interchangeably.

Each subject and object must have an associated label with attributes at all times, because this is part of the operating system's access-decision criteria. Each subject and object does not require a physically unique label, but can be logically associated. For example, all subjects and objects on Server 1 can share the same label of secret clearance and classification.

This type of model is used in environments where information classification and confidentiality is of utmost importance, such as a military institution. Special types of Unix systems are developed based on the MAC model. A company cannot simply choose to turn on either DAC or MAC. It has to purchase an operating system that has been specifically designed to enforce MAC rules. DAC systems do not understand security labels, classifications, or clearances, and thus cannot be used in institutions that require this type of structure for access control. The most recently released MAC system is SE Linux, developed by the NSA and Secure Computing. Trusted Solaris is a product based on the MAC model that most people are familiar with (relative to other MAC products).

Sensitivity Labels

I am very sensitive. Can I have a label?
Response: Nope.

When the MAC model is being used, every subject and object must have a sensitivity label, also called a security label. It contains a classification and different categories. The classification indicates the sensitivity level, and the categories enforce need-to-know rules. Figure 4-14 illustrates a sensitivity label.

The classifications follow a hierarchical structure, one level being more trusted than another. However, the categories do not follow a hierarchical scheme, because they represent compartments of information within a system. The categories can correspond to departments (UN, Information Warfare, Treasury), projects (CRM, AirportSecurity, 2003Budget), or management levels. In a military environment, the classifications could be top secret, secret, confidential, and unclassified. Each classification is more trusted than the one below it. A commercial organization might use confidential, proprietary, corporate, and sensitive. The definition of the classification is up to the organization and should make sense for the environment in which it is used.

The categories portion of the label enforces need-to-know rules. Just because someone has a top-secret clearance does not mean she now has access to all top-secret information. She must also have a need to know. As shown in Figure 4-14, if Cheryl has a top-secret clearance but does not have a need to know that is sufficient to access any of the listed categories (Dallas, Max, Cricket), she cannot look at this object.

NOTE In MAC implementations, the system makes access decisions by comparing the subject's clearance and need-to-know level to that of the security label. In DAC, the system compares the subject's identity to the ACL on the resource.

Software and hardware guards allow the exchange of data between trusted (high assurance) and less trusted (low assurance) systems and environments. For instance, if you were working on a MAC system (working in dedicated security mode of secret) and you needed it to communicate to a MAC database (working in multilevel security mode, which goes up to top secret), the two systems would provide different levels of protection. If a system with lower assurance can directly communicate with a system of high assurance, then security vulnerabilities and compromises could be introduced. A software guard is really just a front-end product that allows interconnectivity between systems working at different security levels. Different types of guards can be used to carry out filtering, processing requests, data blocking, and data sanitization. A hardware guard can be implemented, which is a system with two NICs connecting the two systems that need to communicate with one another. Guards can be used to connect different MAC systems working in different security modes, and they can be used to connect different networks working at different security levels. In many cases, the less trusted system can send messages to the more trusted system and can only receive acknowledgments back. This is common when e-mail messages need to go from less trusted systems to more trusted classified systems.

Role-Based Access Control

I am in charge of chalk, thus I need full control of all servers!
Response: Good try.

A *role-based access control (RBAC)* model, also called *nondiscretionary access control*, uses a centrally administered set of controls to determine how subjects and objects interact. This type of model lets access to resources be based on the role the user

Figure 4-14
A sensitivity label
is made up of a
classification and
categories.

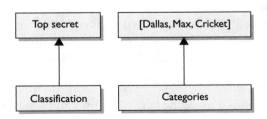

holds within the company. It is referred to as nondiscretionary because assigning a user to a role is unavoidably imposed. This means that if you are assigned only to the Contractor role in a company, there is nothing you can do about it. You don't have the discretion to determine what role you will be assigned.

The more traditional access control administration is based on just the DAC model, where access control is specified at the object level with ACLs. This approach is more complex because the administrator must translate an organizational authorization policy into permission when configuring ACLs. As the number of objects and users grows within an environment, users are bound to be granted unnecessary access to some objects, thus violating the least-privilege rule and increasing the risk to the company. The RBAC approach simplifies access control administration by allowing permissions to be managed in terms of user job roles.

In an RBAC model, a role is defined in terms of the operations and tasks the role will carry out, whereas a DAC model outlines which subjects can access what objects.

Let's say we need a research and development analyst role. We develop this role not only to allow an individual to have access to all product and testing data, but also, and more importantly, to outline the tasks and operations that the role can carry out on this data. When the analyst role makes a request to access the new testing results on the file server, in the background the operating system reviews the role's access levels before allowing this operation to take place.

 NOTE Introducing roles also introduces the difference between rights being assigned explicitly and implicitly. If rights and permissions are assigned explicitly, it indicates they are assigned directly to a specific individual. If they are assigned implicitly, it indicates they are assigned to a role or group and the user inherits those attributes.

An RBAC model is the best system for a company that has high employee turnover. If John, who is mapped to the contractor role, leaves the company, then Chrissy, his replacement, can be easily mapped to this role. That way, the administrator does not need to continually change the ACLs on the individual objects. He only needs to create a role (contractor), assign permissions to this role, and map the new user to this role.

As discussed in the "Identity Management" section, organizations are moving more toward role-based access models to properly control identity and provisioning activities. The formal RBAC model has several approaches to security that can be used in software and organizations.

Core RBAC

This component will be integrated in every RBAC implementation, because it is the foundation of the model. Users, roles, permissions, operations, and sessions are defined and mapped according to the security policy.

- Has a many-to-many relationship among individual users and privileges
- Session is a mapping between a user and a subset of assigned roles
- Accommodates traditional but robust group-based access control

Many users can belong to many groups with various privileges outlined for each group. When the user logs in (this is a session), the various roles and groups this user has been assigned will be available to the user at one time. If I am a member of the Accounting role, RD group, and Administrative role, when I log on, all of the permissions assigned to these various groups are available to me.

This model provides robust options because it can include other components when making access decisions, instead of just basing the decision on a credential set. The RBAC system can be configured to also include time of day, location of role, day of the week, and so on. This means other information, not just the user ID and credential, is used for access decisions.

Hierarchical RBAC

This component allows the administrator to set up an organizational RBAC model that maps to the organizational structures and functional delineations required in a specific environment. This is very useful since businesses are already set up in a personnel hierarchical structure. In most cases, the higher you are in the chain of command, the more access you will most likely have.

1. Role relation defining user membership and privilege inheritance. For example, the nurse role can access a certain amount of files, and the lab technician role can access another set of files. The doctor role inherits the permissions and access rights of these two roles and has more elevated rights already assigned to the doctor role. So hierarchical is an accumulation of rights and permissions of other roles.

2. Reflects organizational structures and functional delineations.

3. Two types of hierarchies:

    a. Limited hierarchies—Only one level of hierarchy is allowed (Role 1 inherits from Role 2 and no other role)

    b. General hierarchies—Allows for many levels of hierarchies (Role 1 inherits Role 2 and Role 3's permissions)

Hierarchies are a natural means of structuring roles to reflect an organization's lines of authority and responsibility. Role hierarchies define an inheritance relation among roles. Different separations of duties are provided under this model.

- **Static Separation of Duty (SSD) Relations through RBAC** This would be used to deter fraud by constraining the combination of privileges (such as, the user cannot be a member of both the Cashier and Accounts Receivable groups).

- **Dynamic Separation of Duties (DSD) Relations through RBAC** This would be used to deter fraud by constraining the combination of privileges that can be activated in any session (for instance, the user cannot be in both the Cashier and Cashier Supervisor roles at the same time, but the user can be a member of both). This one is a little more confusing. It means Joe is a member of both the Cashier and Cashier Supervisor. If he logs in as a Cashier, the Supervisor role is unavailable to him during that session. If he logs in as Cashier Supervisor, the Cashier role is unavailable to him during that session.

> ## RBAC, MAC, DAC
>
> A lot of confusion exists regarding whether RBAC is a type of DAC model or a type of MAC model. Different sources claim different things, but in fact it is a model in its own right. In the 1960s and 1970s, the U.S. military and NSA did a lot of research on the MAC model. DAC, which also sprang to life in the '60s and '70s, has its roots in the academic and commercial research laboratories. The RBAC model, which started gaining popularity in the 1990s, can be used in combination with MAC and DAC systems. For the most up-to-date information on the RBAC model, go to http://csrc.nist.gov/rbac, which has documents that describe an RBAC standard and independent model, with the goal of clearing up this continual confusion.

Role-based access control can be managed in the following ways:

- **Non-RBAC**   Users are mapped directly to applications and no roles are used.
- **Limited RBAC**   Users are mapped to multiple roles and mapped directly to other types of applications that do not have role-based access functionality.
- **Hybrid RBAC**   Users are mapped to multi-application roles with only selected rights assigned to those roles.
- **Full RBAC**   Users are mapped to enterprise roles.

 NOTE   The privacy of many different types of data needs to be protected, which is why many organizations have privacy officers and privacy policies today. The current access control models (MAC, DAC, RBAC) do not lend themselves to protecting data of a given sensitivity level, but instead limit the functions that the users can carry out. For example, managers may be able to access a Privacy folder, but there needs to be more detailed access control that indicates, for example, that they can access customers' home addresses but not Social Security numbers. This is referred to as *Privacy Aware Role Based Access Control.*

Access Control Techniques and Technologies

Once an organization determines what type of access control model it is going to use, it needs to identify and refine its technologies and techniques to support that model. The following sections describe the different access controls and technologies available to support different access control models.

Rule-Based Access Control

Everyone will adhere to my rules.
Response: Who are you again?

   Rule-based access control uses specific rules that indicate what can and cannot happen between a subject and an object. It is based on the simple concept of "if X then Y" programming rules, which can be used to provide finer-grained access control to resources. Before a subject can access an object in a certain circumstance, it must meet a set of predefined rules. This can be simple and straightforward, as in "if the user's ID matches the unique user ID value in the provided digital certificate, then the user can gain access." Or there could be a set of complex rules that must be met before a subject can access an object. For example, "If the user is accessing the system between Monday and Friday and between 8 A.M. and 5 P.M., and if the user's security clearance equals or dominates the object's classification, and if the user has the necessary need to know, then the user can access the object."

Rule-based access control is not necessarily identity-based. The DAC model is identity-based. For example, an identity-based control would stipulate that Tom Jones can read File1 and modify File2. So when Tom attempts to access one of these files, the operating system will check his identity and compare it to the values within an ACL to see if Tom can carry out the operations he is attempting. In contrast, here is a rule-based example: a company may have a policy that dictates that e-mail attachments can only be 5MB or smaller. This rule affects all users. If rule-based was identity-based, it would mean that Sue can accept attachments of 10MB and smaller, Bob can accept attachments 2MB and smaller, and Don can only accept attachments 1MB and smaller. This would be a mess and too confusing. Rule-based access controls simplify this by setting a rule that will affect all users across the board—no matter what their identity is.

Rule-based access allows a developer to define specific and detailed situations in which a subject can or cannot access an object, and what that subject can do once access is granted. Traditionally, rule-based access control has been used in MAC systems as an enforcement mechanism of the complex rules of access that MAC systems provide. Today, rule-based access is used in other types of systems and applications as well. Content filtering uses If-Then programming languages, which is a way to compare data or an activity to a long list of rules. For example, "If an e-mail message contains the word 'Viagra,' then disregard. If an e-mail message contains the words 'sex' and 'free,' then disregard," and so on.

Many routers and firewalls use rules to determine which types of packets are allowed into a network and which are rejected. Rule-based access control is a type of compulsory control, because the administrator sets the rules and the users cannot modify these controls.

Access Control Models

The main characteristics of the three different access control models are important to understand.

- **DAC** Data owners decide who has access to resources, and ACLs are used to enforce the security policy.

- **MAC** Operating systems enforce the system's security policy through the use of security labels.

- **RBAC** Access decisions are based on each subject's role and/or functional position.

Constrained User Interfaces

Constrained user interfaces restrict users' access abilities by not allowing them to request certain functions or information, or to have access to specific system resources. Three major types of restricted interfaces exist: menus and shells, database views, and physically constrained interfaces.

When menu and shell restrictions are used, the options users are given are the commands they can execute. For example, if an administrator wants users to be able to execute only one program, that program would be the only choice available on the menu. This limits the users' functionality. A *shell* is a type of virtual environment within a system. It is the user's interface to the operating system and works as a command interpreter. If restricted shells were used, the shell would contain only the commands the administrator wants the users to be able to execute.

Many times, a database administrator will configure a database so users cannot see fields that require a level of confidentiality. **Database views** are mechanisms used to restrict user access to data contained in databases. If the database administrator wants managers to be able to view their employees' work records but not their salary information, then the salary fields would not be available to these types of users. Similarly, when payroll employees look at the same database, they will be able to view the salary information but not the work history information. This example is illustrated in Figure 4-15.

Physically constraining a user interface can be implemented by providing only certain keys on a keypad or certain touch buttons on a screen. You see this when you get money from an ATM machine. This device has a type of operating system that can accept all kinds of commands and configuration changes, but you are physically constrained from being able to carry out these functions. You are presented with buttons that only enable you to withdraw, view your balance, or deposit funds. Period.

Access Control Matrix

The matrix—let's see, should I take the red pill or the blue pill?

An **access control matrix** is a table of subjects and objects indicating what actions individual subjects can take upon individual objects. Matrices are data structures that programmers implement as table lookups that will be used and enforced by the operating system. Table 4-1 provides an example of an access control matrix.

This type of access control is usually an attribute of DAC models. The access rights can be assigned directly to the subjects (capabilities) or to the objects (ACLs).

Capability Tables

A *capability table* specifies the access rights a certain subject possesses pertaining to specific objects. A capability table is different from an ACL because the subject is bound to the capability table, whereas the object is bound to the ACL.

The capability corresponds to the subject's row in the access control matrix. In Table 4-1, Diane's capabilities are File1: read and execute; File2: read, write, and execute; File3: no access. This outlines what Diane is capable of doing to each resource. An example of a capability-based system is Kerberos. In this environment, the user is given a ticket, which is his capability table. This ticket is bound to the user and dictates what

Harris, D	$45,000	8am-5pm
Torkelson, T	$60,000	6pm-2am
Kowtko, J	$45,000	8am-5pm
Swenson, J	$65,000	6pm-2am

Payroll database view

Harris, D	Work history	8am-5pm
Torkelson, T	Work history	6pm-2am
Kowtko, J	Work history	8am-5pm
Swenson, J	Work history	6pm-2am

Manager database view

Figure 4-15 Different database views of the same tables

objects that user can access and to what extent. The access control is based on this ticket, or capability table. Figure 4-16 shows the difference between a capability table and an ACL.

A capability can be in the form of a token, ticket, or key. When a subject presents a capability component, the operating system (or application) will review the access rights and operations outlined in the capability component and allow the subject to carry out just those functions. A capability component is a data structure that contains a unique object identifier and the access rights the subject has to that object. The object may be a file, array, memory segment, or port. Each user, process, and application in a capability system has a list of capabilities.

Access Control Lists

Access control lists (ACLs) are used in several operating systems, applications, and router configurations. They are lists of subjects that are authorized to access a specific object, and they define what level of authorization is granted. Authorization can be specified to an individual or group.

ACLs map values from the access control matrix to the object. Whereas a capability corresponds to a row in the access control matrix, the ACL corresponds to a column of the matrix. The ACL for File1 in Table 4-1 is shown in Table 4-2.

User	File1	File2	File3
Diane	Read and execute	Read, write, and execute	No access
Katie	Read and execute	Read	No access
Chrissy	Read, write, and execute	Read and execute	Read
John	Read and execute	No access	Read and write

Table 4-1 An Example of an Access Control Matrix

Access Control Matrix

	Subject	File 1	File 2	File 3	File 4
	Larry	Read	Read, write	Read	Read, write
Capability	Curly	Full control	No access	Full control	Read
	Mo	Read, write	No access	Read	Full control
	Bob	Full control	Full control	No access	No access

ACL

Capability = row in matrix
ACL = column in matrix

Figure 4-16 A capability table is bound to a subject, whereas an ACL is bound to an object.

Content-Dependent Access Control

This is sensitive information, so only Bob and I can look at it.
Response: Well, since Bob is your imaginary friend, I think I can live by that rule.

As the name suggests, with *content-dependent access control*, access to objects is determined by the content within the object. The earlier example pertaining to database views showed how content-dependent access control can work. The content of the database fields dictates which users can see specific information within the database tables.

Content-dependent filtering is used when corporations employ e-mail filters that look for specific strings, such as "confidential," "social security number," "top secret," and any other types of words the company deems suspicious. Corporations also have this in place to control web surfing—where filtering is done to look for specific words—to try to figure out whether employees are gambling or looking at pornography.

Context-Dependent Access Control

First you kissed a parrot, then you threw your shoe, and then you did a jig. That's the right sequence, you are allowed access.

Context-dependent access control differs from content-dependent access control in that it makes access decisions based on the context of a collection of information rather than on the sensitivity of the data. A system that is using context-dependent access control "reviews the situation" and then makes a decision. For example, firewalls make context-based access decisions when they collect state information on a packet before allowing it into the network. A stateful firewall understands the necessary steps of communication for specific protocols. For example, in a TCP connection, the sender sends an SYN packet, the receiver sends an SYN/ACK, and then the sender acknowledges that packet with an ACK packet. A stateful firewall understands these different steps and will

Table 4-2 The ACL for File1	User	File1
	Diane	Read and execute
	Katie	Read and execute
	Chrissy	Read, write, and execute
	John	Read and execute

not allow packets to go through that do not follow this sequence. So, if a stateful firewall receives a SYN/ACK and there was not a previous SYN packet that correlates with this connection, the firewall understands this is not right and disregards the packet. This is what stateful means—something that understands the necessary steps of a dialog session. And this is an example of context-dependent access control, where the firewall understands the *context* of what is going on and includes that as part of its access decision.

Access Control Administration

Once an organization develops a security policy, supporting procedures, standards, and guidelines (described in Chapter 3), it must choose the type of access control model: DAC, MAC, or role-based. After choosing a model, the organization must select and implement different access control technologies and techniques. Access control matrices, restricted interfaces, and content-dependent, context-dependent, and rule-based controls are just a few of the choices.

If the environment does not require a high level of security, the organization will choose discretionary and/or role-based. The DAC model enables data owners to allow other users to access their resources, so an organization should choose the DAC model only if it is fully aware of what it entails. If an organization has a high turnover rate and/ or requires a more centralized access control method, the role-based model is more appropriate. If the environment requires a higher security level and only the administrator should be able to grant access to resources, then a MAC model is the best choice.

What is left to work out is how the organization will administer the access control model. Access control administration comes in two basic flavors: centralized and decentralized. The decision makers should understand both approaches so they choose and implement the proper one to achieve the level of protection required.

Access Control Techniques

Access control techniques are used to support the access control models.

- **Access control matrix** Table of subjects and objects that outlines their access relationships
- **ACL** Bound to an object and indicates what subjects can access it
- **Capability table** Bound to a subject and indicates what objects that subject can access
- **Content-based access** Bases access decisions on the sensitivity of the data, not solely on subject identity
- **Context-based access** Bases access decisions on the state of the situation, not solely on identity or content sensitivity
- **Restricted interface** Limits the user's environment within the system, thus limiting access to objects
- **Rule-based access** Restricts subjects' access attempts by predefined rules

Centralized Access Control Administration

I control who can touch the carrots and who can touch the peas.
Response: Could you leave now?

A *centralized access control administration* method is basically what it sounds like: one entity (department or individual) is responsible for overseeing access to all corporate resources. This entity (security administrator) configures the mechanisms that enforce access control, processes any changes that are needed to a user's access control profile, disables access when necessary, and completely removes these rights when a user is terminated, leaves the company, or moves to a different position. This type of administration provides a consistent and uniform method of controlling users' access rights. It supplies strict control over data because only one entity (department or individual) has the necessary rights to change access control profiles and permissions. Although this provides for a more consistent and reliable environment, it can be a slow one, because all changes must be processed by one entity.

The following sections present some examples of centralized remote access control technologies. Each of these authentication protocols is referred to as an AAA protocol, which stands for authentication, authorization, and auditing. (Some resources have the last *A* stand for accounting, but it is the same functionality—just a different name.)

Depending upon the protocol, there are different ways to authenticate a user in this client/server architecture. The traditional authentication protocols are Password Authentication Protocol (PAP), Challenge Handshake Authentication Protocol (CHAP), and a newer method referred to as Extensible Authentication Protocol (EAP). Each of these authentication protocols is discussed at length in Chapter 7.

RADIUS

So, I have to run across half of a circle to be authenticated?
Response: Don't know. Give it a try.

Remote Authentication Dial-In User Service (RADIUS) is a network protocol and provides client/server authentication and authorization, and audits remote users. A network may have access servers, a modem pool, DSL, ISDN, or T1 line dedicated for remote users to communicate through. The access server requests the remote user's logon credentials and passes them back to a RADIUS server, which houses the usernames and password values. The remote user is a client to the access server, and the access server is a client to the RADIUS server.

Most ISPs today use RADIUS to authenticate customers before they are allowed access to the Internet. The access server and customer's software negotiate, through a handshake procedure, and agree upon an authentication protocol (PAP, CHAP, or EAP). The customer provides to the access server a username and password. This communication takes place over a PPP connection. The access server and RADIUS server communicate over the RADIUS protocol. Once the authentication is completed properly, the customer's system is given an IP address and connection parameters, and is allowed access to the Internet. The access server notifies the RADIUS server when the session starts and stops, for billing purposes.

RADIUS is also used within corporate environments to provide road warriors and home users access to network resources. RADIUS allows companies to maintain user profiles in a central database. When a user dials in and is properly authenticated, a preconfigured profile is assigned to him to control what resources he can and cannot access. This technology allows companies to have a single administered entry point, which provides standardization in security and a simplistic way to track usage and network statistics.

RADIUS was developed by Livingston Enterprises for its network access server product series, but was then published as standards. This means it is an open protocol that any vendor can use and manipulate so it will work within its individual products. Because RADIUS is an open protocol, it can be used in different types of implementations. The format of configurations and user credentials can be held in LDAP servers, various databases, or text files. Figure 4-17 shows some examples of possible RADIUS implementations.

TACACS

Terminal Access Controller Access Control System (TACACS) has a very funny name. Not funny ha-ha, but funny "huh?" TACACS has been through three generations: TACACS, Extended TACACS (XTACACS), and TACACS+. TACACS combines its authentication and authorization processes, XTACACS separates authentication, authorization, and auditing processes, and TACACS+ is XTACACS with extended two-factor user authentication. TACACS uses fixed passwords for authentication, while TACACS+ allows users to employ dynamic (one-time) passwords, which provides more protection.

 NOTE   TACACS+ is really not a new generation of TACACS and XTACACS; it is a brand-new protocol that provides similar functionality and shares the same naming scheme. Because it is a totally different protocol, it is not backward-compatible with TACACS or XTACACS.

TACACS+ provides basically the same functionality as RADIUS with a few differences in some of its characteristics. First, TACACS+ uses TCP as its transport protocol, while RADIUS uses UDP. "So what?" you may be thinking. Well, any software that is developed to use UDP as its transport protocol has to be "fatter" with intelligent code that will look out for the items that UDP will not catch. Since UDP is a connectionless protocol, it will not detect or correct transmission errors. So RADIUS must have the necessary code to detect packet corruption, long timeouts, or dropped packets. Since the developers of TACACS+ choose to use TCP, the TACACS+ software does not have to have the extra code to look for and deal with these transmission problems. TCP is a connection-oriented protocol, and that is its job and responsibility.

RADIUS encrypts the user's password only as it is being transmitted from the RADIUS client to the RADIUS server. Other information, as in the username, accounting, and authorized services, is passed in cleartext. This is an open invitation for attackers to capture session information for replay attacks. Vendors who integrate RADIUS into their products need to understand these weaknesses and integrate other security mechanisms to protect against these types of attacks.

TACACS+ encrypts all of this data between the client and server and thus does not have the vulnerabilities inherent in the RADIUS protocol.

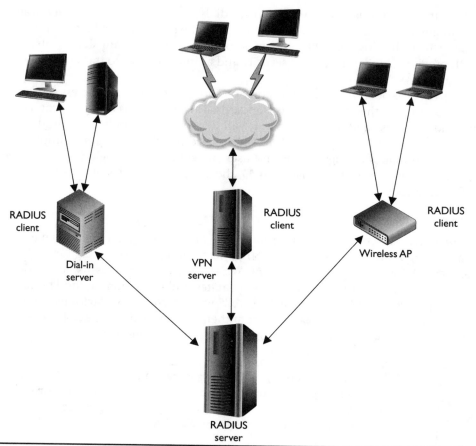

Figure 4-17 Environments can implement different RADIUS infrastructures.

The RADIUS protocol combines the authentication and authorization functionality. TACACS+ uses a true Authentication, Authorization, and Accounting/Audit (AAA) architecture, which separates the authentication, authorization, and accounting functionalities. This gives a network administrator more flexibility in how remote users are authenticated. For example, if Tom is a network administrator and has been assigned the task of setting up remote access for users, he must decide between RADIUS and TACACS+. If the current environment already authenticates all of the local users through a domain controller using Kerberos, then Tom can configure the remote users to be authenticated in this same manner, as shown in Figure 4-18. Instead of having to maintain a remote access server database of remote user credentials and a database within Active Directory for local users, Tom can just configure and maintain one database. The separation of authentication, authorization, and accounting functionality provides this capability. TACACS+ also enables the network administrator to define more granular user profiles, which can control the actual commands users can carry out.

Remember that RADIUS and TACACS+ are both protocols, and protocols are just agreed-upon ways of communication. When a RADIUS client communicates with a RADIUS server, it does so through the RADIUS protocol, which is really just a set of defined fields that will accept certain values. These fields are referred to as attribute-value pairs (AVPs). As an analogy, suppose I send you a piece of paper that has several different boxes drawn on it. Each box has a headline associated with it: first name, last name, hair color, shoe size. You fill in these boxes with your values and send it back to me. This is basically how protocols work; the sending system just fills in the boxes (fields) with the necessary information for the receiving system to extract and process.

Since TACACS+ allows for more granular control on what users can and cannot do, TACACS+ has more AVPs, which allows the network administrator to define ACLs, filters, user privileges, and much more. Table 4-3 points out the differences between RADIUS and TACACS+.

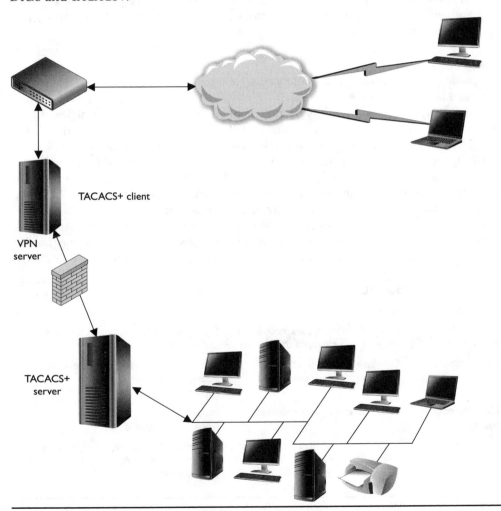

TACACS+ client

VPN
server

TACACS+
server

Figure 4-18   TACACS+ works in a client/server model.

> ## Watchdog
>
> Watchdog timers are commonly used to detect software faults, such as a process ending abnormally or hanging. The watchdog functionality sends out a type of "heartbeat" packet to determine whether a service is responding. If it is not, the process can be terminated or reset. This guards against software deadlocks, infinite loops, and process prioritization problems. This functionality can be used in AAA protocols to determine whether packets need to be re-sent and whether connections experiencing problems should be closed and reopened.

So, RADIUS is the appropriate protocol when simplistic username/password authentication can take place and users only need an Accept or Deny for obtaining access, as in ISPs. TACACS+ is the better choice for environments that require more sophisticated authentication steps and tighter control over more complex authorization activities, as in corporate networks.

Diameter

If we create our own technology, we get to name it any goofy thing we want!
Response: I like Snizzernoodle.

   Diameter is a protocol that has been developed to build upon the functionality of RADIUS and overcome many of its limitations. The creators of this protocol decided to call it Diameter as a play on the term RADIUS—as in *the diameter is twice the radius.*

   Diameter is another AAA protocol that provides the same type of functionality as RADIUS and TACACS+ but also provides more flexibility and capabilities to meet the new demands of today's complex and diverse networks. At one time, all remote communication took place over PPP and SLIP connections and users authenticated themselves through PAP or CHAP. Those were simpler, happier times when our parents had to walk uphill both ways to school wearing no shoes. As with life, technology has become much more complicated and there are more devices and protocols to choose

	RADIUS	TACACS+
Packet delivery	UDP	TCP
Packet encryption	Encrypts only the password from the RADIUS client to the server.	Encrypts all traffic between the client and server.
AAA support	Combines authentication and authorization services.	Uses the AAA architecture, separating authentication, authorization, and auditing.
Multiprotocol support	Works over PPP connections.	Supports other protocols, such as AppleTalk, NetBIOS, and IPX.
Responses	Uses single-challenge response when authenticating a user, which is used for all AAA activities.	Uses multiple-challenge response for each of the AAA processes. Each AAA activity must be authenticated.

Table 4-3 Specific Differences Between These Two AAA Protocols

Mobile IP

This technology allows a user to move from one network to another and still use the same IP address. It is an improvement upon the IP protocol because it allows a user to have a *home IP address*, associated with his home network, and a *care-of address*. The care-of address changes as he moves from one network to the other. All traffic that is addressed to his home IP address is forwarded to his care-of address.

from than ever before. Today, we want our wireless devices and smart phones to be able to authenticate themselves to our networks and we use roaming protocols, Mobile IP, Ethernet over PPP, Voice over IP (VoIP), and other crazy stuff that the traditional AAA protocols cannot keep up with. So in came the smart people with a new AAA protocol, Diameter, that can deal with these issues and many more.

Diameter protocol consists of two portions. The first is the base protocol, which provides the secure communication among Diameter entities, feature discovery, and version negotiation. The second is the extensions, which are built on top of the base protocol to allow various technologies to use Diameter for authentication.

Up until the conception of Diameter, IETF has had individual working groups who defined how Voice over IP (VoIP), Fax over IP (FoIP), Mobile IP, and remote authentication protocols work. Defining and implementing them individually in any network can easily result in too much confusion and interoperability. It requires customers to roll out and configure several different policy servers and increases the cost with each new added service. Diameter provides a base protocol, which defines header formats, security options, commands, and AVPs. This base protocol allows for extensions to tie in other services, such as VoIP, FoIP, Mobile IP, wireless, and cell phone authentication. So Diameter can be used as an AAA protocol for all of these different uses.

As an analogy, consider a scenario in which ten people all need to get to the same hospital, which is where they all work. They all have different jobs (doctor, lab technician, nurse, janitor, and so on), but they all need to end up at the same location. So, they can either all take their own cars and their own routes to the hospital, which takes up more hospital parking space and requires the gate guard to authenticate each and every car, or they can take a bus. The bus is the common element (base protocol) to get the individuals (different services) to the same location (networked environment). Diameter provides the common AAA and security framework that different services can work within, as illustrated in Figure 4-19.

 NOTE Roaming Operations (ROAMOPS) allows PPP users to gain access to the Internet without the need of dialing into their home service provider. The individual service providers, who have roaming agreements, carry out cross-authentication for their customers so users can dial into any service provider's point of presence and gain Internet access.

RADIUS and TACACS+ are client/server protocols, which means the server portion cannot send unsolicited commands to the client portion. The server portion can only speak when spoken to. Diameter is a peer-based protocol that allows either end to initi-

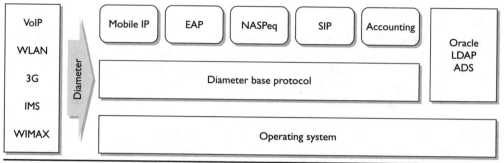

Figure 4-19 Diameter provides an AAA architecture for several services.

ate communication. This functionality allows the Diameter server to send a message to the access server to request the user to provide another authentication credential if she is attempting to access a secure resource.

Diameter is not directly backward-compatible with RADIUS but provides an upgrade path. Diameter uses TCP and AVPs, and provides proxy server support. It has better error detection and correction functionality than RADIUS, as well as better failover properties, and thus provides better network resilience. Diameter also provides end-to-end security through the use of IPSec or TLS, which is not available in RADIUS.

Diameter has the functionality and ability to provide the AAA functionality for other protocols and services because it has a large AVP set. RADIUS has 2^8 (256) AVPs, while Diameter has 2^{32} (a whole bunch). Recall from earlier in the chapter that AVPs are like boxes drawn on a piece of paper that outline how two entities can communicate back and forth. So, more AVPs allow for more functionality and services to exist and communicate between systems. Diameter provides the following AAA functionality:

- **Authentication**
  - PAP, CHAP, EAP
  - End-to-end protection of authentication information
  - Replay attack protection
- **Authorization**
  - Redirects, secure proxies, relays, and brokers
  - State reconciliation
  - Unsolicited disconnect
  - Reauthorization on demand
- **Accounting**
  - Reporting, ROAMOPS accounting, event monitoring

You may not be familiar with Diameter, because it is relatively new. It probably won't be taking over the world tomorrow, but it will be used by environments that need to provide the type of services being demanded of them, and then slowly seep down into corporate networks as more products are available. RADIUS has been around for a long time and has served its purpose well, so don't expect it to exit the stage any time soon.

Decentralized Access Control Administration

Okay, everyone just do whatever you want.

A *decentralized access control administration* method gives control of access to the people closer to the resources—the people who may better understand who should and should not have access to certain files, data, and resources. In this approach, it is often the functional manager who assigns access control rights to employees. An organization may choose to use a decentralized model if its managers have better judgment regarding which users should be able to access different resources, and there is no business requirement that dictates strict control through a centralized body is necessary.

Changes can happen faster through this type of administration because not just one entity is making changes for the whole organization. However, there is a possibility that conflicts of interest could arise that may not benefit the organization. Because no single entity controls access as a whole, different managers and departments can practice security and access control in different ways. This does not provide uniformity and fairness across the organization. One manager could be too busy with daily tasks and decide it is easier to let everyone have full control over all the systems in the department. Another department may practice a stricter and detail-oriented method of control by giving employees only the level of permissions needed to fulfill their tasks.

Also, certain controls can overlap, in which case actions may not be properly proscribed or restricted. If Mike is part of the accounting group and recently has been under suspicion for altering personnel account information, the accounting manager may restrict his access to these files to read-only access. However, the accounting manager does not realize that Mike still has full-control access under the network group he is also a member of. This type of administration does not provide methods for consistent control, as a centralized method would. Another issue that comes up with decentralized administration is lack of proper consistency pertaining to the company's protection. For example, when Sean is fired for looking at pornography on his computer, some of the groups Sean is a member of may not disable his account. So, Sean may still have access after he is terminated, which could cause the company heartache if Sean is vindictive.

Access Control Methods

Access controls can be implemented at various layers of a network and individual systems. Some controls are core components of operating systems or embedded into applications and devices, and some security controls require third-party add-on packages. Although different controls provide different functionality, they should all work together to keep the bad guys out and the good guys in, and to provide the necessary quality of protection.

Most companies do not want people to be able to walk into their building arbitrarily, sit down at an employee's computer, and access network resources. Companies also don't want every employee to be able to access all information within the company, as in human resource records, payroll information, and trade secrets. Companies want some assurance that employees who can access confidential information will have some restrictions put upon them, making sure, say, a disgruntled employee does not have the ability to delete financial statements, tax information, and top-secret data that would put the company at risk. Several types of access controls prevent these things from happening, as discussed in the sections that follow.

Access Control Layers

Access control consists of three broad categories: administrative, technical, and physical. Each category has different access control mechanisms that can be carried out manually or automatically. All of these access control mechanisms should work in concert with each other to protect an infrastructure and its data.

Each category of access control has several components that fall within it, as shown next:

- **Administrative Controls**
  - Policy and procedures
  - Personnel controls
  - Supervisory structure
  - Security-awareness training
  - Testing
- **Physical Controls**
  - Network segregation
  - Perimeter security
  - Computer controls
  - Work area separation
  - Data backups
  - Cabling
  - Control zone
- **Technical Controls**
  - System access
  - Network architecture
  - Network access
  - Encryption and protocols
  - Auditing

The following sections explain each of these categories and components and how it relates to access control.

Administrative Controls

Senior management must decide what role security will play in the organization, including the security goals and objectives. These directives will dictate how all the supporting mechanisms will fall into place. Basically, senior management provides the skeleton of a security infrastructure and then appoints the proper entities to fill in the rest.

The first piece to building a security foundation within an organization is a security policy. It is management's responsibility to construct a security policy and delegate the development of the supporting procedures, standards, and guidelines, indicate which personnel controls should be used, and specify how testing should be carried out to ensure all pieces fulfill the company's security goals. These items are *administrative controls* and work at the top layer of a hierarchical access control model. (Administrative controls are examined in detail in Chapter 3, but are mentioned here briefly to show the relationship to logical and physical controls pertaining to access control.)

Personnel Controls

Personnel controls indicate how employees are expected to interact with security mechanisms and address noncompliance issues pertaining to these expectations. These controls indicate what security actions should be taken when an employee is hired, terminated, suspended, moved into another department, or promoted. Specific procedures must be developed for each situation, and many times the human resources and legal departments are involved with making these decisions.

Supervisory Structure

Management must construct a supervisory structure in which each employee has a superior to report to, and that superior is responsible for that employee's actions. This forces management members to be responsible for employees and take a vested interest in their activities. If an employee is caught hacking into a server that holds customer credit card information, that employee *and* her supervisor will face the consequences. This is an administrative control that aids in fighting fraud and enforcing proper control.

Security-Awareness Training

How do you know they know what they are supposed to know?

In many organizations, management has a hard time spending money and allocating resources for items that do not seem to affect the bottom line: profitability. This is why training traditionally has been given low priority, but as computer security becomes more and more of an issue to companies, they are starting to recognize the value of security-awareness training.

A company's security depends upon technology and people, and people are usually the weakest link and cause the most security breaches and compromises. If users understand how to properly access resources, why access controls are in place, and the ramifications for not using the access controls properly, a company can reduce many types of security incidents.

Testing

All security controls, mechanisms, and procedures must be tested on a periodic basis to ensure they properly support the security policy, goals, and objectives set for them. This testing can be a drill to test reactions to a physical attack or disruption of the network, a penetration test of the firewalls and perimeter network to uncover vulnerabilities, a query to employees to gauge their knowledge, or a review of the procedures and standards to make sure they still align with implemented business or technology changes. Because change is constant and environments continually evolve, security procedures and practices should be continually tested to ensure they align with management's expectations and stay up-to-date with each addition to the infrastructure. It is management's responsibility to make sure these tests take place.

Physical Controls

We will go much further into physical security in Chapter 6, but it is important to understand certain physical controls must support and work with administrative and technical (logical) controls to supply the right degree of access control. Examples of physical controls include having a security guard verify individuals' identities prior to entering a facility, erecting fences around the exterior of the facility, making sure server rooms and wiring closets are locked and protected from environmental elements (humidity, heat, and cold), and allowing only certain individuals to access work areas that contain confidential information. Some physical controls are introduced next, but again, these and more physical mechanisms are explored in depth in Chapter 6.

Network Segregation

I have used my Lego set to outline the physical boundaries between you and me.
Response: Can you make the walls a little higher please?

Network segregation can be carried out through physical and logical means. A network might be physically designed to have all AS400 computers and databases in a certain area. This area may have doors with security swipe cards that allow only individuals who have a specific clearance to access this section and these computers. Another section of the network may contain web servers, routers, and switches, and yet another network portion may have employee workstations. Each area would have the necessary physical controls to ensure that only the permitted individuals have access into and out of those sections.

Perimeter Security

How perimeter security is implemented depends upon the company and the security requirements of that environment. One environment may require employees to be authorized by a security guard by showing a security badge that contains a picture identification before being allowed to enter a section. Another environment may require no authentication process and let anyone and everyone into different sections. Perimeter security can also encompass closed-circuit TVs that scan the parking lots and waiting areas, fences surrounding a building, the lighting of walkways and parking areas, motion detectors, sensors, alarms, and the location and visual appearance of a building. These are examples of perimeter security mechanisms that provide physical access control by providing protection for individuals, facilities, and the components within facilities.

Computer Controls

Each computer can have physical controls installed and configured, such as locks on the cover so the internal parts cannot be stolen, the removal of the floppy and CD-ROM drives to prevent copying of confidential information, or implementation of a protection device that reduces the electrical emissions to thwart attempts to gather information through airwaves.

Work Area Separation

Some environments might dictate that only particular individuals can access certain areas of the facility. For example, research companies might not want office personnel to be able to enter laboratories so they can't disrupt experiments or access test data. Most network administrators allow only network staff in the server rooms and wiring closets, to reduce the possibilities of errors or sabotage attempts. In financial institutions, only certain employees can enter the vaults or other restricted areas. These examples of work area separation are physical controls used to support access control and the overall security policy of the company.

Cabling

Different types of cabling can be used to carry information throughout a network. Some cable types have sheaths that protect the data from being affected by the electrical interference of other devices that emit electrical signals. Some types of cable have protection material around each individual wire to ensure there is no crosstalk between the different wires. All cables need to be routed throughout the facility so they are not in the way of employees or are exposed to any dangers like being cut, burnt, crimped, or eavesdropped upon.

Control Zone

The company facility should be split up into zones depending upon the sensitivity of the activity that takes place per zone. The front lobby could be considered a public area, the product development area could be considered top secret, and the executive offices could be considered secret. It does not matter what classifications are used, but it should be understood that some areas are more sensitive than others, which will require different access control based on the needed protection level. The same is true of the company network. It should be segmented, and access controls should be chosen for each zone based on the criticality of devices and the sensitivity of data being processed.

Technical Controls

Technical controls are the software tools used to restrict subjects' access to objects. They are core components of operating systems, add-on security packages, applications, network hardware devices, protocols, encryption mechanisms, and access control matrixes. These controls work at different layers within a network or system and need to maintain a synergistic relationship to ensure there is no unauthorized access to resources and that the resources' availability, integrity, and confidentiality are guaranteed. Technical controls protect the integrity and availability of resources by limiting the number of subjects that can access them and protecting the confidentiality of resources by preventing disclosure to unauthorized subjects. The following sections explain how some technical controls work and where they are implemented within an environment.

System Access

Different types of controls and security mechanisms control how a computer is accessed. If an organization is using a MAC architecture, the clearance of a user is identified and compared to the resource's classification level to verify that this user can access the requested object. If an organization is using a DAC architecture, the operating system checks to see if a user has been granted permission to access this resource. The sensitivity of data, clearance level of users, and users' rights and permissions are used as logical controls to control access to a resource.

Many types of technical controls enable a user to access a system and the resources within that system. A technical control may be a username and password combination, a Kerberos implementation, biometrics, public key infrastructure (PKI), RADIUS, TACACS, or authentication using a smart card through a reader connected to a system. These technologies verify the user is who he says he is by using different types of authentication methods. Once a user is properly authenticated, he can be authorized and allowed access to network resources. These technologies are addressed in further detail in future chapters, but for now understand that system access is a type of technical control that can enforce access control objectives.

Network Architecture

The architecture of a network can be constructed and enforced through several logical controls to provide segregation and protection of an environment. Whereas a network can be segregated physically by walls and location, it can also be segregated logically through IP address ranges and subnets and by controlling the communication flow between the segments. Often, it is important to control how one segment of a network communicates with another segment.

Figure 4-20 is an example of how an organization may segregate its network and determine how network segments can communicate. This example shows that the organization does not want the internal network and the demilitarized zone (DMZ) to have open and unrestricted communication paths. There is usually no reason for internal users to have direct access to the systems in the DMZ, and cutting off this type of communication reduces the possibilities of internal attacks on those systems. Also, if an attack comes from the Internet and successfully compromises a system on the DMZ, the attacker must not be able to easily access the internal network, which this type of logical segregation protects against.

This example also shows how the management segment can communicate with all other network segments, but those segments cannot communicate in return. The segmentation is implemented because the management consoles that control the firewalls and IDSs reside in the management segment, and there is no reason for users, other than the administrator, to have access to these computers.

A network can be segregated physically and logically. This type of segregation and restriction is accomplished through logical controls.

Network Access

Systems have logical controls that dictate who can and cannot access them and what those individuals can do once they are authenticated. This is also true for networks. Routers, switches, firewalls, and bridges all work as technical controls to enforce access

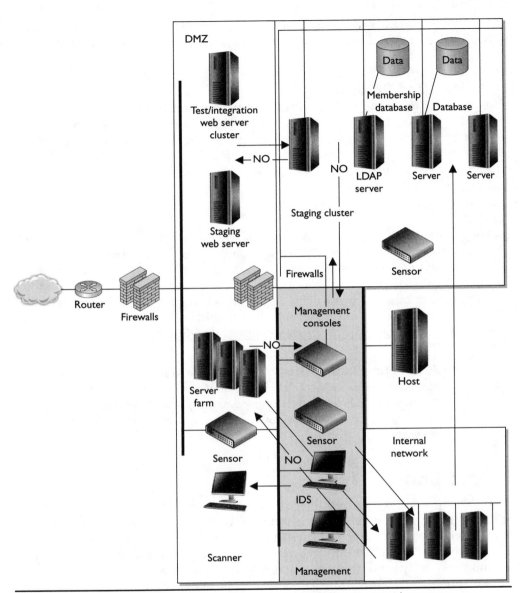

Figure 4-20 Technical network segmentation controls how different network segments communicate.

restriction into and out of a network, and access to the different segments within the network. If an attacker from the Internet wants to gain access to a specific computer, chances are she will have to hack through a firewall, router, and a switch just to be able to start an attack on a specific computer that resides within the internal network. Each device has its own logical controls that make decisions about what entities can access them and what type of actions they can carry out.

Access to different network segments should be granular in nature. Routers and firewalls can be used to ensure that only certain types of traffic get through to each segment.

Encryption and Protocols

Encryption and protocols work as technical controls to protect information as it passes throughout a network and resides on computers. They ensure that the information is received by the correct entity, and that it is not modified during transmission. These logical controls can preserve the confidentiality and integrity of data and enforce specific paths for communication to take place. (Chapter 8 is dedicated to cryptography and encryption mechanisms.)

Auditing

Auditing tools are technical controls that track activity within a network, on a network device, or on a specific computer. Even though auditing is not an activity that will deny an entity access to a network or computer, it will track activities so a network administrator can understand the types of access that took place, identify a security breach, or warn the administrator of suspicious activity. This information can be used to point out weaknesses of other technical controls and help the administrator understand where changes must be made to preserve the necessary security level within the environment.

 NOTE Many of the subjects touched on in these sections will be fully addressed and explained in later chapters. What is important to understand is that there are administrative, technical, and physical controls that work toward providing access control, and you should know several examples of each for the exam.

Access Control Types

As previously stated, access control types (administrative, physical, and technical) work at different levels, but different levels of what? They work together at different levels within their own categories. A security guard is a type of control used to scare off attackers and ensure that only authorized personnel enter a building. If an intruder gets around the security guard in some manner, he could be faced with motion detectors, locks on doors, and alarms. These layers are depicted in Figure 4-21.

Each control works at a different level of granularity, but it can also perform different functionalities. The different functionalities of access controls are *preventive, detective, corrective, deterrent, recovery, compensating,* and *directive.*

By having a better understanding of the different control functionalities, you will be able to make more informed decisions about what controls will be best used in

Figure 4-21
Security should be implemented in layers, which provide several barriers to attackers.

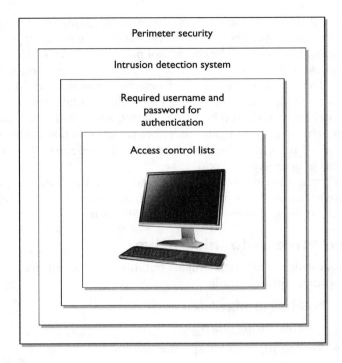

specific kinds of situations. The seven different access control functionalities are as follows:

- **Deterrent**   Intended to discourage a potential attacker
- **Preventive**   Intended to avoid an incident from occurring
- **Corrective**   Fixes components or systems after an incident has occurred
- **Recovery**   Intended to bring controls back to regular operations
- **Detective**   Helps identify an incident's activities
- **Compensating**   Controls that provide for an alternative measure of control
- **Directive**   Mandatory controls that have been put in place due to regulations or environmental requirements

Once you understand fully what the different controls do, you can use them in the right locations for specific risks—or you can just put them where they would look the prettiest.

When looking at a security structure of an environment, it is most productive to use a preventive model and then use detective, recovery, and corrective mechanisms to help support this model. Basically, you want to stop any trouble before it starts, but you must be able to quickly react and combat trouble if it does find you. All security controls should be built on the concept of preventive security. However, it is not feasible to prevent everything; therefore, what you cannot prevent, you should be able to quickly detect. That's why preventive and detective controls should always be implemented together and should complement each other. To take this concept further, what you can't prevent, you should be able to detect, and if you detect something, it means you weren't able to prevent it, and therefore you should take corrective action to make sure it is indeed prevented the next time around. Therefore, all three types work together: preventive, detective, and corrective.

The control types described next (administrative, physical, and technical) are preventive in nature. These are important to understand when developing a security access control model and when taking the CISSP exam.

Preventive: Administrative

The following are *soft* mechanisms put into place to enforce access control and protect the organization as a whole:

- Policies and procedures
- Effective hiring practices
- Pre-employment background checks
- Controlled termination processes
- Data classification and labeling
- Security awareness

 NOTE One best practice that can be incorporated would require individuals to sign a statement outlining what expectations are regarding the access they are being granted. This in turn can be used for either termination of the individual from the work environment, and possibly prosecution under the governing laws such as the Computer Fraud and Abuse Act. The improper administration and management of access controls is the main cause for most unauthorized access compromises.

Preventive: Physical

The following can physically restrict access to a facility, specific work areas, or computer systems:

- Badges, swipe cards
- Guards, dogs
- Fences, locks, mantraps

Preventive: Technical

The following are logical controls that are part of operating systems, third-party application add-ons, or hardware units:

- Passwords, biometrics, smart cards
- Encryption, protocols, call-back systems, database views, constrained user interfaces
- Antivirus software, ACLs, firewalls, routers, clipping levels

Table 4-4 shows how these categories of access control mechanisms perform different security functions. However, Table 4-4 does not necessarily cover all the possibilities. For example, a fence can provide preventive and deterrent measures by making it harder for intruders to access a facility, but it could also be a compensative control. If a company cannot afford a security guard, it might erect a fence to act as the compensative physical control. Each control is able to meet more requirements than those listed in the table. Table 4-4 is only an example to show the relationships among the different controls and the security attributes they could provide.

 NOTE   Locks are usually considered delay mechanisms because they only delay a determined intruder. The goal is to delay access long enough to allow law enforcement or the security guard to respond to the situation.

Any control can really end up being a compensating control. An organization would choose a compensating control if another control is too expensive but protection is still needed. For example, a company can't afford a security guard staff, so they erect fences, which would be the compensating control. Another reason to use a compensating control is business needs. If the security team recommends closing a specific port on a firewall, but the business requires that service to be available to external users, then the compensating control could be to implement an intrusion prevention system (IPS) that would closely monitor the traffic coming in from that port.

Several types of security mechanisms exist, and they all need to work together. The complexity of the controls and of the environment they are in can cause the controls to contradict each other or leave gaps in security. This can introduce unforeseen holes in the company's protection not fully understood by the implementers. A company may have very strict technical access controls in place and all the necessary administrative controls up to snuff, but if any person is allowed to physically access any system in the facility, then clear security dangers are present within the environment. Together, these controls should work in harmony to provide a healthy, safe, and productive environment.

Type of Control:	Preventive — Avoid undesirable events from occurring	Detective — Identify undesirable events that have occurred	Corrective — Correct undesirable events that have occurred	Deterrent — Discourage security violations	Recovery — Restore resources and capabilities	Compensative — Provide alternatives to other controls
Category of Control:						
Physical						
Fences				X		X
Locks	X					X
Badge system	X					X
Security guard	X					X
Biometric system	X					X
Mantrap doors	X					X
Lighting				X		X
Motion detectors		X				X
Closed-circuit TVs		X				X
Offsite facility					X	X
Administrative						
Security policy	X					X
Monitoring and supervising		X				X

Table 4-4 Service That Security Controls Provide

Type of Control:	Preventive	Detective	Corrective	Deterrent	Recovery	Compensative
Separation of duties	X					X
Job rotation		X				X
Information classification	X					X
Personnel procedures	X					X
Investigations		X				X
Testing	X					X
Security-awareness training	X					X
Technical						
ACLs	X					X
Routers	X					X
Encryption	X					X
Audit logs		X				X
IDS		X				X
Antivirus software	X		X			X
Server images			X			X
Smart cards	X					X
Dial-up call-back systems	X					X
Data backup					X	X

Table 4-4 Service That Security Controls Provide (*continued*)

Accountability

Auditing capabilities ensure users are accountable for their actions, verify that the security policies are enforced, and can be used as investigation tools. There are several reasons why network administrators and security professionals want to make sure accountability mechanisms are in place and configured properly: to be able to track bad deeds back to individuals, detect intrusions, reconstruct events and system conditions, provide legal recourse material, and produce problem reports. Audit documentation and log files hold a mountain of information—the trick is usually deciphering it and presenting it in a useful and understandable format.

Accountability is tracked by recording user, system, and application activities. This recording is done through auditing functions and mechanisms within an operating system or application. Audit trails contain information about operating system activities, application events, and user actions. Audit trails can be used to verify the health of a system by checking performance information or certain types of errors and conditions. After a system crashes, a network administrator often will review audit logs to try and piece together the status of the system and attempt to understand what events could be attributed to the disruption.

Audit trails can also be used to provide alerts about any suspicious activities that can be investigated at a later time. In addition, they can be valuable in determining exactly how far an attack has gone and the extent of the damage that may have been caused. It is important to make sure a proper chain of custody is maintained to ensure any data collected can later be properly and accurately represented in case it needs to be used for later events such as criminal proceedings or investigations.

It is a good idea to keep the following in mind when dealing with auditing:

- Store the audits securely.
- The right audit tools will keep the size of the logs under control.
- The logs must be protected from any unauthorized changes in order to safeguard data.
- Train the right people to review the data in the right manner.
- Make sure the ability to delete logs is only available to administrators.
- Logs should contain activities of all high-privileged accounts (root, administrator).

An administrator configures what actions and events are to be audited and logged. In a high-security environment, the administrator would configure more activities to be captured and set the threshold of those activities to be more sensitive. The events can be reviewed to identify where breaches of security occurred and if the security policy has been violated. If the environment does not require such levels of security, the events analyzed would be fewer, with less demanding thresholds.

Items and actions to be audited can become an endless list. A security professional should be able to assess an environment and its security goals, know what actions should be audited, and know what is to be done with that information after it is captured—without wasting too much disk space, CPU power, and staff time. The following gives a broad overview of the items and actions that can be audited and logged:

- **System-level events**
  - System performance
  - Logon attempts (successful and unsuccessful)
  - Logon ID
  - Date and time of each logon attempt
  - Lockouts of users and terminals
  - Use of administration utilities
  - Devices used
  - Functions performed
  - Requests to alter configuration files
- **Application-level events**
  - Error messages
  - Files opened and closed
  - Modifications of files
  - Security violations within application
- **User-level events**
  - Identification and authentication attempts
  - Files, services, and resources used
  - Commands initiated
  - Security violations

The threshold (clipping level) and parameters for each of these items must be configured. For example, an administrator can audit each logon attempt or just each failed logon attempt. System performance can look only at the amount of memory used within an eight-hour period, or the memory, CPU, and hard drive space used within an hour.

Intrusion detection systems (IDSs) continually scan audit logs for suspicious activity. If an intrusion or harmful event takes place, audit logs are usually kept to be used later to prove guilt and prosecute if necessary. If severe security events take place, many times the IDS will alert the administrator or staff member so they can take proper actions to end the destructive activity. If a dangerous virus is identified, administrators may take the mail server offline. If an attacker is accessing confidential information within the database, this computer may be temporarily disconnected from the network or Internet. If an attack is in progress, the administrator may want to watch the actions taking place so she can track down the intruder. IDSs can watch for this type of activity during real time and/or scan audit logs and watch for specific patterns or behaviors.

Review of Audit Information

It does no good to collect it if you don't look at it.

Audit trails can be reviewed manually or through automated means—either way, they must be reviewed and interpreted. If an organization reviews audit trails manually, it needs to establish a system of how, when, and why they are viewed. Usually audit logs are very popular items right after a security breach, unexplained system action, or system disruption. An administrator or staff member rapidly tries to piece together the activities that led up to the event. This type of audit review is event-oriented. Audit trails can also be viewed periodically to watch for unusual behavior of users or systems, and to help understand the baseline and health of a system. Then there is a real-time, or near real-time, audit analysis that can use an automated tool to review audit information as it is created. Administrators should have a scheduled task of reviewing audit data. The audit material usually needs to be parsed and saved to another location for a certain time period. This retention information should be stated in the company's security policy and procedures.

Reviewing audit information manually can be overwhelming. There are applications and audit trail analysis tools that reduce the volume of audit logs to review and improve the efficiency of manual review procedures. A majority of the time, audit logs contain information that is unnecessary, so these tools parse out specific events and present them in a useful format.

An *audit-reduction tool* does just what its name suggests—reduces the amount of information within an audit log. This tool discards mundane task information and records system performance, security, and user functionality information that can be useful to a security professional or administrator.

Keystroke Monitoring

Oh, you typed an L. Let me write that down. Oh, and a P, and a T, and an S…hey, slow down!

Keystroke monitoring is a type of monitoring that can review and record keystrokes entered by a user during an active session. The person using this type of monitoring can have the characters written to an audit log to be reviewed at a later time. This type of auditing is usually done only for special cases and only for a specific amount of time, because the amount of information captured can be overwhelming and/or unimportant. If a security professional or administrator is suspicious of an individual and his activities, she may invoke this type of monitoring. In some authorized investigative stages, a keyboard dongle may be unobtrusively inserted between the keyboard and the computer to capture all the keystrokes entered, including power-on passwords.

A hacker can also use this type of monitoring. If an attacker can successfully install a Trojan horse on a computer, the Trojan horse can install an application that captures data as it is typed into the keyboard. Typically, these programs are most interested in user credentials and can alert the attacker when credentials have been successfully captured.

Privacy issues are involved with this type of monitoring, and administrators could be subject to criminal and civil liabilities if it is done without proper notification to the employees and authorization from management. If a company wants to use this type of auditing, it should state so in the security policy, address the issue in security-awareness training, and present a banner notice to the user warning that the activities at that computer may be monitored in this fashion. These steps should be taken to protect the company from violating an individual's privacy, and they should inform the users where their privacy boundaries start and stop pertaining to computer use.

Protecting Audit Data and Log Information

If an intruder breaks into your house, he will do his best to cover his tracks by not leaving fingerprints or any other clues that can be used to tie him to the criminal activity. The same is true in computer fraud and illegal activity. The intruder will work to cover his tracks. Attackers often delete audit logs that hold this incriminating information. (Deleting specific incriminating data within audit logs is called *scrubbing*.) Deleting this information can cause the administrator to not be alerted or aware of the security breach, and can destroy valuable data. Therefore, audit logs should be protected by strict access control.

Only certain individuals (the administrator and security personnel) should be able to view, modify, and delete audit trail information. No other individuals should be able to view this data, much less modify or delete it. The integrity of the data can be ensured with the use of digital signatures, message digest tools, and strong access controls. Its confidentiality can be protected with encryption and access controls, if necessary, and it can be stored on *write-once media* (CD-ROMs) to prevent loss or modification of the data. Unauthorized access attempts to audit logs should be captured and reported.

Audit logs may be used in a trial to prove an individual's guilt, demonstrate how an attack was carried out, or corroborate a story. The integrity and confidentiality of these logs will be under scrutiny. Proper steps need to be taken to ensure that the confidentiality and integrity of the audit information is not compromised in any way.

Access Control Practices

The fewest number of doors open allows the fewest number of flies in.

We have gone over how users are identified, authenticated, and authorized, and how their actions are audited. These are necessary parts of a healthy and safe network environment. You also want to take steps to ensure there are no unnecessary open doors and that the environment stays at the same security level you have worked so hard to achieve. This means you need to implement good access control practices. Not keeping up with daily or monthly tasks usually causes the most vulnerabilities in an environment. It is hard to put out all the network fires, fight the political battles, fulfill all the users' needs, and still keep up with small maintenance tasks. However, many companies have found that not doing these small tasks caused them the greatest heartache of all.

The following is a list of tasks that must be done on a regular basis to ensure security stays at a satisfactory level:

- Deny access to systems by undefined users or anonymous accounts.
- Limit and monitor the usage of administrator and other powerful accounts.

- Suspend or delay access capability after a specific number of unsuccessful logon attempts.
- Remove obsolete user accounts as soon as the user leaves the company.
- Suspend inactive accounts after 30 to 60 days.
- Enforce strict access criteria.
- Enforce the need-to-know and least-privilege practices.
- Disable unneeded system features, services, and ports.
- Replace default password settings on accounts.
- Limit and monitor global access rules.
- Ensure logon IDs are not descriptive of job function.
- Remove redundant resource rules from accounts and group memberships.
- Remove redundant user IDs, accounts, and role-based accounts from resource access lists.
- Enforce password rotation.
- Enforce password requirements (length, contents, lifetime, distribution, storage, and transmission).
- Audit system and user events and actions and review reports periodically.
- Protect audit logs.

Even if all of these countermeasures are in place and properly monitored, data can still be lost in an unauthorized manner in other ways. The next section looks at these issues and their corresponding countermeasures.

Unauthorized Disclosure of Information

Several things can make information available to others for whom it is not intended, which can bring about unfavorable results. Sometimes this is done intentionally; other times, unintentionally. Information can be disclosed unintentionally when one falls prey to attacks that specialize in causing this disclosure. These attacks include social engineering, covert channels, malicious code, and electrical airwave sniffing. Information can be disclosed accidentally through object reuse methods, which are explained next. (Social engineering was discussed in Chapter 3, while covert channels will be discussed in Chapter 5.)

Object Reuse

Can I borrow this thumb drive?
Response: Let me destroy it first.

Object reuse issues pertain to reassigning to a subject media that previously contained one or more objects. Huh? This means before someone uses a hard drive, USB drive, or tape, it should be cleared of any residual information still on it. This concept also applies to objects reused by computer processes, such as memory locations, variables, and registers. Any sensitive information that may be left by a process should be securely cleared before allowing another process the opportunity to access the object. This ensures that information not intended for this individual or any other subject is not disclosed. Many times, USB drives are exchanged casually in a work environment. What if a supervisor lent a USB drive to an employee without erasing it and it contained confidential employee performance reports and salary raises forecasted for the next year? This could prove to be a bad decision and may turn into a morale issue if the information was passed around. Formatting a disk or deleting files only removes the pointers to the files; it does not remove the actual files. This information will still be on the disk and available until the operating system needs that space and overwrites those files. So, for media that holds confidential information, more extreme methods should be taken to ensure the files are actually gone, not just their pointers.

Sensitive data should be classified (secret, top secret, confidential, unclassified, and so on) by the data owners. How the data are stored and accessed should also be strictly controlled and audited by software controls. However, it does not end there. Before allowing someone to use previously used media, it should be erased or degaussed. (This responsibility usually falls on the operations department.) If media holds sensitive information and cannot be purged, steps should be created describing how to properly destroy it so no one else can obtain this information.

 NOTE Sometimes hackers actually configure a sector on a hard drive so it is marked as bad and unusable to an operating system, but that is actually fine and may hold malicious data. The operating system will not write information to this sector because it thinks it is corrupted. This is a form of data hiding. Some boot-sector virus routines are capable of putting the main part of their code (payload) into a specific sector of the hard drive, overwriting any data that may have been there, and then protecting it as a bad block.

Emanation Security

Quick, cover your computer and your head in tinfoil!

All electronic devices emit electrical signals. These signals can hold important information, and if an attacker buys the right equipment and positions himself in the right place, he could capture this information from the airwaves and access data transmissions as if he had a tap directly on the network wire.

Several incidents have occurred in which intruders have purchased inexpensive equipment and used it to intercept electrical emissions as they radiated from a computer. This equipment can reproduce data streams and display the data on the intruder's monitor, enabling the intruder to learn of covert operations, find out military strategies, and uncover and exploit confidential information. This is not just stuff found in spy novels. It really happens. So, the proper countermeasures have been devised.

TEMPEST TEMPEST started out as a study carried out by the DoD and then turned into a standard that outlines how to develop countermeasures that control spurious electrical signals emitted by electrical equipment. Special shielding is used on equipment to suppress the signals as they are radiated from devices. TEMPEST equipment is implemented to prevent intruders from picking up information through the airwaves with listening devices. This type of equipment must meet specific standards to be rated as providing TEMPEST shielding protection. TEMPEST refers to standardized technology that suppresses signal emanations with shielding material. Vendors who manufacture this type of equipment must be certified to this standard.

The devices (monitors, computers, printers, and so on) have an outer metal coating, referred to as a *Faraday cage*. This is made of metal with the necessary depth to ensure only a certain amount of radiation is released. In devices that are TEMPEST rated, other components are also modified, especially the power supply, to help reduce the amount of electricity used.

Even allowable limits of emission levels can radiate and still be considered safe. The approved products must ensure only this level of emissions is allowed to escape the devices. This type of protection is usually needed only in military institutions, although other highly secured environments do utilize this kind of safeguard.

Many military organizations are concerned with stray radio frequencies emitted by computers and other electronic equipment because an attacker may be able to pick them up, reconstruct them, and give away secrets meant to stay secret.

TEMPEST technology is complex, cumbersome, and expensive, and therefore only used in highly sensitive areas that really need this high level of protection.

Two alternatives to TEMPEST exist: use white noise or use a control zone concept, both of which are explained next.

 NOTE TEMPEST is the name of a program, and now a standard, that was developed in the late 1950s by the U.S. and British governments to deal with electrical and electromagnetic radiation emitted from electrical equipment, mainly computers. This type of equipment is usually used by intelligence, military, government, and law enforcement agencies, and the selling of such items is under constant scrutiny.

White Noise A countermeasure used to keep intruders from extracting information from electrical transmissions is white noise. White noise is a uniform spectrum of random electrical signals. It is distributed over the full spectrum so the bandwidth is constant and an intruder is not able to decipher real information from random noise or random information.

Control Zone Another alternative to using TEMPEST equipment is to use the zone concept, which was addressed earlier in this chapter. Some facilities use material in their walls to contain electrical signals. This prevents intruders from being able to access information emitted via electrical signals from network devices. This control zone creates a type of security perimeter and is constructed to protect against unauthorized access to data or the compromise of sensitive information.

Access Control Monitoring

Access control monitoring is a method of keeping track of who attempts to access specific company resources. It is an important detective mechanism, and different technologies exist that can fill this need. It is not enough to invest in antivirus and firewall solutions. Companies are finding that monitoring their own internal network has become a way of life.

Intrusion Detection

Intrusion detection systems (IDSs) are different from traditional firewall products because they are designed to detect a security breach. *Intrusion detection* is the process of detecting an unauthorized use of, or attack upon, a computer, network, or telecommunications infrastructure. IDSs are designed to aid in mitigating the damage that can be caused by hacking, or breaking into sensitive computer and network systems. The basic intent of the IDS tool is to spot something suspicious happening on the network and sound an alarm by flashing a message on a network manager's screen, or possibly sending a page or even reconfiguring a firewall's ACL setting. The IDS tools can look for sequences of data bits that might indicate a questionable action or event, or monitor system log and activity recording files. The event does not need to be an intrusion to sound the alarm—any kind of "non-normal" behavior may do the trick.

Although different types of IDS products are available, they all have three common components: sensors, analyzers, and administrator interfaces. The sensors collect traffic and user activity data and send them to an analyzer, which looks for suspicious activity. If the analyzer detects an activity it is programmed to deem as fishy, it sends an alert to the administrator's interface.

IDSs come in two main types: *network-based*, which monitor network communications, and *host-based*, which can analyze the activity within a particular computer system.

IDSs can be configured to watch for attacks, parse audit logs, terminate a connection, alert an administrator as attacks are happening, protect system files, expose a hacker's techniques, illustrate which vulnerabilities need to be addressed, and possibly help track down individual hackers.

Network-Based IDSs

All the sailors love NIDS, because they are always in promiscuous mode.

A network-based IDS (NIDS) uses sensors, which are either host computers with the necessary software installed or dedicated appliances—each with its network interface card (NIC) in promiscuous mode. Normally, NICs watch for traffic that has the address of its host system, broadcasts, and sometimes multicast traffic. The NIC driver copies the data from the transmission medium and sends it up the network protocol stack for processing. When an NIC is put into promiscuous mode, the NIC driver captures all traffic, makes a copy of all packets, and then passes one copy to the TCP stack and one copy to an analyzer to look for specific types of patterns.

An NIDS monitors network traffic and cannot "see" the activity going on inside a computer itself. To monitor the activities within a computer system, a company would need to implement a host-based IDS.

Host-Based IDSs

A host-based IDS (HIDS) can be installed on individual workstations and/or servers to watch for inappropriate or anomalous activity. HIDSs are usually used to make sure users do not delete system files, reconfigure important settings, or put the system at risk in any other way. So, whereas the NIDS understands and monitors the network traffic, a HIDS's universe is limited to the computer itself. A HIDS does not understand or review network traffic, and a NIDS does not "look in" and monitor a system's activity. Each has its own job and stays out of the other's way.

In most environments, HIDS products are installed only on critical servers, not on every system on the network, because of the resource overhead and the administration nightmare that such an installation would cause.

Just to make life a little more confusing, HIDS and NIDS can be one of the following types:

- Signature-based
  - Pattern matching
  - Stateful matching
- Anomaly-based
  - Statistical anomaly–based
  - Protocol anomaly–based
  - Traffic anomaly–based
  - Rule- or Heuristic-based

Knowledge- or Signature-Based Intrusion Detection

Knowledge is accumulated by the IDS vendors about specific attacks and how they are carried out. Models of how the attacks are carried out are developed and called *signatures*. Each identified attack has a signature, which is used to detect an attack in progress or determine if one has occurred within the network. Any action that is not recognized as an attack is considered acceptable.

NOTE Signature-based is also known as pattern matching.

An example of a signature is a packet that has the same source and destination IP address. All packets should have a different source and destination IP address, and if they have the same address, this means a Land attack is under way. In a Land attack, a hacker modifies the packet header so that when a receiving system responds to the sender, it is responding to its own address. Now that seems as though it should be benign enough, but vulnerable systems just do not have the programming code to know what to do in this situation, so they freeze or reboot. Once this type of attack was discovered, the signature-based IDS vendors wrote a signature that looks specifically for packets that contain the same source and destination address.

Signature-based IDSs are the most popular IDS products today, and their effectiveness depends upon regularly updating the software with new signatures, as with antivirus software. This type of IDS is weak against new types of attacks because it can recognize only the ones that have been previously identified and have had signatures written for them. Attacks or viruses discovered in production environments are referred to as being "in the wild." Attacks and viruses that exist but that have not been released are referred to as being "in the zoo." No joke.

State-Based IDSs

Before delving too deep into how a state-based IDS works, you need to understand what the state of a system or application actually is. Every change that an operating system experiences (user logs on, user opens application, application communicates to another application, user inputs data, and so on) is considered a state transition. In a very technical sense, all operating systems and applications are just lines and lines of instructions written to carry out functions on data. The instructions have empty variables, which is where the data is held. So when you use the calculator program and type in 5, an empty variable is instantly populated with this value. By entering that value, you change the state of the application. When applications communicate with each other, they populate empty variables provided in each application's instruction set. So, a state transition is when a variable's value changes, which usually happens continuously within every system.

Specific state changes (activities) take place with specific types of attacks. If an attacker will carry out a remote buffer overflow, then the following state changes will occur:

1. The remote user connects to the system.
2. The remote user sends data to an application (the data exceed the allocated buffer for this empty variable).
3. The data are executed and overwrite the buffer and possibly other memory segments.
4. A malicious code executes.

So, *state* is a snapshot of an operating system's values in volatile, semipermanent, and permanent memory locations. In a state-based IDS, the initial state is the state prior to the execution of an attack, and the compromised state is the state after successful penetration. The IDS has rules that outline which state transition sequences should sound an alarm. The activity that takes place between the initial and compromised state is what the state-based IDS looks for, and it sends an alert if any of the state-transition sequences match its preconfigured rules.

This type of IDS scans for attack signatures in the context of a stream of activity instead of just looking at individual packets. It can only identify known attacks and requires frequent updates of its signatures.

Statistical Anomaly–Based IDS

Through statistical analysis I have determined I am an anomaly in nature.
Response: You have my vote.

A *statistical anomaly–based IDS* is a behavioral-based system. Behavioral-based IDS products do not use predefined signatures, but rather are put in a learning mode to build a profile of an environment's "normal" activities. This profile is built by continually sampling the environment's activities. The longer the IDS is put in a learning mode, in most instances, the more accurate a profile it will build and the better protection it will provide. After this profile is built, all future traffic and activities are compared to it. The same type of sampling that was used to build the profile takes place, so the same type of data is being compared. Anything that does not match the profile is seen as an attack, in response to which the IDS sends an alert. With the use of complex statistical algorithms, the IDS looks for anomalies in the network traffic or user activity. Each packet is given an anomaly score, which indicates its degree of irregularity. If the score is higher than the established threshold of "normal" behavior, then the preconfigured action will take place.

The benefit of using a statistical anomaly–based IDS is that it can react to new attacks. It can detect "0 day" attacks, which means an attack is new to the world and no signature or fix has been developed yet. These products are also capable of detecting the "low and slow" attacks, in which the attacker is trying to stay under the radar by sending packets little by little over a long period of time. The IDS should be able to detect these types of attacks because they are different enough from the contrasted profile.

Now for the bad news. Since the only thing that is "normal" about a network is that it is constantly changing, developing the correct profile that will not provide an overwhelming number of false positives can be difficult. Many IT staff members know all too well this dance of chasing down alerts that end up being benign traffic or activity. In fact, some environments end up turning off their IDS because of the amount of time these activities take up. (Proper education on tuning and configuration will reduce the number of false positives.)

If an attacker detects there is an IDS on a network, she will then try to detect the type of IDS it is so she can properly circumvent it. With a behavioral-based IDS, the attacker could attempt to integrate her activities into the behavior pattern of the network traffic. That way, her activities are seen as "normal" by the IDS and thus go undetected. It is a good idea to ensure no attack activity is underway when the IDS is in learning mode. If this takes place, the IDS will never alert you of this type of attack in the future because it sees this traffic as typical of the environment.

If a corporation decides to use a statistical anomaly–based IDS, it must ensure that the staff members who are implementing and maintaining it understand protocols and packet analysis. Because this type of an IDS sends generic alerts, compared to other types of IDSs, it is up to the network engineer to figure out what the actual issue is. For example, a signature-based IDS reports the type of attack that has been identified, while a rule-based IDS identifies the actual rule the packet does not comply with. In a statistical anomaly–based IDS, all the product really understands is that something "abnormal" has happened, which just means the event does not match the profile.

NOTE A behavior-based IDS is also referred to as a heuristic IDS. The term heuristic means to create new information from different data sources. The IDS gathers different "clues" from the network or system and calculates the probability an attack is taking place. If the probability hits a set threshold, then the alarm sounds.

Attack Techniques

It is common for hackers to first identify whether an IDS is present on the network they are preparing to attack. If one is present, that attacker may implement a Denial-of-Service attack to bring it offline. Another tactic is to send the IDS incorrect data, which will make the IDS send specific alerts indicating a certain attack is under way, when in truth it is not. The goal of these activities is either to disable the IDS or to distract the network and security individuals so they will be busy chasing the wrong packets, while the real attack takes place.

Determining the proper thresholds for statistically significant deviations is really the key for the successful use of a behavioral-based IDS. If the threshold is set too low, nonintrusive activities are considered attacks (false positives). If the threshold is set too high, some malicious activities won't be identified (false negatives).

Once an IDS discovers an attack, several things can happen, depending upon the capabilities of the IDS and the policy assigned to it. The IDS can send an alert to a console to tell the right individuals an attack is being carried out; send an e-mail or page to the individual assigned to respond to such activities; kill the connection of the detected attack; or reconfigure a router or firewall to try to stop any further similar attacks. A modifiable response condition might include anything from blocking a specific IP address to redirecting or blocking a certain type of activity.

Protocol Anomaly–Based IDS

A statistical anomaly–based IDS can use protocol anomaly–based filters. These types of IDSs have specific knowledge of each protocol they will monitor. A protocol anomaly pertains to the format and behavior of a protocol. The IDS builds a model (or profile) of each protocol's "normal" usage. Keep in mind, however, that protocols have *theoretical* usage, as outlined in their corresponding RFCs, and *real-world* usage, which refers to the fact that vendors seem to always "color outside the boxes" and don't strictly follow the RFCs in their protocol development and implementation. So, most profiles of individual protocols are a mix between the official and real-world versions of the protocol and its usage. When the IDS is activated, it looks for anomalies that do not match the profiles built for the individual protocols.

Although several vulnerabilities within operating systems and applications are available to be exploited, many more successful attacks take place by exploiting vulnerabilities in the protocols themselves. At the OSI data link layer, the Address Resolution Protocol (ARP) does not have any protection against ARP attacks where bogus data is inserted into its table. At the network layer, the Internet Control Message Protocol

What's in a Name?

Signature-based IDSs are also known as misuse-detection systems, and behavioral-based IDSs are also known as profile-based systems.

(ICMP) can be used in a Loki attack to move data from one place to another, when this protocol was designed to only be used to send status information—not user data. IP headers can be easily modified for spoofed attacks. At the transport layer, TCP packets can be injected into the connection between two systems for a session hijacking attack.

 NOTE When an attacker compromises a computer and loads a backdoor on the system, he will need to have a way to communicate to this computer through this backdoor and stay "under the radar" of the network firewall and IDS. Hackers have figured out that a small amount of code can be inserted into an ICMP packet, which is then interpreted by the backdoor software loaded on a compromised system. Security devices are usually not configured to monitor this type of traffic because ICMP is a protocol that is supposed to be used just to send status information—not commands to a compromised system.

Because every packet formation and delivery involves many protocols, and because more attack vectors exist in the protocols than in the software itself, it is a good idea to integrate protocol anomaly–based filters in any network behavioral-based IDS.

Traffic Anomaly–Based IDS

Most behavioral-based IDSs have traffic anomaly–based filters, which detect changes in traffic patterns, as in DoS attacks or a new service that appears on the network. Once a profile is built that captures the baselines of an environment's ordinary traffic, all future traffic patterns are compared to that profile. As with all filters, the thresholds are tunable to adjust the sensitivity, and to reduce the number of false positives and false negatives. Since this is a type of statistical anomaly–based IDS, it can detect unknown attacks.

Rule-Based IDS

A rule-based IDS takes a different approach than a signature-based or statistical anomaly–based system. A signature-based IDS is very straightforward. For example, if a signature-based IDS detects a packet that has all of its TCP header flags with the bit value of 1, it knows that an xmas attack is under way—so it sends an alert. A statistical anomaly–based IDS is also straightforward. For example, if Bob has logged on to his computer at 6 A.M. and the profile indicates this is abnormal, the IDS sends an alert, because this is seen as an activity that needs to be investigated. Rule-based intrusion detection gets a little trickier, depending upon the complexity of the rules used.

Rule-based intrusion detection is commonly associated with the use of an expert system. An expert system is made up of a knowledge base, inference engine, and rule-based programming. Knowledge is represented as rules, and the data to be analyzed are referred to as facts. The knowledge of the system is written in rule-based programming (IF *situation* THEN *action*). These rules are applied to the facts, the data that comes in from a sensor, or a system that is being monitored. For example, in scenario 1 the IDS pulls data from a system's audit log and stores it temporarily in its fact database, as illustrated in Figure 4-22. Then, the preconfigured rules are applied to this data to indicate whether anything suspicious is taking place. In our scenario, the rule states "IF *a root user creates File1* AND *creates File2* SUCH THAT *they are in the same directory* THEN *there is a call to Administrative Tool1* TRIGGER *send alert.*" This rule has been defined such that if a root user creates two files in the same directory and then makes a call to a specific administrative tool, an alert should be sent.

It is the inference engine that provides some artificial intelligence into this process. An inference engine can infer new information from provided data by using inference rules. To understand what inferring means in the first place, let's look at the following:

Socrates is a man.

All men are mortals.

Thus, we can infer that Socrates is mortal. If you are asking "What does this have to do with a hill of beans?" just hold on to your hat—here we go.

Regular programming languages deal with the "black and white" of life. The answer is either yes or no, not maybe this or maybe that. Although computers can carry out complex computations at a much faster rate than humans, they have a harder time guessing, or inferring, answers because they are very structured. The fifth-generation programming languages (artificial intelligence languages) are capable of dealing with the grayer areas of life and can attempt to infer the right solution from the provided data.

So, in a rule-based IDS founded on an expert system, the IDS gathers data from a sensor or log, and the inference engine uses its preprogrammed rules on it. If the characteristics of the rules are met, an alert or solution is provided.

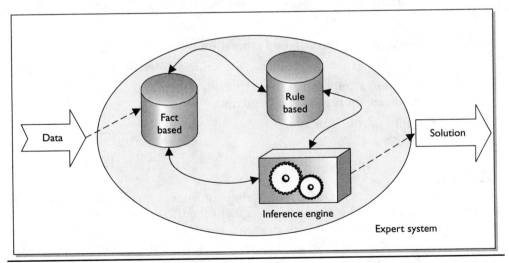

Figure 4-22 Rule-based IDS and expert system components

IDS Types

It is important to understand the characteristics that make the different types of IDS technologies distinct. The following is a summary:

- **Signature-based**
  - Pattern matching, similar to antivirus software
  - Signatures must be continuously updated
  - Cannot identify new attacks
  - Two types:
    - **Pattern matching** Compares packets to signatures
    - **Stateful matching** Compares patterns to several activities at once
- **Anomaly-based**
  - Behavioral-based system that learns the "normal" activities of an environment
  - Can detect new attacks
  - Also called behavior- or heuristic-based
  - Three types:
    - **Statistical anomaly–based** Creates a profile of "normal" and compares activities to this profile
    - **Protocol anomaly–based** Identifies protocols used outside of their common bounds
    - **Traffic anomaly–based** Identifies unusual activity in network traffic
- **Rule-based**
  - Use of IF/THEN rule-based programming within expert systems
  - Use of an expert system allows for artificial intelligence characteristics
  - The more complex the rules, the more demands on software and hardware processing requirements
  - Cannot detect new attacks

IDS Sensors

Network-based IDSs use sensors for monitoring purposes. A sensor, which works as an analysis engine, is placed on the network segment the IDS is responsible for monitoring. The sensor receives raw data from an event generator, as shown in Figure 4-23, and compares it to a signature database, profile, or model, depending upon the type of IDS. If there is some type of a match, which indicates suspicious activity, the sensor works with the response module to determine what type of activity must take place (alerting through instant messaging, paging, or by e-mail, carrying out firewall reconfiguration, and so on). The sensor's role is to filter received data, discard irrelevant information, and detect suspicious activity.

Switched Environments

NIDSs have a harder time working on a switched network, compared to traditional nonswitched environments, because data are transferred through independent virtual circuits and not broadcasted, as in nonswitched environments. The IDS sensor acts as a sniffer and does not have access to all the traffic in these individual circuits. So, we have to take all the data on each individual virtual private connection, make a copy of it, and put the copies of the data on one port (spanning port) where the sensor is located. This allows the sensor to have access to all the data going back and forth on a switched network.

A monitoring console monitors all sensors and supplies the network staff with an overview of the activities of all the sensors in the network. These are the components that enable network-based intrusion detection to actually work. Sensor placement is a critical part of configuring an effective IDS. An organization can place a sensor outside of the firewall to detect attacks and place a sensor inside the firewall (in the perimeter network) to detect actual intrusions. Sensors should also be placed in highly sensitive areas, DMZs, and on extranets. Figure 4-24 shows the sensors reporting their findings to the central console.

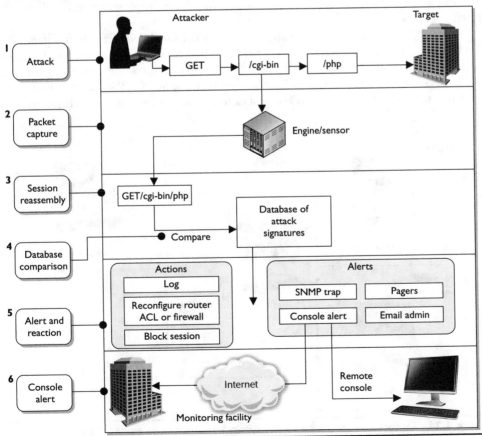

Figure 4-23   The basic architecture of an NIDS

The IDS can be centralized, as firewall products that have IDS functionality integrated within them, or distributed, with multiple sensors throughout the network.

Network Traffic

If the network traffic volume exceeds the IDS system's threshold, attacks may go unnoticed. Each vendor's IDS product has its own threshold, and you should know and understand that threshold before you purchase and implement the IDS.

In very high-traffic environments, multiple sensors should be in place to ensure all packets are investigated. If necessary to optimize network bandwidth and speed, different sensors can be set up to analyze each packet for different signatures. That way, the analysis load can be broken up over different points.

Intrusion Prevention Systems

An ounce of prevention does something good.
Response: Yeah, causes a single point of failure.

In the industry, there is constant frustration with the inability of existing products to stop the bad guys from accessing and manipulating corporate assets. This has created a market demand for vendors to get creative and come up with new, innovative technologies and new products for companies to purchase, implement, and still be frustrated with.

The next "big thing" in the IDS arena has been the *intrusion prevention system (IPS)*. The traditional IDS only detects that something bad may be taking place and sends an alert. The goal of an IPS is to detect this activity and not allow the traffic to gain access to the target in the first place, as shown in Figure 4-25. So, an IPS is a preventative and proactive technology, whereas an IDS is a detective and after-the-fact technology.

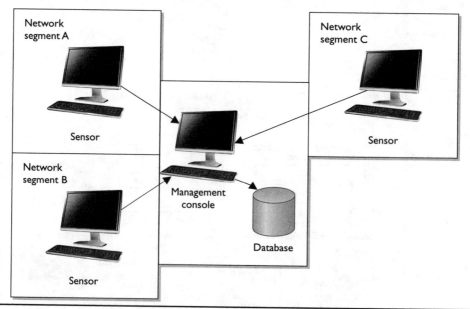

Figure 4-24   Sensors must be placed in each network segment to be monitored by the IDS.

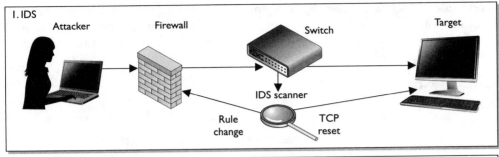

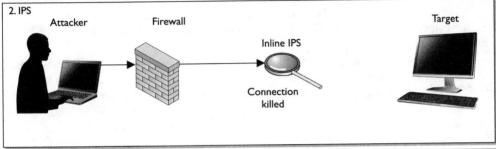

Figure 4-25 IDS vs. IPS architecture

Honeypot

Hey, curious, ill-willed, and destructive attackers, look at this shiny new vulnerable computer.

A *honeypot* is a computer set up as a sacrificial lamb on the network. The system is not locked down and has open ports and services enabled. This is to entice a would-be attacker to this computer instead of attacking authentic production systems on a network. The honeypot contains no real company information, and thus will not be at risk if and when it is attacked.

This enables the administrator to know when certain types of attacks are happening so he can fortify the environment and perhaps track down the attacker. The longer the hacker stays at the honeypot, the more information will be disclosed about her techniques.

It is important to draw a line between *enticement* and *entrapment* when implementing a honeypot system. Legal and liability issues surround each. If the system only has open ports and services that an attacker might want to take advantage of, this would be an example of enticement. If the system has a web page indicating the user

Intrusion Responses

Most IDSs and IPSs are capable of several types of response to a triggered event. An IDS can send out a special signal to drop or kill the packet connections at both the source and destinations. This effectively disconnects the communication and does not allow it to be transmitted. An IDS might block a user from accessing a resource on a host system, if the threshold is set to trigger this response. An IDS can send alerts of an event trigger to other hosts, IDS monitors, and administrators.

can download files, and once the user does this the administrator charges this user with trespassing, it would be entrapment. Entrapment is where the intruder is induced or tricked into committing a crime. Entrapment is illegal and cannot be used when charging an individual with hacking or unauthorized activity.

Network Sniffers

I think I smell a packet!

Response: Nope. It's my feet.

A packet or network *sniffer* is a general term for programs or devices able to examine traffic on a LAN segment. Traffic that is being transferred over a network medium is transmitted as electrical signals, encoded in binary representation. The sniffer has to have a protocol-analysis capability to recognize the different protocol values to properly interpret their meaning.

The sniffer has to have access to a network adapter that works in promiscuous mode, and a driver that captures the data. This data can be overwhelming, so it must be properly filtered. The filtered data are stored in a buffer, and this information is displayed to a user and/or captured in logs. Some utilities have sniffer and packet-modification capabilities, which is how some types of spoofing and man-in-the-middle attacks are carried out.

Network sniffers are used by the people in the white hats (administrators and security professionals) usually to try and track down a recent problem with the network. But the guys in the black hats (attackers and crackers) can use them to learn about what type of data is passed over a specific network segment and to modify data in an unauthorized manner. Black hats usually use sniffers to obtain credentials as they pass over the network medium.

 NOTE Sniffers are dangerous because they are very hard to detect and their activities are difficult to audit.

A Few Threats to Access Control

As a majority of security professionals know, there is more risk and a higher probability of an attacker causing mayhem from within an organization than from outside it. However, many people within organizations do not know this fact, because they only hear stories about the outside attackers who defaced a web server or circumvented a firewall to access confidential information.

An attacker from the outside can enter through remote access entry points, enter through firewalls and web servers, physically break in, or exploit a partner communication path (extranet, vendor connection, and so on). An insider has legitimate reasons for using the systems and resources, but can misuse his privileges and launch an actual attack also. The danger of insiders is that they have already been given a wide range of access that a hacker would have to work to obtain; they probably have intimate knowledge of the environment; and, generally, they are trusted. We have discussed many different types of access control mechanisms that work to keep the outsiders outside and restrict insiders' abilities to a minimum and audit their actions. Now we will look at some specific attacks commonly carried out in environments today by insiders or outsiders.

Dictionary Attack

Several programs can enable an attacker (or proactive administrator) to identify user credentials. This type of program is fed lists (dictionaries) of commonly used words or combinations of characters, and then compares these values to capture passwords. In other words, the program hashes the dictionary words and compares the resulting message digest with the system password file that also stores its passwords in a one-way hashed format. If the hashed values match, it means a password has just been uncovered. Once the right combination of characters is identified, the attacker can use this password to authenticate herself as a legitimate user. Because many systems have a threshold that dictates how many failed logon attempts are acceptable, the same type of activity can happen to a captured password file. The dictionary-attack program hashes the combination of characters and compares it to the hashed entries in the password file. If a match is found, the program has uncovered a password.

The dictionaries come with the password cracking programs, and extra dictionaries can be found on several sites on the Internet.

NOTE Passwords should never be transmitted or stored in cleartext. Most operating systems and applications put the passwords through hashing algorithms, which result in hash values, also referred to as message digest values.

Countermeasures

To properly protect an environment against dictionary and other password attacks, the following practices should be followed:

- Do not allow passwords to be sent in cleartext.
- Encrypt the passwords with encryption algorithms or hashing functions.
- Employ one-time password tokens.
- Use hard-to-guess passwords.
- Rotate passwords frequently.
- Employ an IDS to detect suspicious behavior.
- Use dictionary cracking tools to find weak passwords chosen by users.
- Use special characters, numbers, and upper- and lowercase letters within the password.
- Protect password files.

Brute Force Attacks

I will try over and over until you are defeated.
Response: Okay, wake me when you are done.

Several types of **brute force attacks** can be implemented, but each continually tries different inputs to achieve a predefined goal. Brute force is defined as "trying every possible combination until the correct one is identified." So in a brute force password attack, the software tool will see if the first letter is an "a" and continue through the alphabet until that single value is uncovered. Then the tool moves on to the second value, and so on.

The most effective way to uncover passwords is through a hybrid attack, which combines a dictionary attack and a brute force attack. If a dictionary tool has found that a user's password starts with Dallas, then the brute force tool will try Dallas1, Dallas01, Dallasa1, and so on until a successful logon credential is uncovered. (A brute force attack is also known as an exhaustive attack.)

These attacks are also used in **wardialing** efforts, in which the wardialer inserts a long list of phone numbers into a wardialing program in hopes of finding a modem that can be exploited to gain unauthorized access. A program is used to dial many phone numbers and weed out the numbers used for voice calls and fax machine services. The attacker usually ends up with a handful of numbers he can now try to exploit to gain access into a system or network.

So, a brute force attack perpetuates a specific activity with different input parameters until the goal is achieved.

Countermeasures

For phone brute force attacks, auditing and monitoring of this type of activity should be in place to uncover patterns that could indicate a wardialing attack:

- Perform brute force attacks to find weaknesses and hanging modems.
- Make sure only necessary phone numbers are made public.
- Provide stringent access control methods that would make brute force attacks less successful.
- Monitor and audit for such activity.
- Employ an IDS to watch for suspicious activity.
- Set lockout thresholds.

Spoofing at Logon

So, what are your credentials again?

An attacker can use a program that presents to the user a fake logon screen, which often tricks the user into attempting to log on. The user is asked for a username and password, which are stored for the attacker to access at a later time. The user does not know this is not his usual logon screen because they look exactly the same. A fake error message can appear, indicating that the user mistyped his credentials. At this point, the fake logon program exits and hands control over to the operating system, which prompts the user for a username and password. The user assumes he mistyped his information and doesn't give it a second thought, but an attacker now knows the user's credentials.

Phishing

Hello, this is your bank. Hand over your SSN, credit card number, and your shoe size.
Response: Okay, that sounds honest enough.

Phishing is a type of social engineering with the goal of obtaining personal information, credentials, credit card number, or financial data. The attackers lure, or fish, for sensitive data through various different methods.

The term *phishing* was coined in 1996 when hackers started stealing America Online (AOL) passwords. The hackers would pose as AOL staff members and send messages to victims asking them for their passwords in order to verify correct billing information or verify information about the AOL accounts. Once the password was provided, the hacker authenticated as that victim and used his e-mail account for criminal purposes, as in spamming, pornography, and so on.

Although phishing has been around since the 1990s, many people did not fully become aware of it until mid-2003 when these types of attacks spiked. Phishers created convincing e-mails requesting potential victims to click a link to update their bank account information.

Victims click these links and are presented with a form requesting bank account numbers, Social Security numbers, credentials, and other types of data that can be used in identity theft crimes. These types of phishing e-mail scams have increased dramatically in recent years with some phishers masquerading as large banking companies, PayPal, eBay, Amazon.com, and other well-known Internet entities.

Phishers also create web sites that look very similar to legitimate sites and lure victims to them through e-mail messages and other web sites to gain the same type of information. Some sites require the victims to provide their Social Security numbers, date of birth, and mother's maiden name for authentication purposes before they can update their account information.

The nefarious web sites not only have the look and feel of the legitimate web site, but attackers would provide URLs with domain names that look very similar to the legitimate site's address. For example, www.amazon.com might become www.amzaon.com. Or use a specially placed @ symbol. For example, www.msn.com@notmsn.com would actually take the victim to the web site notmsn.com and provide the username of www.msn.com to this web site. The username www.msn.com would not be a valid username for notmsn.com, so the victim would just be shown the home page of notmsn.com. Now, notmsn.com is a nefarious site and created to look and feel just like www.msn.com. The victim feels comfortable he is at a legitimate site and logs on with his credentials.

Some JavaScript commands are even designed to show the victim an incorrect web address. So let's say Bob is a suspicious and vigilant kind of a guy. Before he inputs his username and password to authenticate and gain access to his online bank account, he always checks the URL values in the address bar of his browser. Even though he closely inspects it to make sure he is not getting duped, there could be a JavaScript replacing the URL www.evilandwilltakeallyourmoney.com with www.citibank.com so he thinks things are safe and life is good.

 NOTE There have been fixes to the previously mentioned attack dealing with URLs, but it is important to know that attackers will continually come up with new ways of carrying out these attacks. Just knowing about phishing doesn't mean you can properly detect or prevent it. As a security professional, you must keep up with the new and tricky strategies deployed by attackers.

Some attacks use pop-up forms when a victim is at a legitimate site. So if you were at your bank's actual web site and a pop-up window appeared asking you for some sensitive information, this probably wouldn't worry you since you were communicating with your actual bank's web site. You may believe the window came from your bank's web server, so you fill it out as instructed. Unfortunately, this pop-up window could be from another source entirely, and your data could be placed right in the attacker's hands, not your bank's.

With this personal information, phishers can create new accounts in the victim's name, gain authorized access to bank accounts, and make illegal credit card purchases or cash advances.

 CAUTION Attackers also install key loggers on systems to gather victims' credentials, Social Security numbers, and bank account information. Key loggers are pieces of software that capture all the keystrokes a user types in.

As more people have become aware of these types of attacks and grown wary of clicking embedded links in e-mail messages, phishers have varied their attack methods. For instance, they began sending e-mails that indicate to the user that they have won a prize or that there is a problem with a financial account. The e-mail instructs the person to call a number, which has an automated voice asking the victim to type in their credit card number or Social Security number for authentication purposes.

In 2006, at least 35 phishing web sites were identified that carried out attacks on many banks' token-based authentication systems. Federal guidelines requested that financial institutions implement two-factor authentication for online transactions. To meet this need, some banks provided their customers with token devices that created one-time passwords. Countering, phishers set up fake web sites that looked like the financial institution, duping victims into typing their one-time passwords. The web sites would then send these credentials to the actual bank web site, authenticate as this user, and gain access to their account.

A similar type of attack is called *pharming*, which redirects a victim to a seemingly legitimate, yet fake, web site. In this type of attack, the attacker carries out something called DNS poisoning, in which a DNS server resolves a host name into an incorrect IP address. When you type www.logicalsecurity.com into the address bar of your web browser, your computer really has no idea what this data is. So an internal request is made to review your TCP/IP network setting, which contains the IP address of the DNS server your computer is supposed to use. Your system then sends a request to this DNS server basically asking "Do you have the IP address for www.logicalsecurity.com?" The

DNS server reviews its resource records and if it has one with this information in it, it sends the IP address for the server that is hosting www.logicalsecurity.com to your computer. Your browser then shows the home page of this web site you requested.

Now, what if an attacker poisoned this DNS server so the resource record has the wrong information? When you type in www.logicalsecurity.com and your system sends a request to the DNS server, the DNS server will send your system the IP address that it has recorded, not knowing it is incorrect. So instead of going to www.logicalsecurity .com, you are sent to www.bigbooty.com. This could make you happy or sad, depending upon your interests, but you are not at the site you requested.

So, let's say the victim types in a web address of www.nicebank.com, as illustrated in Figure 4-26. The victim's system sends a request to a poisoned DNS server, which points the victim to a different web site. This different web site looks and feels just like the requested web site, so the user enters his username and password and may even be presented with web pages that look legitimate.

The benefit of a pharming attack to the attacker is that it can affect a large amount of victims without the need for sending out e-mails, and the victims usually fall for this more easily since they are requesting to go to a web site themselves.

Identity Theft

I'm glad someone stole my identity. I'm tired of being me.

Identity theft refers to a situation where someone obtains key pieces of personal information such as a driver's license number, bank account number, credentials, or Social Security number, and then uses that information to impersonate someone else.

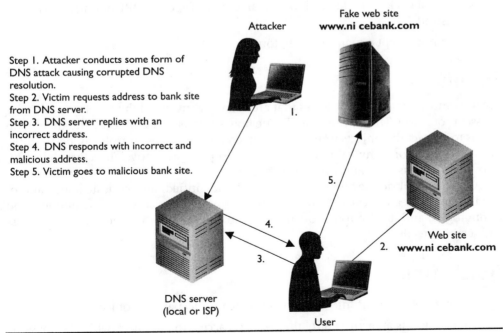

Step 1. Attacker conducts some form of DNS attack causing corrupted DNS resolution.
Step 2. Victim requests address to bank site from DNS server.
Step 3. DNS server replies with an incorrect address.
Step 4. DNS responds with incorrect and malicious address.
Step 5. Victim goes to malicious bank site.

Figure 4-26 Pharming has been a common attack over the last couple of years.

Typically, identity thieves will use the personal information to obtain credit, merchandise, services in the name of the victim, or false credentials for the thief. This can result in such things as ruining the victim's credit rating, generating false criminal records, and issuing arrest warrants for the wrong individuals. Identity theft is categorized in two ways: true name and account takeover. True name identity theft means the thief uses personal information to open new accounts. The thief might open a new credit card account, establish cellular phone service, or open a new checking account in order to obtain blank checks. Account takeover identity theft means the imposter uses personal information to gain access to the person's existing accounts. Typically, the thief will change the mailing address on an account and run up a huge bill before the person, whose identity has been stolen, realizes there is a problem. The Internet has made it easier for an identity thief to use the information they've stolen because transactions can be made without any personal interaction.

Countermeasures to phishing attacks include the following:

- Be skeptical of e-mails indicating you must make changes to your accounts, or warnings stating an account will be terminated if you don't perform some online activity.
- Call the legitimate company to find out if this is a fraudulent message.
- Review the address bar to see if the domain name is correct.
- When submitting any type of financial information or credential data, an SSL connection should be set up, which is indicated in the address bar (https://) and a closed-padlock icon in the browser at the bottom-right corner.
- Do not click an HTML link within an e-mail. Type the URL out manually instead.
- Do not accept e-mail in HTML format.

Summary

Access controls are security features that are usually considered the first line of defense in asset protection. They are used to dictate how subjects access objects, and their main goal is to protect the objects from unauthorized access. These controls can be administrative, physical, or technical in nature and can supply preventive, detective, deterrent, recovery, compensative, and corrective services.

Access control defines how users should be identified, authenticated, and authorized. These issues are carried out differently in different access control models and technologies, and it is up to the organization to determine which best fits its business and security needs.

Quick Tips

- Access is a flow of information between a subject and an object.
- A subject is an active entity that requests access to an object, which is a passive entity.

- A subject can be a user, program, or process.
- Confidentiality is the assurance that information is not disclosed to unauthorized subjects.
- Some security mechanisms that provide confidentiality are encryption, logical and physical access control, transmission protocols, database views, and controlled traffic flow.
- Identity management solutions include directories, web access management, password management, legacy single sign-on, account management, and profile update.
- Password synchronization reduces the complexity of keeping up with different passwords for different systems.
- Self-service password reset reduces help-desk call volumes by allowing users to reset their own passwords.
- Assisted password reset reduces the resolution process for password issues for the help-desk department.
- IdM directories contain all resource information, users' attributes, authorization profiles, roles, and possibly access control policies so other IdM applications have one centralized resource from which to gather this information.
- An automated workflow component is common in account management products that provide IdM solutions.
- User provisioning refers to the creation, maintenance, and deactivation of user objects and attributes, as they exist in one or more systems, directories, or applications.
- The HR database is usually considered the authoritative source for user identities because that is where it is first developed and properly maintained.
- There are three main access control models: discretionary, mandatory, and nondiscretionary.
- Discretionary access control (DAC) enables data owners to dictate what subjects have access to the files and resources they own.
- Mandatory access control (MAC) uses a security label system. Users have clearances, and resources have security labels that contain data classifications. MAC compares these two attributes to determine access control capabilities.
- Nondiscretionary access control uses a role-based method to determine access rights and permissions.
- Role-based access control is based on the user's role and responsibilities within the company.
- Three main types of restricted interface measurements exist: menus and shells, database views, and physically constrained interfaces.
- Access control lists are bound to objects and indicate what subjects can use them.

- A capability table is bound to a subject and lists what objects it can access.
- Access control can be administered in two main ways: centralized and decentralized.
- Some examples of centralized administration access control technologies are RADIUS, TACACS+, and Diameter.
- A decentralized administration example is a peer-to-peer working group.
- Examples of administrative controls are a security policy, personnel controls, supervisory structure, security-awareness training, and testing.
- Examples of physical controls are network segregation, perimeter security, computer controls, work area separation, data backups, and cable.
- Examples of technical controls are system access, network architecture, network access, encryption and protocols, and auditing.
- Access control mechanisms provide one or more of the following functionalities: preventive, detective, corrective, deterrent, recovery, or compensative.
- For a subject to be able to access a resource, it must be identified, authenticated, and authorized, and should be held accountable for its actions.
- Authentication can be accomplished by biometrics, a password, a passphrase, a cognitive password, a one-time password, or a token.
- A Type I error in biometrics means the system rejected an authorized individual, and a Type II error means an imposter was authenticated.
- A memory card cannot process information, but a smart card can.
- Access controls should default to no access.
- Least-privilege and need-to-know principles limit users' rights to only what is needed to perform tasks of their job.
- Single sign-on technology requires a user to be authenticated to the network only one time.
- Single sign-on capabilities can be accomplished through Kerberos, SESAME, domains, and thin clients.
- In Kerberos, a user receives a ticket from the KDC so they can authenticate to a service.
- The Kerberos user receives a ticket granting ticket (TGT), which allows him to request access to resources through the ticket granting service (TGS). The TGS generates a new ticket with the session keys.
- Types of access control attacks include denial of service, spoofing, dictionary, brute force, and wardialing.
- Audit logs can track user activities, application events, and system events.
- Keystroke monitoring is a type of auditing that tracks each keystroke made by a user.

- Audit logs should be protected and reviewed.
- Object reuse can unintentionally disclose information.
- Just removing pointers to files is not always enough protection for proper object reuse.
- Information can be obtained via electrical signals in airwaves. The ways to combat this type of intrusion are TEMPEST, white noise, and control zones.
- User authentication is accomplished by what someone knows, is, or has.
- One-time password-generating token devices can use synchronous or asynchronous methods.
- Strong authentication requires two of the three user authentication attributes (what someone knows, is, or has).
- Kerberos addresses privacy and integrity but not availability.
- The following are weaknesses of Kerberos: the KDC is a single point of failure; it is susceptible to password guessing; session and secret keys are locally stored; KDC needs to always be available; and there must be management of secret keys.
- IDSs can be statistical (monitor behavior) or signature-based (watch for known attacks).
- Degaussing is a safeguard against disclosure of confidential information because it returns media back to its original state.
- Phishing is a type of social engineering with the goal of obtaining personal information, credentials, credit card number, or financial data.

Questions

Please remember that these questions are formatted and asked in a certain way for a reason. Remember that the CISSP exam is asking questions at a conceptual level. Questions may not always have the perfect answer, and the candidate is advised against always looking for the perfect answer. Instead, the candidate should look for the best answer in the list.

1. Which of the following statements correctly describes biometric methods?

    A. They are the least expensive and provide the most protection.

    B. They are the most expensive and provide the least protection.

    C. They are the least expensive and provide the least protection.

    D. They are the most expensive and provide the most protection.

2. What is derived from a passphrase?

    A. Personal password

    B. Virtual password

    C. User ID

    D. Valid password

3. Which of the following statements correctly describes passwords?

 A. They are the least expensive and most secure.

 B. They are the most expensive and least secure.

 C. They are the least expensive and least secure.

 D. They are the most expensive and most secure.

4. What is the reason for enforcing the separation of duties?

 A. No one person can complete all the steps of a critical activity.

 B. It induces an atmosphere for collusion.

 C. It increases dependence on individuals.

 D. It makes critical tasks easier to accomplish.

5. Which of the following is not a logical access control?

 A. Encryption

 B. Network architecture

 C. ID badge

 D. Access control matrix

6. An access control model should be applied in a _____ manner.

 A. Detective

 B. Recovery

 C. Corrective

 D. Preventive

7. Which access control policy is enforced when an environment uses a nondiscretionary model?

 A. Rule-based

 B. Role-based

 C. Identity-based

 D. Mandatory

8. How is a challenge/response protocol utilized with token device implementations?

 A. This protocol is not used; cryptography is used.

 B. An authentication service generates a challenge, and the smart token generates a response based on the challenge.

 C. The token challenges the user for a username and password.

 D. The token challenges the user's password against a database of stored credentials.

9. Which access control method is user-directed?

 A. Nondiscretionary

B. Mandatory

C. Identity-based

D. Discretionary

10. Which provides the best authentication?

    A. What a person knows

    B. What a person is

    C. What a person has

    D. What a person has and knows

11. Which item is not part of a Kerberos authentication implementation?

    A. Message authentication code

    B. Ticket granting service

    C. Authentication service

    D. Users, programs, and services

12. Which model implements access control matrices to control how subjects interact with objects?

    A. Mandatory

    B. Centralized

    C. Decentralized

    D. Discretionary

13. What does authentication mean?

    A. Registering a user

    B. Identifying a user

    C. Validating a user

    D. Authorizing a user

14. If a company has a high turnover rate, which access control structure is best?

    A. Role-based

    B. Decentralized

    C. Rule-based

    D. Discretionary

15. A password is mainly used for what function?

    A. Identity

    B. Registration

    C. Authentication

    D. Authorization

16. The process of mutual authentication involves _____.

   A. A user authenticating to a system and the system authenticating to the user

   B. A user authenticating to two systems at the same time

   C. A user authenticating to a server and then to a process

   D. A user authenticating, receiving a ticket, and then authenticating to a service

17. Reviewing audit logs is an example of which security function?

   A. Preventive

   B. Detective

   C. Deterrence

   D. Corrective

18. In discretionary access control security, who has delegation authority to grant access to data?

   A. User

   B. Security office

   C. Security policy

   D. Owner

19. Which could be considered a single point of failure within a single sign-on implementation?

   A. Authentication server

   B. User's workstation

   C. Logon credentials

   D. RADIUS

20. What role does biometrics play in access control?

   A. Authorization

   B. Authenticity

   C. Authentication

   D. Accountability

21. What determines if an organization is going to operate under a discretionary, mandatory, or nondiscretionary access control model?

   A. Administrator

   B. Security policy

   C. Culture

   D. Security levels

22. What type of attack attempts all possible solutions?

   A. Dictionary

    B. Brute force

    C. Man-in-the-middle

    D. Spoofing

23. Spoofing can be described as which of the following?

    A. Eavesdropping on a communication link

    B. Working through a list of words

    C. Session hijacking

    D. Pretending to be someone or something else

24. Which of the following is not an advantage of a centralized access control administration?

    A. Flexibility

    B. Standardization

    C. A higher level of security

    D. No need for different interpretations of a necessary security level

25. Which of the following best describes what role-based access control offers companies in reducing administrative burdens?

    A. It allows entities closer to the resources to make decisions about who can and cannot access resources.

    B. It provides a centralized approach for access control, which frees up department managers.

    C. User membership in roles can be easily revoked and new ones established as job assignments dictate.

    D. It enforces enterprisewide security policies, standards, and guidelines.

26. Which of the following is the best description of directories and how they relate to identity management?

    A. Most are hierarchical and follow the X.500 standard.

    B. Most have a flat architecture and follow the X.400 standard.

    C. Most have moved away from LDAP.

    D. Many use LDA.

27. Which of the following is not part of user provisioning?

    A. Creation and deactivation of user accounts

    B. Business process implementation

    C. Maintenance and deactivation of user objects and attributes

    D. Delegating user administration

28. What is the technology that allows a user to remember just one password?

    A. Password generation

    B. Password dictionaries

    C. Password rainbow tables

    D. Password synchronization

29. Which of the following is not considered an anomaly-based intrusion protection system?

    A. Statistical anomaly–based

    B. Protocol anomaly–based

    C. Temporal anomaly–based

    D. Traffic anomaly–based

30. The next graphic covers which of the following:

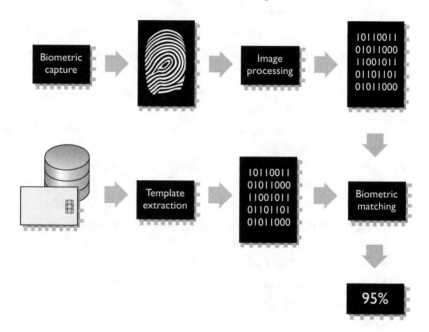

    A. Crossover error rate

    B. Identity verification

    C. Authorization rates

    D. Authentication error rates

31. The diagram shown next explains which of the following concepts:

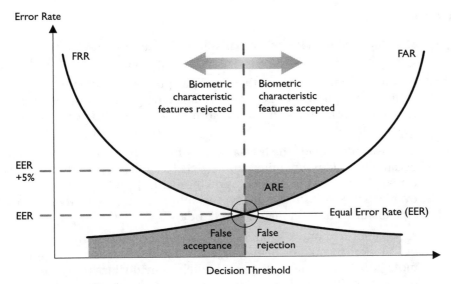

A. Crossover error rate.

B. Type III errors.

C. FAR equals FRR in systems that have a high crossover error rate.

D. Biometrics is a high acceptance technology.

32. The graphic shown here illustrates how which of the following works:

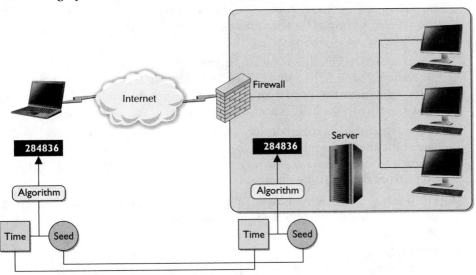

A. Rainbow tables

B. Dictionary attack

C. One-time password

D. Strong authentication

Answers

1. **D**. Compared with the other available authentication mechanisms, biometric methods provide the highest level of protection and are the most expensive.

2. **B**. Most systems do not use the actual passphrase or password the user enters. Instead, they put this value through some type of encryption or hashing function to come up with another format of that value, referred to as a virtual password.

3. **C**. Passwords provide the least amount of protection, but are the cheapest because they do not require extra readers (as with smart cards and memory cards), do not require devices (as do biometrics), and do not require a lot of overhead in processing (as in cryptography). Passwords are the most common type of authentication method used today.

4. **A**. Separation of duties is put into place to ensure one entity cannot carry out a task that could be damaging or risky to the company. It requires two or more people to come together to do their individual tasks to accomplish the overall task. If a person wanted to commit fraud and separation of duties were in place, they would need to participate in collusion.

5. **C**. A logical control is the same thing as a technical control. All of the answers were logical in nature except an ID badge. Badges are used for physical security and are considered physical controls.

6. **D**. The best approach to security is to try to prevent bad things from occurring by putting the necessary controls and mechanisms in place. Detective controls should also be implemented, but a security model should not work from a purely detective approach.

7. **B**. Roles work as containers for users. The administrator or security professional creates the roles and assigns rights to them and then assigns users to the container. The users then inherit the permissions and rights from the containers (roles), which is how implicit permissions are obtained.

8. **B**. An asynchronous token device is based on challenge/response mechanisms. The authentication service sends the user a challenge value, which the user enters into the token. The token encrypts or hashes this value, and the user uses this as her one-time password.

9. **D**. The DAC model allows users, or data owners, the discretion of letting other users access their resources. DAC is implemented by ACLs, which the data owner can configure.

10. **D**. This is considered a strong authentication approach because it is two-factor—it uses two out of the possible three authentication techniques (something a person knows, is, or has).

11. **A**. Message authentication code (MAC) is a cryptographic function and is not a key component of Kerberos. Kerberos is made up of a KDC, a realm of principals (users, services, applications, and devices), an authentication service, tickets, and a ticket granting service.

12. **D.** DAC is implemented and enforced through the use of access control lists (ACLs), which are held in a matrix. MAC is implemented and enforced through the use of security labels.

13. **C.** Authentication means to validate the identity of a user. In most systems, the user must submit some type of public information (username, account number) and a second credential to prove this identity. The second piece of the credential set is private and should not be shared.

14. **A.** It is easier on the administrator if she only has to create one role, assign all of the necessary rights and permissions to that role, and plug a user into that role when needed. Otherwise, she would need to assign and extract permissions and rights on all systems as each individual came and left the company.

15. **C.** As stated in a previous question, passwords are the most common authentication mechanism used today. They are used to validate a user's identity.

16. **A.** Mutual authentication means it is happening in both directions. Instead of just the user having to authenticate to the server, the server also must authenticate to the user.

17. **B.** Reviewing audit logs takes place after the fact, after some type of incident happens. It is detective in nature because the security professional is trying to figure out what exactly happened, how to correct it, and possibly who is responsible.

18. **D.** This question may seem a little confusing if you were stuck between user and owner. Only the data owner can decide who can access the resources she owns. She may be a user and she may not. A user is not necessarily the owner of the resource. Only the actual owner of the resource can dictate what subjects can actually access the resource.

19. **A.** In a single sign-on technology, all users are authenticating to one source. If that source goes down, authentication requests cannot be processed.

20. **C.** Biometrics is a technology that validates an individual's identity by reading a physical attribute. In some cases, biometrics can be used for identification, but that was not listed as an answer choice.

21. **B.** The security policy sets the tone for the whole security program. It dictates the level of risk that management and the company are willing to accept. This in turn dictates the type of controls and mechanisms to put in place to ensure this level of risk is not exceeded.

22. **B.** A brute force attack tries a combination of values in an attempt to discover the correct sequence that represents the captured password or whatever the goal of the task is. It is an exhaustive attack, meaning the attacker will try over and over again until she is successful.

23. **D.** Spoofing is the process of pretending to be another person or process with the goal of obtaining unauthorized access. Spoofing is usually done by using a bogus IP address, but it could be done by using someone else's authentication credentials.

24. **A.** A centralized approach does not provide as much flexibility as decentralized access control administration, because one entity is making all the decisions instead of several entities that are closer to the resources. A centralized approach is more structured in nature, which means there is less flexibility.

25. **C.** An administrator does not need to revoke and reassign permissions to individual users as they change jobs. Instead, the administrator assigns permissions and rights to a role, and users are plugged into those roles.

26. **A.** Most enterprises have some type of directory that contains information pertaining to the company's network resources and users. Most directories follow a hierarchical database format, based on the X.500 standard, and a type of protocol, as in Lightweight Directory Access Protocol (LDAP), that allows subjects and applications to interact with the directory. Applications can request information about a particular user by making an LDAP request to the directory, and users can request information about a specific resource by using a similar request.

27. **B.** User provisioning refers to the creation, maintenance, and deactivation of user objects and attributes as they exist in one or more systems, directories, or applications, in response to business processes. User provisioning software may include one or more of the following components: change propagation, self-service workflow, consolidated user administration, delegated user administration, and federated change control. User objects may represent employees, contractors, vendors, partners, customers, or other recipients of a service. Services may include electronic mail, access to a database, access to a file server or mainframe, and so on.

28. **D.** Password synchronization technologies can allow a user to maintain just one password across multiple systems. The product will synchronize the password to other systems and applications, which happens transparently to the user.

29. C. Behavioral-based system that learns the "normal" activities of an environment. The three types are listed next:

- **Statistical anomaly–based** Creates a profile of "normal" and compares activities to this profile
- **Protocol anomaly–based** Identifies protocols used outside of their common bounds
- **Traffic anomaly–based** Identifies unusual activity in network traffic

30. **B.** These steps are taken to convert the biometric input for identity verification:

  i. A software application identifies specific points of data as match points.

  ii. An algorithm is used to process the match points and translate that information into a numeric value.

  iii. Authentication is approved or denied when the database value is compared with the end user input entered into the scanner.

31. **A.** This rating is stated as a percentage and represents the point at which the false rejection rate equals the false acceptance rate. This rating is the most important measurement when determining a biometric system's accuracy.

    - (Type I error)—rejects authorized individual
      - False Reject Rate (FRR)
    - (Type II error)—accepts impostor
      - False Acceptance Rate (FAR)

32. **C.** Different types of one-time passwords are used for authentication. This graphic illustrates a synchronous token device, which synchronizes with the authentication service by using time or a counter as the core piece of the authentication process.

Security Architecture and Design

This chapter presents the following:

- Computer hardware architecture
- Operating system architectures
- Trusted computing base and security mechanisms
- Protection mechanisms within an operating system
- Various security models
- Assurance evaluation criteria and ratings
- Certification and accreditation processes
- Attack types

Computer and information security covers many areas within an enterprise. Each area has security vulnerabilities and, hopefully, some corresponding countermeasures that raise the security level and provide better protection. Not understanding the different areas and security levels of network devices, operating systems, hardware, protocols, and applications can cause security vulnerabilities that can affect the environment as a whole.

Two fundamental concepts in computer and information security are the security policy and security model. A *security policy* is a statement that outlines how entities access each other, what operations different entities can carry out, what level of protection is required for a system or software product, and what actions should be taken when these requirements are not met. The policy outlines the expectations that the hardware and software must meet to be considered in compliance. A *security model* outlines the requirements necessary to properly support and implement a certain security policy. If a security policy dictates that all users must be identified, authenticated, and authorized before accessing network resources, the security model might lay out an access control matrix that should be constructed so it fulfills the requirements of the security policy. If a security policy states that no one from a lower security level should be able to view or modify information at a higher security level, the supporting security model will outline the necessary logic and rules that need to be implemented to ensure that under no circumstances can a lower-level subject access a higher-level object in an unauthorized manner. A security model provides a deeper explanation of how a computer operating system should be developed to properly support a specific security policy.

 NOTE Individual systems and devices can have their own security policies. These are not the organizational security policies that contain management's directives. The systems' security policies, and the models they use, should enforce the higher-level organizational security policy that is in place. A system policy dictates the level of security that should be provided by the individual device or operating system.

Computer security can be a slippery term because it means different things to different people. Many aspects of a system can be secured, and security can happen at various levels and to varying degrees. As stated in previous chapters, information security consists of the following main attributes:

- **Availability**   Prevention of loss of, or loss of access to, data and resources
- **Integrity**   Prevention of unauthorized modification of data and resources
- **Confidentiality**   Prevention of unauthorized disclosure of data and resources

These main attributes branch off into more granular security attributes, such as authenticity, accountability, nonrepudiation, and dependability. How does a company know which of these it needs, to what degree they are needed, and whether the operating systems and applications they use actually provide these features and protection? These questions get much more complex as one looks deeper into the questions and products themselves. Companies are not just concerned about e-mail messages being encrypted as they pass through the Internet. They are also concerned about the confidential data stored in their databases, the security of their web farms that are connected directly to the Internet, the integrity of data-entry values going into applications that process business-oriented information, internal users sharing trade secrets, external attackers bringing down servers and affecting productivity, viruses spreading, the internal consistency of data warehouses, and much more.

These issues not only affect productivity and profitability, but also raise legal and liability issues with regard to securing data. Companies, and the management that runs them, can be held accountable if any one of the many issues previously mentioned goes wrong. So it is, or at least it should be, very important for companies to know what security they need and how to be properly assured that the protection is actually being provided by the products they purchase.

Many of these security issues must be thought through before and during the design and architectural phases for a product. Security is best if it is designed and built into the foundation of operating systems and applications and not added as an afterthought. Once security is integrated as an important part of the design, it has to be engineered, implemented, tested, audited, evaluated, certified, and accredited. The security that a product provides must be rated on the availability, integrity, and confidentiality it claims to provide. Consumers then use these ratings to determine if specific products provide the level of security they require. This is a long road, with many entities involved with different responsibilities.

This chapter takes you from the steps that are necessary before actually developing an operating system to how these systems are evaluated and rated by governments and other agencies, and what these ratings actually mean. However, before we dive into these concepts, it is important to understand how the basic elements of a computer system work. These elements are the pieces that make up any computer's architecture.

Computer Architecture

Put the processor over there by the plant, the memory by the window, and the secondary storage upstairs.

Computer architecture encompasses all of the parts of a computer system that are necessary for it to function, including the operating system, memory chips, logic circuits, storage devices, input and output devices, security components, buses, and networking components. The interrelationships and internal working of all of these parts can be quite complex, and making them work together in a secure fashion consists of complicated methods and mechanisms. Thank goodness for the smart people who figured this stuff out! Now it is up to us to learn how they did it and why.

The more you understand how these different pieces work and process data, the more you will understand how vulnerabilities actually occur and how countermeasures work to impede and hinder vulnerabilities from being introduced, found, and exploited.

 NOTE This chapter interweaves the hardware and operating system architectures and their components to show you how they work together.

The Central Processing Unit

The CPU seems complex. How does it work?
Response: Black magic. It uses eye of bat, tongue of goat, and some transistors.

The *central processing unit (CPU)* is the brain of a computer. In the most general description possible, it fetches instructions from memory and executes them. Although a CPU is a piece of hardware, it has its own instruction sets (provided by the operating system) that are necessary to carry out its tasks. Each CPU type has a specific architecture and set of instructions that it can carry out. The operating system must be designed to work within this CPU architecture. This is why one operating system may work on a Pentium processor but not on a SPARC processor.

 NOTE Scalable Processor Architecture (SPARC) is a type of Reduced Instruction Set Computing (RISC) chip developed by Sun Microsystems. SunOS, Solaris, and some Unix operating systems have been developed to work on this type of processor.

The chips within the CPU cover only a couple of square inches, but contain over 40 million transistors. All operations within the CPU are performed by electrical signals at different voltages in different combinations, and each transistor holds this voltage, which represents 0's and 1's to the computer. The CPU contains registers that point to memory locations that contain the next instructions to be executed and that enable the CPU to keep status information of the data that need to be processed. A *register* is a temporary storage location. Accessing memory to get information on what instructions and data must be executed is a much slower process than accessing a register, which is a component of the CPU itself. So when the CPU is done with one task, it asks the registers, "Okay, what do I have to do now?" And the registers hold the information that tells the CPU what its next job is.

The actual execution of the instructions is done by the *arithmetic logic unit (ALU)*. The ALU performs mathematical functions and logical operations on data. The ALU can be thought of as the brain of the CPU, and the CPU as the brain of the computer.

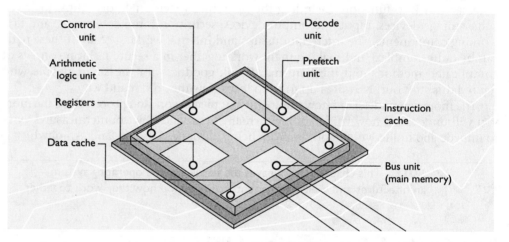

Software holds its instructions and data in memory. When action needs to take place on the data, the instructions and data memory addresses are passed to the CPU registers, as shown in Figure 5-1. When the control unit indicates that the CPU can process them, the instructions and data memory addresses are passed to the CPU for actual processing, number crunching, and data manipulation. The results are sent back to the requesting process's memory address.

An operating system and applications are really just made up of lines and lines of instructions. These instructions contain empty variables, which are populated at run time. The empty variables hold the actual data. There is a difference between instructions and data. The instructions have been written to carry out some type of functionality on the data. For example, let's say you open a Calculator application. In reality, this program is just lines of instructions that allow you to carry out addition, subtraction, division, and other types of mathematical functions that will be executed on the data you provide. So, you type in 3 + 5. The 3 and the 5 are the data values. Once you click the = button, the Calculator program tells the CPU it needs to take the instructions on how to carry out addition and apply these instructions to the two data values 3 and 5. The ALU carries out this instruction and returns the result of 8 to the requesting program. This is when you see the value 8 in the Calculator's field. To users, it seems as though the Calculator program is doing all of this on its own, but it is incapable of this. It depends upon the CPU and other components of the system to carry out this type of activity.

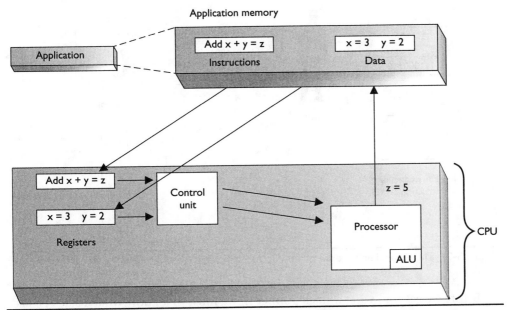

Figure 5-1 Instruction and data addresses are passed to the CPU for processing.

The *control unit* manages and synchronizes the system while different applications' code and operating system instructions are being executed. The control unit is the component that fetches the code, interprets the code, and oversees the execution of the different instruction sets. It determines what application instructions get processed and in what priority and time slice. It controls when instructions are executed, and this execution enables applications to process data. The control unit does not actually process the data. It is like the traffic cop telling traffic when to stop and start again, as illustrated in Figure 5-2. The CPU's time has to be sliced up into individual units and assigned to processes. It is this time slicing that fools the applications and users into thinking the system is actually carrying out several different functions at one time. While the operating system can carry out several different functions at one time (multitasking), in reality the CPU is executing the instructions in a serial fashion (one at a time).

A CPU has several different types of registers, containing information about the instruction set and data that must be executed. *General registers* are used to hold variables and temporary results as the ALU works through its execution steps. The general registers are like the ALU's scratch pad, which it uses while working. *Special registers* (dedicated registers) hold information such as the program counter, stack pointer, and program status word (PSW). The *program counter* register contains the memory address of the next instruction to be fetched. After that instruction is executed, the program counter is updated with the memory address of the next instruction set to be processed. It is similar to a boss and secretary relationship. The secretary keeps the boss on schedule and points her (the boss) to the necessary tasks she must carry out. This allows the boss to just concentrate on carrying out the tasks instead of having to worry about the "busy work" being done in the background.

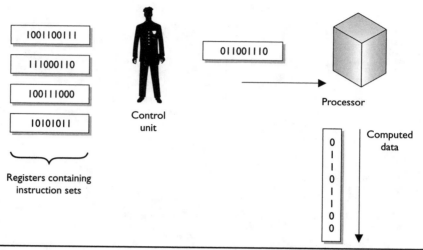

Figure 5-2 The control unit works as a traffic cop, indicating when instructions are sent to the processor.

Before we get into what a stack pointer is, we must first know what a stack is. Each process has its own *stack*, which is a data structure in memory that the process can read from and write to in a last in, first out (LIFO) fashion. Let's say you and I need to communicate through a stack. What I do is put all of the things I need to say to you in a stack of papers. The first paper tells you how you can respond to me when you need to, which is called a *return pointer*. The next paper has some instructions I need you to carry out. The next piece of paper has the data you must use when carrying out these instructions. So, I write down on individual pieces of paper all that I need you to do for me and *stack* them up. When I am done, I tell you to read my stack of papers. You take the first page off the stack and carry out the request. Then you take the second page and carry out that request. You continue to do this until you are at the bottom of the stack, which contains my return pointer. You look at this return pointer (which is my memory address) to know where to send the results of all the instructions I asked you to carry out. This is how processes communicate to other processes and to the CPU. One process stacks up its information that it needs to communicate to the CPU. The CPU has to keep track of where it is in the stack, which is the purpose of the stack pointer. Once the first item on the stack is executed, then the *stack pointer* moves down to tell the CPU where the next piece of data is located.

NOTE The traditional way of explaining how a stack works is to use the analogy of stacking up trays in a cafeteria. When people are done eating, they place their trays on a stack of other trays, and when the cafeteria employees need to get the trays for cleaning, they take the last tray placed on top and work down the stack. This analogy is used to explain how a stack works in the mode of "last in, first out." The process being communicated to takes the last piece of data the requesting process laid down from the top of the stack and works down the stack.

The *program status word (PSW)* holds different condition bits. One of the bits indicates whether the CPU should be working in *user mode* (also called *problem state*) or *privileged mode* (also called *kernel* or *supervisor mode*). The crux of this chapter is to teach you how operating systems protect themselves. They need to protect themselves from applications, utilities, and user activities if they are going to provide a stable and safe environment. One of these protection mechanisms is implemented through the use of these different execution modes. When an *application* needs the CPU to carry out its instructions, the CPU works in user mode. This mode has a lower privilege level, and many of the CPU's instructions and functions are not available to the requesting application. The reason for the extra caution is that the developers of the operating system do not know who developed the application or how it is going to react, so the CPU works in a lower privileged mode when executing these types of instructions. By analogy, if you are expecting visitors who are bringing their two-year-old boy, you move all of the breakables that someone under three feet can reach. No one is ever sure what a two-year-old toddler is going to do, but it usually has to do with breaking something. An operating system and CPU are not sure what applications are going to attempt, which is why this code is executed in a lower privilege.

If the PSW has a bit value that indicates the instructions to be executed should be carried out in privileged mode, this means a trusted process (an operating system process) made the request and can have access to the functionality that is not available in user mode. An example would be if the operating system needed to communicate with a peripheral device. This is a privileged activity that applications cannot carry out. When these types of instructions are passed to the CPU, the PSW is basically telling the CPU, "The process that made this request is an all right guy. We can trust him. Go ahead and carry out this task for him."

Memory addresses of the instructions and data to be processed are held in registers until needed by the CPU. The CPU is connected to an *address bus*, which is a hardwired connection to the RAM chips in the system and the individual input/output (I/O) devices. Memory is cut up into sections that have individual addresses associated with them. I/O devices (CD-ROM, USB device, hard drive, floppy drive, and so on) are also allocated specific unique addresses. If the CPU needs to access some data, either from memory or from an I/O device, it sends down the address of where the needed data are located. The circuitry associated with the memory or I/O device recognizes the address the CPU sent down the address bus and instructs the memory or device to read the requested data and put it on the *data bus*. So the address bus is used by the CPU to indicate the location of the instructions to be processed, and the memory or I/O device responds by sending the data that reside at that memory location through the data bus. This process is illustrated in Figure 5-3.

Once the CPU is done with its computation, it needs to return the results to the requesting program's memory. So, the CPU sends the requesting program's address down the address bus and sends the new results down the data bus with the command `write`. These new data are then written to the requesting program's memory space.

The address and data buses can be 8, 16, 32, or 64 bits wide. Most systems today use a 32-bit address bus, which means the system can have a large address space (2^{32}). Systems can also have a 32-bit data bus, which means the system can move data in parallel

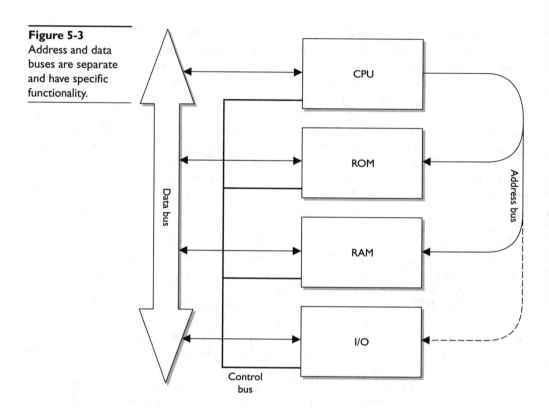

Figure 5-3
Address and data buses are separate and have specific functionality.

Data bus

Address bus

Control bus

back and forth between memory, I/O devices, and the CPU. (A *32-bit data bus* means the size of the chunks of data a CPU can request at a time is 32 bits.)

Multiprocessing

Some specialized computers have more than one CPU, for increased performance. An operating system must be developed specifically to be able to understand and work with more than one processor. If the computer system is configured to work in *symmetric mode*, this means the processors are handed work as needed, as shown with CPU 1 and CPU 2 in Figure 5-4. It is like a load-balancing environment. When a process needs instructions to be executed, a scheduler determines which processor is ready for more work and sends it on. If a processor is going to be dedicated for a specific task or application, all other software would run on a different processor. In Figure 5-4, CPU 4 is dedicated to one application and its threads, while CPU 3 is used by the operating system. When a processor is dedicated as in this example, the system is working in *asymmetric mode*. This usually means the computer has some type of time-sensitive application that needs its own personal processor. So, the system scheduler will send instructions from the time-sensitive application to CPU 4 and send all the other instructions (from the operating system and other applications) to CPU 3. The differences are shown in Figure 5-4.

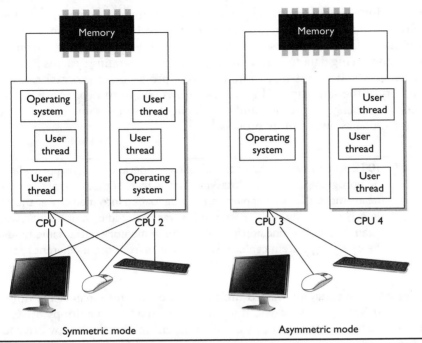

Figure 5-4 Symmetric mode and asymmetric mode

Operating System Architecture

An operating system provides an environment for applications and users to work within. Every operating system is a complex beast, made up of various layers and modules of functionality. It has the responsibility of managing the hardware components, memory management, I/O operations, file system, process management, and providing system services. We next look at each of these responsibilities in every operating system. However, you must realize that whole books are written on just these individual topics, so the discussion here will only be topical.

Process Management

Well just look at all of these processes squirming around like little worms. We need some real organization here!

Operating systems, utilities, and applications in reality are just lines and lines of instructions. They are static lines of code that are brought to life when they are initialized and put into memory. Applications work as individual units, called *processes*, and the operating system has several different processes carrying out various types of functionality. A *process* is the set of instructions that is actually running. A program is not considered a process until it is loaded into memory and activated by the operating system. When a process is created, the operating system assigns resources to it, such as a memory segment, CPU time slot (interrupt), access to system application programming interfaces (APIs), and files to interact with. The *collection* of the instructions and the assigned resources is referred to as a process.

The operating system has many processes, which are used to provide and maintain the environment for applications and users to work within. Some examples of the functionality that individual processes provide include displaying data onscreen, spooling print jobs, and saving data to temporary files. Today's operating systems provide *multiprogramming*, which means that more than one program (or process) can be loaded into memory at the same time. This is what allows you to run your antivirus software, word processor, personal firewall, and e-mail client all at the same time. Each of these applications runs as one or more processes.

 NOTE Many resources state that today's operating systems provide multiprogramming and multitasking. This is true, in that multiprogramming just means more than one application can be loaded into memory at the same time. But in reality, multiprogramming was replaced by multitasking, which means more than one application can be in memory at the same time *and* the operating system can deal with requests from these different applications *simultaneously.*

Earlier operating systems wasted their most precious resource—CPU time. For example, when a word processor would request to open a file on a floppy drive, the CPU would send the request to the floppy drive and then wait for the floppy drive to initialize, for the head to find the right track and sector, and finally for the floppy drive to send the data via the data bus to the CPU for processing. To avoid this waste of CPU time, multitasking was developed, which enabled more than one program to be loaded into memory at one time. Instead of sitting idle waiting for activity from one process, the CPU could execute instructions for other processes, thereby speeding up the necessary processing required for all the different processes.

As an analogy, if you (CPU) put bread in a toaster (process) and just stand there waiting for the toaster to finish its job, you are wasting time. On the other hand, if you put bread in the toaster and then, while it's toasting, feed the dog, make coffee, and come up with a solution for world peace, you are being more productive and not wasting time.

Operating systems started out as cooperative and then evolved into preemptive multitasking. *Cooperative multitasking*, used in Windows 286, 3.*x*, and early Macintosh systems, required the processes to voluntarily release resources they were using. This was not necessarily a stable environment, because if a programmer did not write his code properly to release a resource when his application was done using it, the resource would be committed indefinitely to his application and thus be unavailable to other processes. With *preemptive multitasking*, used in Windows 9*x*, NT, 2000, XP, and in Unix systems, the operating system controls how long a process can use a resource. The system can suspend a process that is using the CPU and allow another process access to it through the use of *time sharing*. So, in operating systems that used cooperative multitasking, the processes had too much control over resource release, and when an application hung, it usually affected all the other applications and sometimes the operating system itself. Operating systems that use preemptive multitasking run the show, and one application does not negatively affect another application as easily.

Different operating system types work within different process models. For example, Unix and Linux systems allow their processes to create new children processes, which is referred to as *forking*. Let's say you are working within a shell of a Linux system. That shell is the command interpreter and an interface that enables the user to interact with the operating system. The shell runs as a process. When you type in a shell the command `cat file1 file2 | grep stuff`, you are telling the operating system to concatenate (`cat`) the two files and then search (`grep`) for the lines that have the value of stuff in them. When you press the ENTER key, the shell forks two children processes—one for the cat command and one for the grep command. Each of these children processes takes on the characteristics of the parent process, but has its own memory space, stack, and program counter values.

A process can run in *running state* (CPU is executing its instructions and data), *ready state* (waiting to send instructions to the CPU), or *blocked state* (waiting for input data, such as keystrokes from a user). These different states are illustrated in Figure 5-5. When a process is blocked, it is waiting for some type of data to be sent to it. In the preceding example of typing the command `cat file1 file2 | grep stuff`, the grep process cannot actually carry out its functionality of searching until the first process (`cat`) is done combining the two files. The grep process will put itself to *sleep* and will be in the blocked state until the cat process is done and sends the grep process the input it needs to work with.

 NOTE   Not all operating systems create and work in the process hierarchy like Unix and Linux systems. Windows systems do not fork new children processes, but instead create new threads that work within the same context of the parent process. This is deeper than what you need to know for the CISSP exam, but life is not just about this exam—right?

The operating system is responsible for creating new processes, assigning them resources, synchronizing their communication, and making sure nothing insecure is taking place. The operating system keeps a *process table*, which has one entry per process. The table contains each individual process's state, stack pointer, memory allocation, program counter, and status of open files in use. The reason the operating system documents all of this status information is that the CPU needs all of it loaded into its registers when it needs to interact with, for example, process 1. When process 1's CPU time slice is over, all of the current status information on process 1 is stored in the process table so that when its time slice is open again, all of this status information can be put back into the CPU registers. So, when it is process 2's time with the CPU, its status information is transferred from the process table to the CPU registers, and transferred back again when the time slice is over. These steps are shown in Figure 5-6.

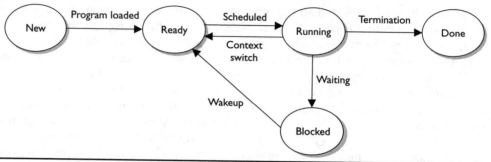

Figure 5-5 Processes enter and exit different states.

How does a process know when it can communicate with the CPU? This is taken care of by using *interrupts*. An operating system fools us, and applications, into thinking it and the CPU are carrying out all tasks (operating system, applications, memory, I/O, and user activities) simultaneously. In fact, this is impossible. Most CPUs can do only

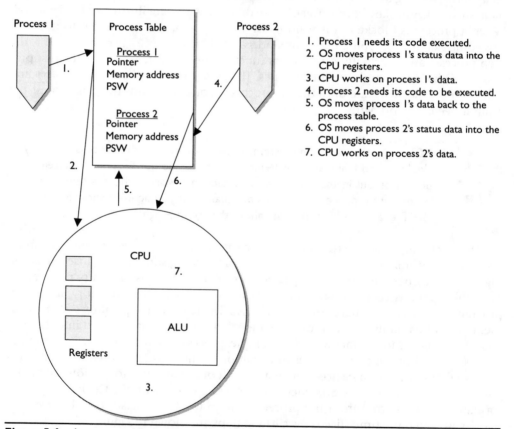

1. Process 1 needs its code executed.
2. OS moves process 1's status data into the CPU registers.
3. CPU works on process 1's data.
4. Process 2 needs its code to be executed.
5. OS moves process 1's data back to the process table.
6. OS moves process 2's status data into the CPU registers.
7. CPU works on process 2's data.

Figure 5-6 A process table contains process status data that the CPU requires.

one thing at a time. So the system has hardware and software interrupts. When a device needs to communicate with the CPU, it has to wait for its interrupt to be called upon. The same thing happens in software. Each process has an interrupt assigned to it. It is like pulling a number at a customer service department in a store. You can't go up to the counter until your number has been called out.

When a process is interacting with the CPU and an interrupt takes place (another process has requested access to the CPU), the current process's information is stored in the process table, and the next process gets its time to interact with the CPU.

 NOTE   Some critical processes cannot afford to have their functionality interrupted by another process. The operating system is responsible for setting the priorities for the different processes. When one process needs to interrupt another process, the operating system compares the priority levels of the two processes to determine if this interruption should be allowed.

There are two categories of interrupts: maskable and non-maskable. A *maskable interrupt* is assigned to an event that may not be overly important and the programmer can indicate that if that interrupt calls, the program does not stop what it is doing. This means the interrupt is ignored. *Non-maskable interrupts* can never be overridden by an application because the event that has this type of interrupt assigned to it is critical. As an example, the reset button would be assigned a non-maskable interrupt. This means that when this button is pushed, the CPU carries out its instructions right away.

As an analogy, a boss can tell her administrative assistant she is not going to take any calls unless the Pope or Elvis phones. This means all other people will be ignored or masked (maskable interrupt), but the Pope and Elvis will not be ignored (non-maskable interrupt). This is probably a good policy. You should always accept calls from either the Pope or Elvis. Just remember not to use any bad words when talking to the Pope.

The *watchdog timer* is an example of a critical process that must always do its thing. This process will reset the system with a warm boot if the operating system hangs and cannot recover itself. For example, if there is a memory management problem and the operating system hangs, the watchdog timer will reset the system. This is one mechanism that ensures the software provides more of a stable environment.

Thread Management
What are all of these hair-like things hanging off of my processes?
Response: Threads.

As described earlier, a process is a program in memory. More precisely, a process is the program's instructions and all the resources assigned to the process by the operating system. It is just easier to group all of these instructions and resources together and control them as one entity, which is a process. When a process needs to send something to the CPU for processing, it generates a thread. A *thread* is made up of an individual instruction set and the data that must be worked on by the CPU.

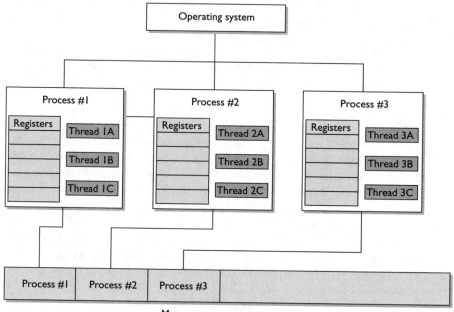

Memory segments

Most applications have several different functions. Word processors can open files, save files, open other programs (such as an e-mail client), and print documents. Each one of these functions requires a thread (instruction set) to be dynamically generated. So, for example, if Tom chooses to print his document, the word processor process generates a thread that contains the instructions of how this document should be printed (font, colors, text, margins, and so on). If he chooses to send a document via e-mail through this program, another thread is created that tells the e-mail client to open and what file needs to be sent. Threads are dynamically created and destroyed as needed. Once Tom is done printing his document, the thread that was generated for this functionality is destroyed.

A program that has been developed to carry out several different tasks at one time (display, print, interact with other programs) is capable of running several different threads simultaneously. An application with this capability is referred to as a *multi-threaded* application.

NOTE Each thread shares the same resources of the process that created it. So, all the threads created by a word processor work in the same memory space and have access to all the same files and system resources.

Process Scheduling

Scheduling and synchronizing various processes and their activities is part of process management, which is a responsibility of the operating system. Several components need to be considered during the development of an operating system, which will dictate how process scheduling will take place. A scheduling policy is created to govern how threads will interact with other threads. Different operating systems can use different schedulers, which are basically algorithms that control the timesharing of the CPU. As stated earlier, the different processes are assigned different priority levels (interrupts) that dictate which processes overrule other processes when CPU time allocation is required. The operating system creates and deletes processes as needed, and oversees them changing state (ready, blocked, running). The operating system is also responsible for controlling deadlocks between processes attempting to use the same resources.

When a process makes a request for a resource (memory allocation, printer, secondary storage devices, disk space, and so on), the operating system creates certain data structures and dedicates the necessary processes for the activity to be completed. Once the action takes place (a document is printed, a file is saved, or data are retrieved from the drive), the process needs to tear down these built structures and release the resources back to the resource pool so they are available for other processes. If this does not happen properly, the system may run out of critical resources (that is, memory).

Another situation to be concerned about is a software deadlock. One example of a deadlock situation is when process A commits resource 1 and needs to use resource 2 to properly complete its task, but process B has committed resource 2 and needs resource 1 to finish its job. So both processes are in deadlock because they do not have the resources they need to finish the function they are trying to carry out. This situation does not take place as often as it used to, as a result of better programming. Also, operating systems now have the intelligence to detect this activity and either release committed resources or control the allocation of resources so they are properly shared between processes.

Operating systems have different methods of dealing with resource requests and releases and solving deadlock situations. In some systems, if a requested resource is unavailable for a certain period of time, the operating system kills the process that is "holding on to" that resource. This action releases the resource from the process that had committed it and restarts the process so it is "clean" and available for use by other applications. Other operating systems might require a program to request all the resources it needs *before* it actually starts executing instructions, or require a program to release its currently committed resources before it may acquire more.

Definitions

The concepts of how computer operating systems work can be overwhelming at times. For test purposes, make sure you understand the following definitions:

- **Multiprogramming** An operating system can load more than one program in memory at one time.
- **Multitasking** An operating system can handle requests from several different processes loaded into memory at the same time.
- **Multithreading** An application has the ability to run multiple threads simultaneously.
- **Multiprocessing** The computer has more than one CPU.

Process Activity

Process 1, go into your room and play with your toys. Process 2, go into your room and play with your toys. No intermingling and no fighting!

Computers can run different applications and processes at the same time. The processes have to share resources and play nice with each other to ensure a stable and safe computing environment that maintains its integrity. Some memory, data files, and variables are actually shared between different processes. It is critical that more than one process do not attempt to read and write to these items at the same time. The operating system is the master program that prevents this type of action from taking place and ensures that programs do not corrupt each other's data held in memory. The operating system works with the CPU to provide time slicing through the use of interrupts to ensure that processes are provided with adequate access to the CPU. This also makes certain that critical system functions are not negatively affected by rogue applications.

To protect processes from each other, operating systems can implement process isolation. **Process isolation** is necessary to ensure that processes do not "step on each other's toes," communicate in an insecure manner, or negatively affect each other's productivity. Older operating systems did not enforce process isolation as well as systems do today. This is why in earlier operating systems, when one of your programs hung, all other programs, and sometimes the operating system itself, hung. With process isolation, if one process hangs for some reason, it will not affect the other software running. (Process isolation is required for preemptive multitasking.) Different methods can be used to carry out process isolation:

- Encapsulation of objects
- Time multiplexing of shared resources
- Naming distinctions
- Virtual mapping

When a process is *encapsulated*, no other process understands or interacts with its internal programming code. When process A needs to communicate with process B, process A just needs to know how to communicate with process B's interface. An interface defines how communication must take place between two processes. As an analogy, think back to how you had to communicate with your third-grade teacher. You had to call her Mrs. So-and-So, say please and thank you, and speak respectfully to get whatever it was you needed. The same thing is true for software components that need to communicate with each other. They must know *how* to communicate properly with each other's interfaces. The interfaces dictate the type of requests a process will accept and the type of output that will be provided. So, two processes can communicate with each other, even if they are written in different programming languages, as long as they know how to communicate with each other's interface. Encapsulation provides *data hiding*, which means that outside software components will not know how a process works and will not be able to manipulate the process's internal code. This is an integrity mechanism and enforces modularity in programming code.

Time multiplexing was already discussed, although we did not use this term. *Time multiplexing* is a technology that allows processes to use the same resources. As stated earlier, a CPU must be shared between many processes. Although it seems as though all applications are running (executing their instructions) simultaneously, the operating system is splitting up time shares between each process. Multiplexing means there are several data sources and the individual data pieces are piped into one communication channel. In this instance, the operating system is coordinating the different requests from the different processes and piping them through the one shared CPU. An operating system must provide proper time multiplexing (resource sharing) to ensure a stable working environment exists for software and users.

Naming distinctions just means that the different processes have their own name or identification value. Processes are usually assigned process identification (PID) values, which the operating system and other processes use to call upon them. If each process is isolated, that means each process has its own unique PID value.

Virtual address space mapping is different from the physical mapping of memory. An application is written such that basically it thinks it is the only program running on an operating system. When an application needs memory to work with, it tells the operating system's memory manager how much memory it needs. The operating system carves out that amount of memory and assigns it to the requesting application. The application uses its own address scheme, which usually starts at 0, but in reality, the application does not work in the *physical* address space it thinks it is working in. Rather, it works in the address space the memory manager assigns to it. The physical memory is the RAM chips in the system. The operating system chops up this memory and assigns portions of it to the requesting processes. Once the process is assigned its own memory space, it can address this portion however it wishes, which is called *virtual address mapping*. Virtual address mapping allows the different processes to have their own memory space; the memory manager ensures no processes improperly interact with another process's memory. This provides integrity and confidentiality.

Memory Management

To provide a safe and stable environment, an operating system must exercise proper memory management—one of its most important tasks. After all, everything happens in memory. It's similar to how we depend on oxygen and gravity for our existence. If either slides out of balance, we're in big trouble.

The goals of memory management are to

- Provide an abstraction level for programmers
- Maximize performance with the limited amount of memory available
- Protect the operating system and applications loaded into memory

Abstraction means that the details of something are hidden. Developers of applications do not know the amount or type of memory that will be available in each and every system their code will be loaded on. If a developer had to be concerned with this type of detail, then her application would be able to work only on the one system that maps to all of her specifications. To allow for portability, the memory manager hides all of the memory issues and just provides the application with a memory segment.

Every computer has a memory hierarchy. Certain small amounts of memory are very fast and expensive (registers, cache), while larger amounts are slower and less expensive (RAM, hard drive). The portion of the operating system that keeps track of how these different types of memory are used is lovingly called the *memory manager*. Its jobs are to allocate and deallocate different memory segments, enforce access control to ensure processes are interacting only with their own memory segments, and swap memory contents from RAM to the hard drive.

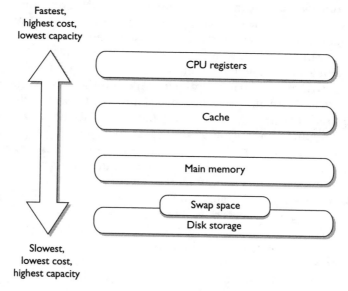

The memory manager has five basic responsibilities:

Relocation

- Swap contents from RAM to the hard drive as needed (explained later in the "Virtual Memory" section of this chapter)
- Provide pointers for applications if their instructions and memory segment have been moved to a different location in main memory

Protection

- Limit processes to interact only with the memory segments assigned to them
- Provide access control to memory segments

Sharing

- Use complex controls to ensure integrity and confidentiality when processes need to use the same shared memory segments
- Allow many users with different levels of access to interact with the same application running in one memory segment

Logical organization

- Allow for the sharing of specific software modules, such as dynamic link library (DLL) procedures

Physical organization

- Segment the physical memory space for application and operating system processes

NOTE A dynamic link library (DLL) is a set of functions that applications can call upon to carry out different types of procedures. For example, the Windows operating system has a crypt32.dll that is used by the operating system and applications for cryptographic functions. Windows has a set of DLLs, which is just a library of functions to be called upon.

How can an operating system make sure a process only interacts with its memory segment? When a process creates a thread, because it needs some instructions and data processed, the CPU uses two registers. A *base register* contains the beginning address that was assigned to the process, and a *limit register* contains the ending address, as illustrated in Figure 5-7. The thread contains an address of where the instruction and data reside that need to be processed. The CPU compares this address to the base and limit registers to make sure the thread is not trying to access a memory segment outside of its bounds. So, the base register makes it impossible for a thread to reference a memory address below its allocated memory segment, and the limit register makes it impossible for a thread to reference a memory address above this segment.

Figure 5-7
Base and limit registers are used to contain a process in its own memory segment.

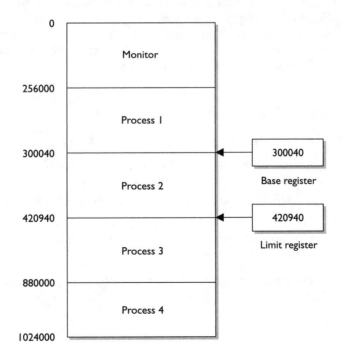

Memory is also protected through the use of user and privileged modes of execution, as previously mentioned, and covered in more detail later in the "CPU Modes and Protection Rings" section of this chapter.

Memory Types

The operating system instructions, applications, and data are held in memory, but so are the basic input/output system (BIOS), device controller instructions, and firmware. They do not all reside in the same memory location or even the same type of memory. The different types of memory, what they are used for, and how each is accessed can get a bit confusing because the CPU deals with several different types for different reasons.

The following sections outline the different types of memory that can be used within computer systems.

Random Access Memory

Random access memory (RAM) is a type of temporary storage facility where data and program instructions can temporarily be held and altered. It is used for read/write activities by the operating system and applications. It is described as volatile because if the computer's power supply is terminated, then all information within this type of memory is lost.

RAM is an integrated circuit made up of millions of transistors and capacitors. The capacitor is where the actual charge is stored, which represents a 1 or 0 to the system. The transistor acts like a gate or a switch. A capacitor that is storing a binary value of 1 has several electrons stored in it, which have a negative charge, whereas a capacitor that is storing a 0 value is empty. When the operating system writes over a 1 bit with a 0 bit, in reality it is just emptying out the electrons from that specific capacitor.

One problem is that these capacitors cannot keep their charge for long. Therefore, a memory controller has to "recharge" the values in the capacitors, which just means it continually reads and writes the same values to the capacitors. If the memory controller

---

Memory Protection Issues

- Every address reference is validated for protection.
- Two or more processes can share access to the same segment with potentially different access rights.
- Different instruction and data types can be assigned different levels of protection.
- Processes cannot generate an unpermitted address or gain access to an unpermitted segment.

All of these issues make it more difficult for memory management to be carried out properly in a constantly changing and complex system. Any time more complexity is introduced, it usually means more vulnerabilities can be exploited.

does not "refresh" the value of 1, the capacitor will start losing its electrons and become a 0 or a corrupted value. This explains how *dynamic RAM (DRAM)* works. The data being held in the RAM memory cells must be continually and dynamically refreshed so your bits do not magically disappear. This activity of constantly refreshing takes time, which is why DRAM is slower than static RAM.

NOTE When we are dealing with memory activities, we use a time metric of nanoseconds (ns), which is a billionth of a second. So if you look at your RAM chip and it states 70 ns, this means it takes 70 nanoseconds to read and refresh each memory cell.

Static RAM (SRAM) does not require this continuous-refreshing nonsense; it uses a different technology, by holding bits in its memory cells without the use of capacitors, but it *does* require more transistors than DRAM. Since SRAM does not need to be refreshed, it is faster than DRAM, but because SRAM requires more transistors, it takes up more space on the RAM chip. Manufacturers cannot fit as many SRAM memory cells on a memory chip as they can DRAM memory cells, which is why SRAM is more expensive. So, DRAM is cheaper and slower, and SRAM is more expensive and faster. It always seems to go that way. SRAM has been used in cache, and DRAM is commonly used in RAM chips.

Because life is not confusing enough, we have many other types of RAM. The main reason for the continual evolution of RAM types is that it directly affects the speed of the computer itself. Many people, mistakenly, think that just because you have a fast processor, your computer will be fast. However, memory type and size and bus sizes are also critical components. Think of memory as pieces of paper used by the system to hold instructions. If the system had small pieces of papers (small amount of memory) to read and write from, it would spend most of its time looking for these pieces and lining them up properly. When a computer spends more time moving data from one small portion of memory to another than actually processing the data, it is referred to as *thrashing*. This causes the system to crawl in speed and your frustration level to increase.

The size of the data bus also makes a difference in system speed. You can think of a data bus as a highway that connects different portions of the computer. If a ton of data must go from memory to the CPU and can only travel over a four-lane highway, compared to a 64-lane highway, there will be delays in processing. So the processor, memory type and amount, and bus speeds are critical components to system performance.

Hardware Segmentation
Systems of a higher trust level may need to implement *hardware segmentation* of the memory used by different processes. This means memory is separated physically instead of just logically. This adds another layer of protection to ensure that a lower-privileged process does not access and modify a higher-level process's memory space.

The following are additional types of RAM you should be familiar with:

- **Synchronous DRAM (SDRAM)** Synchronizes itself with the system's CPU and synchronizes signal input and output on the RAM chip. It coordinates its activities with the CPU clock so the timing of the CPU and the timing of the memory activities are synchronized. This increases the speed of transmitting and executing data.

- **Extended data out DRAM (EDO DRAM)** Is faster than DRAM because DRAM can access only one block of data at a time, whereas EDO DRAM can capture the next block of data while the first block is being sent to the CPU for processing. It has a type of "look ahead" feature that speeds up memory access.

- **Burst EDO DRAM (BEDO DRAM)** Works like (and builds upon) EDO DRAM in that it can transmit data to the CPU as it carries out a read option, but it can send more data at once (burst). It reads and sends up to four memory addresses in a small number of clock cycles.

- **Double data rate SDRAM (DDR SDRAM)** Carries out read operations on the rising and falling cycles of a clock pulse. So instead of carrying out one operation per clock cycle, it carries out two and thus can deliver twice the throughput of SDRAM. Basically, it doubles the speed of memory activities, when compared to SDRAM, with a smaller number of clock cycles. Pretty groovy.

 NOTE These different RAM types require different controller chips to interface with them; therefore, the motherboards that these memory types are used on often are very specific in nature.

Well, that's enough about RAM for now. Let's look at other types of memory that are used in basically every computer in the world.

Read-Only Memory

Read-only memory (ROM) is a *nonvolatile* memory type, meaning that when a computer's power is turned off, the data are still held within the memory chips. When data are inserted into ROM memory chips, the data cannot be altered. Individual ROM chips are manufactured with the stored program or routines designed into it. The software that is stored within ROM is called *firmware*.

Programmable read-only memory (PROM) is a form of ROM that can be modified after it has been manufactured. PROM can be programmed only one time because the voltage that is used to write bits into the memory cells actually burns out the fuses that connect the individual memory cells. The instructions are "burned into" PROM using a specialized PROM programmer device.

Erasable and programmable read-only memory (EPROM) can be erased, modified, and upgraded. EPROM holds data that can be electrically erased or written to. To erase the data on the memory chip, you need your handy-dandy ultraviolet (UV) light device that provides just the right level of energy. The EPROM chip has a quartz window, which is where you point the UV light. Although playing with UV light devices can be fun for the whole family, we have moved on to another type of ROM technology that does not require this type of activity.

To erase an EPROM chip, you must remove the chip from the computer and wave your magic UV wand, which erases *all* of the data on the chip—not just portions of it. So someone invented *electrically erasable programmable read-only memory (EEPROM)*, and we all put our UV light wands away for good.

EEPROM is similar to EPROM, but its data storage can be erased and modified electrically by onboard programming circuitry and signals. This activity erases only one byte at a time, which is slow. And because we are an impatient society, yet another technology was developed that is very similar, but works more quickly.

Flash memory is a special type of memory that is used in digital cameras, BIOS chips, memory cards for laptops, and video game consoles. It is a solid-state technology, meaning it does not have moving parts and is used more as a type of hard drive than memory.

Flash memory basically moves around different levels of voltages to indicate that a 1 or 0 must be held in a specific address. It acts as a ROM technology rather than a RAM technology. (For example, you do not lose pictures stored on your memory stick in your digital camera just because your camera loses power. RAM is volatile and ROM is nonvolatile.) When Flash memory needs to be erased and turned back to its original state, a program initiates the internal circuits to apply an electric field. The erasing function takes place in blocks or on the entire chip instead of erasing one byte at a time.

Flash memory is used as a small disk drive in most implementations. Its benefits over a regular hard drive are that it is smaller, faster, and lighter. So let's deploy Flash memory everywhere and replace our hard drives! Maybe one day. Today it is relatively expensive compared to regular hard drives.

Cache Memory

I am going to need this later, so I will just stick it into cache for now.

Cache memory is a type of memory used for high-speed writing and reading activities. When the system assumes (through its programmatic logic) that it will need to access specific information many times throughout its processing activities, it will store the information in cache memory so it is easily and quickly accessible. Data in cache can be accessed much more quickly than data stored in real memory. Therefore, any information needed by the CPU very quickly, and very often, is usually stored in cache memory, thereby improving the overall speed of the computer system.

An analogy is how the brain stores information it uses often. If one of Marge's primary functions at her job is to order parts, which requires telling vendors the company's address, Marge stores this address information in a portion of her brain from which she can easily and quickly access it. This information is held in a type of cache. If Marge was asked to recall her third-grade teacher's name, this information would not necessarily be held in cache memory, but in a more long-term storage facility within her noggin. The long-term storage within her brain is comparable to a system's hard drive. It takes more time to track down and return information from a hard drive than from specialized cache memory.

NOTE Different motherboards have different types of cache. Level 1 (L1) is faster than Level 2 (L2), and L2 is faster than L3. Some processors and device controllers have cache memory built into them. L1 and L2 are usually built into the processors and the controllers themselves.

Memory Mapping

Okay, here is your memory, here is my memory, and here is Bob's memory. No one use each other's memory!

Because there are different types of memory holding different types of data, a computer system does not want to let every user, process, and application access all types of memory anytime they want to. Access to memory needs to be controlled to ensure data do not get corrupted and that sensitive information is not available to unauthorized processes. This type of control takes place through memory mapping and addressing.

The CPU is one of the most trusted components within a system, and can access memory directly. It uses physical addresses instead of pointers (logical addresses) to memory segments. The CPU has physical wires connecting it to the memory chips within the computer. Because physical wires connect the two types of components, physical addresses are used to represent the intersection between the wires and the transistors on a memory chip. Software does not use physical addresses; instead, it employs logical memory addresses. Accessing memory indirectly provides an access control layer between the software and the memory, which is done for protection and efficiency. Figure 5-8 illustrates how the CPU can access memory directly using physical addresses and how software must use memory indirectly through a memory mapper.

Let's look at an analogy. You would like to talk to Mr. Marshall about possibly buying some acreage in Iowa. You don't know Mr. Marshall personally, and you do not want to give out your physical address and have him show up at your doorstep. Instead, you would like to use a more abstract and controlled way of communicating, so you give Mr. Marshall your phone number so you can talk to him about the land and determine whether you want to meet him in person. The same type of thing happens in computers. When a computer runs software, it does not want to expose itself unnecessarily to software written by good and bad programmers. Computers enable software to access memory indirectly by using index tables and pointers, instead of giving them the right to access the memory directly. This is one way the computer system protects itself.

When a program attempts to access memory, its access rights are verified and then instructions and commands are carried out in a way to ensure that badly written code does not affect other programs or the system itself. Applications, and their processes, can only access the memory allocated to them, as shown in Figure 5-9. This type of memory architecture provides protection and efficiency.

The physical memory addresses that the CPU uses are called *absolute addresses*. The indexed memory addresses that software uses are referred to as *logical addresses*. And *relative addresses* are based on a known address with an offset value applied. As explained previously, an application does not "know" it is sharing memory with other applications. When the program needs a memory segment to work with, it tells the memory manager how much memory it needs. The memory manager allocates this

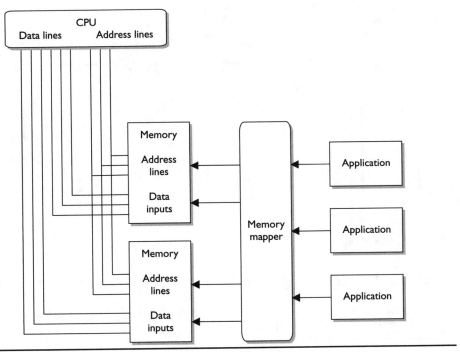

Figure 5-8 The CPU and applications access memory differently.

much physical memory, which could have the physical addressing of 34,000 to 39,000, for example. But the application is not written to call upon addresses in this numbering scheme. It is most likely developed to call upon addresses starting with 0 and extending to, let's say, 5000. So the memory manager allows the application to use its own addressing scheme—the logical addresses. When the application makes a call to one of these "phantom" logical addresses, the memory manager must map this address to the actual physical address. (It's like two people using their own naming scheme. When Bob asks Diane for a ball, Diane knows he really means a stapler. Don't judge Bob and Diane, it works for them.)

The mapping process is illustrated in Figure 5-10. When an application needs its instructions and data processed by the CPU, the physical addresses are loaded into the base and limit registers. When a thread indicates the instruction needs to be processed, it provides a logical address. The memory manager maps the logical address to the physical address, so the CPU knows where the instruction is located. The thread will actually be using a relative address, because the application uses the address space of 0 to 5000. When the thread indicates it needs the instruction at the memory address 3400 to be executed, the memory manager has to work from its mapping of logical address 0 to the actual physical address and then figure out the physical address for the logical address 3400. So the logical address 3400 is relative to the starting address 0.

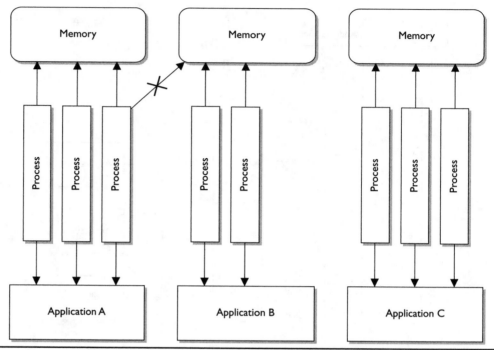

Figure 5-9 Applications, and the processes they use, access their own memory segments only.

As an analogy, if I know you use a different number system than everyone else in the world, and you tell me that you need 14 cookies, I would need to know where to start in *your* number scheme to figure out how many cookies to really give you. So, if you inform me that in "your world" your numbering scheme starts at 5, I would map 5 to 0 and know that the offset is a value of 5. So when you tell me you want 14 cookies (the relative number), I take the offset value into consideration. I know that you start at the value 5, so I map your logical address of 14 to the physical number of 9. (But I would not give you nine cookies, because you made me work too hard to figure all of this out. I will just eat them myself.)

So the application is working in its "own world" using its "own addresses," and the memory manager has to map these values to reality, which means the absolute address values.

Memory Leaks

Oh great, the memory leaked all over me. Does someone have a mop?

When an application makes a request for a memory segment, it is allocated a specific memory amount by the operating system. When the application is done with the memory, it is supposed to tell the operating system to release the memory so it is available to other applications. This is only fair. But some applications are written poorly and do not indicate to the system that this memory is no longer in use. If this happens enough times, the operating system could become "starved" for memory, which would drastically affect the system's performance.

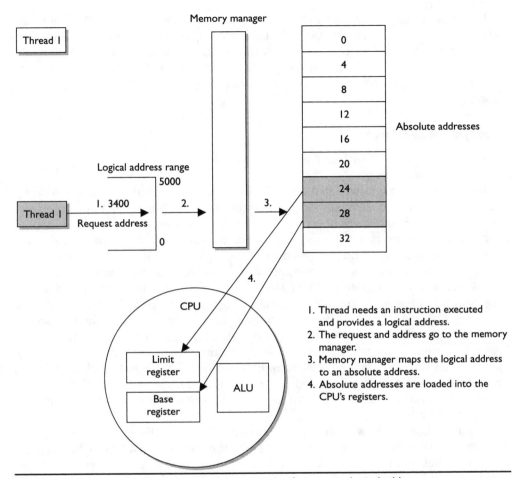

Figure 5-10 The CPU uses absolute addresses, and software uses logical addresses.

When a memory leak is identified in the hacker world, this opens the door to new denial-of-service (DoS) attacks. For example, when it was uncovered that a Unix application and a specific version of a Telnet protocol contained memory leaks, hackers amplified the problem. They continually sent requests to systems with these vulnerabilities. The systems would allocate resources for these network requests, which in turn would cause more and more memory to be allocated and not returned. Eventually the systems would run out of memory and freeze.

 NOTE Memory leaks can be caused by operating systems, applications, and software drivers.

Two main countermeasures can protect against memory leaks: developing better code that releases memory properly, and using a *garbage collector*. A garbage collector is software that runs an algorithm to identify unused committed memory and then tells the operating system to mark that memory as "available." Different types of garbage collectors work with different operating systems, programming languages, and algorithms.

Virtual Memory

My RAM is overflowing! Can I use some of your hard drive space?
Response: No, I don't like you.

Secondary storage is considered nonvolatile storage media and includes such things as the computer's hard drive, floppy disks, and CD-ROMs. When RAM and secondary storage are combined, the result is *virtual memory*. The system uses hard drive space to extend its RAM memory space. *Swap space* is the reserved hard drive space used to extend RAM capabilities. Windows systems use the pagefile.sys file to reserve this space. When a system fills up its volatile memory space, it writes data from memory onto the hard drive. When a program requests access to this data, it is brought from the hard drive back into memory in specific units, called *pages*. This process is called *virtual memory paging*. Accessing data kept in pages on the hard drive takes more time than accessing data kept in memory because physical disk read/write access must take place. Internal control blocks, maintained by the operating system, keep track of what page frames are residing in RAM and what is available "offline," ready to be called into RAM for execution or processing, if needed. The payoff is that it seems as though the system can hold an incredible amount of information and program instructions in memory, as shown in Figure 5-11.

A security issue with using virtual swap space is that when the system is shut down, or processes that were using the swap space are terminated, the pointers to the pages are reset to "available" even though the actual data written to disk is still physically there. These data could conceivably be compromised and captured. On a very secure operating system, there are routines to wipe the swap spaces after a process is done with it, before it is used again. The routines should also erase this data before a system shutdown, at which time the operating system would no longer be able to maintain any control over what happens on the hard drive surface.

 NOTE If a program, file, or data are encrypted and saved on the hard drive, they will be decrypted when used by the controlling program. While these unencrypted data are sitting in RAM, the system could write out the data to the swap space on the hard drive, in their unencrypted state. Attackers have figured out how to gain access to this space in unauthorized manners.

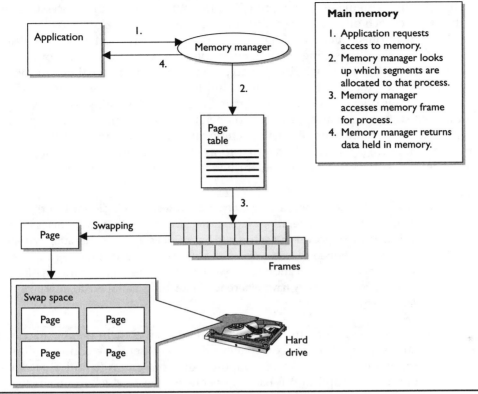

Main memory

1. Application requests access to memory.
2. Memory manager looks up which segments are allocated to that process.
3. Memory manager accesses memory frame for process.
4. Memory manager returns data held in memory.

Figure 5-11   Combining RAM and secondary storage to create virtual memory

CPU Modes and Protection Rings

If I am corrupted, very bad things can happen.
Response: Then you need to go into ring 0.

If an operating system is going to be stable, it must be able to protect itself from its users and their applications. This requires the capability to distinguish between operations performed on behalf of the operating system itself and operations performed on behalf of the users or applications. This can be complex because the operating system software may be accessing memory segments, sending instructions to the CPU for processing, and accessing secondary storage devices at the same time. Each user application (e-mail client, antivirus program, web browser, word processor, personal firewall, and so on) may also be attempting the same types of activities at the same time. The operating system must keep track of all of these events and ensure none of them violates the system's overall security policy.

The operating system has several protection mechanisms to ensure processes do not negatively affect each other or the critical components of the system itself. One has already been mentioned: memory protection. Another security mechanism the system uses is *protection rings*. These rings provide strict boundaries and definitions for what the processes that work within each ring can access and what operations they can successfully execute. The processes that operate within the inner rings have more privileges than the processes operating in the outer rings, because the inner rings only permit the most trusted components and processes to operate within them. Although operating systems may vary in the number of protection rings they use, processes that execute within the inner rings are usually referred to as existing in privileged, or supervisor, mode. The processes working in the outer rings are said to execute in user mode.

NOTE   The actual ring architecture used by a system is dictated by the processor and the operating system. The hardware chip (processor) is constructed to provide a certain number of rings, and the operating system must be developed to also work in this ring structure. This is one reason why an operating system platform may work with an Intel chip but not an Alpha chip, for example. They have different architectures and ways to interpret instruction sets.

Operating system components operate in a ring that gives them the most access to memory locations, peripheral devices, system drivers, and sensitive configuration parameters. Because this ring provides much more dangerous access to critical resources, it is the most protected. Applications usually operate in ring 3, which limits the type of memory, peripheral device, and driver access activity and is controlled through the operating system services or system calls. The different rings are illustrated in Figure 5-12. The type of commands and instructions sent to the CPU from applications in the outer rings are more restrictive in nature. If an application tries to send instructions to the CPU that fall outside its permission level, the CPU treats this violation as an exception and may show a general protection fault or exception error and attempt to shut down the offending application.

Protection rings support the availability, integrity, and confidentiality requirements of multitasking operating systems. The most commonly used architecture provides four protection rings:

- **Ring 0**   Operating system kernel
- **Ring 1**   Remaining parts of the operating system
- **Ring 2**   I/O drivers and utilities
- **Ring 3**   Applications and user activity

These protection rings provide an intermediate layer between subjects and objects, and are used for access control when a subject tries to access an object. The ring determines the access level to sensitive system resources. The lower the number, the greater the amount of privilege given to the process that runs within that ring. Each subject and

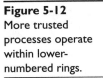

Figure 5-12
More trusted
processes operate
within lower-
numbered rings.

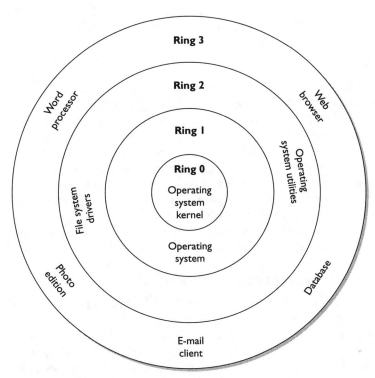

object is logically assigned a number (0 through 3) depending upon the level of trust the operating system assigns it. A subject in ring 3 cannot directly access an object in ring 1, but subjects in ring 1 can directly access an object in ring 3. Entities can only access objects within their own ring and cannot directly communicate with objects in higher rings. When an application needs access to components in rings it is not allowed to directly access, it makes a request of the operating system to perform the necessary tasks. This is handled through system calls, where the operating system executes instructions not allowed in user mode. The request is passed off to an operating system service, which works at a higher privilege level and can carry out the more sensitive tasks.

When the operating system executes instructions for processes in rings 0 and 1, it operates in supervisor mode or privileged mode. When the operating system executes instructions for applications and processes in ring 3, it operates in user mode. User mode provides a much more restrictive environment for the application to work in, which in turn protects the system from misbehaving programs.

If CPU execution modes and protection rings are new to you, think of protection rings as buckets. The operating system has to work within the structure and confines provided by the CPU. The CPU provides the operating system with different buckets, labeled 0 through 3. The operating system must logically place processes into the different buckets, based upon the trust level the operating system has in those processes. Since the operating system kernel is the most trusted component, it and its processes go into bucket 0. The remaining operating system processes go into bucket 1 and all user applications go into bucket 3.

NOTE Many operating systems today do not use the second protection ring very often, if at all.

So, when a process from bucket 0 needs its instructions to be executed by the CPU, the CPU checks the bucket number (ring number) and flips a bit indicating that this process can be fully trusted. This means this process can interact with all of the functionality the CPU provides to processes. Some of the most privileged activities are I/O and memory access attempts. When another process, this time from bucket 3, needs its instructions processed by the CPU, the CPU first looks at what bucket this process came from. Since this process is from bucket 3, the CPU knows the operating system has the least amount of trust in this process and therefore flips a bit that restricts the amount of functionality available to this process.

The CPU dictates how many buckets (rings) there are, and the operating system will be developed to use either two or all of them.

Operating System Architecture

You can't see me and you don't know that I exist, so you can't talk to me.
Response: Fine by me.

Operating systems can be developed by using several types of architecture. The architecture is the framework that dictates how the operating system's services and functions are placed and how they interact. This section looks at the monolithic, layered, and client/server structures.

A *monolithic operating system architecture* is commonly referred to as "The Big Mess" because of its lack of structure. The operating system is mainly made up of various procedures that can call upon each other in a haphazard manner. In these types of systems, modules of code can call upon each other as needed. The communication between the different modules is not as structured and controlled as in a layered architecture, and data hiding is not provided. MS-DOS is an example of a monolithic operating system.

A *layered operating system* architecture separates system functionality into hierarchical layers. For example, a system that followed a layered architecture was, strangely enough, called THE (Technische Hogeschool Eindhoven) multiprogramming system. THE had five layers of functionality. Layer 0 controlled access to the processor and provided multiprogramming functionality: layer 1 carried out memory management; layer 2 provided interprocess communication; layer 3 dealt with I/O devices; and layer 4 was where the applications resided. Layer 5 was the user layer and not implemented directly by THE. The processes at the different layers each had interfaces to be used by processes in layers below and above them.

This is different from a monolithic architecture, in which the different modules can communicate with any other module. Layered operating systems provide *data hiding*, which means that instructions and data (packaged up as procedures) at the various layers do not have direct access to the instructions and data at any other layers. Each procedure at each layer has access only to its own data and a set of functions that it requires to carry out its own tasks. If a procedure can access more procedures than it really needs, this opens the door for more successful compromises. For example, if an attacker is able to compromise and gain control of one procedure, and this procedure has direct access to all other procedures, the attacker could compromise a more privileged procedure and carry out more devastating activities.

A monolithic operating system provides only one layer of security. In a layered system, each layer should provide its own security and access control. If one layer contains the necessary security mechanisms to make security decisions for all the other layers, then that one layer knows too much about (and has access to) too many objects at the different layers. This directly violates the data-hiding concept. Modularizing software and its code increases the assurance level of the system, because if one module is compromised, it does not mean all other modules are now vulnerable. Examples of layered operating systems are THE, VAX/VMS, Multics, and Unix (although THE and Multics are no longer in use).

 NOTE Do not confuse client/server *operating system* architecture with client/server network architecture, which is the traditional association for "client/server." In a *network*, an application works in a client/server model because it provides distributed computing capabilities. The client portion of the application resides on the workstations, and the server portion is usually a back-end database or server.

Another approach to system design works within a client/server architecture, which means that portions of software and functionality that were previously in the monolithic kernel are now at the higher levels of the operating system. The operating system functions are divided into several different processes that run in user mode, instead of kernel mode.

The goal of a client/server architecture is to move as much code as possible from having to work in kernel mode (privileged mode) so the system has a leaner kernel, referred to as the *microkernel*. In this model, the requesting process is referred to as the client, and the process that fulfills the request is called the server. The server process can be file system server, memory server, I/O server, or process server. These servers are commonly called *subsystems*. The client is either a user process or another operating system process.

Domains

Okay, here are all the marbles you can play with. We will call that your domain of resources.

A *domain* is defined as a set of objects that a subject is able to access. This domain can be all the resources a user can access, all the files available to a program, the memory segments available to a process, or the services and processes available to an application. A subject needs to be able to access and use objects (resources) to perform tasks, and the domain defines which objects are available to the subject and which objects are untouchable and therefore unusable by the subject.

 NOTE Remember that a thread is a portion of a process. When the thread is generated, it shares the same domain (resources) as its process.

These domains have to be identified, separated, and strictly enforced. An operating system and CPU work in either privileged mode or user mode. The reason to even use these different modes, which are dictated by the protection ring, is to define different domains. When a process's instructions are being executed in privileged mode, the process has a much larger domain to work with (or more resources to access); thus, it can carry out more activities. When an operating system process works in privileged mode, it can access more memory segments, transfer data from an unprotected domain to a protected domain, and directly access and communicate with hardware devices. An application that functions in user mode cannot access memory directly and has a more limited amount of resources available to it. Only a certain segment of memory is available to this application, and that segment must be accessed in an indirect and controlled fashion.

A process that resides in a privileged domain needs to be able to execute its instructions and process its data with the assurance that programs in a different domain cannot negatively affect its environment. This is referred to as an *execution domain*. Because processes in a privileged domain have access to sensitive resources, the environment must be protected from rogue program code or unexpected activities resulting from programs in other domains. Some systems may only have distinct user and privilege areas, whereas other systems may have complex architectures that contain up to ten execution domains.

An execution domain has a direct correlation to the protection ring that a subject or object is assigned to. The lower the protection ring number, the higher the privilege and the larger the domain. This concept is depicted in Figure 5-13.

Layering and Data Hiding

Although, academically, there are three main types of architectures for operating systems, the terms *layering* and *data hiding* are commonly used when talking about protection mechanisms for operating systems—even ones that follow the client/server architecture, because it also uses layering and data hiding to protect itself.

A layered operating system architecture *mainly* addresses how functionality is laid out and is available to the users and programs. It provides its functionality in a hierarchy, whereas a client/server architecture provides functionality in more of a linear fashion. A request does not have to go through various layers in a client/server architecture. The request just goes to the necessary subsystem. But in terms of security, both architectures use layer and data hiding to protect the critical operating system processes from applications, and applications from other applications.

It is almost too bad that we have so many terms—execution domains, protection rings, layering, data hiding, protection domains, CPU modes, and so on—because in reality they all are different ways to describe the same thing that takes place within every operating system today. When people are first learning these topics, many of these concepts seem discrete and totally unrelated. But in reality, these concepts have to work together in a very orchestrated manner for the whole operating system to work and provide the level of protection it does.

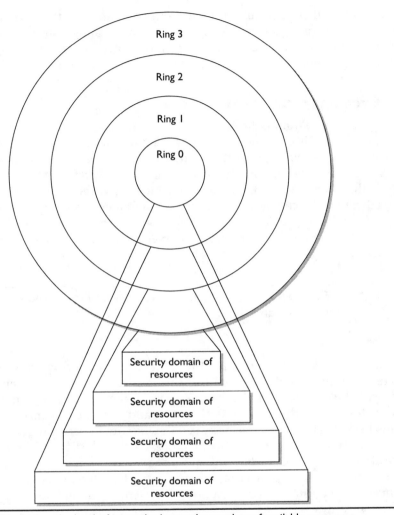

Figure 5-13 The higher the level of trust, the larger the number of available resources.

As previously discussed, the operating system and CPU work within the same architecture, which provides protection rings. A process's protection domain (execution domain) is determined by the protection ring that it resides within. When a process needs the CPU to execute instructions, the CPU works in a specific mode (user or privileged) depending upon what protection ring the process is in. Layering and data hiding are provided by placing the different processes in different protection rings and controlling how communication takes place from the less trusted and the more trusted processes.

So, layering is a way to provide buffers between the more trusted and less trusted processes. The less trusted processes cannot directly communicate with the more trusted processes, but rather must submit their requests to an operating system service. This service acts as a broker or a bouncer that makes sure nothing gains unauthorized access to the more trusted processes. This architecture protects the operating system overall, including all the applications and user activities going on within it.

The Evolution of Terminology

Although *academically* monolithic, layered, and client/server architectures describe how an *operating system* is constructed, these terms have morphed to describe mainly how the kernel is built. What this means is that in the industry, and on the CISSP exam, when you see the term "monolithic system," it is actually referring to the fact that all of the code that makes up the kernel runs in kernel (privileged mode). So the confusing piece is that there is actually an operating system framework called a monolithic framework and there is a specific term that applies only to the kernel (monolithic kernel)— but today these terms have merged. Whenever the term "monolithic system" is used today, it refers to how the kernel is built.

 NOTE Remember that kernel mode, privileged mode, and supervisory mode all mean the same thing.

A monolithic kernel means all of the kernel's activity works in privileged (supervisory) mode, as illustrated in Figure 5-14. This means the operating system's functionality (process, file, memory, I/O management, and more) work in ring 0 of the protection rings we discussed earlier. Windows NT, 2000, and Vista are all considered monolithic systems because all of their operating services execute in kernel mode. On one hand, this causes a security risk, because if one process within the kernel fails, it can affect the whole kernel. It also means that with more code running in this privilege mode, more code can be exploited by attackers, giving them a high level of control of the system. This means that creating a secure monolithic system is complex and it is more difficult to ensure security.

The reason Windows operating systems (and Unix and Linux) have been developed to use a kernel is because of performance. When some kernel components run in user mode and others in kernel mode, it takes a lot longer for the CPU to carry out its execution of instructions because of the changing from user mode to kernel mode and back again.

What this means is that most of the operating systems we work with today mainly use ring 0 and ring 3 of the protection ring architecture described in a previous section. All of the kernel and device drivers are in ring 0 and all user applications are in ring 3. Since drivers run in this privileged mode, it is important the drivers be written properly and not be malicious in any way. Since many device drivers are provided by third parties, it is hard to know if they are developed properly and securely. This is why Microsoft created much stricter requirements for drivers in its Vista operating system. Third-party vendors that write drivers must now meet much more stringent criteria before the operating system will allow them to load.

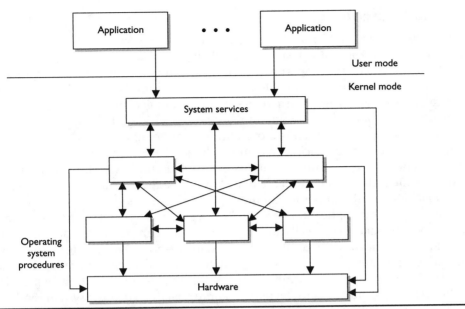

Figure 5-14 Subsystems fulfill the requests of the client processes.

Breaking It Down for the Exam

The following statements summarize many of the critical concepts you need to understand:

- Layering and data hiding provide protection to data and processes by implementing layers of abstraction. Access to sensitive processes and data can only take place through properly formatted requests that are sent to system APIs. This means the communication that takes place between the different layers of trust only happens through well-defined interfaces. Creating and maintaining these different layers helps protect data from other processes that are not authorized to access it.

- If a process does not have an interface with which to communicate to another process at another layer, it cannot have access to its data.

- The protection ring architecture allows for processes to run in either kernel or user mode.

- Processes with a higher trust level (that is, they work in a lower number protection ring) have a larger domain than processes with lower trust levels.

- Execution (protection) domains allow for the isolation of process activity, which provides protection and system stability.

- Monolithic systems have all kernel activities running in supervisory mode, whereas microkernels have only a small subset of kernel activities running in this privileged mode. All other kernel activities run in user mode. Most modern operating systems take a hybrid approach between monolithic and microkernel in design.

Virtual Machines

I would like my own simulated environment so I can have my own world.
Response: No problem. Just slip on this straightjacket first.

If you have been into computers for a while, you might remember computer games that did not have the complex, life-like graphics of today's games. *Pong* and *Asteroids* were what we had to play with when we were younger. In those simpler times, the games were 16-bit and were written to work in a 16-bit MS-DOS environment. When our Windows operating systems moved from 16-bit to 32-bit, the 32-bit operating systems were written to be backward compatible, so someone could still load and play a 16-bit game in an environment that the game did not understand. The continuation of this little life pleasure was available to users because the operating systems created virtual machines for the games to run in.

When a 16-bit application needs to interact with the operating system, it has been developed to make system calls and interact with the computer's memory in a way that would only work within a 16-bit operating system—not a 32-bit system. So, the virtual machine simulates a 16-bit operating system, and when the application makes a request, the operating system converts the 16-bit request into a 32-bit request (this is called *thunking*) and reacts to the request appropriately. When the system sends a reply to this request, it changes the 32-bit reply into a 16-bit reply so the application understands it.

Today, virtual machines are much more advanced. Basic *virtualization* enables single hardware equipment to run multiple operating system environments synchronously, greatly enhancing processing power utilization, among other benefits. Creating virtual instances of operating systems, applications, and storage devices is known as virtualization.

In today's jargon, a virtual instance of an operating system is known as a *virtual machine.* A virtual machine is commonly referred to as a *guest* that is executed in the *host* environment. Virtualization allows a single host environment to execute multiple guests at once, with multiple virtual machines dynamically pooling resources from a common physical system. Computer resources such as RAM, processors, and storage are emulated through the host environment. The virtual machines do not directly access these resources; instead, they communicate with the host environment responsible for managing system resources.

What this means is that you can have one computer running several different operating systems at one time. For example, you can run a system with Windows 2000, Linux, Unix, and Windows 2008 on one computer. Think of a house that has different rooms. Each operating system gets its own room, but each share the same resources that the house provides—a foundation, electricity, water, roof, and so on. An operating system that is "living" in a specific room does not need to know about or interact with another operating system in another room to take advantage of the resources provided by the house. The same concept happens in a computer: Each operating system shares the resources provided by the physical system (as in memory, processor, buses, and so on). They "live" and work in their own "rooms," which are the guest virtual machines. The physical computer itself is the host.

Why do this? One reason is that it is cheaper than having a full physical system for each and every operating system. If they can all live on one system and share the same physical resources, your costs are reduced immensely. This is the same reason people get roommates. The rent can be split among different people, and all can share the same house and resources.

The following useful list, taken from www.kernelthread.com/publications/virtualization, pertains to the different reasons for using virtualization in various environments. It was written years ago, but is still very applicable to today's needs and the CISSP exam.

- *Virtual machines can be used to consolidate the workloads of several under-utilized servers to fewer machines, perhaps a single machine (server consolidation). Related benefits are savings on hardware, environmental costs, management, and administration of the server infrastructure.*

- *The need to run legacy applications is served well by virtual machines. A legacy application might simply not run on newer hardware and/or operating systems. Even if it does, if may under-utilize the server, so it makes sense to consolidate several applications. This may be difficult without virtualization because such applications are usually not written to coexist within a single execution environment.*

- *Virtual machines can be used to provide secure, isolated sandboxes for running untrusted applications. You could even create such an execution environment dynamically—on the fly—as you download something from the Internet and run it. Virtualization is an important concept in building secure computing platforms.*

- *Virtual machines can be used to create operating systems, or execution environments with resource limits, and given the right schedulers, resource guarantees. Partitioning usually goes hand-in-hand with quality of service in the creation of QoS-enabled operating systems.*

- *Virtual machines can provide the illusion of hardware, or hardware configuration that you do not have (such as SCSI devices or multiple processors). Virtualization can also be used to simulate networks of independent computers.*

- *Virtual machines can be used to run multiple operating systems simultaneously: different versions, or even entirely different systems, which can be on hot standby. Some such systems may be hard or impossible to run on newer real hardware.*

- *Virtual machines allow for powerful debugging and performance monitoring. You can put such tools in the virtual machine monitor, for example. Operating systems can be debugged without losing productivity, or setting up more complicated debugging scenarios.*

- *Virtual machines can isolate what they run, so they provide fault and error containment. You can inject faults proactively into software to study its subsequent behavior.*

- *Virtual machines are great tools for research and academic experiments. Since they provide isolation, they are safer to work with. They encapsulate the entire state of a running system: you can save the state, examine it, modify it, reload it, and so on.*

- *Virtualization can make tasks such as system migration, backup, and recovery easier and more manageable.*

- *Virtualization on commodity hardware has been popular in co-located hosting. Many of the above benefits make such hosting secure, cost-effective, and appealing in general.*

Additional Storage Devices

Besides the memory environment discussed previously, many types of physical storage devices should be covered, along with the ramifications of security compromises that could affect them. Many, if not all, of the various storage devices used today enable the theft or compromise of data in an organization. As their sizes have shrunk, their capacities have grown. Floppy disks, while small in relative storage capacity (about 1.44MB of data), have long been known to be a source of viruses and data theft. A thief who has physical access to a computer with an insecure operating system can use a basic floppy disk to boot the system.

Many PCs and Unix workstations have a BIOS that allows the machine to be booted from devices other than the floppy disk, such as a CD-ROM or even a USB thumb drive. Possible ways to harden the environment include password-protecting the BIOS so that a nonapproved medium cannot take over the machine, and controlling access to the physical environment of the computer equipment.

In many instances, removable storage units have unfortunately come up missing. Two noteworthy incidents occurred in July 2004, at which time both Los Alamos National Laboratory and Sandia National Laboratories reported lost storage media containing classified information. This raised enough of a concern at Los Alamos that the military research facility was totally shut down, with no employees allowed to enter, while a thorough search and investigation was performed. Sandia National Laboratories reported it was missing a computer floppy disk marked classified, which it later located.

Rewritable CD/DVDs, mini-disks, optical disks—virtually any portable storage medium—can be used to compromise security. Current technology headaches for the security professional include USB thumb drives and USB-attachable MP3 players capable of storing multiple gigabytes of data. The first step in prevention is to update existing security policies (or implement new ones) to include the new technologies. Even cellular phones can be connected to computer ports for data, sound, image, and video transmission that could be out of bounds of an outdated security policy. Technologies such as Bluetooth, FireWire, and Blackberry all have to be taken into account when addressing security concerns and vulnerabilities.

Input/Output Device Management

Some things come in, some things go out.
Response: We took a vote and would like you to go out.

We have covered a lot of operating system responsibilities up to now, and we are not stopping yet. An operating system also has to control all input/output devices. It sends commands to them, accepts their interrupts when they need to communicate with the CPU, and provides an interface between the devices and the applications.

I/O devices are usually considered block or character devices. A block device works with data in fixed-size blocks, each block with its own unique address. A disk drive is an example of a block device. A character device, such as a printer, network interface card, or mouse, works with streams of characters, without using any fixed sizes. This type of data is not addressable.

When a user chooses to print a document, open a stored file on a word processor, or save files to a jump drive, these requests go from the application the user is working in, through the operating system, and to the device requested. The operating system uses a device driver to communicate with a device controller, which may be a circuit card that fits into an expansion slot. The controller is an electrical component with its own software that provides a communication path that enables the device and operating system to exchange data. The operating system sends commands to the device controller's registers and the controller then writes data to the peripheral device or extracts data to be processed by the CPU, depending on the given commands. If the command is to extract data from the hard drive, the controller takes the bits and puts them into the necessary block size and carries out a checksum activity to verify the integrity of the data. If the integrity is successfully verified, the data are put into memory for the CPU to interact with.

Operating systems need to access and release devices and computer resources properly. Different operating systems handle accessing devices and resources differently. For example, Windows NT is considered a stabler and safer data processing environment than Windows 9x because applications in Windows NT cannot make direct requests to hardware devices. Windows NT and Windows 2000 have a much more controlled method of accessing devices than Windows 9x. This method helps protect the system from badly written code that does not properly request and release resources. Such a level of protection helps ensure the resources' integrity and availability.

Interrupts

When an I/O device has completed whatever task was asked of it, it needs to inform the CPU that the necessary data are now in memory for processing. The device's controller sends a signal down a bus, which is detected by the interrupt controller. (This is what it means to use an interrupt. The device signals the interrupt controller and is basically saying, "I am done and need attention now.") If the CPU is busy *and* the device's interrupt is not a higher priority than whatever job is being processed, then the device has to wait. The interrupt controller sends a message to the CPU, indicating what device needs attention. The operating system has a table (called the *interrupt vector*) of all the I/O devices connected to it. The CPU compares the received number with the values within the interrupt vector so it knows which I/O device needs its services. The table has the memory addresses of the different I/O devices. So when the CPU understands that the hard drive needs attention, it looks in the table to find the correct memory address. This is the new program counter value, which is the initial address of where the CPU should start reading from.

Why Does My Video Card Need to Have Its Own RAM?

The RAM on a video card is really just a type of buffer. The application or operating system writes the pixel values into this RAM space instead of writing to the system's RAM. The pixel values are then displayed to the user on the monitor screen. Graphic-intensive games work better with video cards with a lot of RAM, because storing this display information on the system's RAM takes too long for the read and write procedures. This results in delayed reactions between the user's interaction commands and what is displayed on the screen. We never seemed to have these problems when we all played *Pong*.

One of the main goals of the operating system software that controls I/O activity is to be device independent. This means a developer can write an application to read (open a file) or write (save a file) to any device (floppy disk, jump drive, hard drive, CD-ROM drive). This level of abstraction frees application developers from having to write different procedures to interact with the various I/O devices. If a developer had to write an individual procedure of how to write to a CD-ROM drive, *and* how to write to a floppy disk, how to write to a jump drive, how to write to a hard disk, and so on, each time a new type of I/O device was developed, all of the applications would have to be patched or upgraded.

Operating systems can carry out software I/O procedures in various ways. We will look at the following methods:

- Programmed I/O
- Interrupt-driven I/O
- I/O using DMA
- Premapped I/O
- Fully mapped I/O

Programmable I/O   If an operating system is using programmable I/O, this means the CPU sends data to an I/O device and polls the device to see if it is ready to accept more data. If the device is not ready to accept more data, the CPU wastes time by waiting for the device to become ready. For example, the CPU would send a byte of data (a character) to the printer and then ask the printer if it is ready for another byte. The CPU sends the text to be printed one byte at a time. This is a very slow way of working and wastes precious CPU time. So the smart people figured out a better way: interrupt-driven I/O.

Interrupt-Driven I/O   If an operating system is using interrupt-driven I/O, this means the CPU sends a character over to the printer and then goes and works on another process's request. When the printer is done printing the first character, it sends an interrupt to the CPU. The CPU stops what it is doing, sends another character to the printer, and moves to another job. This process (send character—go do something else—interrupt—send another character) continues until the whole text is printed. Although the CPU is not waiting for each byte to be printed, this method does waste a lot of time dealing with all the interrupts. So we excused those smart people and brought in some smarter people, who came up with I/O using DMA.

I/O Using DMA Direct memory access (DMA) is a way of transferring data between I/O devices and the system's memory without using the CPU. This speeds up data transfer rates significantly. When used in I/O activities, the DMA controller feeds the characters to the printer without bothering the CPU. This method is sometimes referred to as *unmapped I/O*.

Premapped I/O Premapped I/O and fully mapped I/O (described next) do not pertain to performance, as do the earlier methods, but provide two approaches that can directly affect security. In a premapped I/O system, the CPU sends the physical memory address of the requesting process to the I/O device, and the I/O device is trusted enough to interact with the contents of memory directly. So the CPU does not control the interactions between the I/O device and memory. The operating system trusts the device to behave properly. Scary.

Fully Mapped I/O Under fully mapped I/O, the operating system does not fully trust the I/O device. The physical address is not given to the I/O device. Instead, the device works purely with logical addresses and works on behalf (under the security context) of the requesting process. So the operating system does not trust the device to interact with memory directly. The operating system does not trust the process or device and acts as the broker to control how they communicate with each other.

Beam Me Up, Scotty!

A cofounder of Intel, Gordon Moore, came up with Moore's Law, which states that the number of transistors placed inexpensively on an integrated circuit will double every 18 months. No one really paid attention to this until it came to be true every 18 months or so. Now he's right up there with Nostradamus.

So chip makers have continually put an amazing amount of stuff on one tiny piece of silicon, but we will soon hit the wall and have to look for other types of technologies. Today, people are looking at quantum physics to make up tomorrow's processor. In quantum physics, particles are not restricted to holding just two states (1 or 0), but instead can hold these states simultaneously and other states in between. Freaky.

And other individuals are looking to our own personal DNA, which holds the instructions for our bodies. There have already been experiments in which DNA was used for computation processes. It can carry out complex computations in parallel instead of serially like today's processors. But it sounds kind of gross.

You won't find a quantum or DNA computer at Best Buy any time soon, but one day maybe.

System Architecture

Designing a system from the ground up is a complicated task with many intricate and abstract goals that must be achieved through mathematics, logic, design, programming code, and implementation. Fundamental design decisions must be made when constructing a system. Security is only one goal of a system, but it is the goal security professionals are most concerned about.

Availability, integrity, and confidentiality can be enforced at different places within an enterprise. For example, a company may store customer credit card information in a database that many users can access. This information, obviously, requires protection to ensure it is not accessed or modified in an unauthorized manner. We should start with general questions and gradually drill down into the details. Where should this protection be placed? Should there be access controls that screen users when they log in and assign them their rights at that point, dictating which data they can and cannot access? Should the data files holding the credit card information be protected at the file system level? Should protection be provided by restricting users' operations and activities? Or should there be a combination of all of these? The first and most general question is, Where should the protection take place: at the user's end, where the data are stored, or by restricting user activities within the environment? This is illustrated in Figure 5-15.

The same type of questions have to be answered when building an operating system. Once these general questions have been answered, the placement of the mechanisms needs to be addressed. Security mechanisms can be placed at the hardware, kernel, operating system, services, and program layers. At which layer(s) should security mechanisms be implemented? If protection is implemented at the hardware layer, then a broad level of protection is provided, because it provides a baseline of security for all the components that work on top of the hardware layer. If the protection mechanisms are closer to the user (in the higher levels of the operating system architecture), the security is more detail-oriented and focused than mechanisms that work at the lower levels of the architecture.

No matter where the security mechanism is placed within the operating system architecture, the more complex the security mechanism becomes, the less assurance it usually provides. The reason is that greater complexity of the mechanism demands more technical understanding from the individuals who install, test, maintain, and use it. The more complex the security mechanism, the harder it is to fully test it under all possible conditions. On the other hand, simplistic mechanisms may not be able to provide the desired richness of functionality and options, although they are easier to install, maintain, use, and test. So the trade-offs between functionality and assurance must be fully understood to make the right security mechanism choices when designing a system.

Once the designers have an idea of what the security mechanisms should focus on (users, operations, or data), what layer(s) the mechanisms should be placed at (hardware, kernel, operating system, services, or program), and how complex each mechanism is, they need to build and integrate the mechanisms in such a way that they have a proper relationship with other parts of the system.

First, the design team needs to decide what system mechanisms to trust and place in protection ring 0. Then, the team must specify how these modules of code can interact in a secure manner. Although it might seem that you would want to trust all the compo-

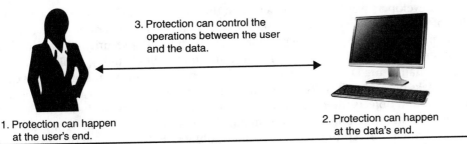

Figure 5-15 Security can take place in three main areas.

nents within the system, this would cause too much overhead, complexity, and performance bottlenecks. For a mechanism to be trusted, it must perform in a predictable and secure manner and not adversely affect other trusted or untrusted mechanisms. In return, these trusted components have access to more privileged services, have direct access to memory, usually have higher priority when requesting CPU processing time, and have more control over system resources. So the trusted subjects and objects need to be identified and distinguished from the untrusted ones and placed into defined subsets.

Defined Subsets of Subjects and Objects

I totally trust you. You can do whatever you want.
Response: I want to leave.

As stated previously, not all components need to be trusted and therefore not all components fall within the *trusted computing base (TCB)*. The TCB is defined as the total combination of protection mechanisms within a computer system. The TCB includes hardware, software, and firmware. These are part of the TCB because the system is sure these components will enforce the security policy and not violate it.

The components that do fall within the TCB need to be identified and their accepted capabilities need to be defined. For example, a system that does not require a high level of trust may permit all authenticated users to access and modify all files on the computer. This subset of subjects and objects is large and the relationship between them is loose and relaxed. A system that requires a higher level of trust may permit only two subjects to access all files on a computer system, and permit only one of those subjects to actually modify all the files. This subset is much smaller and the rules being enforced are more stringent and detailed.

Security Architecture

The security architecture is one component of a product's overall architecture and is developed to provide guidance during the design of the product. It should outline the level of assurance required and the potential impacts this level of security could have during the development stages and on the product overall. As the software development project moves from architecture, to design, to specifications, and then code development, the security architecture and requirements become more granular with each step.

If developers want to develop a system that achieves an Orange Book assurance rating of D (very low), then what makes up the TCB is not much of an issue because the system will not be expected to provide a very high level of security. However, if the developers want to develop a system with an Orange Book rating of B2 or B1 (much higher than rating D), they will need to ensure that all components of the TCB carry out their tasks properly. These TCB components need to enforce strict rules that dictate how subjects and objects interact. The developers also need to ensure these components are identified, audited, and react in a predictable manner, because these are the components that will be scrutinized, tested, and evaluated before a rating of B2 or B1 can be given. (The Orange Book is an evaluation criterion and is addressed in the section "The Orange Book" later in the chapter.)

Trusted Computing Base

The term "trusted computing base," which originated from the Orange Book, does not address the level of security a system provides, but rather the level of trust a system provides, albeit in a security sense. This is because no computer system can be totally secure. The types of attacks and vulnerabilities change and evolve over time, and with enough time and resources, most attacks become successful. However, if a system meets a certain criteria, it is looked upon as providing a certain level of trust, meaning it will react predictably in different types of situations.

The TCB does not address *only* operating system components, because a computer system is not made up of *only* an operating system. The TCB addresses hardware, software components, and firmware. Each can affect the computer's environment in a negative or positive manner, and each has a responsibility to support and enforce the security policy of that particular system. Some components and mechanisms have direct responsibilities in supporting the security policy, such as firmware that will not let a user boot a computer from a floppy disk, or the memory manager that will not let processes overwrite other processes' data. Then there are components that do not enforce the security policy but must behave properly and not violate the trust of a system. Examples of the ways in which a component could violate the system's security policy include an application that attempts to make a direct call to a piece of hardware instead of using the proper system calls through the operating system, a program that attempts to read data outside of its approved memory space, or a piece of software that does not properly release resources after use.

A TCB is usually a very abstract concept for people who are not system designers, and many books and papers do not make it any easier to fully understand what this term means. If an operating system is using a TCB, this means the system has a hardened kernel that compartmentalizes system processes. The kernel is made up of hardware, software, and firmware, so in a sense the kernel is the TCB. But the TCB can include other components, such as trusted commands, programs, and configuration files that can directly interact with the kernel. For example, when installing a Unix system, the administrator can choose to install the TCB during the setup procedure. If the TCB is enabled, then the system has a trusted path, a trusted shell, and system integrity–checking capabilities. A *trusted path* is a communication channel between the user, or program, and the kernel. The TCB provides protection resources to ensure this channel cannot be compromised in any way. A *trusted shell* means that someone who is working in that shell cannot "bust out of it," and other processes cannot "bust into it."

Several Unix commands are part of the TCB, such as `setuid` (set process ID) and `setguid` (set process group ID). Only a privileged user, as in root, should be able to change process ID information.

Earlier operating systems (MS-DOS, Windows 3.11, and Novell Netware release 3, for example) did not have TCBs. Windows 95 had a TCB, but it can be used only while working in 32-bit mode. Windows NT was the first version of Windows that truly incorporated the idea of a TCB. Microsoft is using the words "Trustworthy Computing" a lot, but this is not just a Microsoft concept. Several vendors came together to develop a better TCB by agreeing to improve methods on how to protect software from being compromised. Microsoft is just the first vendor to implement it, in its Windows 2003 product.

NOTE To understand Microsoft's Windows 7 kernel, visit http://channel9 .msdn.com/shows/Going+Deep/Mark-Russinovich-Inside-Windows-7/.

Every operating system has specific components that would cause the system grave danger if they were compromised. The TCB provides extra layers of protection around these mechanisms to help ensure they are *not* compromised, so the system will always run in a safe and predictable manner.

How does the TCB do its magic? The processes within the TCB are the components that protect the system overall. So the developers of the operating system must make sure these processes have their own *execution domain*. This means they reside in ring 0, their instructions are executed in privileged state, and no less trusted processes can directly interact with them. The developers need to ensure the operating system maintains an isolated execution domain, so their processes cannot be compromised or tampered with. The resources that the TCB processes use must also be isolated, so tight access control can be provided and all access requests and operations can be properly audited. So basically, the operating system tells all the other processes they cannot play with the TCB processes and that they cannot play with the TCB's resources.

The four basic functions of the TCB are process activation, execution domain switching, memory protection, and I/O operations. We have really covered all of these things already throughout previous sections without using this exact terminology, so here's a recap. *Process activation* deals with the activities that must take place when a process is going to have its instructions and data processed by the CPU. As described earlier, the CPU fills its registers with information about the requesting process (program counter, base and limit addresses, user or privileged mode, and so on). A process is "activated" when its interrupt is called upon, enabling it to interact with the CPU. A process is "deactivated" when its instructions are completely executed by the CPU or when another process with a higher priority calls upon the CPU. When a process is deactivated, the CPU's registers must be filled with new information about the new requesting process. The data that is getting switched in and out of the registers may be sensitive in nature, so the TCB components must make sure all of this is taking place securely.

For an analogy, suppose that five people all want to ask your advice at the same time. There is only one of you, so each person has a certain amount of time that they can spend with you. Person 1 gives you her papers, so you can read through them and figure out her problem in order to give her a proper answer. As you are reading Person 1's papers, Person 2 comes barging into the room claiming he has an emergency. As a result, you put Person 1's papers down on your desk and start reading Person 2's papers to figure out his problem. Eventually, you have five people around you, and you can only spend five seconds with each of them at a time. As you talk to one individual, you must grab the right file from your desk. These files have sensitive information, so you have to make sure to keep all the files straight and make sure these people cannot read one another's files. This is what the TCB and the CPU are doing as they are dealing with several different process requests at one time. Instead of reading stacks of paper, the CPU reads instructions and data on a memory segment stack.

Execution domain switching takes place when a process needs to call upon a process in a higher protection ring. As explained earlier, less trusted processes run in user mode and cannot carry out activities such as communicating with hardware or directly sending requests to the kernel. Therefore, a process running in user mode (ring 3) must make a request to an operating system service, which works in ring 1. The less trusted process will have its information loaded into the CPU's registers and then when the CPU sees that an operating system service has been called, it switches domains and security context. This means the information of the operating system service process is loaded into the CPU's registers and the CPU carries out those instructions in privileged mode. So, execution domain switching refers to when the CPU has to go from executing instructions in user mode to privileged mode and back. All of this must happen properly or a less trusted process might be executed in privileged mode and have direct access to system resources.

Memory protection and I/O operations have been discussed in previous sections, so just realize that these operations are the responsibility of the components within the TCB.

The TCB is responsible for carrying out the TCB memory protection and I/O operations securely. It does this by compartmentalizing these activities into discrete units, which are the processes that make up the kernel. This ensures that if a kernel process is compromised, it does not mean all the processes are now under the control of the attacker.

Not every part of a system needs to be trusted. Part of evaluating the trust level of a system is to identify the architecture, security services, and assurance mechanisms that make up the TCB. During the evaluation process, the tests must show how the TCB is protected from accidental or intentional tampering and compromising activity. For systems to achieve a higher trust level rating, they must meet well-defined TCB requirements, and the details of their operational states, developing stages, testing procedures, and documentation will be reviewed with more granularity than systems attempting to achieve a lower trust rating.

By using specific security criteria, trust can be built into a system, evaluated, and certified. This approach can provide a measurement system for customers to use when comparing one product to another. It also gives vendors guidelines on what expectations are put upon their systems and provides a common assurance rating metric so when one group talks about a C2 rating, everyone else understands what that term means.

The Orange Book is one of these evaluation criteria. It defines a trusted system as hardware and software that utilize measures to protect unclassified or classified data for a range of users without violating access rights and the security policy. It looks at all protection mechanisms within a system that enforce the security policy and provide an environment that will behave in a manner expected of it. This means each layer of the system must trust the underlying layer to perform the expected functions, provide the expected level of protection, and operate in an expected manner under many different situations. When the operating system makes calls to hardware, it anticipates that data will be returned in a specific data format and behave in a consistent and predictable manner. Applications that run on top of the operating system expect to be able to make certain system calls, receive the required data in return, and operate in a reliable and dependable environment. Users expect the hardware, operating system, and applications to perform in particular fashions and provide a certain level of functionality. For all of these actions to behave in such predicable manners, the requirements of a system must be addressed in the planning stages of development, not afterward.

Security Perimeter

Now, whom do we trust?
Response: Anyone inside the security perimeter.

As stated previously, not every process and resource falls within the TCB, so some of these components fall outside of an imaginary boundary referred to as the *security perimeter*. A security perimeter is a boundary that divides the trusted from the untrusted. For the system to stay in a secure and trusted state, precise communication standards must be developed to ensure that when a component within the TCB needs to communicate with a component outside the TCB, the communication cannot expose the system to unexpected security compromises. This type of communication is handled and controlled through interfaces.

For example, a resource that is within the boundary of the TCB, or security perimeter, must not allow less trusted components access to critical system resources. The processes within the TCB must also be careful about the commands and information they accept from less trusted resources. These limitations and restrictions are built into the interfaces that permit this type of communication to take place and are the mechanisms that enforce the security perimeter. Communication between trusted components and untrusted components needs to be controlled to ensure that the system stays stable and safe.

 NOTE The TCB and security perimeter are not physical entities, but conceptual constructs used by system developers to delineate between trusted and untrusted components.

Reference Monitor and Security Kernel

Up to now, our computer system architecture developers have accomplished many things in developing their system. They have defined where the security mechanisms will be located (hardware, kernel, operating system, services, or programs), the processes that are within the TCB, and how the security mechanisms and processes will interact with each other. They have defined the security perimeter that separates the trusted and untrusted components. They have developed proper interfaces for these entities to communicate securely. Now they need to develop and implement a mechanism that ensures that the subjects that access objects have been given the necessary permissions to do so. This means the developers need to develop and implement a reference monitor and security kernel.

The *reference monitor* is an abstract machine that mediates all access subjects have to objects, both to ensure that the subjects have the necessary access rights and to protect the objects from unauthorized access and destructive modification. For a system to achieve a higher level of trust, it must require subjects (programs, users, or processes) to be fully authorized prior to accessing an object (file, program, or resource). A subject must not be allowed to use a requested resource until the subject has proven it has been granted access privileges to use the requested object. The reference monitor is an access control concept, not an actual physical component, which is why it is normally referred to as the "reference monitor concept" or an "abstract machine."

The *security kernel* is made up of hardware, software, and firmware components that fall within the TCB, and it implements and enforces the reference monitor concept. The security kernel mediates all access and functions between subjects and objects. The security kernel is the core of the TCB and is the most commonly used approach to building trusted computing systems. The security kernel has three main requirements:

- It must provide isolation for the processes carrying out the reference monitor concept, and the processes must be tamperproof.

- It must be invoked for every access attempt and must be impossible to circumvent. Thus, the security kernel must be implemented in a complete and foolproof way.

- It must be small enough to be tested and verified in a complete and comprehensive manner.

These are the requirements of the reference monitor; therefore, they are the requirements of the components that provide and enforce the reference monitor concept—the security kernel.

These issues work in the abstract but are implemented in the physical world of hardware devices and software code. The assurance that the components are enforcing the abstract idea of the reference monitor is proved through testing and functionality.

 NOTE The reference monitor is a concept in which an abstract machine mediates all access to objects by subjects. The security kernel is the hardware, firmware, and software of a TCB that implements this concept. The TCB is the totality of protection mechanisms within a computer system that work together to enforce a security policy. The TCB contains the security kernel and all other security protection mechanisms.

The following is a quick analogy to show you the relationship between the processes that make up the kernel, the kernel itself, and the reference monitor concept. Individuals make up a society. The individuals represent the processes, and the society represents the kernel. For a society to have a certain standard of living, its members must interact in specific ways, which is why we have laws. The laws represent the reference monitor, which enforces proper activity. Each individual is expected to stay within the bounds of the laws and act in specific ways so society as a whole is not adversely affected and the standard of living is not threatened. The components within a system must stay within the bounds of the reference monitor's laws so they will not adversely affect other components and threaten the security of the system.

Security Policy

As previously stated, the TCB contains components that directly enforce the security policy, but what is a security policy? A security policy is a set of rules and practices that dictates how sensitive information and resources are managed, protected, and distributed. A security policy expresses exactly what the security level should be by setting the goals of what the security mechanisms are supposed to accomplish. This is an important element that has a major role in defining the design of the system. The security policy is a foundation for the specifications of a system and provides the baseline for evaluating a system.

Chapter 3 examined security policies in depth, but those policies were directed toward the company itself. The security policies being addressed here are for operating systems, devices, and applications. The different policies are similar but have different targets: an organization as opposed to an individual computer system.

A system provides trust by fulfilling and enforcing the security policy and oversees the communication between subjects and objects. The policy must indicate which subjects can access individual objects and which actions are acceptable and unacceptable. The security policy provides the framework for the system's security architecture.

For a system to provide an acceptable level of trust, it must be based on an architecture that provides the capabilities to protect itself from untrusted processes, intentional or accidental compromises, and attacks at different layers of the system. A majority of the trust ratings obtained through formal evaluations require a defined subset of subjects and objects, explicit domains, and the isolation of processes so their access can be controlled and the activities performed on them can be audited.

Let's regroup. We know that a system's trust is defined by how it enforces its own security policy. When a system is tested against specific criteria, a rating is assigned to the system and this rating is used by customers, vendors, and the computing society as a whole. The criteria will determine if the security policy is being properly supported and enforced. The security policy lays out the rules and practices pertaining to how a system will manage, protect, and allow access to sensitive resources. The reference monitor is a concept that says all subjects must have proper authorization to access objects, and this concept is implemented by the security kernel. The security kernel comprises all the resources that supervise system activity in accordance with the system's security policy and is part of the operating system that controls access to system resources. For the security kernel to work correctly, the individual processes must be isolated from each other and domains must be defined to dictate which objects are available to which subjects.

Security policies that prevent information from flowing from a high security level to a lower security level are called *multilevel security policies*. These types of policies permit a subject to access an object only if the subject's security level is higher than or equal to the object's classification.

As previously stated, the concepts covered in the previous sections are abstract ideas that will be manifested in physical hardware components, firmware, software code, and activities through designing, building, and implementing a system. These ideas are like abstract goals and dreams we would like to accomplish, which are obtained by our physical hard work and discipline.

Least Privilege

Once resources and processes are isolated properly, *least privilege* needs to be enforced. This means that a process has no more privileges than necessary to be able to fulfill its functions. Only processes that *need* to carry out critical system functions should be allowed to, and other, less privileged processes should call upon the more privileged processes to carry out these types of activities when necessary. This type of indirect activity protects the system from poorly written or misbehaving code. Processes should possess a level of privilege only as long as they really need it. If a process needs to have its status elevated so it can interact directly with a system resource, as soon as its tasks are complete, the process's status should be dropped to a lower privilege to ensure that another mechanism cannot use it to adversely affect the system. Only processes that need complete system privileges are located in the kernel—other, less privileged processes call upon them to process sensitive or delicate operations.

As an example of least privilege access control, the system backup program may have read access on the files, but it does not need to be able to modify the files. Similarly, the restore program would be allowed to write files to the disk, but not to read them.

Security Models

An important concept in the design and analysis of secure systems is the security model, because it incorporates the security policy that should be enforced in the system. A model is a symbolic representation of a policy. It maps the desires of the policymakers into a set of rules that a computer system must follow.

The reason this chapter has repeatedly mentioned the security policy and its importance is that it is an abstract term that represents the objectives and goals a system must meet and accomplish to be deemed secure and acceptable. How do we get from an abstract security policy to the point at which an administrator is able to uncheck a box on the GUI to disallow David from accessing configuration files on his system? There are many complex steps in between that take place during the system's design and development.

A security model maps the abstract goals of the policy to information system terms by specifying explicit data structures and techniques necessary to enforce the security policy. A security model is usually represented in mathematics and analytical ideas, which are mapped to system specifications and then developed by programmers through programming code. So we have a policy that encompasses security goals such as "each subject must be authorized to access each object." The security model takes this requirement and provides the necessary mathematical formulas, relationships, and structure to be followed to accomplish this goal. From there, specifications are developed per operating system type (Unix, Windows, Macintosh, and so on), and individual vendors can decide how they are going to implement mechanisms that meet these necessary specifications.

So in a very general and simplistic example, if a security policy states that subjects need to be authorized to access objects, the security model would provide the mathematical relationships and formulas explaining how x can access y only through the outlined specific methods. Specifications are then developed to provide a bridge to what this means in a computing environment and how it maps to components and mechanisms that need to be coded and developed. The developers then write the program code to produce the mechanisms that provide a way for a system to use ACLs and give administrators some degree of control. This mechanism presents the network administrator with a GUI that enables the administrator to choose (via check boxes, for example) which subjects can access what objects and to be able to set this configuration within the operating system. This is a rudimentary example, because security models can be very complex, but it is used to demonstrate the relationship between the security policy and the security model.

Some security models, such as the Bell-LaPadula model, enforce rules to provide confidentiality protection. Other models, such as the Biba model, enforce rules to provide integrity protection. Formal security models, such as Bell-LaPadula and Biba, are used to provide high assurance in security. Informal models, such as Clark-Wilson, are used more as a framework to describe how security policies should be expressed and executed.

A security policy outlines goals without regard to how they will be accomplished. A model is a framework that gives the policy form and solves security access problems for particular situations. Several security models have been developed to enforce security policies. The following sections provide overviews of each model.

Relationship Between a Security Policy and a Security Model

If someone tells you to live a healthy and responsible life, this is a very broad, vague, and abstract notion. So when you ask this person how this is accomplished, they outline the things you should and should not do (do not harm others, do not lie, eat your vegetables, and brush your teeth). The security policy provides the abstract goals, and the security model provides the do's and don'ts necessary to fulfill these goals.

State Machine Models

No matter what state I am in, I am always safe.

In *state machine models*, to verify the security of a system, the state is used, which means that all current permissions and all current instances of subjects accessing objects must be captured. Maintaining the state of a system deals with each subject's association with objects. If the subjects can access objects only by means that are concurrent with the security policy, the system is secure. State machines have provided a basis for important security models. A state of a system is a snapshot of a system at one moment of time. Many activities can alter this state, which are referred to as *state transitions*. The developers of an operating system that will implement the state machine model need to look at all the different state transitions that are possible and assess whether a system that starts up in a secure state can be put into an insecure state by any of these events. If all of the activities that are allowed to happen in the system do not compromise the system and put it into an insecure state, then the system executes a secure state machine model.

The state machine model is used to describe the behavior of a system to different inputs. It provides mathematical constructs that represent sets (subjects and objects) and sequences. When an object accepts an input, this modifies a state variable. A simplistic example of a state variable is (Name, Value), as shown in Figure 5-16. This variable is part of the operating system's instruction set. When this variable is called upon to be used, it can be populated with (Color, Red) from the input of a user or program. Let's say the user enters a different value, so now the variable is (Color, Blue). This is a simplistic example of a state transition. Some state transitions are this simple, but complexity comes in when the system must decide if this transition should be allowed. To allow this transition, the object's security attributes and the access rights of the subject must be reviewed and allowed by the operating system.

Developers who implement the state machine model must identify all the initial states (default variable values) and outline how these values can be changed (inputs that will be accepted) so the various number of final states (resulting values) still ensure that the system is safe. The outline of how these values can be changed is often implemented through condition statements: *"if condition then update."*

Formal Models

Using models in software development has not become as popular as once imagined, primarily because vendors are under pressure to get products to market as soon as possible. Using formal models takes more time during the architectural phase of development, extra time that many vendors feel they cannot afford. Formal models are definitely used in the development of systems that cannot allow errors or security breaches, such as air traffic control systems, spacecraft software, railway signaling systems, military classified systems, and medical control systems. This does not mean that these models, or portions of them, are not used in industry products, but rather that industry vendors do not always follow these models in the purely formal and mathematical way that the models were designed for.

A system that has employed a state machine model will be in a secure state in each and every instance of its existence. It will boot up into a secure state, execute commands and transactions securely, allow subjects to access resources only in secure states, and shut down and fail in a secure state. Failing in a secure state is extremely important. It is imperative that if anything unsafe takes place, the system must be able to "save itself" and not make itself vulnerable. When an operating system displays an error message to the user or reboots or freezes, it is executing a safety measure. The operating system has experienced something that is deemed illegal and it cannot take care of the situation itself, so to make sure it does not stay in this insecure state, it reacts in one of these fashions. Thus, if an application or system freezes on you, know that it is simply the system trying to protect itself and your data.

Several points should be considered when developing a product that uses a state machine model. Initially, the developer must define what and where the state variables are. In a computer environment, all data variables could independently be considered state variables, and an inappropriate change to one could conceivably change or corrupt the system or another process's activities. Next, the developer must define a secure state for each state variable. The next step is to define and identify the allowable state transition functions. These functions will describe the allowable changes that can be made to the state variables.

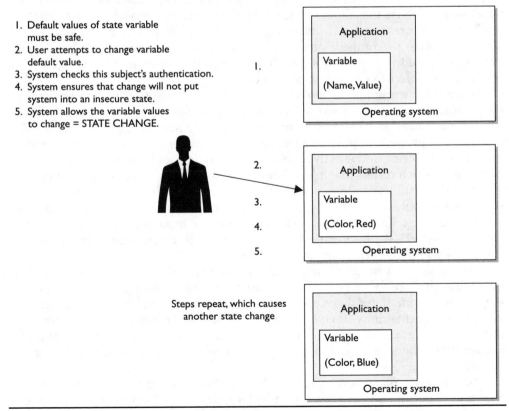

1. Default values of state variable must be safe.
2. User attempts to change variable default value.
3. System checks this subject's authentication.
4. System ensures that change will not put system into an insecure state.
5. System allows the variable values to change = STATE CHANGE.

Figure 5-16 A simplistic example of a state change

After the state transition functions are defined, they must be tested to verify that the overall machine state will not be compromised and that these transition functions will keep the integrity of the system (computer, data, program, or process) intact at all times.

The Bell-LaPadula Model

I don't want anyone to know my secrets.
Response: We need Mr. Bell and Mr. LaPadula in here then.

In the 1970s, the U.S. military used time-sharing mainframe systems and was concerned about the security of these systems and leakage of classified information. The *Bell-LaPadula model* was developed to address these concerns. It was the first mathematical model of a multilevel security policy used to define the concept of a secure state machine and modes of access and outlined rules of access. Its development was funded by the U.S. government to provide a framework for computer systems that would be used to store and process sensitive information. The model's main goal was to prevent secret information from being accessed in an unauthorized manner.

A system that employs the Bell-LaPadula model is called a *multilevel security system* because users with different clearances use the system, and the system processes data with different classifications. The level at which information is classified determines the handling procedures that should be used. The Bell-LaPadula model is a state machine model that enforces the *confidentiality* aspects of access control. A matrix and security levels are used to determine if subjects can access different objects. The subject's clearance is compared to the object's classification and then specific rules are applied to control how subject-to-object interactions can take place.

This model uses subjects, objects, access operations (read, write, and read/write), and security levels. Subjects and objects can reside at different security levels and will have relationships and rules dictating the acceptable activities between them. This model, when properly implemented and enforced, has been mathematically proven to provide a very secure and effective operating system. It is an information-flow security model also, which means that information does not flow in an insecure manner.

The Bell-LaPadula model is a subject-to-object model. An example would be how you (subject) could read a data element (object) from a specific database and write data into that database. The Bell-LaPadula model focuses on ensuring that subjects are properly authenticated—by having the necessary security clearance, need to know, and formal access approval—before accessing an object.

Three main rules are used and enforced in the Bell-LaPadula model: the simple security rule, the *-property (star property) rule, and the strong star property rule. The *simple security rule* states that a subject at a given security level cannot read data that reside at a higher security level. For example, if Bob is given the security clearance of secret, this rule states he cannot *read* data classified as top secret. If the organization wanted Bob to be able to read top-secret data, it would have given him that clearance in the first place.

The **-property rule* (star property rule) states that a subject in a given security level cannot *write* information to a lower security level. The simple security rule is referred to as the "no read up" rule, and the *-property rule is referred to as the "no write down" rule. The third rule, the *strong star property rule*, states that a subject that has read and write capabilities can only perform those functions at the same security level, nothing higher and nothing lower. So, for a subject to be able to read and write to an object, the clearance and classification must be equal.

These three rules indicate what states the system can go into. Remember that a state is the values of the variables in the software at a snapshot in time. If a subject has performed a read operation on an object at a lower security level, the subject now has a variable that is populated with the data that was read, or copied into its variable. If a subject has written to an object at a higher security level, the subject has modified a variable within that object's domain.

NOTE In access control terms, the word *dominate* means to be higher than or equal to. So if you see a statement such as "A subject can only perform a read operation if the access class of the subject dominates the access class of an object," this just means the subject must have a clearance that is higher than or equal to the object. In the Bell-LaPadula model, this is referred to as the *dominance relation*, which is the relationship of the subject's clearance to the object's classification.

The state of a system changes as different operations take place. The Bell-LaPadula model defines a secure state, meaning a secure computing environment and the allowed actions, which are security-preserving operations. This means the model provides a secure state and only permits operations that will keep the system within a secure state and not let it enter into an insecure state. So if 100 people access 2,000 objects in a day using this one system, this system is put through a lot of work and several complex activities must take place. However, at the end of the day, the system is just as secure as it was at the beginning of the day. This is the definition of the *Basic Security Theorem* used in computer science, which states that if a system initializes in a secure state and all allowed state transitions are secure, then every subsequent state will be secure no matter what inputs occur.

NOTE The *tranquility principle*, which is also used in this model, means that subjects and objects cannot change their security levels once they have been instantiated (created).

An important thing to note is that the Bell-LaPadula model was developed to make sure secrets stay secret; thus, it provides and addresses confidentiality only. This model does not address the integrity of the data the system maintains—only who can and cannot access the data and what operations can be carried out.

NOTE Ensuring that information does not flow from a higher security level to a lower level is referred to as *controlling unauthorized downgrading of information*, which would take place through a "write down" operation. An actual compromise occurs if and when a user at a lower security level reads this data.

So what does this mean and why does it matter? Chapter 4 discussed mandatory access control (MAC) systems versus discretionary access control (DAC) systems. All MAC systems are based on the Bell-LaPadula model, because it allows for multilevel security to be integrated into the code. Subjects and objects are assigned labels. The subject's label contains its clearance label (top secret, secret, or confidential) and the object's label contains its classification label (top secret, secret, or confidential). When a subject attempts to access an object, the system compares the subject's clearance label and the object's classification label and looks at a matrix to see if this is a legal and secure activity. In our scenario, it is a perfectly fine activity, and the subject is given access to the object. Now, if the subject's clearance label is top secret and the object's classification label is secret, the subject cannot write to this object, because of the *-property rule, which makes sure that subjects cannot accidentally or intentionally share confidential information by writing to an object at a lower security level. As an example, suppose that a busy and clumsy general (who has top-secret clearance) in the army opens up a briefing letter (which has a secret classification) that will go to all clerks at all bases around the world. He attempts to write that the United States is attacking Cuba. The Bell-LaPadula model will come into action and not permit this general to write this information to this type of file because his clearance is higher than that of the memo.

Likewise, if a nosey military staff clerk tried to read a memo that was available only to generals and above, the Bell-LaPadula model would stop this activity. The clerk's clearance is lower than that of the object (the memo), and this violates the simple security rule of the model. It is all about keeping secrets secret.

NOTE It is important that MAC operating systems and MAC databases follow these rules. In Chapter 11, we will look at how databases can follow these rules by the use of polyinstantiation.

CAUTION You may run into the Bell-LaPadula rule called *Discretionary Security Property (ds-property)*, which is another property of this model. This rule is based on named subjects and objects. It specifies that specific permissions allow a subject to pass on permissions at its own discretion. These permissions are stored in an access matrix. This just means that mandatory and discretionary access control mechanisms can be implemented in one operating system.

The Biba Model

The *Biba model* was developed after the Bell-LaPadula model. It is a state machine model and is very similar to the Bell-LaPadula model. Biba addresses the *integrity* of data within applications. The Bell-LaPadula model uses a lattice of security levels (top secret, secret, sensitive, and so on). These security levels were developed mainly to ensure that sensitive data were only available to authorized individuals. The Biba model is not concerned with security levels and confidentiality, so it does not base access decisions upon this type of lattice. The Biba model uses a lattice of integrity levels.

Rules to Know

The main rules of the Bell-LaPadula model that you need to understand are:

- **Simple security rule** A subject cannot read data within an object that resides at a higher security level (the "no read up" rule).
- ***- property rule** A subject cannot write to an object at a lower security level (the "no write down" rule).
- **Strong star property rule** For a subject to be able to read and write to an object, the subject's clearance and the object's classification must be equal.

If implemented and enforced properly, the Biba model prevents data from any *integrity* level from flowing to a higher integrity level. Biba has three main rules to provide this type of protection:

- ***-integrity axiom** A subject cannot write data to an object at a higher integrity level (referred to as "no write up").
- **Simple integrity axiom** A subject cannot read data from a lower integrity level (referred to as "no read down").
- **Invocation property** A subject cannot request service (invoke) to subjects of higher integrity.

The name "simple integrity axiom" might sound a little goofy, but this rule protects the subject and data at a higher integrity level from being corrupted by data at a lower integrity level. This is all about trusting the source of the information. Another way to look at it is that trusted data are "clean" data and untrusted data (from a lower integrity level) are "dirty" data. Dirty data should not be mixed with clean data, because that could ruin the integrity of the clean data.

The simple integrity axiom applies not only to subjects creating the data, but also to processes. A process of lower integrity should not be writing to trusted data of a higher integrity level. The areas of the different integrity levels are compartmentalized within the application that is based on the Biba model.

An analogy would be if you were writing an article for *The New York Times* about the security trends over the last year, the amount of money businesses lost, and the cost/benefit ratio of implementing firewalls, IDSs, and vulnerability scanners. You do not want to get your data and numbers from any old web site without knowing how those figures were calculated and the sources of the information. Your article (data at a higher integrity level) can be compromised if mixed with unfounded information from a bad source (data at a lower integrity level).

When you are first learning about the Bell-LaPadula and Biba models, they may seem very similar, and the reasons for their differences may be somewhat confusing. The Bell-LaPadula model was written for the U.S. government, and the government is very paranoid about leakage of its secret information. In its model, a user cannot write to a lower level because that user might let out some secrets. Similarly, a user at a lower level cannot read anything at a higher level because that user might learn some secrets. However, not everyone is so worried about confidentiality and has such big important secrets to protect. The commercial industry is more concerned about the *integrity* of its data. An accounting firm is more worried about keeping its numbers straight and making sure decimal points are not dropped or extra zeroes are not added in a process carried out by an application. The accounting firm is more concerned about the integrity of these data and is usually under little threat of someone trying to steal these numbers, so the firm would use software that employs the Biba model. Of course, the accounting firm does not look for the name Biba on the back of a product or make sure it is in the design of its application. Which model to use is something that was decided upon and implemented when the application was being designed. The assurance ratings are what consumers use to determine if a system is right for them. So, even if the accountants are using an application that employs the Biba model, they would not necessarily know (and we're not going to tell them).

If you don't have enough rules to understand so far, here's another one. The *invocation property* in the Biba model states that a subject cannot invoke (call upon) a subject at a higher integrity level. Well, how is this different from the other two Biba rules? The *-integrity axiom (no write up) dictates how subjects can *modify* objects. The simple integrity axiom (no read down) dictates how subjects can *read* objects. The invocation property dictates how one subject can communicate with and initialize other subjects at run time. An example of a subject invoking another subject is when a process sends a request to a procedure to carry out some type of task. Subjects are only allowed to invoke tools at a lower integrity level. With the invocation property, the system is making sure a dirty subject cannot invoke a clean tool to contaminate a clean object.

Bell-LaPadula vs. Biba

The Bell-LaPadula model is used to provide *confidentiality*. The Biba model is used to provide *integrity*. The Bell-LaPadula and Biba models are informational flow models because they are most concerned about data flowing from one level to another. Bell-LaPadula uses security levels, and Biba uses integrity levels. It is important for CISSP test takers to know the rules of Biba and Bell-LaPadula. Their rules sound very similar: simple and * rules—one writing one way and one reading another way. A tip for how to remember them is that if the word "simple" is used, the rule is talking about reading. If the rule uses * or "star," it is talking about writing. So now you just need to remember the reading and writing directions per model.

The Clark-Wilson Model

The *Clark-Wilson model* was developed after Biba and takes some different approaches to protecting the integrity of information. This model uses the following elements:

- **Users** Active agents
- **Transformation procedures (TPs)** Programmed abstract operations, such as read, write, and modify
- **Constrained data items (CDIs)** Can be manipulated only by TPs
- **Unconstrained data items (UDIs)** Can be manipulated by users via primitive read and write operations
- **Integrity verification procedures (IVPs)** Check the consistency of CDIs with external reality

Although this list may look overwhelming, it is really quite straightforward. When an application uses the Clark-Wilson model, it separates data into one subset that needs to be highly protected, which is referred to as a constrained data item (CDI), and another subset that does not require a high level of protection, which is called an unconstrained data item (UDI). Users cannot modify critical data (CDI) directly. Instead, the subject (user) must be authenticated to a piece of software, and the software procedures (TPs) will carry out the operations on behalf of the user. For example, when Kathy needs to update information held within her company's database, she will not be allowed to do so without a piece of software controlling these activities. First, Kathy must authenticate to a program, which is acting as a front end for the database, and then the program will control what Kathy can and cannot do to the information in the database. This is referred to as *access triple*: subject (user), program (TP), and object (CDI). A user cannot modify CDI without using a TP.

So, Kathy is going to input data, which is supposed to overwrite some original data in the database. The software (TP) has to make sure this type of activity is secure and will carry out the write procedures for Kathy. Kathy (and any type of subject) is not trusted enough to manipulate objects directly.

The CDI must have its integrity protected by the TPs. The UDI does not require such a high level of protection. For example, if Kathy did her banking online, the data on her bank's servers and databases would be split into UDI and CDI categories. The CDI category would contain her banking account information, which needs to be highly protected. The UDI data could be her customer profile, which she can update as needed. TPs would not be required when Kathy needed to update her UDI information.

In some cases, a system may need to change UDI data into CDI data. For example, when Kathy updates her customer profile via the web site to show her new correct address, this information will need to be moved into the banking software that is responsible for mailing out bank account information. The bank would not want Kathy to interact directly with that banking software, so a piece of software (TP) is responsible for copying that data and updating this customer's mailing address. At this stage, the TP is changing the state of the UDI data to CDI. These concepts are shown in Figure 5-17.

Remember that this is an integrity model, so it must have something that ensures that specific integrity rules are being carried out. This is the job of the IVP. The IVP ensures that all critical data (CDI) follow the application's defined integrity rules. What usually turns people's minds into spaghetti when they are first learning about models is that models are theoretical and abstract. Thus, when they ask the common question, "What are these defined integrity rules that the CDI must comply with?" they are told, "Whatever the vendor chooses them to be."

A model is made up of constructs, mathematical formulas, and other PhD kinds of stuff. The model provides the framework that can be used to build a certain characteristic into software (confidentiality, integrity, and so on). So the model does not stipulate what integrity rules the IVP must enforce; it just provides the framework, and the vendor chooses the integrity rules. The vendor implements integrity rules that its customer base needs the most. So if a vendor is developing an application for a financial institution, the UDI could be customer profiles that they are allowed to update and the CDI could be the bank account information, usually held on a mainframe. The UDI data do not need to be as highly protected and can be located on the same system or another system. A user can have access to UDI data without the use of a TP, but when the user needs to access CDI, they must use TP. So the vendor who develops the product will determine what type of data is considered UDI and what type of data is CDI and develop the TPs to control and orchestrate how the software enforces the integrity of the CDI values.

In a banking application, the IVP would ensure that the CDI represents the correct value. For example, if Kathy has $2,000 in her account and then deposits $50, the CDI for her account should now have a value of $2,050. The IVP ensures the consistency of the data. So after Kathy carries out this transaction and the IVP validates the integrity of

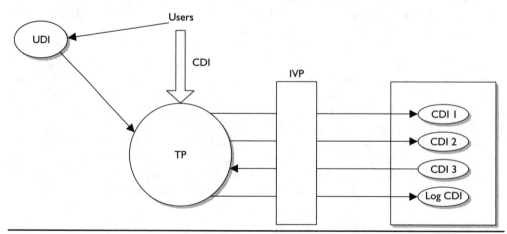

Figure 5-17 Subjects cannot modify CDI without using TP.

the CDI (new bank account value is correct), then the CDI is considered to be in a *consistent state*. TPs are the only components allowed to modify the state of the CDIs. In our example, TPs would be software procedures that carry out deposit, withdrawal, and transfer functionalities. Using TPs to modify CDIs is referred to as a ***well-formed transaction***.

A well-formed transaction is a series of operations that are carried out to transfer the data from one consistent state to the other. If Kathy transfers money from her checking account to her savings account, this transaction is made up of two operations: subtract money from one account and add it to a different account. By making sure the new values in her checking and savings accounts are accurate and their integrity is intact, the IVP maintains internal and external consistency. The Clark-Wilson model also outlines how to incorporate ***separation of duties*** into the architecture of an application. If we follow our same example of banking software, if a customer needs to withdraw over $10,000, the application may require a supervisor to log in and authenticate this transaction. This is a countermeasure to potential fraudulent activities. The model provides the rules that the developers must follow to properly implement and enforce separation of duties through software procedures.

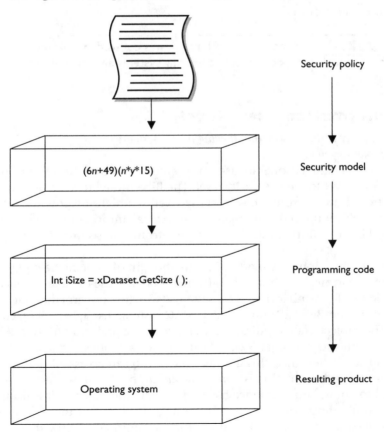

Goals of Integrity Models

The following are the three main goals of integrity models:

- Prevent unauthorized users from making modifications
- Prevent authorized users from making improper modifications (separation of duties)
- Maintain internal and external consistency (well-formed transaction)

Clark-Wilson addresses each of these goals in its model. Biba only addresses the first goal.

Internal and external consistency is provided by the IVP, which ensures that what is stored in the system as CDI properly maps to the input value that modified its state. So if Kathy has $2,500 in her account and she withdraws $2,000, the resulting value in the CDI is $500.

To summarize, the Clark-Wilson model enforces the three goals of integrity by using access triple (subject, software [TP], object), separation of duties, and auditing. This model enforces integrity by using well-formed transactions (through access triple) and separation of user duties.

 NOTE The access control matrix was covered in Chapter 4. This is another commonly used model in operating systems and applications.

The Information Flow Model

Now, which way is the information flowing in this system?
Response: Not to you.

The Bell-LaPadula model focuses on preventing information from flowing from a high security level to a low security level. The Biba model focuses on preventing information from flowing from a low integrity level to a high integrity level. Both of these models were built upon the *information flow model*. Information flow models can deal with any kind of information flow, not only from one security (or integrity) level to another.

In the information flow model, data are thought of as being held in individual and discrete compartments. In the Bell-LaPadula model, these compartments are based on security levels. Remember that MAC systems (which you learned about in Chapter 4) are based on the Bell-LaPadula model. MAC systems use labels on each subject and object. The subject's label indicates the subject's clearance and need to know. The object's label indicates the object's classification and categories. If you are in the army and have a top-secret clearance, this does not mean you can access all of the army's top-secret information. Information is *compartmentalized* based on two factors—classification and need to know. Your clearance has to dominate the object's classification and your security profile must contain one of the categories listed in the object's label, which enforces need to know. So Bell-LaPadula is an information flow model that ensures that information cannot flow from one compartment to another in a way that threatens the confidentiality of the data. Biba compartmentalizes data based on integrity levels. It is an information flow model that controls information flow in a way that is intended to protect the integrity of the most trusted information.

How can information flow within a system? The answer is in *many* ways. Subjects can access files. Processes can access memory segments. When data are moved from the hard drive's swap space into memory, information flows. Data are moved into and out of registers on a CPU. Data are moved into different cache memory storage devices. Data are written to the hard drive, thumb drive, CD-ROM drive, and so on. Properly controlling all of these ways of how information flows can be a very complex task. This is why the information flow model exists—to help architects and developers make sure their software does not allow information to flow in a way that can put the system or data in danger. One way that the information flow model provides this type of protection is by ensuring that covert channels do not exist in the code.

Covert Channels

I have my decoder ring, cape, and pirate's hat on. I will communicate to my spy buddies with this tribal drum and a whistle.

A *covert channel* is a way for an entity to receive information in an unauthorized manner. It is an information flow that is not controlled by a security mechanism. This type of information path was not developed for communication; thus, the system does not properly protect this path, because the developers never envisioned information being passed in this way. Receiving information in this manner clearly violates the system's security policy.

The channel to transfer this unauthorized data is the result of one of the following conditions:

- Improper oversight in the development of the product
- Improper implementation of access controls within the software
- Existence of a shared resource between the two entities

Covert channels are of two types: storage and timing. In a *covert storage channel*, processes are able to communicate through some type of storage space on the system. For example, System A is infected with a Trojan horse that has installed software that will be able to communicate to another process in a limited way. System A has a very sensitive file (File 2) that is of great interest to a particular attacker. The software the Trojan horse installed is able to read this file and it needs to send the contents of the file to the attacker, which can only happen one bit at a time. The intrusive software is going to communicate to the attacker by locking a specific file (File 3). When the attacker attempts to access File 3 and finds it has a software lock enabled on it, the attacker interprets this to mean the first bit in the sensitive file is a 1. The second time the attacker attempts to access File 3 it is not locked. The attacker interprets this value to be zero. This continues until all of the data in the sensitive file are sent to the attacker. In this example, the software the Trojan horse installed is the messenger. It can access the sensitive data and it uses another file that is on the hard drive to send signals to the attacker.

Other Types of Covert Channels

Although we are looking at covert channels within programming code, covert channels can be used in the outside world as well. Let's say you are going to attend one of my lectures. Before the lecture begins, you and I agree on a way of communicating that no one else in the audience will understand. I tell you that if I twiddle a pen between my fingers in my right hand, that means there will be a quiz at the end of class. If I twiddle a pen between my fingers in my left hand, there will be no quiz. It is a covert channel, because this is not a normal way of communicating and it is secretive. (In this scenario, I would twiddle the pen in both hands to confuse you and make you stay after class to take the quiz all by yourself. Shame on you for wanting to be forewarned about a quiz!)

Another way that a covert storage channel attack can take place is through file creation. A system has been compromised and has software that can create and delete files within a specific directory and has read access to a sensitive file. When the intrusive software sees that the first bit of the data within the sensitive file is 1, it will create a file named Temp in a specific directory. The attacker will try and create (or upload) a file with the exact same name, and the attacker will receive a message indicating there is already a file with that name that exists in that directory. The attacker will know this means the first bit in the sensitive file is a 1. The attacker tries to create the same file again, and when the system allows this it means the intrusive software on the system deleted that file, which means the second bit is a 0.

Information flow models produce rules on how to ensure that covert channels do not exist. But there are many ways information flows within a system, so identifying and rooting out covert channels is usually more difficult than one would think at first glance.

 NOTE An overt channel is a channel of communication that was developed specifically for communication purposes. Processes should be communicating through overt channels, not covert channels.

In a *covert timing channel*, one process relays information to another by modulating its use of system resources. The two processes that are communicating to each other are using the same shared resource, which is time. So in our example, Process A is a piece of nefarious software that was installed via a Trojan horse. In a multitasked system, each process is offered access to interact with the CPU. When this function is offered to Process A, it rejects it—which indicates a 1 to the attacker. The next time Process A is offered access to the CPU, it uses it, which indicates a 0 to the attacker. Think of this as a type of Morse code, but using some type of system resource.

Countermeasures Because all operating systems have some type of covert channel, it is not always feasible to get rid of them all. The number of acceptable covert channels usually depends on the assurance rating of a system. A system that has a Common Criteria rating of EAL 6 has fewer covert channels than a system with an EAL rating of 3, because an EAL 6 rating represents a higher assurance level of providing a particular protection level when compared to the EAL 3 rating. There is not much a user can do to counteract these channels; instead, the channels must be addressed when the system is constructed and developed.

NOTE In the Orange Book, covert channels in operating systems are not addressed until security level B2 and above because these are the systems that would be holding data sensitive enough for others to go through all the necessary trouble to access data in this fashion.

The Noninterference Model

Stop touching me. Stop touching me. You are interfering with me!

Multilevel security properties can be expressed in many ways, one being *noninterference*. This concept is implemented to ensure any actions that take place at a higher security level do not affect, or interfere with, actions that take place at a lower level. This type of model does not concern itself with the flow of data, but rather with what a subject knows about the state of the system. So if an entity at a higher security level performs an action, it cannot change the state for the entity at the lower level.

If a lower-level entity was aware of a certain activity that took place by an entity at a higher level and the state of the system changed for this lower-level entity, the entity might be able to deduce too much information about the activities of the higher state, which in turn is a way of leaking information.

Users at a lower security level should not be aware of the commands executed by users at a higher level and should not be affected by those commands in any way.

Let's say that Tom and Kathy are both working on a multilevel mainframe at the same time. Tom has the security clearance of secret and Kathy has the security clearance of top secret. Since this is a central mainframe, the terminal Tom is working at has the context of secret, and Kathy is working at her own terminal, which has a context of top secret. This model states that nothing Kathy does at her terminal should directly or indirectly affect Tom's domain (available resources and working environment). So whatever commands she executes or whichever resources she interacts with should not affect Tom's experience of working with the mainframe in any way. This sounds simple enough, until you actually understand what this model is *really* saying.

It seems very logical and straightforward that when Kathy executes a command, it should not affect Tom's terminal. But the real intent of this model is to address covert channels and inference attacks. The model looks at the shared resources that the different users of a system will use and tries to identify how information can be passed from a process working at a higher security clearance to a process working at a lower security clearance. Since Tom and Kathy are working on the same system at the same time, they will most likely have to share some type of resources. So the model is made up of rules to ensure that Kathy cannot pass data to Tom through covert storage or timing channels.

The other security breach this model addresses is the inference attack. An *inference attack* occurs when someone has access to some type of information and can infer (or guess) something that he does not have the clearance level or authority to know. For example, let's say Tom is working on a file that contains information about supplies that are being sent to Russia. He closes out of that file and one hour later attempts to open the same file. During this time, this file's classification has been elevated to top secret, so when Tom attempts to access it, he is denied. Tom can infer that some type of top-secret mission is getting ready to take place with Russia. He does not have clearance to know this, thus it would be an inference attack or "leaking information." (Inference attacks are further explained in Chapter 11.)

The Lattice Model

A lattice is a mathematical construct that is built upon the notion of a group. The most common definition of the **lattice model** is "a structure consisting of a finite partially ordered set together with least upper and greatest lower bound operators on the set."

Two things are wrong with this type of explanation. First, "a structure consisting of a finite partially ordered set together with least upper and greatest lower bound operators on the set" can only be understood by someone who understands the model in the first place. This is similar to the common definition of metadata: "data about data." Only *after* you really understand what metadata are does this definition make any sense to you. So this definition of lattice model is not overly helpful.

The problem with the mathematical explanation is that it is in weird alien writings that only people who obtain their master's or PhD degree in mathematics can understand. This model needs to be explained in everyday language so even Homer Simpson can understand it. So let's give it a try.

The MAC model was explained in Chapter 4 and then built upon in this chapter. In this model, the subjects and objects have labels. Each subject's label contains the clearance and need-to-know categories that this subject can access. Suppose Kathy's security clearance is top secret and she has been formally granted access to the compartments named Iraq and Korea, based on her need to know. So Kathy's security label states the following: TS {Iraq, Korea}. Table 5-1 shows the different files on the system in this scenario. The system is based on the MAC model, which means the operating system is making access decisions based on security label contents.

Kathy attempts to access File B; since her clearance is greater than File B's classification, she can read this file but not write to it. This is where the *"partially ordered set together with least upper and greatest lower bound* operators on the set" comes into play. A set is a subject (Kathy) and an object (file). It is a partially ordered set because all of the access controls are not completely equal. The system has to decide between read, write, full control, modify, and all the other types of access permissions used in this operating system. So, "partially ordered" means the system has to apply the most restrictive access controls to this set, and "least upper bound" means the system looks at one access control's statement (Kathy can read the file) and the other access control's statement (Kathy cannot write to the file) and takes the least *upper* bound value. Since no write is

Kathy's Security Label	File B's Security Label	File C's Security Label	File D's Security Label
Top Secret {Iraq, Korea}	Secret {Iraq}	Top Secret {Iraq, Korea}	Secret {Iraq, Korea, Iran}

Table 5-1 Security Access Control Elements

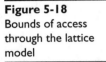

Figure 5-18
Bounds of access through the lattice model

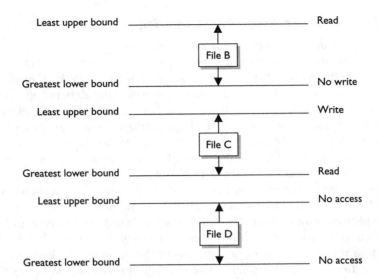

more restrictive than read, Kathy's *least upper bound* access to this file is read and her greatest lower bound is no write. Figure 5-18 illustrates the bounds of access. This is just a confusing way of saying, "The most that Kathy can do with this file is read it. The least she can do is *not* write to it."

Let's figure out the least upper bound and greatest lower bound access levels for Kathy and File C. Kathy's clearance equals File C's classification. Under the Bell-LaPadula model, this is when the strong star property would kick in. (Remember that the strong star property states that a subject can read and write to an object of the same security level.) So the least upper bound is write and the greatest lower bound is read.

If we look at File D's security label, we see it has a category that Kathy does not have in her security label, which is Iran. This means Kathy does not have the necessary need to know to be able to access this file. Kathy's least upper bound and greatest lower bound access permission is no access.

So why does this model state things in a very confusing way when in reality it describes pretty straightforward concepts? First, I am describing this model in the most simplistic and basic terms possible so you can get the basic meaning of the purpose of the model. These seemingly straightforward concepts build in complexity when you think about all the subject-to-object communications that go on within an operating system during any one second. Also, this is a formal model, which means it can be proven mathematically to provide a specific level of protection if all of its rules are followed properly. Learning these models is similar to learning the basics of chemistry. A student first learns about the components of an atom (protons, neutrons, and electrons) and how these elements interact with each other. This is the easy piece. Then the student gets into organic chemistry and has to understand how these components work together in complex organic systems (weak and strong attractions, osmosis, and ionization). The student then goes to quantum physics to learn that the individual elements of an atom actually have several different subatomic particles (quarks, leptons, and mesons). In this book, you are just learning the basic components of the models. Much more complexity lies under the covers.

The Brewer and Nash Model

A wall separates our stuff so you can't touch my stuff.
Response: Your stuff is green and smells funny. I don't want to touch it.

The **Brewer and Nash model**, also called the **Chinese Wall model**, was created to provide access controls that can change dynamically depending upon a user's previous actions. The main goal of the model is to protect against conflicts of interest by users' access attempts. For example, if a large marketing company provides marketing promotions and materials for two banks, an employee working on a project for Bank A should not look at the information the marketing company has on its other bank customer, Bank B. Such action could create a conflict of interest because the banks are competitors. If the marketing company's project manager for the Bank A project could view information on Bank B's new marketing campaign, he may try to trump its promotion to please his more direct customer. The marketing company would get a bad reputation if it allowed its internal employees to behave so irresponsibly. This marketing company could implement a product that tracks the different marketing representatives' access activities and disallows certain access requests that would present this type of conflict of interest. In Figure 5-19, we see that when a representative accesses Bank A's information, the system automatically makes Bank B's information off limits. If the representative accessed Bank B's data, Bank A's information would be off limits. These access controls change dynamically depending upon the user's authorizations, activities, and previous access requests.

The Chinese Wall model is also based on an information flow model. No information can flow between subjects and objects in a way that would result in a conflict of interest. The model states that a subject can write to an object if, and only if, the subject cannot read another object that is in a different dataset. So if we stay with our example,

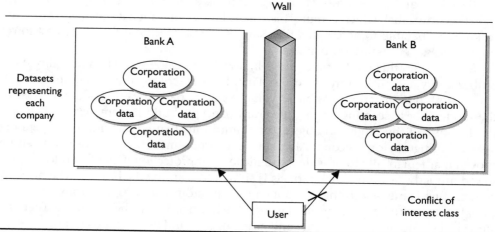

Figure 5-19 The Chinese Wall model provides dynamic access controls.

the project manager could not write to any objects within the Bank A dataset if he currently has read access to any objects in the Bank B dataset.

This is only one example of how this model can be used. Other industries will have their own possible conflicts of interest. If you were Martha's stockbroker, you should not be able to read a dataset that indicates a stock's price is getting ready to go down *and* be able to write to Martha's account indicating she should sell the stock she has.

The Graham-Denning Model

Remember that these are all models, so they are not very specific in nature. Each individual vendor must decide upon how it is going to actually meet the rules outlined in the chosen model. Bell-LaPadula and Biba don't define how the security and integrity ratings are defined and modified, nor do they provide a way to delegate or transfer access rights. The *Graham-Denning model* addresses these issues and defines a set of basic rights in terms of commands that a specific subject can execute on an object. This model has eight primitive protection rights, or rules of how these types of functionalities should take place securely, which are outlined next:

- How to securely create an object
- How to securely create a subject
- How to securely delete an object
- How to securely delete a subject
- How to securely provide the read access right
- How to securely provide the grant access right
- How to securely provide the delete access right
- How to securely provide transfer access rights

These things may sound insignificant, but when you're building a secure system, they are critical.

The Harrison-Ruzzo-Ullman Model

The Harrison-Ruzzo-Ullman (HRU) model deals with access rights of subjects and the integrity of those rights. A subject can carry out only a finite set of operations on an object. Since security loves simplicity, it is easier for a system to allow or disallow authorization of operations if one command is restricted to a single operation. For example, if a subject sent command X, which only required the operation of Y, this is pretty straightforward and allows the system to allow or disallow this operation to take place. But, if a subject sent a command M, and to fulfill that command, operations N, B, W, and P had to be carried out, then there is much more complexity for the system to decide if this command should be authorized.

Security Models Recap

All of these different models can get your head spinning. Most people are not familiar with all of them, which can make it all even harder to absorb. The following are the core concepts of the different models:

- **The Bell-LaPadula Model** This confidentiality model describes the allowable information flows and formalizes the military security policy. It is the first mathematical model of a multilevel security policy that defines the concept of a secure state and necessary modes of access.

  - **The simple security rule** A subject cannot read data at a higher security level (no read up).

  - **The *-property rule** A subject cannot write data to an object at a lower security level (no write down).

  - **The strong star property rule** A subject can perform read and write functions only to the objects at its same security level.

- **The Biba Model** This model protects the integrity of the information within a system and the activities that take place. It addresses the first goal of integrity.

  - **The simple integrity axiom** A subject cannot read data at a lower integrity level (no read down).

  - **The *-integrity axiom** A subject cannot modify an object in a higher integrity level (no write up).

- **The Clark-Wilson Model** This integrity model is implemented to protect the integrity of data and to ensure that properly formatted transactions take place. It addresses all three goals of integrity.

  - Subjects can access objects only through authorized programs (access triple).

  - Separation of duties is enforced.

  - Auditing is required.

- **The Access Control Matrix Model** This is a model in which access decisions are based on objects' ACLs and subjects' capability tables.

- **The Information Flow Model** This is a model in which information is restricted in its flow to only go to and from entities in a way that does not negate the security policy.

- **The Noninterference Model** This model states that commands and activities performed at one security level should not be seen by, or affect, subjects or objects at a different security level.

- **The Brewer and Nash Model** This model allows for dynamically changing access controls that protect against conflicts of interest. Also known as the Chinese Wall model.

- **The Graham-Denning Model** This model shows how subjects and objects should be created and deleted. It also addresses how to assign specific access rights.

Security Modes of Operation

A system can operate in different modes depending on the sensitivity of the data being processed, the clearance level of the users, and what those users are authorized to do. The mode of operation describes the security conditions under which the system actually functions.

These modes are used in MAC systems, which hold one or more classifications of data. Several things come into play when determining the mode the operating system should be working in:

- The types of users who will be directly or indirectly connecting to the system
- The type of data (classification levels, compartments, and categories) processed on the system
- The clearance levels, need to know, and formal access approvals the users will have

The following sections describe the different security modes that operating systems can be developed and configured to work in.

Dedicated Security Mode

Our system only holds secret data and we can all access it.

A system is operating in a ***dedicated security mode*** if *all* users have a clearance for, and a formal need to know about, *all* data processed within the system. All users have been given formal access approval for *all* information on the system and have signed nondisclosure agreements (NDAs) pertaining to this information. The system can handle a single classification level of information.

Many military systems have been designed to handle only one level of security, which works in dedicated security mode. This requires everyone who uses the system to have the highest level of clearance required by any and all data on the system. If a system holds top-secret data, only users with that clearance can use the system. Other military systems work with multiple security levels, which is done by compartmentalizing the data. These types of systems can support users with high and low clearances simultaneously.

System High-Security Mode

Our system only holds secret data, but only some of us can access all of it.

A system is operating in *system high-security mode* when all users have a security clearance to access the information but not necessarily a need to know for all the information processed on the system. So, unlike in the dedicated security mode, in which all users have a need to know pertaining to *all* data on the system, in system high-security mode, all users have a need to know pertaining to *some* of the data.

This mode also requires all users to have the highest level of clearance required by any and all data on the system. However, even though a user has the necessary security level to access an object, the user may still be restricted if he does not have a need to know pertaining to that specific object.

Compartmented Security Mode

Our system has various classifications of data, and each individual has the clearance to access all of the data, but not necessarily the need to know.

A system is operating in *compartmented security mode* when all users have the clearance to access all the information processed by the system in a system high-security configuration, but might not have the need to know and formal access approval. This means that if the system is holding secret and top-secret data, all users must have at least a top-secret clearance to gain access to this system. This is how compartmented and multilevel security modes are different. Both modes require the user to have a valid need to know, NDA, and formal approval, but compartmented security mode requires the user to have a clearance that dominates (above or equal to) any and all data on the system, whereas multilevel security mode just requires the user to have clearance to access the data she will be working with.

In compartmented security mode, users are restricted from accessing some information because they do not need to access it to perform the functions of their jobs and they have not been given formal approval to access it. This would be enforced by having on all objects security labels that reflect the sensitivity (classification level, classification category, and handling procedures) of the information. In this mode, users can access a compartment, of data only, enforced by mandatory access controls.

The objective is to ensure that the minimum possible number of people learn of information at each level. Compartments are categories of data with a limited number of subjects cleared to access data at each level. *Compartmented mode workstations (CMWs)* enable users to process multiple compartments of data at the same time, if they have the necessary clearance.

Multilevel Security Mode

Our system has various classifications of data, and each individual has the clearance and need to know to access only individual pieces of data.

A system is operating in *multilevel security mode* when it permits two or more classification levels of information to be processed at the same time when not all of the users have the clearance or formal approval to access all the information being processed by the system. So all users must have formal approval, NDA, need to know, and the necessary clearance to access the data that they need to carry out their jobs. In this mode, the user cannot access all of the data on the system, only what she is cleared to access.

The Bell-LaPadula model is an example of a multilevel security model because it handles multiple information classifications at a number of different security levels within one system simultaneously.

Guards

Software and hardware guards allow the exchange of data between trusted (high assurance) and less trusted (low assurance) systems and environments. Let's say you are working on a MAC system (working in dedicated security mode of secret) and you need the system to communicate with a MAC database (working in multilevel security mode, which goes up to top secret). These two systems provide different levels of protection.

As previously stated, if a system with lower assurance could directly communicate with a system of higher assurance, then security vulnerabilities and compromises could be introduced. So, a software guard can be implemented, which is really just a front-end product that allows interconnectivity between systems working at different security levels. (The various types of guards available can carry out filtering, processing requests, data blocking, and data sanitization.) Or a hardware guard can be implemented, which is a system with two NICs connecting the two systems that need to communicate. The guard is an add-on piece that provides a level of strict access control between different systems.

The guard accepts requests from the system of lower assurance, reviews the request to make sure it is allowed, and then submits the request to the system of higher assurance. The goal is to ensure that information does not flow from a high security level to a low security level in an unauthorized manner.

Guards can be used to connect different MAC systems working in different security modes and to connect different networks working at different security levels. In many cases, the less trusted system can send messages to the more trusted system but can only receive acknowledgments in return. This is common when e-mail messages need to go from less trusted systems to more trusted classified systems.

Security Modes Recap

Many times it is easier to understand these different modes when they are laid out in a clear and simplistic format. Pay attention to the words in italics because they emphasize the differences among the various modes.

Dedicated Security Mode   All users must have . . .

- Proper clearance for all information on the system
- Formal access approval for all information on the system
- A signed NDA for all information on the system
- A valid need to know for *all* information on the system
- All users can access all data.

System High-Security Mode   All users must have . . .

- Proper clearance for all information on the system
- Formal access approval for all information on the system
- A signed NDA for all information on the system
- A valid need to know for *some* information on the system
- All users can access some data, based on their need to know.

Compartmented Security Mode   All users must have . . .

- Proper clearance for the highest level of data classification on the system
- Formal access approval for all information they will access on the system
- A signed NDA for all information they will access on the system

- A valid need to know for *some* of the information on the system
- All users can access some data, based on their need to know and formal access approval.

Multilevel Security Mode   All users must have . . .

- Proper clearance for all information they will access on the system
- Formal access approval for all information they will access on the system
- A signed NDA for all information they will access on the system
- A valid need to know for *some* of the information on the system
- All users can access some data, based on their need to know, clearance, and formal access approval.

Trust and Assurance

I trust that you will act properly, thus I have a high level of assurance in you.
Response: You are such a fool.

As discussed earlier in the section "Trusted Computing Base," no system is really secure because, with enough resources, attackers can compromise almost any system in one way or another; however, systems can provide levels of trust. The trust level tells the customer how much protection he can expect out of this system and the *assurance* that the system will act in a correct and predictable manner in each and every computing situation.

The TCB comprises all the protection mechanisms within a system (software, hardware, firmware). All of these mechanisms need to work in an orchestrated way to enforce all the requirements of a security policy. When evaluated, these mechanisms are tested, their designs are inspected, and their supporting documentation is reviewed and evaluated. How the system is developed, maintained, and even delivered to the customer are all under review when the trust for a system is being gauged. All of these different components are put through an evaluation process and assigned an assurance rating, which represents the level of trust and assurance the testing team has in the product. Customers then use this rating to determine which system best fits their security needs.

Assurance and trust are similar in nature, but slightly different with regard to product ratings. In a trusted system, all protection mechanisms work together to process sensitive data for many types of uses, and will provide the necessary level of protection per classification level. Assurance looks at the same issues but in more depth and detail. Systems that provide higher levels of assurance have been tested extensively and have had their designs thoroughly inspected, their development stages reviewed, and their technical specifications and test plans evaluated. You can buy a car and you can trust it, but you have a much deeper sense of assurance of that trust if you know how the car was built, what it was built with, who built it, what tests it was put through, and how it performed in many different situations.

In the Trusted Computer System Evaluation Criteria (TCSEC), commonly known as the Orange Book (addressed shortly), the lower assurance level ratings look at a system's protection mechanisms and testing results to produce an assurance rating, but the higher assurance level ratings look more at the system design, specifications, development procedures, supporting documentation, and testing results. The protection mechanisms in the higher assurance level systems may not necessarily be much different from those in the lower assurance level systems, but the way they were designed and built is under much more scrutiny. With this extra scrutiny comes higher levels of assurance of the trust that can be put into a system.

Systems Evaluation Methods

A *security evaluation* examines the security-relevant parts of a system, meaning the TCB, access control mechanisms, reference monitor, kernel, and protection mechanisms. The relationship and interaction between these components are also evaluated. There are different methods of evaluating and assigning assurance levels to systems. Two reasons explain why more than one type of assurance evaluation process exists: methods and ideologies have evolved over time, and various parts of the world look at computer security differently and rate some aspects of security differently. Each method will be explained and compared.

Why Put a Product Through Evaluation?

Submitting a product to be evaluated against the Orange Book, Information Technology Security Evaluation Criteria, or Common Criteria is no walk in the park for a vendor. In fact, it is a really painful and long process, and no one wakes up in the morning thinking, "Yippee! I have to complete all of the paperwork that the National Computer Security Center requires so my product can be evaluated!" So, before we go through these different criteria, let's look at *why* anyone would even put themselves through this process.

If you were going shopping to buy a firewall, how would you know what level of protection each provides and which is the best product for your environment? You could listen to the vendor's marketing hype and believe the salesperson who informs you that a particular product will solve all of your life problems in one week. Or you could listen to the advice of an independent third party who has fully tested the product and does not have any bias toward the product. If you choose the second option, then you join a world of people who work within the realm of assurance ratings in one form or another.

In the United States, the National Computer Security Center (NCSC) is an organization within the National Security Agency (NSA) that is responsible for evaluating computer systems and products. It has a group, called the Trusted Product Evaluation Program (TPEP), that oversees the testing by approved evaluation entities of commercial products against a specific set of criteria.

So, a vendor creates a product and submits it to an approved evaluation entity that is compliant with the TPEP guidelines. The evaluation entity has groups of testers who will follow a set of criteria (for many years it was the Orange Book but now it is moving toward the Common Criteria) to test the vendor's product. Once the testing is over, the product is assigned an assurance rating. So, instead of having to trust the marketing hype of the financially motivated vendor, you as a consumer can take the word of an objective third-party entity that fully tested the product.

This evaluation process is very time-consuming and expensive for the vendor. Not every vendor puts its product through this process, because of the expense and delayed date to get it to market. Typically, a vendor would put its product through this process if its main customer base will be making purchasing decisions based on assurance ratings. In the United States, the Department of Defense *is* the largest customer, so major vendors put their main products through this process with the hope that the Department of Defense (and others) will purchase their products.

The Orange Book

The U.S. Department of Defense developed the *Trusted Computer System Evaluation Criteria (TCSEC)*, which is used to evaluate operating systems, applications, and different products. These evaluation criteria are published in a book with an orange cover, which is called, appropriately, the *Orange Book*. (We like to keep things simple in security!) Customers use the assurance rating that the criteria present as a metric when comparing different products. It also provides direction for manufacturers so they know what specifications to build to, and provides a one-stop evaluation process so customers do not need to have individual components within the systems evaluated.

The Orange Book is used to evaluate whether a product contains the security properties the vendor claims it does and whether the product is appropriate for a specific application or function. The Orange Book is used to review the functionality, effectiveness, and assurance of a product during its evaluation, and it uses classes that were devised to address typical patterns of security requirements.

TCSEC provides a classification system that is divided into hierarchical divisions of assurance levels:

- A. Verified protection
- B. Mandatory protection
- C. Discretionary protection
- D. Minimal security

Classification A represents the highest level of assurance, and D represents the lowest level of assurance.

Each division can have one or more numbered classes with a corresponding set of requirements that must be met for a system to achieve that particular rating. The classes with higher numbers offer a greater degree of trust and assurance. So B2 would offer more trust than B1, and C2 would offer more trust than C1.

The criteria include four main topics—security policy, accountability, assurance, and documentation—but these actually break down into seven different areas:

- **Security policy** The policy must be explicit and well defined and enforced by the mechanisms within the system.
- **Identification** Individual subjects must be uniquely identified.

- **Labels**   Access control labels must be associated properly with objects.
- **Documentation**   Documentation must be provided, including test, design, and specification documents, user guides, and manuals.
- **Accountability**   Audit data must be captured and protected to enforce accountability.
- **Life-cycle assurance**   Software, hardware, and firmware must be able to be tested individually to ensure that each enforces the security policy in an effective manner throughout their lifetimes.
- **Continuous protection**   The security mechanisms and the system as a whole must perform predictably and acceptably in different situations continuously.

These categories are evaluated independently, but the rating assigned at the end does not specify these different objectives individually. The rating is a sum total of these items.

Each division and class incorporates the requirements of the ones below it. This means that C2 must meet its criteria requirements and all of C1's requirements, and B3 has its requirements to fulfill along with those of C1, C2, B1, and B2. Each division or class ups the ante on security requirements and is expected to fulfill the requirements of all the classes and divisions below it.

So, when a vendor submits a product for evaluation, it submits it to the NCSC. The group that oversees the processes of evaluation is called the Trusted Products Evaluation Program (TPEP). Successfully evaluated products are placed on the Evaluated Products List (EPL) with their corresponding rating. When consumers are interested in certain products and systems, they can check the appropriate EPL to find out their assigned security levels.

Isn't the Orange Book Dead?

We are moving from the Orange Book to the Common Criteria in the industry, so a common question is, "Why do I have to study this Orange Book stuff?" Just because we are going through this transition, does not make the Orange Book unimportant. It was the first evaluation criteria and was used for 20 years. Many of the basic terms and concepts that have carried through originated in the Orange Book. And we still have several products with these ratings that eventually will go through the Common Criteria evaluation process.

The CISSP exam is moving steadily from the Orange Book to the Common Criteria all the time, but don't count the Orange Book out yet.

As a follow-on observation, many people are new to the security field. It is a booming market, which means a flood of not-so-experienced people will be jumping in and attempting to charge forward without a real foundation of knowledge. To some readers, this book will just be a nice refresher and something that ties already known concepts together. To other readers, many of these concepts are new and more challenging. If a lot of this stuff is new to you—you are new to the market. That is okay, but knowing how we got where we are today is very beneficial because it broadens your view of *deep* understanding—instead of just memorizing for an exam.

Division D: Minimal Protection

There is only one class in Division D. It is reserved for systems that have been evaluated but fail to meet the criteria and requirements of the higher divisions.

Division C: Discretionary Protection

The C rating category has two individual assurance ratings within it, which are described next. The higher the number of the assurance rating, the greater the protection.

C1: Discretionary Security Protection Discretionary access control is based on individuals and/or groups. It requires a separation of users and information, and identification and authentication of individual entities. Some type of access control is necessary so users can ensure their data will not be accessed and corrupted by others. The system architecture must supply a protected execution domain so privileged system processes are not adversely affected by lower-privileged processes. There must be specific ways of validating the system's operational integrity. The documentation requirements include design documentation, which shows that the system was built to include protection mechanisms, test documentation (test plan and results), a facility manual (so companies know how to install and configure the system correctly), and user manuals.

The type of environment that would require this rating is one in which users are processing information at the same sensitivity level; thus, strict access control and auditing measures are not required. It would be a trusted environment with low security concerns.

C2: Controlled Access Protection Users need to be identified individually to provide more precise access control and auditing functionality. Logical access control mechanisms are used to enforce authentication and the uniqueness of each individual's identification. Security-relevant events are audited, and these records must be protected from unauthorized modification. The architecture must provide resource, or object, isolation so proper protection can be applied to the resource and any actions taken upon it can be properly audited. The object reuse concept must also be invoked, meaning that any medium holding data must not contain any remnants of information after it is released for another subject to use. If a subject uses a segment of memory, that memory space must not hold any information after the subject is done using it. The same is true for storage media, objects being populated, and temporary files being created—all data must be efficiently erased once the subject is done with that medium.

This class requires a more granular method of providing access control. The system must enforce strict logon procedures and provide decision-making capabilities when subjects request access to objects. A C2 system cannot guarantee it will not be compromised, but it supplies a level of protection that would make attempts to compromise it harder to accomplish.

The type of environment that would require systems with a C2 rating is one in which users are trusted but a certain level of accountability is required. C2, overall, is seen as the most reasonable class for commercial applications, but the level of protection is still relatively weak.

Division B: Mandatory Protection

Mandatory access control is enforced by the use of security labels. The architecture is based on the Bell-LaPadula security model, and evidence of reference monitor enforcement must be available.

B1: Labeled Security Each data object must contain a classification label and each subject must have a clearance label. When a subject attempts to access an object, the system must compare the subject's and object's security labels to ensure the requested actions are acceptable. Data leaving the system must also contain an accurate security label. The security policy is based on an informal statement, and the design specifications are reviewed and verified.

This security rating is intended for environments that require systems to handle classified data.

NOTE Security labels are not required until security rating B; thus, C2 does not require security labels but B1 does.

B2: Structured Protection The security policy is clearly defined and documented, and the system design and implementation are subjected to more thorough review and testing procedures. This class requires more stringent authentication mechanisms and well-defined interfaces among layers. Subjects and devices require labels, and the system must not allow covert channels. A trusted path for logon and authentication processes must be in place, which means the subject communicates directly with the application or operating system, and no trapdoors exist. There is no way to circumvent or compromise this communication channel. Operator and administration functions are separated within the system to provide more trusted and protected operational functionality. Distinct address spaces must be provided to isolate processes, and a covert channel analysis is conducted. This class adds assurance by adding requirements to the design of the system.

The type of environment that would require B2 systems is one that processes sensitive data that require a higher degree of security. This type of environment would require systems that are relatively resistant to penetration and compromise.

B3: Security Domains In this class, more granularity is provided in each protection mechanism, and the programming code that is not necessary to support the security policy is excluded. The design and implementation should not provide too much complexity, because as the complexity of a system increases, so must the skill level of the individuals who need to test, maintain, and configure it; thus, the overall security can be threatened. The reference monitor components must be small enough to test properly and be tamperproof. The security administrator role is clearly defined, and the system must be able to recover from failures without its security level being compromised. When the system starts up and loads its operating system and components, it must be done in an initial secure state to ensure that any weakness of the system cannot be taken advantage of in this slice of time.

The type of environment that requires B3 systems is a highly secured environment that processes very sensitive information. It requires systems that are highly resistant to penetration.

Division A: Verified Protection

Formal methods are used to ensure that all subjects and objects are controlled with the necessary discretionary and mandatory access controls. The design, development, implementation, and documentation are looked at in a formal and detailed way. The security mechanisms between B3 and A1 are not very different, but the way the system was designed and developed is evaluated in a much more structured and stringent procedure.

A1: Verified Design   The architecture and protection features are not much different from systems that achieve a B3 rating, but the assurance of an A1 system is higher than a B3 system because of the formality in the way the A1 system was designed, the way the specifications were developed, and the level of detail in the verification techniques. Formal techniques are used to prove the equivalence between the TCB specifications and the security policy model. A more stringent change configuration is put in place with the development of an A1 system, and the overall design can be verified. In many cases, even the way in which the system is delivered to the customer is under scrutiny to ensure there is no way of compromising the system before it reaches its destination.

The type of environment that would require A1 systems is the most secure of secured environments. This type of environment deals with top-secret information and cannot adequately trust anyone using the systems without strict authentication, restrictions, and auditing.

 NOTE   TCSEC addresses confidentiality, but not integrity. Functionality of the security mechanisms and the assurance of those mechanisms are not evaluated separately, but rather are combined and rated as a whole.

The Orange Book and the Rainbow Series

Why are there so many colors in the rainbow?
Response: Because there are so many product types that need to be evaluated.

The Orange Book mainly addresses government and military requirements and expectations for their computer systems. Many people within the security field have pointed out several deficiencies in the Orange Book, particularly when it is being applied to systems that are to be used in commercial areas instead of government organizations. The following list summarizes a majority of the troubling issues that security practitioners have expressed about the Orange Book:

- It looks specifically at the operating system and not at other issues like networking, databases, and so on.
- It focuses mainly on one attribute of security—confidentiality—and not on integrity and availability.

- It works with government classifications and not the protection classifications commercial industries use.
- It has a relatively small number of ratings, which means many different aspects of security are not evaluated and rated independently.

The Orange Book places great emphasis on controlling which users can access a system and virtually ignores controlling what those users do with the information once they are authorized. Authorized users can, and usually do, cause more damage to data than outside attackers. Commercial organizations have expressed more concern about the integrity of their data, whereas military organizations stress that their top concern is confidentiality. Because of these different goals, the Orange Book is a better evaluation tool for government and military systems.

Because the Orange Book focuses on the operating system, many other areas of security were left out. The Orange Book provides a broad framework for building and evaluating trusted systems, but it leaves many questions about topics other than operating systems unanswered. So, more books were written to extend the coverage of the Orange Book into other areas of security. These books provide detailed information and interpretations of certain Orange Book requirements and describe the evaluation processes. These books are collectively called the *Rainbow Series* because the cover of each is a different color.

The Red Book

The Orange Book addresses single-system security, but networks are a combination of systems, and each network needs to be secure without having to fully trust each and every system connected to it. The *Trusted Network Interpretation (TNI)*, also called the *Red Book* because of the color of its cover, addresses security evaluation topics for networks and network components. It addresses isolated local area networks and wide area internetwork systems.

Like the Orange Book, the Red Book does not supply specific details about how to implement security mechanisms. Instead, it provides a framework for securing different types of networks. A network has a security policy, architecture, and design, as does an operating system. Subjects accessing objects on the network need to be controlled, monitored, and audited. In a network, the subject could be a workstation and an object could be a network service on a server.

The Red Book rates confidentiality of data and operations that happen within a network and the network products. Data and labels need to be protected from unauthorized modification, and the integrity of information as it is transferred needs to be ensured. The source and destination mechanisms used for messages are evaluated and tested to ensure modification is not allowed.

Encryption and protocols are components that provide a lot of the security within a network, and the Red Book measures their functionality, strength, and assurance.

The following is a brief overview of the security items addressed in the Red Book:

- **Communication integrity**
  - **Authentication** Protects against masquerading and playback attacks. Mechanisms include digital signatures, encryption, timestamp, and passwords.

- **Message integrity**   Protects the protocol header, routing information, and packet payload from being modified. Mechanisms include message authentication and encryption.

- **Nonrepudiation**   Ensures that a sender cannot deny sending a message. Mechanisms include encryption, digital signatures, and notarization.

- **Denial-of-service prevention**

  - **Continuity of operations**   Ensures that the network is available even if attacked. Mechanisms include fault-tolerant and redundant systems and the capability to reconfigure network parameters in case of an emergency.

  - **Network management**   Monitors network performance and identifies attacks and failures. Mechanisms include components that enable network administrators to monitor and restrict resource access.

- **Compromise protection**

  - **Data confidentiality**   Protects data from being accessed in an unauthorized method during transmission. Mechanisms include access controls, encryption, and physical protection of cables.

  - **Traffic flow confidentiality**   Ensures that unauthorized entities are not aware of routing information or frequency of communication via traffic analysis. Mechanisms include padding messages, sending noise, or sending false messages.

  - **Selective routing**   Routes messages in a way to avoid specific threats. Mechanisms include network configuration and routing tables.

Assurance is derived by comparing how things actually work to a theory of how things should work. Assurance is also derived by testing configurations in many different scenarios, evaluating engineering practices, and validating and verifying security claims.

TCSEC was introduced in 1985 and retired in December 2000. It was the first methodical and logical set of standards developed to secure computer systems. It was greatly influential to several countries that based their evaluation standards on the TCSEC guidelines. TCSEC was finally replaced with the Common Criteria.

Information Technology Security Evaluation Criteria

The *Information Technology Security Evaluation Criteria (ITSEC)* was the first attempt at establishing a single standard for evaluating security attributes of computer systems and products by many European countries. The United States looked to the Orange Book and Rainbow Series, and Europe employed ITSEC to evaluate and rate computer systems. (Today, everyone is migrating to the Common Criteria, explained in the next section.)

ITSEC evaluates two main attributes of a system's protection mechanisms: functionality and assurance. When the functionality of a system's protection mechanisms is being evaluated, the services that are provided to the subjects (access control mechanisms, auditing, authentication, and so on) are examined and measured. Protection mechanism functionality can be very diverse in nature because systems are developed differently just to provide different functionality to users. Nonetheless, when functionality is evaluated, it is tested to see if the system's protection mechanisms deliver what its vendor says they deliver. Assurance, on the other hand, is the degree of confidence in the protection mechanisms, and their effectiveness and capability to perform consistently. Assurance is generally tested by examining development practices, documentation, configuration management, and testing mechanisms.

It is possible for two systems' protection mechanisms to provide the same type of functionalities and have very different assurance levels. This is because the underlying mechanisms providing the functionality can be developed, engineered, and implemented differently. System A and System B may have protection mechanisms that provide the same type of functionality for authentication, in which case both products would get the same rating for functionality. But System A's developers could have been sloppy and careless when developing their authentication mechanism, in which case their product would receive a lower assurance rating. ITSEC actually separates these two attributes (functionality and assurance) and rates them separately, whereas TCSEC clumps them together and assigns them one rating (D through A1).

The following list shows the different types of functionalities and assurance items tested during an evaluation:

- Security functional requirements
- Identification and authentication
- Audit
- Resource utilization
- Trusted paths/channels
- User data protection
- Security management
- Product access
- Communications
- Privacy
- Protection of the product's security functions
- Cryptographic support
- Security assurance requirements
- Guidance documents and manuals

- Configuration management
- Vulnerability assessment
- Delivery and operation
- Life-cycle support
- Assurance maintenance
- Development
- Testing

Consider again our example of two systems that provide the same functionality (pertaining to the protection mechanisms) but have very different assurance levels. Using the TCSEC approach, the difference in assurance levels will be hard to distinguish because the functionality and assurance level are rated together. Under the ITSEC approach, the functionality is rated separately from the assurance, so the difference in assurance levels will be more noticeable. In the ITSEC criteria, classes F1 to F10 rate the functionality of the security mechanisms, whereas E0 to E6 rate the assurance of those mechanisms.

So a difference between ITSEC and TCSEC is that TCSEC bundles functionality and assurance into one rating, whereas ITSEC evaluates these two attributes separately. The other differences are that ITSEC was developed to provide more flexibility than TCSEC, and ITSEC addresses integrity, availability, and confidentiality, whereas TCSEC addresses only confidentiality. ITSEC also addresses networked systems, whereas TCSEC deals with stand-alone systems.

Table 5-2 is a general mapping of the two evaluation schemes to show you their relationship to each other.

As you can see, a majority of the ITSEC ratings can be mapped to the Orange Book ratings, but then ITSEC took a step farther and added F6 through F10 for specific needs consumers might have that the Orange Book does not address.

ITSEC is criteria for operating systems and other products, which it refers to individually as the *target of evaluation (TOE)*. So if you are reading literature discussing the ITSEC rating of a product and it states the TOE has a rating of F1 and E5, you know the TOE is the product that was evaluated and that it has a low functionality rating and a high assurance rating.

The ratings pertain to assurance, which is the correctness and effectiveness of the security mechanism, and functionality. Functionality is viewed in terms of the system's security objectives, security functions, and security mechanisms. The following are some examples of the functionalities that are tested: identification and authentication, access control, accountability, auditing, object reuse, accuracy, reliability of service, and data exchange.

ITSEC	TCSEC
E0	= D
FI + EI	= CI
F2 + E2	= C2
F3 + E3	= BI
F4 + E4	= B2
F5 + E5	= B3
F5 + E6	= AI
F6	= Systems that provide high integrity
F7	= Systems that provide high availability
F8	= Systems that provide data integrity during communication
F9	= Systems that provide high confidentiality (like cryptographic devices)
FI0	= Networks with high demands on confidentiality and integrity

Table 5-2   ITSEC and TCSEC Mapping

Common Criteria

"TCSEC is too hard, ITSEC is too soft, but the Common Criteria is just right," said the baby bear.

The Orange Book and the Rainbow Series provide evaluation schemes that are too rigid for the business world. ITSEC attempted to provide a more flexible approach by separating the functionality and assurance attributes and considering the evaluation of entire systems. However, this flexibility added complexity because evaluators could mix and match functionality and assurance ratings, which resulted in too many classifications to keep straight. Because we are a species that continues to try to get it right, the next attempt for an effective and usable evaluation criteria was the *Common Criteria*.

In 1990, the International Organization for Standardization (ISO) identified the need of international standard evaluation criteria to be used globally. The Common Criteria project started in 1993 when several organizations came together to combine and align existing and emerging evaluation criteria (TCSEC, ITSEC, Canadian Trusted Computer Product Evaluation Criteria [CTCPEC], and the Federal Criteria). The Common Criteria was developed through a collaboration among national security standards organizations within the United States, Canada, France, Germany, the United Kingdom, and the Netherlands.

The benefit of having a globally recognized and accepted set of criteria is that it helps consumers by reducing the complexity of the ratings and eliminating the need to understand the definition and meaning of different ratings within various evaluation schemes. This also helps manufacturers, because now they can build to one specific set of requirements if they want to sell their products internationally, instead of having to meet several different ratings with varying rules and requirements.

The Orange Book evaluates all systems by how they compare to the Bell-LaPadula model. The Common Criteria provides more flexibility by evaluating a product against a protection profile, which is structured to address a real-world security need. So while the Orange Book says, "Everyone march in this direction in this form using this path," the Common Criteria asks, "Okay, what are the threats we are facing today and what are the best ways of battling them?"

Under the Common Criteria model, an evaluation is carried out on a product and it is assigned an *Evaluation Assurance Level (EAL)*. The thorough and stringent testing increases in detailed-oriented tasks as the assurance levels increase. The Common Criteria has seven assurance levels. The range is from EAL1, where functionality testing takes place, to EAL7, where thorough testing is performed and the system design is verified. The different EAL packages are listed next:

- **EAL1**   Functionally tested
- **EAL2**   Structurally tested
- **EAL3**   Methodically tested and checked
- **EAL4**   Methodically designed, tested, and reviewed
- **EAL5**   Semiformally designed and tested
- **EAL6**   Semiformally verified design and tested
- **EAL7**   Formally verified design and tested

NOTE   When a system is "formally verified," this means it is based on a model that can be mathematically proven.

The Common Criteria uses *protection profiles* in its evaluation process. This is a mechanism used to describe a real-world need of a product that is not currently on the market. The protection profile contains the set of security requirements, their meaning and reasoning, and the corresponding EAL rating that the intended product will require. The protection profile describes the environmental assumptions, the objectives, and the functional and assurance level expectations. Each relevant threat is listed along with how it is to be controlled by specific objectives. The protection profile also justifies the assurance level and requirements for the strength of each protection mechanism.

The protection profile provides a means for a consumer, or others, to identify specific security needs; this is the security problem to be conquered. If someone identifies a security need that is not currently being addressed by any current product, that person can write a protection profile describing the product that would be a solution for this real-world problem. The protection profile goes on to provide the necessary goals and protection mechanisms to achieve the required level of security, as well as a list of things that could go wrong during this type of system development. This list is used by the engineers who develop the system, and then by the evaluators to make sure the engineers dotted every *i* and crossed every *t*.

The Common Criteria was developed to stick to evaluation classes but also to retain some degree of flexibility. Protection profiles were developed to describe the functionality, assurance, description, and rationale of the product requirements.

Like other evaluation criteria before it, the Common Criteria works to answer two basic questions about products being evaluated: what does its security mechanisms do (functionality), and how sure are you of that (assurance)? This system sets up a framework that enables consumers to clearly specify their security issues and problems; developers to specify their security solution to those problems; and evaluators to unequivocally determine what the product actually accomplishes.

A protection profile contains the following five sections:

- **Descriptive elements**   Provides the name of the profile and a description of the security problem to be solved.

- **Rationale**   Justifies the profile and gives a more detailed description of the real-world problem to be solved. The environment, usage assumptions, and threats are illustrated along with guidance on the security policies that can be supported by products and systems that conform to this profile.

- **Functional requirements**   Establishes a protection boundary, meaning the threats or compromises within this boundary to be countered. The product or system must enforce the boundary established in this section.

- **Development assurance requirements**   Identifies the specific requirements the product or system must meet during the development phases, from design to implementation.

- **Evaluation assurance requirements**   Establishes the type and intensity of the evaluation.

The evaluation process is just one leg of determining the functionality and assurance of a product. Once a product achieves a specific rating, it only applies to that particular version and only to certain configurations of that product. So if a company buys a firewall product because it has a high assurance rating, the company has no guarantee the next version of that software will have that rating. The next version will need to go through its own evaluation review. If this same company buys the firewall product and installs it with configurations that are not recommended, the level of security the company was hoping to achieve can easily go down the drain. So, all of this rating stuff is a formalized method of reviewing a system being evaluated in a lab. When the product is implemented in a real environment, factors other than its rating need to be addressed and assessed to ensure it is properly protecting resources and the environment.

NOTE   When a product is assigned an assurance rating, this means it has the *potential* of providing this level of protection. The customer has to properly configure the product to actually obtain this level of security. The vendor should provide the necessary configuration documentation, and it is up to the customer to keep the product properly configured at all times.

Certification vs. Accreditation

We have gone through the different types of evaluation criteria that a system can be appraised against to receive a specific rating. This is a very formalized process, following which the evaluated system or product will be placed on an EPL indicating what rating it achieved. Consumers can check this listing and compare the different products and systems to see how they rank against each other in the property of protection. However, once a consumer buys this product and sets it up in their environment, security is not guaranteed. Security is made up of system administration, physical security, installation, and configuration mechanisms within the environment, and other security issues. To fairly say a system is secure, all of these items must be taken into account. The rating is just one piece in the puzzle of security.

Different Components of the Common Criteria

The different components of the Common Criteria are shown and described next:

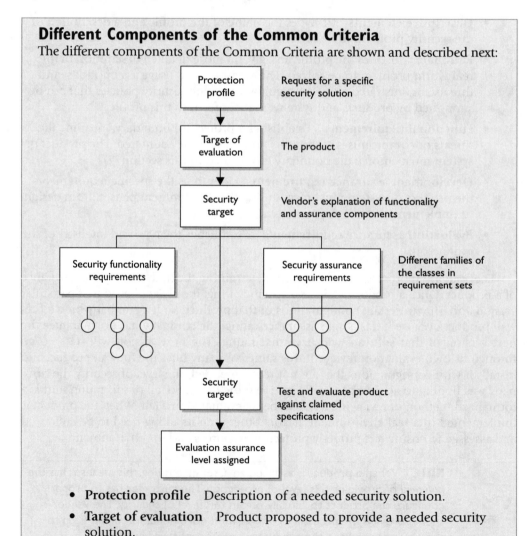

- **Protection profile**   Description of a needed security solution.
- **Target of evaluation**   Product proposed to provide a needed security solution.

- **Security target** Vendor's written explanation of the security functionality and assurance mechanisms that meet the needed security solution—in other words, "This is what our product does and how it does it."

- **Packages—EALs** Functional and assurance requirements are bundled into packages for reuse. This component describes what must be met to achieve specific EAL ratings.

Certification

How did you certify this product?

Response: It came in a very pretty box. Let's keep it.

Certification is the comprehensive technical evaluation of the security components and their compliance for the purpose of accreditation. A certification process may use safeguard evaluation, risk analysis, verification, testing, and auditing techniques to assess the appropriateness of a specific system. For example, suppose Dan is the security officer for a company that just purchased new systems to be used to process its confidential data. He wants to know if these systems are appropriate for these tasks and if they are going to provide the necessary level of protection. He also wants to make sure they are compatible with his current environment, do not reduce productivity, and do not open doors to new threats—basically, he wants to know if these are the right products for his company. He could pay a company that specializes in these matters to perform the necessary procedures to certify the systems, or it can be carried out internally. The evaluation team will perform tests on the software configurations, hardware, firmware, design, implementation, system procedures, and physical and communication controls.

The goal of a certification process is to ensure that a system, product, or network is right for the customer's purposes. Customers will rely upon a product for slightly different reasons, and environments will have various threat levels. So a particular product is not necessarily the best fit for every single customer out there. (Of course, vendors will try to convince you otherwise.) The product has to provide the right functionality and security for the individual customer, which is the whole purpose of a certification process.

The certification process and corresponding documentation will indicate the good, the bad, and the ugly about the product and how it works within the given environment. Dan will take these results and present them to his management for the accreditation process.

Accreditation

Accreditation is the formal acceptance of the adequacy of a system's overall security and functionality by management. The certification information is presented to management, or the responsible body, and it is up to management to ask questions, review the reports and findings, and decide whether to accept the product and whether any corrective action needs to take place. Once satisfied with the system's overall security as presented, management makes a formal accreditation statement. By doing this, management is stating it understands the level of protection the system will provide in its current environment and understands the security risks associated with installing and maintaining this system.

> ### No More Pencil Whipping
>
> Many organizations are taking the accreditation process more seriously than they did in the past. Unfortunately, sometimes when a certification process is completed and the documentation is sent to management for review and approval, management members just blindly sign the necessary documentation without really understanding what they are signing. Accreditation means management is accepting the *risk* that is associated with allowing this new product to be introduced into the organization's environment. When large security compromises take place, the buck stops at the individual who signed off on the offending item. So as these management members are being held more accountable for what they sign off on and as more regulations make executives personally responsible for security, the pencil whipping of accreditation papers is decreasing, but has not stopped.

 NOTE Certification is a technical review that assesses the security mechanisms and evaluates their effectiveness. Accreditation is management's official acceptance of the information in the certification process findings.

Because software, systems, and environments continually change and evolve, the certification and accreditation should also continue to take place. Any major addition of software, changes to the system, or modification of the environment should initiate a new certification and accreditation cycle.

Open vs. Closed Systems

Computer systems can be developed to integrate easily with other systems and products (open systems) or can be developed to be more proprietary in nature and work with only a subset of other systems and products (closed systems). The following sections describe the difference between these approaches.

Open Systems

I want to be able to work and play well with others.
Response: But no one wants to play with you.

Systems described as *open* are built upon standards, protocols, and interfaces that have published specifications, which enable third-party vendors to develop add-on components and devices. This type of architecture provides interoperability between products created by different vendors. This interoperability is provided by all the vendors involved who follow specific standards and provide interfaces that enable each system to easily communicate with other systems and allow add-ons to hook into the system easily.

A majority of the systems in use today are open systems. The reason an administrator can have Windows XP, Windows 2000, Macintosh, and Unix computers communicating easily on the same network is because these platforms are open. If a software vendor creates a closed system, it is restricting its potential sales to proprietary environments.

NOTE In Chapter 11, we will look at the standards that support interoperability, including CORBA, DCOM, J2EE, and more.

Closed Systems

I only want to play with you and him.
Response: Just play with him.

Systems referred to as *closed* use an architecture that does not follow industry standards. Interoperability and standard interfaces are not employed to enable easy communication between different types of systems and add-on features. Closed systems are proprietary, meaning the system can only communicate with like systems.

A closed architecture can provide more security to the system because it does not have as many doorways in, and it operates in a more secluded environment than open environments. Because a closed system is proprietary, there are not as many tools to thwart the security mechanisms and not as many people who understand its design, language, and security weaknesses and thus exploit them. A majority of the systems today are built with open architecture to enable them to work with other types of systems, easily share information, and take advantage of the functionality that third-party add-ons bring. However, this opens the doors to more hacks, cracks, and attacks. You can't have your cake and eat it too it seems.

Enterprise Architecture

Up until now we have covered many operating system and application items and concepts. We started with the architecture of a system and went through the many components that must be securely built in to help ensure the necessary level of protection required from it. The system *security architecture* is a high-level design that works as a framework. The architecture lays out what needs to be in place to ensure that the system's security policy and protection level are met. Great, so what is an enterprise security architecture?

Organizations have a choice when attempting to secure their environment as a whole. They can just toss in products here and there, which are referred to as point solutions or stovepipe solutions, and hope the ad hoc approach magically works in a manner that secures the environment evenly and covers all of the enterprise's vulnerabilities. Or the organization can take the time to understand the environment, understand the security requirements of the business and environment, and lay out an overarching framework and strategy that maps the two together. Most organizations choose option one, which is the "constantly putting out fires" approach. This is a lovely way to keep stress levels elevated, and security requirements unmet, and to let confusion and chaos be the norm.

The second approach would be to define an enterprise security architecture, allow it to be the guide when implementing solutions to ensure needs are met, provide standard protection across the environment, and reduce the amount of security surprises the organization will run into. Although implementing an enterprise security architecture will not necessarily promise pure utopia, it does tame the chaos and gets the security staff, and organization, into a more proactive and mature mindset when dealing with security as a whole.

An *enterprise security architecture* defines the information security strategy that consists of layers of policy, standards, solutions, and procedures and the way they are linked across an enterprise strategically, tactically, and operationally. This is different from the infrastructure architecture. Infrastructure is the underlying technology and hardware needed to support the enterprise security architecture. So basically you can have an infrastructure (switches, cables, routers, nodes, and so on), but it requires the software, people, and processes to work together in a cohesive and secure manner to have an actual enterprise architecture. Besides security, this type of architecture allows organizations to better achieve interoperability, integration, ease-of-use, standardization, and governance.

How do you know if an organization does not have an enterprise security architecture in place? If the answer is "yes" to most of the following questions, this type of architecture is not in place.

- Does identifying new vulnerabilities and exposures take more than 15 days?
- When user access requirements increase because of business needs, does the security or network administrator just modify the access controls without the user manager's documented approval?
- When a new product is being rolled out, do unexpected interoperability issues pop up that require more time and money to fix?
- Do many "one-off" efforts take place instead of following standardized procedures when security issues arise?
- Are the business unit managers unaware of their security responsibilities and how their responsibilities map to legal and regulatory requirements?
- Is "sensitive data" defined in a policy, but the necessary controls are not fully implemented and monitored?
- Are stovepipe (point) solutions implemented instead of enterprise-wide solutions?
- Are the same expensive mistakes continuing to take place?
- Is there a continual disconnect between senior management and the security staff?
- Is security governance currently unavailable because the enterprise is not viewed or monitored in a standardized and holistic manner?
- Are business decisions made without taking security into account?
- Are security personnel usually putting out fires with no real time to look at and develop strategic approaches?
- Are more and more security personnel seeking out shrinks and going on anti-depressant or anti-anxiety medication?

If many of these answers are "yes," no useful architecture is in place. Now, the following is something very interesting the author has seen over several years. Most organizations have the problems listed earlier and yet they focus on each item as if they were unconnected. What the CSO, CISO, and/or security administrator do not understand is that these are just *symptoms* of a treatable disease. The "treatment" is to put one person in charge of a team that develops a phased-approach enterprise security architecture rollout plan. The goals are to shift from technology-oriented to business-centric security processes; link administrative, technical, and physical controls to properly manage risk; and integrate these processes into the IT infrastructure, business processes, and the organization's culture. Following this, you can move on to implementing world peace, solving global hunger, and making all politicians tell the truth.

The main reason organizations do not develop and roll out an enterprise security architecture is because they do not fully understand what one is and it seems like an overwhelming task. Fighting fires is more understandable and straightforward, so many companies stay with this familiar approach.

If you'll remember, in Chapter 3 we went through how to set up a security program where the following outline of tasks was provided:

- Plan and Organize
  - Establish management commitment
  - Establish oversight steering committee
  - Assess business drivers
  - Carry out a threat profile on the organization
  - Carry out a risk assessment
  - Develop security architectures at an organizational, application, network, and component level
  - Identify solutions per architecture level
  - Obtain management approval to move forward
- Implement
  - Assign roles and responsibilities
  - Develop and implement security policies, procedures, standards, baselines, and guidelines
  - Identify sensitive data at rest and in transit
  - Implement the following blueprints:
    - Asset identification and management
    - Risk management
    - Vulnerability management
    - Compliance
    - Identity management and access control
    - Change control
    - Software development life cycle
    - Business continuity planning
    - Awareness and training
    - Physical security
    - Incident response

- Implement solutions (administrative, technical, physical) per blueprint
  - Develop auditing and monitoring solutions per blueprint
  - Establish goals, service level agreements (SLAs), and metrics per blueprint
- Operate and Maintain
  - Follow procedures to ensure all baselines are met in each implemented blueprint
  - Carry out internal and external audits
  - Carry out tasks outlined per blueprint
  - Manage service level agreements per blueprint
- Monitor and Evaluate
  - Review logs, audit results, collected metric values, and SLAs per blueprint
  - Assess goal accomplishments per blueprint
  - Carry out quarterly meetings with steering committee
  - Develop improvement steps and integrate into the Plan and Organize phase

 NOTE The CISSP exam may use the term "plan" instead of blueprint.

These are also the basic steps of setting up an enterprise security architecture, because a security program and the security architecture must follow the same model. The security program is often considered the administrative components, as in policies, standards, risk management, personnel security, data classification, and so on. Basically, every main concept covered in Chapter 3 is a component of a security program. An enterprise security architecture goes deeper than the security program and provides more granularity. For example, if the security policy dictates that network access control must be implemented and enforced, the architecture would cover the network schematic, network zones based on trust levels and business needs, external connections, security mechanisms, tools, processes, and roles involved at each level. The architecture works its way down from the policy level to the component level.

As an analogy, let's say Shannon tells a builder she wants a ranch-style house, with four bedrooms, whose size should be 2,500 square feet. This is a high-level description (policy) and the builder is not going to just wing it and see if he can build this from scratch. The builder will use a blueprint to follow (architecture), which will provide more detailed requirements that must be met to fulfill Shannon's request.

Almost all robust enterprise security architectures work with the structure provided by the Zachman architecture framework in one way or another. Table 5-3 shows you the makeup of this architectural framework. (In order to see the full framework, go to www .zifa.com.) The Zachman framework has been around for many years and has been used by many organizations to build or better define their business environment. This framework is not security-oriented, but it is a good template to work with because it offers direction on how to understand an actual enterprise in a modular fashion.

Order	Layer	What (Data)	How (Function)	Where (Network)	Who (People)	When (Time)	Why (Motivation)
1	Scope context boundary • Planner	List of things important to the business	List of processes the business performs	List of locations in which the business operates	List of organizations important to the business	List of events significant to the business	List of business goals/strategies
2	Business model concepts • Owner	e.g., semantic or entity-relationship model	e.g., business process model	e.g., business logistics model	e.g., workflow model	e.g., master schedule	e.g., business plan
3	System model logic • Designer	e.g., logical data model	e.g., application architecture	e.g., distributed system architecture	e.g., human interface architecture	e.g., processing structure	e.g., business rule model
4	Technology model physics • Builder	e.g., physical data model	e.g., system design	e.g., technology architecture	e.g., presentation architecture	e.g., control structure	e.g., rule design
5	Component configuration • Implementer	e.g., data definition	e.g., program	e.g., network architecture	e.g., security architecture	e.g., timing definition	e.g., rule specification
6	Functioning enterprise instances • Worker	e.g., data	e.g., function	e.g., network	e.g., organization	e.g., schedule	e.g., strategy

Table 5-3 Zachman Framework for Enterprise Architecture

NOTE The Zachman framework is used as a model for *robust* security architectures, which means it deals with many components throughout the organization. Many people are familiar with *technical* security architectures, which just deal with a network and the systems within that network. These are two totally different things. The robust security architecture encompasses the technical architecture and much more, as you can see in Table 5-3.

The Zachman framework is a two-dimensional model that uses six basic communication interrogatives (What, How, Where, Who, When, and Why) intersecting with different levels (Planner, Owner, Designer, Builder, Implementer, and Worker) to give a holistic view of the enterprise. This framework was developed in the 1980s and is based on the principles of classical business architecture that contain rules that govern an ordered set of relationships.

Based on the author's experience, most technical people have a negative visceral reaction to models like this. They feel it's too much work, that it's a lot of fluff, is not directly relevant, and so on. If you handed the same group of people a network schematic with firewalls, IDSs, and VPNs, they would say, "Now were talking about security!" This is because they are technology focused and they do not understand all the other components of security, which are just as (or more) important than technology.

Working at the enterprise level requires different thinking than working just at the system or technical level. Not only do the solutions need to apply to the whole enterprise in a standardized manner, they need to map to business needs. For example, when thinking about access control—instead of just thinking about Kerberos, domain controllers, ACLs, and credentials—you must also consider what regulations and laws the company must comply with. If the company must comply with Sarbanes-Oxley (SOX), for example, the company needs many of these processes documented and access must be approved by managers. This may require identity management solutions instead of just depending upon Microsoft's domain authentication technology.

When an enterprise security architecture is being developed, the following items must be understood and followed: strategic alignment, process enhancement, business enablement, and security effectiveness.

Strategic alignment means the business drivers and the regulatory and legal requirements are being met by the security architecture. The current security posture must be understood. This means an enterprise risk assessment was carried out so the company could understand its current threats and their ability to deal with these threats. There should be a consensus regarding the vulnerabilities and threats within the organization. It also means an acceptable risk level was set based on the company's risk tolerance. Great, but what does this really mean? Well, strategic alignment means, "What assets do we have to protect?," "How well are our security initiatives tied to business needs?," "What is the definition of 'enough security'?," and "Is senior management on board with all of this?"

The result of these efforts is to come up with an agreed-upon current risk profile and a desired profile. A three-year security plan should be developed that outlines how the organization will get to, and achieve, the desired profile, and also should detail a phased approach regarding how the full security enterprise will be built.

SABSA

A group developed the Sherwood Applied Business Security Architecture (SABSA), as shown in the following table, which is based on the Zachman framework. When building a security architecture, you can visit www.sabsa-institute.org/home.aspx to learn more about this approach. While the SABSA is not exam-oriented, the Zachman framework is. So you might want to dig into this model after your CISSP exam.

	Assets (What)	Motivation (Why)	Process (How)	People (Who)	Location (Where)	Time (When)
Contextual	The business	Business risk model	Business process model	Business organization and relationships	Business geography	Business time dependencies
Conceptual	Business attributes profile	Control objectives	Security strategies and architectural layering	Security entity model and trust framework	Security domain model	Security-related lifetimes and deadlines
Logical	Business information model	Security policies	Security services	Entity schema and privilege profiles	Security domain definitions and associations	Security processing cycle
Physical	Business data model	Security rules, practices, and procedures	Security mechanisms	Users, applications, and user interface	Platform and network infrastructure	Control structure execution
Component	Detailed data structures	Security standards	Security products and tools	Identities, functions, actions, and ACLs	Processes, nodes, addresses, and protocols	Security step timing and sequencing
Operational	Assurance of operation continuity	Operation risk management	Security service management and support	Application and user management and support	Security of sites, networks, and platforms	Security operations schedule

 NOTE The preceding information may seem very obvious as to what needs to first take place, but unfortunately many companies just start plugging in firewalls, configuring ACLs, and rolling out encryption solutions without setting up an overall plan. It gets everybody busy, but often they're marching down different paths with no agreed-upon goal for everyone to be working toward.

A few other items approached at the strategic stage are

- Stakeholders and their requirements are defined.
- Owners and custodians are identified and assigned responsibilities.
- Responsibility, accountability, and authority are defined and assigned.
- Someone buys a beer keg to get through the rest of the phases.

Senior management must be actively involved at this stage and provide the necessary resources and support. Without management support, the effort will limp along with no real success in the end.

When looking at the *business enablement* part of the architecture, we need to remind ourselves that companies are in business to make money. Companies and organizations do not exist for the sole purpose of being secure. Security cannot stand in the way of business processes, but should be implemented to better enable them. Many of the critical business processes deal with end-to-end transaction integrity and are commonly a large focus when security must enable business activities.

Business enablement means the core business processes are integrated into the security operating model—they are standards-based and follow a risk tolerance–based criteria. What does this mean in the real world? Let's say a company's bean counters have figured out that if they allow the customer service and support staff to work from home, the company would save a lot of money on office rent, utilities, and overhead—plus, their insurance is cheaper. The company could move into this new model with the use of VPNs, firewalls, content filtering, and so on. If a financial institution wants to allow their customers the ability to view bank account information and carry out money transfers, it can offer this service if the correct security mechanisms were put in place. Security should help the organization thrive by providing the mechanisms to do new things safely.

The *process enhancement* piece can be quite beneficial to an organization if it takes advantage of this capability. When an organization is serious about securing their environment, it means they will have to take a close look at many of the business processes that take place on an ongoing process. Many times these processes are viewed through the eyeglasses of security, because that's the reason for the activity, but this is a perfect chance to enhance and improve upon the same processes to increase productivity. When you look at many business processes taking place in all types of organizations, you commonly find a duplication of efforts, manual steps that can be easily automated, or ways to streamline and reduce time and effort that are involved in certain tasks. This is commonly referred to as *process reengineering*.

When an organization is developing its security blueprints, those blueprints must be integrated into the business processes to be effective. This can allow for process management to be refined and calibrated. This allows for security to be integrated in system life cycles and day-to-day operations.

Security effectiveness deals with metrics, meeting service level agreement (SLA) requirements, return on investment (ROI), meeting set baselines, and providing management with a dashboard or balanced scorecard system. These are ways to determine how useful the current security solutions and architecture as a whole are performing.

Many organizations are just getting to this point of their architecture, because there is a need to ensure that the countermeasures in place are providing the necessary level of protection and that finite funds are being used properly. Once baselines are set, then metrics can be developed to verify baseline compliancy. These metrics are then rolled up to management in a format they can understand that shows them the health of the organization's security posture and compliance levels. This also allows management to make informed business decisions. Security affects almost everything today in business, so this information should be readily available to senior management in a form they can actually use. All these items (strategic alignment, process enhancement, business enablement, and security effectiveness) can only take place if there is a strong foundation of supporting security blueprints. The blueprints outline the actual security mechanisms that will be used to provide the organization with the level of protection it needs. Blueprints that can be in place include access control, identity management, asset management, incident response, infrastructure security, application security, and so on. Without a strong and supporting security foundation, none of the other goals can actually be accomplished. It would be like trying to build a house on sand.

Figure 5-20 shows how organizations are commonly evolving in their security maturity.

 NOTE An enterprise security foundation cannot be built without established *security zones*. This provides boundaries based on trust and specifies what actually needs to be protected. This will allow protection and risk management to be carried out in a standardized manner across the enterprise.

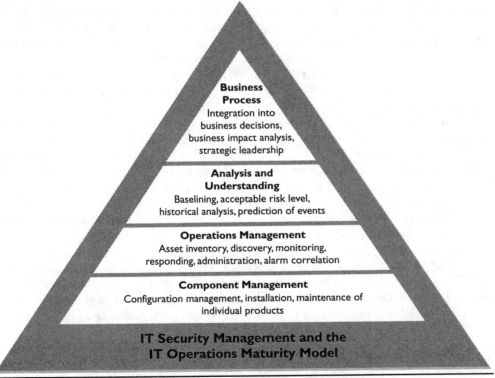

Figure 5-20 IT Security Management and the IT Operations Maturity Model

A Few Threats to Review

Now that we have talked about how everything is supposed to work, let's take a quick look at some of the things that can go wrong when designing a system.

Software almost always has bugs and vulnerabilities. The rich functionality demanded by users brings about deep complexity, which usually opens the doors to problems in the computer world. Also, vulnerabilities are always around because attackers continually find ways of using system operations and functionality in a negative and destructive way. Just like there will always be cops and robbers, there will always be attackers and security professionals. It is a game of trying to outwit each other and seeing who will put the necessary effort into winning the game.

 NOTE Carnegie Mellon University estimates there are 5 to 15 bugs in every 1,000 lines of code. Windows 2000 has 40–60 million lines of code.

Maintenance Hooks

In the programming world, *maintenance hooks* are a type of backdoor. They are instructions within software that only the developer knows about and can invoke, and which give the developer easy access to the code. They allow the developer to view and edit the code without having to go through regular access controls. During the development phase of the software, these can be very useful, but if they are not removed before the software goes into production, they can cause major security issues.

The maintenance hook is usually initiated by a random sequence of keystrokes that provides access into the software without having to go through normal access control and security checks and mechanisms.

An application that has a maintenance hook enables the developer to execute commands by using a specific sequence of keystrokes. Once this is done successfully, the developer can be inside the application looking directly at the code or configuration files. She might do this to watch problem areas within the code, check variable population, export more code into the program, or fix problems she sees taking place. Although this sounds nice and healthy, if an attacker finds out about this maintenance hook, he can take more sinister actions. So all maintenance hooks need to be removed from software before it goes into production.

 NOTE Many would think that since security is more in the minds of people today, that maintenance hooks would be a thing of the past. This is not true. Developers are still using maintenance hooks, because of their lack of understanding or care of security issues, and many maintenance hooks still reside in older software that organizations are using.

Countermeasures

Because maintenance hooks are usually inserted by programmers, they are the ones who usually have to take them out before the programs go into production. Code reviews and unit and quality assurance testing should always be on the lookout for backdoors, in case the programmer overlooked extracting them. Because maintenance hooks are within the code of an application or system, there is not much a user can do to prevent their presence, but when a vendor finds out a backdoor exists in its product, it usually develops and releases a patch to reduce this vulnerability. Because most vendors sell their software without including the associated source code, it may be very difficult for companies who have purchased software to identify backdoors. The following lists some preventive measures against backdoors:

- Use a host intrusion detection system to watch for any attackers using backdoors into the system.
- Use file system encryption to protect sensitive information.
- Implement auditing to detect any type of backdoor use.

Time-of-Check/Time-of-Use Attacks

Specific attacks can take advantage of the way a system processes requests and performs tasks. A *time-of-check/time-of-use (TOC/TOU) attack* deals with the sequence of steps a system uses to complete a task. This type of attack takes advantage of the dependency on the timing of events that take place in a multitasking operating system.

As stated previously, operating systems and applications are in reality just lines and lines of instructions. An operating system must carry out instruction 1, then instruction 2, then instruction 3, and so on. This is how it is written. If an attacker can get in between instructions 2 and 3 and manipulate something, she can control the result of these activities.

An example of a TOC/TOU attack is if process 1 validates the authorization of a user to open a noncritical text file and process 2 carries out the open command. If the attacker can change out this noncritical text file with a password file while process 1 is carrying out its task, she has just obtained access to this critical file. (It is a flaw within the code that allows this type of compromise to take place.)

NOTE   This type of attack is also referred to as an *asynchronous attack*. Asynchronous describes a process in which the timing of each step may vary. The attack gets in between these steps and modifies something. Race conditions are also considered TOC/TOU attacks by some in the industry.

A *race condition* is when two different processes need to carry out their tasks on one resource. The processes need to follow the correct sequence. Process 1 needs to carry out its work before process 2 accesses the same resource and carries out its tasks. If process 2 goes before process 1, the outcome could be very different. If an attacker can manipulate the processes so process 2 does its task first, she can control the outcome of the processing procedure. Let's say process 1's instructions are to add 3 to a value and process 2's instructions are to divide by 15. If process 2 carries out its tasks before process 1, the outcome would be different. So if an attacker can make process 2 do its work before process 1, she can control the result.

Looking at this issue from a security perspective, there are several types of race condition attacks that are quite concerning. If a system splits up the authentication and authorization steps, an attacker could be authorized before she is even authenticated. For example, in the normal sequence, process 1 verifies the authentication before allowing a user access to a resource, and process 2 authorizes the user to access the resource. If the attacker makes process 2 carry out its tasks before process 1, she can access a resource without the system making sure she has been authenticated properly.

So although the terms "race condition" and "TOC/TOU attack" are sometimes used interchangeably, in reality they are two different things. A race condition is an attack in which an attacker makes processes execute out of sequence to control the result. A TOC/TOU attack is when an attacker jumps in between two tasks and modifies something to control the result.

Countermeasures

It would take a dedicated attacker with great precision to perform these types of attacks, but it is possible and has been done. To protect against race condition attacks, it is best to *not* split up critical tasks that can have their sequence altered. This means the system should use atomic operations where only one system call is used to check authentication and then grant access in one task. This would not give the processor the opportunity to switch to another process in between two tasks. Unfortunately, using these types of atomic operations is not always possible.

To avoid TOC/TOU attacks, it is best if the operating system can apply software locks to the items it will use when it is carrying out its "checking" tasks. So if a user requests access to a file, while the system is validating this user's authorization, it should put a software lock on the file being requested. This ensures the file cannot be deleted and replaced with another file. Applying locks can be carried out easily on files, but it is more challenging to apply locks to database components and table entries to provide this type of protection.

Buffer Overflows

My cup runneth over and so does my buffer.

Today, many people know the term "buffer overflow" and the basic definition, but it is important for security professionals to understand what is going on beneath the covers.

A *buffer overflow* takes place when too much data are accepted as input to an application or operating system. A buffer is an allocated segment of memory. A buffer can be overflowed arbitrarily with too much data, but for it to be of any use to an attacker, the code inserted into the buffer must be of a specific length, followed up by commands the attacker wants executed. So, the purpose of a buffer overflow may be either to make a mess, by shoving arbitrary data into various memory segments, or to accomplish a specific task, by pushing into the memory segment a carefully crafted set of data that will accomplish a specific task. This task could be to open a command shell with administrative privilege or execute malicious code.

Let's take a deeper look at how this is accomplished. Software may be written to accept data from a user, web site, database, or another application. The accepted data needs something to happen to it, because it has been inserted for some type of manipulation or calculation, or to be used as a parameter to be passed to a procedure. A procedure is code that can carry out a specific type of function on the data and return the result to the requesting software, as shown in Figure 5-21.

When a programmer writes a piece of software that will accept data, this data will be stored in a variable. When this software calls upon a procedure to carry out some type of functionality, it stacks the necessary instructions and data in a memory segment for the procedure to read from. (Memory stacks were explained earlier in the chapter, but we will go over them again in this section.)

The data accepted from an outside entity is placed in a variable. This variable must have a place to live in memory, which is called a buffer. A buffer is like a memory container for data. The buffer needs to be the right size to accept the inputted data. So if the input is supposed to be one character, the buffer should be one byte in size. If a programmer does not ensure that only one byte of data is being inserted into the software, then someone can input several characters at once and thus overflow that specific buffer.

The buffers hold data, which are placed on a memory stack. You can think of a buffer as a small bucket to hold water (data). We have several of these small buckets stacked on top of one another (memory stack), and if too much water is poured into the top bucket, it spills over into the buckets below it (buffer overflow) and overwrites the instructions and data on the memory stack.

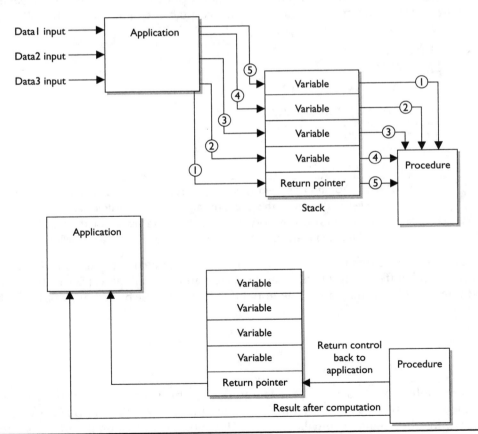

Figure 5-21   A memory stack has individual buffers to hold instructions and data.

What Is a Stack and How Does It Work?

If you are interacting with an application that calculates mortgage rates, you have to put in the parameters that need to be calculated—years of loan, percentage of interest rate, and amount of loan. These parameters are passed into empty variables and put in a linear construct (memory stack), which acts like a queue for the procedure to pull from when it carries out this calculation. The first thing your mortgage rate application lays down on the stack is its return pointer. This is a pointer to the requesting application's memory address that tells the procedure to return control to the requesting application after the procedure has worked through all the values on the stack. The mortgage rate application then places on top of the return pointer the rest of the data you have input and sends a request to the procedure to carry out the necessary calculation, as illustrated in Figure 5-21. The procedure takes the data off the stack starting at the top, so they are first in, last off (FILO). The procedure carries out its functions on all the data and returns the result and control back to the requesting mortgage rate application once it hits the return pointer in the stack.

So the stack is just a segment in memory that allows for communication between the requesting application and the procedure or subroutine. The potential for problems comes into play when the requesting application does not carry out proper **bounds checking** to ensure the inputted data are of an acceptable length. Look at the following C code to see how this could happen:

```
#include<stdio.h>
int main(int argc, char **argv)
{
        char buf1 [5] = "1111";
        char buf2 [7] = "222222";
        strcpy (buf2, "3333333333");
        printf ("%s\n", buf2);
        printf ("%s\n", buf1);
        return 0;
}
```

 CAUTION You do not need to know C programming for the CISSP exam. We are digging deep into this topic because buffer overflows are so common and have caused grave security breaches over the years. For the CISSP exam, you just need to understand the overall concept of a buffer overflow.

Here, we are setting up a buffer (buf1) to hold four characters and a NULL value, and a second buffer (buf2) to hold six characters and a NULL value. (The NULL values indicate the buffer's end place in memory.) If we viewed these buffers, we would see the following:

```
Buf2
\0 2 2 2 2 2 2
Buf1
\0 1 1 1 1
```

The application then accepts ten 3s into buf2, which can only hold six characters. So the six variables in buf2 are filled and then the four variables in buf1 are filled, overwriting the original contents of buf1. This took place because the strcpy command did not make sure the buffer was large enough to hold that many values. So now if we looked at the two buffers, we would see the following:

```
Buf2
\0 3 3 3 3 3 3
Buf1
\0 3 3 3 3
```

But what gets even more interesting is when the actual return pointer is written over, as shown in Figure 5-22. In a carefully crafted buffer overflow attack, the stack is filled properly so the return pointer can be overwritten and control is given to the malicious instructions that have been loaded onto the stack instead of back to the requesting application. This allows the malicious instructions to be executed in the security context of the requesting application. If this application is running in a privileged mode, the attacker has more permissions and rights to carry out more damage.

The attacker must know the size of the buffer to overwrite and must know the addresses that have been assigned to the stack. Without knowing these addresses, she could not lay down a new return pointer to her malicious code. The attacker must also write this dangerous payload to be small enough so it can be passed as input from one procedure to the next.

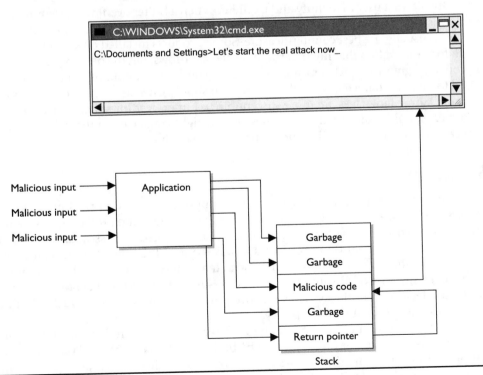

Figure 5-22 A buffer overflow attack

Windows' core is written in the C language and has layers and layers of object-oriented code on top of it. When a procedure needs to call upon the operating system to carry out some type of task, it calls upon a system service via an API call. The API works like a doorway to the operating system's functionality.

The C language is susceptible to buffer overflow attacks because it allows for direct pointer manipulations to take place. Specific commands can provide access to low-level memory addresses without carrying out bounds checking. The C functions that do perform the necessary boundary checking include `strncpy()`, `strncat()`, `snprintf()`, and `vsnprintf()`.

An operating system must be written to work with specific CPU architectures. These architectures dictate system memory addressing, protection mechanisms, and modes of execution, and work with specific instruction sets. This means a buffer overflow attack that works on an Intel chip will not necessarily work on a Motorola or a SPARC processor. These different processors set up the memory address of the stacks differently, so the attacker may have to craft a different buffer overflow code for different platforms. This is usually not an obstacle since most times the code is already written and available via different hacking web sites.

Countermeasures

Buffer overflows are in the source code of various applications and operating systems. They have been around since programmers started developing software. This means it is very difficult for a user to identify and fix them. When a buffer overflow is identified, the vendor usually sends out a patch. So keeping systems current on updates, hotfixes, and patches is usually the best countermeasure. Some products installed on systems can also watch for input values that might result in buffer overflows. But the best countermeasure is proper programming. This means use bounds checking. If an input value is only supposed to be nine characters, then the application should only accept nine characters and no more. Some languages are more susceptible to buffer overflows than others. So programmers should understand these issues, use the right languages for the right purposes, and carry out code review to identify buffer overflow vulnerabilities.

Summary

The architecture of a computer system is very important and comprises many topics. The system has to ensure that memory is properly segregated and protected, ensure that only authorized subjects access objects, ensure that untrusted processes cannot perform activities that would put other processes at risk, control the flow of information, and define a domain of resources for each subject. It also must ensure that if the computer experiences any type of disruption, it will not result in an insecure state. Many of these issues are dealt with in the system's security policy, and the security model is built to support the requirements of this policy.

Once the security policy, model, and architecture have been developed, the computer operating system, or product, must be built, tested, evaluated, and rated. An evaluation is done by comparing the system to predefined criteria. The rating assigned to the system depends upon how it fulfills the requirements of the criteria. Customers use this rating to understand what they are really buying and how much they can trust this new product. Once the customer buys the product, it must be tested within their own environment to make sure it meets their company's needs, which takes place through certification and accreditation processes.

Quick Tips

- Two systems can have the exact same hardware, software components, and applications, but provide different levels of protection because of the different security policies and security models the two systems were built upon.

- A CPU contains a control unit, which controls the timing of the execution of instructions and data, and an ALU, which performs mathematical functions and logical operations.

- Most systems use protection rings. The more privileged processes run in the lower-numbered rings and have access to all or most of the system resources. Applications run in higher-numbered rings and have access to a smaller amount of resources.

- Operating system processes are executed in privileged or supervisor mode, and applications are executed in user mode, also known as "problem state."

- Secondary storage is nonvolatile and can be a hard drive, CD-ROM drive, floppy drive, tape backup, or a jump drive.

- Virtual storage combines RAM and secondary storage so the system seems to have a larger bank of memory.

- A deadlock situation occurs when two processes are trying to access the same resource at the same time.

- Security mechanisms can focus on different issues, work at different layers, and vary in complexity.

- The more complex a security mechanism is, the less amount of assurance it can usually provide.

- Not all system components fall under the trusted computing base (TCB), which includes only those system components that enforce the security policy directly and protect the system. These components are within the security perimeter.

- Components that make up the TCB are hardware, software, and firmware that provide some type of security protection.

- A security perimeter is an imaginary boundary that has trusted components within it (those that make up the TCB) and untrusted components outside it.

- The reference monitor concept is an abstract machine that ensures all subjects have the necessary access rights before accessing objects. Therefore, it mediates all accesses to objects by subjects.

- The security kernel is the mechanism that actually enforces the rules of the reference monitor concept.

- The security kernel must isolate processes carrying out the reference monitor concept, must be tamperproof, must be invoked for each access attempt, and must be small enough to be properly tested.

- A security domain is all the objects available to a subject.

- Processes need to be isolated, which can be done through segmented memory addressing, encapsulation of objects, time multiplexing of shared resources, naming distinctions, and virtual mapping.

- The level of security a system provides depends upon how well it enforces the security policy.

- A multilevel security system processes data at different classifications (security levels), and users with different clearances (security levels) can use the system.

- Processes should be assigned least privilege so they have just enough system privileges to fulfill their tasks and no more.

- Some systems provide security at different layers of their architectures, which is called layering. This separates the processes and provides more protection for them individually.

- Data hiding occurs when processes work at different layers and have layers of access control between them. Processes need to know how to communicate only with each other's interfaces.

- A security model maps the abstract goals of a security policy to computer system terms and concepts. It gives the security policy structure and provides a framework for the system.

- A closed system is often proprietary to the manufacturer or vendor, whereas the open system allows for more interoperability.

- The Bell-LaPadula model deals only with confidentiality, while the Biba and Clark-Wilson models deal only with integrity.

- A state machine model deals with the different states a system can enter. If a system starts in a secure state, all state transitions take place securely, and the system shuts down and fails securely, the system will never end up in an insecure state.

- A lattice model provides an upper bound and a lower bound of authorized access for subjects.

- An information flow security model does not permit data to flow to an object in an insecure manner.

- The Bell-LaPadula model has a simple security rule, which means a subject cannot read data from a higher level (no read up). The *-property rule means a subject cannot write to an object at a lower level (no write down). The strong star property rule dictates that a subject can read and write to objects at its own security level.

- The Biba model does not let subjects write to objects at a higher integrity level (no write up), and it does not let subjects read data at a lower integrity level (no read down). This is done to protect the integrity of the data.

- The Bell-LaPadula model is used mainly in military systems. The Biba and Clark-Wilson models are used in the commercial sector.

- The Clark-Wilson model dictates that subjects can only access objects through applications. This model also illustrates how to provide functionality for separation of duties and requires auditing tasks within software.

- If a system is working in a dedicated security mode, it only deals with one level of data classification, and all users must have this level of clearance to be able to use the system.

- Compartmented and multilevel security modes enable the system to process data classified at different classification levels.

- Trust means that a system uses all of its protection mechanisms properly to process sensitive data for many types of users. Assurance is the level of confidence you have in this trust and that the protection mechanisms behave properly in all circumstances predictably.

- The Orange Book, also called Trusted Computer System Evaluation Criteria (TCSEC), was developed to evaluate systems built to be used mainly by the military. Its use was expanded to evaluate other types of products.

- In the Orange Book, D classification means a system provides minimal protection and is used for systems that were evaluated but failed to meet the criteria of higher divisions.

- In the Orange Book, the C division deals with discretionary protection, and the B division deals with mandatory protection (security labels).

- In the Orange Book, the A classification means the system's design and level of protection are verifiable and provide the highest level of assurance and trust.

- In the Orange Book, C2 requires object reuse protection and auditing.

- In the Orange Book, B1 is the first rating that requires security labels.

- In the Orange Book, B2 requires security labels for all subjects and devices, the existence of a trusted path, routine covert channel analysis, and the provision of separate administrator functionality.

- The Orange Book deals mainly with stand-alone systems, so a range of books were written to cover many other topics in security. These books are called the Rainbow Series.

- ITSEC evaluates the assurance and functionality of a system's protection mechanisms separately, whereas TCSEC combines the two into one rating.

- The Common Criteria was developed to provide globally recognized evaluation criteria and is in use today. It combines sections of TCSEC, ITSEC, CTCPEC, and the Federal Criteria.

- The Common Criteria uses protection profiles and ratings from EAL1 to EAL7.

- Certification is the technical evaluation of a system or product and its security components. Accreditation is management's formal approval and acceptance of the security provided by a system.

- A covert channel is an unintended communication path that transfers data in a way that violates the security policy. There are two types: timing and storage covert channels.

- A covert timing channel enables a process to relay information to another process by modulating its use of system resources.

- A covert storage channel enables a process to write data to a storage medium so another process can read it.

- A maintenance hook is developed to let a programmer into the application quickly for maintenance. This should be removed before the application goes into production or it can cause a serious security risk.

- An execution domain is where instructions are executed by the CPU. The operating system's instructions are executed in a privileged mode, and applications' instructions are executed in user mode.

- Process isolation ensures that multiple processes can run concurrently and the processes will not interfere with each other or affect each other's memory segments.

- The only processes that need complete system privileges are located in the system's kernel.

- TOC/TOU stands for time-of-check/time-of-use. This is a class of asynchronous attacks.

- The Biba model addresses the first goal of integrity, which is to prevent unauthorized users from making modifications.

- The Clark-Wilson model addresses all three integrity goals: prevent unauthorized users from making modifications, prevent authorized users from making improper modifications, and maintain internal and external consistency.

- In the Clark-Wilson model, users can only access and manipulate objects through programs. It uses access triple, which is subject-program-object.

Questions

Please remember that these questions are formatted and asked in a certain way for a reason. Keep in mind that the CISSP exam is asking questions at a conceptual level. Questions may not always have the perfect answer, and the candidate is advised against always looking for the perfect answer. Instead, the candidate should look for the best answer in the list.

1. What flaw creates buffer overflows?

   A. Application executing in privileged mode

   B. Inadequate memory segmentation

    C. Inadequate protection ring use

    D. Insufficient bounds checking

2. The operating system performs all except which of the following tasks?

    A. Memory allocation

    B. Input and output tasks

    C. Resource allocation

    D. User access to database views

3. If an operating system allows sequential use of an object without refreshing it, what security issue can arise?

    A. Disclosure of residual data

    B. Unauthorized access to privileged processes

    C. Data leakage through covert channels

    D. Compromise of the execution domain

4. What is the final step in authorizing a system for use in an environment?

    A. Certification

    B. Security evaluation and rating

    C. Accreditation

    D. Verification

5. What feature enables code to be executed without the usual security checks?

    A. Temporal isolation

    B. Maintenance hook

    C. Race conditions

    D. Process multiplexing

6. If a component fails, a system should be designed to do which of the following?

    A. Change to a protected execution domain

    B. Change to a problem state

    C. Change to a more secure state

    D. Release all data held in volatile memory

7. What security advantage does firmware have over software?

    A. It is difficult to modify without physical access.

    B. It requires a smaller memory segment.

    C. It does not need to enforce the security policy.

    D. It is easier to reprogram.

8. Which is the first level of the Orange Book that requires classification labeling of data?

   A. B3

   B. B2

   C. B1

   D. C2

9. Which of the following best describes the security kernel?

   A. A software component that monitors activity and writes security events to an audit log

   B. A software component that determines whether a user is authorized to perform a requested operation

   C. A software component that isolates processes and separates privileged and user modes

   D. A software component that works in the center protection ring and provides interfaces between trusted and untrusted objects

10. The Information Technology Security Evaluation Criteria was developed for which of the following?

    A. International use

    B. U.S. use

    C. European use

    D. Global use

11. A security kernel contains which of the following?

    A. Software, hardware, and firmware

    B. Software, hardware, and system design

    C. Security policy, protection mechanisms, and software

    D. Security policy, protection mechanisms, and system design

12. What is the purpose of base and limit registers?

    A. Countermeasure buffer overflows

    B. Time sharing of system resources, mainly the CPU

    C. Process isolation

    D. TCB enforcement

13. A guard is commonly used with a classified system. What is the main purpose of implementing and using a guard?

    A. To ensure that less trusted systems only receive acknowledgments and not messages

    B. To ensure proper information flow

    C. To ensure that less trusted and more trusted systems have open architectures and interoperability

    D. To allow multilevel and dedicated mode systems to communicate

14. The trusted computing base (TCB) controls which of the following?

    A. All trusted processes and software components

    B. All trusted security policies and implementation mechanisms

    C. All trusted software and design mechanisms

    D. All trusted software and hardware components

15. What is the imaginary boundary that separates components that maintain security from components that are not security related?

    A. Reference monitor

    B. Security kernel

    C. Security perimeter

    D. Security policy

16. Which model deals only with confidentiality?

    A. Bell-LaPadula

    B. Clark-Wilson

    C. Biba

    D. Reference monitor

17. What is the best description of a security kernel from a security point of view?

    A. Reference monitor

    B. Resource manager

    C. Memory mapper

    D. Security perimeter

18. When is the security of a system most effective and economical?

    A. When it is designed and implemented from the beginning of the development of the system

    B. When it is designed and implemented as a secure and trusted front end

    C. When it is customized to fight specific types of attacks

    D. When the system is optimized before security is added

19. In secure computing systems, why is there a logical form of separation used between processes?

   A. Processes are contained within their own security domains so each does not make unauthorized accesses to other processes or their resources.

   B. Processes are contained within their own security perimeter so they can only access protection levels above them.

   C. Processes are contained within their own security perimeter so they can only access protection levels equal to them.

   D. The separation is hardware and not logical in nature.

20. What type of attack is taking place when a higher-level subject writes data to a storage area and a lower-level subject reads it?

   A. TOC/TOU

   B. Covert storage attack

   C. Covert timing attack

   D. Buffer overflow

21. What type of rating does the Common Criteria give to products?

   A. PP

   B. EPL

   C. EAL

   D. A–D

22. Which best describes the *-integrity axiom?

   A. No write up in the Biba model

   B. No read down in the Biba model

   C. No write down in the Bell-LaPadula model

   D. No read up in the Bell-LaPadula model

23. Which best describes the simple security rule?

   A. No write up in the Biba model

   B. No read down in the Biba model

   C. No write down in the Bell-LaPadula model

   D. No read up in the Bell-LaPadula model

24. Which of the following was the first mathematical model of a multilevel security policy used to define the concepts of a security state and mode of access, and to outline rules of access?

   A. Biba

   B. Bell-LaPadula

   C. Clark-Wilson

   D. State machine

25. Which of the following is a true statement pertaining to memory addressing?

    A. The CPU uses absolute addresses. Applications use logical addresses. Relative addresses are based on a known address and an offset value.

    B. The CPU uses logical addresses. Applications use absolute addresses. Relative addresses are based on a known address and an offset value.

    C. The CPU uses absolute addresses. Applications use relative addresses. Logical addresses are based on a known address and an offset value.

    D. The CPU uses absolute addresses. Applications use logical addresses. Absolute addresses are based on a known address and an offset value.

Answers

1. **D.** A buffer overflow takes place when too much data are accepted as input. Programmers should implement the correct security controls to ensure this does not take place. This means they need to perform bounds checking and parameter checking to ensure that only the allowed amount of data is actually accepted and processed by the system.

2. **D.** The operating system has a long list of responsibilities, but implementing database views is not one of them. This is the responsibility of the database management software.

3. **A.** If an object has confidential data and these data are not properly erased before another subject can access them, this leftover or residual data can be accessible. This can compromise the data and system's security by disclosing this confidential information. This is true of media (hard drives) and memory segments.

4. **C.** Certification is a technical review of a product, and accreditation is management's formal approval of the findings of the certification process. This question asked you which step was the final step in authorizing a system before it is used in an environment, and that is what accreditation is all about.

5. **B.** Maintenance hooks get around the system's or application's security and access control checks by allowing whomever knows the key sequence to access the application and most likely its code. Maintenance hooks should be removed from any code before it gets into production.

6. **C.** The state machine model dictates that a system should start up securely, carry out secure state transitions, and even fail securely. This means that if the system encounters something it deems unsafe, it should change to a more secure state for self-preservation and protection.

7. **A.** Firmware is a type of software that is held in a ROM or EROM chip. It is usually used to allow the computer to communicate with some type of peripheral device. The system's BIOS instructions are also held in firmware on the motherboard. In most situations, firmware cannot be modified unless someone has physical access to the system. This is different from other types of software that may be modified remotely or through logical means.

8. **C.** These assurance ratings are from the Orange Book. B levels on up require security labels be used, but the question asks which is the first level to require this. B1 comes before B2 and B3, so it is the correct answer.

9. **B.** A security kernel is the software component that enforces access control for the operating system. A reference monitor is the abstract machine that holds all of the rules of access for the system. The security kernel is the active entity that enforces the reference monitor's rules. They control the access attempts of any and all subjects; a user is just one example of a subject.

10. **C.** In ITSEC, the *I* does not stand for international, it stands for information. This set of criteria was developed to be used by European countries to evaluate and rate their products.

11. **A.** The security kernel makes up the main component of the TCB, which is composed of software, hardware, and firmware. The security kernel performs a lot of different activities to protect the system. Enforcing the reference monitor's access rules is just one of those activities.

12. **C.** The CPU has base and limit registers that contain the starting and ending memory addresses a process is allowed to work within. This ensures the process is isolated from other processes in that it cannot interact with another process's memory segment.

13. **B.** The guard accepts requests from the less trusted entity, reviews the request to make sure it is allowed, and then submits the request on behalf of the less trusted system. The goal is to ensure that information does not flow from a high security level to a low security level in an unauthorized manner.

14. **D.** The TCB contains and controls all protection mechanisms within the system, whether they are software, hardware, or firmware.

15. **C.** The security perimeter is a boundary between items that are within the TCB and items that are outside the TCB. It is just a mark of delineation between these two groups of items.

16. **A.** The Bell-LaPadula model was developed for the U.S. government with the main goal of keeping sensitive data unreachable to those who were not authorized to access and view the same. This model was the first mathematical model of a multilevel security policy used to define the concepts of a security state and mode of access and to outline rules of access. The Biba and Clark-Wilson models do not deal with confidentiality, but with integrity instead.

17. **A.** The security kernel is a portion of the operating system's kernel and enforces the rules outlined in the reference monitor. It is the enforcer of the rules and is invoked each time a subject makes a request to access an object.

18. **A.** It is difficult to add useful and effective security at the end of developing a product or to add security as a front end to an existing product. Adding security at the end of a project is usually more expensive because it will break items, and the team will need to go back to the drawing board and redesign and recode portions of the product.

19. **A.** Processes are assigned their own variables, system resources, and memory segments, which make up their domain. This is done so they do not corrupt each other's data or processing activities.

20. **B.** A covert channel is being used when something is using a resource for communication purposes, and that is not the reason this resource was created. A process can write to some type of shared media or storage place that another process will be able to access. The first process writes to this media and the second process reads it. This action goes against the security policy of the system.

21. **C.** The Common Criteria uses a different assurance rating system than the previously used criteria. It has packages of specifications that must be met for a product to obtain the corresponding rating. These ratings and packages are called Evaluation Assurance Levels (EALs). Once a product achieves any type of rating, customers can view this information on an Evaluated Products List (EPL).

22. **A.** The *-integrity axiom (or star integrity axiom) indicates that a subject of a lower integrity level cannot write to an object of a higher integrity level. This rule is put into place to protect the integrity of the data that resides at the higher level.

23. **D.** The simple security rule is implemented to ensure that any subject at a lower security level cannot view data that resides at a higher level. The reason this type of rule is put into place is to protect the confidentiality of the data that resides at the higher level. This rule is used in the Bell-LaPadula model. Remember that if you see "simple" in a rule, it pertains to reading, while * or "star" pertains to writing.

24. **B.** This is a formal definition of the Bell-LaPadula model, which was created and implemented to protect government and military confidential information.

25. **A.** The physical memory addresses that the CPU uses are called absolute addresses. The indexed memory addresses that software uses are referred to as logical address

6

Physical and Environmental Security

This chapter presents the following:

- Administrative, technical, and physical controls
- Facility location, construction, and management
- Physical security risks, threats, and countermeasures
- Electric power issues and countermeasures
- Fire prevention, detection, and suppression
- Intrusion detection systems

Security is very important to organizations and their infrastructures, and physical security is no exception. Hacking is not the only way information and their related systems can be compromised. Physical security encompasses a different set of threats, vulnerabilities, and risks than the other types of security we've addressed so far. Physical security mechanisms include site design and layout, environmental components, emergency response readiness, training, access control, intrusion detection, and power and fire protection. Physical security mechanisms protect people, data, equipment, systems, facilities, and a long list of company assets.

Introduction to Physical Security

The physical security of computers and their resources in the 1960s and 1970s was not as challenging as it is today because computers were mostly mainframes that were locked away in server rooms, and only a handful of people knew what to do with them anyway. Today, a computer sits on almost every desk in every company, and access to devices and resources is spread throughout the environment. Companies have several wiring closets and server rooms, and remote and mobile users take computers and resources out of the facility. Properly protecting these computer systems, networks, facilities, and employees has become an overwhelming task to many companies.

Theft, fraud, sabotage, vandalism, and accidents are raising costs for many companies because environments are becoming more complex and dynamic. Security and complexity are at the opposite ends of the spectrum. As environments and technology become more complex, more vulnerabilities are introduced that allow for compromises to take place. Most companies have had memory or processors stolen from workstations, while some have had computers and laptops taken. Even worse, many companies have been victims of more dangerous crimes, such as robbery at gunpoint, a shooting rampage by a disgruntled employee, anthrax, bombs, and terrorist activities. Many companies may have implemented security guards, closed-circuit TV (CCTV) surveillance, intrusion detection systems (IDSs), and requirements for employees to maintain a higher level of awareness of security risks. These are only some of the items that fall within the physical security boundaries. If any of these does not provide the necessary protection level, it could be the weak link that causes potentially dangerous security breaches.

Most people in the information security field do not think as much about *physical* security as they do about *computer* security and the associated hackers, ports, viruses, and technology-oriented security countermeasures. But information security without proper physical security could be a waste of time.

Even people within the physical security market do not always have a holistic view of physical security. There are so many components and variables to understand, people have to specialize in specific fields, such as secure facility construction, risk assessment and analysis, secure data center implementation, fire protection, IDS and CCTV implementation, personnel emergency response and training, legal and regulatory aspects of physical security, and so on. Each has its own focus and skill set, but for an organization to have a solid physical security program, all of these areas must be understood and addressed.

Just as most software is built with functionality as the number one goal, with security somewhere farther down the priority list, many facilities and physical environments are built with functionality and aesthetics in mind, with not as much concern for providing levels of protection. Many thefts and deaths could be prevented if all organizations were to implement physical security in an organized, mature, and holistic manner. Most people are not aware of many of the crimes that happen every day. Many people also are not aware of all the civil lawsuits that stem from organizations not practicing due diligence and due care pertaining to physical security. The following is a short list of some examples of things companies are sued for pertaining to improper physical security implementation and maintenance:

- An apartment complex does not respond to a report of a broken lock on a sliding glass door, and subsequently a woman who lives in that apartment is raped by an intruder.
- Bushes are growing too close to an ATM, allowing criminals to hide behind them and attack individuals as they withdraw money from their accounts.
- A portion of an underground garage is unlit, which allows an attacker to sit and wait for an employee who works late.
- A gas station's outside restroom has a broken lock, which allows an attacker to enter after a female customer and kill her.

- A convenience store hangs too many advertising signs and posters on the exterior windows, prompting thieves to choose this store because the signs hide any crimes taking place inside the store from people driving or walking by.

Many examples like this take place every day. These crimes might make it to our local news outlets, but there are too many incidents to be reported in national newspapers or on network news programs. It is important for security professionals to evaluate security from the standpoint of a potential criminal, and to detect and remedy any points of vulnerability that could be exploited by the same. Just as many people are unaware of many of these "smaller" crimes that happen every day, they are also unaware of all the civil suits brought about because organizations are not practicing due diligence and due care regarding physical security. While many different security-related crimes occur every day, these kinds of crimes may be overshadowed by larger news events or be too numerous to report. A security professional needs to regard security as a holistic process, and as such it must be viewed from all angles and approaches. Danger can come from anywhere and take any different number of shapes, formats, and levels of severity.

Physical security has a different set of vulnerabilities, threats, and countermeasures from that of computer and information security. The set for physical security has more to do with physical destruction, intruders, environmental issues, theft, and vandalism. When security professionals look at *information* security, they think about how someone can enter an environment in an unauthorized manner through a port, modem, or wireless access point. When security professionals look at *physical* security, they are concerned with how people can physically enter an environment and cause an array of damages.

The threats that an organization faces fall into these broad categories:

- **Natural environmental threats** Floods, earthquakes, storms and tornadoes, fires, extreme temperature conditions, and so forth

- **Supply system threats** Power distribution outages, communications interruptions, and interruption of other natural energy resources such as water, steam, gas, and so on

- **Manmade threats** Unauthorized access (both internal and external), explosions, damage by angry employees, employee errors and accidents, vandalism, fraud, theft, and others

- **Politically motivated threats** Strikes, riots, civil disobedience, terrorist attacks, bombings, and so forth

In all situations, the primary consideration, above all else, is that nothing should impede *life safety* goals. When we discuss life safety, protecting human life is the first priority. Good planning helps balance life safety concerns and other security measures. For example, barring a door to prevent unauthorized physical intrusion might prevent individuals from being able to escape in the event of a fire.

NOTE Life safety goals should always take precedence over all other types of goals.

A physical security program should comprise safety and security mechanisms. Safety deals with the protection of life and assets against fire, natural disasters, and devastating accidents. Security addresses vandalism, theft, and attacks by individuals. Many times an overlap occurs between the two, but both types of threat categories must be understood and properly planned for. This chapter addresses both safety and security mechanisms that every security professional should be aware of.

Physical security must be implemented based on a *layered defense model*, which means that physical controls should work together in a tiered architecture. The concept is that if one layer fails, other layers will protect the valuable asset. Layers would be implemented moving from the perimeter toward the asset. For example, you would have a fence, then your facility walls, then an access control card device, then a guard, then an IDS, and then locked computer cases and safes. This series of layers will protect the company's most sensitive assets, which would be placed in the innermost control zone of the environment. So if the bad guy were able to climb over your fence and outsmart the security guard, he would still have to circumvent several layers of controls before getting to your precious resources and systems.

Security needs to protect all the assets of the organization and enhance productivity by providing a secure and predictable environment. Good security enables employees to focus on their tasks at hand and encourages attackers to move on to an easier target. This is the hope, anyway. Keeping in mind the AIC security triad that has been presented in previous chapters, we look at physical security that can affect the *availability* of company resources, the *integrity* of the assets and environment, and the *confidentiality* of the data and business processes.

The Planning Process

Okay, so what are we doing and why?
Response: We have no idea.

A designer, or team of designers, needs to be identified to create or improve upon an organization's current physical security program. The team must work with management to define the objectives of the program, design the program, and develop performance-based metrics and evaluation processes to ensure the objectives are continually being met.

The objectives of the physical security program depend upon the level of protection required for the various assets and the company as a whole. And this required level of protection, in turn, depends upon the organization's acceptable risk level. This acceptable risk level should be derived from the laws and regulations with which the organization must comply and from the threat profile of the organization overall. This requires identifying who and what could damage business assets, identifying the types of attacks and crimes that could take place, and understanding the business impact of these threats. The type of physical countermeasures required and their adequacy or inadequacy needs to be measured against the organization's threat profile. A financial institution has a much different threat profile, and thus a much different acceptable risk level, when compared to a grocery store. The threat profile of a hospital is different from the threat profile of a military base or a government agency. The team must understand the types of adversaries it must consider, the capabilities of these adversaries, and the resources and tactics these individuals would use. (Review Chapter 3 for a discussion of acceptable risk level concepts.)

Physical security is a combination of people, processes, procedures, and equipment to protect resources. The design of a solid physical security program should be methodical and should weigh the objectives of the program and the available resources. Although every organization is different, the approach to constructing and maintaining a physical security program is the same. The organization must first define the vulnerabilities, threats, threat agents, and targets.

 NOTE Remember that a vulnerability is a weakness and a threat is the potential that someone will identify this weakness and use it against you. The threat agent is the person or mechanism that actually exploits this identified vulnerability.

Threats can be grouped into categories such as internal and external threats. Inside threats may include misbehaving devices, fire hazards, or employees who aim to damage the company in some way. Employees have intimate knowledge of the company's facilities and assets, which is usually required to perform tasks and responsibilities— but this makes it easier for the insider to carry out damaging activity without being noticed. Unfortunately, a large threat to companies can be their own security guards, which is usually not realized until it is too late. These people have keys and access codes to all portions of a facility and usually work during employee off-hours. This gives the guards ample windows of opportunity to carry out their crimes. It is critical for a company to carry out a background investigation, or to pay a company to perform this service, before hiring a security guard. If you hire a wolf to guard the chicken coop, things can get ugly.

External threats come in many different forms as well. Government buildings are usually chosen targets for some types of political revenge. If a company performs abortions or conducts animal research, then activists are usually a large and constant threat. And, of course, banks and armored cars are tempting targets for organized crime members.

A threat that is even trickier to protect against is *collusion*, in which two or more people work together to carry out fraudulent activity. Many criminal cases have uncovered insiders working with outsiders to defraud or damage a company. The types of controls for this type of activity are procedural protection mechanisms, which were described at length in Chapter 3. This may include separation of duties, preemployment background checks, rotations of duties, and supervision.

As with any type of security, most attention and awareness surrounds the exciting and headline-grabbing tidbits about large crimes being carried out and criminals being captured. In information security, most people are aware of viruses and hackers but not of the components that make up a corporate security program. The same is true for physical security. Many people talk about current robberies, murders, and other criminal activity at the water cooler, but do not pay attention to the necessary framework that should be erected and maintained to reduce these types of activities. An organization's physical security program should address the following goals:

- **Crime and disruption prevention through deterrence**   Fences, security guards, warning signs, and so forth
- **Reduction of damage through the use of delaying mechanisms**   Layers of defenses that slow down the adversary, such as locks, security personnel, and barriers
- **Crime or disruption detection**   Smoke detectors, motion detectors, CCTV, and so forth
- **Incident assessment**   Response of security guards to detected incidents and determination of damage level
- **Response procedures**   Fire suppression mechanisms, emergency response processes, law enforcement notification, and consultation with outside security professionals

So, an organization should try to prevent crimes and disruptions from taking place, but must also plan to deal with them when they do happen. A criminal should be delayed in her activities by having to penetrate several layers of controls before gaining access to a resource. All types of crimes and disruptions should be able to be detected through components that make up the physical security program. Once an intrusion is discovered, a security guard should be called upon to assess the situation. The security guard must then know how to properly respond to a large range of potentially dangerous activities. The emergency response activities could be carried out by the organization's internal security team or by outside experts.

This all sounds straightforward enough, until the team responsible for developing the physical security program looks at all the possible threats, the finite budget that the team has to work with, and the complexity of choosing the right combination of countermeasures and ensuring that they all work together in a manner that ensures no gaps of protection. All of these components must be understood in depth before the design of a physical security program can begin.

As with all security programs, it is possible to determine how beneficial and effective your physical security program is only if it is monitored through a performance-based approach. This means you should devise measurements and metrics to gauge the effectiveness of your countermeasures. This enables management to make informed business decisions when investing in the protection of the organization's physical security. The goal is to increase the performance of the physical security program and decrease the risk to the company in a cost-effective manner. You should establish a baseline of performance and thereafter continually evaluate performance to make sure that the company's protection objectives are being met. The following list provides some examples of possible performance metrics:

- Number of successful crimes
- Number of successful disruptions

- Number of unsuccessful crimes or disruptions
- Time between detection, assessment, and recovery steps
- Business impact of disruptions
- Number of false-positive detection alerts
- Time it took for a criminal to defeat a control
- Time it took to restore the operational environment

Capturing and monitoring these types of metrics enables the organization to identify deficiencies, evaluate improvement measures, and perform cost/benefit analyses.

The physical security team needs to carry out a risk analysis, which will identify the organization's vulnerabilities, threats, and business impacts. The team should present these findings to management and work with them to define an acceptable risk level for the physical security program. From there, the team must develop baselines (minimum levels of security) and metrics in order to evaluate and determine if the baselines are being met by the implemented countermeasures. Once the team identifies and implements the countermeasures, the performance of these countermeasures should be continually evaluated and expressed in the previously created metrics. These performance values are compared to the set baselines. If the baselines are continually maintained, then the security program is successful, because the company's acceptable risk level is not being exceeded. This is illustrated in Figure 6-1.

So, before an effective physical security program can be rolled out, the following steps must be taken:

- Identify a team of internal employees and/or external consultants who will build the physical security program through the following steps.
- Carry out a risk analysis to identify the vulnerabilities and threats and to calculate the business impact of each threat.
- Work with management to define an acceptable risk level for the physical security program.
- Derive the required performance baselines from the acceptable risk level.
- Create countermeasure performance metrics.
- Develop criteria from the results of the analysis, outlining the level of protection and performance required for the following categories of the security program:
  - Deterrence
  - Delaying
  - Detection
  - Assessment
  - Response
- Identify and implement countermeasures for each program category.
- Continuously evaluate countermeasures against the set baselines to ensure the acceptable risk level is not exceeded.

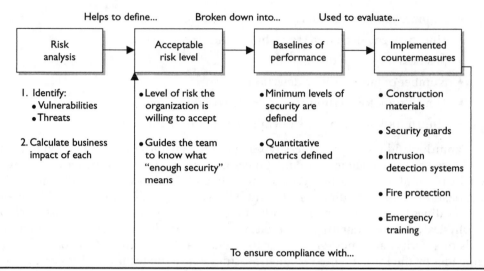

Figure 6-1 Relationships of risk, baselines, and countermeasures

Once these steps have taken place (or continue to take place, as in the case of the last step), then the team is ready to move forward in its actual design phase. The design will incorporate the controls required for each category of the program: deterrence, delaying, detection, assessment, and response. We will dig deeper into these categories and their corresponding controls later in the chapter in the "Designing a Physical Security Program" section.

One of the most commonly used approaches in physical security program development is described in the following section.

Crime Prevention Through Environmental Design

This place is so nice and pretty and welcoming. No one would want to carry out crimes here.

Crime Prevention Through Environmental Design (CPTED) is a discipline that outlines how the proper design of a physical environment can reduce crime by directly affecting human behavior. It provides guidance in loss and crime prevention through proper facility construction and environmental components and procedures.

CPTED concepts were developed in the 1960s. They have been built upon and have matured as our environments and crime types have evolved. CPTED has been used not just to develop corporate physical security programs, but also for large-scale activities such as development of neighborhoods, towns, and cities. It addresses landscaping, entrances, facility and neighborhood layouts, lighting, road placement, and traffic circulation patterns. It looks at microenvironments, such as offices and restrooms, and macroenvironments, like campuses and cities. The crux of CPTED is that the physical environment can be manipulated to create behavioral effects that will reduce crime and the fear of crime. It looks at the components that make up the relationship between humans and their environment. This encompasses the physical, social, and psychological needs of the users of different types of environments and predictable behaviors of these users and offenders.

CPTED provides guidelines on items some of us might not consider. For example, hedges and planters around a facility should not be higher than 2.5 feet tall, so they cannot be used to gain access to a window. A data center should be located at the center of a facility, so the facility's walls will absorb any damages from external forces, instead of the data center. Street furnishings (benches and tables) encourage people to sit and watch what is going on around them, which discourages criminal activity. A corporation's landscape should not include wooded areas or other places where intruders can hide. Ensure that CCTV cameras are mounted in full view, so criminals know their activities will be captured, and other people know the environment is well monitored and thus safer.

CPTED and target hardening are two different approaches. *Target hardening* focuses on denying access through physical and artificial barriers (alarms, locks, fences, and so on). Traditional target hardening can lead to restrictions on the use, enjoyment, and aesthetics of an environment. Sure, we can implement hierarchies of fences, locks, and intimidating signs and barriers—but how pretty would that be? If your environment is a prison, this look might be just what you need. But if your environment is an office building, you're not looking for Fort Knox décor. Nevertheless, you still must provide the necessary levels of protection, but your protection mechanisms should be more subtle and unobtrusive.

Let's say your organization's team needs to protect a side door at your facility. The traditional target-hardening approach would be to put locks, alarms, and cameras on the door, install an access control mechanism, such as a proximity reader, and instruct security guards to monitor this door. The CPTED approach would be to ensure there is no sidewalk leading to this door from the front of the building if you don't want customers using it. The CPTED approach would also ensure no tall trees or bushes block the ability to view someone using this door. Barriers such as trees and bushes may make intruders feel more comfortable in attempting to break in through a secluded door.

Similarities in Approaches

The risk analysis steps are very similar to the steps outlined in Chapter 3 for the development of an organizational security program and the steps outlined in Chapter 9 for a business impact analysis, because each of these processes (development of an information security program, a physical security program, or a business continuity plan) accomplishes goals that are similar to the goals of the other two processes, but with different focuses. Each process requires a team to carry out a risk analysis to determine the company's threats and risks. An information security program looks at the internal and external threats to resources and data through business processes and technological means. Business continuity looks at how natural disasters and disruptions could damage the organization, while physical security looks at internal and external physical threats to the company resources.

Each requires a solid risk analysis process. Review Chapter 3 to understand the core components of every risk analysis.

The best approach is usually to build an environment from a CPTED approach and then apply the target-hardening components on top of the design where needed.

If a parking garage were developed using the CPTED approach, the stair towers and elevators within the garage might have glass windows instead of metal walls, so people feel safer, and potential criminals will not carry out crimes in this more visible environment. Pedestrian walkways would be created such that people could look out across the rows of cars and see any suspicious activities. The different rows for cars to park in would be separated by low walls and structural pillars, instead of solid walls, to allow pedestrians to view activities within the garage.

CPTED provides three main strategies to bring together the physical environment and social behavior to increase overall protection: natural access control, natural surveillance, and natural territorial reinforcement.

Natural Access Control

Natural access control is the guidance of people entering and leaving a space by the placement of doors, fences, lighting, and even landscaping. For example, an office building may have external bollards with lights in them, as shown in Figure 6-2. These bollards actually carry out different safety and security services. The bollards themselves protect the facility from physical destruction by preventing people from driving their cars into the building. The light emitted helps ensure that criminals do not have a dark place to hide. And the lights and bollard placement guide people along the sidewalk to the entrance, instead of using signs or railings. As shown in Figure 6-2, the landscape, sidewalks, lighted bollards, and clear sight lines are used as natural access controls. They work together to give individuals a feeling of being in a safe environment and help dissuade criminals by working as deterrents.

Figure 6-2 Sidewalks, lights, and landscaping can be used for protection.

NOTE Bollards are short posts commonly used to prevent vehicular access and to protect a building or people walking on a sidewalk from vehicles. They can also be used to direct foot traffic.

Clear lines of sight and transparency can be used to discourage potential offenders, because of the absence of places to hide or carry out criminal activities.

The CPTED model shows how *security zones* can be created. An environment's space should be divided into zones with different security levels, depending upon who needs to be in that zone and the associated risk. The zones can be labeled as controlled, restricted, public, or sensitive. This is conceptually similar to information classification, as described in Chapter 3. In a data classification program, different classifications are created, along with data handling procedures and the level of protection that each classification requires. The same is true of physical zones. Each zone should have a specific protection level required of it, which will help dictate the types of controls that should be put into place.

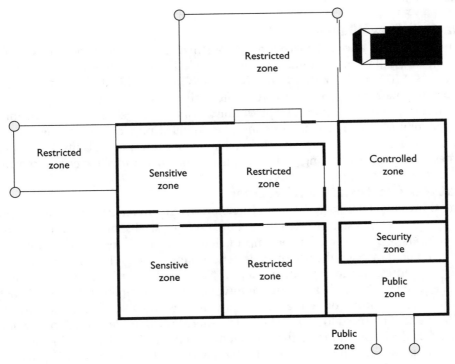

Access control should be in place to control and restrict individuals from going from one security zone to the next. Access control should also be in place for all facility entrances and exits. The security program development team needs to consider other ways in which intruders can gain access to buildings, such as by climbing adjacent trees to access skylights, upper-story windows, and balconies. The following controls are commonly used for access controls within different organizations:

- Limit the number of entry points.
- Force all guests to go to a front desk and sign in before entering the environment.
- Reduce the number of entry points even further after hours or during the weekend, when not as many employees are around.
- Have a security guard validate a picture ID before allowing entrance.
- Require guests to sign in and be escorted.
- Encourage employees to question strangers.

Access barriers can be naturally created (cliffs, rivers, hills), existing manmade elements (railroad tracks, highways), or artificial forms designed specifically to impede movement (fences, closing streets).

Natural Surveillance

Surveillance can also take place through organized means (security guards), mechanical means (CCTV), and natural strategies (straight lines of sight, low landscaping, raised entrances). The goal of *natural surveillance* is to make criminals feel uncomfortable by providing many ways observers could potentially see them and to make all other people feel safe and comfortable, by providing an open and well-designed environment.

Natural surveillance is the use and placement of physical environmental features, personnel walkways, and activity areas in ways that maximize visibility. Figure 6-3 illustrates a stairway in a parking garage designed to be open and allow easy observation.

Natural Territorial Reinforcement

The third CPTED strategy is natural *territorial reinforcement*, which creates physical designs that emphasize or extend the company's physical sphere of influence so legitimate users feel a sense of ownership of that space. Territorial reinforcement can be implemented through the use of walls, fences, landscaping, light fixtures, flags, clearly marked addresses, and decorative sidewalks. The goal of territorial reinforcement is to create a sense of a dedicated community. Companies implement these elements so employees feel proud of their environment and have a sense of belonging, which they will defend if required to do so. These elements are also implemented to give potential offenders the impression that they do not belong there, that their activities are at risk of being observed, and that their illegal activities will not be tolerated or ignored.

Most corporate environments use a mix of the CPTED and target-hardening approaches. CPTED deals mainly with the construction of the facility, its internal and external designs, and exterior components such as landscaping and lighting. If the environment is built based on CPTED, then the target hardening is like icing on the cake. The target-hardening approach applies more granular protection mechanisms, such as locks and motion detectors. The rest of the chapter looks at physical controls that can be used in both models.

Figure 6-3 Open areas reduce the likelihood of criminal activity.

Designing a Physical Security Program

Our security guards should wear pink uniforms and throw water balloons at intruders.
Response: Very scary environment indeed!

If a team is organized to assess the protection level of an existing facility, it needs to investigate the following:

- HVAC systems
- Construction materials of walls and ceilings
- Power distribution systems
- Communication paths and types (copper, telephone, fiber)
- Surrounding hazardous materials

- Exterior components:
  - Topography
  - Proximity to airports, highways, railroads
  - Potential electromagnetic interference from surrounding devices
  - Climate
  - Soil
  - Existing fences, detection sensors, cameras, barriers
  - Working hours of employees
  - Operational activities that depend upon physical resources
  - Vehicle activity
  - Neighbors

To properly obtain this information, the team should do surveys and interview various employees. All of this collected data will help the team to evaluate the current controls, identify weaknesses, and ensure operational productivity is not negatively affected by implementing new controls.

Although there are usually written policies and procedures on what *should* be taking place pertaining to physical security, policies and reality do not always match up. It is important for the team to observe how the facility is used, note daily activities that could introduce vulnerabilities, and determine how the facility is protected. This information should be documented and compared to the information within the written policy and procedures. In most cases, existing gaps must be addressed and fixed. Just writing out a policy helps no one if it is not actually followed.

Every organization must comply with various regulations, whether they be safety and health regulations; fire codes; state and local building codes; Departments of Defense, Energy, or Labor requirements; or some other agency's regulations. The organization may also have to comply with requirements of the Occupational Safety and Health Administration (OSHA) and the Environmental Protection Agency (EPA), if it is operating in the United States, or with the requirements of equivalent organizations within another country. The physical security program development team must understand all the regulations the organization must comply with and how to reach compliance through physical security and safety procedures.

Activity Support

CPTED also encourages activity support, which is planned activities for the areas to be protected. These activities are designed to get people to work together to increase the overall awareness of acceptable and unacceptable activities in the area. The activities could be neighborhood watch groups, company barbeques, block parties, or civic meetings. This strategy is sometimes the reason for particular placement of basketball courts, soccer fields, or baseball fields in open parks. The increased activity will hopefully keep the bad guys from milling around doing things the community does not welcome.

Legal issues must be understood and properly addressed, also. These issues may include access availability for the disabled, liability issues, the failure to protect assets and people, excessive force used by security guards, and so on. This long laundry list of items can get a company into legal trouble if it is not doing what it is supposed to. Occasionally, the legal trouble may take the form of a criminal case—for example, if doors default to being locked when power is lost and, as a result, several employees are trapped and killed during a fire, criminal negligence may be alleged. Legal trouble can also come in the form of civil cases—for instance, if a company does not remove the ice on its sidewalks and a pedestrian falls and breaks his ankle, the pedestrian may sue the company. The company may be found negligent and held liable for damages.

Every organization should have a *facility safety officer*, whose main job is to understand all the components that make up the facility and what the company needs to do to protect its assets and stay within compliance. This person should oversee facility management duties day in and day out, but should also be heavily involved with the team that has been organized to evaluate the organization's physical security program.

A physical security program is a collection of controls that are implemented and maintained to provide the protection levels necessary to be in compliance with the physical security policy. The policy should embody all the regulations and laws that must be adhered to and should set the risk level the company is willing to accept.

By this point, the team has carried out a risk analysis, which consisted of identifying the company's vulnerabilities, threats, and business impact pertaining to the identified threats. The program design phase should begin with a structured outline, which will evolve into a framework. This framework will then be fleshed out with the necessary controls and countermeasures. The outline should contain the program categories and the necessary countermeasures. The following is a simplistic example:

I. Deterrence of criminal activity
   A. Fences
   B. Warning signs
   C. Security guards
   D. Dogs
II. Delay of intruders to help ensure they can be caught
   A. Locks
   B. Defense-in-depth measures
   C. Access controls
III. Detection of intruders
   A. External intruder sensors
   B. Internal intruder sensors
IV. Assessment of situations
   A. Security guard procedures
   B. Communication structure (calling tree)

     V. Response to intrusions and disruptions

        A. Response force

        B. Emergency response procedures

        C. Police, fire, medical personnel

The team can then start addressing each phase of the security program, usually starting with the facility.

Facility

I can't see the building.
Response: That's the whole idea.

When a company decides to erect a building, it should consider several factors before pouring the first batch of concrete. Of course, land prices, customer population, and marketing strategies are reviewed, but as security professionals, we are more interested in the confidence and protection that a specific location can provide. Some organizations that deal with top-secret or confidential information make their facilities unnoticeable so they do not attract the attention of would-be attackers. The building may be hard to see from the surrounding roads, the company signs and logos may be small and not easily noticed, and the markings on the building may not give away any information that pertains to what is going on inside that building. It is a type of urban camouflage that makes it harder for the enemy to seek out that company as a target.

A company should evaluate how close the facility would be to a police station, fire station, and medical facilities. Many times, the proximity of these entities raises the real estate value of properties, but for good reason. If a chemical company that manufactures highly explosive materials needs to build a new facility, it may make good business sense to put it near a fire station. (Although the fire station might not be so happy.) If another company that builds and sells expensive electronic devices is expanding and needs to move operations into another facility, police reaction time may be looked at when choosing one facility location over another. Each of these issues—police station, fire station, and medical facility proximity—can also reduce insurance rates and must be looked at carefully. Remember that the ultimate goal of physical security is to ensure the safety of personnel. Always keep that in mind when implementing any sort of physical security control. Protect your fellow humans, be your brother's keeper, and *then* run.

Some buildings are placed in areas surrounded by hills or mountains to help prevent eavesdropping of electrical signals emitted by the facility's equipment. In some cases, the organization itself will build hills or use other landscaping techniques to guard against eavesdropping. Other facilities are built underground or right into the side of a mountain for concealment and disguise in the natural environment, and for protection from radar tools, spying activities, and aerial bomb attacks.

Construction

We need a little more than glue, tape, and a stapler.

Physical construction materials and structure composition need to be evaluated for their appropriateness to the site environment, their protective characteristics, their utility, and their costs and benefits. Different building materials provide different levels of

Issues with Selecting a Facility Site

When selecting a location for a facility, some of the following items are critical to the decision-making process:

- **Visibility**
  - Surrounding terrain
  - Building markings and signs
  - Types of neighbors
  - Population of the area
- **Surrounding area and external entities**
  - Crime rate, riots, terrorism attacks
  - Proximity to police, medical, and fire stations
  - Possible hazards from surrounding area
- **Accessibility**
  - Road access
  - Traffic
  - Proximity to airports, train stations, and highways
- **Natural disaster**
  - Likelihood of floods, tornadoes, earthquakes, or hurricanes
  - Hazardous terrain (mudslides, falling rock from mountains, or excessive snow or rain)

fire protection and have different rates of combustibility, which correlate with their fire ratings. When making structural decisions, the decision of what type of construction material to use (wood, concrete, or steel) needs to be considered in light of what the building is going to be used for. If an area will be used to store documents and old equipment, it has far different needs and legal requirements than if it is going to be used for employees to work in every day.

The *load* (how much weight can be held) of a building's walls, floors, and ceilings needs to be estimated and projected to ensure the building will not collapse in different situations. In most cases, this may be dictated by local building codes. The walls, ceilings, and floors must contain the necessary materials to meet the required fire rating and to protect against water damage. The windows (interior and exterior) may need to provide ultraviolet (UV) protection, may need to be shatterproof, or may need to be translucent or opaque, depending on the placement of the window and the contents of the building. The doors (exterior and interior) may need to have directional openings, have the same fire rating as the surrounding walls, prohibit forcible entries, display emergency egress markings, and—depending on placement—have monitoring and attached alarms. In most buildings, raised floors are used to hide and protect wires and pipes, but in turn the floors' outlets need to be electrically grounded because they are raised.

Building codes may regulate all of these issues, but there are still many options within each category that the physical security program development team should review for extra security protection. The right options should accomplish the company's security and functionality needs and still be cost-effective.

When designing and building a facility, the following major items need to be addressed from a physical security point of view:

- **Walls**
  - Combustibility of material (wood, steel, concrete)
  - Fire rating
  - Reinforcements for secured areas
- **Doors**
  - Combustibility of material (wood, pressed board, aluminum)
  - Fire rating
  - Resistance to forcible entry
  - Emergency marking
  - Placement
  - Locked or controlled entrances
  - Alarms
  - Secure hinges
  - Directional opening
  - Electric door locks that revert to an unlocked state for safe evacuation in power outages
  - Type of glass—shatterproof or bulletproof glass requirements
- **Ceilings**
  - Combustibility of material (wood, steel, concrete)
  - Fire rating
  - Weight-bearing rating
  - Drop-ceiling considerations
- **Windows**
  - Translucent or opaque requirements
  - Shatterproof
  - Alarms
  - Placement
  - Accessibility to intruders

- Flooring
  - Weight-bearing rating
  - Combustibility of material (wood, steel, concrete)
  - Fire rating
  - Raised flooring (electrical grounding)
  - Nonconducting surface and material
- **Heating, ventilation, and air conditioning**
  - Positive air pressure
  - Protected intake vents
  - Dedicated power lines
  - Emergency shutoff valves and switches
  - Placement
- **Electric power supplies**
  - Backup and alternate power supplies
  - Clean and steady power source
  - Dedicated feeders to required areas
  - Placement and access to distribution panels and circuit breakers
- **Water and gas lines**
  - Shutoff valves—labeled and brightly painted for visibility
  - Positive flow (material flows out of building, not in)
  - Placement—properly located and labeled
- **Fire detection and suppression**
  - Placement of sensors and detectors
  - Placement of suppression systems
  - Type of detectors and suppression agents

Ground

If you are holding a power cord plug that has two skinny metal pieces and one fatter, rounder metal piece, which all go into the outlet—what is that fatter, rounder piece for? It is a ground connector, which is supposed to act as the conduit for any excess current to ensure that people and devices are not negatively affected by a spike in electrical current. So, in the wiring of a building, where do you think this ground should be connected? Yep, to the ground. Old mother earth. But many buildings are not wired properly, and the ground connector is connected to nothing. This can be very dangerous, since the extra current has nowhere to escape but into our equipment or ourselves.

The risk analysis results will help the team determine the type of construction material that should be used when constructing a new facility. Several grades of building construction are available. For example, *light frame construction material* provides the least amount of protection against fire and forcible entry attempts. It is composed of untreated lumber that would be combustible during a fire. Light frame construction material is usually used to build homes, primarily because it is cheap, but also because homes typically are not under the same types of fire and intrusion threats that office buildings are.

Heavy timber construction material is commonly used for office buildings. Combustible lumber is still used in this type of construction, but there are requirements on the thickness and composition of the materials to provide more protection from fire. The construction materials must be at least four inches in thickness. More dense woods are used and are fastened with metal bolts and plates. Whereas light frame construction material has a fire survival rate of 30 minutes, the heavy timber construction material has a fire rate of one hour.

A building could be made up of *incombustible material*, such as steel, which provides a higher level of fire protection than the previously mentioned materials, but loses its strength under extreme temperatures, something that may cause the building to collapse. So, although the steel will not burn, it may melt and weaken. If a building consists of *fire-resistant material*, the construction material is fire-retardant and has steel rods encased inside of concrete walls and support beams. This provides the most protection against fire and forced entry attempts.

The team should choose its construction material based on the identified threats of the organization and the fire codes to be complied with. If a company is just going to have some office workers in a building and has no real adversaries interested in destroying the facility, then the light frame or heavy timber construction material would be used. Facilities for government organizations, which are under threat by domestic and foreign terrorists, would be built with fire-resistant materials. A financial institution would also use fire-resistant and reinforcement material within its building. This is especially true for its exterior walls, through which thieves may attempt to drive vehicles to gain access to the vaults.

Calculations of approximate penetration times for different types of explosives and attacks are based on the thickness of the concrete walls and the gauge of rebar used. (*Rebar* refers to the steel rods encased within the concrete.) So even if the concrete were damaged, it would take longer to actually cut or break through the rebar. Using thicker rebar and properly placing it within the concrete provides even more protection.

Reinforced walls, rebar, and the use of double walls can be used as delaying mechanisms. The idea is that it will take the bad guy longer to get through two reinforced walls, which gives the response force sufficient time to arrive at the scene and stop the attacker, we hope.

Entry Points

Understanding the company needs and types of entry points for a specific building is critical. The various types of entry points may include doors, windows, roof access, fire escapes, chimneys, and service delivery access points. Second and third entry points must also be considered, such as internal doors that lead into other portions of the building and to exterior doors, elevators, and stairwells. Windows at the ground level should be fortified, because they could be easily broken. Fire escapes, stairwells to the roof, and chimneys are many times overlooked as potential entry points.

NOTE Ventilation ducts and utility tunnels can also be used by intruders and thus must be properly protected with sensors and access control mechanisms.

The weakest portion of the structure, usually its doors and windows, will likely be attacked first. With regard to doors, the weaknesses usually lie within the frames, hinges, and door material. The bolts, frames, hinges, and material that make up the door should all provide the same level of strength and protection. For example, if a company implements a heavy, nonhollow steel door but uses weak hinges that could be easily extracted, the company is just wasting money. The attacker can just remove the hinges and remove this strong and heavy door.

The door and surrounding walls and ceilings should also provide the same level of strength. If another company has an extremely fortified and secure door, but the surrounding wall materials are made out of regular light frame wood, then it is also wasting money on doors. There is no reason to spend a lot of money on one countermeasure that can be easily circumvented by breaking a weaker countermeasure in proximity.

Doors   Different door types for various functionalities include the following:

- Vault doors
- Personnel doors
- Industrial doors
- Vehicle access doors
- Bullet-resistant doors

Doors can be hollow-core or solid-core. The team needs to understand the various entry types and the potential forced-entry threats, which will help them determine what type of door should be implemented. Hollow-core doors can be easily penetrated by kicking or cutting them; thus, they are usually used internally. The team also has a choice of solid-core doors, which are made up of various materials to provide different fire ratings and protection from forced entry. As stated previously, the fire rating and protection level of the door needs to match the fire rating and protection level of the surrounding walls.

Bulletproof doors are also an option if there is a threat that damage could be done to resources by shooting through the door. These types of doors are constructed in a manner that involves sandwiching bullet-resistant and bulletproof material between wood or steel veneers to still give the door some aesthetic qualities while providing the necessary levels of protection.

Hinges and strike plates should be secure, especially on exterior doors or doors used to protect sensitive areas. The hinges should have pins that cannot be removed, and the door frames must provide the same level of protection as the door itself.

Fire codes dictate the number and placement of doors with panic bars on them. These are the crossbars that release an internal lock to allow a locked door to open. Panic bars can be on regular entry doors and also on emergency exit doors. Those are the ones that usually have the sign that indicates the door is not an exit point and that an alarm will go off if the door is opened. It might seem like fun and a bit tempting to see if the alarm will *really* go off or not—but don't try it. You're just asking for lots of yelling and dirty looks from the facility management group.

Mantraps and turnstiles can be used so unauthorized individuals entering a facility cannot get in or out if it is activated. A *mantrap* is a small room with two doors. The first door is locked; a person is identified and authenticated by a security guard, biometric system, smart card reader, or swipe card reader. Once the person is authenticated and access is authorized, the first door opens and allows the person into the mantrap. The first door locks and the person is trapped. The person must be authenticated again before the second door unlocks and allows him or her into the facility. Some mantraps use biometric systems that weigh the person who enters, to ensure only one person at a time is entering the mantrap area. This is a control to counter piggybacking.

Doorways with automatic locks can be configured to be fail-safe or fail-secure. A *fail-safe* setting means that if a power disruption occurs that affects the automated locking system, the doors default to being unlocked. Fail-safe deals directly with protecting people. If people work in an area and there is a fire or the power is lost, it is not a good idea to lock them in. This would not make you many friends. A *fail-secure* configuration means that the doors default to being locked if there are any problems with the power.

Windows Windows should be properly placed (this is where security and aesthetics can come to blows) and should have frames of the proper strengths, the necessary glazing material, and possibly have a protective covering. The glazing material, which is applied to the windows as they are being made, may be standard, tempered, acrylic, wire, or laminated on glass. Standard glass windows are commonly used in residential homes and are easily broken. Tempered glass is made by heating the glass and then suddenly cooling it. This increases its mechanical strength, which means it can handle more stress and is harder to break. It is usually five to seven times stronger than standard glass.

Acrylic glass can be made out of polycarbonate acrylic, which is stronger than standard glass but produces toxic fumes if burned. Polycarbonate acrylics are stronger than regular acrylics, but both are made out of a type of transparent plastic. Because of their combustibility, their use may be prohibited by fire codes. The strongest window material is glass-clad polycarbonate. It is resistant to a wide range of threats (fire, chemical, breakage), but of course is much more expensive. These types of windows would be used in areas that are under the greatest threat.

Some windows are made out of glass that has *embedded wires*—in other words, it actually has two sheets of glass, with the wiring in between. The wires help reduce the likelihood of the window being broken or shattering.

Laminated glass has two sheets of glass with a plastic film in between. This added plastic makes it much more difficult to break the window. As with other types of glass, laminated glass can come in different depths. The greater the depth (more glass and plastic), the more difficult it is to break.

A lot of window types have a film on them that provides efficiency in heating and cooling. They filter out UV rays and are usually tinted, which can make it harder for the bad guy to peep in and monitor internal activities. Some window types have a different kind of film applied that makes it more difficult to break them, whether by explosive, storm, or intruder.

Internal Compartments

Many components that make up a facility must be looked at from a security point of view. *Internal partitions* are used to create barriers between one area and another. These partitions can be used to segment separate work areas, but should never be used in protected areas that house sensitive systems and devices. Many buildings have dropped ceilings, meaning the interior partitions do not extend to the true ceiling—only to the dropped ceiling. An intruder can lift a ceiling panel and climb over the partition. This example of intrusion is shown in Figure 6-4. In many situations, this would not require forced entry, specialized tools, or much effort. (In some office buildings, this may even be possible from a common public-access hallway.) These types of internal partitions should not be relied upon to provide protection for sensitive areas.

Computer and Equipment Rooms

It used to be necessary to have personnel within the computer rooms for proper maintenance and operations. Today, most servers, routers, switches, mainframes, and other equipment housed in computer rooms can be controlled remotely. This enables computers to live in rooms that have fewer people milling around and spilling coffee. Because the computer rooms no longer have personnel sitting and working in them for long periods, the rooms can be constructed in a manner that is efficient for equipment instead of people.

Window Types

A security professional may be involved with the planning phase of building a facility, and each of these items comes into play when constructing a secure building and environment. The following sums up the types of windows that can be used:

- **Standard**   No extra protection. The cheapest and lowest level of protection.
- **Tempered**   Glass is heated and then cooled suddenly to increase its integrity and strength.
- **Acrylic**   A type of plastic instead of glass. Polycarbonate acrylics are stronger than regular acrylics.
- **Wired**   A mesh of wire is embedded between two sheets of glass. This wire helps prevent the glass from shattering.
- **Laminated**   The plastic layer between two outer glass layers. The plastic layer helps increase its strength against breakage.
- **Solar window film**   Provides extra security by being tinted and offers extra strength due to the film's material.
- **Security film**   Transparent film is applied to the glass to increase its strength.

Smaller systems can be stacked vertically to save space. They should be mounted on racks or placed inside equipment cabinets. The wiring should be close to the equipment to save on cable costs and to reduce tripping hazards.

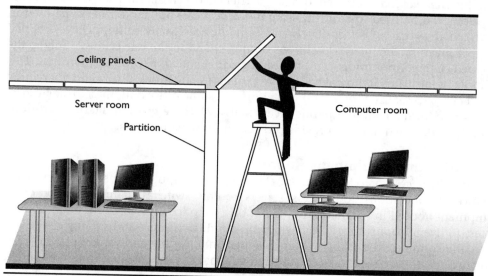

Figure 6-4   An intruder can lift ceiling panels and enter a secured area with little effort.

Data centers, server rooms, and wiring closets should be located in the core areas of a facility, near wiring distribution centers. Strict access control mechanisms and procedures should be implemented for these areas. The access control mechanisms may be smart card readers, biometric readers, or combination locks, as described in Chapter 4. These restricted areas should have only one *access* door, but fire code requirements typically dictate there must be at least two doors to most data centers and server rooms. Only one door should be used for daily entry and exit, and the other door should be used only in emergency situations. This second door should not be an access door, which means people should not be able to come in through this door. It should be locked, but should have a panic bar that will release the lock if pressed.

These restricted areas ideally should not be directly accessible from public areas like stairways, corridors, loading docks, elevators, and restrooms. This helps ensure that the people who are by the doors to secured areas have a specific purpose for being there, versus being on their way to the restroom or standing around in a common area gossiping about the CEO.

Because data centers usually hold expensive equipment and the company's critical data, their protection should be thoroughly thought out before implementation. Data centers should not be located on the top floors because it would be more difficult for an emergency crew to access it in a timely fashion in case of a fire. By the same token, data centers should not be located in basements where flooding can affect the systems. And if a facility is in a hilly area, the data center should be located well above ground level. Data centers should be located at the core of a building, to provide protection from natural disasters or bombs and to provide easier access to emergency crews if necessary.

Which access controls and security measures should be implemented for the data center depends upon the sensitivity of the data being processed and the protection level required. Alarms on the doors to the data processing center should be activated during off-hours, and there should be policies dictating how to carry out access control during normal business hours, after hours, and during emergencies. If a combination lock is used to enter the data processing center, the combination should be changed at least every six months and also after an employee who knows the code leaves the company.

The various controls discussed next are shown in Figure 6-5. The team responsible for designing a new data center (or evaluating a current data center) should understand all the controls shown in Figure 6-5 and be able to choose what is needed.

The data processing center should be constructed as one room rather than different individual rooms. The room should be away from any of the building's water pipes in case a break in a line causes a flood. The vents and ducts from the HVAC system should be protected with some type of barrier bars and should be too small for anyone to crawl through and gain access to the center. The data center must have positive air pressure, so no contaminants can be sucked into the room and into the computers' fans.

In many data centers, an emergency Off switch is situated next to the door so someone can turn off the power if necessary. If a fire occurs, this emergency Off switch should be flipped as employees are leaving the room and before the fire suppression agent is released. This is critical if the suppression agent is water, because water and electricity are *not* a good match—especially during a fire. A company can install a fire suppression system that is tied into this switch, so when a fire is detected, the electricity

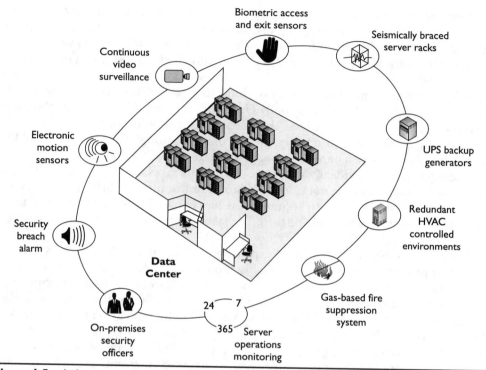

Figure 6-5 A data center should have many physical security controls.

is automatically shut off right before the suppression material is released. (The suppression material could be a type of gas, such as halon, or FM-200, or water. Gases are usually a better choice for environments filled with computers. We will cover different suppression agents in the "Fire Prevention, Detection, and Suppression" section later in the chapter.)

Portable fire extinguishers should be located close to the equipment and should be easy to see and access. Smoke detectors or fire sensors should be implemented, and water sensors should be placed under the raised floors. Since most of the wiring and cables run under the raised floors, it is important that water does not get to these places and, if it does, that an alarm sound if water is detected.

 NOTE If there is any type of water damage in a data center or facility, mold and mildew could easily become a problem. Instead of allowing things to "dry out on their own," many times it is better to use industry-strength dehumidifiers, water movers, and sanitizers to ensure secondary damage does not occur.

Water can cause extensive damage to equipment, flooring, walls, computers, and facility foundations. It is important that an organization be able to detect leaks and unwanted water. The detectors should be under raised floors and on dropped ceilings (to detect leaks from the floor above it). The location of the detectors should be documented and their position marked for easy access. As smoke and fire detectors should be tied to an alarm system, so should water detectors. The alarms usually just alert the necessary staff members and not everyone in the building. The staff members who are responsible for following up when an alarm sounds should be trained properly on how to reduce any potential water damage. Before any poking around to see where water is or is not pooling in places it does not belong, the electricity for that particular zone of the building should be temporarily turned off.

Water detectors can help prevent damage to

- Equipment
- Flooring
- Walls
- Computers
- Facility foundations

Location of water detectors should be

- Under raised floors
- On dropped ceilings

It is important to maintain the proper temperature and humidity levels within data centers, which is why an HVAC system should be implemented specifically for this room. Too high a temperature can cause components to overheat and turn off; too low a temperature can cause the components to work more slowly. If the humidity is high, then corrosion of the computer parts can take place; if humidity is low, then static electricity can be introduced. Because of this, the data center must have its own temperature and humidity controls, which are separate from the rest of the building.

It is best if the data center is on a different electrical system than the rest of the building, if possible. Thus, if anything negatively affects the main building's power, it will not carry over and affect the center. The data center may require redundant power supplies, which means two or more feeders coming in from two or more electrical substations. The idea is that if one of the power company's substations were to go down, the company would still be able to receive electricity from the other feeder. But just because a company has two or more electrical feeders coming into its facility does not mean true redundancy is automatically in place. Many companies have paid for two feeders to come into their building, only to find out both feeders were coming from the same substation! This defeats the whole purpose of having two feeders in the first place.

Data centers need to have their own backup power supplies, either an uninterrupted power supply (UPS) or generators. The different types of backup power supplies are discussed later in the chapter, but it is important to know at this point that the power backup must be able to support the load of the data center.

Many companies choose to use large glass panes for the walls of the data center so personnel within the center can be viewed at all times. This glass should be shatter-resistant since the window is acting as an exterior wall. The center's doors should not be hollow, but rather secure solid-core doors. Doors should open out rather than in so they don't damage equipment when opened. Best practices indicate that the door frame should be fixed to adjoining wall studs and that there should be at least three hinges per door. These characteristics would make the doors much more difficult to break down.

Protecting Assets

The main threats that physical security components combat are theft, interruptions to services, physical damage, compromised system and environment integrity, and unauthorized access.

Real loss is determined by the cost to replace the stolen items, the negative effect on productivity, the negative effect on reputation and customer confidence, fees for consultants that may need to be brought in, and the cost to restore lost data and production levels. Many times, companies just perform an inventory of their hardware and provide value estimates that are plugged into risk analysis to determine what the cost to the company would be if the equipment were stolen or destroyed. However, the information held within the equipment may be much more valuable than the equipment itself, and proper recovery mechanisms and procedures also need to be plugged into the risk assessment for a more realistic and fair assessment of cost.

Laptop theft is increasing at incredible rates each year. They have been stolen for years, but in the past they were stolen mainly to sell the hardware. Now laptops are also being stolen to gain sensitive data for identity theft crimes. What is important to understand is that this is a rampant, and potentially very dangerous, crime. Many people claim, "My whole life is on my laptop" or possibly their PDA. Since employees use laptops as they travel, they may have extremely sensitive company or customer data on their systems that can easily fall into the wrong hands. The following list provides many of the protection mechanisms that can be used to protect laptops and the data they hold:

- Inventory all laptops, including serial numbers so they can be properly identified if recovered.
- Harden the operating system.
- Password protect the BIOS.
- Register all laptops with the vendor, and file a report when one is stolen. If a stolen laptop is sent in for repairs, it will be flagged by the vendor.
- Do not check a laptop as luggage when flying.
- Never leave a laptop unattended, and carry it in a nondescript carrying case.
- Engrave the laptop with a symbol or number for proper identification.
- Use a slot lock with a cable to connect a laptop to a stationary object.
- Back up the data from the laptop and store it on a stationary PC or backup media.
- Use specialized safes if storing laptops in vehicles.
- Encrypt all sensitive data.

Tracing software can be installed so that your laptop can "phone home" if it is taken from you. Several products offer this tracing capability. Once installed and configured, the software periodically sends in a signal to a tracking center. If you report that your laptop has been stolen, the vendor of this software will work with service providers and law enforcement to track down and return your laptop.

A company may have need for a safe. Safes are commonly used to store backup data tapes, original contracts, or other types of valuables. The safe should be penetration-resistant and provide fire protection. The types of safes an organization can choose from are

- **Wall safe**   Embedded into the wall and easily hidden
- **Floor safe**   Embedded into the floor and easily hidden
- **Chests**   Stand-alone safes
- **Depositories**   Safes with slots, which allow the valuables to be easily slipped in
- **Vaults**   Safes that are large enough to provide walk-in access

If a safe has a combination lock, it should be changed periodically, and only a small subset of people should have access to the combination or key. The safe should be in a visible location, so anyone who is interacting with the safe can be seen. The goal is to uncover any unauthorized access attempts. Some safes have passive or thermal relocking functionality. If the safe has a *passive relocking* function, it can detect when someone attempts to tamper with it, in which case extra internal bolts will fall into place to ensure it cannot be compromised. If a safe has a *thermal relocking* function, when a certain temperature is met (possibly from drilling), an extra lock is implemented to ensure the valuables are properly protected.

Internal Support Systems

This place has no air conditioning or water. Who would want to break into it anyway?

Having a fortified facility with secure compartmentalized areas and protected assets is nice, but having lights, air conditioning, and water within this facility is even better. Physical security needs to address these support services, because their malfunction or disruption could negatively affect the organization in many ways.

Although there are many incidents of various power losses here and there for different reasons (storms, hurricanes, California nearly running out of electricity), one of the most notable power losses took place in August 2003, when eight East Coast states and portions of Canada lost power for several days. Although there were rumors about a worm causing this disruption, it was found to be a software bug in GE Energy's XA/21 system. This disaster left over 50 million people without power for days, caused four nuclear power plants to be shut down, and put a lot of companies in insecure and chaotic condition. Security professionals need to be able to help organizations handle both the small bumps in the road, such as power surges or sags, and the gigantic sinkholes, such as what happened in the United States and Canada on August 14, 2003.

Electric Power

We don't need no stinkin' power supply. Just rub these two sticks together.

Because computing and communication have become so essential in the corporate world, power failure is a much more devastating event than it was 10 to 15 years ago. The need for good plans to fall back on is crucial to ensure that a business will not be drastically affected by storms, high winds, hardware failure, lightning, or other events that can stop or disrupt power supplies. A continuous supply of electricity assures the availability of company resources; thus, a security professional must be familiar with the threats to electric power and the corresponding countermeasures.

Several types of power backup capabilities exist. Before a company chooses one, it should calculate the total cost of anticipated downtime and its effects. This information can be gathered from past records and other businesses in the same area on the same power grid. The total cost per hour for backup power is derived by dividing the annual expenditures by the annual standard hours of use.

Large and small issues can cause power failure or fluctuations. The effects manifest in variations of voltage that can last a millisecond to days. A company can pay to have two different supplies of power to reduce its risks, but this approach can be costly. Other, less expensive mechanisms are to have generators or UPSs in place. Some generators have sensors to detect power failure and will start automatically upon failure. Depending on the type and size of the generator, it might provide power for hours or days. UPSs are usually short-term solutions compared to generators.

Power Protection

Protecting power can be done in three ways: through UPSs, power line conditioners, and backup sources. UPSs use battery packs that range in size and capacity. A UPS can be online or standby. **Online UPS systems** use AC line voltage to charge a bank of batteries. When in use, the UPS has an inverter that changes the DC output from the batteries into the required AC form and that regulates the voltage as it powers computer devices. This conversion process is shown in Figure 6-6. Online UPS systems have the normal primary power passing through them day in and day out. They constantly provide power from their own inverters, even when the electric power is in proper use. Since the environment's electricity passes through this type of UPS all the time, the UPS device is able to quickly detect when a power failure takes place. An online UPS can provide the necessary electricity and picks up the load after a power failure much more quickly than a standby UPS.

Standby UPS devices stay inactive until a power line fails. The system has sensors that detect a power failure, and the load is switched to the battery pack. The switch to the battery pack is what causes the small delay in electricity being provided. So an on-line UPS picks up the load much more quickly than a standby UPS, but costs more of course.

Backup power supplies are necessary when there is a power failure and the outage will last longer than a UPS can last. Backup supplies can be a redundant line from another electrical substation or from a motor generator and can be used to supply main power or to charge the batteries in a UPS system.

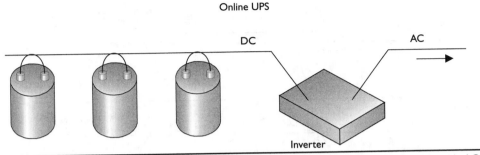

Figure 6-6   A UPS device converts DC current from its internal or external batteries to usable AC by using an inverter.

A company should identify critical systems that need protection from interrupted power supplies, and then estimate how long secondary power would be needed and how much power is required per device. Some UPS devices provide just enough power to allow systems to shut down gracefully, whereas others allow the systems to run for a longer period. A company needs to determine whether systems should only have a big enough power supply to allow them to shut down properly or whether they need a system that keeps them up and running so critical operations remain available.

Just having a generator in the closet should not give a company that warm fuzzy feeling of protection. An alternate power source should be tested periodically to make sure it works, and to the extent expected. It is never good to find yourself in an emergency only to discover the generator does not work, or someone forgot to buy the gas necessary to keep the thing running.

Electric Power Issues

Electric power enables us to be productive and functional in many different ways, but if it is not installed, monitored, and respected properly, it can do us great harm.

When *clean* power is being provided, the power supply contains no interference or voltage fluctuation. The possible types of interference (*line noise*) are *electromagnetic interference (EMI)* or *radio frequency interference (RFI)*, which is disturbance to the flow of electric power while it travels across a power line, as shown in Figure 6-7. EMI can be created by the difference between three wires: hot, neutral, and ground, and the magnetic field they create. Lightning and electrical motors can induce EMI, which could then interrupt the proper flow of electrical current as it travels over wires to, from, and within buildings. RFI can be caused by anything that creates radio waves. Fluorescent lighting is one of the main causes of RFI within buildings today, so does that mean we need to rip out all the fluorescent lighting? That's one choice, but we could also just use shielded cabling where fluorescent lighting could cause a problem. If you take a break from your reading, climb up into your office's dropped ceiling, and look around, you would probably see wires bundled and tied up to the *true* ceiling. If your office is using fluorescent lighting, the power and data lines should not be running over, or on top of, the fluorescent lights. This is because the radio frequencies being given off can interfere with the data or power current as it travels through these wires. Now, get back down from the ceiling. We have work to do.

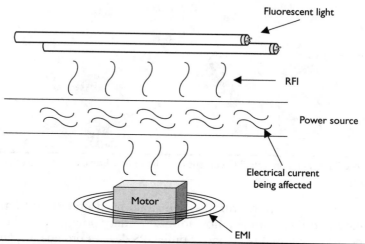

Figure 6-7 RFI and EMI can cause line noise on power lines.

Interference interrupts the flow of an electrical current, and fluctuations can actually deliver a different level of voltage than what was expected. Each fluctuation can be damaging to devices and people. The following explains the different types of voltage fluctuations possible with electric power:

- **Power excess**
  - **Spike** Momentary high voltage
  - **Surge** Prolonged high voltage
- **Power loss**
  - **Fault** Momentary power outage
  - **Blackout** Prolonged, complete loss of electric power
- **Power degradation**
  - **Sag/dip** Momentary low-voltage condition, from one cycle to a few seconds
  - **Brownout** Prolonged power supply that is below normal voltage
- **In-rush current** Initial surge of current required to start a load

Electric Power Definitions

The following list summarizes many of the electric power concepts discussed so far:

- **Ground** The pathway to the earth to enable excessive voltage to dissipate
- **Noise** Electromagnetic or frequency interference that disrupts the power flow and can cause fluctuations
- **Transient noise** A short duration of power line disruption
- **Clean power** Electrical current that does not fluctuate
- **EMI** Electromagnetic interference
- **RFI** Radio frequency interference

When an electrical device is turned on, it can draw a large amount of current, which is referred to as *in-rush current*. If the device sucks up enough current, it can cause a *sag* in the available power for surrounding devices. This could negatively affect their performance. As stated earlier, it is a good idea to have the data processing center and devices on a different electrical wiring segment from that of the rest of the facility, if possible, so the devices will not be affected by these issues. For example, if you are in a building or house without efficient wiring and you turn on a vacuum cleaner or microwave, you may see the lights quickly dim because of this in-rush current. The drain on the power supply caused by in-rush currents still happens in other environments when these types of electrical devices are used—you just might not be able to see the effects. Any type of device that would cause such a dramatic in-rush current should not be used on the same electrical segment as data processing systems.

Surge   A surge is a prolonged rise in voltage from a power source. Surges can cause a lot of damage very quickly. A surge is one of the most common power problems and is controlled with surge protectors. These protectors use a device called a metal oxide varistor, which moves the excess voltage to ground when a surge occurs. Its source can be from a strong lightning strike, a power plant going online or offline, a shift in the commercial utility power grid, and electrical equipment within a business starting and stopping. Most computers have a built-in surge protector in their power supplies, but these are baby surge protectors and cannot provide protection against the damage that larger surges (say, from storms) can cause. So, you need to ensure all devices are properly plugged into larger surge protectors, whose only job is to absorb any extra current before it is passed to electrical devices.

Blackout   A blackout is when the voltage drops to zero. This can be caused by lightning, a car taking out a power line, storms, or failure to pay the power bill. It can last for seconds or days. This is when a backup power source is required for business continuity.

Brownout   When power companies are experiencing high demand, they frequently reduce the voltage in an electrical grid, which is referred to as a brownout. Constant-voltage transformers can be used to regulate this fluctuation of power. They can use different ranges of voltage and only release the expected 120 volts of alternating current to devices.

Noise   Noise on power lines can be a result of lightning, the use of fluorescent lighting, a transformer being hit by an automobile, or other environmental or human activities. Frequency ranges overlap, which can affect electrical device operations. Lightning sometimes produces voltage spikes on communications and power lines, which can destroy equipment or alter data being transmitted. When generators are switched on because power loads have increased, they too can cause voltage spikes that can be harmful and disruptive. Storms and intense cold or heat can put a heavier load on generators and cause a drop in voltage. Each of these instances is an example of how normal environmental behaviors can affect power voltage, eventually adversely affecting equipment, communications, or the transmission of data.

Because these and other occurrences are common, mechanisms should be in place to detect unwanted power fluctuations and protect the integrity of your data processing environment. *Voltage regulators* and *line conditioners* can be used to ensure a clean and smooth distribution of power. The primary power runs through a regulator or conditioner. They have the capability to absorb extra current if there is a spike, and to store energy to add current to the line if there is a sag. The goal is to keep the current flowing at a nice, steady level so neither motherboard components nor employees get fried.

Many data centers are constructed to take power-sensitive equipment into consideration. Because surges, sags, brownouts, blackouts, and voltage spikes frequently cause data corruption, the centers are built to provide a high level of protection against these events. Other types of environments usually are not built with these things in mind and do not provide this level of protection. Offices usually have different types of devices connected and plugged into the same outlets. Outlet strips are plugged into outlet strips, which are connected to extension cords. This causes more line noise and a reduction of voltage to each device. Figure 6-8 depicts an environment that can cause line noise, voltage problems, and possibly a fire hazard.

Preventive Measures and Good Practices

Don't stand in a pool of water with a live electrical wire.
Response: Hold on, I need to write that one down.

When dealing with electric power issues, the following items can help protect devices and the environment:

- Plug in every device to a surge protector to protect from excessive current.
- Shut down devices in an orderly fashion to help avoid data loss or damage to devices due to voltage changes.
- Employ power line monitors to detect frequency and voltage amplitude changes.
- Use regulators to keep voltage steady and the power clean.
- Protect distribution panels, master circuit breakers, and transformer cables with access controls.
- Provide protection from magnetic induction through shielded lines.
- Use shielded cabling for long cable runs.
- Do not run data or power lines directly over fluorescent lights.
- Use three-prong connections or adapters if using two-prong connections.
- Do not plug outlet strips and extension cords into each other.

Environmental Issues

Improper environmental controls can cause damage to services, hardware, and lives. Interruption of some services can cause unpredicted and unfortunate results. Power, heating, ventilation, air-conditioning, and air-quality controls can be complex and contain many variables. They all need to be operating properly and to be monitored regularly.

Figure 6-8
This configuration
can cause a lot of
line noise and poses
a fire hazard.

During facility construction, the physical security team must make certain that water, steam, and gas lines have proper shutoff valves, as shown in Figure 6-9, and *positive drains*, which means their contents flow out instead of in. If there is ever a break in a main water pipe, the valve to shut off water flow must be readily accessible. Similarly, in case of fire in a building, the valve to shut off the gas lines must be readily accessible. In case of a flood, a company wants to ensure that material cannot travel up through the water pipes and into its water supply or facility. Facility, operations, and security personnel should know where these shutoff valves are, and there should be strict procedures to follow in these types of emergencies. This will help reduce the potential damage.

Figure 6-9
Water, steam, and
gas lines should have
emergency shutoff
valves.

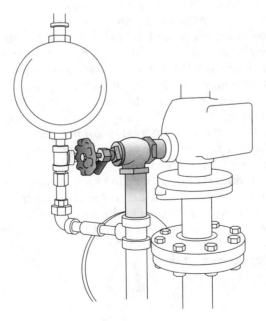

Most electronic equipment must operate in a climate-controlled atmosphere. Although it is important to keep the atmosphere at a proper working temperature, it is important to understand that the components within the equipment can suffer from overheating even in a climate-controlled atmosphere if the internal computer fans are not cleaned or are blocked. When devices are overheated, the components can expand and contract, which causes components to change their electronic characteristics, reducing their effectiveness or damaging the system overall.

NOTE The climate issues involved with a data processing environment are why it needs its own separate HVAC system. Maintenance procedures should be documented and properly followed. HVAC activities should be recorded and reviewed annually.

Maintaining appropriate temperature and humidity is important in any facility, especially facilities with computer systems. Improper levels of either can cause damage to computers and electrical devices. High humidity can cause corrosion, and low humidity can cause excessive static electricity. This static electricity can short out devices, cause the loss of information, or provide amusing entertainment for unsuspecting employees.

NOTE Humidity should be kept between 40% and 60%, and the temperature should be between 70°F and 74°F.

Lower temperatures can cause mechanisms to slow or stop, and higher temperatures can cause devices to use too much fan power and eventually shut down. Table 6-1 lists different components and their corresponding damaging temperature levels.

In drier climates, or during the winter, the air contains less moisture, which can cause static electricity when two dissimilar objects touch each other. This electricity usually travels through the body and produces a spark from a person's finger that can release several thousand volts. This can be more damaging than you would think. Usually the charge is released on a system casing and is of no concern, but sometimes it is released directly to an internal computer component and causes damage. People who work on the internal parts of a computer usually wear antistatic armbands to reduce the chance of this happening.

In more humid climates, or during the summer, more humidity is in the air, which can also affect components. Particles of silver can begin to move away from connectors onto copper circuits, which cement the connectors into their sockets. This can adversely affect the electrical efficiency of the connection. A *hygrometer* is usually used to monitor humidity. It can be manually read, or an automatic alarm can be set up to go off if the humidity passes a set threshold.

Preventive Steps Against Static Electricity

The following are some simple measures to prevent static electricity:

- Use antistatic flooring in data processing areas.
- Ensure proper humidity.
- Have proper grounding for wiring and outlets.
- Don't have carpeting in data centers, or have static-free carpets if necessary.
- Wear antistatic bands when working inside computer systems.

Ventilation

Can I smoke in the server room?
Response: Security!

Ventilation has several requirements that must be met to ensure a safe and comfortable environment. A closed-loop recirculating air-conditioning system should be installed to maintain air quality. "Closed-loop" means the air within the building is reused after it has been properly filtered, instead of bringing outside air in. Positive pressurization and ventilation should also be implemented to control contamination. *Positive pressurization* means that when an employee opens a door, the air goes out, and outside air does not come in. If a facility were on fire, you would want the smoke to go out the doors instead of being pushed back in when people are fleeing.

The assessment team needs to understand the various types of contaminants, how they can enter an environment, the damage they could cause, and the steps to ensure that a facility is protected from dangerous substances or high levels of average contaminants. Airborne material and particle concentrations must be monitored for inappropriate levels. Dust can affect a device's functionality by clogging up the fan that is supposed to be cooling the device. Excessive concentrations of certain gases can accelerate corrosion and cause performance issues or failure of electronic devices. Although most disk drives are hermetically sealed, other storage devices can be affected by airborne contaminants. Air-quality devices and ventilation systems deal with these issues.

Table 6-1 Components Affected by Specific Temperatures	Material or Component	Damaging Temperature
	Computer systems and peripheral devices	175°F
	Magnetic storage devices	100°F
	Paper products	350°F

Fire Prevention, Detection, and Suppression

We can either try to prevent fires or have one really expensive weenie-roast.

The subject of physical security would not be complete without a discussion on fire safety. A company must meet national and local standards pertaining to fire prevention, detection, and suppression methods. *Fire prevention* includes training employees on how to react properly when faced with a fire, supplying the right equipment and ensuring it is in working order, making sure there is an easily reachable fire suppression supply, and storing combustible elements in the proper manner. Fire prevention may also include using proper noncombustible construction materials and designing the facility with containment measures that provide barriers to minimize the spread of fire and smoke. These thermal or fire barriers can be made up of different types of construction material that is noncombustible and has a fire-resistant coating applied to them.

Fire detection response systems come in many different forms. Manual detection response systems are the red pull boxes you see on many building walls. Automatic detection response systems have sensors that react when they detect the presence of fire or smoke. We will review different types of detection systems in the next section.

Fire suppression is the use of a suppression agent to put out a fire. Fire suppression can take place manually through handheld portable extinguishers, or automatically through automated systems such as water sprinkler systems, or halon or CO_2 discharge systems. The upcoming "Fire Suppression" section reviews the different types of suppression agents and where they are best used. Automatic sprinkler systems are widely used and highly effective in protecting buildings and their contents. When deciding upon the type of fire suppression systems to install, a company needs to evaluate many factors, including an estimate of the occurrence rate of a possible fire, the amount of damage that could result, the types of fires that would most likely take place, and the types of suppression systems to choose from.

Fire protection processes should consist of implementing early smoke or fire detection devices and shutting down systems until the source of the heat is eliminated. A warning signal may be sounded by a smoke or fire detector before the suppression agent is released, so that if it is a false alarm or a small fire that can be handled without the automated suppression system, someone has time to shut down the suppression system.

Types of Fire Detection

Fires present a dangerous security threat because they can damage hardware and data and risk human life. Smoke, high temperatures, and corrosive gases from a fire can cause devastating results. It is important to evaluate the fire safety measurements of a building and the different sections within it.

A fire begins because something ignited it. Ignition sources can be failure of an electrical device, improper storage of combustible materials, carelessly discarded cigarettes, malfunctioning heating devices, and arson. A fire needs fuel (paper, wood, liquid, and so on) and oxygen to continue to burn and grow. The more fuel per square

Fire Resistant Ratings

Fire resistant ratings are the result of tests carried out in laboratories using specific configurations of environmental settings. The American Society for Testing and Materials (ASTM) is the organization that creates the standards that dictate how these tests should be performed and how to properly interpret the test results. ASTM accredited testing centers carry out the evaluations in accordance with these standards and assign fire resistant ratings that are then used in federal and state fire codes. The tests evaluate the fire resistance of different types of materials in various environmental configurations. Fire resistance represents the ability of a laboratory-constructed assembly to contain a fire for a specific period of time. For example, a 5/8-inch-thick drywall sheet installed on each side of a wood stud provides a one-hour rating. If the thickness of this drywall is doubled, then this would be given a two-hour rating. The rating system is used to classify different building components.

meter, the more intense the fire will become. A facility should be built, maintained, and operated to minimize the accumulation of fuels that can feed fires.

There are four classes (A, B, C, and D) of fire, which are explained in the "Fire Suppression" section. You need to know the differences between the types of fire so you know how to properly extinguish each type. Portable fire extinguishers have markings that indicate what type of fire they should be used on, as illustrated in Figure 6-10. The markings denote what types of chemicals are within the canisters and what types of fires they have been approved to be used on. Portable extinguishers should be located within 50 feet of any electrical equipment, and also near exits. The extinguishers should be marked clearly, with an unobstructed view. They should be easily reachable and operational by employees, and inspected quarterly.

A lot of computer systems are made of components that are not combustible but that will melt or char if overheated. Most computer circuits use only two to five volts of direct current, which usually cannot start a fire. If a fire does happen in a computer room, it will most likely be an electrical fire caused by overheating of wire insulation or by overheating components that ignite surrounding plastics. Prolonged smoke usually occurs before combustion.

Several types of detectors are available, each of which works in a different way. The detector can be activated by smoke or heat.

Smoke Activated Smoke-activated detectors are good for early-warning devices. They can be used to sound a warning alarm before the suppression system activates. A photoelectric device, also referred to as an optical detector, detects the variation in light intensity. The detector produces a beam of light across a protected area, and if the beam is obstructed, the alarm sounds. Figure 6-11 illustrates how a photoelectric device works.

Another type of photoelectric device samples the surrounding air by drawing air into a pipe. If the light source is obscured, the alarm will sound.

Figure 6-10 Portable extinguishers are marked to indicate what type of fire they should be used on.

Heat Activated Heat-activated detectors can be configured to sound an alarm either when a predefined temperature (fixed temperature) is reached or when the temperature increases over a period of time (rate-of-rise). Rate-of-rise temperature sensors usually provide a quicker warning than fixed-temperature sensors because they are more sensitive, but they can also cause more false alarms. The sensors can either be spaced uniformly throughout a facility, or implemented in a line type of installation, which is operated by a heat-sensitive cable.

It is not enough to have these fire and smoke detectors installed in a facility; they must be installed in the right places. Detectors should be installed both on and above suspended ceilings and raised floors, because companies run many types of wires in both places that could start an electrical fire. No one would know about the fire until it broke through the floor or dropped ceiling if detectors were not placed in these areas.

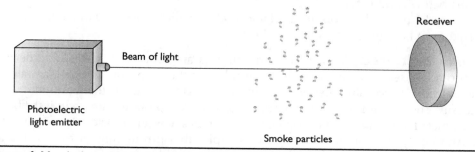

Figure 6-11 A photoelectric device uses a light emitter and a receiver.

Automatic Dial-Up Alarm

Fire detection systems can be configured to call the local fire station, and possibly the police station, to report a detected fire. The system plays a prerecorded message that gives the necessary information so officials can properly prepare for the stated emergency and arrive at the right location.

Detectors should also be located in enclosures and air ducts, because smoke can gather in these areas before entering other spaces. It is important that people are alerted about a fire as quickly as possible so damage may be reduced, fire suppression activities may start quickly, and lives may be saved. Figure 6-12 illustrates the proper placement of smoke detectors.

Fire Suppression

How about if I just spit on the fire?
Response: I'm sure that will work just fine.

It is important to know the different types of fires and what should be done to properly suppress them. Each fire type has a rating that indicates what materials are

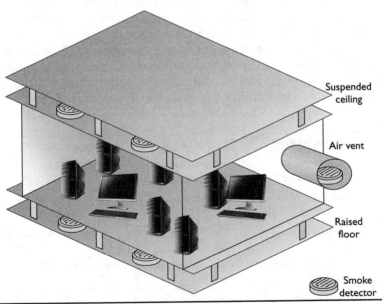

Figure 6-12   Smoke detectors should be located above suspended ceilings, below raised floors, and in air vents.

> ### Plenum Area
>
> Wiring and cables are strung through *plenum areas*, such as the space above dropped ceilings, the space in wall cavities, and the space under raised floors. Plenum areas should have fire detectors. Also, only plenum-rated cabling should be used in plenum areas, which is cabling that is made out of material that does not let off hazardous gases if it burns.

burning. Table 6-2 shows the four types of fire and their suppression methods, which all employees should know.

You can suppress a fire in several ways, all of which require that certain precautions be taken. In many buildings, suppression agents located in different areas are designed to initiate after a specific trigger has been set off. Each agent has a zone of coverage, meaning an area that the agent supplier is responsible for. If a fire ignites within a certain zone, it is the responsibility of that suppression agent device to initiate, and then suppress that fire. Different types of suppression agents available include water, halon, foams, CO_2, and more. CO_2 is good for putting out fires but bad for many types of life forms. If an organization uses CO_2, the suppression releasing device should have a delay mechanism within it that makes sure the agent does not start applying CO_2 to the area until after an audible alarm has sounded and people have been given time to evacuate. CO_2 is a colorless, odorless substance that is potentially lethal because it removes oxygen from the air. Gas masks do not provide protection against CO_2. This type of fire suppression mechanism is best used in unattended facilities and areas.

For Class B and C fires, specific types of dry powders can be used, which include sodium or potassium bicarbonate, calcium carbonate, or monoammonium phosphate. The first three powders interrupt the chemical combustion of a fire. Monoammonium phosphate melts at low temperatures and excludes oxygen from the fuel.

Fire Class	Type of Fire	Elements of Fire	Suppression Method
A	Common combustibles	Wood products, paper, and laminates	Water, foam
B	Liquid	Petroleum products and coolants	Gas, CO_2, foam, dry powders
C	Electrical	Electrical equipment and wires	Gas, CO_2, dry powders
D	Combustible metals	Magnesium, sodium, potassium	Dry powder

Table 6-2 Four Types of Fire and Their Suppression Methods

Foams are mainly water-based and contain a foaming agent that allows them to float on top of a burning substance to exclude the oxygen.

NOTE There is actually a Class K fire, for commercial kitchens. These fires should be put out with a wet chemical, which is usually a solution of potassium acetate. This chemical works best when putting out cooking oil fires.

A fire needs fuel, oxygen, and high temperatures. Table 6-3 shows how different suppression substances interfere with these elements of fire.

By law, companies that have halon extinguishers do not have to replace them, but the extinguishers cannot be refilled. So, companies that have halon extinguishers do not have to replace them right away, but when the extinguisher's lifetime runs out, FM-200 extinguishers or other EPA-approved chemicals should be used.

NOTE Halon has not been manufactured since January 1, 1992, by international agreement. The Montreal Protocol banned halon in 1987, and countries were given until 1992 to comply with these directives. The most effective replacement for halon is FM-200, which is similar to halon but does not damage the ozone.

The HVAC system should be connected to the fire alarm and suppression system so it properly shuts down if a fire is identified. A fire needs oxygen, and this type of system can feed oxygen to the fire. Plus, the HVAC can spread deadly smoke into all areas of the building. Many fire systems can configure the HVAC to shut down if a fire alarm is triggered.

Water Sprinklers

I'm hot. Go pull that red thingy on the wall. I need some water.
Water sprinklers typically are simpler and less expensive than halon and FM-200 systems but can cause water damage. In an electrical fire, the water can increase the inten-

Combustion Elements	Suppression Methods	How Suppression Works
Fuel	Soda acid	Removes fuel
Oxygen	Carbon dioxide	Removes oxygen
Temperature	Water	Reduces temperature
Chemical combustion	Gas—Halon or Halon substitute	Interferes with the chemical reactions between elements

Table 6-3 How Different Substances Interfere with Elements of Fire

Halon

Halon is a gas that was widely used in the past to suppress fires because it interferes with the chemical combustion of the elements within a fire. It mixes quickly with the air and does not cause harm to computer systems and other data processing devices. It was used mainly in data centers and server rooms.

It was discovered that halon has chemicals (chlorofluorocarbons) that deplete the ozone and that concentrations greater than 10 percent are dangerous to people. Halon used on extremely hot fires degrades into toxic chemicals, which is even more dangerous to humans.

Some really smart people figured that the ozone was important to keep around, which caused halon to be federally restricted, and no companies are allowed to purchase and install new halon extinguishers. Companies that still have halon systems have been instructed to replace them with nontoxic extinguishers.

The following are some of the EPA-approved replacements for Halon:

- FM-200
- NAF-S-III
- CEA-410
- FE-13
- Inergen
- Argon
- Argonite

sity of the fire, because it can work as a conductor for electricity—only making the situation worse. If water is going to be used in any type of environment with electrical equipment, the electricity must be turned off before the water is released. Sensors should be used to shut down the electric power before water sprinklers activate. Each sprinkler head should activate individually to avoid wide-area damage, and there should be shutoff valves so the water supply can be stopped if necessary.

A company should take great care in deciding which suppression agent and system is best for it. Four main types of water sprinkler systems are available: wet pipe, dry pipe, preaction, and deluge.

- **Wet pipe** *Wet pipe systems* always contain water in the pipes and are usually discharged by temperature control level sensors. One disadvantage of wet pipe systems is that the water in the pipes may freeze in colder climates. Also, if there is a nozzle or pipe break, it can cause extensive water damage. These types of systems are also called *closed head systems*.

- **Dry pipe** In *dry pipe systems*, the water is not actually held in the pipes. The water is contained in a "holding tank" until it is released. The pipes hold pressurized air, which is reduced when a fire or smoke alarm is activated, allowing the water valve to be opened by the water pressure. Water is not allowed into the pipes that feed the sprinklers until an actual fire is detected. First, a heat or smoke sensor is activated; then, the water fills the pipes leading to the sprinkler heads, the fire alarm sounds, the electric power supply is disconnected, and finally water is allowed to flow from the sprinklers. These pipes are best used in colder climates because the pipes will not freeze. Figure 6-13 depicts a dry pipe system.

- **Preaction** *Preaction systems* are similar to dry pipe systems in that the water is not held in the pipes, but is released when the pressurized air within the pipes is reduced. Once this happens, the pipes are filled with water, but it is not released right away. A thermal-fusible link on the sprinkler head has to melt before the water is released. The purpose of combining these two techniques is to give people more time to respond to false alarms or to small fires that can be handled by other means. Putting out a small fire with a handheld extinguisher is better than losing a lot of electrical equipment to water damage. These systems are usually used only in data processing environments rather than the whole building, because of the higher cost of these types of systems.

- **Deluge** A *deluge system* has its sprinkler heads wide open to allow a larger volume of water to be released in a shorter period. Because the water being released is in such large volumes, these systems are usually not used in data processing environments.

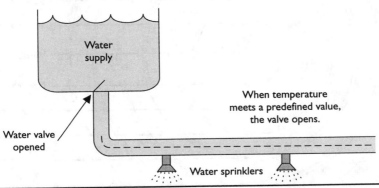

Figure 6-13 Dry pipe systems do not hold water in the pipes.

Perimeter Security

Halt! Who goes there?

The first line of defense is perimeter control at the site location, to prevent unauthorized access to the facility. As mentioned earlier in this chapter, physical security should be implemented by using a layered defense approach. For example, before an intruder can get to the written recipe for your company's secret barbeque sauce, she will need to climb or cut a fence, slip by a security guard, pick a door lock, circumvent a biometric access control reader that protects access to an internal room, and then break into the safe that holds the recipe. The idea is that if an attacker breaks through one control layer, there will be others in her way before she can obtain the company's crown jewels.

NOTE It is also important to have a diversity of controls. For example, if one key works on four different door locks, the intruder has to obtain only one key. Each entry should have its own individual key or authentication combination.

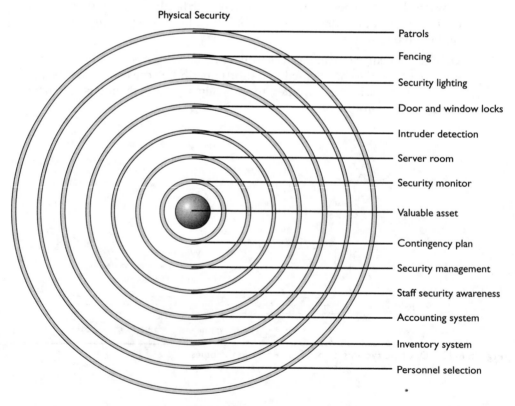

This defense model should work in two main modes: one mode during normal facility operations and another mode during the time the facility is closed. When the facility is closed, all doors should be locked with monitoring mechanisms in strategic positions to alert security personnel of suspicious activity. When the facility is in operation, security gets more complicated because authorized individuals need to be distinguished from unauthorized individuals. Perimeter security deals with facility and personnel access controls, external boundary protection mechanisms, intrusion detection, and corrective actions. The following sections describe the elements that make up these categories.

Facility Access Control

Access control needs to be enforced through physical and technical components when it comes to physical security. Physical access controls use mechanisms to identify individuals who are attempting to enter a facility or area. They make sure the right individuals get in and the wrong individuals stay out, and provide an audit trail of these actions. Having personnel within sensitive areas is one of the best security controls because they can personally detect suspicious behavior. However, they need to be trained on what activity is considered suspicious and how to report such activity.

Before a company can put into place the proper protection mechanisms, it needs to conduct a detailed review to identify which individuals should be allowed into what areas. Access control points can be identified and classified as external, main, and secondary entrances. Personnel should enter and exit through a specific entry, deliveries should be made to a different entry, and sensitive areas should be restricted. Figure 6-14 illustrates the different types of access control points into a facility. After a company has identified and classified the access control points, the next step is to determine how to protect them.

Locks

Locks are inexpensive access control mechanisms that are widely accepted and used. They are considered delaying devices to intruders. The longer it takes to break or pick a lock, the longer a security guard or police officer has to arrive on the scene if the intruder has been detected. Almost any type of a door can be equipped with a lock, but keys can be easily lost and duplicated, and locks can be picked or broken. If a company depends solely on a lock-and-key mechanism for protection, an individual who has the key can come and go as he likes without control and can remove items from the premises without detection. Locks should be used as part of the protection scheme, but should not be the sole protection scheme.

Locks vary in functionality. Padlocks can be used on chained fences, preset locks are usually used on doors, and programmable locks (requiring a combination to unlock) are used on doors or vaults. Locks come in all types and sizes. It is important to have the right type of lock so it provides the correct level of protection.

To the curious mind or a determined thief, a lock is considered a little puzzle to solve, not a deterrent. In other words, locks may be merely a challenge, not necessarily something to stand in the way of malicious activities. Thus, you need to make the challenge difficult, through the complexity, strength, and quality of the locking mechanisms.

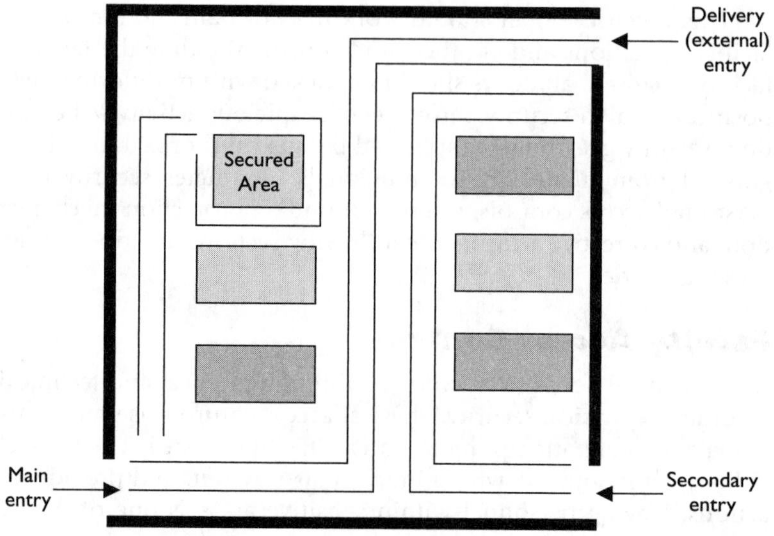

Figure 6-14
Access control
points should be
identified, marked,
and monitored
properly.

Delivery
(external)
entry

Secured
Area

Main
entry

Secondary
entry

NOTE The delay time provided by the lock should match the penetration
resistance of the surrounding components (door, door frame, hinges). A smart
thief takes the path of least resistance, which may be to pick the lock, remove
the pins from the hinges, or just kick down the door.

Mechanical Locks   Two main types of mechanical locks are available: the warded
lock and the tumbler lock. The warded lock is the basic padlock, as shown in Figure
6-15. It has a spring-loaded bolt with a notch cut in it. The key fits into this notch and
slides the bolt from the locked to the unlocked position. The lock has wards in it, which
are metal projections around the keyhole, as shown in Figure 6-16. The correct key for
a specific warded lock has notches in it that fit in these projections and a notch to slide
the bolt back and forth. These are the cheapest locks, because of their lack of any real
sophistication, and are also the easiest to pick.

The *tumbler lock* has more pieces and parts than a ward lock. As shown in Figure
6-17, the key fits into a cylinder, which raises the lock metal pieces to the correct height
so the bolt can slide to the locked or unlocked position. Once all of the metal pieces are
at the correct level, the internal bolt can be turned. The proper key has the required size
and sequences of notches to move these metal pieces into their correct position.

The three types of tumbler locks are the pin tumbler, wafer tumbler, and lever tumbler. The *pin tumbler* lock, shown in Figure 6-17, is the most commonly used tumbler
lock. The key has to have just the right grooves to put all the spring-loaded pins in the
right position so the lock can be locked or unlocked.

Figure 6-15
A warded lock

Wafer tumbler locks (also called disc tumbler locks) are the small, round locks you usually see on file cabinets. They use flat discs (wafers) instead of pins inside the locks. They often are used as car and desk locks. This type of lock does not provide much protection because it can be easily circumvented.

NOTE Some locks have interchangeable cores, which allow for the core of the lock to be taken out. You would use this type of lock if you wanted one key to open several locks. You would just replace all locks with the same core.

Figure 6-16
A key fits into a notch to turn the bolt to unlock the lock.

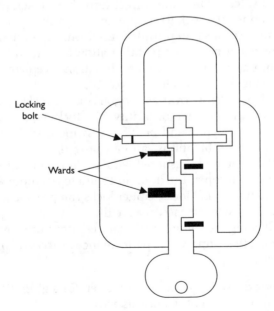

Locking bolt

Wards

Figure 6-17
Tumbler lock

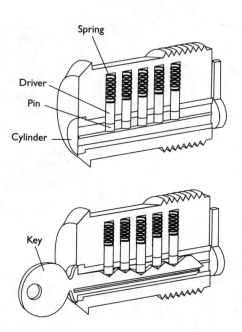

Combination locks, of course, require the correct combination of numbers to unlock them. These locks have internal wheels that have to line up properly before being unlocked. A user spins the lock interface left and right by so many clicks, which lines up the internal wheels. Once the correct turns have taken place, all the wheels are in the right position for the lock to release and open the door. The more wheels within the locks, the more protection provided. Electronic combination locks do not use internal wheels, but rather have a keypad that allows a person to type in the combination instead of turning a knob with a combination faceplate. An example of an electronic combination lock is shown in Figure 6-18.

Cipher locks, also known as programmable locks, are keyless and use keypads to control access into an area or facility. The lock requires a specific combination to be entered into the keypad and possibly a swipe card. They cost more than traditional locks, but their combinations can be changed, specific combination sequence values can be locked out, and personnel who are in trouble or under duress can enter a specific code that will open the door and initiate a remote alarm at the same time. Thus, compared to traditional locks, cipher locks can provide a much higher level of security and control over who can access a facility.

The following are some functionalities commonly available on many cipher combination locks that improve the performance of access control and provide for increased security levels:

- **Door delay** If a door is held open for a given time, an alarm will trigger to alert personnel of suspicious activity.

- **Key override** A specific combination can be programmed to be used in emergency situations to override normal procedures or for supervisory overrides.

- **Master keying**   Enables supervisory personnel to change access codes and other features of the cipher lock.
- **Hostage alarm**   If an individual is under duress and/or held hostage, a combination he enters can communicate this situation to the guard station and/or police station.

If a door is accompanied by a cipher lock, it should have a corresponding visibility shield so a bystander cannot see the combination as it is keyed in. Automated cipher locks must have a backup battery system and be set to unlock during a power failure so personnel are not trapped inside during an emergency.

NOTE   It is important to change the combination of locks and to use random combination sequences. Often, people do not change their combinations or clean the keypads, which allows an intruder to know what key values are used in the combination, because they are the dirty and worn keys. The intruder then just needs to figure out the right combination of these values.

Some cipher locks require all users to know and use the same combination, which does not allow for any individual accountability. Some of the more sophisticated cipher locks permit specific codes to be assigned to unique individuals. This provides more accountability, because each individual is responsible for keeping his access code secret, and entry and exit activities can be logged and tracked. These are usually referred to as *smart locks*, because they are designed to allow only authorized individuals access at certain doors at certain times.

NOTE   Hotel key cards are also known as smart cards. They are programmed by the nice hotel guy or gal behind the counter. The access code on the card can allow access to a hotel room, workout area, business area, and better yet—the mini bar.

Figure 6-18
An electronic
combination lock

Device Locks Unfortunately, hardware has a tendency to "walk away" from facilities; thus, device locks are necessary to thwart these attempts. Cable locks consist of a vinyl-coated steel cable that can secure a computer or peripheral to a desk or other stationary components, as shown in Figure 6-19.

The following are some of the device locks available and their capabilities:

- **Switch controls** Cover on/off power switches
- **Slot locks** Secure the system to a stationary component by the use of steel cable that is connected to a bracket mounted in a spare expansion slot
- **Port controls** Block access to disk drives or unused serial or parallel ports
- **Peripheral switch controls** Secure a keyboard by inserting an on/off switch between the system unit and the keyboard input slot
- **Cable traps** Prevent the removal of input/output devices by passing their cables through a lockable unit

Administrative Responsibilities It is important for a company not only to choose the right type of lock for the right purpose, but also to follow proper maintenance and procedures. Keys should be assigned by facility management, and this assignment should be documented. Procedures should be written out detailing how keys are to be assigned, inventoried, and destroyed when necessary, and what should happen if and when keys are lost. Someone on the company's facility management team should be assigned the responsibility of overseeing key and combination maintenance.

Most organizations have master keys and submaster keys for the facility management staff. A master key opens all the locks within the facility, and the submaster keys open one or more locks. Each lock has its own individual unique keys as well. So if a

Figure 6-19
FMJ/PAD.LOCK's notebook security cable kit secures a notebook by enabling the user to attach the device to a stationary component within an area.

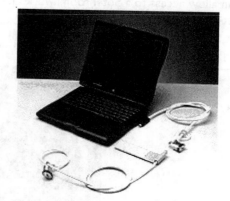

facility has 100 offices, the occupant of each office can have his or her own key. A master key allows access to all offices for security personnel and for emergencies. If one security guard is responsible for monitoring half the facility, the guard can be assigned one of the submaster keys for just those offices.

Since these master and submaster keys are powerful, they must be properly guarded and not widely shared. A security policy should outline what portions of the facility and which device types need to be locked. As a security professional, you should understand what type of lock is most appropriate for each situation, the level of protection provided by various types of locks, and how these locks can be circumvented.

Circumventing Locks Each lock type has corresponding tools that can be used to pick it (open it without the key). A tension wrench is a tool shaped like an L and is used to apply tension to the internal cylinder of a lock. The lock picker uses a lock pick to manipulate the individual pins to their proper placement. Once certain pins are "picked" (put in their correct place), the tension wrench holds these down while the lock picker figures out the correct settings for the other pins. After the intruder determines the proper pin placement, the wrench is used to then open the lock.

Intruders may carry out another technique, referred to as *raking*. To circumvent a pin tumbler lock, a lock pick is pushed to the back of the lock and quickly slid out while providing upward pressure. This movement makes many of the pins fall into place. A tension wrench is also put in to hold the pins that pop into the right place. If

Lock Strengths

Basically, three grades of locks are available:

- **Grade 1**   Commercial and industrial use
- **Grade 2**   Heavy-duty residential/light-duty commercial
- **Grade 3**   Residential/consumer expendable (that is, "throwaway" locks)

The cylinders within the locks fall into three main categories:

- **Low security**   No pick or drill resistance provided (can fall within any of the three grades of locks)
- **Medium security**   A degree of pick resistance protection provided (uses tighter and more complex keyways [notch combination]; can fall within any of the three grades of locks)
- **High security**   Pick resistance protection through many different mechanisms (only used in grade 1 and 2 locks)

all the pins do not slide to the necessary height for the lock to open, the intruder holds the tension wrench and uses a thinner pick to move the rest of the pins into place.

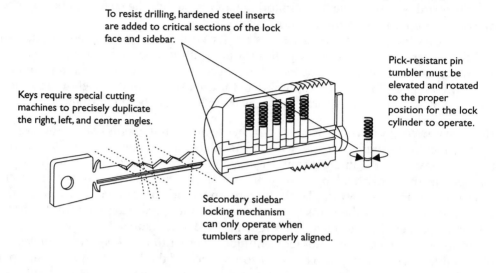

To resist drilling, hardened steel inserts are added to critical sections of the lock face and sidebar.

Pick-resistant pin tumbler must be elevated and rotated to the proper position for the lock cylinder to operate.

Keys require special cutting machines to precisely duplicate the right, left, and center angles.

Secondary sidebar locking mechanism can only operate when tumblers are properly aligned.

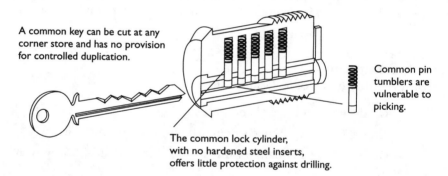

A common key can be cut at any corner store and has no provision for controlled duplication.

Common pin tumblers are vulnerable to picking.

The common lock cylinder, with no hardened steel inserts, offers little protection against drilling.

Lock bumping is a tactic that intruders can use to force the pins in a tumbler lock to their open position by using a special key called a bump key. The stronger the material that makes up the lock, the smaller the chance that this type of lock attack would be successful.

Now, if this is all too much trouble for the intruder, she can just drill the lock, use bolt cutters, attempt to break through the door or the doorframe, or remove the hinges. There are just so many choices for the bad guys.

Personnel Access Controls

Proper identification needs to verify whether the person attempting to access a facility or area should actually be allowed in. Identification and authentication can be verified by matching an anatomical attribute (biometric system), using smart or memory cards (swipe cards), presenting a photo ID to a security guard, using a key, or providing a card and entering a password or PIN.

A common problem with controlling authorized access into a facility or area is called *piggybacking*. This occurs when an individual gains unauthorized access by using someone else's legitimate credentials or access rights. Usually an individual just follows another person closely through a door without providing any credentials. The best preventive measures against piggybacking are to have security guards at access points and to educate employees about good security practices.

If a company wants to use a card badge reader, it has several types of systems to choose from. Individuals usually have cards that have embedded magnetic strips that contain access information. The reader can just look for simple access information within the magnetic strip, or it can be connected to a more sophisticated system that scans the information, makes more complex access decisions, and logs badge IDs and access times.

If the card is a memory card, then the reader just pulls information from it and makes an access decision. If the card is a smart card, the individual may be required to enter a PIN or password, which the reader compares against the information held within the card or in an authentication server. (Memory and smart cards are covered in Chapter 4.)

These access cards can be used with *user-activated readers*, which just means the user actually has to do something—swipe the card or enter a PIN. *System sensing access control readers*, also called *proximity devices* or *transponders*, recognize the presence of an approaching object within a specific area. This type of system does not require the user to swipe the card through the reader. The reader sends out interrogating signals and obtains the access code from the card without the user having to do anything.

NOTE *Electronic access control (EAC) tokens* is a generic term used to describe proximity authentication devices, such as proximity readers, programmable locks, or biometric systems, which identify and authenticate users before allowing them entrance into physically controlled areas.

External Boundary Protection Mechanisms

Let's build a fort and let only the people who know the secret handshake inside!

Proximity protection components are usually put into place to provide one or more of the following services:

- Control pedestrian and vehicle traffic flows
- Various levels of protection for different security zones
- Buffers and delaying mechanisms to protect against forced entry attempts
- Limit and control entry points

These services can be provided by using the following control types:

- **Access control mechanisms** Locks and keys, an electronic card access system, personnel awareness
- **Physical barriers** Fences, gates, walls, doors, windows, protected vents, vehicular barriers

- **Intrusion detection** Perimeter sensors, interior sensors, annunciation mechanisms
- **Assessment** Guards, CCTV cameras
- **Response** Guards, local law enforcement agencies
- **Deterrents** Signs, lighting, environmental design

Several types of perimeter protection mechanisms and controls can be put into place to protect a company's facility, assets, and personnel. They can deter would-be intruders, detect intruders and unusual activities, and provide ways of dealing with these issues when they arise. Perimeter security controls can be natural (hills, rivers) or manmade (fencing, lighting, gates). Landscaping is a mix of the two. In the beginning of this chapter, we explored CPTED and how this approach is used to reduce the likelihood of crime. Landscaping is a tool employed in the CPTED method. Sidewalks, bushes, and created paths can point people to the correct entry points, and trees and spiky bushes can be used as natural barriers. These bushes and trees should be placed such that they cannot be used as ladders or accessories to gain unauthorized access to unapproved entry points. Also, there should not be an overwhelming number of trees and bushes, which could provide intruders with places to hide. In the following sections, we look at the manmade components that can work within the landscaping design.

Fencing

I just want a little fence to keep out all the little mean people.

Fencing can be quite an effective physical barrier. Although the presence of a fence may only delay dedicated intruders in their access attempts, it can work as a psychological deterrent by telling the world that your company is serious about protecting itself.

Fencing can provide crowd control and helps control access to entrances and facilities. However, fencing can be costly and unsightly. Many companies plant bushes or trees in front of the fence that surrounds their buildings for aesthetics and to make the building less noticeable. But this type of vegetation can damage the fencing over time or negatively affect its integrity. The fencing needs to be properly maintained, because if a company has a sagging, rusted, pathetic fence, it is equivalent to telling the world that the company is not truly serious and disciplined about protection. But a nice, shiny, intimidating fence can send a different message—especially if the fencing is topped with three rungs of barbed wire.

When deciding upon the type of fencing, several factors should be considered. The gauge of the metal should correlate to the types of physical threats the company would most likely face. After carrying out the risk analysis (covered earlier in the chapter), the physical security team should understand the probability of enemies attempting to cut the fencing, drive through it, or climb over or crawl under it. Understanding these threats will help the team determine the necessary gauge and mesh sizing of the fence wiring.

The risk analysis results will also help indicate what height of fencing the organization should implement. Fences come in varying heights, and each height provides a different level of security:

- Fences *three to four feet high* only deter casual trespassers.

- Fences *six to seven feet high* are considered too high to climb easily.

- Fences *eight feet high* (possibly with strands of barbed or razor wire at the top) means you are serious about protecting your property. They often deter the more determined intruder.

The barbed wire on top of fences can be tilted in or out, which also provides extra protection. If the organization is a prison, it would have the barbed wire on top of the fencing pointed in, which makes it harder for prisoners to climb and escape. If the organization is a military base, the barbed wire would be tilted out, making it harder for someone to climb over the fence and gain access to the premises.

Critical areas should have fences at least eight feet high to provide the proper level of protection. The fencing should not sag in any areas and must be taut and securely connected to the posts. The fencing should not be easily circumvented by pulling up its posts. The posts should be buried sufficiently deep in the ground and should be secured with concrete to ensure the posts cannot be dug up or tied to vehicles and extracted. If the ground is soft or uneven, this might provide ways for intruders to slip or dig under the fence. In these situations, the fencing should actually extend into the dirt to thwart these types of attacks.

Fences work as "first line of defense" mechanisms. A few other controls can be used also. Strong and secure gates need to be implemented. It does no good to install a highly fortified and expensive fence and then have an unlocked or weenie gate that allows easy access.

Gauges and Mesh Sizes

The gauge of fence wiring is the thickness of the wires used within the fence mesh. The lower the gauge number, the larger the wire diameter:

- **11 gauge** = 0.0907-inch diameter

- **9 gauge** = 0.1144-inch diameter

- **6 gauge** = 0.162-inch diameter

The mesh sizing is the minimum clear distance between the wires. Common mesh sizes are 2 inches, 1 inch, and 3/8 inch. It is more difficult to climb or cut fencing with smaller mesh sizes, and the heavier gauged wiring is harder to cut. The following list indicates the strength levels of the most common gauge and mesh sizes used in chain-link fencing today:

- **Extremely high security**   3/8-inch mesh, 11 gauge

- **Very high security**   1-inch mesh, 9 gauge

- **High security**   1-inch mesh, 11 gauge

- **Greater security**   2-inch mesh, 6 gauge

- **Normal industrial security**   2-inch mesh, 9 gauge

PIDAS Fencing

Perimeter Intrusion Detection and Assessment System (PIDAS) is a type of fencing that has sensors located on the wire mesh and at the base of the fence. It is used to detect if someone attempts to cut or climb the fence. It has a passive cable vibration sensor that sets off an alarm if an intrusion is detected. PIDAS is very sensitive and can cause many false alarms.

Gates basically have four distinct classifications:

- **Class I**   Residential usage.

- **Class II**   Commercial usage, where general public access is expected; examples include a public parking lot entrance, a gated community, or a self-storage facility.

- **Class III**   Industrial usage, where limited access is expected; an example is a warehouse property entrance not intended to serve the general public.

- **Class IV**   Restricted access; this includes a prison entrance that is monitored either in person or via closed circuitry.

Each gate classification has its own long list of implementation and maintenance guidelines in order to ensure the necessary level of protection. These classifications and guidelines are developed by Underwriters Laboratory (UL), a nonprofit organization that tests, inspects, and classifies electronic devices, fire protection equipment, and specific construction materials. This is the group that certifies these different items to ensure they are in compliance with national building codes. Their specific code, UL-325, deals with garage doors, drapery, gates, and louver and window operators and systems.

So, whereas in the information security world we look to NIST for our best practices and industry standards, in the physical security world, we look to UL for the same type of direction.

 NOTE   UL standards can be found at www.ul.com. A good introduction to the UL-325 standard, which deals with gates, can be found at www.abrpaint .com/services/GatesFencing/ul325intro.htm.

Bollards

Bollards usually look like small concrete pillars outside a building. Sometimes companies try to dress them up by putting flowers or lights in them to soften the look of a protected environment. They are placed by the sides of buildings that have the most immediate threat of someone driving a vehicle through the exterior wall. They are usually placed between the facility and a parking lot and/or between the facility and a road that runs close to an exterior wall. Within the United States after September 11, 2001, many military and government institutions, which did not have bollards, hauled in huge boulders to surround and protect sensitive buildings. They provided the same type of protection that bollards would provide. These were not overly attractive, but provided the sense that the government was serious about protecting those facilities.

Lighting

Many of the items mentioned in this chapter are things people take for granted day in and day out during our usual busy lives. Lighting is certainly one of those items you would probably not give much thought to, unless it wasn't there. Unlit (or improperly lit) parking lots and parking garages have invited many attackers to carry out criminal activity that they may not have engaged in otherwise with proper lighting. Breaking into cars, stealing cars, and attacking employees as they leave the office are the more common types of attacks that take place in such situations. A security professional should understand that the right illumination needs to be in place, that no dead spots (unlit areas) should exist between the lights, and that all areas where individuals may walk should be properly lit. A security professional should also understand the various types of lighting available and where they should be used.

Wherever an array of lights is used, each light covers its own zone or area. The zone each light covers depends upon the illumination of light produced, which usually has a direct relationship to the wattage capacity of the bulbs. In most cases, the higher the lamp's wattage, the more illumination it produces. It is important that the zones of illumination coverage overlap. For example, if a company has an open parking lot, then light poles must be positioned within the correct distance of each other to eliminate any dead spots. If the lamps that will be used provide a 30-foot radius of illumination, then the light poles should be erected less than 30 feet apart so there is an overlap between the areas of illumination.

NOTE Critical areas need to have illumination that reaches at least eight feet with the illumination of two foot-candles.

If an organization does not implement the right types of lights and ensure they provide proper coverage, it increases the probability of criminal activity, accidents, and lawsuits.

Exterior lights that provide protection usually require less illumination intensity than interior working lighting, except for areas that require security personnel to inspect identification credentials for authorization. It is also important to have the correct lighting when using various types of surveillance equipment. The correct contrast between a potential intruder and background items needs to be provided, which only happens with the correct illumination and placement of lights. If the light is going to bounce off of dark, dirty, or darkly painted surfaces, then more illumination is required for the necessary contrast between people and the environment. If the area has clean concrete and light-colored painted surfaces, then not as much illumination is required. This is because when the same amount of light falls on an object and the surrounding background, an observer must depend on the contrast to tell them apart.

When lighting is installed, it should be directed toward areas where potential intruders would most likely be coming from and directed away from the security force posts. For example, lighting should be pointed at gates or exterior access points, and the guard locations should be more in the shadows, or under a lower amount of illumination. This is referred to as *glare protection* for the security force. If you are familiar with military operations, you might know that when you are approaching a military entry point, there is a fortified guard building with lights pointing toward the oncoming cars. A large sign instructs you to turn off your headlights, so the guards are not temporarily blinded by your lights and have a clear view of anything coming their way.

Lights used within the organization's security perimeter should be directed outward, which keeps the security personnel in relative darkness and allows them to easily view intruders beyond the company's perimeter.

An array of lights that provides an even amount of illumination across an area is usually referred to as *continuous lighting*. Examples are the evenly spaced light poles in a parking lot, light fixtures that run across the outside of a building, or series of fluorescent lights used in parking garages. If the company building is relatively close to another company's property, a railway, an airport, or a highway, the owner may need to ensure the lighting does not "bleed over" property lines in an obtrusive manner. Thus, the illumination needs to be *controlled*, which just means an organization should erect lights and use illumination in such a way that does not blind its neighbors or any passing cars, trains, or planes.

You probably are familiar with the special home lighting gadgets that turn certain lights on and off at predetermined times, giving the illusion to potential burglars that a house is occupied even when the residents are away. Companies can use a similar technology, which is referred to as *standby lighting*. The security personnel can configure the times that different lights turn on and off, so potential intruders think different areas of the facility are populated.

 NOTE Redundant or backup lights should be available in case of power failures or emergencies. Special care must be given to understand what type of lighting is needed in different parts of the facility in these types of situations. This lighting may run on generators or battery packs.

Responsive area illumination takes place when an IDS detects suspicious activities and turns on the lights within a specific area. When this type of technology is plugged into automated IDS products, there is a high likelihood of false alarms. Instead of continuously having to dispatch a security guard to check out these issues, a CCTV camera can be installed to scan the area for intruders.

If intruders want to disrupt the security personnel or decrease the probability of being seen while attempting to enter a company's premises or building, they could attempt to turn off the lights or cut power to them. This is why lighting controls and switches should be in protected, locked, and centralized areas.

Surveillance Devices

Usually, installing fences and lights does not provide the necessary level of protection a company needs to protect its facility, equipment, and employees. Areas need to be under surveillance so improper actions are noticed and taken care of before damage occurs. Surveillance can happen through visual detection or through devices that use sophisticated means of detecting abnormal behavior or unwanted conditions. It is important that every organization have a proper mix of lighting, security personnel, IDSs, and surveillance technologies and techniques.

Visual Recording Devices

Because surveillance is based on sensory perception, surveillance devices usually work in conjunction with guards and other monitoring mechanisms to extend their capabilities and range of perception. A *closed-circuit TV (CCTV)* system is a commonly used monitoring device in most organizations, but before purchasing and implementing a CCTV, you need to consider several items:

- **The purpose of CCTV** To detect, assess, and/or identify intruders
- **The type of environment the CCTV camera will work in** Internal or external areas
- **The field of view required** Large or small area to be monitored
- **Amount of illumination of the environment** Lit areas, unlit areas, areas affected by sunlight
- **Integration with other security controls** Guards, IDSs, alarm systems

The reason you need to consider these items before you purchase a CCTV product is that there are so many different types of cameras, lenses, and monitors that make up the different CCTV products. You must understand what is expected of this physical security control, so that you purchase and implement the right type.

CCTVs are made up of cameras, transmitters, receivers, a recording system, and a monitor. The camera captures the data and transmits it to a receiver, which allows the data to be displayed on a monitor. The data are recorded so they can be reviewed at a later time if needed. Figure 6-20 shows how multiple cameras can be connected to one multiplexer, which allows several different areas to be monitored at one time. The multiplexer accepts video feed from all the cameras and interleaves these transmissions over one line to the central monitor. This is more effective and efficient than the older systems that require the security guard to physically flip a switch from one environment to the next. In these older systems, the guard can view only one environment at a time, which of course makes it more likely that suspicious activities will be missed.

A CCTV sends the captured data from the camera's transmitter to the monitor's receiver, usually through a coaxial cable, instead of broadcasting the signals over a public network. This is where the term "closed-circuit" comes in. This circuit should be tamperproof, which means an intruder cannot manipulate the video feed that the security guard is monitoring. The most common type of attack is to replay previous recordings without the security personnel knowing it. For example, if an attacker is able to compromise a company's CCTV and play the recording from the day before, the security guard would not know an intruder is in the facility carrying out some type of crime. This is one reason why CCTVs should be used in conjunction with intruder detection controls, which we address in the next section.

NOTE CCTVs should have some type of recording system. Digital recorders save images to hard drives and allow advanced search techniques that are not possible with videotape recorders. Digital recorders use advanced compression techniques, which drastically reduce the storage media requirements.

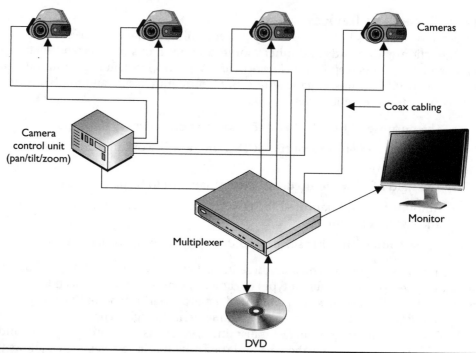

Figure 6-20   Several cameras can be connected to a multiplexer.

Most of the CCTV cameras in use today employ light-sensitive chips called *charged-coupled devices (CCDs)*. The CCD is an electrical circuit that receives input light from the lens and converts it into an electronic signal, which is then displayed on the monitor. Images are focused through a lens onto the CCD chip surface, which forms the electrical representation of the optical image. It is this technology that allows for the capture of extraordinary detail of objects and precise representation, because it has sensors that work in the infrared range, which extends beyond human perception. The CCD sensor picks up this extra "data" and integrates it into the images shown on the monitor to allow for better granularity and quality in the video.

CCDs are also used in fax machines, photocopiers, bar code readers, and even telescopes. CCTVs that use CCDs allow more granular information within an environment to be captured and shown on the monitor compared to the older CCTV technology that relied upon cathode ray tubes (CRTs).

Two main types of lenses are used in CCTV: fixed focal length and zoom (varifocal). The *focal length* of a lens defines its effectiveness in viewing objects from a horizontal and vertical view. The focal length value relates to the angle of view that can be achieved. Short focal length lenses provide wider-angle views, while long focal length lenses provide a narrower view. The size of the images shown on a monitor, along with the area covered by one camera, is defined by the focal length. For example, if a company implements a CCTV camera in a warehouse, the focal length lens values should be between 2.8 and 4.3 millimeters (mm) so the whole area can be captured. If the company implements another CCTV camera that monitors an entrance, that lens value should be around 8mm, which allows a smaller area to be monitored.

NOTE   Fixed focal length lenses are available in various fields of views: wide, medium, and narrow. A lens that provides a "normal" focal length creates a picture that approximates the field of view of the human eye. A wide-angle lens has a short focal length, and a telephoto lens has a long focal length. When a company selects a fixed focal length lens for a particular view of an environment, it should understand that if the field of view needs to be changed (wide to narrow), the lens must be changed.

So, if we need to monitor a large area, we use a lens with a smaller focal length value. Great, but what if a security guard hears a noise or thinks he sees something suspicious? A fixed focal length lens is stationary, meaning the guard cannot move the camera from one point to the other and properly focus the lens automatically. The *zoom* lenses provide flexibility by allowing the viewer to change the field of view to different angles and distances. The security personnel usually have a remote-control component integrated within the centralized CCTV monitoring area that allows them to move the cameras and zoom in and out on objects as needed. When both wide scenes and close-up captures are needed, a zoom lens is best. This type of lens allows the focal length to change from wide angle to telephoto while maintaining the focus of the image.

To understand the next characteristic, depth of field, think about pictures you might take while on vacation with your family. For example, if you want to take a picture of your spouse with the Grand Canyon in the background, the main object of the picture is your spouse. Your camera is going to zoom in and use a *shallow depth of focus*. This provides a softer backdrop, which will lead the viewers of the photograph to the foreground, which is your spouse. Now, let's say you get tired of taking pictures of your spouse and want to get a scenic picture of just the Grand Canyon itself. The camera would use a *greater depth of focus*, so there is not such a distinction between objects in the foreground and background.

The depth of field is necessary to understand when choosing the correct lenses and configurations for your company's CCTV. The **depth of field** refers to the portion of the environment that is in focus when shown on the monitor. The depth of field varies depending upon the size of the lens opening, the distance of the object being focused on, and the focal length of the lens. The depth of field increases as the size of the lens opening decreases, the subject distance increases, or the focal length of the lens decreases. So, if you want to cover a large area and not focus on specific items, it is best to use a wide-angle lens and a small lens opening.

CCTV lenses have *irises*, which control the amount of light that enters the lens. *Manual iris lenses* have a ring around the CCTV lens that can be manually turned and controlled. A lens with a manual iris would be used in areas that have fixed lighting, since the iris cannot self-adjust to changes of light. An **auto iris lens** should be used in environments where the light changes, as in an outdoor setting. As the environment brightens, this is sensed by the iris, which automatically adjusts itself. Security personnel will configure the CCTV to have a specific fixed exposure value, which the iris is responsible for maintaining. On a sunny day, the iris lens closes to reduce the amount of light entering the camera, while at night, the iris opens to capture more light—just like our eyes.

When choosing the right CCTV for the right environment, you must determine the amount of light present in the environment. Different CCTV camera and lens products have specific illumination requirements to ensure the best quality images possible. The illumination requirements are usually represented in the *lux* value, which is a metric used to represent illumination strengths. The illumination can be measured by using a light meter. The intensity of light (illumination) is measured and represented in measurement units of lux or foot-candles. (The conversion between the two is one foot-candle = 10.76 lux.) The illumination measurement is not something that can be accurately provided by the vendor of a light bulb, because the environment can directly affect the illumination. This is why illumination strengths are most effectively measured where the light source is implemented.

Next, you need to consider the mounting requirements of the CCTV cameras. The cameras can be implemented in a *fixed mounting* or in a mounting that allows the cameras to move when necessary. A fixed camera cannot move in response to security personnel commands, whereas cameras that provide *PTZ capabilities* can pan, tilt, or zoom as necessary.

So, buying and implementing a CCTV system may not be as straightforward as it seems. As a security professional, you would need to understand the intended use of the CCTV, the environment that will be monitored, and the functionalities that will be required by the security staff that will use the CCTV on a daily basis. The different components that can make up a CCTV product are shown in Figure 6-21.

Great—your assessment team has done all of its research and bought and implemented the correct CCTV system. Now it would be nice if someone actually watched the monitors for suspicious activities. Realizing that monitor watching is a mentally deadening activity may lead your team to implement a type of *annunciator system*. Different types of annunciator products are available that can either "listen" for noise and activate electrical devices, such as lights, sirens, or CCTV cameras, or detect movement. Instead of expecting a security guard to stare at a CCTV monitor for eight hours straight, the guard can carry out other activities and be alerted by an annunciator if movement is detected on a screen.

Intrusion Detection Systems

Surveillance techniques are used to watch for unusual behaviors, whereas intrusion detection devices are used to sense changes that take place in an environment. Both are monitoring methods, but they use different devices and approaches. This section addresses the types of technologies that can be used to detect the presence of an intruder. One such machine, a perimeter scanning device, is shown in Figure 6-22.

IDSs are used to detect unauthorized entries and to alert a responsible entity to respond. These systems can monitor entries, doors, windows, devices, or removable coverings of equipment. Many work with magnetic contacts or vibration-detection devices that are sensitive to certain types of changes in the environment. When a change is detected, the IDS device sounds an alarm either in the local area, or in both the local area and a remote police or guard station.

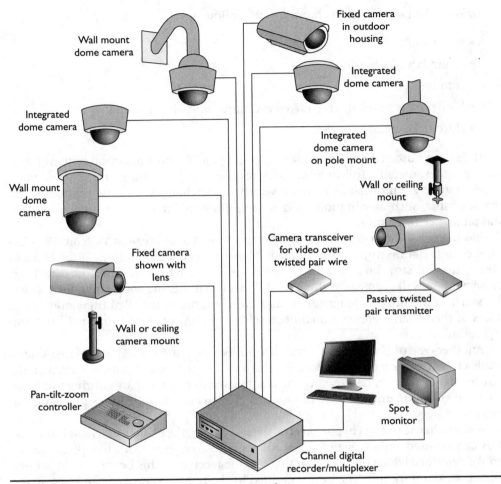

Figure 6-21 A CCTV product can comprise several components.

Figure 6-22
Different perimeter
scanning devices
work by covering a
specific area.

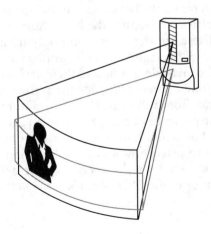

IDSs can be used to detect changes in the following:

- Beams of light
- Sounds and vibrations
- Motion
- Different types of fields (microwave, ultrasonic, electrostatic)
- Electrical circuit

IDSs can be used to detect intruders by employing electromechanical systems (magnetic switches, metallic foil in windows, pressure mats) or volumetric systems. Volumetric systems are more sensitive because they detect changes in subtle environmental characteristics, such as vibration, microwaves, ultrasonic frequencies, infrared values, and photoelectric changes.

Electromechanical systems work by detecting a change or break in a circuit. The electrical circuits can be strips of foil embedded or connected to windows. If the window breaks, the foil strip breaks, which sounds an alarm. Vibration detectors can detect movement on walls, screens, ceilings, and floors when the fine wires embedded within the structure are broken. Magnetic contact switches can be installed on windows and doors. If the contacts are separated because the window or door is opened, an alarm will sound.

Another type of electromechanical detector is a pressure pad. This is placed underneath a rug or portion of the carpet and is activated after hours. If someone steps on the pad, an alarm initiates, because no one is supposed to be in this area during this time.

Types of volumetric IDSs are photoelectric, acoustical-seismic, ultrasonic, and microwave.

A *photoelectric system* (or *photometric system*) detects the change in a light beam and thus can be used only in windowless rooms. These systems work like photoelectric smoke detectors, which emit a beam that hits the receiver. If this beam of light is interrupted, an alarm sounds. The beams emitted by the photoelectric cell can be cross-sectional and can be invisible or visible beams. *Cross-sectional* means that one area can have several different light beams extending across it, which is usually carried out by using hidden mirrors to bounce the beam from one place to another until it hits the light receiver. These are the most commonly used systems in the movies. You have probably seen James Bond and other noteworthy movie spies or criminals use night-vision goggles to see the invisible beams and then step over them.

A *passive infrared system (PIR)* identifies the changes of heat waves in an area it is configured to monitor. If the particles' temperature within the air rises, it could be an indication of the presence of an intruder, so an alarm is sounded.

An *acoustical detection system* uses microphones installed on floors, walls, or ceilings. The goal is to detect any sound made during a forced entry. Although these systems are easily installed, they are very sensitive and cannot be used in areas open to sounds of storms or traffic. *Vibration sensors* are very similar and are also implemented to detect forced entry. Financial institutions may choose to implement these types of sensors on exterior walls, where bank robbers may attempt to drive a vehicle through. They are also commonly used around the ceiling and flooring of vaults to detect someone trying to make an unauthorized bank withdrawal.

Wave-pattern motion detectors differ in the frequency of the waves they monitor. The different frequencies are microwave, ultrasonic, and low frequency. All of these devices generate a wave pattern that is sent over a sensitive area and reflected back to a receiver. If the pattern is returned undisturbed, the device does nothing. If the pattern returns altered, because something in the room is moving, an alarm sounds.

A *proximity detector*, or *capacitance detector*, emits a measurable magnetic field. The detector monitors this magnetic field, and an alarm sounds if the field is disrupted. These devices are usually used to protect specific objects (artwork, cabinets, or a safe) versus protecting a whole room or area. Capacitance change in an electrostatic field can be used to catch a bad guy, but first you need to understand what capacitance change means. An electrostatic IDS creates an electrostatic magnetic field, which is just an electric field associated with static electric charges. All objects have a static electric charge. They are all made up of many subatomic particles, and when everything is stable and static, these particles constitute one holistic electric charge. This means there is a balance between the electric capacitance and inductance. Now, if an intruder enters the area, his subatomic particles will mess up this lovely balance in the electrostatic field, causing a capacitance change, and an alarm will sound. So if you want to rob a company that uses these types of detectors, leave the subatomic particles that make up your body at home.

The type of motion detector that a company chooses to implement, its power capacity, and its configurations dictate the number of detectors needed to cover a sensitive area. Also, the size and shape of the room and the items within the room may cause barriers, in which case more detectors would be needed to provide the necessary level of coverage.

Intrusion Detection Systems Characteristics

IDSs are very valuable controls to use in every physical security program, but several issues need to be understood before their implementation.

- They are expensive and require human intervention to respond to the alarms.
- A redundant power supply and emergency backup power are necessary.
- They can be linked to a centralized security system.
- They should have a fail-safe configuration, which defaults to "activated."
- They should detect, and be resistant to, tampering.

IDSs are support mechanisms intended to detect and announce an attempted intrusion. They will not prevent or apprehend intruders, so they should be seen as an aid to the organization's security forces.

Patrol Force and Guards

One of the best security mechanisms is a security guard and/or a patrol force to monitor a facility's grounds. This type of security control is more flexible than other security mechanisms, provides good response to suspicious activities, and works as a great deterrent. However, it can be a costly endeavor, because it requires a salary, benefits, and time off. People sometimes are unreliable. Screening and bonding is an important part of selecting a security guard, but this only provides a certain level of assurance. One issue is if the security guard decides to make exceptions for people who do not follow the organization's approved policies. Because basic human nature is to trust and help people, a seemingly innocent favor can put an organization at risk.

IDSs and physical protection measures ultimately require human intervention. Security guards can be at a fixed post or can patrol specific areas. Different organizations will have different needs from security guards. They may be required to check individual credentials and enforce filling out a sign-in log. They may be responsible for monitoring IDSs and expected to respond to alarms. They may need to issue and recover visitor badges, respond to fire alarms, enforce rules established by the company within the building, and control what materials can come into or go out of the environment. The guard may need to verify that doors, windows, safes, and vaults are secured; report identified safety hazards; enforce restrictions of sensitive areas; and escort individuals throughout facilities.

The security guard should have clear and decisive tasks that she is expected to fulfill. The guard should be fully trained on the activities she is expected to perform and on the responses expected from her in different situations. She should also have a central control point to check in to, two-way radios to ensure proper communication, and the necessary access into areas she is responsible for protecting.

The best security has a combination of security mechanisms and does not depend on just one component of security. Thus, a security guard should be accompanied by other surveillance and detection mechanisms.

Dogs

Dogs have proven to be highly useful in detecting intruders and other unwanted conditions. Their hearing and sight outperform those of humans, and their intelligence and loyalty can be used for protection.

The best security dogs go through intensive training to respond to a wide range of commands and to perform many tasks. Dogs can be trained to hold an intruder at bay until security personnel arrive or to chase an intruder and attack. Some dogs are trained to smell smoke so they can alert others to a fire.

Of course, dogs cannot always know the difference between an authorized person and an unauthorized person, so if an employee goes into work after hours, he can have more on his hands than expected. Dogs can provide a good supplementary security mechanism, or a company can ask the security guard to bare his teeth at the sight of an unknown individual instead. Whatever works.

Auditing Physical Access

Physical access control systems can use software and auditing features to produce audit trails or access logs pertaining to access attempts. The following information should be logged and reviewed:

- The date and time of the access attempt
- The entry point at which access was attempted
- The user ID employed when access was attempted
- Any unsuccessful access attempts, especially if during unauthorized hours

As with audit logs produced by computers, access logs are useless unless someone actually reviews them. A security guard may be required to review these logs, but a security professional or a facility manager should also review these logs periodically. Management needs to know where entry points into the facility exist and who attempts to use them.

Audit and access logs are detective, not preventive. They are used to piece together a situation after the fact instead of attempting to prevent an access attempt in the first place.

Testing and Drills

Having fire detectors, portable extinguishers, and suppressions agents is great, but people also need to be properly trained on what to do when a fire (or other type of emergency) takes place. An evacuation and emergency response plan must be developed and actually put into action. The plan needs to be documented and to be easily accessible in times of crisis. People who are assigned specific tasks must be taught and informed how to fulfill those tasks, and dry runs must be done to walk people through different emergency situations. The drills should take place at least once a year, and the entire program should be continually updated and improved.

The tests and drills prepare personnel for what they may be faced with and provide a controlled environment to learn the tasks expected of them. These tests and drills also point out issues that may not have been previously thought about and addressed in the planning process.

The exercise should have a predetermined scenario that the company may indeed be faced with one day. Specific parameters and a scope of the exercise must be worked out before sounding the alarms. The team of testers must agree upon what exactly is getting tested and how to properly determine success or failure. The team must agree upon the timing and duration of the exercise, who will participate in the exercise, who will receive which assignments, and what steps should be taken. During evacuation, specific people should be given lists of employees that they are responsible for ensuring they have escaped the building. This is the only way the organization will know if someone is still left inside and who that person is.

- Tests and drills:
  - Prepare personnel.
  - Provide a controlled environment.
- Evacuation and emergency response plans:
  - Need to be developed.
  - Must be put into action.
  - Need to be documented.
  - Must be put in easily accessible places.
  - People must be assigned specific tasks.
  - People should be taught and informed how to fulfill those tasks.
- Drills should take place at least once a year.
- The entire program should be continually updated and improved.
- Agree upon parameters for drills and tests:
  - The timing and duration of the exercise
  - Who will participate in the exercise
  - Who will receive which assignments
  - What steps should be taken

Summary

Our distributed environments have put much more responsibility on the individual user, facility management, and administrative procedures and controls than in the old days. Physical security is not just the night guard who carries around a big flashlight. Now, security can be extremely technical, comes in many forms, and raises many liability and legal issues. Natural disasters, fires, floods, intruders, vandals, environmental issues, construction materials, and power supplies all need to be planned for and dealt with.

Every organization should develop, implement, and maintain a physical security program that contains the following control categories: deterrence, delay, detection, assessment, and response. It is up to the organization to determine its acceptable risk level and the specific controls required to fulfill the responsibility of each category.

Physical security is not often considered when people think of organizational security and company asset protection, but real threats and risks need to be addressed and planned for. Who cares if a hacker can get through an open port on the web server if the building is burning down?

Quick Tips

- Physical security is usually the first line of defense against environmental risks and unpredictable human behavior.

- Crime Prevention Through Environmental Design (CPTED) combines the physical environment and sociology issues that surround it to reduce crime rates and the fear of crime.

- The value of property within the facility and the value of the facility itself need to be ascertained to determine the proper budget for physical security so that security controls are cost-effective.

- Automated environmental controls help minimize the resulting damage and speed the recovery process. Manual controls can be time-consuming and error-prone, and require constant attention.

- Construction materials and structure composition need to be evaluated for their protective characteristics, their utility, and their costs and benefits.

- Some physical security controls may conflict with the safety of people. These issues need to be addressed; human life is always more important than protecting a facility or the assets it contains.

- When looking at locations for a facility, consider local crime, natural disaster possibilities, and distance to hospitals, police and fire stations, airports, and railroads.

- The HVAC system should maintain the appropriate temperature and humidity levels and provide closed-loop recirculating air-conditioning and positive pressurization and ventilation.

- High humidity can cause corrosion, and low humidity can cause static electricity.

- Dust and other air contaminants may adversely affect computer hardware, and should be kept to acceptable levels.

- Administrative controls include drills and exercises of emergency procedures, simulation testing, documentation, inspections and reports, prescreening of employees, post-employment procedures, delegation of responsibility and rotation of duties, and security-awareness training.

- Emergency procedure documentation should be readily available and periodically reviewed and updated.

- Proximity identification devices can be user-activated (action needs to be taken by a user) or system sensing (no action needs to be taken by the user).

- A transponder is a proximity identification device that does not require action by the user. The reader transmits signals to the device, and the device responds with an access code.

- Exterior fencing can be costly and unsightly, but can provide crowd control and help control access to the facility.
- If interior partitions do not go all the way up to the true ceiling, an intruder can remove a ceiling tile and climb over the partition into a critical portion of the facility.
- Intrusion detection devices include motion detectors, CCTVs, vibration sensors, and electromechanical devices.
- Intrusion detection devices can be penetrated, are expensive to install and monitor, require human response, and are subject to false alarms.
- CCTV enables one person to monitor a large area, but should be coupled with alerting functions to ensure proper response.
- Security guards are expensive but provide flexibility in response to security breaches and can deter intruders from attempting an attack.
- A cipher lock uses a keypad and is programmable.
- Company property should be marked as such, and security guards should be trained how to identify when these items leave the facility in an improper manner.
- Media should be protected from destruction, modification, theft, unauthorized copying, and disclosure.
- Floors, ceilings, and walls need to be able to hold the necessary load and provide the required fire rating.
- Water, steam, and gas lines need to have shutoff valves and positive drains (substance flows out instead of in).
- The threats to physical security are interruption of services, theft, physical damage, unauthorized disclosure, and loss of system integrity.
- The primary power source is what is used in day-to-day operations, and the alternate power source is a backup in case the primary source fails.
- Power companies usually plan and implement brownouts when they are experiencing high demand.
- Power noise is a disturbance of power and can be caused by electromagnetic interference (EMI) or radio frequency interference (RFI).
- EMI can be caused by lightning, motors, and the current difference between wires. RFI can be caused by electrical system mechanisms, fluorescent lighting, and electrical cables.
- Power transient noise is disturbance imposed on a power line that causes electrical interference.
- Power regulators condition the line to keep voltage steady and clean.
- UPS factors that should be reviewed are the size of the electrical load the UPS can support, the speed with which it can assume the load when the primary source fails, and the amount of time it can support the load.

- Shielded lines protect from electrical and magnetic induction, which causes interference to the power voltage.

- Perimeter protection is used to deter trespassing and to enable people to enter a facility through a few controlled entrances.

- Smoke detectors should be located on and above suspended ceilings, below raised floors, and in air ducts to provide maximum fire detection.

- A fire needs high temperatures, oxygen, and fuel. To suppress it, one or more of those items needs to be reduced or eliminated.

- Gases, like Halon, FM-200, and other Halon substitutes, interfere with the chemical reaction of a fire.

- The HVAC system should be turned off before activation of a fire suppressant to ensure it stays in the needed area and that smoke is not distributed to different areas of the facility.

- Portable fire extinguishers should be located within 50 feet of electrical equipment and should be inspected quarterly.

- CO_2 is a colorless, odorless, and potentially lethal substance because it removes the oxygen from the air in order to suppress fires.

- Piggybacking, when unauthorized access is achieved to a facility via another individual's legitimate access, is a common concern with physical security.

- Halon is no longer available because it depletes the ozone. FM-200 or other similar substances are used instead of halon.

- Proximity systems require human response, can cause false alarms, and depend on a constant power supply, so these protection systems should be backed up by other types of security systems.

- Dry pipe systems reduce the accidental discharge of water because the water does not enter the pipes until an automatic fire sensor indicates there is an actual fire.

- In locations with freezing temperatures where broken pipes cause problems, dry pipes should be used.

- A preaction pipe delays water release.

- CCTVs are best used in conjunction with other monitoring and intrusion alert methods.

Questions

Please remember that these questions are formatted and asked in a certain way for a reason. You must remember that the CISSP exam is asking questions at a conceptual level. Questions may not always have the perfect answer, and the candidate is advised against always looking for the perfect answer. The candidate should look for the best answer in the list.

1. What is the first step that should be taken when a fire has been detected?

   A. Turn off the HVAC system and activate fire door releases.

   B. Determine which type of fire it is.

   C. Advise individuals within the building to leave.

   D. Activate the fire suppression system.

2. A company needs to implement a CCTV system that will monitor a large area outside the facility. Which of the following is the correct lens combination for this?

   A. A wide-angle lens and a small lens opening

   B. A wide-angle lens and a large lens opening

   C. A wide-angle lens and a large lens opening with a small focal length

   D. A wide-angle lens and a large lens opening with a large focal length

3. When should a Class C fire extinguisher be used instead of a Class A fire extinguisher?

   A. When electrical equipment is on fire

   B. When wood and paper are on fire

   C. When a combustible liquid is on fire

   D. When the fire is in an open area

4. Which of the following is not a true statement about CCTV lenses?

   A. Lenses that have a manual iris should be used in outside monitoring.

   B. Zoom lenses will carry out focus functionality automatically.

   C. Depth of field increases as the size of the lens opening decreases.

   D. Depth of field increases as the focal length of the lens decreases.

5. How does Halon fight fires?

   A. It reduces the fire's fuel intake.

   B. It reduces the temperature of the area and cools the fire out.

   C. It disrupts the chemical reactions of a fire.

   D. It reduces the oxygen in the area.

6. What is a mantrap?

   A. A trusted security domain

   B. A logical access control mechanism

   C. A double-door facility used for physical access control

   D. A fire suppression device

7. What is true about a transponder?

    A. It is a card that can be read without sliding it through a card reader.

    B. It is a passive proximity device.

    C. It is a card that a user swipes through a card reader to gain access to a facility.

    D. It exchanges tokens with an authentication server.

8. When is a security guard the best choice for a physical access control mechanism?

    A. When discriminating judgment is required

    B. When intrusion detection is required

    C. When the security budget is low

    D. When access controls are in place

9. Which of the following is not a characteristic of an electrostatic intrusion detection system?

    A. It creates an electrostatic field and monitors for a capacitance change.

    B. It can be used as an intrusion detection system for large areas.

    C. It produces a balance between the electric capacitance and inductance of an object.

    D. It can detect if an intruder comes within a certain range of an object.

10. What is a common problem with vibration-detection devices used for perimeter security?

    A. They can be defeated by emitting the right electrical signals in the protected area.

    B. The power source is easily disabled.

    C. They cause false alarms.

    D. They interfere with computing devices.

11. Which of the following is an example of glare protection?

    A. Using automated iris lenses with short focal lengths

    B. Using standby lighting, which is produced by a CCTV camera

    C. Directing light toward entry points and away from a security force post

    D. Ensuring that the lighting system uses positive pressure

12. Which of the following is not a main component of CPTED?

    A. Natural access control

    B. Natural surveillance

    C. Territorial reinforcement

    D. Target hardening

13. Which problems may be caused by humidity in an area with electrical devices?

    A. High humidity causes excess electricity, and low humidity causes corrosion.

    B. High humidity causes corrosion, and low humidity causes static electricity.

    C. High humidity causes power fluctuations, and low humidity causes static electricity.

    D. High humidity causes corrosion, and low humidity causes power fluctuations.

14. What does positive pressurization pertaining to ventilation mean?

    A. When a door opens, the air comes in.

    B. When a fire takes place, the power supply is disabled.

    C. When a fire takes place, the smoke is diverted to one room.

    D. When a door opens, the air goes out.

15. Which of the following answers contains a category of controls that does not belong in a physical security program?

    A. Deterrence and delaying

    B. Response and detection

    C. Assessment and detection

    D. Delaying and lighting

16. Which is not an administrative control pertaining to emergency procedures?

    A. Intrusion detection systems

    B. Awareness and training

    C. Drills and inspections

    D. Delegation of duties

17. If an access control has a fail-safe characteristic but not a fail-secure characteristic, what does that mean?

    A. It defaults to no access.

    B. It defaults to being unlocked.

    C. It defaults to being locked.

    D. It defaults to sounding a remote alarm instead of a local alarm.

18. Which of the following is not considered a delaying mechanism?

    A. Locks

    B. Defense-in-depth measures

    C. Warning signs

    D. Access controls

19. What are the two general types of proximity identification devices?

    A. Biometric devices and access control devices

    B. Swipe card devices and passive devices

    C. Preset code devices and wireless devices

    D. User-activated devices and system sensing devices

20. Which of the following answers best describes the relationship between a risk analysis, acceptable risk level, baselines, countermeasures, and metrics?

    A. The risk analysis output is used to determine the proper countermeasures required. Baselines are derived to measure these countermeasures. Metrics are used to track countermeasure performance to ensure baselines are being met.

    B. The risk analysis output is used to help management understand and set an acceptable risk level. Baselines are derived from this level. Metrics are used to track countermeasure performance to ensure baselines are being met.

    C. The risk analysis output is used to help management understand and set baselines. An acceptable risk level is derived from these baselines. Metrics are used to track countermeasure performance to ensure baselines are being met.

    D. The risk analysis output is used to help management understand and set an acceptable risk level. Baselines are derived from the metrics. Metrics are used to track countermeasure performance to ensure baselines are being met.

21. Most of today's CCTV systems use charged-coupled devices. Which of the following is not a characteristic of these devices?

    A. Receives input through the lenses and converts them into an electronic signal

    B. Captures signals in the infrared range

    C. Provides better-quality images

    D. Records data on hard drives instead of tapes

22. Which is not a drawback to installing intrusion detection and monitoring systems?

    A. It's expensive to install.

    B. It cannot be penetrated.

    C. It requires human response.

    D. It's subject to false alarms.

23. What is a cipher lock?

    A. A lock that uses cryptographic keys

    B. A lock that uses a type of key that cannot be reproduced

    C. A lock that uses a token and perimeter reader

    D. A lock that uses a keypad

24. If a cipher lock has a door delay option, what does that mean?

    A. After a door is open for a specific period, the alarm goes off.

    B. It can only be opened during emergency situations.

    C. It has a hostage alarm capability.

    D. It has supervisory override capability.

25. Which of the following best describes the difference between a warded lock and a tumbler lock?

    A. A tumbler lock is more simplistic and easier to circumvent than a warded lock.

    B. A tumbler lock uses an internal bolt, and a warded lock uses internal cylinders.

    C. A tumbler lock has more components than a warded lock.

    D. A warded lock is mainly used externally, and a tumbler lock is used internally.

Answers

1. **C.** Human life takes precedence. Although the other answers are important steps in this type of situation, the first step is to warn others and save as many lives as possible.

2. **A.** The depth of field refers to the portion of the environment that is in focus when shown on the monitor. The depth of field varies depending upon the size of the lens opening, the distance of the object being focused on, and the focal length of the lens. The depth of field increases as the size of the lens opening decreases, the subject distance increases, or the focal length of the lens decreases. So if you want to cover a large area and not focus on specific items, it is best to use a wide-angle lens and a small lens opening.

3. **A.** A Class C fire is an electrical fire. Thus, an extinguisher with the proper suppression agent should be used. The following table shows the fire types, their attributes, and suppression methods:

Fire Class	Type of Fire	Elements of Fire	Suppression Method
A	Common combustibles	Wood products, paper, and laminates	Water, foam
B	Liquid	Petroleum products and coolants	Gas, CO_2, foam, dry powders
C	Electrical	Electrical equipment and wires	Gas, CO_2, dry powders
D	Combustible metals	Magnesium, sodium, potassium	Dry powder

4. **A.** Manual iris lenses have a ring around the CCTV lens that can be manually turned and controlled. A lens that has a manual iris would be used in an area that has fixed lighting, since the iris cannot self-adjust to changes of light. An auto iris lens should be used in environments where the light changes, such as an outdoor setting. As the environment brightens, this is sensed by the iris, which automatically adjusts itself. Security personnel will configure the CCTV to have a specific fixed exposure value, which the iris is responsible for maintaining. The other answers are true.

5. **C.** Halon is a type of gas used to interfere with the chemical reactions between the elements of a fire. A fire requires fuel, oxygen, high temperatures, and chemical reactions to burn properly. Different suppressant agents have been developed to attack each aspect of a fire: CO_2 displaces the oxygen, water reduces the temperature, and soda acid removes the fuel.

6. **C.** A mantrap is a small room with two doors. The first door is locked; a person is identified and authenticated by a security guard, biometric system, smart card reader, or swipe card reader. Once the person is authenticated and access is authorized, the first door opens and allows the person into the mantrap. The first door locks and the person is trapped. The person must be authenticated again before the second door unlocks and allows him or her into the facility.

7. **A.** A transponder is a type of physical access control device that does not require the user to slide a card through a reader. The reader and card communicate directly. The card and reader have a receiver, transmitter, and battery. The reader sends signals to the card to request information. The card sends the reader an access code.

8. **A.** Although many effective physical security mechanisms are on the market today, none can look at a situation, make a judgment about it, and decide what the next step should be. A security guard is employed when a company needs to have a countermeasure that can think and make decisions in different scenarios.

9. **B.** An electrostatic IDS creates an electrostatic field, which is just an electric field associated with static electric charges. The IDS creates a balanced electrostatic field between itself and the object being monitored. If an intruder comes within a certain range of the monitored object, there is capacitance change. The IDS can detect this change and sound an alarm.

10. **C.** This type of system is sensitive to sounds and vibrations and detects the changes in the noise level of an area it is placed within. This level of sensitivity can cause many false alarms. These devices do not emit any waves; they only listen for sounds within an area and are considered passive devices.

11. **C.** When lighting is installed, it should be directed toward areas where potential intruders would most likely be coming from, and directed away from the security force posts. For example, lighting should be pointed at gates or exterior access points, and the guard locations should be in the shadows, or under a lower amount of illumination. This is referred to as "glare protection" for the security force.

12. **D.** Natural access control is the use of the environment to control access to entry points, such as using landscaping and bollards. An example of natural surveillance is the construction of pedestrian walkways so there is a clear line of sight of all the activities in the surroundings. Territorial reinforcement gives people a sense of ownership of a property, giving them a greater tendency to protect it. These concepts are all parts of CPTED. Target hardening has to do with implementing locks, security guards, and proximity devices.

13. **B.** High humidity can cause corrosion, and low humidity can cause excessive static electricity. Static electricity can short-out devices or cause loss of information.

14. **D.** Positive pressurization means that when someone opens a door, the air goes out, and outside air does not come in. If a facility were on fire and the doors were opened, positive pressure would cause the smoke to go out instead of being pushed back into the building.

15. **D.** The categories of controls that should make up any physical security program are deterrence, delaying, detection, assessment, and response. Lighting is a control itself, not a category of controls.

16. **A.** Awareness and training, drills and inspections, and delegation of duties are all items that have a direct correlation to proper emergency procedures. It is management's responsibility to ensure that these items are in place, properly tested, and carried out. Intrusion detection systems are technical controls.

17. **B.** A fail-safe setting means that if a power disruption were to affect the automated locking system, the doors would default to being unlocked. A fail-secure configuration means a door would default to being locked if there were any problems with the power.

18. **C.** Every physical security program should have delaying mechanisms, which have the purpose of slowing down an intruder so security personnel can be

alerted and arrive at the scene. A warning sign is a deterrence control, not a delaying control.

19. **D.** A user-activated system requires the user to do something: swipe the card through the reader and/or enter a code. A system sensing device recognizes the presence of the card and communicates with it without the user needing to carry out any activity.

20. **B.** The physical security team needs to carry out a risk analysis, which will identify the organization's vulnerabilities, threats, and business impacts. The team should present these findings to management and work with them to define an acceptable risk level for the physical security program. From there, the team should develop baselines (minimum levels of security) and metrics to properly evaluate and determine whether the baselines are being met by the implemented countermeasures. Once the team identifies and implements the countermeasures, the countermeasures' performance should be continually evaluated and expressed in the previously created metrics. These performance values are compared against the set baselines. If the baselines are continually maintained, then the security program is successful because the company's acceptable risk level is not being exceeded.

21. **D.** The CCD is an electrical circuit that receives input light from the lens and converts it into an electronic signal, which is then displayed on the monitor. Images are focused through a lens onto the CCD chip surface, which forms the electrical representation of the optical image. This technology allows the capture of extraordinary details of objects and precise representation because it has sensors that work in the infrared range, which extends beyond human perception. The CCD sensor picks up this extra "data" and integrates it into the images shown on the monitor, to allow for better granularity and quality in the video. CCD does not record data.

22. **B.** Monitoring and intrusion detection systems are expensive, require someone to respond when they set off an alarm, and, because of their level of sensitivity, can cause several false alarms. Like any other type of technology or device, they have their own vulnerabilities that can be exploited and penetrated.

23. **D.** Cipher locks, also known as programmable locks, use keypads to control access into an area or facility. The lock can require a swipe card and a specific combination that's entered into the keypad.

24. **A.** A security guard would want to be alerted when a door has been open for an extended period. It may be an indication that something is taking place other than a person entering or exiting the door. A security system can have a threshold set so that if the door is open past this period, an alarm sounds.

25. **C.** The tumbler lock has more pieces and parts than a warded lock. The key fits into a cylinder, which raises the lock metal pieces to the correct height so the bolt can slide to the locked or unlocked position. A warded lock is easier to circumvent than a tumbler lock.

Telecommunications and Network Security

This chapter presents the following:

- OSI model
- TCP/IP and many other protocols
- LAN, WAN, MAN, intranet, and extranet technologies
- Cable types and data transmission types
- Network devices and services
- Communications security management
- Telecommunications devices
- Remote access methods and technologies
- Wireless technologies

Telecommunications and networking use various mechanisms, devices, software, and protocols that are interrelated and integrated. Networking is one of the more complex topics in the computer field, mainly because so many technologies and concepts are involved. A network administrator or engineer must know how to configure networking software, protocols and services, and devices; deal with interoperability issues; install, configure, and interface with telecommunications software and devices; and troubleshoot effectively. A security professional must understand these issues and be able to analyze them a few levels deeper to recognize fully where vulnerabilities can arise within networks. This can be an overwhelming and challenging task. However, if you are someone who enjoys challenges and appreciates the intricacies of technology, then maintaining security and networking infrastructures may be more fun than work.

As a security professional, you cannot advise others on how to secure an environment if you do not fully understand how to do so yourself. To secure an application that contains a buffer overflow, for example, you must understand what a buffer overflow is, what the outcome of the exploit is, how to identify a buffer overflow properly, and possibly how to write program code to remove this weakness from the program. To secure a network architecture, you must understand the various networking platforms involved, the network devices, and how data flows through a network. You must understand how various protocols work, their purposes, their interactions with other protocols, how they may provide exploitable vulnerabilities, and how to choose and implement the appropriate types of protocols in a given environment. You must also understand the different types of firewalls, routers, switches, and bridges, when one is more appropriate than the other, where they are to be placed, their interactions with other devices, and the degree of security each provides.

The many different types of devices, protocols, and security mechanisms within an environment provide different functionality, but they also provide a layered approach to security. Layers within security are important, so that if an attacker is able to bypass one layer, another layer stands in the way to protect the internal network. Many networks have routers, firewalls, intrusion detection systems (IDSs), antivirus software, and more. Each specializes in a certain piece of security, but they all should work in concert to provide a layered approach to security.

Although networking and telecommunications are complicated topics to understand, it is that complexity that makes it the most fun for those who truly enjoy these fields. However, complexity can be the enemy of security. It is important to understand the components within an environment and their relationships to other components that make up the environment as a whole. This chapter addresses several of the telecommunications and networking aspects included in many networks.

Telecommunications is the electrical transmission of data among systems, whether through analog, digital, or wireless transmission types. The data can flow across copper wires, coaxial cable, fiber, or airwaves, the telephone company's public-switched telephone network (PSTN), or a service provider's fiber cables, switches, and routers. Definitive lines exist between the media used for transmission, the technologies, the protocols, and whose equipment is being used. However, the definitive lines get blurry when one follows how data created on a user's workstation flows within seconds through a complex path of Ethernet cables, to a router that divides the company's network and the rest of the world, through the Asynchronous Transfer Mode (ATM) switch provided by the service provider, to the many switches the packets transverse throughout the ATM cloud, on to another company's network, through its router, and to another user's workstation. Each piece is interesting, but when they are all integrated and work together, it is awesome.

Telecommunications usually refers to telephone systems, service providers, and carrier services. Most telecommunications systems are regulated by governments and international organizations. In the United States, telecommunications systems are regulated by the Federal Communications Commission (FCC), which includes voice and data transmissions. In Canada, agreements are managed through Spectrum, Information Technologies and Telecommunications (SITT), Industry Canada. Globally, organizations develop policies, recommend standards, and work together to provide standardization and the capability for different technologies to properly interact.

The main standards organizations are the International Telecommunication Union (ITU) and the International Standards Organization (ISO). Their models and standards have shaped our technology today, and the technological issues governed by these organizations are addressed throughout this chapter.

NOTE Do not get overwhelmed with the size of this chapter and the amount of information within it. This chapter, as well as the others, attempts to teach you the concepts and meanings behind the definitions and answers you will need for the CISSP exam. This book is not intended to give you one-liners to remember for the exam, but rather it teaches you the meaning behind the answers. The "Quick Tips" section at the end of the chapter, as well as the questions, helps you zero in on the most important concepts for the exam itself.

Open Systems Interconnection Reference Model

I don't understand what all of these protocols are doing.
Response: Okay, let's make a model to explain it then.

ISO is a worldwide federation that works to provide international standards. In the early 1980s, ISO worked to develop a protocol set that would be used by all vendors throughout the world to allow the interconnection of network devices. This movement was fueled with the hopes of ensuring that all vendor products and technologies could communicate and interact across international and technical boundaries. The actual protocol set did not catch on as a standard, but the model of this protocol set, the OSI model, was adopted and is used as an abstract framework to which most operating systems and protocols adhere.

Many people think that the OSI reference model arrived at the beginning of the computing age as we know it and helped shape and provide direction for many, if not all, networking technologies. However, this is not true. In fact, it was introduced in 1984, at which time the basics of the Internet had already been developed and implemented, and the basic Internet protocols had been in use for many years. The Transmission Control Protocol/Internet Protocol (TCP/IP) suite actually has its own model that is often used today when examining and understanding networking issues. Figure 7-1 shows the differences between the OSI and TCP/IP networking models. In this chapter, we will focus more on the OSI model.

NOTE The host-to-host layer is sometimes called the transport layer in the TCP/IP model.

Protocol

A network *protocol* is a standard set of rules that determines how systems will communicate across networks. Two different systems that use the same protocol can communicate and understand each other despite their differences, similar to how two people can communicate and understand each other by using the same language.

The OSI reference model, as described by ISO Standard 7498, provides important guidelines used by vendors, engineers, developers, and others. The model segments the networking tasks, protocols, and services into different layers. Each layer has its own responsibilities regarding how two computers communicate over a network. Each layer

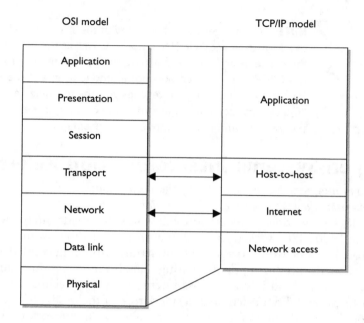

Figure 7-1
The OSI and TCP/IP
networking models

has certain functionalities, and the services and protocols that work within that layer fulfill them.

The OSI model's goal is to help others develop products that will work within an open network architecture. An *open network* architecture is one that no vendor owns, that is not proprietary, and that can easily integrate various technologies and vendor implementations of those technologies. Vendors have used the OSI model as a jumping-off point for developing their own networking frameworks. These vendors used the OSI model as a blueprint and developed their own protocols and interfaces to produce functionality that is different from, or overlaps, that of other vendors. However, because these vendors use the OSI model as their starting place, integration of other vendor products is an easier task, and the interoperability issues are less burdensome than if the vendors had developed their own networking framework from scratch.

Although computers communicate in a physical sense (electronic signals are passed from one computer over a wire to the other computer), they also communicate through logical channels. Each protocol at a specific OSI layer on one computer communicates with a corresponding protocol operating at the same OSI layer on another computer. This happens through *encapsulation*.

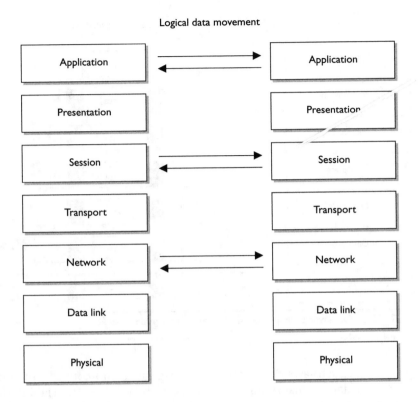

Logical data movement

Here's how encapsulation works: A message is constructed within a program on one computer and then passed down through the protocol's stack. A protocol at each layer adds its own information to the message; thus, the message grows in size as it goes down the protocol stack. The message is then sent to the destination computer, and the encapsulation is reversed by taking the packet apart through the same steps used by the source computer that encapsulated it. At the data link layer, only the information pertaining to the data link layer is extracted, and the message is sent up to the next layer. Then at the network layer, only the network layer data are stripped and processed and the packet is again passed up to the next layer, and so on. This is how computers communicate logically. The information stripped off at the destination computer informs it how to interpret and process the packet properly. Data encapsulation is shown in Figure 7-2.

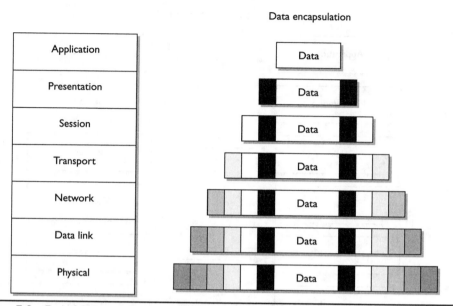

Figure 7-2 Each OSI layer adds its own information to the data packet.

A protocol at each layer has specific responsibilities and control functions it performs, as well as data format syntaxes it expects. Each layer has a special interface (connection point) that allows it to interact with three other layers: (1) communications from the interface of the layer above it, (2) communications to the interface of the layer below it, and (3) communications with the same layer in the interface of the target packet address. The control functions, added by the protocols at each layer, are in the form of headers and trailers of the packet.

The benefit of modularizing these layers, and the functionality within each layer, is that various technologies, protocols, and services can interact with each other and provide the proper interfaces to enable communications. This means a computer can use an application protocol developed by Novell, a transport protocol developed by Apple, and a data link protocol developed by IBM to construct and send a message over the network. The protocols, technologies, and computers that operate within the OSI model are considered *open systems*. Open systems are capable of communicating with other open systems because they implement international standard protocols and interfaces. The specification for each layer's interface is very structured, while the actual code that makes up the internal part of the software layer is not defined. This makes it easy for vendors to write plug-ins in a modularized manner. Systems are able to integrate the plug-ins into the network stack seamlessly, gaining the vendor-specific extensions and functions.

Understanding the functionalities that take place at each OSI layer and the corresponding protocols that work at those layers helps you understand the overall communication process between computers. Once you understand this process, a more detailed look at each protocol will show you the full range of options each protocol provides and the security weaknesses embedded into each of those options.

Application Layer

Hand me your information. I will take it from here.

The *application layer*, layer 7, works closest to the user and provides file transmissions, message exchanges, terminal sessions, and much more. This layer does not include the actual applications but rather the protocols that support the applications. When an application needs to send data over the network, it passes instructions and the data to the protocols that support it at the application layer. This layer processes and properly formats the data and passes the same down to the next layer within the OSI model. This happens until the data the application layer constructed contain the essential information from each layer necessary to transmit the data over the network. The data are then put on the network cable and are transmitted until they arrive at the destination computer.

Some examples of the protocols working at this layer are the Simple Mail Transfer Protocol (SMTP), Hypertext Transfer Protocol (HTTP), Line Printer Daemon (LPD), File Transfer Protocol (FTP), Telnet, and Trivial File Transfer Protocol (TFTP). Figure 7-3 shows how applications communicate with the underlying protocols through application programming interfaces (APIs). If a user makes a request to send an e-mail message through her e-mail client Outlook, the e-mail client sends this information to SMTP. SMTP adds its information to the user's information and passes it down to the presentation layer.

 NOTE The application layer in the TCP/IP architecture model is equivalent to a combination of the application, presentation, and session layers in the OSI model (refer to Figure 7-1).

Presentation Layer

You will now be transformed into something that everyone can understand.

The *presentation layer*, layer 6, receives information from the application layer protocols and puts it in a format all computers following the OSI model can understand. This layer provides a common means of representing data in a structure that can be

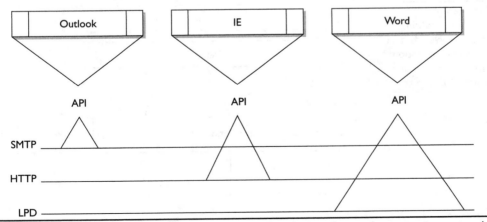

Figure 7-3 Applications send requests to an API, which is the interface to the supporting protocol.

properly processed by the end system. This means that when a user constructs a Word document and sends it out to several people, it does not matter whether the receiving computers have different word processing programs; each of these computers will be able to receive this file and understand and present it to its user as a document. It is the data representation processing that is done at the presentation layer that enables this to take place. For example, when a Windows XP computer receives a file from another computer system, information within the file's header explains what type of file it is. The Windows XP operating system has a list of file types it understands and a table describing what program should be used to open and manipulate each of these file types. For example, the sender could create a Word file in Word 2000, while the receiver uses Open Office. The receiver can open this file because the presentation layer on the sender's system converted the file to American Standard Code for Information Interchange (ASCII), and the receiver's computer knows it opens these types of files with its word processor, Open Office.

The presentation layer is not concerned with the meaning of data, but with the syntax and format of those data. It works as a translator, translating the format an application is using to a standard format used for passing messages over a network. If a user uses a Corel application to save a graphic, for example, the graphic could be a Tagged Image File Format (TIFF), Graphic Interchange Format (GIF), or Joint Photographic Experts Group (JPEG) format. The presentation layer adds information to tell the destination computer the file type and how to process and present it. This way, if the user sends this graphic to another user who does not have the Corel application, the user's operating system can still present the graphic because it has been saved into a standard format. Figure 7-4 illustrates the conversion of a file into different standard file types.

This layer also handles data compression and encryption issues. If a program requests a certain file to be compressed and encrypted before being transferred over the network, the presentation layer provides the necessary information for the destination computer. It includes instructions on the encryption or compression type used and

Figure 7-4
The presentation layer receives data from the application layer and puts it into a standard format.

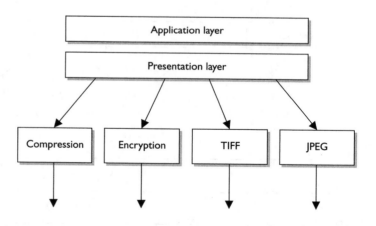

how to properly present it to the user. Instructions are added to the data package that tell the receiving system how to decrypt or decompress the data properly.

Session Layer

I don't want to talk to a computer. I want to talk to an application.

When two applications need to communicate, or transfer information, a connection session may need to be set up between them. The *session layer*, layer 5, is responsible for establishing a connection between the two applications, maintaining it during the transfer of data, and controlling the release of this connection. A good analogy for the functionality within this layer is a telephone conversation. When Kandy wants to call a friend, she uses the telephone. The telephone network circuitry and protocols set up the connection over the telephone lines and maintain that communication path, and when Kandy hangs up, they release all the resources they were using to keep that connection open.

Similar to how telephone circuitry works, the session layer works in three phases: connection establishment, data transfer, and connection release. It provides session restart and recovery if necessary and provides the overall maintenance of the session. When the conversation is over, this path is broken down and all parameters are set back to their original settings. This process is known as *dialog management*. Figure 7-5 depicts the three phases of a session. Some protocols that work at this layer are Network File System (NFS), Structured Query Language (SQL), NetBIOS, and remote procedure call (RPC).

Figure 7-5
The session layer sets up the connection, maintains it, and tears it down once communication is completed.

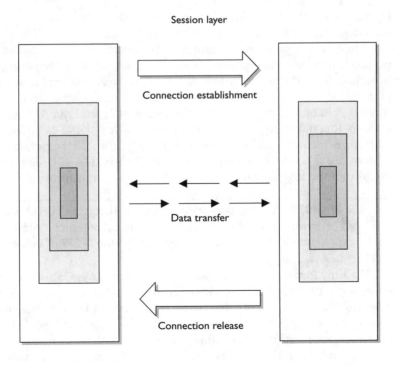

Session layer

Connection establishment

Data transfer

Connection release

The session layer protocol can enable communication between two applications to happen in three different modes:

- **Simplex**   Communication takes place in one direction.
- **Half-duplex**   Communication takes place in both directions, but only one application can send information at a time.
- **Full-duplex**   Communication takes place in both directions, and both applications can send information at the same time.

Many people have a hard time understanding the difference between what takes place at the session layer versus the transport layer, because their definitions sound similar. Session layer protocols control application-to-application communication, whereas the transport layer protocols handle computer-to-computer communication. For example, if you are using a product that is working in a client/server model, in reality you have a small piece of the product on your computer (client portion) and the larger piece of the software product is running on a different computer (server portion). The communication between these two pieces of the same software product needs to be controlled, which is why session layer protocols even exist. Session layer protocols take on the functionality of middleware, which allows software on two different computers to communicate. The next section will dive into the functionality of the transport layer protocols.

Transport Layer

How do I know if I lose a piece of the message?
Response: The transport layer will fix it for you.

When two computers are going to communicate through a connection-oriented protocol, they will first agree on how much information each computer will send at a time, how to verify the integrity of the data once received, and how to determine whether a packet was lost along the way. The two computers agree on these parameters through a handshaking process at the *transport layer*, layer 4. The agreement on these issues before transferring data helps provide more reliable data transfer, error detection, correction, recovery, and flow control, and it optimizes the network services needed to perform these tasks. The transport layer provides end-to-end data transport services and establishes the logical connection between two communicating computers.

 NOTE   Connection-oriented protocols, such as TCP, provide reliable data transmission when compared to connectionless protocols, such as UDP. This distinction is covered in more detail in the "TCP/IP" section, later in the chapter.

The functionality of the session and transport layers is similar insofar as they both set up some type of session or virtual connection for communication to take place. The difference is that protocols that work at the session layer set up connections between *applications,* whereas protocols that work at the transport layer set up connections between *computer systems.* For example, we can have three different applications on computer A communicating to three applications on computer B. The session layer protocols keep track of these different sessions. You can think of the transport layer protocol as the bus. It does not know or care what applications are communicating with each other. It just provides the mechanism to get the data from one system to another.

The transport layer receives data from many different applications and assembles the data into a stream to be properly transmitted over the network. The main protocols that work at this layer are TCP, User Datagram Protocol (UDP), and Sequenced Packet Exchange (SPX). Information is passed down from different entities at higher layers to the transport layer, which must assemble the information into a stream, as shown in Figure 7-6. The stream is made up of the various data segments passed to it. Just like a bus can carry a variety of people, the transport layer protocol can carry a variety of application data types. (The host-to-host, or transport, layer in the TCP/IP architecture model is equivalent to the transport layer in the OSI model. Refer to Figure 7-1.)

NOTE   Different references can place specific protocols at different layers. For example, many references place the Secure Sockets Layer (SSL) protocol in the session layer, while other references place it in the transport layer. It is not that one is right or wrong. The OSI model tries to draw boxes around reality, but some protocols straddle the different layers. SSL is made up of two protocols—one works in the lower portion of the session layer and the other works in the transport layer. For purposes of the CISSP exam, SSL resides in the transport layer.

Network Layer

Many roads lead to Rome.

The main responsibilities of the *network layer*, layer 3, are to insert information into the packet's header so it can be properly addressed and routed, and then to actually route the packets to their proper destination. In a network, many routes can lead to one destination. The protocols at the network layer must determine the best path for the packet to take. Routing protocols build and maintain their routing tables at this layer.

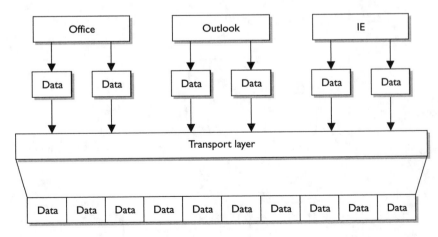

Figure 7-6   TCP formats data from applications into a stream to be prepared for transmission.

These tables are maps of the network, and when a packet must be sent from computer A to computer M, the protocols check the routing table, add the necessary information to the packet's header, and send it on its way.

The protocols that work at this layer do not ensure the delivery of the packets. They depend on the protocols at the transport layer to catch any problems and resend packets if necessary. IP is a common protocol working at the network layer, although other routing and routed protocols work there as well. Some of the other protocols are the Internet Control Message Protocol (ICMP), Routing Information Protocol (RIP), Open Shortest Path First (OSPF), Border Gateway Protocol (BGP), and Internet Group Management Protocol (IGMP). Figure 7-7 shows that a packet can take many routes and that the network layer enters routing information into the header to help the packet arrive at its destination. (The Internet layer in the TCP/IP architecture model is equivalent to the network layer in the OSI model. Refer to Figure 7-1.)

Data Link Layer

As we continue down the protocol stack, we are getting closer to the actual network wire over which all these data will travel. The outer format of the data packet changes slightly at each layer, and it comes to a point where it needs to be translated into local area network (LAN) or wide area network (WAN) technology binary format for proper line transmission. This happens at the *data link layer*, layer 2.

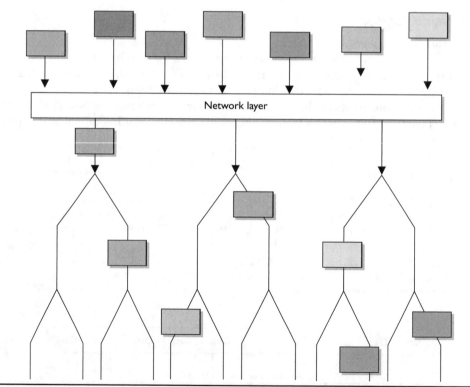

Figure 7-7 The network layer determines the most efficient path for each packet to take.

NOTE APSTNDP—To remember all the layers within the OSI model in the correct order, memorize "All People Seem To Need Data Processing." Remember that you are starting at layer 7, the application layer, at the top.

LAN and WAN technologies can use different protocols, network interface cards (NICs), cables, and transmission methods. Each of these technologies has different data format structures, and they interpret electricity voltages in different ways. The data link layer is where the network stack knows what format the data frame must be in to transmit properly over Token Ring, Ethernet, ATM, or Fiber Distributed Data Interface (FDDI) networks. If the network is an Ethernet network, for example, all the computers will expect the header to be a certain length, the flags to be positioned in a certain place within the packet, and the trailer information to be in a certain place with specific fields. On a Token Ring network, the computers would expect most of these parameters to be in different places and the frames to have particular formats. The data link layer is responsible for proper communication within these technologies and for changing the data into the necessary format for the physical layer. It will also manage to reorder frames that are received out of sequence, and notify upper-layer protocols when there are transmission error conditions.

The data link layer is divided into two functional sublayers: the *Logical Link Control (LLC)* and the *Media Access Control (MAC)*. The LLC, defined in the IEEE 802.2 specification, communicates with the protocol immediately above it, the network layer. The MAC will have the appropriately loaded protocols to interface with the protocol requirements of the physical layer. The IEEE MAC specification for Ethernet is 802.3, Token Ring is 802.5, wireless LAN is 802.11, and so on. So when you see a reference to an IEEE standard, such as 802.11, 802.16, 802.3, and so on, it refers to the protocol working at the MAC sublayer of the data link layer of a protocol stack.

Some of the protocols that work at the data link layer are the Serial Line Internet Protocol (SLIP), Point-to-Point Protocol (PPP), Reverse Address Resolution Protocol (RARP), Layer 2 Forwarding (L2F), Layer 2 Tunneling Protocol (L2TP), FDDI, and Integrated Services Digital Network (ISDN). Figure 7-8 shows how the data link layer converts the information into bits, and the physical layer converts those bits into electrical signals. (The network interface layer in the TCP/IP architecture model is equivalent to a combination of the data link and physical layers in the OSI model. Refer to Figure 7-1.)

Each network technology (Ethernet, Token Ring, and so on) defines the compatible physical transmission type (coaxial, twisted pair, or fiber) that is required to enable network communication. Each network technology also has defined electronic signaling and bit patterns. This means, for example, that a signal of 0.5 volts may represent a 0 on one technology and a 1 on another technology. The data link layer protocol specifies the proper bit patterns, and the physical layer protocol translates this information into electrical encoding and electricity state transitions. Network cards bridge the data link and physical layers. Information is passed down through the first six layers and reaches the network card driver at the data link layer. Depending on the network technology being used (Ethernet, Token Ring, FDDI, and so on), the network card driver encodes the bits at the data link layer, which are then turned into electricity states at the physical layer and placed onto the wire for transmission.

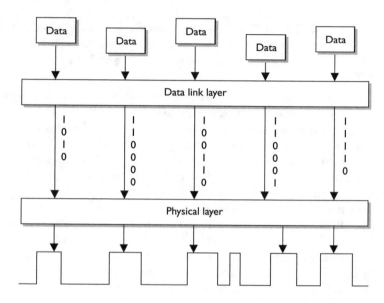

Figure 7-8
The data link layer converts the data into bits for the physical layer.

Physical Layer

Everything ends up as electrical signals anyway.

The *physical layer*, layer 1, converts bits into voltage for transmission. Signals and voltage schemes have different meanings for different LAN and WAN technologies. If a user sends data through his dial-up software and out his modem onto a telephone line, the data format, electrical signals, and control functionality are much different than if that user sends data through the NIC and onto a unshielded twisted pair (UTP) wire for LAN communication. The mechanisms that control this data going onto the telephone line, or the UTP wire, work at the physical layer. This layer controls synchronization, data rates, line noise, and medium access. Specifications for the physical layer include the timing of voltage changes, voltage levels, and the physical connectors for electrical, optical, and mechanical transmission.

Functions and Protocols in the OSI Model

For the exam, you will need to know the functionality that takes place at the different layers of the OSI model, along with specific protocols that work at each layer. The following is a quick overview of each layer and its components.

Application

The protocols at the application layer handle file transfer, virtual terminals, network management, and fulfilling networking requests of applications. A few of the protocols that work at this layer include

- File Transfer Protocol (FTP)
- Trivial File Transfer Protocol (TFTP)
- Simple Network Management Protocol (SNMP)
- Simple Mail Transfer Protocol (SMTP)

- Telnet
- Hypertext Transfer Protocol (HTTP)

Presentation

The services of the presentation layer handle translation into standard formats, data compression and decompression, and data encryption and decryption. No protocols work at this layer, just services. The following lists some of the presentation layer standards:

- American Standard Code for Information Interchange (ASCII)
- Extended Binary-Coded Decimal Interchange Mode (EBCDIC)
- Tagged Image File Format (TIFF)
- Joint Photographic Experts Group (JPEG)
- Motion Picture Experts Group (MPEG)
- Musical Instrument Digital Interface (MIDI)

Session

The session layer protocols set up connections between applications, maintain dialog control, and negotiate, establish, maintain, and tear down the communication channel. Some of the protocols that work at this layer include

- Network File System (NFS)
- NetBIOS
- Structured Query Language (SQL)
- Remote procedure call (RPC)

Transport

The protocols at the transport layer handle end-to-end transmission and segmentation into a data stream. The following protocols work at this layer:

- Transmission Control Protocol (TCP)
- User Datagram Protocol (UDP)
- Secure Sockets Layer (SSL)/Transport Layer Security (TLS)
- Sequenced Packet Exchange (SPX)

Network

The responsibilities of the network layer protocols include internetworking service, addressing, and routing. The following lists some of the protocols that work at this layer:

- Internet Protocol (IP)
- Internet Control Message Protocol (ICMP)
- Internet Group Management Protocol (IGMP)
- Routing Information Protocol (RIP)
- Open Shortest Path First (OSPF)
- Novel Internetwork Packet Exchange (IPX)

Data Link

The protocols at the data link layer convert data into LAN or WAN frames for transmission, convert messages into bits, and define how a computer accesses a network. This layer is divided into the Logical Link Control (LLC) and the Media Access Control (MAC) sublayers. Some protocols that work at this layer include the following:

- Address Resolution Protocol (ARP)
- Reverse Address Resolution Protocol (RARP)
- Point-to-Point Protocol (PPP)
- Serial Line Internet Protocol (SLIP)

Physical

Network interface cards and drivers convert bits into electrical signals and control the physical aspects of data transmission, including optical, electrical, and mechanical requirements. The following are some of the standard interfaces at this layer:

- High-Speed Serial Interface (HSSI)
- X.21
- EIA/TIA-232 and EIA/TIA-449

 NOTE The security services defined in the OSI security model include data integrity (protection from modification and destruction), data confidentiality (protection from disclosure), authentication (verification of identity of the communication source), and access control services (enable mechanisms to allow or restrict access).

Tying the Layers Together

Pick up all of these protocols from the floor and put them into a stack—a network stack.

The OSI model is used as a framework for many products and many types of vendors. Various types of devices and protocols work at different parts of this seven-layer model. Whereas computers can interpret and process data at each of the seven layers, routers can understand information only up to the network layer, because a router's main function is to route packets, which does not require knowledge about any further information within the packet. A router peels back the header information until it reaches the network layer data, where the routing and IP address information is located. The router looks at this information to make its decisions on where the packet should be sent next. Bridges understand only up to the data link layer, and repeaters understand data only at the physical layer. Figure 7-9 shows what level of the OSI model each type of device understands.

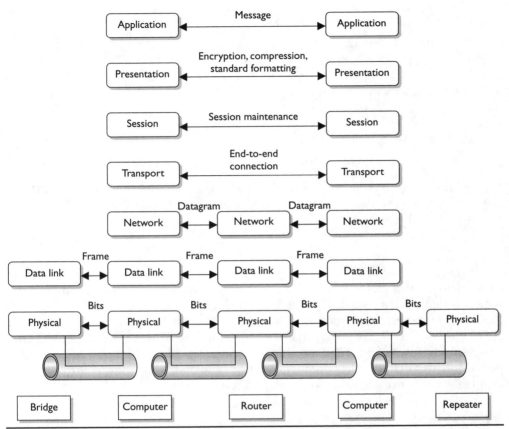

Figure 7-9 Each device works at a particular layer within the OSI model.

TCP/IP

Transmission Control Protocol/Internet Protocol (TCP/IP) is a suite of protocols that governs the way data travel from one device to another. Besides its eponymous two main protocols, TCP/IP includes other protocols as well. IP is a network layer protocol and provides datagram routing services. IP's main task is to support internetwork addressing and packet routing. It is a connectionless protocol that envelopes data passed to it from the transport layer. The IP protocol addresses the datagram with the source and destination IP addresses. The protocols within the TCP/IP suite work together to break down the data passed from the application layer into pieces that can be moved along a network. They work with other protocols to transmit the data to the destination computer and then reassemble the data back into a form that the application layer can understand and process.

IP

IP is a connectionless protocol that provides the addressing and routing capabilities for each package of data.

The data, IP, and network relationship can be compared to the relationship between a letter and the postal system:

- Data = Letter
- IP = Addressed envelope
- Network = Postal system

The message is the letter, which is enveloped and addressed by IP, and the network and its services enable the message to be sent from its origin to its destination, like the postal system.

Two main protocols work at the transport layer: TCP and UDP. *TCP* is a reliable and *connection-oriented protocol*, which means it ensures packets are delivered to the destination computer. If a packet is lost during transmission, TCP has the ability to identify this issue and re-send the lost or corrupted packet. TCP also supports packet sequencing (to ensure each and every packet was received), flow and congestion control, and error detection and correction. *UDP*, on the other hand, is a *best-effort* and *connectionless protocol*. It has neither packet sequencing nor flow and congestion control, and the destination does not acknowledge every packet it receives.

TCP

TCP is referred to as a connection-oriented protocol because, before any user data are actually sent, handshaking takes place between the two systems that want to communicate. Once the handshaking completes successfully, a virtual connection is set up between the two systems. UDP is considered a connectionless protocol because it does not go through these steps. Instead, UDP sends out messages without first contacting the destination computer and does not know if the packets were received properly or dropped. Figure 7-10 shows the difference between a connection-oriented and a connectionless protocol.

UDP and TCP sit together on the transport layer, and developers can choose which to use when coding applications. Many times, TCP is the transport protocol of choice because it provides reliability and ensures the packets are delivered. For example, SMTP is used to transmit e-mail messages and uses TCP because it must make sure the data are delivered. TCP provides a full-duplex, reliable communication mechanism, and if

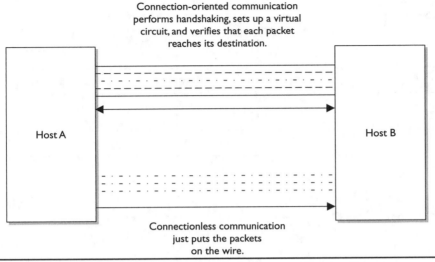

Figure 7-10   Connection-oriented versus connectionless protocol functionality

any packets are lost or damaged, they are re-sent; however, TCP requires a lot of system overhead.

If a programmer knows data dropped during transmission is not detrimental to the application, he may choose to use UDP because it is faster and requires fewer resources. For example, UDP is a better choice than TCP when a server sends status information to all listening nodes on the network. A node will not be negatively affected if, by some chance, it did not receive this status information, because the information will be re-sent every 30 minutes.

UDP and TCP are transport protocols that applications use to get their data across a network. They both use ports to communicate with upper OSI layers and to keep track of various conversations that take place simultaneously. The ports are also the mechanism used to identify how other computers access services. When a TCP or UDP message is formed, a source and destination port are contained within the header information along with the source and destination IP addresses. This makes up a *socket,* and is how packets know where to go (by the address) and how to communicate with the right service or protocol on the other computer (by the port number). The IP address acts as the doorway to a computer, and the port acts as the doorway to the actual protocol or service. To communicate properly, the packet needs to know these doors. Figure 7-11 shows how packets communicate with applications and services through ports.

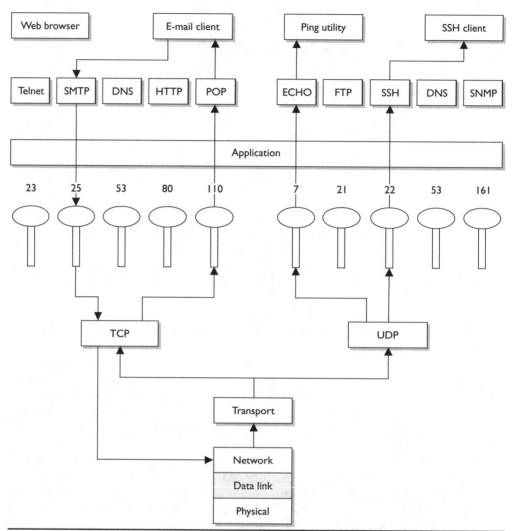

Figure 7-11   The packet can communicate with upper-layer protocols and services through a port.

Well-Known Ports

Port numbers up to 1023 (0–1023) are called well-known ports, and almost every computer in the world has the exact same protocol mapped to the exact same port number. That is why they are called well known—everyone follows this same standardized approach. This means that on almost every computer, port 25 is mapped to SMTP, port 21 is mapped to FTP, port 80 is mapped to HTTP, and so on. This mapping between lower-numbered ports and specific protocols is a de facto standard, which just means that we all do this and that we do not have a standards body telling us this is how it should be done. The fact that almost everyone follows this approach translates to more interoperability among systems all over the world. (Note that ports 0 to 1023 can be used only by privileged system or root processes.)

Because this is a de facto standard and not a standard that absolutely must be followed, administrators can map different protocols to different port numbers if that fits their purpose.

The following shows some of the most commonly used protocols and the ports to which they are usually mapped:

- Telnet port 23
- SMTP port 25
- HTTP port 80
- SNMP ports 161 and 162
- FTP ports 21 and 20

The difference between TCP and UDP can also be seen in the message formats. Because TCP offers more services than UDP, it must contain much more information within its packet header format, as shown in Figure 7-12. Table 7-1 lists the major differences between TCP and UDP.

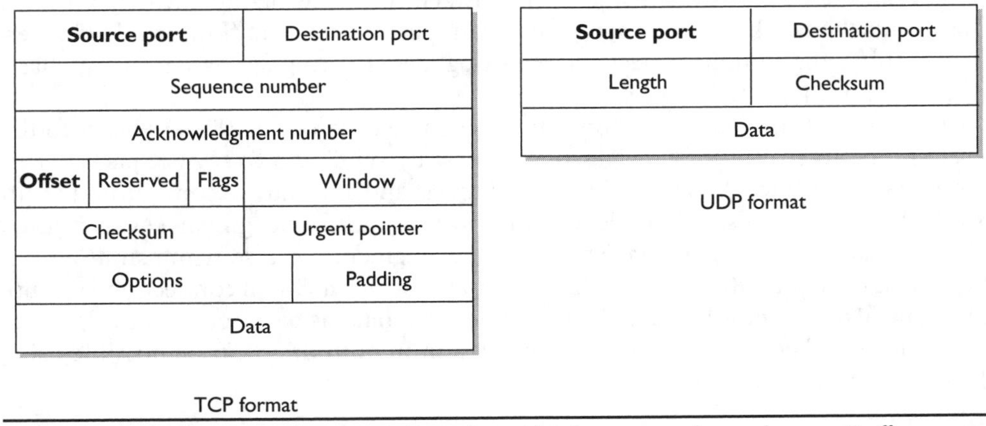

Source port		Destination port
Sequence number		
Acknowledgment number		
Offset	Reserved	Flags	Window
Checksum		Urgent pointer
Options		Padding
Data		

TCP format

Source port	Destination port
Length	Checksum
Data	

UDP format

Figure 7-12 TCP carries a lot more information within its segment format because it offers more services than UDP.

Service	TCP	UDP
Reliability	Ensures that packets reach their destinations, returns ACKs when packets are received, and is a reliable protocol.	Does not return ACKs and does not guarantee that a packet will reach its destination. Is an unreliable protocol.
Connection	Connection-oriented. It performs handshaking and develops a virtual connection with the destination computer.	Connectionless. It does no handshaking and does not set up a virtual connection.
Packet sequencing	Uses sequence numbers within headers to make sure each packet within a transmission is received.	Does not use sequence numbers.
Congestion controls	The destination computer can tell the source if it is overwhelmed and thus slow the transmission rate.	The destination computer does not communicate back to the source computer about flow control through UDP.
Usage	Used when reliable delivery is required.	Used when reliable delivery is not required, such as in streaming video and status broadcasts.
Speed and overhead	Uses a considerable amount of resources and is slower than UDP.	Uses fewer resources and is faster than TCP.

Table 7-1 Major Differences Between TCP and UDP

The TCP Handshake

Every proper dialog begins with a polite handshake.

TCP must set up a virtual connection between two hosts before any data are sent. This means the two hosts must agree on certain parameters, data flow, windowing, error detection, and options. These issues are negotiated during the handshaking phase, as shown in Figure 7-13.

The host that initiates communication sends a synchronous (SYN) packet to the receiver. The receiver acknowledges this request by sending a SYN/ACK packet. This packet translates into, "I have received your request and am ready to communicate with you." The sending host acknowledges this with an acknowledgment (ACK) packet, which translates into, "I received your acknowledgment. Let's start transmitting our data." This completes the handshaking phase, after which a virtual connection is set up, and actual data can now be passed. The connection that has been set up at this point is considered *full duplex*, which means transmission in both directions is possible using the same transmission line.

Data Structures

What's in a name?

As stated earlier, the message is usually formed and passed to the application layer from a program and sent down through the protocol stack. Each protocol at each layer adds its own information to the message and passes it down to the next level. This con-

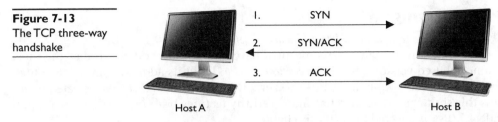

Figure 7-13
The TCP three-way
handshake

cept is usually referred to as *encapsulation*. As the message is passed down the stack, it goes through a sort of evolution, and each stage has a specific name that indicates what is taking place. When an application formats data to be transmitted over the network, the data are called a *message*. The message is sent to the transport layer, where TCP does its magic on the data. The bundle of data is now a *segment*. The segment is sent to the network layer. The network layer adds routing and addressing, and now the bundle is called a *datagram*. The network layer passes off the datagram to the data link layer, which frames the datagram with a header and a trailer, and now it is called a *frame*. Figure 7-14 illustrates these stages.

Sometimes when an author refers to a datagram, she is specifying the stage in which the data are located within the protocol stack. If the literature is describing routers, which work at the network layer, the author might use the word "datagram" because the data at this level have routing and addressing information attached. If an author is describing network traffic and flow control, she might use the word "frame" because all data actually end up in the frame format before they are put on the network wire. However, sometimes an author simply refers to all data packages as *packets*.

The important thing here is that you understand the various steps a data package goes through when it moves up and down the protocol stack, and that just because an author refers to data as a *packet* does not necessarily mean she is indicating the data structure.

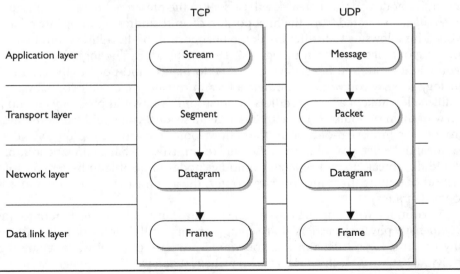

Figure 7-14 The data go through their own evolutionary stages as they pass through the layers within the network stack.

IP Addressing

Take a right at the router and a left at the access server. I live at 10.10.2.3.

Each node on the same network must have a unique IP address. Today, the most commonly used version of IP is *IP version 4 (IPv4)*, but its addresses are in such high demand that their supply has started to run out. *IP version 6 (IPv6)* was created to address this shortage. (IPv6 also has many security features built into it that are not part of IPv4.) IPv6 is covered later in this chapter.

IPv4 uses 32 bits for its addresses, whereas IPv6 uses 128 bits; thus, IPv6 provides more possible addresses with which to work. Each address has a host portion and a network portion, and the addresses are grouped into *classes* and then into *subnets*. The subnet mask of the address differentiates the groups of addresses that define the subnets of a network. IPv4 address classes are listed in the following table:

Class A	0.0.0.0 to 127.255.255.255	The first byte is the network portion and the remaining three bytes are the host portion.
Class B	128.0.0.0 to 191.255.255.255	The first two bytes are the network portion and the remaining two bytes are the host portion.
Class C	192.0.0.0 to 223.255.255.255	The first three bytes are the network portion and the remaining one byte is the host portion.
Class D	224.0.0.0 to 239.255.255.255	Used for multicast addresses.
Class E	240.0.0.0 to 255.255.255.255	Reserved for research.

For any given network within an organization, all nodes connected to the network can have different host addresses but a common network address. The host address identifies every individual node, whereas the network address is the identity of the network they are all connected to; therefore, it is the same for each one of them. Any traffic meant for nodes on this network will be sent to the prescribed network address.

A *subnet* is created from the host portion of an IP address to designate a "sub" network. This allows us to further break the host portion of the address into two or more logical groupings, as shown in Figure 7-15. A network can be logically partitioned to reduce administration headaches, traffic performance, and potentially security. As an analogy, let's say you work at Toddlers R Us and you are responsible for babysitting 100 toddlers. If you kept all 100 toddlers in one room, you would probably end up killing a few of them or yourself. To better manage these kids, you could break them up into groups. The three-year-olds go in the yellow room, the four-year-olds go in the green room, and the five-year-olds go in the blue room. This is what a network administrator would do—break up and separate computer nodes to be able to better control them. Instead of putting them into physical rooms, the administrator puts them into logical rooms (subnets).

To continue with our analogy, when you put your toddlers in different rooms, you would have physical barriers that separate them—walls. Network subnetting is not physical, it is logical. This means you would not have physical walls separating your individual subnets, so how do you keep them separate? This is where subnet masks come into play. A subnet mask defines smaller networks inside a larger network, just like individual rooms are defined within a building.

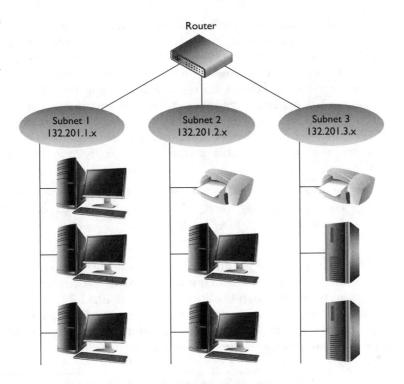

Figure 7-15
Subnets create
logical partitions

Subnetting allows large IP ranges to be divided into smaller, logical, and more tangible network segments. Consider an organization with several divisions, such as IT, Accounting, HR, and so on. Creating subnets for each division breaks the networks into logical partitions that route traffic directly to recipients without dispersing data all over the network. This drastically reduces the traffic load across the network, reducing the possibility of network congestion and excessive broadcast packets in the network. Implementing network security policies is also much more effective across logically categorized subnets with a demarcated perimeter, as compared to a large, cluttered, and complex network.

Subnetting is particularly beneficial in keeping down routing table sizes because external routers can directly send data to the actual network segment without having to worry about the internal architecture of that network and getting the data to individual hosts. This job can be handled by the internal routers, which can determine the individual hosts in a subnetted environment and save the external routers the hassle of analyzing all the 32 bits of an IP address and just look at the "masked" bits.

NOTE To really understand subnetting, you need to dig down into how IP addresses work at the binary level. You should not have to calculate any subnets for the CISSP exam, but for better understanding of how this stuff works under the hood, visit http://compnetworking.about.com/od/workingwithipaddresses/a/subnetmask.htm.

If the traditional subnet masks are used, they are referred to as classful or classical IP addresses. If an organization needs to create subnets that do not follow these traditional sizes, then it would use classless IP addresses. This just means a different subnet mask would be used to define the network and host portions of the addresses. After it became clear that available IP addresses were running out as more individuals and corporations participated on the Internet, classless interdomain routing (CIDR) was created. A Class B address range is usually too large for most companies, and a class C address range is too small, so CIDR provides the flexibility to increase or decrease the class sizes as necessary. CIDR is the method to specify more flexible IP address classes.

 NOTE To better understand CIDR, visit the following resource: www .tcpipguide.com/free/t_IPClasslessAddressingClasslessInterDomainRoutingCI .htm.

Although each node has an IP address, people usually refer to their hostname rather than their IP address. Hostnames, such as www.logicalsecurity.com, are easier for humans to remember than IP addresses, such as 10.13.84.4. However, the use of these two nomenclatures requires mapping between the hostnames and IP addresses, because the computer understands only the numbering scheme. This process is addressed in the "Domain Name Service" section later in this chapter.

 NOTE IP provides addressing, packet fragmentation, and packet timeouts. To ensure that packets do not continually traverse a network forever, IP provides a Time to Live (TTL) value that is decremented every time the packet passes through a router. IP can also provide a Type of Service (ToS) capability, which means it can prioritize different packets for time-sensitive functions.

IPv6

What happened to version 5?
Response: It smelled funny.

IPv6, also called **IP next generation (IPng)**, not only has a larger address space than IPv4 to support more IP addresses, it has many other capabilities that IPv4 does not. All of the specifics of the new functions within IPv6 are beyond the scope of this book, but we will look at a few of them, because IPv6 is the way of the future. IPv6 allows for scoped addresses, which enables an administrator to restrict specific addresses for file servers or file and print sharing, for example. IPv6 has IPSec integrated into the protocol stack, which provides end-to-end secure transmission and authentication. The protocol offers autoconfiguration, which makes administration much easier, and it does not require network address translation (NAT) to extend its address space.

NAT was developed because IPv4 addresses were running out. Although the NAT technology is extremely useful, it has caused a lot of overhead and transmission problems because it breaks the client/server model that many applications use today. IPv6 has more flexibility and routing capabilities and allows for Quality of Service (QoS) priority values to be assigned to time-sensitive transmissions.

Another reason the industry did not jump on the IPv6 bandwagon when it came out years ago is that NAT was developed, which reduced the speed at which IP addresses were being depleted. Although the conversion rate from IPv4 to IPv6 is slow and the implementation process is quite complicated, the industry is making the shift because of all the benefits that IPv6 brings to the table.

 NOTE NAT is covered in the "Network Address Translation" section later in this chapter.

The IPv6 specification, as outlined in RFC 2460, lays out the differences and benefits of IPv6 over IPv4.

- IPv6 increases the IP address size from 32 bits to 128 bits, to support more levels of addressing hierarchy, a much greater number of addressable nodes, and simpler autoconfiguration of addresses.

- The scalability of multicast routing is improved by adding a "scope" field to multicast addresses. Also, a new type of address called an *anycast address* is defined, which is used to send a packet to any one of a group of nodes.

- Some IPv4 header fields have been dropped or made optional, to reduce the common-case processing cost of packet handling and to limit the bandwidth cost of the IPv6 header. This is illustrated in Figure 7-16.

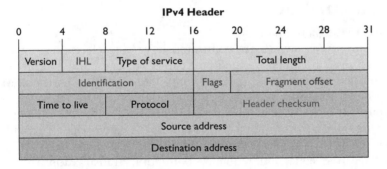

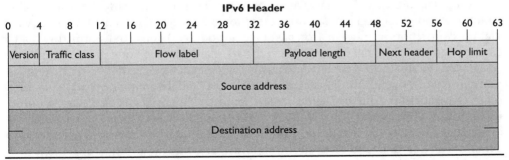

Figure 7-16 IPv4 versus IPv6 headers

- Changes in the way IP header options are encoded allow for more efficient forwarding, less stringent limits on the length of options, and greater flexibility for introducing new options in the future.

- A new capability is added to enable the labeling of packets belonging to particular traffic "flows" for which the sender requests special handling, such as nondefault QoS or "real-time" service.

- Extensions to support authentication, data integrity, and (optional) data confidentiality are also specified for IPv6.

IPv4 does not provide any type of security as in authentication, data integrity, or confidentiality—so how does IPv6? IP security (IPSec) is the answer. IPSec is a protocol suite that protects data that travels over IP networks. Although IPSec is available to be used in IPv4, it is not fully integrated into the IP network stack as it is with IPv6. Refer to Chapter 8 for an extensive review of IPSec.

Types of Transmission

Data transmission can happen in different ways (analog or digital), can use different controlling schemes (synchronous or asynchronous), and can use either one sole channel over a wire (baseband) or several different channels over one wire (broadband). These transmission types and their characteristics are described in the following sections.

Analog and Digital

Would you like your signals wavy or square?

Analog transmission signals are continuously varying electromagnetic waves that can be carried over air, water, twisted-pair cable, coaxial cable, or fiber-optic cable. Through a process of *modulation,* data are combined with a carrier signal of a specific frequency. The modulation of a signal differs in *amplitude* (height of the signal) and *frequency* (number of waves in a defined period of time), as shown in Figure 7-17. This means data are put on the back of a carrier signal. The carrier signals provide many radio stations, frequency ranges, and communication channels. Each radio station is given a certain carrier signal and frequency to use for its transmission. This is how three different country stations can exist on three different radio channels, for example.

Computers use digital signals when moving data from one component to another within the computer itself. When this computer is connected to a telephone line via a dial-up connection, a modem (for *modulate/demo*dulate) must transform this digital data into an analog signal because this is the standard on telephone lines. The modem actually modulates the digital data into an analog signal. Once the data reach the destination computer, they must be transformed back into a digital state so the destination computer can understand them. *Digital signals* represent binary digits as electrical pulses. Each individual pulse is a signal element and represents either a 1 or a 0. *Bandwidth* in digital transmissions refers to the number of electrical pulses that can be transmitted over a link within a second, and these electrical pulses carry individual *bits* of information.

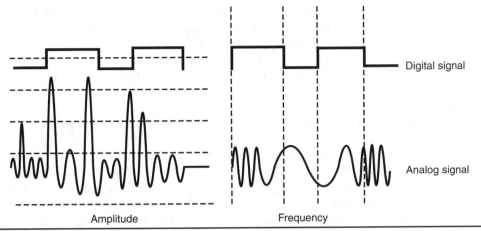

Figure 7-17 Analog signals are measured in amplitude and frequency, whereas digital signals represent binary digits as electrical pulses.

Digital signals are more reliable than analog signals over a long distance and provide a clear-cut and efficient signaling method because the voltage is either *on* (1) or *not on* (0), compared to interpreting the waves of an analog signal. Digital signals can easily be extracted from noise and retransmitted. It is more difficult to extract analog signals from background noise because the amplitudes and frequency of the waves slowly lose form. This is because an analog signal could have an infinite number of values or states, whereas a digital signal exists in discrete states. A digital signal is a square wave, which does not have all of the possible values of the different amplitudes and frequencies of an analog signal. Digital systems are superior to analog systems in that they can transport more calls and data transmissions on the same line at higher quality over longer distances.

Voice and data transmissions used to be transmitted mainly via analog signals over telecommunications links, but today most communication is digitized. Telephone companies digitize telephone networks, and many corporate telephone systems are digitized. Other than radio waves used by radio stations, ham radios, and the like, the only communication that is still analog is what goes from a residential house or business to the telephone company's central office. This section of the telecommunications network is referred to as the *local loop* or *last mile*.

Asynchronous and Synchronous

It's all about timing.

Two devices can communicate through asynchronous or synchronous means, depending on the type of communication and whether the two systems are synchronized in any way. *Asynchronous communication* is used when the two devices are not synchronized in any way.

The sender can send data at any time, and the receiving end must always be ready. *Synchronous communication* takes place between two devices that are synchronized, usually via a clocking mechanism.

Usually, when two devices have a large amount of data to transfer, they use synchronous transmission. With a small amount of data, they use asynchronous transmission. This does not mean one device can decide, "Huh, this is a big heap of data. I better send it through my synchronous route instead of asynchronously." Instead, systems that usually transfer large amounts of data are developed and configured with synchronous communication mechanisms, and systems that transfer smaller amounts of data are developed with asynchronous means.

One example of asynchronous communication takes place between a terminal and a terminal server. If a user is using a system that has terminal-emulation software running, she uses the desktop that the terminal server wants her to use. She sees only her desktop on her computer, while all processing actually takes place on the terminal server. This means every mouse click, keystroke, and command she initiates travels over the networking cable to the terminal server, where the server performs the actions that correspond with these commands. The results are transmitted back to the user's desktop so it seems to her that her computer did the work—when in fact it was done on the terminal server, which could be on another floor or at another location altogether. This type of technology usually transmits a small amount of data at a time; thus, it uses asynchronous data transmission.

Modems also use asynchronous data transmission. Because the data can travel at any time and be any length, stop and start delimiters must be used to tell the receiving end when to start processing a request and when to stop. Each character, which is really just a string of 1's and 0's, has a start-of-character bit and a stop bit attached before and after the character byte. This produces a lot of overhead and extra bits, but it's necessary in asynchronous communication.

Synchronous communication, on the other hand, transfers data as a stream of bits instead of framing it in start and stop bits. The synchronization can happen between two systems using the same clocking mechanism, or a signal can be encoded into the data stream to let the receiver synchronize with the sender of the message. This synchronization needs to take place before the first message is sent. The sending system can transmit a digital clock pulse to the receiving system, which translates into, "We will start here and work in this type of synchronization scheme."

Broadband and Baseband

How many channels can you shove into this one wire?

Baseband uses the entire communication channel for its transmission, whereas *broadband* divides the communication channel into individual and independent channels so different types of data can be transmitted simultaneously. Baseband permits only one signal to be transmitted at a time, whereas broadband carries several signals over different channels. For example, a coaxial cable TV (CATV) system is a broadband technology that delivers multiple television channels over the same cable. This system can also provide home users with Internet access, but these data are transmitted at a different frequency spectrum than the TV channels. Ethernet is a baseband technology that uses the entire wire for just one channel.

Broadband encompasses many different types of technologies, but one general rule is that it provides data transmissions higher than 56 Kbps, which is what a standard modem dial-up connection line provides. Broadband communications provide channels for data transmission and can be used by many users. The types of broadband communication systems available today are leased lines (T1, T3), Broadband ISDN, ATM, Digital Subscriber Line (DSL), broadband wireless, and CATV.

LAN Networking

We really need to connect all of these resources together.

The following are the four main reasons to have a network:

- To allow communication between computers
- To share information
- To share resources
- To provide central administration

Most users on a network need to use the same type of resources, such as information, printers, file servers, plotters, fax machines, Internet connections, and so on. Why not just string all the computers together and have these resources available to all? Great idea! We'll call it *networking!*

Networking has made amazing advances in just a short period of time. In the beginning of the computer age, mainframes were the name of the game. They were isolated powerhouses, and many had "dumb" terminals hanging off them. However, this was not true networking. In the late 1960s and early 1970s, some technical researchers came up with ways of connecting all the mainframes and Unix systems to enable them to communicate. This marked the Internet's baby steps.

Microcomputers evolved and were used in many offices and work areas. Slowly, dumb terminals got a little smarter and more powerful as users needed to share office resources. And *bam!* Ethernet was developed, which allowed for true networking. There was no turning back after this.

 NOTE   Identification and authentication are a large part of networking and are covered extensively in Chapter 4. However, it is important to note that node authentication, by itself, should not be used to establish trustworthiness of a user within the network. Within a distributed network, knowing whom to trust is a major security issue.

Network Topology

Okay, so where is everything?

The physical arrangement of computers and devices is called a **network topology**. Topology refers to the manner in which a network is *physically* connected and shows the layout of resources and systems. A difference exists between the physical network topology and the logical topology. A network can be configured as a physical star but work logically as a ring, as in the Token Ring technology.

The best topology for a particular network depends on such things as how nodes are supposed to interact; which protocols are used; the types of applications that are available; the reliability, expandability, and physical layout of a facility; existing wiring;

and the technologies implemented. The wrong topology or combination of topologies can negatively affect the network's performance, productivity, and growth possibilities.

This section describes the basic types of network topologies. Most networks are much more complex and are usually implemented using a combination of topologies.

Ring Topology

A *ring topology* has a series of devices connected by unidirectional transmission links, as shown in Figure 7-18. These links form a closed loop and do not connect to a central system, as in a star topology (discussed a little later). In a physical ring formation, each node is dependent upon the preceding nodes. In simple networks, if one system fails, all other systems could be negatively affected because of this interdependence. Today, most networks have redundancy in place or other mechanisms that will protect a whole network from being affected by just one workstation misbehaving, but one disadvantage of using a ring topology is that this possibility exists.

Bus Topology

In a simple *bus topology*, a single cable runs the entire length of the network. Nodes are attached to the network through drop points on this cable. Data communications transmit the length of the medium, and each packet transmitted has the capability of being "looked at" by all nodes. Each node decides to accept or ignore the packet, depending upon the packet's destination address.

Bus topologies are of two main types: linear and tree. The *linear bus topology* has a single cable with nodes attached. A *tree topology* has branches from the single cable, and each branch can contain many nodes.

In simple implementations of a bus topology, if one workstation fails, other systems can be negatively affected because of the degree of interdependence. In addition, because all nodes are connected to one main cable, the cable itself becomes a potential single point of failure. Traditionally, Ethernet uses bus and star topologies.

Star Topology

In a *star topology*, all nodes connect to a central device such as a switch. Each node has a dedicated link to the central device. The central device needs to provide enough

Figure 7-18
A ring topology forms a closed-loop connection.

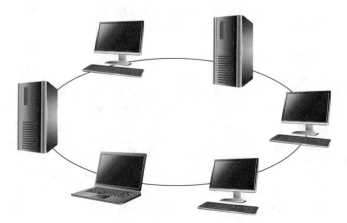

throughput that it does not turn out to be a detrimental bottleneck for the network as a whole. Because a central device is required, it is a potential single point of failure, so redundancy may need to be implemented. Switches can be configured in flat or hierarchical implementations so larger organizations can use them.

When one workstation fails on a star topology, it does not affect other systems, as in the ring or bus topologies. In a star topology, each system is not as dependent on others as it is dependent on the central connection device. This topology generally requires less cabling than other types of topologies. As a result, cut cables are less likely, and detecting cable problems is an easier task.

Not many networks use true linear bus and ring topologies anymore within LAN environments. A ring topology can be used for a backbone network, but most LANs are constructed in a star topology because it enables the network to be more resilient and not as affected if an individual node experiences a problem. Remember that there is a difference between media access methods and the physical topology. Even though a network is Token Ring or Ethernet, this describes only how each node accesses the media and deals with traffic. Although Token Ring is usually thought of as a ring and Ethernet is considered a bus implementation, these descriptions apply only to how they work logically, which takes place at the data link layer. They can easily be physically implemented as a star, and they usually are.

Mesh Topology

This network is a mess!
Response: We like to call it a mesh.

In a *mesh topology*, all systems and resources are connected to each other in a way that does not follow the uniformity of the previous topologies, as shown in Figure 7-19. This arrangement is usually a network of interconnected routers and switches that provides multiple paths to all the nodes on the network. In a full mesh topology, every node is directly connected to every other node, which provides a great degree of redundancy. In a partial mesh topology, every node is not directly connected. The Internet is an example of a partial mesh topology.

Figure 7-19
In a mesh topology, each node is connected to all other nodes, which provides for redundant paths.

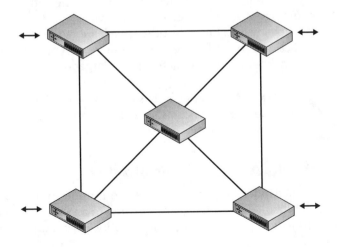

Topology	Characteristics	Problems	Common Technologies
Bus	Uses a linear, single cable for all computers attached. All traffic travels the full cable and can be viewed by all other computers.	If one station experiences a problem, it can negatively affect surrounding computers on the same cable.	Ethernet
Ring	All computers are connected by a unidirectional transmission link, and the cable is in a closed loop.	If one station experiences a problem, it can negatively affect surrounding computers on the same ring.	FDDI
Star	All computers are connected to a central device, which provides more resilience for the network.	The central device is a single point of failure.	Logical bus (Ethernet) and ring topologies (Token Ring)
Tree	A bus topology that does not have one linear cable, but instead uses branches of cables.		Ethernet
Mesh	Computers are connected to each other, which provides redundancy.	Requires more expense in cabling and extra effort to track down cable faults.	Internet

Table 7-2 Summary of Network Topologies

A summary of the different network topologies and their important characteristics is provided in Table 7-2.

No matter what topology is used, most LANs have a backbone in place, which is a cable and protocol combination that connects network segments together. The backbone works at a higher speed than the individual network segments, which allows data to quickly move from one network to the other. Whereas the network segments would most likely be using UTP and Ethernet, the backbone could be using FDDI or Fast Ethernet. An analogy is a city's streets and highways. On the streets (network segments), cars (data) move more slowly, but the streets are connected to a highway (backbone), which enables cars to get from one location to a second distant location very quickly. Similarly, a backbone allows data to cover a larger distance very quickly.

 NOTE   When a ring or bus topology is used, all nodes between the source and destination systems have access to this data transmission. This means it is easier for an attacker to gain access to a lot of potentially sensitive data.

LAN Media Access Technologies

A *LAN* is a network that provides shared communication and resources in a relatively small area. What defines a LAN, as compared to a WAN, depends on the physical medium, encapsulation protocols, and functionality. For example, a LAN could use 10Base-T

> ## Q&A
> **Question**   A LAN is said to cover a relatively small geographical area. When is a LAN no longer a LAN?
>
> **Answer**   When two distinct LANs are connected by a router, the result is an internetwork, not a larger LAN. Each distinct LAN has its own addressing scheme, broadcast domain, and communication mechanisms. If two LANs are connected by a different data link layer technology, such as frame relay or X.25, they are considered a WAN.

cabling, IPX/SPX protocols, and routing protocols, and it could enable users who are in the same local building to communicate. A WAN, on the other hand, could use fiber-optic cabling and the L2TP encapsulation protocol, and could enable users from one building to communicate with users in another building in another state (or country). A WAN connects LANs over great distances geographically. Most of the differences between these technologies are found at the data link layer.

The term "local" in the context of a LAN refers not so much to the geographical area as to the limitations of a LAN with regard to the shared medium, the number of devices and computers that can be connected to it, the transmission rates, the types of cable that can be used, and the compatible devices. If a network administrator develops a very large LAN that would more appropriately be multiple LANs, too much traffic could result in a big performance hit, or the cabling could be too long, in which case *attenuation* (signal loss) becomes a factor. Environments where there are too many nodes, routers, bridges, and switches may be overwhelmed, and administration of these networks could get complex, which opens the door for errors, collisions, and security holes. The network administrator should follow the specifications of the technology he is using, and once he has maxed out these numbers, he should consider implementing two or more LANs instead of one large LAN. LANs are defined by their physical topologies, data link layer technologies, protocols, and devices used. The following sections cover these topics and how they interrelate.

Ethernet

Ethernet is a LAN-sharing technology that enables several devices to communicate on the same network. Ethernet usually uses a bus or star topology. If a linear bus topology is used, all devices connect to one cable. If a star topology is used, each device is connected to a cable that is connected to a centralized device, such as a switch. Ethernet was developed in the 1970s, became commercially available in 1980, and was named the IEEE 802.3 standard.

Ethernet has seen quite an evolution in its short history, from purely coaxial cable installations that worked at 10 Mbps to mostly Category 5 twisted-pair cable that works at speeds of 100 Mbps, 1,000 Mbps (1 Gbps), and 10 Gbps.

Ethernet is defined by the following characteristics:

- Shares media. (All devices must take turns using the same media, and collisions can take place.)
- Uses broadcast and collision domains.

- Uses the carrier sense multiple access with collision detection (CSMA/CD) access method.
- Supports full duplex on twisted-pair implementations.
- Can use coaxial or twisted-pair media.
- Is defined by standard IEEE 802.3.

Ethernet addresses how computers share a common network and how they deal with collisions, data integrity, communication mechanisms, and transmission controls. These are the common characteristics of Ethernet, but Ethernet does vary in the type of cabling schemes and transfer rates it can supply. Several types of Ethernet implementations are available, as outlined in Table 7-3. The following sections discuss 10Base2, 10Base5, and 10Base-T, which are common implementations.

10Base2 10Base2, ThinNet, uses coaxial cable. It has a maximum cable length of 185 meters, provides 10-Mbps transmission rates, and requires British Naval Connectors (BNCs) to network devices.

10Base5 10Base5, ThickNet, uses a thicker coaxial cable that is not as flexible as ThinNet and is more difficult to work with. However, ThickNet can have longer cable segments than ThinNet and is often used as the network backbone. ThickNet is more resistant to electrical interference than ThinNet and is usually preferred when stringing wire through electrically noisy environments that contain heavy machinery and magnetic fields. ThickNet also requires BNCs because it uses coaxial cables.

10Base-T 10Base-T uses twisted-pair copper wiring instead of coaxial cabling. Twisted-pair wiring uses one wire to transmit data and the other to receive data. 10Base-T is usually implemented in a star topology, which provides easy network configuration. In a star topology, all systems are connected to centralized devices, which can be in a flat or hierarchical configuration.

10Base-T networks have RJ-45 connector faceplates to which the computer connects. The wires usually run behind a wall and connect the faceplate to a punchdown block within a wiring closet. The punchdown block is often connected to a 10Base-T hub that serves as a doorway to the network's backbone cable or to a central switch. This type of configuration is shown in Figure 7-20.

Ethernet Type	Cable Type	Speed
10Base2, ThinNet	Coaxial	10 Mbps
10Base5, ThickNet	Coaxial	10 Mbps
10Base-T	UTP	10 Mbps
100Base-TX, Fast Ethernet	UTP	100 Mbps
1000Base-T, Gigabit Ethernet	UTP	1,000 Mbps

Table 7-3 Types of Ethernet

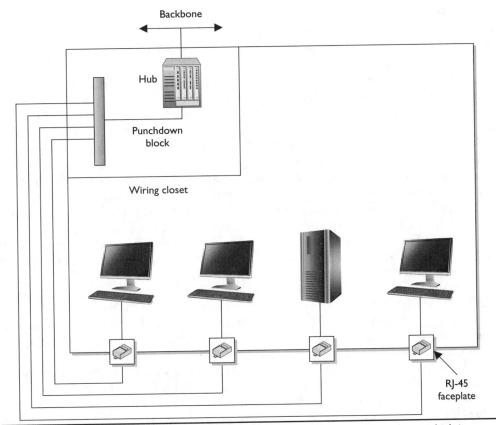

Figure 7-20 Ethernet hosts connect to a punchdown block within the wiring closet, which is connected to the backbone via a hub or switch.

Fast Ethernet: Ethernet in Overdrive   Not surprisingly, 10 Mbps was considered heaven-sent when it first arrived on the networking scene, but soon many users were demanding more speed and power. The smart people had to gather into small rooms and hit the whiteboards with ideas, calculations, and new technologies. The result of these meetings, computations, engineering designs, and testing was Fast Ethernet.

Fast Ethernet is regular Ethernet, except that it runs at 100 Mbps over twisted-pair wiring instead of at 10 Mbps. Around the same time Fast Ethernet arrived, another 100-Mbps technology was developed: 100-VG-AnyLAN. This technology did not use Ethernet's traditional CSMA/CD and did not catch on like Fast Ethernet did.

Fast Ethernet uses the traditional CSMA/CD (explained in the "CSMA" section later in the chapter) and the original frame format of Ethernet. This is why it is used in many enterprise LAN environments today. One environment can run 10- and 100-Mbps network segments that can communicate via 10/100 hubs or switches.

Four main types of Fast Ethernet exist today; their differences pertain to the cabling and transmission distances.

Token Ring

Where's my magic token? I have something to say.
Response: We aren't giving it to you.

Like Ethernet, *Token Ring* is a LAN technology that enables the communication and sharing of networking resources. The Token Ring technology was originally developed by IBM and is now defined by the IEEE 802.5 standard. It uses a token-passing technology with a star-configured topology. The *ring* part of the name pertains to how the signals travel, which is in a logical ring. Each computer is connected to a central hub, called a *Multistation Access Unit (MAU)*. Physically, the topology can be a star, but the signals and transmissions are passed in a logical ring.

A *token-passing technology* is one in which a device cannot put data on the network wire without having possession of a *token*, a control frame that travels in a logical circle and is "picked up" when a system needs to communicate. This is different from Ethernet, in which all the devices attempt to communicate at the same time. This is why Ethernet is referred to as a "chatty protocol" and has collisions. Token Ring does not endure collisions, since only one system can communicate at a time, but this also means communication takes place more slowly compared to Ethernet.

At first, Token Ring technology had the ability to transmit data at 4 Mbps. Later, it was improved to transmit at 16 Mbps. When a frame is put on the wire, each computer looks at it to see whether the frame is addressed to it. If the frame does not have that specific computer's address, the computer puts the frame back on the wire, properly amplifies the message, and passes it to the next computer on the ring.

Token Ring employs a couple of mechanisms to deal with problems that can occur on this type of network. The *active monitor* mechanism removes frames that are continually circulating on the network. This can occur if a computer locks up or is taken offline for one reason or another and cannot properly receive a token destined for it. With the *beaconing* mechanism, if a computer detects a problem with the network, it sends a beacon frame. This frame generates a failure domain, which is between the computer that issued the beacon and its neighbor downstream. The computers and devices within this failure domain will attempt to reconfigure certain settings to try to work around the detected fault. Figure 7-21 depicts a Token Ring network in a physical star configuration.

Token Ring networks were popular in the 1980s and 1990s, and although some are still around, Ethernet has become much more popular and has taken over the LAN networking market.

Q&A

Question   Where do the differences between Ethernet, Token Ring, and FDDI lie?

Answer   These technologies are data link layer technologies. The data link layer is actually made up of a MAC sublayer and an LLC sublayer. These technologies live at the MAC layer and have to interface to the LLC layer. These LAN technologies differ in how they communicate to the protocol stack and what type of functionalities they can provide.

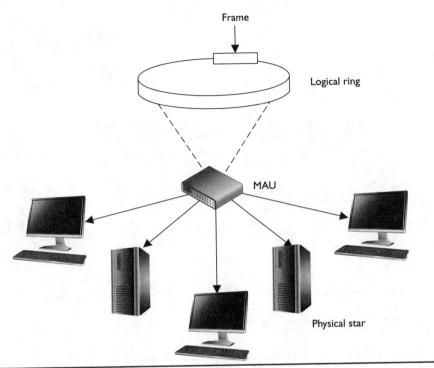

Figure 7-21 A Token Ring network

FDDI

Fiber Distributed Data Interface (FDDI) technology, developed by the American National Standards Institute (ANSI), is a high-speed token-passing media access technology. FDDI has a data transmission speed of up to 100 Mbps and is usually used as a backbone network using fiber-optic cabling. FDDI also provides fault tolerance by offering a second counter-rotating fiber ring. The primary ring has data traveling clockwise and is used for regular data transmission. The second ring transmits data in a counterclockwise fashion and is invoked only if the primary ring goes down. Sensors watch the primary ring and, if it goes down, invoke a ring *wrap* so the data will be diverted to the second ring. Each node on the FDDI network has relays that are connected to both rings, so if a break in the ring occurs, the two rings can be joined.

When FDDI is used as a backbone network, it usually connects several different networks, as shown in Figure 7-22.

Before Fast Ethernet and Gigabit Ethernet hit the market, FDDI was used mainly as campus and service provider backbones. Because FDDI can be employed for distances up to 100 kilometers, it was often used in metropolitan area networks (MANs). The benefit of FDDI is that it can work over long distances and at high speeds with minimal interference. It enables several tokens to be present on the ring at the same time, causing more communication to take place simultaneously, and it provides predictable delays that help connected networks and devices know what to expect and when.

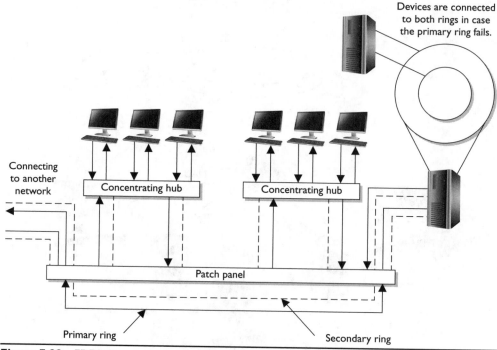

Figure 7-22 FDDI rings can be used as backbones to connect different LANs.

A version of FDDI, Copper Distributed Data Interface (CDDI), can work over UTP cabling. Whereas FDDI would be used more as a MAN, CDDI can be used within a LAN environment to connect network segments.

 NOTE FDDI-2 provides fixed bandwidth that can be allocated for specific applications. This makes it work more like a broadband connection, which allows for voice, video, and data to travel over the same lines.

Table 7-4 sums up the important characteristics of the technologies described in the preceding sections.

Cabling

Why are cables so important?
Response: Without them, our electrons would fall onto the floor.

Network cabling and wiring are important when setting up a network or extending an existing one. Particular types of cables must be used with specific data link layer technologies. Cable types vary in speeds, maximum lengths, and connectivity issues with NICs. In the 1970s and 1980s, coaxial cable was the way to go, but in the late 1980s, twisted-pair wiring hit the scene and today it is the most popular networking cable used.

LAN Implementation	IEEE Standard	Characteristics
Ethernet	802.3	- Uses broadcast and collision domains. - Uses CSMA/CD access method. - Can use coaxial or twisted-pair media. - Transmission speeds of 10 Mbps to 1 Gbps.
Token Ring	802.5	- Token-passing media access method. - Transmission speeds of 4–16 Mbps. - Uses an active monitor and beaconing.
FDDI	802.8	- Dual counter-rotating rings for fault tolerance. - Transmission speeds of 100 Mbps. - Operates over long distances at high speeds and is therefore used as a backbone. - CDDI works over UTP.

Table 7-4 LAN Media Access Methods

Electrical signals travel as currents through cables and can be negatively affected by many factors within the environment, such as motors, fluorescent lighting, magnetic forces, and other electrical devices. These items can corrupt the data as it travels through the cable, which is why cable standards are used to indicate cable type, shielding, transmission rates, and cable distances.

Cabling has bandwidth and data throughput rate values associated with it. Although these two terms are related, they are indeed different. The *bandwidth* of a cable indicates the highest frequency range it uses—for instance, 10Base-T uses 10 MHz and 100Base-TX uses 80 MHz. This is different from the actual amount of data that can be pushed through a cable. The *data throughput rate* is the actual amount of data that goes through the wire after compression and encoding have been used. 10Base-T has a data rate of 10 Mbps, and 100Base-TX has a data rate of 100 Mbps. The bandwidth can be thought of as the size of the pipe, and the data throughput rate is the actual amount of data that travels through that pipe.

Coaxial Cable

Coaxial cable has a copper core that is surrounded by a shielding layer and grounding wire, as shown in Figure 7-23. This is all encased within a protective outer jacket. Compared to twisted-pair cable, coaxial cable is more resistant to electromagnetic interference (EMI), provides a higher bandwidth, and supports the use of longer cable lengths. So, why is twisted-pair cable more popular? Twisted-pair cable is cheaper and easier to work with, and the move to switched environments that provide hierarchical wiring schemes has overcome the cable-length issue of twisted-pair cable.

The two main types of coaxial cable used within LAN environments are 50-ohm cable (used for digital signaling) and 75-ohm cable (used for high-speed digital signaling and analog signaling). The coaxial cable types are 10Base2 (ThinNet) and 10Base5 (ThickNet). Coaxial cable can transmit using either a *baseband* method, whereby the cable carries only one channel, or a *broadband* method, whereby the cable carries several channels.

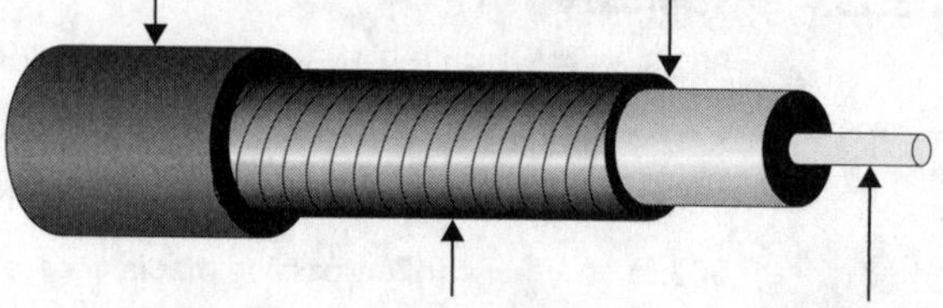

Figure 7-23
Coaxial cable

Sheath

Insulation (PVC, Teflon)

Braided shielding

Conducting core

Figure 7-23
Coaxial cable

Twisted-Pair Cable

This cable is kind of flimsy. Why do we use it?
Response: It's cheap and easy to work with.

Twisted-pair cabling has insulated copper wires surrounded by an outer protective jacket. If the cable has an outer foil shielding, it is referred to as *shielded twisted pair (STP)*, which adds protection from radio frequency interference and electromagnetic interference. Another type of twisted-pair cabling does not have this extra outer shielding and is called *unshielded twisted pair (UTP)*.

The cable contains copper wires that twist around each other, as shown in Figure 7-24. This twisting of the wires protects the signals they carry from radio frequency and electromagnetic interference, as well as crosstalk. Each wire forms a balanced circuit, because the voltage in each pair uses the same amplitude, just with opposite phases. The tighter the twisting of the wires, the more resistant the cable is to interference and attenuation. UTP has several categories of cabling, each of which has its own unique characteristics. The difference in the category ratings is based on how tightly wound the cables are.

The twisting of the wires, the type of insulation used, the quality of the conductive material, and the shielding of the wire determine the rate at which data can be transmitted. The UTP ratings indicate which of these components were used when the cables were manufactured. Some types are more suitable and effective for specific uses and environments. Table 7-5 lists the cable ratings.

Copper cable has been around for many years. It is inexpensive and easy to use. A majority of the telephone systems today use copper cabling with the rating of voice grade. Twisted-pair wiring is the preferred network cabling, but it also has its drawbacks. Copper actually resists the flow of electrons, which causes a signal to degrade after it has traveled a certain distance. This is why cable lengths are recommended for copper cables; if these recommendations are not followed, a network could experience signal loss and data corruption. Copper also radiates energy, which means information can be monitored and captured by intruders. UTP is the least secure networking cable compared to coaxial and fiber. If a company requires higher speed, higher security, and cables to have longer runs than what is allowed in copper cabling, fiber-optic cable may be a better choice.

Figure 7-24
Twisted-pair cabling
uses copper wires.

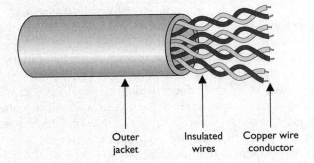

Outer
jacket

Insulated
wires

Copper wire
conductor

Fiber-Optic Cable

Hey, I can't tap into this fiber cable.
Response: Exactly.

Twisted-pair cable and coaxial cable use copper wires as their data transmission media, but fiber-optic cable uses a type of glass that carries light waves, which represent the data being transmitted. The glass core is surrounded by a protective cladding, which in turn is encased within an outer jacket.

UTP Category	Characteristics	Usage
Category 1	Voice-grade telephone cable	Not recommended for network use, but modems can communicate over it.
Category 2	Data transmission up to 4 Mbps	Used in mainframe and minicomputer terminal connections, but not recommended for high-speed networking.
Category 3	10 Mbps for Ethernet and 4 Mbps for Token Ring	Used in 10Base-T network installations.
Category 4	16 Mbps	Usually used in Token Ring networks.
Category 5	100 Mbps for 100Base-TX and CDDI networks; has high twisting and thus low crosstalk	Used in 100Base-TX, CDDI, Ethernet, and ATM installations; most widely used in new network installations.
Category 6	10 Gbps	Used in new network installations requiring high-speed transmission. Standard for Gigabit Ethernet.
Category 7	10 Gbps	Used in new network installations requiring higher-speed transmission.

Table 7-5   UTP Cable Ratings

Because it uses glass, fiber-optic cabling has higher transmission speeds that allow signals to travel over longer distances. Fiber cabling is not as affected by attenuation and EMI when compared to cabling that uses copper. It does not radiate signals, as does UTP cabling, and is difficult to eavesdrop on; therefore, fiber-optic cabling is much more secure than UTP, STP, or coaxial.

Using fiber-optic cable sounds like the way to go, so you might wonder why you would even bother with UTP, STP, or coaxial. Unfortunately, fiber-optic cable is extremely expensive and difficult to work with. It is usually used in backbone networks and environments that require high data transfer rates. Most networks use UTP and connect to a backbone that uses fiber.

Cabling Problems

Cables are extremely important within networks, and when they experience problems, the whole network could experience problems. This section addresses some of the more common cabling issues many networks experience.

Noise   Noise on a line is usually caused by surrounding devices or by characteristics of the wiring's environment. Noise can be caused by motors, computers, copy machines, fluorescent lighting, and microwave ovens, to name a few. This background noise can combine with the data being transmitted over the cable and distort the signal, as shown in Figure 7-25. The more noise there is interacting with the cable, the more likely the receiving end will not receive the data in the form originally transmitted. (How these issues affect power lines is discussed in Chapter 6.)

Attenuation   *Attenuation* is the loss of signal strength as it travels. The longer a cable, the more attenuation is introduced, which causes the signal carrying the data to deteriorate. This is why standards include suggested cable run lengths—once data travels over a certain distance, the resistance of electron flow aggregates and destroys the integrity of the signal.

The effects of attenuation increase with higher frequencies; thus, 100Base-TX at 80MHz has a higher attenuation rate than 10Base-T at 10MHz. This means that cables used to transmit data at higher frequencies should have shorter cable runs to ensure attenuation does not become an issue.

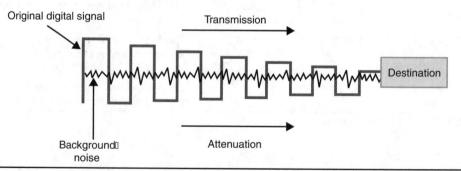

Figure 7-25   Background noise can merge with an electronic signal and alter the signal's integrity.

Backbone

If a UTP cable is used and a cable segment is longer than 185 meters, attenuation may occur. Basically, the data are in the form of electrons, and these electrons have to "swim" through a copper wire. However, this is more like swimming upstream, because there is a lot of resistance on the electrons working in this media. After a certain distance, the electrons start to slow down and their encoding format loses form. If the form gets too degraded, the receiving system cannot interpret them any longer. This is why the standard stipulates a maximum of 185 meters. If a network administrator needs to run a cable longer than this, she needs to integrate a repeater or some type of device that will amplify the signal and ensure it gets to its destination in the right encoding format.

Attenuation can also be caused by cable breaks and malfunctions. This is why cables should be tested. If a cable is suspected of attenuation problems, cable testers can inject signals into the cable and read the results at the end of the cable.

Crosstalk   As previously mentioned, UTP is susceptible to crosstalk, which occurs when electrical signals of one wire spill over to another wire. When the different electrical signals mix, their integrity degrades and data corruption can occur. UTP is much more vulnerable to crosstalk than STP or coaxial because it does not have extra layers of shielding to help protect against it.

As stated earlier, the two-wire pairs within twisted-pair cables form a balanced circuit because they both have the same amplitude, just with different phases. Crosstalk and background noise can throw off this balance, and the wire can actually start to act like an antenna, which means it will be more susceptible to picking up other noises in the environment.

The Fire Rating of Cables

This cable smells funny when it's on fire.

Just as buildings must meet certain fire codes, so must wiring schemes. A lot of companies string their network wires in drop ceilings—the space between the ceiling and the next floor—or under raised floors. This hides the cables and prevents people from tripping over them. However, when wires are strung in places like this, they are more likely to catch on fire without anyone knowing about it. Some cables produce hazardous gases when on fire that would spread throughout the building quickly. Network cabling that is placed in these types of areas, called *plenum space*, must meet a specific fire rating to ensure it will not produce and release harmful chemicals in case of a fire. A building's ventilation system usually is located in this plenum space, so if toxic chemicals were to get into that area, they could be easily spread throughout the building in minutes.

Nonplenum cables usually have a polyvinyl chloride (PVC) jacket covering, whereas plenum-rated cables have jacket covers made of fluoropolymers. When setting up a network or extending an existing network, it is important you know which wire types are required in which situation.

You must consider the following factors when choosing cabling for a network: the company's budget for the network, the ease of handling, possible signal interference, the distance of the cable run, the necessary speed of transmission, security, and the fire rating.

Cables should be installed in unexposed areas so they are not easily tripped over, damaged, or eavesdropped upon. The cables should be strung behind walls and in the protected spaces between the ceiling and next floor. In some situations, wires are encapsulated within *pressurized conduits* so if someone attempts to access a wire, the pressure of the conduit will change, causing an alarm to sound and a message to be sent to the administrator.

In environments where heavy machinery or other devices that create electromagnetic fields are used, STP or fiber-optic cable should be installed. If security is a top priority to a company, fiber-optic cable should be used.

Transmission Methods

A packet may need to be sent to only one workstation, to a set of workstations, or to all workstations on a particular subnet. If a packet needs to go from the source computer to one particular system, a *unicast* transmission method is used. If the packet needs to go to a specific group of systems, the sending system uses the *multicast* method. If a system wants all computers on its subnet to receive a message, it will use the *broadcast* method.

Unicast is pretty simple because it has a source address and a destination address. The data go from point A to Z, it is a one-to-one transmission, and everyone is happy. Multicast is a bit different in that it is a one-to-many transmission. Multicasting enables one computer to send data to a selective group of computers. A good example of multicasting is tuning into a radio station on a computer. Some computers have software that enables the user to determine whether she wants to listen to country western, pop, Christian, or head-banging rock, for example. Once the user selects one of these genres, the software must tell the NIC driver to pick up not only packets addressed to its specific MAC address, but also packets that contain a specific multicast address.

The difference between broadcast and multicast is that in a broadcast one-to-all transmission, everyone gets the data, whereas in a multicast, only the few who have chosen to receive the data actually get it. So how does a server three states away multicast to one particular computer on a specific network and no other networks in between? Good question, glad you asked. The user who elects to receive a multicast actually has to tell her local router she wants to get frames with this particular multicast address passed her way. The local router must tell the router upstream, and this process continues so each router between the source and destination knows where to pass this multicast data. This ensures that the user can get her head-banging rock music without other networks being bothered with this extra data. (The user does not actually need to tell her local router anything; the software on her computer communicates to a routing protocol to handle and pass along the information.)

IP multicast protocols use a Class D address, which is a special address space designed especially for multicasting. It can be used to send out information, multimedia data, and even real-time video and voice clips.

Internet Group Management Protocol (IGMP) is used to report multicast group memberships to routers. When a user chooses to accept multicast traffic, she becomes a member of a particular multicast group. IGMP is the mechanism that allows her computer to inform the local routers that she is part of this group and to send traffic with a specific multicast address to her system.

Media Access Technologies

The physical topology of a network is the lower layer, or foundation, of a network. It determines what type of media will be used and how the media will be connected between different systems. Media access technologies deal with how these systems communicate over this media and are usually represented in protocols, NIC drivers, and interfaces. LAN access technologies set up the rules of how computers will communicate on a network, how errors are handled, what physical medium is to be used, the maximum transmission unit (MTU) size of frames, and much more. These rules enable all computers and devices to communicate and recover from problems, and enable users to be productive in accomplishing their networking tasks. Each participating entity needs to know how to communicate properly so all other systems will understand the transmissions, instructions, and requests. This is taken care of by the LAN media access technology.

Transmission Definitions

The following is a summary of many of the concepts we have addressed so far:

- **Digital signals**   Represent binary digits as discrete electrical pulses
- **Analog signals**   Continuous signals that vary by amplification and frequency
- **Asynchronous communication**   Transfers data sequentially, uses start and stop bits, and requires that communicating devices communicate at the same speed
- **Synchronous communication**   High-speed transmission controlled by electronic clock timing signals
- **Baseband transmission**   Uses the full bandwidth for only one channel and has a low data transfer rate
- **Broadband transmission**   Divides the bandwidth into many channels, enabling different types of data to be transmitted, and provides a high data transfer rate
- **Unicast transmission**   Occurs when a packet is sent from one source computer to one destination computer
- **Multicast transmission**   Occurs when a packet is sent from one source computer to several specific computers
- **Broadcast transmission**   Occurs when a packet is sent from one source computer to all computers on a certain network segment

NOTE An MTU is a parameter that indicates how much data a frame can carry on a specific network. Different types of network technologies may require different MTU sizes, which is why frames are sometimes fragmented.

Token Passing

A *token* is a 24-bit control frame used to control which computers communicate at what intervals. The token is passed from computer to computer, and only the computer that has the token can actually put frames onto the wire. The token grants a computer the right to communicate. The token contains the data to be transmitted and source and destination address information. When a system has data it needs to transmit, it has to wait to receive the token. The computer then connects its message to the token and puts it on the wire. Each computer checks this message to determine whether it is addressed to it, which continues until the destination computer receives the message. The destination computer makes a copy of the message and flips a bit to tell the source computer it did indeed get its message. Once this gets back to the source computer, it removes the frames from the network. The destination computer makes a copy of the message, but only the originator of the message can remove the message from the token and the network.

If a computer that receives the token does not have a message to transmit, it sends the token to the next computer on the network. An empty token has a header, data field, and trailer, but a token that has an actual message has a new header, destination address, source address, and a new trailer.

This type of network access method is used by Token Ring and FDDI technologies.

 NOTE Some applications and network protocol algorithms work better if they can communicate at determined intervals, instead of "whenever the data arrives." In token-passing technologies, traffic arrives in this type of deterministic nature because not all systems can communicate at one time; only the system that has control of the token can communicate.

CSMA

Ethernet protocols define how nodes are to communicate, recover from errors, and access the shared network cable. Ethernet uses CSMA as an access method to the network cable. There are two distinct types of CSMA: CSMA/CD and CSMA/CA.

A transmission is called a *carrier*, so if a computer is transmitting frames, it is performing a carrier activity. When computers use the *carrier sense multiple access with collision detection (CSMA/CD)* protocol, they monitor the transmission activity, or carrier activity, on the wire so they can determine when would be the best time to transmit data. Each node monitors the wire continuously and waits until the wire is free before it transmits its data. As an analogy, consider several people gathered in a group talking here and there about this and that. If a person wants to talk, she usually listens to the current conversation and waits for a break before she proceeds to talk. If she does not wait for the first person to stop talking, she will be speaking at the same time as the other person, and the people around them may not be able to understand fully what each is trying to say.

When using the CSMA/CD access method, computers listen for the absence of a carrier tone on the cable, which indicates that no one else is transmitting data. If two computers sense this absence and transmit data at the same time, contention and a collision can take place. *Contention* means that the nodes have to compete for the same shared medium. A *collision* happens when two or more frames collide, which most likely corrupts both frames. If a computer puts frames on the wire and its frames collide with another computer's frames, it will abort its transmission and alert all other stations that a collision just took place. All stations will execute a random collision timer to force a delay before they attempt to transmit data. This random collision timer is called the *back-off algorithm*. (Collisions are usually reduced by dividing a network with bridges or switches.)

Carrier sense multiple access with collision avoidance (CSMA/CA) is an access method in which each computer signals its intent to transmit data before it actually does so. This tells all other computers on the network not to transmit data right now because doing so could cause a collision. Basically, a system listens to the shared medium to determine whether it is busy or free. Once the system identifies that the "coast is clear" and it can put its data on the wire, it sends out a broadcast to all other systems, telling them it is going to transmit information. It is similar to saying, "Everyone shut up. I am going to talk now." Each system will wait a period of time before attempting to transmit data, to ensure collisions do not take place. The wireless LAN technology, 802.11, uses CSMA/CA for its media access functionality.

Collision Domains

As indicated in the preceding section, a collision occurs on Ethernet networks when two computers transmit data at the same time. Other computers on the network detect this collision because the overlapping signals of the collision increase the voltage of the signal above a specific threshold. The more devices on a contention-based network, the more likely collisions will occur, which increases network *latency* (data transmission delays). A *collision domain* is a group of computers that are contending, or competing, for the same shared communication medium.

An unacceptable amount of collisions can be caused by a highly populated network, a damaged cable or connector, too many repeaters, or cables that exceed the recommended length. If a cable is longer than what is recommended by the Ethernet specification, two computers on opposite ends of the cable may transmit data at the same time. Because the computers are so far away from each other, they may both transmit data and not realize that a collision took place. The systems then go merrily along

Carrier-Sensing and Token-Passing Access Methods

Overall, carrier-sensing access methods are faster than token-passing access methods, but the former do have the problem of collisions. A network segment with many devices can cause too many collisions and slow down the network's performance. Token-passing technologies do not have problems with collisions, but they do not perform at the speed of carrier-sensing technologies. Network switches can help significantly in isolating the network resources, for both the CSMA/CD and the token-passing methods, because they reduce contention.

with their business, unaware that their packets have been corrupted. If the cable is too long, the computers may not listen long enough for evidence of a collision. If the destination computers receive these corrupted frames, they then have to send a request to the source system to retransmit the message, causing even more traffic.

These types of problems are dealt with mainly by implementing collision domains. An Ethernet network can have broadcast and collision domains. One subnet will be on the same broadcast and collision domain if it is not separated by routers or bridges. If the same subnet is divided by bridges, the bridges can enable the broadcast traffic to pass between the different parts of a subnet, but not the collisions, as shown in Figure 7-26. This is how collision domains are formed. Isolating collision domains reduces the amount of collisions that take place on a network and increases its overall performance.

Another benefit of restricting and controlling broadcast and collision domains is that it makes sniffing the network and obtaining useful information more difficult for an intruder as he traverses the network. A useful tactic for attackers is to install a Trojan horse that sets up a network sniffer on the compromised computer. The sniffer is usually configured to look for a specific type of information, such as usernames and passwords. If broadcast and collision domains are in effect, the compromised system will have access only to the broadcast and collision traffic within its specific subnet or broadcast domain. The compromised system will not be able to listen to traffic on other broadcast and collision domains, and this can greatly reduce the amount of traffic and information available to an attacker.

Polling
Hi. Do you have anything you would like to say?

The third type of LAN media access method is polling. In an environment where a *polling* LAN media access method is used, some systems are configured as primary stations and others are configured as secondary stations. At predefined intervals, the pri-

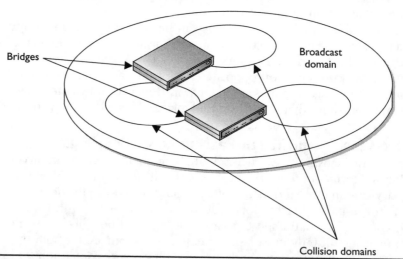

Figure 7-26   Collision domains within one broadcast domain

mary station asks the secondary station if it has anything to transmit. This is the only time a secondary station can communicate.

Polling is a method of monitoring multiple devices and controlling network access transmission. If polling is used to monitor devices, the primary device communicates with each secondary device in an interval to check its status. The primary device then logs the response it receives and moves on to the next device. If polling is used for network access, the primary station asks each device if it has something to communicate to another device. Network access transmission polling is used mainly with mainframe environments.

LAN Protocols

Some protocols, such as UDP, TCP, and IP, were addressed in earlier sections. Networks are made up of these and many other types of protocols that provide an array of functionality. Several of the most widely used TCP/IP protocols—ARP, DHCP, and ICMP—are discussed in the following sections.

Address Resolution Protocol

This IP does me no good! I need a MAC!

On a TCP/IP network, each computer and network device requires a unique IP address and a unique physical hardware address. Each NIC has a unique physical address that is programmed into the ROM chips on the card by the manufacturer. The physical address is also referred to as the *Media Access Control (MAC)* address. The network layer works with and understands IP addresses, and the data link layer works with and understands physical MAC addresses. So, how do these two types of addresses work together since they operate at different layers?

NOTE A MAC address is unique because the first 24 bits represent the manufacturer code and the last 24 bits represent the unique serial number assigned by the manufacturer.

When data comes from the application layer, it goes to the transport layer for sequence numbers, session establishment, and streaming. The data are then passed to the network layer, where routing information is added to each packet and the source and destination IP addresses are attached to the data bundle. Then this goes to the data link layer, which must find the MAC address and add it to the header portion of the frame. When a frame hits the wire, it only knows what MAC address it is heading toward. At this lower layer of the OSI model, the mechanisms do not even understand IP addresses. So if a computer cannot resolve the IP address passed down from the network layer to the corresponding MAC address, it cannot communicate with that destination computer.

NOTE A frame is data that are fully encapsulated, with all of the necessary headers and trailers.

MAC and IP addresses must be properly mapped so they can be correctly resolved. This happens through the *Address Resolution Protocol (ARP)*. When the data link layer receives a frame, the network layer has already attached the destination IP address to it, but the data link layer cannot understand the IP address and thus invokes ARP for help. ARP broadcasts a frame requesting the MAC address that corresponds with the destination IP address. Each computer on the subnet receives this broadcast frame, and all but the computer that has the requested IP address ignore it. The computer that has the destination IP address responds with its MAC address. Now ARP knows what hardware address corresponds with that specific IP address. The data link layer takes the frame, adds the hardware address to it, and passes it on to the physical layer, which enables the frame to hit the wire and go to the destination computer. ARP maps the hardware address and associated IP address and stores this mapping in its table for a predefined amount of time. This caching is done so that when another frame destined for the same IP address needs to hit the wire, ARP does not need to broadcast its request again. It just looks in its table for this information.

Sometimes attackers alter a system's ARP table so it contains incorrect information. This is called *ARP table poisoning*. The attacker's goal is to receive packets intended for another computer. This is a type of *masquerading* attack. For example, if computer A has an IP address of 10.19.34.3 and a MAC address of *x*, and computer B has this mapping in its ARP table, an attacker can alter the ARP table to indicate that IP address 10.19.34.3 is mapped to MAC address *y* (the attacker's MAC address), so any packets computer B tries to send to computer A actually go to the attacker's computer.

Dynamic Host Configuration Protocol

Can you just throw out addresses as necessary? I am too tired to do it manually.

A computer can receive its IP addresses in a few different ways when it first boots up. If it has a statically assigned address, nothing needs to happen. If a computer depends upon a Dynamic Host Configuration Protocol (DHCP) server to assign it the correct IP address, it boots up and makes a request to the DHCP server. The DHCP server assigns the IP address, and everyone is happy.

DHCP is a UDP-based protocol that allows servers to assign IP addresses to network clients in real time. Unlike static IP addresses, where IP addresses are manually configured, the DHCP automatically checks for available IP addresses and correspondingly assigns an IP address to the client. This eliminates the possibility of IP address conflicts that occur if two systems are assigned identical IP addresses, which could cause loss of service. On the whole, DHCP considerably reduces the effort involved in managing large-scale IP networks.

The DHCP assigns IP addresses in real time from a specified range when a client connects to the network; this is different from static addresses, where each system is individually assigned a specific IP address when coming on-line. In a standard DHCP-based network, the client computer broadcasts a *DHCP*DISCOVER message on the network in search of the DHCP server. Once the respective DHCP server receives the *DHCP*DISCOVER request, the server responds with a *DHCP*OFFER packet, offering the client an IP address. The server assigns the IP address based on the subject to the availability of an IP address and in compliance with its network administration policies. The *DHCP*OFFER packet that the server responds with contains the assigned IP address information and configuration settings for client-side services.

Once the client receives the settings sent by the server through the *DHCP*OFFER, it responds the server with a *DHCP*REQUEST packet confirming it acceptance of the allotted settings. The server now acknowledges with a *DHCP*ACK packet, mentioning the validity period *(lease)* for the allocated parameters.

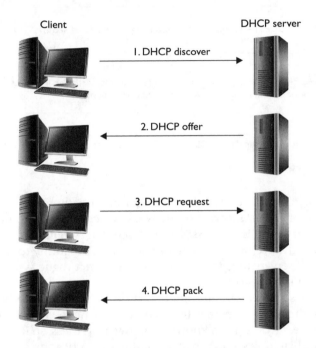

So as shown in Figure 7-27, the DHCP client yells out to the network, "Who can help me get an address?" The DHCP server responds with an offer: "Here is an address and the parameters that go with it." The client accepts this gracious offer, with the *DHCP*REQUEST message, and the server acknowledges this message. Now the client can start interacting with other devices on the network and the user can waste his valuable time on Facebook.

Unfortunately, both the client and server segments of the DHCP are vulnerable to falsified identity. On the client end, attackers can masquerade their systems to appear as valid network clients. This enables rogue systems to become a part of an organization's network and potentially infiltrate into other systems on the network. An attacker may create an unauthorized DHCP server on the network and start responding to clients searching for a DHCP server. A DHCP server controlled by an attacker can compromise client system configurations, carry out man-in-the-middle attacks, route traffic to unauthorized networks, and a lot more, with the end result of jeopardizing the entire network.

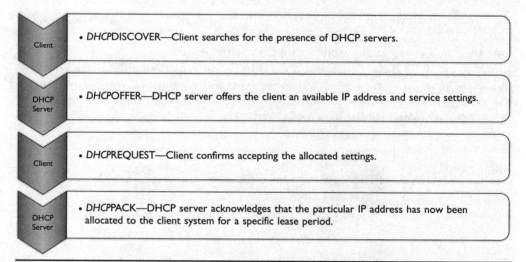

Figure 7-27   The four stages of the Discover, Offer, Request and Acknowledgment (D-O-R-A) process

An effective method to shield networks from unauthenticated DHCP clients is through the use of *DHCP snooping* on network switches. DHCP snooping ensures that DHCP servers can assign IP addresses to only selected systems, identified by their MAC addresses. Also, advance network switches now have capability to direct clients toward legitimate DHCP servers to get IP addresses and restrict rogue systems from becoming DHCP servers on the network.

Diskless workstations have just enough code to know how to boot up and broadcast for an IP address, and they may have a pointer to the server that holds the operating system. The diskless workstation knows its hardware address, so it broadcasts this information so that a listening server can assign it the correct IP address. As with ARP, *Reverse Address Resolution Protocol (RARP)* frames go to all systems on the subnet, but only the RARP server responds. Once the RARP server receives this request, it looks in its table to see which IP address matches the broadcast hardware address. The server then sends a message that contains its IP address back to the requesting computer. The system now has an IP address and can function on the network.

The *Boot Protocol (BOOTP)* was created after RARP to enhance the functionality that RARP provides for diskless workstations. The diskless workstation can receive its IP address, the name server address for future name resolutions, and the default gateway address from the BOOTP server. BOOTP usually provides more functionality to diskless workstations than RARP.

The evolution of this protocol has unfolded as follows: RARP evolved into BOOTP, which evolved into DHCP.

The Difference Between ARP and RARP

ARP knows the IP address and broadcasts to find the matching hardware address, the MAC address. RARP knows the hardware address and broadcasts to find the IP address.

Internet Control Message Protocol

The *Internet Control Message Protocol (ICMP)* is basically IP's "messenger boy." ICMP delivers status messages, reports errors, replies to certain requests, reports routing information, and is used to test connectivity and troubleshoot problems on IP networks.

The most commonly understood use of ICMP is through the use of the *ping* utility. When a person wants to test connectivity to another system, he may ping it, which sends out ICMP ECHO REQUEST frames. The replies on his screen that are returned to the ping utility are called ICMP ECHO REPLY frames and are responding to the ECHO REQUEST frames. If a reply is not returned within a predefined time period, the ping utility sends more ECHO REQUEST frames. If there is still no reply, ping indicates the host is unreachable.

ICMP also indicates when problems occur with a specific route on the network and tells surrounding routers about better routes to take based on the health and congestion of the various pathways. Routers use ICMP to send messages in response to datagrams that could not be delivered. The router selects the proper ICMP response and sends it back to the requesting host, indicating that problems were encountered with the transmission request.

ICMP is used by other connectionless protocols, not just IP, because connectionless protocols do not have any way of detecting and reacting to transmission errors, as do connection-oriented protocols. In these instances, the connectionless protocol may use ICMP to send error messages back to the sending system to indicate networking problems.

Loki Attack

The ICMP protocol was developed to send status messages, not to hold or transmit user data. But someone figured out how to insert some data inside of an ICMP packet, which can be used to communicate to an already compromised system. Loki is actually a client/server program used by hackers to set up backdoors on systems. The attacker targets a computer and installs the server portion of the Loki software. This server portion "listens" on a port, which is the backdoor an attacker can use to access the system. To gain access and open a remote shell to this computer, an attacker sends commands inside of ICMP packets. This is usually successful, because most routers are configured to allow ICMP traffic to come and go out of the network, based on the assumption that this is safe because ICMP was developed to not hold any data or a payload.

Routing Protocols

I have protocols that will tell you where to go.
Response: I would like to tell YOU where to go.

Individual networks on the Internet are referred to as ***autonomous systems (ASs)***. These ASs are independently controlled by different corporations and organizations. An AS is made up of routers, which are administered by a single entity and use a common Interior Gateway Protocol (IGP) within the boundaries of the AS. The boundaries of these ASs are delineated by border routers. These routers connect to the border routers of other ASs and run interior and exterior routing protocols. Internal routers connect to other routers within the same AS and run interior routing protocols. So, in reality, the Internet is just a network made up of ASs and routing protocols.

The architecture of the Internet that supports these various ASs is created so no entity that needs to connect to a specific AS has to know or understand the interior protocols that are being used. Instead, for ASs to communicate, they just have to be using the same exterior routing protocols (see Figure 7-28). As an analogy, suppose you want to deliver a package to a friend who lives in another state. You give the package to your brother, who is going to take a train to the edge of the state and hand it to the postal system at that junction. Thus, you know how your brother will arrive at the edge of the state—by train. You do not know how the postal system will then deliver your package to your friend's house (truck, car, bus), but that is not your concern. It will get to its destination without your participation. Similarly, when one network communicates with another network, the first network puts the data packet (package) on an exterior protocol (train), and when the data packet gets to the border router (edge of the state), the data are transferred to whatever interior protocol is being used on the receiving network. The routing protocols are used by routers to identify a path between the source and destination systems.

Routing protocols can be dynamic or static. A ***dynamic routing protocol*** can discover routes and build a routing table. Routers use these tables to make decisions on the best route for the packets they receive. A dynamic routing protocol can change the entries in the routing table based on changes that take place to the different routes. When a router that is using a dynamic routing protocol finds out that a route has gone down or is congested, it sends an update message to the other routers around it. The other routers use this information to update their routing table, with the goal of providing efficient routing functionality. A ***static routing protocol*** requires the administrator to manually configure the router's routing table.

Route flapping refers to the constant changes in the availability of routes. Also, if a router does not receive an update that a link has gone down, the router will continue to forward packets to that route, which is referred to as a *black hole*.

Two main types of routing protocols are used: distance-vector and link-state routing. ***Distance-vector routing protocols*** make their routing decisions based on the distance (or number of hops) and a vector (a direction). The protocol takes these variables and uses them with an algorithm to determine the best route for a packet. ***Link-state routing protocols*** build a more accurate routing table because they build a topology database of the network. These protocols look at more variables than just the number of hops between two destinations. They use packet size, link speed, delay, loading, and reliability as the variables in their algorithms to determine the best routes for packets to take.

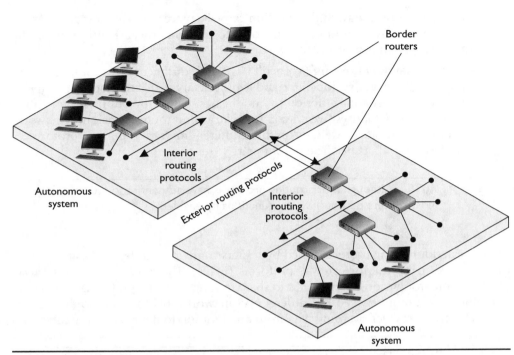

Figure 7-28 Autonomous systems

So, a distance-vector routing protocol only looks at the number of hops between two destinations and considers each hop to be equal. A link-state routing protocol sees more pieces to the puzzle than just the number of hops, but understands the status of each of those hops and makes decisions based on these factors also. As you will see, RIP is an example of a distance-vector routing protocol, and OSPF is an example of a link-state routing protocol. OSPF is preferred and is used in large networks. RIP is still around but should only be used in smaller networks.

De facto and proprietary interior protocols are being used today. The following are just a few of them:

- **Routing Information Protocol** RIP is a standard that outlines how routers exchange routing table data and is considered a distance-vector protocol, which means it calculates the shortest distance between the source and destination. It is considered a legacy protocol, because of its slow performance and lack of functionality. It should only be used in small networks. RIP version 1 has no authentication, and RIP version 2 sends passwords in cleartext or hashed with MD5.

- **Open Shortest Path First** OSPF uses link-state algorithms to send out routing table information. The use of these algorithms allows for smaller, more frequent routing table updates to take place. This provides a more stable network than RIP, but requires more memory and CPU resources to support this extra processing. OSPF allows for a hierarchical routing network that has a backbone link connecting all subnets together. OSPF has replaced RIP in many networks today. Authentication can take place with cleartext passwords or hashed passwords, or you can choose to configure no authentication on the routers using this protocol.

- **Interior Gateway Routing Protocol** IGRP is a distance-vector routing protocol that was developed by, and is proprietary to, Cisco Systems. Whereas RIP uses one criterion to find the best path between the source and destination, IGRP uses five criteria to make a "best route" decision. A network administrator can set weights on these different metrics so that the protocol works best in that specific environment.

 NOTE Although most routing protocols have authentication functionality, most routers do not have this functionality enabled.

The exterior routing protocols used by routers connecting different ASs are generically referred to as exterior gateway protocols (EGPs). The *Border Gateway Protocol (BGP)* enables routers on different ASs to share routing information to ensure effective and efficient routing between the different AS networks. BGP is commonly used by Internet service providers to route data from one location to the next on the Internet.

 NOTE There is an exterior routing protocol called Exterior Gateway Protocol, but it has been widely replaced by BGP, and now the term "exterior gateway protocol" and the acronym EGP are used to refer generically to a type of protocol rather than to specify the outdated protocol.

BGP uses a combination of link-state and distance-vector routing algorithms. It creates a network topology by using its link-state functionality and transmits updates on a periodic basis instead of continuously, which is how distance-vector protocols work. Network administrators can apply weights to the different variables used by link-state routing protocols when determining the best routes. These configurations are collectively called the *routing policy*.

Several types of attacks can take place on routers through their routing protocols. A majority of the attacks have the goal of misdirecting traffic through the use of spoofed ICMP messages. An attacker can masquerade as another router and submit routing table information to the victim router. After the victim router integrates this new information, it may be sending traffic to the wrong subnets or computers, or even to a nonexistent address (black hole). These attacks are successful mainly when routing protocol authentication is not enabled. When authentication is not required, a router can accept routing updates without knowing whether or not the sender is a legitimate router. An attacker could divert a company's traffic to review confidential information or to just disrupt traffic, which would be considered a DoS attack.

Other types of DoS attacks exist, such as flooding a router port, buffer overflows, and SYN floods. Since there are many different types of attacks that can take place, there are just as many countermeasures to be aware of to thwart these types of attacks. Most of these countermeasures involve authentication and encryption of routing data as it is

Wormhole Attack

An attacker can capture a packet at one location in the network and tunnel it to another location in the network. In this type of attack, there are two attackers, one at each end of the tunnel (referred to as a wormhole). Attacker A could capture an authentication token that is being sent to an authentication server, and then send this token to the other attacker, who then uses it to gain unauthorized access to a resource. This can take place on a wired or wireless network, but it is easier to carry out on a wireless network because the attacker does not need to actually penetrate a physical wire.

The countermeasure to this type of attack is to use a leash, which is just data that are put into a header of the individual packets. The leash restricts the packet's maximum allowed transmission distance. The leash can be either *geographical*, which ensures that a packet stays within a certain distance of the sender, or *temporal*, which limits the lifetime of the packet.

It is like the idea of invisible fences used on animals. You put a collar (leash) on your dog (packet) and it prevents him from leaving your yard (network segment).

transmitted back and forth through the use of shared keys or IPSec. For a good description of how these attacks can take place and their corresponding countermeasures, take a look at the Cisco Systems whitepaper "SAFE: Best Practices for Securing Routing Protocols" (www.cisco.com/warp/public/cc/so/neso/vpn/prodlit/sfblp_wp.pdf).

Networking Devices

Several types of devices are used in LANs, MANs, and WANs to provide intercommunication between computers and networks. The use of these devices varies according to their functionality, capabilities, intelligence, and network placement. We will look at the following devices:

- Repeaters
- Bridges
- Routers
- Switches

Repeaters

A *repeater* provides the simplest type of connectivity, because it only repeats and amplifies electrical signals between cable segments, which enables it to extend a network.

Repeaters work at the physical layer and are add-on devices for extending a network connection over a greater distance. The device amplifies signals because signals attenuate the farther they have to travel.

Repeaters can also work as line conditioners by actually cleaning up the signals. This works much better when amplifying digital signals than when amplifying analog signals, because digital signals are discrete units, which makes extraction of background noise from them much easier for the amplifier. If the device is amplifying analog signals, any accompanying noise often is amplified as well, which may further distort the signal.

A *hub* is a multiport repeater. A hub is often referred to as a *concentrator* because it is the physical communication device that allows several computers and devices to communicate with each other. A hub does not understand or work with IP or MAC addresses. When one system sends a signal to go to another system connected to it, the signal is broadcast to all the ports, and thus to all the systems connected to the concentrator.

Bridges

Is this like a bridge over troubled waters?
Response: You are so not funny.

A *bridge* is a LAN device used to connect LAN segments. It works at the data link layer and therefore works with MAC addresses. A repeater does not work with addresses; it just forwards all signals it receives. When a frame arrives at a bridge, the bridge determines whether or not the MAC address is on the local network segment. If the MAC address is not on the local network segment, the bridge forwards the frame to the necessary network segment.

A bridge is used to divide overburdened networks into smaller segments to ensure better use of bandwidth and traffic control. A bridge amplifies the electrical signal, as does a repeater, but it has more intelligence than a repeater and is used to extend a LAN and enable the administrator to filter frames so she can control which frames go where.

When using bridges, you have to watch carefully for **broadcast storms**. Because bridges can forward all traffic, they forward all broadcast packets as well. This can overwhelm the network and result in a broadcast storm, which degrades the network bandwidth and performance.

Three main types of bridges are used: local, remote, and translation. A *local bridge* connects two or more LAN segments within a local area, which is usually a building. A *remote bridge* can connect two or more LAN segments over a MAN by using telecommunications links. A remote bridge is equipped with telecommunications ports, which enable it to connect two or more LANs separated by a long distance and can be brought together via telephone lines. A *translation bridge* is needed if the two LANs being connected are different types and use different standards and protocols. For example, consider a connection between a Token Ring network and an Ethernet network. The frames on each network type are different sizes, the fields contain different protocol information, and the two networks transmit at different speeds. If a regular bridge were put into place, Ethernet frames would go to the Token Ring network, and vice versa, and neither would be able to understand messages that came from the other network segment. A translation bridge does what its name implies—it translates between the two network types.

The following list outlines the functions of a bridge:

- Segments a large network into smaller, more controllable pieces.
- Uses filtering based on MAC addresses.
- Joins different types of network links while retaining the same broadcast domain.

- Isolates collision domains within the same broadcast domain.

- Bridging functionality can take place locally within a LAN or remotely to connect two distant LANs.

- Can translate between protocol types.

NOTE Do not confuse routers with bridges. Routers work at the network layer and filter packets based on IP addresses, whereas bridges work at the data link layer and filter frames based on MAC addresses. Routers usually do not pass broadcast information, but bridges *do* pass broadcast information.

Forwarding Tables

You go that way. And you—you go this way!

A bridge must know how to get a frame to its destination—that is, it must know to which port the frame must be sent and where the destination host is located. Years ago, network administrators had to type route paths into bridges so the bridges had static paths indicating where to pass frames that were headed for different destinations. This was a tedious task and prone to errors. Today, bridges use *transparent bridging*.

If transparent bridging is used, a bridge starts to learn about the network's environment as soon as it is powered on and as the network changes. It does this by examining frames and making entries in its forwarding tables. When a bridge receives a frame from a new source computer, the bridge associates this new source address and the port on which it arrived. It does this for all computers that send frames on the network. Eventually, the bridge knows the address of each computer on the various network segments and to which port each is connected. If the bridge receives a request to send a frame to a destination that is not in its forwarding table, it sends out a query frame on each network segment except for the source segment. The destination host is the only one that replies to this query. The bridge updates its table with this computer address and the port to which it is connected, and forwards the frame.

Many bridges use the *Spanning Tree Algorithm (STA)*, which adds more intelligence to the bridges. STA ensures that frames do not circle networks forever, provides redundant paths in case a bridge goes down, assigns unique identifiers to each bridge, assigns priority values to these bridges, and calculates path costs. This creates much more efficient frame-forwarding processes by each bridge. STA also enables an administrator to indicate whether he wants traffic to travel certain paths instead of others.

If *source routing* is used instead of transparent bridging, the packets contain the necessary information within them to tell the bridge where they should go. The frames hold the forwarding information so they can find their way to their destination without needing bridges and routers to dictate their paths. If the computer wants to dictate its forwarding information instead of depending on a bridge, how does it know the correct route to the destination computer? The source computer sends out explorer packets that arrive at the destination computer. These packets contain the route information the packets had to take to get to the destination, including what bridges they had to pass through. The destination computer then sends these packets back to the source computer, and the source computer strips out the routing information, inserts it into the packets, and sends them on to the destination.

> **Q&A**
>
> **Question** What is the difference between two LANs connected via a bridge versus two LANs connected via a router?
>
> **Answer** If two LANs are connected with a bridge, the LANs have been extended, because they are both in the same broadcast domain. A router can be configured not to forward broadcast information, so if two LANs are connected with a router, an internetwork results. An internetwork is a group of networks connected in a way that enables any node on any network to communicate with any other node. The Internet is an example of an internetwork.

 NOTE External devices and border routers should not accept packets with source routing information within their headers, because that information will override what is laid out in the forwarding and routing tables configured on the intermediate devices. You want to control how traffic traverses your network; you don't want packets to have this type of control and be able to go wherever they want. Source routing can be used by attackers to get around certain bridge and router filtering rules.

Routers

We are going up the chain of the OSI layers while discussing various networking devices. Repeaters work at the physical layer, bridges work at the data link layer, and routers work at the network layer. As we go up each layer, each corresponding device has more intelligence and functionality because it can look deeper into the frame. A repeater looks at the electrical signal. The bridge can look at the MAC address within the header. The router can peel back the first header information and look farther into the frame and find out the IP address and other routing information. The farther a device can look into a frame, the more decisions it can make based on the information within the frame. We will see later that gateways can look all the way to the application layer—not just at addresses and routing information.

Routers are layer 3, or network layer, devices that are used to connect similar or different networks. (For example, they can connect two Ethernet LANs or an Ethernet LAN to a Token Ring LAN.) A router is a device that has two or more interfaces and a routing table so it knows how to get packets to their destinations. It can filter traffic based on access control lists (ACLs), and it fragments packets when necessary. Because routers have more network-level knowledge, they can perform higher-level functions, such as calculating the shortest and most economical path between the sending and receiving hosts.

A router discovers information about routes and changes that take place in a network through its routing protocols (RIP, BGP, OSPF, and others). These protocols tell routers if a link has gone down, if a route is congested, and if another route is more economical. They also update routing tables and indicate if a router is having problems or has gone down.

A bridge uses the same network address for all of its ports, but a router assigns a new address per port, which enables it to connect different networks together.

The router may be a dedicated appliance or a computer running a networking operating system that is dual-homed. When packets arrive at one of the interfaces, the router compares those packets to its ACLs. This list indicates what packets are allowed in and what packets are denied. Access decisions are based on source and destination IP addresses, protocol type, and source and destination ports. An administrator may block all packets coming from the 10.10.12.0 network, any FTP requests, or any packets headed toward a specific port on a specific host, for example. This type of control is provided by the ACLs, which the administrator must program and update as necessary.

What actually happens inside the router when it receives a packet? Let's follow the steps:

1. A frame is received on one of the interfaces of a router. The router views the routing data.

2. The router retrieves the destination IP network address from the datagram.

3. The router looks at its routing table to see which port matches the requested destination IP network address.

4. If the router does not have information in its table about the destination address, it sends out an ICMP error message to the sending computer indicating that the message could not reach its destination.

5. If the router does have a route in its routing table for this destination, it decrements the TTL value and sees whether the MTU is different for the destination network. If the destination network requires a smaller MTU, the router fragments the datagram.

6. The router changes header information in the frame so the frame can go to the next correct router, or if the destination computer is on a connecting network, the changes made enable the frame to go directly to the destination computer.

7. The router sends the frame to its output queue for the necessary interface.

Table 7-6 provides a quick review of the differences between routers and bridges.

When is it best to use a repeater, bridge, or router? A repeater is used if an administrator needs to expand a network and amplify signals so they do not weaken on longer cables. However, a repeater will forward collision and broadcast information because it does not have the intelligence to decipher among different types of traffic.

Bridges work at the data link layer and have a bit more intelligence than a repeater. Bridges can do simple filtering, and they separate collision domains, not broadcast domains. A bridge should be used when an administrator wants to divide a network into segments to reduce traffic congestion and excessive collisions.

A router splits up a network into collision domains and broadcast domains. A router gives more of a clear-cut division between network segments than repeaters or bridges. A router should be used if an administrator wants to have more defined control of where the traffic goes, because more sophisticated filtering is available with routers, and when a router is used to segment a network, the result is more controllable sections.

Bridge	Router
Reads header information, but does not alter it	Creates a new header for each frame
Builds forwarding tables based on MAC addresses	Builds routing tables based on IP addresses
Uses the same network address for all ports	Assigns a different network address per port
Filters traffic based on MAC addresses	Filters traffic based on IP addresses
Forwards broadcast packets	Does not forward broadcast packets
Forwards traffic if a destination address is unknown to the bridge	Does not forward traffic that contains a destination address unknown to the router

Table 7-6   Main Differences Between Bridges and Routers

A router is used when an administrator wants to divide a network along the lines of departments, workgroups, or other business-oriented divisions. A bridge divides segments based more on the traffic type and load.

Switches

I want to talk to you privately. Let's talk through this switch.

Switches combine the functionality of a repeater and the functionality of a bridge. A switch amplifies the electrical signal, like a repeater, and has the built-in circuitry and intelligence of a bridge. It is a multiport connection device that provides connections for individual computers or other hubs and switches. Any device connected to one port can communicate with a device connected to another port with its own virtual private link. How does this differ from the way in which devices communicate using a bridge or a hub? When a frame comes to a hub, the hub sends the frame out through all of its ports. When a frame comes to a bridge, the bridge sends the frame to the port to which the destination network segment is connected. When a frame comes to a switch, the switch sends the frame directly to the destination computer or network, which results in a reduction of traffic. Figure 7-29 illustrates a network configuration that has computers directly connected to their corresponding switches.

On Ethernet networks, computers have to compete for the same shared network medium. Each computer must listen for activity on the network and transmit its data when it thinks the coast is clear. This contention and the resulting collisions cause traffic delays and use up precious bandwidth. When switches are used, contention and collisions are not issues, which results in more efficient use of the network's bandwidth and decreased latency. Switches reduce or remove the sharing of the network medium and the problems that come with it.

A switch is a multiport bridging device, and each port provides dedicated bandwidth to the device attached to it. A port is bridged to another port so the two devices have an end-to-end private link. The switch employs full-duplex communication, so one wire pair is used for sending and another pair is used for receiving. This ensures the two connected devices do not compete for the same bandwidth.

Basic switches work at the data link layer and forward traffic based on MAC addresses. However, today's layer 3, layer 4, and other layer switches have more enhanced

Figure 7-29
Switches enable devices to communicate with each other via their own virtual link.

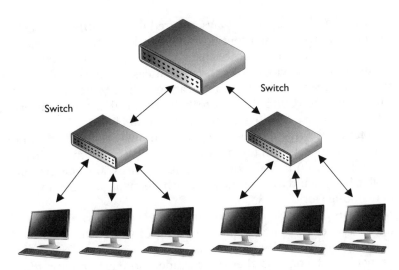

Switch

Switch

functionality than layer 2 switches. These higher-level switches offer routing functionality, packet inspection, traffic prioritization, and QoS functionality. These switches are referred to as *multilayered switches* because they combine data link layer, network layer, and other layer functionalities.

Multilayered switches use hardware-based processing power, which enables them to look deeper within the packet, to make more decisions based on the information found within the packet, and then provide routing and traffic management tasks. Usually this amount of work creates a lot of overhead and traffic delay, but multilayered switches perform these activities within an application-specific integrated circuit (ASIC). This means that most of the functions of the switch are performed at the hardware and chip level rather than at the software level, making it a much quicker method.

Layer 3 and 4 Switches

I want my switch to do everything, even make muffins.

Layer 2 switches only have the intelligence to forward a frame based on its MAC address and do not have a higher understanding of the network as a whole. A layer 3 switch has the intelligence of a router. It not only can route packets based on their IP addresses, but also can choose routes based on availability and performance. A layer 3 switch is basically a router on steroids because it moves the route lookup functionality to the more efficient switching hardware level.

The basic distinction between layer 2, 3, and 4 switches is the header information the device looks at to make forwarding or routing decisions (data link, network, or transport OSI layers). But layer 3 and 4 switches can use tags, which are assigned to each destination network or subnet. When a packet reaches the switch, the switch compares the destination address with its Tag Information Base, which is a list of all the subnets and their corresponding tag numbers. The switch appends the tag to the packet and sends it to the next switch. All the switches in between this first switch and the destination host just review this tag information to determine which route it needs to take, instead of analyzing the full header. Once the packet reaches the last router or switch, this tag is removed and the packet is sent to the destination. This process increases the speed of routing of packets from one location to another.

The use of these types of tags, referred to as *Multiprotocol Label Switching (MPLS)*, not only allows for faster routing, but also addresses service requirements for the different packet types. Some time-sensitive traffic (such as video conferencing) requires a certain level of service (QoS) that guarantees a minimum rate of data delivery to meet the requirements of a user or application. When MPLS is used, different priority information is placed into the tags to help ensure that time-sensitive traffic has a higher priority than less-sensitive traffic, as shown in Figure 7-30.

Many enterprises today use a switched network in which computers are connected to dedicated ports on Ethernet switches, Gigabit Ethernet switches, ATM switches, and more. This evolution of switches, added services, and the capability to incorporate repeater, bridge, and router functionality have made switches an important part of today's networking world.

Because security requires control over who can access specific resources, more intelligent devices can provide a higher level of protection because they can make more detail-oriented decisions regarding who can access resources. When devices can look deeper into the packets, they can consider more information to make access decisions, which provides more granular access control.

As previously stated, switching makes it more difficult for intruders to sniff and monitor network traffic because no broadcast and collision information is continually traveling throughout the network. Switches provide a security service that other devices cannot provide. *Virtual LANs (VLANs)* are also an important part of switching networks, because they enable administrators to have more control over their environment and they can isolate users and groups into logical and manageable entities. VLANs are described in the next section.

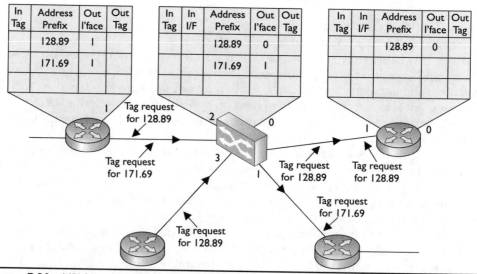

Figure 7-30   MPLS used in time-sensitive traffic

VLANs

What does the V stand for?
Response: Varmint!

The technology behind switches has introduced the capability to use virtual LANs (VLANs). VLANs enable administrators to separate and group computers logically based on resource requirements, security, or business needs instead of the standard physical location of the systems. When repeaters, bridges, and routers are used, systems and resources are grouped in a manner dictated by their physical location. Figure 7-31 shows how computers that are physically located next to each other can be grouped logically into different VLANs. Administrators can form these groups based on the users' and company's needs instead of the physical location of systems and resources.

An administrator may want to place the computers of all users in the Marketing department in the same VLAN network, for example, so all users receive the same broadcast messages and can access the same types of resources. This arrangement could get tricky if a few of the users are located in another building or on another floor, but VLANs provide the administrator with this type of flexibility. VLANs also enable an administrator to apply particular security policies to respective logical groups. This way, if tighter security is required for the payroll department, for example, the administrator

Figure 7-31
VLANs enable administrators to put systems into logical networks.

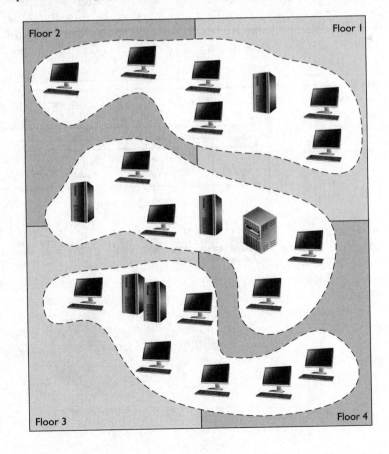

can develop a policy, add all payroll systems to a specific VLAN, and apply the security policy only to the payroll VLAN.

A VLAN exists on top of the physical network, as shown in Figure 7-32. If workstation P1 wants to communicate with workstation D1, the message has to be routed—even though the workstations are physically next to each other—because they are on different logical networks.

Gateways

Gateway is a general term for software running on a device that connects two different environments and which many times acts as a translator for them or somehow restricts their interactions. Usually a gateway is needed when one environment speaks a different language, meaning it uses a certain protocol that the other environment does not understand. The gateway can translate Internetwork Packet Exchange (IPX) protocol packets to IP packets, accept mail from one type of mail server and format it so another type of mail server can accept and understand it, or connect and translate different data link technologies such as FDDI to Ethernet.

Gateways perform much more complex tasks than connection devices such as routers and bridges. However, some people refer to routers as gateways when they connect two unlike networks (Token Ring and Ethernet) because the router has to translate between the data link technologies. Figure 7-33 shows how a network access server (NAS) functions as a gateway between telecommunications and network connections.

Figure 7-32
VLANs exist on a higher level than the physical network and are not bound to it.

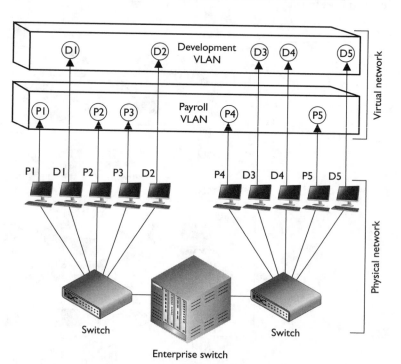

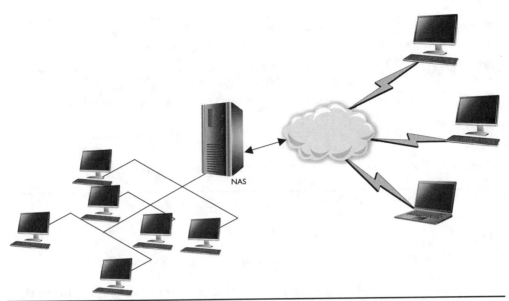

Figure 7-33 Several types of gateways can be used in a network. An NAS is one example.

When networks connect to a backbone, a gateway can translate the different technologies and frame formats used on the backbone network versus the connecting LAN protocol frame formats. If a bridge were set up between an FDDI backbone and an Ethernet LAN, the computers on the LAN would not understand the FDDI protocols and frame formats. In this case, a LAN gateway would be needed to translate the protocols used between the different networks.

A popular type of gateway is an *electronic mail* gateway. Because several e-mail vendors have their own syntax, message format, and way of dealing with message transmission, e-mail gateways are needed to convert messages between e-mail server software. For example, suppose that David, whose corporate network uses Sendmail, writes an e-mail message to Dan, whose corporate network uses Microsoft Exchange. The e-mail gateway will convert the message into a standard that all mail servers understand—usually X.400—and pass it on to Dan's mail server.

Another example of a gateway is a voice and media gateway. Recently, there has been a drive to combine voice and data networks. This provides for a lot of efficiency because the same media can be used for both types of data transfers. However, voice is a streaming technology, whereas data are usually transferred in packets. So, this shared media eventually has to communicate with two different types of networks: the telephone company's PSTN, and routers that will take the packet-based data off to the Internet. This means that a gateway must separate the combined voice and data information and put it into a form that each of the networks can understand.

Table 7-7 lists the devices covered in this "Networking Devices" section and points out their important characteristics.

Device	OSI Layer	Functionality
Repeater	Physical	Amplifies the signal and extends networks.
Bridge	Data Link	Forwards packets and filters based on MAC addresses; forwards broadcast traffic, but not collision traffic.
Router	Network	Separates and connects LANs creating internetworks; routers filter based on IP addresses.
Switch	Data Link	Provides a private virtual link between communicating devices; allows for VLANs; reduces collisions; impedes network sniffing.
Gateway	Application	Connects different types of networks; performs protocol and format translations.

Table 7-7 Network Device Differences

PBXs

I have to dial a 9 to get an outside line. Does that mean the CIA is watching me?
Response: Yep.

Telephone companies use switching technologies to transmit phone calls to their destinations. A telephone company's central office houses the switches that connect towns, cities, and metropolitan areas through the use of optical fiber rings. So, for example, when Dusty makes a phone call from his house, the call first hits the local central office of the telephone company that provides service to Dusty, and then the switch within that office decides whether it is a local or long-distance call and where it needs to go from there. A *Private Branch Exchange (PBX)* is a private telephone switch that is located on a company's property. This switch performs some of the same switching tasks that take place at the telephone company's central office. The PBX has a dedicated connection to its local telephone company's central office, where more intelligent switching takes place.

A PBX can interface with several types of devices and provides a number of telephone services. The data are multiplexed onto a dedicated line connected to the telephone company's central office. Figure 7-34 shows how data from different data sources can be placed on one line at the PBX and sent to the telephone company's switching facility.

PBXs use digital switching devices that can control analog and digital signals. Older PBXs may support only analog devices, but most PBXs have been updated to digital. This move to digital systems and signals has reduced a number of the PBX and telephone security vulnerabilities that used to exist. However, that in no way means PBX fraud does not take place today. Many companies, for example, have modems hanging off their PBX (or other transmission access methods) to enable the vendor to dial in and perform maintenance to the system. These modems are usually unprotected doorways into a company's network. The modem should be activated only when a problem requires the vendor to dial in. It should be disabled otherwise.

In addition, many PBX systems have default system manager passwords that are hardly ever changed. These passwords are set by default; therefore, if 100 companies purchased and implemented 100 PBX systems from the PBX vendor ABC and they do not reset the password, a *phreaker* (a phone hacker) who knows this default password

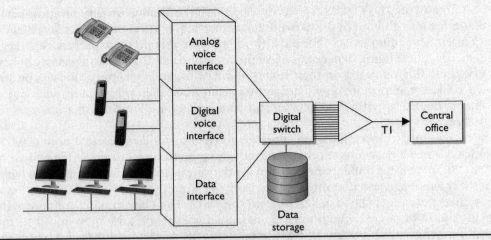

Figure 7-34 A PBX combines different types of data on the same lines.

would now have access to 100 PBX systems. Once a phreaker breaks into a PBX system, she can cause mayhem by rerouting calls, reconfiguring switches, or configuring the system to provide her and her friends with free long-distance calls. This type of fraud happens more often than most companies realize, because many companies do not closely watch their phone bills.

PBX systems are also vulnerable to brute force and other types of attacks, in which phreakers use scripts and dictionaries to guess the necessary credentials to gain access to the system. In some cases, phreakers have listened to and changed people's voice messages. So, for example, when people call to leave Bob a message, they might not hear his usual boring message, but a new message that is screaming obscenities and insults.

Firewalls

A wall that is on fire will stop anyone.
Response: That's the idea.

  Firewalls are used to restrict access to one network from another network. Most companies use firewalls to restrict access to their networks from the Internet. They may also use firewalls to restrict one internal network segment from accessing another internal segment. For example, if the network administrator wants to make sure employees cannot access the Research and Development network, he would place a firewall between this network and all other networks and configure the firewall to allow only the type of traffic he deems acceptable.

  A firewall device supports and enforces the company's network security policy. An organizational security policy provides high-level instructions on acceptable and unacceptable actions as they pertain to security. The firewall has a more defined and granular security policy that dictates what services are allowed to be accessed, what IP addresses and ranges are to be restricted, and what ports can be accessed. The firewall is described as a "choke point" in the network, because all communication should flow through it, and this is where traffic is inspected and restricted.

A firewall may be a router, server, or specialized hardware device. It monitors packets coming into and out of the network it is protecting. It filters out the packets that do not meet the requirements of the security policy. It can discard these packets, repackage them, or redirect them, depending upon the firewall configuration and security policy. Packets are filtered based on their source and destination addresses and ports by service, packet type, protocol type, header information, sequence bits, and much more. Vendors can use specific functionality and parameters for identification and access restriction.

Many times, companies set up firewalls to construct a *demilitarized zone (DMZ)*, which is a network segment located between the protected and unprotected networks. The DMZ provides a buffer zone between the dangerous Internet and the goodies within in the internal network that the company is trying to protect. As shown in Figure 7-35, two firewalls are usually installed to form the DMZ. The DMZ usually contains web, mail, and DNS servers, which must be hardened systems because they would be the first in line for attacks. Many DMZs also have an IDS sensor that listens for malicious and suspicious behavior.

Many different types of firewalls are available, because each environment may have unique requirements and security goals. Firewalls have gone through an evolution of their own and have grown in sophistication and functionality. The following sections describe the various types of firewalls.

The types of firewalls we will review are

- Packet filtering
- Stateful
- Proxy
- Dynamic packet filtering
- Kernel proxy

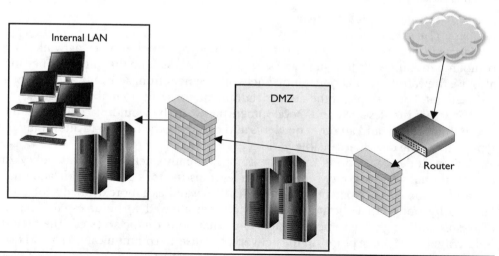

Figure 7-35   At least two firewalls, or firewall interfaces, are generally used to construct a DMZ.

We will then dive into the three main firewall architectures, which are

- Screened host
- Dual-home
- Screened subnet

Then, we will look at honeypots and their uses, so please return all seats to their upright position and lock your tray tables in front of you—we will be taking off shortly.

Packet-Filtering Firewalls

I don't like this packet. Oh, but I like this packet. I don't like this packet. This other packet is okay.

Packet filtering is a security method of controlling what data can flow into and out of a network. Packet filtering takes place by using ACLs, which are developed and applied to a device. ACLs are lines of text, called *rules*, that the device applies to each packet it receives. The lines of text provide specific information pertaining to what packets can be accepted and what packets must be denied. For instance, an ACL may have one line that states that any packets coming from the IP range 172.168.0.0 must be denied; a second line that indicates no packets using the Telnet service are allowed to enter the network; a third line indicating that no traffic headed toward port 443 is allowed; and a fourth line that indicates all traffic on port 80 is acceptable and should be routed to a specific IP address, which is the web server. Each time the device receives a packet, it compares the information in the packet's header to each line in the ACL. If the packet indicates it is using Telnet or requests to make a connection to port 443, it is discarded. If the packet header information indicates it wants to communicate through port 80 using HTTP over TCP, the packet is accepted and redirected to the web server.

This filtering is based on network layer information, which means the device cannot look too far into the packet itself. It can make decisions based on header information only, which is limited. Most routers use ACLs to act as a type of firewall and use a router table to carry out routing decisions, but they do not provide the level of protection offered by other types of firewalls, which look deeper into the packet. Because packet filtering looks only at the header information, it is not application dependent, as many proxy firewalls are. Packet-filtering firewalls also do not keep track of the state of a connection, which takes place in a stateful-inspection firewall (discussed next). Packet filtering is the method used by the first-generation firewall—that is, it was the first type created and used, while other types subsequently developed fall into later generations.

Some of the weaknesses of packet-filtering firewalls are listed next:

- They cannot prevent attacks that employ application-specific vulnerabilities or functions.
- The logging functionality present in packet-filtering firewalls is limited.
- Most packet-filtering firewalls do not support advanced user authentication schemes.
- Many packet-filtering firewalls cannot detect a network packet in which the OSI layer 3 addressing information has been altered (spoofed).

- Due to the small number of variables used in access control decisions, packet-filtering firewalls are susceptible to security breaches caused by improper configurations.

The advantages to using packet-filtering firewalls are that they are scalable, they are not application dependent, and they have high performance because they do not carry out extensive processing on the packets.

Stateful Firewalls

This packet came from Texas, so it is okay.
Response: That's a different type of state.

When packet filtering is used, a packet arrives at the router, and the router runs through its ACLs to determine whether this packet should be allowed or denied. If the packet is allowed, it is passed on to the destination host, or to another router, and the router forgets about the packet. This is different from stateful inspection filtering, which remembers and keeps track of what packets went where until each particular connection is closed.

Stateful filtering is like a nosy neighbor who gets into people's business and conversations. She keeps track of who said what and when. This can be annoying until your house is burglarized. Then you and the police will want to talk to the nosy neighbor, because she knows everything going on in the neighborhood and would be the one most likely to know something unusual happened. A stateful-inspection firewall is nosier than a regular filtering device, because it keeps track of what computers say to each other. This requires that the firewall maintain a *state table*, which is like a score sheet of who said what to whom.

Stateful-inspection firewalls also make decisions on what packets to allow or disallow, but their functionality goes a step further. For example, a regular packet-filtering device may deny any UDP packets requesting service on port 25, and a stateful packet-filtering device may have a rule to allow UDP packets through only if they are responses to outgoing requests. So, for example, if Mitchell sends a request to a computer on a different network, this request is logged in the firewall's state table to indicate that Mitchell's computer made a request and that packets should be coming back to Mitchell. When the computer on the Internet responds to Mitchell, these packets are compared to the data in the state table at the firewall. Because the state table has information about a previous request for these packets, the firewall allows the packets to pass through. If, on the other hand, Mitchell had not made any requests and packets were coming in from the Internet to him, the firewall would see that no previous request for this information was received and then would look at its ACLs to see if these packets should be allowed.

Regular packet filtering compares incoming packets to rules defined in the firewall's ACLs. When a stateful-inspection firewall receives a packet, it first looks in its state table to see whether a connection has already been established and whether these data were requested. If there was no previous connection and the state table holds no information about the packet, the packet is compared to the device's ACLs. If the ACL allows this type of traffic, the packet is allowed to access the network. If that type of traffic is not allowed, the packet is dropped.

Most stateful-inspection firewalls work at the network and transport layers. It depends upon the product, but many times when a connection begins, the firewall investigates all layers of the packet (all headers, payload, and trailers). Once the initial packets go through this in-depth inspection, the firewall then just reviews the network and transport header portions for the rest of the session. Scaling down the inspection in this manner is done to increase performance.

Although stateful inspection provides an extra step of protection, it also adds more complexity because this device must now keep a dynamic state table and remember connections. Stateful-inspection firewalls unfortunately have been the victims of many types of Denial-of-Service (DoS) attacks. Several types of attacks are aimed at flooding the state table with bogus information. The state table is a resource, similar to a system's hard drive space, memory, and CPU. When the state table is stuffed full of bogus information, the device may either freeze or reboot. In addition, if this firewall must be rebooted for some reason, it will lose its information on all recent connections; thus, it may deny legitimate packets.

Proxy Firewalls

Meet my proxy. He will be our middleman.

A *proxy* is a middleman. It intercepts and inspects messages before delivering them to the intended recipients. Suppose you need to give a box and a message to the president of the United States. You couldn't just walk up to the president and hand over these items. Instead, you would have to go through a middleman, likely the Secret Service, who would accept the box and message and thoroughly inspect the box to ensure nothing dangerous was inside. This is what a proxy firewall does—it accepts messages either entering or leaving a network, inspects them for malicious information, and, when it decides the messages are okay, passes the data on to the destination computer. Proxy firewalls are second-generation firewalls.

A proxy firewall stands between a trusted and untrusted network and makes the connection, each way, on behalf of the source. So, if a user on the Internet requests to send data to a computer on the internal protected network, the proxy firewall gets this request first and looks it over for suspicious information. The request does not automatically go to the destination computer—instead, the proxy firewall accepts the request on behalf of

Stateful-Inspection Firewall Characteristics

The following lists some important characteristics of a stateful-inspection firewall:

- Maintains a state table that tracks each and every communication channel
- Provides a high degree of security and does not introduce the performance hit that application proxy firewalls introduce
- Is scalable and transparent to users
- Provides data for tracking connectionless protocols such as UDP and ICMP
- Stores and updates the state and context of the data within the packets
- Is considered a third-generation firewall

the computer it is protecting. If the proxy firewall decides the packet is safe, it sends it on to the destination computer. When the destination computer replies, the reply goes back to the proxy firewall, which repackages the packet to contain the source address of the proxy firewall, not the host system on the internal network. What is important is that a proxy firewall breaks the communication channel; there is no direct connection to internal computers.

This type of firewall makes a copy of each accepted packet before transmitting it. It repackages the packet to hide the packet's true origin. If an attacker attempts to scan or probe a company's network, he will receive only information that has been intercepted and repackaged by the proxy firewall. The returned packets will have only the IP address of the firewall, and the information released will be sparse; thus, the internal network is protected and hidden.

The proxy firewall is the only machine that talks to the outside world. This ensures no computer has direct access to internal computers. This also means the proxy firewall is the only computer that needs a valid public IP address. The rest of the computers on the internal network can use private (nonroutable IP addresses on the Internet) addresses, because no computers on the outside will see their addresses anyway.

Many firewalls are *multihomed*, meaning they have more than one NIC. This allows the company to create several independent DMZs. One interface is connected to the untrusted network (usually the Internet), another interface is connected to the trusted network (internal company network), and the other interfaces can segment different DMZs. One DMZ may have the company's web servers, while the other DMZ has the company's public mail and DNS server.

Other types of firewalls can reside and work on a dual-homed firewall—proxy firewalls being one of them. These firewall architectures are discussed in the "Firewall Architecture" section later in the chapter.

Two types of proxy firewalls can be used: application-level and circuit-level, which are described next.

Pros and Cons of Proxy Firewalls

Pros:

- Looks at the information within a packet, possibly all the way up to the application layer.
- Provides better security than packet filtering.
- Breaks the connection between trusted and untrusted systems.

Cons:

- Some proxy firewalls support only a limited number of applications.
- Degrades traffic performance.
- Application-based proxy firewalls may have scalability and performance issues.
- Breaks the client/server model, which is good for security but sometimes bad for functionality.

Application- and Circuit-Level Proxies Proxies have been described as middlemen between untrusted external hosts and trusted internal hosts. However, there are more issues to understand when looking at the two different types of proxy firewalls available. *Application-level proxies* inspect the packet up through the application layer and make access decisions based on the content of the packet. They understand various services and protocols and the commands that are used by them. An application-level proxy can distinguish between an FTP GET command and an FTP PUT command, for example, and make access decisions based on this granular level of information; on the other hand, packet-filtering firewalls can allow or deny FTP requests only as a whole, not by the commands used within the FTP protocol.

An application-level proxy works for one service or protocol. A computer can have many types of services and protocols (FTP, NTP, SMTP, Telnet, and so on). Thus, one application-level proxy per service is required. This does not mean one proxy firewall per service is required, but rather that one portion of the firewall product is dedicated to understanding how a specific protocol works and how to properly filter it for suspicious data.

A *circuit-level proxy* creates a circuit between the client computer and the server and provides protection at the session layer. It does not understand or care about the higher-level issues an application-level proxy deals with. It knows the source and destination addresses and makes access decisions based on this type of header information.

Providing application-level proxy services can be a tricky undertaking. The proxy must totally understand how specific protocols work and what commands within that protocol are legitimate. This is a lot to know and look at during the transmission of data. As an analogy, picture a screening station at an airport that is made up of many employees, all with the job of interviewing people before they are allowed into the airport and onto an airplane. These employees have been trained to ask specific questions and detect suspicious answers and activities, and have the skill set and authority to detain suspicious individuals. Now, suppose each of these employees speaks a different language, because the people they interview come from different parts of the world. So, one employee who speaks German could not understand and identify suspicious answers of a person from Italy, because they do not speak the same language. This is the same for an application-level proxy firewall. Each proxy is a piece of software that has been designed to understand how a specific protocol "talks" and how to identify suspicious data within a transmission using that protocol.

 NOTE Any type of proxy firewall deconstructs the packets it receives. This means it takes the packet apart and analyzes the pieces for suspicious activity.

If the application-level proxy firewall does not understand a certain protocol or service, it cannot protect this type of communication. In this scenario, a circuit-level proxy is useful because it does not deal with such complex issues. An advantage of a circuit-level proxy is that it can handle a wider variety of protocols and services than an application-level proxy, but the downfall is that the circuit-level proxy cannot provide the degree of granular control an application-level proxy provides. Life is just full of compromises.

A circuit-level proxy works similar to a packet filter in that it makes access decisions based on address, port, and protocol type. It looks at the data within the packet header rather than the data at the application layer of the packet. It does not know whether the contents within the packet are safe or unsafe.

An application-level proxy, on the other hand, is dedicated to a particular protocol or service. At least one proxy is used per protocol because one proxy could not properly interpret all the commands of all the protocols coming its way. A circuit-level proxy works at a lower layer of the OSI model and does not require one proxy per protocol because it does not look at such detailed information.

SOCKS is an example of a circuit-level proxy gateway that provides a secure channel between two computers. When a SOCKS-enabled client sends a request to access a computer on the Internet, this request actually goes to the network's SOCKS proxy firewall, as shown in Figure 7-36, which inspects the packets for malicious information and checks its policy rules to see whether this type of connection is allowed. If the packet is acceptable and this type of connection is allowed, the SOCKS firewall sends the message to the destination computer on the Internet. When the computer on the Internet responds, it sends its packets to the SOCKS firewall, which again inspects the data and then passes the packets on to the client computer.

The SOCKS firewall can screen, filter, audit, log, and control data flowing in and out of a protected network. Because of its popularity, many applications and protocols have been configured to work with SOCKS in a manner that takes less configuration on the administrator's part, and various firewall products have integrated SOCKS software to provide circuit-based protection.

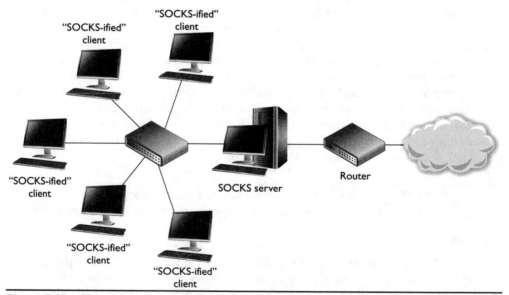

Figure 7-36 The SOCKS server usually sits behind a router, and each SOCKS client must have SOCKS software installed.

Application-Level vs. Circuit-Level Proxy Firewall Characteristics

Characteristics of application-level proxy firewalls:

- Have a different proxy required for each service allowed
- Provide more intricate control than circuit-level proxy firewalls
- Require more processing per packet and thus are slower than a circuit-level proxy firewall

Characteristics of circuit-level proxy firewalls:

- Do not require a proxy for each and every service
- Do not provide the detailed access control an application-level proxy firewall provides
- Provide security for a wider range of protocols

Because SOCKS is a circuit-level proxy, it does not provide detailed, protocol-specific control. The SOCKS product includes the SOCKS server software, which can run on Unix servers, a SOCKS client library, "SOCKS-ified" versions of several applications and protocols, and SOCKS wrappers for utilities such as traceroute and ping.

The benefits of using application-level proxy firewalls are laid out in the following:

- They have extensive logging capabilities due to the firewall being able to examine the entire network packet rather than just the network addresses and ports.
- User authentication is deemed appropriate for a given enterprise infrastructure. Application-layer proxy gateways are capable of authenticating users directly, as opposed to packet-filtering firewalls and stateful-inspection packet-filtering firewalls, which can only carry out system authentication.
- Since application-layer proxy gateway firewalls are not simply layer 3 devices, they can address spoofing attacks and other sophisticated attacks.

SOCKS Proxy Firewall Characteristics

The following are some important characteristics of a SOCKS firewall:

- It is a circuit-level proxy firewall.
- It requires clients to be "SOCKS-ified" with SOCKS client software.
- It can be resource intensive.
- It provides authentication and encryption features similar to other VPN protocols, but is not considered a traditional VPN protocol.

Some of the disadvantages of using application-level proxy firewalls include the following:

- Are not generally well suited to high-bandwidth or real-time applications.
- Tend to be limited in terms of support for new network applications and protocols.
  - Most application-layer proxy gateway firewall vendors provide generic proxy agents to support undefined network protocols or applications.
  - Generic agents tend to negate many of the strengths of the application-layer proxy gateway architecture and thus simply allow traffic to "tunnel" through the firewall.

Dynamic Packet Filtering

When an internal system needs to communicate to an entity outside its trusted network, it must choose a source port so the receiving system knows how to respond properly. The receiving system requires an IP address and a port number so its response can find its way to the sender's computer. Ports up to 1023 are called *well-known ports* and are reserved for server-side services. The sender must choose a dynamic port higher than 1023 when it sets up a connection with another entity. The dynamic packet-filtering firewall then creates an ACL that allows the external entity to communicate with the internal system via this high port. If this were not an available option for your dynamic packet-filtering firewall, you would have to allow "punch holes" in your firewalls for all ports above 1023, because the client side chooses these ports dynamically and the firewall would never know exactly on which port to allow or disallow traffic.

 NOTE The standard port for HTTP is 80, which means a server will have a service listening on port 80 for HTTP traffic. HTTP (and most other protocols) works in a type of client/server model. The server portion uses the well-known ports (FTP uses 20 and 21; SMTP uses 25) so everyone knows how to connect to those services. A client will not use one of these well-known port numbers for itself, but will choose a random, high port number.

An internal system could choose a source port of 11,111 for its message to the outside system. This frame goes to the dynamic packet-filtering firewall, which builds an ACL, as illustrated in Figure 7-37, that indicates a response from the destination computer to this internal system's IP address and port 11,111 is to be allowed. When the destination system sends a response, the firewall allows it. These ACLs are dynamic in nature, so once the connection is finished (either an FIN or RST packet is received), the ACL is removed from the list. On connectionless protocols, such as UDP, the connection times out and then the ACL is pulled.

The benefit of a dynamic packet-filtering firewall, which is a fourth-generation firewall, is that it gives you the option of allowing any type of traffic outbound and permitting only response traffic inbound.

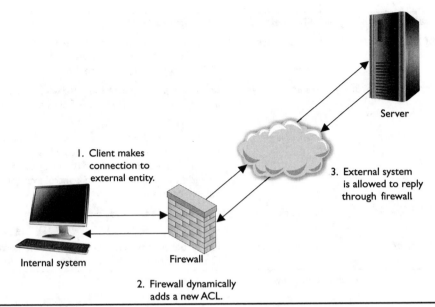

1. Client makes connection to external entity.

Internal system

Firewall

2. Firewall dynamically adds a new ACL.

Server

3. External system is allowed to reply through firewall

Figure 7-37 Dynamic packet filtering adds ACLs when connections are created.

Kernel Proxy Firewalls

This firewall is made from kernels of corn.
Response: Why are you here?

A **kernel proxy firewall** is considered a fifth-generation firewall. It differs from all the previously discussed firewall technologies because it creates dynamic, customized TCP/IP stacks when a packet needs to be evaluated.

When a packet arrives at a kernel proxy firewall, a new virtual network stack is created, which is made up of only the protocol proxies necessary to examine this specific packet properly. If it is an FTP packet, only the FTP proxy is loaded in the stack. The packet is scrutinized at every layer of the stack. This means the data link header will be evaluated along with the network header, transport header, session layer information, and the application layer data. If anything is deemed unsafe at any of these layers, the packet is discarded.

Kernel proxy firewalls are faster than application-layer proxy firewalls because all of the inspection and processing takes place in the kernel and does not need to be passed up to a higher software layer in the operating system. It is still a proxy-based system, so the connection between the internal and external entity is broken by the proxy acting as a middleman, and it can perform NAT by changing the source address, as do the preceding proxy-based firewalls.

Table 7-8 lists the important concepts and characteristics of the firewall types discussed in the preceding sections. Although various firewall products can provide a mix of these services and work at different layers of the OSI model, it is important you understand the basic definitions and functionalities of these firewall types.

Firewall Type	OSI Layer	Characteristics
Packet filtering	Network layer	Looks at destination and source addresses, ports, and services requested. Routers using ACLs dictate acceptable access to a network.
Application-level proxy	Application layer	Looks deep into packets and makes granular access control decisions. It requires one proxy per service.
Circuit-level proxy	Session layer	Looks only at the header packet information. It protects a wider range of protocols and services than an application-level proxy, but does not provide the detailed level of control available to an application-level proxy.
Stateful	Network layer	Looks at the state and context of packets. Keeps track of each conversation using a state table.
Kernel proxy	Application layer	Faster because processing is done in the kernel. One network stack is created for each packet.

Table 7-8 Differences Between Firewalls

The following are some best practices that should be carried out with any firewall type:

- Block ICMP redirect traffic.
- ACLs should be simple and direct.
- Disallow source routing.
- Close unnecessary ports with dangerous services.
- Disable unused interfaces.
- Block directed IP broadcasts.
- Block incoming packets with internal address (they are spoofed).
- Block multicast traffic if not needed.
- Enable logging.

Appliances

A firewall may take the form of either software installed on a regular computer using a regular operating system or a dedicated hardware appliance that has its own operating system. The second choice is usually more secure, because the vendor uses a stripped-down version of an operating system (usually Linux or BSD Unix). Operating systems are full of code and functionality that are not necessary for a firewall. This extra complexity opens the doors for vulnerabilities. If a hacker can exploit and bring down a company's firewall, then the company is very exposed and in danger.

Data Inspection

Data is the "new gold" most organizations must protect today for security, legal, regulatory, and competitive reasons. Because of this, an added functionality or product typically carries out data inspection. This inspection can happen at different communication layers and different protocol types. Some products can only inspect packet payload within SMTP traffic, while others can inspect packet payloads that travel over SMTP, FTP, HTTP, and more. This content monitoring can be looking for suspicious activity (viruses, mobile code, ActiveX, and so on) or for sensitive data that should not be leaving the network (trade secrets, confidential data, Social Security numbers, and others).

Firewall Architecture

Firewalls are great, but where do we put *them?*

Firewalls can be placed in a number of areas on a network to meet particular needs. They can protect an internal network from an external network and act as a choke point for all traffic. A firewall can be used to segment network sections and enforce access controls between two or more subnets. Firewalls can also be used to provide a DMZ between an internal network and an external network.

Firewall software should be installed on a locked-down system, which is called a bastion host.

Bastion Host *Bastion host* is just another name for a locked-down (or hardened) system. A bastion host is usually a highly exposed device, because it is the front line in a network's security and its existence is known on the Internet. This means the device must be extremely secure—no unnecessary services should be running, unused subsystems must be disabled, vulnerabilities must be patched, unnecessary user accounts must be disabled, and any unneeded ports must be closed. A bastion host is not tied to firewall software and activities. It is just a system that is properly locked down. Any system that resides within the DMZ should be installed on a bastion host since it is closer to the Internet and most likely closer to those who would like to do it harm. If firewall software is not installed on a locked-down operating system, or bastion host, the firewall is vulnerable.

Dual-Homed Firewall *Dual-homed* refers to a device that has two interfaces: one facing the external network and the other facing the internal network. If firewall software is installed on a dual-homed device, and it usually is, the underlying operating system should have packet forwarding and routing turned off, for security reasons. If they are enabled, the computer will not apply the necessary ACLs, rules, or other restrictions required of a firewall. When a packet comes to the external NIC from an untrusted network on a dual-homed firewall, and the operating system has forwarding enabled, the operating system will forward the traffic instead of passing it up to the firewall software for inspection.

Many network devices today are *multihomed*, which just means they have several NICs that are used to connect several different networks. Multihomed devices are commonly used to house firewall software, since the job of a firewall is to control the traffic as it goes from one network to another. A common multihomed firewall architecture allows a company to have several DMZs, as described earlier. One DMZ may hold devices that are shared between companies in an extranet, another DMZ may house the company's DNS and mail servers, and yet another DMZ may hold the company's web servers. Different DMZs are used for two reasons: to control the different traffic types (for example, make sure HTTP traffic only goes toward the web servers, and ensure DNS requests go toward the DNS server), and to ensure that if one system on one DMZ is compromised, the other systems in the rest of the DMZs are not accessible to this attacker.

Screened Host   A *screened host* is a firewall that communicates directly with a perimeter router and the internal network. Figure 7-38 shows this type of architecture.

Traffic received from the Internet is first filtered via packet filtering on the outer router. The traffic that makes it past this phase is sent to the screened-host firewall, which applies more rules to the traffic and drops the denied packets. Then the traffic moves to the internal destination hosts. The screened host (the firewall) is the only device that receives traffic directly from the router. No traffic goes directly from the Internet, through the router, and to the internal network. The screened host is always part of this equation.

If the firewall is an application-based system, protection is provided at the network layer by the router, and at the application layer by the proxy. This arrangement offers a high degree of security, because for an attacker to be successful, she would have to compromise two systems.

What does the word "screening" mean in this context? As shown in Figure 7-38, the router is a screening device and the firewall is the screened host. This just means there is a layer that scans the traffic and gets rid of a lot of the "junk" before it is directed toward the firewall. A screened host is different from a screened subnet, which is described next.

Screened Subnet   A *screened-subnet* architecture adds another layer of security to the screened-host architecture. The external firewall screens the data entering the DMZ network. However, instead of the firewall then redirecting the traffic to the internal network, an interior firewall also filters the traffic. The use of these two physical firewalls creates a DMZ.

In an environment with only a screened host, if an attacker successfully breaks through the firewall, nothing lies in her way to prevent her from having full access to the internal network. In an environment using a screened subnet, the attacker would

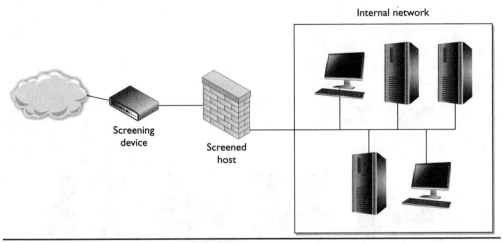

Figure 7-38 A screened host is a firewall that is screened by a router.

have to hack through another router (or firewall) to gain access. In this layered approach to security, the more layers provided, the better the protection. Figure 7-39 shows a simple example of a screened subnet.

The examples shown in the figures are simple in nature. Often, more complex networks and DMZs are implemented in real-world systems. Figures 7-40 and 7-41 show some other possible architectures of screened subnets and their configurations.

The screened-subnet approach provides more protection than a stand-alone firewall or a screened-host firewall because three devices are working together and all three

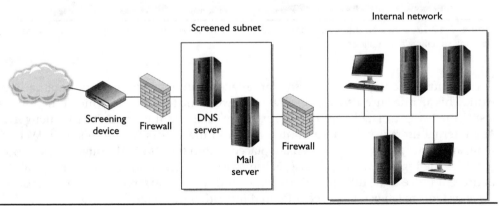

Figure 7-39 With a screened subnet, two firewalls are used to create a DMZ.

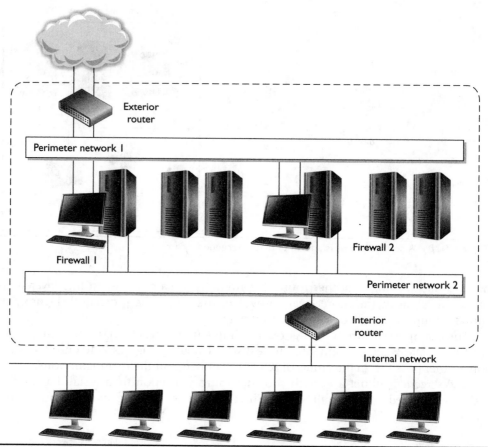

Figure 7-40 A screened subnet can have different networks within it and different firewalls that filter for specific vulnerabilities.

devices must be compromised before an attacker can gain access to the internal network. This architecture also sets up a DMZ between the two routers, which functions as a small network isolated among the trusted internal and untrusted external networks. The internal users usually have limited access to the servers within this area. Web, e-mail, and other public servers often are placed within the DMZ. Although this solution provides the highest security, it also is the most complex. Configuration and maintenance can prove to be difficult in this setup, and when new services need to be added, three systems may need to be reconfigured instead of just one.

The complexity and configuration of the DMZ, perimeter network, and screened hosts and subnets are dictated by the company security policy. The required level of security, and the services that need to be available to internal and external users, should be clearly outlined in this policy.

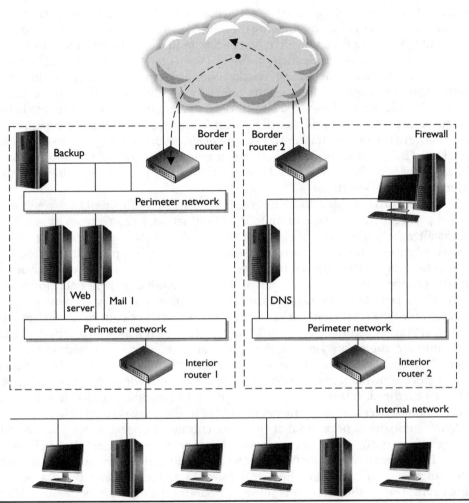

Figure 7-41 Some architectures have separate screened subnets with different server types in each.

 NOTE Sometimes a screened-host architecture is referred to as a single-tiered configuration and a screened subnet is referred to as a two-tiered configuration. If three firewalls create two separate DMZs, this may be called a three-tiered configuration.

The "Shoulds" of Firewalls

Look both ways before crossing the street, and always floss.
Response: Wrong rule set.

The default action of any firewall should be to implicitly deny any packets not explicitly allowed. This means that if no rule states that the packet can be accepted, that packet should be denied, no questions asked. Any packets entering the network that have a source address of an internal host should be denied. *Masquerading,* or *spoofing,* is a popular attacking trick in which the attacker modifies a packet header to have the source address of a host inside the network she wants to attack. This packet is spoofed and illegitimate. There is no reason a packet coming from the Internet should have an internal source network address, so the firewall should deny it. The same is true for outbound traffic. No traffic should be allowed to leave a network that does not have an internal source address. If this occurs, it means someone, or some program, on the internal network is spoofing traffic. This is how *zombies* work—the agents used in distributed DoS (DDos) attacks. If packets are leaving a network with different source addresses, these packets are spoofed and the network is most likely being used as an accomplice in a DDoS attack.

When security is a top priority for a company, its firewalls should reassemble fragmented packets before being sent on to their destination. In some types of attacks, the hackers alter the packets and make them seem to be something they are not. When a fragmented packet comes to a firewall, the firewall is seeing only part of the picture. It will make its best guess as to whether this piece of a packet is malicious or not. Because these fragments contain only a part of the full packet, the firewall is making a decision without having all the facts. Once all fragments are allowed through to a host computer, they can be reassembled into malicious packages that can cause a lot of damage. In environments that require higher security, the firewall should accept each fragment, assemble the fragments into a complete packet, and then make an access decision based on the whole packet. The drawback to this, however, is that firewalls that do reassemble packet fragments before allowing them to go on to their destination computer cause traffic delay and more overhead. It is up to the security officer and company to decide whether this configuration is necessary and whether the added traffic delay is acceptable.

Many companies choose to deny network entrance to packets that contain source routing information, which was mentioned earlier. *Source routing* means the packet decides how to get to its destination, not the routers in between the source and destination computer. Source routing moves a packet throughout a network on a predetermined path. The sending computer must know about the topology of the network and how to route data properly. This is easier for the routers and connection mechanisms in between, because they do not need to make any decisions on how to route the packet. However, it can also pose a security risk. When a router receives a packet that contains source routing information, it figures the packet knows what needs to be done and passes it on. In some cases, not all filters may be applied to the packet, and a network administrator may want packets to be routed only through a certain path and not the route a particular packet dictates. To make sure none of this misrouting happens, many firewalls are configured to check for source routing information within the packet and deny it if it is present.

Unfortunately, once a company erects a firewall, it may have a false sense of security. Firewalls are only one piece of the puzzle, and security has a lot of pieces.

Firewall Architecture Characteristics

It is important to understand the following characteristics of these firewall architecture types:

Dual-homed:

- A single computer with separate NICs connected to each network.
- Used to divide an internal trusted network from an external untrusted network.
- Must disable a computer's forwarding and routing functionality so the two networks are truly segregated.

Screened host:

- Router filters (screens) traffic before it is passed to the firewall.

Screened subnet:

- External router filters (screens) traffic before it enters the subnet. Traffic headed toward the internal network then goes through two firewalls.

The following list addresses some of the disadvantages of firewalls:

- Most of the time a distributed approach needs to be used to control all network access points, which cannot happen through the use of just one firewall.
- Firewalls can present a potential bottleneck to the flow of traffic.
- Firewalls can restrict desirable services that users may want to access. (This is a disadvantage to the users, but an advantage to the security professional.)
- Most firewalls do not provide protection from viruses being downloaded or passed through e-mail, and hooks to virus-detection techniques are needed.
- Border firewalls provide little protection against the inside attacker.
- Firewalls do not protect against rogue modems in listening mode.
- Firewalls do not protect against rogue wireless access points (APs).

The role of firewalls is becoming more and more complex as they evolve and take on more functionality and responsibility. At times, this complexity works against the network administrator and security professional because it requires them to understand and properly implement additional functionality. Without an understanding of the different types of firewalls and architectures available, many more security holes can be introduced, which lays out the welcome mat for attackers.

Honeypot

Hey! Here is a vulnerable system to attack!

A *honeypot* system is a computer that usually sits in the screened subnet, or DMZ, and attempts to lure attackers to it instead of to actual production computers. To make a honeypot system lure attackers, administrators may enable services and ports that are popular to exploit. However, the administrator must be careful to ensure this box is isolated in such a way that, when it is attacked, the hacker is not successful at accessing other computers on the network. Some honeypot systems have services *emulated*, meaning the actual service is not running but software that acts like those services is available. In Chapter 10, honeypot systems are discussed in the context of *enticement versus entrapment*. A legal honeypot can entice attackers to access the computer and attempt to hack into it, but it cannot entrap them. The example given in Chapter 10 shows that having a banner on one system indicating that free MP3s are available to download on the honeypot system is entrapment, because this sets up the user to access the honeypot for reasons other than the intent to harm. If services are running, ports are open, and banners are available for viewing, this will be quite enough to entice, not entrap, attackers.

Some network administrators want to keep the attackers away from their other systems and set up honeypots as decoys. Other administrators want to go after those who hurt them. These administrators would keep detailed logs, enable auditing, and perform different degrees of forensics in the hopes of turning over the attackers to the authorities for prosecution.

Network Segregation and Isolation

Chapter 2 covers network segregation and isolation, but it is an important component that interrelates with the topics in this chapter and thus merits brief mention here. It is important you segregate networks and subnets from each other. This usually means implementing routers that do not pass on broadcast and collision domain information and using different address schemes for different segments. Many networks today use Ethernet technology, which continually broadcasts information that can be useful to inside and outside attackers. Because data are so freely broadcasted in these environments, you must make sure that networks that house sensitive information are properly segmented from other network sections.

The architecture of a network should be clearly thought out, fully documented, and fully tested. A network administrator may not want everyone to be able to talk directly to a mainframe that holds critical information, for example. This traffic should be ported through one channel and filtered by a router or firewall. An administrator also may not want everyone on the network to be able to access the administrator's subnet, which holds the management consoles for all the routers, IDSs, logging servers, and auditing systems. The computers within this subnet need to talk to different systems throughout the network, but there is really no good reason that regular users should be able to access this subnet freely. The subnet should be isolated by ACLs enforced by surrounding routers (or firewalls) and properly segregated.

Also, it is one thing to document what one *thinks* the architecture of a network is, but just because it is on paper does not make it true. If the network schematic indicates that no one from subnet A can contact subnet B because of a specific firewall setting, this needs to be tested and penetration attacks should be launched to determine whether this is indeed true.

Networking Services and Protocols

So far, we have touched on protocols, technologies, topologies, and devices that can be used within a LAN environment. These services are not used in LAN environments only, however; they are also used in MAN and WAN infrastructures. The purpose of splitting the discussion into LAN and WAN sections is to provide a clear-cut explanation of the differences between these networking concepts. As stated earlier in this chapter, a network is set up to enable users to communicate with each other, create central administration, and share resources. The resources usually come in the form of networking services, and the following sections address some of the most popular services in LAN environments.

Domain Name Service

Imagine how hard it would be to use the Internet if we had to remember actual specific IP addresses. The *Domain Name Service (DNS)* is a method of resolving hostnames to IP addresses so names can be used instead of IP addresses when referencing unique hosts on the Internet. Not too many years ago, when the Internet was made up of about 100 computers (versus over 1 billion now), a list used to be kept that mapped every user's hostname to their IP address. This list was kept on an FTP server so everyone could access it. It did not take long for the task of maintaining this list to become overwhelming, and the computing community looked to automate it.

A hierarchical system for domain names was developed, and in 1992 the National Science Foundation (NSF) awarded Network Solutions, Inc. (NSI) the contract to manage and maintain domain names and the registration process of those names. NSI handled the name registration and a hostname resolution directory of DNS servers. It also maintained the authoritative databases of the Internet, which are the root DNS servers. An authoritative root DNS server contained 13 files, one for each of the top-level domain servers.

Until 1999, the Internet Assigned Numbers Authority (IANA) maintained and coordinated the allocation of IP addresses. Large Internet service providers (ISPs) would apply to the registries for blocks of these IP addresses and allocate the blocks to smaller ISPs or individual users. However, after 1999, the Internet Corporation for Assigned Names and Numbers (ICANN) took over the responsibilities of IP address block allocation, DNS management, and root server system management. NSI still maintains the authoritative root databases.

Wonderful. We have had a history lesson, but how does DNS work and what is its place in a network?

When a user types a uniform resource locator (URL) into his web browser, the URL is made up of words or letters that are in a sequence that makes sense to that user, such as www.logicalsecurity.com. However, these words are only for humans—computers work with IP addresses. So after the user enters this URL and presses ENTER, behind the scenes his computer is actually being directed to a DNS server that will resolve this URL, or hostname, into an IP address that the computer understands. Once the hostname has been resolved to an IP address, the computer knows how to get to the web server holding the requested web page.

Many companies have their own DNS servers to resolve their internal hostnames. These companies usually also use the DNS servers at their ISPs to resolve hostnames on the Internet. An internal DNS server can be used to resolve hostnames on the entire network, but usually more than one DNS server is used so the load can be split up and so redundancy and fault tolerance are in place.

Within DNS servers, DNS namespaces are split up administratively into *zones*. One zone may contain all hostnames for the marketing and accounting departments, and another zone may contain hostnames for the administration, research, and legal departments. The DNS server that holds the files for one of these zones is said to be the *authoritative* name server for that particular zone. A zone may contain one or more domains, and the DNS server holding those host records is the authoritative name server for those domains.

The DNS server contains records that map hostnames to IP addresses, which are referred to as *resource records*. When a user's computer needs to resolve a hostname to an IP address, it looks to its TCP/IP settings to find its DNS server. The computer then sends a request, containing the hostname, to the DNS server for resolution. The DNS server looks at its resource records and finds the record with this particular hostname, retrieves the address, and replies to the computer with the corresponding IP address.

It is recommended that a *primary* and a *secondary* DNS server be placed in each zone. The primary DNS server contains the actual resource records for a zone, and the secondary DNS server contains copies of those records. Users can use the secondary DNS server to resolve names, which takes a load off of the primary server. If the primary server goes down for any reason or is taken offline, users can still use the secondary server for name resolution. Having both a primary and secondary DNS server provides fault tolerance and redundancy to ensure users can continue to work if something happens to one of these servers.

The primary and secondary DNS servers synchronize their information through a *zone transfer*. After changes take place to the primary DNS server, those changes must be replicated to the secondary DNS server. It is important to configure the DNS server to allow zone transfers to take place only between the specific servers. For years now, attackers have been carrying out zone transfers to gather very useful network information from victims' DNS servers. Unauthorized zone transfers can take place if the DNS servers are not properly configured to restrict this type of activity.

Internet DNS and Domains

Networks on the Internet are connected in a hierarchical structure, as are the different DNS servers, as shown in Figure 7-42. While performing routing tasks, if a router does not know the necessary path to the requested destination, that router passes the packet up to a router above it. The router above it knows about all the routers below it. This router has a broader view of the routing that takes place on the Internet and has a better chance of getting the packet to the correct destination. This holds true with DNS servers also. If one DNS server does not know which DNS server holds the necessary resource record to resolve a hostname, it can pass the request up to a DNS server above it.

The naming scheme of the Internet resembles an inverted tree with the root servers at the top. Lower branches of this tree are divided into top-level domains, with second-level domains under each. The most common top-level domains are listed next:

- **COM**   Commercial
- **EDU**   Education
- **MIL**   U.S. military organization
- **INT**   International treaty organization
- **GOV**   Government
- **ORG**   Organizational
- **NET**   Networks

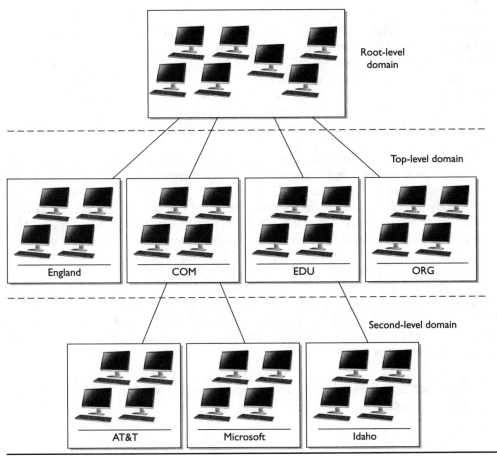

Figure 7-42   The DNS naming hierarchy is similar to the routing hierarchy on the Internet.

So how do all of these DNS servers play together in the Internet playground? When a user types in a URL to access a web site that sells computer books, for example, his computer asks its DNS server if it can resolve this hostname to an IP address. If the primary DNS cannot resolve the host or domain name, it must query a higher-level DNS server, ultimately ending at an authoritative DNS server for the specified domain. Because this web site is most likely not on the corporate network, this particular DNS server will not usually know the necessary IP address of that web site. The DNS server does not just reject the user's request, but rather passes it on to another DNS on the Internet. The request for this hostname resolution continues through different DNS servers until it reaches one that knows the IP address. This information is reported back to the user's computer. The user's computer then attempts to access the web site using the IP address, and soon the user is buying computer books, happy as a clam.

DNS server and hostname resolution is extremely important in corporate networking and Internet use. Without it, users would have to remember and type in the IP address for each web site and individual system, instead of the name. That would be a mess.

DNS Threats

As stated earlier, not every DNS server knows the IP address of every hostname it is asked to resolve. When a request for a hostname-to-IP address mapping arrives at a DNS server (server A), the server reviews its resource records to see if it has the necessary information to fulfill this request. If the server does not have a resource record for this hostname, it forwards the request to another DNS server (server B), which in turn reviews its resource records and, if it has the mapping information, sends the information back to server A. Server A caches this hostname-to-IP address mapping in its memory (in case another client requests it) and sends the information on to the requesting client.

With the preceding information in mind, consider a sample scenario. Andy the attacker wants to make sure that any time one of his competitor's customers tries to visit the competitor's web site, the customer is instead pointed to Andy's web site. Therefore, Andy installs a tool that listens for requests that leave DNS server A asking other DNS servers if they know how to map the competitor's hostname to its IP address. Once Andy sees that server A sends out a request to server B to resolve the competitor's hostname, Andy quickly sends a message to server A indicating that the competitor's hostname resolves to Andy's web site's IP address. Server A's software accepts the first response it gets, so server A caches this mapping information and sends it on to the requesting client. Now when the client tries to reach Andy's competitor's web site, she is instead pointed to Andy's web site. This will happen subsequently to any user who uses server A to resolve the competitor's hostname to an IP address, because this information is cached on server A.

 NOTE Please review Chapter 4 to understand how DNS pharming attacks take place.

Previous vulnerabilities that have allowed this type of activity to take place have been addressed, but this type of attack is still taking place because when server A receives a response to its request, it does not authenticate the sender.

Mitigating DNS threats consists of numerous measures, the most important of which is the use of stronger authentication mechanisms such as the *DNSSEC* (DNS security, which is part of the many current implementations of DNS server software). If DNSSEC were enabled on server A, then server A would, upon receiving a response, validate the digital signature on the message before accepting the information, to make sure that the response is from an authorized DNS server. This sounds simple enough, but for DNSSEC to be rolled out properly, all of the DNS servers on the Internet would have to participate in a PKI to be able to validate digital signatures. (Digital signatures and PKI are covered in Chapter 8.)

Despite the fact that DNSSEC requires greater resources than the traditional DNS, more and more organizations globally are opting to use DNSSEC. The U.S. Government has committed to use DNSSEC for all its top-level domains (.gov, .mil, and so on). Countries such as Brazil, Sweden, and Bulgaria have already implemented DNSSEC on their top-level domains. In addition, Internet Corporation for Assigned Names and Numbers (ICANN) has made an agreement with VeriSign to implement DNSSEC on all of its top-level domains (.com, .net, .org, and so on) by 2011.

NOTE Organizations should implement split DNS, which means a DNS server in the DMZ handles external resolution requests, while an internal DNS server handles only internal requests. This helps ensure that the internal DNS has layers of protection and is not exposed by being "Internet facing."

Now let's discuss another (indirectly related) predicament in securing DNS traffic—that is, the manipulation of the *host file*, a technique frequently used by malware. The host file is used by the operating system to map hostnames to IP addresses. The host file is a plain-text file located in the *%system root%\system32\i386\drivers\etc* folder in Windows and at */etc/hosts* in UNIX/Linux systems. The host file simply consists of a list of IP addresses with their corresponding hostnames.

Depending on its configuration, the computer refers to the host file before issuing a DNS request to a DNS server. Most operating systems give preference to host file–returned IP addresses' details rather than the ones from the DNS server, because the host file is generally under the direct control of the system administrator.

As covered previously, in the early days of the Internet and prior to the conception of the DNS, host files were the primary source of determining a host's network addresses from its hostname. With the gradual increase in the number of hosts connected to the Internet, maintaining host files became next to impossible and ultimately lead to the creation of the Domain Name System.

Due to the important role of host files, they are frequently targeted by malwares to propagate across systems connected on a local network. Once a malicious program takes over the host file, it can divert traffic from its intended destination to web sites hosting malicious content, for example. A common example of host file manipulation carried out by malware involves blocking users from visiting antivirus update websites.

This is usually done by mapping target hostnames to the loopback interface IP address 127.0.0.1. The most effective technique for preventing host file intrusions is to set it as a read-only file.

Attackers don't always have to go into all this technical hustle to divert traffic onto rogue destinations. They can also use some very simple techniques that are surprisingly effective in routing naive users to unintended destinations. The most common approach is known as *URL hiding*. HTML documents and e-mails allow users to attach or embed *hyperlinks* in any given text (such as the "Click Here" links abundantly found on most web pages). Attackers misuse hyperlinks to deceive unsuspecting users into clicking on rogue links.

Let's say a malicious attacker creates an unsuspicious text, *www.good.site*, but embeds the link to an abusive website, *www.bad.site*. People are likely to click on the www .good.site link without knowing that they are actually being taken to the bad site. In addition, attackers also use character encoding to obscure web addresses that may arouse user suspicion.

We'll now have a look at some legal aspects of domain registration. Although these do not pose a direct security risk to your DNS servers or your IT infrastructure, ignorance of them may risk your very domain name on the Internet, thus jeopardizing your entire online presence. Awareness of *domain grabbing* and *cyber squatting* issues will help you better plan out your online presence and allow you to steer clear of these traps.

The Internet Corporation for Assigned Names and Numbers (ICANN) promotes a governance model that follows a first-come, first-serve policy when registering domain names, regardless of trademarks considerations. This has led to a race among individuals on securing attractive and prominent domains. Among these are *cyber squatters*, individuals who register prominent or established names, hoping to sell these later to real-world businesses that may require these names to establish their online presence.

Another tactic employed by cyber squatters is to sift through expired domains just in case the original owner decides to reregister them. They also search for domains that may have the potential for rebranding in the future.

To protect your organization from these threats, it is essential that you register a domain as soon as your company conceives of launching a new brand or applies for a new trademark. Registering important domains for longer periods, such as for five or ten years, instead of annually renewing them reduces the chances of domains slipping out to cyber squatters. Another technique is to register nearby domains as well. For example, if you own the domain logicalsecurity.com, registering logical-security.com and logicalsecurity.net may be a good idea because this will prevent someone else from occupying these domains for furtive purpose.

Directory Services

A *directory service* has a hierarchical database of users, computers, printers, resources, and attributes of each. The directory is mainly used for lookup operations, which enable users to track down resources and other users easily to facilitate access. Most directory service databases are built on the X.500 model and use the Lightweight Directory Access Protocol (LDAP) to access the directory database. (LDAP is discussed in the next section.)

Directory services are often compared to telephone white and yellow pages where, if you want to know how to contact someone, you can easily look through the white or yellow pages and find the necessary contact information. The same is true about directory services, although usually they contain much more than just phone numbers. (Actually, DNS is a type of directory service.)

The directory itself uses classes of objects and subclasses of those objects to provide organization to the directory repository, which is usually a database. Then, the administrator can apply policies to these objects in a centralized manner. The entities within objects may be users, their location, and peripheral information, resources, profiles, electronic commerce information, network services, and much more. The administrator can then develop access control, security, and auditing policies that dictate how and by whom these objects can be accessed, after which each of these actions can be audited. Policies can also be developed and applied to control bandwidth management, firewall filtering, VPN access, and QoS.

Many different directories are developed and maintained by the IT department. These directories can be based on business or security needs, and they can have different security policies, access controls, and profiles applied to them. When more than one directory is in use, the directories need a way to communicate with each other; this takes place through *meta-directories*. *Metadata* are data about data. A meta-directory holds top-level information about the directory itself, which enables a user in one directory to quickly locate an object he is looking for in a totally different directory.

Each directory follows a specific *schema*, like regular databases. The schema provides structure to the directory repository and defines how objects and their relationships are to be represented. Each directory service vendor has a baseline schema that enables administrators to define their own objects and corresponding attributes. However, like many other types of products, interoperability issues may occur between vendors' schemas, in which case they cannot easily communicate with each other. If one company buys another company and needs to merge their networks and combine their directory services, for example, this can turn into a tricky and hairy project.

Directory services offer rich services to users, administrators, and networks as a whole. They enable administrators to maintain and control all resources and users within an environment. The directory database acts as a holding place for almost all of the network's important information and enables users to track down needed services or resources easily and quickly. Two examples of directory services are Microsoft Active Directory and Novell Directory Services (NDS). Although both are based on the X.500 model, they do not easily communicate with each other.

Many services are made available to users within a network, which is a big reason for constructing a network in the first place. This section described DNS and directory services, but a network offers much more—for example, many networks offer print services that enable many users to share local and remote printers. The administrators have centralized network management services that let them view the network as a whole from one graphical application, permit them to add and delete users, troubleshoot network issues, audit activities, add and remove services, control remote user access, and more. Some networks have terminal-emulation services, which enable users to have a lower-powered workstation that sees only the desktop. The operating system actually sits on a server somewhere else and does all the processor-intensive activities.

Networks and networking are interesting, confusing, and rewarding constructs of today's computing world. However, networking complexity causes many errors, security holes, and vulnerabilities to occur, and this is what potential attackers are counting on. The more you know and understand about networking, and how each component works with other components, the more efficiently you can apply security mechanisms and provide a higher level of protection.

Lightweight Directory Access Protocol

Lightweight Directory Access Protocol (LDAP) is a client/server protocol used to access network directories such as Microsoft Active Directory or NDS. These directories follow the X.500 standard. The first iteration of this protocol, Directory Access Protocol (DAP), was created to be a front-end client for X.500 directory services. The idea was that it would be the interface for every service provided by a directory that followed the X.500 standard. Well, the X.500 standard ended up being too complex to actually fully implement, and DAP also was extremely complex and resource hungry. So today, our directory services follow a portion of the X.500 standard and we use a slimmed-down ("lightweight") version of DAP.

The LDAP specification works with directories that organize their database in a hierarchical tree structure. The tree has leaves (entries) with unique distinguished names (DNs). These names are hierarchical and describe the object's place within the tree. The entries can define network resources, computers, people, wireless devices, and more. Each entry has an attribute and a value. The attributes are like the columns in a relational database and provide descriptive information about the entry. For example, if the entry is a printer, then the attributes could be the IP address, the name of the printer, the MAC address, and a description. The values are the data items that fill in these fields. So the attribute provides the field, and when the field is populated with data, this is that attribute's value. Each company defines its own directory structure, attributes, and values so they best meet the company's needs.

 NOTE   The newest LDAP version, version 3, has an extensive security model embedded that supports Internet security standards such as transport layer security (TLS).

Network Address Translation

I have one address I would like to share with everyone!

When computers need to communicate with each other, they must use the same type of addressing scheme so everyone understands how to find and talk to one another. The Internet uses the IP address scheme, and any computer or network that wants to communicate with other users on the network must conform to this scheme; otherwise, that computer will sit in a virtual room with only itself to talk to.

However, IP addresses have become scarce (until the full adoption of IPv6) and expensive. So some smart people came up with *network address translation (NAT)*, which enables a network that does not follow the Internet's addressing scheme to communicate over the Internet.

Private IP addresses have been reserved for internal LAN address use, as outlined in RFC 1918. These addresses can be used within the boundaries of a company, but they cannot be used on the Internet because they will not be properly routed. NAT enables a company to use these private addresses and still be able to communicate transparently with computers on the Internet.

The following lists current private IP address ranges:

- **10.0.0.0–10.255.255.255**   Class A network
- **172.16.0.0–172.31.255.255**   16 contiguous Class B networks
- **192.168.0.0–192.168.255.255**   256 contiguous Class C networks

NAT is a gateway that lies between a network and the Internet (or another network) that performs transparent routing and address translation. Because IP addresses were depleting fast, IPv6 was developed in 1999, and was intended to be the long-term fix to the address shortage problem. NAT was developed as the short-term fix to enable more companies to participate on the Internet. However, to date, IPv6 is slow in acceptance and implementation, while NAT has caught on like wildfire. Many firewall vendors have implemented NAT into their products, and it has been found that NAT actually provides a great security benefit. When attackers want to hack a network, they first do what they can to learn all about the network and its topology, services, and addresses. Attackers cannot easily find out a company's address scheme and its topology when NAT is in place, because NAT acts like a large nightclub bouncer by standing in front of the network and hiding the true IP scheme.

NAT hides internal addresses by centralizing them on one device, and any frames that leave that network have only the source address of that device, not of the actual computer that sends the message. So when a message comes from an internal computer with the address of 10.10.10.2, for example, the message is stopped at the device running NAT software, which happens to have the IP address of 1.2.3.4. NAT changes the header of the frame from the internal address, 10.10.10.2, to the valid IP address of the NAT device, 1.2.3.4. (Yes, I know 1.2.3.4 isn't valid, but I think you get the concept.) When a computer on the Internet replies to this message, it replies to the address 1.2.3.4. The NAT device changes the header on this reply message to 10.10.10.2 and puts it on the wire for the internal user to receive.

Three basic types of NAT implementations can be used:

- **Static mapping**   The NAT software has a pool of public IP addresses configured. Each private address is statically mapped to a specific public address. So computer A always receives the public address x, computer B always receives the public address y, and so on. This is generally used for servers that need to keep the same public address at all times.

- **Dynamic mapping**   The NAT software has a pool of IP addresses, but instead of statically mapping a public address to a specific private address, it works on a first-come, first-served basis. So if Bob needs to communicate over the Internet, his system makes a request to the NAT server. The NAT server takes the first IP on the list and maps it to Bob's private address. The balancing act is to estimate how many computers will most likely need to communicate outside the internal network at one time. This estimate is the number of public addresses the company purchases, instead of purchasing one public address for each computer.

- **Port address translation (PAT)** The company owns and uses only one public IP address for all systems that need to communicate outside the internal network. How in the world could all computers use the exact same IP address? Good question. Here's an example: The NAT device has an IP address of 127.50.41.3. When computer A needs to communicate with a system on the Internet, the NAT device documents this computer's private address and source port number (10.10.44.3; port 43,887). The NAT device changes the IP address in the computer's packet header to 127.50.41.3, with the source port 40,000. When computer B also needs to communicate with a system on the Internet, the NAT device documents the private address and source port number (10.10.44.15; port 23,398) and changes the header information to 127.50.41.3 with source port 40,001. So when a system responds to computer A, the packet first goes to the NAT device, which looks up the port number 40,000 and sees that it maps to computer A's real information. So the NAT device changes the header information to address 10.10.44.3 and port 43,887 and sends it to computer A for processing. A company can save a lot more money by using PAT, because the company needs to buy only a few public IP addresses, which are used by all systems in the network.

Most NAT implementations are *stateful*, meaning they keep track of a communication between the internal host and an external host until that session is ended. The NAT device needs to remember the internal IP address and port to send the reply messages back. This stateful characteristic is similar to stateful-inspection firewalls, but NAT does not perform scans on the incoming packets to look for malicious characteristics. Instead, NAT is a service usually performed on routers or firewalls within a company's screened subnet.

Although NAT was developed to provide a quick fix for the depleting IP address problem, it has actually put the problem off for quite some time. The more companies that implement private address schemes, the less likely IP addresses will become scarce. This has been helpful to NAT and the vendors that implement this technology, but it has put the acceptance and implementation of IPv6 much farther down the road.

Intranets and Extranets

We kind of trust you, but not really. We're going to put you on the extranet.

Web technologies and their uses have exploded with functionality, capability, and popularity. Companies set up internal web sites for centralized business information such as employee phone numbers, policies, events, news, and operations instructions. Many companies have also implemented web-based terminals that enable employees to perform their daily tasks, access centralized databases, make transactions, collaborate on projects, access global calendars, use videoconferencing tools and whiteboard applications, and obtain often-used technical or marketing data.

Web-based clients are different from workstations that log into a network and have their own desktop. Web-based clients limit a user's ability to access the computer's system files, resources, and hard drive space, access back-end systems, and perform other tasks. The web-based client can be configured to provide a GUI with only the buttons, fields, and pages necessary for the users to perform tasks. This gives all users a standard universal interface with similar capabilities.

When a company uses the Internet and web-based technologies inside its networks, it is using an *intranet*, a "private" network that uses Internet technologies, such as TCP/IP. The company has web servers and client machines using web browsers, and it uses the TCP/IP protocol suite. The web pages are written in HTML or XML and are accessed via HTTP.

Using web-based technologies has many pluses. They have been around for quite some time, they are easy to implement, no major interoperability issues occur, and with just the click of a link, a user can be taken to the location of the requested resource. Web-based technologies are not platform dependent, meaning all web sites and pages may be maintained on a Unix server, and all different flavors of client workstations can access them—they only need a web browser.

An *extranet* extends outside the bounds of the company's network to enable two or more companies to share common information and resources. Business partners commonly set up extranets to accommodate business-to-business communication. An extranet enables business partners to work on projects together, share marketing information, communicate and work collaboratively on issues, post orders, and share catalogs, pricing structures, and information on upcoming events. Trading partners often use electronic data interchange (EDI), which provides structure and organization to electronic documents, orders, invoices, purchase orders, and a data flow. EDI has evolved into web-based technologies to provide easy access and easier methods of communication.

For many businesses, an extranet can create a weakness or hole in their security if the extranet is not implemented and maintained properly. Properly configured firewalls need to be in place to control who can use the extranet communication channels. Extranets used to be based mainly on dedicated links, which are more difficult for attackers to infiltrate, but today many extranets are set up over the Internet, which requires properly configured VPNs and security policies.

Value-Added Networks

Many different types of companies use EDI for internal communication and for communication with other companies. A very common implementation is between a company and its supplier. For example, some supplier companies provide inventory to many different companies, such as Target, Wal-Mart, and Kmart. Many of these supplies are made in China and then shipped to a warehouse somewhere in the United States. When Wal-Mart needs to order more inventory, it sends its request through an EDI network, which is basically an electronic form of our paper-based world. Instead of using paper purchase orders, receipts, and forms, EDI provides all of this digitally. A value-added network (VAN) is an EDI infrastructure developed and maintained by a service bureau. A Wal-Mart store tracks its inventory by having employees scan bar codes on individual items. When the inventory of an item becomes low, a Wal-Mart employee sends a request for more of that specific item. This request goes to a mailbox at a VAN that Wal-Mart pays to use, and the request is then pushed out to a supplier that provides this type of inventory for Wal-Mart. Because Wal-Mart (and other stores) deals with thousands of suppliers, using a VAN simplifies the ordering process: instead of an employee having to track down the right supplier and submit a purchase order, this all happens in the background through an automated EDI network, which is managed by a VAN company (called a *service bureau*) for use by other companies.

EDI is moving away from proprietary VAN EDI structures to standardized communication structures to allow more interoperability and easier maintenance. This means that XML, SOAP, and web services are being used. Don't worry, currently these types of technologies are not on the CISSP exam—yet.

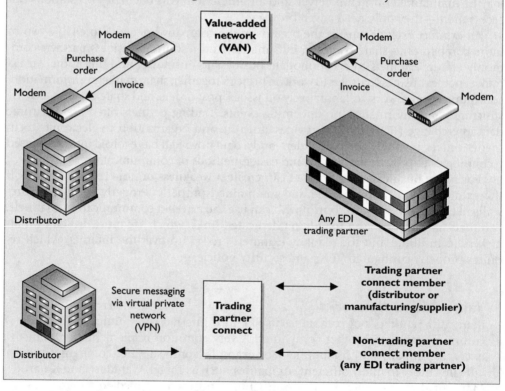

Metropolitan Area Networks

Behind every good man...
Response: Wrong MAN.

A *metropolitan area network (MAN)* is usually a backbone that connects LANs to each other and LANs to WANs, the Internet, and telecommunications and cable networks. A majority of today's MANs are *Synchronous Optical Networks (SONETs)* or FDDI rings provided by the telecommunications service providers. (FDDI technology was discussed earlier in the chapter.) These rings cover a large area, and businesses can connect to the rings via T1, fractional T1, and T3 lines. Figure 7-43 illustrates two companies connected via a SONET ring and the devices usually necessary to make this type of communication possible. This is a simplified example of a MAN. In reality, several businesses are usually connected to one ring.

SONET is actually a standard for telecommunications transmissions over fiber-optic cables. Carriers and telephone companies have deployed SONET networks for North America, and if they follow the SONET standards properly, these various networks can communicate with little difficulty.

SONET is *self-healing*, meaning that if a break in the line occurs, it can use a backup redundant ring to ensure transmission continues. All SONET lines and rings are fully redundant. The redundant line waits in the wings in case anything happens to the primary ring.

SONET networks can transmit voice, video, and data over optical networks. Slower-speed SONET networks often feed into larger, faster SONET networks, as shown in Figure 7-44. This enables businesses in different cities and regions to communicate.

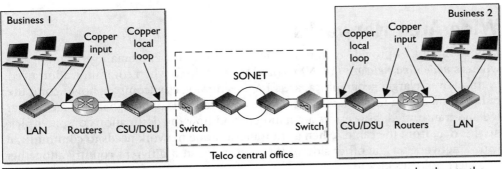

Figure 7-43   A MAN covers a large area and enables businesses to connect to each other, to the Internet, or to other WAN connections.

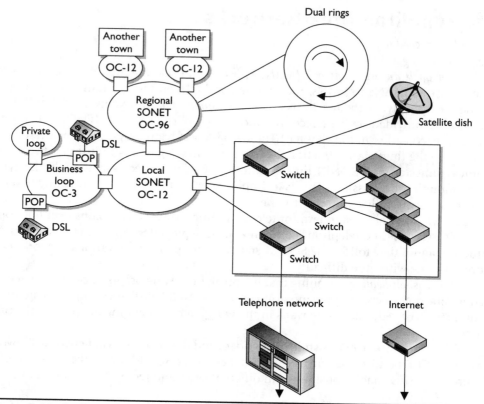

Figure 7-44   Smaller SONET rings connect to larger SONET rings to construct individual MANs.

Wide Area Networks

LAN technologies provide communication capabilities over a small geographic area, whereas *wide area network (WAN)* technologies are used when communication needs to travel over a larger geographical area. LAN technologies encompass how a computer puts its data onto a network cable, the rules and protocols of how that data are formatted and transmitted, how errors are handled, and how the destination computer picks up this data from the cable. When a computer on one network needs to communicate with a network on the other side of the country or in a different country altogether, WAN technologies kick in.

The network must have some avenue to other networks, which is most likely a router that communicates with the company's service provider's routers or telephone company facilities. Just as several types of technologies lie within the LAN arena, several technologies lie within the WAN arena. This section touches on many of these WAN technologies.

Telecommunications Evolution

On the eighth day, God created the telephone.

Telephone systems have been around for about 100 years, and they started as copper-based analog systems. Central switching offices connected individual telephones manually (via human operators) at first, and later by using electronic switching equipment. After two telephones were connected, they had an end-to-end connection, or an end-to-end circuit. Multiple phone calls were divided up and placed on the same wire, which is called multiplexing. *Multiplexing* is a method of combining multiple channels of data over a single transmission path. The transmission is so fast and efficient that the ends do not realize they are sharing a line with many other entities. They think they have the line all to themselves.

In the mid-1960s, digital phone systems emerged with T1 trunks, which carried 24 voice communication calls over two pairs of copper wires. This provided a 1.544-Mbps transmission rate, which brought quicker service but also the capability to put more multiplexed calls on one wire. When calls take place between switching offices (say, local phone calls), they are multiplexed on T1 lines. When a longer-distance call needs to take place, the calls coming in on the T1 lines are multiplexed on T3 lines, which can carry up to 28 T1 lines. This is shown in Figure 7-45.

The next entity to join the telecommunications party was fiber optics, which enabled even more calls to be multiplexed on one trunk line over longer distances. Then came optical carrier technologies such as SONET, which transmitted digitized voice signals in packets. SONET is the standard for telecommunications transmission over fiber-optic cables. This standard sets up the necessary parameters for transporting digital information over optical systems. Telecommunications carriers used this technology to multiplex lower-speed optical links into higher-speed links, similar to how lower-speed LANs connect to higher-speed WAN links today. Figure 7-46 shows an example of SONET rings connected together.

Figure 7-46 shows how telecommunications carriers can provide telephone and Internet access to companies and individuals in large areas. The SONET standard enables all carriers to interconnect.

LAN and WAN Protocols

Communication error rates are lower in LAN environments than in WAN environments, which makes sense when you compare the complexity of each environment. WAN traffic may have to travel hundreds or thousands of miles and pass through several different types of devices, cables, and protocols. Because of this difference, most LAN MAC protocols are connectionless and most WAN communication protocols are connection oriented. Connection-oriented protocols provide reliable transmission, because they have the capability of error detection and correction.

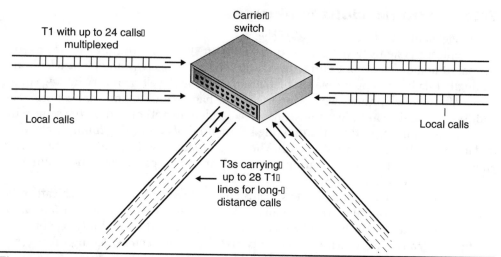

Figure 7-45 Local calls are multiplexed on T1 lines and longer-distance calls are moved from T1 lines to T3 multiplexed lines.

The next evolutionary step in telecommunications history is Asynchronous Transfer Mode (ATM). ATM encapsulates data in fixed cells and can be used to deliver data over the SONET network. The analogy of a highway and cars is used to describe the SONET and ATM relationship. SONET is the highway that provides the foundation (or network) for the cars—the ATM packets—to travel on.

ATM is a high-speed network technology that is used in LAN and WAN implementations by carriers, ISPs, and telephone companies. ATM uses a fixed cell size instead of the variable frame size employed by earlier technologies. This fixed size provides better performance and a reduced overhead for error handling. (More information on ATM technology is provided in the "ATM" section a little later.)

The following is a quick snapshot of telecommunications history:

- Copper lines carry purely analog signals.
- T1 lines carry up to 24 conversations.
- T3 lines carry up to 28 T1 lines.
- Fiber optics and the SONET network used.
- ATM over SONET used.

SONET was developed in the United States to achieve a data rate around 50 Mbps to support the data flow from T1 lines (1.544 Mbps) and T3 lines (44.736 Mbps). Data travels over these T-carriers as electronic voltage to the edge of the SONET network. Then the voltage must be converted into light to run over the fiber-optic carrier lines, known as optical carrier (OC) lines. Each OC-1 frame runs at a signaling rate of 51.84 Mbps, with a throughput of 44.738 Mbps.

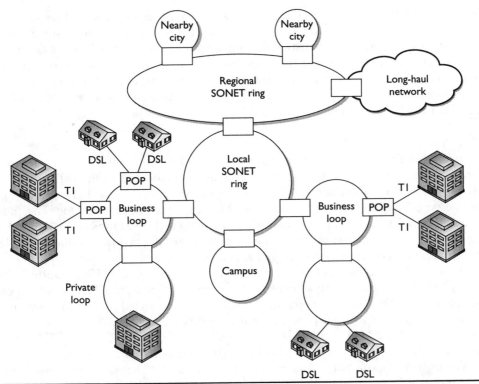

Figure 7-46 SONET technology enables several optical communication loops to communicate.

NOTE Optical carrier lines can provide different bandwidth values: OC-1 = 51.84 Mbps, OC-3 = 155.52 Mbps, OC-12 = 622.08 Mbps, and so on.

The Europeans have a different infrastructure and chose to use Synchronous Digital Hierarchy (SDH), which supports E1 lines (2.048 Mbps) and E3 lines (34.368 Mbps). SONET is the standard for North America, while SDH is the standard for the rest of the world. SDH and SONET are similar but just different enough to be incompatible. For communication to take place between SDH and SONET lines, a gateway must do the proper signaling translation.

You've had only a quick glimpse at an amazing complex giant referred to as *telecommunications*. Many more technologies are being developed and implemented to increase the amount of data that can be efficiently delivered in a short period of time.

Dedicated Links

A *dedicated link* is also called a *leased line* or *point-to-point* link. It is one single link that is pre-established for the purposes of WAN communications between two destinations. It is *dedicated*, meaning only the destination points can communicate with each other. This link is not shared by any other entities at any time. This was the main way companies communicated in the past, because not as many choices were available as there are today. Establishing a dedicated link is a good idea for two locations that will communicate often and require fast transmission and a specific bandwidth, but it is expensive compared to other possible technologies that enable several companies to share the same bandwidth and also share the cost. This does not mean that dedicated lines are not in use; they definitely are used, but many other options are now available, including X.25, frame relay, and ATM technologies.

T-Carriers

T-carriers are dedicated lines that can carry voice and data information over trunk lines. They were developed by AT&T and were initially implemented in the early 1960s to support pulse-code modulation (PCM) voice transmission. This was first used to digitize the voice over a dedicated, two-point, high-capacity connection line. The most commonly used T-carriers are T1 lines that provide up to 1.544 Mbps and T3 lines that provide up to 45 Mbps, as mentioned earlier. Both are digital circuits that multiplex several individual channels into a higher-speed channel.

These lines perform multiplex functionality through time-division multiplexing (TDM). What does this multiplexing stuff really mean? Consider a T1 line, which can multiplex up to 24 channels. If a company has a PBX connected to a T1 line, which in turn connects to the telephone company switching office, 24 calls can be chopped up and placed on the T1 line and transferred to the switching office. If this company did not use a T1 line, it would need 24 individual twisted pairs of wire to handle this many calls.

As shown in Figure 7-47, data are input into these 24 channels and transmitted. Each channel gets to insert up to eight bits into its established time slot. Twenty-four of these eight-bit time slots make up a T1 frame. That does not sound like much information, but 8,000 frames are built per second. Because this happens so quickly, the receiving end does not notice a delay and does not know it is sharing its connection and bandwidth with up to 23 other devices.

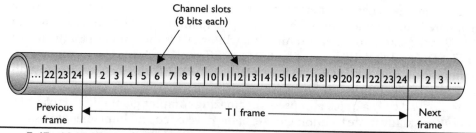

Figure 7-47 Multiplexing puts several phone calls, or data transmissions, on the same wire.

Carrier	# of T1s	# Voice Channels	Speed (Mbps)
Fractional	1/24	1	0.064
T1	1	24	1.544
T2	4	96	6.312
T3	28	672	44.736
T4	168	4,032	274.760

Table 7-9 A T-Carrier Hierarchy Summary Chart

Originally, T1 and T3 lines were used by the carrier companies, but they have been replaced mainly with optical lines. Now T1 and T3 lines feed data into these powerful and super-fast optical lines. The T1 and T3 lines are leased to companies and ISPs that need high-capacity transmission capability. Sometimes, T1 channels are split up between companies who do not really need the full bandwidth of 1.544 Mbps. These are called *fractional* T lines. The different carrier lines and their corresponding characteristics are listed in Table 7-9.

As mentioned earlier, dedicated lines have their drawbacks. They are expensive and inflexible. If a company moves to another location, a T1 line cannot easily follow it. A dedicated line is expensive because companies have to pay for a dedicated connection with a lot of bandwidth even when they do not use the bandwidth. Not many companies require this level of bandwidth 24 hours a day. Instead, they may have data to send out here and there, but not continuously.

The cost of a dedicated line is determined by the distance to the destination. A T1 line run from one building to another building two miles away is much cheaper than a T1 line that covers 50 miles or a full state.

More Multiplexing

Here are some other types of multiplexing functionalities you should be aware of:

Statistical time-division multiplexing (STDM)

- Transmits several types of data simultaneously across a single transmission cable or line (such as a T1 or T3 line), as illustrated next.
- STDM analyzes statistics related to the typical workload of each input device (printer, fax, computer) and determines in real time how much time each device should be allocated for data transmission.

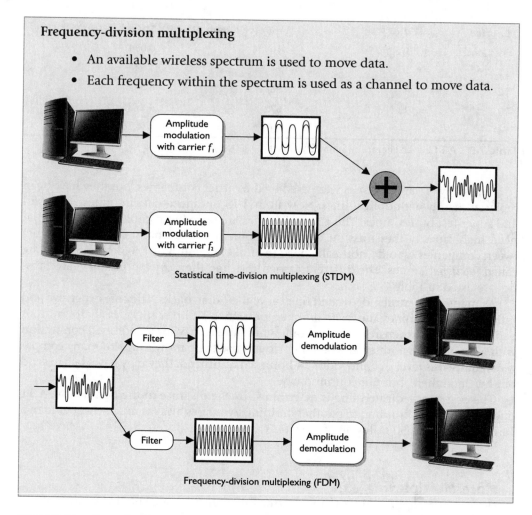

Frequency-division multiplexing

- An available wireless spectrum is used to move data.
- Each frequency within the spectrum is used as a channel to move data.

Statistical time-division multiplexing (STDM)

Frequency-division multiplexing (FDM)

WAN Technologies

I can't throw my packets that far!
Response: We have technology for that.

WAN technologies, as I am sure you have guessed, are used to enable networks to communicate over long distances. Several varieties of WAN technologies are available to companies today. The information that a company evaluates to decide which is the most appropriate WAN technology for it usually includes functionality, bandwidth demands, service level agreements, required equipment, cost, and what is available from service providers. The following sections go over some of the WAN technologies available today.

CSU/DSU

A *Channel Service Unit/Data Service Unit (CSU/DSU)* is required when digital equipment will be used to connect a LAN to a WAN. This connection can take place with T1 and T3 lines, as shown in Figure 7-48. A CSU/DSU is necessary because the signals and frames can vary between the LAN equipment and the WAN equipment used by service providers.

The DSU device converts digital signals from routers, bridges, and multiplexers into signals that can be transmitted over the telephone company's digital lines. The DSU device ensures that the voltage levels are correct and that information is not lost during the conversion. The CSU connects the network directly to the telephone company's line. The CSU/DSU is not always a separate device and can be part of a networking device.

The CSU/DSU provides a digital interface for Data Terminal Equipment (DTE), such as terminals, multiplexers, or routers, and an interface to the Data Circuit-Terminating Equipment (DCE) device, such as a carrier's switch. The CSU/DSU basically works as a translator and, at times, as a line conditioner.

Switching

Dedicated links have one single path to traverse; thus, there is no complexity when it comes to determining how to get packets to different destinations. Only two points of reference are needed when a packet leaves one network and heads toward the other. It gets much more complicated when thousands of networks are connected to each other, which is often when switching comes into play.

Two main types of switching can be used: circuit switching and packet switching. *Circuit switching* sets up a virtual connection that acts like a dedicated link between two systems. ISDN and telephone calls are examples of circuit switching, which is shown in the lower half of Figure 7-49.

When the source system makes a connection with the destination system, they set up a communication channel. If the two systems are local to each other, fewer devices need to be involved with setting up this channel. The farther the two systems are from each other, the more the devices are required to be involved with setting up the channel and connecting the two systems.

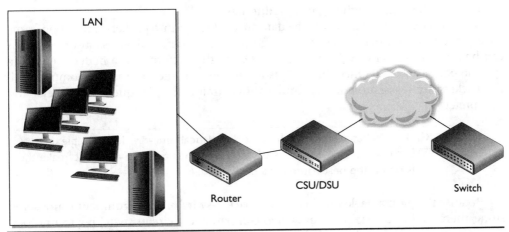

Figure 7-48 A CSU/DSU is required for digital equipment to communicate with telecommunications lines.

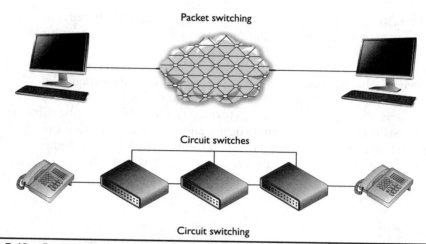

Figure 7-49 Circuit switching provides one road for a communication path, whereas packet switching provides many different possible roads.

An example of how a circuit-switching system works is daily telephone use. When one person calls another, the same type of dedicated virtual communication link is set up. Once the connection is made, the devices supporting that communication channel do not dynamically move the call through different devices, which is what takes place in a packet-switching environment. The channel remains configured at the original devices until the call, or connection, is done and torn down.

Packet switching, on the other hand, does not set up a dedicated virtual link, and packets from one connection can pass through a number of different individual devices (see the top of Figure 7-49), instead of all of them following one another through the same devices. Some examples of packet-switching technologies are the Internet, X.25, and frame relay. The infrastructure that supports these methods is made up of routers and switches of different types. They provide multiple paths to the same destinations, which offers a high degree of redundancy.

In a packet-switching network, the data are broken up into packets containing frame check sequence numbers. These packets go through different devices, and their paths can be dynamically altered by a router or switch that determines a better route for a specific packet to take. Once the packets are received at the destination computer, all the packets are reassembled, according to their frame check sequence numbers, and interpreted.

 NOTE Packet switching is based on statistical time-division multiplexing (STDM), which analyzes statistics on the various possible routes to make the decision on the best route for a packet.

Because the path a packet will take on a packet-switching environment is not set in stone, there could be variable delays when compared to a circuit-switching technology. This is okay, because packet-switching networks usually carry data rather than voice.

Because voice connections clearly detect these types of delays, in many situations a circuit-switching network is more appropriate for voice connections. Voice calls usually provide a steady stream of information, whereas a data connection is "burstier" in nature. When you talk on the phone, the conversation keeps a certain rhythm. You and your friend do not talk extremely fast and then take a few minutes in between conversations to stop talking and create a void with complete silence. However, this is usually how a data connection works. A lot of data are sent from one end to the other at one time, and then dead time occurs until it is time to send more data.

NOTE Voice over IP (VoIP) does move voice data over packet-switched environments. This technology is covered in the section "Multiservice Access Technologies," later in the chapter.

Frame Relay

Why are there so many paths to choose from?

For a long time, many companies used dedicated links to communicate with other companies. Company A had a pipeline to company B that provided a certain bandwidth 24 hours a day and was not used by any other entities. This was great because only the two companies could use the line, so a certain level of bandwidth was always available, but it was expensive and most companies did not use the full bandwidth each and every hour the link was available. Thus, the companies spent a lot of money for a service they did not use all the time. Today, instead of using dedicated lines, companies are turning to frame relay.

Circuit Switching vs. Packet Switching

The following points provide a concise summary of the differences between circuit- and packet-switching technologies:

Circuit switching:

- Connection-oriented virtual links.
- Traffic travels in a predictable and constant manner.
- Fixed delays.
- Usually carries voice-oriented data.

Packet switching:

- Packets can use many different dynamic paths to get to the same destination.
- Traffic is usually bursty in nature.
- Variable delays.
- Usually carries data-oriented data.

Frame relay is a WAN protocol that operates at the data link layer. It is a WAN solution that uses packet-switching technology to let multiple companies and networks share the same WAN media. Whereas direct point-to-point links have a cost based on the distance between the endpoints, the frame relay cost is based on the amount of bandwidth used. Because several companies and networks use the same media and devices (routers and switches), the cost can be greatly reduced per company compared to dedicated links.

If a company knows it will usually require *x* amount of bandwidth each day, it can pay a certain fee to make sure this amount of bandwidth is always available to it. If another company knows it will not have a high bandwidth requirement, it can pay a lower fee that does not guarantee the higher bandwidth allocation. This second company will have the higher bandwidth available to it anyway—at least until that link gets busy, and then the bandwidth level will decrease. (Companies that pay more to ensure that a higher level of bandwidth will always be available pay a *committed information rate*, or *CIR*.)

Two main types of equipment are used in frame relay connections: Data Terminal Equipment (DTE) and Data Circuit-Terminating Equipment (DCE). The DTE is usually a customer-owned device, such as a router or switch, that provides connectivity between the company's own network and the frame relay network. DCE is the service provider's device, or telecommunications company's device, that does the actual data transmission and switching in the frame relay cloud. So the DTE is a company's ramp onto the frame relay network, and the DCE devices actually do the work within the frame relay cloud.

The frame relay cloud is the collection of DCEs that provides switching and data communications functionality. Several service providers offer this type of service, and some providers use other providers' equipment—it can all get confusing because a packet can take so many different routes. This collection is called a *cloud* to differentiate it from other types of networks, and because when a packet hits this cloud, users do not usually know the route their frames will take. The frames will be sent either through permanent or switched virtual circuits that are defined within the DCE or through carrier switches.

Frame relay is an any-to-any service that is shared by many users. As stated earlier, this is beneficial because the costs are much lower than those of dedicated leased lines. Because frame relay is shared, if one subscriber is not using its bandwidth, it is available for others to use. On the other hand, when traffic levels increase, the available bandwidth decreases. This is why subscribers who want to ensure a certain bandwidth is always available to them pay a higher committed rate.

Figure 7-50 shows five sites being connected via dedicated lines versus five sites connected through the frame relay cloud. The first solution requires many dedicated lines that are expensive and not flexible. The second solution is cheaper and provides companies much more flexibility.

Virtual Circuits

Frame relay (and X.25) forwards frames across virtual circuits. These circuits can be either *permanent*, meaning they are programmed in advance, or *switched*, meaning the circuit is quickly built when it is needed and torn down when it is no longer needed.

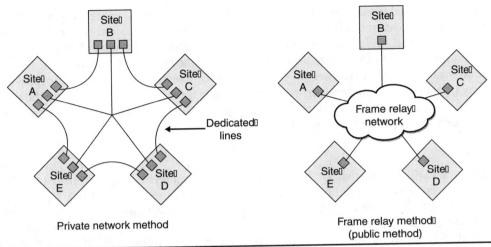

Figure 7-50 A private network connection requires several expensive dedicated links. Frame relay enables users to share a public network.

The *permanent virtual circuit (PVC)* works like a private line for a customer with an agreed-upon bandwidth availability. When a customer decides to pay for the committed rate, a PVC is programmed for that customer to ensure it will always receive a certain amount of bandwidth.

Unlike PVCs, *switched virtual circuits (SVCs)* require steps similar to a dial-up and connection procedure. The difference is that a permanent path is set up for PVC frames, whereas when SVCs are used, a circuit must be built. It is similar to setting up a phone call over the public network. During the setup procedure, the required bandwidth is requested, the destination computer is contacted and must accept the call, a path is determined, and forwarding information is programmed into each switch along the SVC's path. SVCs are used for teleconferencing, establishing temporary connections to remote sites, data replication, and voice calls. Once the connection is no longer needed, the circuit is torn down and the switches forget it ever existed.

Although a PVC provides a guaranteed level of bandwidth, it does not have the flexibility of an SVC. If a customer wants to use her PVC for a temporary connection, as mentioned earlier, she must call the carrier and have it set up, which can take hours.

X.25

X.25 is an older WAN protocol that defines how devices and networks establish and maintain connections. Like frame relay, X.25 is a switching technology that uses carrier switches to provide connectivity for many different networks. It also provides an any-to-any connection, meaning many users use the same service simultaneously. Subscribers are charged based on the amount of bandwidth they use, unlike dedicated links, for which a flat fee is charged.

Data are divided into 128 bytes and encapsulated in High-level Data Link Control (HDLC) frames. The frames are then addressed and forwarded across the carrier switches. Much of this sounds the same as frame relay—and it is, but frame relay is much more advanced and efficient when compared to X.25, because the X.25 protocol was developed and released in the 1970s. During this time, many of the devices connected to networks were dumb terminals and mainframes, the networks did not have built-in functionality and fault tolerance, and the Internet overall was not as foundationally stable and resistant to errors as it is today. When these characteristics were not part of the Internet, X.25 was required to compensate for these deficiencies and to provide many layers of error checking, error correcting, and fault tolerance. This made the protocol fat, which was required back then, but today it slows down data transmission and provides a lower performance rate than frame relay or ATM.

ATM

Asynchronous Transfer Mode (ATM) is another switching technology, but instead of being a packet-switching method, it uses a cell-switching method. ATM is a high-speed networking technology used for LAN, MAN, WAN, and service provider connections. Like frame relay, it is a connection-oriented switching technology, and creates and uses a fixed channel. IP is an example of a connectionless technology. Within the TCP/IP protocol suite, IP is connectionless and TCP is connection oriented. This means IP segments can be quickly and easily routed and switched without each router or switch in between having to worry about whether the data actually made it to its destination—that is TCP's job. TCP works at the source and destination ends to ensure data were properly transmitted, and it re-sends data that ran into some type of problem and did not get delivered properly. When using ATM or frame relay, the devices in between the source and destination have to be more conscious of data and whether those data get to where they need to go, unlike when a purely connectionless protocol is being used.

ATM is a cell-switching technology rather than a packet-switching technology. Data are segmented into fixed-size cells of 53 bytes, instead of variable-size packets. This provides for more efficient and faster use of the communication paths. ATM sets up virtual circuits, which act like dedicated paths between the source and destination. These virtual circuits can guarantee bandwidth and QoS. For these reasons, ATM is a good carrier for voice and video transmission.

ATM technology is used by carriers and service providers and makes up part of the core technology of the Internet, but ATM technology can also be used for a company's private use in backbones and connections to the service provider's networks.

Traditionally, companies used dedicated lines, usually T-carrier lines, to connect to the public networks. However, companies have also moved to implementing an ATM switch on their network, which connects them to the carrier infrastructure. Because the fee is based on bandwidth used instead of a continual connection, it can be much cheaper. Some companies have replaced their Fast Ethernet and FDDI backbones with ATM. When ATMs are used as private backbones, the companies have ATM switches that take the Ethernet, or whatever data link technology is being used, and frame them into the 53-byte ATM cells.

Quality of Service

Quality of Service (QoS) is a capability that allows a protocol to distinguish between different classes of messages and assign priority levels. Some applications, such as video conferencing, are time sensitive, meaning delays would cause unacceptable performance of the application. A technology that provides QoS allows an administrator to assign a priority level to time-sensitive traffic. The protocol then ensures this type of traffic has a specific or minimum rate of delivery.

QoS allows a service provider to guarantee a level of service to its customers. QoS began with ATM and then was integrated into other technologies and protocols responsible for moving data from one place to another. Four different types of ATM QoS services (listed next) are available to customers. Each service maps to a specific type of data that will be transmitted.

- **Constant Bit Rate (CBR)**   A connection-oriented channel that provides a consistent data throughput for time-sensitive applications, such as voice and video applications. Customers specify the necessary bandwidth requirement at connection setup.

- **Variable Bit Rate (VBR)**   A connection-oriented channel best used for delay-insensitive applications because the data throughput flow is uneven. Customers specify their required peak and sustained rate of data throughput.

- **Unspecified Bit Rate (UBR)**   A connectionless channel that does not promise a specific data throughput rate. Customers cannot, and do not need to, control their traffic rate.

- **Available Bit Rate (ABR)**   A connection-oriented channel that allows the bit rate to be adjusted. Customers are given the bandwidth that remains after a guaranteed service rate has been met.

ATM supports various interfaces to provide this type of flexibility and use. A DSU device is used to connect a LAN to the public ATM network. This architecture is used when a company's network is connected to the ATM network via a router or bridge. The DSU device is necessary to make sure the digital signals are converted to a signal type the ATM network can understand.

ATM sets up a fixed channel for all data to transfer through during a transmission. The fixed channels are preprogrammed into the switches along that particular communication path.

ATM was the first protocol to provide true QoS, but as the computing society has increased its desire to send time-sensitive data throughout many types of networks, developers have integrated QoS into other technologies.

QoS has three basic levels:

- **Best-effort service**   No guarantee of throughput, delay, or delivery. Traffic that has priority classifications goes before traffic that has been assigned this classification. Most of the traffic that travels on the Internet has this classification.

- **Differentiated service**   Compared to best-effort service, traffic that is assigned this classification has more bandwidth, shorter delays, and fewer dropped frames.

- **Guaranteed service**   Ensures specific data throughput at a guaranteed speed. Time-sensitive traffic (voice and video) is assigned this classification.

Administrators can set the classification priorities (or use a policy manager product) for the different traffic types, which the protocols and devices then carry out.

SMDS

Switched Multimegabit Data Service (SMDS) is a high-speed packet-switched technology used to enable customers to extend their LANs across MANs and WANs. When a company has an office in one state that needs to communicate with an office in a different state, for example, the two LANs can use this packet-switching protocol to communicate across the already established public network. This protocol is connectionless and can provide bandwidth on demand.

Although some companies still use this technology, it has been greatly replaced with frame relay. Service providers usually maintain only the networks that currently use this technology instead of offering it to new customers.

SDLC

Synchronous Data Link Control (SDLC) protocol is based on networks that use dedicated, leased lines with permanent physical connections. It is used mainly for communications with IBM hosts within a Systems Network Architecture (SNA). Developed by IBM in the 1970s, SDLC is a bit-oriented, synchronous protocol that has evolved into other communication protocols such as HDLC, Link Access Procedure (LAP), and Link Access Procedure-Balanced (LAPB).

SDLC was developed to enable mainframes to communicate with remote locations. The environments that use SDLC usually have primary systems that control secondary stations' communication. SDLC provides the polling media access technology, which is the mechanism that enables secondary stations to communicate on the network. Figure 7-51 shows the primary and secondary stations on an SDLC network.

HDLC

High-level Data Link Control (HDLC) protocol is also a bit-oriented link layer protocol used for transmission over synchronous lines. HDLC is an extension of SDLC, which is mainly used in SNA environments. HDLC provides high throughput, because it supports full-duplex transmissions, and is used in point-to-point and multipoint connections.

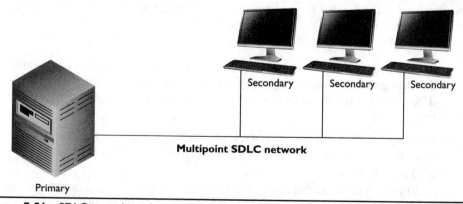

Secondary   Secondary   Secondary

Multipoint SDLC network

Primary

Figure 7-51   SDLC is used mainly in mainframe environments within an SNA network.

Like SDLC, HDLC works with primary stations that contact secondary stations to establish data transmission. Vendors have developed their own parameters within their versions of HDLC, which has resulted in interoperability issues between vendors' HDLC implementations.

HSSI

High-Speed Serial Interface (HSSI) is an interface used to connect multiplexers and routers to high-speed communications services such as ATM and frame relay. It supports speeds up to 52 Mbps, as in T3 WAN connections, which are usually integrated with router and multiplex devices to provide serial interfaces to the WAN.

These interfaces define the electrical and physical interfaces to be used by DTE/DCE devices; thus, HSSI works at the physical layer. The interface was developed by Cisco and T3plus Networking.

Multiservice Access Technologies

Voice in a packet. What will they think of next?

Multiservice access technologies combine several types of communication categories (data, voice, and video) over one transmission line. This provides higher performance, reduced operational costs, and greater flexibility, integration, and control for administrators. The regular phone system is based on a circuit-switched, voice-centric network, referred to as the *public-switched telephone network (PSTN)*. The PSTN uses circuit switching instead of packet switching. When a phone call is made, the call is placed at the PSTN interface, which is the user's telephone. This PSTN is connected to the telephone company's local loop via copper wiring. Once the signals for this phone call reach the telephone company's central office (the end of the local loop), they are part of the telephone company's circuit-switching world. A connection is made between the source and the destination, and as long as the call is in session, the data flows through the same switches.

When a phone call is made, the connection has to be set up, signaling has to be controlled, and the session has to be torn down. This takes place through the Signaling System 7 (SS7) protocol. When *Voice over IP (VoIP)* is used, it employs the *Session Initiation Protocol (SIP)*, which sets up and breaks down the call sessions, just as SS7 does for non-IP phone calls. SIP is an application layer protocol that can work over TCP or UDP. SIP provides the foundation to allow the more complex phone-line features that SS7 provides, such as causing a phone to ring, dialing a phone number, generating busy signals, and so on.

The PSTN is being replaced by data-centric, packet-oriented networks that can support voice, data, and video. The new VoIP networks use different switches, protocols, and communication links. This means VoIP has to go through a tricky transition stage that enables the old systems and infrastructures to communicate with the new systems until the old systems are dead and gone.

High-quality compression is used with VoIP technology, and the identification numbers (phone numbers) are IP addresses. This technology gets around some of the barriers present in the PSTN today. The interface devices (telephones) have embedded functions and logic that make it more difficult to implement different types of services that the network as a whole can support. In VoIP, the interface to the network can be a computer, server, PBX, or anything else that runs a telephone application. This provides more flexibility when it comes to adding new services and provides a lot more control and intelligence to the interfacing devices.

Because this is a packet-oriented switching technology, latency delays are possible. This manifests as longer delays within a conversation and a slight loss of synchronicity in the conversation. When someone using VoIP for a phone call experiences these types of lags in the conversation, it means the packets holding the other person's voice message got queued somewhere within the network and are on their way. This is referred to as *jittering*, but protocols are developed to help smooth out these issues and provide a more continuous telephone call experience.

 NOTE Applications that are time sensitive, such as voice and video signals, need to work over an isochronous network. An isochronous network contains the necessary protocols and devices that guarantee continuous bandwidth without interruption.

Four main components are needed for VoIP: an IP telephony device, a call-processing manager, a voicemail system, and a voice gateway. The *IP telephony device* is just a phone that has the necessary software that allows it to work as a network device. Traditional phone systems require a "smart network" and a "dumb phone." In VoIP, the phone must be "smart" by having the necessary software to take analog signals, digitize them, break them into packets, and create the necessary headers and trailers for the packets to find their destination. The *voicemail system* is a storage place for messages and provides user directory lookups and call-forwarding functionality. A *voice gateway* carries out packet routing and provides access to legacy voice systems and backup calling processes.

When a user makes a call, his "smart phone" will send a message to the *call-processing manager* to indicate a call needs to be set up. When the person at the destination takes her phone off the hook, this notifies the call-processing manager that the call has been accepted. The call-processing manager notifies both the sending and receiving phones that the channel is active, and voice data are sent back and forth over a traditional data network line.

Moving voice data through packets is more involved than moving regular data through packets. This is because data are usually sent in bursts, in which voice data are sent as a constant stream. A delay in data transmission is not noticed as much as is a delay in voice transmission. The VoIP technology, and its supporting protocols, has advanced to provide voice data transmission with improved bandwidth, variability in delay, round-trip delay, and packet loss issues.

Using VoIP means a company has to pay for and maintain only one network, instead of one network dedicated to data transmission and another network dedicated to voice transmission. This saves money and administration overhead, but certain security issues must be understood and dealt with.

 NOTE A media gateway is the translation unit between disparate telecommunications networks. VoIP Media Gateways perform the conversion between Time Division Multiplexing (TDM) voice to Voice over Internet Protocol (VoIP).

Lawful Interception

It is now compulsory for many organizations to have lawful interception capability of voice and data communications. This helps law enforcement agencies to monitor and track suspected criminal activities. The implementation of lawful interception in VoIP networks is not as easy as it is in traditional PSTN networks. Various solutions are available to fulfill this need, but a proper network needs to be designed to ensure that effective monitoring can take place. A lawful interception solution should be undetectable to the user as well as have proper management interface and effective security controls.

 NOTE Voice data can travel over IP, frame relay, and ATM transmission protocols.

H.323 Gateways

The ITU-T recommendations cover a wide variety of multimedia communication services. H.323 is part of this family of recommendations, but it is also a standard that deals with video, real-time audio, and data packet–based transmissions where multiple users can be involved with the data exchange. An H.323 environment features terminals, which can be telephones or computers with telephony software, gateways that connect this environment to the PSTN, multipoint control units, and gatekeepers that manage calls and functionality.

Like any type of gateway, H.323 gateways connect different types of systems and devices and provide the necessary translation functionality. The H.323 terminals are connected to these gateways, which in turn can be connected to the PSTN. These gateways translate protocols used on the circuit-based telephone network and the packet-based VoIP network. The gateways also translate the circuit-oriented traffic into packet-oriented traffic and vice versa as required.

Today, it is necessary to implement the gateways that enable the new technology to communicate with the old, but soon the old PSTN may be a thing of the past and all communication may take place over packets instead of circuits.

The newer technology looks to provide transmission mechanisms that will involve much more than just voice. Although we have focused mainly on VoIP, other technologies support the combination of voice and data over the same network, such as Voice over ATM (VoATM) and Voice over Frame Relay (VoFR). ATM and frame relay are connection-oriented protocols, and IP is connectionless. This means frame relay and ATM commonly provide better QoS and less jittering and latency.

What's in a Name?

The terms "IP telephony" and "Voice over IP" (VoIP) are used interchangeably:

- VoIP is widely used for the actual services offered: Caller ID, QoS, voice mail, and so on.
- IP telephony is an umbrella term for all real-time applications over IP, including voice over instant messaging (IM) and videoconferencing.

The best of both worlds is to combine IP over ATM or frame relay. This allows for packet-oriented communication over a connection-oriented network that will provide an end-to-end connection. IP is at the network layer and is media independent—it can run over a variety of data link layer protocols and technologies.

Traditionally, a company has on its premises a PBX, which is a switch between the company and the PSTN, and T1 or T3 lines connecting the PBX to the telephone company's central office, which houses switches that act as ramps onto the PSTN. When WAN technologies are used instead of accessing the PSTN through the central office switches, the data are transmitted over the frame relay, or ATM, cloud. An example of this configuration is shown in Figure 7-52.

Because frame relay and ATM utilize PVCs and SVCs, they both have the ability to use SVCs for telephone calls. Remember that a CIR is used when a company wants to ensure it will always have a certain bandwidth available. When a company pays for this guaranteed bandwidth, it is paying for a PVC for which the switches and routers are programmed to control its connection and for that connection to be maintained. SVCs, on the other hand, are set up on demand and are temporary in nature. They are perfect for making telephone calls or transmitting video during videoconferencing.

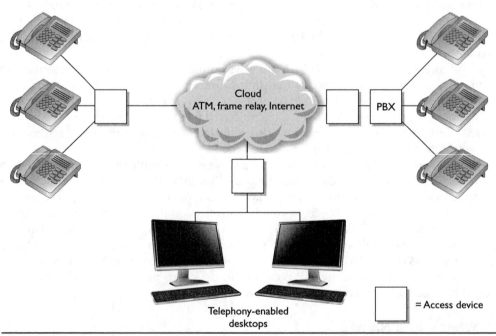

Figure 7-52 Regular telephone calls connect phones to the PSTN. Voice over WAN technologies connect calls to a WAN.

Digging Deeper into SIP

As stated earlier, the *SIP (Session Initiation Protocol)* is a signaling protocol widely used for VoIP communications sessions. It is used in applications such as video conferencing, multimedia, instant messaging, and online gaming. It is analogous to the SS7 protocol used in PSTN networks and supports features present in traditional telephony systems.

SIP consists of two major components: the *User Agent Client (UAC)* and *User Agent Server (UAS)*. The UAC is the application that creates the SIP requests for initiating a communication session. UACs are generally messaging tools and soft-phone applications that are used to place VoIP calls. The UAS is the SIP server, which is responsible for handling all routing and signaling involved in VoIP calls.

SIP relies on a three-way-handshake process to initiate a session. To illustrate how an SIP-based call kicks off, let's look at an example of two people, Bill and John, trying to communicate using their VoIP phones. Bill's system starts by sending an INVITE packet to John's system. Since Bill's system is unaware of John's location, the INVITE packet is sent to the SIP server, which looks up John's address in the SIP *registrar* server. Once the location of John's system has been determined, the INVITE packet is forwarded to him. During this entire process, the server keeps the caller (Bill) updated by sending him a TRYING packet, indicating the process is underway. Once the INVITE packet reaches John's system, it starts ringing. While John's system rings and waits for John to respond, it sends a RINGING packet to Bill's system, notifying Bill that the INVITE packet has been received and John's system is waiting for John to accept the call. As soon as John answers the call, an OK packet is sent to Bill's system (through the server). Bill's system now issues an ACK packet to begin call setup. It is important to note here that SIP itself is not used to stream the conversation because it's just a signaling protocol. The actual voice stream is carried on media protocols such as the *Real-time Transport Protocol (RTP)*. Once Bill and John are done communicating, a BYE message is sent from the system terminating the call. The other system responds with an OK, acknowledging the session has ended. This handshake is illustrated in Figure 7-53.

The SIP architecture consists of three different types of servers, which play an integral role in the entire communication process of the VoIP system. These servers are the *proxy* server, the *registrar* server, and the *redirect* server. The proxy server is used to relay packets within a network between the UACs and the UAS. It also forwards requests generated by callers to their respective recipients. Proxy servers are also generally used for name mapping, which allows the proxy server to interlink an external SIP system to an internal SIP client.

The registrar server keeps a centralized record of the updated locations of all the users on the network. These addresses are stored on a location server. The redirect server allows SIP devices to retain their SIP identities despite changes in their geographic location. This allows a device to remain accessible when its location is physically changed and hence while it moves through different networks. The use of redirect servers allows clients to remain within reach while they move through numerous network coverage zones. This configuration is generally known as an *intraorganizational* configuration. Intraorganizational routing enables SIP traffic to be routed within a VoIP network without being transmitted over the PSTN or external network, thus allowing secure communication sessions.

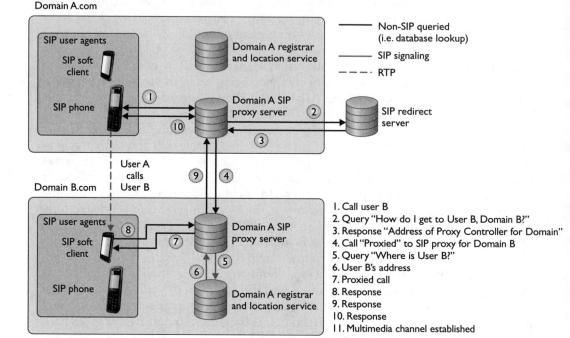

Skype is a popular Internet telephony application that uses a peer-to-peer communication model rather than the traditional client/server approach of VoIP systems. The Skype network does not rely on centralized servers to maintain its user directories. Instead, user records are maintained across distributed member nodes. This is the reason the network can quickly accommodate user surges without having to rely on expensive central infrastructure and computing resources.

IP Telephony Issues

VoIP's integration with the TCP/IP protocol has brought about immense security challenges because it allows malicious users to bring their TCP/IP experience into this relatively new platform, where they can probe for flaws in both the architecture and the VoIP systems. Also involved are the traditional security issues associated with networks, such as unauthorized access, exploitation of communication protocols, and the spreading of malware. Even the prime reasons behind VoIP exploitations remain akin to the traditional hacker psychology of gaining infamy. In addition, the promise of financial benefit derived from stolen call time is a strong incentive for most attackers. In short, the VoIP telephony network faces all the flaws that traditional computer networks have faced.

Moreover, VoIP devices follow an architecture similar to traditional computers—that is, they use operating systems, communicate through Internet protocols, and provide a combination of services and applications.

SIP-based signaling suffers from the lack of encrypted call channels and authentication of control signals. Attackers can tap into the SIP server and client communication

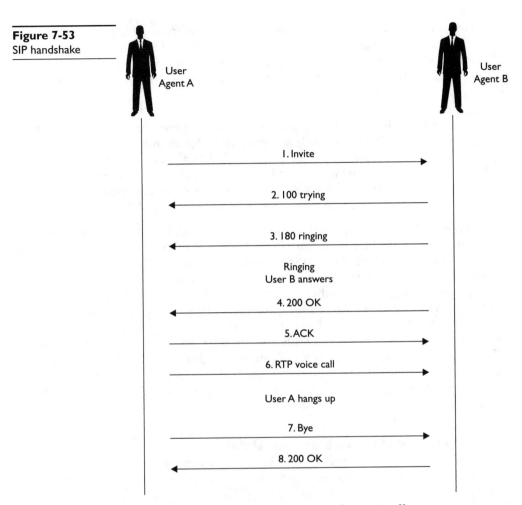

Figure 7-53
SIP handshake

User Agent A

User Agent B

1. Invite

2. 100 trying

3. 180 ringing

Ringing
User B answers

4. 200 OK

5. ACK

6. RTP voice call

User A hangs up

7. Bye

8. 200 OK

to sniff out login IDs, passwords/PINs, and phone numbers. Needless to say, once an attacker gets a hold of such information, he can use it to place unauthorized calls on the network using the victim's funds. Toll fraud is considered to be the most significant threat that VoIP networks face. VoIP network implementations will need to ensure that VoIP–PSTN gateways are secure from intrusions to prevent these instances of fraud.

Attackers can also masquerade identities by redirecting SIP control packets from a caller to a forged destination to mislead the caller into communicating with an unintended end system. Like in any networked system, VoIP devices are also vulnerable to DoS attacks. Just as attackers would flood TCP servers with SYN packets on a TCP/IP network to exhaust a device' resources, attackers can flood RTP servers with call requests in order to overwhelm its processing capabilities. Attackers have also been known to connect laptops simulating IP phones to the Ethernet interfaces that IP phones use. These systems can then be used to carry out intrusions and DoS attacks. In addition to these circumstances, if attackers are able to intercept voice packets, they may eavesdrop onto ongoing conversations as well. Attackers can also intercept RTP packets containing the media stream of a communication session to inject arbitrary audio/video data that may be a cause of annoyance to the actual participants.

Attackers can also impersonate a server and issue commands such as bye, checksync, and reset to VoIP clients. The bye command causes VoIP devices to close down while in a conversation, the checksync command can be used to reboot VoIP terminals, and the reset command causes the server to reset and reestablish the connection, which takes considerable time.

NOTE Recently, a new variant to traditional e-mail spam has emerged on VoIP networks, commonly known as *SPIT (Spam over Internet Telephony)*. SPIT causes serious loss of VoIP bandwidth and is a time-wasting nuisance for the people on the attacked network. Because SPIT cannot be deleted like spam on first sight, the victim has to go through the entire message. SPIT is also a major cause of overloaded voicemail servers.

Combating VoIP security threats requires a well-thought-out infrastructure implementation plan. With the convergence of traditional and VoIP networks, balancing security while maintaining unconstrained traffic flow is crucial. The use of authorization on the network is an important step in limiting the possibilities of rogue and unauthorized entities on the network. Authorization of individual IP terminals ensures that only pre-listed devices are allowed to access the network. Although not absolutely foolproof, this method is a first layer of defense in preventing possible rogue devices from connecting and flooding the network with illicit packets. In addition to this preliminary measure, it is essential for two communicating VoIP devices to be able to authenticate their identities. Device identification may occur on the basis of fixed hardware identification parameters, such as MAC addresses or other "soft" codes that may be assigned by servers (for example, layered encryption techniques).

VoIP Security Measures Broken Down

Hackers can intercept incoming and outgoing calls, carry out DoS attacks, spoof phone calls, and eavesdrop on sensitive conversations. Many of the countermeasures to these types of attacks are the same ones used with traditional data-oriented networks:

- Keep patches updated on each network device involved with VoIP transmissions:
  - The call manager server.
  - The voicemail server.
  - The gateway server.
- Identify unidentified or rogue telephony devices.
  - Implement authentication so only authorized telephony devices are working on the network.
- Install and maintain
  - Stateful firewalls.
  - VPN for sensitive voice data.
  - Intrusion detection.

- Filter unnecessary ports on routers, switches, PCs, and IP telephones.
- Employ real-time monitoring that looks for attacks, tunneling, and abusive call patterns through IDS/IPS.
- Employ content monitoring.
- Use encryption when data (voice, fax, video) cross an untrusted network.
  - Use a two-factor authentication requirement.
  - Limit the number of calls via media gateways.
  - Close the media sessions after completion.

The use of secure cryptographic protocols such as *Transport Layer Security (TLS)* ensures that all SIP packets are conveyed within an encrypted and secure tunnel. The use of TLS can provide a secure channel for VoIP client/server communication and prevents the possibility of eavesdropping and packet manipulation.

WAN Technology Summary

We have covered several WAN technologies in the previous sections. Table 7-10 provides a snapshot of the important characteristics of each.

WAN Technology	Characteristics
Dedicated line	- Dedicated, leased line that connects two locations - Expensive compared to other WAN options - Secure because only two locations are using the same media
Frame relay	- High-performance WAN protocol that uses packet-switching technology, which works over public networks - Shared media among companies - Uses SVCs and PVCs - Fee based on bandwidth used
X.25	- First packet-switching technology developed to work over public networks - Shared media among companies - Lower speed than frame relay because of its extra overhead - International standard and used more in countries other than the U.S. - Uses SVCs and PVCs
SMDS	- High-speed swtiching technology used over public network
ATM	- High-speed bandwidth switching and multiplexing technology that has a low delay - Uses 53-byte fixed-size cells - Very fast because of the low overhead
SDLC	- Enables mainframes to communicate with remote offices - Provides polling mechanism to allow primary and secondary stations to communicate
HDLC	- New and improved SDLC protocol - A data encapsulation method for synchronous serial links - Point-to-point and multipoint communication

Table 7-10   Characteristics of WAN Technologies

WAN Technology	Characteristics
HSSI	- DTE/DCE interface to enable high-speed communication over WAN links
VoIP	- Combines voice and data over the same IP network media and protocol - Reduces the costs of implementing and maintaining two different networks

Table 7-10 Characteristics of WAN Technologies *(continued)*

Remote Access

I need to talk to you, but I am way over here!

Remote access covers several technologies that enable remote and home users to connect to networks that will grant them access to network resources that help them perform their tasks. Most of the time, these users must first gain access to the Internet through an ISP, which sets up a connection to the destination network.

For many corporations, remote access is a necessity because it enables users to obtain up-to-date information, it reduces networking costs by using the Internet as the access media instead of expensive dedicated lines, and it extends the workplace for employees to their homes or on the road. Remote access can streamline access to resources and information through Internet connections and provides a competitive advantage by letting partners, suppliers, and customers have closely controlled links. The most common types of remote connectivity methods used are VPNs, dial-up connections, ISDN, cable modems, and DSL connections.

Dial-Up and RAS

Remote access is usually gained by connecting to a remote access server (RAS), which acts as a gateway and can be an endpoint to a PPP session. Users dial into a RAS, which performs authentication by comparing the provided credentials with the database of credentials it maintains. A type of access authentication technology used in remote-connection situations is RADIUS, which is covered in Chapter 4. An administrator can set several configurations to dictate what actions take place when a remote user attempts to connect to the RAS. Usually a request for a username and password takes place, and the RAS may hang up the call to call the user back at a predefined phone number. This security activity is used to try to ensure that only authenticated users are given access to the network, and it reverses the long-distance charges back to the company. Even if an attacker finds out the logon credentials necessary to gain remote access, it is unlikely the attacker will also be at the predefined phone number. However, this security measure can be compromised if someone implements call forwarding.

When attackers are trying to find an entry point into a network, they often target remote access methods. They realize that many companies who have a stack of modems (or other types of access points) to provide remote access to their network are under the false impression that their firewall that monitors Internet traffic somehow magically protects all access to their network. If such a company has not implemented any (or strong) access control over the RAS, attackers can easily walk into its network without ever having to bother with the firewall.

Wardialing is used by many attackers to identify remote access modems. Specially written program tools can be used to dial a large bank of phone numbers that is fed to them.

The tools log valid data connections (modems used for data transmission) and attempt to identify the system on the other end of the phone line. Some of these tools have the option of performing a dictionary attack, which attempts many possible username and password combinations in the hopes of being authorized and allowed access to the network. Wardialing enables an attacker to find all the modems that provide remote access into a network. Once the attacker finds a modem, she attempts to access the network through this entry point. If unprotected modems (or any remote access technology) are used within an infrastructure, they are usually much easier to compromise than a firewall.

Companies often have modems hanging off of workstations here or there without much ado. Employees may install them or the IT staff may install them and then forget about them. Therefore, it is important for companies to perform wardialing on their own network to make sure no unaccounted-for modems are attached. Some corporate PBX phone systems have the capability to detect modem signals on analog phone lines and audit/record their usage. This feature can be implemented to support the appropriate security policy of "no unauthorized devices are to be attached to the data and telephone network."

When you are looking at the security angle of remote access, the three most important rules to enforce are the following:

- All users on the remote access equipment must be fully authenticated to proceed with its use.
- No covert or inappropriate access to the communication circuits is allowed.
- After authentication, users shall have access to those authorized services to which they are entitled, and no more.

ISDN

Integrated Services Digital Network (ISDN) is a communications protocol provided by telephone companies and ISPs. This protocol and the necessary equipment enable data, voice, and other types of traffic to travel over a medium in a digital manner previously used only for analog voice transmission. Telephone companies went all digital many years ago, except for the local loops, which consist of the copper wires that connect houses and businesses to their carrier provider's central offices. These central offices contain the telephone company's switching equipment, and it is here the analog-to-digital transformation takes place. However, the local loop is always analog, and is therefore slower. ISDN was developed to replace the aging telephone analog systems, but it has yet to catch on to the level expected.

ISDN uses the same wires and transmission media used by analog dial-up technologies, but it works in a digital fashion. If a computer uses a modem to communicate with an ISP, the modem converts the data from digital to analog to be transmitted over the phone line. If that same computer was configured and had the necessary equipment to utilize ISDN, it would not need to convert the data from digital to analog, but would keep it in a digital form. This, of course, means the receiving end would also require the necessary equipment to receive and interpret this type of communication properly. Communicating in a purely digital form provides higher bit rates that can be sent more economically.

ISDN is a set of telecommunications services that can be used over public and private telecommunications networks. It provides a digital point-to-point circuit-switched medium and establishes a circuit between the two communicating devices. An ISDN connection can be used for anything a modem can be used for, but it provides more functionality and higher bandwidth. This switched digital service can provide bandwidth on an as-needed basis and can be used for LAN-to-LAN on-demand connectivity, instead of using an expensive dedicated link.

As stated earlier, analog uses a full channel for communication, but ISDN can break up this channel into multiple channels to provide full-duplex communication and a higher level of control and error handling. ISDN provides two basic home and business services: *Basic Rate Interface (BRI)* and *Primary Rate Interface (PRI)*. BRI has two B channels that enable data to be transferred and one D channel that provides for call setup, connection management, error control, caller ID, and more. The bandwidth available with BRI is 144 Kbps, whereas the top modems can provide only 56 Kbps.

The D channel provides for a quicker call setup and process in making a connection. An ISDN connection may require a setup connection time of only two to five seconds, whereas a modem may require a timeframe of 45 to 90 seconds. This D channel is an out-of-band communication link between the local loop equipment and the user's terminal. It is out of band because the control data are not mixed in with the user communication data. This makes it more difficult for a would-be defrauder to send bogus instructions back to the service provider's equipment in hopes of causing a DoS, obtaining services not paid for, or conducting some other type of destructive behavior.

The BRI service is common for residential use and the PRI, which has 23 B channels and one D channel, is more commonly used in corporations. ISDN is not usually the primary telecommunications connection for companies, but it can be used as a backup in case the primary connection goes down. A company can also choose to implement dial-on-demand routing (DDR), which can work over ISDN. DDR allows a company to send WAN data over its existing telephone lines and use the public circuit-switched network as a temporary type of WAN link. It is usually implemented by companies that

ISDN Examined

ISDN breaks the telephone line into different channels and transmits data in a digital form rather than the old analog form. Three ISDN implementations are in use:

- **BRI ISDN**   This implementation operates over existing copper lines at the local loop and provides digital voice and data channels. It uses two B channels and one D channel with a combined bandwidth of 144 Kbps and is generally used for home subscribers.

- **PRI ISDN**   This implementation has up to 23 B channels and 1 D channel, at 64 Kbps per channel. The total bandwidth is equivalent to a T1, which is 1.544 Mbps. This would be more suitable for a company that requires a higher amount of bandwidth.

- **Broadband ISDN (BISDN)**   This implementation can handle many different types of services simultaneously and is mainly used within telecommunications carrier backbones. When BISDN is used within a backbone, ATM is employed to encapsulate data at the data link layer into cells, which travel over a SONET network.

send out only a small amount of WAN traffic and is a much cheaper solution than a real WAN implementation. The connection activates when it is needed and then idles out.

DSL

Digital Subscriber Line (DSL) is another type of high-speed connection technology used to connect a home or business to the service provider's central office. It can provide 6 to 30 times higher bandwidth speeds than ISDN and analog technologies. It uses existing phone lines and provides a 24-hour connection to the Internet. This does indeed sound better than sliced bread, but only certain people can get this service because you have to be within a 2.5-mile radius of the DSL service provider's equipment. As the distance between a residence and the central office increases, the transmission rates for DSL decrease.

DSL is a broadband technology that can provide up to a 52-Mbps transmission speed without replacing the carrier's copper wire. The end user and the carrier's equipment do need to be upgraded for DSL, though, and this is why many companies and residents cannot use this service at this time. The user and carrier must have DSL modems that use the same modulation techniques.

DSL provides faster transmission rates because it uses all of the available frequencies available on a voice-grade UTP line. When you call someone, your voice data travels down this UTP line and the service provider "cleans up" the transmission by removing the high and low frequencies. Humans do not use these frequencies when they talk, so if there is anything on these frequencies, it is considered line noise and thus removed. So in reality, the available bandwidth of the line that goes from your house to the telephone company's central office is artificially reduced. When DSL is used, this does not take place and therefore the high and low frequencies can be used for data transmission.

DSL offers several types of services. With *symmetric services,* traffic flows at the same speed upstream and downstream (to and from the Internet or destination). With *asymmetric services,* the downstream speed is much higher than the upstream speed. In most situations, an asymmetric connection is fine for residence users because they usually download items from the Web much more often than they upload data.

Cable Modems

We already have a cable running to your house, so just buy this extra service.

The cable television companies have been delivering television services to homes for years, and then they started delivering data transmission services for users who have cable modems and want to connect to the Internet at high speeds.

Cable modems provide high-speed access, up to 50 Mbps, to the Internet through existing cable coaxial and fiber lines. The cable modem provides upstream and downstream conversions.

Not all cable companies provide Internet access as a service, mainly because they have not upgraded their infrastructure to move from a one-way network to a two-way network. Once this conversion takes place, data can come down from a central point (referred to as the head) to a residential home and back up to the head and onto the Internet.

xDSL

Many different flavors of DSL are available, each with its own characteristics and specific uses.

- **Symmetrical DSL (SDSL)** Data travel upstream and downstream at the same rate. Bandwidth can range between 192 Kbps to 1.1 Mbps. Used mainly for business applications that require high speeds in both directions.

- **Asymmetrical DSL (ADSL)** Data travel downstream faster than upstream. Upstream speeds are 128 Kbps to 384 Kbps, and downstream speeds can be as fast as 768 Kbps. Generally used by residential users.

- **ISDN DSL (IDSL)** Provides DSL for customers who cannot get SDSL or ADSL because of their distance from the central office. It is capable of reaching customers who are up to 36,000 feet (almost 7 miles) from the provider's central office. IDSL operates at a symmetrical speed of 128 Kbps.

- **High-bit-rate DSL (HDSL)** Provides T1 (1.544 Mbps) speeds over regular copper phone wire without the use of repeaters. Requires two twisted pairs of wires, which many voice-grade UTP lines do not have.

Coaxial and fiber cables are used to deliver hundreds of television stations to users, and one or more of the channels on these lines are dedicated to carrying data. The bandwidth is shared between users in a local area; therefore, it will not always stay at a static rate. So, for example, if Mike attempts to download a program from the Internet at 5:30 P.M., he most likely will have a much slower connection than if he had attempted it at 10:00 A.M., because many people come home from work and hit the Internet at the same time. As more people access the Internet within his local area, Mike's Internet access performance drops.

Always Connected

Unlike modem connections, DSL lines and cable modems are connected to the Internet all the time. No dial-up steps are required. This can cause a huge security issue because many hackers look for just these types of connections. Systems using these types of connections are always online and available for scanning, probing, hacking, and attacking. These systems are also often used in DDoS attacks. Because the systems are on all the time, attackers plant Trojan horses that lie dormant until they get the command from the attacker to launch an attack against a victim. Many of the DDoS attacks use as their accomplices systems with DSL and cable modems, and usually the owner of the computer has no idea their system is being used to attack another system.

Sharing the same media brings up a slew of security concerns, because users with network sniffers can easily view their neighbors' traffic and data as both travel to and from the Internet. Many cable companies are now encrypting the data that go back and forth over shared lines through a type of data link encryption.

VPN

Here's the secret handshake. Now you can use the secret tunnel.

A *virtual private network (VPN)* is a secure, private connection through a public network or an otherwise unsecure environment, as shown in Figure 7-54. It is a *private* connection because the encryption and tunneling protocols are used to ensure the confidentiality and integrity of the data in transit. It is important to remember that VPN technology requires a tunnel to work and it assumes encryption. The protocols that can be used for VPNs are Point-to-Point Tunneling Protocol (PPTP), IPSec, and L2TP.

The sending and receiving ends must have the necessary hardware and software to set up an encrypted tunnel, which provides the private link. The tunneling encryption protocol used encrypts the data and protects that information as it travels through the untrusted public network, usually the Internet.

Remote users, or road warriors, can use VPNs to connect to their company network to access their e-mail, network resources, and corporate assets. A remote user must have the necessary software loaded on his computer to use a VPN. The user first makes a PPP connection to an ISP, and the ISP makes a full connection for the user to the destination network. PPP encapsulates datagrams to be properly transmitted over a telecommunication link. Once this connection has been made, the user's software initiates a VPN connection with the destination network. Because data exchanged between the two entities will be encrypted, the two entities go through a handshaking phase to agree upon the type of encryption that will be used and the key that will be employed to encrypt their data. The ISP is involved with the creation of the PPP connection, which is a type of foundation for the VPN connection. Once the PPP connection is set up, the ISP is out of the picture and the VPN parameters are negotiated and decided upon by the user and the destination network. After this is complete, the user and network can then communicate securely through their newly created virtual connection.

VPN connections can be used not only by remote users to access a network but also to provide a connection between two routers (many times called a gateway-to-gateway connection). It is a flexible connection, and the only requirements are that each entity must have a connection, VPN software, the necessary protocols, and the same encryption mechanisms. Once the VPN connection is made, the user can access network resources.

Up to this point, we have been discussing a VPN that exists over dial-up and Internet connections, but a VPN can also take place between firewalls that have VPN functionality. Within a network, the VPN device sits on the outer edge of the security domain. When a company implements a firewall that has VPN functionality embedded, the company can centralize administration for the VPN and firewall. In this type of configuration, packets that enter the network can come in encrypted through the VPN connection and must be decrypted to allow the firewall to inspect the packets and either allow or deny them. Because extra work is being done on the packets as they

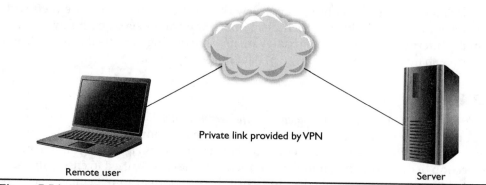

Figure 7-54   A VPN provides a virtual dedicated link between two entities across a public network.

enter and leave a network, much more overhead is generated, which causes degradation in performance. However, today most of the processing that takes place is being moved to hardware and integrated circuits, which can work at much faster speeds than pure software.

Tunneling Protocols

How do we get our message through this sea of packets?
Response: Create a tunnel.

As previously mentioned, VPNs use tunneling protocols, but what the heck are they anyway? A *tunnel* is a virtual path across a network that delivers packets that are encapsulated and possibly encrypted. Encapsulation and encryption sound alike, but they describe two different reasons a tunnel would be used in the first place.

If one network uses NetBIOS Enhanced User Interface (NetBEUI) and needs to be connected to another network that also uses NetBEUI, but they are two states apart, what is the problem? NetBEUI is nonroutable. So for these two networks to communicate, the NetBEUI packets must be encapsulated within a routable protocol, such as IP. This type of encapsulation happens all the time on the Internet and between networks. When an Ethernet network is connected to an FDDI backbone, that FDDI network does not understand the Ethernet frame format; thus, the packets must be encapsulated within the FDDI protocol when they are sent over the FDDI network. If two networks use IPX and need to communicate across the Internet, these messages must also be encapsulated in a protocol that the Internet can understand, such as IP.

The second variation to a tunnel is one that uses encapsulation *and* encryption. The encapsulation reasons stay the same, and the encryption is used to protect the data's confidentiality and integrity as it travels through untrusted environments. These are both ways of tunneling through another network.

Tunneling is the main ingredient to a VPN because that is how the VPN creates its connection. Three main tunneling protocols are used in VPN connections: PPTP, L2TP, and IPSec. (IPSec is described in depth in Chapter 8.)

IPSec

IPSec is fully covered in Chapter 8, but let's take a quick look at some configuration possibilities for this protocol suite.

IPSec can be configured to provide transport adjacency, which just means that more than one security protocol (ESP and AH) is applied to a packet. IPSec can also be configured to provide iterated tunneling, in which an IPSec tunnel is tunneled through another IPSec tunnel, as shown in the following diagram. Iterated tunneling would be used if the traffic needed different levels of protection at different junctions of its path. For example, if the IPSec tunnel started from an internal host to an internal border router, this may not require encryption, so only the AH protocol would be used. But when that data travels from that border router throughout the Internet to another network, then the data require more protection. So the first packets travel through a semisecure tunnel until they get ready to hit the Internet and then they go through a very secure second tunnel.

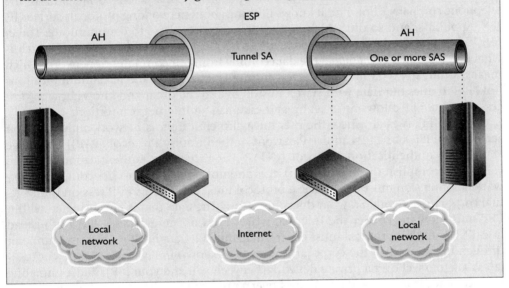

PPP   Before we dig too deeply into true tunneling protocols, let's take a look at an encapsulation protocol again. Tunneling and encapsulation protocols sound very similar, because tunneling protocols use encapsulation. Encapsulation just means that an extra header, and possibly a trailer, has been added to a frame. A tunneling protocol adds these headers and trailers so the packets can be transmitted over a certain network type. So, if you needed to get packets using the network and transport protocols of IPX/SPX over the Internet, a gateway would add the necessary TCP/IP headers and trailers, which are required to be routable on the Internet. Once these packets get to their destination, these headers and trailers are removed and the packets are sent to their designated host.

Point-to-Point Protocol (PPP) is not really a tunneling protocol, but an encapsulation protocol. It does not need to wrap up current frames with special headers and trailers, which will be taken off at the destination. Instead, it allows TCP/IP traffic to be transmitted over a medium developed for telephone voice data.

PPP is used to encapsulate messages and transmit them over a serial line. Therefore, it allows TCP/IP and other protocols to be carried across telecommunications lines. PPP is used to establish telecommunication connections between routers, from user to router, and from user to user. It is also employed to establish an Internet connection between a computer and an Internet *point of presence (PoP)*—usually a bank of modems and access servers at an ISP location. The user dials into this PoP over a telecommunications line and communicates using PPP.

When you connect to the Internet, you may be using a serial asynchronous dial-up connection or a point-to-point connection, such as a T1 line. A T1 line is a *serial* connection, meaning one bit follows the one in front of it, compared to a *parallel* connection, where channels of bits travel simultaneously. This serial connection is the telephone company's line, and it knows nothing about networking protocols such as IP, IPX, AppleTalk, and so on, which is what our computers use to communicate. Therefore, this traffic needs to be encapsulated before it is put onto this serial link, which is what PPP does. PPP *encapsulates* the data coming from our computer or network, which means it puts the data into the correct format to travel over the telecommunications link. PPP frames our data with start and stop bits so the other end knows how to process the data. PPP allows us to set up and establish an Internet connection.

Once a link is established, the user must authenticate to a network authentication server at the ISP site. PPP can use Password Authentication Protocol (PAP), Challenge Handshake Authentication Protocol (CHAP), or Extensible Authentication Protocol (EAP) to accomplish this task. If the user is attempting to dial into her company's network, another step must take place: a protocol must deliver this PPP session to the actual corporate network. So what does this mean? The data that is encapsulated within PPP must now travel over the Internet, which does not understand PPP, but instead uses IP. So another protocol must encapsulate the PPP data in IP packets and tunnel it through the Internet to the corporate network, as shown in Figure 7-55. PPP encapsulates data to travel over a private network (between you and your ISP), and a tunneling protocol encapsulates the data to travel over a public network, such as the Internet.

Three of the main tunneling protocols used today for setting up a VPN are IPSec, PPTP, and L2TP. They reduce the cost of remote networking because the user can connect to a local ISP instead of dialing directly to the corporate network, which may accrue long-distance charges.

PPP has, for the most part, replaced *Serial Line Internet Protocol (SLIP)*, an older protocol that was used to encapsulate data to be sent over serial connection links. PPP has several capabilities that SLIP does not have:

- Implements header and data compression for efficiency and better use of bandwidth
- Has error correction

Figure 7-55
A VPN connection
can be used to
extend a PPP
connection securely.

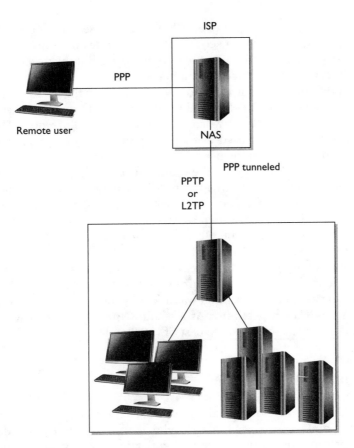

- Supports different authentication methods
- Can encapsulate protocols other than just IP
- Does not require both ends to have an IP address assigned before data transfer can occur

PPTP

The Internet does not understand my dial-up packets.
Response: Wrap them up in PPTP.

Why do we need tunneling protocols? Because some protocols cannot be properly routed over specific networks. We have been talking specifically about PPP frames, which are not routable over the Internet, but the Internet does not understand some other protocols, such as IPX, NetBEUI, and AppleTalk. Alone, these frames could not find their way to the ultimate destination they are seeking when crossing the Internet, so they need a hand. That's what the tunneling protocol does. Imagine a ferry taking cars across a body of water. The car cannot get to the other side by itself because it isn't built to deal with water, but the ferry can move and navigate in the water, just as the tunneling protocol can move in the IP-based Internet.

PPTP, a Microsoft protocol, allows remote users to set up a PPP connection to a local ISP and then create a secure VPN to their destination. PPTP has been the de facto industry-standard tunneling protocol for years, but the new de facto standard for VPNs is IPSec, which is covered in Chapter 8.

Although tunneling does not by default mean the user's data are encrypted, in most implementations tunneling and encryption are both used. When PPTP is used, the PPP payload is encrypted with Microsoft Point-to-Point Encryption (MPPE) using MS-CHAP or EAP-TLS. The keys used in encrypting this data are generated during the authentication process between the user and the authentication server.

Along with encryption, the frame must be encapsulated as well. A series of encapsulations takes place in this technology. The user's data are encapsulated within PPP, and then this frame is encapsulated by PPTP with a Generic Routing Encapsulation (GRE) header and IP header, as shown in Figure 7-56. This encapsulation allows the resulting frame to be routable over public networks, such as the Internet.

One limitation of PPTP is that it can work only over IP networks, so other protocols must be used to move data over frame relay, X.25, and ATM links. Cisco started to develop a protocol, Layer 2 Forwarding (L2F), that would tunnel PPP traffic through these other types of networks, but it was asked by the IETF to combine its work with PPTP for the sake of interoperability. As a result, Cisco developed Layer 2 Tunneling Protocol (L2TP), which combines the best of PPTP and L2F.

L2TP

L2TP was R2D2's little cousin.
Response: You are still not funny.

L2TP provides the functionality of PPTP, but it can work over networks other than just IP, and it provides a higher level of security when combined with IPSec. L2TP does not provide any encryption or authentication services, so it needs to be combined with IPSec if those services are required.

The processes that L2TP uses for encapsulation are similar to those used by PPTP. The PPP frame is encapsulated with L2TP.

When the destination system receives the L2TP frame, it processes the headers. Once it gets to the IPSec trailer, it verifies the integrity and authentication of the frame. Then it uses the information in the ESP header to decrypt the rest of the headers and data payload properly.

The following items outline the differences between PPTP and L2TP:

- PPTP can run only within IP networks. L2TP, on the other hand, can run within and tunnel through networks that use other protocols, such as frame relay, X.25, and ATM.

- PPTP is an encryption protocol and L2TP is not; therefore, L2TP lacks the security to be called a *true* VPN solution. L2TP is often used in conjunction with IPSec to provide the necessary encryption.

- L2TP supports TACACS+ and RADIUS, while PPTP does not.

Figure 7-56
PPTP encapsulates
a PPP frame.

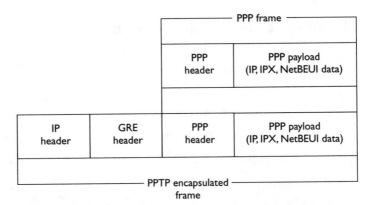

Authentication Protocols

Hey, how do I know you are who you say you are?

   Password Authentication Protocol (PAP) is used by remote users to authenticate over PPP lines. It provides identification and authentication of the user who is attempting to access a network from a remote system. This protocol requires a user to enter a password before being authenticated. The password and the username credentials are sent over the network to the authentication server after a connection has been established via PPP. The authentication server has a database of user credentials that are compared to the supplied credentials to authenticate users.

   PAP is one of the least secure authentication methods, because the credentials are sent in cleartext, which renders them easy to capture by network sniffers. Although it is not recommended, some systems revert to PAP if they cannot agree on any other authentication protocol. During the handshake process of a connection, the two entities negotiate how authentication is going to take place, what connection parameters to use, the speed of data flow, and other factors. Both entities will try to negotiate and agree upon the most secure method of authentication; they may start with EAP, and if one computer does not have EAP capabilities, they will try to agree upon CHAP; if one of the computers does not have CHAP capabilities, they may be forced to use PAP. If this type of authentication is unacceptable, the administrator will configure the RAS to accept only CHAP authentication and higher, and PAP cannot be used at all.

   Challenge Handshake Authentication Protocol (CHAP) addresses some of the vulnerabilities found in PAP. It uses a challenge/response mechanism to authenticate the user instead of sending a password. When a user wants to establish a PPP connection and both ends have agreed that CHAP will be used for authentication purposes, the user's computer sends the authentication server a logon request. The server sends the user a challenge, which is a random value. This challenge is encrypted with the use of a predefined password as an encryption key, and the encrypted challenge value is returned to the server. The authentication server also uses the predefined password as an encryption key and decrypts the challenge value, comparing it to the original value sent. If the two results are the same, the authentication server deduces that the user must have entered the correct password, and authentication is granted. The steps that take place in CHAP are depicted in Figure 7-57.

A Summary of Tunneling Protocols

Point-to-Point Tunneling Protocol (PPTP):

- Designed for client/server connectivity
- Sets up a single point-to-point connection between two computers
- Works at the data link layer
- Transmits over IP networks only

Layer 2 Forwarding (L2F):

- Created before L2TP by Cisco
- Merged with PPTP, which resulted in L2TP
- Provides mutual authentication
- No encryption

Layer 2 Tunneling Protocol (L2TP):

- Hybrid of L2F and PPTP
- Sets up a single point-to-point connection between two computers
- Works at the data link layer
- Transmits over multiple types of networks, not just IP
- Combined with IPSec for security

IPSec:

- Handles multiple connections at the same time
- Provides secure authentication and encryption
- Supports only IP networks
- Focuses on LAN-to-LAN communication rather than user-to-user
- Works at the network layer, and provides security on top of IP
- Can work in *tunnel mode*, meaning the payload and the header are protected, or *transport mode*, meaning only the payload is protected

Please review Chapter 8 for a full understanding of the IPSec protocol suite.

Extensible Authentication Protocol (EAP) is also supported by PPP. Actually, EAP is not a specific authentication mechanism as are PAP and CHAP. Instead, it provides a framework to enable many types of authentication techniques to be used during PPP connections. As the name states, it extends the authentication possibilities from the norm (PAP and CHAP) to other methods such as one-time passwords, token cards, biometrics, Kerberos, and future mechanisms. So when a user connects to an authentication server and both have EAP capabilities, they can negotiate between a longer list of possible authentication methods.

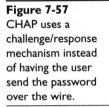

Figure 7-57
CHAP uses a challenge/response mechanism instead of having the user send the password over the wire.

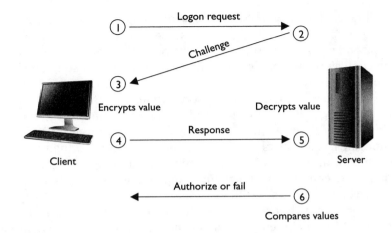

Remote Access Guidelines

Remote users should be identified and authenticated and their activities audited to ensure no malicious activity is taking place and that no one is abusing access rights. All remote users should be justified in their right to access the network, and their access privileges should be reviewed on an annual basis. For example, if Brian worked in the software development group and required remote access to work from home, and then six months later he was moved into the logistics group, he might not require remote access any longer; therefore, remote access should no longer be available to him.

PAP vs. CHAP

PAP characteristics:

- Sends credentials in cleartext during transmission.
- Use has decreased because it does not provide a high level of security.
- Supported by most networks and NASs.

CHAP characteristics:

- Used the same way PAP is used but provides a higher degree of security.
- Authenticates using a challenge/response method.
- Used by remote users, routers, and NASs to provide authentication before providing connectivity.

PAP is vulnerable to sniffing because it sends the password and data in plaintext, but it is also vulnerable to man-in-the-middle attacks. CHAP is not vulnerable to man-in-the-middle attacks because it continues this challenge/response activity throughout the connection to ensure the authentication server is still communicating with a user who holds the necessary credentials.

Expected activity and behavior pertaining to remote access should be within the company's security policy or in an issue-specific policy that outlines who should do what and when. This policy should be presented and available to all users to help clear up confusion and enable the company to take steps if someone is abusing their use of remote access.

The access modems should be set to answer after the fourth ring. Wardialers are often configured to move to another phone number if the number they are dialing rings longer than two or three times, because connections that ring more than three times are usually telephone lines and not data lines. Configuring the modem to answer on the fourth ring or higher is done in the hope that attackers will not be able to tell that the telephone line is actually being used for remote data access.

The remote access facilities should be consolidated when possible. This means all access servers are housed in the same server room and administered by the same person or group. This helps ensure consistency in how remote entry points are maintained and monitored, and helps make certain that when changes take place, they happen to all entry points. This also facilitates centralized auditing and logging, and makes it more difficult for administrators to forget all the ways the company is allowing users to access the environment.

Strong two-factor user authentication should be used via RADIUS or TACACS+ servers, which are explained in Chapter 4. If the data that users and the company will be transmitting are confidential or sensitive, users should connect via a VPN. Various levels of security should be provided to various types of users entering the network to help ensure each user has only the necessary access rights and permissions he needs.

Companies may restrict access based on the address of the source computer that is trying to gain access. If the address is unknown or not on the ACL, the connection should be denied. A firewall should be implemented to ensure remote users access only the services and ports the network administrator wants them to access.

Caller ID and callback settings, as well as two-factor authentication, can be configured on the RAS server. The *caller ID* functionality can view the source telephone number and allow or deny access based on a predefined list of approved phone numbers. For an attacker to get around this, she must call from a preauthorized telephone number or compromise the telephone company's central office equipment. The *callback* option requires the RAS to call the user requesting access in return. With callback configured, after a user authenticates to the RAS, the RAS drops the connection and calls the user back at a preconfigured telephone number.

Caller ID and callback options are great, but they are usually not practical because they require users to call in from a static phone number each time they access the network. Most users who are accessing the network remotely are doing so because they are on the road and moving from place to place.

Wireless Technologies

Look, Ma, no wires!

Wireless communications take place much more often than we think, and a wide range of broadband wireless data transmission technologies are used in various frequency ranges. Broadband wireless signals occupy frequency bands that may be shared with microwave, satellite, radar, and ham radio use, for example. We use these technologies for television transmissions, cellular phones, satellite transmissions, spying, surveillance, and garage door openers. This section focuses on how wireless technologies are used in LAN environments.

Wireless Communications

When two people are talking, they are using wireless communication because their vocal cords are altering airwaves, which are signals that travel with no cables attached to another person. Wireless communication involves transmitting signals via radio waves through air and space, which also alters airwaves.

Signals are measured in *frequency* and *amplitudes*. The frequency of a signal dictates the amount of data that can be carried and how far. The higher the frequency, the more data the signal can carry, but the higher the frequency, the more susceptible the signal is to atmospheric interference. A higher frequency can carry more data but over a shorter distance.

In a wired network, each computer and device has its own cable connecting it to the network in some fashion. In wireless technologies, each device must instead share the allotted radio frequency spectrum with all other wireless devices that need to communicate. This spectrum of frequencies is finite in nature, which means it cannot grow if more and more devices need to use it. The same thing happens with Ethernet—all the computers on a segment share the same medium, and only one computer can send data at any given time. Otherwise, a collision can take place. Wired networks using Ethernet employ the CSMA/CD (collision detection) technology. Wireless technology is actually very similar to Ethernet, but it uses CSMA/CA (collision avoidance). The wireless device sends out a broadcast indicating it is going to transmit data. This is received by other devices on the shared medium, which causes them to hold off on transmitting information. It is all about trying to eliminate or reduce collisions. (The two versions of CSMA are explained earlier in this chapter in the section "CSMA.")

A number of technologies have been developed to allow wireless devices to access and share this limited amount of medium for communication purposes. We will look at two different types of spread spectrum techniques: frequency hopping and direct sequence. The goal of each of these wireless technologies is to split the available frequency into usable portions, since it is a limited resource, and to allow the devices to share them efficiently.

Spread Spectrum

Can I spread these signals with a butter knife?
Response: Whatever.

In wireless technologies, certain technologies and industries are allocated specific *spectrums*, or frequency ranges, to be used for transmissions. In the United States, the FCC decides upon this allotment of frequencies and enforces its own restrictions. *Spread spectrum* means that something is distributing individual signals across the allocated frequencies in some fashion. So when a spread spectrum technology is used, the sender spreads its data across the frequencies over which it has permission to communicate. This allows for more effective use of the available bandwidth, because the sending system can use more than one frequency at a time. Think of it in terms of serial versus parallel communication. In serial transmissions, all the bits have to be fed into one channel, one after the other. In parallel transmissions, the bits can take several channels to arrive at their destination. Parallel is a faster approach because more channels can be used at one time. This is similar to checkout lanes in a grocery store. We have all been in the situation where there was just one checkout lane open, which drastically slows down the amount of traffic (people and their food) that can get properly processed in a short period of time. Once the manager calls more checkers to the front to open their lanes, then parallel processing can be done and the grumbling stops. So spreading the signal allows the data to travel in a parallel fashion by allowing the sender and receiver to send data over more than one frequency.

We will look at two types of spread spectrum: frequency hopping spread spectrum (FHSS) and direct sequence spread spectrum (DSSS).

Frequency Hopping Spread Spectrum　Frequency hopping spread spectrum (FHSS) takes the total amount of bandwidth (spectrum) and splits it into smaller sub-channels. The sender and receiver work at one of these channels for a specific amount of time and then move to another channel. The sender puts the first piece of data on one frequency, the second on a different frequency, and so on. The FHSS algorithm determines the individual frequencies that will be used and in what order, and this is referred to as the sender and receiver's hop sequence.

Interference is a large issue in wireless transmissions because it can corrupt signals as they travel. Interference can be caused by other devices working in the same frequency space. The devices' signals step on each other's toes and distort the data being sent. The FHSS approach to this is to hop between different frequencies so if another device is operating at the same frequency, it will not be drastically affected. Consider another analogy: Suppose George and Marge have to work in the same room. They could get into each other's way and affect each other's work. But if they periodically change rooms, the probability of them interfering with each other is reduced.

A hopping approach also makes it much more difficult for eavesdroppers to listen in on and reconstruct the data being transmitted when used in technologies other than WLAN. FHSS has been used extensively in military wireless communications devices because the only way the enemy could intercept and capture the transmission is by knowing the hopping sequence. But in today's WLAN devices, the hopping sequence is known and does not provide any security. The receiver has to know the sequences to be able to obtain the data.

So how does this FHSS stuff work? The sender and receiver hop from one frequency to another based on a predefined hop sequence. Several pairs of senders and receivers can move their data over the same set of frequencies because they are all using different hop sequences. Let's say you and I share a hop sequence of 1, 5, 3, 2, 4, and Nicole and Ed have a sequence of 4, 2, 5, 1, 3. I send my first message on frequency 1, and Nicole sends her first message on frequency 4 at the same time. My next piece of data is sent on frequency 5, the next on 3, and so on until each reaches its destination, which is your wireless device. So your device listens on frequency 1 for a half second, and then listens on frequency 5, and so on, until it receives all of the pieces of data that are on the line on those frequencies at that time. Ed's device is listening to the same frequencies but at different times and in a different order, so his device ignores my message because it is out of sync with his predefined sequence. Without knowing the right code, Ed treats my messages as background noise and does not process it.

Direct Sequence Spread Spectrum   Direct sequence spread spectrum (DSSS) takes a different approach by applying sub-bits to a message. The sub-bits are used by the sending system to generate a different format of the data before the data are transmitted. The receiving end uses these sub-bits to reassemble the signal into the original data format. The sub-bits are called *chips* and the sequence of how the sub-bits are applied is referred to as the *chipping* code.

When the sender's data are combined with the chip, to anyone who does not know the chipping sequence, these signals appear as random noise. This is why the sequence is sometimes called a pseudo-noise sequence. Once the sender combines the data with the chipping sequence, the new form of the information is modulated with a radio carrier signal, and it is shifted to the necessary frequency and transmitted. What the heck does that mean? When using wireless transmissions, the data are actually moving over radio signals that work in specific frequencies. Any data to be moved in this fashion must have a carrier signal, and this carrier signal works in its own specific range, which is a frequency. So you can think of it this way: once the data are combined with the chipping code, it is put into a car (carrier signal), and the car travels down its specific road (frequency) to get to its destination.

The receiver basically reverses the process, first by demodulating the data from the carrier signal (removing it from the car). The receiver must know the correct chipping sequence to change the received data into its original format. This means the sender and receiver must be properly synchronized.

The sub-bits provide error-recovery instructions, just as parity does in RAID technologies. If a signal is corrupted using FHSS, it must be re-sent; but by using DSSS, even if the message is somewhat distorted, the signal can still be regenerated because it can be rebuilt from the chipping code bits. The use of this code allows for prevention of interference, allows for tracking of multiple transmissions, and provides a level of error correction.

FHSS vs. DSSS   FHSS uses only a portion of the total bandwidth available at any one time, while the DSSS technology uses all of the available bandwidth continuously. DSSS spreads the signals over a wider frequency band, whereas FHSS uses a narrow band carrier.

Since DSSS sends data across all frequencies at once, it has a higher data throughput than FHSS. The first WAN standard, 802.11, used FHSS, but as bandwidth requirements increased, DSSS was implemented. By using FHSS, the 802.11 standard can provide a data throughput of only 1 to 2 Mbps. By using DSSS instead, 802.11b provides a data throughput of up to 11 Mbps.

WLAN Components

A wireless LAN (WLAN) uses a transceiver, called an *access point (AP)*, which connects to an Ethernet cable that is the link wireless devices use to access resources on the wired network, as shown in Figure 7-58. When the AP is connected to the LAN Ethernet by a wired cable, it is the component that connects the wired and the wireless worlds. The

Spread Spectrum Types

This technology transmits data by "spreading" it over a broad range of frequencies.

- Frequency hopping spread spectrum (FHSS) moves data by changing frequencies.

- Direct sequence spread spectrum (DSSS) takes a different approach by applying sub-bits to a message and uses all of the available frequencies at the same time.

- Orthogonal frequency-division multiplexing (OFDM) is a digital multicarrier modulation scheme that compacts multiple modulated carriers tightly together, reducing the required bandwidth. The modulated signals are orthogonal (perpendicular) and do not interfere with each other. OFDM uses a composite of narrow channel bands to enhance its performance in high frequency bands.

APs are in fixed locations throughout a network and work as communication *beacons*. Let's say a wireless user has a device with a wireless NIC, which modulates her data onto radio frequency signals that are accepted and processed by the AP. The signals transmitted from the AP are received by the wireless NIC and converted into a digital format, which the device can understand.

When APs are used to connect wireless and wired networks, this is referred to as an *infrastructure WLAN*, which is used to extend an existing wired network. When there is just one AP and it is not connected to a wired network, it is considered to be in *stand-alone* mode and just acts as a wireless hub.

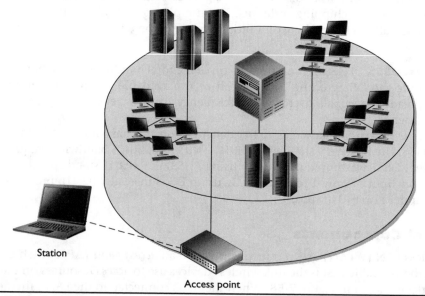

Station

Access point

Figure 7-58 A wireless device must authenticate with an access point.

For a wireless device and AP to communicate, they must be configured to communicate over the same channel. A *channel* is a certain frequency within a given frequency band. The AP is configured to transmit over a specific channel, and the wireless device will "tune" itself to be able to communicate over this same frequency.

Any hosts that wish to participate within a particular WLAN must be configured with the proper *Service Set ID (SSID)*. Various hosts can be segmented into different WLANs by using different SSIDs. The reasons to segment a WLAN into portions are the same reasons wired systems are segmented on a network: the users require access to different resources, have different business functions, or have different levels of trust.

An *ad hoc WLAN* has no APs; the wireless devices communicate with each other through their wireless NICs instead of going through a centralized device. To construct an ad hoc network, wireless client software is installed on contributing hosts and configured for peer-to-peer operation mode. Then, the user clicks Network Neighborhood in a Windows platform, and the software searches for other hosts operating in this similar mode and shows them to the user.

NOTE   When wireless devices work in infrastructure mode, the AP and wireless clients form a group referred to as a Basic Service Set (BSS). This group is assigned a name, which is the SSID value.

The SSID is usually required when a wireless device wants to authenticate to an AP. For the device to prove it should be allowed to communicate with the wired network, it must first provide a valid SSID value. The SSID should not be seen as a reliable security mechanism because many APs broadcast their SSIDs, which can be easily sniffed and used by attackers.

The wireless device can authenticate to the AP in two main ways: *open system authentication (OSA)* and *shared key authentication (SKA)*. OSA does not require the wireless device to prove to the AP it has a specific cryptographic key to allow for authentication purposes. In many cases, the wireless device needs to provide only the correct SSID value. In OSA implementations, all transactions are in cleartext because no encryption is involved. So an intruder can sniff the traffic, capture the necessary steps of authentication, and walk through the same steps to be authenticated and associated to an AP.

NOTE   OSA just means the device does not need to prove it has a specific cryptographic key for authentication. Depending upon the product and the configuration, a network administrator can also limit access to specific MAC addresses. This would still be considered OSA.

When an AP is configured to use SKA, the AP sends a random value to the wireless device. The device encrypts this value with its cryptographic key and returns it. The AP decrypts and extracts the response, and if it is the same as the original value, the device is authenticated. In this approach, the wireless device is authenticated to the network by proving it has the necessary encryption key. This method is based on the *Wired Equivalent Privacy (WEP)* protocol, which also enables data transfers to be encrypted.

WEP is usually disabled by default on the commonly purchased wireless AP devices. If a nonsecurity-educated individual or employee purchases one of these devices on his own, he may not be familiar with setting up the interoperating devices in a secure fashion. With WEP disabled, there is no privacy, and the AP is broadcasting its location and identity.

A long list of deficiencies in this protocol has been uncovered. The new solutions being developed to remedy these deficiencies are explained in the upcoming "802.11i" section.

Wireless Standards

We don't need no stinking standards!
Response: Uh, yeah we do.

Standards are developed so that many different vendors can create various products that will work together seamlessly. Standards are usually developed on a consensus basis among the different vendors in a specific industry. The Institute of Electrical and Electronics Engineers (IEEE) develops standards for a wide range of technologies— wireless being one of them.

The first WLAN standard, 802.11, was developed in 1997 and provided a 1- to 2-Mbps transfer rate. It worked in the 2.4GHz frequency range. This fell into the available range unlicensed by the FCC, which means that companies and users do not need to pay to use this range.

The 802.11 standard outlines how wireless clients and APs communicate, lays out the specifications of their interfaces, dictates how signal transmission should take place, and describes how authentication, association, and security should be implemented.

Now just because life is unfair, a long list of standards actually fall under the 802.11 main standard. You may have seen this alphabet soup (802.11a, 802.11b, 802.11i, 802.11g, 802.11h, and so on) and not clearly understood the differences among them. IEEE created several task groups to work on specific areas within wireless communications. Each group had its own focus and was required to investigate and develop standards for its specific section. The letter suffixes indicate the order in which they were proposed and accepted.

802.11b

This standard was the first extension to the 802.11 WLAN standard and is the most common standard used today. (Although 802.11a was conceived and approved first, it was not released first because of the technical complexity involved with this proposal.) 802.11b provides a transfer rate of up to 11 Mbps and works in the 2.4GHz frequency range. It uses DSSS and is backward-compatible with 802.11 implementations.

802.11a

This standard uses a different method of modulating data onto the necessary radio carrier signals. Whereas 802.11b uses DSSS, 802.11a uses OFDM and works in the 5GHz frequency band. Because of these differences, 802.11a is not backward-compatible with 802.11b or 802.11. Several vendors have developed products that can work with both 802.11a and 802.11b implementations; the devices must be properly configured or may be able to sense the technology already being used and configure themselves appropriately.

OFDM is a modulation scheme (FHSS and DSSS are two other examples of modulation schemes) that splits a signal over several narrowband channels. The channels are then modulated and sent over specific frequencies. Because the data is divided across these different channels (spectrum), any interference from the environment will degrade only a small portion of the signal. This allows for greater throughput. Like FHSS and DSSS, OFDM is a physical layer specification. It can be used to transmit high-definition digital audio and video broadcasting as well as WLAN traffic.

This technology offers advantages in two areas: speed and frequency. 802.11a provides up to 54 Mbps, and it does not work in the already very crowded 2.4GHz spectrum. The 2.4GHz frequency band is referred to as a "dirty" frequency because several devices already work there—microwaves, cordless phones, baby monitors, and so on. In many situations, this means that contention for access and use of this frequency can cause loss of data or inadequate service. But because 802.11a works at a higher frequency, it does not provide the same range as the 802.11b and 802.11g standards. The maximum speed for 802.11a is attained at short distances from the AP, up to 25 feet.

One downfall of using the 5GHz frequency range is that other countries have not necessarily allocated this band for use of WLAN transmissions. So 802.11a products may work in the United States, but they may not necessarily work in other countries around the world.

802.11e

This working group has provided QoS and proper support of multimedia traffic. Multimedia and other types of time-sensitive applications have a lower tolerance for delays in data transmission. QoS provides the capability to prioritize traffic, and affords guaranteed delivery. This specification and its capabilities may open the door to allow many different types of data to be transmitted over wireless connections.

802.11f

When a user moves around in a WLAN, her wireless device often needs to communicate with different APs. An AP can cover only a certain distance, and as the user moves out of the range of the first AP, another AP needs to pick up and maintain her signal to ensure she does not lose network connectivity. This is referred to as *roaming*, and for this to happen seamlessly, the APs need to communicate with each other. If the second AP must take over this user's communication, it will need to be assured that this user has been properly authenticated and must know the necessary settings for this user's connection. This means the first AP would need to be able to convey this information to the second AP. The conveying of this information between the different APs during roaming is what 802.11f deals with. It outlines how these data can be properly shared.

802.11g

We are never happy with what we have; we always need more functions, more room, and more speed. The 802.11g standard provides for higher data transfer rates—up to 54 Mbps. This is basically a speed extension for current 802.11b products. If a product meets the specifications of 802.11b, its data transfer rates are up to 11 Mbps, and if a product is based on 802.11g, that new product can be backward-compatible with older equipment but work at a much higher transfer rate.

So do we go with 802.11g or with 802.11a? They both provide higher bandwidth. 802.11g is backward-compatible with 802.11b, so that is a good thing if you already have a current infrastructure. But 802.11g still works in the 2.4GHz range, which is continually getting more crowded. 802.11a works in the 5GHz band and may be a better bet if you use other devices in the other, more crowded frequency range. But working at higher frequency means a device's signal cannot cover as wide a range. Your decision will also come down to what standard wins out in the standards war. Most likely, one or the other standard will eventually be ignored by the market, so you will not have to worry about making this decision. Only time will tell which one will be the keeper.

802.11h

As stated earlier, 802.11a works in the 5GHz range, which is not necessarily available in countries other than the United States for this type of data transmission. The 802.11h standard builds upon the 802.11a specification to meet the requirements of European wireless rules so products working in this range can be properly implemented in European countries.

802.11i

A wide range of security flaws have been documented in 802.11, which has reduced the possible implementations of WLANs and has caused serious security breaches for those who chose to implement them anyway. Each of the mentioned WLAN standards is based on the same security model, so they have all inherited the same deficiencies.

Security Wireless Standard

The first WLAN standard, IEEE 802.11, has a tremendous number of security flaws. These are found within the core standard itself, as well as in different implementations of this technology. To address these issues, a new IEEE Task Group has been developed to improve upon the standard and close the holes that the current wireless implementations are faced with. The deficiencies within the original 802.11 standard include no user authentication, no mutual authentication between the wireless device and AP, and a flawed encryption protocol. The encryption protocol allows for specific bits to be modified without the receiver recognizing it, and the different encryption components (key and initialization vectors) do not provide enough randomness to the encryption process. This lack of randomness allows for encrypted wireless traffic to be easily broken with free downloadable tools available on different web sites.

 NOTE Many of the cryptography topics in this section are clearly defined in Chapter 8. It may be beneficial to re-read this section after completing Chapter 8 if you are new to cryptography.

The use of Extensible Authentication Protocol (EAP) and 802.1X (introduced later in this section) to enforce user authentication and mutual authentication has been integrated into the new WLAN standard, 802.11i. To detect modifications of bits during transmission, Message Integrity Code (MIC) was also integrated. And the *Temporal Key Integrity Protocol (TKIP)* generates random values used in the encryption process, which makes it much harder for an attacker to break. To allow for an even higher level of encryption protection, the standard also includes the new Advanced Encryption Standard (AES) algorithm to be used in new WLAN implementations.

This section looks at these different components and their relationships to one another.

What Is Wrong with WEP Implementations?

The types of attacks that can be carried out on devices and networks that just depend upon WEP are numerous and unnerving. Current implementations are vulnerable to this long laundry list of attacks if they use products that are based purely on the original 802.11 standard. Wireless traffic can be easily sniffed, data can be modified during transmission without the receiver being notified, rogue APs can be erected (that users can authenticate to and communicate with, not knowing it is a malicious entity), and encrypted wireless traffic can be decrypted quickly and easily. Unfortunately, these vulnerabilities usually provide doorways to the actual wired network where the more destructive attacks can begin.

Many vendors who produce WLAN products have developed their own security techniques and technologies to overcome the 802.11 security flaws and issues, but this usually amounts to just wrapping Band-Aids around the crux of the problem, which is a poorly constructed and implemented standard and technology. When vendors are forced to develop their own solutions, there are always many interoperability issues customers have to deal with.

The 802.11i standard employs two different approaches that provide much more security and protection than the protocol used in the original 802.11 standard, WEP. This enhancement of security and protection is accomplished through specific protocols, technologies, and algorithms. The first protocol is TKIP, and it is backward-compatible for the many WLAN products and networks currently implemented in networks everywhere. TKIP actually works with WEP by feeding it keying material, which is data to be used for generating new dynamic keys. WEP uses the RC4 encryption algorithm, and the current implementation of the algorithm provides very little protection. More complexity is added to the key generation process with the use of TKIP, which makes it much more difficult for attackers to uncover the encryption keys. The IEEE working group provided TKIP so customers would only need to obtain firmware or software updates instead of purchasing new equipment for this type of protection.

802.11i has another capability of providing encryption protection with the use of the AES algorithm in counter mode with CBC-MAC (CCM), which is referred to as the *CCM Protocol (CCMP)*. AES is a more appropriate algorithm for wireless than RC4 but requires more processing power. AES is not backward-compatible with current WLAN products, so customers should implement this configuration only if they have not yet deployed a WLAN in their network.

NOTE   Cipher Block Chaining (CBC) mode is explained in Chapter 8.

The algorithms, technologies, and protocols that make up the new wireless standard are complex. It is important to understand each component and how they all work together to provide a higher degree of confidence and protection for our future WLAN environments.

In the next section, we will look at the different encryption processes in the 802.11i standard (CCMP and TKIP), and the following sections will cover the other components that make up this standard that are not included in the original 802.11 standard.

802.1X

The 802.11i standard can be understood as three main components in two specific layers. The lower layer contains the improved encryption algorithms (TKIP and CCMP), while the layer that resides on top of it contains 802.1X. They work together to provide more layers of protection than the current 802.11 standard provides.

So what is 802.1X anyway? The *802.1X* standard is a port-based network access control that ensures a user cannot make a full network connection until he is properly authenticated. This means a user cannot access network resources and no traffic is allowed to pass, other than authentication traffic, from the wireless device to the network until the user is properly authenticated. An analogy is having a chain on your front door that enables you to open the door slightly to identify a person who knocks before you allow him to enter your house.

By incorporating 802.1X, the new standard allows for the *user* to be authenticated, whereas using only WEP provides *system* authentication. User authentication provides a higher degree of confidence and protection than system authentication.

The 802.1X technology actually provides an authentication framework and a method of dynamically distributing encryption keys. The three main entities in this framework are the supplicant (wireless device), the authenticator (AP), and the authentication server (usually a RADIUS server). If the environment does not have an authentication server, the AP can fulfill the roles of authenticator and authentication server.

The AP usually does not have much intelligence and acts like a middleman by passing frames between the wireless device and the authentication server. This is usually a good approach, since this does not require a lot of processing overhead for the AP, and the AP can deal with controlling several connections at once instead of having to authenticate each and every user.

The AP controls all communication and allows the wireless device to communicate with the authentication server and wired network only when all authentication steps are completed successfully. This means the wireless device cannot send or receive HTTP, DHCP, SMTP, or any other type of traffic until the user is properly authorized. WEP does not provide this type of strict access control. This is just one example of more security being provided by 802.11i.

Another disadvantage of the original 802.11 standard is that mutual authentication is not possible. When using WEP alone, the wireless device can authenticate to the AP, but the authentication server is not required to authenticate to the wireless device. This means a rogue AP can be set up to capture users' credentials and traffic without the users being aware of this type of attack. 802.11i deals with this issue by using EAP. EAP allows for mutual authentication to take place between the authentication server and wireless device, and provides flexibility in that users can be authenticated by using passwords, tokens, one-time passwords, certificates, smart cards, or Kerberos. This allows wireless users to be authenticated using the current infrastructure's existing authentication technology. The wireless device and authentication server that are 802.11i-compliant have different authentication modules that plug into 802.1X to allow for these different options. So, 802.1X provides the framework that allows for the different EAP modules to be added by a network administrator. The two entities (supplicant and authenticator) agree upon one of these authentication methods (EAP modules) during their initial handshaking process.

The 802.11i standard does not deal with the full protocol stack but addresses only what is taking place at the data link layer of the OSI model. Authentication protocols reside at a higher layer than this, so 802.11i does not specify particular authentication protocols. The use of EAP, however, allows different protocols to be used by different vendors. For example, Cisco uses a purely password-based authentication framework called Lightweight Extensible Authentication Protocol (LEAP). Other vendors, including Microsoft, use EAP and Transport Layer Security (EAP-TLS), which carries out authentication through digital certificates. And yet another choice is Protective EAP (PEAP), where only the server uses a digital certificate.

If EAP-TLS is being used, the authentication server and wireless device exchange digital certificates for authentication purposes. If PEAP is being used instead, the user of the wireless device sends the server a password and the server authenticates to the wireless device with its digital certificate. In both cases, some type of public key infrastructure (PKI) needs to be in place. If a company does not have a PKI currently implemented, it can be an overwhelming and costly task to deploy a PKI just to secure wireless transmissions.

When EAP-TLS is being used, the steps the server takes to authenticate to the wireless device are basically the same as when an SSL connection is being set up between a web server and web browser. Once the wireless device receives and validates the server's digital certificate, it creates a master key, encrypts it with the server's public key, and sends it over to the authentication server. Now the wireless device and authentication server have a master key, which they use to generate individual symmetric session keys. Both entities use these session keys for encryption and decryption purposes, and it is the use of these keys that sets up a secure channel between the two devices.

Companies may choose to use PEAP instead of EAP-TLS because they don't want the hassle of installing and maintaining digital certificates on every wireless device. Before you purchase a WLAN product, you should understand the requirements and complications of each method to ensure you know what you are getting yourself into and if it is the right fit for your environment.

As stated earlier, Cisco took a different approach to this authentication game. It implemented LEAP, which is based purely on passwords. This means no PKI is required and the wireless device and server authenticate to each other by exchanging predetermined passwords.

A large concern with current WLANs using just WEP is that if individual wireless devices are stolen, they can easily be authenticated to the wired network. 802.11i has added steps to require the user to authenticate to the network instead of just requiring the wireless device to authenticate. By using EAP, the user must send some type of credential set that is tied to his identity. When using only WEP, the wireless device authenticates itself by proving it has a symmetric key that was manually programmed into it. Since the user does not need to authenticate using WEP, a stolen wireless device can allow an attacker easy access to your precious network resources.

Dynamic Keys and the Use of Initialization Vectors

The three core deficiencies with WEP are the use of static encryption keys, the ineffective use of initialization vectors, and the lack of packet integrity assurance. The WEP protocol uses the RC4 algorithm, which is a stream symmetric cipher. *Symmetric* means the sender and receiver must use the exact same key for encryption and decryption purposes. The 802.11 standard does not stipulate how to update these keys through an automated process, so in most environments, the RC4 symmetric keys are never changed out. And usually all of the wireless devices and the AP share the exact same key. This is like having everyone in your company use the exact same password. Not a good idea. So that is the first issue—static WEP encryption keys on all devices.

The next flaw is how initialization vectors (IVs) are used. An IV is a numeric seeding value that is used with the symmetric key and RC4 algorithm to provide more randomness to the encryption process. Randomness is extremely important in encryption because any patterns can give the bad guys insight into how the process works, which may allow them to uncover the encryption key that was used. The key and IV value are inserted into the RC4 algorithm to generate a key stream. The values (1's and 0's) of the key stream are XORed with the binary values of the individual packets. The result is ciphertext, or encrypted packets.

In most WEP implementations, the same IV values are used over and over again in this process, and since the same symmetric key (or shared secret) is generally used, there is no way to provide effective randomness in the key stream that is generated by the algorithm. The appearance of patterns allows attackers to reverse-engineer the process to uncover the original encryption key, which can then be used to decrypt future encrypted traffic.

So now we are onto the third mentioned weakness, which is the integrity assurance issue. WLAN products that use only the 802.11 standard introduce a vulnerability that is not always clearly understood. An attacker can actually change data within the wireless packets by flipping specific bits and altering the Integrity Check Value (ICV) so the receiving end is oblivious to these changes. The ICV works like a CRC function; the sender calculates an ICV and inserts it into a frame's header. The receiver calculates his own ICV and compares it with the ICV sent with the frame. If the ICVs are the same, the receiver can be assured that the frame was not modified during transmission. If the ICVs are different, it indicates a modification did indeed take place and thus the receiver discards the frame. In WEP, there are certain circumstances in which the receiver cannot detect whether an alteration to the frame has taken place; thus, there is no true integrity assurance.

So the problems identified with the 802.11 standard include poor authentication, static WEP keys that can be easily obtained by attackers, IV values that are repetitive and do not provide the necessary degree of randomness, and a lack of data integrity. The use of the 802.1X technology in the new 802.11i standard provides access control by restricting network access until full authentication and authorization have been completed, and provides a robust authentication framework that allows for different EAP modules to be plugged in. These two technologies (802.1X and EAP) work together to enforce mutual authentication between the wireless device and authentication server. So what about the static keys, IV value, and integrity issues?

TKIP addresses the deficiencies of WEP pertaining to static WEP keys and inadequate use of IV values. Two very useful and powerful programs, AirSnort and WEP-Crack, can be used to easily crack WEP's encryption by taking advantage of these weaknesses and the ineffective use of the key scheduling algorithm within the WEP protocol. If a company is using products that implement only WEP encryption and is not using a third-party encryption solution (such as a VPN), these programs can break its encrypted traffic within minutes to hours. There is no "maybe" pertaining to breaking WEP's encryption. Using these tools means it will be broken no matter whether a 40-bit or 128-bit key is being used. This is one of the most serious and dangerous vulnerabilities pertaining to the original 802.11 standard.

The use of TKIP provides the ability to rotate encryption keys to help fight against these types of attacks. The protocol increases the length of the IV value and ensures each and every frame has a different IV value. This IV value is combined with the transmitter's MAC address and the original WEP key, so even if the WEP key is static, the resulting encryption key will be different for each and every frame. (WEP key + IV value + MAC address = new encryption key.) So what does that do for us? This brings more randomness to the encryption process, and it is randomness that is necessary to properly thwart cryptanalysis and attacks on cryptosystems. The changing IV values and resulting keys make the resulting key stream less predictable, which makes it much harder for the attacker to reverse-engineer the process and uncover the original key.

TKIP also deals with the integrity issues by using a MIC instead of an ICV function. If you are familiar with a message authentication code (MAC) function, this is the same thing. A symmetric key is used with a hashing function, which is similar to a CRC function but stronger. The use of MIC instead of ICV ensures the receiver will be properly alerted if changes to the frame take place during transmission. The sender and receiver calculate their own separate MIC values. If the receiver generates a MIC value different than the one sent with the frame, the frame is seen as compromised and it is discarded.

 NOTE These cryptography concepts and technologies are covered in Chapter 8.

The Answer to All Our Prayers?

Up to now, if a company required more protection than what was provided in the original 802.11 standard, it had to place a firewall between the AP and the wired network. Also, the wireless devices could have VPN software installed to provide another, stronger layer of encryption. And as stated earlier, different vendors have come up with their own proprietary security solutions. But hopefully with 802.11i, continual Band-Aids won't need to be applied on top of this wireless technology. Instead, the security will be provided from the core of the technology itself.

So does the use of EAP, 802.1X, AES, and TKIP result in secure and highly trusted WLAN implementations? Maybe, but we need to understand what we are dealing with here. TKIP was created as a quick fix to WEP's overwhelming problems. It does not provide an overhaul for the wireless standard itself because WEP and TKIP are still based on the RC4 algorithm, which is not the best fit for this type of technology. The use of AES is closer to an actual overhaul, but it is not backward-compatible with current 802.11 implementations. In addition, we should understand that using all of these new components and mixing them with the current 802.11 components will add more complexity and steps to the process. Security and complexity do not usually get along. The highest security is usually accomplished with simplistic and elegant solutions to ensure all of the entry points are clearly understood and protected. These new technologies add more flexibility to how vendors can choose to authenticate users and authentication servers, but can also bring us interoperability issues because the vendors will not all choose the same methods. This means that if a company buys an AP from company A, then the wireless cards it buys from companies B and C may not work seamlessly.

So does that mean all of this work has been done for naught? No. 802.11i provides much more protection and security than WEP ever did. The working group has had very knowledgeable people involved and some very large and powerful companies aiding in the development of these new solutions. But the customers who purchase these new products need to understand what will be required of them *after* the purchase order is made out. For example, with the use of EAP-TLS, each wireless device needs its own digital certificate. Are your current wireless devices programmed to handle certificates? How will the certificates be properly deployed to all the wireless devices? How will the certificates be maintained? Will the devices and authentication server verify that certificates have not been revoked by periodically checking a certificate revocation list (CRL)? What if a rogue authentication server or AP was erected with a valid digital certificate? The wireless device would just verify this certificate and trust that this server is the entity it is supposed to be communicating with. And if the certificate authority is ever compromised, the whole EAP-TLS infrastructure is compromised, as with any PKI environment.

The original 802.11 standard has received so much bad press and attention that it is very likely the new working group put extra effort into ensuring all of the *i*'s were dotted and all of the *t*'s were crossed pertaining to this new release. But time will tell through rounds of testing and real-life implementations. This new and improved standard will get us much further down the security road than we are now, but there are two other things to keep in mind concerning new products being developed and released. First, the vendors need to properly interpret and adhere to the standards to provide the level of assurance and security promised by the standard itself. Second, customers need to have awareness and intelligence about what they are purchasing and implementing into their environments. Many times products and technologies are installed without the company knowing exactly what this newcomer does and how to properly test and secure it. True security is based on education, knowledge, and experience. So the ultimate goals are to have a solid standard that is used to develop a secure product and to ensure that the customer is knowledgeable about this new product so the overall level of protection is actually achieved. If one of these components does not meet its own individual goal, it can bring havoc to the overall efforts.

New Products

Today, new WLAN products are already being developed following the stipulations of this new wireless standard. Many products will straddle the fence by providing TKIP for backward-compatibility with current WLAN implementations and AES for companies that are just now thinking about extending their current wired environments with a wireless component. Customers should review the Wi-Fi Alliance's certification findings before buying wireless products since it has already started assessing systems against the 802.11i proposed standard. Table 7-11 breaks down the characteristics of the different wireless security structures currently used.

802.11j

Many countries have been developing their own wireless standards, which inevitably causes massive interoperability issues. This can be frustrating for the customer because he cannot use certain products, and it can be frustrating and expensive for vendors because they have a laundry list of specifications to meet if they want to sell their products in various countries. If vendors are unable to meet these specifications, whole customer bases are unavailable to them. The 802.11j task group has been working on bringing together many of the different standards and streamlining their development to allow for better interoperability across borders.

802.11n

The proposal for 802.11n by the World Wide Spectrum Efficiency (WWiSE) is an attempt to replace the current mix of various Wi-Fi technologies. 802.11n is designed to be much faster, with throughput at 100 Mbps, and it works at the same frequency range of 802.11a (5GHz). The intent is to maintain some backward-compatibility with current Wi-Fi standards, while combining a mix of the current technologies. The proposals for this standard use a concept called *multiple input, multiple output (MIMO)* to increase the throughput. This will necessitate the use of two receive and two transmit antennas to broadcast in parallel using a 20MHz channel.

Not enough different wireless standards for you? You say you want more? Okay, here you go!

	802.1x Dynamic WEP	Wi-Fi Protected Access (WPA)	Wi-Fi Protected Access 2 (WPA2)
Access Control	802.1x	802.1x or pre-shared key	802.1x or pre-shared key
Authentication	EAP methods	EAP methods or pre-shared key	EAP methods or pre-shared key
Encryption	WEP	TKIP (RC4)	CCMP (AES Counter Mode)
Integrity	None	Michael MIC	CCMP (AES CBC-MAC)

Table 7-11   Characteristics of Wireless Security Structures Currently in Use

802.16

All the wireless standards covered so far are WLAN-oriented standards. 802.16 is a metropolitan area network (MAN) wireless standard, which allows for wireless traffic to cover a much wider geographical area. This technology is also referred to as *broadband wireless access*.

802.15

This standard deals with a much smaller geographical network, which is referred to as a *wireless personal area network (WPAN)*. This technology allows for connectivity to take place among local devices, such as a computer communicating with a PDA, a cellular phone communicating with a computer, or a headset communicating with another device. The goal here—as with all wireless technologies—is to allow for data transfer without all of those pesky cables.

Bluetooth Wireless

The *Bluetooth wireless* technology is actually a portion of the 802.15 standard. It has a 1- to 3-Mbps transfer rate and works in a range of approximately ten meters. If you have a cell phone and a PDA that are both Bluetooth-enabled, and both have calendar functionality, you could have them update each other without any need to connect them physically. If you added some information to your cell phone contacts list and task list, for example, you could just place the phone close to your PDA. The PDA would sense that the other device was nearby, and it would then attempt to set up a network connection with it. Once the connection is made, synchronization between the two devices would take place and the PDA would add the new contacts list and task list data. This sounds very much like a *Jetsons* scenario, but several types of devices already work this way. Bluetooth works in the frequency range of other 802.11 devices (2.4GHz).

Real security risks exist when transferring unprotected data via Bluetooth in a public area, because any device within a certain range can capture this type of data transfer.

Another attack that Bluetooth is vulnerable to is referred to as *Bluejacking*. In this attack, someone sends an unsolicited message to a device that is Bluetooth-enabled. Bluejackers look for a receiving device (phone, PDA, laptop) and then send a message to it. Often, the Bluejacker is trying to send someone else their business card, which will be added to the victim's contact list in their address book. The countermeasure is to put the Bluetooth-enabled device into nondiscoverable mode so others cannot identify this device in the first place. If you receive some type of message this way, just look around you. Bluetooth only works within a ten-meter distance, so it is coming from someone close by.

 NOTE Some of these standards are still being developed, and not all of these standards and technologies will survive. It will take time to see which catch on and are accepted by vendors and customers alike. Wireless is still an immature technology that is currently undergoing painful growth spurts, and it is difficult to determine at this stage of the game the true future of each standard. But wireless has caught on like wildfire, and it will be interesting to watch it grow and consume the market.

WAP

There is a hole in this security.
Response: Yep, we call it the gap in the WAP.

Wireless Application Protocol (WAP) is not a standard per se. Instead, WAP is a de facto market and industry-driven protocol stack. What's the difference? When a governing body, such as IEEE, determines there's a need for a new technology, it creates a working group to develop the corresponding standard. This standard works as a blueprint for all of the vendors that want to develop this type of technology. If no recognized standard is in place, organizations can come together and outline specifications for the new technology for all to follow.

WAP provides a common architecture for wireless devices to be able to communicate over the Internet. It enables wireless devices to send and receive data (in addition to voice data), meaning cell phones and PDAs can connect to content providers on the Internet and find out stock quotes, get weather updates, access e-mail, and more. It also opened the door for new types of wireless devices to be created and sold.

Some of these wireless devices do not have the full resources PCs and laptops have—they do not have the same amount of processing power, memory, storage space, and supporting circuitry. This means these devices cannot use the same protocol stack (as in TCP/IP) used by these more powerful systems, and they cannot run the same type of applications. The WAP protocol stack was developed to be used with the limited resources and applications that have been created to work in this new environment.

WAP is a set of communications protocols used to standardize the way wireless devices interface with each other and the Internet. The WAP model contains protocols that perform similar functionalities to those performed by protocols in the TCP/IP stack. Because wireless can be a web-based technology, WAP provides a way to present web pages. Personal computers and servers use HTML or XML to present web-based material and JavaScript to perform the processing in the background. WAP uses an XML-compliant Wireless Markup Language (WML) and WMLScript to perform these similar tasks. WAP has its own session and transport protocols and a transport layer security protocol called *Wireless Transport Layer Security (WTLS)*, which is similar to TLS and SSL. The wireless device has a WAP microbrowser that displays the web pages to the user.

The vision for developing this type of technology and these devices is to provide users with the functionality to check e-mail, voice messages, a calendar, and more from anywhere without needing physically to plug into any network. A user can watch the stock market on her PDA while riding a bus and hit a few buttons when she wants to sell her stocks because of a dip in the market. Users can also transfer funds from one bank account to another on their mobile phones, receive the daily news, and much more. The devices could be used to communicate with financial institutions or other organizations that provide information and wireless capabilities through the Internet.

Because these devices use a different set of protocols, a gateway is required to translate between WAP and the Internet's protocols and application types, as shown in Figure 7-59. Service providers can provide this gateway much as they can provide the service for users and companies to access the Internet today.

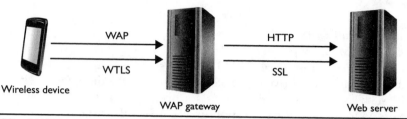

Figure 7-59 A WAP gateway is required to translate WAP protocols to Internet protocols.

When data comes from the wireless mobile device, it can be encrypted with WTLS, which must be translated into TLS or SSL by the gateway. Because the wireless devices use the Internet for transmission, and the Internet does not understand WTLS, WTLS must be translated into a protocol the Internet does understand. This translation takes place at the service provider's gateway.

A security concern is that these data will be decrypted at the service provider's site and then encrypted with SSL or TLS. That means for a second or two, the data are not protected. This is referred to as the *gap in the WAP*, and it has caused a lot of concern for businesses and security professionals and is still one of the issues that needs to be dealt with.

WTLS works similarly to SSL/TLS, by encrypting data and allowing for authentication to take place between the communicating devices. WTLS has three classes that define how authentication takes place between a wireless device and a gateway server:

Class 1	Anonymous authentication	The wireless device and server do not authenticate to each other.
Class 2	Server authentication	The server authenticates to the wireless device.
Class 3	Two-way client and server authentication	The server and the wireless device authenticate to each other.

In most cases, the gateway server dictates which type of authentication will be used, but the wireless device must be properly configured so it can actually work in this type of implementation.

i-Mode

WAP and *i-Mode* are the two main protocols used for wireless Internet transmissions by cell phones and other PDA-like devices. WAP was developed by a consortium of companies with the goal of allowing people to carry out business-oriented activities. i-Mode was developed by a company in Japan (NTT DoCoMo) and is geared more toward providing an entertainment platform than toward providing functionality for business-oriented individuals.

i-Mode works with a slimmed-down version of HTML, called Compact HTML (cHTML), while WAP uses Wireless Markup Language (WML), a markup language based on XML. Both i-Mode and WAP employ an architecture consisting of a content server, gateway, and user terminal. The server can be a WAP or HTTP server, and the gateway translates the protocols so they can be understood and work over the Internet. The user terminal is a cell phone or mobile device that has a microbrowser, which interprets and presents the web content to the user.

i-Mode has exploded in popularity in Japan and is currently spreading throughout Asia and parts of Europe. WAP is currently in its second version and is used mainly in North America. They are both relatively new technologies that will continue to advance because we just love to be on the Internet anywhere we go!

Mobile Phone Security

No matter what technology is being used on mobile phones and PDAs, the same types of security breaches seem to take place. Most corporations do not incorporate the use of these types of technologies into their security policies. This was all right when phones were just phones, but today they are small computers that can connect to computers and networks, and thus are new entry points for malicious activities. Since they are computers with operating systems, many employees save sensitive data on them, such as credentials, contacts, company files, and more, none of which is usually encrypted. And since many cell phones also have a camera functionality, organizations should be aware that this is a new way that sensitive data and activities can be captured and released to the world. Every organization should include this new technology and source of security breaches into their policies and security program.

Another common security issue with cell phones is that the cell phone must authenticate to a base station before it is allowed to make a call, but the base station is not required to authenticate to the cell phone. This has opened the door for attackers to set up rogue base stations. When a cell phone sends authentication data to this rogue base station, the attacker captures it and can now use it to authenticate and gain unauthorized access to the cellular network.

Cell phone cloning has been around for many years, and this activity won't stop any time soon. A regular cell phone can be stolen and then reprogrammed with someone else's access credentials. This is a common activity used by organized crime rings and drug dealers who do not want their information readily available to law enforcement. Global System Mobile (GSM) phones use a Subscriber Identity Module (SIM) chip, which contains authentication data, phone numbers, saved messages, and more. Before a GSM phone can gain access to the cellular network, the SIM must be present in the phone. Attackers are cloning these SIM chips so they can make fraudulent calls on the cell phone owner's account.

It is important to be aware that cell phones move their data over the airwaves and then the data are put on a wired network by the telephone company or service provider. So, a portion of the distance that the traffic must travel over is wireless, but then the remaining distance may take place over a wired environment. Thus, if someone encrypts their data and sends it on their cell phone, typically it is encrypted only while it is traveling over the wireless portion of the network. Once it hits the wired portion of the network, it may no longer be encrypted. So encrypting data for transmission on a cell phone or PDA does not necessarily promise end-to-end encryption.

Unfortunately, these types of attacks on cell phones will never really stop. We will come up with more countermeasures and the bad guys will come up with new ways to exploit vulnerabilities that we did not think of. It is the same cat and mouse game that is carried out in the traditional network world. But the main issue pertaining to cell phone attacks is that they are not usually included in a corporation's security program or even recognized as a threat. This will change as more attacks take place through this new entry point and more viruses are written and spread through the interactions of cell phones and PDAs and the corporate network. The following are some of the issues with using mobile devices in an enterprise:

- False base stations can be created.
- Confidential data can be stolen.
- Use of camera functionality.
- Access to the Internet and bypassing company firewalls.
- Short message spamming.
- Malicious code can be downloaded.
- Encryption can be weak and not end-to-end.

 NOTE Universal Mobile Telecommunications System is a proposed new standard for third-generation mobile communications. The Internet Engineering Consortium provides a good introduction to *Universal Mobile Telecommunications System (UMTS) Protocols and Protocol Testing* at www.iec.org/ online/tutorials/umts/.

Cell phone firewall products are available that can be implemented to protect against the following types of security issues:

- VoIP signaling and DoS attacks
- Toll fraud
- VoIP bandwidth abuses
- Virus infections
- Restricting file transfer
- Voice mail and PBX attacks
- Unauthorized employee connections
- Wardialing

Implementation of these types of firewalls is rare today, but will probably be more common as additional companies experience these types of threats.

War Driving for WLANs

A common attack on wireless networks is *war driving,* which is when one or more people either walk or drive around with a wireless device equipped with the necessary equipment and software with the intent of identifying APs and breaking into them.

Traditionally, this activity has taken place by using a laptop and driving in the proximity of buildings that have WLANs implemented, but today even PDAs can be used for this type of attack.

Kismet and NetStumbler are programs that sniff (monitor) for APs. When one of these programs identifies an AP's signal, it logs the network name, the SSID, the MAC address of the AP, the manufacturer of the AP, the channel it was heard on, the signal strength, the signal-to-noise ratio, and whether WEP is enabled. Attackers drive around in their cars with a laptop running NetStumbler, actively looking for APs. They can usually find APs within a range of up to 350 feet, but with a more powerful antenna, the attacker can locate APs much farther away. NetStumbler broadcasts probes once each second, waiting for APs to respond. Airsnarf, AirSnort, and WEP-Crack are utilities that can be used to break and capture the WEP encryption keys, if WEP is enabled.

NOTE Inventive individuals have used Pringles cans and beverage cans as inexpensive antennas for war-driving endeavors. These antennas can focus on an AP from well over a mile away.

Some of the best practices pertaining to WLAN implementations are listed next:

- *Enable an 802.11i implementation technology as in WPA.*

- *Change default SSID.* Each AP comes with a preconfigured default SSID value.

- *Disable "broadcast SSID" on the AP.* Most APs allow for this to be turned off.

- *Implement another layer of authentication (RADIUS, Kerberos).* Before the user can access the network, require him to authenticate.

- *Physically put the AP at the center of the building.* The AP has a specific zone of coverage it can provide.

- *Logically put the AP in a DMZ with a firewall between the DMZ and internal network.* Allow the firewall to investigate the traffic before it gets to the wired network.

- *Implement VPN for wireless devices to use.* This adds another layer of protection for data being transmitted.

- *Configure the AP to allow only known MAC addresses into the network.* Allow only known devices to authenticate. But remember that these MAC addresses are sent in cleartext, so an attacker could capture them and masquerade himself as an authenticated device.

- *Assign static IP addresses to wireless devices and disable DHCP.* If an attacker gains access and DHCP is enabled, you have just given the attacker a valid working IP address to use.

- *Carry out penetration tests on the WLAN.* Use the tools described in this section to identify APs and attempt to break the current encryption scheme being used.

- *Move to a product that follows the 802.11i standard.*

Satellites

Today, satellites are used to provide wireless connectivity between different locations. For two different locations to communicate via satellite links, they must be within the satellite's line of sight and *footprint* (area covered by the satellite). The sender of information (ground station) modulates the data onto a radio signal that is transmitted to the satellite. A transponder on the satellite receives this signal, amplifies it, and relays it to the receiver. The receiver must have a type of antenna—one of those circular, dish-like things we see on top of buildings. The antenna contains one or more microwave receivers, depending upon how many satellites it is accepting data from.

Satellites provide broadband transmission that is commonly used for television channels and PC Internet access. If a user is receiving TV data, then the transmission is set up as a one-way network. If a user is using this connection for Internet connectivity, then the transmission is set up as a two-way network. The available bandwidth depends upon the antenna and terminal type and the service provided by the service provider. Time-sensitive applications can suffer from the delays experienced as the data go to and from the satellite. These types of satellites are placed into a low Earth orbit, which means there is not as much distance between the ground stations and the satellites as in other types of satellites. In turn, this means smaller receivers can be used, which makes low Earth orbit satellites ideal for two-way paging, international cellular communication, TV stations, and Internet use.

NOTE   As of this writing, there are around 12 million satellite subscribers in the United States and 30 million in Europe, mainly digital TV subscribers.

The size of the footprint depends upon the type of satellite being used. It can be as large as a country or only a few hundred feet in circumference. The footprint covers an area on the Earth for only a few hours or less, so the service provider usually has a large number of satellites dispatched to provide constant coverage at strategic areas.

In most cases, satellite broadband is a hybrid system that uses a regular phone line and modem for data and requests sent from the user's machine, but employs a satellite link to send data to the user, as shown in Figure 7-60.

3G Wireless Communication

The third generation in mobile telephony is a technology often referred to as *broadband wireless*. The first generation dealt with analog transmissions of voice-only data over circuit-switched networks. The second generation allows for digitally encoded voice

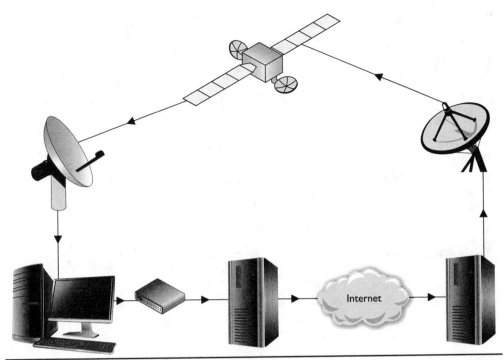

Figure 7-60 Satellite broadband

and data to be transmitted between wireless devices, such as cell phones, and content providers. This generation provides a throughput of around 19.2 Kbps. Time Division Multiple Access (TDMA), Code Division Multiple Access (CDMA), Global System for Mobile Communications (GSM), and Personal Communications Services (PCS) all fall under the umbrella of 2G mobile telephony. This technology can transmit data over circuit-switched networks and supports data encryption, fax transmissions, and short message services (SMSs).

Table 7-12 provides a breakdown of their different characteristics.

WARNING It is now critical that you understand more detailed information about broadband wireless communication for the CISSP exam. Please review the article "Broadband Wireless Communication" at http://www .logicalsecurity.com/resources/resources_articles.html.

	1G	2G	3G	4G
Spectrum	900MHz	1,800MHz	2GHz	40GHz and 60GHZ
Multiplexing Type	Analog FDMA	TDMA	CDMA	OFDM
Voice Support	Basic telephony	Caller ID and voice mail	Conference calls and low-quality video	Telepresence and high-definition video
Messaging Features	None	Text only	Graphics and formatted text	Full unified messaging
Data Support	None	Circuit switched (packet switched in 2.5G)	Packet switched	Native IPv6
Target Data Rate	N/A	14.4 Kbps (approx. 115 Kbps in 2.5G)	2 Mbps (10 Mbps in 3.5G) 14 Mbps with HSPA+	100 Mbps
Real Data Rate	2.4 Kbps	9.6 Kbps (approx. 40 Kbps in 2.5G)	64 Kbps	Unknown
Interface with Other Devices	Acoustic coupler	RS232 serial cable or IrDA	IEEE 802.11 or Bluetooth	Seamless connection via multiple methods
Timeline	1980–1994	1995–2001	2002–2005	2006–2010

Table 7-12 Telephony Generation Basic Characteristics

Mobile Technology Generations

Like many technologies, the mobile communication technology has gone through several different generations.

First generation (1G):

- Analog services.
- Voice service only.

Second generation (2G):

- Primarily voice, some low-speed data (circuit switched).
- Phones were smaller in size.
- Added functionality of e-mail, paging, and caller ID.

Generation 2½ (2.5G):

- Higher bandwidth than 2G.
- "Always on" technology for e-mail and pages.

Third generation (3G):

- Integration of voice and data.
- Packet-switched technology, instead of circuit-switched.

Rootkits

Just leave your tools here. So when you want to come back and attack me again, it will be much easier.

Many times, when a computer is successfully compromised, a hacker will attempt to elevate his privileges to obtain administrator- or root user–level access. Working in the security context of these types of privileged users allows the attacker to carry out more dangerous activities. Once the level of access is achieved, the attacker can upload a bundle of tools, collectively called a *rootkit*. The first thing that is usually installed is a backdoor program, which allows the attacker to enter the system at any time without having to go through any authentication steps. (A backdoor is just a service that listens on a specific port.) The other tools in the rootkit may vary, but they usually comprise utilities that are used to cover the attacker's tracks. For example, every operating system has basic utilities that a root or administrator user can use to detect the presence of the rootkit, an installed sniffer, and the backdoor. The hacker replaces these default utilities with new utilities, which share the same name. They are referred to as "Trojaned programs" because they carry out the intended functionality but do some devious activity in the background. For example, on a Unix system, the ps (process status) utility lists all the processes running on the system and their status. The top utility lists the processes, their status, and the amount of memory each process is using. Most rootkits have Trojaned programs that replace these utilities, because the root user could run ps or top and see there is a backdoor service running, and thus detect the presence of an attack. But when this user runs one of these Trojaned programs, the program lists all other services except the backdoor process. Most rootkits also contain sniffers, so the data can be captured and reviewed by the attacker. For a sniffer to work, the system's NIC must be put into promiscuous mode, which just means it can "hear" all the traffic on the network link. The default ipconfig utility allows the root user to employ a specific parameter to see whether or not the NIC is running in promiscuous mode. So, the rootkit also contains a Trojaned ipconfig program, which hides the fact that the NIC is in promiscuous mode.

NOTE ipconfig is a utility used in Windows environments to view network configurations. In Unix\Linux, this utility is called ifconfig.

Rootkits usually contain "log scrubbers" that remove traces of the attacker's activities from the system logs. They can also contain Trojaned programs that replace `find` and `ls` Unix utilities, so that when a user does a listing of what is in a specific directory, the rootkit will not be listed.

Some of the more powerful rootkits actually update the kernel of the system, instead of just replacing individual utilities. The kernel is the brain of the operating system, so modifying its code gives the attacker much more control over a system. It is also very difficult to detect kernel updates, compared to replaced utilities, because most host IDS products look at changes to file sizes and modification dates, which would apply to utilities and programs but not necessarily to the kernel of the operating system.

NOTE Ironically, sometimes when an attacker compromises a system and installs a rootkit, he fortifies the system against other attackers. This means that when the attacker gets onto the system, he does all the things the administrator should have done, such as disabling unnecessary services and user accounts, patching the system, and so on. The attacker does this so no other attacker can use this system or the installed rootkit.

The countermeasures to rootkits include properly hardening the system and running updated antivirus and antispyware software. Another protection mechanism is to use a host-based IDS (covered in Chapter 4), which looks for suspicious activities and keeps track of the integrity of the system. As stated earlier, however, the functionality of the HIDS usually cannot detect modifications to the kernel. Therefore, the best defense is to use a monolithic kernel rather than individual kernel modules. If you are familiar with working in Unix and Linux, you know you can install the operating system within individual kernel modules or use one big kernel. A kernel rootkit loads itself as a kernel module. It cannot (or it is more difficult to) modify or affect the kernel if it is one unit. Any system that is providing some type of protection (proxy server, firewall, IDS) that is running on a Linux or Unix system should be installed with a monolithic kernel.

Spyware and Adware

The terms "spyware" and "adware" vary in definition, depending upon whom you ask. In general terms, both are some type of software installed on a computer without the user knowing about it. The software usually collects some type of data that can be used by a vendor to better market its products to the user, or it may collect data for a hacker. *Adware* is usually the term used when companies want to track a user's buying and browsing habits through the use of cookies, so a merchant knows how to effectively market to this user. Some adware is software installed on your system that causes pop-up ads to appear continuously as you are surfing the Web. The software could be part of another software package you installed, or a stealth installation could have taken place.

Spyware is usually considered more dangerous than adware because it may be written to capture keystrokes, capture system information, or install a backdoor on a system. Through the use of keyloggers, spyware can capture passwords, credit card information, or other sensitive data. The use of spyware is increasing the frequency of identity fraud, because hackers are gathering account numbers, Social Security numbers, PIN numbers, and more. Unfortunately, not all antivirus software can detect adware and spyware. Antivirus software looks for specific virus signatures and reproduction activities, but adware and spyware do not currently attempt to reproduce and spread themselves as viruses, so they could be doing their devious work even after antivirus software has scanned your system and told you everything is happy and healthy.

NOTE Products have been developed to identify adware and spyware, and antivirus vendors are starting to incorporate this functionality into their products.

WARNING It is now critical that you understand more detailed information about e-mail threats for the CISSP exam. Please review the article "Email Threats" at http://www.logicalsecurity.com/resources/resources_articles.html.

Instant Messaging

Instant messaging (IM) allows people to communicate with one another through a type of real-time and personal chat room. It alerts individuals when someone who is on their "buddy list" has accessed the Internet so they can send text messages back and forth in real time. The technology also allows for files to be transferred from system to system. The technology is made up of clients and servers. The user installs an IM client (AOL, ICQ, Yahoo! Messenger, and so on) and is assigned a unique identifier. This user gives out this unique identifier to people whom she wants to communicate with via IM.

Because of the lack of strong authentication, accounts can be spoofed so the receiver accepts information from a malicious user instead of the legitimate sender. Also, numerous buffer overflow and malformed packet attacks have been successful with different IM clients. These attacks are usually carried out with the goal of obtaining unauthorized access to the victim's system.

Many firewalls do not have the capability to scan for this type of traffic to uncover suspicious activity. Blocking specific ports on the firewalls is not usually effective because the IM traffic may be using common ports that need to be open (HTTP port 80 and FTP port 21). Many of the IM clients autoconfigure themselves to work on another port if their default port is unavailable and blocked by the firewall.

Even with all of these issues and potential vulnerabilities, many companies allow their employees to use this technology because it allows quick and effective communication to take place. So, if you absolutely have to allow this technology in your environment, there are some things you should do to help reduce your threat level. The

Instant Messaging Spam

Instant messaging spam (SPIM) is a type of spamming that uses instant messengers for this malicious act. Although this kind of spamming isn't as common as e-mail spamming, it is certainly increasing over time. The fact that firewalls are unable to block SPIM has made it more attractive for spammers. One way to prevent SPIM is to enable the option of receiving instant messages only from a known list of users.

following are best practices for protecting an environment from these types of security breaches:

- Establish a security policy specifying IM usage restrictions.
- Implement an integrated antivirus/firewall product on all computers.
- Configure firewalls to block IM traffic.
- Upgrade IM software to more secure versions.
- Implement corporate IM servers so internal employees communicate within the organization's network only.
- Another alternative is to not allow employees to use this functionality and force them to communicate the old-fashioned way—through e-mail and by phone.

Summary

This chapter touched on many of the different technologies within different types of networks, including how they work together to provide an environment in which users can communicate, share resources, and be productive. Each piece of networking is important to security, because almost any piece can introduce unwanted vulnerabilities and weaknesses into the infrastructure. It is important you understand how the various devices, protocols, authentication mechanisms, and services work individually and how they interface and interact with other entities. This may appear to be an overwhelming task because of all the possible technologies involved. However, knowledge and hard work will keep you up to speed and, hopefully, one step ahead of the hackers and attackers.

Quick Tips

- Dual-homed firewalls can be compromised if the operating system does not have packet forwarding or routing disabled.
- A protocol is a set of rules that dictates how computers communicate over networks.
- The application layer, layer 7, has services and protocols required by the user's applications for networking functionality.
- The presentation layer, layer 6, formats data into a standardized format and deals with the syntax of the data, not the meaning.
- Routers work at the network layer, layer 3.
- The session layer, layer 5, sets up, maintains, and breaks down the dialog (session) between two applications. It controls the dialog organization and synchronization.
- The transport layer, layer 4, provides end-to-end transmissions.
- The network layer, layer 3, provides routing, addressing, and fragmentation of packets. This layer can determine alternative routes to avoid network congestion.

- The data link layer, layer 2, prepares data for the network medium by framing it. This is where the different LAN and WAN technologies live.

- The physical layer, layer 1, provides physical connections for transmission and performs the electrical encoding of data. This layer transforms bits to electrical signals.

- TCP/IP is a suite of protocols that is the de facto standard for transmitting data across the Internet. TCP is a reliable, connection-oriented protocol, while IP is an unreliable, connectionless protocol.

- Data are encapsulated as they travel down the OSI model on the source computer, and the process is reversed on the destination computer. During encapsulation, each layer adds its own information so the corresponding layer on the destination computer knows how to process the data.

- The data link layer defines how the physical layer transmits the network layer packets. ARP and RARP are two protocols at this layer.

- Two main protocols at the transport layer are TCP and UDP.

- UDP is a connectionless protocol that does not send or receive acknowledgments when a datagram is received. It does not ensure data arrives at its destination. It provides "best-effort" delivery.

- TCP is a connection-oriented protocol that sends and receives acknowledgments. It ensures data arrives at its destination.

- ARP translates the IP address into a MAC address (physical Ethernet address), while RARP translates a MAC address into an IP address.

- ICMP works at the network layer and informs hosts, routers, and devices of network or computer problems. It is the major component of the ping utility.

- DNS resolves hostnames into IP addresses and has distributed databases all over the Internet to provide name resolution.

- Altering an ARP table so an IP address is mapped to a different MAC address is called *ARP poisoning* and can redirect traffic to an attacker's computer or an unattended system.

- Packet filtering (screening routers) is accomplished by ACLs and is a first-generation firewall. Traffic can be filtered by addresses, ports, and protocol types.

- Tunneling protocols move frames from one network to another by placing them inside of routable encapsulated frames.

- Packet filtering provides application independence, high performance, and scalability, but it provides low security and no protection above the network layer.

- Firewalls that use proxies transfer an isolated copy of each approved packet from one network to another network.

- An application proxy requires a proxy for each approved service and can understand and make access decisions on the protocols used and the commands within those protocols.

- Circuit-level firewalls also use proxies but at a lower layer. Circuit-level firewalls do not look as deep within the packet as application proxies do.

- A proxy firewall is the middleman in communication. It does not allow anyone to connect directly to a protected host within the internal network. Proxy firewalls are second-generation firewalls.

- Application proxy firewalls provide good security and have full application-layer awareness, but they have poor performance, limited application support, and poor scalability.

- Stateful inspection keeps track of each communication session. It must maintain a state table that contains data about each connection. It is a third-generation firewall.

- VPN uses tunneling protocols and encryption to provide a secure network link between two networks or hosts. A private and secure connection can be made across an unsecure network.

- VPN can use PPTP, L2TP, or IPSec as a tunneling protocol.

- PPTP works at the data link layer. IPSec works at the network layer and can handle multiple tunnels at the same time.

- Dedicated links are usually the most expensive type of WAN connectivity method because the fee is based on the distance between the two destinations rather than on the amount of bandwidth used. T1 and T3 are examples of dedicated links.

- Frame relay and X.25 are packet-switched WAN technologies that use virtual circuits instead of dedicated ones.

- A hub (concentrator) in star topologies serves as the central meeting place for all cables from computers and devices.

- A bridge divides networks into more controllable segments to ensure more efficient use of bandwidth. Bridges work at the data link layer and understand MAC addresses, not IP addresses.

- A switch is a device with combined repeater and bridge technology. It works at the data link layer and understands MAC addresses.

- Routers link two or more network segments, where each segment can function as an independent network. A router works at the network layer, works with IP addresses, and has more network knowledge than bridges, switches, or repeaters.

- A bridge filters by MAC addresses and forwards broadcast traffic. A router filters by IP addresses and does not forward broadcast traffic.

- Layer 3 switching combines switching and routing technology.

- Attenuation is the loss of signal strength when a cable exceeds its maximum length.

- STP and UTP are twisted-pair cabling types that are the most popular, cheapest, and easiest to work with. However, they are the easiest to tap into, have crosstalk issues, and are vulnerable to electromagnetic interference (EMI).

- Coaxial cable is more expensive than UTP and STP, is more resistant to EMI, and can carry baseband and broadband technologies.

- Fiber-optic cabling carries data as light waves, is expensive, can transmit data at high speeds, is difficult to tap into, and is resistant to EMI. If security is extremely important, fiber cabling should be used.

- ATM transfers data in fixed cells, is a WAN technology, and transmits data at very high rates. It supports voice, data, and video applications.

- FDDI is a LAN and MAN technology, usually used for backbones, that uses token-passing technology and has redundant rings in case the primary ring goes down.

- Ethernet, 802.3, is the most commonly used LAN implementation today and can operate at 10 to 1,000 Mbps.

- Token Ring, 802.5, is an older LAN implementation that uses a token-passing technology.

- Ethernet uses CSMA/CD, which means all computers compete for the shared network cable, listen to learn when they can transmit data, and are susceptible to data collisions.

- Circuit-switching technologies set up a circuit that will be used during a data transmission session. Packet-switching technologies do not set up circuits—instead, packets can travel along many different routes to arrive at the same destination.

- A permanent virtual circuit (PVC) is programmed into WAN devices, whereas a switched virtual circuit (SVC) is temporary. SVCs are set up and then torn down quickly when no longer needed.

- CSU/DSU is used when a LAN device needs to communicate with WAN devices. It ensures the necessary electrical signaling and format are used. It interfaces between a DTE and a DCE.

- ISDN has a BRI rate that uses two B channels and one D channel, and a PRI rate that uses up to 23 B channels. They support voice, data, and video.

- Frame relay is a WAN protocol that works at the data link layer and performs packet switching. It is an economical choice because the fee is based on bandwidth usage.

- PPP is an encapsulation protocol for telecommunication connections. It replaced SLIP and is ideal for connecting different types of devices over serial lines.

- DSL transmits high-speed bandwidth over existing phone lines.

- Remote access servers can be configured to call back remote users, but this can be compromised by enabling call forwarding.

- PAP sends credentials in cleartext, and CHAP authenticates using a challenge/response mechanism and therefore does not send passwords over the network.

- SOCKS is a proxy-based firewall solution. It is a circuit-based proxy firewall and does not use application-based proxies.

- IPSec tunnel mode protects the payload and header information of a packet, while IPSec transport mode protects only the payload.

- A screened-host firewall lies between the perimeter router and the LAN.

- A screened subnet is a DMZ created by two physical firewalls.

- NAT is used when companies do not want systems to know internal hosts' addresses, and it enables companies to use private, nonroutable IP addresses.

- The 802.11 standard is a WLAN technology and has several variations—802.11a, 802.11b, 802.11f, 802.11g, and 802.11i.

- The 802.15 standard outlines wireless personal area network (WPAN) technologies, and 802.16 addresses wireless MAN technologies.

- WAP is a protocol stack used instead of TCP/IP on wireless devices.

- Environments can be segmented into different WLANs by using different SSIDs.

- The 802.11b standard works in the 2.4GHz range at 11 Mbps, and 802.11a works in the 5GHz range at 54 Mbps.

- IPv4 uses 32 bits for its addresses, whereas IPv6 uses 128 bits; thus, IPv6 provides more possible addresses with which to work.

- Subnetting allows large IP ranges to be divided into smaller, logical and easier to maintain network segments.

- SIP (Session Initiation Protocol) is a signaling protocol widely used for VoIP communications sessions.

- A new variant to the traditional e-mail spam has emerged on VoIP networks, commonly known as SPIT (Spam over Internet Telephony).

- Open relay is a SMTP server that is configured in such a way that it can transmit e-mail messages from any source to any destination.

Questions

Please remember that these questions are formatted and asked in a certain way for a reason. Keep in mind that the CISSP exam is asking questions at a conceptual level. Questions may not always have the perfect answer, and the candidate is advised against always looking for the perfect answer. The candidate should look for the best answer in the list.

1. What does it mean if someone says they were a victim of a Bluejacking attack?

   A. An unsolicited message was sent.

   B. A cell phone was cloned.

   C. An IM channel introduced a worm.

   D. Traffic was analyzed.

2. How does TKIP provide more protection for WLAN environments?

   A. It uses the AES algorithm.

    B. It decreases the IV size and uses the AES algorithm.

    C. It adds more keying material.

    D. It uses MAC and IP filtering.

3. Which of the following is not a characteristic of the IEEE 802.11a standard?

    A. It works in the 5GHz range.

    B. It uses the OFDM spread spectrum technology.

    C. It provides 52 Mbps in bandwidth.

    D. It covers a smaller distance than 802.11b.

4. What can be used to compromise and defeat callback security?

    A. Passive wiretapping

    B. Call forwarding

    C. Packet spoofing

    D. A brute force attack

5. Which is not considered a firewall architecture used to protect networks?

    A. A screened host

    B. A screened subnet

    C. A NAT gateway

    D. A two-tiered DMZ

6. Why are switched infrastructures safer environments than routed networks?

    A. It is more difficult to sniff traffic since the computers have virtual private connections.

    B. They are just as unsafe as nonswitched environments.

    C. The data link encryption does not permit wiretapping.

    D. Switches are more intelligent than bridges and implement security mechanisms.

7. What functionality hangs up on a remote caller and looks at a table of predefined valid phone numbers?

    A. Caller ID

    B. RAS

    C. Callback

    D. NOS

8. Which of the following protocols is considered connection-oriented?

    A. IP

    B. ICMP

    C. UDP

    D. TCP

9. Which of the following best describes Ethernet transmissions over a LAN?

  A. Traffic is sent to a gateway that sends it to the destination system.

  B. Traffic is bursty in nature and broadcasts data to all hosts on the subnet.

  C. Traffic streams and does not broadcast data.

  D. Traffic is contained within collision domains but not broadcast domains.

10. Which of the following proxies cannot make access decisions on protocol commands?

  A. Application

  B. Packet filtering

  C. Circuit

  D. Stateful

11. A security concern that is prevalent in distributed environments and systems is _____.

  A. Knowing the proper proxy and default gateway

  B. Knowing whom to trust

  C. Knowing what authentication method is most appropriate

  D. Knowing how to resolve hostnames

12. Which protocol is commonly used to authenticate users on dial-up connections?

  A. PPTP

  B. IPSec

  C. CHAP

  D. L2F

13. Which of the following shows the layer sequence as layers 2, 5, 7, 4, and 3?

  A. Data link, session, application, transport, and network

  B. Data link, transport, application, session, and network

  C. Network, session, application, network, and transport

  D. Network, transport, application, session, and presentation

14. What is another name for a VPN?

  A. Transport session

  B. Tunnel

  C. End-to-end connection

  D. Bandwidth

15. When security is a high priority, why is fiber cabling used?

  A. It has high data transfer rates and is less vulnerable to EMI.

  B. It multiplexes data, which can confuse attackers.

C. It has a high degree of data detection and correction.

D. Data interception is very difficult.

16. Why are mainframe environments considered more secure than LAN environments?

    A. They usually have fewer entry points.

    B. They have stronger authentication mechanisms.

    C. They have more auditing and encryption implemented.

    D. They are actually weaker than LANs.

17. What does it mean when computers communicate logically and physically with each other?

    A. They speak physically through headers and trailers and logically through physical connections.

    B. They speak physically through PVCs and logically through SVCs.

    C. They speak physically when connected to a backbone network and logically when they speak to each other within the same LAN.

    D. They speak physically through electrons and network cables and logically through layers in the OSI model.

18. How does data encapsulation and the protocol stack work?

    A. Each protocol or service at each layer in the OSI model multiplexes other packets to the data as they are passed down the protocol stack.

    B. Each protocol or service at each layer in the OSI model adds its own information to the data as they are passed down the protocol stack.

    C. The packet is encapsulated and grows as it hops from router to router.

    D. The packet is encapsulated and grows when it is passed up the protocol stack.

19. Systems that are built on the OSI framework are considered open systems. What does this mean?

    A. They do not have authentication mechanisms configured by default.

    B. They have interoperability issues.

    C. They are built with internationally accepted protocols and standards so they can easily communicate with other systems.

    D. They are built with international protocols and standards so they can choose what types of systems they will communicate with.

20. Which of the following protocols work in the following layers: application, data link, network, and transport?

    A. FTP, ARP, TCP, and UDP

    B. FTP, ICMP, IP, and UDP

    C. TFTP, ARP, IP, and UDP

    D. TFTP, RARP, IP, and ICMP

21. What is the purpose of the presentation layer?

 A. Addressing and routing

 B. Data syntax and formatting

 C. End-to-end connection

 D. Framing

22. What is the purpose of the data link layer?

 A. End-to-end connection

 B. Dialog control

 C. Framing

 D. Data syntax

23. What takes place at the session layer?

 A. Dialog control

 B. Routing

 C. Packet sequencing

 D. Addressing

24. At what layer does a bridge work?

 A. Session

 B. Network

 C. Transport

 D. Data link

25. Which best describes the IP protocol?

 A. A connectionless protocol that deals with dialog establishment, maintenance, and destruction

 B. A connectionless protocol that deals with the addressing and routing of packets

 C. A connection-oriented protocol that deals with the addressing and routing of packets

 D. A connection-oriented protocol that deals with sequencing, error detection, and flow control

Answers

1. A. Bluejacking occurs when someone sends an unsolicited message to a device that is Bluetooth-enabled. Bluejackers look for a receiving device (phone, PDA, laptop) and then send a message to it. Often, the Bluejacker is trying to send someone else their business card, which will be added to the victim's contact list in their address book.

2. **C.** The TKIP protocol actually works with WEP by feeding it keying material, which is data to be used for generating random keystreams. TKIP increases the IV size, ensures it is random for each packet, and adds the sender's MAC address to the keying material.

3. **C.** The IEEE standard 802.11a uses the OFDM spread spectrum technology, works in the 5GHz frequency band, and provides bandwidth of up to 54 Mbps.

4. **B.** A remote access server can be configured to drop a remote user's connection and call him back at a predefined number. If call forwarding is enabled, this security measure can be compromised.

5. **C.** The other answers describe basic firewall architectures, meaning where they can be placed within an environment. Network address translation (NAT) maps public addresses to private addresses and does not provide traffic monitoring capabilities. Some firewalls provide NAT services, but the goals of the services are different.

6. **A.** Switched environments use switches to allow different network segments and/or systems to communicate. When this communication takes place, a virtual connection is set up between the communicating devices. Since it is a dedicated connection, broadcast and collision data are not available to other systems, as in an environment that uses purely bridges and routers.

7. **C.** The goal of a callback system is to provide another layer of authentication. For an attacker to compromise this setup successfully and obtain unauthorized access, she would need to be at the preconfigured phone number or reconfigure the telephone company's equipment to forward the call to her.

8. **D.** TCP is the only connection-oriented protocol listed. A connection-oriented protocol provides reliable connectivity and data transmission, while a connectionless protocol provides unreliable connections and does not promise or ensure data transmission.

9. **B.** Ethernet is a very "chatty" protocol because it allows all systems to hear each other's broadcasts, and the technology has many collisions because all systems have to share the same medium.

10. **C.** Application and circuit are the only types of proxy-based firewall solutions listed here. The others do not use proxies. Circuit-based proxy firewalls make decisions based on header information, not the protocol's command structure. Application-based proxies are the only ones that understand this level of granularity about the individual protocols.

11. **B.** Distributed environments bring about a lot more complexity and drastically increase the difficulty of access control. Since you now have many different applications, devices, services, and users, it is much more difficult to know which entities to trust and to what degree.

12. **C.** The other protocols listed are used for tunneling and/or VPN connectivity, not user authentication. CHAP uses the challenge-response method of authenticating a user.

13. **A.** The OSI model is made up of seven layers: application (layer 7), presentation (layer 6), session (layer 5), transport (layer 4), network (layer 3), data link (layer 2), and physical (layer 1).

14. **B.** A VPN sets up a private and secure tunnel by encapsulating and encrypting data. This allows data to be safely transmitted over untrusted networks.

15. **D.** It is difficult to tap into a fiber line, and fiber does not radiate signals as other cable types do.

16. **A.** This is a relative and general statement. Mainframes are more closed systems and work in more closed environments compared to the distributed environments we work in today. Mainframes usually have a smaller number of entry points, which are generally very controlled.

17. **D.** Systems, of course, communicate physically using network cables or airwaves. But they also communicate logically. An FTP protocol on one system "speaks" to the FTP protocol on another system and is not aware that any other protocols, devices, and cables are involved. Protocols, services, and applications communicate logically, and this communication is transmitted over physical means.

18. **B.** Data encapsulation means a piece of data is put inside another type of data. This usually means that individual protocols apply their own instruction set in the form of headers and trailers. As a data package goes down the OSI layers, or protocol stack, of a system, each protocol involved adds its own instructions. This process is reversed at the destination.

19. **C.** An open system is a system that has been developed based on standardized protocols and interfaces. Following these standards allows the systems to interoperate more effectively with other systems that follow the same standards.

20. **C.** Different protocols have different functionalities. The OSI model is an attempt to describe conceptually where these different functionalities take place in a networking stack. The model attempts to draw boxes around reality to help people better understand the stack. Each layer has a specific functionality and has several different protocols that can live at that layer and carry out that specific functionality.

21. **B.** No protocols work at the presentation layer, but services that carry out data formatting, compression/decompression, and encryption/decryption processes do occur at that layer. Putting data into a standardized format allows for a large subset of applications to be able to understand and interpret it.

22. **C.** The data link layer, in most cases, is the only layer that understands the environment in which the system is working, whether it be Ethernet, Token Ring, wireless, or a connection to a WAN link. This layer adds the necessary headers and trailers to the frame. Other systems on the same type of network using the same technology understand only the specific header and trailer format used in their data link technology.

23. **A.** The session layer is responsible for controlling how applications communicate, not how computers communicate. Not all applications use protocols that work at the session layer, so this layer is not always used in networking functions. A session layer protocol will set up the connection to the other application logically and control the dialog going back and forth. Session layer protocols allow applications to keep track of the dialog.

24. **D.** A bridge will read header information only in the data link layer and no higher because it makes forwarding and filtering decisions based on what is held within this header, which is the MAC address.

25. **B.** The IP protocol is connectionless and works at the network layer. It adds source and destination addresses to a packet as it goes through its data encapsulation process. IP can also make routing decisions based on the destination address.

Cryptography

This chapter presents the following:

- History of cryptography
- Cryptography components and their relationships
- Government involvement in cryptography
- Symmetric and asymmetric key algorithms
- Public key infrastructure (PKI) concepts and mechanisms
- Hashing algorithms and uses
- Types of attacks on cryptosystems

Cryptography is a method of storing and transmitting data in a form that only those it is intended for can read and process. It is considered a science of protecting information by encoding it into an unreadable format. Cryptography is an effective way of protecting sensitive information as it is stored on media or transmitted through untrusted network communication paths.

One of the goals of cryptography, and the mechanisms that make it up, is to hide information from unauthorized individuals. However, with enough time, resources, and motivation, hackers can break most algorithms and reveal the encoded information. So a more realistic goal of cryptography is to make obtaining the information too work-intensive or time-consuming to be worthwhile to the attacker.

The first encryption methods date back to 4,000 years ago and were considered more of an art form. Encryption was later adapted as a tool to use in warfare, commerce, government, and other arenas in which secrets needed to be safeguarded. With the relatively recent birth of the Internet, encryption has gained new prominence as a vital tool in everyday transactions. Throughout history, individuals and governments have worked to protect communication by encrypting it. As a result, the encryption algorithms and the devices that use them have increased in complexity, new methods and algorithms have been continually introduced, and encryption has become an integrated part of the computing world.

Cryptography has had an interesting history and has undergone many changes down through the centuries. Keeping secrets has proven very important to the workings of civilization. It gives individuals and groups the ability to hide their true intentions, gain a competitive edge, and reduce vulnerability, among other things.

The changes that cryptography has undergone closely follow advances in technology. The earliest cryptography methods involved a person carving messages into wood or stone, which was then delivered to the intended individual who had the necessary means to decipher the messages. Cryptography has come a long way since then. Now it is inserted into streams of binary code that pass over network wires, Internet communication paths, and airwaves.

The History of Cryptography

Look, I scrambled up the message so no one can read it.
Response: Yes, but now neither can we.

Cryptography has roots that begin around 2000 B.C. in Egypt, when hieroglyphics were used to decorate tombs to tell the life story of the deceased. The intention of the practice was not so much about hiding the messages themselves; rather, the hieroglyphics were intended to make the life story seem more noble, ceremonial, and majestic.

Encryption methods evolved from being mainly for show into practical applications used to hide information from others.

A Hebrew cryptographic method required the alphabet to be flipped so each letter in the original alphabet was mapped to a different letter in the flipped, or shifted, alphabet. The encryption method was called *atbash*, which was used to hide the true meaning of messages. An example of an encryption key used in the atbash encryption scheme is shown next:

```
ABCDEFGHIJKLMNOPQRSTUVWXYZ
ZYXWVUTSRQPONMLKJIHGFEDCBA
```

For example, the word "security" is encrypted into "hvxfirgb." What does "xrhhk" come out to be?

This is an example of a *substitution cipher*, because each character is replaced with another character. This type of substitution cipher is referred to as a *monoalphabetic substitution cipher* because it uses only one alphabet, whereas a *polyalphabetic substitution cipher* uses multiple alphabets.

 NOTE   Cipher is another term for algorithm.

This simplistic encryption method worked for its time and for particular cultures, but eventually more complex mechanisms were required.

Around 400 B.C., the Spartans used a system of encrypting information in which they would write a message on a sheet of papyrus (a type of paper) that was wrapped around a staff (a stick or wooden rod), which was then delivered and wrapped around a different staff by the recipient. The message was only readable if it was wrapped around the correct size staff, which made the letters properly match up, as shown in Figure 8-1. This is referred to as the *scytale cipher*. When the papyrus was not wrapped around the staff, the writing appeared as just a bunch of random characters.

Later, in Rome, Julius Caesar (100–44 B.C.) developed a simple method of shifting letters of the alphabet, similar to the atbash scheme. He simply shifted the alphabet by three positions. The following example shows a standard alphabet and a shifted alphabet. The alphabet serves as the algorithm, and the key is the number of locations it has been shifted during the encryption and decryption process.

Standard Alphabet:
ABCDEFGHIJKLMNOPQRSTUVWXYZ

Cryptographic Alphabet:
DEFGHIJKLMNOPQRSTUVWXYZABC

As an example, suppose we need to encrypt the message "Logical Security." We take the first letter of this message, *L*, and shift up three locations within the alphabet. The encrypted version of this first letter is *O*, so we write that down. The next letter to be encrypted is *O*, which matches *R* when we shift three spaces. We continue this process for the whole message. Once the message is encrypted, a carrier takes the encrypted version to the destination, where the process is reversed.

Plaintext:
LOGICAL SECURITY

Ciphertext:
ORJLFDO VHFXULWB

Today, this technique seems too simplistic to be effective, but in the time of Julius Caesar, not very many people could read in the first place, so it provided a high level of protection. The Caesar cipher is an example of a monoalphabetic cipher. Once more people could read and reverse-engineer this type of encryption process, the cryptographers of that day increased the complexity by creating polyalphabetic ciphers.

Figure 8-1
The scytale was used by the Spartans to decipher encrypted messages.

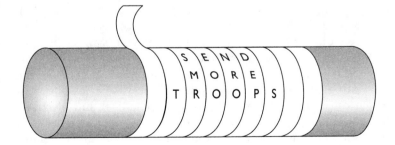

ROT13

A more recent encryption method used in the 1980s, *ROT13*, was really the same thing as a Caesar cipher. Instead of shifting three spaces in the alphabet, the encryption process shifted 13 spaces. It was not really used to protect data, because our society could already easily handle this task. Instead, it was used in online forums (or bulletin boards) when "inappropriate" material, as in nasty jokes, were shared among users. The idea was that if you were interested in reading something potentially "offensive" you could simply use the shift 13 approach and read the material. Other people who did not want to view it would not be offended, because they would just leave the text and not decrypt it.

In the 16th century in France, Blaise de Vigenere developed a polyalphabetic substitution cipher for Henry III. This was based on the Caesar cipher, but it increased the difficulty of the encryption and decryption process.

As shown in Figure 8-2, we have a message that needs to be encrypted, which is SYSTEM SECURITY AND CONTROL. We have a key with the value of SECURITY. We also have a Vigenere table, or algorithm, which is really the Caesar cipher on steroids. Whereas the Caesar cipher used one shift alphabet (letters were shifted up three places), the Vigenere cipher has 27 shift alphabets and the letters are shifted up only one place.

 NOTE Plaintext is the readable version of a message. After an encryption process, the resulting text is referred to as *ciphertext*.

So, looking at the example in Figure 8-2, we take the first value of the key, *S*, and, starting with the first alphabet in our algorithm, trace over to the *S* column. Then we look at the first value of plaintext that needs to be encrypted, which is *S*, and go down to the *S* row. We follow the column and row and see that they intersect on the value *K*. That is the first encrypted value of our message, so we write down *K*. Then we go to the next value in our key, which is *E*, and the next value of plaintext, which is *Y*. We see that the *E* column and the *Y* row intersect at the cell with the value of *C*. This is our second encrypted value, so we write that down. We continue this process for the whole message (notice that the key repeats itself, since the message is longer than the key). The resulting ciphertext is the encrypted form that is sent to the destination. The destination must have the same algorithm (Vigenere table) and the same key (SECURITY) to properly reverse the process to obtain a meaningful message.

The evolution of cryptography continued as countries refined their practices using new methods, tools, and practices throughout the Middle Ages. By the late 1800s, cryptography was commonly used in the methods of communication between military factions.

During World War II, encryption devices were used for tactical communication, which drastically improved with the mechanical and electromechanical technology that provided the world with telegraphic and radio communication. The rotor cipher machine, which is a device that substitutes letters using different rotors within the machine, was a huge breakthrough in military cryptography that provided complexity that proved difficult to break. This work gave way to the most famous cipher machine in

Vigenere Table

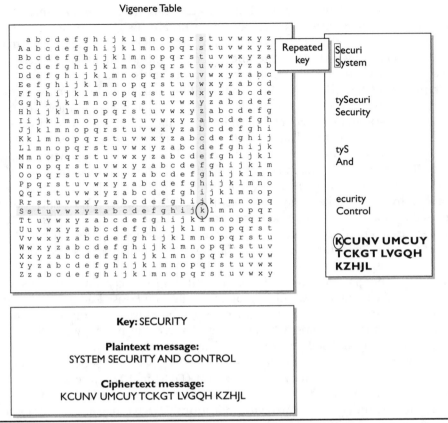

Figure 8-2 Polyalphabetic algorithms were developed to increase encryption complexity.

history to date: Germany's *Enigma* machine. The Enigma machine had separate rotors, a plug board, and a reflecting rotor.

The originator of the message would configure the Enigma machine to its initial settings before starting the encryption process. The operator would type in the first letter of the message, and the machine would substitute the letter with a different letter and present it to the operator. This encryption was done by moving the rotors a predefined number of times. So, if the operator typed in a *T* as the first character, the Enigma machine might present an *M* as the substitution value. The operator would write down the letter *M* on his sheet. The operator would then advance the rotors and enter the next letter. Each time a new letter was to be encrypted, the operator would advance the rotors to a new setting. This process was followed until the whole message was encrypted. Then the encrypted text was transmitted over the airwaves, most likely to a German U-boat. The chosen substitution for each letter was dependent upon the rotor setting, so the crucial and secret part of this process (the key) was the initial setting and how the operators advanced the rotors when encrypting and decrypting a message. The operators at each end needed to know this sequence of increments to advance each rotor in order to enable the German military units to properly communicate.

Although the mechanisms of the Enigma were complicated for the time, a team of Polish cryptographers broke its code and gave Britain insight into Germany's attack plans and military movement. It is said that breaking this encryption mechanism shortened World War II by two years. After the war, details about the Enigma machine were published—one of the machines is exhibited at the Smithsonian Institute.

Cryptography has a deep, rich history. Mary, Queen of Scots, lost her life in the 16th century when an encrypted message she sent was intercepted. During the Revolutionary War, Benedict Arnold used a codebook cipher to exchange information on troop movement and strategic military advancements. Militaries have always played a leading role in using cryptography to encode information and to attempt to decrypt the enemy's encrypted information. William Frederick Friedman, who published *The Index of Coincidence and Its Applications in Cryptography* in 1920, is called the "Father of Modern Cryptography" and broke many messages intercepted during WWII. Encryption has been used by many governments and militaries and has contributed to great victory for some because it enabled them to execute covert maneuvers in secrecy. It has also contributed to great defeat for others, when their cryptosystems were discovered and deciphered.

When computers were invented, the possibilities for encryption methods and devices expanded exponentially and cryptography efforts increased dramatically. This era brought unprecedented opportunity for cryptographic designers to develop new encryption techniques. The most well-known and successful project was *Lucifer*, which was developed at IBM. Lucifer introduced complex mathematical equations and functions that were later adopted and modified by the U.S. National Security Agency (NSA) to establish the U.S. Data Encryption Standard (DES) in 1976, a federal government standard. DES has been used worldwide for financial and other transactions, and was embedded into numerous commercial applications. DES has had a rich history in computer-oriented encryption and has been in use for over 25 years.

A majority of the protocols developed at the dawn of the computing age have been upgraded to include cryptography and to add necessary layers of protection. Encryption is used in hardware devices and in software to protect data, banking transactions, corporate extranet transmissions, e-mail messages, web transactions, wireless communications, the storage of confidential information, faxes, and phone calls.

The code breakers and cryptanalysis efforts and the amazing number-crunching capabilities of the microprocessors hitting the market each year have quickened the evolution of cryptography. As the bad guys get smarter and more resourceful, the good guys must increase their efforts and strategy. *Cryptanalysis* is the science of studying and breaking the secrecy of encryption processes, compromising authentication schemes, and reverse-engineering algorithms and keys. Cryptanalysis is an important piece of cryptography and cryptology. When carried out by the "good guys," cryptanalysis is intended to identify flaws and weaknesses so developers can go back to the drawing board and improve the components. It is also performed by curious and motivated hackers, to identify the same types of flaws, but with the goal of obtaining the encryption key for unauthorized access to confidential information.

NOTE Cryptanalysis is a very sophisticated science that encompasses a wide variety of tests and attacks. We will cover these types of attacks at the end of this chapter. Cryptology, on the other hand, is the study of cryptanalysis and cryptography.

Different types of cryptography have been used throughout civilization, but today cryptography is deeply rooted in every part of our communications and computing world. Automated information systems and cryptography play a huge role in the effectiveness of militaries, the functionality of governments, and the economics of private businesses. As our dependency upon technology increases, so does our dependency upon cryptography, because secrets will always need to be kept.

Cryptography Definitions and Concepts

Why can't I read this?
Response: It is in ciphertext.

Encryption is a method of transforming readable data, called *plaintext*, into a form that appears to be random and unreadable, which is called *ciphertext*. Plaintext is in a form that can be understood either by a person (a document) or by a computer (executable code). Once it is transformed into ciphertext, neither human nor machine can properly process it until it is decrypted. This enables the transmission of confidential information over insecure channels without unauthorized disclosure. When data are stored on a computer, they are usually protected by logical and physical access controls. When this same sensitive information is sent over a network, it can no longer take these controls for granted, and the information is in a much more vulnerable state.

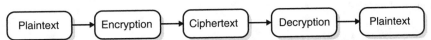

A system or product that provides encryption and decryption is referred to as a *cryptosystem* and can be created through hardware components or program code in an application. The cryptosystem uses an encryption algorithm (which determines how simple or complex the encryption process will be), keys, and the necessary software components and protocols. Most algorithms are complex mathematical formulas that are applied in a specific sequence to the plaintext. Most encryption methods use a secret value called a *key* (usually a long string of bits), which works with the algorithm to encrypt and decrypt the text.

The *algorithm*, the set of rules also known as the cipher, dictates how enciphering and deciphering take place. Many of the mathematical algorithms used in computer systems today are publicly known and are not the secret part of the encryption process. If the internal mechanisms of the algorithm are not a secret, then something must be. The secret piece of using a well-known encryption algorithm is the key. A common analogy used to illustrate this point is the use of locks you would purchase from your local hardware store. Let's say 20 people bought the same brand of lock. Just because these people share the same type and brand of lock does not mean they can now unlock each other's doors and gain access to their private possessions. Instead, each lock comes with its own key, and that one key can only open that one specific lock.

In encryption, the *key* (cryptovariable) is a value that comprises a large sequence of random bits. Is it just any random number of bits crammed together? Not really. An algorithm contains a *keyspace*, which is a range of values that can be used to construct a key. When the algorithm needs to generate a new key, it uses random values from this keyspace. The larger the keyspace, the more available values can be used to represent different keys—and the more random the keys are, the harder it is for intruders to figure them out. For example, if an algorithm allows a key length of 2 bits, the keyspace for that algorithm would be 4, which indicates the total number of different keys that would be possible. (Remember that we are working in binary and that 2^2 equals 4.) That would not be a very large keyspace, and certainly it would not take an attacker very long to find the correct key that was used.

A large keyspace allows for more possible keys. (Today, we are commonly using key sizes of 128, 256, 512, or even 1,024 bits and larger. So a key size of 512 bits would provide a 2^{512} possible combinations (the keyspace). The encryption algorithm should use the entire keyspace and choose the values to make up the keys as randomly as possible. If a smaller keyspace were used, there would be fewer values to choose from when generating a key, as shown in Figure 8-3. This would increase an attacker's chances of figuring out the key value and deciphering the protected information.

If an eavesdropper captures a message as it passes between two people, she can view the message, but it appears in its encrypted form and is therefore unusable. Even if this attacker knows the algorithm that the two people are using to encrypt and decrypt their information, without the key, this information remains useless to the eavesdropper, as shown in Figure 8-4.

Kerckhoffs' Principle

Auguste Kerckhoffs published a paper in 1883 stating that the only secrecy involved with a cryptography system should be the key. He claimed that the algorithm should be publicly known. He asserted that if security were based on too many secrets, there would be more vulnerabilities to possibly exploit.

Cryptosystems

A cryptosystem encompasses all of the necessary components for encryption and decryption to take place. Pretty Good Privacy (PGP) is just one example of a cryptosystem. A cryptosystem is made up of at least the following:

- Software
- Protocols
- Algorithms
- Keys

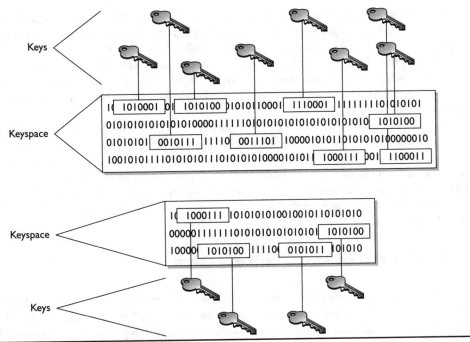

Figure 8-3 Larger keyspaces permit a greater number of possible key values.

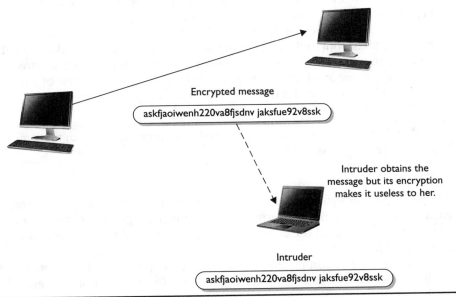

Figure 8-4 Without the right key, the captured message is useless to an attacker.

So, why do we care what some guy said over 120 years ago? Because this debate is still going on. Cryptographers in the private and academic sectors agree with Kerckhoffs' principle, because making an algorithm publicly available means that many more people can view the source code, test it, and uncover any type of flaws or weaknesses. It is the attitude of "many heads are better than one." Once someone uncovers some type of flaw, the developer can fix the issue, and provide society with a much stronger algorithm.

But, not everyone agrees with this philosophy. Governments around the world create their own algorithms that are not released to the public. Their stance is that if a smaller number of people know how the algorithm actually works, then a smaller number of people will know how to possibly break it. Cryptographers in the private sector do not agree with this practice and do not trust algorithms they cannot examine.

It is basically the same as the open-source versus compiled software debate that is in full force today.

The Strength of the Cryptosystem

You are the weakest link. Goodbye!

The *strength* of an encryption method comes from the algorithm, the secrecy of the key, the length of the key, the initialization vectors, and how they all work together within the cryptosystem. When strength is discussed in encryption, it refers to how hard it is to figure out the algorithm or key, whichever is not made public. Attempts to break a cryptosystem usually involve processing an amazing number of possible values in the hopes of finding the one value (key) that can be used to decrypt a specific message. The strength of an encryption method correlates to the amount of necessary processing power, resources, and time required to break the cryptosystem or to figure out the value of the key. Breaking a cryptosystem can be accomplished by a brute force attack, which means trying every possible key value until the resulting plaintext is meaningful. Depending on the algorithm and length of the key, this can be an easy task or one that is close to impossible. If a key can be broken with a Pentium II processor in three hours, the cipher is not strong at all. If the key can only be broken with the use of a thousand multiprocessing systems over 1.2 million years, then it is pretty darn strong.

NOTE Initialization vectors are explained in the section with the same name later in this chapter.

The goal when designing an encryption method is to make compromising it too expensive or too time-consuming. Another name for cryptography strength is *work factor*, which is an estimate of the effort and resources it would take an attacker to penetrate a cryptosystem.

How strong a protection mechanism is required depends on the sensitivity of the data being protected. It is not necessary to encrypt information about a friend's Saturday barbeque with a top-secret encryption algorithm. Conversely, it is not a good idea to send intercepted spy information using PGP. Each type of encryption mechanism has its place and purpose.

Even if the algorithm is very complex and thorough, other issues within encryption can weaken encryption methods. Because the key is usually the secret value needed to actually encrypt and decrypt messages, improper protection of the key can weaken the encryption. Even if a user employs an algorithm that has all the requirements for strong encryption, including a large keyspace and a large and random key value, if she shares her key with others, the strength of the algorithm becomes almost irrelevant.

Important elements of encryption are to use an algorithm without flaws, use a large key size, use all possible values within the keyspace, and to protect the actual key. If one element is weak, it could be the link that dooms the whole process.

Services of Cryptosystems

Cryptosystems can provide the following services:

- **Confidentiality**   Renders the information unintelligible except by authorized entities.

- **Integrity**   Data has not been altered in an unauthorized manner since it was created, transmitted, or stored.

- **Authentication**   Verifies the identity of the user or system that created information.

- **Authorization**   Upon proving identity, the individual is then provided with the key or password that will allow access to some resource.

- **Nonrepudiation**   Ensures that the sender cannot deny sending the message.

As an example of how these services work, suppose your boss sends you a message telling you that you will be receiving a raise that doubles your salary. The message is encrypted, so you can be sure it really came from your boss (authenticity), that someone did not alter it before it arrived at your computer (integrity), that no one else was able to read it as it traveled over the network (confidentiality), and that your boss cannot deny sending it later when he comes to his senses (nonrepudiation).

Different types of messages and transactions require higher or lower degrees of one or all of the services that cryptography methods can supply. Military and intelligence agencies are very concerned about keeping information confidential, so they would choose encryption mechanisms that provide a high degree of secrecy. Financial institutions care about confidentiality, but they also care about the integrity of the data being transmitted, so the encryption mechanism they would choose may differ from the military's encryption methods. If messages were accepted that had a misplaced decimal point or zero, the ramifications could be far reaching in the financial world. Legal agencies may care most about the authenticity of the messages they receive. If information received ever needed to be presented in a court of law, its authenticity would certainly be questioned; therefore, the encryption method used must ensure authenticity, which confirms who sent the information.

NOTE If David sends a message and then later claims he did not send it, this is an act of repudiation. When a cryptography mechanism provides nonrepudiation, the sender cannot later deny he sent the message (well, he can try to deny it, but the cryptosystem proves otherwise). It's a way of keeping the sender honest.

The types and uses of cryptography have increased over the years. At one time, cryptography was mainly used to keep secrets secret (confidentiality), but today we use cryptography to ensure the integrity of data, to authenticate messages, to confirm that a message was received, for access control, and much more. Throughout this chapter, we will cover the different types of cryptography that provide these different types of functionality, along with any related security issues.

Cryptography Definitions

The following definitions are critical for your understanding of cryptography:

- **Access control**   Restricting and controlling subject and object access attempts
- **Algorithm**   Set of mathematical rules used in encryption and decryption
- **Cipher**   Another name for algorithm
- **Cryptography**   Science of secret writing that enables you to store and transmit data in a form that is available only to the intended individuals
- **Cryptosystem**   Hardware or software implementation of cryptography that transforms a message to ciphertext and back to plaintext
- **Cryptanalysis**   Practice of breaking cryptic systems
- **Cryptology**   The study of both cryptography and cryptanalysis
- **Data origin authentication**   Proving the source of a message (system-based authentication)
- **Encipher**   Act of transforming data into an unreadable format
- **Entity authentication**   Proving the identity of the entity that sent a message
- **Decipher**   Act of transforming data into a readable format
- **Key**   Secret sequence of bits and instructions that governs the act of encryption and decryption
- **Key clustering**   Instance when two different keys generate the same ciphertext from the same plaintext
- **Keyspace**   A range of possible values used to construct keys
- **Plaintext**   Data in readable format, also referred to as cleartext
- **Receipt**   Acknowledgment that a message has been received
- **Work factor**   Estimated time, effort, and resources necessary to break a cryptosystem

If some of these terms do not make sense now, just hold on. We will cover them all in the following sections.

One-Time Pad

I want to use my one-time pad three times.
Response: Not a good idea.

A *one-time pad* is a perfect encryption scheme because it is considered unbreakable if implemented properly. It was invented by Gilbert Vernam in 1917, so sometimes it is referred to as the Vernam cipher.

This cipher does not use shift alphabets, as do the Caesar and Vigenere ciphers discussed earlier, but instead uses a pad made up of random values, as shown in Figure 8-5. Our plaintext message that needs to be encrypted has been converted into bits, and our one-time pad is made up of random bits. This encryption process uses a binary mathematic function called exclusive-OR, usually abbreviated as XOR.

XOR is an operation that is applied to two bits and is a function commonly used in binary mathematics and encryption methods. When combining the bits, if both values are the same, the result is 0 (1 XOR 1 = 0). If the bits are different from each other, the result is 1 (1 XOR 0 = 1). For example:

Message stream `1001010111`

Keystream `0011101010`

Ciphertext stream `1010111101`

So in our example, the first bit of the message is XORed to the first bit of the one-time pad, which results in the ciphertext value 1. The second bit of the message is XORed with the second bit of the pad, which results in the value 0. This process continues until the whole message is encrypted. The result is the encrypted message that is sent to the receiver.

In Figure 8-5, we also see that the receiver must have the same one-time pad to decrypt the message, by reversing the process. The receiver takes the first bit of the encrypted message and XORs it with the first bit of the pad. This results in the plaintext value. The receiver continues this process for the whole encrypted message, until the entire message is decrypted.

The one-time pad encryption scheme is deemed unbreakable only if the following things are true about the implementation process:

- *The pad must be used only one time.* If the pad is used more than one time, this might introduce patterns in the encryption process that will aid the evildoer in his goal of breaking the encryption.

- *The pad must be as long as the message.* If it is not as long as the message, the pad will need to be reused to cover the whole message. This would be the same thing as using a pad more than one time, which could introduce patterns.

- *The pad must be securely distributed and protected at its destination.* This is a very cumbersome process to accomplish, because the pads are usually just individual pieces of paper that need to be delivered by a secure courier and properly guarded at each destination.

- *The pad must be made up of truly random values.* This may not seem like a difficult task, but even our computer systems today do not have truly random number generators; rather, they have pseudorandom number generators.

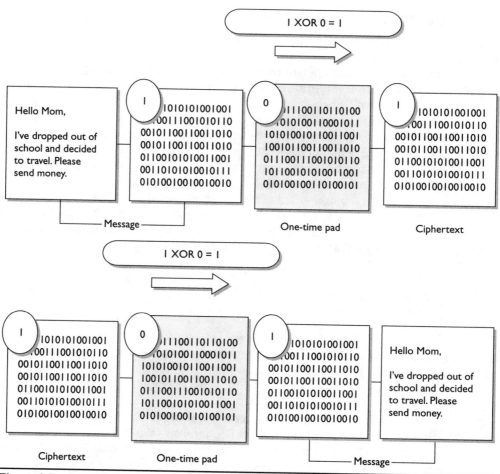

Figure 8-5 A one-time pad

 NOTE A *number generator* is used to create a stream of random values and must be seeded by an initial value. This piece of software obtains its seeding value from some component within the computer system (time, CPU cycles, and so on). Although a computer system is complex, it is a predictable environment, so if the seeding value is predictable in any way, the resulting values created are not truly random—but *pseudorandom*.

Although the one-time pad approach to encryption can provide a very high degree of security, it is impractical in most situations because of all of its different requirements. Each possible pair of entities that might want to communicate in this fashion must receive, in a secure fashion, a pad that is as long as, or longer than, the actual message. This type of key management can be overwhelming and may require more over-

---

One-Time Pad Requirements

For a one-time pad encryption scheme to be considered unbreakable, each pad in the scheme must be:

- Made up of truly random values
- Used only one time
- Securely distributed to its destination
- Secured at sender's and receiver's sites
- At least as long as the message

---

head than it is worth. The distribution of the pad can be challenging, and the sender and receiver must be perfectly synchronized so each is using the same pad.

One-time pads have been used throughout history to protect different types of sensitive data. Today, they are still in place for many types of militaries as a backup encryption option if current encryption processes (that require computers and a power source) are unavailable for reasons of war or attacks.

Running and Concealment Ciphers

I have my decoder ring, spyglasses, and secret handshake. Now let me figure out how I will encrypt my messages.

Two spy-novel-type ciphers are the running key cipher and the concealment cipher. The *running key cipher* could use a key that does not require an electronic algorithm and bit alterations, but cleverly uses components in the physical world around you. For instance, the algorithm could be a set of books agreed upon by the sender and receiver. The key in this type of cipher could be a book page, line number, and column count. If I get a message from my supersecret spy buddy and the message reads "14916c7.29913 c7.91115c8," this could mean for me to look at the 1st book in our predetermined series of books, the 49th page, 6th line down the page, and the 7th column. So I write down the letter in that column, which is *m*. The second set of numbers starts with 2, so I go to the 2nd book, 99th page, 3rd line down, and then to the 7th column, which is *p*. The last letter I get from the 9th book, 11th page, 5th line, 8th column, which is *t*. So now I have come up with my important secret message, which is *mpt*. This means nothing to me, and I need to look for a new spy buddy. Running key ciphers can be used in different and more complex ways, but I think you get the point.

A *concealment cipher* is a message within a message. If my other supersecret spy buddy and I decide our key value is every third word, then when I get a message from him, I will pick out every third word and write it down. Suppose he sends me a message that reads, "The saying, 'The time is right' is not cow language, so is now a dead subject." Because my key is every third word, I come up with "The right cow is dead." This again means nothing to me, and I am now turning in my decoder ring.

NOTE A concealment cipher, also called a null cipher, is a type of steganography method. Steganography is described later in this chapter.

No matter which of these two types of cipher is used, the roles of the algorithm and key are the same, even if they are not mathematical equations. In the running key cipher, the algorithm may be a predefined set of books. The key indicates the book, page, line, and word within that line. In substitution ciphers, the algorithm dictates that substitution will take place using a predefined alphabet or sequence of characters, and the key indicates that each character will be replaced with another character, as in the third character that follows it in that sequence of characters. In actual mathematical structures, the algorithm is a set of mathematical functions that will be performed on the message, and the key can indicate in which order these functions take place. So even if an attacker knows the algorithm, and we have to assume he does, if he does not know the key, the message is still useless to him.

Steganography

Where's the top-secret message?
Response: In this picture of my dogs.

Steganography is a method of hiding data in another media type so the very existence of the data is concealed as illustrated in Figure 8-6. Only the sender and receiver are supposed to be able to see the message because it is secretly hidden in a graphic, wave file, document, or other type of media. The message is not encrypted, just hidden. Encrypted messages can draw attention because it tells the bad guy, "This is something sensitive." A message hidden in a picture of your grandmother would not attract this type of attention, even though the same secret message can be embedded into this image. Steganography is a type of security through obscurity.

Steganography includes the concealment of information within computer files. In digital steganography, electronic communications may include steganographic coding inside of a document file, image file, program, or protocol. Media files are ideal for steganographic transmission because of their large size. As a simple example, a sender might start with an innocuous image file and adjust the color of every 100th pixel to correspond to a letter in the alphabet, a change so subtle that someone not specifically looking for it is unlikely to notice it.

Let's look at the components that are involved with steganography, which are listed next:

- **Carrier** A signal, data stream, or file that has hidden information (payload) inside of it

- **Stego-medium** The medium in which the information is hidden

- **Payload** The information that is to be concealed and transmitted

So if you want to secretly send a message to me that says, "This book is so big I can kill someone with it" and want to get it past my editor—the message would be the payload. If you send this message embedded in the picture of your grandmother, the picture would be the carrier file and the stego-medium would be a JPEG.

A method of embedding the message into some type of medium is to use the *least significant bit (LSB)*. Many types of files have some bits that can be modified and not affect the file they are in, which is where secret data can be hidden without altering the file in a visible manner. In the LSB approach, graphics with a high resolution or an audio file that has many different types of sounds (high bit rate) are the most successful for hiding information within. There is commonly no noticeable distortion, and the file is usually not increased to a size that can be detected. A 24-bit bitmap file will have 8 bits representing each of the three color values, which are red, green, and blue. These 8 bits are within each pixel. If we consider just the blue, there will be 2^8 different values of blue. The difference between 11111111 and 11111110 in the value for blue intensity is likely to be undetectable by the human eye. Therefore, the least significant bit can be used for something other than color information.

A digital graphic is just a file that shows different colors and intensities of light. The larger the file, the more bits that can be modified without much notice or distortion.

Several different types of tools can be used to hide messages within the carrier. Figure 8-7 illustrates one such tool that allows the user to encrypt the message along with hiding it within a file.

Figure 8-6
Main components of steganography

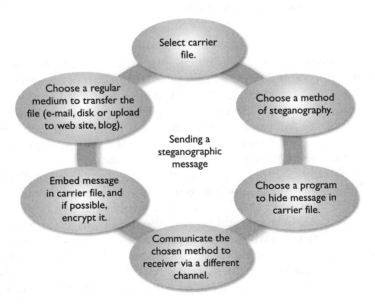

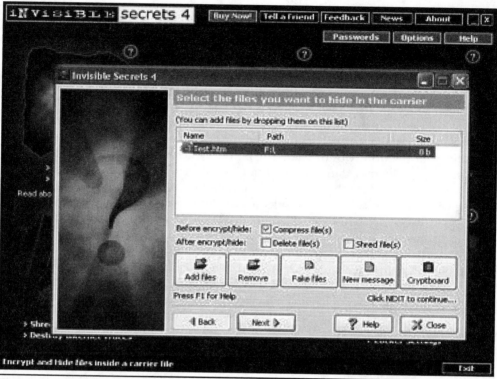

Figure 8-7 Embedding secret material

A concealment cipher (null cipher), explained earlier, is an example of a type of steganography method. The null values are not part of the secret message, but are used to hide the secret message. Let's look at an example. If I send you the message used in the example earlier, "The saying, 'The time is right' is not cow language, so is now a dead subject," you would think I was nuts. If you knew the secret message was made up of every third word, you would be able to extract the secret message from the null values. So the secret message is "The right cow is dead."

What if you wanted to get a secret message to me in a nondigital format? So you use a physical method of sending secret messages instead of our computers. You could write the message in invisible ink, and I would need to have the necessary chemical to make it readable. You could create a very small photograph of the message, called a *microdot*, and put it within the ink of a stamp. Another physical steganography method is to send me a very complex piece of art, which has the secret message in it that can be seen if it is held at the right angle and has a certain type of light shown on it. These are just some examples of the many ways that steganography can be carried out.

Digital Watermarking

Have you ever tried to copy something that was not yours that had an embedded logo or trademark of another company? (If so, shame on you!) The embedded logo or trademark is called a *digital watermark*. Instead of having a secret message within a graphic that is supposed to be invisible to you, digital watermarks are usually visible. These are put into place to deter people from using material that is not theirs. This type of steganography is referred to as **Digital Rights Management (DRM)**. The goal is to restrict the usage of material that is owned by a company or individual.

Secret message hidden in the picture. → Weapons are stockpiled in the hills.

Types of Ciphers

Symmetric encryption ciphers come in two basic types: substitution and transposition (permutation). The *substitution cipher* replaces bits, characters, or blocks of characters with different bits, characters, or blocks. The *transposition cipher* does not replace the original text with different text, but rather moves the original values around. It rearranges the bits, characters, or blocks of characters to hide the original meaning.

Substitution Ciphers

Give me your A and I will change it out for an M. Now, no one can read your message. Response: That will fool them.

A substitution cipher uses a key to dictate how the substitution should be carried out. In the *Caesar cipher*, each letter is replaced with the letter three places beyond it in the alphabet. The algorithm is the alphabet, and the key is the instruction "shift up three."

As a simple example, if George uses the Caesar cipher with the English alphabet to encrypt the important message "meow," the encrypted message would be "phrz." Substitution is used in today's symmetric algorithms, but it is extremely complex compared to this example, which is only meant to show you the concept of how a substitution cipher works in its most simplistic form.

Transposition Ciphers

In a transposition cipher, the values are scrambled, or put into a different order. The key determines the positions the values are moved to, as illustrated in Figure 8-8.

This is a simplistic example of a transposition cipher and only shows one way of performing transposition. When implemented with complex mathematical functions, transpositions can become quite sophisticated and difficult to break. Symmetric algorithms employed today use both long sequences of complicated substitutions and transpositions on messages. The algorithm contains the possible ways that substitution and transposition processes *can* take place (represented in mathematical formulas). The key is used as the instructions for the algorithm, dictating exactly how these processes *will* happen and in what order. To understand the relationship between an algorithm and a key, let's look at Figure 8-9. Conceptually, an algorithm is made up of different boxes, each of which has a different set of mathematical formulas that dictates the substitution and transposition steps that will take place on the bits that enter the box. To encrypt our message, the bit values must go through these different boxes. If

Figure 8-8
A transposition
cipher

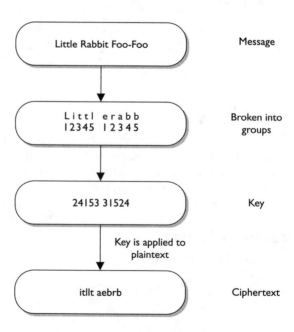

each of our messages goes through each of these different boxes in the same order with the same values, the evildoer will be able to easily reverse-engineer this process and uncover our plaintext message.

To foil an evildoer, we use a key, which is a set of values that indicates which box should be used, in what order, and with what values. So if message A is encrypted with key 1, the key will make the message go through boxes 1, 6, 4, and then 5. When we need to encrypt message B, we will use key 2, which will make the message go through boxes 8, 3, 2, and then 9. It is the key that adds the randomness and the secrecy to the encryption process.

Simple substitution and transposition ciphers are vulnerable to attacks that perform *frequency analysis*. In every language, some words and patterns are used more often than others. For instance, in the English language, the most commonly used letter is E. If Mike is carrying out frequency analysis on a message, he will look for the most frequently repeated pattern of eight bits (which make up a character). So, if Mike sees that there are 12 patterns of eight bits and he knows that E is the most commonly used letter in the language, he will replace these bits with this vowel. This allows him to gain a foothold on the process, which will allow him to reverse-engineer the rest of the message.

Today's symmetric algorithms use substitution and transposition methods in their encryption processes, but the mathematics used are (or should be) too complex to allow for simplistic frequency-analysis attacks to be successful.

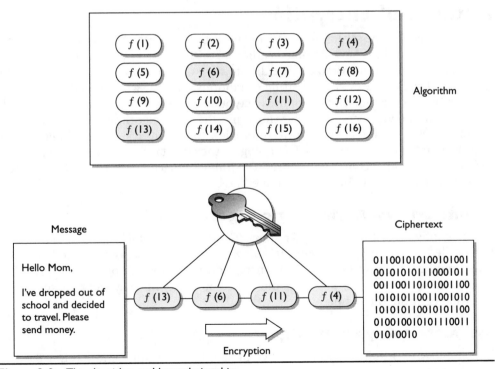

Figure 8-9 The algorithm and key relationship

Key Derivation Functions

For complex keys to be generated, commonly a master key is created, and then symmetric keys are generated from it. For example, if an application is responsible for creating a session key for each subject that requests one, it should not be giving out the same instance of that one key. Different subjects need to have different symmetric keys to ensure that the window for the bad guy to capture and uncover that key is smaller than if the same key were to be used over and over again. When two or more keys are created from a master key, they are called *subkeys*.

Key Derivation Functions (KDFs) are used to generate keys that are made up of random values. Different values can be used independently or together as random key material. The algorithm is created to use specific hash, password, and/or salt values, which will go through a certain number of rounds of mathematical functions dictated by the algorithm. The more rounds that this keying material goes through, the more assurance and security for the cryptosystem overall.

NOTE Remember that the algorithm stays static, and the randomness provided by cryptography is mainly by means of the keying material.

Methods of Encryption

Although there can be several pieces to an encryption process, the two main pieces are the algorithms and the keys. As stated earlier, algorithms used in computer systems are complex mathematical formulas that dictate the rules of how the plaintext will be turned into ciphertext. A key is a string of random bits that will be used by the algorithm to add to the randomness of the encryption process. For two entities to be able to communicate via encryption, they must use the same algorithm and, many times, the same key. In some encryption technologies, the receiver and the sender use the same key, and in other encryption technologies, they must use different but related keys for encryption and decryption purposes. The following sections explain the differences between these two types of encryption methods.

Symmetric vs. Asymmetric Algorithms

Cryptography algorithms are either *symmetric algorithms*, which use symmetric keys (also called secret keys), or *asymmetric algorithms*, which use asymmetric keys (also called public and private keys). As if encryption were not complicated enough, the terms used to describe the key types only make it worse. Just pay close attention and you will get through this fine.

Symmetric Cryptography

In a cryptosystem that uses symmetric cryptography, the sender and receiver use two instances of the same key for encryption and decryption, as shown in Figure 8-10. So the key has dual functionality, in that it can carry out both encryption and decryption processes. Symmetric keys are also called *secret* keys, because this type of encryption relies on each user to keep the key a secret and properly protected. If an intruder were to get this key, they could decrypt any intercepted message encrypted with it.

Each pair of users who want to exchange data using symmetric key encryption must have two instances of the same key. This means that if Dan and Iqqi want to communicate, both need to obtain a copy of the same key. If Dan also wants to communicate using symmetric encryption with Norm and Dave, he needs to have three separate keys, one for each friend. This might not sound like a big deal until Dan realizes that he may communicate with hundreds of people over a period of several months, and keeping track and using the correct key that corresponds to each specific receiver can become a daunting task. If ten people needed to communicate securely with each other using symmetric keys, then 45 keys would need to be kept track of. If 100 people were going to communicate, then 4,950 keys would be involved. The equation used to calculate the number of symmetric keys needed is

$$N(N - 1)/2 = \text{number of keys}$$

When using symmetric algorithms, the sender and receiver use the same key for encryption and decryption functions. The security of the symmetric encryption method is completely dependent on how well users protect the key. This should raise red flags for you if you have ever had to depend on a whole staff of people to keep a secret. If a key is compromised, then all messages encrypted with that key can be decrypted and read by an intruder. This is complicated further by how symmetric keys are actually shared and updated when necessary. If Dan wants to communicate with Norm for the first time, Dan has to figure out how to get the right key to Norm securely. It is not safe to just send it in an e-mail message, because the key is not protected and can be easily intercepted and used by attackers. Thus, Dan must get the key to Norm through an *out-of-band method*. Dan can save the key on a thumb drive and walk over to Norm's desk, or have a secure courier deliver it to Norm. This is a huge hassle, and each method is very clumsy and insecure.

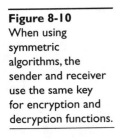

Figure 8-10
When using symmetric algorithms, the sender and receiver use the same key for encryption and decryption functions.

Symmetric encryption uses the same keys.

Because both users employ the same key to encrypt and decrypt messages, symmetric cryptosystems can provide confidentiality, but they cannot provide authentication or nonrepudiation. There is no way to prove through cryptography who actually sent a message if two people are using the same key.

If symmetric cryptosystems have so many problems and flaws, why use them at all? Because they are very fast and can be hard to break. Compared with asymmetric systems, symmetric algorithms scream in speed. They can encrypt and decrypt relatively quickly large amounts of data that would take an unacceptable amount of time to encrypt and decrypt with an asymmetric algorithm. It is also difficult to uncover data encrypted with a symmetric algorithm if a large key size is used. For many of our applications that require encryption, symmetric key cryptography is the only option.

The following list outlines the strengths and weakness of symmetric key systems:

Strengths

- Much faster (less computationally intensive) than asymmetric systems.
- Hard to break if using a large key size.

Weaknesses

- Requires a secure mechanism to deliver keys properly.
- Each pair of users needs a unique key, so as the number of individuals increases, so does the number of keys, possibly making key management overwhelming.
- Provides confidentiality but not authenticity or nonrepudiation.

The following are examples of symmetric algorithms, which will be explained later in the "Block and Stream Ciphers" section:

- Data Encryption Standard (DES)
- Triple-DES (3DES)
- Blowfish
- IDEA (International Data Encryption Algorithm)
- RC4, RC5, and RC6
- Advanced Encryption Standard (AES)

Asymmetric Cryptography

Some things you can tell the public, but some things you just want to keep private.

In symmetric key cryptography, a single secret key is used between entities, whereas in public key systems, each entity has different keys, or *asymmetric keys*. The two different asymmetric keys are mathematically related. If a message is encrypted by one key, the other key is required in order to decrypt the message.

In a public key system, the pair of keys is made up of one public key and one private key. The *public key* can be known to everyone, and the *private key* must be known and used only by the owner. Many times, public keys are listed in directories and databases of e-mail addresses so they are available to anyone who wants to use these keys to encrypt or decrypt data when communicating with a particular person. Figure 8-11 illustrates the use of the different keys.

The public and private keys of an asymmetric cryptosystem are mathematically related, but if someone gets another person's public key, she should not be able to figure out the corresponding private key. This means that if an evildoer gets a copy of Bob's public key, it does not mean she can employ some mathematical magic and find out Bob's private key. But if someone got Bob's private key, then there is big trouble—no one other than the owner should have access to a private key.

If Bob encrypts data with his private key, the receiver must have a copy of Bob's public key to decrypt it. The receiver can decrypt Bob's message and decide to reply to Bob in an encrypted form. All she needs to do is encrypt her reply with Bob's public key, and then Bob can decrypt the message with his private key. It is not possible to encrypt and decrypt using the same key when using an asymmetric key encryption technology because, although mathematically related, the two keys are not the same key, as they are in symmetric cryptography. Bob can encrypt data with his private key, and the receiver can then decrypt it with Bob's public key. By decrypting the message with Bob's public key, the receiver can be sure the message really came from Bob. A message can be decrypted with a public key only if the message was encrypted with the corresponding private key. This provides authentication, because Bob is the only one who is supposed to have his private key. If the receiver wants to make sure Bob is the only one that can read her reply, she will encrypt the response with his public key. Only Bob will be able to decrypt the message because he is the only one who has the necessary private key.

The receiver can also choose to encrypt data with her private key instead of using Bob's public key. Why would she do that? Authentication—she wants Bob to know that the message came from her and no one else. If she encrypted the data with Bob's public key, it does not provide authenticity because anyone can get Bob's public key. If she uses her private key to encrypt the data, then Bob can be sure the message came from her and no one else. Symmetric keys do not provide authenticity because the same key is used on both ends. Using one of the secret keys does not ensure the message originated from a specific individual.

Figure 8-11
An asymmetric
cryptosystem

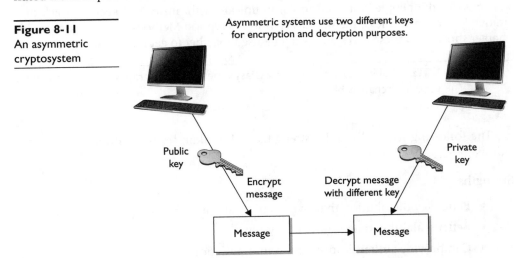

Asymmetric systems use two different keys
for encryption and decryption purposes.

Public key

Private key

Encrypt message

Decrypt message with different key

Message

Message

If confidentiality is the most important security service to a sender, she would encrypt the file with the receiver's public key. This is called a *secure message format* because it can only be decrypted by the person who has the corresponding private key.

If authentication is the most important security service to the sender, then she would encrypt the data with her private key. This provides assurance to the receiver that the only person who could have encrypted the data is the individual who has possession of that private key. If the sender encrypted the data with the receiver's public key, authentication is not provided because this public key is available to anyone.

Encrypting data with the sender's private key is called an *open message format* because anyone with a copy of the corresponding public key can decrypt the message. Confidentiality is not ensured.

Each key type can be used to encrypt and decrypt, so do not get confused and think the public key is only for encryption and the private key is only for decryption. They both have the capability to encrypt and decrypt data. However, if data are encrypted with a private key, they cannot be decrypted with a private key. If data are encrypted with a private key, they must be decrypted with the corresponding public key.

An asymmetric algorithm works much more slowly than a symmetric algorithm, because symmetric algorithms carry out relatively simplistic mathematical functions on the bits during the encryption and decryption processes. They substitute and scramble (transposition) bits, which is not overly difficult or processor-intensive. The reason it is hard to break this type of encryption is that the symmetric algorithms carry out this type of functionality over and over again. So a set of bits will go through a long series of being substituted and scrambled.

Asymmetric algorithms are slower than symmetric algorithms because they use much more complex mathematics to carry out their functions, which requires more processing time. Although they are slower, asymmetric algorithms can provide authentication and nonrepudiation, depending on the type of algorithm being used. Asymmetric systems also provide for easier and more manageable key distribution than symmetric systems and do not have the scalability issues of symmetric systems. The reason for these differences is that, with asymmetric systems, you can send out your public key to all of the people you need to communicate with, instead of keeping track of a unique key for each one of them. The "Hybrid Encryption Methods" section later in this chapter shows how these two systems can be used together to get the best of both worlds.

NOTE Public key cryptography is asymmetric cryptography. The terms can be used interchangeably.

The following list outlines the strengths and weaknesses of asymmetric key algorithms:

Strengths

- Better key distribution than symmetric systems
- Better scalability than symmetric systems
- Can provide authentication and nonrepudiation

Weaknesses

- Works much more slowly than symmetric systems
- Mathematically intensive tasks

The following are examples of asymmetric key algorithms:

- RSA (Rivest-Shamir-Adleman)
- Elliptic curve cryptosystem (ECC)
- Diffie-Hellman
- El Gamal
- Digital Signature Algorithm (DSA)
- Merkle-Hellman Knapsack

These algorithms will be explained further in the "Types of Asymmetric Systems" section later in the chapter.

Table 8-1 summarizes the differences between symmetric and asymmetric algorithms.

 NOTE Digital signatures will be discussed later in the section "Digital Signatures." (We like to keep it simple around here.)

Block and Stream Ciphers

Which should I use, the stream cipher or the block cipher?
Response: The stream cipher, because it makes you look skinnier.

The two main types of symmetric algorithms are block ciphers, which work on blocks of bits, and stream ciphers, which work on one bit at a time.

Attribute	Symmetric	Asymmetric
Keys	One key is shared between two or more entities.	One entity has a public key, and the other entity has the corresponding private key.
Key exchange	Out-of-band through secure mechanisms.	A public key is made available to everyone, and a private key is kept secret by the owner.
Speed	Algorithm is less complex and faster.	The algorithm is more complex and slower.
Use	Bulk encryption, which means encrypting files and communication paths.	Key distribution and digital signatures.
Security service provided	Confidentiality.	Authentication and nonrepudiation.

Table 8-1 Differences Between Symmetric and Asymmetric Systems

Block Ciphers

When a *block cipher* is used for encryption and decryption purposes, the message is divided into blocks of bits. These blocks are then put through mathematical functions, one block at a time. Suppose you need to encrypt a message you are sending to your mother and you are using a block cipher that uses 64 bits. Your message of 640 bits is chopped up into 10 individual blocks of 64 bits. Each block is put through a succession of mathematical formulas, and what you end up with is 10 blocks of encrypted text. You send this encrypted message to your mother. She has to have the same block cipher and key, and those 10 ciphertext blocks go back through the algorithm in the reverse sequence and end up in your plaintext message.

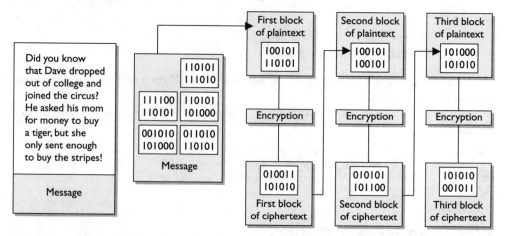

A strong cipher contains the right level of two main attributes: confusion and diffusion. *Confusion* is commonly carried out through substitution, while *diffusion* is carried out by using transposition. For a cipher to be considered strong, it must contain both of these attributes, to ensure that reverse-engineering is basically impossible. The randomness of the key values and the complexity of the mathematical functions dictate the level of confusion and diffusion involved.

In algorithms, diffusion takes place as individual bits of a block are scrambled, or diffused throughout that block. Confusion is provided by carrying out complex substitution functions so the bad guy cannot figure out how to substitute the right values and come up with the original plaintext. Suppose I have 500 wooden blocks with individual letters written on them. I line them all up to spell out a paragraph (plaintext). Then I substitute 300 of them with another set of 300 blocks (confusion through substitution). Then I scramble all of these blocks up (diffusion through transposition) and leave them in a pile. For you to figure out my original message, you would have to substitute the correct blocks and then put them back in the right order. Good luck.

Confusion pertains to making the relationship between the key and resulting ciphertext as complex as possible so the key cannot be uncovered from the ciphertext. Each ciphertext value should depend upon several parts of the key, but this mapping between the key values and the ciphertext values should seem completely random to the observer.

Diffusion, on the other hand, means that a single plaintext bit has influence over several of the ciphertext bits. Changing a plaintext value should change many ciphertext values, not just one. In fact, in a strong block cipher, if one plaintext bit is changed, it will change every ciphertext bit with the probability of 50 percent. This means that if one plaintext bit changes, then about half of the ciphertext bits will change.

Block ciphers use diffusion and confusion in their methods. Figure 8-12 shows a conceptual example of a simplistic block cipher. It has four block inputs, and each block is made up of four bits. The block algorithm has two layers of four-bit substitution boxes called *S-boxes*. Each S-box contains a lookup table used by the algorithm as instructions on how the bits should be encrypted.

Figure 8-12 shows that the key dictates what S-boxes are to be used when scrambling the original message from readable plaintext to encrypted nonreadable cipher text. Each S-box contains the different substitution methods that can be performed on each block. This example is simplistic—most block ciphers work with blocks of 32, 64, or 128 bits in size, and many more S-boxes are usually involved.

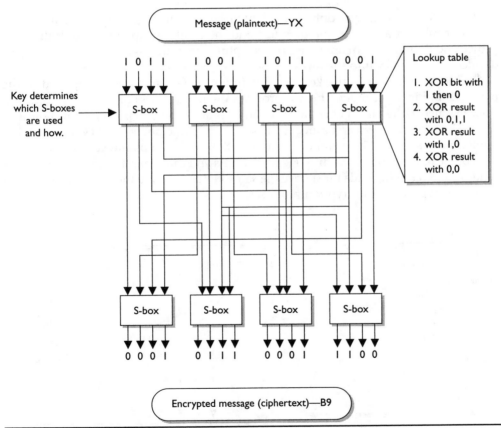

Figure 8-12 A message is divided into blocks of bits, and substitution and transposition functions are performed on those blocks.

Stream Ciphers

As stated earlier, a block cipher performs mathematical functions on blocks of bits. A stream cipher, on the other hand, does not divide a message into blocks. Instead, a *stream cipher* treats the message as a stream of bits and performs mathematical functions on each bit individually.

When using a stream cipher, a plaintext bit will be transformed into a different ciphertext bit each time it is encrypted. Stream ciphers use *keystream generators*, which produce a stream of bits that is XORed with the plaintext bits to produce ciphertext, as shown in Figure 8-13.

 NOTE This process is very similar to the one-time pad explained earlier. The individual bits in the one-time pad are used to encrypt the individual bits of the message through the XOR function, and in a stream algorithm the individual bits created by the keystream generator are used to encrypt the bits of the message through XOR also.

If the cryptosystem were only dependent upon the symmetric stream algorithm, an attacker could get a copy of the plaintext and the resulting ciphertext, XOR them together, and find the keystream to use in decrypting other messages. So the smart people decided to stick a key into the mix.

In block ciphers, it is the key that determines what functions are applied to the plaintext and in what order. The key provides the randomness of the encryption process. As stated earlier, most encryption algorithms are public, so people know how they work. The secret to the secret sauce is the key. In stream ciphers, the key also provides randomness, so that the stream of bits that is XORed to the plaintext is as random as possible. This concept is shown in Figure 8-14. As you can see in this graphic, both the sending and receiving ends must have the same key to generate the same keystream for proper encryption and decryption purposes.

Figure 8-13
With stream ciphers, the bits generated by the keystream generator are XORed with the bits of the plaintext message.

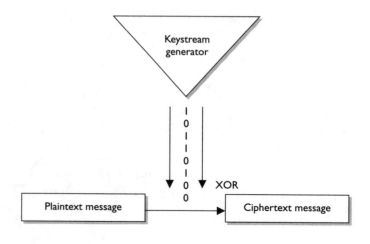

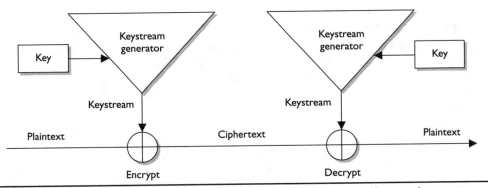

Figure 8-14   The sender and receiver must have the same key to generate the same keystream.

Initialization Vectors

Initialization vectors (IVs) are random values that are used with algorithms to ensure patterns are not created during the encryption process. They are used with keys and do not need to be encrypted when being sent to the destination. If IVs are not used, then two identical plaintext values that are encrypted with the same key will create the same ciphertext. Providing attackers with these types of patterns can make their job easier in breaking the encryption method and uncovering the key. For example, if we have the plaintext value of "See Spot run" two times within our message, we need to make sure that even though there is a pattern in the plaintext message, a pattern in the resulting ciphertext will not be created. So the IV and key are both used by the algorithm to provide more randomness to the encryption process.

A strong and effective stream cipher contains the following characteristics:

- **Long periods of no repeating patterns within keystream values**   Bits generated by the keystream must be random.

- **Statistically unpredictable keystream**   The bits generated from the keystream generator cannot be predicted.

- **A keystream not linearly related to the key**   If someone figures out the keystream values, that does not mean she now knows the key value.

- **Statistically unbiased keystream (as many 0's as 1's)**   There should be no dominance in the number of 0's or 1's in the keystream.

Stream ciphers require a lot of randomness and encrypt individual bits at a time. This requires more processing power than block ciphers require, which is why stream ciphers are better suited to be implemented at the hardware level. Because block ciphers do not require as much processing power, they can be easily implemented at the software level.

   NOTE   We do have block ciphers that work at the silicon level, and stream ciphers that work at the software level. The previous statement is just a "best practice" or guideline when it comes to development and implementation.

> ## Stream Ciphers vs. One-Time Pads
> Stream ciphers were developed to provide the same type of protection one-time pads do, which is why they work in such a similar manner. In reality, stream ciphers cannot provide the level of protection one-time pads do, but because stream ciphers are implemented through software and automated means, they are much more practical.

Hybrid Encryption Methods

Up to this point, we have figured out that symmetric algorithms are fast but have some drawbacks (lack of scalability, difficult key management, and they provide only confidentiality). Asymmetric algorithms do not have these drawbacks but are very slow. We just can't seem to win. So we turn to a hybrid system that uses symmetric and asymmetric encryption methods together.

Asymmetric and Symmetric Algorithms Used Together

Public key cryptography uses two keys (public and private) generated by an asymmetric algorithm for protecting encryption keys and key distribution, and a secret key is generated by a symmetric algorithm and used for bulk encryption. Then there is a hybrid use of the two different algorithms: asymmetric and symmetric. Each algorithm has its pros and cons, so using them together can be the best of both worlds.

In the hybrid approach, the two technologies are used in a complementary manner, with each performing a different function. A symmetric algorithm creates keys used for encrypting bulk data, and an asymmetric algorithm creates keys used for automated key distribution.

When a symmetric key is used for bulk data encryption, this key is used to encrypt the message you want to send. When your friend gets the message you encrypted, you want him to be able to decrypt it, so you need to send him the necessary symmetric key to use to decrypt the message. You do not want this key to travel unprotected, because if the message were intercepted and the key were not protected, an evildoer could intercept the message that contains the necessary key to decrypt your message and read your information. If the symmetric key needed to decrypt your message is not protected, there is no use in encrypting the message in the first place. So we use an asymmetric algorithm to encrypt the symmetric key, as depicted in Figure 8-15. Why do we use the symmetric key on the message and the asymmetric key on the symmetric key? As stated earlier, the asymmetric algorithm takes longer because the math is more complex. Because your message is most likely going to be longer than the length of the key, we use the faster algorithm (symmetric) on the message and the slower algorithm (asymmetric) on the key.

How does this actually work? Let's say Bill is sending Paul a message that Bill wants only Paul to be able to read. Bill encrypts his message with a secret key, so now Bill has ciphertext and a symmetric key. The key needs to be protected, so Bill encrypts the symmetric key with an asymmetric key. Remember that asymmetric algorithms use private and public keys, so Bill will encrypt the symmetric key with Paul's public key. Now Bill has ciphertext from the message and ciphertext from the symmetric key. Why did Bill encrypt the symmetric key with Paul's public key instead of his own private key? Because if Bill encrypted it with his own private key, then anyone with Bill's public key could decrypt it and retrieve the symmetric key. However, Bill does not want anyone who has his public key to read his message to Paul. Bill only wants Paul to be able to read it. So Bill encrypts the symmetric key with Paul's public key. If Paul has done a good job protecting his private key, he will be the only one who can read Bill's message.

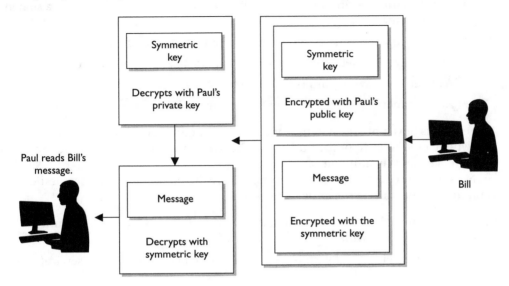

Paul receives Bill's message and Paul uses his private key to decrypt the symmetric key. Paul then uses the symmetric key to decrypt the message. Paul then reads Bill's very important and confidential message that asks Paul how his day is.

Now when I say that Bill is using this key to encrypt and that Paul is using that key to decrypt, those two individuals do not necessarily need to find the key on their hard drive and know how to properly apply it. We have software to do this for us—thank goodness.

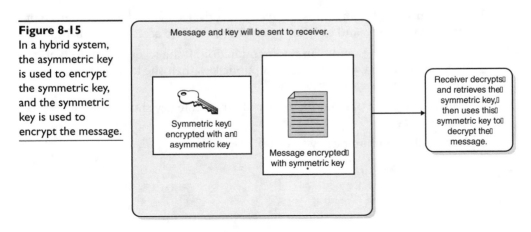

Figure 8-15 In a hybrid system, the asymmetric key is used to encrypt the symmetric key, and the symmetric key is used to encrypt the message.

If this is your first time with these issues and you are struggling, don't worry. I remember when I first started with these concepts, and they turned my brain into a pretzel. Just remember the following points:

- An asymmetric algorithm performs encryption and decryption by using public and private keys that are related to each other mathematically.
- A symmetric algorithm performs encryption and decryption by using a shared secret or key.
- A symmetric key is used to encrypt and/or decrypt the actual message.
- Public keys are used to encrypt the symmetric key for secure key exchange.
- A secret key is synonymous to a symmetric key.
- An asymmetric key refers to a public or private key.

So, that is how a hybrid system works. The symmetric algorithm creates a secret key that will be used to encrypt the bulk, or the message, and the asymmetric key encrypts the secret key for transmission.

Now to ensure that some of these concepts are driven home, ask these questions of yourself without reading the answers provided:

1. If a symmetric key is encrypted with a receiver's public key, what security service(s) is provided?
2. If data are encrypted with the sender's private key, what security service(s) is provided?
3. If the sender encrypts data with the receiver's private key, what security services(s) is provided?
4. Why do we encrypt the message with the symmetric key?
5. Why don't we encrypt the symmetric key with another symmetric key?
6. What is the meaning of life?

Answers

1. Confidentiality, because only the receiver's private key can be used to decrypt the symmetric key, and only the receiver should have access to this private key.
2. Authenticity of the sender and nonrepudiation. If the receiver can decrypt the encrypted data with the sender's public key, then she knows the data was encrypted with the sender's private key.
3. None, because no one but the owner of the private key should have access to it. Trick question.
4. Because the asymmetric key algorithm is too slow.

5. We need to get the necessary symmetric key to the destination securely, which can only be carried out through asymmetric cryptography through the use of public and private keys to provide a mechanism for secure transport of the symmetric key.

6. 42.

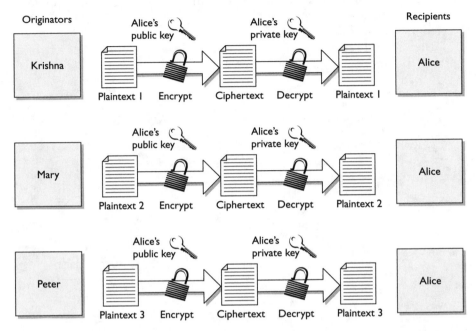

Session Keys

Hey, I have a disposable key!
Response: Amazing. Now go away.

A *session key* is a single-use symmetric key that is used to encrypt messages between two users during a communication session. A session key is no different from the symmetric key described in the previous section, but it is only good for one communication session between users.

If Tanya has a symmetric key she uses to always encrypt messages between Lance and herself, then this symmetric key would not be regenerated or changed. They would use the same key every time they communicated using encryption. However, using the same key repeatedly increases the chances of the key being captured and the secure communication being compromised. If, on the other hand, a new symmetric key were generated each time Lance and Tanya wanted to communicate, as shown in Figure 8-16, it would be used only during their one dialogue and then destroyed. If they wanted to communicate an hour later, a new session key would be created and shared.

Digital Envelopes

When cryptography is new to people, the process of using symmetric and asymmetric cryptography together can be a bit confusing. But it is important to understand these concepts, because they really are the core, fundamental concepts of all cryptography. This process is not just used in an e-mail client or in a couple of products—this is how it is done when data and a symmetric key must be protected in transmission.

The use of these two technologies together can be referred to as a hybrid approach, but more commonly as a *digital envelope*.

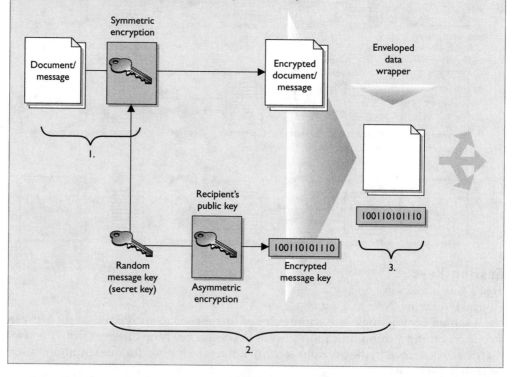

A session key provides more protection than static symmetric keys because it is valid for only one session between two computers. If an attacker were able to capture the session key, she would have a very small window of time to use it to try to decrypt messages being passed back and forth.

In cryptography, almost all data encryption takes place through the use of session keys. When you write an e-mail and encrypt it before sending it over the wire, it is actually being encrypted with a session key. If you write another message to the same person one minute later, a brand-new session key is created to encrypt that new message. So if an evildoer happens to figure out one session key, that does not mean she has access to all other messages you write and send off.

When two computers want to communicate using encryption, they must first go through a handshaking process. The two computers agree on the encryption algorithms

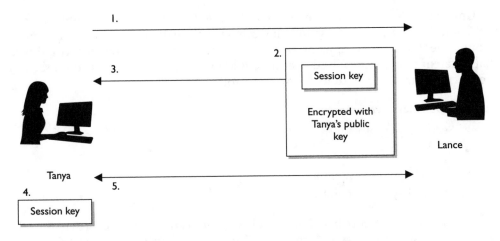

1) Tanya sends Lance her public key.
2) Lance generates a random session key and encrypts it using Tanya's public key.
3) Lance sends the session key, encrypted with Tanya's public key, to Tanya.
4) Tanya decrypts Lance's message with her private key and now has a copy of the session key.
5) Tanya and Lance use this session key to encrypt and decrypt messages to each other.

Figure 8-16 A session key is generated so all messages can be encrypted during one particular session between users.

that will be used and exchange the session key that will be used for data encryption. In a sense, the two computers set up a virtual connection between each other and are said to be in session. When this session is done, each computer tears down any data structures it built to enable this communication to take place, releases the resources, and destroys the session key. These things are taken care of by operating systems and applications in the background, so a user would not necessarily need to be worried about using the wrong type of key for the wrong reason. The software will handle this, but it is important for security professionals to understand the difference between the key types and the issues that surround them.

NOTE Private and symmetric keys should not be available in cleartext. This may seem obvious to you, but there have been several implementations over time that have allowed for this type of compromise to take place.

Wireless Security Woes

We covered the different 802.11 standards and the Wired Equivalent Privacy (WEP) protocol in Chapter 7. Among the long laundry list of security problems with WEP, not using unique session keys for data encryption is one of them. If only WEP is being used to encrypt wireless traffic, then in most implementations, just one static symmetric key is being used over and over again to encrypt the packets. This is one of the changes and advancements in the 802.11i standard, which makes sure each packet is encrypted with a unique session key.

Unfortunately, we don't always seem to be able to call an apple an apple. In many types of technology, the exact same thing can have more than one name. This could be because the different inventors of the technology had schizophrenia or it could mean that different terms just evolved over time that overlapped. Sadly, you could see symmetric cryptography referred to as any of the following:

- Single key cryptography
- Secret key cryptography
- Session key cryptography
- Private key cryptography
- Shared-key cryptography

We know the difference between secret keys (static) and session keys (dynamic), but what is this "single key" and "private key" mess? Well, using the term "single key" makes sense, because the sender and receiver are using one single key. I (the author) am saddened that the term "private key" can be used to describe symmetric cryptography because it only adds more confusion to the difference between symmetric cryptography (where one symmetric key is used) and asymmetric cryptography (where both a private and public key are used). But no one asked for or cares about my opinion, so we just need to remember this little quirk and still understand the difference between symmetric and asymmetric cryptography.

Types of Symmetric Systems

Several types of symmetric algorithms are used today. They have different methods of providing encryption and decryption functionality. The one thing they all have in common is that they are symmetric algorithms, meaning the sender and receiver are using two instances of the same key.

In this section, we will be walking through many of the following algorithms and their characteristics:

- Data Encryption Standard (DES)
- 3DES (Triple DES)
- Blowfish
- Twofish
- IDEA (International Data Encryption Algorithm)
- RC4, RC5, RC6
- AES (Advanced Encryption Standard)
- SAFER (Secure and Fast Encryption Routine)
- Serpent

Data Encryption Standard

Data Encryption Standard (DES) has had a long and rich history within the computer community. The National Institute of Standards and Technology (NIST) researched the need for the protection of sensitive but unclassified data during the 1960s and initiated a cryptography program in the early 1970s. NIST invited vendors to submit data encryption algorithms to be used as a cryptographic standard. IBM had already been developing encryption algorithms to protect financial transactions. In 1974, IBM's 128-bit algorithm, named *Lucifer*, was submitted and accepted. The NSA modified this algorithm to use a key size of 64 bits (with eight bits used for parity, resulting in an effective key length of 56 bits) instead of the original 128 bits, and named it the *Data Encryption Algorithm (DEA)*. Controversy arose about whether the NSA weakened Lucifer on purpose to enable it to decrypt messages not intended for it, but in the end the modified Lucifer became a national cryptographic standard in 1977 and an American National Standards Institute (ANSI) standard in 1978.

 NOTE   DEA is the algorithm that fulfills DES, which is really just a standard. So DES is the standard and DEA is the algorithm, but in the industry we usually just refer to it as DES. The CISSP exam may refer to the algorithm by either name, so remember both.

DES has been implemented in a majority of commercial products using cryptography functionality and in the applications of almost all government agencies. It was tested and approved as one of the strongest and most efficient cryptographic algorithms available. The continued overwhelming support of the algorithm is what caused the most confusion when the NSA announced in 1986 that, as of January 1988, the agency would no longer endorse DES and that DES-based products would no longer fall under compliance with Federal Standard 1027. The NSA felt that because DES had been so popular for so long, it would surely be targeted for penetration and become useless as an official standard. Many researchers disagreed, but NSA wanted to move on to a newer, more secure, and less popular algorithm as the new standard.

The NSA's decision to drop its support for DES caused major concern and negative feedback. At that time, it was shown that DES still provided the necessary level of protection; that projections estimated a computer would require thousands of years to crack DES; that DES was already embedded in thousands of products; and that there was no equivalent substitute. NSA reconsidered its decision and NIST ended up recertifying DES for another five years.

In 1998, the Electronic Frontier Foundation built a computer system for $250,000 that broke DES in three days by using a brute force attack against the keyspace. It contained 1,536 microprocessors running at 40MHz, which performed 60 million test decryptions per second per chip. Although most people do not have these types of systems to conduct such attacks, as Moore's Law holds true and microprocessors increase in processing power, this type of attack will become more feasible for the average attacker. This brought about 3DES, which provides stronger protection, as discussed later in the chapter.

DES was later replaced by the Rijndael algorithm as the *Advanced Encryption Standard (AES)* by NIST. This means that Rijndael is the new approved method of encrypting sensitive but unclassified information for the U.S. government; it has been accepted by, and is widely used in, the public arena today.

How Does DES Work?

How does DES work again?
Response: With voodoo magic and a dead chicken.

DES is a symmetric block encryption algorithm. When 64-bit blocks of plaintext go in, 64-bit blocks of ciphertext come out. It is also a symmetric algorithm, meaning the same key is used for encryption and decryption. It uses a 64-bit key: 56 bits make up the true key, and 8 bits are used for parity.

When the DES algorithm is applied to data, it divides the message into blocks and operates on them one at a time. The blocks are put through 16 rounds of transposition and substitution functions. The order and type of transposition and substitution functions depend on the value of the key used with the algorithm. The result is 64-bit blocks of ciphertext.

What Does It Mean When an Algorithm Is Broken?

I dropped my algorithm.
Response: Well, now it's broken.

As described in an earlier section, DES was finally broken with a dedicated computer lovingly named the DES Cracker (also known as Deep Crack). But what does "broken" really mean?

In most instances, an algorithm is broken if someone is able to uncover a key that was used during an encryption process. So let's say Kevin encrypted a message and sent it to Valerie. Marc captures this encrypted message and carries out a brute force attack on it, which means he tries to decrypt the message with different keys until he uncovers the right one. Once he identifies this key, the algorithm is considered broken. So does that mean the algorithm is worthless? It depends on who your enemies are.

If an algorithm is broken through a brute force attack, this just means the attacker identified the one key that was used for one instance of encryption. But in proper implementations, we should be encrypting data with session keys, which are good only for that one session. So even if the attacker uncovers one session key, it may be useless to the attacker, in which case he now has to work to identify a new session key.

If your information is of sufficient value that enemies or thieves would exert a lot of resources to break the encryption (as may be the case for financial transactions or military secrets), you would not use an algorithm that has been broken. If you are encrypting messages to your mother about a meatloaf recipe, you likely are not going to worry about whether the algorithm has been broken.

So breaking an algorithm can take place through brute force attacks or by identifying weaknesses in the algorithm itself. Brute force attacks have increased in potency because of the increased processing capacity of computers today. An algorithm that uses a 40-bit key has around 1 trillion possible key values. If a 56-bit key is used, then there are approximately 72 quadrillion different key values. This may seem like a lot, but relative to today's computing power, these key sizes do not provide much protection at all.

On a final note, algorithms are built on the current understanding of mathematics. As the human race advances in mathematics, the level of protection that today's algorithms provide may crumble.

DES Modes

Block ciphers have several modes of operation. Each mode specifies how a block cipher will operate. One mode may work better in one type of environment for specific functionality, whereas another mode may work better in another environment with totally different requirements. It is important that vendors who employ DES (or any block cipher) understand the different modes and which one to use for which purpose.

DES and other symmetric block ciphers have several distinct modes of operation that are used in different situations for different results. You just need to understand five of them:

- Electronic Code Book (ECB)
- Cipher Block Chaining (CBC)
- Cipher Feedback (CFB)
- Output Feedback (OFB)
- Counter Mode (CTR)

Electronic Code Book Mode   ECB mode operates like a code book. A 64-bit data block is entered into the algorithm with a key, and a block of ciphertext is produced. For a given block of plaintext and a given key, the same block of ciphertext is always produced. Not all messages end up in neat and tidy 64-bit blocks, so ECB incorporates padding to address this problem. ECB is the easiest and fastest mode to use, but as we will see, it has its dangers.

A key is basically instructions for the use of a code book that dictates how a block of text will be encrypted and decrypted. The code book provides the recipe of substitutions and permutations that will be performed on the block of plaintext. The security issue that comes up with using ECB mode is that each block will be encrypted with the exact same key, and thus the exact same code book. So, two bad things can happen here: an attacker could uncover the key and thus have the key to decrypt all the blocks of data, or an attacker could gather the ciphertext and plaintext of each block and build the code book that was used, without needing the key.

The crux of the problem is that there is not enough randomness to the process of encrypting the independent blocks, so if this mode is used to encrypt a large amount of data, it could be cracked more easily than the other modes that block ciphers can work in. So the next question to ask is, why even use this mode? This mode is the fastest and easiest, so we use it to encrypt small amounts of data, such as PINs, challenge-response values in authentication processes, and encrypting keys.

Because this mode works with blocks of data independently, data within a file does not have to be encrypted in a certain order. This is very helpful when using encryption in databases. A database has different pieces of data accessed in a random fashion. If it is encrypted in ECB mode, then any record or table can be added, encrypted, deleted, or decrypted independently of any other table or record. Other DES modes are dependent upon the text encrypted before them. This dependency makes it harder to encrypt and decrypt smaller amounts of text, because the previous encrypted text would need to be decrypted first. (Once we cover chaining in the next section, this dependency will make more sense.)

Because ECB mode does not use chaining, you should not use it to encrypt large amounts of data, because patterns would eventually show themselves.

Cipher Block Chaining Mode   In ECB mode, a block of plaintext and a key will always give the same ciphertext. This means that if the word "balloon" were encrypted and the resulting ciphertext were "hwicssn," each time it was encrypted using the same key, the same ciphertext would always be given. This can show evidence of a pattern, enabling an evildoer, with some effort, to discover the pattern and get a step closer to compromising the encryption process.

Cipher Block Chaining (CBC) does not reveal a pattern, because each block of text, the key, and the value based on the previous block are processed in the algorithm and applied to the next block of text, as shown in Figure 8-17. This results in more random ciphertext. Ciphertext is extracted and used from the previous block of text. This provides dependence between the blocks, in a sense chaining them together. This is where the name Cipher Block Chaining comes from, and it is this chaining effect that hides any patterns.

The results of one block are XORed with the next block before it is encrypted, meaning each block is used to modify the following block. This chaining effect means that a particular ciphertext block is dependent upon all blocks before it, not just the previous block.

As an analogy, let's say you have five buckets of marbles. Each bucket contains a specific color of marbles: red, blue, yellow, black, and green. The first bucket of red marbles (block of bits) you shake and tumble around (encrypt) to get them all mixed up. Then you take the second bucket of marbles, which are blue, and pour in the red marbles and go through the same exercise of shaking and tumbling them. You pour this bucket of marbles into your next bucket and shake them all up. This illustrates the incorporated randomness that is added when using chaining in a block encryption process.

When we encrypt our very first block using CBC, we do not have a previous block of ciphertext to "dump in" and use to add the necessary randomness to the encryption process. If we do not add a piece of randomness when encrypting this first block, then the bad guys could identify patterns, work backward, and uncover the key. So, we use an initialization vector (IVs were introduced previously in the "Initialization Vectors" section). The 64-bit IV is XORed with the first block of plaintext, and then it goes through its encryption process. The result of that (ciphertext) is XORed with the second block of plaintext, and then the second block is encrypted. This continues for the whole message. It is the chaining that adds the necessary randomness that allows us to use CBC mode to encrypt large files. Neither the individual blocks nor the whole message will show patterns that will allow an attacker to reverse-engineer and uncover the key.

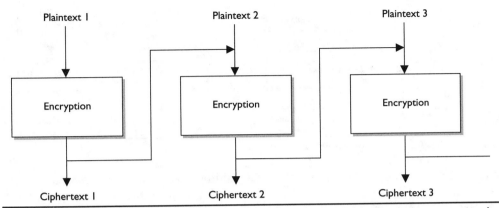

Figure 8-17 In CBC mode, the ciphertext from the previous block of data is used in encrypting the next block of data.

If we choose a different IV each time we encrypt a message, even if it is the same message, the ciphertext will always be unique. This means that if you send the same message out to 50 people and encrypt each one using a different IV, the ciphertext for each message will be different. Pretty nifty.

Cipher Feedback Mode   Sometimes block ciphers can emulate a stream cipher. Before we dig into how this would happen, let's first look at why. If you are going to send an encrypted e-mail to your boss, your e-mail client will use a symmetric block cipher working in CBC mode. The e-mail client would not use ECB mode, because most messages are long enough to show patterns that can be used to reverse-engineer the process and uncover the encryption key. The CBC mode is great to use when you need to send large chunks of data at a time. But what if you are not sending large chunks of data at one time, but instead are sending a steady stream of data to a destination? If you are working on a terminal that communicates with a back-end terminal server, what is really going on is that each keystroke and mouse movement you make is sent to the backend server in chunks of eight bits to be processed. So even though it seems as though the computer you are working on is carrying out your commands and doing the processing you are requesting, it is not—this is happening on the server. Thus, if you need to encrypt the data that go from your terminal to the terminal server, you could not use CBC mode because it only encrypts blocks of data 64 bits in size. You have blocks of eight bits you need to encrypt. So what do you know? We have just the mode for this type of situation!

Figure 8-18 illustrates how CFB mode works, which is really a combination of a block cipher and a stream cipher. For the first block of eight bits that needs to be encrypted, we do the same thing we did in CBC mode, which is to use an IV. Recall how stream ciphers work: The key and the IV are used by the algorithm to create a keystream, which is just a random set of bits. This set of bits is XORed to the block of plaintext, which results in the same size block of ciphertext. So the first block (eight bits) is XORed to the set of bits created through the keystream generator. Two things take place with this resulting eight-bit block of ciphertext. One copy goes over the wire to the destination (in our scenario, to the terminal server), and another copy is used to

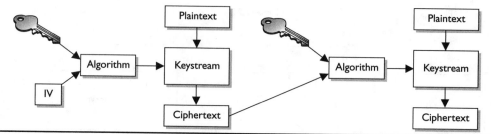

Figure 8-18 A block cipher working in CFB mode

encrypt the next block of eight-bit plaintext. Adding this copy of ciphertext to the encryption process of the next block adds more randomness to the encryption process.

We walked through a scenario where eight-bit blocks needed to be encrypted, but in reality CFB mode can be used to encrypt any size blocks, even blocks of just one bit. But since most of our encoding maps eight bits to one character, using CFB to encrypt eight-bit blocks is very common.

NOTE When using CBC mode, it is a good idea to use a unique IV value per message, but this is not necessary since the message being encrypted is usually very large. When using CFB mode, we are encrypting a smaller amount of data, so it is imperative a new IV value be used to encrypt each new stream of data.

Output Feedback Mode As you have read, you can use ECB mode for the process of encrypting small amounts of data, such as a key or PIN value. These components will be around 64 bits or more, so ECB mode works as a true block cipher. You can use CBC mode to encrypt larger amounts of data, in block sizes of 64 bits. In situations where you need to encrypt a smaller amount of data, you need the cipher to work like a stream cipher and to encrypt individual bits of the blocks, as in CFB. In some cases, you still need to encrypt a small amount of data at a time (one to eight bits), but you need to ensure possible errors do not affect your encryption and decryption processes.

If you look back at Figure 8-18, you see that the ciphertext from the previous block is used to encrypt the next block of plaintext. What if a bit in the first ciphertext gets corrupted? Then we have corrupted values going into the process of encrypting the next block of plaintext, and this problem just continues because of the use of chaining in this mode. Now look at Figure 8-19. It looks terribly similar to Figure 8-18, but notice that the values used to encrypt the next block of plaintext are coming directly from the keystream, not from the resulting ciphertext. This is the difference between the two modes.

If you need to encrypt something that would be very sensitive to these types of errors, such as digitized video or digitized voice signals, you should not use CFB mode. You should use OFB mode instead, which reduces the chance that these types of bit corruptions can take place.

So OFB is a mode that a block cipher can work in when it needs to emulate a stream, because it encrypts small amounts of data at a time, but it has a smaller chance of creating and extending errors throughout the full encryption process.

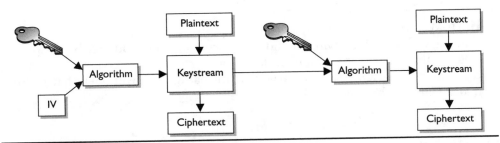

Figure 8-19   A block cipher working in OFB mode

To ensure OFB and CFB are providing the most protection possible, the size of the ciphertext (in CFB) or keystream values (in OFB) needs to be the same size as the block of plaintext being encrypted. This means that if you are using CFB and are encrypting eight bits at a time, the ciphertext you bring forward from the previous encryption block needs to be eight bits. Otherwise, you are repeating values over and over, which introduces patterns. (This is the same reason why a one-time pad should be used only one time and should be as long as the message itself.)

Counter Mode   Counter Mode (CTR) is very similar to OFB mode, but instead of using a randomly unique IV value to generate the keystream values, this mode uses an IV counter that increments for each plaintext block that needs to be encrypted. The unique counter ensures that each block is XORed with a unique keystream value.

The other difference is that there is no chaining involved, which means no ciphertext is brought forward to encrypt the next block. Since there is no chaining, the encryption of the individual blocks can happen in parallel, which increases the performance. The main reason CTR would be used instead of the other modes is performance.

This mode has been around for quite some time and is used in encrypting ATM cells for virtual circuits, in IPSec, and is now integrated in the new wireless security standard, 802.11i. A developer would choose to use this mode in these situations because individual ATM cells or packets going through an IPSec tunnel or over radio frequencies may not arrive at the destination in order. Since chaining is not involved, the destination can decrypt and begin processing the packets without having to wait for the full message to arrive and *then* decrypt all the data.

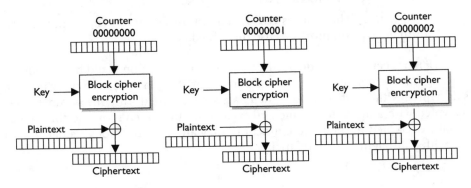

> ### Here We Are
> If this is your first time trying to understand cryptography, you may be exasperated by now. Don't get too uptight. Many people are new to cryptography, because all of this magic just seems to work in the background without us having to understand it or mess with it.

Triple-DES

We went from DES to Triple-DES (3DES), so it might seem we skipped Double-DES. We did. Double-DES has a key length of 112 bits, but there is a specific attack against Double-DES that reduces its work factor to about the same as DES. Thus, it is no more secure than DES. So let's move on to 3DES.

Many successful attacks against DES and the realization that the useful lifetime of DES was about up brought much support for 3DES. NIST knew that a new standard had to be created, which ended up being AES, but a quick fix was needed in the meantime to provide more protection for sensitive data. The result: 3DES (also known as TDEA—Triple Data Encryption Algorithm).

3DES uses 48 rounds in its computation, which makes it highly resistant to differential cryptanalysis. However, because of the extra work 3DES performs, there is a heavy performance hit. It can take up to three times longer than DES to perform encryption and decryption.

Although NIST has selected the Rijndael algorithm to replace DES as the AES, NIST and others expect 3DES to be around and used for quite some time.

3DES can work in different modes, and the mode chosen dictates the number of keys used and what functions are carried out:

- **DES-EEE3** Uses three different keys for encryption, and the data are encrypted, encrypted, encrypted.
- **DES-EDE3** Uses three different keys for encryption, and the data are encrypted, decrypted, and encrypted.
- **DES-EEE2** The same as DES-EEE3 but uses only two keys, and the first and third encryption processes use the same key.
- **DES-EDE2** The same as DES-EDE3 but uses only two keys, and the first and third encryption processes use the same key.

EDE may seem a little odd at first. How much protection could be provided by encrypting something, decrypting it, and encrypting it again? The decrypting portion here is decrypted with a different key. When data are encrypted with one symmetric key and decrypted with a different symmetric key, it is jumbled even more. So the data are not actually decrypted in the middle function, they are just run through a decryption process with a different key. Pretty tricky.

The Advanced Encryption Standard

After DES was used as an encryption standard for over 20 years and it was cracked in a relatively short time once the necessary technology was available, NIST decided a new standard, the Advanced Encryption Standard (AES), needed to be put into place. In January 1997, NIST announced its request for AES candidates and outlined the requirements in FIPS PUB 197. AES was to be a symmetric block cipher supporting key sizes of 128, 192, and 256 bits. The following five algorithms were the finalists:

- **MARS**   Developed by the IBM team that created Lucifer
- **RC6**   Developed by RSA Laboratories
- **Serpent**   Developed by Ross Anderson, Eli Biham, and Lars Knudsen
- **Twofish**   Developed by Counterpane Systems
- **Rijndael**   Developed by Joan Daemen and Vincent Rijmen

Out of these contestants, Rijndael was chosen. The block sizes that Rijndael supports are 128, 192, and 256 bits. The number of rounds depends upon the size of the block and the key length:

- If both the key and block size are 128 bits, there are 10 rounds.
- If both the key and block size are 192 bits, there are 12 rounds.
- If both the key and block size are 256 bits, there are 14 rounds.

Rijndael works well when implemented in software and hardware in a wide range of products and environments. It has low memory requirements and has been constructed to easily defend against timing attacks.

Rijndael was NIST's choice to replace DES. It is now the algorithm required to protect sensitive but unclassified U.S. government information.

 NOTE   DEA is the algorithm used within DES, and Rijndael is the algorithm used in AES. In the industry, we refer to these as DES and AES instead of by the actual algorithms.

International Data Encryption Algorithm

International Data Encryption Algorithm (IDEA) is a block cipher and operates on 64-bit blocks of data. The 64-bit data block is divided into 16 smaller blocks, and each has eight rounds of mathematical functions performed on it. The key is 128 bits long, and IDEA is faster than DES when implemented in software.

The IDEA algorithm offers different modes similar to the modes described in the DES section, but it is considered to be harder to break than DES because it has a longer key size. IDEA is used in the PGP and other encryption software implementations. It was thought to replace DES, but it is patented, meaning that licensing fees would have to be paid to use it.

As of this writing, there have been no successful practical attacks against this algorithm, although there have been numerous attempts.

Blowfish

One fish, two fish, red fish, blowfish.
Response: Hmm, I thought it was blue fish.

Blowfish is a block cipher that works on 64-bit blocks of data. The key length can be anywhere from 32 bits up to 448 bits, and the data blocks go through 16 rounds of cryptographic functions. It was intended as a replacement to the aging DES. While many of the other algorithms have been proprietary and thus encumbered by patents or kept as government secrets, this wasn't the case with Blowfish. Bruce Schneier, the creator of Blowfish, has stated, "Blowfish is un-patented, and will remain so in all countries. The algorithm is hereby placed in the public domain, and can be freely used by anyone."

RC4

RC4 is one of the most commonly implemented stream ciphers. It has a variable key size, is used in the SSL protocol, and was (improperly) implemented in the 802.11 WEP protocol standard. RC4 was developed in 1987 by Ron Rivest and was considered a trade secret of RSA Data Security, Inc. until someone posted the source code on a mailing list. Since the source code was released nefariously, the stolen algorithm is sometimes implemented and referred to as ArcFour or ARC4 because the title RC4 is trademarked.

The algorithm is very simple, fast, and efficient, which is why it became so popular.

RC5

RC5 is a block cipher that has a variety of parameters it can use for block size, key size, and the number of rounds used. It was created by Ron Rivest and analyzed by RSA Data Security, Inc. The block sizes used in this algorithm are 32, 64, or 128 bits, and the key size goes up to 2,048 bits. The number of rounds used for encryption and decryption is also variable. The number of rounds can go up to 255.

RC6

RC6 is a block cipher that was built upon RC5, so it has all the same attributes as RC5. The algorithm was developed mainly to be submitted as AES, but Rijndael was chosen instead. There were some modifications of the RC5 algorithm to increase the overall speed, the result of which is RC6.

Cryptography Notation

In some resources, you may run across *rc5-w/r/b* or *RC5-32/12/16*. This is a type of shorthand that describes the configuration of the algorithm.

- w = Word size, in bits, which can be 16, 32, or 64 bits in length
- r = Number of rounds, which can be 0 to 255

So *RC5-32/12/16* would mean the following:

- 32-bit words, which means it encrypts 64-bit data blocks
- Using 12 rounds
- With a 16-byte (128-bit) key

A developer configures these parameters (words, number of rounds, key size) for the algorithm for specific implementations. The existence of these parameters gives developers extensive flexibility.

Types of Asymmetric Systems

As described earlier in the chapter, using purely symmetric key cryptography has three drawbacks, which affect the following:

- **Security services** Purely symmetric key cryptography provides confidentiality only, not authentication or nonrepudiation.
- **Scalability** As the number of people who need to communicate increases, so does the number of symmetric keys required, meaning more keys must be managed.
- **Secure key distribution** The symmetric key must be delivered to its destination through a secure courier.

Despite these drawbacks, symmetric key cryptography was all that the computing society had available for encryption for quite some time. Symmetric and asymmetric cryptography did not arrive on the same day or even in the same decade. We dealt with the issues surrounding symmetric cryptography for quite some time, waiting for someone smarter to come along and save us from some of this grief.

The Diffie-Hellman Algorithm

The first group to address the shortfalls of symmetric key cryptography decided to attack the issue of secure distribution of the symmetric key. Whitfield Diffie and Martin Hellman worked on this problem and ended up developing the first asymmetric key agreement algorithm, called, naturally, Diffie-Hellman.

To understand how Diffie-Hellman works, consider an example. Let's say that Tanya and Erika would like to communicate over an encrypted channel by using Diffie-Hellman. They would both generate a private and public key pair and exchange public keys. Tanya's software would take her private key (which is just a numeric value) and Erika's public key (another numeric value) and put them through the Diffie-Hellman algorithm. Erika's software would take her private key and Tanya's public key and insert them into the Diffie-Hellman algorithm on her computer. Through this process, Tanya and Erika derive the same shared value, which is used to create instances of symmetric keys.

So, Tanya and Erika exchanged information that did not need to be protected (their public keys) over an untrusted network, and in turn generated the exact same symmetric key on each system. They both can now use these symmetric keys to encrypt, transmit, and decrypt information as they communicate with each other.

NOTE The preceding example describes key *agreement*, which is different from key *exchange*, the functionality used by the other asymmetric algorithms that will be discussed in this chapter. With key exchange functionality, the sender encrypts the symmetric key with the receiver's public key before transmission.

The Diffie-Hellman algorithm enables two systems to exchange a symmetric key securely without requiring a previous relationship or prior arrangements. The algorithm allows for key distribution, but does not provide encryption or digital signature functionality. The algorithm is based on the difficulty of calculating discrete logarithms in a finite field.

The original Diffie-Hellman algorithm is vulnerable to a man-in-the-middle attack, because no authentication occurs before public keys are exchanged. In our example, when Tanya sends her public key to Erika, how does Erika really know it is Tanya's public key? What if Lance spoofed his identity, told Erika he was Tanya, and sent over his key? Erika would accept this key, thinking it came from Tanya. Let's walk through the steps of how this type of attack would take place, as illustrated in Figure 8-20:

1. Tanya sends her public key to Erika, but Lance grabs the key during transmission so it never makes it to Erika.

2. Lance spoofs Tanya's identity and sends over his public key to Erika. Erika now thinks she has Tanya's public key.

3. Erika sends her public key to Tanya, but Lance grabs the key during transmission so it never makes it to Tanya.

4. Lance spoofs Erika's identity and sends over his public key to Tanya. Tanya now thinks she has Erika's public key.

5. Tanya combines her private key and Lance's public key and creates symmetric key S1.

6. Lance combines his private key and Tanya's public key and creates symmetric key S1.

7. Erika combines her private key and Lance's public key and creates symmetric key S2.

8. Lance combines his private key and Erika's public key and creates symmetric key S2.

9. Now Tanya and Lance share a symmetric key (S1) and Erika and Lance share a different symmetric key (S2). Tanya and Erika think they are sharing a key between themselves and do not realize Lance is involved.

10. Tanya writes a message to Erika, uses her symmetric key (S1) to encrypt the message, and sends it.

11. Lance grabs the message and decrypts it with symmetric key S1, reads or modifies the message and re-encrypts it with symmetric key S2, and then sends it to Erika.

12. Erika takes symmetric key S2 and uses it to decrypt and read the message.

The countermeasure to this type of attack is to have authentication take place before accepting someone's public key, which usually happens through the use of digital signatures and digital certificates.

NOTE Although the Diffie-Hellman algorithm is vulnerable to a man-in-the-middle attack, it does not mean this type of compromise can take place anywhere this algorithm is deployed. Most implementations include another piece of software or a protocol that compensates for this vulnerability. But some do not. As a security professional, you should understand these issues.

Figure 8-20
A man-in-the-middle
attack

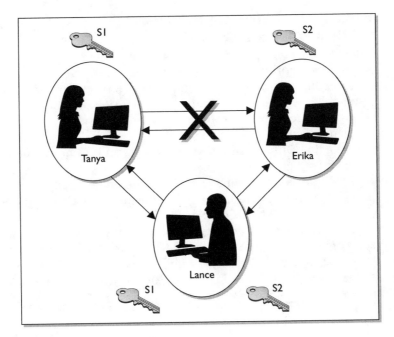

NOTE MQV (Menezes-Qu-Vanstone) is an authentication key agreement cryptography function very similar to Diffie-Hellman. The users' public keys are exchanged to create session keys. It provides protection from an attacker figuring out the session key because she would need to have both users' private keys.

RSA

Give me an R, give me an S, give me an . . . How do you spell "RSA" again?
Response: Sigh.

RSA, named after its inventors Ron Rivest, Adi Shamir, and Leonard Adleman, is a public key algorithm that is the most popular when it comes to asymmetric algorithms. RSA is a worldwide de facto standard and can be used for digital signatures, key exchange, and encryption. It was developed in 1978 at MIT and provides authentication as well as key encryption.

The security of this algorithm comes from the difficulty of factoring large numbers. The public and private keys are functions of a pair of large prime numbers, and the necessary activity required to decrypt a message from ciphertext to plaintext using a private key is comparable to factoring a product into two prime numbers.

NOTE A prime number is a positive whole number with no proper divisors, meaning the only numbers that can divide a prime number are 1 and the number itself.

What Is the Difference Between Public Key Cryptography and Public Key Infrastructure?

Public key cryptography is the use of an asymmetric algorithm. Thus, the terms asymmetric algorithm and public key cryptography are interchangeable and mean the same thing. Examples of asymmetric algorithms are RSA, elliptic curve cryptosystem (ECC), Diffie-Hellman, El Gamal, LUC, and Knapsack. These algorithms are used to create public/private key pairs, perform key exchange or agreement, and generate and verify digital signatures.

Note that Diffie-Hellman can only perform key agreement and cannot generate or verify digital signatures.

Public key infrastructure (PKI) is a different animal. It is not an algorithm, a protocol, or an application—it is an infrastructure based on public key cryptography. Let's look at why we even need PKIs today. When Erika needs to send Tanya a symmetric key securely, she must obtain Tanya's public key. Erika could get the key from a public repository that holds public keys for many individuals, but if Lance has switched out Tanya's public key and inserted his own, when Erika acquires a key she thinks is Tanya's, she actually receives Lance's key and Erika has no idea.

One advantage of using RSA is that it can be used for encryption and digital signatures. Using its one-way function, RSA provides encryption and signature verification, and the inverse direction performs decryption and signature generation.

RSA has been implemented in applications; in operating systems by Microsoft, Apple, Sun, and Novell; and at the hardware level in network interface cards, secure telephones, and smart cards. It can be used as a *key exchange protocol*, meaning it is used to encrypt the symmetric key to get it securely to its destination. RSA has been most commonly used with the symmetric algorithm DES, which is quickly being replaced with AES. So, when RSA is used as a key exchange protocol, a cryptosystem generates a symmetric key using either the DES or AES algorithm. Then the system encrypts the symmetric key with the receiver's public key and sends it to the receiver. The symmetric key is protected because only the individual with the corresponding private key can decrypt and extract the symmetric key.

Diving into Numbers

Cryptography is really all about using mathematics to scramble bits into an undecipherable form and then using the same mathematics in reverse to put the bits back into a form that can be understood by computers and people. RSA's mathematics are based on the difficulty of factoring a large integer into its two prime factors. Put on your nerdy hat with the propeller and let's look at how this algorithm works.

The algorithm creates a public key and a private key from a function of large prime numbers. When data are encrypted with a public key, only the corresponding private key can decrypt the data. This act of decryption is basically the same as factoring the product of two prime numbers. So, let's say I have a secret (encrypted message), and for you to be able to uncover the secret, you have to take a specific large number and factor it and come up with the two numbers I have written down on a piece of paper. This may sound simplistic, but the number you must properly factor can be 2^{300} in size. Not as easy as you may think.

The following sequence describes how the RSA algorithm comes up with the keys in the first place:

1. Choose two random large prime numbers, p and q.

2. Generate the product of these numbers: $n = pq$.

   Choose a random integer to be the encryption key, e. Make sure that e and $(p - 1)(q - 1)$ are relatively prime.

3. Compute the decryption key, d. This is $ed = 1 \mod (p - 1)(q - 1)$ or $d = e^{-1} \mod ([p - 1][q - 1])$.

4. The public key = (n, e).

5. The private key = (n, d).

6. The original prime numbers p and q are discarded securely.

We now have our public and private keys, but how do they work together?

If you need to encrypt message *m* with your public key (*e*, *n*), the following formula is carried out:

$C = m^e \bmod n$

Then you need to decrypt the message with your private key (*d*), so the following formula is carried out:

$M = c^d \bmod n$

You may be thinking, "Well, I don't understand these formulas, but they look simple enough. Why couldn't someone break these small formulas and uncover the encryption key?" Maybe someone will one day. As the human race advances in its understanding of mathematics and as processing power increases and cryptanalysis evolves, the RSA algorithm may be broken one day. If we were to figure out how to quickly and more easily factor large numbers into their original prime values, all of these cards would fall down, and this algorithm would no longer provide the security it does today. But we have not hit that bump in the road yet, so we are all happily using RSA in our computing activities.

One-Way Functions

A *one-way function* is a mathematical function that is easier to compute in one direction than in the opposite direction. An analogy of this is when you drop a glass on the floor. Although dropping a glass on the floor is easy, putting all the pieces back together again to reconstruct the original glass is next to impossible. This concept is similar to how a one-way function is used in cryptography, which is what the RSA algorithm, and all other asymmetric algorithms, is based upon.

The easy direction of computation in the one-way function that is used in the RSA algorithm is the process of multiplying two large prime numbers. Multiplying the two numbers to get the resulting product is much easier than factoring the product and recovering the two initial large prime numbers used to calculate the obtained product, which is the difficult direction. RSA is based on the difficulty of factoring large numbers that are the product of two large prime numbers. Attacks on these types of cryptosystems do not necessarily try every possible key value, but rather try to factor the large number, which will give the attacker the private key.

When a user encrypts a message with a public key, this message is encoded with a one-way function (breaking a glass). This function supplies a *trapdoor* (knowledge of how to put the glass back together), but the only way the trapdoor can be taken advantage of is if it is known about and the correct code is applied. The private key provides this service. The private key knows about the trapdoor, knows how to derive the original prime numbers, and has the necessary programming code to take advantage of this secret trapdoor to unlock the encoded message (reassembling the broken glass). Knowing about the trapdoor and having the correct functionality to take advantage of it are what make the private key private.

When a one-way function is carried out in the easy direction, encryption and digital signature verification functionality are available. When the one-way function is carried out in the hard direction, decryption and signature generation functionality are available. This means only the public key can carry out encryption and signature verification and only the private key can carry out decryption and signature generation.

As explained earlier in this chapter, *work factor* is the amount of time and resources it would take for someone to break an encryption method. In asymmetric algorithms, the work factor relates to the difference in time and effort that carrying out a one-way function in the easy direction takes compared to carrying out a one-way function in the hard direction. In most cases, the larger the key size, the longer it would take for the bad guy to carry out the one-way function in the hard direction (decrypt a message).

The crux of this section is that all asymmetric algorithms provide security by using mathematical equations that are easy to perform in one direction and next to impossible to perform in the other direction. The "hard" direction is based on a "hard" mathematical problem. RSA's hard mathematical problem requires factoring large numbers into their original prime numbers. Diffie-Hellman and El Gamal are based on the difficulty of calculating logarithms in a finite field.

El Gamal

El Gamal is a public key algorithm that can be used for digital signatures, encryption, and key exchange. It is based not on the difficulty of factoring large numbers but on calculating discrete logarithms in a finite field. El Gamal is actually an extension of the Diffie-Hellman algorithm.

Although El Gamal provides the same type of functionality as some of the other asymmetric algorithms, its main drawback is performance. When compared to other algorithms, this algorithm is usually the slowest.

Elliptic Curve Cryptosystems

Elliptic curves. That just sounds like fun.

Elliptic curves are rich mathematical structures that have shown usefulness in many different types of applications. An *elliptic curve cryptosystem (ECC)* provides much of the same functionality RSA provides: digital signatures, secure key distribution, and encryption. One differing factor is ECC's efficiency. ECC is more efficient than RSA and any other asymmetric algorithm.

Figure 8-21 is an example of an elliptic curve. In this field of mathematics, points on the curves compose a structure called a group. These points are the values used in mathematical formulas for ECC's encryption and decryption processes. The algorithm computes discrete logarithms of elliptic curves, which is different from calculating discrete logarithms in a finite field (which is what Diffie-Hellman and El Gamal use).

Some devices have limited processing capacity, storage, power supply, and bandwidth, such as wireless devices and cellular telephones. With these types of devices, efficiency of resource use is very important. ECC provides encryption functionality, requiring a smaller percentage of the resources needed by RSA and other algorithms, so it is used in these types of devices.

In most cases, the longer the key, the more protection that is provided, but ECC can provide the same level of protection with a key size that is shorter than what RSA requires. Because longer keys require more resources to perform mathematical tasks, the smaller keys used in ECC require fewer resources of the device.

Figure 8-21
Elliptic curves

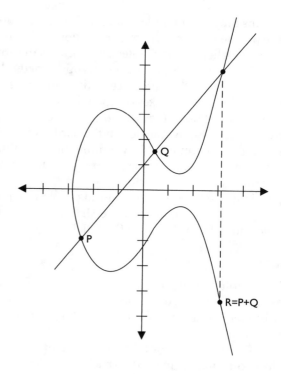

LUC

This algorithm is based on "Lucas sequences" and implements a discrete logarithm in a finite field, but by using the Lucas sequences, computation may take place more quickly.

Knapsack

Over the years, different versions of knapsack algorithms have arisen. The first to be developed, Merkle-Hellman, could be used only for encryption, but it was later improved upon to provide digital signature capabilities. These types of algorithms are based on the "knapsack problem," a mathematical dilemma that poses the following question: If you have several different items, each having its own weight, is it possible to add these items to a knapsack so the knapsack has a specific weight?

This algorithm was discovered to be insecure and is not currently used in cryptosystems.

Zero Knowledge Proof

Total knowledge zero. Yep, that's how I feel after reading all of this cryptography stuff!
Response: Just put your head between your knees and breathe slowly.

When military representatives are briefing the news media about some big world event, they have one goal in mind: to tell the story that the public is supposed to hear and nothing more. Do not provide extra information that someone could use to infer more information than they are supposed to know. The military has this goal because it knows that not just the good guys are watching CNN. This is an example of *zero knowledge proof*. You tell someone just the information they need to know without "giving up the farm."

Zero knowledge proof is used in cryptography also. If I encrypt something with my private key, you can verify my private key was used by decrypting the data with my public key. By encrypting something with my private key, I am proving to you I have my private key—but I do not give or show you my private key. I do not "give up the farm" by disclosing my private key. In a zero knowledge proof, the verifier cannot prove to another entity that this proof is real, because he does not have the private key to prove it. So, only the owner of the private key can prove he has possession of the key.

Message Integrity

My message was altered, thus it has character flaws.
Response: So do you.

Parity bits and cyclic redundancy check (CRC) functions have been used in protocols to detect modifications in streams of bits as they are passed from one computer to another, but they can usually detect only unintentional modifications. Unintentional modifications can happen if a spike occurs in the power supply, if there is interference or attenuation on a wire, or if some other type of physical condition happens that causes the corruption of bits as they travel from one destination to another. Parity bits cannot identify whether a message was captured by an intruder, altered, and then sent on to the intended destination. The intruder can just recalculate a new parity value that includes his changes, and the receiver would never know the difference. For this type of protection, hash algorithms are required to successfully detect intentional and unintentional unauthorized modifications to data. We will now dive into hash algorithms and their characteristics.

The One-Way Hash

Now, how many times does the one-way hash run again?
Response: One, brainiac.

A *one-way hash* is a function that takes a variable-length string and a message and produces a fixed-length value called a hash value. For example, if Kevin wants to send a message to Maureen and he wants to ensure the message does not get altered in an unauthorized fashion while it is being transmitted, he would calculate a hash value for the message and append it to the message itself. When Maureen receives the message, she performs the same hashing function Kevin used and then compares her result with the hash value sent with the message. If the two values are the same, Maureen can be sure the message was not altered during transmission. If the two values are different, Maureen knows the message was altered, either intentionally or unintentionally, and she discards the message.

The hashing algorithm is not a secret—it is publicly known. The secrecy of the one-way hashing function is its "one-wayness." The function is run in only one direction, not the other direction. This is different from the one-way function used in public key cryptography, in which security is provided based on the fact that, without knowing a trapdoor, it is very hard to perform the one-way function backward on a message and come up with readable plaintext. However, one-way hash functions are never used in reverse; they create a hash value and call it a day. The receiver does not attempt to reverse the process at the other end, but instead runs the same hashing function one way and compares the two results.

The hashing one-way function takes place without the use of any keys. This means, for example, that if Cheryl writes a message, calculates a message digest, appends the digest to the message, and sends it on to Scott, Bruce can intercept this message, alter Cheryl's message, recalculate another message digest, append it to the message, and send it on to Scott. When Scott receives it, he verifies the message digest, but never knows the message was actually altered by Bruce. Scott thinks the message came straight from Cheryl and it was never modified, because the two message digest values are the same. If Cheryl wanted more protection than this, she would need to use *message authentication code (MAC)*.

A MAC function is an authentication scheme derived by applying a secret key to a message in some form. This does not mean the symmetric key is used to encrypt the message, though. You should be aware of three basic types of MACs: a hash MAC (HMAC) and a CBC-MAC.

HMAC

In the previous example, if Cheryl were to use an HMAC function instead of just a plain hashing algorithm, a symmetric key would be concatenated with her message. The result of this process would be put through a hashing algorithm, and the result would be a MAC value. This MAC value is then appended to her message and sent to Scott. If Bruce were to intercept this message and modify it, he would not have the necessary symmetric key to create the MAC value that Scott will attempt to generate. Figure 8-22 walks through these steps.

Why Can't We Call an Apple an Apple?

The idea of a hashing function is simple. You run a message through a hashing algorithm, which in turn generates a hashing value. It must have been too simple, because someone threw in a lot of terms to make it more confusing:

- A hashing value can also be called a *message digest* or *fingerprint*.
- Hashing algorithms are also called *nonkeyed message digests*.
- Two types of message authentication code (MAC) exist: hashed MAC (HMAC) and CBC-MAC.
- MAC is also sometimes called *message integrity code (MIC)* or *modification detection code (MDC)*.

Good luck, and may the force be with you.

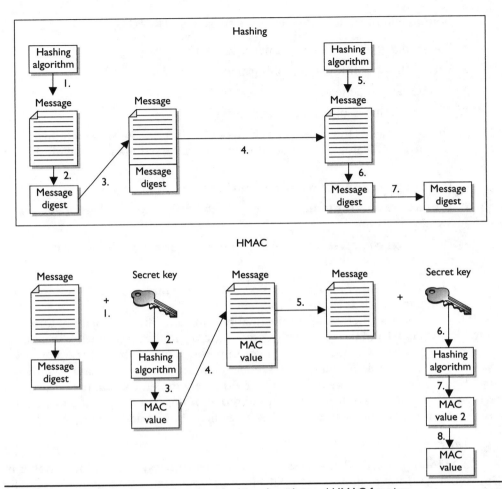

Figure 8-22 The steps involved in using a hashing algorithm and HMAC function

The top portion of Figure 8-22 shows the steps of a hashing process:

1. The sender puts the message through a hashing function.
2. A message digest value is generated.
3. The message digest is appended to the message.
4. The sender sends the message to the receiver.
5. The receiver puts the message through a hashing function.
6. The receiver generates her own message digest value.
7. The receiver compares the two message digest values. If they are the same, the message has not been altered.

The bottom half of Figure 8-22 shows the steps of an HMAC:

1. The sender concatenates a symmetric key with the message.
2. The result is put through a hashing algorithm.
3. A MAC value is generated.
4. The MAC value is appended to the message.
5. The sender sends the message to the receiver. (Just the message with the attached MAC value. The sender does not send the symmetric key with the message.)
6. The receiver concatenates a symmetric key with the message.
7. The receiver puts the results through a hashing algorithm and generates her own MAC value.
8. The receiver compares the two MAC values. If they are the same, the message has not been modified.

Now, when we say that the message is concatenated with a symmetric key, we don't mean a symmetric key is used to encrypt the message. The message is not encrypted in an HMAC function, so there is no confidentiality being provided. Think about throwing a message in a bowl and then throwing a symmetric key in the same bowl. If you dump the contents of the bowl into a hashing algorithm, the result will be a MAC value.

This type of technology requires the sender and receiver to have the same symmetric key. The HMAC function does not involve getting the symmetric key to the destination securely. That would have to happen through one of the other technologies we have discussed already (Diffie-Hellman and key agreement, or RSA and key exchange).

CBC-MAC

If a CBC-MAC is being used, the message is encrypted with a symmetric block cipher in CBC mode, and the output of the final block of ciphertext is used as the MAC. The sender does not send the encrypted version of the message, but instead sends the plaintext version and the MAC attached to the message. The receiver receives the plaintext message and encrypts it with the same symmetric block cipher in CBC mode and calculates an independent MAC value. The receiver compares the new MAC value with the MAC value sent with the message. This method does not use a hashing algorithm as does HMAC.

The use of the symmetric key ensures that the only person who can verify the integrity of the message is the person who has a copy of this key. No one else can verify the data's integrity, and if someone were to make a change to the data, he could not generate the MAC value (HMAC or CBC-MAC) the receiver would be looking for. Any modifications would be detected by the receiver.

Now the receiver knows that the message came from the system that has the other copy of the same symmetric key, so MAC provides a form of authentication. It provides *data origin authentication*, sometimes referred to as *system authentication*. This is different from user authentication, which would require the use of a private key. A private key is bound to an individual; a symmetric key is not. MAC authentication provides the weakest form of authentication because it is not bound to a user, just to a computer or device.

> **NOTE** The same key should not be used for authentication and encryption.

As with most things in security, the industry found some security issues with CBC-MAC and created *Cipher-Based Message Authentication Code (CMAC)*. CMAC provides the same type of data origin authentication and integrity as CBC-MAC, but more secure mathematically. CMAC is a variation of CBC-MAC. It is approved to work with AES and Triple DES. CRCs are used to identify data modifications, but these are commonly used lower in the network stack. Since these functions work lower in the network stack, they are used to identify modifications (as in corruption) when the packet is transmitted from one computer to another. HMAC, CBC-MAC, and CMAC work higher in the network stack and can identify not only transmission errors (accidental), but also more nefarious modifications, as in an attacker messing with a message for her own benefit. This mean all of these technologies (except CRC) can identify intentional, unauthorized modifications and accidental changes—three in one!

So here is how CMAC works: the symmetric algorithm (AES or 3DES) creates the symmetric key. This key is used to create subkeys. The subkeys are used individually to encrypt the individual blocks of a message as shown in Figure 8-23. This is the exactly how CBC-MAC works, but with some better magic that works underneath the hood. The magic that is underneath is mathematically based and really too deep for the CISSP exam. To understand more about this mathematical magic, please visit http://csrc.nist.gov/publications/nistpubs/800-38B/SP_800-38B.pdf

Although digging into the CMAC mathematics is too deep for the CISSP exam, what you do need to know is that it is a block cipher–based message authentication code algorithm. This means that it can provide the authentication of the data origin (as in the computer it was sent from) but not the person who sent it.

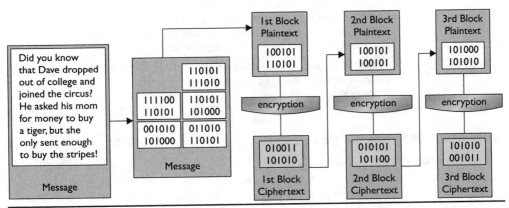

Figure 8-23 Cipher block chaining mode process

Hashes, HMACs, CBC-MACs, CMACs—Oh My!

MACs and hashing processes can be confusing. The following table simplifies the differences between them.

Function	Steps	Security Service Provided
Hash	1. Sender puts a message through a hashing algorithm and generates a message digest (MD) value. 2. Sender sends message and MD value to receiver. 3. Receiver runs just the message through the same hashing algorithm and creates an independent MD value. 4. Receiver compares both MD values. If they are the same, the message was not modified.	Integrity; not confidentiality or authentication. Can detect only unintentional modifications.
HMAC	1. Sender concatenates a message and secret key and puts the result through a hashing algorithm. This creates a MAC value. 2. Sender appends the MAC value to the message and sends it to the receiver. 3. The receiver takes just the message and concatenates it with her own symmetric key. This results in an independent MAC value. 4. The receiver compares the two MAC values. If they are the same, the receiver knows the message was not modified and knows from which system it came.	Integrity and data origin authentication; confidentiality is not provided.
CBC-MAC	1. Sender encrypts a message with a symmetric block algorithm in CBC mode. 2. The last block is used as the MAC. 3. The plaintext message and the appended MAC are sent to the receiver. 4. The receiver encrypts the message, creates a new MAC, and compares the two values. If they are the same, the receiver knows the message was not modified and from which system it came.	Data origin authentication and integrity.
CMAC	CMAC works the same way as the CBC-MAC, but is based on more complex logic and mathematical functions.	

Various Hashing Algorithms

As stated earlier, the goal of using a one-way hash function is to provide a fingerprint of the message. If two different messages produce the same hash value, it would be easier for an attacker to break that security mechanism, because patterns would be revealed.

A strong one-hash function should not provide the same hash value for two or more different messages. If a hashing algorithm takes steps to ensure it does not create the same hash value for two or more messages, it is said to be *collision free*.

Good cryptographic hash functions should have the following characteristics:

- The hash should be computed over the entire message.
- The hash should be a one-way function so messages are not disclosed by their values.
- Given a message and its hash value, computing another message with the same hash value should be impossible.
- The function should be resistant to birthday attacks (explained in the upcoming section "Attacks Against One-Way Hash Functions").

Table 8-2 and the following sections quickly describe some of the available hashing algorithms used in cryptography today.

MD2

MD2 is a one-way hash function designed by Ron Rivest that creates a 128-bit message digest value. It is not necessarily any weaker than the other algorithms in the "MD" family, but it is much slower.

MD4

MD4 is a one-way hash function designed by Ron Rivest. It also produces a 128-bit message digest value. It is used for high-speed computation in software implementations and is optimized for microprocessors.

MD5

MD5 was also created by Ron Rivest and is the newer version of MD4. It still produces a 128-bit hash, but the algorithm is more complex, which makes it harder to break.

MD5 added a fourth round of operations to be performed during the hashing functions and makes several of its mathematical operations carry out more steps or more complexity to provide a higher level of security. Recent research has shown MD5 to be subject to collision attacks, and it is therefore no longer suitable for applications like SSL certificates and digital signatures that require collision attack resistance.

SHA

SHA was designed by NSA and published by NIST to be used with the Digital Signature Standard (DSS). SHA was designed to be used in digital signatures and was developed when a more secure hashing algorithm was required for U.S. government applications.

SHA produces a 160-bit hash value, or message digest. This is then inputted into an asymmetric algorithm, which computes the signature for a message.

Algorithm	Description
Message Digest 2 (MD2) algorithm	One-way function. Produces a 128-bit hash value. Much slower than MD4 and MD5.
Message Digest 4 (MD4) algorithm	One-way function. Produces a 128-bit hash value.
Message Digest 5 (MD5) algorithm	One-way function. Produces a 128-bit hash value. More complex than MD4.
HAVAL	One-way function. Variable-length hash value. Modification of MD5 algorithm that provides more protection against attacks that affect MD5.
Secure Hash Algorithm (SHA)	One-way function. Produces a 160-bit hash value. Used with DSA.
SHA-1, SHA-256, SHA-384, SHA-512	Updated version of SHA. SHA-1 produces a 160-bit hash value, SHA-256 creates a 256-bit value, and so on.

Table 8-2 Various Hashing Algorithms Available

SHA is similar to MD4. It has some extra mathematical functions and produces a 160-bit hash instead of a 128-bit hash, which makes it more resistant to brute force attacks, including birthday attacks.

SHA was improved upon and renamed SHA-1. Recently, newer versions of this algorithm (collectively known as the SHA-2 family) have been developed and released: SHA-256, SHA-384, and SHA-512.

HAVAL

HAVAL is a variable-length one-way hash function and is a modification of MD5. It processes message blocks twice the size of those used in MD5; thus, it processes blocks of 1,024 bits. HAVAL can produce hashes from 128 to 256 bits in length.

Tiger

Ross Anderson and Eli Biham developed a hashing algorithm called Tiger in 1995. It was designed to carry out hashing functionalities on 64-bit systems and to be faster than MD5 and SHA-1. The resulting hash value is 192 bits. Designwise most hash algorithms (MD5, RIPEMD, SHA-0, and SHA-1) are derivatives or have been built upon the MD4 architecture. Tiger was built upon a different type of architecture with the goal of not being vulnerable to the same type of attacks that could be successful toward the other hashing algorithms. To fully understand how tested attacks have been carried out on the Tiger algorithm, you can view the document at http://th.informatik.uni-mannheim.de/People/Lucks/papers/Tiger_FSE_v10.pdf.

 NOTE A European project called RIPE (RACE Integrity Primitives Evaluation) developed a hashing algorithm with the purpose of replacing MD4. This algorithm is called RIPEMD and is very similar to MD4, but did not gain much attention.

Attacks Against One-Way Hash Functions

A good hashing algorithm should not produce the same hash value for two different messages. If the algorithm does produce the same value for two distinctly different messages, this is called a *collision*. An attacker can attempt to force a collision, which is referred to as a *birthday attack*. This attack is based on the mathematical birthday paradox that exists in standard statistics. Now hold on to your hat while we go through this—it is a bit tricky:

How many people must be in the same room for the chance to be greater than even that another person has the same birthday as you?

Answer: 253

How many people must be in the same room for the chance to be greater than even that at least two people share the same birthday?

Answer: 23

This seems a bit backward, but the difference is that in the first instance, you are looking for someone with a specific birthday date that matches yours. In the second instance, you are looking for any two people who share the same birthday. There is a higher probability of finding two people who share a birthday than of finding another person who shares your birthday. Or, stated another way, it is easier to find two matching values in a sea of values than to find a match for just one specific value.

Why do we care? The birthday paradox can apply to cryptography as well. Since any random set of 23 people most likely (at least a 50 percent chance) includes two people who share a birthday, by extension, if a hashing algorithm generates a message digest of 60 bits, there is a high likelihood that an adversary can find a collision using only 2^{30} inputs.

The main way an attacker can find the corresponding hashing value that matches a specific message is through a brute force attack. If he finds a message with a specific hash value, it is equivalent to finding someone with a specific birthday. If he finds two messages with the same hash values, it is equivalent to finding two people with the same birthday.

The output of a hashing algorithm is n, and to find a message through a brute force attack that results in a specific hash value would require hashing 2^n random messages. To take this one step further, finding two messages that hash to the same value would require review of only $2^{n/2}$ messages.

How Would a Birthday Attack Take Place?

Sue and Joe are going to get married, but before they do, they have a prenuptial contract drawn up that states if they get divorced, then Sue takes her original belongings and Joe takes his original belongings. To ensure this contract is not modified, it is hashed and a message digest value is created.

One month after Sue and Joe get married, Sue carries out some devious activity behind Joe's back. She makes a copy of the message digest value without anyone knowing. Then she makes a new contract that states that if Joe and Sue get a divorce, Sue owns both her own original belongings and Joe's original belongings. Sue hashes this new contract and compares the new message digest value with the message digest value that correlates with the contract. They don't match. So Sue tweaks her contract ever so slightly and creates another message digest value and compares them. She continues to tweak her contract until she forces a collision, meaning her contract creates the same message digest value as the original contract. Sue then changes out the original contract with her new contract and quickly divorces Joe. When Sue goes to collect Joe's belongings and he objects, she shows him that no modification could have taken place on the original document because it still hashes out to the same message digest. Sue then moves to an island.

Hash algorithms usually use message digest sizes (the value of n) that are large enough to make collisions difficult to accomplish, but they are still possible. An algorithm that has 160-bit output, like SHA-1, may require approximately 2^{80} computations to break. This means there is a less than 1 in 2^{80} chance that someone could carry out a successful birthday attack.

The main point of discussing this paradox is to show how important longer hashing values truly are. A hashing algorithm that has a larger bit output is less vulnerable to brute force attacks such as a birthday attack. This is the primary reason why the new versions of SHA have such large message digest values.

Digital Signatures

To do a digital signature, do I sign my name on my monitor screen?
Response: Sure.

A digital signature is a hash value that has been encrypted with the sender's private key. The act of signing means encrypting the message's hash value with a private key, as shown in Figure 8-24.

From our earlier example in the section "The One-Way Hash," if Kevin wants to ensure that the message he sends to Maureen is not modified *and* he wants her to be sure it came only from him, he can digitally sign the message. This means that a one-way hashing function would be run on the message, and then Kevin would encrypt that hash value with his private key.

When Maureen receives the message, she will perform the hashing function on the message, and come up with her own hash value. Then she will decrypt the sent hash value (digital signature) with Kevin's public key. She then compares the two values, and if they are the same, she can be sure the message was not altered during transmission. She is also sure the message came from Kevin because the value was encrypted with his private key.

The hashing function ensures the integrity of the message, and the signing of the hash value provides authentication and nonrepudiation. The act of signing just means the value was encrypted with a private key.

We need to be clear on all the available choices within cryptography, because different steps and algorithms provide different types of security services:

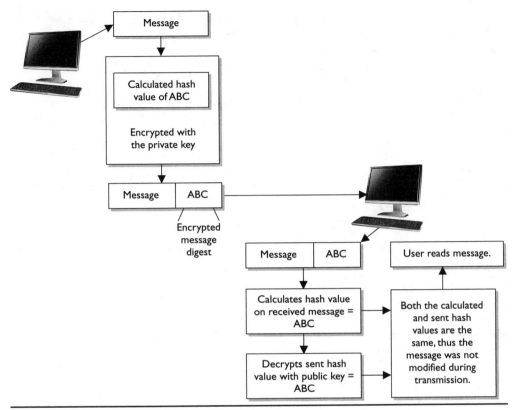

Figure 8-24   Creating a digital signature for a message

- A message can be encrypted, which provides confidentiality.
- A message can be hashed, which provides integrity.
- A message can be digitally signed, which provides authentication, nonrepudiation, and integrity.
- A message can be encrypted and digitally signed, which provides confidentiality, authentication, nonrepudiation, and integrity.

Some algorithms can only perform encryption, whereas others support digital signatures and encryption. When hashing is involved, a hashing algorithm is used, not an encryption algorithm.

It is important to understand that not all algorithms can necessarily provide all security services. Most of these algorithms are used in some type of combination to provide all the necessary security services required of an environment. Table 8-3 shows the services provided by the algorithms.

Algorithm Type	Encryption	Digital Signature	Hashing Function	Key Distribution
Asymmetric Key Algorithms				
RSA	X	X		X
ECC	X	X		X
Diffie-Hellman				X
El Gamal	X	X		X
DSA		X		
LUC	X	X		X
Knapsack	X	X		X
Symmetric Key Algorithms				
DES	X			
3DES	X			
Blowfish	X			
IDEA	X			
RC4	X			
SAFER	X			
Hashing Algorithms				
Ronald Rivest family of hashing functions: MD2, MD4, and MD5			X	
SHA			X	
HAVAL (variable-length hash values using a one-way function design)			X	

Table 8-3 Various Functions of Different Algorithms

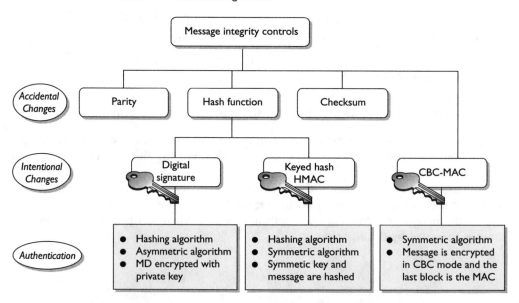

Digital Signature Standard

Because digital signatures are so important in proving who sent which messages, the U.S. government decided to establish standards pertaining to their functions and acceptable use. In 1991, NIST proposed a federal standard called the *Digital Signature Standard (DSS)*. It was developed for federal departments and agencies, but most vendors also designed their products to meet these specifications. The federal government requires its departments to use DSA, RSA, or the elliptic curve digital signature algorithm (ECDSA) and SHA. SHA creates a 160-bit message digest output, which is then inputted into one of the three mentioned digital signature algorithms. SHA is used to ensure the integrity of the message, and the other algorithms are used to digitally sign the message. This is an example of how two different algorithms are combined to provide the right combination of security services.

RSA and DSA are the best known and most widely used digital signature algorithms. DSA was developed by the NSA. Unlike RSA, DSA can be used only for digital signatures, and DSA is slower than RSA in signature verification. RSA can be used for digital signatures, encryption, *and* secure distribution of symmetric keys.

Public Key Infrastructure

Let's put all of these cryptography pieces in a bowl and figure out how they all work together.

Public key infrastructure (PKI) consists of programs, data formats, procedures, communication protocols, security policies, and public key cryptographic mechanisms working in a comprehensive manner to enable a wide range of dispersed people to communicate in a secure and predictable fashion. In other words, a PKI establishes a level of trust within an environment. PKI is an ISO authentication framework that uses public key cryptography and the X.509 standard. The framework was set up to enable authentication to happen across different networks and the Internet. Particular protocols and algorithms are not specified, which is why PKI is called a framework and not a specific technology.

PKI provides authentication, confidentiality, nonrepudiation, and integrity of the messages exchanged. PKI is a *hybrid* system of symmetric and asymmetric key algorithms and methods, which were discussed in earlier sections.

There is a difference between public key cryptography and PKI. Public key cryptography is another name for asymmetric algorithms, while PKI is what its name states—it is an infrastructure. The infrastructure assumes that the receiver's identity can be positively ensured through certificates and that an asymmetric algorithm will automatically carry out the process of key exchange. The infrastructure therefore contains the pieces that will identify users, create and distribute certificates, maintain and revoke certificates, distribute and maintain encryption keys, and enable all technologies to communicate and work together for the purpose of encrypted communication and authentication.

Public key cryptography is one piece in PKI, but many other pieces make up this infrastructure. An analogy can be drawn with the e-mail protocol Simple Mail Transfer Protocol (SMTP). SMTP is the technology used to get e-mail messages from here to there, but many other things must be in place before this protocol can be productive. We need e-mail clients, e-mail servers, and e-mail messages, which together build a type of infrastructure—an e-mail infrastructure. PKI is made up of many different parts: certificate authorities, registration authorities, certificates, keys, and users. The following sections explain these parts and how they all work together.

Each person who wants to participate in a PKI requires a digital certificate, which is a credential that contains the public key for that individual along with other identifying information. The certificate is created and signed (digital signature) by a trusted third party, which is a certificate authority (CA). When the CA signs the certificate, it binds the individual's identity to the public key, and the CA takes liability for the authenticity of that individual. It is this trusted third party (the CA) that allows people who have never met to authenticate to each other and to communicate in a secure method. If Kevin has never met Dave, but would like to communicate securely with him, and they both trust the same CA, then Kevin could retrieve Dave's digital certificate and start the process.

Certificate Authorities

How do I know I can trust you?
Response: The CA trusts me.

A CA is a trusted organization (or server) that maintains and issues digital certificates. When a person requests a certificate, the registration authority (RA) verifies that individual's identity and passes the certificate request off to the CA. The CA constructs the certificate, signs it, sends it to the requester, and maintains the certificate over its lifetime. When another person wants to communicate with this person, the CA will basically vouch for that person's identity. When Dave receives a digital certificate from Kevin, Dave will go through steps to validate it. Basically, by providing Dave with his digital certificate, Kevin is stating, "I know you don't know or trust me, but here is this document that was created by someone you do know and trust. The document says I am a good guy and you should trust me."

Once Dave validates the digital certificate, he extracts Kevin's public key, which is embedded within it. Now Dave knows this public key is bound to Kevin. He also knows that if Kevin uses his private key to create a digital signature and Dave can properly decrypt it using this public key, it did indeed come from Kevin.

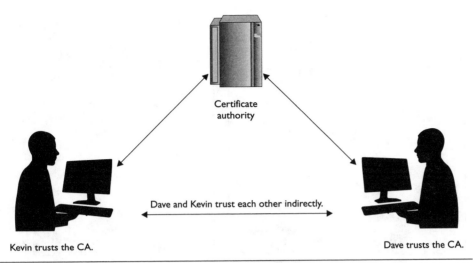

Certificate authority

Dave and Kevin trust each other indirectly.

Kevin trusts the CA.   Dave trusts the CA.

NOTE Remember the man-in-the-middle attack covered earlier in the section "The Diffie-Hellman Algorithm"? This attack is possible if two users are not working in a PKI environment and do not truly know the identity of the owners of the public keys.

The CA can be internal to an organization. Such a setup would enable the company to control the CA server, configure how authentication takes place, maintain the certificates, and recall certificates when necessary. Other CAs are organizations dedicated to this type of service, and other individuals and companies pay them to supply it. Some well-known CAs are Entrust and VeriSign. Many browsers have several well-known CAs configured by default.

NOTE More and more organizations are setting up their own internal PKIs. When these independent PKIs need to interconnect to allow for secure communication to take place (either between departments or between different companies), there must be a way for the two root CAs to trust each other. The two CAs do not have a CA above them they can both trust, so they must carry out cross certification. A *cross certification* is the process undertaken by CAs to establish a trust relationship in which they rely upon each other's digital certificates and public keys as if they had issued them themselves. When this is set up, a CA for one company can validate digital certificates from the other company and vice versa.

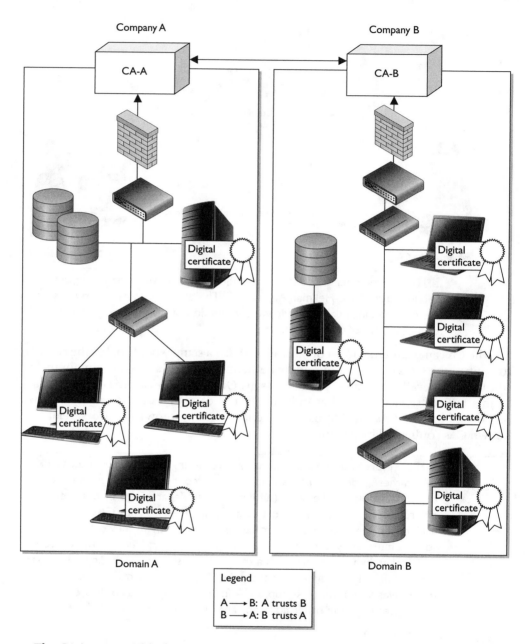

The CA is responsible for creating and handing out certificates, maintaining them, and revoking them if necessary. Revocation is handled by the CA, and the revoked certificate information is stored on a *certificate revocation list (CRL)*. This is a list of every certificate that has been revoked. This list is maintained and updated periodically. A certificate may be revoked because the key holder's private key was compromised or because the CA discovered the certificate was issued to the wrong person. An analogy for the use of a CRL is how a driver's license is used by a police officer. If an officer pulls over Sean for speeding, the officer will ask to see Sean's license. The officer will then run a check on the license to find out if Sean is wanted for any other infractions of the law and to verify the license has not expired. The same thing happens when a person compares a certificate to a CRL. If the certificate became invalid for some reason, the CRL is the mechanism for the CA to let others know this information.

NOTE CRLs are the thorn in the side of many PKI implementations. They are challenging for a long list of reasons. It is interesting to know that, by default, web browsers do not check a CRL to ensure that a certificate is not revoked. So when you are setting up an SSL connection to do e-commerce over the Internet, you could be relying on a certificate that has actually been revoked. Not good.

Online Certificate Status Protocol (OCSP) is being used more and more rather than the cumbersome CRL approach. When using just a CRL, the user's browser must either check a central CRL to find out if the certification has been revoked or continually push out CRL values to the clients to ensure they have an updated CRL. If OCSP is implemented, it does this work automatically in the background. It carries out real-time validation of a certificate and reports back to the user whether the certificate is valid, invalid, or unknown. OCSP checks the CRL that is maintained by the CA. So the CRL is still being used, but now we have a protocol developed specifically to check the CRL during a certificate validation process.

Certificates

One of the most important pieces of a PKI is its digital certificate. A *certificate* is the mechanism used to associate a public key with a collection of components in a manner that is sufficient to uniquely identify the claimed owner. The standard for how the CA creates the certificate is X.509, which dictates the different fields used in the certificate and the valid values that can populate those fields. We are currently at version 4 of this standard, which is often denoted as X.509v4. Many cryptographic protocols use this type of certificate, including SSL.

The certificate includes the serial number, version number, identity information, algorithm information, lifetime dates, and the signature of the issuing authority, as shown in Figure 8-25.

The Registration Authority

The *registration authority (RA)* performs the certification registration duties. The RA establishes and confirms the identity of an individual, initiates the certification process with a CA on behalf of an end user, and performs certificate life-cycle management functions. The RA cannot issue certificates, but can act as a broker between the user and the CA. When users need new certificates, they make requests to the RA, and the RA verifies all necessary identification information before allowing a request to go to the CA.

NOTE A few years ago, VeriSign assigned some very powerful certificates to two individuals who claimed to work for Microsoft. They did not work for Microsoft, and this opened the door to a lot of potential security compromises.

PKI Steps

Now that we know some of the main pieces of a PKI and how they actually work together, let's walk through an example. First, suppose that John needs to obtain a digital certificate for himself so he can participate in a PKI. The following are the steps to do so:

1. John makes a request to the RA.

2. The RA requests certain identification information from John, such as a copy of his driver's license, his phone number, his address, and other identifying information.

3. Once the RA receives the required information from John and verifies it, the RA sends his certificate request to the CA.

4. The CA creates a certificate with John's public key and identity information embedded. (The private/public key pair is generated either by the CA or on John's machine, which depends on the systems' configurations. If it is created at the CA, his private key needs to be sent to him by secure means. In most cases, the user generates this pair and sends in his public key during the registration process.)

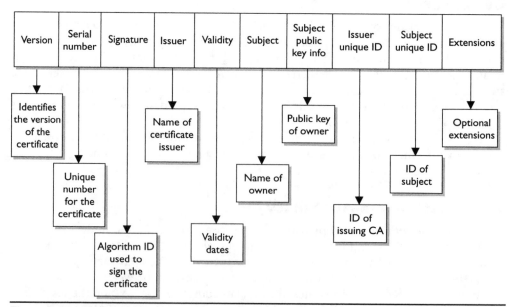

Figure 8-25 Each certificate has a structure with all the necessary identifying information in it.

Now John is registered and can participate in a PKI. John and Diane decide they want to communicate, so they take the following steps, shown in Figure 8-26.

5. John requests Diane's public key from a public directory.

6. The directory, sometimes called a repository, sends Diane's digital certificate.

7. John verifies the digital certificate and extracts her public key. John uses this public key to encrypt a session key that will be used to encrypt their messages. John sends the encrypted session key to Diane. John also sends his certificate, containing his public key, to Diane.

8. When Diane receives John's certificate, her browser looks to see if it trusts the CA that digitally signed this certificate. Diane's browser trusts this CA and, after she verifies the certificate, both John and Diane can communicate using encryption.

A PKI may be made up of the following entities and functions:

- CA
- RA
- Certificate repository
- Certificate revocation system
- Key backup and recovery system
- Automatic key update
- Management of key histories
- Timestamping
- Client-side software

Figure 8-26
CA and user
relationships

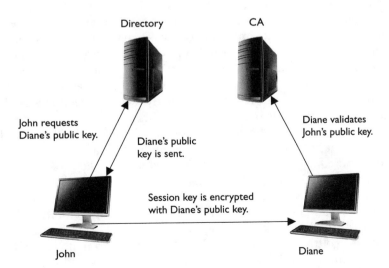

PKI supplies the following security services:

- Confidentiality
- Access control
- Integrity
- Authentication
- Nonrepudiation

A PKI must retain a key history, which keeps track of all the old and current public keys that have been used by individual users. For example, if Kevin encrypted a symmetric key with Dave's old public key, there should be a way for Dave to still access this data. This can only happen if the CA keeps a proper history of Dave's old certificates and keys.

 NOTE Another important component that must be integrated into a PKI is a reliable time source that provides a way for secure timestamping. This comes into play when true nonrepudiation is required.

Key Management

I am the manager of all keys!
Response: I feel so sorry for you.

Cryptography can be used as a security mechanism to provide confidentiality, integrity, and authentication, but not if the keys are compromised in any way. The keys can be captured, modified, corrupted, or disclosed to unauthorized individuals. Cryptography is based on a trust model. Individuals must trust each other to protect their own keys, trust the administrator who is maintaining the keys, and trust a server that holds, maintains, and distributes the keys.

Many administrators know that key management causes one of the biggest headaches in cryptographic implementation. There is more to key maintenance than using them to encrypt messages. The keys must be distributed securely to the right entities and updated continuously. They must also be protected as they are being transmitted and while they are being stored on each workstation and server. The keys must be generated, destroyed, and recovered properly. Key management can be handled through manual or automatic processes.

The keys are stored before and after distribution. When a key is distributed to a user, it does not just hang out on the desktop. It needs a secure place within the file system to be stored and used in a controlled method. The key, the algorithm that will use the key, configurations, and parameters are stored in a module that also needs to be protected. If an attacker is able to obtain these components, she could masquerade as another user and decrypt, read, and re-encrypt messages not intended for her.

Historically, physical cryptographic keys were kept in secured boxes and delivered by escorted couriers. The keys could be distributed to a main server, and then the local administration would distribute them, or the courier would visit each computer individually. Some implementations distributed a master key to a site, and then that key was used to generate unique secret keys to be used by individuals at that location. Today, most key distributions are handled by a protocol through automated means and not manually by an individual. A company must evaluate the overhead of key management, the required security level, and cost-benefit issues to decide how it will conduct key management, but overall, automation provides a more accurate and secure approach.

When using the Kerberos protocol (described in Chapter 4), a Key Distribution Center (KDC) is used to store, distribute, and maintain cryptographic session and secret keys. This method provides an automated method of key distribution. The computer that wants to access a service on another computer requests access via the KDC. The KDC then generates a session key to be used between the requesting computer and the computer providing the requested resource or service. The automation of this process reduces the possible errors that can happen through a manual process, but if the ticket granting service (TGS) portion of the KDC gets compromised in any way, then all the computers and their services are affected and possibly compromised.

In some instances, keys are still managed through manual means. Unfortunately, although many companies use cryptographic keys, they rarely if ever change them, either because of the hassle of key management or because the network administrator is already overtaxed with other tasks or does not realize the task actually needs to take place. The frequency of use of a cryptographic key has a direct correlation to how often the key should be changed. The more a key is used, the more likely it is to be captured and compromised. If a key is used infrequently, then this risk drops dramatically. The necessary level of security and the frequency of use can dictate the frequency of key updates. A mom-and-pop diner might only change its cryptography keys every month, whereas an information warfare military unit might change them every day or every week. The important thing is to change the keys using a secure method.

Key management is the most challenging part of cryptography and also the most crucial. It is one thing to develop a very complicated and complex algorithm and key method, but if the keys are not securely stored and transmitted, it does not really matter how strong the algorithm is.

Key Management Principles

Keys should not be in cleartext outside the cryptography device. As stated previously, many cryptography algorithms are known publicly, which puts more stress on protecting the secrecy of the key. If attackers know how the actual algorithm works, in many cases all they need to figure out is the key to compromise a system. This is why keys should not be available in cleartext—the key is what brings secrecy to encryption.

These steps, and all of key distribution and maintenance, should be automated and hidden from the user. These processes should be integrated into software or the operating system. It only adds complexity and opens the doors for more errors when processes are done manually and depend upon end users to perform certain functions.

Keys are at risk of being lost, destroyed, or corrupted. Backup copies should be available and easily accessible when required. If data are encrypted and then the user accidentally loses the necessary key to decrypt it, this information would be lost forever if there were not a backup key to save the day. The application being used for cryptography may have key recovery options, or it may require copies of the keys to be kept in a secure place.

Different scenarios highlight the need for key recovery or backup copies of keys. For example, if Bob has possession of all the critical bid calculations, stock value information, and corporate trend analysis needed for tomorrow's senior executive presentation, and Bob has an unfortunate confrontation with a bus, someone is going to need to access this data after the funeral. As another example, if an employee leaves the company and has encrypted important documents on her computer before departing, the company would probably still want to access that data later. Similarly, if the vice president did not know that running a large magnet over the floppy disk that holds his private key was not a good idea, he would want his key replaced immediately instead of listening to a lecture about electromagnetic fields and how they rewrite sectors on media.

Of course, having more than one key increases the chance of disclosure, so a company needs to decide whether it wants to have key backups and, if so, what precautions to put into place to protect them properly. A company can choose to have multiparty control for emergency key recovery. This means that if a key must be recovered, more than one person is needed for this process. The key recovery process could require two or more other individuals to present their private keys or authentication information. These individuals should not all be members of the IT department. There should be a member from management, an individual from security, and one individual from the IT department. All of these requirements reduce the potential for abuse and would require collusion for fraudulent activities to take place.

Rules for Keys and Key Management

Key management is critical for proper protection. The following are responsibilities that fall under the key management umbrella:

- The key length should be long enough to provide the necessary level of protection.
- Keys should be stored and transmitted by secure means.
- Keys should be extremely random, and the algorithm should use the full spectrum of the keyspace.
- The key's lifetime should correspond with the sensitivity of the data it is protecting. (Less secure data may allow for a longer key lifetime, whereas more sensitive data might require a shorter key lifetime.)
- The more the key is used, the shorter its lifetime should be.
- Keys should be backed up or escrowed in case of emergencies.
- Keys should be properly destroyed when their lifetime comes to an end.

Link Encryption vs. End-to-End Encryption

Encryption can be performed at different communication levels, each with different types of protection and implications. Two general modes of encryption implementation are link encryption and end-to-end encryption. *Link encryption* encrypts all the data along a specific communication path, as in a satellite link, T3 line, or telephone circuit. Not only is the user information encrypted, but the header, trailers, addresses, and routing data that are part of the packets are also encrypted. The only traffic not encrypted in this technology is the data link control messaging information, which includes instructions and parameters that the different link devices use to synchronize communication methods. Link encryption provides protection against packet sniffers and eavesdroppers. In *end-to-end encryption*, the headers, addresses, routing, and trailer information are not encrypted, enabling attackers to learn more about a captured packet and where it is headed.

Link encryption, which is sometimes called *online encryption*, is usually provided by service providers and is incorporated into network protocols. All of the information is encrypted, and the packets must be decrypted at each hop so the router, or other intermediate device, knows where to send the packet next. The router must decrypt the header portion of the packet, read the routing and address information within the header, and then re-encrypt it and send it on its way.

With end-to-end encryption, the packets do not need to be decrypted and then encrypted again at each hop, because the headers and trailers are not encrypted. The devices in between the origin and destination just read the necessary routing information and pass the packets on their way.

End-to-end encryption is usually initiated by the user of the originating computer. It provides more flexibility for the user to be able to determine whether or not certain messages will get encrypted. It is called "end-to-end encryption" because the message stays encrypted from one end of its journey to the other. Link encryption has to decrypt the packets at every device between the two ends.

Link encryption occurs at the data link and physical layers, as depicted in Figure 8-27. Hardware encryption devices interface with the physical layer and encrypt all data that passes through them. Because no part of the data is available to an attacker, the attacker cannot learn basic information about how data flows through the environment. This is referred to as *traffic-flow security.*

NOTE A *hop* is a device that helps a packet reach its destination. It is usually a router that looks at the packet address to determine where the packet needs to go next. Packets usually go through many hops between the sending and receiving computers.

Encryption at Different Layers

In reality, encryption can happen at different layers of an operating system and network stack. The following are just a few examples:

- End-to-end encryption happens within the applications.
- SSL encryption takes place at the transport layer.
- PPTP encryption takes place at the data link layer.
- Link encryption takes place at the data link and physical layers.

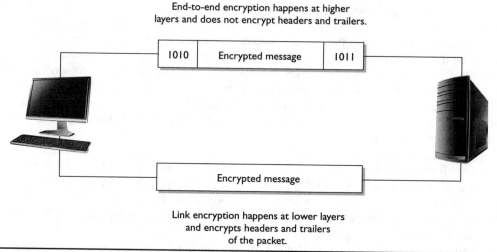

End-to-end encryption happens at higher
layers and does not encrypt headers and trailers.

| 1010 | Encrypted message | 1011 |

Encrypted message

Link encryption happens at lower layers
and encrypts headers and trailers
of the packet.

Figure 8-27 Link and end-to-end encryption happen at different OSI layers.

The following list outlines the advantages and disadvantages of end-to-end and link encryption methods.

Advantages of end-to-end encryption include the following:

- It provides more flexibility to the user in choosing what gets encrypted and how.
- Higher granularity of functionality is available because each application or user can choose specific configurations.
- Each hop computer on the network does not need to have a key to decrypt each packet.

Disadvantages of end-to-end encryption include the following:

- Headers, addresses, and routing information are not encrypted, and therefore not protected.

Advantages of link encryption include the following:

- All data are encrypted, including headers, addresses, and routing information.
- Users do not need to do anything to initiate it. It works at a lower layer in the OSI model.

Disadvantages of link encryption include the following:

- Key distribution and management are more complex because each hop device must receive a key, and when the keys change, each must be updated.
- Packets are decrypted at each hop; thus, more points of vulnerability exist.
- Link encryption defeats traffic analysis

Hardware vs. Software Cryptography Systems

Encryption can be done through software or hardware, and there are trade-offs with each. Generally, software is less expensive and provides a slower throughput than hardware mechanisms. Software cryptography methods can be more easily modified and disabled compared to hardware systems, but it depends on the application and the hardware product.

If a company needs to perform high-end encryption functions at a higher speed, the company will most likely implement a hardware solution.

E-mail Standards

Like other types of technologies, cryptography has industry standards and de facto standards. Standards are necessary because they help ensure interoperability among vendor products. Standards usually mean that a certain technology has been under heavy scrutiny and properly tested and accepted by many similar technology communities. A company still needs to decide on what type of standard to follow and what type of technology to implement.

A company needs to evaluate the functionality of the technology and perform a cost-benefit analysis on the competing products within the chosen standards. For a cryptography implementation, the company would need to decide what must be protected by encryption, whether digital signatures are necessary, how key management should take place, what types of resources are available to implement and maintain the technology, and what the overall cost will amount to.

If a company only needs to encrypt some e-mail messages here and there, then PGP may be the best choice. If the company wants all data encrypted as it goes throughout the network and to sister companies, then a link encryption implementation may be the best choice. If a company wants to implement a single sign-on environment where users need to authenticate to use different services and functionality throughout the network, then implementing a PKI or Kerberos might serve it best. To make the most informed decision, the network administrators should understand each type of technology and standard, and should research and test each competing product within the chosen technology before making the final purchase. Cryptography, including how to implement and maintain it, can be a complicated subject. Doing homework versus buying into buzzwords and flashy products might help a company reduce its headaches down the road.

The following sections briefly describe some of the most popular e-mail standards in use.

Multipurpose Internet Mail Extension

Multipurpose Internet Mail Extension (MIME) is a technical specification indicating how multimedia data and e-mail attachments are to be transferred. The Internet has mail standards that dictate how mail is to be formatted, encapsulated, transmitted, and opened. If a message or document contains a binary attachment, MIME dictates how that portion of the message should be handled.

When an attachment contains an audio clip, graphic, or some other type of multi-media component, the e-mail client will send the file with a header that describes the file type. For example, the header might indicate that the MIME type is Image and that the subtype is jpeg. Although this will be in the header, many times systems also use the file's extension to identify the MIME type. So, in the preceding example, the file's name might be stuff.jpeg. The user's system will see the extension .jpeg, or see the data in the header field, and look in its association list to see what program it needs to initialize to open this particular file. If the system has JPEG files associated with the Explorer application, then Explorer will open and present the picture to the user.

Sometimes systems either do not have an association for a specific file type or do not have the helper program necessary to review and use the contents of the file. When a file has an unassociated icon assigned to it, it might require the user to choose the Open With command and choose an application in the list to associate this file with that program. So when the user double-clicks that file, the associated program will initialize and present the file. If the system does not have the necessary program, the web site might offer the necessary helper program, like Acrobat or an audio program that plays WAV files.

MIME is a specification that dictates how certain file types should be transmitted and handled. This specification has several types and subtypes, enables different computers to exchange data in varying formats, and provides a standardized way of presenting the data. So if Sean views a funny picture that is in GIF format, he can be sure that when he sends it to Debbie, it will look exactly the same.

Secure MIME (S/MIME) is a standard for encrypting and digitally signing electronic mail and for providing secure data transmissions. S/MIME extends the MIME standard by allowing for the encryption of e-mail and attachments. The encryption and hashing algorithms can be specified by the user of the mail package, instead of having it dictated to them. S/MIME follows the Public Key Cryptography Standards (PKCS). S/MIME provides confidentiality through encryption algorithms, integrity through hashing algorithms, authentication through the use of X.509 public key certificates, and nonrepudiation through cryptographically signed message digests.

Privacy-Enhanced Mail

Privacy-Enhanced Mail (PEM) is an Internet standard to provide secure e-mail over the Internet and for inhouse communication infrastructures. The protocols within PEM provide authentication, message integrity, encryption, and key management. This standard was developed to provide compatibility with many types of key-management processes and symmetric and public key methods of encryption. It was also designed to be compatible with PKCS.

PEM is a series of message authentication and encryption technologies developed by several governing groups. PEM can use AES for encryption and RSA for sender authentication and key management. It also provides support for nonrepudiation. The following are specific components that can be used in PEM:

- Messages encrypted with AES in CBC mode
- Public key management, provided by using RSA
- X.509 standard, used for certification structure and format

PEM has not caught on to the extent the developers had planned. The main issue is that PEM provides too much structure for different environments that require more flexibility in their secure communication infrastructure.

Message Security Protocol

The military has its own way of securing messages.
Response: It has its own way of doing most things.

The *Message Security Protocol (MSP)* is the military's PEM. Developed by the NSA, it is an X.400-compatible application-level protocol used to secure e-mail messages. MSP can be used to sign and encrypt messages and to perform hashing functions. Like PEM, applications that incorporate MSP enable different algorithms and parameters to be used to provide greater flexibility.

Pretty Good Privacy

Pretty Good Privacy (PGP) was designed by Phil Zimmerman as a freeware e-mail security program and was released in 1991. It was the first widespread public key encryption program. PGP is a complete cryptosystem that uses cryptographic protection to protect e-mail and files. It can use RSA public key encryption for key management and use IDEA symmetric cipher for bulk encryption of data, although the user has the option of picking different types of algorithms for these functions. PGP can provide confidentiality by using the IDEA encryption algorithm, integrity by using the MD5 hashing algorithm, authentication by using the public key certificates, and nonrepudiation by using cryptographically signed messages. PGP uses its own type of digital certificates rather than what is used in PKI, but they both have similar purposes.

The user's private key is generated and encrypted when the application asks the user to randomly type on her keyboard for a specific amount of time. Instead of using passwords, PGP uses passphrases. The passphrase is used to encrypt the user's private key that is stored on her hard drive.

PGP does not use a hierarchy of CAs, or any type of formal trust certificates, but instead relies on a "web of trust" in its key management approach. Each user generates and distributes his or her public key, and users sign each other's public keys, which creates a community of users who trust each other. This is different from the CA approach, where no one trusts each other; they only trust the CA. For example, if Mark and Joe want to communicate using PGP, Mark can give his public key to Joe. Joe signs Mark's key and keeps a copy for himself. Then, Joe gives a copy of his public key to Mark so they can start communicating securely. Later, Mark would like to communicate with Sally, but Sally does not know Mark and does not know if she can trust him. Mark sends Sally his public key, which has been signed by Joe. Sally has Joe's public key, because they have communicated before, and she trusts Joe. Because Joe signed Mark's public key, Sally now also trusts Mark and sends her public key and begins communicating with him.

So, basically, PGP is a system of "I don't know you, but my buddy Joe says you are an all right guy, so I will trust you on Joe's word."

Each user keeps in a file, referred to as a *key ring*, a collection of public keys he has received from other users. Each key in that ring has a parameter that indicates the level of trust assigned to that user and the validity of that particular key. If Steve has known Liz for many years and trusts her, he might have a higher level of trust indicated on her stored public key than on Tom's, whom he does not trust much at all. There is also a field indicating who can sign other keys within Steve's realm of trust. If Steve receives a key from someone he doesn't know, like Kevin, and the key is signed by Liz, he can look at the field that pertains to whom he trusts to sign other people's keys. If the field indicates that Steve trusts Liz enough to sign another person's key, Steve will accept Kevin's key and communicate with him because Liz is vouching for him. However, if Steve receives a key from Kevin and it is signed by untrustworthy Tom, Steve might choose to not trust Kevin and not communicate with him.

These fields are available for updating and alteration. If one day Steve really gets to know Tom and finds out he is okay after all, he can modify these parameters within PGP and give Tom more trust when it comes to cryptography and secure communication.

Because the web of trust does not have a central leader, such as a CA, certain standardized functionality is harder to accomplish. If Steve were to lose his private key, he would need to notify everyone else trusting his public key that it should no longer be trusted. In a PKI, Steve would only need to notify the CA, and anyone attempting to verify the validity of Steve's public key would be told not to trust it upon looking at the most recently updated CRL. In the PGP world, this is not as centralized and organized. Steve can send out a key revocation certificate, but there is no guarantee it will reach each user's key ring file.

PGP is a public domain software that uses public key cryptography. It has not been endorsed by the NSA, but because it is a great product and free for individuals to use, it has become somewhat of an encryption de facto standard on the Internet.

 NOTE PGP is considered a cryptosystem because it has all the necessary components: symmetric key algorithms, asymmetric key algorithms, message digest algorithms, keys, protocols, and the necessary software components.

Quantum Cryptography

Gee, cryptography just isn't complex enough. Let's mix some quantum physics in with it.

Today, we have very sophisticated and strong algorithms that are more than strong enough for most uses, even financial transactions and exchanging your secret meatloaf recipe. Some communication data are so critical and so desired by other powerful entities that even our current algorithms may be broken. This type of data might be spy interactions, information warfare, government espionage, and so on. When a whole country wants to break another country's encryption, a great deal of resources will be put behind such efforts—which can put our current algorithms at risk of being broken.

Because of the need to always build a better algorithm, some very smart people have mixed quantum physics and cryptography, which has resulted in a system (if built correctly) that is unbreakable and where any eavesdroppers can be detected. In traditional cryptography, we try to make it very hard for an eavesdropper to break an algorithm and uncover a key, but we cannot detect that an eavesdropper is on the line. In quantum cryptography, however, not only is the encryption very strong, but an eavesdropper *can* be detected.

Quantum cryptography can be carried out using various methods. So, we will walk through one version to give you an idea of how all this works.

Let's say Tom and Kathy are spies and need to send their data back and forth with the assurance it won't be captured. To do so, they need to establish a symmetric encryption key on both ends, one for Tom and one for Kathy.

In *quantum cryptography*, photon polarization is commonly used to represent bits (1 or 0). *Polarization* is the orientation of electromagnetic waves, which is what photons are. Photons are the particles that make up light. The electromagnetic waves have an orientation of horizontal or vertical, or left hand or right hand. Think of a photon as a jellybean. As a jellybean flies through the air, it can be vertical (standing up straight), horizontal (lying on its back), left handed (tilted to the left), or right handed (tilted to the right). (This is just to conceptually get your head around the idea of polarization.)

Now both Kathy and Tom each have their own photon gun, which they will use to send photons (information) back and forth to each other. They also have a mapping between the polarization of a photon and a binary value. The polarizations can be represented as vertical (|), horizontal (–), left (\), or right (/), and since we only have two values in binary, there must be some overlap.

In this example, a photon with a vertical (|) polarization maps to the binary value of 0. A left polarization (\) maps to 1, a right polarization (/) maps to 0, and a horizontal polarization (–) maps to 1. This mapping (or encoding) is the binary values that make up an encryption key. Tom must have the same mapping to interpret what Kathy sends to him. Tom will use this as his map so when he receives a photon with the polarization of (\), he will write down a 1. When he receives a photon with the polarization of (|), he will write down a 0. He will do this for the whole key, and use these values as the key to decrypt a message Kathy sends him.

NOTE   If it helps, think about it this way. Tom receives a jellybean that is horizontal and he writes down a 1. The next jellybean he receives is tilted to the right, so he writes down 0. The next jellybean is vertical, so he writes down 1. He does this for all of the jellybeans Kathy sends his way. Now he has a string of binary values that is the encryption key his system will use to decrypt the messages Kathy sends to him.

So they both have to agree upon a key, which is the mapping between the polarization states of the photons and how those states are represented in a binary value. This happens at the beginning of a communication session over a dedicated fiber line. Once the symmetric key is established, it can be used by Kathy and Tom to encrypt and decrypt messages that travel over a more public communication path, like the Internet. The randomness of the polarization and the complexity of creating a symmetric key in this manner help ensure that an eavesdropper will not uncover the encryption key.

Since this type of cryptography is based on quantum physics and not strictly mathematics, the sender and receiver can be confident that no eavesdropper is listening to the communication path used to establish their key and that a man-in-the-middle attack is not being carried out. This is because, at the quantum level, even "looking" at an atom or a subatomic particle changes its attributes. This means that if there is an eavesdropper carrying out a passive attack, such as sniffing, the receiver would know because just this simple act changes the characteristics (polarization) of the photons.

 NOTE This means that as the jellybeans are sent from Kathy to Tom, if Sean tries to view the jellybeans, the ones that were traveling in a horizontal manner could be tilting left, and ones that were traveling in a vertical manner could now be traveling horizontally.

 CAUTION This is a very quick explanation of quantum cryptography. To fully understand it, you would need to understand both cryptography and quantum physics in greater depth—and not use jellybeans.

Some people in the industry think quantum cryptography is used between the U.S. White House and the Pentagon and between some military bases and defense contractor locations. This type of information is classified Top Secret by the U.S. government, and unless you know the secret handshake and have the right decoder ring, you will not be privy to this type of information.

Internet Security

Is the Internet tied up into a web?
Response: Well, kind of.

The Web is not the Internet. The Web runs on top of the Internet, in a sense. The Web is the collection of HTTP servers that hold and process web sites we see. The Internet is the collection of physical devices and communication protocols used to traverse these web sites and interact with them. (These issues were touched upon in Chapter 2.) The web sites look the way they do because their creators used a language that dictates the look, feel, and functionality of the page. Web browsers enable users to read web pages by enabling them to request and accept web pages via HTTP, and the user's browser converts the language (HTML, DHTML, and XML) into a format that can be viewed on the monitor. The browser is the user's window to the World Wide Web.

Browsers can understand a variety of protocols and have the capability to process many types of commands, but they do not understand them all. For those protocols or commands the user's browser does not know how to process, the user can download and install a viewer or plug-in, a modular component of code that integrates itself into the system or browser. This is a quick and easy way to expand the functionality of the browser. However, this can cause serious security compromises, because the payload of the module can easily carry viruses and malicious software that users don't discover until it's too late.

Start with the Basics

Why do we connect to the Internet? At first, this seems a basic question, but as we dive deeper into the query, complexity creeps in. We connect to download MP3s, check e-mail, order security books, look at web sites, communicate with friends, and perform various other tasks. But what are we really doing? We are using services provided by a computer's protocols and software. The services may be file transfers provided by FTP, remote connectivity provided by Telnet, Internet connectivity provided by HTTP, secure connections provided by SSL, and much, much more. Without these protocols, there would be no way to even connect to the Internet.

Management needs to decide what functionality employees should have pertaining to Internet use, and the administrator must implement these decisions by controlling services that can be used inside and outside the network. Services can be restricted in various ways, such as allowing certain services to only run on a particular system and to restrict access to that system; employing a secure version of a service; filtering the use of services; or blocking services altogether. These choices determine how secure the site will be and indicate what type of technology is needed to provide this type of protection.

Let's go through many of the technologies and protocols that make up the World Wide Web.

HTTP

TCP/IP is the protocol suite of the Internet, and HTTP is the protocol of the Web. HTTP sits on top of TCP/IP. When a user clicks a link on a web page with her mouse, her browser uses HTTP to send a request to the web server hosting that web site. The web server finds the corresponding file to that link and sends it to the user via HTTP. So where is TCP/IP in all of this? The TCP protocol controls the handshaking and maintains the connection between the user and the server, and the IP protocol makes sure the file is routed properly throughout the Internet to get from the web server to the user. So, the IP protocol finds the way to get from A to Z, TCP makes sure the origin and destination are correct and that no packets are lost along the way, and, upon arrival at the destination, HTTP presents the payload, which is a web page.

HTTP is a stateless protocol, which means the client and web server make and break a connection for each operation. When a user requests to view a web page, that web server finds the requested web page, presents it to the user, and then terminates the connection. If the user requests a link within the newly received web page, a new connection must be set up, the request goes to the web server, and the web server sends the requested item and breaks the connection. The web server never "remembers" the users that ask for different web pages, because it would have to commit a lot of resources to the effort.

HTTP Secure

HTTP Secure (HTTPS) is HTTP running over SSL. (HTTP works at the application layer and SSL works at the transport layer.) *Secure Sockets Layer (SSL)* uses public key encryption and provides data encryption, server authentication, message integrity, and optional client authentication. When a client accesses a web site, that web site may have both secured and public portions. The secured portion would require the user to be authenticated in some fashion. When the client goes from a public page on the web site to a secured page, the web server will start the necessary tasks to invoke SSL and protect this type of communication.

The server sends a message back to the client, indicating a secure session should be established, and the client in response sends its security parameters. The server compares those security parameters to its own until it finds a match. This is the handshaking phase. The server authenticates to the client by sending it a digital certificate, and if the client decides to trust the server, the process continues. The server can require the client to send over a digital certificate for mutual authentication, but that is rare.

The client generates a session key and encrypts it with the server's public key. This encrypted key is sent to the web server, and they both use this symmetric key to encrypt the data they send back and forth. This is how the secure channel is established.

SSL keeps the communication path open until one of the parties requests to end the session. The session is usually ended when the client sends the server a FIN packet, which is an indication to close out the channel.

SSL requires an SSL-enabled server and browser. SSL provides security for the connection but does not offer security for the data once received. This means the data are encrypted while being transmitted, but not after the data are received by a computer. So if a user sends bank account information to a financial institution via a connection protected by SSL, that communication path is protected, but the user must trust the financial institution that receives this information, because at this point, SSL's job is done.

The user can verify that a connection is secure by looking at the URL to see that it includes https://. The user can also check for a padlock or key icon, depending on the browser type, which is shown at the bottom corner of the browser window.

In the protocol stack, SSL lies beneath the application layer and above the network layer. This ensures SSL is not limited to specific application protocols and can still use the communication transport standards of the Internet. Different books and technical resources place SSL at different layers of the OSI model, which may seem confusing at first. But the OSI model is a conceptual construct that attempts to describe the reality of networking. This is like trying to draw nice neat boxes around life—some things don't fit perfectly and hang over the sides. SSL is actually made up of two protocols: one works at the lower end of the session layer, and the other works at the top of the transport layer. This is why one resource will state that SSL works at the session layer and another resource puts it in the transport layer. For the purposes of the CISSP exam, we'll use the latter definition: the SSL protocol works at the transport layer.

Although SSL is almost always used with HTTP, it can also be used with other types of protocols. So if you see a common protocol that is followed by an s, that protocol is using SSL to encrypt its data.

SSL is currently at version 3.0. Since SSL was developed by Netscape, it is not an open-community protocol. This means the technology community cannot easily extend SSL to interoperate and expand in its functionality. If a protocol is proprietary in nature, as SSL is, the technology community cannot directly change its specifications and functionality. If the protocol is an open-community protocol, then its specifications can be modified by individuals within the community to expand what it can do and what technologies it can work with. So the open-community version of SSL is Transport Layer Security (TLS). The differences between SSL 3.0 and TLS is slight, but TLS is more extensible and is backward compatible with SSL.

Secure HTTP

Though their names are very similar, there is a difference between *Secure HTTP (S-HTTP)* and HTTP Secure (HTTPS). S-HTTP is a technology that protects each message sent between two computers, while HTTPS protects the communication channel between two computers, messages and all. HTTPS uses SSL/TLS and HTTP to provide a protected circuit between a client and server. So, S-HTTP is used if an individual message needs to be encrypted, but if all information that passes between two computers must be encrypted, then HTTPS is used, which is SSL over HTTP.

Secure Electronic Transaction

Secure Electronic Transaction (SET) is a security technology proposed by Visa and MasterCard to allow for more secure credit card transaction possibilities than what is currently available. SET has been waiting in the wings for full implementation and acceptance as a standard for quite some time. Although SET provides an effective way of transmitting credit card information, businesses and users do not see it as efficient because it requires more parties to coordinate their efforts, more software installation and configuration for each entity involved, and more effort and cost than the widely used SSL method.

SET is a cryptographic protocol and infrastructure developed to send encrypted credit card numbers over the Internet. The following entities would be involved with a SET transaction, which would require each of them to upgrade their software, and possibly their hardware:

- **Issuer (cardholder's bank)** The financial institution that provides a credit card to the individual.
- **Cardholder** The individual authorized to use a credit card.
- **Merchant** The entity providing goods.

- **Acquirer (merchant's bank)** The financial institution that processes payment cards.
- **Payment gateway** This processes the merchant payment. It may be an acquirer.

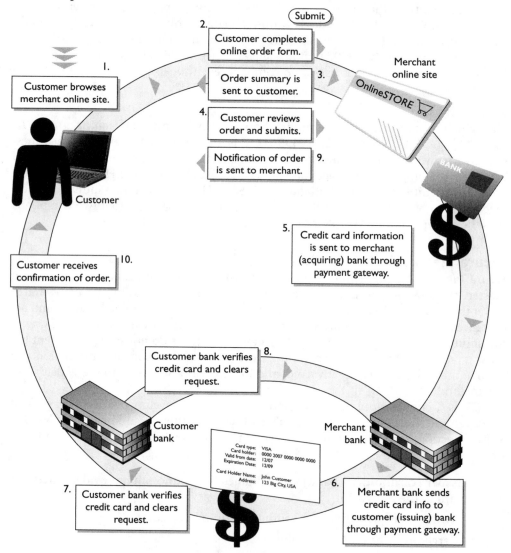

To use SET, a user must enter her credit card number into her electronic wallet software. This information is stored on the user's hard drive or on a smart card. The software then creates a public key and a private key that are used specifically for encrypting financial information before it is sent.

Let's say Tanya wants to use her electronic credit card to buy her mother a gift from a web site. When she finds the perfect gift and decides to purchase it, she sends her encrypted credit card information to the merchant's web server. The merchant does not decrypt the credit card information, but instead digitally signs it and sends it on to its processing bank. At the bank, the payment server decrypts the information, verifies that Tanya has the necessary funds, and transfers the funds from Tanya's account to the merchant's account. Then the payment server sends a message to the merchant telling it to finish the transaction, and a receipt is sent to Tanya and the merchant. At each step, an entity verifies a digital signature of the sender and digitally signs the information before it is sent to the next entity involved in the process. This would require all entities to have digital certificates and to participate in a PKI.

This is basically a very secure way of doing business over the Internet, but today everyone seems to be happy enough with the security SSL provides. They do not feel motivated enough to move to a different and more encompassing technology. The lack of motivation comes from all of the changes that would need to take place to our current processes and the amount of money these changes would require.

Cookies

Hey, I found a web site that's giving out free cookies!
Response: Great, I'll bring the milk!

Cookies are text files that a browser maintains on a user's hard drive. Cookies have different uses, and some are used for demographic and advertising information. As a user travels from site to site on the Internet, the sites could be writing data to the cookies stored on the user's system. The sites can keep track of the user's browsing and spending habits and the user's specific customization for certain sites. For example, if Emily goes to mainly gardening sites on the Internet, those sites will most likely record this information and the types of items in which she shows most interest. Then, when Emily returns to one of the same or similar sites, it will retrieve her cookies, find she has shown interest in gardening books in the past, and present her with its line of gardening books. This increases the likelihood of Emily purchasing a book of her liking. This is a way of zeroing in on the right marketing tactics for the right person.

The servers at the web site determine how cookies are actually used. When a user adds items to his shopping cart on a site, such data are usually added to a cookie. Then, when the user is ready to check out and pay for his items, all the data in this specific cookie are extracted and the totals are added.

As stated before, HTTP is a stateless protocol, meaning a web server has no memory of any prior connections. This is one reason to use cookies. They retain the memory between HTTP connections by saving prior connection data to the client's computer.

For example, if you carry out your banking activities online, your bank's web server keeps track of your activities through the use of cookies. When you first go to its site and are looking at public information, such as branch locations, hours of operation, and CD rates, no confidential information is being transferred back and forth. Once you make a request to access your bank account, the web server sets up an SSL connection and requires you to send credentials. Once you send your credentials and are authenticated, the server generates a cookie with your authentication and account information in it. The server sends it to your browser, which either saves it to your hard drive or keeps it in memory.

NOTE Some cookies are stored as text files on your hard drive. These files should not contain any sensitive information, such as account numbers and passwords. In most cases, cookies that contain sensitive information stay resident in memory and are not stored on the hard drive.

So, suppose you look at your checking account, do some work there, and then request to view your savings account information. The web server sends a request to see if you have been properly authenticated for this activity by checking your cookie.

Most online banking software also periodically requests your cookie, to ensure no man-in-the-middle attacks are going on and that someone else has not hijacked the session.

It is also important to ensure that secure connections time out. This is why cookies have timestamps within them. If you have ever worked on a site that has an SSL connection set up for you and it required you to reauthenticate, the reason is that your session has been idle for a while and, instead of leaving a secure connection open, the web server software closed it out.

A majority of the data within a cookie is meaningless to any entities other than the servers at specific sites, but some cookies can contain usernames and passwords for different accounts on the Internet. The cookies that contain sensitive information should be encrypted by the server at the site that distributes them, but this does not always happen, and a nosey attacker could find this data on the user's hard drive and attempt to use it for mischievous activity. Some people who live on the paranoid side of life do not allow cookies to be downloaded to their systems (controlled through browser security controls). Although this provides a high level of protection against different types of cookie abuse, it also reduces their functionality on the Internet. Some sites require cookies because there is specific data within the cookies that the site must utilize correctly in order to provide the user with the services she requested.

 NOTE Some third-party products can limit the type of cookies downloaded, hide the user's identities as he travels from one site to the next, and mask the user's e-mail addresses and the mail servers he uses if he is concerned about concealing his identity and his tracks.

Secure Shell

Secure Shell (SSH) functions as a type of tunneling mechanism that provides terminal-like access to remote computers. SSH is a program and a protocol that can be used to log into another computer over a network. For example, the program can let Paul, who is on computer A, access computer B's files, run applications on computer B, and retrieve files from computer B without ever physically touching that computer. SSH provides authentication and secure transmission over vulnerable channels like the Internet.

 NOTE SSH can also be used for secure channels for file transfer and port redirection.

SSH should be used instead of Telnet, FTP, rlogin, rexec, or rsh, which provide the same type of functionality SSH offers but in a much less secure manner. SSH is a program and a set of protocols that work together to provide a secure tunnel between two computers. The two computers go through a handshaking process and exchange (via Diffie-Hellman) a session key that will be used during the session to encrypt and protect the data sent. The steps of an SSH connection are outlined in Figure 8-28.

Once the handshake takes place and a secure channel is established, the two computers have a pathway to exchange data with the assurance that the information will be encrypted and its integrity will be protected.

Internet Protocol Security

Hey, is there a really complex protocol that can provide me with network layer protection?
Response: Yep, IPSec.

The *Internet Protocol Security (IPSec)* protocol suite provides a method of setting up a secure channel for protected data exchange between two devices. The devices that share this secure channel can be two servers, two routers, a workstation and a server, or two gateways between different networks. IPSec is a widely accepted standard for providing network layer protection. It can be more flexible and less expensive than end-to-end and link encryption methods.

IPSec has strong encryption and authentication methods, and although it can be used to enable tunneled communication between two computers, it is usually employed to establish virtual private networks (VPNs) among networks across the Internet.

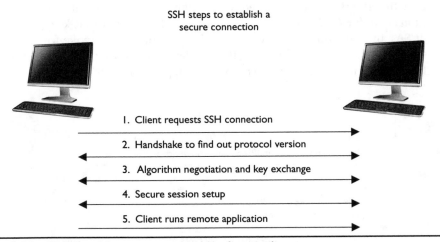

Figure 8-28 SSH is used for remote terminal-like functionality.

IPSec is not a strict protocol that dictates the type of algorithm, keys, and authentication method to use. Rather, it is an open, modular framework that provides a lot of flexibility for companies when they choose to use this type of technology. IPSec uses two basic security protocols: *Authentication Header (AH)* and *Encapsulating Security Payload (ESP)*. AH is the authenticating protocol, and ESP is an authenticating and encrypting protocol that uses cryptographic mechanisms to provide source authentication, confidentiality, and message integrity.

IPSec can work in one of two modes: *transport mode*, in which the payload of the message is protected, and *tunnel mode*, in which the payload and the routing and header information are protected. ESP in transport mode encrypts the actual message information so it cannot be sniffed and uncovered by an unauthorized entity. Tunnel mode provides a higher level of protection by also protecting the header and trailer data an attacker may find useful. Figure 8-29 shows the high-level view of the steps of setting up an IPSec connection.

Each device will have at least one *security association (SA)* for each secure connection it uses. The SA, which is critical to the IPSec architecture, is a record of the configurations the device needs to support an IPSec connection. When two devices complete their handshaking process, which means they have agreed upon a long list of parameters they will use to communicate, these data must be recorded and stored somewhere, which is in the SA. The SA can contain the authentication and encryption keys, the agreed-upon algorithms, the key lifetime, and the source IP address. When a device receives a packet via the IPSec protocol, it is the SA that tells the device what to do with the packet. So if device B receives a packet from device C via IPSec, device B will look to the corresponding SA to tell it how to decrypt the packet, how to properly authenticate the source of the packet, which key to use, and how to reply to the message if necessary.

SAs are directional, so a device will have one SA for outbound traffic and a different SA for inbound traffic for each individual communication channel. If a device is connecting to three devices, it will have at least six SAs, one for each inbound and outbound connection per remote device. So how can a device keep all of these SAs organized and ensure that the right SA is invoked for the right connection? With the mighty *security parameter index (SPI)*, that's how. Each device has an SPI that keeps track of the different SAs and tells the device which one is appropriate to invoke for the different packets it receives. The SPI value is in the header of an IPSec packet, and the device reads this value to tell it which SA to consult, as depicted in Figure 8-30.

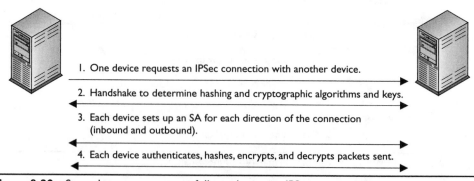

1. One device requests an IPSec connection with another device.

2. Handshake to determine hashing and cryptographic algorithms and keys.

3. Each device sets up an SA for each direction of the connection (inbound and outbound).

4. Each device authenticates, hashes, encrypts, and decrypts packets sent.

Figure 8-29   Steps that two computers follow when using IPSec

IPSec can authenticate the sending devices of the packet by using MAC (covered in the earlier section, "The One-Way Hash"). The ESP protocol can provide authentication, integrity, and confidentiality if the devices are configured for this type of functionality. So if a company just needs to make sure it knows the source of the sender and must be assured of the integrity of the packets, it would choose to use AH. If the company would like to use these services and also have confidentiality, it would use the ESP protocol because it provides encryption functionality. In most cases, the reason ESP is employed is because the company must set up a secure VPN connection.

It may seem odd to have two different protocols that provide overlapping functionality. AH provides authentication and integrity, and ESP can provide those two functions *and* confidentiality. Why even bother with AH then? In most cases, the reason has to do with whether the environment is using network address translation (NAT). IPSec will generate an integrity check value (ICV), which is really the same thing as a MAC value, over a portion of the packet. Remember that the sender and receiver generate their own values. In IPSec, it is called an ICV value. The receiver compares her ICV value with the one sent by the sender. If the values match, the receiver can be assured the packet has not been modified during transmission. If the values are different, the packet has been altered and the receiver discards the packet.

The AH protocol calculates this ICV over the data payload, transport, and network headers. If the packet then goes through a NAT device, the NAT device changes the IP address of the packet. That is its job. This means a portion of the data (network header) that was included to calculate the ICV value has now changed, and the receiver will generate an ICV value that is different from the one sent with the packet, which means the packet will be discarded automatically.

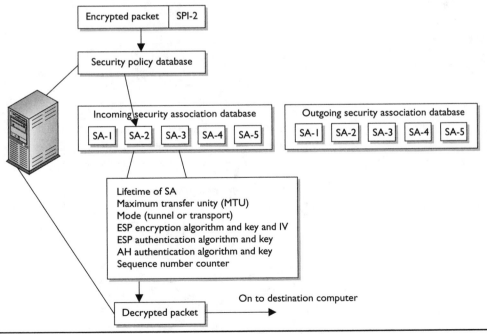

Figure 8-30   The SPI and SA help the system process IPSec packets.

The ESP protocol follows similar steps, except it does not include the network header portion when calculating its ICV value. When the NAT device changes the IP address, it will not affect the receiver's ICV value because it does not include the network header when calculating the ICV. The differences are shown in Figure 8-31.

Because IPSec is a framework, it does not dictate which hashing and encryption algorithms are to be used or how keys are to be exchanged between devices. Key management can be handled manually or automated by a key management protocol. The de facto standard for IPSec is to use Internet Key Exchange (IKE), which is a combination of the ISAKMP and OAKLEY protocols. The *Internet Security Association and Key Management Protocol (ISAKMP)* is a key exchange architecture that is independent of the type of keying mechanisms used. Basically, ISAKMP provides the framework of what can be negotiated to set up an IPSec connection (algorithms, protocols, modes, keys). The OAKLEY protocol is the one that carries out the negotiation process. You can think of ISAKMP as providing the playing field (the infrastructure) and OAKLEY as the guy running up and down the playing field (carrying out the steps of the negotiation).

 NOTE Simple Key Management Protocol for IP (SKIP) is another key exchange protocol that provides basically the same functionality as IKE. It is important to know that all of these protocols work at the network layer.

IPSec is very complex with all of its components and possible configurations. This complexity is what provides for a great degree of flexibility, because a company has many different configuration choices to achieve just the right level of protection. If this

Figure 8-31
AH and ESP use
different portions
of the packet to
calculate the ICVs.

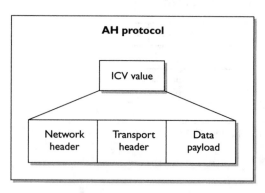

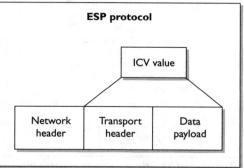

is all new to you and still confusing, please review one or more of the following references to help fill in the gray areas.

Attacks

Eavesdropping and sniffing data as it passes over a network are considered *passive attacks* because the attacker is not affecting the protocol, algorithm, key, message, or any parts of the encryption system. Passive attacks are hard to detect, so in most cases methods are put in place to try to prevent them rather than to detect and stop them.

Altering messages, modifying system files, and masquerading as another individual are acts that are considered *active attacks* because the attacker is actually doing something instead of sitting back and gathering data. Passive attacks are usually used to gain information prior to carrying out an active attack. The following sections address some active attacks that relate to cryptography.

Cipher-Only Attacks

In this type of attack, the attacker has the ciphertext of several messages. Each of the messages has been encrypted using the same encryption algorithm. The attacker's goal is to discover the key used in the encryption process. Once the attacker figures out the key, she can decrypt all other messages encrypted with the same key.

A ciphertext-only attack is the most common type of active attack because it is very easy to get ciphertext by sniffing someone's traffic, but it is the hardest attack to actually be successful at because the attacker has so little information about the encryption process.

Known-Plaintext Attacks

In known-plaintext attacks, the attacker has the plaintext and corresponding ciphertext of one or more messages. Again, the goal is to discover the key used to encrypt the messages so other messages can be deciphered and read.

Messages usually start with the same type of beginning and close with the same type of ending. An attacker might know that each message a general sends out to his commanders always starts with certain greetings and ends with specific salutations and the general's name and contact information. In this instance, the attacker has some of the plaintext (the data that are the same on each message) and can capture an encrypted message, and therefore capture the ciphertext. Once a few pieces of the puzzle are discovered, the rest is accomplished by reverse-engineering, frequency analysis, and brute force attempts. Known-plaintext attacks were used by the United States against the Germans and the Japanese during World War II.

Chosen-Plaintext Attacks

In chosen-plaintext attacks, the attacker has the plaintext and ciphertext, but can choose the plaintext that gets encrypted to see the corresponding ciphertext. This gives her more power and possibly a deeper understanding of the way the encryption process works so she can gather more information about the key being used. Once the key is discovered, other messages encrypted with that key can be decrypted.

How would this be carried out? I can e-mail a message to you that I think you not only will believe, but that you will also panic about, encrypt, and send to someone else. Suppose I send you an e-mail that states, "The meaning of life is 42." You may think you have received an important piece of information that should be concealed from others, everyone except your friend Bob, of course. So you encrypt my message and send it to Bob. Meanwhile I am sniffing your traffic and now have a copy of the plaintext of the message, because I wrote it, and a copy of the ciphertext.

Chosen-Ciphertext Attacks

In chosen-ciphertext attacks, the attacker can choose the ciphertext to be decrypted and has access to the resulting decrypted plaintext. Again, the goal is to figure out the key. This is a harder attack to carry out compared to the previously mentioned attacks, and the attacker may need to have control of the system that contains the cryptosystem.

 NOTE   All of these attacks have a derivative form, the names of which are the same except for putting the word "adaptive" in front of them: such as adaptive chosen-plaintext and adaptive chosen-ciphertext. What this means is that the attacker can carry out one of these attacks and, depending upon what she gleaned from that first attack, modify her next attack. This is the process of reverse-engineering or cryptanalysis attacks: using what you learned to improve your next attack.

Differential Cryptanalysis

This type of attack also has the goal of uncovering the key that was used for encryption purposes. This attack looks at ciphertext pairs generated by encryption of plaintext pairs with specific differences and analyzes the effect and result of those differences. One

Public vs. Secret Algorithms

The public mainly uses algorithms that are known and understood versus the secret algorithms where the internal processes and functions are not released to the public. In general, cryptographers in the public sector feel as though the strongest and best-engineered algorithms are the ones released for peer review and public scrutiny, because a thousand brains are better than five, and many times some smarty-pants within the public population can find problems within an algorithm that the developers did not think of. This is why vendors and companies have competitions to see if anyone can break their code and encryption processes. If someone does break it, that means the developers must go back to the drawing board and strengthen this or that piece.

Not all algorithms are released to the public, such as the ones developed by the NSA. Because the sensitivity level of what the NSA encrypts is so important, it wants as much of the process to be as secret as possible. The fact that the NSA does not release its algorithms for public examination and analysis does not mean its algorithms are weak. Its algorithms are developed, reviewed, and tested by many of the top cryptographic smarty-pants around, and are of very high quality.

such attack was invented in 1990 as an attack against DES, and it turned out to be an effective and successful attack against DES and other block algorithms.

The attacker takes two messages of plaintext and follows the changes that take place to the blocks as they go through the different S-boxes. (Each message is being encrypted with the same key.) The differences identified in the resulting ciphertext values are used to map probability values to different possible key values. The attacker continues this process with several more sets of messages and reviews the common key probability values. One key will continue to show itself as the most probable key used in the encryption processes. Since the attacker chooses the different plaintext messages for this attack, it is considered to be a type of chosen-plaintext attack.

Linear Cryptanalysis

Linear cryptanalysis is another type of attack that carries out functions to identify the highest probability of a specific key employed during the encryption process using a block algorithm. The attacker carries out a known-plaintext attack on several different messages encrypted with the same key. The more messages the attacker can use and put through this type of attack, the higher the confidence level in the probability of a specific key value.

The attacker evaluates the input and output values for each S-box. He evaluates the probability of input values ending up in a specific combination. Identifying specific output combinations allows him to assign probability values to different keys until one shows a continual pattern of having the highest probability.

Side-Channel Attacks

All of the attacks we have covered thus far have been based mainly on the mathematics of cryptography. Using plaintext and ciphertext involves high-powered mathematical tools that are needed to uncover the key used in the encryption process.

But what if we took a different approach? Let's say we see something that looks like a duck, walks like a duck, sounds like a duck, swims in water, and eats bugs and small fish. We could confidently conclude that this is a duck. Similarly, in cryptography, we can review facts and infer the value of an encryption key. For example, we could detect how much power consumption is used for encryption and decryption (the fluctuation of electronic voltage). We could also intercept the radiation emissions released and then calculate how long the processes take. Looking around the cryptosystem, or its attributes and characteristics, is different from looking into the cryptosystem and trying to defeat it through mathematical computations.

If I want to figure out what you do for a living, but I don't want you to know I am doing this type of reconnaissance work, I won't ask you directly. Instead, I will find out when you go to work and come home, the types of clothing you wear, the items you carry, whom you talk to . . . or I can just follow you to work. These are examples of side channels.

So, in cryptography, gathering "outside" information with the goal of uncovering the encryption key is just another way of attacking a cryptosystem.

An attacker could measure power consumption, radiation emissions, and the time it takes for certain types of data processing. With this information, he can work backward by reverse-engineering the process to uncover an encryption key or sensitive data. A power attack reviews the amount of heat released. This type of attack has been successful in uncovering confidential information from smart cards. In 1995, RSA private keys were uncovered by measuring the relative time cryptographic operations took.

The idea is that, instead of attacking a device head on, just watch how it performs to figure out how it works. In biology, scientists can choose to carry out a noninvasive experiment, which will watch an organism eat, sleep, mate, and so on. This type of approach learns about the organism through understanding its behaviors instead of killing it and looking at it from the inside out.

Replay Attacks

A big concern in distributed environments is the *replay attack*, in which an attacker captures some type of data and resubmits it with the hopes of fooling the receiving device into thinking it is legitimate information. Many times, the data captured and resubmitted are authentication information, and the attacker is trying to authenticate herself as someone else to gain unauthorized access.

Timestamps and sequence numbers are two countermeasures to replay attacks. Packets can contain sequence numbers, so each machine will expect a specific number on each receiving packet. If a packet has a sequence number that has been previously used, this is an indication of a replay attack. Packets can also be timestamped. A threshold can be set on each computer to only accept packets within a certain timeframe. If a packet is received that is past this threshold, it can help identify a replay attack.

Just in case there aren't enough attacks here for you, we have three more, introduced quickly in the following sections.

Algebraic Attacks

Algebraic attacks analyze the vulnerabilities in the mathematics used within the algorithm and exploit the intrinsic algebraic structure. For instance, attacks on the "textbook" version of the RSA cryptosystem exploit properties of the algorithm such as the fact that the encryption of a raw "0" message is "0".

Analytic Attacks

Analytic attacks identify algorithm structural weaknesses or flaws, as opposed to brute force attacks, which simply exhaust all possibilities without respect to the specific properties of the algorithm. Examples = Double DES attack and RSA factoring attack.

Statistical Attacks

Statistical attacks identify statistical weaknesses in algorithm design for exploitation—for example, if statistical patterns are identified, as in the number of 0's compared to the number of 1's. For instance, a random number generator may be biased. If keys are taken directly from the output of the RNG, then the distribution of keys would also be biased. The statistical knowledge about the bias could be used to reduce the search time for the keys.

Summary

Cryptography has been used in one form or another for over 4,000 years, and the attacks on cryptography have probably been in place for 3,999 years and 364 days. As one group of people works to find new ways to hide and transmit secrets, another group of people is right on their heels finding holes in the newly developed ideas and products. This can be viewed as evil and destructive behavior, or as the thorn in the side of the computing world that pushes it to build better and more secure products and environments.

Cryptographic algorithms provide the underlying tools to most security protocols used in today's infrastructures. The algorithms work off of mathematical functions and provide various types of functionality and levels of security. A big leap was made when encryption went from purely symmetric key use to public key cryptography. This evolution provided users and maintainers much more freedom and flexibility when it came to communicating with a variety of users all over the world.

Encryption can be supplied at different layers of the OSI model by a range of applications, protocols, and mechanisms. Today, not much thought has to be given to cryptography and encryption because it is taken care of in the background by many operating systems, applications, and protocols. However, for administrators who maintain these environments, for security professionals who propose and implement security solutions, and for those interested in obtaining a CISSP certification, knowing the ins and outs of cryptography is essential.

Quick Tips

- Cryptography is the science of protecting information by encoding it into an unreadable format.
- The most famous rotor encryption machine is the Enigma used by the Germans in WWII.
- A readable message is in a form called plaintext, and once it is encrypted, it is in a form called ciphertext.
- Cryptographic algorithms are the mathematical rules that dictate the functions of enciphering and deciphering.
- Cryptanalysis is the study of breaking cryptosystems.
- Nonrepudiation is a service that ensures the sender cannot later falsely deny sending a message.
- Key clustering is an instance in which two different keys generate the same ciphertext from the same plaintext.
- The range of possible keys is referred to as the keyspace. A larger keyspace and the full use of the keyspace allow for more random keys to be created. This provides more protection.

- The two basic types of encryption mechanisms used in symmetric ciphers are substitution and transposition. Substitution ciphers change a character (or bit) out for another, while transposition ciphers scramble the characters (or bits).

- A polyalphabetic cipher uses more than one alphabet to defeat frequency analysis.

- Steganography is a method of hiding data within another media type, such as a graphic, WAV file, or document. This method is used to hide the existence of the data.

- A key is a random string of bits inserted into an encryption algorithm. The result determines what encryption functions will be carried out on a message and in what order.

- In symmetric key algorithms, the sender and receiver use the same key for encryption and decryption purposes.

- In asymmetric key algorithms, the sender and receiver use different keys for encryption and decryption purposes.

- Symmetric key processes provide barriers of secure key distribution and scalability. However, symmetric key algorithms perform much faster than asymmetric key algorithms.

- Symmetric key algorithms can provide confidentiality, but not authentication or nonrepudiation.

- Examples of symmetric key algorithms include DES, 3DES, Blowfish, IDEA, RC4, RC5, RC6, and AES.

- Asymmetric algorithms are used to encrypt keys, and symmetric algorithms are used to encrypt bulk data.

- Asymmetric key algorithms are much slower than symmetric key algorithms, but can provide authentication and nonrepudiation services.

- Examples of asymmetric key algorithms include RSA, ECC, Diffie-Hellman, El Gamal, Knapsack, and DSA.

- Two main types of symmetric algorithms are stream and block ciphers. Stream ciphers use a keystream generator and encrypt a message one bit at a time. A block cipher divides the message into groups of bits and encrypts them.

- Block ciphers are usually implemented in software, and stream ciphers are usually implemented in hardware.

- Many algorithms are publicly known, so the secret part of the process is the key. The key provides the necessary randomization to encryption.

- Data Encryption Standard (DES) is a block cipher that divides a message into 64-bit blocks and employs S-box-type functions on them.

- Because technology has allowed the DES keyspace to be successfully broken, Triple-DES (3DES) was developed to be used instead. 3DES uses 48 rounds of computation and up to three different keys.

- International Data Encryption Algorithm (IDEA) is a symmetric block cipher with a key of 128 bits.
- RSA is an asymmetric algorithm developed by Rivest, Shamir, and Adleman and is the de facto standard for digital signatures.
- Elliptic curve cryptosystems (ECCs) are used as asymmetric algorithms and can provide digital signature, secure key distribution, and encryption functionality. They use much less resources, which makes them better for wireless device and cell phone encryption use.
- When symmetric and asymmetric key algorithms are used together, this is called a hybrid system. The asymmetric algorithm encrypts the symmetric key, and the symmetric key encrypts the data.
- A session key is a symmetric key used by the sender and receiver of messages for encryption and decryption purposes. The session key is only good while that communication session is active and then it is destroyed.
- A public key infrastructure (PKI) is a framework of programs, procedures, communication protocols, and public key cryptography that enables a diverse group of individuals to communicate securely.
- A certificate authority (CA) is a trusted third party that generates and maintains user certificates, which hold their public keys.
- The CA uses a certification revocation list (CRL) to keep track of revoked certificates.
- A certificate is the mechanism the CA uses to associate a public key to a person's identity.
- A registration authority (RA) validates the user's identity and then sends the request for a certificate to the CA. The RA cannot generate certificates.
- A one-way function is a mathematical function that is easier to compute in one direction than in the opposite direction.
- RSA is based on a one-way function that factors large numbers into prime numbers. Only the private key knows how to use the trapdoor and how to decrypt messages that were encrypted with the corresponding public key.
- Hashing algorithms provide data integrity only.
- When a hash algorithm is applied to a message, it produces a message digest, and this value is signed with a private key to produce a digital signature.
- Some examples of hashing algorithms include SHA-1, MD2, MD4, MD5, and HAVAL.
- HAVAL produces a variable-length hash value, whereas the other hashing algorithms mentioned produce a fixed-length value.
- SHA-1 produces a 160-bit hash value and is used in DSS.
- A birthday attack is an attack on hashing functions through brute force. The attacker tries to create two messages with the same hashing value.

- A one-time pad uses a pad with random values that are XORed against the message to produce ciphertext. The pad is at least as long as the message itself and is used once and then discarded.

- A digital signature is the result of a user signing a hash value with a private key. It provides authentication, data integrity, and nonrepudiation. The act of signing is the actual encryption of the value with the private key.

- Examples of algorithms used for digital signatures include RSA, El Gamal, ECDSA, and DSA.

- Key management is one of the most challenging pieces of cryptography. It pertains to creating, maintaining, distributing, and destroying cryptographic keys.

- The Diffie-Hellman protocol is a key agreement protocol and does not provide encryption for data and cannot be used in digital signatures.

- TLS is the "next version" of SSL and is an open-community protocol, which allows for expansion and interoperability with other technologies.

- Link encryption encrypts the entire packet, including headers and trailers, and has to be decrypted at each hop. End-to-end encryption does not encrypt the headers and trailers, and therefore does not need to be decrypted at each hop.

- Privacy-Enhanced Mail (PEM) is an Internet standard that provides secure e-mail over the Internet by using encryption, digital signatures, and key management.

- Message Security Protocol (MSP) is the military's PEM.

- Pretty Good Privacy (PGP) is an e-mail security program that uses public key encryption. It employs a web of trust instead of the hierarchical structure used in PKI.

- S-HTTP provides protection for each message sent between two computers, but not the actual link. HTTPS protects the communication channel. HTTPS is HTTP that uses SSL for security purposes.

- Secure Electronic Transaction (SET) is a proposed electronic commerce technology that provides a safer method for customers and merchants to perform transactions over the Internet.

- In IPSec, AH provides integrity and authentication, and ESP provides those plus confidentiality.

- IPSec protocols can work in transport mode (the data payload is protected) or tunnel mode (the payload and headers are protected).

- IPSec uses IKE as its key exchange protocol. IKE is the de facto standard and is a combination of ISAKMP and OAKLEY.

- DEA is the algorithm used for the DES standard.

Questions

Please remember that these questions are formatted and asked in a certain way for a reason. Keep in mind that the CISSP exam is asking questions at a conceptual level. Questions may not always have the perfect answer, and the candidate is advised against always looking for the perfect answer. The candidate should look for the best answer in the list.

1. What is the goal of cryptanalysis?

    A. To determine the strength of an algorithm

    B. To increase the substitution functions in a cryptographic algorithm

    C. To decrease the transposition functions in a cryptographic algorithm

    D. To determine the permutations used

2. The frequency of brute force attacks has increased because

    A. The use of permutations and transpositions in algorithms has increased.

    B. As algorithms get stronger, they get less complex, and thus more susceptible to attacks.

    C. Processor speed and power has increased.

    D. Key length reduces over time.

3. Which of the following is not a property or characteristic of a one-way hash function?

    A. It converts a message of arbitrary length into a value of fixed length.

    B. Given the digest value, it should be computationally infeasible to find the corresponding message.

    C. It should be impossible or rare to derive the same digest from two different messages.

    D. It converts a message of fixed length to an arbitrary length value.

4. What would indicate that a message had been modified?

    A. The public key has been altered.

    B. The private key has been altered.

    C. The message digest has been altered.

    D. The message has been encrypted properly.

5. Which of the following is a U.S. federal government algorithm developed for creating secure message digests?

    A. Data Encryption Algorithm

    B. Digital Signature Standard

    C. Secure Hash Algorithm

    D. Data Signature Algorithm

6. Which of the following best describes the difference between HMAC and CBC-MAC?

   A. HMAC creates a message digest and is used for integrity; CBC-MAC is used to encrypt blocks of data for confidentiality.

   B. HMAC uses a symmetric key and a hashing algorithm; CBC-MAC uses the first block for the checksum.

   C. HMAC provides integrity and data origin authentication; CBC-MAC uses a block cipher for the process of creating a MAC.

   D. HMAC encrypts a message with a symmetric key and then puts the result through a hashing algorithm; CBC-MAC encrypts the whole message.

7. What is an advantage of RSA over the DSA?

   A. It can provide digital signature and encryption functionality.

   B. It uses fewer resources and encrypts faster because it uses symmetric keys.

   C. It is a block cipher rather than a stream cipher.

   D. It employs a one-time encryption pad.

8. Many countries restrict the use or exportation of cryptographic systems. What is the reason given when these types of restrictions are put into place?

   A. Without standards, there would be many interoperability issues when trying to employ different algorithms in different programs.

   B. The systems can be used by some countries against their local people.

   C. Criminals could use encryption to avoid detection and prosecution.

   D. Laws are way behind, so adding different types of encryption would confuse the laws more.

9. What is used to create a digital signature?

   A. The receiver's private key

   B. The sender's public key

   C. The sender's private key

   D. The receiver's public key

10. Which of the following best describes a digital signature?

    A. A method of transferring a handwritten signature to an electronic document

    B. A method to encrypt confidential information

    C. A method to provide an electronic signature and encryption

    D. A method to let the receiver of the message prove the source and integrity of a message

11. How many bits make up the effective length of the DES key?

    A. 56

    B. 64

C. 32

D. 16

12. Why would a certificate authority revoke a certificate?

   A. If the user's public key has become compromised

   B. If the user changed over to using the PEM model that uses a web of trust

   C. If the user's private key has become compromised

   D. If the user moved to a new location

13. What does DES stand for?

   A. Data Encryption System

   B. Data Encryption Standard

   C. Data Encoding Standard

   D. Data Encryption Signature

14. Which of the following best describes a certificate authority?

   A. An organization that issues private keys and the corresponding algorithms

   B. An organization that validates encryption processes

   C. An organization that verifies encryption keys

   D. An organization that issues certificates

15. What does DEA stand for?

   A. Data Encoding Algorithm

   B. Data Encoding Application

   C. Data Encryption Algorithm

   D. Digital Encryption Algorithm

16. Who was involved in developing the first public key algorithm?

   A. Adi Shamir

   B. Ross Anderson

   C. Bruce Schneier

   D. Martin Hellman

17. What process usually takes place after creating a DES session key?

   A. Key signing

   B. Key escrow

   C. Key clustering

   D. Key exchange

18. DES performs how many rounds of permutation and substitution?

    A. 16

    B. 32

    C. 64

    D. 56

19. Which of the following is a true statement pertaining to data encryption when it is used to protect data?

    A. It verifies the integrity and accuracy of the data.

    B. It requires careful key management.

    C. It does not require much system overhead in resources.

    D. It requires keys to be escrowed.

20. If different keys generate the same ciphertext for the same message, what is this called?

    A. Collision

    B. Secure hashing

    C. MAC

    D. Key clustering

21. What is the definition of an algorithm's work factor?

    A. The time it takes to encrypt and decrypt the same plaintext

    B. The time it takes to break the encryption

    C. The time it takes to implement 16 rounds of computation

    D. The time it takes to apply substitution functions

22. What is the primary purpose of using one-way hashing on user passwords?

    A. It minimizes the amount of primary and secondary storage needed to store passwords.

    B. It prevents anyone from reading passwords in plaintext.

    C. It avoids excessive processing required by an asymmetric algorithm.

    D. It prevents replay attacks.

23. Which of the following is based on the fact that it is hard to factor large numbers into two original prime numbers?

    A. ECC

    B. RSA

    C. DES

    D. Diffie-Hellman

24. Which of the following describes the difference between the Data Encryption Standard and the Rivest-Shamir-Adleman algorithm?

    A. DES is symmetric, while RSA is asymmetric.

    B. DES is asymmetric, while RSA is symmetric.

    C. They are hashing algorithms, but RSA produces a 160-bit hashing value.

    D. DES creates public and private keys, while RSA encrypts messages.

25. Which of the following uses a symmetric key and a hashing algorithm?

    A. HMAC

    B. Triple-DES

    C. ISAKMP-OAKLEY

    D. RSA

26. The generation of keys that are made up of random values is referred to as Key Derivation Functions (KDFs). What values are not commonly used in this key generation process?

    A. Hashing values

    B. Asymmetric values

    C. Salts

    D. Passwords

Answers

1. **A.** Cryptanalysis is the process of trying to reverse engineer a cryptosystem with the possible goal of uncovering the key used. Once this key is uncovered, all other messages encrypted with this key can be accessed. Cryptanalysis is carried out by the white hats to test the strength of the algorithm.

2. **C.** A brute force attack is resource intensive. It guesses values until the correct one is obtained. As computers have more powerful processors added to them, attackers can carry out more powerful brute force attacks.

3. **D.** A hashing algorithm will take a string of variable length, the message can be any size, and compute a fixed-length value. The fixed-length value is the message digest. The MD family creates the fixed-length value of 128 bits, and SHA creates one of 160 bits.

4. **C.** Hashing algorithms generate message digests to detect whether modification has taken place. The sender and receiver independently generate their own digests, and the receiver compares these values. If they differ, the receiver knows the message has been altered.

5. **C.** SHA was created to generate secure message digests. Digital Signature Standard (DSS) is the standard to create digital signatures, which dictates that SHA must be used. DSS also outlines the digital signature algorithms that can be used with SHA: RSA, DSA, and ECDSA.

6. **C.** In an HMAC operation, a message is concatenated with a symmetric key and the result is put through a hashing algorithm. This provides integrity and system or data authentication. CBC-MAC uses a block cipher to create a MAC, which is the last block of ciphertext.

7. **A.** RSA can be used for data encryption, key exchange, and digital signatures. DSA can be used only for digital signatures.

8. **C.** The U.S. government has greatly reduced its restrictions on cryptography exportation, but there are still some restrictions in place. Products that use encryption cannot be sold to any country the United States has declared is supporting terrorism. The fear is that the enemies of the country would use encryption to hide their communication, and the government would be unable to break this encryption and spy on their data transfers.

9. **C.** A digital signature is a message digest that has been encrypted with the sender's private key. A sender, or anyone else, should never have access to the receiver's private key.

10. **D.** A digital signature provides authentication (knowing who really sent the message), integrity (because a hashing algorithm is involved), and nonrepudiation (the sender cannot deny sending the message).

11. **A.** DES has a key size of 64 bits, but 8 bits are used for parity, so the true key size is 56 bits. Remember that DEA is the algorithm used for the DES standard, so DEA also has a true key size of 56 bits, because we are actually talking about the same algorithm here. DES is really the standard and DEA is the algorithm. We just call it DES in the industry because it is easier.

12. **C.** The reason a certificate is revoked is to warn others who use that person's public key that they should no longer trust the public key because, for some reason, that public key is no longer bound to that particular individual's identity. This could be because an employee left the company, or changed his name and needed a new certificate, but most likely it is because the person's private key was compromised.

13. **B.** Data Encryption Standard was developed by NIST and the NSA to encrypt sensitive but unclassified government data.

14. **D.** A registration authority (RA) accepts a person's request for a certificate and verifies that person's identity. Then the RA sends this request to a certificate authority (CA), which generates and maintains the certificate. Some companies are in business solely for this purpose—Entrust and VeriSign are just two examples.

15. **C.** DEA is the algorithm that fulfilled the DES standard. So DEA has all of the attributes of DES: a symmetric block cipher that uses 64-bit blocks, 16 rounds, and a 56-bit key.

16. **D.** The first released public key cryptography algorithm was developed by Whitfield Diffie and Martin Hellman.

17. **D.** After a session key has been created, it must be exchanged securely. In most cryptosystems, an asymmetric key (the receiver's public key) is used to encrypt this session key, and it is sent to the receiver.

18. **A.** DES carries out 16 rounds of mathematical computation on each 64-bit block of data it is responsible for encrypting. A round is a set of mathematical formulas used for encryption and decryption processes.

19. **B.** Data encryption always requires careful key management. Most algorithms are so strong today it is much easier to go after key management rather than to launch a brute force attack. Hashing algorithms are used for data integrity, encryption does require a good amount of resources, and keys do not have to be escrowed for encryption.

20. **D.** Message A was encrypted with key A and the result is ciphertext Y. If that same message A were encrypted with key B, the result should not be ciphertext Y. The ciphertext should be different since a different key was used. But if the ciphertext is the same, this occurrence is referred to as key clustering.

21. **B.** The work factor of a cryptosystem is the amount of time and resources necessary to break the cryptosystem or its encryption process. The goal is to make the work factor so high that an attacker could not be successful at this type of attack.

22. **B.** Passwords are usually run through a one-way hashing algorithm so the actual password is not transmitted across the network or stored on the authentication server in plaintext. This greatly reduces the risk of an attacker being able to obtain the actual password.

23. **B.** The RSA algorithm's security is based on the difficulty of factoring large numbers into their original prime numbers. This is a one-way function. It is easier to calculate the product than it is to identify the prime numbers used to generate that product.

24. **A.** DES is a symmetric algorithm. RSA is a public key algorithm. DES is used to encrypt data, and RSA is used to create public/private key pairs.

25. **A.** When an HMAC function is used, a symmetric key is combined with the message, and then that result is put though a hashing algorithm. The result is an HMAC value. HMAC provides data origin authentication and data integrity.

26. **B.** Different values can be used independently or together to play the role of random key material. The algorithm is created to use specific hash, passwords, and\or salt values, which will go through a certain number of rounds of mathematical functions dictated by the algorithm.

Business Continuity and Disaster Recovery

This chapter presents the following:

- Project initiation steps
- Recovery and continuity planning requirements
- Business impact analysis
- Selecting, developing, and implementing disaster and continuity plans
- Backup and offsite facilities
- Types of drills and tests

We can't prepare for every possibility, as recent events have proved. In 2005, Hurricane Katrina wreaked extensive damage. Businesses were not merely affected—their buildings were destroyed and lives were lost. The catastrophic Indian Ocean tsunami in December 2004 struck with little warning. The World Trade Center towers coming down after terrorists crashed planes into them affected many surrounding businesses, people, the government, and the world in a way that most people would have never imagined. Every year, thousands of businesses are affected by floods, fires, tornadoes, terrorist attacks, and vandalism. The companies that survive these traumas are the ones that thought ahead, planned for the worst, estimated the possible damages that could occur, and put the necessary controls in place to protect themselves. This is a very small percentage of businesses today. Most businesses affected by these events have to close their doors forever. The companies that have survived these negative eventualities had a measured, approved set of advance arrangements and procedures

An organization depends upon resources, personnel, and tasks that are performed on a daily basis in order to stay healthy, happy, and profitable. Most organizations have tangible resources, intellectual property, employees, computers, communication links, facilities, and facility services. If any one of these is damaged or inaccessible for one reason or another, the company can be crippled. If more than one is damaged, the company may be in a darker situation. The longer these items are unusable, the longer it will probably take for an organization to get back on its feet. Some companies are never able to recover after certain disasters. However, the companies that thought ahead, planned for the possible disasters, and did not put all of their eggs in one basket have had a better chance of resuming business and staying in the market.

Business Continuity and Disaster Recovery

What do we do if everything blows up? And how can we still make our widgets?

The goal of *disaster recovery* is to minimize the effects of a disaster and to take the necessary steps to ensure that the resources, personnel, and business processes are able to resume operation in a timely manner. This is different from continuity planning, which provides methods and procedures for dealing with longer-term outages and disasters. The goal of a disaster recovery plan is to handle the disaster and its ramifications right after the disaster hits; the disaster recovery plan is usually very information technology (IT) focused.

A disaster recovery plan is carried out when everything is still in emergency mode and everyone is scrambling to get all critical systems back online. A business continuity plan (BCP) takes a broader approach to the problem. It includes getting critical systems to another environment while repair of the original facilities is under way, getting the right people to the right places, and performing business in a different mode until regular conditions are back in place. It also involves dealing with customers, partners, and shareholders through different channels until everything returns to normal. So, disaster recovery deals with, "Oh my goodness, the sky is falling," and continuity planning deals with, "Okay, the sky fell. Now, how do we stay in business until someone can put the sky back where it belongs?"

A continual theme runs through many of the chapters in this book: availability, integrity, and confidentiality. Because each chapter deals with a different topic, each looks at these three security characteristics in a slightly different way. In Chapter 4, for example, which discussed access control, availability meant that resources should be available to users and subjects in a controlled and secure manner. The access control method should protect the integrity and/or confidentiality of a resource. In fact, the access control method must take many steps to ensure the resource is kept confidential and that there is no possibility its contents can be altered while they are being accessed. In this chapter, we point out that integrity and confidentiality must be considered not only in everyday procedures, but also in those procedures undertaken immediately after a disaster or disruption. For instance, it may not be appropriate to leave a server that holds confidential information in one building while everyone else moves to another building.

It is also important to note that a company may be much more vulnerable *after* a disaster hits, because the security services used to protect it may be unavailable or operating at a reduced capacity. Therefore, it is important that if the business has secret stuff, it stays secret and that the integrity of data and systems is ensured even when people and the company are in dire straits. Availability is one of the main themes behind business continuity planning in that it ensures that the resources required to keep the business going will continue to be available to the people and systems that rely upon them. This may mean backups need to be done religiously and that redundancy needs to be factored into the architecture of the systems, networks, and operations. If communication lines are disabled or if a service is rendered unusable for any significant period of time, there must be a quick and tested way of establishing alternate communications and services.

When looking at business continuity planning, some companies focus mainly on backing up data and providing redundant hardware. Although these items are extremely important, they are just small pieces of the company's overall operations pie. Hardware and computers need people to configure and operate them, and data is usually not useful unless it is accessible by other systems and possibly outside entities. Thus, a larger picture of how the various processes within a business work together needs to be understood. Planning must include getting the right people to the right places, documenting the necessary configurations, establishing alternate communications channels (voice and data), providing power, and making sure all dependencies, including processes and applications, are properly understood and taken into account. For example, there may be no point in bringing a server back online if the DNS server is not working on the network.

It is also important to understand how automated tasks can be carried out manually, if necessary, and how business processes can be safely altered to keep the operation of the company going. This may be critical in ensuring the company survives the event with the least impact to its operations. Without this type of vision and planning, when a disaster hits, a company could have its backup data and redundant servers physically available at the alternate facility, but the people responsible for activating them may be standing around in a daze not knowing where to start or how to perform in such a different environment.

Business Continuity Planning

Preplanned procedures allow an organization to

- Provide an immediate and appropriate response to emergency situations
- Protect lives and ensure safety
- Reduce business impact
- Resume critical business functions
- Work with outside vendors during the recovery period
- Reduce confusion during a crisis
- Ensure survivability of the business
- Get "up and running" quickly after a disaster

Part of business decisions today should include the following:

- Letting business partners know your company is prepared
- Reassuring shareholders and boards of trustees about your company's readiness
- Making sure a BCP is in place if industry regulations require it

Business Continuity Steps

Although no specific scientific equation must be followed to create continuity plans, certain best practices have proven themselves over time. The National Institute of Standards and Technology (NIST) is responsible for developing these best practices and documenting them so they are easily available to all. NIST outlines the following steps in its Special Publication 800-34, *Continuity Planning Guide for Information Technology Systems* (http://csrc.nist.gov/publications/nistpubs/800-34/sp800-34.pdf):

1. *Develop the continuity planning policy statement.* Write a policy that provides the guidance necessary to develop a BCP and that assigns authority to the necessary roles to carry out these tasks.

2. *Conduct the business impact analysis (BIA).* Identify critical functions and systems and allow the organization to prioritize them based on necessity. Identify vulnerabilities, threats, and calculate risks.

3. *Identify preventive controls.* Once threats are recognized, identify and implement controls and countermeasures to reduce the organization's risk level in an economical manner.

4. *Develop recovery strategies.* Formulate methods to ensure systems and critical functions can be brought online quickly.

5. *Develop the contingency plan.* Write procedures and guidelines for how the organization can still stay functional in a crippled state.

6. *Test the plan and conduct training and exercises.* Test the plan to identify deficiencies in the BCP, and conduct training to properly prepare individuals on their expected tasks.

7. *Maintain the plan.* Put in place steps to ensure the BCP is a living document that is updated regularly.

Different companies and guidelines include the previous information, but may have different names for the steps. (ISC)[2] has the following steps with the same information:

1. Project initiation
2. BIA
3. Recovery strategy
4. Plan design and development
5. Implementation
6. Testing
7. Continual maintenance

Understanding the Organization First

A company has no real hope of rebuilding itself and its processes after a disaster if it does not have a good understanding of how the company works in the first place. This notion might seem absurd at first. You might think, "Well, of course a company knows how it works." But you would be surprised at how truly difficult it is to fully understand an organization down to the level of detail required to rebuild it if necessary. Each individual knows and understands their little world within the company, but hardly anyone at any company can fully explain how each and every business process takes place. It is out of the scope of this book to go into business processes and enterprise architecture, but you can review a mature and useful model at www.intervista-institute.com/resources/zachman-poster .html. This is one of the most comprehensive approaches to understanding a company's architecture and all the pieces and parts that make it up. This model breaks down the core portions of a corporate enterprise to illustrate the various requirements of every business process. It looks at the data, function, network, people, time, and motivation components of the enterprise's infrastructure and how they are tied to the roles within the company. The beauty of this model is that it dissects business processes down to the atomic level and shows the necessary interdependencies that exist, all of which must be working correctly for effective and efficient processes to be carried out.

Note that this link points to a poster that illustrates the comprehensive model, which helps companies classify the various components of the enterprise. This site also contains other resources pertaining to this model.

It would be very beneficial for a BCP team to use this type of model to understand the core components of an organization, because the team's responsibility is to make sure the organization can be rebuilt if need be.

The necessary steps required to roll out a business continuity planning process are illustrated in Figure 9-1.

Although the NIST 800-34 document deals specifically with IT contingency plans, these steps are the same when creating enterprisewide BCPs. This chapter steps you through these different phases and what you should do to build an effective and useful BCP.

Making BCP Part of the Security Policy and Program

Why do we need to combine business continuity and security plans anyway? Response: They both protect the business, unenlightened one.

As explained in Chapter 3, every company should have security policies, procedures, standards, and guidelines. Having these in place is part of a well-managed environment and yields operational and cost-savings benefits. Together, they provide the framework of a security program for an organization. As such, the program needs to be a living entity. As a company goes through changes, so should the program, thereby ensuring it stays current, usable, and effective.

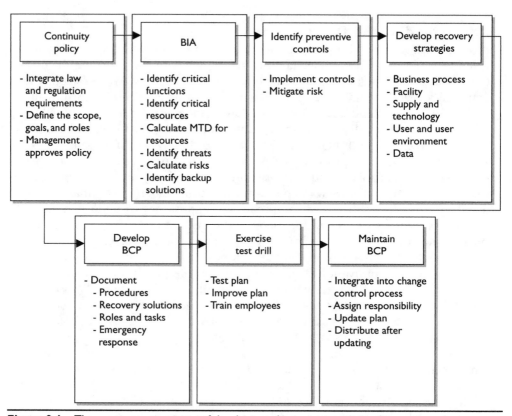

Figure 9-1 The process components of developing a business continuity plan

Business continuity should be a part of the security program and business decisions, as opposed to being an entity that stands off in a corner by itself. When properly integrated with change management processes, it stands a much better chance of being continually updated and improved upon. Business continuity is a foundational piece of an effective security program and is critical to ensuring relevance in time of need.

A very important question to ask when first developing a BCP is *why* it is being developed. This may seem silly and the answer may at first appear obvious, but that is not always the case. You might think that the reason to have these plans is to deal with an unexpected disaster and to get people back to their tasks as quickly and as safely as possible, but the full story is often a bit different. Why are most companies in business? To make money and be profitable. If these are usually the main goals of businesses, then any BCP needs to be developed to help achieve and, more importantly, maintain these goals. The main reason to develop these plans in the first place is to reduce the risk of financial loss by improving the company's ability to recover and restore operations. This encompasses the goals of mitigating the effects of the disaster.

Not all organizations are businesses that exist to make profits. Government agencies, military units, nonprofit organizations, and the like exist to provide some type of protection or service to a nation or society. While a company must create its BCP to ensure that revenue continues to come in so it can stay in business, other types of organizations must create their BCPs to make sure they can still carry out their critical tasks. Although the focus and business drivers of the organizations and companies may differ, their BCPs often will have similar constructs—which is to get their critical processes up and running.

Protecting what is most important to a company is rather difficult if what is most important is not first identified. Senior management is usually involved with this step because it has a point of view that extends beyond each functional manager's focus area of responsibility. The company's business plan usually defines the company's critical mission and business function. The functions must have priorities set upon them to indicate which is most crucial to a company's survival.

For many companies, financial operations are most critical. As an example, an automotive company would be impacted far more seriously if its credit and loan services were unavailable for a day than if, say, an assembly line went down for a day, since credit and loan services are where it generates the biggest revenues. For other organizations, customer service might be the most critical area. For example, if a company makes heart pacemakers and its physician services department is unavailable at a time when an operating room surgeon needs to contact it because of a complication, the results could be disastrous for the patient. The surgeon and the company would likely be sued, and the company would likely never be able to sell another pacemaker to that surgeon, her colleagues, or perhaps even the patient's HMO ever again. It would be very difficult to rebuild a reputation and sales after something like that happened.

Advanced planning for emergencies covers issues that were thought of and foreseen. Many other problems may arise that are not covered in the plan; thus, flexibility in the plan is crucial. The plan is a systematic way of providing a checklist of actions that should take place right after a disaster. These actions have been thought through to help the people involved be more efficient and effective in dealing with traumatic situations.

The most critical part of establishing and maintaining a current continuity plan is management support. Management must be convinced of the necessity of such a plan. Therefore, a business case must be made to obtain this support. The business case may include current vulnerabilities, regulatory and legal obligations, the current status of recovery plans, and recommendations. Management is mostly concerned with cost/benefit issues, so preliminary numbers need to be gathered and potential losses estimated. The decision of how a company should recover is purely a business decision and should always be treated as such.

Project Initiation

Before everyone runs off in 2,000 different directions at one time, let's understand what needs to be done in the project initiation phase. This is the phase in which the company really needs to figure out what it is doing and why. So, after someone gets the donuts and coffee, let's get down to business.

Once management's support is solidified, a *business continuity coordinator* must be identified. This person will be the leader for the BCP team and will oversee the development, implementation, and testing of the continuity and disaster recovery plans. It is best if this person has good social skills, is somewhat of a politician, and has a cape, because he will need to coordinate a lot of different departments and busy individuals who have their own agendas. This person needs to have direct access to management and have the credibility and authority to carry out leadership tasks.

A leader needs a team, so a BCP committee needs to be put together. Management and the coordinator should work together to appoint specific, qualified people to be on this committee. The team must comprise people who are familiar with the different departments within the company, because each department is unique in its functionality and has distinctive risks and threats. The best plan is when all issues and threats are brought to the table and discussed. This cannot be done effectively with a few people who are familiar with only a couple of departments. Representatives from each department must be involved with not only the planning stages but also the testing and implementation stages.

The committee should be made up of representatives from *at least* the following departments:

- Business units
- Senior management
- IT department
- Security department
- Communications department
- Legal department

If the BCP coordinator is a good management leader, she will understand that it is best to make these team members feel a sense of ownership pertaining to their tasks and roles. The people who develop the BCP should also be the ones who execute it. If you knew that in a time of crisis you would be expected to carry out some critical tasks, you might pay more attention during the planning and testing phases.

The team must then work with the management staff to develop the ultimate goals of the plan, identify the critical parts of the business that must be dealt with first during a disaster, and ascertain the priorities of departments and tasks. Management needs to help direct the team on the scope of the project and the specific objectives. At first glance, it might seem as though the scope and objectives are quite clear—protect the company. But it is not that simple. Is the team supposed to develop a BCP for just one facility or for more than one facility? Is the plan supposed to cover just large potential threats (hurricanes, tornadoes, floods) or deal with smaller issues as well (loss of a communications line, power failure, Internet connection failure)? Should the plan address possible terrorist attacks and bomb threats? What is the threat profile of the company? If the scope of the project is not properly defined, how do you know when you are done?

 NOTE Most companies outline the scope of their BCP to encompass only the larger threats. The smaller threats are then covered by independent departmental contingency plans.

At this phase, the team works with management to develop the *continuity planning policy statement*. This statement lays out the scope of the BCP project, the team member roles, and the goals of the project. Basically, it is a document that outlines what needs to be accomplished after the team communicates with management and comes to agreement on the terms of the project. The document should be returned to management to make sure there are no assumptions or omissions and that everyone is in agreement.

The BCP coordinator would then need to implement some good old-fashioned project management skills; see Table 9-1. A project plan should be developed that has the following components:

- Objective-to-task mapping
- Resource-to-task mapping
- Milestones
- Budget estimates
- Success factors
- Deadlines

Once the project plan is completed, it should be presented to management for written approval before any further steps are taken. It is important there are no assumptions in the plan and that the coordinator obtains permission to use the necessary resources to move forward.

Business Continuity Planning Requirements

A major requirement for anything that has such far-reaching ramifications as business continuity planning is management support. It is critical that management understands what the real threats are to the company, the consequences of those threats, and the

BCP Activity	Start Date	Required Completion Date	Completed? Initials/Date	Approved? Initials/Date
Initiating the project				
Continuity policy statement				
Business impact analysis				
Identify preventive controls				
Recovery strategies				
Develop BCP and DRP documents				
Test plans				
Maintain plans				

Table 9-1 Steps to Be Documented and Approved

potential loss values for each threat. Without this understanding, management may only give lip service to continuity planning, and in some cases that is worse than not having any plans at all because of the false sense of security it creates. Without management support, the necessary resources, funds, and time will not be devoted, which could result in bad plans that, again, may instill a false sense of security. Failure of these plans usually means a failure in management understanding, vision, and due-care responsibilities.

Executives may be held responsible and liable under various laws and regulations. They could be sued by stockholders and customers if they do not practice due diligence and due care and fulfill all of their responsibilities when it comes to disaster recovery and business continuity items. Organizations that work within specific industries have strict regulatory rules and laws that they must abide by, and these should be researched and integrated into the plan from the beginning. For example, banking and investment organizations must ensure that even if a disaster occurs, their customers' confidential information will not be disclosed to unauthorized individuals or be altered or vulnerable in any way. Disaster recovery, continuity development, and planning work best in a top-down approach, not a bottom-up approach. This means that management, not the staff, should be driving the project.

Many companies are running so fast to try to keep up with a dynamic and changing business world that they may not see the immediate benefit of spending time and resources on disaster recovery issues. Those individuals who *do* see the value in these efforts may have a hard time convincing top management if management does not see a potential profit margin or increase in market share as a result. But if a disaster does hit and they did put in the effort to properly prepare, the result can literally be priceless. Today's business world requires two important characteristics: the drive to produce a great product or service and get it to the market, and the insight and wisdom to know that unexpected trouble can easily find its way to your doorstep.

It is important that management set the overall goals of continuity planning, and it should help set the priorities of what should be dealt with first. Once management sets the goals, policies, and priorities, other staff members who are responsible for these plans can fill in the rest. However, management's support does not stop there. It needs to make sure the plans and procedures developed are actually implemented. Management must make sure the plans stay updated and represent the real priorities—not simply those perceived—of a company, which change over time.

Business Impact Analysis

How bad is it going to hurt and how long can we deal with this level of pain?

Business continuity planning deals with uncertainty and chance. What is important to note here is that even though you cannot predict whether or when a disaster will happen, that doesn't mean you can't plan for it. Just because we are not planning for an earthquake to hit us tomorrow morning at 10 A.M. doesn't mean we can't plan the activities required to successfully survive when an earthquake (or a similar disaster) does hit. The point of making these plans is to try to think of all the possible disasters that could take place, estimate the potential damage and loss, categorize and prioritize the potential disasters, and develop viable alternatives in case those events do actually happen.

A *business impact analysis (BIA)* is considered a *functional analysis,* in which a team collects data through interviews and documentary sources; documents business functions, activities, and transactions; develops a hierarchy of business functions; and finally applies a classification scheme to indicate each individual function's criticality level. But how do we determine a classification scheme based on criticality levels? The BCP committee must identify the threats to the company and map them to the following characteristics:

- Maximum tolerable downtime
- Operational disruption and productivity
- Financial considerations
- Regulatory responsibilities
- Reputation

The committee will not truly understand all business processes, the steps that must take place, or the resources and supplies these processes require. So the committee must gather this information from the people who do know—department managers and specific employees throughout the organization. The committee starts by identifying the people who will be part of the BIA data-gathering sessions. The committee needs to identify how it will collect the data from the selected employees, be it surveys, interviews, or workshops. Next, the team needs to collect the information by actually conducting surveys, interviews, and workshops. Data points obtained as part of the information gathering will be used later during analysis. It is important that the team members ask about how different tasks—whether processes, transactions, or services, along with any relevant dependencies—get accomplished within the organization. Process flow diagrams should be built, which will be used throughout the BIA and plan development stages.

Upon completion of the data collection phase, the BCP committee needs to conduct an analysis to establish which processes, devices, or operational activities are critical. If a system stands on its own, doesn't affect other systems, and is of low criticality, then it can be classified as a tier two or three recovery step. This means these resources will not be dealt with during the recovery stages until the most critical (tier one) resources are up and running. This analysis can be completed using standard risk assessment and analysis methodologies. (For a full examination of risk analysis, refer to Chapter 3.)

Threats can be manmade, natural, or technical. A manmade threat may be an arsonist, a terrorist, or a simple mistake that can have serious outcomes. Natural threats may be tornadoes, floods, hurricanes, or earthquakes. Technical threats may be data corruption, loss of power, device failure, or loss of a data communications line. It is important to identify all possible threats and estimate the probability of them happening. Some issues may not immediately come to mind when developing these plans, such as an employee strike, vandals, disgruntled employees, or hackers, but they do need to be identified. These issues are often best addressed in a group with scenario-based exercises. This ensures that if a threat becomes reality, the plan includes the ramifications on *all* business tasks, departments, and critical operations. The more issues that are thought of and planned for, the better prepared a company will be if and when these events take place.

BIA Steps

The more detailed and granular steps of a BIA are outlined here:

1. Select individuals to interview for data gathering.

2. Create data-gathering techniques (surveys, questionnaires, qualitative and quantitative approaches).

3. Identify the company's critical business functions.

4. Identify the resources these functions depend upon.

5. Calculate how long these functions can survive without these resources.

6. Identify vulnerabilities and threats to these functions.

7. Calculate the risk for each different business function.

8. Document findings and report them to management.

We cover each of these steps in this chapter, but many times it is easier to comprehend the BIA process when it is clearly outlined in this fashion.

The committee needs to step through scenarios that could produce the following results:

- Equipment malfunction or unavailable equipment
- Unavailable utilities (HVAC, power, communications lines)
- Facility becomes unavailable
- Critical personnel become unavailable
- Vendor and service providers become unavailable
- Software and/or data corruption

The next step in the risk analysis is to assign a value to the assets that could be affected by each threat. This helps establish economic feasibility of the overall plan. As discussed in Chapter 3, assigning values to assets is not as straightforward as it seems. The value of an asset is not just the amount of money paid for it. The asset's role in the company has to be considered, along with the labor hours that went into creating it if it is a piece of software. The value amount could also encompass the liability issues that surround the asset if it were damaged or insecure in any manner. (Review Chapter 3 for an in-depth description and criteria for calculating asset value.)

Qualitative and quantitative impact information should be gathered and then properly analyzed and interpreted. The goal is to see exactly how a business will be affected by different threats. The effects can be economical, operational, or both. Upon completion of the data analysis, it should be reviewed with the most knowledgeable people within the company to ensure that the findings are appropriate and describe the real risks and impacts the organization faces. This will help flush out any additional data points not originally obtained and will give a fuller understanding of all the possible business impacts.

Loss criteria must be applied to the individual threats that were identified. The criteria may include the following:

- Loss in reputation and public confidence
- Loss of competitive advantages
- Increase in operational expenses
- Violations of contract agreements
- Violations of legal and regulatory requirements
- Delayed income costs
- Loss in revenue
- Loss in productivity

These costs can be direct or indirect and must be properly accounted for.

So if the BCP team is looking at the threat of a terrorist bombing, it is important to identify which business function most likely would be targeted, how all business functions could be affected, and how each bulleted item in the loss criteria would be directly or indirectly involved. The timeliness of the recovery can be critical for business processes and the company's survival. For example, it may be acceptable to have the customer support functionality out of commission for two days, whereas five days may leave the company in financial ruin.

After identifying the critical functions, it is necessary to find out exactly what is required for these individual business processes to take place. The resources that are required for the identified business processes are not necessarily just computer systems, but may include personnel, procedures, tasks, supplies, and vendor support. It must be understood that if one or more of these support mechanisms is not available, the critical function may be doomed. The team must determine what type of effect unavailable resources and systems will have on these critical functions.

The BIA identifies which of the company's critical systems are needed for survival and estimates the outage time that can be tolerated by the company as a result of various unfortunate events. The outage time that can be endured by a company is referred to as the *maximum tolerable downtime (MTD)*.

The following are some MTD estimates that may be used within an organization:

- **Nonessential**   30 days
- **Normal**   Seven days
- **Important**   72 hours
- **Urgent**   24 hours
- **Critical**   Minutes to hours

Each business function and asset should be placed in one of these categories, depending upon how long the company can survive without it. These estimates will help the company determine what backup solutions are necessary to ensure the availability of these resources. For example, if being without a T1 communication line for three hours would cost the company $130,000, the T1 line would be considered critical and thus the company should put in a backup T1 line from a different carrier. If a server going down and being unavailable for ten days will only cost the company $250 in revenue, this would fall into the normal category, and thus the company may not need to have a fully redundant server waiting to be swapped out. Instead, the company may choose to count on its vendor service level agreement (SLA), which, for example, may promise to have it back online in eight days.

The BCP team must try to think of all possible events that might occur that could turn out to be detrimental to a company. The BCP team also must understand it cannot possibly contemplate all events, and thus protection may not be available for every scenario introduced. Being properly prepared specifically for a flood, earthquake, terrorist attack, or lightning strike is not as important as being properly prepared to respond to *anything* that damages or disrupts critical business functions.

All of the previously mentioned disasters could cause these results, but so could a meteor strike, a tornado, or a wing falling off of a plane passing overhead. So the moral to the story is to be prepared for the loss of any or all business resources, instead of focusing on the events that could cause the loss.

 NOTE   A BIA is performed at the beginning of business continuity planning to identify the areas that would suffer the greatest financial or operational loss in the event of a disaster or disruption. It identifies the company's critical systems needed for survival and estimates the outage time that can be tolerated by the company as a result of a disaster or disruption.

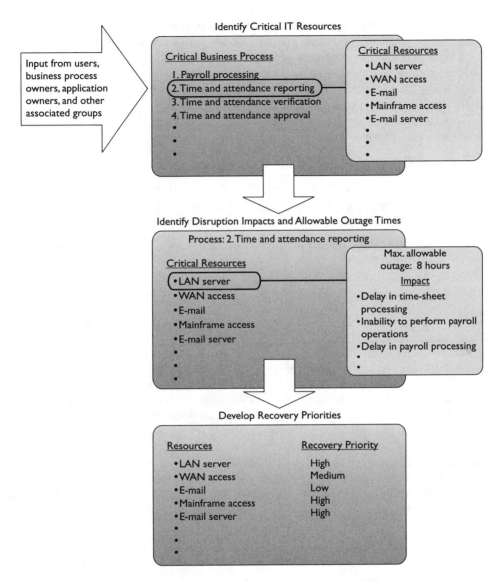

Identify Critical IT Resources

Critical Business Process
1. Payroll processing
2. Time and attendance reporting
3. Time and attendance verification
4. Time and attendance approval

Critical Resources
•LAN server
•WAN access
•E-mail
•Mainframe access
•E-mail server

Input from users, business process owners, application owners, and other associated groups

Identify Disruption Impacts and Allowable Outage Times

Process: 2. Time and attendance reporting

Critical Resources
•LAN server
•WAN access
•E-mail
•Mainframe access
•E-mail server

Max. allowable outage: 8 hours
Impact
•Delay in time-sheet processing
•Inability to perform payroll operations
•Delay in payroll processing

Develop Recovery Priorities

Resources
•LAN server
•WAN access
•E-mail
•Mainframe access
•E-mail server

Recovery Priority
High
Medium
Low
High
High

Interdependencies

Operations depend on manufacturing, manufacturing depends on R&D, payroll depends on accounting, and they all depend on IT.
Response: Hold on. I need to write this down.

It is important to look at a company as a complex animal instead of a static two-dimensional entity. It comprises many types of equipment, people, tasks, departments, communications mechanisms, and interfaces to the outer world. The biggest challenge of true continuity planning is understanding all of these intricacies and their interrelationships. A team may develop plans to back up and restore data, implement redundant data processing equipment, educate employees on how to carry out automated tasks manually, and obtain redundant power supplies. But if all of these components don't know how to work together in a different environment to get the products out the door, it might all be a waste of time.

The following interrelation and interdependency tasks should be carried out by the BCP team and addressed in the resulting plan:

- Define essential business functions and supporting departments.
- Identify interdependencies between these functions and departments.
- Discover all possible disruptions that could affect the mechanisms necessary to allow these departments to function together.
- Identify and document potential threats that could disrupt interdepartmental communication.
- Gather quantitative and qualitative information pertaining to those threats.
- Provide alternative methods of restoring functionality and communication.
- Provide a brief statement of rationale for each threat and corresponding information.

The main goal of business continuity is to resume business as quickly as possible, spending the least amount of money. The overall business interruption and resumption plan should cover all organizational elements, identify critical services and functions, provide alternatives for emergency operations, and integrate each departmental plan. This can be accomplished by in-house appointed employees, outside consultants, or a combination of both. A combination can bring many benefits to the company, because the consultants are experts in this field and know the necessary steps, questions to ask, and issues to look for, and offer general reasonable advice, whereas in-house employees know their company intimately and have a full understanding of how certain threats can affect operations. It is good to cover all the necessary ground, and many times a combination of consultants and employees provides just the right recipe.

Enterprisewide

The agreed-upon scope of the BCP will indicate if one or more facilities will be included in the plan. Most BCPs are developed to cover the enterprise as a whole, instead of dealing with only portions of the organization. In larger organizations, it can be helpful for each department to have its own specific contingency plan that will address its specific needs during recovery. These individual plans need to be compatible with the enterprisewide BCP.

Up until now, we have established management's responsibilities as the following:

- Committing fully to the BCP
- Setting policy and goals
- Making available the necessary funds and resources
- Taking responsibility for the outcome of the development of the BCP
- Appointing a team for the process

The BCP team's responsibilities are as follows:

- Identifying regulatory and legal requirements that must be met
- Identifying all possible vulnerabilities and threats
- Estimating the possibilities of these threats and the loss potential
- Performing a BIA
- Outlining which departments, systems, and processes must be up and running before any others
- Developing procedures and steps in resuming business after a disaster

Several software tools are available for developing a BCP that simplify the process. Automation of these procedures can quicken the pace of the project and allow easier gathering of the massive amount of information. Many of the necessary items are provided in the boilerplate templates.

This information, along with other data explained in previous sections, should be presented to senior management. Management usually wants information stated in monetary, quantitative terms, not in subjective, qualitative terms. It is one thing to know that if a tornado were to hit, the result would be *really bad*, but it is another to know that if a tornado were to hit and affect 65 percent of the facility, the company could be at risk of losing computing capabilities for up to 72 hours, power supply for up to 24 hours, and a full stop of operations for 76 hours, which would equate to a loss of $125,000 each day. Management has a much harder time dealing with *really bad* than with real numbers.

It is important to realize that up until now, the BCP team has not actually developed any of its BCP. It has been collecting data, carrying out analysis on this data, and presenting it to management. Management must review these findings and give the "okay" for the team to move forward and actually develop the plan. In our scenario, we will assume that management has given the thumbs up, and the team will now move into the next stages.

Preventive Measures

Let's just wait and see if a disaster hits.
Response: How about we be more proactive?

During the BIA, the BCP team identified the maximum tolerable downtime for the critical resources. This was done to understand the business impact that would be caused if the assets were unavailable for one reason or another. It only makes sense that the team would try to reduce this impact and mitigate these risks by implementing preventive measures. Not implementing preventive measures would be analogous to going to a doctor, being told to stop eating 300 candy bars a day, increase physical activities, and start taking blood pressure medicine, and then choosing not to follow any of these preventive measures. Why go to the doctor in the first place? The same concept holds true with companies. If a team has been developed to identify risks and has come up with solutions, but the company does not implement at least some of these solutions, why put this team together in the first place?

So, instead of just waiting for a disaster to hit to see how the company holds up, countermeasures should be integrated to better fortify the company from the impacts that were recognized. Appropriate and cost-effective preventive methods and proactive measures are more preferable than reactionary methods. Which types of preventive mechanisms should be put in place depends upon the results of the BIA, but they may include some of the following components:

- Fortification of the facility in its construction materials
- Redundant servers and communications links
- Power lines coming in through different transformers
- Redundant vendor support
- Purchasing of insurance
- Purchasing of UPS and generators
- Data backup technologies
- Media protection safeguards
- Increased inventory of critical equipment
- Fire detection and suppression systems

 NOTE Many of these controls are discussed in this chapter, but others are covered in Chapter 6 and Chapter 12.

Recovery Strategies

Up to this point, the BCP team has carried out the project initiation phase. In this phase, the team obtained management support, the necessary resources, laid out the scope of the project, and identified the BCP team. It also completed the BIA phase. This means that the committee carried out a risk assessment and analysis, which resulted in a report of the real risk level the company faces.

The BCP committee already had to figure out how the organization works as a whole in its BIA phase. It drilled down into the organization and identified the critical functions that absolutely have to be up and running for the company to continue operating. It identified the resources these functions require and calculated MTD values for the individual resources and the functions themselves. So it may seem as though the

BIA phase is already completed. But when the BCP committee carried out these tasks, it was in the "risk assessment" phase of the BCP process. Its goals were to figure out how badly the company could be hurt in different disaster scenarios.

In the recovery strategy stage, the team approaches this information from a different perspective. It now has to figure out what the company needs to do to actually recover the items it has identified as being so important to the organization overall. The BIA provides the blueprint for the recovery strategies for all the components, because the business processes are totally dependent upon these other recovery strategies taking place properly.

At this point, the findings from the BIA have been reported to management, and management has allocated the necessary resources to move into the next phases. The BCP committee now must discover the most cost-effective recovery mechanisms that need to be implemented to address the threats identified in the BIA stage. Remember that in the BIA phase, the team calculated the potential losses for each identified threat. (If the facility was unavailable, it would cost the organization $200,000 a day; if the Internet connection went down, it would cost the company $12,000 per hour, and so on.) The team will use these values in its cost-benefit analysis when reviewing and choosing the necessary recovery solutions that need to be put into place to mitigate the organization's risk level.

So what does the BCP team need to accomplish in the recovery strategy stage? The team needs to actually define the recovery strategies, which are a set of predefined activities that will be implemented and carried out in response to a disaster. Sounds simple enough, but in reality this phase requires just as much work as the BIA phase.

In the BIA, the team has calculated the necessary *recovery times* that must be met for the different critical business functions and the resources those functions rely upon. For example, let's say the team has figured out it would cost the company $200,000 per day in lost revenue if its facility were destroyed and unusable. Now the team knows that the company *has* to be up and running within five to six hours, or the company could be financially crippled. This would mean that the company needs to obtain a hot site or redundant facility that would allow it to be up and running in this amount of time.

What Is the Difference Between Preventive Measures and Recovery Strategies?

Preventive mechanisms are put into place to try to reduce the possibility of the company experiencing a disaster and, if a disaster does hit, to lessen the amount of damage that will take place. Although the company cannot stop a tornado from coming, it could choose to move its facility from tornado valley in Kansas. The company cannot stop a car from plowing into and taking out a transformer, but it can have a separate feed from a different transformer in case this happens.

Recovery strategies are processes on how to rescue the company after a disaster takes place. These processes will integrate mechanisms such as establishing alternate sites for facilities, implementing emergency response procedures, and possibly activating the preventive mechanisms that have already been implemented.

The team has figured out these types of timelines for the individual business functions, operations, and resources. Now it has to identify the recovery mechanisms and strategies that must be implemented to make sure everything is up and running within the timelines it has calculated. The team needs to break down these recovery strategies into the following sections:

- Business process recovery
- Facility recovery
- Supply and technology recovery
- User environment recovery
- Data recovery

Business Process Recovery

A business process is a set of interrelated steps linked through specific decision activities to accomplish a specific task. Business processes have starting and ending points and are repeatable. The processes should encapsulate the knowledge of services, resources, and operations provided by a company. For example, when a customer requests to buy a car via an organization's e-commerce site, a set of steps must be followed, such as these:

1. Validate that the car is available.
2. Validate where the car is located and how long it would take to ship it to the destination.
3. Provide the customer with the price and delivery date.
4. Accept the customer's credit card information.
5. Validate and process the credit card order.
6. Send a receipt and tracking number to the customer.
7. Send the order to the car inventory location.
8. Restock inventory.
9. Send the order to accounting.

The BCP team needs to understand these different steps of the company's most critical steps. The data are usually presented as a workflow document that contains the roles and resources needed for each process. The BCP team must understand the following about critical business processes:

- Required roles
- Required resources
- Input and output mechanisms
- Workflow steps
- Required time for completion
- Interfaces with other processes

This will allow the team to identify threats and the controls to ensure the least amount of process interruption.

Facility Recovery

That mean storm hurt our office. Let's go find another building to work in.

Disruptions are of three main types: nondisasters, disasters, and catastrophes. A *nondisaster* is a disruption in service due to a device malfunction or failure. The solution could include hardware, software, or file restoration. A *disaster* is an event that causes the entire facility to be unusable for a day or longer. This usually requires the use of an alternate processing facility and restoration of software and data from offsite copies. The alternate site must be available to the company until its main facility is repaired and usable. A *catastrophe* is a major disruption that destroys the facility altogether. This requires both a short-term solution, which would be an offsite facility, and a long-term solution, which may require rebuilding the original facility.

Disasters and catastrophes are rare compared to nondisasters, thank goodness. Nondisasters can usually be taken care of by replacing a device or restoring files from onsite backups. The BCP team needs to think through onsite backup requirements and make well-informed decisions. The team must identify the critical equipment and estimate the mean time between failures (MTBF) and the mean time to repair (MTTR) to provide the necessary statistics of when a device may be meeting its maker and a new device may be required.

NOTE   MTBF is the estimated lifetime of a piece of equipment and is calculated by the vendor of the equipment or a third party. The reason for using this value is to know approximately when a particular device will need to be replaced. MTTR is an estimate of how long it will take to fix a piece of equipment and get it back into production. These concepts are further explained in Chapter 12.

For larger disasters that affect the primary facility, an offsite backup facility must be accessible. Generally, contracts are established with third-party vendors to provide such services. The client pays a monthly fee to retain the right to use the facility in a time of need and then incurs a large activation fee when the facility actually has to be used. In addition, there would be a daily or hourly fee imposed for the duration of the stay. This is why subscription services for backup facilities should be considered a short-term solution, not a long-term solution.

It is important to note that most recovery site contracts do not promise to house the company in need at a specific location, but rather promise to provide what has been contracted for somewhere within the company's locale. On, and subsequent to, September 11, 2001, many organizations with Manhattan offices were surprised when they were redirected by their backup site vendor not to sites located in New Jersey (which were already full), but rather to sites located in Boston, Chicago, or Atlanta. This adds yet another level of complexity to the recovery process, specifically the logistics of transporting people and equipment to locations originally unplanned for.

Companies can choose from three main types of leased or rented offsite facilities:

- **Hot site**   A facility that is leased or rented and is fully configured and ready to operate within a few hours. The only missing resources from a hot site are usually the data, which will be retrieved from a backup site, and the people who will be processing the data. The equipment and system software must absolutely be compatible with the data being restored from the main site and must not cause any negative interoperability issues. These sites are a good choice for a company that needs to ensure a site will be available for it as soon as possible. Most hot-site facilities support annual tests that can be done by the company to ensure the site is functioning in the necessary state. This is the most expensive of the three types of offsite facilities and can have problems if a company requires proprietary or unusual hardware or software.

NOTE   The vendor of a hot site will provide the most commonly used hardware and software products to attract the largest customer base. This will most likely not include one specific customer's proprietary or unusual hardware or software products.

- **Warm site**   A leased or rented facility that is usually partially configured with some equipment, but not the actual computers. In other words, a warm site is usually a hot site without the expensive equipment. Staging a facility with duplicate hardware and computers configured for immediate operation is extremely expensive, so a warm site provides an alternate facility with some peripheral devices. This is the most widely used model. It is less expensive than a hot site and can be up and running within a reasonably acceptable time period. It may be a better choice for companies that depend upon proprietary and unusual hardware and software, because they will bring their own hardware and software with them to the site after the disaster hits. The odds of finding a remote site vendor that would have a Cray supercomputer readily available in a time of need are pretty slim. The drawback, however, is that the annual testing available with hot-site contracts is not usually available with warm-site contracts, and thus a company cannot be certain that it will in fact be able to return to an operating state within hours.

- **Cold site**   A leased or rented facility that supplies the basic environment, electrical wiring, air conditioning, plumbing, and flooring, but none of the equipment or additional services. It may take weeks to get the site activated and ready for work. The cold site could have equipment racks and dark fiber (fiber that does not have the circuit engaged) and maybe even desks, but would require the receipt of equipment from the client, since it does not provide any. The cold site is the least expensive option, but takes the most time and effort to actually get up and functioning right after a disaster. Cold sites are often used as backups for call centers, manufacturing plants, and other services that either can be moved lock, stock, and barrel in one shot or would require extensive retooling and building.

NOTE It is important to understand that the different site types listed here are provided by service bureaus, meaning a company pays a monthly subscription fee to another company for this space and service. A *hot* site is a subscription service. A *redundant* site is a site owned and maintained by the company, meaning the company does not pay anyone else for the site. A redundant site might be "hot" in nature, meaning it is ready for production quickly, but the CISSP exam differentiates between a hot site (subscription service) and a redundant site (owned by the company).

Most companies use *warm sites*, which have some devices such as disk drives, tape drives, and controllers, but very little else. These companies usually cannot afford a hot site, and the extra downtime would not be considered detrimental. A warm site can provide a longer-term solution than a hot site. Companies that decide to go with a *cold site* must be able to be out of operation for a week or two. The cold site usually includes power, raised flooring, climate control, and wiring.

The following provides a quick overview of the differences between offsite facilities:

Hot Site Advantages

- Ready within hours for operation
- Highly available
- Usually used for short-term solutions, but available for longer stays
- Annual testing available

Hot Site Disadvantages

- Very expensive
- Limited on hardware and software choices

Warm and Cold Site Advantages

- Less expensive
- Available for longer timeframes because of the reduced costs
- Practical for proprietary hardware or software use

Warm and Cold Site Disadvantages

- Not immediately available
- Operational testing not usually available
- Resources for operations not immediately available

Tertiary Sites

During the BIA phase, the team may recognize the danger of the primary backup facility not being available when needed, which could require a tertiary site. This is a secondary backup site, just in case the primary backup site is unavailable. The secondary backup site is sometimes referred to as a "backup to the backup." This is basically plan B if plan A does not work out.

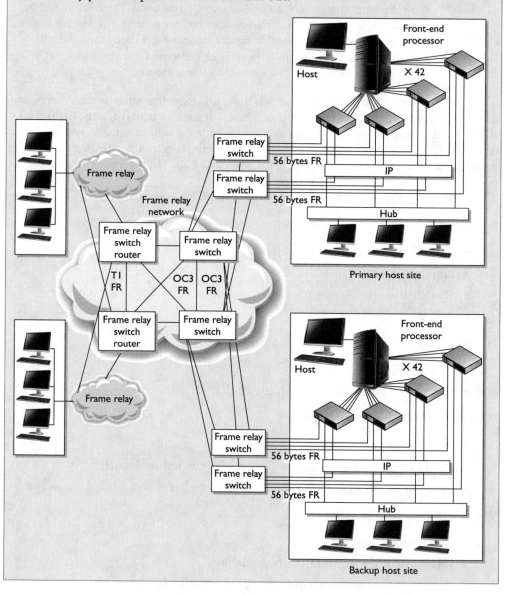

Backup tapes or other media should be tested periodically on the equipment kept at the hot site to make sure the media is readable by those systems. If a warm site is used, the tapes should be brought to the *original* site and tested on those systems. The reason for the difference is that when a company uses a hot site, it depends on the systems located at the hot site; therefore, the media needs to be readable by those systems. If a company depends on a warm site, it will most likely bring its original equipment with it, so the media needs to be readable by the company's systems.

Reciprocal Agreements

If my facility is destroyed, can I come over to yours?
Response: Only if you bring hot cocoa and popcorn.

Another approach to alternate offsite facilities is to establish a *reciprocal agreement*, also referred to as mutual aid, with another company. This means that company A agrees to allow company B to use its facilities if company B is hit by a disaster, and vice versa. This is a cheaper way to go than the other offsite choices, but it is not always the best choice. Most environments are maxed out pertaining to the use of facility space, resources, and computing capability. To allow another company to come in and work out of the same shop could prove to be detrimental to both companies. The stress of two companies working in the same environment could cause tremendous levels of tension. If it did work out, it would only provide a short-term solution. Configuration management could be a nightmare, and the mixing of operations could introduce many security issues.

If you allow another company to move into your facility and work from there, you may have a solid feeling about your friend, the CEO, but what about all of her employees whom you do not know? Now you have a new subset of people who may need to have privileged and direct access to your resources in the shared environment. This other company could be your competitor in the business world, so many of the employees may see you and your company more as a threat than one that is offering a helping hand in need. Close attention needs to be paid when assigning these other people access rights and permissions to your critical assets and resources, if they need access at all.

Offsite Location

When choosing a backup facility, it should be far enough away from the original site so one disaster does not take out both locations. In other words, it is not logical to have the backup site only a few miles away if the company is concerned about tornado damage, because the backup site could also be affected or destroyed. There is a rule of thumb that suggests that alternate facilities should be at a bare minimum at least five miles away from the primary site, while 15 miles is recommended for most low-to-medium critical environments, and 50–200 miles is recommended for critical operations to give maximum protection in cases of regional disasters.

Reciprocal agreements have been known to work well in specific businesses, such as newspaper printing. These businesses require very specific technology and equipment that will not be available through any subscription service. These agreements follow a "you scratch my back and I'll scratch yours" mentality. For most other organizations, they are generally, at best, a secondary option for disaster protection. The other issue to consider is that these agreements are not enforceable. This means that although company A said company B could use its facility when needed, when the need arises, company A legally does not have to fulfill this promise. However, there are still many companies who do opt for this solution either because of the appeal of low cost or, as noted earlier, because it may be the only viable solution in some cases.

Important issues need to be addressed before a disaster hits if a company decides to participate in a reciprocal agreement with another company:

- How long will the facility be available to the company in need?
- How much assistance will the staff supply in integrating the two environments and ongoing support?
- How quickly can the company in need move into the facility?
- What are the issues pertaining to interoperability?
- How many of the resources will be available to the company in need?
- How will differences and conflicts be addressed?
- How does change control and configuration management take place?
- How often can drills and testing take place?
- How can critical assets of both companies be properly protected?

Redundant Sites

It's mine and mine alone.
Response: Okay, keep it then.

Some companies choose to have **redundant sites**, meaning one site is equipped and configured exactly like the primary site, which serves as a redundant environment. These sites are owned by the company and are mirrors of the original production environment. This is one of the most expensive backup facility options, because a full environment must be maintained even though it usually is not used for regular production activities until after a disaster takes place that triggers the relocation of services to the redundant site. But expensive is relative here. If the company would lose a million dollars if it were out of business for just a few hours, the loss potential would override the cost of this option. Many organizations are subjected to regulations that dictate they must have redundant sites in place, so expense is not an issue in these situations.

Another type of facility-backup option is a **rolling hot site**, or mobile hot site, where the back of a large truck or a trailer is turned into a data processing or working area. The trailer has all of the necessary power, telecommunications, and systems to allow for processing to take place right away. The trailer can be brought to the company's parking lot or another location. Another, similar solution is a prefabricated building that can be easily and quickly put together. Military organizations and large insurance companies typically have rolling hot sites or trucks preloaded with equipment because they often need the flexibility to quickly relocate some or all of their processing facilities to different locations around the world depending on where the need arises.

Another option for organizations is to have *multiple processing centers*. An organization may have ten different facilities throughout the world, which may include products and technologies that would move all data processing from one facility to another in a matter of seconds when an interruption is detected. This technology can be implemented within the organization or from one facility to a third-party facility. Certain service bureaus provide this type of functionality to their customers. So if a company's data processing is interrupted, all or some of the processing can be moved to the service bureau's servers.

It is best if a company is aware of all available options for hardware and facility backups, to ensure it makes the best decision for its specific business and critical needs.

Supply and Technology Recovery

At this point, the BCP team has mapped out the necessary business functions that need to be up and running and the specific backup facility option that is best for its organization. Now the team needs to dig down into the more granular items, such as backup solutions for the following:

- Network and computer equipment
- Voice and data communications resources
- Human resources
- Transportation of equipment and personnel
- Environment issues (HVAC)
- Data and personnel security issues
- Supplies (paper, forms, cabling, and so on)
- Documentation

The organization's current technical environment must be understood. This means the planners have to know the intimate details of the network, communications technologies, computers, network equipment, and software requirements that are necessary to get the critical functions up and running. What is surprising to some people is that many organizations do not *totally* understand how their network is configured and how it actually works, because the network was most likely established five to ten years ago and has kept growing like a teenage boy going through puberty. New devices are added, new computers are added, new software packages are added, VoIP may have been integrated, and the demilitarized zone (DMZ) may have been split up into three DMZs, with an extranet for the company's partners. Maybe the company bought and merged with another company and network. Over ten years, a number of technology refreshes most likely have taken place, and the individuals who are maintaining the environment now are not the same people who built it ten years ago. Many IT departments experience employee turnover every one to five years. And most organizational network schematics are notoriously out of date, because everyone is busy with their current tasks or will come up with new tasks just to get out of having to update the schematic.

So the BCP team has to make sure that if the networked environment is partially or totally destroyed, the recovery team has the knowledge and skill to properly rebuild it.

 NOTE Many organizations are moving to Voice over IP (VoIP), which means that if the network goes down, network and voice capability are unavailable. The team should address the possible need of redundant voice systems.

The BCP team needs to take into account several things that are commonly overlooked, such as hardware replacements, software products, documentation, environmental needs, and human resources.

Hardware Backups

I have an extra floppy, video card, and some gum.
Response: I am sure that's all we will need.

The team has identified the equipment required to keep the critical functions up and running. This may include servers, user workstations, routers, switches, tape backup devices, hubs, and more. The needed inventory may seem simple enough, until the team drills down into more detail. If the recovery team is planning to use images to rebuild newly purchased servers and workstations (because the original ones were destroyed), will the images work on the new computers? Using images instead of building systems from scratch can be a time-saving task, unless the team finds out that the replacement equipment is a newer version and thus the images cannot be used. The BCP team should plan for the recovery team to use the company's current images, but also have a manual process of how to build each critical system from scratch with the necessary configurations.

The BCP team also needs to identify how *long* it will take for new equipment to arrive. For example, if the organization has identified Gateway as its equipment replacement supplier, how long will it take this vendor to send 20 servers and 30 workstations to the offsite facility? After a disaster hits, the company could be in its offsite facility only to find that its equipment will take three weeks to be delivered. So, the SLA for the identified vendors needs to be investigated to make sure the company is not further damaged by delays. Once the parameters of the SLA are understood, the team must make a decision between depending upon the vendor or purchasing redundant systems and storing them as backups in case the primary equipment is destroyed. As described earlier, when potential company risks are identified, it is better to take preventive steps to reduce the potential damage. After the calculation of the MTD values, the team will know how long the company can be without a specific device. This data should be used to make the decision regarding whether the company should depend on the vendor's SLA or make readily available a hot-swappable redundant system. If the company will lose $50,000 per hour if a particular server were to go down, then the team should elect to implement redundant systems and technology.

If an organization is using any legacy computers and hardware and a disaster hits tomorrow, where would it find replacements for this legacy equipment? The team should identify legacy devices and understand the risk the organization is under if replacements are unavailable. This type of finding has caused many companies to move from legacy systems to commercial off the shelf (COTS) products to ensure that replacement is possible.

NOTE Different types of backup tape technologies can be used (digital linear tape, digital audio tape, advanced intelligent tape). The team needs to make sure it knows the type of technology that is used by the company and identify the necessary vendor in case the tape-reading device needs to be replaced.

Software Backups

I have a backup server and my backed-up data, but no operating system or applications.
Response: Good luck.

Most companies' IT departments have their array of software disks and licensing information here or there—or possibly in one centralized location. If the facility were destroyed and the IT department's current environment had to be rebuilt, how would it gain access to these software packages? The BCP team should make sure to have an inventory of the necessary software required for mission-critical functions and have backup copies at an offsite facility. Hardware is usually not worth much to a company without the software required to run on it. The software that needs to be backed up can be in the form of applications, utilities, databases, and operating systems. The continuity plan must have provisions to back up and protect these items along with hardware and data.

The BCP team should make sure there are at least two copies of the company's operating system software and critical applications. One copy should be stored onsite and the other copy should be stored at a secure offsite location. These copies should be tested periodically and re-created when new versions are rolled out.

It is common for organizations to work with software developers to create customized software programs. For example, in the banking world, individual financial institutions need software that will allow their bank tellers to interact with accounts, hold account information in databases and mainframes, provide online banking, carry out data replication, and perform a thousand other types of bank-like functionalities. This specialized type of software is developed and available through a handful of software vendors that specialize in this market. When bank A purchases this type of software for all of its branches, the software has to be specially customized for their environment and needs. Once this banking software is installed, the whole organization depends upon it for its minute-by-minute activities.

When bank A receives the specialized and customized banking software from the software vendor, bank A does not receive the source code. Instead, the software vendor provides bank A with a compiled version. Now, what if this software vendor goes out of business because of a disaster or bankruptcy? Then bank A will require a new vendor to maintain and update this banking software; thus, the new vendor will need access to the source code.

The protection mechanism that bank A should implement is called *software escrow*. Software escrow means that a third party holds the source code, backups of the compiled code, manuals, and other supporting materials. A contract between the software vendor, customer, and third party outlines who can do what and when with the source code. This contract usually states that the customer can have access to the source code only if and when the vendor goes out of business, is unable to carry out stated responsibilities, or is in breach of the original contract. If any of these activities takes place, then the customer is protected because it can still gain access to the source code and other materials through the third-party escrow agent.

Many companies have been crippled by not implementing software escrow. Such a company would have paid a software vendor to develop specialized software, and when the software vendor went belly up, the customer did not have access to the code that its whole company ran on.

The BCP committee needs to identify this issue as a vulnerability during its analysis and implement a preventive countermeasure—software escrow.

Documentation

We came up with a great plan six months ago. Did anyone write it down?

Documentation seems to be a dreaded task to most people, who will find many other tasks to take on to ensure they are not the ones stuck with documenting processes and procedures. However, a company may do a great and responsible job of backing up hardware and software to an offsite facility, maintaining it, and keeping everything up-to-date and current; but without documentation, when a disaster hits, no one will know how to put Humpty Dumpty back together again.

Restoration of files can be challenging, but restoring a whole environment that was swept away in a flood can be overwhelming, if not impossible. Procedures need to be documented because when they are actually needed, it will most likely be a chaotic and frantic atmosphere with a demanding time schedule. The documentation may need to include information on how to install images, configure operating systems and servers, and properly install utilities and proprietary software. Other documentation could include a calling tree, which outlines who should be contacted, in what order, and who is responsible for doing the calling. The documentation must also contain contact information for specific vendors, emergency agencies, offsite facilities, and any other entity that may need to be contacted in a time of need.

Most network environments evolve over time. Software has been installed on top of other software, configurations have been altered over the years to properly work in a unique environment, and service packs and patches have been installed to fix this problem or that issue. To expect one person or a group of people to go through all of these steps during a crisis and end up with an environment that looks and behaves exactly like the original environment and in which all components work together seamlessly may be a lofty dream.

So, the dreaded task of documentation may be the saving grace one day. It is an essential piece of business, and therefore an essential piece in disaster recovery and business continuity.

It is important to make one or more roles responsible for proper documentation. As with all the items addressed in this chapter, simply saying "All documentation will be kept up-to-date and properly protected" is the easy part—saying and doing are two different things. Once the BCP team identifies tasks that must be done, the tasks must be assigned to individuals and those individuals have to be accountable. If these steps are not taken, the BCP team could have wasted a lot of time and resources defining these tasks, and the company could be in grave danger if a disaster occurs.

NOTE An organization may need to solidify communications channels and relationships with government officials and emergency response groups. The goal of this activity is to solidify proper protocol in case of a city- or regionwide disaster. During the BIA phase, local authorities should be contacted so the team understands the risks of its geographical location and how to access emergency zones. If the company has to initiate its BCP, many of these emergency response groups will need to be contacted during the recovery stage.

Human Resources

We have everything up and running now—where are all the people to run these systems?

One of the resources commonly left out of the equation is people. A company may restore its networks and critical systems and get business functions up and running, only to realize it doesn't know the answer to the question, "Who will take it from here?" Human resources is a critical component to any recovery and continuity process, and it needs to be fully thought out and integrated into the plan.

What happens if we have to move to an offsite facility that is 250 miles away? We cannot expect people to drive back and forth from home to work. Should we pay for temporary housing for the necessary employees? Do we have to pay their moving costs? Do we need to hire new employees in the area of the offsite facility? If so, what skill set do we need from them? The BCP team should go through a long succession of these types of questions.

Plans

Once the business continuity and disaster recovery plans are completed, where do you think they should be stored? Should the company have only one copy and keep it safely in a file cabinet next to Bob so that he feels safe? Nope. There should be two or three copies of these plans. One copy may be at the primary location, but the other copies should be at other locations in case the primary facility is destroyed. Typically, a copy is stored at the BCP coordinator's home, and another copy is stored at the offsite facility. This reduces the risk of not having access to the plans when needed.

These plans should not be stored in a file cabinet, but rather in a fire-resistant safe. When they are stored offsite, they need to be stored in a way that provides just as much protection as the primary site would provide.

If a large disaster takes place that affects not only the company's facility but also surrounding areas, including housing, do you think your employees will be more worried about your company or their families? Some companies assume that employees will be ready and available to help them get back into production, when in fact they may need to be at home because they have responsibilities to their families.

Regrettably, some employees may be killed in the disaster, and the team may need to look at how it will be able to replace employees quickly through a temporary agency or a headhunter. This is extremely unfortunate, but it is part of reality. The team that identifies all threats and is responsible for identifying solutions needs to think about all of these issues and many more.

Organizations should already have *executive succession planning* in place. This means that if someone in a senior executive position retires, leaves the company, or is killed, the organization has predetermined steps to carry out to protect the company. The loss of a senior executive could tear a hole in the company's fabric, creating a leadership vacuum that must be filled quickly with the right individual. The line of succession plan defines who would step in and assume responsibility for this role. Many organizations have "deputy" roles. For example, an organization may have a deputy CIO, deputy CFO, and deputy CEO ready to take over the necessary tasks if the CIO, CFO, or CEO becomes unavailable.

Often, larger organizations also have a policy indicating that two or more of the senior staff cannot be exposed to a particular risk at the same time. For example, the CEO and president cannot travel on the same plane. If the plane went down and both individuals were killed, then the company could be in danger. This is why you don't see the president of the United States and the vice president together too often. It is not because they don't like each other and thus keep their distance from each other. It is because there is a policy indicating that to protect the United States, its top leaders cannot be under the same risk at the same time.

The End-User Environment

Do you think the users could just use an abacus for calculations and fire for light?

Because the end users are usually the worker bees of a company, they must be provided a functioning environment as soon as possible after a disaster hits. This means that the BCP team must understand the current operational and technical functioning environment and examine critical pieces so they can be replicated.

The first issue pertaining to users is how they will be notified of the disaster and who will tell them where to go and when. A tree structure of managers can be developed so that once a disaster hits, the person at the top of the tree calls two managers, and they in turn call three managers, and so on until all managers are notified. Each manager would be responsible for notifying the people he is responsible for until everyone is on the same page. Then, one or two people must be in charge of coordinating the issues pertaining to users. This could mean directing them to a new facility, making sure they have the necessary resources to complete their tasks, restoring data, and being a liaison between the different groups. The folks in charge of directing should be readily identifiable—by wearing an emergency hat and vest, for example—and should be located in areas where they can be seen by all. This will help ease confusion and reduce panic during difficult and strenuous times.

In most situations, after a disaster, only a skeleton crew is put back to work. The BCP committee identified the most critical functions of the company during the analysis stage, and the employees who carry out those functions must be put back to work first. So the recovery process for the user environment should be laid out in different stages. The first stage is to get the most critical departments back online, the next stage is to get the second most important back online, and so on.

The BCP team needs to identify user requirements, such as whether users can work on stand-alone PCs or need to be connected in a network to fulfill specific tasks. For example, in a financial institution, users who work on stand-alone PCs might be able to accomplish some small tasks like filling out account forms, word processing, and accounting tasks, but they would need to be connected to a host system to update customer profiles and to interact with the database.

The BCP team also needs to identify how current automated tasks can be carried out manually if that becomes necessary. If the network is going to be down for 12 hours, could the necessary tasks be carried out through traditional pen and paper methods? If the Internet connection is going to be down for five hours, could the necessary communications take place through phone calls? Instead of transmitting data through the internal mail system, could couriers be used to run information back and forth? Today, we are extremely dependent upon technology, but we often take for granted that it will always be there for us to use. It is up to the BCP team to realize that technology may be unavailable for a period of time and to come up with solutions for those situations.

Data Backup Alternatives

As we have discussed so far, backup alternatives are needed for hardware, software, personnel, and offsite facilities. It is up to each company and its continuity team to decide if all of these components are necessary for its survival and the specifics for each type of backup needed.

Data have become one of the most critical assets to nearly all organizations. These data may include financial spreadsheets, blueprints on new products, customer information, product inventory, trade secrets, and more. In Chapter 3, we stepped through risk analysis procedures and data classification processes. The BCP team should not be responsible for setting up and maintaining the company's data classification procedures, but the team may recognize that the company is at risk because it does not have these procedures in place. This should be seen as a vulnerability that is reported to management. Management would need to establish another group of individuals who would identify the company's data, define a loss criterion, and establish the classification structure and processes.

The BCP team's responsibility is to provide solutions to protect this data and identify ways to restore it after a disaster. In this section, we look at different ways data can be protected and restored when needed.

Data usually changes more often than hardware and software, so these backup procedures must happen on a continual basis. The data backup process must make sense and be reasonable and effective. If data in the files changes several times a day, backup procedures should happen a few times a day or nightly to ensure all the changes are captured and kept. If data is changed once a month, backing up data every night is a waste of time and resources. Backing up a file and its corresponding changes is usually more desirable than having multiple copies of that one file. Online backup technologies usually have the changes to a file made to a transaction log, which is separate from the original file.

The operations team is responsible for defining which data get backed up and how often. These backups can be full, differential, or incremental backups and are usually used in some type of combination with each other. Most files are not altered every day, so, to save time and resources, it is best to devise a backup plan that does not continually back up data that has not been modified. So, how do we know which data have changed and need to be backed up without having to look at every file's modification date? This is accomplished by an archive bit. Operating systems' file systems keep track of what files have been modified by setting an archive bit. If a file is modified or created, the file system sets the archive bit to 1. Backup software has been created to review this bit setting when making its determination on what gets backed up and what does not.

The first step is to do a *full backup*, which is just what it sounds like—all data are backed up and saved to some type of storage media. During a full backup, the archive bit is cleared, which means that it is set to 0. A company can choose to do full backups only, in which case the restoration process is just one step, but the backup and restore processes could take a long time.

Most companies choose to combine a full backup with a differential or incremental backup. A *differential process* backs up the files that have been modified since the *last full backup*. When the data need to be restored, the full backup is laid down first, and then the most recent differential backup is put down on top of it. The differential process does not change the archive bit value.

An *incremental process* backs up all the files that have changed since the *last full or incremental backup* and sets the archive bit to 0. When the data need to be restored, the full backup data are laid down, and then each incremental backup is laid down on top of it in the proper order (see Figure 9-2). If a company experienced a disaster and it used the incremental process, it would first need to restore the full backup on its hard drives and lay down every incremental backup that was carried out before the disaster took place (and after the last full backup). So, if the full backup was done six months ago and the operations department carried out an incremental backup each month, the restoration team would restore the full backup and start with the older incremental backups taken since the full backup and restore each one of them until they were all restored.

Which backup process is best? If a company wants the backup and restoration processes to be simplistic and straightforward, it can carry out just full backups—but this may require a lot of hard drive space and time. Although using differential and incremental backup processes is more complex, it requires less resources and time. A differential backup takes more time in the backing up phase than an incremental backup, but it also takes less time to restore than an incremental backup, because carrying out restoration of a differential backup happens in two steps, whereas in an incremental backup every incremental backup must be restored in the correct sequence.

Whatever the organization chooses, it is important to not mix differential and incremental backups. This overlap could cause files to be missed, since the incremental backup changes the archive bit, and the differential backup does not.

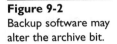

Figure 9-2
Backup software may alter the archive bit.

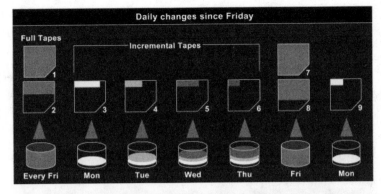

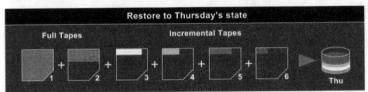

Critical data should be backed up and stored at an onsite area *and* an offsite area. The onsite backup copies should be easily accessible in case of nondisasters and should provide a quick restore process so operations can return to normal. However, onsite backup copies are not enough to provide real protection. The data should also be held in an offsite facility in case of actual disasters or catastrophes. One choice that needs to be made is where the offsite location should be in reference to the main facility. The closer the offsite backup storage site is, the easier it is to access, but this can put the backup copies in danger if a large-scale disaster manages to take out the company's main facility and the backup facility. It may be wiser to choose a backup facility farther away, which makes accessibility harder but reduces the risk. Some companies choose to have more than one backup facility: one that is close and one that is farther away.

The onsite backup information should be stored in a fire-resistant, heat-resistant, and waterproof safe. The procedures for backing up and restoring data should be easily accessible and comprehensible even to operators or administrators who are not intimately familiar with a specific system. In an emergency situation, the same guy who always does the backing up and restoring may not be around, or outsourced consultants may need to be temporarily hired in order to meet the restoration time constraints.

A backup strategy must take into account that failure can take place at any step of the process, so if there is a problem during the backup or restoration process that could corrupt the data, there should be a graceful way of backing out or reconstructing the data from the beginning.

Can we actually restore data? Backing up data is a wonderful thing in life, but making sure it can be properly restored is even better. Many organizations have developed a false sense of security based on the fact that they have a very organized and effective process of backing up their data. That sense of security can disappear in seconds when a company realizes in a time of crisis that its restore processes do not work. For example, one company had paid an offsite backup facility to use a courier to collect its weekly backup tapes and transport them to the offsite facility for safekeeping. What the company did not realize was that this courier used the subway and many times set the tapes on the ground while waiting for the subway train. A subway has many large engines that create their own magnetic field. This can have the same effect on media as large magnets, meaning that the data can be erased or corrupted. The company never tested its restore processes and eventually experienced a disaster. Much to its surprise, it found out that three years of data was corrupted and unusable.

Many other stories and experiences like this are out there. Don't let your organization end up as an anecdote in someone else's book because it failed to verify that its backups could be restored.

Electronic Backup Solutions

Manually backing up systems and data can be time-consuming, error-prone, and costly. Several technologies serve as automated backup alternatives. Although these technologies are usually more expensive, they are quicker and more accurate, which may be necessary for online information that changes often.

Among the many technologies and ways to back up data electronically is *disk shadowing*, which is very similar to data mirroring.

 NOTE   *Disk duplexing* means there is more than one disk controller. If one disk controller fails, the other is ready and available.

Disk shadowing is used to ensure the availability of data and to provide a fault-tolerant solution by duplicating hardware and maintaining more than one copy of the information. The data are dynamically created and maintained on two or more identical disks. If only disk mirroring is used, then each disk would have a corresponding mirrored disk that contains the exact same information. If shadow sets are used, the data can be stored as images on two or more disks.

Systems that need to interact with this data are connected to all the drives at the same time. All of these drives "look" like just one drive to the user. This provides transparency to the user so that when she needs to retrieve a file, she does not have to worry about which drive to go to for this process. When a user writes data to be stored on this media, the data are written to all disks in the shadow set.

Disk shadowing provides online backup storage, which can either reduce or replace the need for periodic offline manual backup operations. Another benefit to this solution is that it can boost read operation performance. Multiple paths are provided to duplicate data, and a shadow set can carry out multiple read requests in parallel.

Disk shadowing is commonly seen as an expensive solution, because two or more hard drives are used to hold the exact same data. If a company has data that will fill up 100 hard drives, it must purchase and maintain at least 200 hard drives. A company would choose this solution if fault tolerance were required.

If a disk drive fails, at least one shadow set is still available. A new disk can be assigned to this set through proper configurations, and the data can be copied from the shadow set. The copying can take place offline, but this means the data are unavailable for a period of time. Most products that provide disk-shadowing functionality allow for online copying, where disks are hot swapped into the set and can carry out the necessary copy functions without having to bring the drives offline.

Electronic vaulting and remote journaling are other solutions that companies should be aware of. *Electronic vaulting* makes copies of files as they are modified and periodically transmits them to an offsite backup site. The transmission does not happen in real time, but is carried out in batches. So, a company can choose to have all files that have been changed sent to the backup facility every hour, day, week, or month. The information can be stored in an offsite facility and retrieved from that facility in a short time.

This form of backup takes place in many financial institutions, so when a bank teller accepts a deposit or withdrawal, the change to the customer's account is made locally to that branch's database and to the remote site that maintains the backup copies of all customer records.

Electronic vaulting is a method of transferring bulk information to offsite facilities for backup purposes. *Remote journaling* is another method of transmitting data offsite, but this usually only includes moving the journal or transaction logs to the offsite facility, not the actual files. These logs contain the *deltas* (changes) that have taken place to the individual files. If and when data are corrupted and need to be restored, the bank can retrieve these logs, which are used to rebuild the lost data. Journaling is efficient for database recovery, where only the reapplication of a series of changes to individual records is required to resynchronize the database.

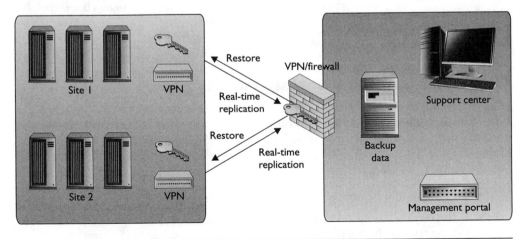

NOTE Remote journaling takes place in real time and transmits only the file deltas. Electronic vaulting takes place in batches and moves the entire file that has been updated.

It may be necessary to keep different versions of software and files, especially in a software development environment. The object and source code should be backed up along with libraries, patches, and fixes. The offsite facility should mirror the onsite facility, meaning it does not make sense to keep all of this data at the onsite facility and only the source code at the offsite facility. Each site should have a full set of the most current and updated information and files.

Another software backup technology we will discuss is referred to as tape vaulting. Many businesses back up their data to tapes that are then manually transferred to an offsite facility by a courier or an employee. With automatic *tape vaulting*, the data are sent over a serial line to a backup tape system at the offsite facility. The company that maintains the offsite facility maintains the systems and changes out tapes when necessary. Data can be quickly backed up and retrieved when necessary. This technology reduces the manual steps in the traditional tape backup procedures.

Basic vaulting of tape data is sending backup tapes to an offsite location, but a manual process can be error-prone. Electronic tape vaulting transmits data over a network to tape devices located at an alternate data center. Electronic tape vaulting improves recovery speed and reduces errors, and backups can be run more frequently.

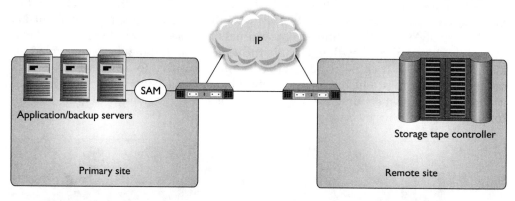

Choosing a Software Backup Facility

I like this facility because it is pink.

A company needs to address several issues and ask specific questions when it is deciding upon a storage facility for its backup materials. The following provides a list of just some of the issues that need to be thought through before committing to a specific vendor for this service:

- Can the media be accessed in the necessary timeframe?
- Is the facility closed on weekends and holidays, and does it only operate during specific hours of the day?
- Are the access control mechanisms tied to an alarm and/or the police station?
- Does the facility have the capability to protect the media from a variety of threats?
- What is the availability of a bonded transport service?

- Are there any geographical environmental hazards such as floods, earthquakes, tornadoes, and so on?
- Is there a fire detection and suppression system?
- Does the facility provide temperature and humidity monitoring and control?
- What type of physical, administrative, and logical access controls are used?

The questions and issues that need to be addressed will vary depending on the type of company, its needs, and the requirements of a backup facility.

Which Data Recovery Solution?

Data classification based on business criticality should have been performed by now.

- The BCP project team needs to divide the data by importance of fast recovery.
- Critical data that need to be continuously available can be restored via electronic vaulting (or remote journaling).
- Other data types can be restored via tapes or mirror systems.

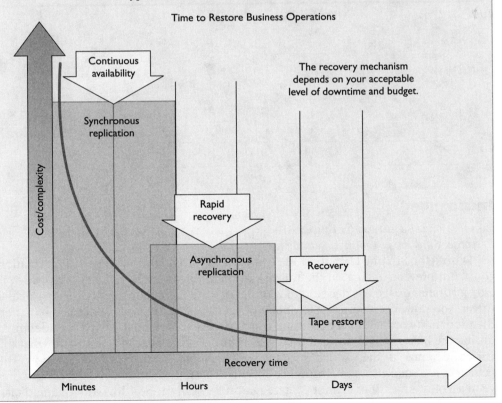

Asynchronous replication means the primary and secondary data volumes are only a few milliseconds out of sync, so the replication is nearly real-time. With synchronous replication, the primary and secondary copies are always in sync, which provides true real-time duplication. Synchronous means replication does not take place in real time, such as in electronic vaulting or batch jobs.

The team must balance the cost to recover against the cost of the disruption. The balancing point becomes the recovery time objective.

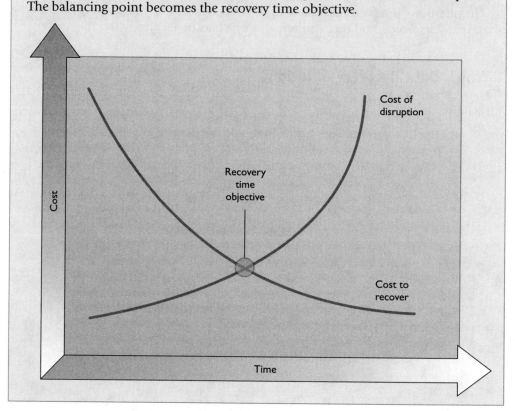

Insurance

Can someone else just pay for this mess?
Response: Sure, we just need a monthly fee.

During the BIA, the team most likely uncovered several threats that the organization could not prevent. Taking on the full risk of these threats often is dangerous, which is why insurance exists. The decision of whether or not to obtain insurance for a particular threat, and how much coverage to obtain when choosing to insure, should be based on the probability of the threat becoming real and the loss potential, which was identified during the BIA. The BCP team should work with management to understand what the current coverage is, the various insurance options, and the limits of each option. The goal here is to make sure the insurance coverage fills in the gap of what the current preventive countermeasures cannot protect against. We can eat healthy, work out, and take our vitamins—but these things cannot prevent death. We purchase life insurance so that after we die, our loved ones are taken care of. (Seems more appropriate to call this death insurance, but that would really hurt marketing efforts of insurance companies.)

Just as people are given different premiums on health and life insurance, companies are given different premiums on the type of insurance they purchase. Different types of insurance policies can be purchased by companies, cyberinsurance being one of them. *Cyberinsurance* is a new type of coverage that insures losses caused by denial-of-service attacks, malware damages, hackers, electronic theft, privacy-related lawsuits, and more. While a person is asked how old he is, previous health issues, if he smokes, and so on, to determine his health insurance premium, companies are asked questions about their security program, such as whether they have an IDS, antivirus software, firewalls, and other security measures.

A company could also choose to purchase a *business interruption insurance* policy. With this type of policy, if the company is out of business for a certain length of time, the insurance company will pay for specified expenses and lost earnings. Another policy that can be bought insures accounts receivable. If a company cannot collect on its accounts receivable for one reason or another, this type of coverage covers part or all of the losses and costs.

The company's insurance should be reviewed annually, because threat levels may change and the company may expand into new ventures that need to be properly covered. Purchasing insurance should not lull a company into a false sense of security, though. Insurance coverage has its limitations, and if the company does not practice due care, the insurance company may not be legally obligated to pay if a disaster hits. It is important to read and understand the fine print when it comes to insurance and to make sure you know what is expected of your company—not just what is expected from the insurance organization.

Recovery and Restoration

Now, who is going to fix everything?
Response: We thought you were.

The BCP coordinator needs to define several different teams that should be properly trained and available if a disaster hits. The types of teams an organization needs depends upon the organization. The following are some examples of teams that a company may need to construct:

- Damage assessment team
- Legal team
- Media relations team
- Network recovery team
- Relocation team
- Restoration team
- Salvage team
- Security team
- Telecommunications team

The BCP coordinator should have an understanding of the needs of the company and the types of teams that need to be developed and trained. Employees should be assigned to the specific teams based on their knowledge and skill set. Each team needs to have a designated leader, who will direct the members and their activities. These team leaders will be responsible not only for ensuring that their team's objectives are met, but also for communicating with each other to make sure each team is working in parallel phases.

The *restoration team* should be responsible for getting the alternate site into a working and functioning environment, and the *salvage team* should be responsible for starting the recovery of the original site. Both teams must know how to do many tasks, such as install operating systems, configure workstations and servers, string wire and cabling, set up the network and configure networking services, and install equipment and applications. Both teams must also know how to restore data from backup facilities, and how to do so in a secure manner that ensures the system's and data's confidentiality, integrity, and availability are not compromised.

The BCP must outline the specific teams, their responsibilities, and notification procedures. The plan must indicate the methods that should be used to contact team leaders during business hours and after business hours.

A role, or a team, needs to be created to carry out a *damage assessment* once a disaster has taken place. The assessment procedures should be properly documented and include the following steps:

- Determine the cause of the disaster.
- Determine the potential for further damage.
- Identify the affected business functions and areas.
- Identify the level of functionality for the critical resources.
- Identify the resources that must be replaced immediately.
- Estimate how long it will take to bring critical functions back online.
- If it will take longer than the previously estimated MTD values to restore operations, then a disaster should be declared, and the BCP should be put into action.

After this information is collected and assessed, it will indicate what teams need to be called to action and whether the BCP actually needs to be activated. The BCP coordinator and team must develop activation criteria. After the damage assessment, if one or more of the situations outlined in the criteria have taken place, then the team is moved into recovery mode.

Different organizations have different criteria, because the business drivers and critical functions will vary from organization to organization. The criteria may comprise some or all of the following elements:

- Danger to human life
- Danger to state or national security
- Damage to facility

- Damage to critical systems
- Estimated value of downtime that will be experienced

Once the damage assessment is completed and the plan is activated, various teams must be deployed, which signals the company's entry into the recovery phase. Each team has its own tasks—for example, the restoration team prepares the offsite facility (if needed), the network team rebuilds the network and systems, and the relocation team starts organizing the staff to move into a new facility.

The recovery process needs to be as organized as possible to get the company up and running as soon as possible. This is much easier to state in a book than to carry out in reality. This is why written procedures are critical. During the BIA, the critical functions and their resources were identified. These are the things that the teams need to work together on getting up and running first. Templates should be developed during the plan development stage. These templates are used by the different teams to step them through the necessary phases and to document their findings. For example, if one step could not be completed until new systems were purchased, this should be indicated on the template. If a step is partially completed, this should be documented so the team does not forget to go back and finish that step when the necessary part arrives. These templates keep the teams on task and also quickly tell the team leaders about the progress, obstacles, and potential recovery time.

 NOTE Examples of possible templates can be found in NIST's *Contingency Planning Guide for Information Technology Systems*, which is available online at http://csrc.nist.gov/publications/nistpubs/800-34/sp800-34.pdf.

When it is time for the company to move back into its original site or a new site, the company enters the *reconstitution phase*. A company is not out of an emergency state until it is back in operation at the original primary site or a new site that was constructed to replace the primary site, because the company is always vulnerable while operating in a backup facility. Many logistical issues need to be considered as to when a company must return from the alternate site to the original site. The following lists a few of these issues:

- Ensuring the safety of employees
- Ensuring an adequate environment is provided (power, facility infrastructure, water, HVAC)
- Ensuring that the necessary equipment and supplies are present and in working order
- Ensuring proper communications and connectivity methods are working
- Properly testing the new environment

Once the coordinator, management, and salvage team sign off on the readiness of the facility, the salvage team should carry out the following steps:

- Back up data from the alternate site and restore it within the new facility.

- Carefully terminate contingency operations.
- Securely transport equipment and personnel to the new facility.

The least critical functions should be moved back first, so if there are issues in network configurations or connectivity, or important steps were not carried out, the critical operations of the company are not negatively affected. Why go through the trouble of moving the most critical systems and operations to a safe and stable site, only to return it to a main site that is untested? Let the less critical departments act as the canary. If they survive, then move over the more critical components of the company.

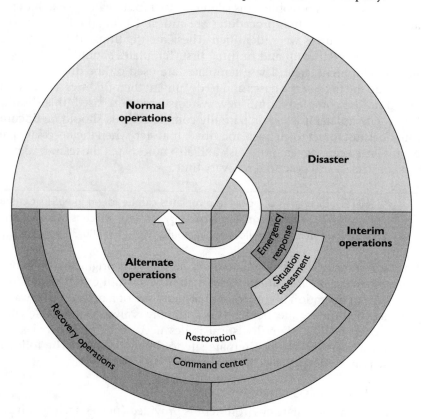

Up to now, the BCP team has covered the following steps:

1. Developed the continuity planning policy statement
   - Outlined the scope and goals of the BCP and roles of the BCP team
2. Performed the business impact analysis (BIA)
   - Identified critical business functions, their resources, and MTD values
   - Identified threats and calculated the impact of these threats
   - Identified solutions
   - Presented findings to management

3. Identified and implemented preventive controls

   - Put controls into place to reduce the company's identified risks

   - Bought more insurance, implemented facility structural reinforcements, rolled out backup solutions for data, installed redundant and fault-tolerant mechanisms, and so on

4. Developed recovery strategies

   - Implemented processes of getting the company up and running in the necessary time

   - Created the necessary teams, developed goals and procedures for each team, created notification steps and planned activation criteria, identified alternate backup solutions, and so on

So, the BCP team has worked long and hard and has all of the previous items figured out. Now it needs to put all of these solutions and steps in the plan itself, test the plan, train the people, and lay out strategies of how the plan is to be maintained and kept up-to-date. No rest for the weary . . . let's march on!

Developing Goals for the Plans

My goals are to own a boat, retire at 55, and grow more hair.
Response: Great, we will integrate this into our BCP.

If you do not have established goals, how do you know when you are done and whether your efforts were actually successful? Goals are established so everyone knows the ultimate objectives. Establishing goals is important for any task, but especially for business continuity and recovery plans. The definition of the goals helps direct the

---

BCP Development Products

Since there is so much work in collecting, analyzing, and maintaining DRP and BCP data, using a product that automates these tasks can prove to be extremely helpful.

"Automated" plan development can help you create

- Customizable questionnaires through the use of expert-system templates
- Timetables for disaster recovery procedures
- What-if scenario modeling
- Reports on financial and operational impact analysis
- Graphic representations of the analysis results
- Sample questionnaires, forms, and templates
- Permission-based plan maintenance
- Central version control and integration
- Regulatory compliancy

proper allocation of resources and tasks, develops necessary strategies, and assists in economical justification of the plans and program overall. Once the goals are set, they provide a guide to the development of the actual plans themselves. Anyone who has been involved in large projects that entail many small, complex details knows that at times it is easy to get off track and not actually accomplish the major goals of the project. Goals are established to keep everyone on track and to ensure that the efforts pay off in the end.

Great, we have established that goals are important. But the goal could be, "Keep the company in business if an earthquake hits." Good goal, but not overly useful without more clarity and direction. To be useful, a goal must contain certain key information, such as the following:

- **Responsibility**   Each individual involved with recovery and continuity should have their responsibilities spelled out in writing to ensure a clear understanding in a chaotic situation. Each task should be assigned to the individual most logically situated to handle it. These individuals must know what is expected of them, which is done through training, drills, communication, and documentation. So, for example, instead of just running out of the building screaming, an individual must know that he is responsible for shutting down the servers before he can run out of the building screaming.

- **Authority**   In times of crisis, it is important to know who is in charge. Teamwork is important in these situations, and almost every team does much better with an established and trusted leader. Such leaders must know that they are expected to step up to the plate in a time of crisis and understand what type of direction they should provide to the rest of the employees. Clear-cut authority will aid in reducing confusion and increasing cooperation.

- **Priorities**   It is extremely important to know what is critical versus what is merely nice to have. Different departments provide different functionality for an organization. The critical departments must be singled out from the departments that provide functionality that the company can live without for a week or two. It is necessary to know which department must come online first, which second, and so on. That way, the efforts are made in the most useful, effective, and focused manner. Along with the priorities of departments, the priorities of systems, information, and programs must be established. It may be necessary to ensure that the database is up and running before working to bring the file server online. The general priorities must be set by the management with the help of the different departments and IT staff.

- **Implementation and testing**   It is great to write down very profound ideas and develop plans, but unless they are actually carried out and tested, they may not add up to a hill of beans. Once a continuity plan is developed, it actually has to be put into action. It needs to be documented and put in places that are easily accessible in times of crisis. The people who are assigned specific tasks need to be taught and informed how to fulfill those tasks, and dry runs must be done to walk people through different situations. The drills should take place at least once a year, and the entire program should be continually updated and improved.

Studies have shown that 65 percent of businesses that lose computing capabilities for over one week are never able to recover and subsequently go out of business. Not being able to bounce back quickly or effectively by setting up shop somewhere else can make a company lose business and, more importantly, its reputation. In such a competitive world, customers have a lot of options. If one company is not prepared to bounce back after a disruption or disaster, customers may go to another vendor and stay there.

Implementing Strategies

Once the strategies have been decided upon, they need to be documented and put into place by the BCP team. This moves the efforts from a purely planning stage to an actual implementation and action phase.

As stated previously, copies of the plans need to be kept in one or more locations other than the primary site, so that if the primary site is destroyed or negatively affected, the continuity plan is still available to the teams. It is also critical that different formats of the plan be available to the team, including both electronic and paper versions. An electronic version of the plan is not very useful if you don't have any electricity to run a computer. In addition to having copies of the recovery documents located at their offices and homes, key individuals should also have easily accessible versions of critical procedures and call tree information. One simple way to accomplish this is to publish the call tree data on cards that can be affixed to personnel badges or kept in a wallet. In an emergency situation, valuable minutes are better spent responding to an incident than looking for a document or having to wait for a laptop to power up.

The plan should address in detail all of the topics we have covered so far. The actual format of the plan will depend on the environment, the goals of the plan, priorities, and identified threats. After each of those items is examined and documented, the topics of the plan can be divided into the necessary categories.

A commonly accepted structure for a BCP is illustrated in Figure 9-3. Each organization's BCP looks different, but these core topics should be covered in some fashion. We walked through these different components earlier in this chapter. The role of the plan is to provide preplanned and sequenced structure to these different processes. The plan also needs to integrate a degree of flexibility, because no one knows exactly what type of disaster will take place, nor its effects. Although procedures need to be documented for the different phases of the plan, a balance between detail and flexibility must be achieved so the company is not ready for only one type of disaster.

Some organizations develop individual plans for specific tasks and goals. These different plans are described in Table 9-2. It is up to management and the BCP team to determine the number and types of plans that should be developed and implemented.

The BCP team can choose to integrate many of these components into the BCP. It is usually better to include these stand-alone plans as appendixes so each document is clear, concise, and usable.

Figure 9-3
The general
structure of a
business continuity
plan

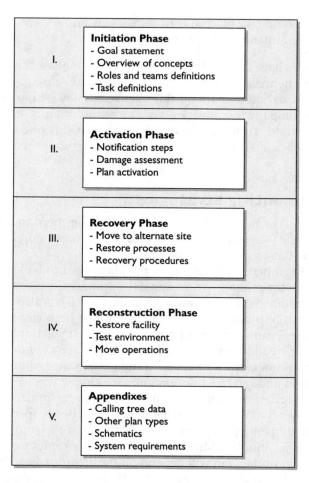

I.
Initiation Phase
- Goal statement
- Overview of concepts
- Roles and teams definitions
- Task definitions

II.
Activation Phase
- Notification steps
- Damage assessment
- Plan activation

III.
Recovery Phase
- Move to alternate site
- Restore processes
- Recovery procedures

IV.
Reconstruction Phase
- Restore facility
- Test environment
- Move operations

V.
Appendixes
- Calling tree data
- Other plan types
- Schematics
- System requirements

Testing and Revising the Plan

We made a plan and tested it and it doesn't work.
Response: Let's just go home then.

The BCP should be tested regularly, because environments continually change. Interestingly, many organizations are moving away from the concept of "testing" because a test naturally leads to a pass or fail score, and in the end, that type of score is not very productive. Instead, many organizations are adopting the concept of exercises, which appear to be less stressful, better focused, and ultimately more productive. Each time the plan is exercised or tested, improvements and efficiencies are generally uncovered, yielding better and better results over time. The responsibility of establishing periodic exercises and the maintenance of the plan should be assigned to a specific person or persons who will have overall ownership responsibilities for the business continuity initiatives within the organization.

As noted earlier, the plan's maintenance should be incorporated into change management procedures so any changes in the environment are reflected in the plan itself.

Plan Type	Description
Business resumption plan	Focuses on how to re-create the necessary business processes that need to be reestablished instead of focusing on IT components (i.e., process oriented instead of procedural oriented).
Continuity of operations plan (COOP)	Establishes senior management and a headquarters after a disaster. Outlines roles and authorities, orders of succession, and individual role tasks.
IT contingency plan	Plan for systems, networks, and major applications recovery procedures after disruptions. A contingency plan should be developed for each major system and application.
Crisis communications plan	Includes internal and external communications structure and roles. Identifies specific individuals who will communicate with external entities. Contains predeveloped statements that are to be released.
Cyber incident response plan	Focuses on malware, hackers, intrusions, attacks, and other security issues. Outlines procedures for incident response.
Disaster recovery plan	Focuses on how to recover various IT mechanisms after a disaster. Whereas a contingency plan is usually for nondisasters, a disaster recovery plan is for disasters that require IT processing to take place at another facility.
Occupant emergency plan	Establishes personnel safety and evacuation procedures.

Table 9-2 Different Types of Recovery Plans

Tests and disaster recovery drills and exercises should be performed at least once a year. A company should have no real confidence in a developed plan until it has actually been tested. The tests and drills prepare personnel for what they may be faced with and provide a controlled environment to learn the tasks expected of them. These tests and drills also point out issues to the planning team and management that may not have been previously thought about and addressed as part of the planning process. The exercises, in the end, demonstrate whether a company can actually recover after a disaster.

The exercise should have a predetermined scenario that the company may indeed be faced with one day. Specific parameters and a scope of the exercise must be worked out before sounding the alarms. The team of testers must agree upon what exactly is getting tested and how to properly determine success or failure. The team must agree upon the timing and duration of the exercise, who will participate in the exercise, who will receive which assignments, and what steps should be taken. Also, the team needs to determine whether hardware, software, personnel, procedures, and communications lines are going to be tested, and whether it is some, all, or a subset combination. If the test will include moving some equipment to an alternate site, then transportation, extra equipment, and alternate site readiness must be addressed and assessed.

Most companies cannot afford for these exercises to interrupt production or productivity, so the exercises may need to take place in sections or at specific times, which will require logistical planning. Written exercise plans should be developed that will test for specific weaknesses in the overall disaster recovery plan. The first exercise should not include all employees, but rather a small group of people here and there until each learns his or her responsibilities. Then, larger drills can take place so overall operations will not be negatively affected. The people carrying out these drills should expect problems and mistakes. This is why they are having the drills in the first place. A company would rather have employees make mistakes during a drill so they can learn from them and perform their tasks more effectively during a real disaster.

NOTE After a disaster, telephone service may not be available. For communications purposes, there should be alternatives in place, such as cell phones or walkie-talkies.

A few different types of drills and tests can be used, each with its own pros and cons. The following sections explain the different types of drills.

Checklist Test
Okay, did we forget anything?

In this type of test, copies of the BCP are distributed to the different departments and functional areas for review. This is done so each functional manager can review the plan and indicate if anything has been left out or if some approaches should be modified or deleted. This is a method that ensures that some things have not been taken for granted or omitted. Once the departments have reviewed their copies and made suggestions, the planning team then integrates those changes into the master plan.

NOTE The checklist test is also called the desk check test.

Structured Walk-Through Test
Let's get in a room and talk about this.

In this test, representatives from each department or functional area come together to go over the plan to ensure its accuracy. The group reviews the objectives of the plan, discusses the scope and assumptions of the plan, reviews the organization and reporting structure, and evaluates the testing, maintenance, and training requirements described. This gives the people responsible for making sure a disaster recovery happens effectively and efficiently a chance to review what has been decided upon and what is expected of them.

The group walks through different scenarios of the plan from beginning to end to make sure nothing was left out. This also raises the awareness of team members about the recovery procedures.

Simulation Test
Everyone take your places. Okay, action!

This type of test takes a lot more planning and people. In this situation, all employees who participate in operational and support functions, or their representatives, come together to practice executing the disaster recovery plan based on a specific scenario. The scenario is used to test the reaction of each operational and support representative.

Again, this is done to ensure specific steps were not left out and that certain threats were not overlooked. It acts as a catalyst to raise the awareness of the people involved.

The drill includes only those materials that will be available in an actual disaster, to portray a more realistic environment. The simulation test continues up to the point of actual relocation to an offsite facility and actual shipment of replacement equipment.

Parallel Test

Let's do a little processing here and a little processing there.

A parallel test is done to ensure that the specific systems can actually perform adequately at the alternate offsite facility. Some systems are moved to the alternate site and processing takes place. The results are compared with the regular processing that is done at the original site. This points out any necessary tweaking, reconfiguring, or steps that need to take place.

Full-Interruption Test

Shut down and move out!

This type of test is the most intrusive to regular operations and business productivity. The original site is actually shut down, and processing takes place at the alternate site. The recovery team fulfills its obligations in preparing the systems and environment for the alternate site. All processing is done only on devices at the alternate offsite facility.

This is a full-blown drill that takes a lot of planning and coordination, but it can reveal many holes in the plan that need to be fixed before an actual disaster hits. Full-interruption tests should be performed only after all other types of tests have been successful. They are the most risky and can impact the business in very serious and devastating ways if not managed properly; therefore, senior management approval needs to be obtained prior to performing full-interruption tests.

The type of organization and its goals will dictate what approach to the training exercise is most effective. Each organization may have a different approach and unique aspects. If detailed planning methods and processes are going to be taught, then specific training may be required, rather than general training that provides an overview. Higher-quality training will result in an increase of employee interest and commitment.

During and after each type of test, a record of the significant events should be documented and reported to management so it is aware of all outcomes of the test.

Other Types of Training

I think I stopped breathing. Quick, blow into my mouth!
Response: Leave me alone.

Employees need to be trained on other issues besides disaster recovery, including first aid and CPR, how to properly use a fire extinguisher, evacuation routes and crowd control methods, emergency communications procedures, and how to properly shut down equipment in different types of disasters.

The more technical employees may need to know how to redistribute network resources and how to use different telecommunications lines if the main one goes down. A redundant power supply needs to be investigated, and the procedures for how to move critical systems from one power supply to the next should be understood and tested.

Emergency Response

You must save your fellow man before any equipment.
Response: But I love my computer more than anyone I know.

Often, the initial response to an emergency affects the ultimate outcome. Emergency response procedures are the prepared actions that are developed to help people in a crisis situation better cope with the disruption. These procedures are the first line of defense when dealing with a crisis situation.

People who are up-to-date on their knowledge of disaster recovery will perform the best, which is why training and drills are very important. Emergencies are unpredictable, and no one knows when they will be called upon to perform.

Protection of life is of the utmost importance and should be dealt with first before looking to save material objects. Training and drills should show the people in charge how to evacuate personnel safely (see Table 9-3). All personnel should know their designated emergency exits and destinations. Emergency gathering spots should take into consideration the effects of seasonal weather. One person in each designated group is often responsible for making sure all people are accounted for. One person in particular should be responsible for notifying the appropriate authorities: the police department, security guards, fire department, emergency rescue, and management. With proper training, employees will be better equipped to handle emergencies rather than just running to the exit.

If the situation is not life threatening, systems should be shut down in an orderly fashion, and critical data files or resources, along with critical personal items like purses and wallets, should be removed during evacuation. There is a reason for the order of activities. As with all processes, there are dependencies with everything we do. Deciding to skip steps or add steps could in fact cause more harm than good.

Once things have approached a reasonable plateau of activity, one or more people will most likely be required to interface with external entities, such as the press, customers, shareholders, and civic officials. One or more people should be prepped in their reaction and response to the recent disaster so a uniform and reasonable response is given to explain the circumstances, how the company is dealing with the disaster, and what customers and others should now expect from the company. The company should quickly present this information instead of having others come to their own conclusions and start false rumors. At least one person should be available to the press to ensure proper messages are being reported and sent out.

Another, unfortunate issue needs to be addressed prior to an emergency: potential looting, vandalism, and fraud opportunities from both a physical and logical perspective. After a company is hit with a large disturbance or disaster is usually when it is most vulnerable, and others may take advantage of this vulnerability. Careful thought and planning needs to take place so these issues can be dealt with properly and so the necessary and expected level of protection is provided at all times.

Procedure: Personnel Evacuation Description	Location	Names of Staff Trained to Carry Out Procedure	Date Last Carried Out
Each floor within the building must have two individuals who will ensure that all personnel have been evacuated from the building after a disaster. These individuals are responsible for performing employee head count, communicating with the BCP coordinator, and assessing emergency response needs for their employees.	West wing parking lot	David Miller Mike Lester	Drills were carried out on May 4, 2005.
Comments: These individuals are responsible for maintaining an up-to-date listing of employees on their specific floor. These individuals must have a company-issued walkie-talkie and proper training for this function.			

Table 9-3   Sample Emergency Response Procedure

Maintaining the Plan

Wow, this plan was developed in 1958!

Response: I am sure it is still fine. Not much has changed since then.

Unfortunately, the various plans that have been covered in this chapter can become quickly out of date. An out-of-date BCP may provide a company with a false sense of security, which could be devastating if and when a disaster actually takes place.

The main reasons plans become outdated include the following:

- The business continuity process is not integrated into the change management process.
- Infrastructure and environment changes occur.
- Reorganization of the company, layoffs, or mergers occur.
- Changes in hardware, software, and applications occur.
- After the plan is constructed, people feel their job is done.
- Personnel turns over.

- Large plans take a lot of work to maintain.
- Plans do not have a direct line to profitability.

Organizations can keep the plan updated by taking the following actions:

- Make business continuity a part of every business decision.
- Insert the maintenance responsibilities into job descriptions.
- Include maintenance in personnel evaluations.
- Perform internal audits that include disaster recovery and continuity documentation and procedures.
- Perform regular drills that use the plan.
- Integrate the BCP into the current change management process.

One of the simplest and most cost-effective and process-efficient ways to keep a plan up-to-date is to incorporate it within the change management process of the organization. When you think about it, it makes a lot of sense. Where do you document new applications, equipment, or services? Where do you document updates and patches? Your change management process should be updated to incorporate fields and triggers that alert the BCP team when a significant change will occur and should provide a means to update the recovery documentation. What's the point of removing the dust bunnies off a plan if it has your configurations from three years ago? There is nothing worse than that feeling at the pit of your stomach when you realize the one thing you thought was going to save you will in fact only serve to keep a fire stoked with combustible material.

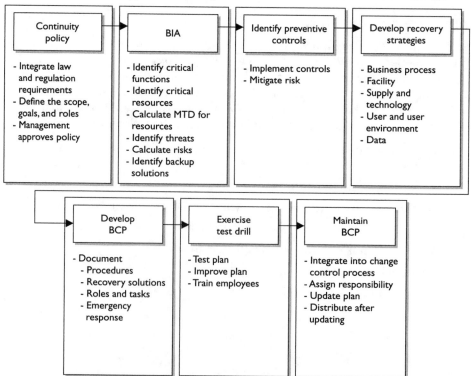

Life Cycles

Remember that the DRP and BCP have life cycles. Understanding and maintaining each step of the life cycle is critical if these plans are to be useful to the organization.

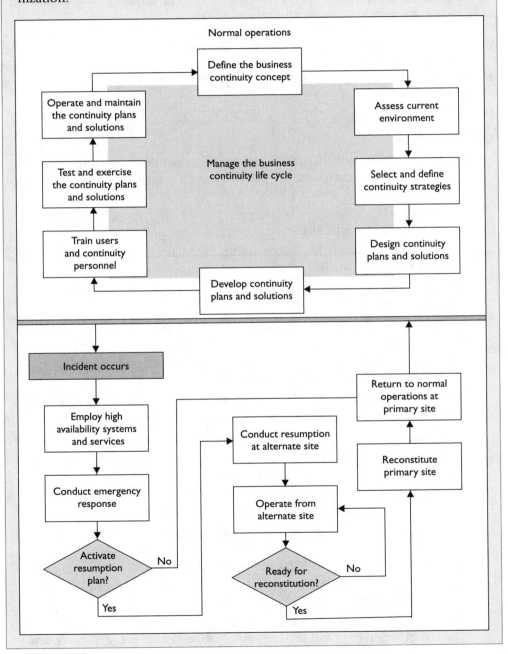

Summary

Although business continuity planning is usually given low priority in most organizations today, that does not mean it is not important and crucial. Unfortunately, many companies have to experience the pain of a disaster to understand how it could have circumvented or mitigated the events that caused the pain.

To develop and carry out business continuity efforts successfully, plenty of thought, planning, time, and effort must go into the different phases of this activity. The real threats must be identified and understood, reasonable countermeasures must be put into place, and detailed plans must be outlined for the unfortunate but anticipated day when they are needed.

Quick Tips

- A business continuity plan (BCP) contains strategy documents that provide detailed procedures that ensure critical business functions are maintained and that help minimize losses of life, operations, and systems.

- A BCP provides procedures for emergency responses, extended backup operations, and post-disaster recovery.

- A BCP should reach enterprisewide, with individual organizational units each having their own detailed continuity and contingency plans.

- A BCP needs to prioritize critical applications and provide a sequence for efficient recovery.

- A BCP requires senior executive management support for initiating the plan and final approval.

- BCPs can quickly become outdated due to personnel turnover, reorganizations, and undocumented changes.

- Executives may be held liable if proper BCPs are not developed and used.

- Threats can be natural, manmade, or technical.

- The steps of recovery planning include initiating the project; performing business impact analyses; developing a recovery strategy; developing a recovery plan; and implementing, testing, and maintaining the plan.

- The project initiation phase involves getting management support, developing the scope of the plan, and securing funding and resources.

- The business impact analysis is one of the most important first steps in the planning development. Qualitative and quantitative data needs to be gathered, analyzed, interpreted, and presented to management.

- Executive commitment and support are the most critical elements in developing the BCP.

- A business case must be presented to gain executive support. This is done by explaining regulatory and legal requirements, exposing vulnerabilities, and providing solutions.

- Plans should be prepared by the people who will actually carry them out.
- The planning group should comprise representatives from all departments or organizational units.
- The BCP team should identify the individuals who will interact with external entities such as the press, shareholders, customers, and civic officials. Response to the disaster should be done quickly and honestly, and should be consistent with any other employee response.
- Disaster recovery and continuity planning should be brought into normal business decision-making procedures.
- The loss criteria for disasters include much more than direct dollar loss. They may include added operational costs, loss in reputation and public confidence, loss of competitive advantage, violation of regulatory or legal requirements, loss in productivity, delayed income, interest costs, and loss in revenue.
- A survey should be developed and given to the most knowledgeable people within the company to obtain the most realistic information pertaining to a company's risk and recovery procedures.
- The plan's scope can be determined by geographical, organizational, or functional means.
- Many things need to be understood pertaining to the working environment so it can be replicated at an alternate site after a disaster.
- Subscription services can supply hot, warm, or cold sites.
- A reciprocal agreement is one in which a company promises another company it can move in and share space if it experiences a disaster and vice versa. Reciprocal agreements are very tricky to implement and are unenforceable. However, they are cheap and sometimes the only choice.
- A hot site is fully configured with hardware, software, and environmental needs. It can usually be up and running in a matter of hours. It is the most expensive option, but some companies cannot be out of business longer than a day without detrimental results.
- A warm site does not have computers, but it does have some peripheral devices such as disk drives, controllers, and tape drives. This option is less expensive than a hot site, but takes more effort and time to get operational.
- A cold site is just a building with power, raised floors, and utilities. No devices are available. This is the cheapest of the three options, but can take weeks to get up and operational.
- When returning to the original site, the least critical organizational units should go back first.
- An important part of the disaster recovery and continuity plan is to communicate its requirements and procedures to all employees.
- Testing, drills, and exercises demonstrate the actual ability to recover and can verify the compatibility of backup facilities.

- Before tests are performed, there should be a clear indication of what is being tested, how success will be determined, and how mistakes should be expected and dealt with.

- A checklist test is one in which copies of the plan are handed out to each functional area to ensure the plan properly deals with the area's needs and vulnerabilities.

- A structured walk-through test is one in which representatives from each functional area or department get together and walk through the plan from beginning to end.

- A simulation test is one in which a practice execution of the plan takes place. A specific scenario is established, and the simulation continues up to the point of actual relocation to the alternate site.

- A parallel test is one in which some systems are actually run at the alternate site.

- A full-interruption test is one in which regular operations are stopped and where processing is moved to the alternate site.

- Remote journaling involves transmitting the journal or transaction log offsite to a backup facility.

Questions

Please remember that these questions are formatted and asked in a certain way for a reason. Keep in mind that the CISSP exam is asking questions at a conceptual level. Questions may not always have the perfect answer, and the candidate is advised against always looking for the perfect answer. Instead, the candidate should look for the best answer in the list.

1. What procedures should take place to restore a system and its data files after a system failure?

    A. Restore from storage media backup.

    B. Perform a parallel test.

    C. Implement recovery procedures.

    D. Perform a walk-through test.

2. What is one of the first steps in developing a business continuity plan?

    A. Identify backup solution.

    B. Decide whether the company needs to perform a walk-through, parallel, or simulation test.

    C. Perform a business impact analysis.

    D. Develop a business resumption plan.

3. How often should a business continuity plan be tested?

    A. At least every ten years

    B. Only when the infrastructure or environment changes

    C. At least every two years

    D. Whenever there are significant changes in the organization

4. During a test recovery procedure, one important step is to maintain records of important events that happen during the procedure. What other step is just as important?

    A. Schedule another test to address issues that took place during that procedure.

    B. Make sure someone is prepared to talk to the media with the appropriate responses.

    C. Report the events to management.

    D. Identify essential business functions.

5. Which of the following actions is least important when quantifying risks associated with a potential disaster?

    A. Gathering information from agencies that report the probability of certain natural disasters taking place in that area

    B. Identifying the company's key functions and business requirements

    C. Identifying critical systems that support the company's operations

    D. Estimating the potential loss and impact the company would face based on how long the outage lasted

6. The purpose of initiating emergency actions right after a disaster takes place is to prevent loss of life and injuries, and to _____.

    A. Secure the area to ensure that no looting or fraud takes place.

    B. Mitigate further damage.

    C. Protect evidence and clues.

    D. Investigate the extent of the damages.

7. Which of the following is the best way to ensure that the company's backup tapes can be restored and used at a warm site?

    A. Retrieve the tapes from the offsite facility, and verify that the equipment at the original site can read them.

    B. Ask the offsite vendor to test them, and label the ones that were properly read.

    C. Test them on the vendor's machine, which won't be used during an emergency.

    D. Inventory each tape kept at the vendor's site twice a month.

8. Which best describes a hot-site facility versus a warm- or cold-site facility?

    A. A site that has disk drives, controllers, and tape drives

    B. A site that has all necessary PCs, servers, and telecommunications

    C. A site that has wiring, central air, and raised flooring

    D. A mobile site that can be brought to the company's parking lot

9. Which is the best description of remote journaling?

   A. Backing up bulk data to an offsite facility

   B. Backing up transaction logs to an offsite facility

   C. Capturing and saving transactions to two mirrored servers in-house

   D. Capturing and saving transactions to different media types

10. Which of the following is something that should be required of an offsite backup facility that stores backed-up media for companies?

    A. The facility should be within 10 to 15 minutes of the original facility to ensure easy access.

    B. The facility should contain all necessary PCs and servers and should have raised flooring.

    C. The facility should be protected by an armed guard.

    D. The facility should protect against unauthorized access and entry.

11. Which item will a business impact analysis not identify?

    A. Whether the company is best suited for a parallel or full-interrupt test

    B. What areas would suffer the greatest operational and financial loss in the event of a particular disaster or disruption

    C. What systems are critical for the company and must be highly protected

    D. What amount of outage time a company can endure before it is permanently crippled

12. Which areas of a company are recovery plans recommended for?

    A. The most important operational and financial areas

    B. The areas that house the critical systems

    C. All areas

    D. The areas that the company cannot survive without

13. Who has the final approval of the business continuity plan?

    A. The planning committee

    B. Each representative of each department

    C. Management

    D. External authority

14. Which are the proper steps for developing a continuity plan?

    A. Project initiation, strategy development, business impact analysis, plan development, implementation, testing, and maintenance

    B. Strategy development, project initiation, business impact analysis, plan development, implementation, testing, and maintenance

    C. Implementation and testing, project initiation, strategy development, business impact analysis, and plan development

    D. Plan development, project initiation, strategy development, business impact analysis, implementation, testing, and maintenance

15. What is the most crucial piece of developing a business continuity plan?

    A. Business impact analysis

    B. Implementation, testing, and following through

    C. Participation from each and every department

    D. Management support

16. During development, testing, and maintenance of the continuity plan, a high degree of interaction and communications is crucial to the process. Why?

    A. This is a regulatory requirement of the process.

    B. The more people who talk about it and are involved, the more awareness will increase.

    C. This is not crucial to the plan and should not be interactive because it will most likely affect operations.

    D. Management will more likely support it.

17. To get proper management support and approval of the plan, a business case must be made. Which of the following is least important to this business case?

    A. Regulatory and legal requirements

    B. Company vulnerabilities to disasters and disruptions

    C. How other companies are dealing with these issues

    D. The impact the company can endure if a disaster hits

18. Which of the following describes a parallel test?

    A. It is performed to ensure that some systems will run at the alternate site.

    B. All departments receive a copy of the disaster recovery plan and walk through it.

    C. Representatives from each department come together and go through the test collectively.

    D. Normal operations are shut down.

19. Which of the following describes a structured walk-through test?

    A. It is performed to ensure that critical systems will run at the alternate site.

    B. All departments receive a copy of the disaster recovery plan and walk through it.

    C. Representatives from each department come together and go through the test collectively.

    D. Normal operations are shut down.

20. When is the emergency actually over for a company?
    A. When all people are safe and accounted for
    B. When all operations and people are moved back into the primary site
    C. When operations are safely moved to the offsite facility
    D. When a civil official declares that all is safe

21. Which of the following does not describe a reciprocal agreement?
    A. The agreement is enforceable.
    B. It is a cheap solution.
    C. It may be able to be implemented right after a disaster.
    D. It could overwhelm a current data processing site.

22. Which of the following describes a cold site?
    A. Fully equipped and operational in a few hours
    B. Partially equipped with data processing equipment
    C. Expensive and fully configured
    D. Provides environmental measures but no equipment

23. Which of the following best describes what a disaster recovery plan should contain?
    A. Hardware, software, people, emergency procedures, recovery procedures
    B. People, hardware, offsite facility
    C. Software, media interaction, people, hardware, management issues
    D. Hardware, emergency procedures, software, identified risk

24. Which of the following is not an advantage of a hot site?
    A. Offers many hardware and software choices.
    B. Is readily available.
    C. Can be up and running in hours.
    D. Annual testing is available.

25. Disaster recovery plans can stay updated by doing any of the following except:
    A. Making disaster recovery a part of every business decision
    B. Making sure it is part of employees' job descriptions
    C. Performing regular drills that use the plan
    D. Making copies of the plan and storing them in an offsite facility

26. What is the second step that is missing in the following graphic?

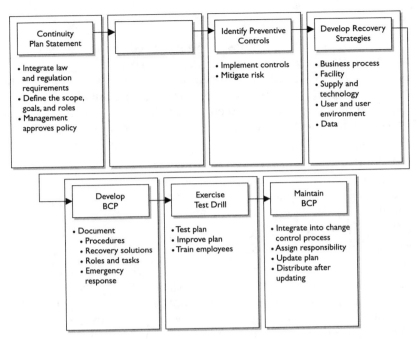

A. Business impact analysis

B. NIST standard

C. Management approval and resource allocation

D. Change control

27. What would the items in the following graphic best be collectively called?

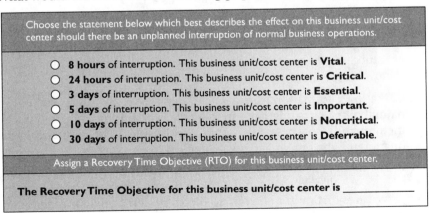

A. Business impact values

B. Activation phase values

C. Maximum tolerable downtime values

D. Reconstitution impact times and values

Answers

1. **C.** In this and similar situations, recovery procedures should be followed, which most likely include recovering data from the backup media. Recovery procedures could include proper steps for rebuilding a system from the beginning, applying the necessary patches and configurations, and ensuring that what needs to take place to ensure productivity is not affected. Some type of redundant system may need to be put into place.

2. **C.** A business impact analysis includes identifying critical systems and functions of a company and interviewing representatives from each department. Once management's support is solidified, a business impact analysis needs to be performed to identify the threats the company faces and the potential costs of these threats.

3. **D.** The plans should be tested if there have been substantial changes to the company or the environment. They should also be tested at least once a year.

4. **C.** When recovery procedures are carried out, the outcome of those procedures should be reported to the individuals who are responsible for this type of activity, which is usually some level of management. If the procedures worked properly, management should know it, and if problems were encountered, management should definitely be made aware of them. Members of management are the ones who are responsible overall for fixing the recovery system and will be the ones to delegate this work and provide the necessary funding and resources.

5. **A.** The question asked you about quantifying the risks, which means to calculate the potential business impact of specific disasters. The core components of a business impact analysis are

   - Identifying the company's key functions and business requirements
   - Identifying critical systems that support the company's operations
   - Estimating the potential loss and impact the company would face based on how long the outage lasted

   Gathering information from agencies that report the probability of certain natural disasters taking place in that area is an important piece in determining the probability of these threats, but it is considered least necessary when quantifying the potential damage that could be experienced.

6. **B.** The main goal of disaster recovery and business continuity plans is to mitigate all risks that could be experienced by a company. Emergency procedures first need to be carried out to protect human life, and then other procedures need to be executed to reduce the damage from further threats.

7. **A.** A warm site is a facility that will not be fully equipped with the company's main systems. The goal of using a warm site is that, if a disaster takes place, the company will bring its systems with it to the warm site. If the company cannot bring the systems with it because they are damaged, the company

must purchase new systems that are exactly like the original systems. So, to properly test backups, the company needs to test them by recovering the data on its original systems at its main site.

8. **B.** A hot site is a facility that is fully equipped and properly configured so that it can be up and running within hours to get a company back into production. Answer B gives the best definition of a fully functionally environment.

9. **B.** Remote journaling is a technology used to transmit data to an offsite facility, but this usually only includes moving the journal or transaction logs to the offsite facility, not the actual files.

10. **D.** This question addresses a facility that is used to store backed-up data; it is not talking about an offsite facility used for disaster recovery purposes. The facility should not be only 10–15 minutes away because some types of disaster could destroy both the company's main facility and this facility if they are that close together, in which case the company would lose all of its information. The facility should have the same security standards as the company's security, including protection against unauthorized access.

11. **A.** All the other answers address the main components of a business impact analysis. Determining the best type of exercise or drill to carry out is not covered under this type of analysis.

12. **C.** It is best if every department within the company has its own contingency plan and procedures in place. These individual plans would "roll up" into the overall BCP enterprise plan.

13. **C.** Management really has the final approval over everything within a company, including these plans.

14. **A.** These steps outline the processes that should take place from beginning to end pertaining to these types of plans.

15. **D.** Management's support is the first thing to obtain before putting any real effort into developing these plans. Without management's support, the effort will not receive the necessary attention, resources, funds, or enforcement.

16. **B.** Communication not only spreads awareness of these plans and their contents, but also allows more people to discuss the possible threats and solutions, which may lead to ideas that the original team did not consider.

17. **C.** The other three answers are key components when building a business case. Although it is a good idea to investigate and learn about how other companies are dealing with similar issues, it is the least important of the four items listed.

18. **A.** In a parallel test, some systems are run at the alternate site, and the results are compared with how processing takes place at the primary site. This is to ensure that the systems work in that area and productivity is not affected. This also extends the previous test and allows the team to walk through the steps of setting up and configuring systems at the offsite facility.

19. **C.** During a structured walk-through test, functional representatives review the plan to ensure its accuracy and that it correctly and accurately reflects the company's recovery strategy.

20. **B.** The emergency is not actually over until the company moves back into its primary site. The company is still vulnerable and at risk while it is operating in an altered or crippled state. This state of vulnerability is not over until the company is operating in the way it was prior to the disaster. Of course, this may mean that the primary site has to be totally rebuilt if it was destroyed.

21. **A.** A reciprocal agreement is not enforceable, meaning that the company that agreed to let the damaged company work out of its facility can decide not to allow this to take place. A reciprocal agreement is a better secondary backup option if the original plan falls through.

22. **D.** A cold site only provides environmental measures—wiring, air conditioning, raised floors—basically a shell of a building and no more.

23. **A.** The recovery plan should contain information about how to deal with people, hardware, software, emergency procedures, recovery procedures, facility issues, and supplies.

24. **A.** Because hot sites are fully equipped, they do not allow for a lot of different hardware and software choices. The subscription service offers basic software and hardware products and does not usually offer a wide range of proprietary items.

25. **D.** The plan should be part of normal business activities. A lot of time and resources go into creating disaster recovery plans, after which they are usually stored away and forgotten about. They need to be updated continuously as the environment changes to ensure that the company can properly react to any type of disaster or disruption.

26. **A.** The missing step is the business impact analysis (BIA). The steps of the BIA are listed next:

    - Identify company's critical business functions.
    - Decide on information-gathering techniques: interviews, surveys, qualitative or quantitative questionnaires.
    - Identify resources these functions depend upon.
    - Calculate how long these functions can be without these resources.
    - Identify vulnerabilities and threats to these functions.
    - Calculate risk for each different business function.
    - Develop backup solutions for resources based on tolerable outage times.
    - Develop recovery solutions for the company's individual departments and for the company as a whole.

27. **C.** Maximum tolerable downtime values. This is the timeframe between an unplanned interruption of business operations and the resumption

of business at a reduced level of service. The BIA identifies which of the company's critical systems are needed for survival, and estimates the outage time that can be tolerated by the company as a result of various unfortunate events. The outage time that can be endured by a company is referred to as the maximum tolerable downtime.

Legal, Regulations, Compliance, and Investigations

This chapter presents the following:

- Computer crimes and computer laws
- Motives and profiles of attackers
- Various types of evidence
- Laws and acts put into effect to fight computer crime
- Computer crime investigation process and evidence collection
- Incident-handling procedures
- Ethics pertaining to information security professionals and best practices

Computer and associated information crimes are the natural response of criminals to society's increasing use of, and dependence upon, technology. For example, stalking can now take place in the virtual world with stalkers pursuing victims through social web sites or chat rooms. However, crime has always taken place, with or without a computer. A computer is just another tool and, like other tools before it, it can be used for good or evil.

Fraud, theft, and embezzlement have always been part of life, but the computer age has brought new opportunities for thieves and crooks. Organized crime can take advantage of the Internet to exploit people through phishing attacks, 419 scams (also called Nigerian Letter scams) and financial dealings. A new degree of complexity has been added to accounting, recordkeeping, communications, and funds transfer. This degree of complexity brings along its own set of vulnerabilities, which many crooks are all too eager to take advantage of.

Companies are being blackmailed by cybercriminals who discover vulnerabilities in their networks. Company trade secrets and confidential information are being stolen when security breaches take place. Online banks are seeing a rise in fraud, and retailers' databases are being attacked and robbed of their credit card information. In addition, identity theft is the fastest growing white-collar crime as of the writing of this book.

As e-commerce and online business become enmeshed in today's business world, these types of issues become more important and more dangerous. Hacking and attacks are continually on the rise, and companies are well aware of it. The legal system and law enforcement are behind in their efforts to track down cybercriminals and successfully prosecute them (although they are getting better each year). New technologies to fight many types of attacks are on the way, but a great need still exists for proper laws, policies, and methods in actually catching the perpetrators and making them pay for the damage they cause. This chapter looks at some of these issues.

The Many Facets of Cyberlaw

Legal issues are very important to companies because a violation of legal commitments can be damaging to a company's bottom line and its reputation. A company has many ethical and legal responsibilities it is liable for in regard to computer fraud. The more knowledge one has about these responsibilities, the easier it is to stay within the proper boundaries.

These issues may fall under laws and regulations pertaining to incident handling, privacy protection, computer abuse, control of evidence, or the ethical conduct expected of companies, their management, and their employees. This is an interesting time for law and technology because technology is changing at an exponential rate. Legislators, judges, law enforcement, and lawyers are behind the eight ball because of their inability to keep up with technological changes in the computing world and the complexity of the issues involved. Law enforcement needs to know how to capture a cybercriminal, properly seize and control evidence, and hand that evidence over to the prosecutorial and defense teams. Both teams must understand what actually took place in a computer crime, how it was carried out, and what legal precedents to use to prove their points in court. Many times, judges and juries are confused by the technology, terms, and concepts used in these types of trials, and laws are not written fast enough to properly punish the guilty cybercriminals. Law enforcement, the court system, and the legal community are definitely experiencing growth pains as they are being pulled into the technology of the twenty-first century.

Many companies are doing business across state lines and in different countries. This brings even more challenges when it comes to who has to follow what laws. Different states can interpret the same law differently or they have their own set of laws. One country may not consider a particular action against the law at all, whereas another country may determine that the same action demands five years in prison. One of the complexities in these issues is jurisdiction. If a hacker from another country steals a bunch of credit card numbers from a U.S. financial institution and he is caught, a U.S. court would want to prosecute him. His homeland may not see this issue as illegal at all or have laws restricting such activities. Although the attackers are not restricted or hampered by country borders, the laws are restricted to borders in many cases.

Despite all of this confusion, companies do have some clear-cut responsibilities pertaining to computer security issues and specifics on how companies are expected to prevent, detect, and report crimes.

The Crux of Computer Crime Laws

Computer crime laws (sometimes referred to as *cyberlaw*) around the world deal with some of the core issues: unauthorized modification or destruction, discloser of sensitive information, unauthorized access, and the use of malware (malicious software).

Although we usually only think of the victims and their systems that were attacked during a crime, laws have been created to combat three categories of crimes. A *computer-assisted crime* is where a computer was used as a tool to help carry out a crime. A *computer-targeted crime* concerns incidents where a computer was the victim of an attack crafted to harm it (and its owners) specifically. The last type of crime is where a computer is not necessarily the attacker or the attackee, but just happened to be involved when a crime was carried out. This category is referred to as *computer is incidental*.

Some examples of computer-assisted crimes are

- Attacking financial systems to carry out theft of funds and/or sensitive information

- Obtaining military and intelligence material by attacking military systems

- Carrying out industrial spying by attacking competitors and gathering confidential business data

- Carrying out information warfare activities by attacking critical national infrastructure systems

- Carrying out hactivism, which is protesting a government or company's activities by attacking their systems and/or defacing their web sites

Some examples of computer-targeted crimes include

- Distributed Denial-of-Service (DDoS) attacks

- Capturing passwords or other sensitive data

- Installing malware with the intent to cause destruction

- Installing rootkits and sniffers for malicious purposes

- Carrying out a buffer overflow to take control of a system

NOTE The main issues addressed in computer crime laws are unauthorized modification, disclosure, destruction, or access, and inserting malicious programming code.

Some confusion typically exists between the two categories—computer-assisted crimes and computer-targeted crimes—because intuitively it would seem any attack would fall into both of these categories. One system is carrying out the attacking, while the other system is being attacked. The difference is that in computer-assisted crimes, the computer is only being used as a tool to carry out a traditional type of crime. Without computers, people still steal, cause destruction, protest against companies (for example, companies that carry out experiments upon animals), obtain competitor information, and go to war. So these crimes would take place anyway; it is just that the computer is simply one of the tools available to the evildoer. As such, it helps the evildoer become more efficient at carrying out a crime. Computer-assisted crimes are usually covered by regular criminal laws in that they are not always considered a "computer crime." One way to look at it is that a computer-*targeted* crime could not take place without a computer, whereas a computer-*assisted* crime could. Thus, a computer-targeted crime is one that did not, and could not, exist before computers became of common use. In other words, in the good old days, you could not carry out a buffer overflow on your neighbor, or install malware on your enemy's system. These crimes require that computers be involved.

If a crime falls into the "computer is incidental" category, this means a computer just happened to be involved in some secondary manner, but its involvement is still insignificant. For example, if you had a friend who worked for a company that runs the state lottery and he gives you a printout of the next three winning numbers and you type them into your computer, your computer is just the storage place. You could have just kept the piece of paper and not put the data in a computer. Another example is child pornography. The actual crime is obtaining and sharing child pornography pictures or graphics. The pictures could be stored on a file server or they could be kept in a physical file in someone's desk. So if a crime falls within this category, the computer is not attacking another computer, and a computer is not being attacked, but the computer is still used in some significant manner.

You may say, "So what? A crime is a crime. Why break it down into these types of categories?" The reason these types of categories are created is to allow current laws to apply to these types of crimes, even though they are in the digital world. Let's say someone is on your computer just looking around, not causing any damage, but she should not be there. Should the legislation have to create a new law stating, "Thou shall not browse around in someone else's computer," or should we just use the already created trespassing law? What if a hacker got into a system that made all of the traffic lights turn green at the exact same time? Should the government go through the hassle of creating a new law for this type of activity, or should the courts use the already created (and understood) manslaughter and murder laws? Remember, a crime is a crime, and a computer is just a new tool to carry out traditional criminal activities.

By allowing the use of current laws, this makes it easier for a judge to know what the proper sentencing (punishments) are for these specific crimes. Sentencing guidelines have been developed by the government to standardize punishments for the same types of crimes throughout federal courts. To use a simplistic description, the guidelines utilize a point system. For example, if you kidnap someone, you receive 10 points. If you take that person over state boundary lines, you get another 2 points. If you hurt this person, you get another 4 points. The higher the points, the more severe the punishment.

So if you steal money from someone's financial account by attacking a bank's mainframe, you may get 5 points. If you use this money to support a terrorist group, you get another 5 points. If you do not claim this revenue on your tax returns, there will be no points. The IRS just takes you behind a building and shoots you in the head.

Now, this in no way means countries can just depend upon the laws on the books and that every computer crime can be countered by an existing law. Many countries have had to come up with new laws that deal specifically with different types of computer crimes. For example, the following are just some of the laws that have been created or modified in the United States to cover the various types of computer crimes:

- 18 USC 1029: Fraud and Related Activity in Connection with Access Devices
- 18 USC 1030: Fraud and Related Activity in Connection with Computers
- 18 USC 2510 et seq.: Wire and Electronic Communications Interception and Interception of Oral Communications
- 18 USC 2701 et seq.: Stored Wire and Electronic Communications and Transactional Records Access
- The Digital Millennium Copyright Act
- The Cyber Security Enhancement Act of 2002

NOTE You do not need to know these laws for the CISSP exam; they are just examples.

Complexities in Cybercrime

Since we have a bunch of laws to get the digital bad guys, this means we have this whole cybercrime thing under control, right?

Alas, hacking, cracking, and attacking have only increased over the years and will not stop anytime soon. Several issues deal with why these activities have not been properly stopped or even curbed. These include proper identification of the attackers, the necessary level of protection for networks, and successful prosecution once an attacker is captured.

Most attackers are never caught because they spoof their addresses and identities and use methods to cover their footsteps. Many attackers break into networks, take whatever resources they were after, and clean the logs that tracked their movements and activities. Because of this, many companies do not even know they have been violated. Even if an attacker's activities trigger an intrusion detection system (IDS) alert, it does not usually find the true identity of the individual, though it does alert the company that a specific vulnerability was exploited.

Attackers commonly hop through several systems before attacking their victim so that tracking them down will be more difficult. Many of these criminals use innocent people's computers to carry out the crimes for them. The attacker will install malicious software on a computer using many types of methods: e-mail attachments, a user downloading a Trojan horse from a web site, exploiting a vulnerability, and so on. Once the software is loaded, it stays dormant until the attacker tells it what systems to attack and when. These compromised systems are called *zombies*, the software installed on them are called *bots*, and when an attacker has several compromised systems, this is known as a *botnet*. The botnet can be used to carry out DDoS attacks, transfer spam or pornography, or do whatever the attacker programs the bot software to do. These items are covered more in-depth in Chapter 11, but are discussed here to illustrate how attackers easily hide their identity.

Local law enforcement departments, the FBI, and the Secret Service are called upon to investigate a range of computer crimes. Although each of these entities works to train its people to identify and track computer criminals, collectively they are very far behind the times in their skills and tools, and are outnumbered by the number of hackers actively attacking networks. Because the attackers use tools that are automated, they can perform several serious attacks in a short timeframe. When law enforcement is called in, its efforts are usually more manual—checking logs, interviewing people, investigating hard drives, scanning for vulnerabilities, and setting up traps in case the attacker comes back. Each agency can spare only a small number of people for computer crimes, and generally they are behind in their expertise compared to many hackers. Because of this, most attackers are never found, much less prosecuted.

This in no way means all attackers get away with their misdeeds. Law enforcement is continually improving its tactics, and individuals are being prosecuted every month. The following site shows all of the current and past prosecutions that have taken place in the U.S.: www.cybercrime.gov. The point is that this is still a small percentage of people who are carrying out digital crimes.

Really only a handful of laws deal specifically with computer crimes, making it more challenging to successfully prosecute the attackers who are caught. Many companies that are victims of an attack usually just want to ensure that the vulnerability the attacker exploited is fixed, instead of spending the time and money to go after and prosecute the attacker. This is a huge contributing factor as to why cybercriminals get away with their activities. Some regulated organizations—for instance, federal institutions—by law, must report breaches. However, most organizations do not have to report breaches or computer crimes. No company wants their dirty laundry out in the open for everyone to see. The customer base will lose confidence, as will the shareholders and investors. We do not actually have true computer crime statistics because most are not reported.

Although regulations, laws, and attacks help make senior management more aware of security issues, when their company ends up in the headlines and it's told how they lost control of over 100,000 credit card numbers, security suddenly becomes very important to them.

CAUTION   Even though financial institutions must, by law, report security breaches and crimes, that does not mean they all *follow* this law. Some of these institutions, just like many other organizations, often simply fix the vulnerability and sweep the details of the attack under the carpet.

Electronic Assets

Another complexity that the digital world has brought upon society is defining what has to be protected and to what extent. We have gone through a shift in the business world pertaining to assets that need to be protected. Fifteen years ago and more, the assets that most companies concerned themselves with protecting were tangible ones (equipment, building, manufacturing tools, inventory). Now companies must add data to their list of assets, and data are usually at the very top of that list: product blueprints, Social Security numbers, medical information, credit card numbers, personal information, trade secrets, military deployment and strategies, and so on. Although the military has always had to worry about keeping their secrets secret, they have never had so many entry points to the secrets that had to be controlled. Companies are still having a hard time not only protecting their data in digital format, but defining what constitutes sensitive data and where that data should be kept.

NOTE In many countries, to deal more effectively with computer crime, legislative bodies have broadened the definition of property to include data.

As many companies have discovered, protecting intangible assets (that is, data, reputation) is much more difficult than protecting tangible assets.

The Evolution of Attacks

About ten years ago, and even further back, hackers were mainly made up of people who just enjoyed the thrill of hacking. It was seen as a challenging game without any real intent of harm. Hackers used to take down large web sites (Yahoo!, MSN, Excite) so their activities made the headlines and they won bragging rights among their fellow hackers. Back then, virus writers created viruses that simply replicated or carried out some benign activity, instead of the more malicious actions they could have carried out. Unfortunately, today, these trends have taken on more sinister objectives.

Although we still have script kiddies and people who are just hacking for the fun of it, organized criminals have appeared on the scene and really turned up the heat regarding the amount of damage done. In the past, script kiddies would scan thousands and thousands of systems looking for a specific vulnerability so they could exploit it. It did not matter if the system was on a company network, a government system, or a home user system. The attacker just wanted to exploit the vulnerability and "play" on the system and network from there. Today's attackers are not so noisy, however, and they certainly don't want any attention drawn to themselves. These organized criminals are after specific targets for specific reasons, usually profit-oriented. They try and stay under the radar and capture credit card numbers, Social Security numbers, and personal information to carry out fraud and identity theft.

NOTE Script kiddies are hackers who do not necessarily have the skill to carry out specific attacks without the tools provided for them on the Internet and through friends. Since these people do not necessarily understand how the attacks are actually carried out, they most likely do not understand the extent of damage they can cause.

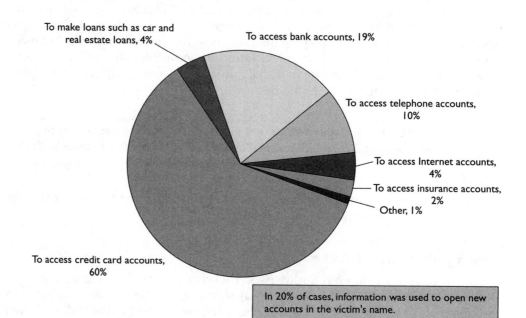

How Stolen Information Was Used

To make loans such as car and real estate loans, 4%

To access bank accounts, 19%

To access telephone accounts, 10%

To access Internet accounts, 4%

To access insurance accounts, 2%

Other, 1%

To access credit card accounts, 60%

In 20% of cases, information was used to open new accounts in the victim's name.

Source: Federal Trade Commission, Identity Theft Survey Report

Common Internet Crime Schemes

- Auction fraud
- Counterfeit cashier's check
- Debt elimination
- Parcel courier e-mail scheme
- Employment/business opportunities

- Escrow services fraud
- Investment fraud
- Lotteries
- Nigerian letter, or "419"
- Ponzi/pyramid
- Reshipping
- Third-party receiver of funds

Find out how these types of computer crimes are carried out by visiting www.ic3.gov/crimeschemes.aspx.

We have already seen a decrease in the amount of viruses created just to populate as many systems as possible, and it is predicted that this benign malware activity will continue to decrease, while more dangerous malware increases. This more dangerous malware has more focused targets and more powerful payloads—usually installing backdoors, bots, and/or loading rootkits.

So while the sophistication of the attacks continues to increase, so does the danger of these attacks. Isn't that just peachy?

Up until now, we have listed some difficulties of fighting cybercrime: the anonymity the Internet provides the attacker; attackers are organizing and carrying out more sophisticated attacks; the legal system is running to catch up with these types of crimes; and companies are just now viewing their data as something that must be protected. All these complexities aid the bad guys, but what if we throw in the complexity of attacks taking place between different countries?

Do You Trust Your Neighbor?

Because an attacker must have access to the systems that hold the wanted resources, it is usually easier for insiders than outsiders to access resources that companies fight to protect. In this sense, employees present a greater potential for computer crimes than outsiders trying to get in. Many statistics and security professionals have indeed indicated that employees cause more security breaches and computer fraud than outside attackers, but the media usually only touts stories about external hackers and crackers. Therefore, fighting off that group of people receives more attention and effort than fighting the threat of employees taking advantage of their position and access.

Different Countries

If a hacker in Ukraine attacked a bank in France, whose legal jurisdiction is that? How do these countries work together to identify the criminal and carry out justice? Which country is required to track down the criminal? And which country should take this person to court? Well, we don't really know. We are still working this stuff out.

When computer crime crosses international boundaries, the complexity of such issues shoots up exponentially, and the chances of the criminal being brought to any court decreases. This is because different countries have different legal systems, some countries have no laws pertaining to computer crime, jurisdiction disputes may erupt, and some governments may not want to play nice with each other. For example, if someone in Iran attacked a system in Israel, do you think the Iranian government would help Israel track down the attacker? What if someone in North Korea attacked a military system in the U.S.? Do you think these two countries would work together to find the hacker? Maybe or maybe not—or perhaps the attack was carried out by their specific government.

There have been efforts to standardize the different countries' approach to computer crimes, because they happen so easily over international boundaries. Although it is very easy for an attacker in China to send packets through the Internet to a bank in Saudi Arabia, it is very difficult (because of legal systems, cultures, and politics) to motivate these governments to work together.

The *Council of Europe (CoE) Convention on Cybercrime* is one example of an attempt to create a standard international response to cybercrime. In fact, it is the first international treaty seeking to address computer crimes by coordinating national laws and improving investigative techniques and international cooperation. The Convention's objectives include the creation of a framework for establishing jurisdiction and extradition of the accused. For example, extradition can only take place when the event is a crime in both jurisdictions.

Many companies communicate internationally every day through e-mail, telephone lines, satellites, fiber cables, and long-distance wireless transmission. It is important for a company to research the laws of different countries pertaining to information flow and privacy.

Global organizations that move data across other country boundaries must be aware of and follow the *Organisation for Economic Co-operation and Development (OECD) Guidelines* and *transborder information flow* rules, which were addressed in Chapter 3. Since most countries have a different set of laws pertaining to the definition of private data and how it should be protected, international trade and business gets more convoluted and can negatively affect the economy of nations. The OECD is an international organization that helps different governments come together and tackle the economic, social, and governance challenges of a globalized economy. Because of this, the OECD came up with guidelines for the various countries to follow so that data are properly protected and everyone follows the same type of rules.

The seven core principles defined by the OECD are as follows:

- Collection of personal data should be limited, obtained by lawful and fair means, and with the knowledge of the subject.

- Personal data should be kept complete and current, and be relevant to the purposes for which it is being used.

- Subjects should be notified of the reason for the collection of their personal information at the time that it is collected, and organizations should only use it for that stated purpose.

- Only with the consent of the subject or by the authority of law should personal data be disclosed, made available, or used for purposes other than those previously stated.

- Reasonable safeguards should be put in place to protect personal data against risks such as loss, unauthorized access, modification, and disclosure.

- Developments, practices, and policies regarding personal data should be openly communicated. In addition, subjects should be able to easily establish the existence and nature of personal data, its use, and the identity and usual residence of the organization in possession of that data.

- Subjects should be able to find out whether an organization has their personal information and what that information is, to correct erroneous data, and to challenge denied requests to do so.

- Organizations should be accountable for complying with measures that support the previous principles.

NOTE Information on OECD Guidelines can be found at www.oecd.org/ document/18/0,2340,en_2649_34255_1815186_1_1_1_1,00.html.

Although the OECD is a great start, we still have a long way to go to standardize how cybercrime is dealt with internationally.

Organizations that are not aware of and/or do not follow these types of rules and guidelines can be fined and sued, their business can be disrupted, or they can go out of business. If your company is expecting to expand globally, it would be wise to have legal council that understands these types of issues so this type of trouble does not find its way to your company's doorstep.

If the organization is exchanging data with European entities, it may need to adhere to the *Safe Harbor* requirements. Europe has always had tighter control over protecting privacy information than the U.S. and other parts of the world. So in the past when U.S. and European companies needed to exchange data, confusion erupted and business was interrupted because the lawyers had to get involved to figure out how to work within the structures of the differing laws. To clear up this mess, a "safe harbor" framework was created, which outlines how any entity that is going to move privacy data to and from Europe must go about protecting it. U.S. companies that deal with European entities can become certified against this rule base so data transfer can happen more quickly and easily.

The European Union (EU) takes individual privacy much more seriously than most other countries in the world, so they have strict laws pertaining to data that are considered private, which are based on the *European Union Principles on Privacy*. This set of principles has six areas that address using and transmitting information considered sensitive in nature. All states in Europe must abide by these six principles to be in compliance.

Types of Laws

As stated earlier, different countries often have different legal systems. In this section, we will cover the core components of these systems and what differentiates them.

- Civil (Code) Law
  - System of law used in continental European countries such as France and Spain.
  - Different from the common law used in the United Kingdom and United States.
  - Civil law is rule-based law not precedence based.
  - For the most part, a civil law system is focused on codified law—or written laws. However, some countries follow an "uncodified" civil law legal system.
  - The history of civil laws dates to the sixth century when the Byzantine emperor Justinian codified the laws of Rome.
  - Civil law was reborn due to the work of Italian legal scholars and spread throughout Europe, as exemplified by the Napoleonic Code of France and the French Civil Code of 1804.
  - Civil legal systems should not be confused with the civil (or tort) laws found in the U.S.
  - Civil law was established by states or nations for self-regulation; thus, civil law can be divided into subdivisions such as French civil law, German civil law, and so on.
  - It is the most widespread legal system in the world and the most common legal system in Europe.
  - Under civil law, lower courts are not compelled to follow the decisions made by higher courts.
- Common Law
  - Developed in England.
  - Based on previous interpretations of laws:
    - In the past, judges would walk throughout the country enforcing laws and settling disputes.
    - They did not have a written set of laws, so they based their laws on custom and precedent.
    - In the twelfth century, the King of England imposed a unified legal system that was "common" to the entire country.

- Reflects the community's morals and expectations.
- Led to the creation of barristers, or lawyers, who actively participate in the litigation process through the presentation of evidence and arguments.
- Today, common law uses judges and juries of peers. If the jury trial is waived, the judge decides the facts.
- Typical systems consist of a higher court, several intermediate appellate courts, and many local trial courts. Precedent flows down through this system. Tradition also allows for "Magistrate's Courts," which address administrative decisions.
- Common law is broken down into the following:
  - Criminal
    - Based on common law, statutory law, or a combination of both.
    - Addresses behavior that is considered harmful to society.
    - Punishment usually involves a loss of freedom, such as incarceration, or monetary fines.
  - Civil/tort
    - Offshoot of criminal law.
    - Under civil law, the defendant owes a legal duty to the victim. In other words, the defendant is obligated to conform to a particular standard of conduct, usually set by what a "reasonable man of ordinary prudence" would do to prevent foreseeable injury to the victim.
    - The defendant's breach of that duty causes injury to the victim; usually physical or financial.
      - Categories of civil law:
        - **Intentional** Examples include assault, intentional infliction of emotional distress, or false imprisonment.
        - **Wrongs against Property** An example is nuisance against landowner.
        - **Wrongs against a Person** Examples include car accidents, dog bites, and a slip and fall.
        - **Negligence** Wrongful death.
        - **Nuisance** Trespassing.
        - **Dignitary Wrongs** Include invasion of privacy and civil rights violations.
        - **Economic Wrongs** Examples include patent, copyright, and trademark infringement.
        - **Strict Liability** Examples include a failure to warn of risks and defects in product manufacturing or design.

- Administrative (regulatory)
  - Laws and legal principles created by administrative agencies to address a number of areas, including international trade, manufacturing, environment, and immigration
- Responsibility is on the prosecution to prove guilt beyond a reasonable doubt (innocent until proven guilty).
- Used in Canada, United Kingdom, Australia, United States, and New Zealand.
- **Customary Law**
  - Deals mainly with personal conduct and patterns of behavior.
  - Based on traditions and customs of the region.
  - Emerged when cooperation of individuals became necessary as communities merged.
  - Not many countries work under a purely customary law system, but instead use a mixed system where customary law is an integrated component. (Codified civil law systems emerged from customary law.)
  - Mainly used in regions of the world that have mixed legal systems (for example, China and India).
  - Restitution is commonly in the form of a monetary fine or service.
- **Religious Law Systems**
  - Based on religious beliefs of the region
    - In Islamic countries, the law is based on the rules of the Koran.
    - The law, however, is different in every Islamic country.
    - Jurists and clerics have a high degree of authority.
  - Cover all aspects of human life, but commonly divided into:
    - Responsibilities and obligations to others
    - Religious duties
  - Knowledge and rules as revealed by God, which define and govern human affairs.
  - Rather than create laws, law makers and scholars attempt to discover the truth of law.
  - Law, in the religious sense, also includes codes of ethics and morality, which are upheld and required by God. For example, Hindu law, Sharia (Islamic law), Halakha (Jewish law), and so on.
- **Mixed Law Systems**
  - Two or more legal systems are used together and apply cumulatively or interactively.
  - Most often mixed law systems consist of civil and common law.

- A combination of systems is used as a result of more or less clearly defined fields of application.

- Civil law may apply to certain types of crimes, while religious law may apply to other types within the same region.

- Examples of mixed law systems include Holland, Canada, and South Africa.

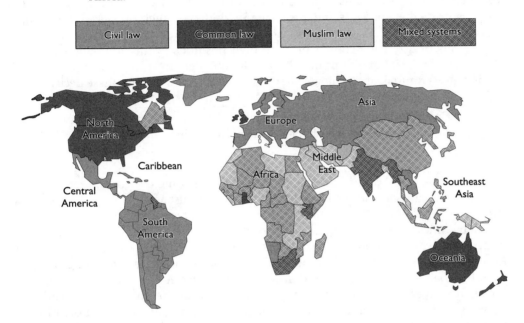

Civil law deals with wrongs against individuals or companies that result in damages or loss. This is referred to as *tort law*. Examples include trespassing, battery, negligence, and products liability. A civil lawsuit would result in financial restitution and/or community service instead of a jail sentence. When someone sues another person in civil court, the jury decides upon liability instead of innocence or guilt. If the jury determines the defendant is liable for the act, then the jury decides upon the punitive damages of the case.

Criminal law is used when an individual's conduct violates the government laws, which have been developed to protect the public. Jail sentences are commonly the punishment for criminal law cases, whereas in civil law cases the punishment is usually an amount of money that the liable individual must pay the victim. For example, in the O.J. Simpson case, he was first tried and found not guilty in the criminal law case, but then was found liable in the civil law case. This seeming contradiction can happen because the burden of proof is lower in civil cases than in criminal cases.

NOTE Civil law generally is derived from common law (case law), cases are initiated by private parties, and the defendant is found "liable" or "not liable" for damages. Criminal law typically is statutory, cases are initiated by government prosecutors, and the defendant is found guilty or not guilty.

Administrative/regulatory law deals with regulatory standards that regulate performance and conduct. Government agencies create these standards, which are usually applied to companies and individuals within those specific industries. Some examples of administrative laws could be that every building used for business must have a fire detection and suppression system, must have easily seen exit signs, and cannot have blocked doors, in case of a fire. Companies that produce and package food and drug products are regulated by many standards so the public is protected and aware of their actions. If a case was made that specific standards were not abided by, high officials in the companies could be held accountable, as in a company that makes tires that shred after a couple of years of use. The people who held high positions in this company were most likely aware of these conditions but chose to ignore them to keep profits up. Under administrative, criminal, and civil law, they may have to pay dearly for these decisions.

 NOTE A map illustrating some of the legal systems in use around the world can be found at www.juriglobe.ca/eng/index.php.

The people who want to be successful in fighting crime over computer wires and airwaves must understand the mentality of the enemy, just as the police officers on the street must understand the mentality of the traditional types of criminal.

Many times, when figuring out a computer crime, or any type of crime, one has to understand why and how crimes are committed. To be a good detective, one would need to know how a criminal thinks, what motivates him to do the things he does, what his goals and demons are, and how these are reflected in the crimes he commits. This is how the detective gets inside the criminal's mind so she can predict his next move as well as understand what circumstances and environments are more prone to fraud and illegal acts. This is true with cybercrime. To properly stop, reduce, or prohibit cybercrime, it is best to know why people do what they do in the first place.

Intellectual Property Laws

Intellectual property laws do not necessarily look at who is right or wrong, but rather how a company can protect what it rightfully owns from unauthorized duplication or use, and what it can do if these laws are violated.

A major issue in many intellectual property cases is what the company did to protect the resources it claims have been violated in one fashion or another. A company must go through many steps to protect resources that it claims to be intellectual property and must show that it exercised due care in its efforts to protect those resources. If an employee sends a file to a friend and the company attempts to terminate the employee based on the activity of illegally sharing intellectual property, it must show the court why this file is so important to the company, what type of damage could be or has been caused as a result of the file being shared, and, most important, what the company had done to protect that file. If the company did not secure the file and tell its employees that they were not allowed to copy and share that file, then the company will most likely lose the case. However, if the company went through many steps to protect that file, explained to its employees that it was wrong to copy and share the information within the file, and that the punishment could be termination, then the company could not be charged with falsely terminating an employee.

Intellectual property can be protected by several different laws, depending upon the type of resource it is. Intellectual property is divided into two categories: industrial property—such as inventions (patents), industrial designs, and trademarks—and copyright, which covers literary and artistic works. These topics are addressed in-depth later in this chapter.

Trade Secret

Trade secret law protects certain types of information or resources from unauthorized use or disclosure. For a company to have its resource qualify as a trade secret, the resource must provide the company with some type of competitive value or advantage. A trade secret can be protected by law if developing it requires special skill, ingenuity, and/or expenditure of money and effort. This means that a company cannot say the sky is blue and call it a trade secret.

A *trade secret* is something that is proprietary to a company and important for its survival and profitability. An example of a trade secret is the formula used for a soft drink, such as Coke or Pepsi. The resource that is claimed to be a trade secret must be confidential and protected with certain security precautions and actions. A trade secret could also be a new form of mathematics, the source code of a program, a method of making the perfect jelly bean, or ingredients for a special secret sauce. A trade secret has no expiration date unless the information is no longer secret or no longer provides economic benefit to the company.

Many companies require their employees to sign a nondisclosure agreement, confirming that they understand its contents and promise not to share the company's trade secrets with competitors. Companies require this both to inform the employees of the importance of keeping certain information secret and to deter them from sharing this information. Having them sign the nondisclosure agreement also gives the company the right to fire the employee or bring charges if the employee discloses a trade secret.

Copyright

In the United States, *copyright law* protects the right of an author to control the public distribution, reproduction, display, and adaptation of his original work. The law covers many categories of work: pictorial, graphic, musical, dramatic, literary, pantomime, motion picture, sculptural, sound recording, and architectural. Copyright law does not cover the specific resource, as does trade secret law. It protects the expression of the idea of the resource instead of the resource itself. A copyright law is usually used to protect an author's writings, an artist's drawings, a programmer's source code, or specific rhythms and structures of a musician's creation. Computer programs and manuals are just two examples of items protected under the Federal Copyright Act. The item is covered under copyright law once the program or manual has been written. Although including a warning and the copyright symbol (©) is not required, doing so is encouraged so others cannot claim innocence after copying another's work.

The protection does not extend to any method of operations, process, concept, or procedure, but it does protect against unauthorized copying and distribution of a work. It protects the form of expression rather than the subject matter. A patent deals more with the subject matter of an invention; copyright deals with how that invention is represented. In that respect, copyright is weaker than patent protection, but the duration of copyright protection is longer. People are provided copyright protection for life plus 50 years.

Computer programs can be protected under the copyright law as literary works. The law protects both the source and object code, which can be an operating system, application, or database. In some instances, the law can protect not only the code, but also the structure, sequence, and organization. The user interface is part of the definition of a software application structure; therefore, one vendor cannot copy the exact composition of another vendor's user interface.

Trademark

My trademark is my stupidity.
Response: Good for you!

A *trademark* is slightly different from a copyright in that it is used to protect a word, name, symbol, sound, shape, color, or combination of these. The reason a company would trademark one of these, or a combination, is that it represents their company (brand identity) to a group of people or to the world. Companies have marketing departments that work very hard in coming up with something new that will cause the company to be noticed and stand out in a crowd of competitors, and trademarking the result of this work with a government registrar is a way of properly protecting it and ensuring others cannot copy and use it.

Companies cannot trademark a number or common word. This is why companies create new names—for example, Intel's Pentium and Standard Oil's Exxon. However, unique colors can be trademarked, as well as identifiable packaging, which is referred to as "trade dress." Thus, Novell Red and UPS Brown are trademarked, as are some candy wrappers.

NOTE In 1883, international harmonization of trademark laws began with the Paris Convention, which in turn prompted the Madrid Agreement of 1891. Today, international trademark law efforts and international registration are overseen by the World Intellectual Property Organization (WIPO), an agency of the United Nations.

Patent

Patents are given to individuals or companies to grant them legal ownership of, and enable them to exclude others from using or copying, the invention covered by the patent. The invention must be novel, useful, and not obvious—which means, for example, that a company could not patent air. Thank goodness. If a company figured out how to patent air, we would have to pay for each and every breath we took!

After the inventor completes an application for a patent and it is approved, the patent grants a limited property right to exclude others from making, using, or selling the invention for a specific period of time. For example, when a pharmaceutical company develops a specific drug and acquires a patent for it, that company is the only one that can manufacture and sell this drug until the stated year in which the patent is up (usually 20 years from the date of approval). After that, the information is in the public domain, enabling all companies to manufacture and sell this product, which is why the price of a drug drops substantially after its patent expires.

This also takes place with algorithms. If an inventor of an algorithm acquires a patent, she has full control over who can use it in their products. If the inventor lets a vendor incorporate the algorithm, she will most likely get a fee and possibly a royalty fee on each instance of the product that is sold.

Similar to trademarks, international patents are overseen by the WIPO. However, the WIPO does not override patent rules, such as time periods, unless the country agrees by treaty to accept the WIPO.

NOTE A patent is the strongest form of intellectual property protection.

Internal Protection of Intellectual Property

Ensuring that specific resources are protected by the previously mentioned laws is very important, but other measures must be taken internally to make sure the resources that are confidential in nature are properly identified and protected.

The resources protected by one of the previously mentioned laws need to be identified and integrated into the company's data classification scheme. This should be directed by management and carried out by the IT staff. The identified resources should have the necessary level of access control protection, auditing enabled, and a proper storage environment. If it is deemed secret, then not everyone in the company should be able to access it. Once the individuals who are allowed to have access are identified, their level of access and interaction with the resource should be defined in a granular method. Attempts to access and manipulate the resource should be properly audited, and the resource should be stored on a protected system with the necessary security mechanisms.

Employees must be informed of the level of secrecy or confidentiality of the resource, and of their expected behavior pertaining to that resource.

If a company fails in one or all of these steps, it may not be covered by the laws described previously, because it may have failed to practice due care and properly protect the resource that it has claimed to be so important to the survival and competitiveness of the company.

Software Piracy

Software piracy occurs when the intellectual or creative work of an author is used or duplicated without permission or compensation to the author. It is an act of infringement on ownership rights, and if the pirate is caught, he could be sued civilly for damages, be criminally prosecuted, or both.

When a vendor develops an application, it usually licenses the program rather than sells it outright. The license agreement contains provisions relating to the use and security of the software and the corresponding manuals. If an individual or company fails to observe and abide by those requirements, the license may be terminated and, depending on the actions, criminal charges may be leveled. The risk to the vendor that develops and licenses the software is the loss of profits it would have earned. Many companies and their employees do not abide by their software licenses, and the employees use the company's software for their home use.

There are four categories of software licensing. *Freeware* is software that is publicly available free of charge and can be used, copied, studied, modified, and redistributed without restriction. *Shareware*, or *trialware*, is used by vendors to market their software. Users obtain a free, trial version of the software. Once the user tries out the program, the user is asked to purchase a copy of it. *Commercial* software is, quite simply, software that is sold for or serves commercial purposes. And, finally, *academic* software is software that is provided for academic purposes at a reduced cost. It can be open source, freeware, or commercial software.

Some software vendors sell bulk licenses, which enable several users to use the product simultaneously. These master agreements define proper use of the software along with restrictions, such as whether corporate software can also be used by employees on their home machines. One other prevalent form of software licensing is the End User Licensing Agreement (EULA). It specifies more granular conditions and restrictions than a master agreement. Other vendors incorporate third-party license-metering software that keeps track of software usability to ensure that the customer stays within the license limit and otherwise complies with the software licensing agreement. The security officer should be aware of all these types of contractual commitments required by software companies. This person needs to be educated on the restrictions the company is under and make sure proper enforcement mechanisms are in place. If a company is found guilty of illegally copying software or using more copies than its license permits, the security officer in charge of this task may be primarily responsible.

Thanks to easy access to high-speed Internet, employees' ability—if not the temptation—to download and use pirated software has greatly increased. A study by the Business Software Alliance (BSA) and International Data Corporation (IDC) found that the frequency of illegal software is 36 percent worldwide. This means that for every two dollars' worth of legal software that is purchased, one dollar's worth is pirated. Software developers often use these numbers to calculate losses resulting from pirated copies. The assumption is that if the pirated copy had not been available, then everyone who is using a pirated copy would have instead purchased it legally.

Not every country recognizes software piracy as a crime, but several international organizations have made strides in curbing the practice. The Software Protection Association (SPA) has been formed by major companies to enforce proprietary rights of software. The association was created to protect the founding companies' software developments, but it also helps others ensure that their software is properly licensed. These are huge issues for companies that develop and produce software, because a majority of their revenue comes from licensing fees.

Other international groups have been formed to protect against software piracy, including the Federation Against Software Theft (FAST), headquartered in London, and the Business Software Alliance (BSA), based in Washington, D.C. They provide similar functionality as the SPA and make efforts to protect software around the world.

One of the offenses an individual or company can commit is to decompile vendor object code. This is usually done to figure out how the application works by obtaining the original source code, which is confidential, and perhaps to reverse-engineer it in the hope of understanding the intricate details of its functionality. Another purpose of reverse-engineering products is to detect security flaws within the code that can later be exploited. This is how some buffer overflow vulnerabilities are discovered.

Many times, an individual decompiles the object code into source code and either finds security holes and can take advantage of them or alters the source code to produce some type of functionality that the original vendor did not intend. In one example, an individual decompiled a program that protects and displays e-books and publications. The vendor did not want anyone to be able to copy the e-publications its product displayed and thus inserted an encoder within the object code of its product that enforced this limitation. The individual decompiled the object code and figured out how to create a decoder that would overcome this restriction and enable users to make copies of the e-publications, which infringed upon those authors' and publishers' copyrights.

The individual was arrested and prosecuted under the new Digital Millennium Copyright Act (DMCA), which makes it illegal to create products that circumvent copyright protection mechanisms. As of this writing, this new act and how it will be enforced have caused many debates and much controversy because of its possible negative effects on free speech and legitimate research.

Interestingly enough, many computer-oriented individuals protested this person's arrest, and the company prosecuting (Adobe) quickly decided to drop all charges.

Privacy

Privacy is becoming more threatened as the world relies more and more on technology. There are several approaches to addressing privacy, including the generic approach and regulation by industry. The generic approach is horizontal enactment. It affects all industries, including government. Regulation by industry is vertical enactment. It defines requirements for specific verticals, such as the financial sector and health care. In both cases, the overall objective is twofold. First, the initiatives seek to protect citizens' personally identifiable information (PII). Second, the initiatives seek to balance the needs of government and businesses to collect and use PII with consideration of security issues.

In response, countries have enacted privacy laws. For example, although the United States already had the Federal Privacy Act of 1974, it has enacted new laws, such as the Gramm-Leach-Bliley Act of 1999 and the Health Insurance Portability and Accountability Act (HIPAA), in response to an increased need to protect personal privacy information. These are examples of a vertical approach to addressing privacy, whereas Canada's Personal Information Protection and Electronic Documents Act and New Zealand's Privacy Act of 1993 are horizontal approaches.

The Federal Privacy Act was put into place to protect U.S. citizens' sensitive information that is collected by government agencies. It states that any data collected must be done in a fair and lawful manner. The data are to be used only for the purposes for which they were collected and held only for a reasonable amount of time. If an agency collects data on a person, that person has the right to receive a report outlining data collected about him if it is requested. Similar laws exist in many countries around the world.

Technology is continually advancing in the amount of data that can be kept in data warehouses, data mining and analysis techniques, and distribution of this mined data. Companies that are data aggregators compile in-depth profiles of personal information on millions of people, even though many individuals have never heard of these specific companies, have never had an account with them, nor have given them permission to obtain personal information. These data aggregators compile, store, and sell personal information. One company (ChoicePoint) has approximately 19 billion records of personal information.

It seems as though putting all of this information together would make sense. It would be easier to obtain, have one centralized source, be extremely robust—and be the delight of identity thieves everywhere. All they have to do is hack into one location and get enough information to steal thousands of identities. One U.S.-based company, LexisNexis, compiles and sells personal and financial data on U.S. consumers.

Laws, Directives, and Regulations

Regulation in computer and information security covers many areas for many different reasons. Some issues that require regulation are data privacy, computer misuse, software copyright, data protection, and controls on cryptography. These regulations can be implemented in various arenas, such as government and private sectors for reasons dealing with environmental protection, intellectual property, national security, personal privacy, public order, health and safety, and prevention of fraudulent activities.

The Increasing Need for Privacy Laws

The following issues have increased the need for more privacy laws and governance:

- **Data aggregation and retrieval technologies advancement**
  - Large data warehouses are continually being created full of private information.
- **Loss of borders (globalization)**
  - Private data flows from country to country for many different reasons.
  - Business globalization.
- **Convergent technologies advancements**
  - Gathering, mining, distributing sensitive information.

Security professionals have so much to keep up with these days, from understanding how the latest worm attacks work and how to properly protect against them, to how new versions of DoS attacks take place and what tools are used to accomplish them. Professionals also need to follow which new security products are released and how they compare to the existing products. This is followed up by keeping track of new technologies, service patches, hotfixes, encryption methods, access control mechanisms, telecommunications security issues, social engineering, and physical security. Laws and regulations have been ascending the list of things that security professionals also need to be aware of. This is because organizations must be compliant with more and more laws and regulations, and noncompliance can result in a fine or a company going out of business, with certain executive management individuals ending up in jail.

Laws, regulations, and directives developed by governments or appointed agencies do not usually provide detailed instructions to follow to properly protect computers and company assets. Each environment is too diverse in topology, technology, infrastructure, requirements, functionality, and personnel. Because technology changes at such a fast pace, these laws and regulations could never successfully represent reality if they were too detailed. Instead, they state high-level requirements that commonly have companies scratching their heads on how to be compliant with them. This is where the security professional comes to the rescue. In the past, security professionals were expected to know how to carry out penetration tests, configure firewalls, and deal only with the technology issues of security. Today, security professionals are being pulled out of the server rooms and asked to be more involved in business-oriented issues. As a security professional, you need to understand the laws and regulations that your company must comply with and what controls must be put in place to accomplish compliance. This means the security professional now must have a foot in both the technical world and the business world.

Over time, the CISSP exam has become more global in nature and less U.S.-centric. Specific questions on U.S. laws and regulations have been taken out of the test, so you do not need to spend a lot of time learning them and their specifics. Be familiar with why laws are developed and put in place and their overall goals, instead of memorizing specific laws and dates.

Thus, the following sections on laws and regulations contain information you do not need to memorize, because you will not be asked questions on these items directly. But remember that the CISSP exam is a *cognitive* exam, so you do need to know the different reasons and motivations for laws and regulations, which is why these sections are provided. This list covers U.S. laws and regulations, but almost every country either has laws similar to these or is in the process of developing them.

The Sarbanes-Oxley Act (SOX)

The Public Company Accounting Reform and Investor Protection Act of 2002, generally referred to as the Sarbanes-Oxley Act (named after the authors of the bill), was created in the wake of corporate scandals and fraud which cost investors billions of dollars and threatened to undermine the economy.

The law, also known as SOX for short, applies to any company that is publicly traded on United States markets. Much of the law governs accounting practices and the methods used by companies to report on their financial status. However, some parts, Section 404 in particular, apply directly to information technology.

SOX provides requirements for how companies must track, manage, and report on financial information. This includes safeguarding the data and guaranteeing its integrity and authenticity. Most companies rely on computer equipment and electronic storage for transacting and archiving data; therefore, processes and controls must be in place to protect the data.

Failure to comply with the Sarbanes-Oxley Act can lead to stiff penalties and potentially significant jail time for company executives, including the Chief Executive Officer (CEO), the Chief Financial Officer (CFO), and others.

The Health Insurance Portability and Accountability Act (HIPAA)

The Health Insurance Portability and Accountability Act (HIPAA), a U.S. federal regulation, has been mandated to provide national standards and procedures for the storage, use, and transmission of personal medical information and health care data. This regulation provides a framework and guidelines to ensure security, integrity, and privacy when handling confidential medical information. HIPAA outlines how security should be managed for any facility that creates, accesses, shares, or destroys medical information.

People's health records can be used and misused in different scenarios for many reasons. As health records migrate from a paper-based system to an electronic system, they become easier to maintain, access, and transfer, but they also become easier to manipulate and access in an unauthorized manner. Traditionally, health care facilities have lagged behind other businesses in their information and network security mechanisms, architecture, and security enforcement because there was no real business need to expend the energy and money to put these items in place. Now there is.

HIPAA mandates steep federal penalties for noncompliance. If medical information is used in a way that violates the privacy standards dictated by HIPAA, even by mistake, monetary penalties of $100 per violation are enforced, up to $25,000 per year, per standard. If protected health information is obtained or disclosed knowingly, the fines can be as much as $50,000 and one year in prison. If the information is obtained or disclosed under false pretenses, the cost can go up to $250,000 with ten years in prison if there is intent to sell or use the information for commercial advantage, personal gain, or malicious harm. This is serious business.

The Gramm-Leach-Bliley Act of 1999 (GLBA)

The Gramm-Leach-Bliley Act of 1999 (GLBA) requires financial institutions to develop privacy notices and give their customers the option to prohibit financial institutions from sharing their information with nonaffiliated third parties. The act dictates that the board of directors is responsible for many of the security issues within a financial institution, that risk management must be implemented, that all employees need to be trained on information security issues, and that implemented security measures must be fully tested. It also requires these institutions to have a written security policy in place.

The Computer Fraud and Abuse Act

The Computer Fraud and Abuse Act, written in 1986 and amended in 1996, is the primary U.S. federal antihacking statute. It prohibits seven forms of activity and makes them federal crimes:

- The knowing access of computers of the federal government to obtain classified information without authorization or in excess of authorization

- The intentional access of a computer to obtain information from a financial institution, the federal government, or any protected computer involved in interstate or foreign communications without authorization or through the use of excess of authorization

- The intentional and unauthorized access of computers of the federal government, or computers used by or for the government when the access affects the government's use of that computer

- The knowing access of a protected computer without authorization or in excess of authorization with the intent to defraud

- Knowingly causing the transmission of a program, information, code, or command and, as a result of such conduct, intentionally causing damage without authorization to a protected computer

- The knowing trafficking of computer passwords with the intent to defraud

- The transmission of communications containing threats to cause damage to a protected computer

These acts range from felonies to misdemeanors with corresponding small to large fines and jail sentences.

The Federal Privacy Act of 1974

In the mid-1960s, a proposal was made that the U.S. government compile and collectively hold in a main federal data bank each individual's information pertaining to the Social Security Administration, the Census Bureau, the Internal Revenue Service, the Bureau of Labor Statistics, and other limbs of the government. The committee that made this proposal saw this as an efficient way of gathering and centralizing data. Others saw it as a dangerous move against individual privacy and too "Big Brother." The federal data bank never came to pass because of strong opposition.

To keep the government in check on gathering information on U.S. citizens and other matters, a majority of its files are considered open to the public. Government files are open to the public unless specific issues enacted by the legislature deem certain files unavailable. This is what is explained in the Freedom of Information Act. This is different from what the Privacy Act outlines and protects. The Privacy Act applies to records and documents developed and maintained by specific branches of the federal government, such as executive departments, government corporations, independent regulatory agencies, and government-controlled corporations. It does not apply to congressional, judiciary, or territorial subdivisions.

An actual *record* is information about an individual's education, medical history, financial history, criminal history, employment, and other similar types of information. Government agencies can maintain this type of information only if it is necessary and relevant to accomplishing the agency's purpose. The Privacy Act dictates that an agency cannot disclose this information without written permission from the individual. However, like most government acts, legislation, and creeds, there is a list of exceptions.

So what does all of this dry legal mumbo-jumbo mean? Basically, agencies can gather information about individuals, but it must be relevant and necessary for its approved cause. In addition, that agency cannot go around town sharing other people's private information. If it does, private citizens have the right to sue the agency to protect their privacy.

This leaks into the computer world because this information is usually held by one type of computer or another. If an agency's computer holds an individual's confidential information, it must provide the necessary security mechanisms to ensure it cannot be compromised or copied in an unauthorized way.

Basel II

The Bank for International Settlements devised a means for protecting banks from overextending themselves and becoming insolvent. The original Basel Capital Accord implemented a system for establishing the minimum amount of capital that member financial institutions were required to keep on hand.

In November 2006, the Basel II Accord went into effect. Basel II takes a more refined approach to determining the actual exposure to risk of each financial institution and taking risk mitigation into consideration to provide an incentive for member institutions to focus on and invest in security measures.

Basel II is built on three main components, called "Pillars." Minimum Capital Requirements measures the risk and spells out the calculation for determining the minimum capital. Supervision provides a framework for oversight and review to continually analyze risk and improve security measures. Market Discipline requires member institutions to disclose their exposure to risk and validate adequate market capital.

Information security is integral to Basel II. Member institutions seeking to reduce the amount of capital they must have on hand must continually assess their exposure to risk and implement security controls or mitigations to protect their data.

Payment Card Industry Data Security Standards (PCI DSS)

Identity theft and credit card fraud are increasingly more common. Not that these things did not occur before, but the advent of the Internet and computer technology have combined to create a scenario where attackers can steal millions of identities at a time.

The credit card industry took proactive steps to curb the problem and stabilize customer trust in credit cards as a safe method of conducting transactions. Visa began their own program, the Cardholder Information Security Protection (CISP) program, while other vendors began similar initiatives.

Eventually, the credit card brands joined forces and devised the Payment Card Industry Data Security Standard (PCI DSS). The PCI Security Standards Council was created as a separate entity to maintain and enforce the PCI Data Security Standard.

The PCI DSS applies to any entity that processes, transmits, stores, or accepts credit card data. Varying levels of compliance and penalties exist and depend on the size of the customer and the volume of transactions. However, credit cards are used by millions and accepted almost anywhere, which means just about every business in the world must comply with the PCI DSS.

The PCI Data Security Standard is made up of 12 main requirements broken down into six major categories. The six categories of PCI DSS are: Build and Maintain a Secure Network, Protect Cardholder Data, Maintain a Vulnerability Management Program, Implement Strong Access Control Measures, Regularly Monitor and Test Networks, and Maintain an Information Security Policy.

The control objectives are implemented via 12 requirements, as stated at https://www.pcisecuritystandards.org/security_standards/pci_dss.shtml:

- Use and maintain a firewall.
- Reset vendor defaults for system passwords and other security parameters.
- Protect cardholder data at rest.
- Encrypt cardholder data when it is transmitted across public networks.
- Use and update antivirus software.
- Systems and applications must be developed with security in mind.
- Access to cardholder data must be restricted by business "need to know."
- Each person with computer access must be assigned a unique ID.
- Physical access to cardholder data should be restricted.
- All access to network resources and cardholder data must be tracked and monitored.
- Security systems and processes must be regularly tested.
- A policy must be maintained that addresses information security.

PCI DSS is a private-sector industry initiative. It is not a law. Noncompliance or violations of the PCI DSS may result in financial penalties or possible revocation of merchant status within the credit card industry, but not jail time. However, Minnesota became the first state to mandate PCI compliance as a law, and other states, as well as the United States federal government, are implementing similar measures.

NOTE As mentioned before, privacy is being dealt with through laws, regulations, self-regulations, and individual protection. PCI is an example of a self-regulation approach. It is not a regulation that came down from the government and that is being governed by a government agency. It is an attempt by the credit card companies to reduce fraud and govern themselves so the government does not have to get involved.

The Computer Security Act of 1987

The Computer Security Act of 1987 requires U.S. federal agencies to identify computer systems that contain sensitive information. The agency must develop a security policy and plan for each of these systems and conduct periodic training for individuals who operate, manage, or use these systems. Federal agency employees must be provided with security-awareness training and be informed of how the agency defines acceptable computer use and practices.

Because the U.S. federal government deals with a lot of important, confidential, and secret information, it wants to make sure all individuals and systems within all federal government agencies meet a certain level of awareness and protection.

The Economic Espionage Act of 1996

Prior to 1996, industry and corporate espionage was taking place with no real guidelines for who could properly investigate the events. The Economic Espionage Act of 1996 provides the necessary structure when dealing with these types of cases and further defines trade secrets to be technical, business, engineering, scientific, or financial. This means that an asset does not necessarily need to be tangible to be protected or be stolen. Thus, this act enables the FBI to investigate industrial and corporate espionage cases.

Employee Privacy Issues

Within a corporation, several employee privacy issues must be thought through and addressed if the company wants to be properly protected. An understanding that each state and country may have different privacy laws should prompt the company to investigate exactly what it can and cannot monitor before it does so.

If a company has learned that the state the facility is located in permits keyboard, e-mail, and surveillance monitoring, it must take the proper steps to ensure that the employees know that these types of monitoring may be put into place. This is the best way for a company to protect itself, make sure it has a legal leg to stand on if necessary, and not present the employees with any surprises.

The monitoring must be work related, meaning that a manager may have the right to listen in on his employees' conversations with customers, but he does not have the right to listen in on personal conversations that are not work related. Monitoring also must happen in a consistent way, such that *all* employees are subjected to monitoring, not just one or two people.

Review on Ways of Dealing with Privacy

Current methods of privacy protection and examples are listed next:

- **Government regulations**   SOX, HIPAA, GLBA, BASEL
- **Self-regulation**   Payment Card Industry (PCI)
- **Individual user**   Passwords, encryption, awareness

Prescreening Personnel

Chapter 3 described why it is important to properly screen individuals before hiring them into a corporation. These steps are necessary to help the company protect itself and to ensure it is getting the type of employee required for the job. This chapter looks at some of the issues from the other side of the table, which deals with that individual's privacy rights.

Limitations exist regarding the type and amount of information that an organization can obtain on a potential employee. The limitations and regulations for background checks vary from jurisdiction to jurisdiction, so the hiring manager needs to consult the legal department. Usually human resources has an outline for hiring managers to follow when it comes to interviews and background checks.

If a company feels it may be necessary to monitor e-mail messages and usage, this must be explained to the employees, first through a security policy and then through a constant reminder such as a computer banner or regular training. It is best to have an employee read a document describing what type of monitoring they could be subjected to, what is considered acceptable behavior, and what the consequences of not meeting those expectations are. The employees should sign this document, which can later be treated as a legally admissible document if necessary. This document is referred to as a waiver of reasonable expectation of privacy (REP). By signing the waiver, employees waive their expectation to privacy.

A company that wants to be able to monitor e-mail should address this point in its security policy and standards. The company should outline who can and cannot read employee messages, describe the circumstances under which e-mail monitoring may be acceptable, and specify where the e-mail can be accessed. Some companies indicate that they will only monitor e-mail that resides on the mail server, whereas other companies declare the right to read employee messages if they reside on the mail server or the employee's computer. A company must not promise privacy to employees that it does not then provide, because that could result in a lawsuit. Although IT and security professionals have access to many parts of computer systems and the network, this does not mean it is ethical and right to overstep the bounds that could threaten a user's privacy. Only the tasks necessary to enforce the security policy should take place, and nothing further that could compromise another's privacy.

Many lawsuits have arisen where an employee was fired for doing something wrong (downloading pornographic material, using the company's e-mail system to send out confidential information to competitors, and so on), and the employee sues the company for improper termination. If the company has not stated that these types of activities were prohibited in its policy and made reasonable effort to inform the employee (through security awareness, computer banners, the employee handbook) of what is considered acceptable and not acceptable, and the resulting repercussions for noncompliance, then the employee could win the suit and receive a large chunk of money from the company. So policies, standards, and security-awareness activities need to spell out these issues; otherwise, the employee's lawyer will claim the employee had an assumed right to privacy.

Personal Privacy Protection

End users are also responsible for their own privacy, especially as it relates to protecting the data that is on their own systems. End users should be encouraged to use common sense and best practices. This includes the use of encryption to protect sensitive personal information, as well as firewalls, antivirus software, and patches to protect computers from becoming infected with malware. Documents containing personal information, such as credit card statements, should also be shredded. Also, it's important for end users to understand that when data is given to a third party, it is no longer under their control.

Liability and Its Ramifications

As legislatures, courts, and law enforcement develop and refine their respective approaches to computer crimes, so too must corporations. Corporations should develop not only their preventive, detective, and corrective approaches, but also their liability and responsibility approaches. As these crimes increase in frequency and sophistication, so do their destruction and lasting effects. In most cases, the attackers are not caught, but there is plenty of blame to be passed around, so a corporation needs to take many steps to ensure that the blame and liability do not land clearly at its doorstep.

The same is true for other types of threats that corporations have to deal with today. If a company has a facility that burns to the ground, the arsonist is only one small piece of this tragedy. The company is responsible for providing fire detection and suppression systems, fire-resistant construction material in certain areas, alarms, exits, fire extinguishers, and backups of all the important information that could be affected by a fire. If a fire burns a company's building to the ground and consumes all the records (customer data, inventory records, and similar information that is necessary to rebuild the business), then the company did not exercise due care to ensure it was protected from such loss (by backing up to an offsite location, for example). In this case, the employees, shareholders, customers, and everyone affected could successfully sue the company. However, if the company did everything expected of it in the previously listed respects, it could not be successfully sued for failure to practice due care (negligence).

Figure 10-1 illustrates the results of a real-world story where a company was found guilty of negligence and fraud.

In the context of security, *due care* means that a company did all it could have reasonably done, under the circumstances, to prevent security breaches, and also took reasonable steps to ensure that if a security breach did take place, proper controls or countermeasures were in place to mitigate the damages. In short, due care means that a company practiced common sense and prudent management and acted responsibly. *Due diligence* means that the company properly investigated all of its possible weaknesses and vulnerabilities.

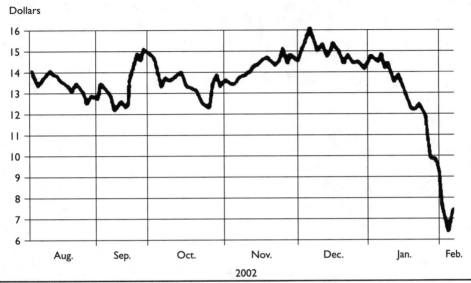

Figure 10-1 One example of the consequences of corporate fraud in 2002

Before you can figure out how to properly protect yourself, you need to find out what it is you are protecting yourself against. This is what due diligence is all about—researching and assessing the current level of vulnerabilities so the true risk level is understood. Only after these steps and assessments take place can effective controls and safeguards be identified and implemented.

The same type of responsibility is starting to be expected of corporations pertaining to computer crime and resource protection. Security is developed and implemented to protect an organization's valuable resources; thus, appropriate safeguards need to be in place to protect the company's mission by protecting its tangible and intangible resources, reputation, employees, customers, shareholders, and legal position. Security is a means to an end and not an end within itself. It is not practiced just for the sake of doing it. It should be practiced in such a way as to accomplish fully understood, planned, and attainable goals.

Senior management has an obligation to protect the company from a long list of activities that can negatively affect it, including protection from malicious code, natural disasters, privacy violation, infractions of the law, and more.

The costs and benefits of security should be evaluated in monetary and nonmonetary terms to ensure that the cost of security does not outweigh the expected benefits. Security should be proportional to potential loss estimates pertaining to the severity, likelihood, and extent of potential damage.

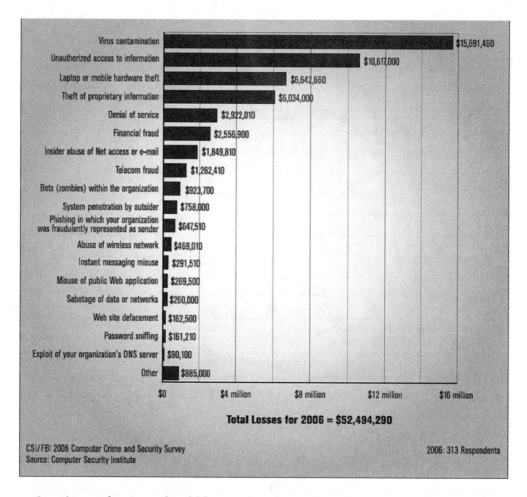

Virus contamination	$15,691,460
Unauthorized access to information	$10,617,000
Laptop or mobile hardware theft	$6,642,660
Theft of proprietary information	$6,034,000
Denial of service	$2,922,010
Financial fraud	$2,556,900
Insider abuse of Net access or e-mail	$1,849,810
Telecom fraud	$1,262,410
Bots (zombies) within the organization	$923,700
System penetration by outsider	$758,000
Phishing in which your organization was fraudulently represented as sender	$647,510
Abuse of wireless network	$469,010
Instant messaging misuse	$291,510
Misuse of public Web application	$269,500
Sabotage of data or networks	$260,000
Web site defacement	$162,500
Password sniffing	$161,210
Exploit of your organization's DNS server	$90,100
Other	$885,000

$0 $4 million $8 million $12 million $16 million

Total Losses for 2006 = $52,494,290

CSI/FBI 2006 Computer Crime and Security Survey
Source: Computer Security Institute

2006: 313 Respondents

Security mechanisms should be employed to reduce the frequency and severity of security-related losses. A sound security program is a smart business practice.

Senior management needs to decide upon the amount of risk it is willing to take pertaining to computer and information security, and implement security in an economical and responsible manner. (These issues are discussed in great detail in Chapter 3.) These risks do not always stop at the boundaries of the organization. Many companies work with third parties, with whom they must share sensitive data. The main company is still liable for the protection of this sensitive data that they own, even if it is on another company's network. This is why more and more regulations are requiring companies to evaluate their third-party's security measures.

When companies come together to work in an integrated manner, special care must be taken to ensure that each party promises to provide the necessary level of protection, liability, and responsibility, which should be clearly defined in the contracts each party signs. Auditing and testing should be performed to ensure that each party is indeed holding up its side of the bargain.

If one of the companies does not provide the necessary level of protection and its negligence affects a partner it is working with, the affected company can sue the upstream company. For example, let's say company A and company B have constructed an extranet. Company A does not put in controls to detect and deal with viruses. Company A gets infected with a destructive virus and it is spread to company B through the extranet. The virus corrupts critical data and causes a massive disruption to company B's production. Therefore, company B can sue company A for being negligent. Both companies need to make sure they are doing their part to ensure their activities, or the lack of them, will not negatively affect another company, which is referred to as *downstream liability*.

NOTE Responsibility generally refers to the obligations and expected actions and behaviors of a particular party. An obligation may have a defined set of specific actions that are required, or a more general and open approach, which enables the party to decide how it will fulfill the particular obligation. Accountability refers to the ability to hold a party responsible for certain actions or inaction.

Each company has different requirements when it comes to their list of due care responsibilities. If these steps are not taken, the company may be charged with negligence if damage arises out of its failure to follow these steps. To prove negligence in court, the plaintiff must establish that the defendant had a *legally recognized obligation*, or duty, to protect the plaintiff from unreasonable risks and that the defendant's failure to protect the plaintiff from an unreasonable risk (breach of duty) was the *proximate cause* of the plaintiff's damages. Penalties for negligence can be either civil or criminal, ranging from actions resulting in compensation for the plaintiff to jail time for violation of the law.

The following are some sample scenarios in which a company could be held liable for negligence in its actions and responsibilities.

Personal Information

A company that holds medical information, Medical Information, Inc., does not have strict procedures on how patient information is disseminated or shared.

A person pretends to be a physician, calls into Medical Information, Inc., and requests medical information on the patient Don Hammy. The receptionist does not question the caller and explains that Don Hammy has a brain tumor. A week later, Don Hammy does not receive the job he interviewed for and finds out that the employer called Medical Information, Inc., for his medical information.

So what was improper about this activity and how would liability be determined? If and when this case went to court, the following items would be introduced and addressed:

- **Legally recognized obligation**
  - Medical Information, Inc., does not have policies and procedures in place to protect patient information.

- The employer does not have the right to make this kind of call and is not able to use medical information against potential employees.

- **Failure to conform to the required standard**
  - Sensitive information was released to an unauthorized person by a Medical Information, Inc., employee.
  - The employer requested information it did not have a right to.

- **Proximate causation and resulting injury or damage**
  - The information provided by Medical Information, Inc., caused Don Hammy great embarrassment and prevented him from obtaining a specific job.
  - The employer made its decision based on information it did not have a right to inquire about in the first place. The employer's illegal acquisition and review of Don's private medical information caused it to not hire him.

The outcome was a long legal battle, but Don Hammy ended up successfully suing both companies, recovered from his brain tumor, bought an island, and has never had to work again.

Hacker Intrusion

A financial institution, Cheapo, Inc., buys the necessary middleware to enable it to offer online bank account transactions for its customers. It does not add any of the necessary security safeguards required for this type of transaction to take place over the Internet.

Within the first two weeks, 22 customers have their checking and savings accounts hacked into, with a combined loss of $439,344.09.

What was improper about this activity and how would liability be determined? If and when this case went to court, the following items would be introduced and addressed:

- **Legally recognized obligation**
  - Cheapo, Inc., did not implement a firewall or IDS, harden the database holding the customer account information, or use encryption for customer transactions.
  - Cheapo, Inc., did not effectively protect its customers' assets.

- **Failure to conform to the required standard**
  - By not erecting the proper security policy and program and implementing the necessary security controls, Cheapo, Inc., broke 12 federal regulations used to govern financial institutions.

- **Proximate causation and resulting injury or damage**
  - The financial institution's failure to practice due care and implement the basic requirements of online banking directly caused 22 clients to lose $439,344.09.

Eventually, a majority of the accounts were attacked and drained, a class action suit was brought against Cheapo, Inc., a majority of the people got most of their money back, and the facility Cheapo, Inc., was using as a financial institution is now used to sell tacos.

These scenarios are simplistic and described in a light-hearted manner, but failure to implement computer and information security properly can expose a company and its board of directors to litigation and legal punishment. Many times people cannot hide behind the corporation and are held accountable individually and personally. The board of directors can compromise its responsibilities to the stockholders, customers, and employees by not ensuring that due care is practiced and that the company was not being negligent in any way.

Investigations

Since computer crimes are only increasing and will never really go away, it is important that all security professionals understand how computer investigations should be carried out. This includes legal requirements for specific situations, understanding the "chain of custody" for evidence, what type of evidence is admissible in court, incident response procedures and escalation processes, and that security professionals are not robo-cops.

When a potential computer crime takes place, it is critical that the investigation steps are carried out properly to ensure that the evidence will be admissible to the court and that it can stand up under the cross-examination and scrutiny that will take place. As a security professional, you should understand that an investigation is not just about potential evidence on a disk drive. The whole environment will be part of an investigation, including the people, network, connected internal and external systems, federal and state laws, management's stance on how the investigation is to be carried out, and the skill set of whomever is carrying out the investigation. Messing up on just one of these components could make your case inadmissible or at least damaging if it is brought to court. So, make sure to watch many more episodes of *CSI* and *Law & Order!*

Incident Response

Many computer crimes go unreported because the victim, in many cases, is not aware of the incident or wants to just patch the hole the hacker came in through and keep the details quiet in order to escape embarrassment or the risk of hurting the company's reputation. This makes it harder to know the real statistics of how many attacks happen each day, the degree of damage caused, and what types of attack and methods are being used.

Although we commonly use the terms "event" and "incident" interchangeably, there are subtle differences between the two. An *event* is a negative occurrence that can be observed, verified, and documented, whereas an *incident* is a series of events that negatively affects the company and/or impacts its security posture. This is why we call reacting to these issues "incident response" (or "incident handling"), because something is negatively affecting the company and causing a security breach.

Many types of incidences (virus, insider attack, terrorist attacks, and so on) exist, and sometimes it is just human error. Indeed, many incident response individuals have received a frantic call in the middle of the night because a system is acting "weird." The reasons could be that a deployed patch broke something, someone misconfigured a device, or the administrator just learned a new scripting language and rolled out some code that caused mayhem and confusion.

When a company endures a computer crime, it should leave the environment and evidence unaltered and contact whoever has been delegated to investigate these types of situations. Someone who is unfamiliar with the proper process of collecting data and evidence from a crime scene could instead destroy that evidence, and thus all hope of prosecuting individuals and achieving a conviction would be lost. Companies should have procedures for many issues in computer security such as enforcement procedures, disaster recovery and continuity procedures, and backup procedures. It is also necessary to have a procedure for dealing with computer incidents because they have become an increasingly important issue of today's information security departments. This is a direct result of attacks against networks and information systems increasing annually. Even though we don't have specific numbers due to a lack of universal reporting and reporting in general, it is clear that the volume of attacks is increasing. Just think about all the spam, phishing scams, malware, distributed denial-of-service and other attacks you see on your own network and hear about in the news.

Unfortunately, many companies do not have a clue as to who to call or what to do right after they have been the victim of a cybercrime. Therefore, all companies should have an incident response policy that indicates who has the authority to initiate an incident response, with supporting procedures set up before an incident takes place. This policy should be managed by the legal department.

The incident response policy should be clear and concise. For example, it should indicate if systems can be taken offline to try to save evidence or if systems have to continue functioning at the risk of destroying evidence. Each system and functionality should have a priority assigned to it. For instance, if the file server is infected, it should be removed from the network, but not shut down. However, if the mail server is infected, it should not be removed from the network or shut down because of the priority the company attributes to the mail server over the file server. Tradeoffs and decisions will have to be made, but it is better to think through these issues before the situation occurs, because better logic is usually possible before a crisis, when there's less emotion and chaos.

All organizations should develop an *incident response team*, as mandated by the incident response policy, to respond to the large array of possible security incidents. The purpose of having an incident response team is to ensure that there is a group of people who are properly skilled, who follow a standard set of procedures, and who are singled out and called upon when this type of event takes place. The team should have proper reporting procedures established, be prompt in their reaction, work in coordination with law enforcement, and be an important element of the overall security program. The team should consist of representatives from various business units, such as the legal department, HR, executive management, the communications department, physical/corporate security, IS security, and information technology.

There are three different types of incident response teams. A *virtual* team is made up of experts who have other duties and assignments within the organization. This type of team introduces a slower response time, and members must neglect their regular duties should an incident occur. As a result, a virtual team can be costly. However, a *permanent* team of folks who are dedicated strictly to incident response can be cost prohibitive to smaller organizations. The third type of incident response team is a *hybrid* of the virtual and permanent models. Certain core members are permanently assigned to the team whereas others are called in as needed.

The incident response team should have the following basic items available:

- A list of outside agencies and resources to contact or report to.
- Roles and responsibilities outlined.
- A call tree to contact these roles and outside entities.
- A list of computer or forensics experts to contact.
- Steps on how to secure and preserve evidence.
- A list of items that should be included on a report for management and potentially the courts.
- A description of how the different systems should be treated in this type of situation. (For example, the systems should be removed from both the Internet and the network and powered down.)

When a suspected crime is reported, the incident response team should follow a set of predetermined steps to ensure uniformity in their approach and make sure no steps are skipped. First, the incident response team should investigate the report and determine that an actual crime has been committed. If the team determines that a crime has been carried out, senior management should be informed immediately. If the suspect is an employee, a human resources representative must be called right away. The sooner the documenting of events begins, the better. If someone is able to document the starting time of the crime, along with the company employees and resources involved, it would provide a good foundation for evidence. At this point, the company must decide if it wants to conduct its own forensics investigation or call in the big guns. If experts are going to be called in, the system that was attacked should be left alone in order to try and preserve as much evidence of the attack as possible. If the company decides to conduct its own forensics investigation, it must deal with many issues and address tricky elements. (Forensics will be discussed later in this chapter.)

Computers networks and business processes face many types of threats, each requiring a specialized type of recovery. However, an incident response team should draft and enforce a basic outline of how *all* incidents are to be handled. This is a much better approach than the way many companies deal with these threats, which is usually in an ad hoc, reactive, and confusing manner. A clearly defined incident-handling process is more cost-effective, enables recovery to happen more quickly, and provides a uniform approach with certain expectation of its results.

Incident handling should be closely related to disaster recovery planning and should be part of the company's disaster recovery plan, usually as an appendix. Both are intended to react to some type of incident that requires a quick response so the company can return to normal operations. Incident handling is a recovery plan that responds to malicious technical threats. The primary goal of incident handling is to contain and mitigate any damage caused by an incident and to prevent any further damage. This is commonly done by detecting a problem, determining its cause, resolving the problem, and documenting the entire process.

Without an effective incident-handling program, individuals who have the best intentions can sometimes make the situation worse by damaging evidence, damaging systems, or spreading malicious code. Many times, the attacker booby-traps the compromised system to erase specific critical files if a user does something as simple as list the files in a directory. A compromised system can no longer be trusted because the internal commands listed in the path could be altered to perform unexpected activities. The system could now have a backdoor for the attacker to enter when he wants, or could have a logic bomb silently waiting for a user to start snooping around only to destroy any and all evidence.

Incident handling should also be closely linked to the company's security training and awareness program to ensure that these types of mishaps do not take place. Past issues that the incident recovery team encountered can be used in future training sessions to help others learn what the company is faced with and how to improve response processes.

Employees need to know how to report an incident. Therefore, the incident response policy should detail an escalation process so that employees understand when evidence of a crime should be reported to higher management, outside agencies, or law enforcement. The process must be centralized, easy to accomplish (or the employees won't bother), convenient, and welcomed. Some employees feel reluctant to report incidents because they are afraid they will get pulled into something they do not want to be involved with or accused of something they did not do. There is nothing like trying to do the right thing and getting hit with a big stick. Employees should feel comfortable about the process, and not feel intimidated by reporting suspicious activities.

The incident response policy should also dictate how employees should interact with external entities, such as the media, government, and law enforcement. This, in particular, is a complicated issue influenced by jurisdiction, the status and nature of the crime, and the nature of the evidence. Jurisdiction alone, for example, depends on the country, state, or federal agency that has control. Given the sensitive nature of public disclosure, communications should be handled by communications, human resources, or other appropriately trained individuals who are authorized to publicly discuss incidents. Public disclosure of an event can lead to two possible outcomes. If not handled correctly, it can compound the negative impact of an incident. For example, given today's information-driven society, denial and "no comment" may result in a backlash. On the other hand, if public disclosure is handled well, it can provide the organization with an opportunity to win back public trust. Some countries and jurisdictions either already have or are contemplating breach disclosure laws that require organizations to notify the public if a security breach involving personally identifiable information is even suspected. So it's to your benefit to make sure you are open and forthright with third parties.

A sound incident-handling program works with outside agencies and counterparts. The members of the team should be on the mailing list of the Computer Emergency Response Team (CERT) so they can keep up to date about new issues and can spot malicious events, hopefully before they get out of hand. CERT is an organization that is responsible for monitoring and advising users and companies about security preparation and security breaches.

 NOTE Resources for CERT can be found at www.cert.org/certcc.html and www.cert.am.

Incident Response Procedures

In the preceding sections, it is repeatedly stated that there should be a standard set of procedures for the team to follow, but what are these procedures? Although different organizations may define these procedures (or stages) a little differently, they should accomplish the exact same thing. To further complicate matters, incident response is a dynamic process. Oftentimes stages are conducted in parallel, even as one stage depends on the output of another. The important thing is that your organization uses a methodical approach. This allows for proper documentation that may be important in later stages of the incident response process or if the case goes to trial and you are asked whether you followed a standard procedure and whether any steps were left out. A documented checklist of your incident response procedure will help ensure admissibility in court.

You should understand the following set of procedures for incidence response:

- Triage
- Investigation
- Containment
- Analysis
- Tracking
- Recovery

When an event has been reported by employees or detected by automated security controls, the first stage carried out by the incident response team should be *triage*. Triage in this sense is very similar to triage conducted by medics when treating people who are injured. The crux of it is, "Is this person really hurt?" "How bad is this person hurt?" "What type of treatment does this person need (surgery, stitches, or just a swift kick in the butt)?"

So that's what we do in the computer world too. We take in the information available, investigate its severity, and set priorities on how to deal with the incident. This begins with an initial screening of the reported event to determine whether it is indeed an incident and whether the incident-handling process should be initiated. A member of the incident response team should be responsible for reviewing an alert to determine if it is a false positive. If the event is a false positive, then it is logged and the incident response process for this particular event is complete. However, if the event is determined to be a real incident, it is identified and classified. Incidents should be categorized according to their level of potential risk, which is influenced by the type of incident, the source (whether it's internal or external), its rate of growth, and the ability to contain the damage. This, in turn, determines what notifications are required during the escalation process, and sets the scope and procedures for the investigation.

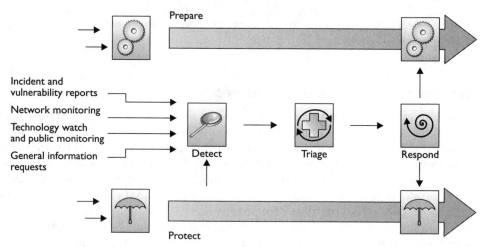

Once we understand the severity of the incident taking place, we move on to the next stage, which is *investigation*. Investigation involves the proper collection of relevant data, which will be used in the analysis and following stages. The goals of these stages are to reduce the impact of the incident, identify the cause of the incident, resume operations as soon as possible, and apply what was learned to prevent the incident from recurring. It is at the analysis stage where computer forensics comes into play. Management must decide if law enforcement should be brought in to carry out the investigation, if evidence should be collected for the purposes of prosecution, or if the hole should just be patched. Most companies do not have a forensics team on staff to carry out these tasks. In such situations, if a suspected crime has occurred and management does not want law enforcement involved but does want a forensics investigation carried out, external forensics experts need to be called in.

We'll go over computer forensics in detail in the next section. For now, it's important to know that an investigation must adhere to company policy as well as applicable laws and regulations.

 NOTE Be careful not to confuse incident response with computer forensics. Although they are both investigative in nature, the terms are not synonymous. Computer forensics has a higher standard of proof than incident response because the assumption is that the evidence must be admissible in a court of law and is handled accordingly.

The next stage is *containment*. In the medical world, if you were found to have tuberculosis, you would be put in an isolation room because no one wants to catch your cooties. In the containment phase, the damage must be mitigated. In the computer world, this could mean that an infected server is taken off the network, firewall configurations are changed to stop an attacker, or the system that is under attack is disconnected from the Internet.

A proper containment strategy buys the incident response team time for a proper investigation and determination of the incident's root cause. The containment strategy should be based on the category of the attack (that is, whether it was internal or external), the assets affected by the incident, and the criticality of those assets. So what kind of containment strategy is best? Well, it depends. Containment strategies can be proactive or reactive. Which is best depends on the environment and the category of the attack. In some cases, the best action might be to disconnect the affected system from the network. However, this reactive approach could cause a denial of service or limit functionality of critical systems. When complete isolation or containment is not a viable solution, you may opt to use network segmentation to virtually isolate a system or systems. Boundary devices can also be used to stop one system from infecting another. Another reactive strategy involves reviewing and revising firewall/filtering router rule configuration. Access control lists can also be applied to minimize exposure. These containment strategies indicate to the attacker that his attack has been noticed and countermeasures are being implemented. But what if, in order to perform a root cause analysis, you need to keep the affected system online and not let on that you've noticed the attack? In this situation, you might consider installing a honeynet or honeypot to provide an area that will contain the attacker but pose minimal risk to the organization. This decision should involve legal counsel and upper management because honeynets and honeypots can introduce liability issues and be used to attack other internal targets.

Once the incident has been contained, we need to figure out what just happened by putting the available pieces together. This is the stage of *analysis*, where more data are gathered (audit logs, video captures, human accounts of activities, system activities) to try and figure out the root cause of the incident. The goals are to figure out who did this, how they did it, when they did it, and why. Management must be continually kept abreast of these activities because they will be the ones making the big decisions on how this whole mess is to be handled.

The group of individuals who make up the analysis team must have a variety of skills. They must also have a solid understanding of the systems affected by the incident, the system and application vulnerabilities, and the network and system configurations. Although formal education is important, real-world applied experience combined with proper training is key for these folks. One of the biggest challenges they face is the dynamic nature of logs. Most ISPs purge or overwrite their logs in a short timeframe, and time is lost the moment the incident occurs. Several hours may pass before an incident is reported or detected. Some countries are considering legislation that would require longer log file retention. However, such laws pose privacy and storage challenges. We can never win.

Once we have as much information as we can get in the last stage and have answered as many questions as we can, we then move to the *tracking* stage. (Tracking may also take place in parallel with the analysis and examination.) We determine whether the source of the incident was internal or external and how the offender penetrated and gained access to the asset. If the attacker was external, the team would contact their ISP to help them in gathering data and possibly help in finding the source of the attack. Many times this is difficult because attackers move from one system to the next, so several ISPs may have to get involved. Thus, it is important that the analysis and tracking team have a good working relationship with third parties such as ISPs, other response teams, and law enforcement.

Once the incident is understood, we move into the *recovery* (or *follow-up*) stage, which means we implement the necessary fix to ensure this type of incident cannot happen again. This may require blocking certain ports, deactivating vulnerable services or functionalities, switching over to another processing facility, or applying a patch. This is properly called "following recovery procedures," because just arbitrarily making a change to the environment may introduce more problems. The recovery procedures may state that a new image needs to be installed, backup data needs to be restored, the system needs to be tested, and all configurations must be properly set.

Regardless of the specifics of the recovery procedures, before an affected system is returned to production, you must first ensure that it can withstand another attack. It doesn't take long for word to get out within the hacker community that a weak system is online. Trained information security personnel should test the system for vulnerabilities to provide information assurance. Vulnerability testing tools that simulate real-world attacks can help the team harden the system against a variety of attacks, including those that were originally directed against it.

 CAUTION An attacked or infected system should never be trusted because you do not necessarily know all the changes that have taken place and the true extent of the damage. Some malicious code could still be hiding somewhere. Systems should be rebuilt to ensure that all of the potential bad mojo has been released by carrying out a proper exorcism.

What Can We Learn from This?

Closure of an incident is determined by the nature or category of the incident, the desired incident response outcome (for example, business resumption or system restoration), and the team's success in determining the incident's source and root cause. Once it is determined that the incident is closed, it is a good idea to have a team briefing that includes all groups affected by the incident to answer the following questions:

- What happened?
- What did we learn?
- How can we do it better next time?

The team should review the incident and how it was handled and carry out a postmortem analysis. The information that comes out of this meeting should indicate what needs to go into the incidence response process and documentation, with the goal of continual improvement. Instituting a formal process for the briefing will provide the team with the ability to start collecting data that can be used to track its performance metrics.

Cops or No Cops?

Management needs to make the decision as to whether law enforcement should be called in to handle the security breach. The following are some of the issues to understand if law enforcement is brought in:

- Company loses control over investigation once law enforcement is involved.

- Secrecy of compromise is not promised; it could become part of public record.

- Effects on reputation need to be considered (the ramifications of this information reaching customers, shareholders, and so on).

- Evidence will be collected and may not be available for a long period of time. It may take a year or so to get into court.

Other issues to think through when a company is developing incident response procedures include deciding how the incident will be explained to the press, customers, and shareholders. This could require the collaboration of the public relations department, management, human resources (if employees are involved), the IT department, and the legal department. A cybercrime may have legal ramifications that are not immediately apparent and must be handled delicately. The company should decide how it will report the matter to outsiders, to ensure that the situation is not perceived in a totally different light.

Computer Forensics and Proper Collection of Evidence

I just spilled coffee on our only evidence.
Response: Case closed. Let's all go home.

Forensics is a science and an art that requires specialized techniques for the recovery, authentication, and analysis of electronic data for the purposes of a criminal act. It is the coming together of computer science, information technology, and engineering with law. When discussing computer forensics with others, you might hear the terms digital forensics, network forensics, electronic data discovery, cyber forensics, and forensic computing. (ISC)² uses computer forensics as a synonym for all of these other terms, so that's what you'll see on the CISSP exam. Computer forensics encompasses all domains in which evidence is in a digital or electronic form, either in storage or on the wire. At one time computer forensics was differentiated from network and code analysis, but now this entire area is referred to as *digital evidence.*

As a forensics discipline, computer forensics is the new kid on the block. This, paired with its complexity, may be the reason why many companies lack skills in this area. Computer forensics does not refer to hardware or software. It is a set of specific processes relating to reconstruction of computer usage, examination of residual data, authentication of data by technical analysis or explanation of technical features of data, and computer usage that must be followed in order for evidence to be admissible in a court of law. This is not something the ordinary network administrator should be carrying out.

The people conducting the forensics investigation must be properly skilled in this trade and know what to look for. If someone reboots the attacked system or inspects various files, this could corrupt viable evidence, change timestamps on key files, and erase footprints the criminal may have left. Most digital evidence has a short lifespan and must be collected quickly in order of volatility. In other words, the most volatile or fragile evidence should be collected first. In most situations, it is best to remove the system from the network, dump the contents of the memory, power down the system, and make a sound image of the attacked system and perform forensic analysis on this copy. Working on the copy instead of the original drive will ensure that the evidence stays unharmed on the original system in case some steps in the investigation actually corrupt or destroy data. Dumping the memory contents to a file before doing any work on the system or powering it down is a crucial step because of the information that could be stored there. This is another method of capturing fragile information. However, this creates a sticky situation because capturing RAM or conducting live analysis can introduce changes to the crime scene because various state changes and operations take place. Whatever method the forensic investigator chooses to collect digital evidence must be documented. This is the most important aspect of evidence handling.

 NOTE The forensics team needs specialized tools, an evidence collection notebook, containers, a camera, and evidence identification tags. The notebook should not be a spiral notebook but rather a notebook that is bound in a way that one can tell if pages have been removed.

International Organization on Computer Evidence

When we covered laws earlier in the chapter, we discussed how important it is to standardize different countries' attitudes and approaches to computer crime since computer crimes often take place over international boundaries. The same thing is true with forensics. Thus, digital evidence must be handled in a similarly careful fashion so it can be used in different courts, no matter what country is prosecuting a suspect. The *International Organization on Computer Evidence (IOCE)* was created to develop international principles dealing with how digital evidence is to be collected and handled so various courts will recognize and use the evidence in the same manner. State-side, we have the *Scientific Working Group on Digital Evidence (SWDGE)*, which also aims to ensure consistency across the forensic community. The principles developed by IOCE and SWDGE for the standardized recovery of computer-based evidence are governed by the following attributes:

- Consistency with all legal systems
- Allowance for the use of a common language
- Durability
- Ability to cross international and state boundaries
- Ability to instill confidence in the integrity of evidence
- Applicability to all forensic evidence
- Applicability at every level, including that of individual, agency, and country

The IOCE/SWDGE principles are listed next:

1. When dealing with digital evidence, all of the general forensic and procedural principles must be applied.

2. Upon the seizing of digital evidence, actions taken should not change that evidence.

3. When it is necessary for a person to access original digital evidence, that person should be trained for the purpose.

4. All activity relating to the seizure, access, storage, or transfer of digital evidence must be fully documented, preserved, and available for review.

5. An individual is responsible for all actions taken with respect to digital evidence while the digital evidence is in their possession.

6. Any agency that is responsible for seizing, accessing, storing, or transferring digital evidence is responsible for compliance with these principles.

So, there you go. Do all of that, and we will finally achieve world peace.

NOTE The Digital Forensic Science Research Workshop (DFSRW) brings together academic researchers and forensic investigators to also address a standardized process for collecting evidence, to research practitioner requirements and incorporate a scientific method as a tenant of digital forensic science. The DFSRW holds an annual workshop in the U.S. Learn more at http://www.dfrws.org/index.shtml.

Motive, Opportunity, and Means

MOM did it.

Today's computer criminals are similar to their traditional counterparts. To understand the "whys" in crime, it is necessary to understand the motive, opportunity, and means—or MOM. This is the same strategy used to determine the suspects in a traditional, noncomputer crime.

Motive is the "who" and "why" of a crime. The motive may be induced by either internal or external conditions. A person may be driven by the excitement, challenge, and adrenaline rush of committing a crime, which would be an internal condition. Examples of external conditions might include financial trouble, a sick family member, or other dire straits. Understanding the motive for a crime is an important piece in figuring out who would engage in such an activity. For example, many hackers attack big-name sites because when the sites go down, it is splashed all over the news. However, once technology advances to the point where attacks cannot bring down these sites, or once these activities are no longer so highly publicized, the individuals will eventually stop initiating these types of attacks because their motive will have been diminished.

Opportunity is the "where" and "when" of a crime. Opportunities usually arise when certain vulnerabilities or weaknesses are present. If a company does not have a firewall, hackers and attackers have all types of opportunities within that network. If a company does not perform access control, auditing, and supervision, employees may have many opportunities to embezzle funds and defraud the company. Once a crime fighter finds out why a person would want to commit a crime (motive), she will look at what could allow the criminal to be successful (opportunity).

Means pertains to the abilities a criminal would need to be successful. Suppose a crime fighter was asked to investigate a complex embezzlement that took place within a financial institution. If the suspects were three people who knew how to use a mouse, keyboard, and a word processing application, but only one of them was a programmer and system analyst, the crime fighter would realize that this person may have the means to commit this crime much more successfully than the other two individuals.

Computer Criminal Behavior

Like traditional criminals, computer criminals have a specific modus operandi (MO). In other words, criminals use a distinct method of operation to carry out their crime that can be used to help identify them. The difference with computer crimes is that the investigator, obviously, must have knowledge of technology. For example, an MO for computer criminals may include the use of specific hacking tools, or targeting specific systems or networks. The method usually involves repetitive signature behaviors, such as sending e-mail messages or programming syntax. Knowledge of the criminal's MO and signature behaviors can be useful throughout the investigative process. Law enforcement can use the information to identify other offenses by the same criminal, for example. The MO and signature behaviors can also provide information that is useful during the interview and interrogation process as well as the trial.

Psychological crime scene analysis (profiling) can also be conducted using the criminal's MO and signature behaviors. Profiling provides insight into the thought processes of the attacker and can be used to identify the attacker or, at the very least, the tool he used to conduct the crime.

 NOTE Locard's Principle of Exchange also provides information that is handy for profiling. The principle states that a criminal leaves something behind and takes something with them. This principle is the foundation of criminalistics. Even in an entirely digital crime scene, Locard's Principle of Exchange can shed light on who the perpetrator(s) may be.

Incident Investigators

Incident investigators are a breed of their own. Many people suspect they come from a different planet, but to date that hasn't been proven. Good incident investigators must be aware of suspicious or abnormal activities that others might normally ignore. This is because, due to their training and experience, they may know what is potentially going on behind some abnormal system activity, while another employee would just respond, "Oh, that just happens sometimes. We don't know why."

The investigator could identify suspicious activities, such as port scans, attempted SQL injections, or evidence in a log that describes a dangerous activity that took place. Identifying abnormal activities is a bit more difficult, because it is more subtle. These activities could be increased network traffic, an employee staying late every night, unusual requests to specific ports on a network server, and so on. As an analogy, if a mother of a teenage boy smelled smoke on his jacket, she might suspect he had taken up smoking. If the teenage boy, who usually plays Xbox games all night, starts going to the library every night, the mother would notice this abnormal activity and, upon snooping around, perhaps discover her son has a new girlfriend he is meeting at the park each night.

On top of being observant, the investigator must understand forensics procedures, evidence collection issues, and how to analyze a situation to determine what is going on, and know how to pick out the clues in system logs.

Different Types of Assessments an Investigator Can Perform

- **Network analysis**
  - Communication analysis
  - Log analysis
  - Path tracing
- **Media analysis**
  - Disk imaging
  - MAC time analysis (Modify, Access, Create)
  - Content analysis
  - Slack space analysis
  - Steganography
- **Software analysis**
  - Reverse engineering
  - Malicious code review
  - Exploit review

The Forensics Investigation Process

To ensure that forensics activities are carried out in a standardized manner, it is necessary for the team to follow specific laid-out steps so nothing is missed and thus ensure the evidence is admissible. Each team or company may commonly come up with their own steps, but all should be essentially accomplishing the same things:

- Identification
- Preservation
- Collection
- Examination
- Analysis
- Presentation
- Decision

Figure 10-2 fills in many of the steps that take place in each phase of the investigation process.

NOTE The principles of criminalistics are included in the forensic investigation process. They are identification of the crime scene, protection of the environment against contamination and loss of evidence, identification of evidence and potential sources of evidence, and the collection of evidence. In regard to minimizing the degree of contamination, it is important to understand that it is impossible not to change a crime scene—be it physical or digital. The key is to minimize changes and document what you did and why, and how the crime scene was affected.

During the examination and analysis process of a forensics investigation, it is critical that the investigator works from an image that contains *all* of the data from the original disk. It must be a bit-level copy, sector by sector, to capture deleted files, slack spaces, and unallocated clusters. These types of images can be created through the use of a specialized tool such as FTK Imager, EnCase, Safeback, or the -dd Unix utility. A file copy tool does not recover all data areas of the device necessary for examination.

Identification	Preservation	Collection	Examination	Analysis	Presentation
Event/crime detection	Case management	Preservation	Preservation	Preservation	Documentation
Resolve signature	Imaging technologies	Approved methods	Traceability	Traceability	Expert testimony
Profile detection	Chain of custody	Approved software	Validation techniques	Statistical	Clarification
Anomalous detection	Time synchronization	Approved hardware	Filtering techniques	Protocols	Mission impact statement
Complaints		Legal authority	Pattern matching	Data mining	Recommended countermeasure
System monitoring		Lossless compression	Hidden data discovery	Timeline	Statistical interpretation
Audit analysis		Sampling	Hidden data extraction	Link	
Etc.		Data reduction		Spatial	
		Recovery techniques			

Figure 10-2 Characteristics of the different phases through an investigation process

Controlling the Crime Scene

Whether the crime scene is physical or virtual, it is important to control who comes in contact with the evidence of the crime to ensure its integrity. The following are just some of the steps that should take place to protect the crime scene:

- Only allow authorized individuals access to the scene. These folks should have knowledge of basic crime scene analysis.
- Document who is at the crime scene.
  - In court, the integrity of the evidence may be in question if there are too many people milling around.
- Document who were the last individuals to interact with the systems.
- If the crime scene does become contaminated, document it. The contamination may not negate the derived evidence, but it will make investigating the crime more challenging.

The original media should have two copies created: a *primary image* (a control copy that is stored in a library) and a *working image* (used for analysis and evidence collection). These should be timestamped to show when the evidence was collected.

Before creating these images, the investigator must make sure the new media has been properly purged, meaning it does not contain any residual data. Some incidents have occurred where drives that were new and right out of the box (shrink-wrapped) contained old data not purged by the vendor.

The investigator works from the duplicate image because it preserves the original evidence, prevents inadvertent alteration of original evidence during examination, and allows re-creation of the duplicate image if necessary. Most media are "magnetic based," and the data are volatile and can be contained in the following:

- Registers and cache
- Process tables and ARP cache
- Contents of system memory
- Temporary file systems
- Data on the disk

So, great care and precision must take place to capture clues from any computer or device. Remember that digital evidence can exist in many more devices than traditional computer systems. PDAs, cell phones, USB jump drives, laptops, GPS devices, and memory cards can be containers of digital evidence as well.

Acquiring evidence on live systems and those using network storage further complicates matters because you cannot turn off the system in order to make a copy of the hard drive. Imagine the reaction you'd receive if you told an IT manager that you needed to shut down a primary database or e-mail system. It wouldn't be favorable. So these systems and others, such as those using on-the-fly encryption, must be imaged while they are running.

To ensure that the original image is not modified, it is important to create message digests for files and directories before and after the analysis to prove the integrity of the original image.

NOTE Logs should be kept detailing all activities, systems, peripherals and their serial numbers, and each team's actions. This will help ensure that the evidence, or the process of collection, can stand up to scrutiny and be used in a court of law. Also be sure to document the role of the system(s) in the organization.

NOTE In most cases, an investigator's notebook cannot be used as evidence in court. It can only be employed by the investigator to refresh his memory during a proceeding.

Forensics Field Kits

When forensics teams are deployed, they should be properly equipped with all of the tools and supplies needed. The following are some of the common items in the forensics field kits:

- **Documentation tools**   Tags, labels, and timelined forms
- **Disassembly and removal tools**   Antistatic bands, pliers, tweezers, screwdrivers, wire cutters, and so on
- **Package and transport supplies**   Antistatic bags, evidence bags and tape, cable ties, and others

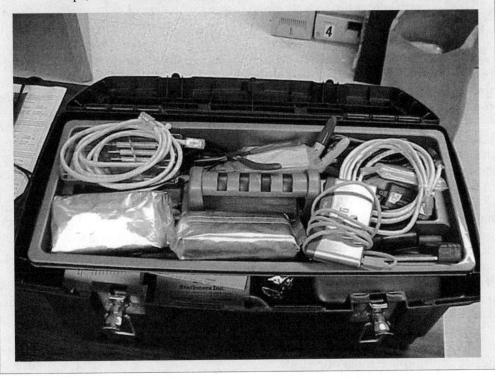

The next crucial piece is to keep a proper *chain of custody* of the evidence. Because evidence from these types of crimes can be very volatile and easily dismissed from court because of improper handling, it is important to follow very strict and organized procedures when collecting and tagging evidence in every single case—no exceptions! Furthermore, the chain of custody should follow evidence through its entire life cycle, beginning with identification and ending with its destruction, permanent archiving, or return to owner.

When copies of data need to be made, this process must meet certain standards to ensure quality and reliability. Specialized software for this purpose can be used. The copies must be able to be independently verified and must be tamperproof.

Each piece of evidence should be marked in some way with the date, time, initials of the collector, and a case number if one has been assigned. Magnetic disk surfaces should not be marked on. The piece of evidence should then be sealed in a container, which should be marked with the same information. The container should be sealed with evidence tape, and if possible the writing should be on the tape so a broken seal can be detected.

NOTE The chain of custody of evidence dictates that all evidence be labeled with information indicating who secured and validated it.

Wires and cables should be labeled, and a photograph of the labeled system should be taken before it is actually disassembled. Media should be write-protected. Storage should be dust free and kept at room temperature without much humidity, and, of course, the media should not be stored close to any strong magnets or magnetic fields.

If possible, the crime scene should be photographed, including behind the computer if the crime involved some type of physical break-in. Documents, papers, and devices should be handled with cloth gloves and placed into containers and sealed. All storage media should be contained, even if it has been erased, because data still may be obtainable.

Because this type of evidence can be easily erased or destroyed and is complex in nature, identification, recording, collection, preservation, transportation, and interpretation are all important. After everything is properly labeled, a chain of custody log should be made of each container and an overall log should be made capturing all events.

For a crime to be successfully prosecuted, solid evidence is required. Computer forensics is the art of retrieving this evidence and preserving it in the proper ways to make it admissible in court. Without proper computer forensics, hardly any computer crimes could ever be properly and successfully presented in court.

The most common reasons for improper evidence collection are no established incident response team, no established incident response procedures, poorly written policy, and a broken chain of custody.

NOTE A chain of custody is a history that shows how evidence was collected, analyzed, transported, and preserved in order to be presented in court. Because electronic evidence can be easily modified, a clearly defined chain of custody demonstrates that the evidence is trustworthy.

The next step is the analysis of the evidence. Forensic investigators use a scientific method that involves

- Determining the characteristics of the evidence, such as whether it's admissible as primary or secondary evidence as well as its source, reliability, and permanence

- Comparing evidence from different sources to determine a chronology of events

- Event reconstruction, including the recovery of deleted files and other activity on the system

This can take place in a controlled lab environment or, thanks to hardware write-blockers and forensic software, in the field. When investigators analyze evidence in a lab, they are dealing with dead forensics; that is, they are working only with static data. Live forensics, which takes place in the field, includes volatile data. If evidence is lacking, then an experienced investigator should be called in to help complete the picture.

Finally, the interpretation of the analysis should be presented to the appropriate party. This could be a judge, lawyer, CEO, or board of directors. Therefore, it is important to present the findings in a format that will be understood by a nontechnical audience. As a CISSP, you should be able to explain these findings in layman's terms using metaphors and analogies. Of course the findings, which are top secret or company confidential, should only be disclosed to authorized parties. This may include the legal department or any outside counsel that assisted with the investigation.

The Australian Computer Emergency Response Team's General Guidelines for Computer Forensics

- Keep the handling and corruption of original data to a minimum.

- Document all actions and explain changes.

- Follow the Five Rules for Evidence (Admissible, Authentic, Complete, Accurate, Convincing).

- Bring in more experienced help when handling and/or analyzing the evidence is beyond your knowledge, skills, or abilities.

- Adhere to your organization's security policy and obtain written permission to conduct a forensics investigation.

- Capture as accurate an image of the system(s) as possible while working quickly.

- Be ready to testify in a court of law.

- Make certain your actions are repeatable.

- Prioritize your actions, beginning with volatile and proceeding to persistent evidence.

- Do not run any programs on the system(s) that are potential evidence.

- Act ethically and in good faith while conducting a forensics investigation, and do not attempt to do any harm.

What Is Admissible in Court?

He is guilty because I don't like him.
Response: Um, I need more than that.

Computer logs are important in many aspects of the IT world. They are generally used to troubleshoot an issue or to try to understand the events that took place at a specific moment in time. When computer logs are to be used as evidence in court, they must be collected in the regular course of business. Most of the time, computer-related documents are considered *hearsay*, meaning the evidence is secondhand evidence. Hearsay evidence is not normally admissible in court unless it has firsthand evidence that can be used to prove the evidence's accuracy, trustworthiness, and reliability, such as the testimony of a businessperson who generated the computer logs and collected them. This person must generate and collect logs as a normal part of his business activities and not just this one time for court. The value of evidence depends upon the genuineness and competence of the source.

It is important to show that the logs, and all evidence, have not been tampered with in any way, which is the reason for the chain of custody of evidence. Several tools are available that run checksums or hashing functions on the logs, which will allow the team to be alerted if something has been modified.

When evidence is being collected, one issue that can come up is the user's expectation of privacy. If an employee is suspected of, and charged with, a computer crime, he might claim that his files on the computer he uses are personal and not available to law enforcement and the courts. This is why it is important for companies to conduct security-awareness training, have employees sign documentation pertaining to the acceptable use of the company's computers and equipment, and have legal banners pop up on every employee's computer when they log on. These are key elements in establishing that a user has no right to privacy when he is using company equipment. The following banner is suggested by CERT Advisory:

> This system is for the use of authorized users only. Individuals using this computer system without authority, or in excess of their authority, are subject to having all of their activities on this system monitored and recorded by system personnel.
>
> In the course of monitoring an individual improperly using this system, or in the course of system maintenance, the activities of authorized users may also be monitored.
>
> Anyone using this system expressly consents to such monitoring and is advised that if such monitoring reveals possible evidence of criminal activity, system personnel may provide the evidence of such monitoring to law enforcement officials.

This explicit warning strengthens a legal case that can be brought against an employee or intruder, because the continued use of the system after viewing this type of warning implies that the person acknowledges the security policy and gives permission to be monitored.

Evidence has its own life cycle, and it is important that the individuals involved with the investigation understand the phases of the life cycle and properly follow them.

The life cycle of evidence includes

- Collection and identification
- Storage, preservation, and transportation
- Presentation in court
- Return of the evidence to the victim or owner

Several types of evidence can be used in a trial, such as written, oral, computer generated, and visual or audio. Oral evidence is testimony of a witness. Visual or audio is usually a captured event during the crime or right after it.

Not all evidence is equal in the eyes of the law, and some types of evidence have more clout, or weight, than others. The following sections quickly describe the different ways evidence can be categorized and valued.

Best Evidence

Best evidence is the primary evidence used in a trial because it provides the most reliability. An example of something that would be categorized as best evidence is an original signed contract. Oral evidence is not considered best evidence because there is no firsthand reliable proof that supports its validity, and it therefore does not have as good a standing as legal documents. Oral evidence cannot be used to dispute a legal document, but it can be used to interpret the document.

Secondary Evidence

Secondary evidence is not viewed as reliable and strong in proving innocence or guilt (or liability in civil cases) when compared to best evidence. Oral evidence, such as a witness's testimony, and copies of original documents are placed in the secondary evidence category.

Direct Evidence

Direct evidence can prove a fact all by itself and does not need backup information to refer to. When direct evidence is used, presumptions are not required. One example of direct evidence is the testimony of a witness who saw a crime take place. Although this oral evidence would be secondary in nature, meaning a case could not rest on just it alone, it is also direct evidence, meaning the lawyer does not necessarily need to provide other evidence to back it up. Direct evidence often is based on information gathered from a witness's five senses.

Conclusive Evidence

Conclusive evidence is irrefutable and cannot be contradicted. Conclusive evidence is very strong all by itself and does not require corroboration.

Circumstantial Evidence

Circumstantial evidence can prove an intermediate fact that can then be used to deduce or assume the existence of another fact. This type of fact is used so the judge or jury will logically assume the existence of a primary fact. For example, if a suspect told a friend he was going to bring down eBay's web site, a case could not rest on that piece of evidence alone because it is circumstantial. However, this evidence can cause the jury to assume that because the suspect said he was going to do it, and hours later it happened, maybe he was the one who did the crime.

Corroborative Evidence

Corroborative evidence is supporting evidence used to help prove an idea or point. It cannot stand on its own but is used as a supplementary tool to help prove a primary piece of evidence.

Opinion Evidence

When a witness testifies, the *opinion rule* dictates that she must testify to only the facts of the issue and not her opinion of the facts. This is slightly different from when an expert witness is used, because an expert is used primarily for his educated opinion. Most lawyers call in expert witnesses to testify and help the defending or prosecuting sides better understand the subject matter so they can help the judge and jury better understand the matters of the case.

Hearsay Evidence

Hearsay evidence pertains to oral or written evidence presented in court that is secondhand and has no firsthand proof of accuracy or reliability. If a witness testifies about something he heard someone else say, it is too far removed from fact and has too many variables that can cloud the truth. If business documents were made during regular business routines, they may be admissible. However, if these records were made just to be presented in court, they could be categorized as hearsay evidence.

The foundation of admissibility is based on the following items:

- Procedures for collecting and maintaining evidence
- Proof of how errors were avoided
- Identification of custodian and skill set
- Reasonable explanations for
  - Why certain actions were taken
  - Why specific procedures were bypassed

It is important that evidence be authentic, complete, sufficient, and reliable to the case at hand. These four characteristics of evidence provide a foundation for a case and help ensure that the evidence is legally permissible.

For evidence to be *authentic*, or relevant, it must have a reasonable and sensible relationship to the findings. If a judge rules that a person's past traffic tickets cannot be brought up in a murder trial, this means the judge has ruled that the traffic tickets are not relevant to the case at hand. Therefore, the prosecuting lawyer cannot even mention them in court.

For evidence to be *complete*, it must present the whole truth. All evidence, even exculpatory evidence, must be handed over.

For the evidence to be *sufficient* or believable, it must be persuasive enough to convince a reasonable person of the validity of the evidence. This means the evidence cannot be subject to personal interpretation. Sufficient evidence also means it cannot be easily doubted.

For evidence to be *reliable*, or accurate, it must be consistent with the facts. Evidence cannot be reliable if it is based on someone's opinion or copies of an original document, because there is too much room for error. Reliable evidence means it is factual and not circumstantial.

 NOTE Don't dismiss the possibility that as an information security professional you will be responsible for entering evidence into court. Most tribunals, commissions, and other semi-legal proceedings have admissibility requirements. Because these requirements can change between jurisdictions, you should seek legal counsel to better understand the specific rules for your jurisdiction.

Surveillance, Search, and Seizure

Two main types of surveillance are used when it comes to identifying computer crimes: physical surveillance and computer surveillance. *Physical surveillance* pertains to security cameras, security guards, and closed-circuit TV (CCTV), which may capture evidence. Physical surveillance can also be used by an undercover agent to learn about the suspect's spending activities, family and friends, and personal habits in the hope of gathering more clues for the case.

Computer surveillance pertains to auditing events, which passively monitors events by using network sniffers, keyboard monitors, wiretaps, and line monitoring. In most jurisdictions, active monitoring may require a search warrant. In most workplace environments, to legally monitor an individual, the person must be warned ahead of time that her activities may be subject to this type of monitoring.

Search and seizure activities can get tricky depending on what is being searched for and where. For example, American citizens are protected by the Fourth Amendment against unlawful search and seizure, so law enforcement agencies must have probable cause and request a search warrant from a judge or court before conducting such a search. The actual search can only take place in the areas outlined by the warrant. The Fourth Amendment does not apply to actions by private citizens unless they are acting as police agents. So, for example, if Kristy's boss warned all employees that the management could remove files from their computers at any time, and her boss was not a police officer or acting as a police agent, she could not successfully claim that her Fourth Amendment rights were violated. Kristy's boss may have violated some specific privacy laws, but he did not violate Kristy's Fourth Amendment rights.

In some circumstances, a law enforcement agent may seize evidence that is not included in the warrant, such as if the suspect tries to destroy the evidence. In other words, if there is an impending possibility that evidence might be destroyed, law enforcement may quickly seize the evidence to prevent its destruction. This is referred to as *exigent circumstances*, and a judge will later decide whether the seizure was proper and legal before allowing the evidence to be admitted. For example, if a police officer had a search warrant that allowed him to search a suspect's living room but no other rooms, and then he saw the suspect dumping cocaine down the toilet, the police officer could seize the cocaine even though it was in a room not covered under his search warrant.

After evidence is gathered, the chain of custody needs to be enacted and enforced to make sure the evidence's integrity is not compromised.

A thin line exists between enticement and entrapment when it comes to capturing a suspect's actions. *Enticement* is legal and ethical, whereas *entrapment* is neither legal nor ethical. In the world of computer crimes, a honeypot is always a good example to show the difference between enticement and entrapment. Companies put systems in their screened subnets that either emulate services that attackers usually like to take advantage of or actually have the services enabled. The hope is that if an attacker breaks into the company's network, she will go right to the honeypot instead of the systems that are actual production machines. The attacker will be enticed to go to the honeypot system because it has many open ports and services running and exhibits vulnerabilities that the attacker would want to exploit. The company can log the attacker's actions and later attempt to prosecute.

The action in the preceding example is legal unless the company crosses the line to entrapment. For example, suppose a web page has a link that indicates that if an individual clicks it, she could then download thousands of MP3 files for free. However, when she clicks that link, she is taken to the honeypot system instead, and the company records all of her actions and attempts to prosecute. Entrapment does not prove that the suspect had the intent to commit a crime; it only proves she was successfully tricked.

Interviewing and Interrogating

Once surveillance and search and seizure activities have been performed, it is very likely that suspects must be interviewed and interrogated. However, interviewing is both an art and a science, and the interview should be conducted by a properly trained professional. Even then, the interview may only be conducted after consultation with legal counsel. This doesn't, however, completely relieve you as an information security professional from responsibility during the interviewing process. You may be asked to provide input or observe an interview in order to clarify technical information that comes up in the course of questioning. When this is needed, there should be one person in charge of the interview or interrogation, with one or two others present. Both the topics of discussion and the questions should be prepared beforehand and asked in a systematic and calm fashion, because the purpose of an interrogation is to obtain evidence for a trial.

The employee interrogator should be in a position that is senior to the employee suspect. A vice president is not going to be very intimidated or willing to spill his guts to the mailroom clerk. The interrogation should be held in a private place, and the suspect should be relatively comfortable and at ease. If exhibits are going to be shown to the suspect, they should be shown one at a time, and otherwise kept in a folder. It is not necessary to read a person their rights before questioning unless law enforcement officers do the interrogation.

What the interrogators do not want to happen during an interrogation is to be deceived by the suspect, to relinquish important information pertaining to the investigation, or to have the suspect flee before a trial date is set.

A Few Different Attack Types

Several categories of computer crimes can be committed and different methods exist to commit those crimes. The following sections go over some of the types of computer fraud and abuses.

Salami

I will take a little bit of your salami, and another little bit of your salami, and a bit more of your salami, and no one will ever notice.

A *salami* attack is one in which the attacker commits several small crimes with the hope that the overall larger crime will go unnoticed. Salami attacks usually take place in the accounting departments of companies, and the most common example of a salami attack involves subtracting a small amount of funds from many accounts with the hope that such an insignificant amount would be overlooked. For example, a bank employee may alter a banking software program to subtract 5 cents from each of the bank's customers' accounts once a month and move this amount to the employee's bank account. If this happened to all of the bank's 50,000 customer accounts, the intruder could make up to $30,000 a year.

Data Diddling

Can I just diddle the data a little?
Response: Nope, it's illegal.

Data diddling refers to the alteration of existing data. Many times, this modification happens before the data is entered into an application or as soon as it completes processing and is outputted from an application. For instance, if a loan processor is entering information for a customer's loan of $100,000, but instead enters $150,000 and then moves the extra approved money somewhere else, this would be a case of data diddling. Another example is if a cashier enters an amount of $40 into the cash register, but really charges the customer $60 and keeps the extra $20.

There are many reasons to enter false information into a system or application, but the usual reason is to overstate revenue and assets and understate expenses and liabilities. Sometimes managers do this to deceive shareholders, creditors, superiors, and partners.

This type of crime is common and one of the easiest to prevent by using access and accounting controls, supervision, auditing, separation of duties, and authorization limits. This is just one example of how insiders can be more dangerous than outsiders.

Excessive Privileges

Excessive privileges is a common security issue that is extremely hard to control in vast and complex environments. It occurs when a user has more computer rights, permissions, and privileges than what is required for the tasks she needs to fulfill. If a user only needs to be able to read and print materials on the file server, she should not be granted full control. A common example of this is when a manager in accounting is granted full control of all files on a specific server, including payroll information. When this person is moved from accounting to the research department, his rights should be revoked or at least reduced, but most companies do not have procedures in place to make sure this happens. (This is referred to as authorization creep.) Now he has full control over the account records and the research records, and thus has excessive privileges. If he ever becomes disgruntled with the company for one reason or another, the company could have much more damage to deal with than if it had properly restricted his access.

Password Sniffing

I think I smell a password!

Password sniffing is just what it sounds like—sniffing network traffic with the hope of capturing passwords being sent between computers. Several tools are available on the Internet that provide this functionality. Capturing a password is tricky, because it is a piece of data that is usually only used when a user wants to authenticate into a domain or access a resource. Some systems and applications do send passwords over the network in cleartext, but a majority of them do not anymore. Instead, the user's workstation performs a one-way hashing function on the password and sends only the resulting value to the authenticating system or service. The authenticating system has a file containing all users' password hash values, not the passwords themselves, and when the authenticating system is asked to verify a user's password, it compares the hashing value sent to what it has in its file.

Many of the tools used to capture passwords can also break the encryption of the password. This is a common way for a computer crime to start.

IP Spoofing

I couldn't have carried out that attack. I have a different address!

Response: I'm not convinced.

Networks and the Internet use IP addresses like we use building numbers and street names to find our way from one place to another. Each computer is assigned an IP address so packets know where they came from and where they are going. However, many attackers do not want anyone to know their real location, so they either manually change the IP address within a packet to show a different address or, more commonly, use a tool that is programmed to provide this functionality for them. This type of activity is referred to as *IP spoofing*. Several attacks that take place use spoofed IP addresses, which give the victim little hope of finding the real system and individual who initiated the attack.

One reason that IP spoofing is so easily accomplished is that the protocol of the Internet, IP, was developed during a time when security was rarely considered. Back then, developers were much more focused on functionality, and probably could not have imagined all the various types of attacks that would be carried out using the protocols they developed.

NOTE Spoofing can be considered a masquerading attack. Masquerading is the act of trying to pretend to be someone else.

Dumpster Diving

I went through your garbage and found your Social Security number, credit card number, network schematics, mother's maiden name, and evidence that you wear funny underwear.

Dumpster diving refers to the concept of rummaging through a company or individual's garbage for discarded documents, information, and other precious items that could then be used in an attack against that company or person. The intruder would have to gain physical access to the premises, but the area where the garbage is kept is usually not highly guarded. Dumpster diving is unethical, but it's not illegal. Trespassing is illegal, however, and may be done in the process of dumpster diving. (Laws concerning this may vary in different states.)

Industrial spies can raid corporate dumpsters to find proprietary and confidential information. Credit card thieves can go through dumpsters to retrieve credit card information from discarded receipts.

Emanations Capturing

Do you think we should be worried about that white van in the parking lot with the huge antenna, large amount of power cords, and the pizzas continually being delivered to it?

Response: Nope.

Emanations, and the way attackers eavesdrop on them, are addressed in Chapter 4 in the "Tempest" section. Basically, every electrical device emits electrical waves into the surrounding environment. These waves contain information, comparable to how wireless technologies work. These waves can be carried over a distance, depending on the strength of the signals and the material and objects in the surrounding area. Attackers have used devices to capture these waves and port them to their own computer systems so they can access information not intended for them.

Attackers need to have specialized tools that tune into the frequency these waves are carried over. They also have to be within close proximity to the building that is emitting the waves. Companies that have information of such sensitive nature that attackers would go through this much trouble usually have special computer systems with shielding that permit only a small amount of electrical signals to be emitted. The companies can also use material within the walls of the building to stop these types of electrical waves from passing through them.

These types of attacks are usually the stuff of spy novels, with three guys in a service van full of high-grade technological devices in the parking lot of a company. However, a certain technology has caused this type of eavesdropping to happen without such spy-like activities: wireless networks. When a company installs a wireless network, certain configurations can be set to prevent outsiders from being able to eavesdrop on its employees' network traffic. Unfortunately, some companies do not employ these configurations for one reason or another. This enables anyone with a laptop and a wireless network interface card (NIC) to drive into a company's parking lot and eavesdrop on network traffic. (Wireless technology and its security ramifications are covered in Chapter 7.)

Wiretapping

Most communications signals are vulnerable to some type of wiretapping or eavesdropping. It can usually be done undetected and is referred to as a passive attack. Tools used to intercept communications include cellular scanners, radio receivers, microphone receivers, tape recorders, network sniffers, and telephone-tapping devices.

NOTE A passive attack is nonintrusive, as in eavesdropping or wiretapping. An active attack, on the other hand, is intrusive, as in DoS or penetration attacks.

It is illegal to intentionally eavesdrop on another person's conversation under many countries' existing wiretap laws. In many cases, this action is only acceptable if the person consents or there is a court order allowing law enforcement to perform these types of activities. Under the latter circumstances, the law enforcement officers must show probable cause to support their allegation that criminal activity is taking place and can only listen to relevant conversations. These requirements are in place to protect an individual's privacy rights.

Ethics

Just because something is not illegal does not make it right.

Ethics are based on many different issues and foundations. They can be relative to different situations and interpreted differently from individual to individual. Therefore, they are often a topic of debate. However, some ethics are less controversial than others, and these types of ethics are easier to expect of all people.

(ISC)^2 requires all certified system security professionals to commit to fully supporting its Code of Ethics. If a CISSP intentionally or knowingly violates this Code of Ethics, he or she may be subject to a peer review panel, which will decide whether the certification should be relinquished.

The full set of (ISC)^2 Code of Ethics for the CISSP is listed on the (ISC)^2 site at https://www.isc2.org/cgi-bin/content.cgi?category=12. The following list is an overview, but each CISSP candidate should read the full version and understand the Code of Ethics before attempting this exam:

- Act honorably, honestly, justly, responsibly, and legally, and protect society.
- Work diligently, provide competent services, and advance the security profession.
- Encourage the growth of research—teach, mentor, and value the certification.
- Discourage unnecessary fear or doubt, and do not consent to bad practices.
- Discourage unsafe practices, and preserve and strengthen the integrity of public infrastructures.

- Observe and abide by all contracts, expressed or implied, and give prudent advice.

- Avoid any conflict of interest, respect the trust that others put in you, and take on only those jobs you are fully qualified to perform.

- Stay current on skills, and do not become involved with activities that could injure the reputation of other security professionals.

An interesting relationship exists between law and ethics. Most often, laws are based on ethics and are put in place to ensure that others act in an ethical way. However, laws do not apply to everything—that is when ethics should kick in. Some things may not be illegal, but that does not necessarily mean they are ethical.

Corporations should have a guide developed on computer and business ethics. This can be part of an employee handbook, used in orientation, posted, and made a part of training sessions.

Certain common ethical fallacies are used by many in the computing world to justify their unethical acts. They exist because people look at issues differently and interpret (or misinterpret) rules and laws that have been put into place. The following are examples of these ethical fallacies:

- Hackers only want to learn and improve their skills. Many of them are not making a profit off of their deeds; therefore, their activities should not be seen as illegal or unethical.

- The First Amendment protects and provides the right for U.S. citizens to write viruses.

- Information should be shared freely and openly; therefore, sharing confidential information and trade secrets should be legal and ethical.

- Hacking does not actually hurt anyone.

The Computer Ethics Institute

The Computer Ethics Institute is a nonprofit organization that works to help advance technology by ethical means.

The Computer Ethics Institute has developed its own Ten Commandments of Computer Ethics:

1. Thou shalt not use a computer to harm other people.

2. Thou shalt not interfere with other people's computer work.

3. Thou shalt not snoop around in other people's computer files.

4. Thou shalt not use a computer to steal.

5. Thou shalt not use a computer to bear false witness.

6. Thou shalt not copy or use proprietary software for which you have not paid.

7. Thou shalt not use other people's computer resources without authorization or proper compensation.

8. Thou shalt not appropriate other people's intellectual output.

9. Thou shalt think about the social consequences of the program you are writing or the system you are designing.

10. Thou shalt always use a computer in ways that ensure consideration and respect for your fellow humans.

The Internet Architecture Board

The *Internet Architecture Board (IAB)* is the coordinating committee for Internet design, engineering, and management. It is responsible for the architectural oversight of the Internet Engineering Task Force (IETF) activities, Internet Standards Process oversight and appeal, and editor of Request for Comments (RFCs). Figure 10-3 illustrates the IAB's place in the hierarchy of entities that help ensure the structure and standardization of the Internet. Otherwise, the Internet would be an unusable big bowl of spaghetti and we would all still be writing letters and buying stamps.

The IAB issues ethics-related statements concerning the use of the Internet. It considers the Internet to be a resource that depends upon availability and accessibility to be useful to a wide range of people. It is mainly concerned with irresponsible acts on the Internet that could threaten its existence or negatively affect others. It sees the Internet as

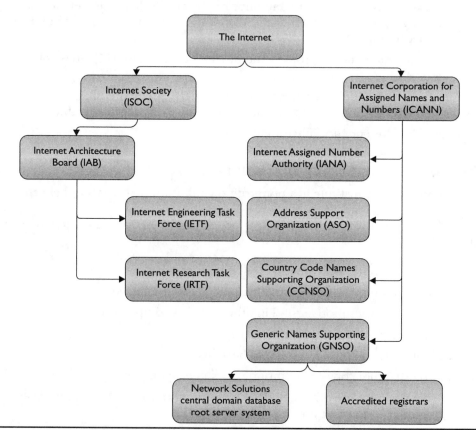

Figure 10-3 Agencies responsible for maintaining order for the components of the Internet

a great gift and works hard to protect it for all who depend upon it. The IAB sees the use of the Internet as a privilege, which should be treated as such and used with respect.

The IAB considers the following acts as unethical and unacceptable behavior:

- Purposely seeking to gain unauthorized access to Internet resources
- Disrupting the intended use of the Internet
- Wasting resources (people, capacity, and computers) through purposeful actions
- Destroying the integrity of computer-based information
- Compromising the privacy of others
- Conducting Internet-wide experiments in a negligent manner

The IAB vows to work with federal agencies to take whatever actions are necessary to protect the Internet. This could be through new technologies, methods, or procedures that are intended to make the Internet more resistant to disruption. A balance exists between enhancing protection and reducing functionality. One of the Internet's main purposes is to enable information to flow freely and not be prohibited; thus, the IAB must be logical and flexible in its approaches, and in the restrictions it attempts to implement. The Internet is everyone's tool, so everyone should work together to protect it.

NOTE RFC 1087 is called "Ethics and the Internet." This RFC outlines the concepts pertaining to what the IAB considers unethical and unacceptable behavior.

Corporate Ethics Programs

More regulations are requiring organizations to have an ethical statement and potentially an ethical program in place. This has been brought on by a lot of slimy things that have taken place in the past that were known about and encouraged by executive management, even if they don't admit it. The ethical program is to serve as the "tone at the top," which means that the executives need to not only ensure that their employees are acting ethically, but that they themselves are following their own rules. The main goal is to ensure that the motto "succeed by any means necessary" is not the spoken or unspoken culture of a work environment. Certain structures can be put into place that provide a breeding ground for unethical behavior. If the CEO gets more in salary based on stock prices, then he may find ways to artificially inflate stock prices, which can directly hurt the investors and shareholders of the company. If managers can only be promoted based on the amount of sales they bring in, these numbers may be fudged and not represent reality. If an employee can only get a bonus if a low budget is maintained, he might be willing to take shortcuts that could hurt company customer service or product development. Although ethics seem like things that float around in the ether and make us feel good to talk about, they have to be actually implemented in the real corporate world through proper business processes and management styles.

The *Federal Sentencing Guidelines for Organizations (FSGO)* created an outline for ethical requirements, and in some cases will reduce the criminal sentencing and liability if ethical programs are put in place. This was updated with requirements that made it much more important for the senior executives and board members of an organization to actively participate and be aware of the ethics program in an organization. The intent is to enforce and foster a sense of due diligence that will detect criminal activity as well as protect against it and deter it from happening. Aspects of the Sarbanes-Oxley Act of 2002 are intended to function in much the same manner but with regard to accounting and truthfulness in corporate reporting.

Summary

Law, ethics, and investigations are very important parts of computer and information security. They are elements that do not usually come to mind when one speaks of information security, but they are a must if a society is serious about controlling this type of crime and punishing the guilty.

In many ways, the laws and courts are in their infancy stages when attempting to deal with computer crimes. They are faced with not having many precedents to fall back on when interpreting what is legal and illegal and what the proper punishments are for each type of computer crime. However, the legal system is quickly developing laws and providing ways to properly interpret them to help all law enforcement agencies and the victims. Over the last few years, hacking and attacking have been performed for fun, mainly by curious computer individuals, but as the punishments increase, such fun may quickly come to an end.

Security professionals should be aware of, and be well versed in, computer security laws and regulations that apply in their environments. They should be able to properly inform their management and customers of expected responsibilities, as well as know what boundaries they are expected to work within themselves.

Quick Tips

- Dumpster diving refers to going through someone's trash to find confidential or useful information. It is legal, unless it involves trespassing, but in all cases it is considered unethical.
- Wiretapping is a passive attack that eavesdrops on communications. It is only legal with prior consent or a warrant.
- Social engineering is the act of tricking or deceiving a person into giving confidential or sensitive information that could then be used against him or his company.
- Civil Law System
    - Uses prewritten rules and is not based on precedence
    - Is different from civil (tort) laws, which work under a common law system
- Common Law System
    - Made up of criminal, civil, and administrative laws

- Customary Law System
  - Addresses mainly personal conduct, and uses regional traditions and customs as the foundations of the laws
  - Is usually mixed with another type of listed legal system rather than being the sole legal system used in a region
- Religious Law System
  - Laws are derived from religious beliefs and address an individual's religious responsibilities; commonly used in Muslim countries or regions.
- Mixed Law System
  - Using two or more legal systems
- Data diddling is the act of willfully modifying information, programs, or documentation in an effort to commit fraud or disrupt production.
- Excessive privileges means an employee has more rights than necessary to complete her tasks.
- Criminal law deals with an individual's conduct that violates government laws developed to protect the public.
- Civil law deals with wrongs committed against individuals or companies that result in injury or damages. Civil law does not use prison time as a punishment, but usually requires financial restitution.
- Administrative, or regulatory, law covers standards of performance or conduct expected by government agencies from companies, industries, and certain officials.
- A patent grants ownership and enables that owner to legally enforce his rights to exclude others from using the invention covered by the patent.
- Copyright protects the expression of ideas rather than the ideas themselves.
- Trademarks protect words, names, product shapes, symbols, colors, or a combination of these used to identify products or a company. These items are used to distinguish products from the competitors' products.
- Trade secrets are deemed proprietary to a company and often include information that provides a competitive edge. The information is protected as long as the owner takes the necessary protective actions.
- Crime over the Internet has brought about jurisdiction problems for law enforcement and the courts.
- Privacy laws dictate that data collected by government agencies must be collected fairly and lawfully, must be used only for the purpose for which they were collected, must only be held for a reasonable amount of time, and must be accurate and timely.
- If companies are going to use any type of monitoring, they need to make sure it is legal in their business sector and must inform all employees that they may be subjected to monitoring.

- Employees need to be informed regarding what is expected behavior pertaining to the use of the company's computer systems, network, e-mail system, and phone system. They need to also know what the ramifications are for not meeting those expectations. These requirements are usually communicated through policies.

- Logon banners should be used to inform users of what could happen if they do not follow the rules pertaining to using company resources. This provides legal protection for the company.

- Countries differ in their view of the seriousness of computer crime and have different penalties for certain crimes. This makes enforcing laws much harder across country borders.

- The three main types of harm addressed in computer crime laws pertain to unauthorized intrusion, unauthorized alteration or destruction, and using malicious code.

- Law enforcement and the courts have a hard time with computer crimes because of the newness of the types of crimes, the complexity involved, jurisdictional issues, and evidence collection. New laws are being written to properly deal with cybercrime.

- If a company does not practice due care in its efforts to protect itself from computer crime, it can be found to be negligent and legally liable for damages.

- Elements of negligence include not fulfilling a legally recognized obligation, failure to conform to a standard of care that results in injury or damage, and proximate causation.

- Most computer crimes are not reported because the victims are not aware of the crime or are too embarrassed to let anyone else know.

- Theft is no longer restricted to physical constraints. Assets are now also viewed as intangible objects that can also be stolen or disclosed via technological means.

- The primary reason for the chain of custody of evidence is to ensure that it will be admissible in court by showing it was properly controlled and handled before being presented in court.

- Companies should develop their own incident response team, which is made up of people from management, IT, legal, human resources, public relations, security, and other key areas of the organization.

- Hearsay evidence is secondhand and usually not admissible in court.

- To be admissible in court, business records have to be made and collected in the normal course of business, not specially generated for a case in court. Business records can easily be hearsay if there is no firsthand proof of their accuracy and reliability.

- The life cycle of evidence includes the identification and collection of the evidence, and its storage, preservation, transportation, presentation in court, and return to the owner.

- Collection of computer evidence is a very complex and detail-oriented task. Only skilled people should attempt it; otherwise, evidence can be ruined forever.

- When looking for suspects, it is important to consider the motive, opportunity, and means (MOM).

- For evidence to be admissible in court, it needs to be relevant, sufficient, and reliable.

- Evidence must be legally permissible, meaning it was seized legally and the chain of custody was not broken.

- In many jurisdictions, law enforcement agencies must obtain a warrant to search and seize an individual's property, as stated in the Fourth Amendment. Private citizens are not required to protect the Fourth Amendment rights of others unless acting as a police agent.

- Enticement is the act of luring an intruder and is legal. Entrapment induces a crime, tricks a person, and is illegal.

- The salami attack is executed by carrying out smaller crimes with the hope that the larger crime will not be noticed. The common salami attack is the act of skimming off a small amount of money.

- After a computer system is seized, the investigators should make a bit mirror image copy of the storage media before doing anything else.

Questions

Please remember that these questions are formatted and asked in a certain way for a reason. Keep in mind that the CISSP exam is asking questions at a conceptual level. Questions may not always have the perfect answer, and the candidate is advised against always looking for the perfect answer. Instead, the candidate should look for the best answer in the list.

1. Which of the following does the IAB consider unethical?

    A. Creating a computer virus

    B. Entering information into a web page

    C. Performing a penetration test on a host on the Internet

    D. Disrupting Internet communications

2. What is the study of computers and surrounding technologies and how they relate to crime?

    A. Computer forensics

    B. Computer vulnerability analysis

    C. Incident handling

    D. Computer information criteria

3. Which of the following does the IAB consider unethical behavior?

    A. Internet users who conceal unauthorized accesses

    B. Internet users who waste computer resources

    C. Internet users who write viruses

    D. Internet users who monitor traffic

4. After a computer forensics investigator seizes a computer during a crime investigation, what is the next step?

    A. Label and put it into a container, and then label the container.

    B. Dust the evidence for fingerprints.

    C. Make an image copy of the disks.

    D. Lock the evidence in the safe.

5. A CISSP candidate signs an ethics statement prior to taking the CISSP examination. Which of the following would be a violation of the (ISC)² Code of Ethics that could cause the candidate to lose his or her certification?

    A. E-mailing information or comments about the exam to other CISSP candidates

    B. Submitting comments on the questions of the exam to (ISC)²

    C. Submitting comments to the board of directors regarding the test and content of the class

    D. Conducting a presentation about the CISSP certification and what the certification means

6. If your company gives you a new PC and you find residual information about confidential company issues, what should you do based on the (ISC)² Code of Ethics?

    A. Contact the owner of the file and inform him about it. Copy it to a disk, give it to him, and delete your copy.

    B. Delete the document because it was not meant for you.

    C. Inform management of your findings so it can make sure this type of thing does not happen again.

    D. E-mail it to both the author and management so everyone is aware of what is going on.

7. Why is it difficult to investigate computer crime and track down the criminal?

    A. Privacy laws are written to protect people from being investigated for these types of crimes.

    B. Special equipment and tools are necessary to detect these types of criminals.

    C. Criminals can hide their identity and hop from one network to the next.

    D. The police have no jurisdiction over the Internet.

8. Protecting evidence and providing accountability for who handled it at different steps during the investigation is referred to as what?

   A. The rule of best evidence

   B. Hearsay

   C. Evidence safety

   D. Chain of custody

9. If an investigator needs to communicate with another investigator but does not want the criminal to be able to eavesdrop on this conversation, what type of communication should be used?

   A. Digitally signed messages

   B. Out-of-band messages

   C. Forensics frequency

   D. Authentication and access control

10. Why is it challenging to collect and identify computer evidence to be used in a court of law?

   A. The evidence is mostly intangible.

   B. The evidence is mostly corrupted.

   C. The evidence is mostly encrypted.

   D. The evidence is mostly tangible.

11. The chain of custody of evidence describes who obtained the evidence and
_____.

   A. Who secured it and stole it

   B. Who controlled it and broke it

   C. Who secured it and validated it

   D. Who controlled it and duplicated it

12. Before shutting down a system suspected of an attack, the investigator should do what?

   A. Remove and back up the hard drive

   B. Dump memory contents to disk

   C. Remove it from the network

   D. Save data in the spooler queue and temporary files

13. Why is computer-generated documentation usually considered unreliable evidence?

   A. It is primary evidence.

   B. It is too difficult to detect prior modifications.

   C. It is corroborative evidence.

   D. It is not covered under criminal law, but it *is* covered under civil law.

14. Which of the following is a necessary characteristic of evidence for it to be admissible?

   A. It must be real.

   B. It must be noteworthy.

   C. It must be reliable.

   D. It must be important.

15. In the United States, what agency usually works with the FBI when investigating computer crimes?

   A. (ISC)²

   B. The Secret Service

   C. The CIA

   D. The state police

16. If a company deliberately planted a flaw in one of its systems in the hope of detecting an attempted penetration and exploitation of this flaw, what would this be called?

   A. Incident recovery response

   B. Entrapment

   C. Illegal

   D. Enticement

17. If an employee is suspected of wrongdoing in a computer crime, what department must be involved?

   A. Human resources

   B. Legal

   C. Audit

   D. Payroll

18. When would an investigator's notebook be admissible in court?

   A. When he uses it to refresh memory

   B. When he cannot be present for testimony

   C. When requested by the judge to learn the original issues of the investigations

   D. When no other physical evidence is available

19. Disks and other media that are copies of the original evidence are considered what?

   A. Primary evidence

   B. Reliable and sufficient evidence

   C. Hearsay evidence

   D. Conclusive evidence

20. If a company does not inform employees that they may be monitored and does not have a policy stating how monitoring should take place, what should a company do?

    A. Don't monitor employees in any fashion.

    B. Monitor during off-hours and slow times.

    C. Obtain a search warrant before monitoring an employee.

    D. Monitor anyway—they are covered by two laws allowing them to do this.

21. What is one reason why successfully prosecuting computer crimes is so challenging?

    A. There is no way to capture electrical data reliably.

    B. The evidence in computer cases does not follow best evidence directives.

    C. These crimes do not always fall into the traditional criminal activity categories.

    D. Wiretapping is hard to do legally.

22. When can executives be charged with negligence?

    A. If they follow the transborder laws

    B. If they do not properly report and prosecute attackers

    C. If they properly inform users that they may be monitored

    D. If they do not practice due care when protecting resources

23. To better deal with computer crime, several legislative bodies have taken what steps in their strategy?

    A. Expanded several privacy laws

    B. Broadened the definition of property to include data

    C. Required corporations to have computer crime insurance

    D. Redefined transborder issues

24. Many privacy laws dictate which of the following rules?

    A. Individuals have a right to remove any data they do not want others to know.

    B. Agencies do not need to ensure that the data is accurate.

    C. Agencies need to allow all government agencies access to the data.

    D. Agencies cannot use collected data for a purpose different from what it was collected for.

25. Which of the following is not true about dumpster diving?

    A. It is legal.

    B. It is illegal.

    C. It is a breach of physical security.

    D. It is gathering data from places people would not expect to be raided.

Answers

1. **D.** The Internet Architecture Board (IAB) is a committee for Internet design, engineering, and management. It considers the use of the Internet to be a privilege that should be treated as such. The IAB considers the following acts unethical and unacceptable behavior:

   - Purposely seeking to gain unauthorized access to Internet resources
   - Disrupting the intended use of the Internet
   - Wasting resources (people, capacity, and computers) through purposeful actions
   - Destroying the integrity of computer-based information
   - Compromising the privacy of others
   - Negligence in the conduct of Internet-wide experiments

2. **A.** Computer forensics is a field that specializes in understanding and properly extracting evidence from computers and peripheral devices for the purpose of prosecution. Collecting this type of evidence requires a skill set and understanding of several relative laws.

3. **B.** This question is similar to question 1. The IAB has declared wasting computer resources through purposeful activities unethical because it sees these resources as assets that are to be available for the computing society.

4. **C.** Several steps need to be followed when gathering and extracting evidence from a scene. Once a computer has been confiscated, the first thing the computer forensics team should do is make an image of the hard drive. The team will work from this image instead of the original hard drive so it stays in a pristine state and the evidence on the drive is not accidentally corrupted or modified.

5. **A.** A CISSP candidate and a CISSP holder should never discuss with others what was on the exam. This degrades the usefulness of the exam to be used as a tool to test someone's true security knowledge. If this type of activity is uncovered, the person could be stripped of their CISSP certification.

6. **C.** When dealing with the possible compromise of confidential company information or intellectual property, management should be informed and be involved as soon as possible. Management members are the ones who are ultimately responsible for this data and who understand the damage its leakage can cause. An employee should not attempt to address and deal with these issues on his own.

7. **C.** Spoofing one's identity and being able to traverse anonymously through different networks and the Internet increase the complexity and difficulty of tracking down criminals who carry out computer crimes. It is very easy to commit many damaging crimes from across the country or world, and this type of activity can be difficult for law enforcement to track down.

8. **D.** Properly following the chain of custody for evidence is crucial for it to be admissible in court. A chain of custody is a history that shows how evidence was collected, analyzed, transported, and preserved in order to establish that it is sufficiently trustworthy to be presented as evidence in court. Because electronic evidence can be easily modified, a clearly defined chain of custody demonstrates that the evidence is trustworthy.

9. **B.** Out-of-band communication means to communicate through some other type of communication channel. For example, if law enforcement agents are investigating a crime on a network, they should not share information through e-mail that passes along this network. The criminal may still have sniffers installed and thus be able to access this data.

10. **A.** The evidence in computer crimes usually comes straight from computers themselves. This means the data are held as electronic voltages, which are represented as binary bits. Some data can be held on hard drives and peripheral devices, and some data may be held in the memory of the system itself. This type of evidence is intangible in that it is not made up of objects one can hold, see, and easily understand. Other types of crimes usually have evidence that is more tangible in nature, and which is easier to handle and control.

11. **C.** The chain of custody outlines a process to ensure that under no circumstance was there a possibility for the evidence to be tampered with. If the chain of custody is broken, there is a high probability that the evidence will not be admissible in court. If it is admitted, it will not carry as much weight.

12. **B.** If the computer was actually attacked or involved in a computer crime, there is a good possibility that useful information could still reside in memory. Specific tools can be used to actually dump this information and save it for analysis before the power is removed.

13. **B.** It can be very difficult to determine if computer-generated material has been modified before it is presented in court. Since this type of evidence can be altered without being detected, the court cannot put a lot of weight on this evidence. Many times, computer-generated evidence is considered hearsay in that there is no firsthand proof backing it up.

14. **C.** For evidence to be admissible, it must be sufficient, reliable, and relevant to the case. For evidence to be reliable, it must be consistent with fact and must not be based on opinion or be circumstantial.

15. **B.** The FBI and Secret Service are both responsible for investigating computer crimes. They have their own jurisdictions and rules outlining who investigates which types of crimes.

16. **D.** Companies need to be very careful about the items they use to entice intruders and attackers, because this may be seen as entrapment by the court. It is best to get the legal department involved before implementing these items. Putting a honeypot in place is usually seen as the use of enticement tools.

17. **A.** It is imperative that the company gets human resources involved if an employee is considered a suspect in a computer crime. This department knows the laws and regulations pertaining to employee treatment and can work to protect the employee and the company at the same time.

18. **A.** Notes that are taken by an investigator will, in most cases, not be admissible in court as evidence. This is not seen as reliable information and can only be used by the investigator to help him remember activities during the investigation.

19. **C.** In most cases, computer-related evidence falls under the hearsay category, because it is seen as copies of the original data that are held in the computer itself and can be modified without any indication. Evidence is considered hearsay when there is no firsthand proof in place to validate it.

20. **A.** Before a company can monitor its employees, it is supposed to inform them that this type of activity can take place. If a company monitors an employee without telling him, this could be seen as an invasion of privacy. The employee had an expected level of privacy that was invaded. The company should implement monitoring capabilities into its security policy and employee security-awareness programs.

21. **C.** We have an infrastructure set up to investigate and prosecute crimes: law enforcement, laws, lawyers, courts, juries, judges, and so on. This infrastructure has a long history of prosecuting "traditional" crimes. Only in the last ten years or so have computer crimes been prosecuted more regularly; thus, these types of crimes are not fully rooted in the legal system with all of the necessary and useful precedents.

22. **D.** Executives are held to a certain standard and are expected to act responsibly when running and protecting a company. These standards and expectations equate to the due care concept under the law. Due care means to carry out activities that a reasonable person would be expected to carry out in the same situation. If an executive acts irresponsibly in any way, she can be seen as not practicing due care and be held negligent.

23. **B.** Many times, what is corrupted, compromised, or taken from a computer is data, so current laws have been updated to include the protection of intangible assets, as in data. Over the years, data and information have become many companies' most valuable asset, which must be protected by the laws.

24. **D.** The Federal Privacy Act of 1974 and the European Union Principles on Privacy were created to protect citizens from government agencies that collect personal data. These acts have many stipulations, including that the information can only be used for the reason for which it was collected.

25. **B.** Dumpster diving is the act of going through someone's trash with the hope of uncovering useful information. Dumpster diving is legal if it does not involve trespassing, but it is unethical.

Application Security

This chapter presents the following:

- Various types of software controls and implementation
- Database concepts and security issues
- Data warehousing and data mining
- Software life-cycle development processes
- Change control concepts
- Object-oriented programming components
- Expert systems and artificial intelligence

Applications and computer systems are usually developed for functionality first, not security first. To get the best of both worlds, security and functionality would have to be designed and developed at the same time. Security should be interwoven into the core of a product and provide protection at different layers. This is a better approach than trying to develop a front end or wrapper that may reduce the overall functionality and leave security holes when the product has to be integrated with other applications.

Software's Importance

Application system controls come in various flavors with many different goals. They can control input, processing, number-crunching methods, interprocess communication, access, output, and interfacing to the system and other programs. They should be developed with potential risks in mind, and many types of threat models and risk analyses should be invoked at different stages of development. The goal is to prevent security compromises and to reduce vulnerabilities and the possibility of data corruption. The controls can be preventive, detective, or corrective. They can come in the form of administrative and physical controls, but are usually more technical in this context.

The specific application controls depend upon the application itself, its objectives, the security goals of the application security policy, the type of data and processing it is to carry out, and the environment the application will be placed in. If an application is purely proprietary and will run only in closed trusted environments, fewer security controls may be needed than those required for applications that will connect businesses over the Internet and provide financial transactions. The trick is to understand the security needs of an application, implement the right controls and mechanisms, thoroughly test the mechanisms and how they integrate into the application, follow structured development methodologies, and provide secure and reliable distribution methods. Seems easy as 1-2-3, right? Nope, the development of a secure application or operating system is very complex and should only be attempted if you have a never-ending supply of coffee, are mentally and physically stable, and have no social life. (This is why we don't have many secure applications.)

Where Do We Place the Security?

"I put mine in my shoe."

Today, many security efforts look to solve security problems through controls such as firewalls, intrusion detection systems (IDSs), sensors, content filtering, antivirus software, vulnerability scanners, and much more. This reliance on a long laundry list of controls occurs mainly because our software contains many vulnerabilities. Our environments are commonly referred to as hard and crunchy on the outside and soft and chewy on the inside. This means our perimeter security is fortified and solid, but our internal environment and software are easy to exploit once access has been obtained.

In reality, the flaws within the software cause a majority of the vulnerabilities in the first place. Several reasons explain why perimeter devices are more often considered than software development for security:

- In the past, it was not crucial to implement security during the software development stages; thus, many programmers today do not practice these procedures.
- Most security professionals are usually not software developers.
- Many software developers do not have security as a main focus
- Software vendors are trying to rush their products to market with their eyes set on functionality, not security.
- The computing community is used to receiving software with bugs and then applying patches.
- Customers cannot control the flaws in the software they purchase, so they must depend upon perimeter protection.

Finger-pointing and quick judgments are neither useful nor necessarily fair at this stage of our computing evolution. Twenty years ago, mainframes did not require much security because only a handful of people knew how to run them, users worked on computers (dumb terminals) that could not introduce malicious code to the mainframe, and environments were closed. The core protocols and framework were developed at a time when threats and attacks were not prevalent. Such stringent security wasn't needed. Then, computer and software evolution took off, and the possibilities splintered into a thousand different directions. The high demand for computer technology and different types of software increased the demand for programmers, system designers, administrators, and engineers. This demand brought in a wave of people who had little experience. Thus, the lack of experience, the high change rate of technology, and the race to market added problems to security measures that are not always clearly understood.

Although it is easy to blame the big software vendors in the sky for producing flawed or buggy software, this is driven by customer demand. For at least a decade, and even today, we have been demanding more and more functionality from software vendors. The software vendors have done a wonderful job in providing these perceived necessities. It has been in the last seven or so years that customers started to also demand security. Our programmers were not properly educated in secure coding, operating systems and applications were not built on secure architectures from the beginning, our software development procedures have not been security oriented, and integrating security as an afterthought makes the process all the clumsier and more costly. So although software vendors should be doing a better job providing us with secure products, we should also understand that this is a relatively new requirement and there is much more complexity when you peek under the covers than most consumers can even comprehend.

This chapter is an attempt to show how to address security at its source, which is at the software and development level. This requires a shift from *reactive* to *proactive* actions toward security problems to ensure they do not happen in the first place, or at least happen to a smaller extent. Figure 11-1 illustrates our current way of dealing with security issues.

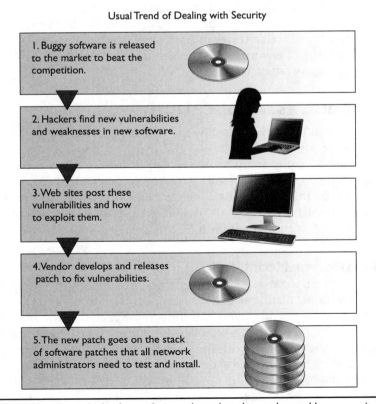

Usual Trend of Dealing with Security

1. Buggy software is released to the market to beat the competition.

2. Hackers find new vulnerabilities and weaknesses in new software.

3. Web sites post these vulnerabilities and how to exploit them.

4. Vendor develops and releases patch to fix vulnerabilities.

5. The new patch goes on the stack of software patches that all network administrators need to test and install.

Figure 11-1   The usual trend of software being released to the market and how security is dealt with

Different Environments Demand Different Security

I demand total and complete security in each and every one of my applications!
Response: Well, don't hold your breath on that one.

Today, network and security administrators are in an overwhelming position of having to integrate different applications and computer systems to keep up with their company's demand for expandable functionality and the new gee-whiz components that executives buy into and demand quick implementation of. This integration is further frustrated by the company's race to provide a well-known presence on the Internet by implementing web sites with the capabilities of taking online orders, storing credit card information, and setting up extranets with partners. This can quickly turn into a confusing ball of protocols, devices, interfaces, incompatibility issues, routing and switching techniques, telecommunications routines, and management procedures—all in all, a big enough headache to make an administrator buy some land in Montana and go raise goats instead.

On top of this, security is expected, required, and depended upon. When security compromises creep in, the finger-pointing starts, liability issues are tossed like hot potatoes, and people might even lose their jobs. An understanding of the environment, what is currently in it, and how it works is required so these new technologies can be implemented in a more controlled and comprehendible fashion.

The days of developing a simple web page and posting it on the Internet to illustrate your products and services are long gone. Today, the customer front end, complex middleware, and three-tiered architectures must be developed and work seamlessly. As the complexity of this type of environment grows, tracking down errors and security compromises becomes an awesome task.

Environment vs. Application

Software controls can be implemented by the operating system, by the application, or through database management controls—and usually a combination of all three is used. Each has its strengths and weaknesses, but if they are all understood and programmed to work in a concerted effort, then many different scenarios and types of compromises can be thwarted. One downside to relying mainly on operating system controls is that although they can control a subject's access to different objects and restrict the actions of that subject within the system, they do not necessarily restrict the

---

The Client/Server Model

Basically, the client/server architecture enables an application system to be divided across multiple platforms that vary in operating systems and hardware. The client requests services and the server fulfills these requests. The server handles the data-processing services and provides the processed result to the client. The client performs the front-end portion of an application, and the server performs the back-end portion, which is usually more labor intensive.

The front end usually includes the user interface and local data-manipulation capabilities, and provides the communications mechanisms that can request services from the server portion of the application.

subject's actions within an application. If an application has a security compromise within its own programming code, it is hard for the operating system to predict and control this vulnerability. An operating system is a broad environment for many applications to work within. It is unfair to expect the operating system to understand all the nuances of different programs and their internal mechanisms.

On the other hand, application controls and database management controls are very specific to their needs and in the security compromises they understand. Although an application might be able to protect data by allowing only certain types of input and not permitting certain users to view data kept in sensitive database fields, it cannot prevent the user from inserting bogus data into the Address Resolution Protocol (ARP) table—this is the responsibility of the operating system and its network stack. Operating system and application controls have their place and limitations. The trick is to find out where one type of control stops so the next type of control can be configured to kick into action.

Security has been mainly provided by security products and perimeter devices rather than controls built into applications. The security products can cover a wide range of applications, can be controlled by a centralized management console, and are further away from application control. However, this approach does not always provide the necessary level of granularity, and does not approach compromises that can take place because of problematic coding and programming routines. Firewalls and access control mechanisms can provide a level of protection by preventing attackers from gaining access to be able to exploit buffer overflows, but the real protection happens at the core of the problem—proper software development and coding practices must be in place.

Complexity of Functionality

Programming is a complex trade—the code itself, routine interaction, global and local variables, input received from other programs, output fed to different applications, attempts to envision future user inputs, calculations, and restrictions form a long list of possible negative security consequences. Many times, trying to account for all the what-ifs and programming on the side of caution can reduce the overall functionality of the application. As you limit the functionality and scope of an application, the market share and potential profitability of that program could be reduced. A balancing act always exists between functionality and security, and in the development world, functionality is usually deemed the most important.

So, programmers and application architects need to find a happy medium between the necessary functionality of the program, the security requirements, and the mechanisms that should be implemented to provide this security. This can add more complexity to an already complex task.

More than one road may lead to enlightenment, but as these roads increase in number, it is hard to know if a path will eventually lead you to bliss or to fiery doom in the underworld. Many programs accept data from different parts of the program, other programs, the system itself, and user input. Each of these paths must be followed in a methodical way, and each possible scenario and input must be thought through and tested to provide a deep level of assurance. It is important that each module be capable of being tested individually and in concert with other modules. This level of understanding and testing will make the product more secure by catching flaws that could be exploited.

Data Types, Format, and Length

I would like my data to be in a small pink rectangle that I can fit in my pocket.
Response: You didn't take your medication today, did you?

We have all heard about the vulnerabilities pertaining to buffer overflows, as if they were new to the programming world. They are not new, but they *are* being exploited nowadays on a recurring basis.

Buffer overflows were discussed in Chapter 5, which explained that attacks are carried out when the software code does not check the length of input that is actually being accepted. Extra instructions could be executed in a privileged mode that would enable an attacker to take control of the system. If a programmer wrote a program that expected the input length to be 5KB, then this needs to be part of the code so the right amount of buffer space is available to hold these data when they actually come in. However, if that program does not make sure the 5KB is accepted—and *only* that 5KB is accepted—an evildoer can input the first 5KB for the expected data to process, and then another 50KB containing malicious instructions can also be processed by the CPU.

Length is not the only thing programmers need to be worried about when it comes to accepting input data. Data also needs to be in the right format and data type. If the program is expecting alpha ASCII characters, it should not accept hexadecimal or UNICODE values.

The accepted value also needs to be reasonable. This means that if an application asks Stacy to enter the amount she would like to transfer from her checking account to her savings account, she should not be able to enter "Bob." This means the data accepted by the program must be in the correct format (numbers versus alphabet characters), but procedures also need to be in place to watch for bogus entries so errors can be stopped at their origin instead of being passed to calculations and logic procedures.

These examples are extremely simplistic compared with what programmers have to face in the real programming world. However, they are presented to show that software needs to be developed to accept the correct data types, format, and length of input data for security and functionality purposes.

Implementation and Default Issues

If I have not said "yes," then the answer is "no."

As many people in the computer field know, out-of-the-box implementations are usually far from secure. Most security has to be configured and turned on after installation—not being aware of this can be dangerous for the inexperienced security person. Windows NT has received its share of criticism for lack of security, but the platform can be secured in many ways. It just comes out of the box in an insecure state, because settings have to be configured to properly integrate into different environments, and this is a friendlier way of installing the product for users. For example, if Mike is installing a new software package that continually throws messages of "Access Denied" when he is attempting to configure it to interoperate with other applications and systems, his patience might wear thin, and he might decide to hate that vendor for years to come because of the stress and confusion inflicted upon him.

Yet again, we are at a hard place for developers and architects. When a security application or device is installed, it should default to "No Access." This means that when Laurel installs a packet-filter firewall, it should not allow any packets to pass into the network that were not specifically granted access. However, this requires Laurel to know how to configure the firewall for it to ever be useful. A fine balance exists between security, functionality, and user-friendliness. If an application is extremely user-friendly, it is probably not as secure. For an application to be user-friendly, it usually requires a lot of extra coding for potential user errors, dialog boxes, wizards, and step-by-step instructions. This extra coding can result in bloated code that can create unforeseeable compromises. So vendors have a hard time winning, but they usually keep making money while trying.

 NOTE   Later versions of Windows have services turned off and require the user to turn them on as needed. This is a step closer to "default with no access," but we still have a ways to go.

Implementation errors and misconfigurations are common issues that cause a majority of the security issues in networked environments. Many people do not realize that various services are enabled when a system is installed. These services can provide evildoers with information that can be used during an attack. Many services provide an actual way into the environment itself. NetBIOS services can be enabled to permit sharing resources in Windows environments, and Telnet services, which let remote users run command shells, and other services can be enabled with no restrictions. Many systems have File Transfer Protocol (FTP), SNMP, and Internet Relay Chat (IRC) services enabled that are not being used and have no real safety measures in place. Some of these services are enabled by default, so when an administrator installs an operating system and does not check these services to properly restrict or disable them, they are available for attackers to uncover and use.

Because vendors have user-friendliness and user functionality in mind, the product will usually be installed with defaults that provide no, or very little, security protection. It would be very hard for vendors to know the security levels required in all the environments the product will be installed in, so they usually do not attempt it. It is up to the person installing the product to learn how to properly configure the settings to achieve the necessary level of protection.

Another problem in implementation and security is the number of unpatched systems. Once security issues are identified, vendors develop patches or updates to address and fix these security holes. However, these often do not get installed on the systems that are vulnerable. The reasons for this vary: administrators may not keep up to date on the recent security vulnerabilities and patches, they may not fully understand the importance of these patches, or they may be afraid the patches will cause other problems. All of these reasons are quite common, but they all have the same result—insecure systems. Many vulnerabilities that are exploited today have had patches developed and released months or years ago.

It is unfortunate that adding security (or service) patches can adversely affect other mechanisms within the system. The patches should be tested for these types of activities before they are applied to production servers and workstations, to help prevent service disruptions that can affect network and employee productivity.

Failure States

Many circumstances are unpredictable and are therefore hard to plan for. However, unpredictable situations can be planned for in a general sense, instead of trying to plan and code for every situation. If an application fails for any reason, it should return to a safe and more secure state. This could require the operating system to restart and present the user with a logon screen to start the operating system from its initialization state. This is why some systems "blue-screen" and/or restart. When this occurs, something is going on within the system that is unrecognized or unsafe, so the system dumps its memory contents and starts all over.

Different system states were discussed in Chapter 5, which described how processes can be executed in a privileged or user mode. If an application fails and is executing in a privileged state, these processes should be shut down properly and released to ensure that disrupting a system does not provide compromises that could be exploited. If a privileged process does not shut down properly and instead stays active, an attacker can figure out how to access the system, using this process, in a privileged state. This means the attacker could have administrative or root access to a system, which opens the door for more severe destruction.

Database Management

From now on I am going to manage the database with ESP.
Response: Well, your crystals, triangles, and tarot cards aren't working.

Databases have a long history of storing important intellectual property and items that are considered valuable and proprietary to companies. Because of this, they usually live in an environment of mystery to all but the database and network administrators. The less anyone knows about the databases, the better. Users generally access databases indirectly through a client interface, and their actions are restricted to ensure the confidentiality, integrity, and availability of the data held within the database and the structure of the database itself.

 NOTE A database management system (DBMS) is a suite of programs used to manage large sets of structured data with ad hoc query capabilities for many types of users. These can also control the security parameters of the database.

The risks are increasing as companies run to connect their networks to the Internet, allow remote user access, and provide more and more access to external entities. A large risk to understand is that these activities can allow indirect access to a back-end database. In the past, employees accessed customer information held in databases instead of customers accessing it themselves. Today, many companies allow their customers to access data in their databases through a browser. The browser makes a connection to the company's middleware, which then connects them to the back-end database. This adds levels of complexity, and the database will be accessed in new and unprecedented ways.

One example is in the banking world, where online banking is all the rage. Many financial institutions want to keep up with the times and add the services they think their customers will want. But online banking is not just another service like being able to order checks. Most banks work in closed (or semiclosed) environments, and opening their environments to the Internet is a huge undertaking. The perimeter network needs to be secured, middleware software has to be developed or purchased, and the database should be behind one, preferably two, firewalls. Many times, components in the business application tier are used to extract data from the databases and process the customer requests.

Access control can be restricted by only allowing roles to interact with the database. The database administrator can define specific roles that are allowed to access the database. Each role will have assigned rights and permissions, and customers and employees are then ported into these roles. Any user who is not within one of these roles is denied access. This means that if an attacker compromises the firewall and other perimeter network protection mechanisms, and then is able to make requests to the database, if he is not in one of the predefined roles, the database is still safe. This process streamlines access control and ensures that no users or evildoers can access the database directly, but must access it indirectly through a role account. Figure 11-2 illustrates these concepts.

Database Management Software

A *database* is a collection of data stored in a meaningful way that enables multiple users and applications to access, view, and modify data as needed. Databases are managed with software that provides these types of capabilities. It also enforces access control restrictions, provides data integrity and redundancy, and sets up different procedures for data manipulation. This software is referred to as a *database management system (DBMS)* and is usually controlled by a database administrator. Databases not only

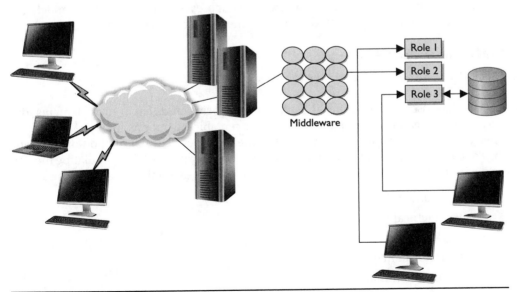

Figure 11-2 One type of database security is to employ roles.

store data, but may also process data and represent it in a more usable and logical form. DBMSs interface with programs, users, and data within the database. They help us store, organize, and retrieve information effectively and efficiently.

A database is the mechanism that provides structure for the data collected. The actual specifications of the structure may be different per database implementation, because different organizations or departments work with different types of data and need to perform diverse functions upon that information. There may be different workloads, relationships between the data, platforms, performance requirements, and security goals. Any type of database should have the following characteristics:

- It centralizes by not having data held on several different servers throughout the network.
- It allows for easier backup procedures.
- It provides transaction persistence.
- It allows for more consistency since all the data are held and maintained in one central location.
- It provides recovery and fault tolerance.
- It allows the sharing of data with multiple users.
- It provides security controls that implement integrity checking, access control, and the necessary level of confidentiality.

 NOTE *Transaction persistence* means the database procedures carrying out transactions are durable and reliable. The state of the database's security should be the same after a transaction has occurred, and the integrity of the transaction needs to be ensured.

Because the needs and requirements for databases vary, different data models can be implemented that align with different business and organizational needs.

Database Models

Ohhh, that database model is very pretty, indeed.
Response: You have problems.

The database model defines the relationships between different data elements, dictates how data can be accessed, and defines acceptable operations, the type of integrity offered, and how the data is organized. A model provides a formal method of representing data in a conceptual form and provides the necessary means of manipulating the data held within the database. Databases come in several types of models, as listed next:

- Relational
- Hierarchical
- Network
- Object-oriented
- Object-relational

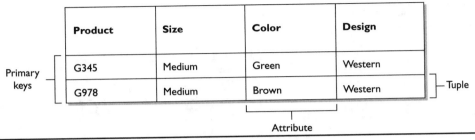

Figure 11-3   Relational databases hold data in table structures.

A *relational database model* uses attributes (columns) and tuples (rows) to contain and organize information (see Figure 11-3). The relational database model is the most widely used model today. It presents information in the form of tables. A relational database is composed of two-dimensional tables, and each table contains unique rows, columns, and cells (the intersection of a row and a column). Each cell contains only one data value that represents a specific attribute value within a given tuple. These data entities are linked by relationships. The relationships between the data entities provide the framework for organizing data. A primary key is a field that links all the data within a record to a unique value. For example, in the table in Figure 11-3, the primary keys are Product G345 and Product G978. When an application or another record refers to this primary key, it is actually referring to all the data within that given row.

A *hierarchical data model* (see Figure 11-4) combines records and fields that are related in a logical tree structure. The structure and relationship between the data elements are different from those in a relational database. In the hierarchical database the parents can have one child, many children, or no children. The tree structure contains branches, and each branch has a number of leaves, or data fields. These databases have well-defined, pre-specified access paths, but are not as flexible in creating relationships between data elements as a relational database. Hierarchical databases are useful for mapping one-to-many relationships.

The hierarchical structured database is one of the first types of database model created, but is not as common as relational databases. To be able to access a certain data entity within a hierarchical database requires the knowledge of which branch to start with and which route to take through each layer until the data are reached. It does not use indexes as relational databases do for searching procedures. Also links (relationships) cannot be created between different branches and leaves on different layers.

The most commonly used implementation of the hierarchical model is in the Lightweight Directory Access Protocol (LDAP) model. You can find this model also used in the Windows registry structure and different file systems, but it is not commonly used in newer database products.

The *network database model* is built upon the hierarchical data model. Instead of being constrained by having to know how to go from one branch to another and then from one parent to a child to find a data element, the network database model allows each data element to have multiple parent and child records. This forms a redundant network-like structure instead of a strict tree structure. (The name does not indicate it is on or distributed throughout a network, it just describes the data element relation-

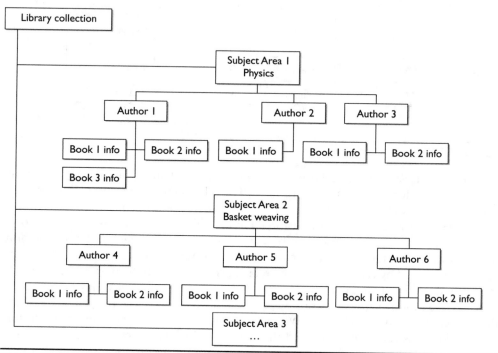

Figure 11-4 A hierarchical data model uses a tree structure and a parent/child relationship.

ships.) If you look at Figure 11-5, you can see how a network model sets up a structure that is similar to a mesh network topology for the sake of redundancy and allows for quick retrieval of data compared to the hierarchical model.

NOTE In Figure 11-5 you will also see a comparison of different database models.

This model uses the constructs of records and sets. A record contains fields, which may lay out in a hierarchical structure. Sets define the one-to-many relationships between the different records. One record can be the "owner" of any number of sets, and the same "owner" can be a member of different sets. This means that one record can be the "top dog" and have many data elements underneath it, or that record can be lower on the totem pole and be beneath a different field that is *its* "top dog." This allows for a lot of flexibility in the development of relationships between data elements.

An *object-oriented database* is designed to handle a variety of data (images, audio, documents, video). An object-oriented database management system (ODBMS) is more dynamic in nature than a relational database, because objects can be created when needed and the data *and* procedure (called method) go with the object when it is requested. In a relational database, the application has to use its own procedures to obtain data

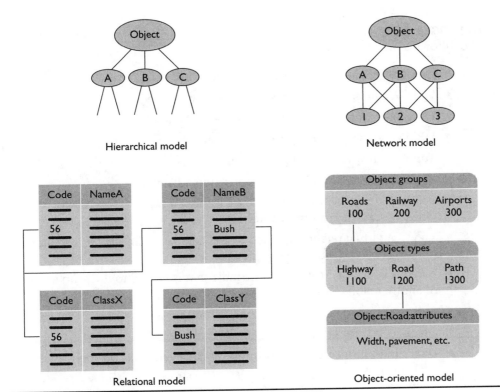

Figure 11-5 Various database models

from the database and then process the data for its needs. The relational database does not actually provide procedures, as object-oriented databases do. The object-oriented database has classes to define the attributes and procedures of its objects.

As an analogy, let's say two different companies provide the same data to their customer bases. If you go to Company A (relational), the person behind the counter will just give you a piece of paper that contains information. Now you have to figure out what to do with that information and how to properly use it for your needs. If you go to Company B (object-oriented), the person behind the counter will give you a box. Within this box is a piece of paper with information on it, but you will also be given a couple of tools to process the data for your needs instead of you having to do it yourself. So in object-oriented databases, when your application queries for some data, what is returned is not only the data but the code to carry out procedures on this data. (When we get to object-oriented programming, you will understand objects, classes, and methods more fully.)

The goal of creating this type of model was to address the limitations that relational databases encountered when large amounts of data must be stored and processed. An object-oriented database also does not depend upon SQL for interactions, so applications that are not SQL clients can work with these types of databases.

Database Jargon

The following are some key database terms:

- **Record**   A collection of related data items.
- **File**   A collection of records of the same type.
- **Database**   A cross-referenced collection of data.
- **DBMS**   Manages and controls the database.
- **Tuple**   A row in a two-dimensional database.
- **Attribute**   A column in a two-dimensional database.
- **Primary key**   Columns that make each row unique. (Every row of a table must include a primary key.)
- **View**   A virtual relation defined by the database administrator in order to keep subjects from viewing certain data.
- **Foreign key**   An attribute of one table that is related to the primary key of another table.
- **Cell**   An intersection of a row and column.
- **Schema**   Defines the structure of the database.
- **Data dictionary**   Central repository of data elements and their relationships.

NOTE   Structured Query Language (SQL) is a standard programming language used to allow clients to interact with a database. Many database products support SQL. It allows clients to carry out operations such as inserting, updating, searching, and committing data. When a client interacts with a database, it is most likely using SQL to carry out requests.

ODBMSs are not as common as relational databases, but are used in niche areas such as engineering and biology, and for some financial sector needs.

Now let's look at object-relational databases, just for the fun of it. An *object-relational database (ORD)* or object-relational database management system (ORDBMS) is a relational database with a software front end that is written in an object-oriented programming language. Why would we create such a silly combination? Well, a relational database just holds data in static two-dimensional tables. When the data are accessed, some type of processing needs to be carried out on it—otherwise, there is really no reason to obtain the data. If we have a front end that provides the procedures (methods) that can be carried out on the data, then each and every application that accesses this database does not need to have the necessary procedures. This means that each and every application does not need to contain the procedures necessary to gain what it really wants from this database.

Different companies will have different business logic that needs to be carried out on the stored data. Allowing programmers to develop this front-end software piece allows the business logic procedures to be used by requesting applications and the data within the database. For example, if we had a relational database that contains inventory data for our company, we might want to be able to use this data for different business purposes. One application can access that database and just check the quantity of widget A products we have in stock. So a front-end object that can carry out that procedure will be created, the data will be grabbed from the database by this object, and the answer will be provided to the requesting application. We also have a need to carry out a trend analysis, which will indicate which products were moved the most from inventory to production. A different object that can carry out this type of calculation will gather the necessary data and present it to our requesting application. We have many different ways we need to view the data in that database: how many products were damaged during transportation, how fast did each vendor fulfill our supply requests, how much does it cost to ship the different products based on their weights, and so on. The data objects in Figure 11-6 contain these different business logic instructions.

Database Programming Interfaces

Data are useless if you can't get to them and use them. Applications need to be able to obtain and interact with the information stored in databases. They also need some type of interface and communication mechanism. The following sections address some of these interface languages:

- **Open Database Connectivity (ODBC)**   An application programming interface (API) that allows an application to communicate with a database either locally or remotely. The application sends requests to the ODBC API. ODBC tracks down the necessary database-specific driver for the database to carry out the translation, which in turn translates the requests into the database commands that a specific database will understand.

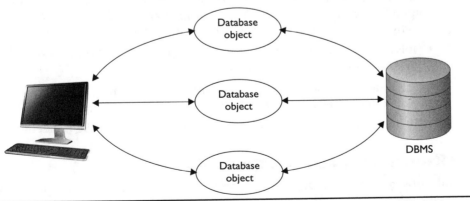

Figure 11-6   The object-relational model allows objects to contain business logic and functions.

- **Object Linking and Embedding Database (OLE DB)** Separates data into components that run as middleware on a client or server. It provides a low-level interface to link information across different databases and provides access to data no matter where it is located or how it is formatted. The following are some characteristics of OLE DB:

  - It's a replacement for ODBC, extending its feature set to support a wider variety of nonrelational databases, such as object databases and spreadsheets that do not necessarily implement SQL.

  - A set of COM-based interfaces provide applications with uniform access to data stored in diverse data sources (see Figure 11-7).

  - Because it is COM-based, OLE DB is limited to use by Microsoft Windows–based client tools. (Unrelated to OLE.)

  - A developer accesses OLE DB services through ActiveX Data Objects (ADO).

  - It allows different applications to access different types and sources of data.

- **ActiveX Data Objects (ADO)** An API that allows applications to access back-end database systems. It is a set of ODBC interfaces that exposes the functionality of data sources through accessible objects. ADO uses the OLE DB interface to connect with the database and can be developed with many different scripting languages. It is commonly used in web applications and other client/server applications. The following are some characteristics of ADO:

  - It's a high-level data access programming interface to an underlying data access technology (such as OLE DB).

  - It's a set of COM objects for accessing data sources, not just database access.

  - It allows a developer to write programs that access data, without knowing how the database is implemented.

  - SQL commands are not required to access a database when using ADO.

- **Java Database Connectivity (JDBC)** An API that allows a Java application to communicate with a database. The application can bridge through ODBC or directly to the database. The following are some characteristics of JDBC:

  - It is an API that provides the same functionality as ODBC but is specifically designed for use by Java database applications.

  - It has database-independent connectivity between the Java platform and a wide range of databases.

  - JDBC is a Java API that enables Java programs to execute SQL statements.

Relational Database Components

Like all software, databases are built with programming languages. Most database languages include a *data definition language (DDL)*, which defines the schema; a *data manipulation language (DML)*, which examines data and defines how the data can be manipulated within the database; a *data control language (DCL)*, which defines the internal

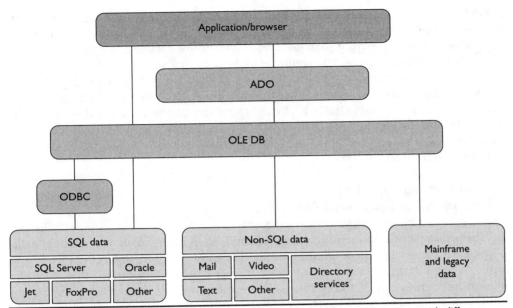

Figure 11-7 OLE DB provides an interface to allow applications to communicate with different data sources.

organization of the database; and an ad hoc *query language (QL)*, which defines queries that enable users to access the data within the database.

Each type of database model may have many other differences, which vary from vendor to vendor. Most, however, contain the following basic core functionalities:

- **Data definition language (DDL)**   Defines the structure and schema of the database. The structure could mean the table size, key placement, views, and data element relationship. The *schema* describes the type of data that will be held and manipulated, and its properties. It defines the structure of the database, access operations, and integrity procedures.

- **Data manipulation language (DML)**   Contains all the commands that enable a user to view, manipulate, and use the database (`view`, `add`, `modify`, `sort`, and `delete` commands).

- **Query language (QL)**   Enables users to make requests of the database.

- **Report generator**   Produces printouts of data in a user-defined manner.

Data Dictionary

Will the data dictionary explain all the definitions of database jargon to me?
Response: Wrong dictionary.

A *data dictionary* is a central collection of data element definitions, schema objects, and reference keys. The schema objects can contain tables, views, indexes, procedures, functions, and triggers. A data dictionary can contain the default values for columns, integrity information, the names of users, the privileges and roles for users, and auditing information. It is a tool used to centrally manage parts of a database by controlling data about the data (referred to as *metadata*) within the database. It provides a cross-reference between groups of data elements and the databases.

The database management software creates and reads the data dictionary to ascertain what schema objects exist and checks to see if specific users have the proper access rights to view them (see Figure 11-8). When users look at the database, they can be restricted by specific views. The different view settings for each user are held within the data dictionary. When new tables, new rows, or new schema are added, the data dictionary is updated to reflect this.

Primary vs. Foreign Key

Hey, my primary key is stuck to my foreign key.
Response: That is the whole idea of their existence.

The *primary key* is an identifier of a row and is used for indexing in relational databases. Each row must have a unique primary key to properly represent the row as one entity. When a user makes a request to view a record, the database tracks this record by its unique primary key. If the primary key were not unique, the database would not know which record to present to the user. In the following illustration, the primary keys for Table A are the dogs' names. Each row (tuple) provides characteristics for each dog (primary key). So when a user searches for Cricket, the characteristics of the type, weight, owner, and color will be provided.

Table A

Dog	Type	Weight	Owner	Color
Dallas	Lab	85 lb	David	Black
Cricket	Terrier	9 lb	George	White
Max	Lab	80 lb	Diane	Yellow
Shannon	Shepherd	72 lb	Marge	Brown

A primary key is different from a foreign key, although they are closely related. If an attribute in one table has a value matching the primary key in another table and there is a relationship set up between the two of them, this attribute is considered a *foreign key*. This foreign key is not necessarily the primary key in its current table. It only has to contain the same information that is held in another table's primary key and be mapped to the primary key in this other table. In the following illustration, a primary key for Table A is Dallas. Because Table B has an attribute that contains the same data as this primary key and there is a relationship set up between these two keys, it is referred to as a foreign key. This is another way for the database to track relationships between the data that it houses.

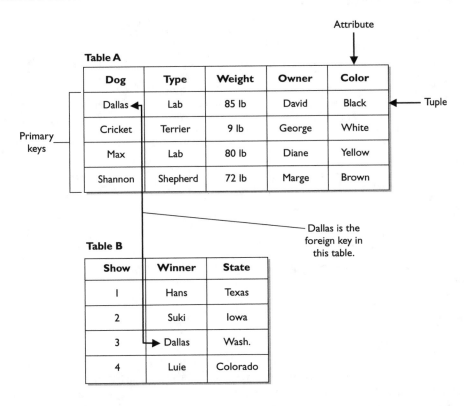

We can think of being presented with a web page that contains the data on Table B. If we want to know more about this dog named Dallas, we double-click that value and the browser presents the characteristics about Dallas that are in Table A.

This allows us to set up our databases with the relationship between the different data elements as we see fit.

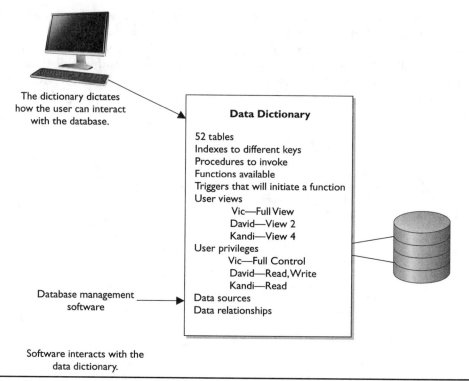

The dictionary dictates how the user can interact with the database.

Data Dictionary

52 tables
Indexes to different keys
Procedures to invoke
Functions available
Triggers that will initiate a function
User views
      Vic—Full View
      David—View 2
      Kandi—View 4
User privileges
      Vic—Full Control
      David—Read, Write
      Kandi—Read
Data sources
Data relationships

Database management software

Software interacts with the data dictionary.

Figure 11-8 The data dictionary is a centralized program that contains information about a database.

Integrity

You just wrote over my table!

Response: Well, my information is more important than yours.

Like other resources within a network, a database can run into *concurrency* problems. Concurrency issues come up when there is a piece of software that will be accessed at the same time by different users and/or applications. As an example of a concurrency problem, suppose that two groups use one price sheet to know how many supplies to order for the next week and also to calculate the expected profit. If Dan and Elizabeth copy this price sheet from the file server to their workstations, they each have a copy of the original file. Suppose that Dan changes the stock level of computer books from 120 to 5, because they sold 115 in the last three days. He also uses the current prices listed in the price sheet to estimate his expected profits for the next week. Elizabeth reduces the price on several software packages on her copy of the price sheet and sees that the stock level of computer books is still over 100, so she chooses not to order any more for next week for her group. Dan and Elizabeth do not communicate this different information to each other, but instead upload their copies of the price sheet to the server for everyone to view and use.

Dan copies his changes back to the file server, and then 30 seconds later Elizabeth copies her changes over Dan's changes. So, the file only reflects Elizabeth's changes.

Because they did not synchronize their changes, they are both now using incorrect data. Dan's profit estimates are off because he does not know that Elizabeth reduced the prices, and next week Elizabeth will have no computer books because she did not know that the stock level had dropped to five.

The same thing happens in databases. If controls are not in place, two users can access and modify the same data at the same time, which can be detrimental to a dynamic environment. To ensure that concurrency issues do not cause problems, processes can *lock* tables within a database, make changes, and then release the software lock. The next process that accesses the table will then have the updated information. Locking ensures that two processes do not access the same table at the same time. Pages, tables, rows, and fields can be locked to ensure that updates to data happen one at a time, which enables each process and subject to work with correct and accurate information.

Database software performs three main types of integrity services: semantic, referential, and entity. A *semantic integrity* mechanism makes sure structural and semantic rules are enforced. These rules pertain to data types, logical values, uniqueness constraints, and operations that could adversely affect the structure of the database. A database has *referential integrity* if all foreign keys reference existing primary keys. There should be a mechanism in place that ensures no foreign key contains a reference to a primary key of a nonexisting record, or a null value. *Entity integrity* guarantees that the tuples are uniquely identified by primary key values. In the previous illustration, the primary keys are the names of the dogs, in which case, no two dogs could have the same name. For the sake of entity integrity, every tuple must contain one primary key. If it does not have a primary key, it cannot be referenced by the database.

The database must not contain unmatched foreign key values. Every foreign key refers to an existing primary key. In the previous illustration, if the foreign key in Table B is Dallas, then Table A must contain a record for a dog named Dallas. If these values do not match, then their relationship is broken, and again the database cannot reference the information properly.

Other configurable operations are available to help protect the integrity of the data within a database. These operations are rollbacks, commits, savepoints, and checkpoints.

The *rollback* is an operation that ends a current transaction and cancels the current changes to the database. These changes could have taken place with the data itself or with schema changes that were typed in. When a rollback operation is executed, the changes are cancelled, and the database returns to its previous state. A rollback can take place if the database has some type of unexpected glitch or if outside entities disrupt its processing sequence. Instead of transmitting and posting partial or corrupt information, the database will roll back to its original state and log these errors and actions so they can be reviewed later.

The *commit* operation completes a transaction and executes all changes just made by the user. As its name indicates, once the commit command is executed, the changes are committed and reflected in the database. These changes can be made to data or schema information. Because these changes are committed, they are then available to all other applications and users. If a user attempts to commit a change and it cannot complete correctly, a rollback is performed. This ensures that partial changes do not take place and that data are not corrupted.

Savepoints are used to make sure that if a system failure occurs, or if an error is detected, the database can attempt to return to a point before the system crashed or hiccupped. For a conceptual example, say Dave typed, "Jeremiah was a bullfrog. He was <savepoint> a good friend of mine." (The system inserted a savepoint.) Then a freak storm came through and rebooted the system. When Dave got back into the database client application, he might see "Jeremiah was a bullfrog. He was," but the rest was lost. Therefore, the savepoint saved some of his work. Databases and other applications will use this technique to attempt to restore the user's work and the state of the database after a glitch, but some glitches are just too large and invasive to overcome.

Savepoints are easy to implement within databases and applications, but a balance must be struck between too many and not enough savepoints. Having too many savepoints can degrade the performance, whereas not having enough savepoints runs the risk of losing data and decreasing user productivity because the lost data would have to be reentered. Savepoints can be initiated by a time interval, a specific action by the user, or the number of transactions or changes made to the database. For example, a database can set a savepoint for every 15 minutes, every 20 transactions completed, each time a user gets to the end of a record, or every 12 changes made to the databases.

So a savepoint restores data by enabling the user to go back in time before the system crashed or hiccupped. This can reduce frustration and help us all live in harmony.

 NOTE   Checkpoints are very similar to savepoints. When the database software fills up a certain amount of memory, a checkpoint is initiated, which saves the data from the memory segment to a temporary file. If a glitch is experienced, the software will try to use this information to restore the user's working environment to its previous state.

A *two-phase commit* mechanism is yet another control that is used in databases to ensure the integrity of the data held within the database. Databases commonly carry out transaction processes, which means the user and the database interact at the same time. The opposite is batch processing, which means that requests for database changes are put into a queue and activated all at once—not at the exact time the user makes the request. In transactional processes, many times a transaction will require that more than one database be updated during the process. The databases need to make sure each database is properly modified, or no modification takes place at all. When a database change is submitted by the user, the different databases initially store these changes temporarily. A transaction monitor will then send out a "pre-commit" command to each database. If all the right databases respond with an acknowledgment, then the monitor sends out a "commit" command to each database. This ensures that all of the necessary information is stored in all the right places at the right time.

Database Security Issues

Oh, I know this and I know that. Now I know the big secret!
Response: Then I am changing the big secret—hold on.

The two main database security issues this section addresses are aggregation and inference. *Aggregation* happens when a user does not have the clearance or permission to access specific information, but she does have the permission to access components of this information. She can then figure out the rest and obtain restricted information. She can learn of information from different sources and combine it to learn something she does not have the clearance to know.

 NOTE Aggregation is the act of combining information from separate sources. The combination of the data forms new information, which the subject does not have the necessary rights to access. The combined information has a sensitivity that is greater than that of the individual parts.

The following is a silly conceptual example. Let's say a database administrator does not want anyone in the Users group to be able to figure out a specific sentence, so he segregates the sentence into components and restricts the Users group from accessing it, as represented in Figure 11-9. However, Emily can access components A, C, and F. Because she is particularly bright, she figures out the sentence and now knows the restricted secret.

To prevent aggregation, the subject, and any application or process acting on the subject's behalf, needs to be prevented from gaining access to the whole collection, including the independent components. The objects can be placed into containers, which are classified at a higher level to prevent access from subjects with lower-level permissions or clearances. A subject's queries can also be tracked, and context-dependent access control can be enforced. This would keep a history of the objects that a subject has accessed and restrict an access attempt if there is an indication that an aggregation attack is under way.

The other security issue is *inference*, which is the intended result of aggregation. The inference problem happens when a subject deduces the full story from the pieces he learned of through aggregation. This is seen when data at a lower security level indirectly portrays data at a higher level.

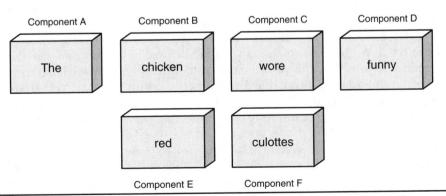

Figure 11-9 Because Emily has access to components A, C, and F, she can figure out the secret sentence through aggregation.

NOTE Inference is the ability to derive information not explicitly available.

For example, if a clerk were restricted from knowing the planned movements of troops based in a specific country, but did have access to food shipment requirements forms and tent allocation documents, he could figure out that the troops were moving to a specific place because that is where the food and tents are being shipped. The food shipment and tent allocation documents were classified as confidential, and the troop movement was classified as top secret. Because of the varying classifications, the clerk could access and ascertain top-secret information he was not supposed to know.

The trick is to prevent the subject, or any application or process acting on behalf of that subject, from indirectly gaining access to the inferable information. This problem is usually dealt with in the development of the database by implementing content- and context-dependent access control rules. *Content-dependent access control* is based on the sensitivity of the data. The more sensitive the data, the smaller the subset of individuals who can gain access to the data.

Context-dependent access control means that the software "understands" what actions should be allowed based upon the state and sequence of the request. So what does that mean? It means the software must keep track of previous access attempts by the user and understand what sequences of access steps are allowed. Content-dependent access control can go like this: "Does Julio have access to File A?" The system reviews the ACL on File A and returns with a response of "Yes, Julio can access the file, but can only read it." In a context-dependent access control situation, it would be more like this: "Does Julio have access to File A?" The system then reviews several pieces of data: What other access attempts has Julio made? Is this request out of sequence of how a safe series of requests takes place? Does this request fall within the allowed time period of system access (8 A.M. to 5 P.M.)? If the answers to all of these questions are within a set of preconfigured parameters, Julio can access the file. If not, he needs to go find something else to do.

Obviously, content-dependent access control is not as complex as context-dependent control because of the amount of items that needs to be processed by the system.

Common attempts to prevent inference attacks are cell suppression, partitioning the database, and noise and perturbation. *Cell suppression* is a technique used to hide specific cells that contain information that could be used in inference attacks. *Partitioning* a database involves dividing the database into different parts, which makes it much harder for an unauthorized individual to find connecting pieces of data that can be brought together and other information that can be deduced or uncovered. *Noise and perturbation* is a technique of inserting bogus information in the hopes of misdirecting an attacker or confusing the matter enough that the actual attack will not be fruitful.

If context-dependent access control is being used to protect against inference attacks, the database software would need to keep track of what the user is requesting. So Julio makes a request to see field 1, then field 5, then field 20, which the system allows, but once he asks to see field 15 the database does not allow this access attempt. The software must be preprogrammed (usually through a rule-based engine) as to what sequence and how much data Julio is allowed to viewed. If he is allowed to view more information, he may have enough data to infer something we don't want him to know.

Often, security is not integrated into the planning and development of a database. Security is an afterthought, and a trusted front end is developed to be used with the database instead. This approach is limited in the granularity of security and in the types of security functions that can take place.

A common theme in security is a balance between effective security and functionality. In many cases, the more you secure something, the less functionality you have. Although this could be the desired result, it is important not to impede user productivity when security is being introduced.

Database Views

Don't show your information to everybody, only a select few.

Databases can permit one group, or a specific user, to see certain information while restricting another group from viewing it altogether. This functionality happens through the use of *database views*, illustrated in Figure 11-10. If a database administrator wants to allow middle management members to see their departments' profits and expenses but not show them the whole company's profits, she can implement views. Senior management would be given all views, which contain all the departments' and the company's profit and expense values, whereas each individual manager would only be able to view his or her department values.

Like operating systems, databases can employ discretionary access control (DAC) and mandatory access control (MAC), which is explained in Chapter 4. Views can be displayed according to group membership, user rights, or security labels. If a DAC system was employed, then groups and users could be granted access through views based on their identity, authentication, and authorization. If a MAC system was in place, then groups and users would be granted access based on their security clearance and the data's classification level.

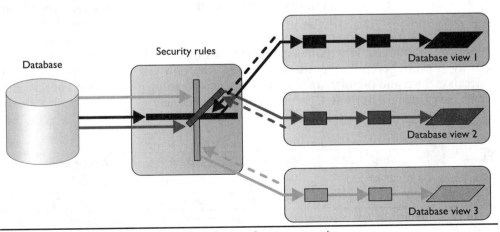

Figure 11-10 Database views are a logical type of access control.

Polyinstantiation

Polyinstantiation.
Response: Gesundheit.

Sometimes a company does not want users at one level to access and modify data at a higher level. This type of situation can be handled in different ways. One approach denies access when a lower-level user attempts to access a higher-level object. However, this gives away information indirectly by telling the lower-level entity that something sensitive lives inside that object at that level.

Another way of dealing with this issue is *polyinstantiation*. This enables a table that contains multiple tuples with the same primary keys, with each instance distinguished by a security level. When this information is inserted into a database, lower-level subjects must be restricted from it. Instead of just restricting access, another set of data is created to fool the lower-level subjects into thinking the information actually means something else. For example, if a naval base has a cargo shipment of weapons going from Delaware to Ukraine via the ship *Oklahoma*, this type of information could be classified as top secret. Only the subjects with the security clearance of top secret and above should know this information, so a dummy file is created that states the *Oklahoma* is carrying a shipment from Delaware to Africa containing food, and it is given a security clearance of unclassified, as shown in Table 11-1. It will be obvious that the *Oklahoma* is gone, but individuals at lower security levels will think the ship is on its way to Africa, instead of Ukraine. This also makes sure no one at a lower level tries to commit the *Oklahoma* for any other missions. The lower-level subjects know that the *Oklahoma* is not available, and they will assign other ships for cargo shipments.

 NOTE Polyinstantiation is a process of interactively producing more detailed versions of objects by populating variables with different values or other variables. It is often used to prevent inference attacks.

In this example, polyinstantiation was used to create two versions of the same object so lower-level subjects did not know the true information, and thus stopping them from attempting to use or change that data in any way. It is a way of providing a cover story for the entities that do not have the necessary security level to know the truth. This is just one example of how polyinstantiation can be used. It is not strictly related to security, however, even though that is its most common use. Whenever a copy of an object is created and populated with different data, meaning two instances of the same object have different attributes, polyinstantiation is in place.

Level	Ship	Cargo	Origin	Destination
Top Secret	Oklahoma	Weapons	Delaware	Ukraine
Unclassified	Oklahoma	Food	Delaware	Africa

Table 11-1 Example of Polyinstantiation to Provide a Cover Story to Subjects at Lower Security Levels

Online Transaction Processing

What if our databases get overwhelmed?

Response: OLTP to the rescue!

Online transaction processing (OLTP) is generally used when databases are clustered to provide fault tolerance and higher performance. OLTP provides mechanisms that watch for problems and deal with them appropriately when they do occur. For example, if a process stops functioning, the monitor mechanisms within OLTP can detect this and attempt to restart the process. If the process cannot be restarted, then the transaction taking place will be rolled back to ensure no data is corrupted or that only part of a transaction happens. Any erroneous or invalid transactions detected should be written to a transaction log. The transaction log also collects the activities of successful transactions. Data is written to the log before and after a transaction is carried out so a record of events exists.

The main goal of OLTP is to ensure that transactions happen properly or they don't happen at all. Transaction processing usually means that individual indivisible operations are taking place independently. If one of the operations fails, the rest of the operations needs to be rolled back to ensure that only accurate data is entered into the database.

The set of systems involved in carrying out transactions are managed and monitored with a software OLTP product to make sure everything takes place smoothly and correctly.

OLTP can load-balance incoming requests if necessary. This means that if requests to update databases increase, and the performance of one system decreases because of the large volume, OLTP can move some of these requests to other systems. This makes sure all requests are handled and that the user, or whoever is making the requests, does not have to wait a long time for the transaction to complete.

When there is more than one database, it is important they all contain the same information. Consider this scenario: Katie goes to the bank and withdraws $6,500 from her $10,000 checking account. Database A receives the request and records a new checking account balance of $3,500, but database B does not get updated. It still shows a balance of $10,000. Then, Katie makes a request to check the balance on her checking account, but that request gets sent to database B, which returns inaccurate information because the withdrawal transaction was never carried over to this database. OLTP makes sure a transaction is not complete until *all databases receive and reflect this change.*

OLTP records transactions as they occur (in real time), which usually updates more than one database in a distributed environment. This type of complexity can introduce many integrity threats, so the database software should implement the characteristics of what's known as the ACID test:

- **Atomicity** Divides transactions into units of work and ensures that all modifications take effect or none takes effect. Either the changes are committed or the database is rolled back.

- **Consistency** A transaction must follow the integrity policy developed for that particular database and ensure all data are consistent in the different databases.

- **Isolation** Transactions execute in isolation until completed, without interacting with other transactions. The results of the modification are not available until the transaction is completed.

- **Durability** Once the transaction is verified as accurate on all systems, it is committed, and the databases cannot be rolled back.

Data Warehousing and Data Mining

Data warehousing combines data from multiple databases or data sources into a large database for the purpose of providing more extensive information retrieval and data analysis. Data from different databases is extracted and transferred to a central data storage device called a warehouse. The data is normalized, which means redundant information is stripped out and data are formatted in the way the data warehouse expects it. This enables users to query one entity rather than accessing and querying different databases.

The data sources the warehouse is built from are used for operational purposes. A data warehouse is developed to carry out analysis. The analysis can be carried out to make business forecasting decisions and identify marketing effectiveness, business trends, and even fraudulent activities.

Data warehousing is not simply a process of mirroring data from different databases and presenting the data in one place. It provides a base of data that is then processed and presented in a more useful and understandable way. Related data are summarized and correlated before being presented to the user. Instead of having every piece of data presented, the user is given data in a more abridged form that best fits her needs.

Although this provides easier access and control, because the data warehouse is in one place, it also requires more stringent security. If an intruder got into the data warehouse, he could access all of the company's information at once.

Data mining is the process of massaging the data held in the data warehouse into more useful information. Data-mining tools are used to find an association and correlation in data to produce *metadata*. Metadata can show previously unseen relationships between individual subsets of information. It can reveal abnormal patterns not previously apparent. A simplistic example in which data mining could be useful is in detecting insurance fraud. Suppose the information, claims, and specific habits of millions of customers are kept in a database warehouse, and a mining tool is used to look for certain patterns in claims. It might find that each time John Smith moved, he had an insurance claim two to three months following the move. He moved in 1967 and two months later had a suspicious fire, then moved in 1973 and had a motorcycle stolen three months after that, and then moved again in 1984 and had a burglar break-in two months afterward. This pattern might be hard for people to manually catch because he had different insurance agents over the years, the files were just updated and not reviewed, or the files were not kept in a centralized place for agents to review.

Data mining can look at complex data and simplify it by using fuzzy logic, a set theory, and expert systems to perform the mathematical functions and look for patterns in data that are not so apparent. In many ways, the metadata is more valuable than the data it was derived from; thus, it must be highly protected. (Fuzzy logic and expert systems are discussed later in this chapter, in the "Artificial Neural Networks" section.)

The goal of data warehouses and data mining is to be able to extract information to gain knowledge about the activities and trends within the organization, as shown in Figure 11-11. With this knowledge, people can detect deficiencies or ways to optimize operations. For example, if we worked at a retail store company, we would want consumers to spend gobs and gobs of money there. We can better get their business if we understood customers' purchasing habits. If candy and other small items are placed at the checkout stand, purchases of those items go up 65 percent compared to if the items were somewhere else in the store. If one store is in a more affluent neighborhood and we see a constant (or increasing) pattern of customers purchasing expensive wines there, that is where we would also sell our expensive cheeses and gourmet items. We would not place our gourmet items at another store that frequently accepts food stamps.

 NOTE Data mining is the process of analyzing a data warehouse using tools that look for trends, correlations, relationships, and anomalies without knowing the meaning of the data. Metadata is the result of storing data within a data warehouse and mining the data with tools. Data goes into a data warehouse and metadata comes out of that data warehouse.

So we would carry out these activities if we want to harness organization-wide data for comparative decision making, workflow automation, and/or competitive advantage.

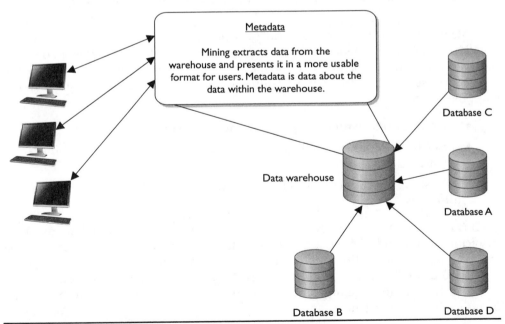

Figure 11-11 Mining tools are used to identify patterns and relationships in data warehouses.

It is not just information-aggregation; management's goals in understanding different aspects of the company are to enhance business value and help employees work more productively.

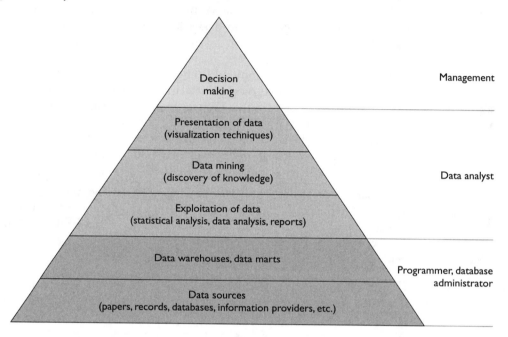

Data mining is also known as *knowledge discovery in database (KDD)*, and is a combination of techniques to identify valid and useful patterns. Different types of data can have various interrelationships, and the method used depends on the type of data and the patterns sought. The following are three approaches used in KDD systems to uncover these patterns:

- **Classification** Groups together data according to shared similarities.
- **Probabilistic** Identifies data interdependencies and applies probabilities to their relationships.
- **Statistical** Identifies relationships between data elements and uses rule discovery.

It is important to keep an eye on the output from the KDD and look for anything suspicious that would indicate some type of internal logic problem. For example, if you wanted a report that outlines the net and gross revenues for each retail store, and instead get a report that states "Bob," there may be an issue you need to look into.

Table 11-2 outlines the different types of systems used, depending on the requirements of the resulting data.

	Data-Based System	Rules-Based System	Knowledge-Based System
Can Process	Data	Data rules	Data rules knowledge
Can Output	Information	Information decisions Real-time decisions	Information decisions Answers Expert advice Recommendations
Commonly Used For	Hard-coded rules	Enterprise rules	Departmental rules
Ideal For	IT/system rules	Simplistic business rules	Complex business rules
Best for These Types of Applications	Traditional information systems	Decisioning compliance	Advising Product selection Recommending Troubleshooting
Domain Scope	—	Broad logic	Deep logic

Table 11-2   Various Types of Systems Based on Capabilities

System Development

Security is most effective if it is planned and managed throughout the life cycle of a system or application versus applying a third-party package as a front end after the development. Many security risks, analyses, and events occur during a product's lifetime, and these issues should be dealt with from the initial planning stage and continue through the design, coding, implementation, and operational stages. If security is added at the end of a project development rather than at each step of the life cycle, the cost and time of adding security increases dramatically. Security should not be looked at as a short sprint, but should be seen as a long run with many hills and obstacles.

Many developers, programmers, and architects know that adding security at a later phase of the system's life cycle is much more expensive and complicated than integrating it into the planning and design phase. Different security components can affect many different aspects of a system, and if they are thrown in at the last moment, they will surely affect other mechanisms negatively, restrict some already developed functionality, and cause the system to perform in unusual and unexpected ways. This approach costs more money because of the number of times the developers have to go back to the drawing board, recode completed work, and rethink different aspects of the system's architecture.

Management of Development

Many developers know that good project management keeps the project moving in the right direction, allocates the necessary resources, provides the necessary information, and plans for the worst yet hopes for the best. Project management is an important part of product development, and security management is an important part of project management.

A security plan should be drawn up at the beginning of a development project and integrated into the functional plan to ensure that security is not overlooked. The first plan is broad, covers a wide base, and refers to documented references for more detailed information. The references could include computer standards (RFCs, IEEE standards, and best practices), documents developed in previous projects, security policies, accreditation statements, incident-handling plans, and national or international guidelines (Orange Book, Red Book, and Common Criteria). This helps ensure that the plan stays on target.

The security plan should have a lifetime of its own. It will need to be added to, subtracted from, and explained in more detail as the project continues. It is important to keep it up to date for future reference. It is always easy to lose track of actions, activities, and decisions once a large and complex project gets underway.

The security plan and project management activities may likely be audited so security-related decisions can be understood. When assurance in the system needs to be guaranteed, indicating that security was fully considered in each phase of the life cycle, the procedures, development, decisions, and activities that took place during the project will be reviewed. The documentation must accurately reflect how the system or product was built and how it operates once implemented into an environment.

Life-Cycle Phases

There is a time to live, a time to die, a time to love . . .
Response: And a time to shut up.

Several types of models are used for system and application development, which include varying life cycles. This section outlines the core components that are common to all of them. Each model basically accomplishes the same thing; the main difference is how the development and lifetime of a system is broken into sections.

A project may start with a good idea, only to have the programmers and engineers just wing it; or, the project may be carefully thought out and structured to follow the necessary life cycles, and the programmers and engineers may stick to the plan. The first option may seem more fun in the beginning, because the team can skip stuffy requirements, blow off documentation, and get the product out the door in a shorter time and under budget. However, the team that takes the time to think through all the scenarios of each phase of the life cycle would actually have more fun, because its product would be more sound and more trusted by the market, and the team would make more money in the long run and would not need to chaotically develop several service and security patches to fix problems missed the first time around.

The different models integrate the following phases in one fashion or another:

- Project initiation
- Functional design analysis and planning
- System design specifications

- Software development
- Installation/implementation
- Operational/maintenance
- Disposal

Security is not listed as an individual bullet point because it should be embedded throughout all phases. Addressing security issues after the product is released costs a lot more money than addressing it during the development of the product. Functionality is the main force driving product development, and several considerations need to take place within that realm, but this section addresses the *security* issues that must be examined at each phase of the product's life cycle.

Project Initiation
So what are we building and why?

This is the phase when everyone involved attempts to understand why the project is needed and what the scope of the project entails. Either a specific customer needs a new system or application or a demand for the product exists in the market. During this phase, the project management team examines the characteristics of the system and proposed functionality, brainstorming sessions take place, and obvious restrictions are reviewed.

A conceptual definition of the project should be initiated and developed to ensure everyone is on the right page and that this is a proper product to develop and will be, hopefully, profitable. This phase could include evaluating products currently on the market and identifying any demands not being met by current vendors. It could also be a direct request for a specific product from a current or future customer.

In either case, because this is for a specific client or market, an initial study of the product needs to be started, and a high-level proposal should be drafted that outlines the necessary resources for the project and the predicted timeline of development. The estimated profit expected from the product also needs to be conducted. This information is submitted to senior management, who will determine whether the next phase should begin or further information is required.

In this phase, user needs are identified and the basic security objectives of the product are acknowledged. It must be determined if the product will be processing sensitive data, and if so, the levels of sensitivity involved should be defined. An initial risk analysis should be initiated that evaluates threats and vulnerabilities to estimate the cost/benefit ratios of the different security countermeasures. Issues pertaining to security integrity, confidentiality, and availability need to be addressed. The level of each security attribute should be focused upon so a clear direction of security controls can begin to take shape.

A basic security framework is designed for the project to follow, and risk management processes are established. Risk management will continue throughout the lifetime of the project. Risk information may start to be gathered and evaluated in the project initiation phase, but it will become more granular in nature as the phases graduate into the functional design and design-specification phase.

Risk Management

Okay, question one. How badly can we screw up?

One of the most important pieces of risk management is to know the right questions to ask. Risk management was discussed in Chapter 3, but that chapter dealt with identifying and mitigating risks that directly affect the business as a whole. Risk management must also be performed when developing and implementing software. Although the two functions are close in concepts, goals, and objectives, they have different specific tasks and focus.

Software development usually focuses on rich functionality and getting the product out the door and on shelves so customers can buy it as soon as possible. Most of the time, security is not part of the process or it quickly falls by the wayside when a deadline seems imminent. It is not just the programmer who should be thinking about coding in a secure manner, but the design of the product should have security integrated and layered throughout the project. Software engineers should address security threat scenarios and solutions during their tasks. It is not just one faction of a development team that might fall down when it comes to security. Security has never really been treated as an important function of the process—that is, until the product is bought by several customers who undergo attacks and compromises that tie directly to how the product was developed and programmed. Then, security is quite a big deal, but it is too late to integrate security into the project. Instead, a patch is developed and released.

The first step in risk management is to identify the threats and vulnerabilities and to calculate the level of risk involved. When all the risks are evaluated, management will decide upon the acceptable level of risk. Of course, it would be nice for management to not accept any risks and for the product to be designed and tested until it is foolproof; however, this would cause the product to be in development for a long time and to be too expensive to purchase. Compromises and intelligent business decisions must be made to provide a balance between risks and economic feasibility.

Risk Analysis

A risk analysis is performed to identify the relative risks and the potential consequences of what a customer can be faced with when using the particular product that is being developed. This process usually involves asking many, many questions to draw up the laundry list of vulnerabilities and threats, the probability of these vulnerabilities being exploited, and the outcome if one of these threats actually becomes real and a compromise takes place. The questions vary from product to product—such as its intended purpose, the expected environment it will be implemented into, the personnel involved, and the types of businesses that would purchase and use this type of product. The following is a short list of the types of questions that should be asked during a software risk analysis:

- What is the possibility of buffer overflows, and how do we avoid and test for them?
- Does the product properly verify the format/validity of all user-supplied input?
- Are there threat agents outside and inside the environment? What are those threat agents?

- What type of businesses would depend on this product, and what type of business loss would arise if the product were to go offline for a specific period?

- Are there covert channel issues that need to be dealt with?

- What type of fault tolerance is to be integrated into the product, and when would it be initiated?

- Is encryption needed? Which type? What strength?

- Are contingency plans needed for emergency issues?

- Would another party (ISP or hosting agency) be maintaining this product for the customer?

- Is mobile code necessary? Why? And if so, how can it be implemented?

- Will this product be in an environment that is connected to the Internet? What effects could this have on the product?

- Does this product need to interface to vulnerable systems?

- How could this product be vulnerable to Denial-of-Service (DoS) attacks?

- How could this product be vulnerable to viruses?

- Are intrusion alert mechanisms necessary?

- Would there be motivation for insiders or outsiders to sabotage this product? Why? And how could such sabotage be accomplished?

- Would competitor companies of the purchaser want to commit fraud via this product? Why? And how could such fraud be accomplished?

- What other systems would be affected if this product failed?

This is a short list, and each question should branch off into other questions to ensure all possible threats and risks are identified and considered.

Once all the risks are identified, the probability of them actually taking place needs to be quantified, and the consequences of these risks need to be properly evaluated to ensure the right countermeasures are implemented within the development phase and the product itself. If a product will only be used to produce word documents, a lower level of security countermeasures and tests would be needed compared with a product that maintains credit card data.

Many of the same risk analysis steps outlined in Chapter 3 can be applied in the risk analysis that must be performed when developing a product. Once the threats are identified by the project team members, the probability of their occurrence is estimated, and their consequences are calculated, the risks can be listed in order of criticality. If the possibility of a DoS taking place is high and could devastate a customer, then this is at the high end of importance. If the possibility of fraud is low, then this is pushed down the priority list. The most probable and potentially devastating risks are approached first, and the less likely and less damaging are dealt with after the more important risks.

These risks need to be addressed in the design and architecture of the product as well as in the functionality the product provides, the implementation procedures, and the required maintenance. A banking software product may need to be designed to have web server farms within a demilitarized zone (DMZ) of the branch, but have the components and databases behind another set of firewalls to provide another layer of protection. This means the architecture of the product would include splitting it among different systems and developing communications methods between the different parts. If the product is going to provide secure e-mail functionality, then all the risks involved with just this service need to be analyzed and properly accounted for. Implementation procedures need to be thought through and addressed. How will the customer set up this product? What are the system and environment requirements? Does this product need to be supplied with a public key infrastructure (PKI)? The level of maintenance required after installation is important to many products. Will the vendor need to keep the customer abreast of certain security issues? Should any logging and auditing take place? The more these things are thought through in the beginning, the less scrambling will be involved at the end of the process.

It is important to understand the difference between project risk analysis and security risk analysis. They often are confused or combined. The project team may do a risk analysis pertaining to the risk of the project failing. This is much different from the security risk analysis, which has different threats and issues. The two should be understood and used, but in a distinctively different manner.

Functional Design Analysis and Planning

I would like to design a boat to carry my yellow ducky.
Response: You are in the wrong meeting.

In this phase, a project plan is developed by the software architectures to define the security activities and create security checkpoints to ensure quality assurance for security controls takes place and that the configuration and change control process is identified. At this point in the project, resources are identified, test schedules start to form, and evaluation criteria are developed to be able to properly test the security controls. A formal functional baseline is formed, meaning the expectations of the product are outlined in a formal manner, usually through documentation. A test plan is developed, which will be updated through each phase to ensure all issues are properly tested.

Security requirements can be derived from several different sources:

- Functional needs of the system or application
- National, international, or organizational standards and guidelines
- Export restrictions
- The sensitivity level of data being processed (militarily strategic data versus private-sector data)
- Relevant security policies
- Cost/benefit analysis results
- Required level of protection to achieve the targeted assurance level rating

The initial risk assessment will most likely be updated throughout the project as more information is uncovered and learned. In some projects, more than one risk analysis needs to be performed at different stages of the life cycle. For example, if the project team knows the product will need to identify and authenticate users in a domain setting that requires a medium level of security, it will perform an initial risk analysis. Later in the life cycle, if it is determined that this product should work with biometric devices and have the capability to integrate with systems that require high security levels, the project team will perform a whole new risk analysis, because new morsels have been added to the mix.

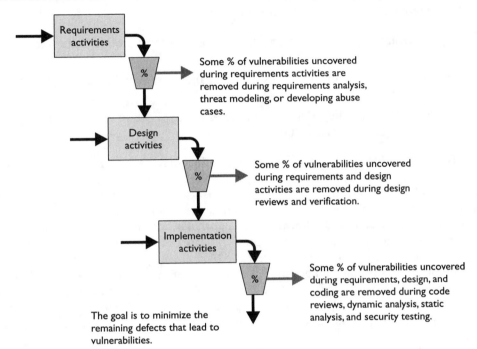

Some % of vulnerabilities uncovered during requirements activities are removed during requirements analysis, threat modeling, or developing abuse cases.

Some % of vulnerabilities uncovered during requirements and design activities are removed during design reviews and verification.

Some % of vulnerabilities uncovered during requirements, design, and coding are removed during code reviews, dynamic analysis, static analysis, and security testing.

The goal is to minimize the remaining defects that lead to vulnerabilities.

This phase addresses the functionality required of the product and is captured in a design document. If the product is being developed for a customer, the design document is used as a tool to explain to the customer what the developing team understands to be the requirements of the product. A design document is usually drawn up by analysts, with the guidance of engineers and architects, and presented to the customer. The customer can then decide if more functionality needs to be added or subtracted, after which the customer and development team can begin hammering out exactly what is expected from the product.

With regard to security issues, this is where high-level questions are asked. Examples of these questions include the following: Are authentication and authorization necessary? Is encryption needed? Will the product need to interface with other systems? Will the product be directly accessed via the Internet?

Many companies skip the functional design phase and jump right into developing specifications for the product. Or a design document is not shared with the customer. This can cause major delays and retooling efforts, because a broad vision of the product needs to be developed before looking strictly at the details. If the customer is not involved at this stage, the customer will most likely think the developers are creating a product that accomplishes X, while the development team thinks the customer wants Y. A lot of time can be wasted developing a product that is not what the customer actually wants, so clear direction and goals must be drawn up before the beginning of coding. This is usually an important function of the project management team.

System Design Specifications

Software requirements come from three models:

- **Informational model**   Dictates the type of information to be processed and how it will be processed

- **Functional model**   Outlines the tasks and functions the application needs to carry out

- **Behavioral model**   Explains the states the application will be in during and after specific transitions take place

For example, an antivirus software application may have an informational model that dictates what information is to be processed by the program, such as virus signatures, modified system files, checksums on critical files, and virus activity. It would also have a functional model that dictates that the application should be able to scan a hard drive, check e-mail for known virus signatures, monitor critical system files, and update itself. The behavioral model would indicate that when the system starts up, the antivirus software application will scan the hard drive. The computer coming online would be the event that changes the state of the application. If a virus were found, the application would change state and deal with the virus appropriately. The occurrence of the virus is the event that would change the state. Each state must be accounted for to ensure that the product does not go into an insecure state and act in an unpredictable way.

The informational, functional, and behavioral model data go into the software design as requirements. What comes out of the design is the data, architectural, and procedural design, as shown in Figure 11-12.

The architects and developers take the data design and the informational model data and transform them into the data structures that will be required to implement the software. The architectural design defines the relationships between the major structures and components of the application. The procedural design transforms structural components into descriptive procedures.

This is the point where access control mechanisms are chosen, subject rights and permissions are defined, the encryption method and algorithm are chosen, the handling of sensitive data is ironed out, the necessary objects and components are identified, the interprocessing communication is evaluated, the integrity mechanism is identified, and any other security specifications are appraised and solutions are determined.

The work breakdown structure (WBS) for future phases needs to be confirmed, which includes the development and implementation stages. This includes a timeline and detailed activities for testing, development, staging, integration testing, and product delivery.

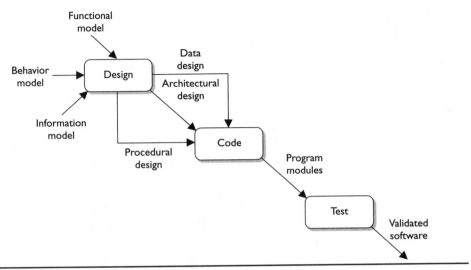

Figure 11-12 Information from three models can go into the design.

The system design is a tool used to describe the user requirements and the internal behavior of a system. It then maps the two elements to show how the internal behavior actually accomplishes the user requirements.

This phase starts to look at more details of the product and the environment it will be implemented within. The required functionality was determined in the last phase. This phase addresses what mechanisms are needed to provide this functionality and determines how it will be coded, tested, and implemented.

The modularity and reusability of the product, or the product components, need to be addressed. Code that provides security-critical functions should be simple in design, to catch errors in a less confusing fashion, and should be small enough to be fully tested in different situations. Components can be called and used by different parts of the product or by other applications. This attribute—reusability—can help streamline the product and provide for a more efficient and structured coding environment.

The product could have portability issues that need to be dealt with and handled at the early stages of the product development. If the product needs to work on Unix or Windows systems, then different coding requirements are needed compared with a product that will be installed only on mainframes. Also, the environment that will implement this product should be considered. Will this product be used by individual users, or will all the users within the network access this product in one fashion or another? Whether the product is a single-user product or a multiuser product has large ramifications on the development of the necessary specifications.

The testability of the product and components needs to be thought about at this early phase instead of at later phases. Programmers can code in *hooks* that show the testers the state of the product at different stages of data processing. Just because the product appears to act correctly and produces the right results at the end of the processing phases does not mean no internal errors exist. This is why testing should happen in modular ways, the flow of data through the product must be followed, and each step should be analyzed.

This phase should look closely at all the questions asked at the project initiation and ensure that specifications are developed for each issue addressed. For example, if authentication is required, this phase will lay out all the details necessary for this process to take place. If fraud is a large risk, then all the necessary countermeasures should be identified, and how they integrate into the product should be shown. If covert channels are a risk, then these issues should be addressed, and pseudocode should be developed to show how covert channels will be reduced or eliminated.

If the product is being developed for a specific customer, the specifications of the product should be shared with the customer to again ensure everyone is still on the same page and headed in the right direction. This is the stage to work out any confusion or misunderstanding before the actual coding begins.

The decisions made during the design phase are pivotal steps to the development phase. The design is the only way customer requirements are translated into software components; thus, software design serves as the foundation, and greatly affects software quality and maintenance. If good product design is not put into place in the beginning of the project, the following phases will be much more challenging.

Software Development

Code jockeys to your cubes and start punching those keys!

This is the phase where the programmers and developers become deeply involved. They are usually involved up to this point for their direction and advice, but at this phase, it is basically dropped into their laps. Let the programming and testing begin!

This is the stage where the programmers should code in a way that does not permit software compromises. Among other issues to address, the programmers need to check input lengths so buffer overflows cannot take place, inspect code to prevent the presence of covert channels, check for proper data types, make sure checkpoints cannot be bypassed by users, verify syntax, and perform checksums. Different attack scenarios should be played out to see how the code could be attacked or modified in an unauthorized fashion. Debugging and code reviews should be carried out by peer developers, and everything should be clearly documented.

Most programmers do not like to document and will find a way to get out of the task. Six to twelve months later, no one will remember specific issues that were addressed, how they were handled, or the solutions to problems that have already been encountered—or the programmer who knew all the details will have gone to work for a competitor or won the lottery and moved to an island. This is another cause of rework and wasted man-hours. Documentation is extremely important, for many different reasons, and can save a company a lot of money in the long run.

Verification vs. Validation

Verification determines if the product accurately represents and meets the specifications. After all, a product can be developed that does not match the original specifications, so this step ensures the specifications are being properly met.

Validation determines if the product provides the necessary solution for the intended real-world problem. In large projects, it is easy to lose sight of the overall goal. This exercise ensures that the main goal of the project is met.

Formal and informal testing should begin as soon as possible. *Unit testing* can start very early in development. After a programmer develops a component, or unit of code, it is tested with several different input values and in many different situations. Unit testing usually continues throughout the development phase. A totally different group of people should carry out the formal testing. This is an example of *separation of duties*. A programmer should not develop, test, and release software. The more eyes that see the code and the more fingers that are punching keys, the greater the chance that bugs will be found before the product is released.

Of course, any software hooks inserted for testing or modification purposes need to be removed from the application prior to being released to production because these can easily provide attackers backdoors into the product.

No cookie-cutter recipe exists for security testing, because the applications and products can be so diverse in functionality and security objectives. It is important to map security risks to test cases and code. Linear thinking can be followed by identifying a vulnerability, providing the necessary test scenario, performing the test, and reviewing the code for how it deals with such a vulnerability. At this phase, tests are conducted in an actual network, which should mirror the production environment to ensure the code does not work only in the labs.

Security attacks and penetrations usually take place during this phase to identify any missed vulnerabilities. Functionality, performance, and penetration resistance are evaluated. All the necessary functionality required of the product should be in a checklist to ensure each function is accounted for.

Security tests should be run to test against the vulnerabilities identified earlier within the project. Buffer overflows should be attempted, the product should be hacked and attacked, interfaces should be hit with unexpected inputs, DoS situations should be tested, unusual user activity should take place, and if a system crashes, the product should react by reverting back to a more secure state. The product should be tested in various environments with different applications, configurations, and hardware platforms. A product may respond fine when installed on a clean Windows 2000 installation on a stand-alone PC, but it may throw unexpected errors when installed on a laptop that is remotely connected to a network and has an SMS client installed.

Separation of Duties

Different environmental types (development, testing, and production) should be properly separated, and functionality and operations should not overlap. Developers should not have access to code used in production. The code should be tested, submitted to the library, and then sent to the production environment. At this stage, issues found in unit and formal testing are relayed to the development team in problem reports. The problems are fixed and retesting occurs. This is a continual process until everyone is satisfied that the product is ready for production. If there is a specific customer, the customer would run through a range of tests before formally accepting the product. Then the product is formally released to the market or customer.

NOTE Sometimes developers enter lines of code in a product that will allow them to do a few keystrokes and get right into the application. This allows them to bypass any security and access controls so they can quickly access the application's code. This is referred to as a "backdoor" or "maintenance hook" and should be removed before the code goes into production.

Installation/Implementation

This product doesn't work.
Response: Try plugging it in.

The implementation stage focuses on how to use and operate the developed system or application. At this phase, the customer has purchased the developed product and installed it into its environment. The product would then be configured for the right level of protection. Functionality and performance tests should be performed, and the results should be analyzed and compared with the company's security requirements.

The configurations should be documented by the vendor and supplied with the product for the customer to use. User guides and operation and maintenance manuals are developed so users know how to properly use the systems and the technical staff knows how to properly configure the product if needed. Security activities need to be monitored to ensure the system or application performs in the manner promised by the service level agreement.

Accreditation should occur between the implementation and the beginning of operational use of the system or application. This process follows the certification process, which formally or informally tests all the security features to determine if they accomplish the required security needs. Certification is the process of reviewing and evaluating security controls and functionality. It is usually a task assigned to an outside, independent reviewer. (Certification and accreditation were covered in detail in Chapter 5.)

The accreditation is the formal acceptance of the system by management and an explicit acceptance of risk. The accreditation looks at the whole system, not just at an application or a newly upgraded feature, because security is a service that takes place at different layers of the system and can be manifested in many ways. The accreditation process forces the management and technical staff to work together to ensure quality and a level of protection provided by purchased and implemented technologies. The technical staff understands operational and mechanical issues, and the management staff understands mission, financial, and liability issues. Together, they can cover a lot of ground during the certification accreditation processes.

Once management is sure of the security provided by the new system and understands and accepts the risk, it should issue a formal accreditation statement.

Auditing needs to be enabled and monitored, and contingency recovery plans and procedures should be developed and tested to make sure the system and product react as planned in the event of a system failure or emergency situation.

Operational and Maintenance

Okay, the thing is out there. Now someone has to take care of that thing.

When you reach this phase, do not think that security is done and under control, and that all you have to do now is sit back and eat donuts. On the contrary, security is just as, or more, important during the operational phase than during earlier phases.

The initial part of this phase includes configuring the new system and inserting it properly into the network and environment. Many times, security controls are not enabled or properly configured for the environment, so even if they were correctly coded from the beginning, it does not really matter if they are not actually used or are used in an unintended way.

Operational assurance is carried out by continually conducting vulnerability tests, monitoring activities, and auditing events. It is through operational assurance activities that an administrator learns of new vulnerabilities or security compromises, so the proper actions can take place.

If major changes happen to the system, product, or environment, a new risk analysis may need to be performed along with a new certification and accreditation process. These major changes could include adding new systems and/or new applications, relocating the facility, or changing data sensitivity or criticality.

Disposal

All good things must come to an end.

When it is time for "out with the old and in with the new," certain steps may need to take place to make sure this transition happens in a secure manner. Depending on the sensitivity level of the data held on a system, various disposal activities may be necessary. Information may need to be archived, backed up to another system, discarded, or destroyed. If the data are sensitive and need to be destroyed, they may need to be purged by overwriting, degaussing, or physically destroying the media. It depends on the data and the company's policy about destroying sensitive information.

If the product being replaced is just a word processor or an antivirus software package, this phase can be easily taken care of. But if the software is integrated into every part of the company's processing infrastructure, properly extracting it without affecting productivity and security can be an overwhelming task.

Testing Types

If we would like the assurance that the software is any good at all, we should probably test it. There are different types of tests the software should go through because there are different potential flaws we will be looking for. The following are some of the most common testing approaches:

- **Unit testing**   Individual component is in a controlled environment where programmers validate data structure, logic, and boundary conditions.
- **Integration testing**   Verifying that components work together as outlined in design specifications.
- **Acceptance testing**   Ensuring that the code meets customer requirements.
- **Regression testing**   After a change to a system takes place, retesting to ensure functionality, performance, and protection.

When testing software, we not only need to think inside and outside the box, we need to throw the box, kick the box, and use it as a whoopee cushion. It is very hard to think of *all* the ways users may potentially harm the software product. It is also hard to think of *all* the ways hackers are going to attempt to break the software. So the following items are just some of the things that should be done to test the software:

- Various types of data should be input.
- Data at the different points within acceptable data ranges should be input.
  - Perform bounds checking to look for buffer overflows.
  - Conduct data validation to ensure the software is only accepting the type of data it should (that is, numbers and not letters, ASCII and not Unicode, and so on).
- Submit data outside of acceptable ranges.
- Test for different user activities.
- Validate data before and after being processed to identify improper changes.
- Prevent object reuse vulnerabilities.
  - Subject may have unauthorized access to residual data in an object or memory space.

Data can be contaminated in many ways—when it is either going into an application or coming out as output, or both. To ensure the data to be processed are accurate, the following input and output controls should be put into place:

- Input controls
  - Error detection and correction
  - Message digest values
  - Transaction and monetary counts
  - Resubmission and self-validating controls
- Output controls
  - Error handling
  - Reconciliation of values
  - Handling procedures
  - Audit trails and logging

Get This Garbage Out of Here!

Garbage collection is an automated way for the operating system to carry out part of its memory management tasks. A *garbage collector* identifies blocks of memory that were once allocated but are no longer in use and deallocates the blocks and marks them as free. It also gathers scattered blocks of free memory and combines them into larger blocks. It helps provide a more stable environment and does not waste precious memory. Some programming languages, such as Java, perform automatic garbage collection; others, such as C, require the developer to perform it manually, thus leaving opportunity for error. We've already covered some of these basic controls. The bad guys, however, will continually attempt to break through any and all of them in one way or another, and only solid programming and testing will help fortify your product against their evil ways.

Postmortem Review

"Lance did it!" "No, Sue did it!" "Fred did it." "The boogeyman did it!"

It is important that the team gather after the completion of a project to exhale, talk about the overall project, and discuss things that should be improved for the next time. If this phase is taken seriously and handled properly, the company can save money and time on future projects, because the team can pass along lessons it has learned so mistakes will not be repeated and the process will be streamlined. All of these activities will help the next project run more smoothly with fewer mistakes and in less time.

This should be a structured event in which someone leads the meeting(s) and someone takes notes, but it should also be a relaxed atmosphere so each team member feels comfortable in expressing opinions and ideas. The review must not become a finger-pointing session or a cesspool of complaining. It is a method of looking at the project from an objective view and identifying issues that could be improved upon the next time around.

Some companies do not see the value in this exercise and just race off to start the next project, which will most likely be cursed with the problems of the prior project. Projects are learning processes, and business is about making the best product in the least amount of time for the least amount of money. It is beneficial for management to understand how the two go together and to make sure a postmortem review is part of every project. The most successful businesses streamline the processes of projects and project management and hone them to become a repeatable procedure that produces the expected level of quality. These businesses continually take the time to look at how processes can be improved and built upon.

System Life-Cycle Phases

The following are the common phases of system and software development along with the core security tasks that take place at each phase:

- **Project initiation**
  - Conception of project definition
  - Proposal and initial study
  - Initial risk analysis
- **Functional design analysis and planning**
  - Requirements uncovered and defined
  - System environment specifications determined
  - Formal design created
- **System design specifications**
  - Functional design review
  - Functionality broken down
  - Detailed planning put into place
  - Code design
- **Software development**
  - Developing and programming software
- **Installation**
  - Product installation and implementation
  - Testing and auditing
- **Maintenance support**
  - Product changes, fixes, and minor modifications
- **Disposal**
  - Replace product with new product

This chapter explains a life cycle containing seven phases. Other models may use different cycles and a different number of phases, but they accomplish the same basic objectives. Table 11-3 illustrates the NIST's software development life cycle (SDLC) model.

	Initiation	Acquisition/Development	Implementation	Operations/Maintenance	Disposition
SDLC	Needs Determination: • Perception of a need • Linkage of need to mission and performance objectives • Assessment of alternatives to capital assets • Preparing for investment review and budgeting	• Functional statement of need • Market research • Feasibility study • Requirements analysis • Alternatives analysis • Cost-benefit analysis • Software conversion study • Cost analysis • Risk management plan • Acquisition planning	• Installation • Inspection • Acceptance testing • Initial user training • Documentation	• Performance measurement • Contract modifications • Operations • Maintenance	• Appropriateness of disposal • Exchange and sale • Internal organization screening • Transfer and donation • Contract closeout
Security Considerations	• Security categorization • Preliminary risk assessment	• Risk assessment • Security functional requirements analysis • Security assurance requirements analysis • Cost considerations and reporting • Security planning • Security control development • Developmental security test and evaluation • Other planning components	• Inspection and acceptance • System integration • Security certification • Security accreditation	• Configuration management and control • Continuous monitoring	• Information preservation • Media sanitization • Hardware and software disposal

Table 11-3 NIST's Breakdown of the SDLC Model They Provide

Software Development Methods

Over the years several Software Development Methods (SDMs) have been created to meet the various requirements of software developers and vendors. These methods help developers through the different stages (analysis, design, programming, maintenance) of program creation. They are commonly referred to as development guidelines, which is in fact what they are. There is a long list of them:

- **Waterfall** A classical method using discrete phases of development that require formal reviews and documentation before moving into the next phase of the project.

- **Spiral** A method that builds upon the waterfall method with an emphasis on risk analysis, prototypes, and simulations at different phases of the development cycle. This method periodically revisits previous stages to update and verify design requirements.

- **Structured Programming Development** A programming methodology that involves the use of logical blocks to achieve system design using procedural programming. A structured program layout minimizes the use of arbitrary transfer control statements such as GOTO and emphasizes single points of entry and exit. This hierarchical approach makes it easier for the program to be understood and modified later on. Structured programming encourages module reuse to allow for better memory utilization.

- **Iterative Development** A method that follows a cyclic approach to software development. Unlike traditional models, iterative development focuses on mapping out project milestones through continually assessing the current state of the project with the initial objectives on the basis of resources, timeframes, and execution plan. Iterative development provides a dynamic method of evaluating a project's overall status and allows corrective amendments to improve project effectiveness.

- **Modified Prototype Model (MPM)** A method specifically designed to confront challenges in web application development, the modified prototype model allows developers to swiftly translate client requirements into a displayable product or prototype. Modified prototypes are generally used when both the developer and the client are unsure of the final nature of the product. Using modifiable prototypes allows the final product to be carved out as the system specifications become less hazy.

- **Exploratory Model** A method that is used in instances where clearly defined project objectives have not been presented. Instead of focusing on explicit tasks, the exploratory model relies on covering a set of specifications that are likely to encase the final product's working. Testing is an important part of exploratory development as it ascertains that the current phase of the project is compliant with likely implementation scenarios.

- **Joint Analysis Development (JAD)** A method that uses a team approach in application development in a workshop-oriented environment.

- **Rapid Application Development (RAD)** A method of determining user requirements and developing systems quickly to satisfy immediate needs.

- **Reuse Model**   A model that approaches software development by using progressively developed models. Reusable programs are evolved by gradually modifying pre-existing prototypes to customer specifications. Since the reuse model does not require programs to be built from scratch, it drastically reduces both development cost and time.

- **Cleanroom**   An approach that attempts to prevent errors or mistakes by following structured and formal methods of developing and testing. This approach is used for high-quality and critical applications that will be put through a strict certification process.

- **Component-Based Development**   A model that refers to the use of independent and standardized modules that are assembled into serviceable programs. Each standard module consists of a functional algorithm or instruction set and is provided with an interface to communicate with one another. A common example of these modules are "objects," which are frequently used in object-oriented programming. Component-based development adds reusability and pluggable functionality to programs and is widely used in modern programming to augment program coherence and substantially reduce software maintenance costs.

- **Extreme Programming**   A methodology that is generally implemented in scenarios requiring rapid adaptations to changing client requirements. Extreme programming emphasizes client feedback to evaluate project outcomes and to analyze project domains that may require further attention. The coding principle of extreme programming throws out the traditional long-term planning carried out for code reuse and instead focuses on creating simple code optimized for the contemporary assignment. Extreme programming recognizes the fact that customer requirements are likely to change significantly throughout the project life cycle and plies the development process to adjust these changes.

Computer-Aided Software Engineering

Computer-aided software engineering (CASE) involves the use of tools to create and manage software. "CASE tools" is a general term for many types of tools used by programmers, developers, project managers, and analysts that help them make application development faster and with fewer errors. This is because many of the manual tasks are taken care of through automation with the use of CASE tools. Different tools provide managerial, administrative, and technical help in software projects.

The first CASE tools were translators, compilers, assemblers, linkers, and loaders. However, as programming and projects became more complex, the need for more complex tools grew. The tools graduated into program editors, debuggers, code analyzers, and version-control mechanisms. These tools aid in keeping more detailed records of requirements, design, and implementation and in testing the program and project overall. A CASE tool is aimed at supporting one or more software engineering tasks and activities in the process of developing software. It applies engineering principles to the development and analysis of specifications using specific tools.

Many vendors can get their products to the market faster because they are "computer aided." The CASE tools enable software engineering to be done correctly and fast, relatively speaking.

When the automation covers the complete life cycle of a product, the tools are referred to as *integrated computer-aided software engineering (I-CASE) tools*, and if tools are used for one specific part of the life cycle, then the tools are termed *CASE tools*.

Prototyping

I would like a prototype of a mini-me.
Response: One of you is enough.

Many times, it is necessary to build for the customer and the developers a model of the gathered requirements of a software product. This model, called a *prototype*, can show the customer where the development team is headed and its interpretation of the customer's stated requirements. This enables the customer to agree on the direction the team is headed and get an idea of what the product will look like, or it enables the customer to make changes and further explain any requirements that were uncertain or confusing. The prototype also enables testing to begin earlier in the development process so errors or problems can be uncovered and addressed.

Some projects are very large and may require the product to be partitioned so each part has its own prototype to be reviewed and built upon. In either case, while partitioning or prototyping the full product, an analyst will develop an abbreviated representation of the requirements for the prototype. The software can be created using prototyping tools, which speed up the process. This enables the design to be translated into executable form.

Security testing can begin at an earlier stage if a prototype is developed. Penetration, vulnerability, and data format tests can be performed at each stage of development and with each prototype developed.

If a software prototype is impractical, paper prototypes can be developed where interaction, queries, displays, and logic are shown on paper for the customer to see and the developers to walk through. A series of storyboard sheets can be used to represent each screenshot and the actions that take place behind the screen.

Secure Design Methodology

Secure design methodology is essential for ensuring the development of secure and reliable computing environments. Secure applications minimize the possibility of vulnerability exploitation by attackers, in turn reducing the risks posed to information assets. Breaches in information security can have disastrous consequences to an organization, such as financial loss, disclosure of trade secrets, damaged reputation, and loss of customer confidence. A secure designing methodology ensures early implementation of security policies and techniques rather than bolting them on as an afterthought.

The fundamentals of secure application design lie in identifying the platforms used in information systems. Once you have identified the platforms used, it's important to analyze their susceptibility to known vulnerabilities and flaws. These are inherent flaws in systems that are frequently utilized by attackers to carry out intrusions.

Attack surface analytics are created once a threat model has been created. The use of attack surface analysis techniques provides a structured process for analyzing program entry points as well. Attack surface analytics focus on documenting possible entry points irrespective of their defined privileges. Once these entry points have been documented, they can be used to specify program granularity as the program matures through its development cycle.

Another aspect that must be considered at design phase is the type of data that the application will be processing; this helps to specify sanitization parameters of the inputs and outputs. Sanitizing inputs and outputs reduces the possibility of attackers using rogue characters to compromise system resources. It is mandatory for the program architect to be well versed with countermeasures needed to mitigate these threats.

Secure Development Methodology

To ensure the creation of a secure application, it is essential to implement secure development practices. A weak development approach can easily jeopardize an otherwise secure design.

Secure development ensures the use of frameworks governing the requirements of the final product. Secure development emphasizes constantly analyzing the developed code for flaws and vulnerabilities, instead of putting it off until the software has been completely developed. In fact, it is a widely accepted fact that most vulnerabilities are cheaper to fix if discovered early during the design or development phase instead of after the software has been rolled out.

An important strategy for securing the development process is incorporating regular code reviews into the programming process. Code reviewing allows for the early identification of vulnerabilities, architectural lapses, and other improvement possibilities. This involves routine code reviews by both standard programmers and security specialists. It is essential that all recommendations created out of a review session be documented irrespective of whether or not they were implemented.

The use of automatic code-auditing tools has also reduced the effort in analyzing large code segments, but it is important to note that code analyzers only highlight code flaws; logical errors may not be detected without human analysis.

Since code review is a collaborative process, it is likely to create multiple instances of a program. With multiple cycles of code reviews and changes made to the original source code, managing updated versions and channeling all developments into a single source becomes both a challenge and a security issue. The introduction of centralized code repositories has simplified the review process. Version control technologies track changes in the source code and automatically channel all development effort into single updated files. An additional benefit of using version control software is that they allow *reversion*—the ability to undo the last changes to a file—thus enabling programmers to revert a program to its original state in case a modification does not work out. Compared to manual backup and tracking techniques, the use of tracking systems reduces the chances of undocumented changes, surreptitious code injections, unnoticed bugs, and other security risks that result from complex program structures.

Security Testing

Security testing is a comprehensive analysis technique that examines programs under artificially created attack scenarios. The objective of security testing is to analyze program behavior through penetration testing procedures. The scope of security testing is to analyze various vulnerabilities that may exist in newly developed applications. Security testing ensures that an application cannot be manipulated into gaining access to critical system processes or assets.

Security testing can evaluate a program for implementation of input validation techniques. Attackers may use various approaches depending on the nature of the software to inject malicious code into the application. Security tests also evaluate a program's strength against buffer overflow flaws that may occur due to misconfigurations and judge program behavior in the event of critical errors.

A well-rounded security test encompasses both manual and automatic tests. Automated tests help locate a wide range of flaws that are generally associated with careless or erroneous code implementations. Automated tests generally use programs known as fuzzers, vulnerability scanners, and code scanners. Fuzzers use complex input to impair program execution. Vulnerability scanning checks for underlying program flaws originating from errors in strongly typed languages, development and configuration faults, transaction sequence faults, and mapping trigger conditions. Automated tests primarily identify starting points that need to be further scrutinized manually.

A manual test is used to analyze aspects of the program that require human intuition and can usually be judged using computing techniques. Testers also try to locate design flaws. These include logical errors, where attackers may manipulate program flow by using shrewdly crafted program sequences to access greater privileges or bypass authentication mechanisms. Manual testing involves code auditing by security-centric programmers who try to modify the logical program structure using rogue inputs and reverse-engineering techniques. Manual tests simulate the live scenarios involved in real-world attacks. Some manual testing also involves the use of social engineering to analyze the human weakness that may lead to system compromise.

Change Control

I am changing stuff left and right.
Response: Was it approved and tested first?

Changes during development or production can cause a lot of havoc if not done properly. Changes could take place for several reasons. During the development phases, a customer may alter requirements and ask that certain functionalities be added, removed, or modified. In production, changes may need to happen because of other changes in the environment, new requirements of a product or system, or newly released patches or upgrades. These changes should be controlled to make sure they are approved, incorporated properly, and do not affect any original functionality in an adverse way. Change control is the process of controlling the life cycle of an application and documenting the necessary change control activities.

A process for dealing with changes needs to be in place at the beginning of a project so everyone knows how changes are dealt with and what is expected of each entity when a change request is made. Some projects have been doomed from the start because proper change control was not put into place and enforced. Many times in development, the customer and vendor agree on the design of the product, the requirements, and the specifications. The customer is then required to sign a contract confirming this is the agreement, and that if they want any further modifications, they will have to pay the vendor for that extra work. If this is not put into place, then the customer can continually request changes, which requires the development team to put in the extra hours to provide these changes, the result of which is that the vendor loses money and the product does not meet its completion deadline.

Other reasons exist to have change control in place. These reasons deal with organization, standard procedures, and expected results. If a product is in the last phase of development and a change request comes in, the team should know how to deal with it. Usually, the team leader must tell the project manager how much extra time will be required to complete the project if this change is incorporated and what steps need to be taken to ensure this change does not affect other components within the product. In addition, security cannot be compromised, and management must approve the change. If these processes are not controlled, one part of a development team could implement the change without another part of the team being aware of it. This could break some of the other development team's software pieces. When the pieces of the product are integrated and it is found that some pieces are incompatible, some jobs may be in jeopardy, because management never approved the change in the first place.

The change must be approved, documented, and tested. Some tests may need to be rerun to ensure the change does not affect the product's capabilities. When a programmer makes a change to source code, it should be done on the test version of the code. Under no conditions should a programmer change the code that is already in production. The changes to the code should be made and tested, and then the new code should go to the librarian. Production code should come only from the librarian and not from a programmer or directly from a test environment.

Official Definitions of Configuration Management

- The procedures used to carry out changes that affect the network, individual systems, or software

- Identifying, controlling, accounting for, and auditing changes made to the baseline trusted computing base (TCB), which includes changes to hardware, software, and firmware

- A system that controls changes and tests documentation through the operational life cycle of a system

Change control should be evaluated during system audits. It is possible to overlook a problem that a change has caused in testing, so the procedures for how change control is implemented and enforced should be examined during a system audit.

The following are some necessary steps for a change control process:

1. Make a formal request for a change.
2. Analyze the request.
   A. Develop the implementation strategy.
   B. Calculate the costs of this implementation.
   C. Review any security implications.
3. Record the change request.
4. Submit the change request for approval.
5. Develop the change.
   A. Recode segments of the product and add or subtract functionality.
   B. Link these changes in the code to the formal change control request.
   C. Submit software for testing and quality approval.
   D. Repeat until quality is adequate.
   E. Make version changes.
6. Report results to management.

The changes to systems may require another round of certification and accreditation. If the changes to a system are significant, then the functionality and level of protection may need to be reevaluated (certified), and management would have to approve the overall system, including the new changes (accreditation).

The Capability Maturity Model

The *Capability Maturity Model (CMM)* describes procedures, principles, and practices that underlie software development process maturity. This model was developed to help software vendors improve their development processes by providing an evolutionary path from an ad hoc "fly by the seat of your pants" approach, to a more disciplined and repeatable method that improves software quality, reduces the life cycle of development, provides better project management capabilities, allows for milestones to be created and met in a timely manner, and takes a more proactive approach than the less effective reactive approach.

This model provides policies, procedures, guidelines, and best practices to allow an organization to develop a standardized approach to software development that can be used across many different groups. The goal is to continue to review and improve upon the processes to optimize output, increase capabilities, and provide higher-quality software at a lower cost.

The model offers a layered framework that enables different organizations to implement continuous improvement. It is a tool for the software development company and one for those wanting to assess a vendor's development consistency and quality. For example, if the company StuffRUs wants a software development company, Software-RUs, to develop an application for it, it can choose to buy into the sales hype about how wonderful SoftwareRUs is, or it can ask for SoftwareRUs to be evaluated against the CMM model. Third-party companies evaluate software development companies to certify organizations' product development processes. Many software companies have this evaluation done so they can use this as a selling point to attract new customers.

Five maturity levels are used:

- **Initial**   Development process is ad hoc or even chaotic. The company does not use effective management procedures and plans. There is no assurance of consistency, and quality is unpredictable.

- **Repeatable**   A formal management structure, change control, and quality assurance are in place. The company can properly repeat processes throughout each project. The company does not have formal process models defined.

- **Defined**   Formal procedures are in place that outline and define processes carried out in each project. The organization has a way to allow for quantitative process improvement.

- **Managed**   The company has formal processes in place to collect and analyze qualitative data, and metrics are defined and fed into the process-improvement program.

- **Optimizing**   The company has budgeted and integrated plans for continuous process improvement.

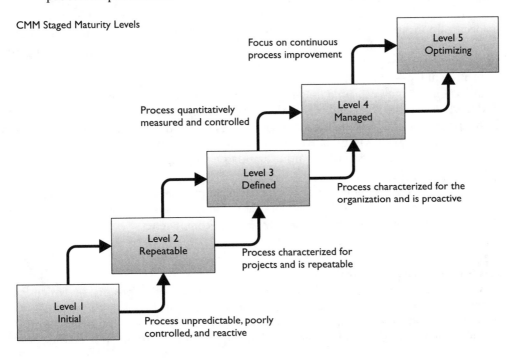

CMM Staged Maturity Levels

Focus on continuous process improvement

Level 5 Optimizing

Process quantitatively measured and controlled

Level 4 Managed

Process characterized for the organization and is proactive

Level 3 Defined

Process characterized for projects and is repeatable

Level 2 Repeatable

Process unpredictable, poorly controlled, and reactive

Level 1 Initial

Software Escrow

Will someone keep a copy of my source code?

If a company pays another company to develop software for it, it should have some type of *software escrow* in place for protection. In a software escrow, a third party keeps a copy of the source code, and possibly other materials, which it will release to the customer only if specific circumstances arise, mainly if the vendor who developed the code goes out of business or for some reason is not meeting its obligations and responsibilities. This procedure protects the customer, because the customer pays the vendor to develop software code for it, and if the vendor goes out of business, the customer otherwise would no longer have access to the actual code. This means the customer code could never be updated or maintained properly.

A logical question would be, "Why doesn't the vendor just hand over the source code to the customer, since the customer paid for it to be developed in the first place?" It does not work that way. The code is the vendor's intellectual property. The vendor employs and pays people with the necessary skills to develop that code, and if the vendor were to just hand it over to the customer, it would be giving away its intellectual property, its secrets. The customer gets compiled code instead of source code. Compiled code is code that has been put through a compiler and is unreadable to humans. Most software profits are based on licensing, which outlines what customers can do with the compiled code.

Application Development Methodology

Applications are written in programming code, which tells the operating system and processor what needs to happen to accomplish the user's requirements when operating a specific application. Programming languages have gone through several generations, each generation building on the next, providing richer functionality and giving the programmers more powerful tools as the languages evolve.

Different types of languages can be used: machine language, assembly language, and high-level languages. *Machine language* is in a form that the processor can understand and work with directly. *Assembly* and *high-level languages* cannot be understood directly by the processor and must be translated, which results in machine language. The process is typically done by a compiler, whose function is to turn human-understandable programming language into machine-understandable language, or object code.

 NOTE Assembly code will be turned into machine code by an assembler program. Assembly code works at the lower layers of a software architecture. Many drivers contain assembly language components.

Source Code vs. Machine Code

When source code is processed by a compiler, the result is object code, which is written for a specific platform and processor. This object code is the executable form of an application that a user purchases from a vendor. When the object code runs, it is in machine code, which is what the processor actually understands.

Generations of Languages

Program languages have evolved over time to provide programmers and systems with more functionality. The following is the current list of software program generations:

- Generation one: machine language
- Generation two: assembly language
- Generation three: high-level language
- Generation four: very high-level language
- Generation five: natural language

 WARNING You will need to know more detailed information about these different software program generations. Please read and understand the article "Programming Languages" at www.logicalsecurity.com/resources/resources_articles.html.

When a customer purchases a program, it is in object code form. The program has already been compiled, and it is ready to be executed and set up on the system. The compiler will put it into a form that specific processors can understand. This is why a program that works on a computer with an Alpha processor may not work on a computer with a Pentium processor. The programs work with different processors and operating systems that require different forms of machine language.

If the program was actually sold in the form of original source code, it would have to be complied on the customer's computer; thus, the customer must have the correct complier. Also, original source code would enable competing vendors to view each other's original ideas and techniques. Source code is considered intellectual property by vendors who develop software, and therefore should be highly protected.

Various programs are used to turn high-level programming code (or source code) into object or machine code. These programs are interpreters, compilers, and assemblers. They work as translators. *Interpreters* translate one command at a time during execution, and *compilers* translate large sections of code at a time. *Assemblers* translate assembly language into machine language. Most applications are compiled, whereas many scripting languages are interpreted.

 WARNING You will need to know more detailed information about different programming languages. Please read and understand the article "Programming Languages" at www.logicalsecurity.com/resources/resources_articles.html.

Object-Oriented Concepts

Objects are so cute, and small, and modular. I will take one in each color!

Software development used to be done by classic input-processing-output methods. This development used an information flow model from hierarchical information structures. Data was input into a program, and the program passed the data from the beginning to end, performed logical procedures, and returned a result.

Object-oriented programming (OOP) methods perform the same functionality but with different techniques that work in a more efficient manner. First, you need to understand the basic concepts of OOP.

OOP works with classes and objects. A real-world object, such as a table, is a member (or an instance) of a larger class of objects called "furniture." The furniture class will have a set of attributes associated with it, and when an object is generated, it inherits these attributes. The attributes may be color, dimensions, weight, style, and cost. These attributes apply if a chair, table, or loveseat object is generated, also referred to as *instantiated*. Because the table is a member of the class furniture, the table inherits all attributes defined for the class (see Figure 11-13).

The programmer develops the class and all of its characteristics and attributes. The programmer does not develop each and every object, which is the beauty of this approach. As an analogy, let's say you developed a super-duper coffee maker with the goal of putting Starbucks out of business. A customer punches the available buttons on your coffee maker interface, which is a large latte, with skim milk, vanilla and raspberry flavoring, and an extra shot of espresso, where the coffee is served at 250 degrees. Your coffee maker does all of this through automation and provides the customer with a lovely cup of coffee exactly to her liking. The next customer wants a mocha frappuccino, with whole milk, and extra foam. (Remember the days when we just asked for a cup of coffee and life wasn't this complicated?) So the goal is to make something once (coffee maker, class), allow it to accept requests through an interface, and create various results (cups of coffee, objects) depending upon the requests submitted.

Figure 11-13
In object-oriented inheritance, each object belongs to a class and takes on the attributes of that class.

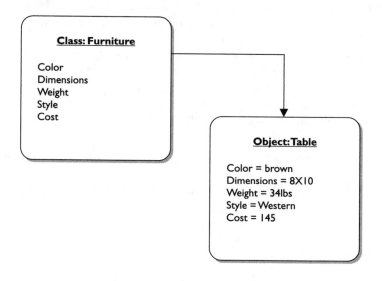

Class: Furniture

Color
Dimensions
Weight
Style
Cost

Object: Table

Color = brown
Dimensions = 8X10
Weight = 34lbs
Style = Western
Cost = 145

But how does the class create objects based on requests? A piece of software that is written in OOP will have a request sent to it, usually from another object. The requesting object wants a new object to carry out some type of functionality. Let's say that object A wants object B to carry out subtraction on the numbers sent from A to B. When this request comes in, an object is built (instantiated) with all of the necessary programming code. Object B carries out the subtraction task and sends the result back to object A. It does not matter what programming language the two objects are written in; what matters is if they know how to communicate with each other. One object can communicate with another object if it knows the application programming code (API) communication requirements. An API is the mechanism that allows objects to talk to each other. Let's say if I want to talk to you, I can only do it by speaking French and I can only use three phrases or less, because that is all you understand. As long as I follow these rules, I can talk to you. If I don't follow these rules, I can't talk to you.

NOTE An object is preassembled code that is a self-contained module.

So what's so great about OOP? If you look at Figure 11-14, you can see the difference between OOP and non-OOP techniques. Non-OOP applications are written as monolithic entities. This means an application is just one big pile of code. If you need to change something in this pile, you would need to go through the whole program's logic functions to figure out what your one change is going to break. If the program contains hundreds or thousands of lines of code, this is not an easy or enjoyable task. Now, if you choose to write your program in an object-oriented language, you don't have one monolithic application, but an application that is made up of smaller components (objects). If you need to make changes or updates to some functionality in your application, you can just change the code within the class that creates the object carrying out that functionality and not worry about everything else the program actually carries out. The following breaks down the benefits of OOP:

- Modularity
  - Autonomous objects, cooperation through exchanges of messages.
- Deferred commitment
  - The internal components of an object can be redefined without changing other parts of the system.
- Reusability
  - Refining classes through inheritance.
  - Other programs using same objects.
- Naturalness
  - Object-oriented analysis, design, and modeling maps to business needs and solutions.

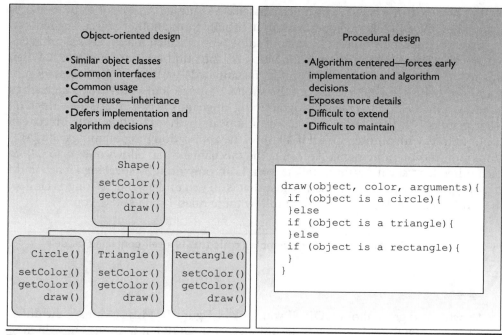

Figure 11-14 Procedural versus object-oriented programming

Most applications have some type of functionality in common. Instead of developing the same code to carry out the same functionality for ten different applications, using OOP allows you to just create the object once and let it be reused in other applications. This reduces development time and saves money.

Now that we understand the concepts, let's figure out the different terminology used. A *method* is the functionality or procedure an object can carry out. An object may be constructed to accept data from a user and to reformat the request so a back-end server can understand and process it. Another object may perform a method that extracts data from a database and populates a web page with this information. Or an object may carry out a withdrawal procedure to allow the user of an ATM to extract money from her account.

The objects encapsulate the attribute values, which means this information is packaged under one name and can be reused as one entity by other objects. Objects need to be able to communicate with each other, and this happens by using *messages* that are sent to the receiving object's API. If object A needs to tell object B that a user's checking account must be reduced by $40, it sends object B a message. The message is made up of the destination, the method that needs to be performed, and the corresponding arguments. Figure 11-15 shows this example.

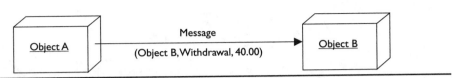

Figure 11-15 Objects communicate via messages.

An object can have a shared portion and a private portion. The shared portion is the interface (API) that enables it to interact with other components. Messages enter through the interface to specify the requested operation, or method, to be performed. The private part of an object is how it actually works and performs the requested operations. Other components need not know how each object works internally—only that it does the job requested of it. This is how *information hiding* is possible. The details of the processing are hidden from all other program elements outside the object. Objects communicate through well-defined interfaces; therefore, they do not need to know how each of their siblings works.

NOTE Data hiding is provided by encapsulation, which protects an object's private data from outside access. No object should be allowed to, or have the need to, access another object's internal data or processes.

These objects can grow to great numbers, so the complexity of understanding, tracking, and analyzing can get a bit overwhelming. Many times, the objects are shown in connection to a reference or pointer in documentation. Figure 11-16 shows how related objects are represented as a specific piece, or reference, in an ATM system. This enables analysts and developers to look at a higher level of operation and procedures without having to view each individual object and its code. Thus, this modularity provides for a more easily understood model.

Abstraction is the capability to suppress unnecessary details so the important, inherent properties can be examined and reviewed. It enables the separation of conceptual aspects of a system. For example, if a software architect needs to understand how data flows through the program, she would want to understand the big pieces of the program and trace the steps the data takes from first being input into the program all the way until it exits the program as output. It would be difficult to understand this concept if the small details of every piece of the program were presented. Instead, through abstraction, all the details are suppressed so she can understand a crucial part of the product. It is like being able to see a forest without having to look at each and every tree.

Messaging can happen in several ways. Two objects can have a single connection (one to one), a multiple connection (one to many), and a mandatory connection or an optional connection. It is important to map these communication paths to identify if information can flow in a way that is not intended. This will help ensure that sensitive data cannot be passed to objects of a lower security level.

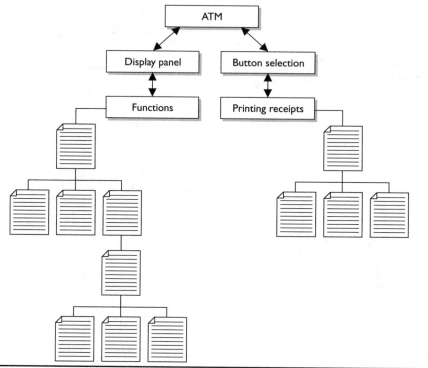

Figure 11-16 Object relationships within a program

Each object should have specifications it should adhere to. This discipline provides cleaner programming and reduces programming errors and omissions. The following list is an example of what should be developed for each object:

- Object name
- Attribute descriptions
- Attribute name
- Attribute content
- Attribute data type
- External input to object
- External output from object
- Operation descriptions
- Operation name
- Operation interface description
- Operation processing description

- Performance issues
- Restrictions and limitations
- Instance connections
- Message connections

The developer creates a class that outlines these specifications. When objects are instantiated, they inherit these attributes.

Each object can be reused as stated previously, which is the beauty of OOP. This enables a more efficient use of resources and the programmer's time. Different applications can use the same objects, which reduces redundant work, and as an application grows in functionality, objects can be easily added and integrated into the original structure.

The objects can be catalogued in a library, which provides an economical way for more than one application to call upon the objects (see Figure 11-17). The library provides an index and pointers to where the objects actually live within the system or on another system.

When applications are developed in a modular approach, like object-oriented methods, components can be reused, complexity is reduced, and parallel development can be done. These characteristics allow for fewer mistakes, easier modification, resource efficiency, and more timely coding than the classic information flow models. OOP also provides functional independence, which means each module addresses a specific subfunction of requirements and has an interface that is easily understood by other parts of the application.

An object is encapsulated, meaning the data structure (the operation's functionality) and the acceptable ways of accessing it are grouped into one entity. Other objects, subjects, and applications can use this object and its functionality by accessing it through controlled and standardized interfaces and sending it messages (see Figure 11-18).

Figure 11-17
Applications locate the necessary objects through a library index.

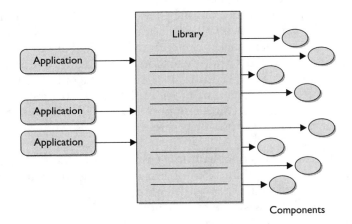

Figure 11-18
The different
components of an
object and the way
it works are hidden
from other objects.

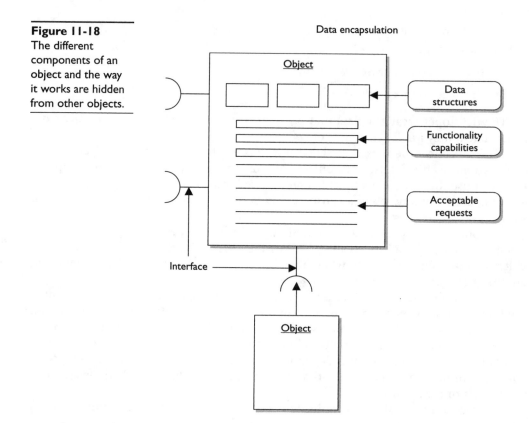

Polymorphism

Polymorphism is a funny name.
Response: You are funny looking.

Polymorphism comes from the Greek meaning "having multiple forms." This concept usually confuses people, so let's jump right into an example. If I developed a program in an OOP language, I can create a variable that can be used in different forms. The application will determine what form to use at the time of execution (run time). So if my variable is named USERID and I develop the object so the variable can accept either an integer or letters, this provides flexibility. This means the user ID can be accepted as a number (account number) or name (characters). If application A uses this object, it can choose to use integers for the user IDs, while application B can choose to use characters.

What confuses people with this term is that (ISC)² commonly uses the following definition or description: "Two objects can receive the same input and have different outputs." Clear as mud.

As a simplistic example of polymorphism, suppose three different objects receive the input "Bob." Object A would process this input and produce the output "43-year-old white male." Object B would receive the input "Bob" and produce the output "Husband of Sally." Object C would produce the output of "Member of User group." Each object received the same input, but responded with a different output.

Polymorphism can also take place in the following example: Object A and Object B are created from the same parent class, but Object B is also under a subclass. Object B would have some different characteristics from Object A because of this inheritance from the parent class *and* the subclass. When Object A and Object B receive the same input, they would result in different outputs because only one of them inherited characteristics from the subclass.

NOTE Polymorphism is when different objects respond to the same command, input, or message in different ways.

From here, the programmer uses OOP to create the components laid out in the design and those that must be tested.

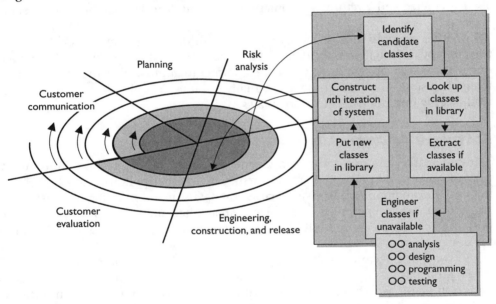

How Do We Know What to Create?

Object-oriented analysis (OOA) is the process of classifying objects that will be appropriate for a solution. A problem is analyzed to determine the classes of objects to be used in the application.

Object-oriented design (OOD) creates a representation of a real-world problem and maps it to a software solution using OOP. The result of an OOD is a design that modularizes data and procedures. The design interconnects data objects and processing operations.

Data Modeling

Let's see. The data went thataway. Oh no, it went thataway. Oops, I lost the data.

The previous paragraphs have provided a simple look at a *structured analysis approach*. A full-structured analysis approach looks at all objects and subjects of an application and maps the interrelationships, communications paths, and inheritance properties. This is different from *data modeling*, which considers data independently of the way the data are processed and of the components that process the data. A data model follows an input value from beginning to end and verifies that the output is correct. OOA is an example of a structured analysis approach. If an analyst is reviewing the OOA of an application, she will make sure all relationships are set up correctly, that the inheritance flows in a predictable and usable manner, that the instances of objects are practical and provide the necessary functionality, and that the attributes of each class cover all the necessary values used by the application. When another analyst does a data model review of the same application, he will follow the data and the returned values after processing takes place. An application can have a perfect OOA structure, but when 1 + 1 is entered and it returns −3, something is wrong. This is what the data modeling looks at.

Another example of data modeling deals with databases. Data modeling can be used to provide insight into the data and the relationships that govern it. A data item in one file structure, or data store, might be a pointer to another file structure or to a different data store. These pointers must actually point to the right place. Data modeling would verify this, not OOA structure analysis.

Software Architecture

Software architecture relates the components that make up a software solution to the parts of a real-world problem. Software architects view the application at a higher level than do the programmers, who are focused on data structures, coding rules, variables, and communication paths between objects. An architectural view looks at how the application actually meets and fulfills the requirements recognized and agreed upon in the design phase.

Software architecture involves the process of partitioning requirements into individual problems that can be solved by individual software solutions. This process is the transition phase between the software requirement analysis and the design of the actual components that make up the resulting application.

If the requirements are that the application will scan hard drives and e-mail messages for viruses, the software architecture will break these requirements into individual units that need to be achieved by functionality within that application. These units may include the following functionalities:

- Virus signature storage
- An agent that compares software strings on hard drives to virus signatures
- A process of parsing an e-mail message before the user can view it
- Procedures necessary if data on a hard drive is compressed

- Actions taken if a virus is found
- Actions taken if an e-mail attachment is encrypted

This way of developing a product provides more control and modularity of issues and solutions. If a group of programmers is told to develop an antivirus software package, the group may sit there like deer caught in headlights. However, if one developer is told to write a piece of the program that holds and updates signature files, another developer is told to determine how data on the hard drive will be compared with the signatures within the signature files, and another developer is instructed to program a way to read compressed files, then the programmers will have set goals and start pounding at the keyboards.

Software architects need to provide this type of direction: a high-level view of the application's objectives and a vision of the overall goals of the project.

Data Structures

A *data structure* is a representation of the logical relationship between elements of data. It dictates the degree of association between elements, methods of access, processing alternatives, and the organization of data elements.

The structure can be simple in nature, like the scalar item, which represents a single element that can be addressed by an identifier and accessed by a single address in storage. The scalar items can be grouped in arrays, which provide access by indexes. Other data structures include hierarchical structures by using multilinked lists that contain scalar items, vectors, and possibly arrays. The hierarchical structure provides categorization and association. If a user can make a request of an application to find all computer books written on security, and that application returns a list, then this application is using a hierarchical data structure of some kind. Figure 11-19 shows simple and complex data structures.

Cohesion and Coupling

I do a bunch of stuff and rely on many other modules.
Response: Low cohesion and high coupling describes you best, then.

 Cohesion reflects how many different types of tasks a module can carry out. If a module carries out only one task (subtraction of values) or several tasks that are very similar (subtract, add, multiply), it is described as having high cohesion, which is a good thing. The higher the cohesion, the easier it is to update or modify and not affect other modules that interact with it. This also means the module is easier to reuse and maintain because it is more straightforward when compared to a module with low cohesion. A model with low cohesion carries out multiple different tasks and increases the complexity of the module, which makes it harder to maintain and reuse.

 Coupling is a measurement that indicates how much interaction one module requires to carry out its tasks. If a module has low (loose) coupling, this means the module does not need to communicate to many other modules to carry out its job. High (tight) coupling means a module depends upon many other modules to carry out its

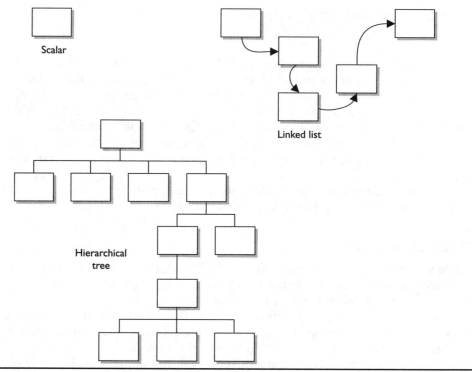

Figure 11-19 Data structures range from very simple to very complex in nature and design.

tasks. Low coupling is more desirable because the modules are easier to understand, easier to reuse, and changes can take place and not affect many modules around it. Low coupling indicates that the programmer created a well-structured module. As an analogy, a company would want their employees to be able to carry out their individual jobs with the least amount of dependencies on other workers. If Joe had to talk with five other people just to get one task done, too much complexity exists, it's too time-consuming, and more places are created where errors can take place.

An example of *low coupling* would be one module passing a variable value to another module. As an example of *high coupling*, Module A would pass a value to Module B, another value to Module C, and yet another value to Module D. Module A cannot complete its tasks until Modules B, C, and D complete their tasks and return results back to Module A.

NOTE Modules should be self-contained and perform a single logical function, which is high cohesion. Modules should not drastically affect each other, which is low coupling.

Distributed Computing

Many of our applications work in a client/server model, which means the smaller part (client) of the application can run on different systems and the larger piece (server) of the application runs on a server. The server portion carries out more functionality and horsepower compared to the clients. The clients will send the server portion requests, and the server will respond with a result. Simple enough, but how do the client and server pieces actually carry out communication with each other?

The three main intercomponent communication architectures used today are Common Object Request Broker Architecture (CORBA), Microsoft COM model, and EJB (Enterprise Java Beans). We will be covering these in the next sections.

A distributed object computing model needs to register the client and server components, which means to find out where they live on the network, what their names or IDs are, and what type of functionality the different components carry out. So the first step is basically, "Where are all the pieces, how do I call upon them when I need them, and what do they do?" This organization must be put in place because the coordination between the components should be controlled and monitored, and requests and results must be able to pass back and forth between the correct components.

Life might be easier if we had just one intercomponent communication architecture for developers to follow, but what fun would that be? The different architectures work a little differently from each other and are necessary to work in different programming environments. Nevertheless, they all perform the basic function of allowing components on the client and server side to communicate with each other.

CORBA and ORBs

Has anyone seen my ORB? I need to track down an object.

If we want components to be able to communicate, this means standardized interfaces and communication methods must be used. This is the only way interoperability can take place.

Common Object Request Broker Architecture (CORBA) is an open object-oriented standard architecture developed by the Object Management Group (OMG). It provides interoperability among the vast array of software, platforms, and hardware in environments today. CORBA enables applications to communicate with one another no matter where the applications are located or who developed them.

This standard defines the APIs, communication protocol, and client/server communication methods to allow heterogeneous applications written in different programming languages and run on various platforms to work together. Sounds just lovely.

The OMG developed the CORBA model for the use of these different services in an environment. The model defines object semantics so the external visible characteristics are standard and are viewed the same by all other objects in the environment. This standardization enables many different developers to write hundreds or thousands of components that can interact with other components in an environment without having to know how the component actually works. The developers know how to communicate with the components because the interfaces are uniform and follow the rules of the model.

In the model, clients request services from objects. The client passes the object a message that contains the name of the object, the requested operation, and any necessary parameters.

The CORBA model provides standards to build a complete distributed environment. It contains two main parts: system-oriented components (*object request brokers [ORBs]* and object services) and application-oriented components (application objects and common facilities). The ORB manages all communications between components and enables them to interact in a heterogeneous and distributed environment, as shown in Figure 11-20. The ORB works independently of the platforms where the objects reside, which provides greater interoperability.

ORB is the middleware that establishes the client/server relationship between objects. When a client needs to access an object on a server for that object to perform an operation or method, the ORB intercepts the request and is responsible for finding the object. Once the object is found, the ORB invokes a method (or operation), passes the parameters, and returns the result to the client. The client software does not need to know where the object resides or go through the trouble of finding it. That is the ORB's job. The objects can be written in different languages and reside on different operating systems and platforms, but the client does not need to worry about any of this (see Figure 11-21).

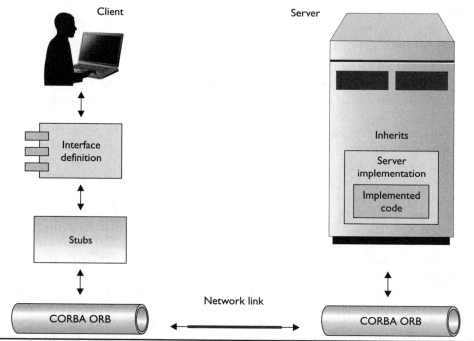

Figure 11-20 The ORB enables different components throughout a network to communicate and work with each other.

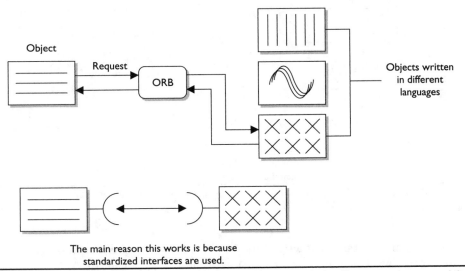

Object

Request

ORB

Objects written
in different
languages

The main reason this works is because
standardized interfaces are used.

Figure 11-21 CORBA provides standard interface definitions, which offer greater interoperability in heterogeneous environments.

When objects communicate with each other, they use *pipes*, which are intercomponent communications services. Different types of pipes are available, such as remote procedure calls (RPCs) and ORBs. ORBs provide communications between distributed objects. If an object on a workstation must have an object on a server process data, it can make a request through the ORB, which will track down the needed object and facilitate the communication path between these two objects until the process is complete. This is the client/server communication pipe used in many networking environments.

ORBs are mechanisms that enable objects to communicate locally or remotely. They enable objects to make requests to objects and receive responses. This happens transparently to the client and provides a type of pipeline between all corresponding objects. Using CORBA enables an application to be usable with many different types of ORBs. It provides portability for applications and tackles many of the interoperability issues that many vendors and developers run into when their products are implemented into different environments.

COM and DCOM

Component Object Model (COM) is a model that allows for interprocess communication within one application or between applications on the same computer system. The model was created by Microsoft and outlines standardized APIs, component naming schemes, and communication standards. So if I am a developer and I want my application to be able to interact with the Windows operating system and the different applications developed for this platform, I will follow the COM outlined standards.

Distributed Component Object Model (DCOM) supports the same model for component interaction, and also supports *distributed* IPC. COM enables applications to use components on the same systems, while DCOM enables applications to access objects

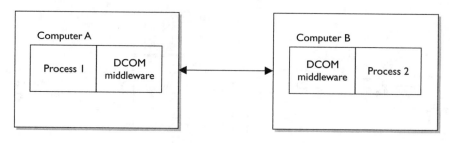

It is the middleware portion of DCOM
that allows different processes
to communicate across a network.

Figure 11-22 Although DCOM provides communication mechanisms in a distributed environment, it still works off of the COM architecture.

that reside in different parts of a network. So this is how the client/server-based activities are carried by COM-based operating systems and/or applications.

Without DCOM, programmers would have to write much more complicated code to find necessary objects, set up network sockets, and incorporate the services necessary to allow communication. DCOM takes care of these issues (and more), and enables the programmer to focus on his tasks of developing the necessary functionality within his application. DCOM has a library that takes care of session handling, synchronization, buffering, fault identification and handling, and data format translation.

DCOM works as the middleware that enables distributed processing and provides developers with services that support process-to-process communications across networks (see Figure 11-22).

Other types of middleware provide similar functionality: ORB, message-oriented middleware (MOM), RPC, ODBC, and so on. DCOM provides ORB-like services, data connectivity services, distributed messaging services, and distributed transaction services layered over its RPC mechanism. DCOM integrates all of these functionalities into one technology that uses the same interface as COM (see Figure 11-23).

Figure 11-23
DCOM provides
several services over
its RPC mechanism
and a COM interface.

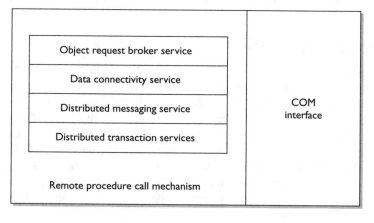

SOAP

What if we need programs running on different operating systems to communicate over web-based communication methods? We would use Simple Object Access Protocol (SOAP). SOAP is an XML-based protocol that encodes messages in a web service setup. So if you have a Windows 2000 computer, for instance, and you need to access a Windows 2008 computer that offers a specific web service, the programs on both systems can communicate using SOAP without running into interoperability issues. This communication most commonly takes place over HTTP because it is readily available in basically all computers today.

When the Windows 2000 computer makes a request of the Windows 2008 computer for some type of service, SOAP encodes the request so that the other program can understand it and then respond with the service that was asked for.

SOAP actually defines an XML schema or a structure of how communication is going to take place. The SOAP XML schema defines how objects communicate directly. One advantage of SOAP is that the program calls will most likely get through firewalls because HTTP communication is commonly allowed. This helps ensure that the client/server model is not broken by getting denied by a firewall in between the communicating entities.

Enterprise JavaBeans

Enterprise JavaBeans (EJB) is a structural design for the development and implementation of distributed applications written in Java. EJB provides interfaces and methods to allow different applications to be able to communicate across a networked environment. By using the Internet Inter-ORB Protocol (IIOP), the client portion does not have to be a program written in Java, but can be any valid CORBA client.

NOTE A Java component is called a Java Bean.

The Java Platform Enterprise Edition has several APIs, EJB being just one of them. EJB is used to encapsulate the business logic of an application on the server (in the client/server model). Just as the COM and CORBA models were created to allow a modular approach to programming code with the goal of interoperability, EJB defines a client/server model that is object-oriented and platform independent. The main goal is to have a standardized method of implementing back-end code that carries out business logic for enterprise-wide applications.

Object Linking and Embedding

Object linking and embedding (OLE) provides a way for objects to be shared on a local personal computer and to use COM as their foundation. OLE enables objects—such as graphics, pictures, and spreadsheets—to be embedded into documents. In this book, many graphics have been placed throughout the text, and OLE technology was used to do so.

> ## OLE
> The capability for one program to call another program is called linking. The capability to place a piece of data inside a foreign program or document is called embedding.

OLE also allows for linking different objects and documents. For example, when Chrissy creates a document that contains a URL, that URL turns blue and is underlined, indicating a user can just double-click it to be taken to the appropriate web site. This is an example of linking capabilities. If Chrissy adds a spreadsheet to her document, this is an instance of embedding. If she needs to edit the spreadsheet, she can double-click the spreadsheet, and the operating system will open the correct environment (which might be Excel) to let her make her changes.

This technology was evolved to work on the World Wide Web and is called ActiveX. The components are like other components, but are meant to be portable. ActiveX components can run on any platform that supports DCOM (using the COM model) or that communicates using DCOM services.

Distributed Computing Environment

Distributed Computing Environment (DCE) is a standard developed by the Open Software Foundation (OSF), also called Open Group. It is basically middleware that is available to many vendors to use within their products. This middleware has the capability to support many types of applications across an enterprise. DCE provides an RPC service, security service, directory service, time service, and distributed file support.

DCE is a set of management services with a communications layer based on RPC. It is a layer of software that sits on the top of the network layer and provides services to the applications above it. DCE and DCOM offer much of the same functionality. DCOM, however, was developed by Microsoft and is more proprietary in nature.

DCE's time service provides host clock synchronization and enables applications to determine sequencing and to schedule events based on this clock synchronization. This time synchronization is for applications. Users cannot access this functionality directly. The directory service enables users, servers, and resources to be contacted anywhere on the network. When the directory service is given the name, it returns the network address of the resource along with other necessary information. DCOM uses a *globally unique identifier (GUID)*, while DCE uses a *universal unique identifier (UUID)*. They are both used to uniquely identify users, resources, and components within an environment. DCE is illustrated in Figure 11-24.

The RPC function collects the arguments and commands from the sending program and prepares them for transmission over the network. RPC determines the network transport protocol to be used and finds the receiving host's address in the directory service. The thread service provides real-time priority scheduling in a multithreading environment. The security services support authentication and authorization services. The distributed file service (DFS), on the other hand, provides a single integrated file system that all DCE users can use to share files. This is important because many environments have different operating systems that cannot understand other file systems. However, if DCE is being used, a DCE local file system exists alongside the native file system.

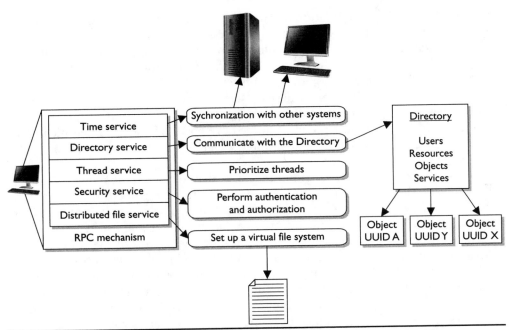

Figure 11-24 DCE provides many services, which are all wrapped into one technology.

Expert Systems and Knowledge-Based Systems

Hey, this computer is smarter than me!
Response: No surprise there.

Expert systems, also called *knowledge-based systems*, use artificial intelligence (AI) to solve problems.

AI software uses nonnumerical algorithms to solve complex problems, recognize hidden patterns, prove theorems, play games, mine data, and help in forecasting and diagnosing a range of issues. The type of computation done by AI software cannot be accomplished by straightforward analyses and regular programming logic techniques.

Expert systems emulate human logic to solve problems that would usually require human intelligence and intuition. These systems represent expert knowledge as data or rules within the software of a system, and this data and these rules are called upon when it is necessary to solve a problem. Knowledge-based systems collect data of human know-how and hold it in some type of database. These fragments of data are used to reason through a problem.

A regular program can deal with inputs and parameters only in the ways in which it has been designed and programmed. Although a regular program can calculate the mortgage payments of a house over 20 years at an 8-percent interest rate, it cannot necessarily forecast the placement of stars in 100 million years because of all the unknowns and possible variables that come into play. Although both programs—a regular program and an expert system—have a finite set of information available to them, the expert system will attempt to "think" like a person, reason through different scenarios, and provide an answer even without all the necessary data. Conventional programming deals with procedural manipulation of data, whereas humans attempt to solve complex problems using abstract and symbolic approaches.

A book may contain a lot of useful information, but a person has to read that book, interpret its meaning, and then attempt to use those interpretations within the real world. This is what an expert system attempts to do.

Professionals in the field of AI develop techniques that provide the modeling of information at higher levels of abstraction. The techniques are part of the languages and tools used, which enable programs to be developed that closely resemble human logic. The programs that can emulate human expertise in specific domains are called *expert systems*.

Rule-based programming is a common way of developing expert systems. The rules are based on if-then logic units and specify a set of actions to be performed for a given situation. This is one way expert systems are used to find patterns, which is called *pattern matching*. A mechanism, called the *inference engine*, automatically matches facts against patterns and determines which rules are applicable. The actions of the corresponding rules are executed when the inference engine is instructed to begin execution.

Huh? Okay, let's say Dr. Gorenz is puzzled by a patient's symptoms and is unable to match the problems the patient is having to a specific ailment and find the right cure. So he uses an expert system to help him in his diagnosis. Dr. Gorenz can initiate the expert system, which will then take him through question-and-answer scenarios. The expert system will use the information gathered through this interaction, and it will go step by step through the facts, looking for patterns that can be tied to known diseases, ailments, and medical issues. Although Dr. Gorenz is very smart and one of the top doctors in his field, he cannot necessarily recall all possible diseases and ailments. The expert system can analyze this information because it is working off of a database that has been stuffed full of medical information that can fill up several libraries.

As the expert system goes through the medical information, it may see that the patient had a case of severe hives six months ago, had a case of ringing in the ears and blurred vision three months ago, and has a history of diabetes. The system will look at the patient's recent complaints of joint aches and tiredness. With each finding, the expert system digs deeper, looking for further information, and then uses all the information obtained and compares it with the knowledge base available to it. In the end, the expert system returns a diagnosis to Dr. Gorenz that says the patient is suffering from a rare disease found only in Brazil that is caused by a specific mold that grows on bananas. Because the patient has diabetes, his sensitivity is much higher to this contaminant. The system spits out the necessary treatment. Then, Dr. Gorenz marches back into the room where the patient is waiting and explains the problem and protects his reputation of being a really smart doctor.

Expert Systems

An expert system is a computer program containing a knowledge base and a set of algorithms and rules used to infer new facts from data and incoming requests.

The system not only uses a database of facts, but also collects a wealth of knowledge from experts in a specific field. This knowledge is captured by using interactive tools that have been engineered specifically to capture human knowledge. This knowledge base is then transferred to automated systems that help in human decisions by offering advice, free up experts from repetitive routine decisions, ensure decisions are made in a consistent and quick manner, and allow a company to retain its organization's expertise even as employees come and go.

An expert system usually consists of two parts: an inference engine and a knowledge base. The inference engine handles the user interface, external files, scheduling, and program-accessing capabilities. The knowledge base contains data pertaining to a specific problem or domain. Expert systems use the inference engine to decide how to execute a program or how the rules should be initiated and followed. The inference engine of a knowledge-based system provides the necessary rules for the system to take the original facts and combine them to form new facts.

The systems employ AI programming languages to allow for real-world decision making. The system is built by a knowledge system builder (programmer), a knowledge engineer (analyst), and subject matter expert(s), as shown in Figure 11-25. It is built on facts, rules of thumb, and expert advice. The information gathered from the expert(s) during the development of the system is kept in a knowledge base and is used during the question-and-answer session with the end user. The system works as a consultant to the end user and can recommend several alternative solutions by considering competing hypotheses at the same time.

Expert systems are commonly used to automate a security log review for an IDS.

 NOTE Expert systems use automatic logical processing, inference engine processing, and general methods of searching for problem solutions.

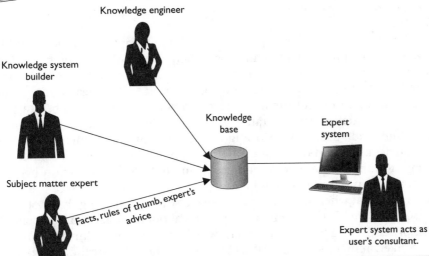

Figure 11-25 What goes into developing an expert system and how the system is used once developed

Artificial Neural Networks

An *artificial neural network (ANN)* is a mathematical or computational model based on the neural structure of the brain. Computers perform activities like calculating large numbers, keeping large ledgers, and performing complex mathematical functions, but they cannot recognize patterns or learn from experience as the brain can. ANNs contain many units that stimulate neurons, each with a small amount of memory. The units work on data that are input through their many connections. Via training rules, the systems are able to learn from examples and have the capability to generalize.

The brain stores information in forms of patterns. People have the ability to recognize another person's face from several different angles. Each angle of that person's face is made up of a complex set of patterns. Even if only half the face is seen or the face is viewed in a shadow or dark lighting, the human brain can insert the missing pieces, and people can recognize their friends and acquaintances. A computer that uses conventional programming and logic would have to have each piece of the pattern and the full face in one particular angle to be able to match or recognize it.

The brain uses neurons to remember, think, apply previous experiences, perform logic, and recognize patterns. The capacity of the brain comes from the large number of neurons and the multiple connections between them. The power of the brain is a result of genetic programming and learning.

ANNs try to replicate the basic functions of neurons and their circuitry to solve problems in a new way. They consist of many simple computational neural units connected to each other. An input value is presented to one, some, or all the units, which in turn perform functions on the data.

The brain has clusters of neurons that process in an interactive and dynamic way. Biologically, neurons have no restrictions of interconnections among themselves; therefore, a neuron can have thousands of connections. In addition, the neurons in the brain work in a three-dimensional world, whereas the electronic units in ANNs have a physical limitation on the possible number of connections and thus operate in a two-dimensional world.

Like the brain, the ANN's real power comes from its capability to learn. Within the brain, when something is learned and used often, the connection path to where that information is stored is strengthened to provide quicker access. This is why sometimes you know something but "can't put your finger on it." This means there is no pronounced pathway to the information stored somewhere in the brain. If a person is asked her phone number, she can rattle it off without any real energy. But if you ask her who her third-grade teacher was, it might take more time and energy. Both facts are held within her brain, but the phone number has a more pronounced connection path and comes to mind more quickly and easily. In an ANN, a connection between two units that are often activated might be strengthened, which is a form of learning.

It is known that when something happens to someone in a highly emotional state, that person is more likely to remember specifics about a situation or incident. If Joyce had a surprise party on her 35th birthday, which was filled with fun and emotion, she will most likely remember that birthday more than her 36th birthday, when her husband only bought her a card. But she and her husband will probably remember her

45th birthday, when her husband forgot her birthday, because the fight that occurred was full of emotion and activity. The reason some memories are more vivid than others is because more emotion is tied to them, or more weight is assigned to them. In ANNs, some inputs have higher weights assigned to them than other inputs, which amplifies the meaning or importance of the inputs, just like emotion does with human beings.

NOTE Decisions by ANNs are only as good as the experiences they are given.

Intuition is a hard quality to replicate in electrical circuits and logic gates. Fuzzy logic and other mathematical disciplines are used for intuition, forecasting, and intelligent guessing. These approaches work with types of probability within mathematics and memberships of different sets. One simple example of the use of fuzzy logic is a washing machine that has built-in intelligence. When a person puts a load of clothes in the washing machine and the tank fills with water, the machine using fuzzy logic sends a beam from one part of the tank to the other. Depending on how much light actually was received at the other end, it can determine how dirty the clothes are because of the density of the dirt in the water. Additional tests can be used to see if the dirt is oily or dry and to check other relevant attributes. The washing machine takes in all this information and estimates the right temperature and the right amount of laundry soap to use. This provides a more efficient way of washing, by saving on water and soap and washing the clothes at the right temperature for the right amount of time. The washing machine does not necessarily know all the facts or know that the information it gathered is 100-percent correct, but it can make guesses that will be pretty close to reality.

ANNs are programmed with the capability to decide and to learn to improve their functionality through massive trial-and-error decision making.

Fuzzy logic is necessary because a regular computer system does not see the world in shades of gray. It cannot differentiate between good, bad, few, and many. Fuzzy logic is an approach to enable the computer to use these vague values that mean something to humans but nothing to computers.

Stock market forecasting and insurance and financial risk assessments are examples of where fuzzy logic can be used and is most beneficial. They require a large number of variables and decision-making information from experts in those particular domains. The system can indicate which insurance or financial risks are good or bad without the user having to input a stack of conditions, if-then statements, and variable values.

Conventional systems see the world in black and white and work in a sea of precision and decimal points. Fuzzy logic enables the computer to incorporate imprecision into the programming language, which opens up a whole new world for computing and attacking complex issues. Neural network researchers attempt to understand more of how the brain works and of nature's capabilities so newly engineered ANN solutions can solve more complex problems than could be solved through traditional computing means.

Web Security

When it comes to the Internet and web-based applications, many situations are unique to this area. Rarely are threats of vandalism an issue in typical computing environments. Also, the potential risk for fraud is higher due to the universal availability of these applications over the Internet. The reason we are using the Internet is to expose our product or service to the widest possible audience. We smartly put these web servers in the DMZ so those who access these servers don't have direct access to our other internal servers. One of the unfortunate issues when using web-based applications is that you need to allow the Internet to access them in order for them to function, so you must open up the ports related to the Web (80 and 443) on your firewall—so now any attack that can come through on these ports is "game on."

The applications themselves are somewhat mysterious to the purveyors of the Internet as well. If you want to sell your homemade pies via the Internet, you'll typically need to display them in graphic form and allow some form of communication for questions (via e-mail or online chat). You'll need some sort of shopping cart if you want to actually collect money for your pies, and typically you'll have to deal with interfacing with shipping and payment processing channels . . . all of this from someone who just wanted to sell pies! If you are a master baker, you probably *aren't* a webmaster, so now you'll have to rely on someone else to set up your web site and load the appropriate applications on it. Should you develop your own PHP- or Java-based application? The benefits could be wonderful, having a customized application that would further automate your business, but the risks of developing an in-house application (especially if it's your first time) are great if you haven't developed the methodology, development process, QA, and change control, as well as identified the risks and vulnerabilities . . . all of this to sell pies? Now you understand why those nice ladies and gents sell them by the roadside—no web application headaches!

The alternative to developing your own web application is using an off-the-shelf variety instead. Many commercial and free options are available for nearly every e-commerce need. These are written in a variety of languages, by a variety of entities, so now the issue is, "Whom should we trust?" Do these developers have the same processes in place that you would have used yourself? Have these applications been developed and tested with the appropriate security in mind? Will these applications introduce any vulnerabilities along with the functionality they provide? Does your webmaster understand the security implications associated with the web application he suggests you use on your site for certain functionality? These are the problems that plague not only those wanting to sell homemade pies on the Internet, but also financial institutions, auction sites, and everyone who is involved in e-commerce.

With all of these issues in mind, let's try to define the most glaring threats associated with having a web server connected to the Internet.

Vandalism

This attack usually involves replacing the legitimate graphics and titles on a web site with ones modified by the attacker. You may wonder why vandalism is a threat to your web server. Actually, many script-kiddies are hacking systems solely for bragging rights. Messing up your pie shop may not be as impressive to the hacking elite as defacing a .gov or .mil site, but any site must be guarded. Public perception is also at risk here: even though technically astute customers can understand that the hacker only replaced a graphic on the front page of your site, everyone else believes that hackers accessed the entire customer database. Remember: perception is reality!

Financial Fraud

Money is a strong motivator to those who would like something for nothing. Whenever transactions are involved, the potential for fraud is present, especially in an anonymous environment like the Internet. The same people who wouldn't dare steal a newspaper from a broken vending machine in public find it easy to rationalize the theft of web-based goods and services over the Internet.

Privileged Access

The Web and its players are distributed all over the planet. You can have employees making pies in Tulsa, a webmaster who lives in Singapore, and your servers hosted in London. This being the case, there has to be a mechanism for remote administrative access, which introduces the risk of someone other than an authorized administrator gaining access to your system. Once an attacker gains access in this way, you can no longer trust the system, the logs, or the transaction information.

Theft of Transaction Information

To collect money, ship goods, and identify one customer from another, you will have to collect and store data. How you collect and store this information will ultimately tell the tale of your success. Of course, transaction information will be a target for hackers who would like to steal identities, sell credit card information to organized crime rings, or simply use the collected information themselves to commit fraud.

Theft of Intellectual Property

Once a web server is compromised, that system can be used to attack the internal network and any system connected to it. This puts an attacker one hop from databases and file stores that may reveal company secrets. Can you afford to lose your competitive advantage?

Denial-of-Service (DoS) Attacks

One of the oldest attacks in the hacker's repertoire is the Denial-of-Service attack. This is the simple but effective technique of overwhelming a system or service with requests that tie up resources to the point that legitimate requests cannot be fulfilled. Some attacks in this genre will cause a system or service to fail in an uncontrolled manner and stop processing—not a good state for a web server.

As mentioned before, web servers and the applications that run on them are widely accessible due to the fact that we want people to access them. Although in the past there have been highly publicized cases of vulnerabilities in web servers themselves (Microsoft's IIS 4.0, for example), the majority of the hacks being performed today are exploiting the web applications running on top of the web servers at the application level. To compound the problem, usually so much traffic is traveling to web servers that logging (and, of course, reviewing) all of the pertinent information is exhausting for most organizations. Firewalls will allow traffic coming in on port 80 to your web server because this is required. Some webmasters believe that using SSL (Secure Sockets Layer), via port 443, for all connections will protect them in some way. This will encrypt the connections of legitimate users and protect them from sniffing attacks, but using SSL will also encrypt the attacker's traffic from any intrusion detection systems and do nothing to protect the web application itself. If we employed intrusion detection in the DMZ, first of all, it would be a full-time job. Second, if it's a standard network-based IDS, it wouldn't provide much help anyway. This is not to say that logging, SSL, firewalls, and IDSs shouldn't be deployed; it's simply that each of these must be evaluated for its effectiveness in your organization's "defense in depth" strategy.

In addition to the countermeasures already mentioned, consider use of the following as safeguards for mitigating security risks to your web-based applications.

Create a Quality Assurance Process

A quality assurance process is quite effective in ensuring that the servers that host your web apps are installed and configured properly. Even the most secure web application can be compromised if the underlying operating system has vulnerabilities. This process should include all aspects of the server, from the operating system to installed patches, the web server, and the removal of unwanted services, documentation, and libraries. To verify that the system meets required criteria, the execution of a web and network scan should be completed before deployment of the system.

Web Application Firewalls

Unlike traditional firewalls that only look at destination/source addresses and port numbers, application-layer firewalls do deep packet inspection, which means they are capable of looking for and blocking specific attack behaviors or anomalies in protocol verbs such as HTTP's POST command.

Intrusion Prevention Systems

An intrusion prevention system (IPS), as opposed to an intrusion detection system, can actually *prevent* attacks it identifies. These types of systems are typically placed inline, which is to say that all traffic must be evaluated and passed through the IPS before it can reach the servers behind it. This raises a concern of performance, which typically raises the cost and hardware requirements. These systems are considered by some to be an extension of intrusion detection systems.

Implement SYN Proxies on the Firewall

If you search the Internet, you will find that, historically, one of the most common Denial-of-Service attacks has been SYN floods. A SYN flood is where attackers send fake SYN requests to servers in an attempt to exhaust the amount of legitimate requests the server can maintain. If the attacker is successful, the server will wait for a predetermined timeout period for the bogus connections to complete (which, of course, never do), and most legitimate requests will be ignored by the server.

By implementing a SYN proxy on the firewall, now the firewall can manage the connections to the server. If a predefined threshold of SYN requests (let's say 500 in a second) occurs, the firewall is on guard. If requests continue to come in, the firewall has the option of dropping the oldest requests that haven't resulted in an *established* connection, thereby allowing legitimate connections to make their way to be processed by the server. Not all firewalls support this option, but those which support connection "state tables" usually will.

All of these solutions are wonderful, but at the core of all of this is the web-based application itself. True web security should start with designing and deploying secure application services and allowing the other controls to mitigate the risk. Now we will dive deeper into some of the specific threats and vulnerabilities associated with this topic.

 NOTE SYN floods are covered in more detail later in this chapter.

Specific Threats for Web Environments

The most common types of vulnerabilities, threats, and complexities are covered in the following sections, which we will attack one at a time:

- Information gathering
- Administrative interfaces
- Authentication and access control
- Configuration management
- Input validation
- Parameter validation
- Session management

Information Gathering

Information gathering is usually the first step in an attacker's methodology. Information gathered may allow an attacker to infer additional information that can be used to compromise systems. Unfortunately, most of the information gathered is from sources that are available to anyone who asks. The big search engines make it even easier for an attacker to gather information because they aggregate information and can return results from the search engine's cache without the attacker ever connecting to the target company's web server.

The majority of the culprits to information disclosure are developers and web server administrators who are just trying to do their jobs. The comments in the HTML source code put in by the developer to explain a routine or the backup files that have been stored on the web server by the admin aren't glaring security issues, but if they can be accessed by unauthorized users, they could reveal much more than an organization would normally allow. Even the error messages returned by the server when an improper request is made can contain physical paths to the database, version numbers, and so on, which can be interpreted by an attacker as a foothold to gain unauthorized access to a system.

More sophisticated attackers go beyond the search engines to explore the contents of all accessible files on a server for possible clues to the structure of the internal network or the connection string used by the web server to connect to the database server.

In order for a web server to provide the active content and common interfaces that web users demand these days, the servers must access data sources, process code, and return the results to the web clients. To employ these mechanisms, the appropriate code must be written and presented to the web browser in the appropriate format. One technology called *server side includes (SSI)* allows web developers to reuse content by inserting the same content into multiple web documents. This typically involves use of an `include` statement in the code and a file (.inc) that is to be included. However, if these files are able to be accessed by an attacker, the code would be visible and could be changed to "include" other files containing sensitive information. Other technologies such as Active Server Pages (ASP; pages that have an .asp file extension) are used to provide an "active" user environment. These files can disclose any contained sensitive code if they were able to be viewed. Developers should avoid using any sensitive code in the SSI file or ASP files (like database connection strings or some proprietary business logic) so in the event the document should ever find itself in anyone's hands unparsed by the server, the code isn't readily available. There have been too many vulnerabilities with these types of files in the past to assume they will not be able to be read.

Another tip that will allow developers to avoid exposing the physical location or passwords used to connect to a database is to use a Data Source Name (DSN). This is a logical name for the data store, rather than the drive letter and directory location of the database, that can be used when programming to the Open Database Connectivity (ODBC) interface. When an ODBC DSN is used to store these values, they are stored in the registry of the system, not in the code itself. This technique actually makes the code easier to modify since the connection strings are a variable stored in the registry, so it would be a good best practice.

The countermeasures to the information-gathering techniques used by attackers are to be aware of the information you are making available to the public and limit its availability to only the minimal amount necessary. Developers should be aware of the potential of their code to be viewed by someone outside of the organization, and administrators should routinely check search engines for references to their web sites, e-mail addresses, file types, and data stores. Many web sites and entire books are dedicated to information gathering via publicly available databases, so it would be a good example of due diligence to check these out.

Administrative Interfaces

Everyone wants to work from the coffee shop or at home in their pajamas. Webmasters and web developers are particularly fond of this concept. Although some systems mandate that administration be carried out from a local terminal, in most cases there is an interface to administer the systems remotely, even over the Web. While this may be "wicked cool" to the webmaster, it also provides an entry point into the system for an unauthorized user.

Since we are talking about the Web, using a web-based *administrative interface* is in most opinions a bad idea. If we've identified the vulnerability and are willing to accept the risk, the administrative interface should be at least (if not more) secure as the web application or service we are hosting.

A bad habit that's found even in high-security environments is hard-coding authentication credentials into the links to the management interfaces, or enabling the "remember password" option. This does make it easier on the administrator but offers up too much access to someone who stumbles across the link regardless of their intentions.

So, let's face the facts: most commercial software and web application servers install some type of administrative console by default. Knowing this and remembering the information-gathering techniques we've already spoken about should be enough for organizations to take this threat seriously. If the interface is not needed, it should be disabled. When custom applications are developed, the existence of management interfaces is less known, so consideration should be given to this in policy and procedures.

The simple countermeasure for this threat requires that the management interfaces be removed, but this may upset your administrators. Using a stronger authentication mechanism would be better than the standard username/password scenario. Controlling which systems are allowed to connect and administer the system is another good technique. Many systems allow specific IP addresses or network IDs to be defined that only allow administrative access from these stations.

Ultimately, the most secure management interface for a system would be one that is out-of-band, meaning a separate channel of communication is used to avoid any vulnerabilities that may exist in the environment that the system operates in. An example of out-of-band would be using a modem connected to a web server to dial in directly and configure it using a local interface, as opposed to connecting via the Internet and using a web interface. This should only be done through an encrypted channel, as in SSH.

Authentication and Access Control

If you've used the Internet for banking, shopping, registering for classes, or working from home, I'd be willing to bet you've had to log in through a web-based application. From the consumer side or the provider side, the topic of *authentication and access control* is an obvious issue. Consumers want an access control mechanism that provides the security and privacy they would expect from a trusted entity, but they also don't want to be too burdened by the process. From the service providers' perspective, they want to provide the highest amount of security to the consumer that performance, compliance, and cost will allow. So, from both of these perspectives, typically usernames and passwords are still used to control access to most web applications.

The problem with using passwords to authenticate users on a web site is probably the same reason you use the Internet to deliver your service in the first place: accessibility. Accessibility is great if all the people accessing your site are legitimate users. Accessibility isn't that great when everyone on the planet who's inclined to attempt unauthorized access to your site can anonymously give it a shot. Passwords don't really prove much. They are used because they are cheap and reasonably effective, but they really don't prove that the user "jsmith" is *really* John Smith; they just prove that the person using the account jsmith has typed in the correct password. That could be anyone! Have you ever used anyone else's account for anything? Tell the truth!

It wouldn't be a stretch to think of a system that held sensitive information (medical, financial, and so on) to be an identified target for attackers. Mining usernames via search engines or simply using common usernames (like jsmith) and attempting to log in to these sites is very common. If you've ever signed up at a web site for access to download a "free" document or file, what username did you use? Is it the same one you use for other sites? Maybe even the same password? Crafty attackers might be mining information via other web sites that seem rather friendly, offering to evaluate your IQ and send you the results, or enter you into a sweepstakes. Remember that untrained, unaware users are an organization's biggest threat. Beware!

Another weakness in authentication (especially when passwords are used) is the fact that illegitimate (as well as legitimate) users can lock out the account after a threshold of bad logon attempts are made. This is a good policy to help prevent password guessing and brute force attacks against your system. As you probably know, brute force attacks attempt every possible combination of characters to get into a system, and web applications are just as vulnerable as other systems. The countermeasure of account lockout does, in fact, keep this attack in check, but if this type of attack attempts to log in as *every* user account on the system, it effectively locks all users out. What would be the impact if this was a financial institution and now 100,000 users suddenly needed the Help Desk to assist them with unlocking their accounts? An administrative nightmare! This may also lead to an evaluation of your organization's account creation and password reset policy. How do you authenticate a user who has lost their password? What do you reset the password to? When an account is created, do you use a default password? All of these should be defined in policy and procedure. Remember, you are only as secure as your weakest link.

The solution to the massive account lockout DoS attack could be to only lock out the account for a limited amount of time—30 minutes for low-risk sites to three hours or even a day depending on the amount of risk. Ultimately, your organization must determine what level of risk you're willing to accept. Using a multifactor authentication mechanism won't necessarily stop these types of attacks either, but it will make the success of unauthorized access less likely.

Log files should be analyzed to determine the offending system or systems, although these will seldom be the actual machines belonging to the attacker. Such analysis will allow your organization to see where the attempts are originating from and adjust the access rules of firewalls and systems accordingly.

Finally, a best practice would be to exchange all authentication information via a secure mechanism. This will typically mean using encryption of the password and credentials or securing the channel of communication. These days, it would seem silly to have to remind web sites that the benefits of using SSL (when your http:// changes to https://) are well worth the price you pay for the server certificate required and the processing related to the encryption/decryption process on each end. Some large sites, however, still don't use encrypted authentication mechanisms and have exposed themselves to the threat of attackers sniffing usernames and passwords.

Configuration Management

Configuration management is simply the concept of managing the configuration of your systems. The default accounts and their passwords, the sample files on the system, and the management interfaces should all be identified and a security baseline defined in a web environment. Before a system goes live in production, there should be a verification process to ensure compliance with the policy. This is, of course, a "perfect world" scenario.

In the real-world arena of web application development, the process may only mean that the requirements for the application are specified; a developer sets up a "test" environment that emulates the production environment (with the same operating system and web server installed); and the developer writes the code, tests the application for functionality, and passes it off to whomever she reports to, whereupon the application is put into production without another thought. This isn't the section of this book where we should to go into the security that surrounds sound development practices, but to iterate briefly: a common mistake is taking the test environment (since everything worked in the test) and making *that* the production environment. The application may certainly work, but the developer almost certainly set up the test environment without the baseline security levels that would be used in the production environment. Too often the company is enticed to get an application online with a focus on availability rather than integrity or confidentiality. This (erroneous) school of thought would be, "Hey, let's see if it works and then we'll lock it down," but this lockdown may be forgotten, and too often this leads to an eventual system compromise.

If an organization doesn't have their own in-house development team and simply acquires an application they want to put into production, there should still be a process in place to identify vulnerabilities and verify that the application is implemented securely. Applications that have been installed with the default configurations are rarely secure. Many applications have default administrative accounts and passwords that are widely known by the hacker community. The presence of error pages or the sample files that are installed to help with an implementation are signs of weakness to attackers. You may be wondering how an attacker would be able to detect these things on your web server: the answer is your favorite search engine.

Search engines (such as Google) are really good at analyzing web pages for the links in them and then following all of the links, cataloguing everything they find along the way. This is a great feature for those of us who use Internet search engines to find recipes, directions, or movie quotes, but hackers using craftily articulated search requests can easily reveal management interfaces, error pages that show misconfigurations, and even areas of your web site that you may not have wanted the world to see.

The solution to all of these threats is to have a defined policy and procedures. The procedures should involve removing default configurations and applying the security patches from vendors in a timely fashion. Another smart approach would be when an application goes from testing to production, all of the system's access control lists (ACLs) should be reviewed to verify that the appropriate security is applied so the most pristine system files are protected. Finally, remove anything and everything on your system that you would not want accessible to the world via search engines. This would include system documentation, internal files, sample files, and default error pages.

Input Validation

Web servers aren't that smart; they just do what they are told to. They are designed to process requests via a certain protocol. The term "protocol" means the rules that are followed in a certain situation to ensure appropriate communication. When a person sits at their web browser and types in a request for http://www.website.com/index.htm, they are using a protocol called Hypertext Transfer Protocol (HTTP) to request the file "index.htm" from the server "www" in the "website.com" namespace. A request in this form is called a Uniform Resource Locator (URL), and it's pretty close to the way we speak—well, at least we can read it. Like many situations in computerland, there is more than one way to request something because computers speak several different "languages"—such as binary, hexadecimal, and many other coding mechanisms—each of which is interpreted and processed by the system as valid commands. Validating that these requests are allowed is part of *input validation* and is usually tied to some coded validation rules. The fact that these rules have to be coded means that it's possible some sneaky requests may slip through the coded validation rules.

Some sneaky examples follow:

- **Path or directory traversal** This attack is also known as the "dot dot slash" because it is perpetrated by inserting the characters "../" several times into a URL to back up or traverse into directories that weren't supposed to be accessible from the Web. The command "../" at the command prompt tells the system to back up to the previous directory (try it, "cd ../"). If a web server's default directory is c:\inetpub\www, a URL requesting http://www.website.com/scripts/../../../../../windows/system32/cmd.exe?/c+dir+c:\ would issue the command to back up several directories to ensure it has gone all the way to the root of the drive and then make the request to change to the operating system directory (windows\ system32) and run the cmd.exe listing the contents of the c: drive.

- **Unicode encoding** Unicode is an industry-standard mechanism developed to represent the entire range of over 100,000 textual characters in the world as a standard coding format. Web servers support Unicode to support different character sets (such as Chinese), and, at one time, many supported it by default. So, even if we told our systems to not allow the "../" directory traversal request mentioned earlier, an attacker using Unicode could effectively make the same directory traversal request without using "/" but with any of the Unicode representation of that character (three exist: %c1%1c, %c0%9v, and %c0%af). That request may slip through unnoticed and be processed.

- **URL encoding** Ever notice a "space" that appears as "%20" in a URL in a web browser? (Why is it only me who notices that?) The "%20" represents the space because spaces aren't allowed characters in a URL. Much like the attacks using Unicode characters, attackers found that they could bypass filtering techniques and make requests by representing characters differently.

Besides just serving static files to users, almost every web application is going to have to accept some input. When you use the Web, you are constantly asked to input information such as usernames, passwords, and credit card information. To a web application, this input is just data that is to be processed like the rest of the code in the application. Usually, this input is used as a variable and fed into some code that will process it based on some logic, such as IF [username input field]=X AND [password input field]=Y THEN Authenticate. This will function well assuming there is always correct information put into the input fields, but what if the wrong information is input? Developers have to cover all the angles. They have to assume that sometimes the wrong input will be given, and they have to handle that situation appropriately. To deal with this, a routine is usually coded in that will tell the system what to do if the input isn't what was expected.

The buffer overflow is probably the most notorious of input validation mistakes. A buffer is an area reserved by an application to store something in it, such as some user input. After the application receives the input, an instruction pointer directs the application to do something with the input that's been put in the buffer. A buffer overflow occurs when an application erroneously allows an invalid amount of input to be written into the buffer area, overwriting the instruction pointer in the code that told the program what to do with the input. Once the instruction pointer is overwritten, whatever code has been placed in the buffer can then be executed, all under the security context of the application.

Client-side validation is when the input validation is done at the client before it is even sent back to the server to process. If you've missed a field in a web form before and after clicking Submit, you immediately receive a message informing you that you've forgotten to fill in one of the fields. Here, you've experienced client-side validation. This is a good idea, rather than sending incomplete requests to the server and the server having to kick back the error. The problem arises when the client-side validation is the *only* validation that takes place. In this situation, the server trusts that the client has done its job correctly and processes the input as if it is valid. In normal situations, accepting this input would be fine, but when an attacker can intercept the traffic between the client and server and modify it or just directly make illegitimate requests to the server without using a client, a compromise is more likely.

In an environment where input validation is weak, an attacker will try to input specific operating system (OS) commands into the input fields instead of what the system was expecting (such as the username and password) in an effort to trick the system into running them. Remember that computers do what they're told, and if an attacker can get them to run an OS command, they will be able to execute them as if they were the application. If the web application is written to access a database, as most are, there is the threat of SQL injection, where instead of valid input the attacker puts actual database commands into the input fields, which are then parsed and run by the application.

SQL (Structured Query Language) statements can be used by attackers to bypass authentication and reveal all records in a database.

Remember that different layers of a system (see Figure 11-26) all have their own vulnerabilities that must be identified and fixed.

A similar sounding attack is cross-site scripting, which, in the security community, has replaced buffer overflows as the biggest threat in web applications. The term "cross-site scripting" (XSS) refers to an attack where a vulnerability is found on a web site that allows an attacker to inject malicious code into a web application. The malicious code can then be executed in the browsers of unsuspecting users as they access the site. Turning off all scripting would fix this vulnerability, but would break a lot of web applications.

All of the attacks in this section have the related issue of erroneously assuming what input data is possible, the effects that specially encoded data has on an application, and believing the input that is received is always valid. The countermeasures to all of these

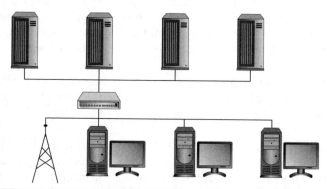

Security policies	Password policy, audit policy, system access policy, user rights…
Web applications	Apache, Internet Explorer, Firefox, Microsoft IIS, FTP, Tomcat WebLogic, ColdFusion, SSH, Telnet…
Third-party applications	Lotus Notes, Microsoft Exchange, Adobe Acrobat, Windows Media, Sendmail…
Databases	Oracle, Microsoft SQL Server, MySQL, IBM DB2, IBM DB/400, Sybase, Lotus Domino…
Operating systems	Microsoft Windows, Linux, Unix, Solaris, Mac OS, BSD, AIX, AS/400, Novell NetWare…
Networks	IPSec, PPTP, Network File System, DHCP, DNS, LDAP, SNMP…
Hardware	Routers, switches, hubs, wireless access points, hardware firewalls…

Figure 11-26 Attacks can take place at many levels within one computer.

would be to filter out all "known" malicious requests, never trust information coming from the client without first validating it, and implement a strong policy to include appropriate parameter checking in all applications.

Parameter Validation

The issue of parameter validation is akin to the issue of input validation mentioned earlier. *Parameter validation* is where the values that are being received by the application are validated to be within defined limits before the server application processes them within the system. The main difference between parameter validation and input validation would have to be whether the application was expecting the user to input a value as opposed to an environment variable that is defined by the application. Attacks in this area deal with manipulating values that the system would assume are beyond the client being able to configure, mainly because there isn't a mechanism provided in the interface to do so. We know that we should never assume—don't make me say the saying—and this is especially true when dealing with computers because they lack the common sense we've been endowed with as humans.

In an effort to provide a rich end-user experience, web application designers have to employ mechanisms to keep track of the thousands of different web browsers that could be connected at any given time. The HTTP protocol by itself doesn't really facilitate managing the state of a user's connection; it really just connects to a server, gets whatever objects (the .htm file, graphics, and so forth) are requested in the HTML code (HTTP's markup language), and then just disconnects or times out. If the browser does, in fact, disconnect or time out, how does the server know how to recognize it when it returns? Would you be irritated if you had to re-enter *all* of your information *again* because you spent too long looking at possible flights while booking a flight online? Since most people would, web developers employ the technique of passing a cookie to the client to help the server remember things about the state of the connection. A cookie isn't a program but rather just some data that are passed and stored in memory (called a session cookie), or locally as a file (called a persistent cookie), to pass state information back to the server. An example of how cookies are employed would be a shopping cart application used on a commercial web site. As you put items into your cart, they are maintained by updating a session cookie on your system. You may have noticed the "Cookies must be enabled" message that some web sites issue as you enter their site.

Since accessing a session cookie in memory is usually beyond the reach of most users, most web developers didn't think about this as a serious threat when designing their systems. It is not uncommon for web developers to enable account lockout after a certain number of unsuccessful login attempts have occurred (something we talked about earlier). If a developer is using a session cookie to keep track of how many times a client has attempted to log in, there may be a vulnerability here. If an application didn't want to allow more than three unsuccessful logins before locking a client out, the server might pass a session cookie to the client, setting a value such as "number of allowed logins = 3." After each unsuccessful attempt, the server would tell the client to decrement the "number of allowed logins" value. When the value reaches 0, the client would be directed to a "Your account has been locked out" page.

A web proxy is a piece of software installed on a system that is designed to intercept all traffic between the local web browser and the web server. Using freely available web proxy software (such as Achilles or Burp Proxy), an attacker could monitor and modify any information as it travels in either direction. In the preceding example, when the server tells the client via a session cookie that the "number of allowed logins = 3," if that information is intercepted by an attacker using one of these proxies and he changes the value to "number of allowed logins = 50000," this would effectively allow a brute force attack on the system if it has no other validation mechanism in place.

Using a web proxy can also exploit the use of hidden fields in web pages. Just like it sounds, a hidden field is not shown in the user interface but contains a value that is passed to the server when the web form is submitted. The exploit of using hidden values can occur when a web developer codes the prices of items on a web page as hidden values instead of referencing the items and their prices on the server. The attacker uses the web proxy to intercept the submitted information from the client and changes the value (the price) before it gets to the server. This is surprisingly easy to do and, assuming no other checks are in place, would allow the perpetrator to see the new values specified in the e-commerce shopping cart.

The countermeasure that would lessen the risk associated with these threats would be *adequate parameter validation*. Adequate parameter validation may include pre-validation and post-validation controls. In a client/server environment, pre-validation controls may be placed on the client side, prior to submitting requests to the server. Even when these are employed, the server should perform parallel pre-validation of input prior to application submission because a client will have fewer controls than a server, and may have been compromised or bypassed.

- **Pre-validation** Input controls verifying data is in appropriate format, and compliant with application specifications, prior to submission to the application. An example of this would be form field validation, where web forms do not allow letters in a field that is expecting to receive a number (currency) value.

- **Post-validation** Ensuring an application's output is consistent with expectations (that is, within predetermined constraints of reasonableness).

Session Management

As highlighted earlier, managing several thousand different clients connecting to a web-based application is a challenge. The aspect of *session management* requires consideration before delivering applications via the Web. Commonly, the most used method of managing client sessions is by assigning unique session IDs to every connection. A session ID is a value sent by the client to the server with every request that uniquely identifies the client to the server or application. In the event that an attacker was able to acquire or even guess an authenticated client's session ID and render it to the server as its own session ID, the server would be fooled and the attacker would have access to the session.

The old "never send anything in clear text" rule certainly applies here. HTTP traffic is unencrypted by default and does nothing to combat an attacker sniffing session IDs off the wire. Because session IDs are usually passed in, and maintained, via the HTTP protocol, they should be protected in some way.

An attacker being able to predict or guess the session IDs would also be a threat in this type of environment. Using sequential session IDs for clients would be a mistake. Random session IDs of an appropriate length would counter session ID prediction. Building in some sort of timestamp or time-based validation will combat *replay attacks*. (A replay attack is simply an attacker capturing the traffic from a legitimate session and replaying it to authenticate his session.) Finally, any cookies that are used to keep state on the connection should also be encrypted.

WARNING It is important for you to understand more in-depth web security concepts and attacks. Please review and understand the article www.logicalsecurity.com/resources/resources_articles.html.

Mobile Code

Code that can be transmitted across a network, to be executed by a system or device on the other end, is called *mobile code*. There are many legitimate reasons to allow mobile code—for example, web browser applets that may execute in the background to download additional content for the web page, such as plug-ins that allow you to view a video.

The cautions arise when a web site downloads code intended to do malicious or compromising actions, especially when the recipient is unaware that the compromising activity is taking place. If a web site is compromised, it can be used as a platform from which to launch attacks against anyone visiting the site and just browsing. On a web browser, having security settings set to high, or disallowing various scripting or active web components, may be an appropriate countermeasure. Some of the common types of mobile code are covered in the next sections.

Java Applets

Java is an object-oriented, platform-independent programming language. It is employed as a full-fledged programming language and is used to write complete programs and short programs, called *applets*, which run in a user's browser.

Other languages are compiled to object code for a specific operating system and processor. This is why a particular application may run on Windows but not on Macintosh. An Intel processor does not necessarily understand machine code compiled for an Alpha processor, and vice versa. Java is platform independent because it creates intermediate code, *bytecode*, which is not processor-specific. The Java Virtual Machine (JVM) then converts the bytecode to the machine code that the processor on that particular system can understand (see Figure 11-27). Let's quickly walk through these steps:

1. A programmer creates a Java applet and runs it through a compiler.

2. The Java compiler converts the source code into bytecode (non-processor-specific).

3. The user downloads the Java applet.

4. The JVM converts the bytecode into machine-level code (processor-specific).

5. The applet runs when called upon.

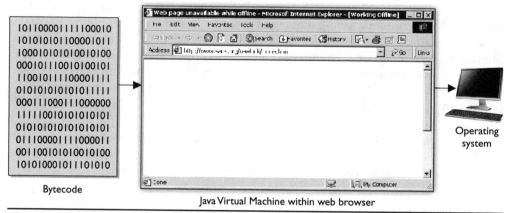

Bytecode

Java Virtual Machine within web browser

Operating system

Figure 11-27   The JVM interprets bytecode to machine code for that specific platform.

When an applet is executed, the JVM will create a virtual machine within an environment called a *sandbox*. This virtual machine is an enclosed environment in which the applet carries out its activities. Applets are commonly sent over within a requested web page, which means the applet executes as soon as it arrives. It can carry out malicious activity on purpose or accidentally if the developer of the applet did not do his part correctly. So the sandbox strictly limits the applet's access to any system resources. The JVM mediates access to system resources to ensure the applet code behaves and stays within its own sandbox. These components are illustrated in Figure 11-28.

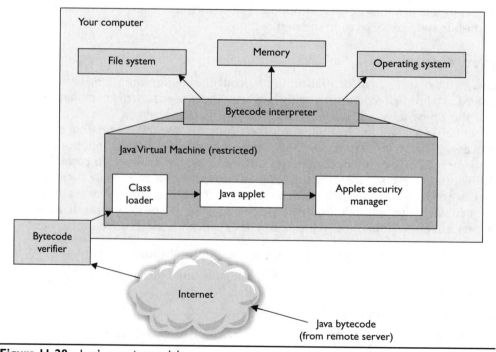

Figure 11-28   Java's security model

Browser Settings

Java applets and the actions they perform can be prevented and controlled by specific browser settings. These settings do not affect full-fledged Java applications running outside of the browser.

NOTE The Java language itself provides protection mechanisms as in garbage collection, memory management, validating address usage, and a component that verifies adherence to predetermined rules.

However, as with many other things in the computing world, the bad guys have figured out how to escape their confines and restrictions. Programmers have figured out how to write applets that enable the code to access hard drives and resources that are supposed to be protected by the Java security scheme. This code can be malicious in nature and cause destruction and mayhem to the user and her system.

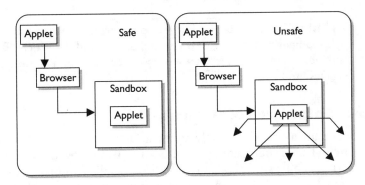

ActiveX Controls

ActiveX is a Microsoft technology composed of a set of OOP technologies and tools based on COM and DCOM. A programmer uses these tools to create ActiveX controls, which are self-sufficient programs similar to Java applets. ActiveX controls can be re-used by many applications within one system, or different systems, on the network. These controls can be downloaded from web sites to add extra functionality (as in providing animations for web pages), but they are also components of Windows operating systems themselves (dynamic link libraries [DLLs]) and carry out common operating system tasks.

Instead of trying to keep ActiveX controls in a safe area for various computations and activities, this technology practices security by informing the user where the program came from. The user can decide whether or not to trust this origin.

ActiveX technology provides security levels and authentication, letting users control the security of the ActiveX components they download. Unlike Java applets, ActiveX components are downloaded to a user's hard drive when he chooses to add the functionality the component provides. This means the ActiveX component has far greater access to the user's system compared to Java applets.

The security level setting of the user's browser dictates whether an ActiveX component is downloaded automatically or whether the user is first prompted with a warning. The security level is configurable by the user via his browser controls. As the security level increases, so too does the browser's sensitivity level to signed and unsigned components and controls, and to the initialization of ActiveX scripts.

The main security difference between Java applets and ActiveX controls is that Java sets up a sandbox for the code to execute in, and this restricts the code's access to resources within the user's computer. ActiveX uses Authenticode technology, which relies on digital certificates and trusting certificate authorities. (Signing, digital certificates, and certificate authorities are explained in detail in Chapter 8.) Although both are good and interesting technologies, they have inherent flaws. Java has not been able to ensure that all code stays within the sandbox, which has caused several types of security compromises. These instances are examples of malware. ActiveX doesn't necessarily provide security—in fact, it often presents annoying dialog boxes to users. Since most users do not understand this technology, they continually click OK because they don't understand the risks involved.

WARNING It is important for you to understand more about programming development issues. Please review and understand the article "Basic Security and Development Issues" at www.logicalsecurity.com/resources/resources_articles.html.

Malicious Software (Malware)

Several types of malicious code or malware exist, such as viruses, worms, Trojan horses, and logic bombs. They usually are dormant until activated by an event the user or system initiates. They can be spread by e-mail, sharing media (jump drives), sharing documents and programs, or downloading things from the Internet, or they can be purposely inserted by an attacker.

Adhering to the usual rule of not opening an e-mail attachment that comes from an unknown source is one of the best ways to combat malicious code. However, recent viruses and worms have infected personal e-mail address books, so this precaution is not a sure thing to protect systems from malicious code. If an address book is infected and used during an attack, the victim gets an e-mail message that seems to have come from a person he knows. Because he knows this person, he will proceed to open the e-mail message and double-click the attachment. And Bam! His computer is now infected and uses the e-mail client's address book to spread the virus to all his friends and acquaintances.

Antivirus software should be installed to watch for known virus signatures, and host intrusion detection software can be used to watch for suspicious activity, file access, and changes to help detect evildoers and their malicious activity.

Malicious code can be detected through the following clues:

- File size increase
- Many unexpected disk accesses

- A change in an update or modified timestamp
- A sudden decrease of hard drive space
- Unexpected and strange activity by applications
- A sudden increase in network activity

The following section quickly looks at a few types of malicious code.

Viruses

A *virus* is a small application, or string of code, that infects applications. The main function of a virus is to reproduce, and it requires a host application to do this. In other words, viruses cannot replicate on their own. A virus infects a file by inserting or attaching a copy of itself to the file. The virus may also cause destruction by deleting system files, displaying graphics, reconfiguring systems, or overwhelming mail servers. Several viruses have been released that achieved self-perpetuation by mailing themselves to every entry in a victim's personal address book. The virus masqueraded as coming from a trusted source. The ILOVEYOU, Melissa, and Naked Wife viruses are older viruses that used the programs Outlook and Outlook Express as their host applications and were replicated when the victim chose to open the message.

Macros are programs written in Word Basic, Visual Basic, or VBScript and are generally used with Microsoft Office products. Macros automate tasks that users would otherwise have to carry out themselves. Users can define a series of activities and common tasks for the application to perform when a button is clicked, instead of doing each of those tasks individually. A *macro virus* is a virus written in one of these macro languages and is platform independent. They infect and replicate in templates and within documents. Macro viruses are common because they are extremely easy to write, and Office products are in wide use.

Some viruses infect the boot sector (*boot sector viruses*) of a computer and either move data within the boot sector or overwrite the sector with new information. Some boot sector viruses have part of their code in the boot sector, which can initiate the virus, and the rest of their code in sectors on the hard drive it has marked off as bad. Because the sectors are marked as bad, the operating system and applications will not attempt to use those sectors; thus, they will not get overwritten.

Other types of viruses append themselves to executables on the system and compress them by using the user's permissions (*compression viruses*). When the user chooses to use that executable, the system automatically decompresses it and the malicious code, which usually causes the malicious code to initialize and perform its dirty deeds.

What Is a Virus?

A virus is a program that searches out other programs and infects them by embedding a copy of itself. When the infected program executes, the embedded virus is executed, which propagates the infection.

A *stealth virus* hides the modifications it has made to files or boot records. This can be accomplished by monitoring system functions used to read files or sectors and forging the results. This means that when an antivirus program attempts to read an infected file or sector, the original uninfected form will be presented instead of the actual infected form. The virus can hide itself by masking the size of the file it is hidden in or actually move itself temporarily to another location while an antivirus program is carrying out its scanning process.

So a stealth virus is a virus that hides its tracks after infecting a system. Once the system is infected, the virus can make modifications to make the computer appear the same as before. The virus can show the original file size of a file it infected instead of the new, larger size to try to trick the antivirus software into thinking no changes have been made.

A *polymorphic virus* produces varied but operational copies of itself. This is done in the hopes of outwitting a virus scanner. Even if one or two copies are found and disabled, other copies may still remain active within the system.

The polymorphic virus can use different encryption schemes requiring different decryption routines. This would require an antivirus scan for several scan strings, one for each possible decryption method, in order to identify all copies of this type of virus.

These viruses can also vary the sequence of their instructions by including *noise*, or bogus instructions, with other useful instructions. They can also use a mutation engine and a random-number generator to change the sequence of their instructions in the hopes of not being detected. A polymorphic virus has the capability to change its own code, enabling the virus to have hundreds or thousands of variants. These activities can cause the virus scanner to not properly recognize the virus and to leave it alone.

A *multipart virus* infects both the boot sector of a hard drive and executable files. The virus first becomes resident in memory and then infects the boot sector. Once it is in memory, it can infect the entire system.

A *self-garbling virus* attempts to hide from antivirus software by garbling its own code. As the virus spreads, it changes the way its code is formatted. A small portion of the virus code decodes the garbled code when activated.

Meme viruses are not actual computer viruses but types of e-mail messages that are continually forwarded around the Internet. They can be chain letters, e-mail hoax virus alerts, religious messages, or pyramid selling schemes. They are replicated by humans, not software, and can waste bandwidth and spread fear. Several e-mails have been passed around describing dangerous viruses, even though the viruses weren't real. People believed the e-mails and felt as though they were doing the right thing by passing them along to tell friends about this supposedly dangerous malware, when really the people were duped and were themselves spreading a meme virus.

Macro Languages

Macro languages enable users to edit, delete, and copy files. Because these languages are so easy to use, many more types of macro viruses are possible.

Script viruses have been quite popular and damaging over the last few years. Scripts are files that are executed by an interpreter—for example, Microsoft Windows Script Host, which interprets different types of scripting languages. Web sites have become more dynamic and interactive through the use of script files written in Visual Basic (VBScript) and Java (Jscript) as well as other scripting languages that are embedded in HTML. When a web page that has these scripts embedded is requested by a web browser, these embedded scripts are executed, and if they are malicious, then everything just blows up. Okay, this a tad overdramatic. The virus will carry out the payload (instructions) that the virus writer has integrated into the script, whether it is sending out copies of itself to everyone in your contact list or deleting critical files. Scripts are just another infection vector used by malware writers to carry out their evil ways.

NOTE The LoveLetter virus is one of the most well-known viruses because of the amount of damage it caused. It was written in VBScript.

Another type of virus, called the *tunneling virus*, attempts to install itself under the antivirus program. When the antivirus goes around doing its health check on critical files, file sizes, modification dates, and so on, it makes a request to the operating system to gather this information. Now, if the virus can put itself between the antivirus and the operating system, when the antivirus sends out a command (system call) for this type of information, the tunneling virus can intercept this call. Instead of the operating system responding to the request, the tunneling virus responds with information that indicates that everything is fine and healthy and that there is no indication of any type of infection.

NOTE An EICAR test is done with antivirus software by introducing a string that all antivirus products recognize as hostile so that testing can be conducted. Antivirus software products have an EICAR.com file and a signature that matches this file. After software configurations are completed, you then put this file on the system to test the antivirus product's reactions to a virus.

Malware Components
It is common for malware to have six main elements, although it is not necessary for them *all* to be in place.

- **Insertion** Installs itself on the victim's system
- **Avoidance** Uses methods to avoid being detected
- **Eradication** Removes itself after the payload has been executed
- **Replication** Makes copies of itself and spreads to other victims
- **Trigger** Uses an event to initiate its payload execution
- **Payload** Carries out its function (that is, deletes files, installs a backdoor, exploits a vulnerability, and so on)

Botnets

A "bot" is short for "robot" and is a piece of code that carries out functionality for its master, who is the author of this code. *Bots* are a type of malware and are being installed on thousands of computers even now as you're reading this sentence. It is a piece of dormant code, also known as a *zombie*, that is used to forward items sent to it. Items sent to bots can be spam, viruses, pornography, or attack code. The reason to send these types of items through bots is to help ensure that the original sender will not be located and identified.

Hackers compromise thousands of systems with this zombie code through many different methods: e-mail attachments, compromised web sites, links embedded in e-mail, Trojan horses, and so on. The zombie code sends a message to the hacker indicating that a specific system has been compromised and the system is now available to be used by the attacker as she wishes. When a hacker has a collection of these compromised systems, it is referred to as a **botnet** (network of bots). The hacker can use all of these systems to carry out powerful DDoS attacks or even rent these systems to spammers.

The owner of this botnet (commonly referred to as the *bot herder*) controls the systems remotely, usually through the Internet relay chat (IRC) protocol.

The common steps of the development and use of a botnet are listed next:

1. A hacker sends out malicious code that has the bot software as its payload.

2. Once installed, the bot logs into an IRC or web server that it is coded to contact. The server then acts as the controlling server of the botnet.

3. A spammer pays the hacker to use these systems and sends instructions to the controller server, which causes all of the infected systems to send out spam messages to mail servers.

Spammers use this method so their messages have a higher likelihood of getting through mail server spam filters since the sending IP addresses are those of the victim's system. Thus, the source IP addresses change constantly. This is how you are constantly updated on the new male enhancement solutions and ways to purchase Viagra.

Figure 11-29 illustrates the life cycle of a botnet. The botnet herder works with, or pays, hackers to develop and spread malware to infect systems that will become part of the botnet. Whoever wants to tell you about a new product they just released, carry out identity theft, or conduct attacks, and so on, will pay the herder to use the botnet for their purposes.

Worms

Worms are different from viruses in that they can reproduce on their own without a host application, and are self-contained programs. A worm can propagate itself by using e-mail, web site downloads, and more. The definitions of a worm and virus are continually merging, and the distinction is becoming more blurred. The ILOVEYOU program was a worm. When the user executed an e-mail attachment, several processes were spawned automatically. The worm was copied and sent to all addresses within the victim's address book. Some files on the hard drive were deleted and replaced. If these were opened, the worm self-propagation started again. ILOVEYOU acts as a virus by

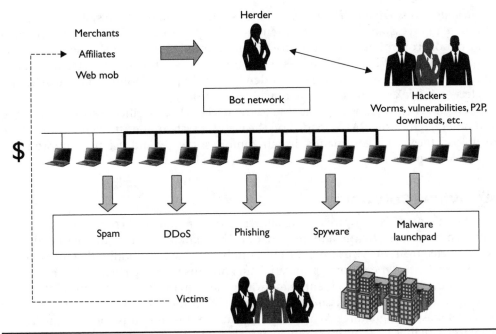

Figure 11-29 The cycle of how botnets are created, maintained, and used

requiring the use of an e-mail client, such as Outlook, and works as a worm by reproducing itself when the user opens infected files that reside on his hard drive.

Logic Bombs

A *logic bomb* executes a program, or string of code, when a certain event happens or a date and time arrives. For example, if a user accesses her bank account software, a logic bomb may be initiated, and a program may be triggered to copy the user's account number and transaction codes. Another example is when a user accesses the Internet through his cable modem. This action can initiate a planted bomb that sends a message to an attacker over the Internet to let him know the user is online and in position for an attack.

Trojan Horses

A *Trojan horse* is a program that is disguised as another program. For example, a Trojan horse can be named Notepad.exe and have the same icon as the regular Notepad program. However, when a user executes Notepad.exe, the program can delete system files. Trojan horses perform a useful functionality in addition to the malicious functionality in the background. So the Trojan horse named Notepad.exe may still run the Notepad program for the user, but in the background it will manipulate files or cause other malicious acts. A host-based IDS can be configured to watch certain files and detect when they grow in size, which is often a sign of a Trojan horse. If the original Notepad.exe was 50KB in size and then grew to 2MB, it may indicate that a Trojan horse has infected that program.

Remote Access Trojans (RATs) are malicious programs that run on systems and allow intruders to access and use a system remotely. They mimic the functionality of legitimate remote control programs used for remote administration, but are used for sinister purposes instead of helpful activities. They are developed to allow for stealth installation and operation, and are usually hidden in some type of mobile code, such as Java applets or ActiveX controls, that are downloaded from web sites.

Several RAT programs are available to the hacker (Back Orifice, SubSeven, Netbus, and others). Once the RAT is loaded on the victim's system, the attacker can download or upload files, send commands, install zombie software, and use the compromised system as he pleases.

Antivirus Software

Traditional antivirus software use signatures to detect malicious code. The signature is a fingerprint created by the antivirus vendor. The signature is a sequence of code that was extracted from the virus itself. Just like our bodies have antibodies that identify and go after a specific type of foreign material, an antivirus software package has an engine that uses these signatures to identify malware. The antivirus software scans files, e-mail messages, and other data passing through specific protocols, and then compares them to its database of signatures. When there is a match, the antivirus software carries out whatever activities it is configured to do, which can be to quarantine the file, attempt to clean the file (remove the virus), provide a warning message dialog box to the user, and/or log the event.

Signature-based detection (also called *fingerprint detection*) is an effective way to detect malicious software, but there is a delayed response time to new threats. Once a virus is detected, the antivirus vendor must study it, develop and test a new signature, release the signature, and all customers must download it. If the malicious code is just sending out silly pictures to all of your friends, this delay is not so critical. If the malicious software is similar to the Slammer worm, this amount of delay can be devastating.

 NOTE The Slammer worm was released in 2003. It took advantage of a buffer overflow within the Microsoft SQL Server 2000 software and caused excessive Denial-of-Service attacks. Several documented accounts have estimated the resulting damages to industry to be over $1 billion.

Since new malware is released daily, it is hard for antivirus software to keep up. The technique of using signatures means this software can only detect viruses that have been identified and where a signature is created. Since virus writers are prolific and busy beasts and because viruses can morph, it is important that the antivirus software have other tricks up its sleeve to detect malicious code.

Another technique that almost all antivirus software products use is referred to as *heuristic detection*. This approach analyzes the overall structure of the malicious code, evaluates the coded instructions and logic functions, and looks at the type of data within the virus or worm. So, it collects a bunch of information about this piece of code and assesses the likelihood of it being malicious in nature. It has a type of "suspiciousness counter," which is incremented as the program finds more potentially malicious attributes. Once a predefined threshold is met, the code is officially considered dangerous and the antivirus software jumps into action to protect the system. This allows antivirus software to detect unknown malware, instead of just relying on signatures.

As an analogy, let's say Barney is the town cop who is employed to root out the bad guys and lock them up (quarantine). If Barney was going to use a signature method, he would compare a stack of photographs to each person he sees on the street. When he sees a match, he quickly throws the bad guy into his patrol car and drives off. If he was going to use the heuristic method, he would be watching for suspicious activity. So if someone with a ski mask was standing outside a bank, Barney would assess the likelihood of this being a bank robber against it just being a cold guy in need of some cash.

 CAUTION Diskless workstations are still vulnerable to viruses, even though they do not have a hard disk and a full operating system. They can still get viruses that load and reside in memory. These systems can be rebooted remotely (remote booting) to bring the memory back to a clean state, which means the virus is "flushed" out of the system.

Some antivirus products create a simulated environment, called a virtual machine or sandbox, and allow some of the logic within the suspected code to execute in the protected environment. This allows the antivirus software to see the code in question in action, which gives it more information as to whether or not it is malicious.

 NOTE The virtual machine or sandbox is also sometimes referred to as an *emulation buffer*. They are all the same thing—a piece of memory that is segmented and protected so that if the code is malicious, the system is protected.

Reviewing information about a piece of code is called *static analysis*, while allowing a portion of the code to run in a virtual machine is called *dynamic analysis*. They are both considered heuristic detection methods.

Immunizers

Don't bother looking over here. We're already infected.

Another approach some antivirus software uses is called *immunization*. Products with this type of functionality would make it look as though a file, program, or disk was already infected. An *immunizer* attaches code to the file or application, which would fool a virus into "thinking" it was already infected. This would cause the virus to not infect this file (or application) and move onto the next file.

Immunizers are usually virus-specific, since a specific virus is going to make a distinct call to a file to uncover if it has been infected. But as the number of viruses (and other malware types) increased and the number of files needed to be protected increased, this approach was quickly overwhelmed. Antivirus vendors do not implement this type of functionality anymore because of this reason.

Now, even though all of these approaches are sophisticated and effective, they are not 100-percent effective because virus writers are crafty. It is a continual cat-and-mouse game that is carried out each and every day. The antivirus industry comes out with a new way of detecting malware and the very next week the virus writers have a way to get around this approach. This means that antivirus vendors have to continually increase the intelligence of their products and you have to buy a new version each and every year.

The next phase in the antivirus software evolution is referred to as *behavior blockers*. Antivirus software that carries out **behavior blocking** actually allows the suspicious code to execute within the operating system unprotected and watches its interactions with the operating system, looking for suspicious activities. The antivirus software would be watching for the following types of actions:

- Writing to startup files or the Run keys in the registry
- Opening, deleting, or modifying files
- Scripting e-mail messages to send executable code
- Connecting to network shares or resources
- Modifying an executable's logic
- Creating or modifying macros and scripts
- Formatting a hard drive or writing to the boot sector

If the antivirus program detects some of these potentially malicious activities, it can terminate the software and provide a message to the user. The newer generation behavior blockers actually analyze sequences of these types of operations before determining the system is infected. (The first-generation behavior blockers only looked for individual actions, which resulted in a large number of false positives.) The newer generation software can intercept a dangerous piece of code and not allow it to interact with other running processes. They can also detect rootkits. In addition, some of these antivirus programs can allow the system to roll back to a state before an infection took place so the damages inflicted can be "erased."

While it sounds like behavior blockers might bring us our well-deserved bliss and utopia, one drawback is that the malicious code must actually execute in real time; otherwise, our systems can be damaged. This type of constant monitoring also requires a high level of system resources. We just can't seem to win.

 TIP Heuristic detection and behavior blocking is considered proactive and can detect new malware, sometimes called "zero day" attacks. Signature-based detection cannot detect new malware.

Most antivirus vendors use a blend of all of these technologies to provide as much protection as possible. The individual anti-malware attack solutions are shown in Figure 11-30.

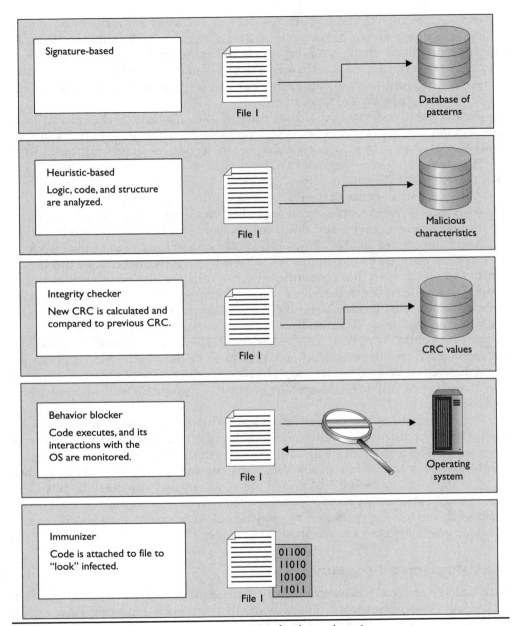

Figure 11-30 Antivirus vendors use various types of malware detection.

Spam Detection

We are all pretty tired of receiving e-mails that try to sell us things we don't need. A great job, a master's degree that requires no studying, and a great sex life are all just a click away (and only $19.99!)—as promised by this continual stream of messages. These e-mails have been given the label *spam*, which is electronic unsolicited junk e-mail. Along with being a nuisance, spam eats up a lot of network bandwidth and can be the source of spreading malware. Many organizations have spam filters on their mail servers and users can configure spam rules within their e-mail clients, but just as virus writers always come up with ways to circumvent antivirus software, spammers come up with clever ways of getting around spam filters.

Detecting spam properly has become a science in itself. One technique used is called *Bayesian filtering*. Many moons ago, a gentleman named Thomas Bayes (a mathematician) developed a way to actually guess the probability of something being true by using math. Now what is fascinating about this is that in mathematics things are either true or they are not. This is the same in software. Software deals with 1's and 0's, on and off, true and false. Software does not deal with the grays (probabilities) of life too well.

Bayesian logic reviews prior events to predict future events, which is basically quantifying uncertainty. Conceptually, this is not too hard to understand. If you run into a brick wall three times and fall down, you should conclude that your future attempts will result in the same painful outcomes. What is more interesting is when this logic is performed on activities that contain many more variables. For example, how does a spam filter ensure you do not receive e-mails trying to sell you Viagra, but it does allow the e-mails from your friend who is obsessed with Viagra and wants to continue e-mailing you about this drug's effects and attributes? A Bayesian filter applies statistical modeling to the words that make up an e-mail message. This means the words that make up the message have mathematical formulas performed on them to be able to fully understand their relationship to one another. The Bayesian filter carries out a frequency analysis on each word and then evaluates the message as a whole to determine whether or not it is spam.

So this filter is not just looking for "Viagra," "manhood," "sex," and other words that cannot be printed in a wholesome book like this one. It is looking at how often these words are used, and in what order, to make a determination as to whether or not this message is spam. Unfortunately, spammers know how these filters work and manipulate the words in the subject line and message to try and fool the spam filter. This is why you can receive messages with misspelled words or words that use symbols instead of characters. The spammers are very dedicated to getting messages promising utopia to your e-mail box because there is big money to be made that way.

Anti-Malware Programs

Detecting and protecting an enterprise from the long list of malware requires more than just rolling out antivirus software. Just as with other pieces of a security program, certain administrative, physical, and technical controls must be deployed and maintained.

The organization should either have an antivirus policy or it should be called out in an existing security policy. There should be standards outlining what type of antivirus software and anti-spyware software should be installed and how they should be configured.

Antivirus information and expected user behaviors should be integrated into the security-awareness program, along with who a user should contact if she discovers a virus. A standard should cover the do's and don'ts when it comes to malware, which are listed next.

- Every workstation, server, and PDA should have antivirus software installed.
- An automated way of updating antivirus signatures should be deployed on each device.
- Users should not be able to disable antivirus software.
- A preplanned virus eradication process should be developed and a contact person designated in case of an infection.
- All external disks (USB drives and so on) should be scanned automatically.
- Backup files should be scanned.
- Antivirus policies and procedures should be reviewed annually.
- Antivirus software should provide boot virus protection.
- Antivirus scanning should happen at a gateway and on each device.
- Virus scans should be automated and scheduled. Do not rely on manual scans.
- Critical systems should be physically protected so malicious software cannot be installed locally.

 TIP Antivirus files that contain updates (that is, new signatures) are called DAT files. It is just a data file with the file extension of .dat.

Since malware has cost organizations millions and billions of dollars in operation costs and productivity hits, many have implemented antivirus solutions at network entry points. The scanning software can be integrated into a mail server, proxy server, or firewall. (They are sometimes referred to as *virus walls*.) This software scans incoming traffic looking for malware so it can be detected and stopped before entering the network. These products can scan SMTP, HTTP, FTP, and possibly other protocols types, but what is important to realize is that the product is only looking at one or two protocols and not *all* of the incoming traffic. This is the reason each server and workstation should also have antivirus software installed.

Patch Management

Vendors are often in too big a hurry to get something released—anything, in fact—that will plug up some hole just found in their product, even if it means breaking a thing or two in the process. That "thing" they might break, or disable, or remove, in the name of counteracting a vulnerability, may bring your business to a standstill. Pick your favorite DBMS or messaging application and take a look at the list of patches, and then the patches-for-the-patches, that were released over the last five years. Ask your DBA how often a patch breaks some obscure function of a critical application. The same obscure function that just happens to be the favorite *function-of-choice* for your developers, and, of course, the one function the critical application can't live without.

You can take steps to reduce the impact of such patches. The best way is to develop, and mature, a *patch management process,* the goal of which is to introduce patches and hotfixes into the production environment in a controlled fashion and to always have a rollback plan. A good patch management process follows a structured six-step methodology, as described next.

Step 1: Infrastructure

You need to put the base *infrastructure* in place for your patch management process. This doesn't just include the physical infrastructure, such as switches, routers, cables, and everything else that allows you to distribute the patch, but *everything* that will allow the *process* to move forward. Create a patch management strategy that will fit your organization and then assemble a team that is responsible for, and that will be held accountable for, the patching of the systems in the organization. Who should this team include? The team members should be representatives from not just the system administration folks, but also the development community and/or the people that support the applications running alongside or on top of the software being patched. And it *is* software we are talking about here, regardless of whether it gets installed to a hard drive or gets burnt into some flash-ROM, as is the case with "firmware." Software gets *patched,* whereas hardware typically gets *replaced or upgraded.* Nevertheless, whether it's software or hardware, some *process* should be followed that responsibly introduces a change into the environment—something that may take some thought.

Step 2: Research

Many a time, the wrong patch gets quickly installed to the wrong system. In a rush to stop the script-kiddie bombardment of a vulnerable server, an administrator misreads the last portion of a patch name, or downloads the patch for a slightly different version of software, and installs it . . . completely breaking the application in the process. Or even worse, an administrator finds a patch for download on a less-than-reputable web site and doesn't bother to check the authenticity or integrity of the file before installing it. This is the quickest way to put Trojan horses and malware onto a system.

The only way to prevent these unfortunate mishaps is to research a patch first, and make sure the source of any downloads is authentic, and that the files are free from corruption by performing some kind of integrity check. Many files are released along with a fingerprint or *digital signature* created by a hash-algorithm such as MD5 or SHA-1. These signatures provide a way for ensuring the integrity of a file by recalculating the signature and comparing.

Step 3: Assess and Test

Before installing on the production systems, it is important to test for any unexpected effects a patch may have. Testing is best done in a test environment, and one that mirrors, as close as possible, the production environment. Testing should be conducted according to a *test plan* that acts as a script designed to walk a system through all the known functions or procedures. A test plan should give a system a thorough "workout" that simulates the activities of the system in production. Finally, any patch management process should fit into the organization's Change Management Process. Patching is certainly *changing* the production environment, and change management is the practice of controlling such changes, reducing the unexpected issues that can arise, and, should issues occur, providing for a rollback strategy.

Step 4: Mitigation ("Rollback")

So even though you researched, tested, and implemented according to change management practices, you may still encounter issues with a particular patch. Your only choice to keep the production systems functioning is to roll back any changes and to reset the production environment to a state that existed before the patch. No test plan can account for everything, and preparing for the unknown ahead of time is the best way to mitigate issues when they arise. The goal of a rollback plan is to research and outline all the steps necessary to get back to the operational state prior to the installation of a patch should you need to.

Step 5: Deployment ("Rollout")

When the time comes to actually deploy the patch, the best thing you can do is run right over to the most critical system first and "push the go button" . . . right? Wrong! Most organizations take a phased approach when possible and start with a *pilot group* of less critical systems. After a period, the next group of more sensitive systems is patched, ending with the most critical of systems. Often, deployment strategies, especially when many systems are concerned, involve the use of automated scripts or deployment tools. These tools help reduce the issues associated with human error by executing a scripted series of steps every time on every system. A common best practice is to conduct patch deployments within a predetermined scheduled *patching window* outside of peak usage times, and with the Patch Management Team present or available for support.

Step 6: Validation, Reporting, and Logging

Finally, in order to keep track of what was done to the environment, there must be some form of auditing of what, where, when, and how patches get deployed. Logs should be kept, and documents and standard builds and configurations should be updated to include the new patches. Once the deployment is complete, confirmation that all systems designated for patching *did* actually get patched should be implemented. This can be done via manual inspection of the systems, or through use of some sort of scanning tool. Tools such as these may use an agent that is installed locally on the systems being evaluated, or employ remote application calls or query-packets to determine the status of a patch on a system. Once all scans are completed and all data are collected, a report should be generated for review and then archived for historical purposes.

Limitations to Patching

Just because you have a mature process that includes all of the six steps listed earlier, it doesn't guarantee success. Patch management can be restricted by failures in the systems or infrastructure involved in distribution of the patches, or from failures in the patching method itself. Often, patching simply takes longer than planned, and extends beyond a patching window, causing some systems to be patched while others remain vulnerable. What's worse, if patched systems become incompatible with unpatched systems, some systems may become inoperable. This sort of issue, where patching takes too long, is often the result of excess network load that starves systems for the precious bandwidth required to deliver patch files.

Best Practices

A good patch management practice involves determining the right solution for the given organization and environment. This, after all, is the real trick to patch management. Anyone can buy the latest patch management tool, but finding the *right* tool and using it in the most efficient way is where the challenges lie.

Some vendors release their own change management and change control processes. Many publish documents that outline a change control methodology, while others merely release patches in accordance with a predictable posted schedule, along with specific procedures for deployment of their patches.

No matter how great you feel your patch management process is, as part of your rollback plan you should always back up systems before patching. That's not to say you should only back up when you plan on patching. Far from it. Backups should be part of the day-to-day operations and administration of the systems in the organization. However, it is best to have backups that are up to date and that provide the best restore options should issues with patches, or any other problems, arise.

Finally, it is good practice to keep an up-to-date inventory of all the software, hardware, and configuration info. This is more challenging than it sounds. Maintaining a library full of installation CD-ROMs, hardware devices, manuals, and update files, can take a lot of work, not to mention a lot of space or storage. In a pinch, such a library is invaluable and almost always outweighs the cost and trouble of maintaining it, however.

Anything Else?

Being able to determine exactly which patches are, and are not, installed on any given system is incredibly useful. One way to track this is with a good configuration management process that requires the maintenance of baseline standard configuration documents. If these are up to date, you shouldn't need to run a scan every time you must determine how many systems need patching.

To reduce the risk to systems, be they patched or not, you should surround such systems with compensating controls that reduce risk to the system from exploit. Server hardening means that unnecessary services are disabled and access controls are tightened to provide only the least privileges required to users and/or processes. Furthermore, systems can be protected by firewalls and other forms of end-point security that limit the exposure of exploitable vectors into a system. None of these negate the need for patch management processes, but they do increase their effectiveness and buy an organization more time to get patches implemented.

Attacks

This section shows how software weaknesses and bugs are used to provide methods of bringing down systems and/or networks. The weaknesses can reside in the applications, the operating system, protocols, and the network stack.

Denial of Service

The network stack is the portion of the operating system that enables devices to communicate over the network. This is where packets are built and sent over the wire and where packets are received and processed. Different operating systems and vendors interpret the Requests for Comments (RFCs) for networking protocols differently, which end up in slightly different network stacks. These differences can contain their own flaws that can be taken advantage of to produce a *Denial-of-S ervice (DoS)* attack. These attacks are performed by sending malformed packets to a system that does not recognize the format and thus does not know how to properly process it. This can cause the system to crash or stop processing other packets (denial of service).

DoS attacks cost businesses millions of dollars each year because of system downtime, lost revenue and productivity, diminished reputation, and the man-hours involved in tracking down the problem and fixing it. DoS attacks can interrupt service or completely deny legitimate users access to needed system resources.

DoS attacks can consume a victim's bandwidth by flooding the network connection either from an attacker with more bandwidth than the victim or from several attackers working together to saturate the victim's network and bring it to its knees. If more than one attack is involved, each attacker amplifies the effects of the other attackers by combining their bandwidth capabilities and overwhelming the victim's network segment.

Another type of DoS attack uses up all of the victim's resources instead of consuming the network's bandwidth. The resources can be processes, file system quotas, memory allocation, and CPU utilization. The following sections discuss some of the possible DoS attacks available.

Smurf

Oh, a cute little blue attack.

The Internet Control Message Protocol (ICMP) is the mini-messenger of IP and can be used to find out what systems are up and running (or alive) when being used within the ping utility. ICMP reports status reports and error messages. When a user pings another computer, the ping utility sends an ICMP ECHO REQUEST message, and if the system is up and running, it responds with an ECHO REPLY message. It basically says, "Hello, computer 10.10.10.1, are you up and running?" and that computer answers back, "Yep."

The *smurf* attack requires three players: the attacker, the victim, and the amplifying network. The attacker spoofs (changes the source IP address in a packet header) to make an ICMP ECHO REQUEST packet seem as though it originated at the victim's system. This ICMP ECHO REQUEST message is broadcast to the amplifying network, which replies to the message in full force. The victim system and network are overwhelmed. The ECHO functions of ICMP are there to determine if a computer is up and running and accepting requests. However, this attack takes advantage of the protocol's lack of certain safety measures, which are built in to protect computers from being overwhelmed with ECHO messages.

Countermeasures

- Disable direct broadcast functionality at border routers to make sure a certain network is not used as an amplifying site.
- Configure perimeter routers to reject as incoming messages any packets that contain internal source IP addresses. These packets are spoofed.
- Allow only the necessary ICMP traffic into and out of an environment.
- Employ a network-based IDS to watch for suspicious activity.
- Some systems are more sensitive to certain types of DoS, and patches have already been released. The appropriate patches should be applied.

Fraggle

Fraggle is an attack that is similar to smurf, but instead of using ICMP, it employs the User Datagram Protocol (UDP) as its weapon of choice. The attacker broadcasts a spoofed UDP packet to the amplifying network, which in turn replies to the victim's system. The larger the amplifying network, the larger the amount of traffic that is pointed at the victim's system.

Different ICMP and UDP packets should be restricted from entering a network for many reasons. An attacker often uses these protocols to learn the topology of a network, locate routers, and learn about the types of systems within the network. Because we want to limit the amount of information available to attackers, the following restrictions should take place at the network's perimeter routers.

Countermeasures

- Disable direct broadcast functionality at perimeter routers to make sure a certain network is not used as an amplifying site.
- Packets that contain internal source IP addresses should not be accepted by perimeter routers as incoming messages. These packets are spoofed.
- Allow only the necessary UDP packets into and out of the environment.
- Employ a network-based IDS to watch for suspicious activity.
- Some systems are more sensitive to certain types of DoS, and certain patches may have already been released. The appropriate patches should thus be applied.

SYN Flood

Wanna talk? Wanna talk? Wanna talk? Wanna talk? Wanna talk? Wanna talk?
Response: This is looking like a SYN attack.

Because TCP is a connection-oriented protocol, it must set up a virtual connection between two computers. This virtual connection calls for handshaking, and when using the TCP protocol, this requires a three-way process. If computer Blah would like to communicate with computer Yuck, Blah will send a synchronize (SYN) packet to a specific port on Yuck that is in a LISTEN state. If Yuck is up, running, and accepting calls, it will reply to Blah with an SYN/ACK acknowledgment message. After receiving that message, Blah will send an ACK message to Yuck, and the connection will be established.

Systems, and their network stack, are expected to only have to deal with a certain number of these types of connections, so they have allocated only a certain amount of resources necessary for these types of functions. A quick analogy is in order. If Katie is only expecting three to five friends to show up at her house for a get-together on Friday night, she will most likely only buy a couple of six packs of beer and munchies. When Friday night comes around and over 100 people show up, the party comes to a standstill when there is no more beer and only a bag of pretzels to go around. The same sort of thing is true within the network stack. Once too many SYN requests are received, the system runs out of resources to process any more requests to set up communications paths.

Attackers can take advantage of this design flaw by continually sending the victim SYN messages with spoofed packets. The victim will commit the necessary resources to set up this communications socket, and it will send its SYN/ACK message, waiting for the ACK message in return. However, the victim will never receive the ACK message, because the packet is spoofed, and the victim system sent the SYN/ACK message to a computer that does not exist. So the victim system receives a SYN message, and it dutifully commits the necessary resources to set up a connection with another computer. This connection is queued waiting for the ACK message, and the attacker sends another SYN message. The victim system does what it is supposed to and commits more resources, sends the SYN/ACK message, and queues this connection. This may only need to happen a dozen times before the victim system no longer has the necessary resources to open up another connection. This makes the victim computer unreachable from legitimate computers, denying other systems service from the victim computer.

The SYN message does not take a lot of bandwidth, and this type of attack can leave the victim computer in this state from about a minute and a half to up to 23 minutes, depending on the TCP/IP stack. Because the SYN packet is spoofed, tracking down the evildoer is more difficult. Vendors have released patches that increase the connection queue and/or decrease the connection establishment timeout period, which enables the system to flush its connection queue.

Countermeasures

- Decrease the connection-established timeout period. (This only lessens the effects of a SYN attack.)
- Increase the size of the connection queue in the IP stack.
- Install vendor-specific patches, where available, to deal with SYN attacks.
- Employ a network-based IDS to watch for this type of activity and alert the responsible parties when this type of attack is under way.
- Install a firewall to watch for these types of attacks and alert the administrator or cut off the connection.

Teardrop

When packets travel through different networks, they may need to be fragmented and recombined depending on the network technology of each specific network. Each network technology has a maximum transmission unit (MTU), which indicates the largest packet size it can process. Some systems make sure that packets are not too large, but do not check to see if a packet is too small. The receiving system, the victim, would receive the fragments and attempt to recombine them, but these fragments have been made in such a way by an attacker that they cannot be properly reassembled. Many systems do not know how to deal with this situation. Attackers can take advantage of this design flaw and send very small packets that would cause a system to freeze or reboot.

Countermeasures

- Install the necessary patch or upgrade the operating system.
- Disallow malformed fragments of packets to enter the environment.
- Use a router that combines all fragments into a full packet prior to routing it to the destination system.

Distributed Denial of Service

A *Distributed Denial-of-Service (DDoS)* attack is a logical extension of the DoS attack that gets more computers involved in the act. DoS attacks overwhelm computers by one computer sending bad packets or continually requesting services until the system's resources are all tied up and cannot honor any further requests. The DDoS attack uses hundreds or thousands of computers to request services from a server or server farm until the system or web site is no longer functional.

The attack can use other computers that knowingly participate, but most likely are unknowingly used as slaves in the process. The attacker creates master controllers that can in turn control slaves, or *zombie* machines. The master controllers are systems an attacker has been able to achieve administrative rights to, so that programs can be loaded that will wait and listen for further instructions. The components of the third tier of computers are referred to as zombies because they do not necessarily know they are involved in an attack. Scripts that have been put on their hard drives execute, and together all the zombies work in concert to overwhelm a victim. An example of a DDoS attack is shown in Figure 11-31.

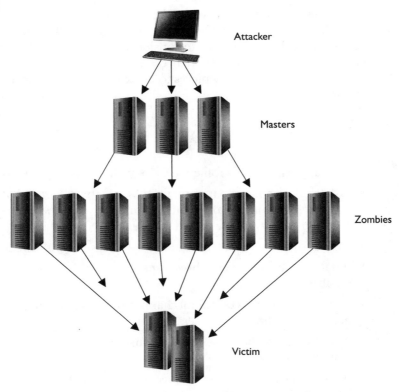

Figure 11-31
In a DDoS attack, the attacker uses masters to control the zombies to overwhelm the victim with requests.

Attacker

Masters

Zombies

Victim

Countermeasures

- Use perimeter routers to restrict unnecessary ICMP and UDP traffic.
- Employ a network-based IDS to watch for this type of suspicious activity.
- Disable unused subsystems and services on computers.
- Rename the administrator account and implement strict password management so systems cannot be used unknowingly.
- Configure perimeter routers to reject as incoming messages any packets that contain internal source IP addresses. These packets are spoofed.

Summary

Although functionality is the first concern when developing software, adding security into the mix before the project starts and then integrating it into every step of the development process would be highly beneficial. Although many companies do not view this as the most beneficial approach to software development, they are becoming convinced of it over time as more security patches and fixes must be developed and released, and as their customers continually demand more secure products.

Software development is a complex task, especially as technology changes at the speed of light, environments evolve, and more expectations are placed upon vendors who wish to be the "king of the mountain" within the software market. This complexity also makes implementing effective security more challenging. For years, programmers and developers did not need to consider security issues within their code, but this trend is changing. Education, experience, awareness, enforcement, and the demands of the consumers are all necessary pieces to bring more secure practices and technologies to the program code we all use.

Quick Tips

- If an application fails for any reason, it should go directly to a secure state.
- A database management system (DBMS) is the software that controls the access restrictions, data integrity, redundancy, and the different types of manipulation available for a database.
- In relational database terminology, a database row is called a tuple.
- A database primary key is how a specific row is located from other parts of the database.
- A view is an access control mechanism used in databases to ensure that only authorized subjects can access sensitive information.
- A relational database uses two-dimensional tables with rows (tuples) and columns (attributes).
- A hierarchical database uses a tree-like structure to define relationships between data elements, using a parent/child relationship.
- Most databases have a data definition language (DDL), a data manipulation language (DML), a query language (QL), and a report generator.
- A data dictionary is a central repository that describes the data elements within a database and their relationships. A data dictionary contains data about a database, which is called metadata.
- Database integrity is provided by concurrency mechanisms. One concurrency control is locking, which prevents users from accessing and modifying data being used by someone else.
- Entity integrity makes sure that a row, or tuple, is uniquely identified by a primary key, and referential integrity ensures that every foreign key refers to an existing primary key.
- A rollback cancels changes and returns the database to its previous state. This takes place if there is a problem during a transaction.
- A commit statement terminates a transaction and saves all changes to the database.
- A checkpoint is used if there is a system failure or problem during a transaction. The user is then returned to the state of the last checkpoint.
- Aggregation can happen if a user does not have access to a group of elements, but has access to some of the individual elements within the group.

Aggregation happens if the user combines the information of these individual elements and figures out the information of the group of data elements, which is at a higher sensitivity level.

- Inference is the capability to derive information that is not explicitly available.

- Common attempts to prevent inference attacks are partitioning the database, cell suppression, and adding noise to the database.

- Polyinstantiation is the process of allowing a table to have multiple rows with the same primary key. The different instances can be distinguished by their security levels or classifications.

- Polymorphism is when different objects are given the same input and react differently.

- The two largest security problems associated with database security are inference and aggregation.

- Data warehousing combines data from multiple databases and data sources.

- Data mining is the process of massaging data held within a data warehouse to provide more useful information to users.

- Data-mining tools produce metadata, which can contain previously unseen relationships and patterns.

- Security should be addressed in each phase of system development. It should not be addressed only at the end of development, because of the added cost, time, and effort and the lack of functionality.

- Systems and applications can use different development models that utilize different life cycles, but all models contain project initiation, functional design analysis and planning, system design specifications, software development, installation, operations and maintenance, and disposal in some form or fashion.

- Risk management and assessments should start at the beginning of a project and continue throughout the lifetime of the product.

- If proper design for a product is not put into place in the beginning, more effort will have to take place in the implementation, testing, and maintenance phases.

- Separation of duties should be practiced in roles, environments, and functionality pertaining to the development of a product.

- A programmer should not have direct access to code in production. This is an example of separation of duties.

- Certification deals with testing and assessing the security mechanism in a system, while accreditation pertains to management formally accepting the system and its associated risk.

- Change control needs to be put in place at the beginning of a project and must be enforced through each phase.

- Changes must be authorized, tested, and recorded. The changes must not affect the security level of the system or its capability to enforce the security policy.

- Iterative development is a software development method that follows a cyclic approach to software development.

- Waterfall development is a software development method that is a classical method using discrete phases of development that require formal reviews and documentation before moving into the next phase of the project.

- Spiral development is a software development method that builds upon the waterfall method with an emphasis on risk analysis, prototypes, and simulations at different phases of the development cycle. This method periodically revisits previous stages to update and verify design requirements.

- Security testing is a comprehensive analysis technique that tests programs under artificially created attack scenarios.

- High-level programming languages are translated into machine languages for the system and its processor to understand.

- Source code is translated into machine code, or object code, by compilers, assemblers, and interpreters.

- Object-oriented programming provides modularity, reusability, and more granular control within the programs themselves.

- Objects are members, or instances, of classes. The classes dictate the objects' data types, structure, and acceptable actions.

- Objects communicate with each other through messages.

- A method is functionality that an object can carry out.

- Data and operations internal to objects are hidden from other objects, which is referred to as data hiding. Each object encapsulates its data and processes.

- Objects can communicate properly because they use standard interfaces.

- Object-oriented design represents a real-world problem and modularizes the problem into cooperating objects that work together to solve the problem.

- If an object does not require much interaction with other modules, it has low coupling.

- The best programming design enables objects to be as independent and modular as possible; therefore, the higher the cohesion and the lower the coupling, the better.

- An object request broker (ORB) manages communications between objects and enables them to interact in a heterogeneous and distributed environment.

- Common Object Request Broker Architecture (CORBA) provides a standardized way for objects within different applications, platforms, and environments to communicate. It accomplishes this by providing standards for interfaces between objects.

- Component Object Model (COM) provides an architecture for components to interact on a local system. Distributed COM (DCOM) uses the same interfaces as COM, but enables components to interact over a distributed, or networked, environment.

- Open Database Connectivity (ODBC) enables several different applications to communicate with several different types of databases by calling the required driver and passing data through that driver.

- Object linking and embedding (OLE) enables a program to call another program (linking) and permits a piece of data to be inserted inside another program or document (embedding).

- Dynamic Data Exchange (DDE) enables applications to work in a client/server model by providing the interprocess communication (IPC) mechanism.

- Distributed Computing Environment (DCE) provides much of the same functionality as DCOM, which enables different objects to communicate in a networked environment.

- DCE uses universal unique identifiers (UUIDs) to keep track of different subjects, objects, and resources.

- An expert system uses a knowledge base full of facts, rules of thumb, and expert advice. It also has an inference machine that matches facts against patterns and determines which rules are to be applied.

- Expert systems are used to mimic human reasoning and replace human experts.

- Expert systems use inference engine processing, automatic logical processing, and general methods of searching for problem solutions.

- Artificial neural networks (ANNs) attempt to mimic a brain by using units that react like neurons.

- ANNs can learn from experiences and can match patterns that regular programs and systems cannot.

- Java security employs a sandbox so the applet is restricted from accessing the user's hard drive or system resources. Programmers have figured out how to write applets that escape the sandbox.

- ActiveX uses a security scheme that includes digital signatures. The browser security settings determine how ActiveX controls are dealt with.

- SOAP allows programs created with different programming languages and running on different operating systems to interact without compatibility issues.

- A virus is an application that requires a host application for replication.

- Macro viruses are common because the languages used to develop macros are easy to use and they infect Office products, which are everywhere.

- A boot sector virus overwrites data in the boot sector and can contain the rest of the virus in a sector it marks as "bad."

- A stealth virus hides its tracks and its actions.

- A polymorphic virus tries to escape detection by making copies of itself and modifying the code and attributes of those copies.

- Multipart viruses can have one part of the virus in the boot sector and another part of the virus on the hard drive.

- A self-garbling virus tries to escape detection by changing, or garbling, its own code.

- A worm does not require a host application to replicate.

- A logic bomb executes a program when a predefined event takes place, or a date and time are met.

- A Trojan horse is a program that performs useful functionality and malicious functionally without the user knowing it.

- Smurf and Fraggle are two examples of DoS attacks that take advantage of protocol flaws and use amplifying networks.

Questions

Please remember that these questions are formatted and asked in a certain way for a reason. Keep in mind that the CISSP exam is asking questions at a conceptual level. Questions may not always have the perfect answer, and the candidate is advised against always looking for the perfect answer. Instead, the candidate should look for the best answer in the list.

1. What is the final stage in the change control management process?

    A. Configure the hardware properly.

    B. Update documentation and manuals.

    C. Inform users of the change.

    D. Report the change to management.

2. Which best describes a logic bomb?

    A. It's used to move assets from one computer to another.

    B. It's an action triggered by a specified condition.

    C. It's self-replicating.

    D. It performs both a useful action and a malicious action.

3. An application is downloaded from the Internet to perform disk cleanup and to delete unnecessary temporary files. The application is also recording network login data and sending it to another party. This application is best described as which of the following?

    A. A virus

    B. A Trojan horse

    C. A worm

    D. A logic bomb

4. Why are macro viruses so prevalent?

    A. They replicate quickly.

    B. They infect every platform in production.

    C. The languages used to write macros are very easy to use.

    D. They are activated by events that happen commonly on each system.

5. Which action is not part of configuration management?

    A. Submitting a formal request

    B. Operating system configuration and settings

    C. Hardware configuration

    D. Application settings and configuration

6. Expert systems are used to automate security log review for what purpose?

    A. To develop intrusion prevention

    B. To ensure best access methods

    C. To detect intrusion

    D. To provide statistics that will not be used for baselines

7. Which form of malware is designed to reproduce itself by utilizing system resources?

    A. A worm

    B. A virus

    C. A Trojan horse

    D. A multipart virus

8. Expert systems use each of the following items except for _____.

    A. Automatic logical processing

    B. General methods of searching for problem solutions

    C. An inference engine

    D. Cycle-based reasoning

9. Which of the following replicates itself by attaching to other programs?

    A. A worm

    B. A virus

    C. A Trojan horse

    D. Malware

10. What is the importance of inference in an expert system?

    A. The knowledge base contains facts, but must also be able to combine facts to derive new information and solutions.

    B. The inference machine is important to fight against multipart viruses.

    C. The knowledge base must work in units to mimic neurons in the brain.

    D. The access must be controlled to prevent unauthorized access.

11. A system has been patched many times and has recently become infected with a dangerous virus. If antivirus software indicates that disinfecting a file may damage it, what is the correct action?

    A. Disinfect the file and contact the vendor.

    B. Back up the data and disinfect the file.

    C. Replace the file with the file saved the day before.

    D. Restore an uninfected version of the patched file from backup media.

12. Which of the following centrally controls the database and manages different aspects of the data?

    A. Data storage

    B. The database

    C. A data dictionary

    D. Access control

13. What is the purpose of polyinstantiation?

    A. To restrict lower-level subjects from accessing low-level information

    B. To make a copy of an object and modify the attributes of the second copy

    C. To create different objects that will react in different ways to the same input

    D. To create different objects that will take on inheritance attributes from their class

14. When a database detects an error, what enables it to start processing at a designated place?

    A. A checkpoint

    B. A data dictionary

    C. Metadata

    D. A data-mining tool

15. Database views provide what type of security control?

    A. Detective

    B. Corrective

    C. Preventive

    D. Administrative

16. If one department can view employees' work history and another group cannot view their work history, what is this an example of?

    A. Context-dependent access control

    B. Content-dependent access control

C. Separation of duties

D. Mandatory access control

17. Which of the following is used to deter database inference attacks?

   A. Partitioning, cell suppression, and noise and perturbation

   B. Controlling access to the data dictionary

   C. Partitioning, cell suppression, and small query sets

   D. Partitioning, noise and perturbation, and small query sets

18. What is a disadvantage of using context-dependent access control on databases?

   A. It can access other memory addresses.

   B. It can cause concurrency problems.

   C. It increases processing and resource overhead.

   D. It can cause deadlock situations.

19. If security was not part of the development of a database, how is it usually handled?

   A. Through cell suppression

   B. By a trusted back end

   C. By a trusted front end

   D. By views

20. What is an advantage of content-dependent access control in databases?

   A. Processing overhead.

   B. It ensures concurrency.

   C. It disallows data locking.

   D. Granular control.

21. Which of the following is used in the Distributed Computing Environment technology?

   A. A globally unique identifier (GUID)

   B. A universal unique identifier (UUID)

   C. A universal global identifier (UGID)

   D. A global universal identifier (GUID)

22. When should security first be addressed in a project?

   A. During requirements development

   B. During integration testing

   C. During design specifications

   D. During implementation

23. Online application systems that detect an invalid transaction should do which of the following?

A. Roll back and rewrite over original data.

B. Terminate all transactions until properly addressed.

C. Write a report to be reviewed.

D. Checkpoint each data entry.

24. What is the final phase of the system development life cycle?

A. Certification

B. Unit testing

C. Development

D. Accreditation

25. Which of the following are rows and columns within relational databases?

A. Rows and tuples

B. Attributes and rows

C. Keys and views

D. Tuples and attributes

Answers

1. **D.** A common CISSP theme is to report to management, get management's buy in, get management's approval, and so on. The change must first be approved by the project or program manager. Once the change is completed, it is reported to senior management, usually as a status report in a meeting or a report that addresses several things at one time, not necessarily just this one item.

2. **B.** A logic bomb is a program that has been coded to carry out some type of activity when a certain event takes place, or when a time and date are met. For example, an attacker may have a computer attack another computer on Michelangelo's birthday, the logic bomb may be set to execute in two weeks and three minutes, or it may initiate after a user strikes specific keys in a certain sequence.

3. **B.** A Trojan horse looks like an innocent and helpful program, but in the background it is carrying out some type of malicious activity unknown to the user. The Trojan horse could be corrupting files, sending the user's password to an attacker, or attacking another computer.

4. **C.** A macro language is written specifically to allow nonprogrammers to program macros. Macros are sequences of steps that can be executed with one keystroke, and were developed to reduce the repetitive activities of users. The language is very simplistic, which is why macro viruses are so easy to write.

5. **A.** Submitting a formal request would fall under the change control umbrella. Most environments have a change control process that dictates how all changes will be handled, approved, and tested. Once the change is approved, there needs to be something in place to make sure the actual configurations implemented to carry out this change take place properly. This is the job of configuration management.

6. **C.** An IDS can be based on an expert system or have an expert system component. The job of the expert system is to identify patterns that would represent an intrusion or an attack that an IDS without this component may not pick up on. The expert system will look at a history of events and identify a pattern that would be otherwise very hard to uncover.

7. **A.** A worm does not need a host to replicate itself, but it does need an environment, which would be an operating system and its resources. A virus requires a host, which is usually a specific application.

8. **D.** An expert system attempts to reason like a person by using logic that works with the gray areas in life. It does this by using a knowledge base, automatic logical processing components, general methods of searching for solutions, and an inference engine. It carries out its logical processing with rule-based programming.

9. **B.** As stated in an earlier answer, a virus requires a host to replicate, which is usually a specific application.

10. **A.** The whole purpose of an expert system is to look at the data it has to work with and what the user presents to it and to come up with new or different solutions. It basically performs data-mining activities, identifies patterns and relationships the user can't see, and provides solutions. This is the same reason you would go to a human expert. You would give her your information, and she would combine it with the information she knows and give you a solution or advice, which is not necessarily the same data you gave her.

11. **D.** Some files cannot be properly sanitized by the antivirus software without destroying them or affecting their functionality. So, the administrator must replace such a file with a known uninfected file. Plus, the administrator needs to make sure he has the patched version of the file, or else he could be introducing other problems. Answer C is not the *best* answer because the administrator may not know the file was clean yesterday, so just restoring yesterday's file may put him right back in the same boat.

12. **C.** A data dictionary holds the schema information about the database. This schema information is represented as metadata. When the database administrator modifies the database attributes, she is modifying the data dictionary because it is the central component that holds this type of information. When a user attempts to access the database, the data dictionary will be consulted to see if this activity is deemed appropriate.

13. **B.** Instantiation is what happens when an object is created from a class. Polyinstantiation is when more than one object is made, and the other copy is modified to have different attributes. This can be done for several reasons. The example given in the chapter was a way to use polyinstantiation for security purposes, to ensure that a lower-level subject could not access an object at a higher level.

14. **A.** Savepoints and checkpoints are similar in nature. A savepoint is used to periodically save the state of the application and the user's information, whereas a checkpoint saves data held in memory to a temporary file. Both are used so that if the application endures a glitch, it has the necessary tools to bring the user back to his working environment without losing any data. You experience this with a word processor when it asks you if you want to review the recovered version of a file you were working on.

15. **C.** A database view is put into place to prevent certain users from viewing specific data. This is a preventive measure, because the administrator is preventing the users from seeing data not meant for them. This is one control to prevent inference attacks.

16. **B.** Content-dependent access control carries out its restrictions based upon the sensitivity of the data. Context-dependent control reviews the previous access requests and makes an access decision based on the previous activities.

17. **A.** Partitioning means to logically split the database into parts. Views then dictate what users can view specific parts. Cell suppression means that specific cells are not viewable by certain users. And noise and perturbation is when bogus information is inserted into the database to try to give potential attackers incorrect information.

18. **C.** Relative to other types of access control, context-dependent control requires a lot of overhead and processing, because it makes decisions based on many different variables.

19. **C.** A trusted front end can be developed to implement more security that the database itself is lacking. It can require a more granular and stringent access control policy by requiring tighter identification and authorization pieces than those inherent in the database. Front ends can also be developed to provide more user friendliness and interoperability with other applications.

20. **D.** As stated in an earlier answer, content-dependent access control bases its access decision on the sensitivity of the data. This provides more granular control, which almost always means more processing is required.

21. **B.** A universal unique identifier (UUID) is used by DCE, and a globally unique identifier (GUID) is used by DCOM. DCE and DCOM both need a naming structure to keep track of their individual components, which is what these different naming schemes provide.

22. **A.** The trick to this question, and any one like it, is that security should be implemented at the first possible phase of a project. Requirements are gathered and developed at the beginning of a project, which is project initiation. The other answers are steps that follow this phase, and security should be integrated right off the bat instead of in the middle or at the end.

23. **C.** This can seem like a tricky question. It is asking you if the system detected an invalid transaction, which is most likely a user error. This error should be logged so it can be reviewed. After the review, the supervisor, or whoever makes this type of decision, will decide whether or not it was a mistake and investigate it as needed. If the system had a glitch, power fluctuation, hang-up, or any other software- or hardware-related error, it would not be an invalid transaction, and in that case the system would carry out a rollback function.

24. **D.** Out of this list, the last phase is accreditation, which is where management formally approves of the product. The question could have had different answers. For example, if it had listed disposal, that would be the right answer because it would be the last phase listed.

25. **D.** In a relational database, a row is referred to as a tuple, whereas a column is referred to as an attribute.

Operations Security

This chapter presents the following:

- Administrative management responsibilities
- Operations department responsibilities
- Configuration management
- Trusted recovery states
- Redundancy and fault-tolerant systems
- E-mail security
- Threats to operations security

Operations security pertains to everything that takes place to keep networks, computer systems, applications, and environments up and running in a secure and protected manner. It consists of ensuring that people, applications, and servers have the proper access privileges to only the resources they are entitled to and that oversight is implemented via monitoring, auditing, and reporting controls. Operations take place after the network is developed and implemented. This includes the continual maintenance of an environment and the activities that should take place on a day-to-day or week-to-week basis. These activities are routine in nature and enable the network and individual computer systems to continue running correctly and securely.

Networks and computing environments are evolving entities; just because they are secure one week does not mean they are still secure three weeks later. Many companies pay security consultants to come in and advise them on how to improve their infrastructure, policies, and procedures. A company can then spend thousands or even hundreds of thousands of dollars to implement the consultant's suggestions and install properly configured firewalls, intrusion detection systems (IDSs), antivirus software, and patch management systems. However, if the IDS and antivirus software do not continually have updated signatures, if the systems are not continually patched, if firewalls and devices are not tested for vulnerabilities, or if new software is added to the network and not added to the operations plan, then the company can easily slip back into an insecure and dangerous place. This can happen if the company does not keep its operations security tasks up-to-date.

Most of the necessary operations security issues have been addressed in earlier chapters. They were integrated with related topics and not necessarily pointed out as actual operations security issues. So instead of repeating what has already been stated, this chapter reviews and points out the operations security topics that are important for organizations and CISSP candidates.

The Role of the Operations Department

I am a very prudent man.
Response: That is debatable.

The continual effort to make sure the correct policies, procedures, standards, and guidelines are in place and being followed is an important piece of the *due care* and *due diligence* efforts that companies need to perform. Due care and due diligence are comparable to the "prudent person" concept. A prudent person is seen as responsible, careful, cautious, and practical, and a company practicing due care and due diligence is seen in the same light. The right steps need to be taken to achieve the necessary level of security, while balancing ease of use, compliance with regulatory requirements, and cost constraints. It takes continued effort and discipline to retain the proper level of security. Operations security is all about ensuring that people, applications, equipment, and the overall environment are properly and adequately secured.

Although operations security is the practice of continual maintenance to keep an environment running at a necessary security level, liability and legal responsibilities also exist when performing these tasks. Companies, and senior executives at those companies, often have legal obligations to ensure that resources are protected, safety measures are in place, and security mechanisms are tested to guarantee they are actually providing the necessary level of protection. If these operations security responsibilities are not fulfilled, the company may have more than antivirus signatures to be concerned about.

An organization must consider many threats, including disclosure of confidential data, theft of assets, corruption of data, interruption of services, and destruction of the physical or logical environment. It is important to identify systems and operations that are sensitive (meaning they need to be protected from disclosure) and critical (meaning they must remain available at all times). (Refer to Chapter 10 to learn more about the legal, regulatory, and ethical responsibilities of companies when it comes to security.)

It is also important to note that while organizations have a significant portion of their operations activities tied to computing resources, they still also rely on physical resources to make things work, including paper documents and data stored on microfilm, tapes, and other removable media. A large part of operations security includes ensuring that the physical and environmental concerns are adequately addressed, such as temperature and humidity controls, media reuse, disposal, and destruction of media containing sensitive information.

Overall, operations security is about configuration, performance, fault tolerance, security, and accounting and verification management to ensure that proper standards of operations and compliance requirements are met.

Administrative Management

I think our tasks should be separated, because I don't trust you.
Response: Fine by me.

Administrative management is a very important piece of operations security. One aspect of administrative management is dealing with personnel issues. This includes separation of duties and job rotation. The objective of *separation of duties* is to ensure that one person acting alone cannot compromise the company's security in any way. High-risk activities should be broken up into different parts and distributed to different individuals or departments. That way, the company does not need to put a dangerously high level of trust in certain individuals. For fraud to take place, collusion would need to be committed, meaning more than one person would have to be involved in the fraudulent activity. Separation of duties, therefore, is a preventive measure that requires collusion to occur in order for someone to commit an act that is against policy.

Table 12-1 shows many of the common roles within organizations and their corresponding job definitions. Each role needs to have a completed and well-defined job description. Security personnel should use these job descriptions when assigning access rights and permissions in order to ensure that individuals have access only to those resources needed to carry out their tasks.

Organizational Role	Core Responsibilities
Control Group	Obtains and validates information obtained from analysts, administrators, and users and passes it on to various user groups.
Systems Analyst	Designs data flow of systems based on operational and user requirements.
Application Programmer	Develops and maintains production software.
Help Desk/Support	Resolves end-user and system technical or operations problems.
IT Engineer	Performs the day-to-day operational duties on systems and applications.
Database Administrator	Creates new database tables and manages the database.
Network Administrator	Installs and maintains the LAN/WAN environment.
Security Administrator	Defines, configures, and maintains the security mechanisms protecting the organization.
Tape Librarian	Receives, records, releases, and protects system and application files backed up on media such as tapes or disks.
Quality Assurance	Can consist of both Quality Assurance (QA) and Quality Control (QC). QA ensures that activities meet the prescribed standards regarding supporting documentation and nomenclature. QC ensures that the activities, services, equipment, and personnel operate within the accepted standards.

Table 12-1 Roles and Associated Tasks

Table 12-1 contains just a few roles with a few tasks per role. Organizations should create a *complete* list of roles used within their environment, with each role's associated tasks and responsibilities. This should then be used by data owners and security personnel when determining who should have access to specific resources and the type of access.

Separation of duties helps prevent mistakes and minimize conflicts of interest that can take place if one person is performing a task from beginning to end. For instance, a programmer should not be the only one to test her own code. Another person with a different job and agenda should perform functionality and integrity testing on the programmer's code, because the programmer may have a focused view of what the program is supposed to accomplish and thus may test only certain functions and input values, and only in certain environments.

Another example of separation of duties is the difference between the functions of a computer user and the functions of a security administrator. There must be clear-cut lines drawn between system administrator duties and computer user duties. These will vary from environment to environment and will depend on the level of security required within the environment. System and security administrators usually have the responsibility of performing backups and recovery procedures, setting permissions, adding and removing users, and developing user profiles. The computer user, on the other hand, may be allowed to install software, set an initial password, alter desktop configurations, and modify certain system parameters. The user should not be able to modify her own security profile, add and remove users globally, or make critical access decisions pertaining to network resources. This would breach the concept of separation of duties.

Job rotation means that, over time, more than one person fulfills the tasks of one position within the company. This enables the company to have more than one person who understands the tasks and responsibilities of a specific job title, which provides backup and redundancy if a person leaves the company or is absent. Job rotation also helps identify fraudulent activities, and therefore can be considered a detective type of control. If Keith has performed David's position, Keith knows the regular tasks and routines that must be completed to fulfill the responsibilities of that job. Thus, Keith is better able to identify whether David does something out of the ordinary and suspicious. (Refer to Chapter 4 for further examples pertaining to job rotation.)

Least privilege and need to know are also administrative-type controls that should be implemented in an operations environment. *Least privilege* means an individual should have just enough permissions and rights to fulfill his role in the company and no more. If an individual has excessive permissions and rights, it could open the door to abuse of access and put the company at more risk than is necessary. For example, if Dusty is a technical writer for a company, he does not necessarily need to have access to the company's source code. So, the mechanisms that control Dusty's access to resources should not let him access source code. This would properly fulfill operations security controls that are in place to protect resources.

Least privilege and need to know have a symbiotic relationship. Each user should have a need to know about the resources that he is allowed to access. If Mike does not have a need to know how much the company paid last year in taxes, then his system rights should not include access to these files, which would be an example of exercising least privilege. The use of new identity management software that combines traditional directories, access control systems, and user provisioning within servers, applications, and systems is becoming the norm within organizations. This software provides the capabilities to ensure that only specific access privileges are granted to specific users and it often includes advanced audit functions that can be used to verify compliance to legal and regulatory directives.

A user's access rights may be a combination of the least-privilege attribute, the user's security clearance, the user's need to know, the sensitivity level of the resource, and the mode in which the computer operates. A system can operate in different modes depending on the sensitivity of the data being processed, the clearance level of the users, and what those users are authorized to do. The mode of operation describes the conditions under which the system actually functions. These are clearly defined in Chapter 5.

Mandatory vacations are another type of administrative control, though the name may sound a bit odd at first. Chapter 3 touches on reasons to make sure employees take their vacations. Reasons include being able to identify fraudulent activities and enabling job rotation to take place. If an accounting employee has been performing a salami attack by shaving off pennies from multiple accounts and putting the money into his own account, a company would have a better chance of figuring this out if that employee is required to take a vacation for a week or longer. When the employee is on vacation, another employee has to fill in. She might uncover questionable documents and clues of previous activities, or the company may see a change in certain patterns once the employee who is committing fraud is gone for a week or two.

It is best for auditing purposes if the employee takes two contiguous weeks off from work to allow more time for fraudulent evidence to appear. Again, the idea behind mandatory vacations is that, traditionally, those employees who have committed fraud are usually the ones who have resisted going on vacation because of their fear of being found out while away.

Security and Network Personnel

The security administrator should not report to the network administrator, because their responsibilities have different focuses. The network administrator is under pressure to ensure high availability and performance of the network and resources and to provide the users with the functionality they request. But many times this focus on performance and user functionality is at the cost of security. Security mechanisms commonly decrease performance in either processing or network transmission because there is more involved: content filtering, virus scanning, intrusion detection prevention, anomaly detection, and so on. Since these are not the areas of focus and responsibility of many network administrators, a conflict of interest could arise. The security administrator should be within a different chain of command from that of the network personnel, to ensure that security is not ignored or assigned a lower priority.

The following list lays out tasks that should be carried out by the security administrator, not the network administrator:

- **Implements and maintains security devices and software** Despite some security vendors' claims that their products will provide effective security with "set it and forget it" deployments, security products require monitoring and maintenance in order to provide their full value. Version updates and upgrades may be required when new capabilities become available to combat new threats, and when vulnerabilities are discovered in the security products themselves.

- **Carries out security assessments**   As a service to the business that the security administrator is working to secure, a security assessment leverages the knowledge and experience of the security administrator to identify vulnerabilities in the systems, networks, software, and in-house developed products used by a business. These security assessments enable the business to understand the risks it faces and to make sensible business decisions about products and services it considers purchasing, and risk mitigation strategies it chooses to fund versus risks it chooses to accept, transfer (by buying insurance), or avoid (by not doing something it had earlier considered doing, but that isn't worth the risk or risk mitigation cost).

- **Creates and maintains user profiles and implements and maintains access control mechanisms**   The security administrator puts into practice the security policies of least privilege, and oversees accounts that exist, along with the permissions and rights they are assigned.

- **Configures and maintains security labels in mandatory access control (MAC) environments**   MAC environments, mostly found in government and military agencies, have security labels set on data objects and subjects. Access decisions are based on comparing the object's classification and the subject's clearance, as covered extensively in Chapter 4. It is the responsibility of the security administrator to oversee the implementation and maintenance of these access controls.

- **Sets initial passwords for users**   New accounts must be protected from attackers who might know patterns used for passwords, or might find accounts that have been newly created without any passwords and take over those accounts before the authorized user accesses the account and changes the password. The security administrator operates automated new password generators, or manually sets new passwords, and then distributes them to the authorized user so attackers cannot guess the initial or default passwords on new accounts, and so new accounts are never left unprotected.

- **Reviews audit logs**   While some of the strongest security protections come from preventive controls (such as firewalls that block unauthorized network activity), detective controls such as reviewing audit logs are also required. The firewall blocked 60,000 unauthorized access attempts yesterday. The only way to know if that's a good thing or an indication of a bad thing is for the security administrator (or automated technology under his control) to review those firewall logs to look for patterns. If those 60,000 blocked attempts were the usual low-level random noise of the Internet, then things are (probably) normal; but if those attempts were advanced and came from a concentrated selection of addresses on the Internet, a more deliberate (and more possibly successful) attack may be underway. The security administrator's review of audit logs detects bad things as they occur and, hopefully, before they cause real damage.

Accountability

You can't prove that I did it.
Response: Ummm, yes we can.

Users' access to resources must be limited and properly controlled to ensure that excessive privileges do not provide the opportunity to cause damage to a company and its resources. Users' access attempts and activities while using a resource need to be properly monitored, audited, and logged. The individual user ID needs to be included in the audit logs to enforce individual responsibility. Each user should understand his responsibility when using company resources and be accountable for his actions.

Capturing and monitoring audit logs helps determine if a violation has actually occurred or if system and software reconfiguration is needed to better capture only the activities that fall outside of established boundaries. If user activities were not captured and reviewed, it would be very hard to determine if users have excessive privileges or if there has been unauthorized access.

Auditing needs to take place in a routine manner. Also, someone needs to review audit and log events. If no one routinely looks at the output, there really is no reason to create logs. Audit and function logs often contain too much cryptic or mundane information to be interpreted manually. This is why products and services are available that parse logs for companies and report important findings. Logs should be monitored and reviewed, through either manual or automatic methods, to uncover suspicious activity and to identify an environment that is shifting away from its original baselines. This is how administrators can be warned of many problems before they become too big and out of control. (See Chapters 3, 6, and 10 for auditing, logging, and monitoring issues.)

When monitoring, administrators need to ask certain questions that pertain to the users, their actions, and the current level of security and access:

- *Are users accessing information and performing tasks that are not necessary for their job description?* The answer would indicate whether users' rights and permissions need to be reevaluated and possibly modified.

- *Are repetitive mistakes being made?* The answer would indicate whether users need to have further training.

- *Do too many users have rights and privileges to sensitive or restricted data or resources?* The answer would indicate whether access rights to the data and resources need to be reevaluated, whether the number of individuals accessing them needs to be reduced, and/or whether the extent of their access rights should be modified.

Clipping Levels

I am going to keep track of how many mistakes you make.

Companies can set predefined thresholds for the number of certain types of errors that will be allowed before the activity is considered suspicious. The threshold is a baseline for violation activities that may be normal for a user to commit before alarms are raised. This baseline is referred to as a *clipping level*. Once this clipping level has been exceeded, further violations are recorded for review. Most of the time, IDS software is used to track these activities and behavior patterns, because it would be too overwhelming for an individual to continually monitor stacks of audit logs and properly identify certain activity patterns. Once the clipping level is exceeded, the IDS can e-mail a message to the network administrator, send a message to his pager, or just add this information to the logs, depending on how the IDS software is configured.

The goal of using clipping levels, auditing, and monitoring is to discover problems before major damage occurs and, at times, to be alerted if a possible attack is underway within the network.

NOTE The security controls and mechanisms that are in place must have a degree of transparency. This enables the user to perform tasks and duties without having to go through extra steps because of the presence of the security controls. Transparency also does not let the user know too much about the controls, which helps prevent him from figuring out how to circumvent them. If the controls are too obvious, an attacker can figure out how to compromise them more easily.

Assurance Levels

When products are evaluated for the level of trust and assurance they provide, many times operational assurance and life-cycle assurance are part of the evaluation process. *Operational assurance* concentrates on the product's architecture, embedded features, and functionality that enable a customer to continually obtain the necessary level of protection when using the product. Examples of operational assurances examined in the evaluation process are access control mechanisms, the separation of privileged and user program code, auditing and monitoring capabilities, covert channel analysis, and trusted recovery when the product experiences unexpected circumstances.

Life-cycle assurance pertains to how the product was developed and maintained. Each stage of the product's life cycle has standards and expectations it must fulfill before it can be deemed a highly trusted product. Examples of life-cycle assurance standards are design specifications, clipping-level configurations, unit and integration testing, configuration management, and trusted distribution. Vendors looking to achieve one of the higher security ratings for their products will have each of these issues evaluated and tested.

The following sections address several of these types of operational assurance and life-cycle assurance issues not only as they pertain to evaluation, but also as they pertain to a company's responsibilities once the product is implemented. A product is just a tool for a company to use for functionality and security. It is up to the company to ensure that this functionality and security are continually available through responsible and proactive steps.

Operational Responsibilities

Operations security encompasses safeguards and countermeasures to protect resources, information, and the hardware on which the resources and information reside. The goal of operations security is to reduce the possibility of damage that could result from unauthorized access or disclosure by limiting the opportunities of misuse.

Some organizations may have an actual operations department that is responsible for activities and procedures required to keep the network running smoothly and to keep productivity at a certain level. Other organizations may have a few individuals who are responsible for these things, but no structured department dedicated just to operations. Either way, the people who hold these responsibilities are accountable for certain activities and procedures and must monitor and control specific issues.

Operations within a computing environment may pertain to software, personnel, and hardware, but an operations department often focuses on the hardware and software aspects. Management is responsible for employees' behavior and responsibilities. The people within the operations department are responsible for ensuring that systems are protected and continue to run in a predictable manner.

The operations department usually has the objectives of preventing recurring problems, reducing hardware and software failures to an acceptable level, and reducing the impact of incidents or disruption. This group should investigate any unusual or unexplained occurrences, unscheduled initial program loads, deviations from standards, or other odd or abnormal conditions that take place on the network.

Unusual or Unexplained Occurrences

Networks, and the hardware and software within them, can be complex and dynamic. At times, conditions occur that are at first confusing and possibly unexplainable. It is up to the operations department to investigate these issues, diagnose the problem, and come up with a logical solution.

One example could be a network that has hosts that are continually kicked off the network for no apparent reason. The operations team should conduct controlled troubleshooting to make sure it does not overlook any possible source for the disruption and that it investigates different types of problems. The team may look at connectivity issues between the hosts and the wiring closet, the hubs and switches that control their connectivity, and any possible cabling defects. The team should work methodically until it finds a specific problem. Central monitoring systems and event management solutions can help pinpoint the root cause of problems and save much time and effort in diagnosing problems.

 NOTE Event management means that a product is being used to collect various logs throughout the network. The product identifies patterns and potentially malicious activities that a human would most likely miss because of the amount of data in the various logs.

Deviations from Standards

In this instance, "standards" pertains to computing service levels and how they are measured. Each device can have certain standards applied to it: the hours of time to be online, the number of requests that can be processed within a defined period of time, bandwidth usage, performance counters, and more. These standards provide a baseline that is used to determine whether there is a problem with the device. For example, if a device usually accepts approximately 300 requests per minute, but suddenly it is only able to accept three per minute, the operations team would need to investigate the deviation from the standard that is usually provided by this device. The device may be failing or under a DoS attack, or be subject to legitimate business use cases that had not been foreseen when the device was first implemented.

Sometimes the standard needs to be recalibrated so it portrays a realistic view of the service level it can provide. If a server was upgraded from a Pentium II to a Pentium III, the memory was quadrupled, the swap file was increased, and three extra hard drives were added, the service level of this server should be reevaluated.

Unscheduled Initial Program Loads (a.k.a. Rebooting)

Initial program load (IPL) is a mainframe term for loading the operating system's kernel into the computer's main memory. On a personal computer, booting into the operating system is the equivalent to IPLing. This activity takes place to prepare the computer for user operation.

The operations team should investigate computers that reboot for no reason—a trait that could indicate the operating system is experiencing major problems, or is possessed by the devil.

Asset Identification and Management

Asset management is easily understood as "knowing what the company owns." In a retail store, this may be called inventory management, and is part of routine operations to ensure that sales records and accounting systems are accurate, and that theft is discovered. While these same principles may apply to an IT environment, there's much more to it than just the physical and financial aspect.

A prerequisite for knowing if hardware (including systems and networks) and software are in a secure configuration is knowing what hardware and software are present in the environment. Asset management includes knowing and keeping up-to-date this complete inventory of hardware (systems and networks) and software.

At a high level, asset management may seem to mean knowing that the company owns 600 desktop PCs of one manufacturer, 400 desktop PCs of another manufacturer, and 200 laptops of a third manufacturer. Is that sufficient to manage the configuration and security of these 1200 systems? No.

Taking it a level deeper, would it be enough to know that those 600 desktop PCs from manufacturer A are model 123, the 400 desktop PCs from manufacturer B are model 456, and the 200 laptops are model C? Still no.

To be fully aware of all of the "moving parts" that can be subject to security risks, it is necessary to know the complete manifest of components within each hardware system, operating system, hardware network device, network device operating system, and software application in the environment. The firmware within a network card inside a computer may be subject to a security vulnerability; certainly the device driver within the operating system that operates that network card may present a risk. Operating systems are a relatively well-known and fairly well manageable aspect of security risk. Less known and increasingly more important are the applications (software): Did an application include a now out-of-date and insecure version of a Java Runtime Environment?

Did an application drop another copy of an operating system library into a nonstandard (and unmanaged) place, just waiting to be found by an old exploit you were sure you had already patched (and did, but only in the usual place where that library exists in the operating system)?

Asset management means knowing everything—hardware, firmware, operating system, language runtime environments, applications, and individual libraries—in the overall environment. Clearly, only an automated solution can fully accomplish this.

Having a complete inventory of everything that exists in the overall environment is necessary, but is not sufficient. One security principle is simplicity: If a component is not needed, it is best for the component to not be present. A component that is not present in the environment cannot cause a security risk to the environment. Sometimes components are bundled and are impractical to remove. In such cases, they simply must be managed along with everything else to ensure they remain in a secure state.

Configuration standards are the expected configuration against which the actual state may be checked. Any change from the expected configuration should be investigated, because it means either the expected configuration is not being accurately kept up-to-date, or that control over the environment is not adequately preventing unauthorized (or simply unplanned) changes from happening in the environment. Automated asset management tools may be able to compare the expected configuration against the actual state of the environment.

Returning to the principle of simplicity, it is best to keep the quantity of configuration standards to the reasonable minimum that supports the business needs. Change Management, or Configuration Management, must be involved in all changes to the environment so configuration standards may be accurately maintained. Keeping the quantity of configuration standards to a reasonable minimum will reduce the total cost of Change Management.

System Controls

System controls are also part of operations security. Within the operating system itself, certain controls must be in place to ensure that instructions are being executed in the correct security context. The system has mechanisms that restrict the execution of certain types of instructions so they can take place only when the operating system is in a privileged or supervisor state. This protects the overall security and state of the system and helps ensure it runs in a stable and predictable manner.

Operational procedures need to be developed that indicate what constitutes the proper operation of a system or resource. This would include a system startup and shutdown sequence, error handling, and restoration from a known good source.

An operating system does not provide direct access to hardware by processes of lower privilege, which are usually processes used by user applications. If a program needs to send instructions to hardware devices, the request is passed off to a process of higher privilege. To execute privileged hardware instructions, a process must be running in a restrictive and protective state. This is an integral part of the operating system's architecture, and the determination of what processes can submit what type of instructions is made based on the operating system's control tables.

Many input/output (I/O) instructions are defined as privileged and can be executed only by the operating system kernel processes. When a user program needs to interact with any I/O activities, it must notify the system's core privileged processes that work at the inner rings of the system. Either these processes (called system services) authorize the user program processes to perform these actions and temporarily increase their privileged state or the system's processes are used to complete the request on behalf of the user program. (Review Chapter 5 for a more in-depth understanding of these types of system controls.)

Trusted Recovery

What if my application or system blows up?
Response: It should do so securely.

When an operating system or application crashes or freezes, it should not put the system in any type of insecure state. The usual reason for a system crash in the first place is that it encountered something it perceived as insecure or did not understand and decided it was safer to freeze, shut down, or reboot than to perform the current activity.

An operating system's response to a type of failure can be classified as one of the following:

- System reboot
- Emergency system restart
- System cold start

A *system reboot* takes place after the system shuts itself down in a controlled manner in response to a kernel (trusted computing base) failure. If the system finds inconsistent object data structures or if there is not enough space in some critical tables, a system reboot may take place. This releases resources and returns the system to a more stable and safer state.

An *emergency system restart* takes place after a system failure happens in an uncontrolled manner. This could be a kernel or media failure caused by lower-privileged user processes attempting to access memory segments that are restricted. The system sees this as an insecure activity that it cannot properly recover from without rebooting. The kernel and user objects could be in an inconsistent state, and data could be lost or corrupted. The system thus goes into a maintenance mode and recovers from the actions taken. Then it is brought back up in a consistent and stable state.

A *system cold start* takes place when an unexpected kernel or media failure happens and the regular recovery procedure cannot recover the system to a more consistent state. The system, kernel, and user objects may remain in an inconsistent state while the system attempts to recover itself, and intervention may be required by the user or administrator to restore the system.

It is important to ensure that the system does not enter an insecure state when it is affected by any of these types of problems, and that it shuts down and recovers properly to a secure and stable state. (Refer to Chapter 5 for more information on TCB and kernel components and activities.)

After a System Crash

When a system goes down, and they will, it is important that the operations personnel know how to troubleshoot and fix the problem. The following are the proper steps that should be taken:

1. **Enter into single-user or safe mode.** When a system cold start takes place, due to the system's inability to automatically recover itself to a secure state, the administrator must be involved. The system will either automatically boot up only so far as a "single user mode" or must be manually booted to a "Recovery Console." These are modes where the systems do not start services for users or the network, file systems typically remain unmounted, and only the local console is accessible. As a result, the administrator must either physically be at the console, or have deployed external technology such as secured dial-in/dial-back modems attached to serial console ports or remote Keyboard Video Mouse (KVM) switches attached to graphic consoles.

2. **Fix issue and recover files.** In single user mode, the administrator salvages file systems from damage that may have occurred as a result of the unclean sudden shutdown of the system, and then attempts to identify the cause of the shutdown to prevent it from recurring. Sometimes the administrator will also have to roll back or roll forward databases or other applications in single user mode. Other times, these will occur automatically when the administrator brings the system out of single user mode, or will be performed manually by the system administrator before applications and services return to their normal state.

3. **Validate critical files and operations.** If the investigation into the cause of the sudden shutdown suggests corruption has occurred (for example, through software or hardware failure, or user/administrator reconfiguration, or some kind of attack), then the administrator must validate the contents of configuration files and ensure system files (operating system program files, shared library files, possibly application program files, and so on) are consistent with their expected state. Cryptographic checksums of these files, verified by programs such as Tripwire, can perform validations of system files. The administrator must verify the contents of system configuration files against the system documentation.

Security Concerns

- **Bootup sequence (C:, A:, D:) should not be available to reconfigure.** To ensure that systems recover to a secure state, the design of the system must prevent an attacker from changing the bootup sequence of the system. For example, on a Windows workstation or server, only authorized users should have access to BIOS settings to allow the user to change the order in which bootable devices are checked by the hardware. If the approved boot order is C: (the main hard drive) only, with no other hard drives and no removable (for example, floppy, CD/DVD, or USB) devices allowed, then the hardware settings must prohibit the user (and the attacker) from changing those device selections and the order in which they are used. If the user or attacker can change the bootable devices selections or order, and can cause the system to reboot (which is always possible with physical access to a system), they can boot their own media and attack the software and/or data on the system.

- **Writing actions to system logs should not be able to be bypassed.** Through separation of duties and access controls, system logs and system state files must be preserved against attempts by users/attackers to hide their actions or change the state to which the system will next restart. If any system configuration file can be changed by an unauthorized user, and then the user can find a way to cause the system to restart, the new—possibly insecure—configuration will take effect.

- **System forced shutdown should not be allowed.** To reduce the possibility of an unauthorized configuration change taking effect, and to reduce the possibility of denial of service through an inappropriate shutdown, only administrators should have the ability to instruct critical systems to shut down.

- **Output should not be able to be rerouted.** Diagnostic output from a system can contain sensitive information. The diagnostic log files, including console output, must be protected by access controls from being read by anyone other than authorized administrators. Unauthorized users must not be able to redirect the destination of diagnostic logs and console output.

Input and Output Controls

Garbage in, garbage out.

What is input into an application has a direct correlation to what that application outputs. Thus, input needs to be monitored for errors and suspicious activity. If a checker at a grocery store continually puts in the amount of $1.20 for each prime rib steak customers buy, the store could eventually lose a good amount of money. This activity could be done either by accident, which would require proper retraining, or on purpose, which would require disciplinary actions.

Because so many companies are extremely dependent upon computers and applications to process their data, input and output controls are very important. Chapter 10 addresses illegal activities that take place when users alter the data going into a program or the output generated by a program, usually for financial gain.

The applications themselves also need to be programmed to only accept certain types of values input into them and to do some type of logic checking about the received input values. If an application requests the user input a mortgage value of a property and the user enters 25 cents, the application should ask the user for the value again so that wasted time and processing is not done on an erroneous input value. Also, if an application has a field that holds only monetary values, a user should not be able to enter "bob" in the field without the application barking. These and many more input and output controls are discussed in Chapter 11.

All the controls mentioned in the previous sections must be in place and must continue to function in a predictable and secure fashion to ensure that the systems, applications, and the environment as a whole continue to be operational. Let's look at a few more issues that can cause problems if not dealt with properly.

- Online transactions must be recorded and timestamped.
- Data entered into a system should be in the correct format and validated to ensure such data are not malicious.
- Ensure output reaches the proper destinations securely.
  - A signed receipt should always be required before releasing sensitive output.
  - A heading and trailing banner should indicate who the intended receiver is.
  - Once output is created, it must have the proper access controls implemented, no matter what its format (paper, digital, tape).
  - If a report has no information (nothing to report), it should contain "no output."

Some people get confused by the last bullet item. The logical question would be, "If there is nothing to report, why generate a report with no information." Let's say each Friday you send me a report outlining that week's security incidents and mitigation steps. One Friday I receive no report. Instead of me having to go and chase you down trying to figure out why you have not fulfilled that task, if I received a report that states "no output," I will be assured the task was indeed carried out and I don't have to come hit you with a stick.

Another type of input to a system could be ActiveX components, plug-ins, updated configuration files, or device drivers. It is best if these are cryptographically signed by the trusted authority before distribution. This allows the administrator manually, and/ or the system automatically, to validate that the files are from the trusted authority (manufacturer, vendor, supplier) before the files are put into production on a system. Microsoft Windows XP and Windows 2000 introduced Driver Signing, whereby the operating system warns the user if a device driver that has not been signed by an entity with a certificate from a trusted Certificate Authority is attempting to install. Windows Mobile devices and newer Windows desktop operating systems, by default, will warn when unsigned application software attempts to install. Note that the fact that an application installer or device driver is signed does not mean it is safe or reliable—it only means the user has a high degree of assurance of the origin of the software or driver. If the user does not trust the origin (the company or developer) that signed the software or driver, or the software or driver is not signed at all, this should be a red flag that stops the user from using the software or driver until its security and reliability can be confirmed by some other channel.

System Hardening

I threw the server down a flight of steps. I think it is pretty hardened.
Response: Well, that should be good enough then.

A recurring theme in security is that controls may be generally described as being physical, administrative, or technical. It has been said that if unauthorized physical access can be gained to a security-sensitive item, then the security of the item is virtually impossible to ensure. (This is why all data on portable devices should be encrypted.) In other words, "If I can get to the console of the computer, I can own it." It is likely obvious that the data center itself must be physically secured. We see guards, gates, fences, barbed wire, lights, locked doors, and so on. This creates a strong physical security perimeter around the facilities where valuable information is stored.

Across the street from that data center is an office building in which hundreds or thousands of employees sit day after day, accessing the valuable information from their desktop PCs, laptops, and handheld devices over a variety of networks. Convergence of data and voice may also have previously unlikely devices such as telephones plugged into this same network infrastructure. In an ideal world, the applications and methods by which the information is accessed would secure the information against any network attack; however, the world is not ideal, and it is the security professional's responsibility to secure valuable information in the real world. Therefore, the physical components that make up those networks through which the valuable information flows also must be secured.

- Wiring closets should be locked.
- Network switches and hubs, when it is not practical to place them in locked wiring closets, should be inside locked cabinets.
- Network ports in public places (for example, kiosk computers and even telephones) should be made physically inaccessible.

Laptops, "thumb drives" (USB removable storage devices), portable hard drives, mobile phones / PDAs, even MP3 players all can contain large amounts of information, some of it sensitive and valuable. Users must know where these devices are at all times, and store them securely when not actively in use. Laptops disappear from airport security checkpoints; thumb drives are tiny and get left behind and forgotten; and mobile phones, PDAs, and MP3 players are stolen every day. So if physical security is in place, do we really still need technical security? Yep.

An application that is not installed, or a system service that is not enabled, cannot be attacked. Even a disabled system service may include vulnerable components that an advanced attack could leverage, so it is better for unnecessary components to not exist at all in the environment. Those components that cannot be left off of a system at installation time, and cannot be practically removed due to the degree of integration into a system, should be disabled so as to make them impractical for anyone except an authorized system administrator to re-enable. Every installed application, and especially every operating service, must be part of the overall Configuration Management database so vulnerabilities in these components may be tracked.

Components that can be neither left off nor disabled must be configured to the most conservative practical setting that still allows the system to operate efficiently for those business purposes that require the system's presence in the environment. Database engines, for example, should run as a nonprivileged user, rather than as root or SYSTEM. If a system will run multiple application services, each one should run under its own least-privileged user ID so a compromise to one service on the system does not grant access to the other services on the system. Just as totally unnecessary services should be left off of a system, unnecessary parts of a single service should be left uninstalled if possible, and disabled otherwise. And for extra protection, wrap everything up with tin foil and duct tape. Although aliens can travel thousands of light years in sophisticated space ships, they can never get through tin foil.

NOTE   Locked down systems are referred to as bastion hosts.

Licensing Issues

Companies have the ethical obligation to use only legitimately purchased software applications. Software makers and their industry representation groups such as the Business Software Alliance (BSA) use aggressive tactics to target companies that use pirated (illegal) copies of software.

Companies are responsible for ensuring that software in the corporate environment is not pirated, and that the licenses (that is, license counts) are being abided by. An operations or configuration management department is often where this capability is located in a company. Automated asset management systems, or more general system management systems, may be able to report on the software installed throughout an environment, including a count of installations of each. These counts should be compared regularly (perhaps quarterly) against the inventory of licensed applications and counts of licenses purchased for each application. Applications that are found in the environment and for which no license is known to have been purchased by the company, or applications found in excess of the number of licenses known to have been purchased, should be investigated. When applications are found in the environment for which the authorized change control and supply chain processes were not followed, they need to be brought under control, and the business area that acquired the application outside of the approved processes must be educated as to the legal and information security risks their actions may pose to the company. Many times, the business unit manager would need to sign a document indicating he understands this risk and is personally accepting it. So if and when things do blow up, we know exactly who to hit with a stick.

Applications for which no valid business need can be found should be removed, and the person who installed them should be educated and warned that future such actions may result in more severe consequences—like a spanking.

Companies should have an *acceptable use policy*, which indicates what software users can install and informs users that the environment will be surveyed from time to time to verify compliance. Technical controls should be emplaced to prevent unauthorized users from being able to install unauthorized software in the environment.

Organizations that are using unlicensed products are often turned in by disgruntled employees as an act of revenge.

Remote Access Security

I have my can that is connected to another can with a string. Can you put the other can up to my computer monitor? I have work to do.

Remote access is a major component of normal operations, and a great enabler of organizational resilience in the face of certain types of disasters. If a regional disaster makes it impractical for large numbers of employees to commute to their usual work site, but the data center—or a remote backup data center—remains operational, remote access to computer resources can allow many functions of a company to continue almost as usual. Remote access can also be a way to reduce normal operational costs by reducing the amount of office space that must be owned or rented, furnished, cleaned, cooled and heated, and provided with parking, since employees will instead be working from home. Remote access may also be the only way to enable a mobile workforce, such as traveling salespeople, who need access to company information while in several different cities each week to meet with current and potential customers.

As with all things that enable business and bring value, remote access also brings risks. Is the person logging in remotely who he claims to be? Is someone physically or electronically looking over his shoulder, or tapping the communication line? Is the client device from which he is performing the remote access in a secure configuration, or has it been compromised by spyware, Trojan horses, and other malicious code?

This has been a thorn in the side of security groups and operation departments for basically every company. It is dangerous to allow computers to be able to directly connect to the corporate network without knowing if they are properly patched, if the virus signatures are updated, if they are infected with malware, and so on. This has been a direct channel used by many attackers to get to the heart of an organization's environment. Because of this needed protection, vendors have been developing technology to quarantine systems and ensure they are properly secured before access to corporate assets is allowed.

Remote Administration

To gain the benefits of remote access without taking on unacceptable risks, remote administration needs to take place securely. The following are just a few of the guidelines to use.

- Commands and data should not take place in cleartext (that is, should be encrypted). For example, SSH should be used, not Telnet.
- Truly critical systems should be administered locally instead of remotely.
- Only a small number of administrators should be able to carry out this remote functionality.
- Strong authentication should be in place for any administration activities.
- Anyone who wears green shoes really should not be able to access these systems. They are weird.

Configuration Management

The only thing that is constant is change.

Every company should have a policy indicating how changes take place within a facility, who can make the changes, how the changes are approved, and how the changes are documented and communicated to other employees. Without these policies in place, people can make changes that others do not know about and that have not been approved, which can result in a confusing mess at the lowest end of the impact scale, and a complete breakdown of operations at the high end. Heavily regulated industries such as finance, pharmaceuticals, and energy have very strict guidelines regarding what specifically can be done and at exactly what time and under which conditions. These guidelines are intended to avoid problems that could impact large segments of the population or downstream partners. Without strict controls and guidelines, vulnerabilities can be introduced into an environment. Tracking down and reversing the changes after everything is done can be a very complicated and nearly impossible task.

The changes can happen to network configurations, system parameters, applications, and settings when adding new technologies, application configurations, or devices, or when modifying the facility's environmental systems. Change control is important not only for an environment, but also for a product during its development and life cycle. Changes must be effective and orderly, because time and money can be wasted by continually making changes that do not meet an ultimate goal.

Some changes can cause a serious network disruption and affect systems' availability. This means changes must be thought through, approved, and carried out in a structured fashion. Backup plans may be necessary in case the change causes unforeseen negative effects. For example, if a facility is changing its power source, there should be backup generators on hand in case the transition does not take place as smoothly as planned. Or if a server is going to be replaced with a different server type, interoperability issues could prevent users from accessing specific resources, so a backup or redundant server should be in place to ensure availability and continued productivity.

Change Control Process

A well-structured change management process should be put into place to aid staff members through many different types of changes to the environment. This process should be laid out in the change control policy. Although the types of changes vary, a standard list of procedures can help keep the process under control and ensure it is carried out in a predictable manner. The following steps are examples of the types of procedures that should be part of any change control policy:

1. **Request for a change to take place** Requests should be presented to an individual or group that is responsible for approving changes and overseeing the activities of changes that take place within an environment.

2. **Approval of the change**   The individual requesting the change must justify the reasons and clearly show the benefits and possible pitfalls of the change. Sometimes the requester is asked to conduct more research and provide more information before the change is approved.

3. **Documentation of the change**   Once the change is approved, it should be entered into a change log. The log should be updated as the process continues toward completion.

4. **Tested and presented**   The change must be fully tested to uncover any unforeseen results. Depending on the severity of the change and the company's organization, the change and implementation may need to be presented to a change control committee. This helps show different sides to the purpose and outcome of the change and the possible ramifications.

5. **Implementation**   Once the change is fully tested and approved, a schedule should be developed that outlines the projected phases of the change being implemented and the necessary milestones. These steps should be fully documented and progress should be monitored.

6. **Report change to management**   A full report summarizing the change should be submitted to management. This report can be submitted on a periodic basis to keep management up-to-date and ensure continual support.

These steps, of course, usually apply to large changes that take place within a facility. These types of changes are typically expensive and can have lasting effects on a company. However, smaller changes should also go through some type of change control process. If a server needs to have a patch applied, it is not good practice to have an engineer just apply it without properly testing it on a nonproduction server, without having the approval of the IT department manager or network administrator, and without having backup and backout plans in place in case the patch causes some negative effect on the production server. Of course, these changes need to be documented.

As stated previously, it is critical that the operations department create approved backout plans before implementing changes to systems or the network. It is very common for changes to cause problems that were not properly identified before the implementation process began. Many network engineers have experienced the headaches of applying poorly developed "fixes" or patches that end up breaking something else in the system. To ensure productivity is not negatively affected by these issues, a backout plan should be developed. This plan describes how the team will restore the system to its original state before the change was implemented.

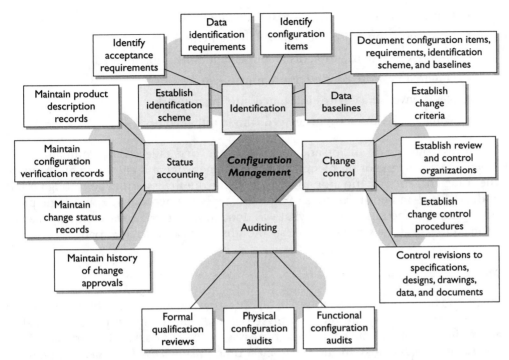

Change Control Documentation

Failing to document changes to systems and networks is only asking for trouble, because no one will remember, for example, what was done to that one server in the DMZ six months ago or how the main router was fixed when it was acting up last year. Changes to software configurations and network devices take place pretty often in most environments, and keeping all of these details properly organized is impossible, unless someone maintains a log of this type of activity.

Numerous changes can take place in a company, some of which are listed next:

- New computers installed
- New applications installed
- Different configurations implemented
- Patches and updates installed
- New technologies integrated

- Policies, procedures, and standards updated
- New regulations and requirements implemented
- Network or system problems identified and fixes implemented
- Different network configuration implemented
- New networking devices integrated into the network
- Company acquired by, or merged with, another company

The list could go on and on and could be general or detailed. Many companies have experienced some major problem that affects the network and employee productivity. The IT department may run around trying to figure out the issue and go through hours or days of trial-and-error exercises to find and apply the necessary fix. If no one properly documents the incident and what was done to fix the issue, the company may be doomed to repeat the same scramble six months to a year down the road.

Media Controls

Media and devices that can be found in an operations environment require a variety of controls to ensure they are properly preserved and that the integrity, confidentiality, and availability of the data held on them are not compromised. For the purposes of this discussion, "media" may include both electronic (disk, CD/DVD, tape, Flash devices such as USB "thumb drives," and so on) and nonelectronic (paper) forms of information; and media libraries may come into custody of media before, during, and/or after the information content of the media is entered into, processed on, and/or removed from systems.

The operational controls that pertain to these issues come in many flavors. The first are controls that prevent unauthorized access (protect confidentiality), which as usual can be physical, administrative, and technical. If the company's backup tapes are to be properly protected from unauthorized access, they must be stored in a place where only authorized people have access to them, which could be in a locked server room or an offsite facility. If media needs to be protected from environmental issues such as humidity, heat, cold, fire, and natural disasters (to maintain availability), the media should be kept in a fireproof safe in a regulated environment or in an offsite facility that controls the environment so it is hospitable to data processing components. These issues are covered in detail in Chapter 6.

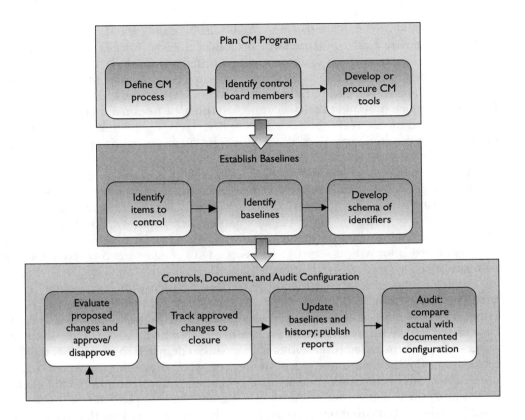

Companies may have a media library with a librarian in charge of protecting its resources. If so, most or all of the responsibilities described in this chapter for the protection of the confidentiality, integrity, and availability of media fall to the librarian. Users may be required to check out specific types of media and resources from the library, instead of having the resources readily available for anyone to access them. This is common when the media library includes the distribution media for licensed software. It provides an accounting (audit log) of uses of media, which can help in demonstrating due diligence in complying with license agreements, and in protecting confidential information (such as personally identifiable information, financial/credit card information, protected health information) in media libraries containing those types of data.

Media should be clearly marked and logged, its integrity should be verified, and it should be properly erased of data when no longer needed. After large investment is made to secure a network and its components, a common mistake is for old computers along with their hard drives and other magnetic storage media to be replaced, and the obsolete equipment shipped out the back door along with all the data the company just spent so much time and money securing. This puts the information on the obsolete equipment and media at risk of disclosure, and violates legal, regulatory, and ethical obligations of the company. Thus, the requirement of erasure is the end of the media life cycle.

When media is erased (cleared of its contents), it is said to be *sanitized*. In military/government classified systems terms, this means erasing information so it is not readily retrieved using routine operating system commands or commercially available forensic/data recovery software. Clearing is acceptable when media will be reused in the same physical environment for the same purposes (in the same compartment of compartmentalized information security) by people with the same access levels for that compartment.

Purging means making information unrecoverable even with extraordinary effort such as physical forensics in a laboratory. Purging is required when media will be removed from the physical confines where the information on the media was allowed to be accessed, or will be repurposed to a different compartment. Media can be sanitized in several ways: *zeroization* (overwriting with a pattern designed to ensure that the data formerly on the media are not practically recoverable), *degaussing* (magnetic scrambling of the patterns on a tape or disk that represent the information stored there), and destruction (shredding, crushing, burning). Deleting files on a piece of media does not actually make the data disappear; it only deletes the pointers to where the data in those files still live on the media. This is how companies that specialize in restoration can recover the deleted files intact after they have been apparently/accidentally destroyed. Even simply overwriting media with new information may not eliminate the possibility of recovering the previously written information. This is why zeroization (see Figure 12-1) and secure overwriting algorithms are required. And, if any part of a piece of media containing highly sensitive information cannot be cleared or purged, then physical destruction must take place.

Not all clearing/purging methods are applicable to all media—for example, optical media is not susceptible to degaussing, and overwriting may not be effective against Flash devices. The degree to which information may be recoverable by a sufficiently motivated and capable adversary must not be underestimated or guessed at in ignorance. For the highest value commercial data, and for all data regulated by government or military classification rules, read and follow the rules and standards.

Data remanence is the residual physical representation of information that was saved and then erased in some fashion. This remanence may be enough to enable the data to be reconstructed and restored to a readable form. This can pose a security threat to a company that thinks it has properly erased confidential data from its media. If the media is reassigned (*object reuse*), then an unauthorized individual could gain access to your sensitive data.

Figure 12-1
Zeroization
overwrites media
to protect sensitive
data.

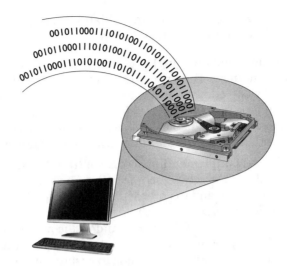

If the media does not hold confidential or sensitive information, overwriting or deleting the files may be the appropriate step to take. (Refer to Chapter 4 for further discussion on these issues.)

The guiding principle for deciding what is the necessary method (and cost) of data erasure is to ensure that the enemies' cost of recovering the data exceeds the value of the data. "Sink the company" (or "sink the country") information has value so high that the destruction of the media, which involves both the cost of the destruction and the total loss of any potential reusable value of the media, is justified. For most other categories of information, multiple or simple overwriting is sufficient. Each company must evaluate the value of its data and then choose the appropriate erasure/disposal method.

Methods were discussed earlier for secure clearing, purging, and destruction of electronic media. Other forms of information, such as paper, microfilm, and microfiche, also require secure disposal. "Dumpster diving" is the practice of searching through trash at homes and businesses to find valuable information that was simply thrown away, without being first securely destroyed through shredding or burning.

Atoms and Data

A device that performs degaussing generates a coercive magnetic force that reduces the magnetic flux density of the storage media to zero. This magnetic force is what properly erases data from media. Data are stored on magnetic media by the representation of the polarization of the atoms. Degaussing changes this polarization (magnetic alignment) by using a type of large magnet to bring it back to its original flux (magnetic alignment).

Media management, whether in a library or managed by other systems or individuals, has the following attributes and tasks:

- **Tracking** (audit logging) who has custody of each piece of media at any given moment. This creates the same kind of audit trail as any audit logging activity—to allow an investigation to determine where information was at any given time, who had it, and, for particularly sensitive information, why they accessed it. This enables an investigator to focus efforts on particular people, places, and time, if a breach is suspected or known to have happened.

- **Effectively implementing access controls** to restrict who can access each piece of media to only those people defined by the owner of the media/information on the media, and to enforce the appropriate security measures based on the classification of the media/information on the media. Certain media, due to the physical type of the media, and/or the nature of the information on the media, may require "special handling." All personnel who are authorized to access media must have training to ensure they understand what is required of such media. An example of special handling for, say, classified information may be that the media may only be removed from the library or its usual storage place under physical guard, and even then may not be removed from the building. Access controls will include *physical* (locked doors, drawers, cabinets, or safes), *technical* (access and authorization control of any automated system for retrieving contents of information in the library), and *administrative* (the actual rules for who is supposed to do what to each piece of information). Finally, the data may need to change format, as in printing electronic data to paper. The data still needs to be protected at the necessary level, no matter what format it is in. Procedures must include how to continue to provide the appropriate protection. For example, sensitive material that is to be mailed should be sent in a sealable inner envelope and use only courier service.

- **Tracking the number and location of backup versions** (both onsite and offsite). This is necessary to ensure proper disposal of information when the information reaches the end of its lifespan; to account for the location and accessibility of information during audits; and to find a backup copy of information if the primary source of the information is lost or damaged.

- **Documenting the history of changes to media**. For example, when a particular version of a software application kept in the library has been deemed obsolete, this fact must be recorded so the obsolete version of the application is not used unless that particular obsolete version is required. Even once no possible need for the actual media or its content remains, retaining a log of the former existence and the time and method of its deletion may be useful to demonstrate due diligence.

- **Ensuring environmental conditions do not endanger media**. Each media type may be susceptible to damage from one or more environmental influences. For example, all media formats are susceptible to fire, and most are susceptible to liquids, smoke, and dust. Magnetic media formats are susceptible to strong magnetic fields. Magnetic and optical media formats are susceptible to variations in temperature and humidity. A media library and any other space where reference copies of information are stored must be physically built so all types of media will be kept within their environmental parameters, and the environment must be monitored to ensure conditions do not range outside of those parameters. Media libraries are particularly useful when large amounts of information must be stored and physically/environmentally protected, so that the high cost of environmental control and media management may be centralized in a small number of physical locations, and so that cost is spread out over the large number of items stored in the library.

- **Ensuring media integrity** by verifying on a media-type and environment-appropriate basis that each piece of media remains usable, and transferring still-valuable information from pieces of media reaching their obsolescence date to new pieces of media. Every type of media has an expected lifespan under certain conditions, after which it can no longer be expected that the media will reliably retain information. For example, a commercially produced CD or DVD stored in good environmental conditions should be reliable for at least ten years, whereas an inexpensive CD-R or DVD-R sitting on a shelf in a home office may become unreliable after just one year. All types of media in use at a company should have a documented (and conservative) expected lifespan. When the information on a piece of media has more remaining lifespan before its scheduled obsolescence/destruction date than does the piece of media on which the information is recorded, then the information must be transcribed to a newer piece or a newer format of media. Even the availability of hardware to read media in particular formats must be taken into account. A media format that is physically stable for decades, but for which no working device remains available to read, is of no value. Additionally, as part of maintaining the integrity of the specific contents of a piece of media, if the information on that media is highly valuable or mandated to be kept by some regulation or law, a cryptographic signature of the contents of the media may be maintained, and the contents of the piece of media verified against that signature on a regular basis.

- **Inventorying the media on a scheduled basis** to detect if any media has been lost/changed. This can reduce the amount of damage a violation of the other media protection responsibilities could cause by detecting such violations sooner rather than later, and is a necessary part of the media management life cycle by which the controls in place are verified as being sufficient.

- **Carrying out secure disposal activities.** Disposition includes the lifetime after which the information is no longer valuable and the minimum necessary measures for the disposal of the media/information. Secure disposal of media/information can add significant cost to media management. Knowing that only a certain percentage of the information must be securely erased at the end of its life may significantly reduce the long-term operating costs of the company. Similarly, knowing that certain information must be disposed of securely can reduce the possibility of a piece of media being simply thrown in a dumpster and then found by someone who publicly embarrasses or blackmails the company over the data security breach represented by that inappropriate disposal of the information. It is the business that creates the information stored on media, not the person, library, or librarian who has custody of the media, that is responsible for setting the lifetime and disposition of that information. The business must take into account the useful lifetime of the information to the business, legal and regulatory restrictions and, conversely, the requirements for retention and archiving, when making these decisions. If a law or regulation requires the information to be kept beyond its normally useful lifetime for the business, then disposition may involve archiving— moving the information from the ready (and possibly more expensive) accessibility of a library to a long-term stable and (with some effort) retrievable format that has lower storage costs.

- **Internal and external labeling** of each piece of media in the library should include

  - Date created
  - Retention period
  - Classification level
  - Who created it
  - Date to be destroyed
  - Name and version

Taken together, these tasks implement the full life cycle of the media and represent a necessary part of the full life cycle of the information stored thereon.

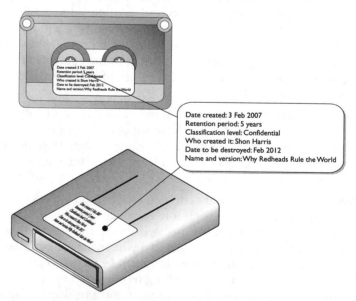

Date created: 3 Feb 2007
Retention period: 5 years
Classification level: Confidential
Who created it: Shon Harris
Date to be destroyed: Feb 2012
Name and version: Why Redheads Rule the World

Media Protection
Now, what is a media librarian responsible for again?

- Marking
- Logging
- Integrity verification
- Physical access protection
- Environmental protection
- Transmittal
- Disposition

Data Leakage

Leaks of personal information can cause large dollar losses. The Ponemon Institute's much-quoted October 2006 study suggests a per-record cost of $186. These costs include investigation, contacting affected individuals to inform them, penalties and fines to regulatory agencies and contract liabilities, and mitigating expenses (such as credit reporting) and direct damages to affected individuals. In addition to financial loss, a company's reputation may be damaged. External to the breached company's direct costs, the people whose information has been breached may face having their identities stolen. In 2006 alone, 785,000 people suffered from leaks of private information.

The most common cause of data breach for a business is a lack of discipline among employees. Negligence led to the overwhelming majority of all leaks (77 percent) in 2006 (*Source: InfoWatch 2006 Survey*).

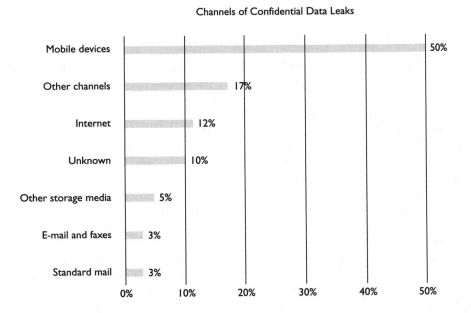

Channels of Confidential Data Leaks

- Mobile devices — 50%
- Other channels — 17%
- Internet — 12%
- Unknown — 10%
- Other storage media — 5%
- E-mail and faxes — 3%
- Standard mail — 3%

While the most common forms of negligent data breaches occur due to the inappropriate removal of information—for instance, from a secure company system to an insecure home computer so that the employee can work from home, or due to simple theft of an insecure laptop or tape from a taxi cab, airport security checkpoint, or shipping box—breaches also occur due to negligent uses of technologies that are inappropriate for a particular use—for example, reassigning some type of medium (say, a page frame, disk sector, or magnetic tape) that contained one or more objects to an unrelated purpose without securely ensuring that the media contained no residual data.

	Activity	Occurred	Affected
1.	Gratis Internet Company collected the personal data of 7 million Americans via the Internet and later resold it to third parties.	March 2006	7 million people
2.	Leak of personal data of U.S. Army veterans and servicemen.	May 2006	28.7 million people
3.	A laptop with personal details of TG customers was lost by an outsourced contractor of Texas Guaranteed.	May 2006	1.3 million people
4.	A laptop of an employee of the Nationwide Building Society was stolen. It contained the personal information of 11 million society members.	August 2006	11 million people
5.	A mobile computer containing personal details of the company's employees was stolen from the office of Affiliated Computer Services (ACS).	October 2006	1.4 million people

Source: InfoWatch 2006 Survey

It would be too easy to simply blame employees for any inappropriate use of information that results in the information being put at risk, followed by breaches. Employees have a job to do, and their understanding of that job is almost entirely based on what their employer tells them. What an employer tells an employee about the job is not limited to, and may not even primarily be in, the "job description." Instead, it will be in the feedback the employee receives on a day-to-day and year-to-year basis regarding their work. If the company in its routine communications to employees and its recurring training, performance reviews, and salary/bonus processes does not include security awareness, then employees will not understand security to be a part of their job.

The increased complexity in the environment and types of media that are now being commonly used in environments require more communication and training to ensure that the environment is well protected.

Further, except in government and military environments, company policies and even awareness training will not stop the most dedicated employees from making the best use of up-to-date consumer technologies, including those technologies not yet integrated into the corporate environment, and even those technologies not yet reasonably secured for the corporate environment or corporate information. Companies must stay aware of new consumer technologies and how employees (wish to) use them in the corporate environment. Just saying "no" will not stop an employee from using, say, a personal digital assistant, a USB thumb drive, a smart phone, or e-mail to forward corporate data to their home e-mail address in order to work on the data when out of the office. Companies must include in their technical security controls the ability to detect and/or prevent such actions through, for example, computer lockdowns, which prevent writing sensitive data to non-company-owned storage devices, such as USB thumb drives, and e-mailing sensitive information to nonapproved e-mail destinations.

Network and Resource Availability

In the triangle of security services, *availability* is one of the foundational components, the other two being *confidentiality* and *integrity*. Network and resource availability often is not fully appreciated until it is gone. That is why administrators and engineers need to implement effective backup and redundant systems to make sure that when something happens (and something will happen), users' productivity will not be drastically affected.

The network needs to be properly maintained to make sure the network and its resources will always be available when they're needed. For example, the cables need to be the correct type for the environment and technology used, and cable runs should not exceed the recommended lengths. Older cables should be replaced with newer ones, and periodic checks should be made for possible cable cuts and malfunctions.

A majority of networks use Ethernet technology, which is very resistant to failure. Token Ring was designed to be fault tolerant and does a good job when all the computers within this topology are configured and act correctly. If one network interface card (NIC) is working at a different speed than the others, the whole ring can be affected and traffic may be disrupted. Also, if two systems have the same MAC address, the whole network can be brought down. These issues need to be considered when maintaining an existing network. If an engineer is installing a NIC on a Token Ring network, she should ensure it is set to work at the same speed as the others and that there is no possibility for duplicate MAC addresses.

As with disposal, device backup solutions and other availability solutions are chosen to balance the value of having information available against the cost of keeping that information available.

- **Redundant hardware** ready for "hot swapping" keeps information highly available by having multiple copies of information (mirroring) or enough extra information available to reconstruct information in case of partial loss (parity, error correction). Hot swapping allows the administrator to replace the failed component while the system continues to run and information remains available; usually degraded performance results, but unplanned downtime is avoided.

- **Fault-tolerant technologies** keep information available against not only individual storage device faults but even against whole system failures. Fault tolerance is among the most expensive possible solutions, and is justified only for the most mission-critical information. All technology will eventually experience a failure of some form. A company that would suffer irreparable harm from any unplanned downtime, or that would accumulate millions of dollars in losses for even a very brief unplanned downtime, can justify paying the high cost for fault-tolerant systems.

- **Service level agreements (SLAs)** help service providers, whether they are an internal IT operation or an outsourcer, decide what type of availability technology is appropriate. From this determination, the price of a service or the budget of the IT operation can be set. The process of developing an SLA with a business is also beneficial to the business. While some businesses have performed this type of introspection on their own, many have not, and being forced to go through the exercise as part of budgeting for their internal IT operations or external sourcing helps the business understand the real value of its information.

- **Solid operational procedures** are also required to maintain availability. The most reliable hardware with the highest redundancy or fault tolerance, designed for the fastest mean time to repair, will mostly be a waste of money if operational procedures, training, and continuous improvement are not part of the operational environment: one slip of the finger by an IT administrator can halt the most reliable system.

We need to understand when system failures are most likely to happen. . . .

Mean Time Between Failures (MTBF)

MTBF is the estimated lifespan of a piece of equipment. MTBF is calculated by the vendor of the equipment or a third party. The reason for using this value is to know approximately when a particular device will need to be replaced. Either based on historical data or scientifically estimated by vendors, it is used as a benchmark for reliability by predicting the average time that will pass in the operation of a component or a system until its final death.

Organizations trending MTBF over time for the device they use may be able to identify types of devices that are failing above the averages promised by manufacturers and take action such as proactively contacting manufacturers under warranty, or deciding that old devices are reaching the end of their useful life and choosing to replace them en masse before larger scale failures and operational disruptions occur.

Mean Time to Repair (MTTR)

You are very mean. I have decided not to repair you.

Mean Time To Repair (MTTR) is the amount of time it will be expected to take to get a device fixed and back into production. For a hard drive in a redundant array, the MTTR is the amount of time between the actual failure and the time when, after noticing the failure, someone has replaced the failed drive and the redundant array has completed rewriting the information on the new drive. This is likely to be measured in hours. For a nonredundant hard drive in a desktop PC, the MTTR is the amount of time between when the user emits a loud curse and calls the help desk, and the time when the replaced

What's the Real Deal?

MTBF can be misleading. Putting aside questions of whether manufacturer-predicted MTBFs are believable, consider a desktop PC with a single hard drive installed, where the hard drive has an MTBF estimate by the manufacturer of 30,000 hours. Thus, 30,000 hours / 8760 hours/year = a little over three years MTBF. This suggests that this model of hard drive, on average, will last over three years before it fails. Put aside the notions of whether the office environment in which that PC is located is temperature-, humidity-, shock-, and coffee spill–controlled, and install a second identical hard drive in that PC. The possibility of failure has now doubled, giving two chances in that three-year period of suffering a failure of a hard drive in the PC. Extrapolate this to a data center with thousands of these hard drives in it, and it becomes clear that a hard drive replacement budget is required each year, along with redundancy for important data.

hard drive has been reloaded with the operating system, software, and any backed-up data belonging to the user. This is likely to be measured in days. For an unplanned re-boot, the MTTR is the amount of time between the failure of the system and the point in time when it has rebooted its operating system, checked the state of its disks (hopefully finding nothing that its file systems cannot handle), and restarted its applications, and its applications have checked the consistency of their data (hopefully finding nothing that their journals cannot handle) and once again begun processing transactions. For well-built hardware running high-quality, well-managed operating systems and software, this may be only minutes. For commodity equipment without high-performance journaling file systems and databases, this may be hours, or, worse, days if automated recovery/rollback does not work and a restore of data from tape is required.

- The MTTR may pertain to fixing a component or the device, or replacing the device, or perhaps refers to a vendor's SLA.
- If the MTTR is too high for a critical device, then redundancy should be used.

The MTBF and MTTR numbers provided by manufacturers are useful in choosing how much to spend on new systems. Systems that can be down for brief periods of time without significant impact may be built from inexpensive components with lower MTBF expectations and modest MTTR. Higher MTBF numbers are often accompanied by higher prices. Systems that cannot be allowed to be down need redundant components. Systems for which no downtime is allowable, or even those brief windows of increased risk experienced when a redundant component has failed and is being replaced, may require fault tolerance.

Single Points of Failure

Don't put all your eggs in one basket, or all your electrons in one device.

A *single point of failure* poses a lot of potential risk to a network, because if the device fails, a segment or even the entire network is negatively affected. Devices that could represent single points of failure are firewalls, routers, network access servers, T1 lines, switches, bridges, hubs, and authentication servers—to name a few. The best defenses against being vulnerable to these single points of failure are proper maintenance, regular backups, redundancy, and fault tolerance.

Multiple paths should exist between routers in case one router goes down, and dynamic routing protocols should be used so each router will be informed when a change to the network takes place. For WAN connections, a failover option should be configured to enable an ISDN to be available if the WAN router fails. Figure 12-2 illustrates a common e-commerce environment that contains redundant devices.

Redundant array of inexpensive disks (RAID) provides fault tolerance for hard drives and can improve system performance. Redundancy and speed are provided by breaking up the data and writing it across several disks so different disk heads can work simultaneously to retrieve the requested information. Control data are also spread across each disk—this is called *parity*—so that if one disk fails, the other disks can work together and restore its data.

Figure 12-2
Each critical device may require a redundant partner to ensure availability.

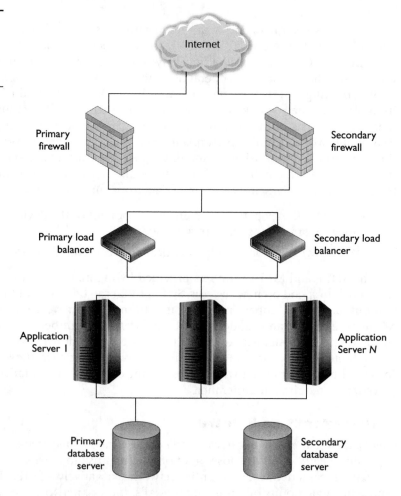

Information that is required to always be available—that is, for which MTTR must be essentially zero and for which significantly degraded performance is unacceptable—should be mirrored or duplexed. In both mirroring (also known as RAID 1) and duplexing, every data write operation occurs simultaneously or nearly simultaneously in more than one physical place. The distinction between mirroring and duplexing is that with mirroring the two (or more) physical places where the data are written may be attached to the same controller, leaving the storage still subject to the single point of failure of the controller itself; in duplexing, two or more controllers are used. Mirroring and duplexing may occur on multiple storage devices that are physically at a distance from one another, providing a degree of disaster tolerance.

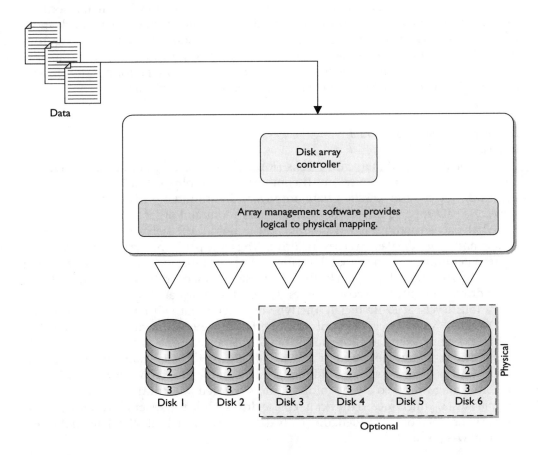

The benefit of mirrors/duplexes is that, for mostly read operations, the read requests may be satisfied from any copy in the mirror/duplex, potentially allowing for multiples of the speed of individual devices. See RAID, which is discussed shortly, for details.

The following sections address other technologies that can be used to help prevent productivity disruption because of single points of failures.

Direct Access Storage Device

Direct Access Storage Device (DASD) is a general term for magnetic disk storage devices, which historically have been used in mainframe and minicomputer (mid-range computer) environments. A redundant array of independent disks (RAID) is a type of DASD. The key distinction between Direct Access and Sequential Access storage devices is that any point on a Direct Access Storage Device may be promptly reached, whereas every point in between the current position and the desired position of a Sequential Access Storage Device must be traversed in order to reach the desired position. Tape drives are Sequential Access Storage Devices. Some tape drives have minimal amounts of Direct Access intelligence built in. These include multitrack tape devices that store at specific points on the tape and cache in the tape drive information about where major sections of data on the tape begin, allowing the tape drive to more quickly reach a track and a point on the track from which to begin the now much shorter traversal of data from that indexed point to the desired point. While this makes such tape drives noticeably faster than their purely sequential peers, the difference in performance between Sequential and Direct Access Storage Devices is orders of magnitude.

RAID

Everyone be calm—this is a raid.
Response: Wrong raid.

Redundant array of inexpensive disks (RAID) is a technology used for redundancy and/or performance improvement. It combines several physical disks and aggregates them into logical arrays. When data are saved, the information is written across all drives. A RAID appears as a single drive to applications and other devices.

When data are written across all drives, the technique of *striping* is used. This activity divides and writes the data over several drives. The write performance is not affected, but the read performance is increased dramatically because more than one head is retrieving data at the same time. It might take the RAID system six seconds to write a block of data to the drives and only two seconds or less to read the same data from the disks.

Various levels of RAID dictate the type of activity that will take place within the RAID system. Some levels deal only with performance issues, while other levels deal with performance and fault tolerance. If fault tolerance is one of the services a RAID level provides, parity is involved. If a drive fails, the parity is basically instructions that tell the RAID system how to rebuild the lost data on the new hard drive. Parity is used to rebuild a new drive so all the information is restored. Most RAID systems have *hot-swapping* disks, which means they can replace drives while the system is running. When a drive is swapped out, or added, the parity data are used to rebuild the data on the new disk that was just added.

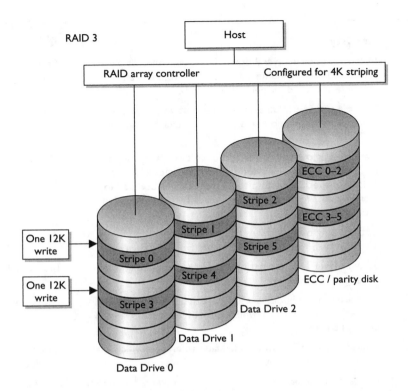

NOTE RAID level 15 is actually a combination of levels 1 and 5, and RAID 10 is a combination of levels 1 and 0.

The most common RAID levels used today are levels 1, 3, and 5. Table 12-2 describes each of the possible RAID levels.

NOTE RAID level 5 is the most commonly used mode.

RAID Level	Activity	Name
0	Data striped over several drives. No redundancy or parity is involved. If one volume fails, the entire volume can be unusable. It is used for performance only.	Striping
1	Mirroring of drives. Data are written to two drives at once. If one drive fails, the other drive has the exact same data available.	Mirroring
2	Data striping over all drives at the bit level. Parity data are created with a hamming code, which identifies any errors. This level specifies that up to 39 disks can be used: 32 for storage and 7 for error recovery data. This is not used in production today.	Hamming code parity
3	Data striping over all drives and parity data held on one drive. If a drive fails, it can be reconstructed from the parity drive.	Byte-level parity
4	Same as level 3, except parity is created at the block level instead of the byte level.	Block-level parity
5	Data are written in disk sector units to all drives. Parity is written to all drives also, which ensures there is no single point of failure.	Interleave parity
6	Similar to level 5 but with added fault tolerance, which is a second set of parity data written to all drives.	Second parity data (or double parity)
10	Data are simultaneously mirrored and striped across several drives and can support multiple drive failures.	Striping and mirroring

Table 12-2 Different RAID Levels

Massive Array of Inactive Disks (MAID)

I have a maid that collects my data and vacuums.
Response: Sure you do.

A relatively recent entrant into the medium scale storage arena (in the hundreds of terabytes) is MAID, a *massive array of inactive disks*. MAID has a particular (possibly large) niche, where up to several hundred terabytes of data storage are needed, but it carries out mostly write operations. Smaller storage requirements generally do not justify the increased acquisition cost and operational complexity of a MAID. Medium to large storage requirements where much of the data are regularly active would not accomplish a true benefit from MAID since the performance of a MAID in such a use case declines rapidly as more drives are needed to be active than the MAID is intended to offer. At the very highest end of storage, with a typical write-mostly use case, tape drives remain the most economical solution due to the lower per-unit cost of tape storage and the decreasing percent of the total media needed to be online at any given time.

In a MAID, rack-mounted disk arrays have all inactive disks powered down, with only the disk controller alive. When an application asks for data, the controller powers up the appropriate disk drive(s), transfers the data, and then powers the drive(s) down again. By powering down infrequently accessed drives, energy consumption is significantly reduced, and the service life of the disk drives may be increased.

Redundant Array of Independent Tapes (RAIT)

How is a rat going to help us store our data?
Response: Who hired you and why?

RAIT (redundant array of independent tapes) is similar to RAID, but uses tape drives instead of disk drives. Tape storage is the lowest cost option for very large amounts of data, but is very slow compared to disk storage. For very large write-mostly storage applications where MAID is not economical and where a higher performance than typical tape storage is desired, or where tape storage provides appropriate performance and higher reliability is required, RAIT may fit.

As in RAID 1 striping, in RAIT, data are striped in parallel to multiple tape drives, with or without a redundant parity drive. This provides the high capacity at low cost typical of tape storage, with higher than usual tape data transfer rates and optional data integrity.

Storage Area Networks

Drawing from the Local Area Network (LAN), Wide Area Network (WAN), and Metropolitan Area Network (MAN) nomenclature, a *Storage Area Network (SAN)* consists of large amounts of storage devices linked together by a high-speed private network and storage-specific switches. This creates a "fabric" that allows users to attach to and interact in a transparent mode. When a user makes a request for a file, he does not need to know which server or tape drive to go to—the SAN software finds it and magically provides it to the user.

Many infrastructures have data spewed all over the network and tracking down the necessary information can be frustrating, but also backing up all of the necessary data can also prove challenging in this setup.

SANs provide redundancy, fault tolerance, reliability, and backups, and allow the users and administrators to interact with the SAN as one virtual entity. Because the network that carries the data in the SAN is separate from a company's regular data network, all of this performance, reliability, and flexibility come without impact to the data networking capabilities of the systems on the network.

SANs are not commonly used in average or mid-sized companies. They are for companies that have to keep track of terabytes of data and have the funds for this type of technology. The storage vendors are currently having a heyday, not only because everything we do business-wise is digital and must be stored, but because government regulations are requiring companies to keep certain types of data for a specific retention period. Imagine storing all of your company's e-mail traffic for seven years . . . that's just one type of data that must be retained.

NOTE Tape drives, optical jukeboxes, and disk arrays may also be attached to, and referenced through, a SAN.

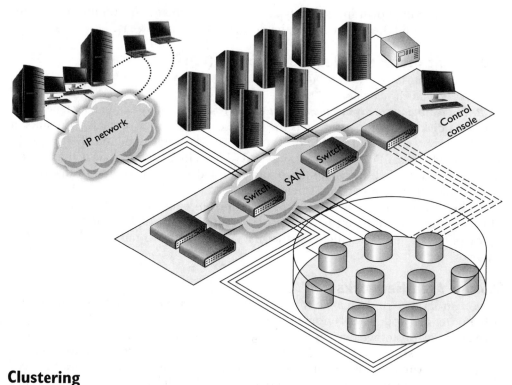

Clustering

Okay, everyone gather over here and perform the same tasks.

Clustering is a fault-tolerant server technology that is similar to redundant servers, except each server takes part in processing services that are requested. A *server cluster* is a group of servers that are viewed logically as one server to users and can be managed as a single logical system. Clustering provides for availability and scalability. It groups physically different systems and combines them logically, which provides immunity to faults and improves performance. Clusters work as an intelligent unit to balance traffic, and users who access the cluster do not know they may be accessing different systems at different times. To the users, all servers within the cluster are seen as one unit. Clusters may also be referred to as server farms.

If one of the systems within the cluster fails, processing continues because the rest pick up the load, although degradation in performance could occur. This is more attractive, however, than having a secondary (redundant) server that waits in the wings in case a primary server fails, because this secondary server may just sit idle for a long period of time, which is wasteful. When clustering is used, all systems are used to process requests and none sits in the background waiting for something to fail. Clustering is a logical outgrowth of redundant servers. Consider a single server that requires high availability, and so has a hot standby redundant server allocated. For each such single server requiring high availability, an additional redundant server must be purchased. Since failure of multiple primary servers at once is unlikely, it would be economically efficient to have a small number of extra servers, any of which could take up the load of any single failed primary server. Thus was born the cluster.

Clustering offers a lot more than just availability. It also provides load balancing (each system takes a part of the processing load), redundancy, and failover (other systems continue to work if one fails).

Grid Computing

I am going to use a bit of the processing power of every computer and take over the world.

Grid computing is another load-balanced parallel means of massive computation, similar to clusters, but implemented with loosely coupled systems that may join and leave the grid randomly. Most computers have extra CPU processing power that is not being used many times throughout the day. So some smart people thought that was wasteful and came up with a way to use all of this extra processing power. Just like the power grid provides electricity to entities on an as-needed basis (if you pay your bill), computers can volunteer to allow their extra processing power to be available to different groups for different projects. The first project to use grid computing was SETI (Search for Extra-Terrestrial Intelligence), where people allowed their systems to participate in scanning the universe looking for aliens who are trying to talk to us.

Although this may sound similar to clustering, where in a cluster a central controller has master control over allocation of resources and users to cluster nodes, and the nodes in the cluster are under central management (in the same trust domain), in grid computing the nodes do not trust each other and have no central control.

Applications that may be technically suitable to run in a grid and that would enjoy the economic advantage of a grid's cheap massive computing power, but which require secrecy, may not be good candidates for a grid computer since the secrecy of the content of a workload unit allocated to a grid member cannot be guaranteed by the grid against the owner of the individual grid member. Additionally, because the grid members are of variable capacity and availability, and do not trust each other, grid computing is not appropriate for applications that require tight interactions and coordinated scheduling among multiple workload units. This means sensitive data should not be processed over a grid, and this is not the proper technology for time-sensitive applications.

A more appropriate use of grid computing is projects like financial modeling, weather modeling, and earthquake simulation. Each of these has an incredible amount of variables and input that need to be continually computed. This approach has also been used to try and crack algorithms and was used to generate Rainbow Tables.

 NOTE Rainbow Tables consist of all possible passwords in hashed formats. This allows attackers to uncover passwords much more quickly than carrying out a dictionary or brute force attack.

Backups

Backing up software and having backup hardware devices are two large parts of network availability. (These issues are covered extensively in Chapters 6 and 9, so they are discussed only briefly here.) You need to be able to restore data if a hard drive fails, a disaster takes place, or some type of software corruption occurs.

A policy should be developed that indicates what gets backed up, how often it gets backed up, and how these processes should occur. If users have important information on their workstations, the operations department needs to develop a method that indicates that backups include certain directories on users' workstations or that users move their critical data to a server share at the end of each day to ensure it gets backed up. Backups may occur once or twice a week, every day, or every three hours. It is up to the company to determine this routine. The more frequent the backups, the more resources will be dedicated to it, so there needs to be a balance between backup costs and the actual risk of potentially losing data.

A company may find that conducting automatic backups through specialized software is more economical and effective than spending IT work-hours on the task. The integrity of these backups needs to be checked to ensure they are happening as expected—rather than finding out right after two major servers blow up that the automatic backups were saving only temporary files. (Review Chapters 6 and 9 for more information on backup issues.)

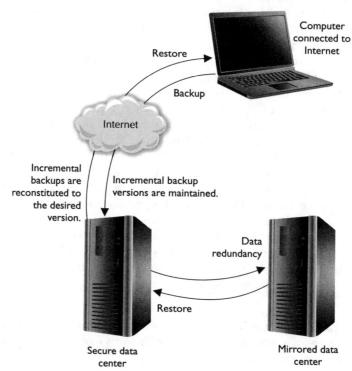

Hierarchical Storage Management (HSM)

HSM (Hierarchical Storage Management) provides continuous online backup functionality. It combines hard disk technology with the cheaper and slower optical or tape jukeboxes. The HSM system dynamically manages the storage and recovery of files, which are copied to storage media devices that vary in speed and cost. The faster media holds the data that are accessed more often, and the seldom-used files are stored on the slower devices, or *near-line* devices, as shown in Figure 12-3. The storage media could

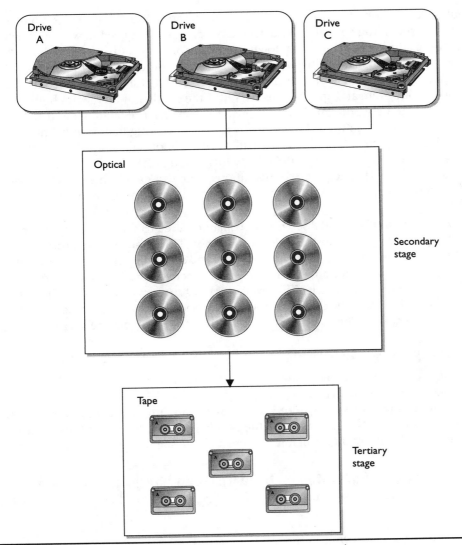

Figure 12-3 HSM provides an economical and efficient way of storing data.

include optical disks, magnetic disks, and tapes. This functionality happens in the background without the knowledge of the user or any need for user intervention.

HSM works, according to tuning based on the trade-off between the cost of storage and the availability of information, by migrating the actual content of less used files to lower-speed, lower-cost storage, while leaving behind a "stub," which looks to the user like it contains the full data of the migrated file. When the user or an application accesses the stub, the HSM uses the information in the stub to find the real location of the information, and then retrieve it transparently for the user.

This type of technology was created to save money and time. If all data were stored on hard drives, that would be expensive. If a lot of the data were stored on tapes, it would take too long to retrieve the data when needed. So HSM provides a terrific approach by providing you with the data you need, when you need it, without having to bother the administrator to track down some tape or optical disk.

Full, incremental, and differential data backup technologies were discussed in Chapter 9, along with software and hardware backups. Backups should include the underlying operating system and applications, as well as the configuration files for both. Systems are attached to networks, and network devices can experience failures and data losses as well. Data loss of a network device usually means the configuration of the network device is lost completely (and the device will not even boot up), or that the configuration of the network device reverts to defaults (which, though it will boot up, does your network little good). Therefore, the configurations of network and other nonsystem devices (for example, the phone system) in the environment are also necessary.

 CAUTION TFTP servers are commonly used to save the configuration settings from network devices. However, TFTP is an insecure protocol, some network settings are sensitive and should be kept confidential, and a coordinated attack is possible against network devices that load their configurations using TFTP by first causing the network device to fail and then attacking the TFTP download of the configuration to cause a malicious configuration to be loaded. Alternatives to TFTP should be sought.

Contingency Planning

What does our contingency plan state?
Response: It says to blame everything on Bob.

When an incident strikes, more is required than simply knowing how to restore data from backups. Also necessary are the detailed procedures that outline the activities to keep the critical systems available and ensure that operations and processing are not

Summary of Technologies Used to Keep the Juices Flowing
The following are the items you will most likely run into when taking the CISSP exam.

- Disk shadowing (mirroring)
- Redundant servers
- RAID, MAID, RAIT
- Clustering
- Backups
- Dual backbones
- Direct Access Storage Device
- Redundant power
- Mesh network topology instead of star, bus, or ring

interrupted. Contingency management defines what should take place during and after an incident. Actions that are required to take place for emergency response, continuity of operations, and dealing with major outages must be documented and readily available to the operations staff. There should be at least three instances of these documents: the original that is onsite; a copy that is also onsite, but in a protective, fireproof safe; and a copy that is at an offsite location.

Contingency plans should not be trusted until they have been tested. Organizations should carry out exercises to ensure that the staff fully understands their responsibilities and how to carry them out. Another issue to consider is how to keep these plans up-to-date. As our dynamic, networked environments change, so must our plans on how to rescue them when necessary.

Although in the security industry "contingency planning" and "business continuity planning (BCP)" are commonly used interchangeably, it is important that you understand the actual difference for the CISSP exam. BCP addresses how to keep the organization in business after a disaster takes place. It is about the survivability of the organization and making sure that critical functions can still take place even after a disaster. Contingency plans address how to deal with small incidents that do not qualify as disasters, as in power outages, server failures, a down communication link to the Internet, or the corruption of software. It is important that organizations be ready to deal with large and small issues that they may run into one day.

Mainframes

What is that massive gray thing in the corner?
Response: No one really knows.

Much of the discussion earlier was devoted to low-end (desktops, laptops, workstations) and mid-range (mini-computer) systems. *Mainframe* computers are still with us, and are likely to remain so for some time. The distinction between a mainframe and a high-end mid-range computer attached to a SAN has been narrowing, but certain attributes still make a mainframe different.

Not because of their hardware architecture, but because of very conservative (and therefore very expensive) engineering practices, mainframes tend to be highly reliable and available. That is, the developers of mainframes trade off the valuable research money and development effort that makes lower-end systems so fast with so many

---

Environmental Controls

The operations department is also responsible for a majority of the items covered in Chapter 6. This includes server room temperature and humidity, fire protection, HVAC, water protection, power sources, positive air pressure to protect against contaminants, and a closed-loop recirculating air-conditioning system.

All of these items have already been covered extensively in Chapter 6. You need to make sure you understand that these responsibilities fall within the operations department responsibilities.

features, for the reliability that lower-end systems almost universally lack. A side effect of this high investment in software quality (including both the operating system and applications) is that the results produced by mainframe processing tend to be more accurate than the commonly used servers and off-the-shelf software.

As a result of this reliability, mainframes are better for critical data needs that must be always "up."

There is a key hardware difference between mainframes and even the highest end mid-range systems: mainframe hardware is designed first and foremost for massive input/output. On a modern desktop PC, the CPU power has increased 1,000,000 times in the past 25 years, but the I/O capability has increased orders of magnitude less than that. This allows mainframes, especially today as they have borrowed from the vast CPU power improvements of PCs, to run huge numbers of processes at once, without each process being input/output starved; that ultra-fast modern PC could run only a small fraction of the number of data-hungry processes at once before I/O bottlenecks brought the PC to a stand-still. This makes mainframes non-processing-specific (as an ultra-fast cheap modern PC can be), and thus excellent general high-volume processing platforms. This also explains what may seem to be a hidden reason for some of the high cost of a mainframe. Mainframes have vast amounts of "processor" power hidden away in their front-end processors (which keep the users' interactions from distracting the central processor), their I/O processors (which move data and communicate with disk and tape drives without loading the central processor), and their network processors (which move data to and from the network, efficiently, without loading the central processor). All of this "hidden" processing power requires hardware, which contributes to the high costs of mainframes.

Another benefit of the reliability of mainframes is that they are not maintenance-intensive. Where patches are released regularly and in quantity for lower-end systems, mainframes have much reduced patch release schedules, and the quantity of patches in each release are much smaller.

Another classical difference between a mainframe and a mid-range system or a PC is the user interface. Today, mainframes still often perform batch processing rather than run interactive programs, and, though the practice is on the decline, they still sometimes accept user jobs as batches requested through Remote Job Entry (RJE) from a mainframe terminal.

A more basic difference, offering interesting possibilities, between mainframes and other types of systems, is that where PCs and mid-range systems have one hardware personality and often just one operating system, mainframes at IPL can be configured with each bootup to be a different kind of system. This allows backward compatibility of newer hardware processors with older operating systems, enabling a company to retain value from a long ago investment in software for many years, where in the PC and mid-range system arena the very old software would simply no longer be usable. Mainframes also were the first commercial-scale use of virtualization, allowing a "single" mainframe computer (which could consist of multiple banks of memory, storage, and CPUs, that today can even be added dynamically) to appear to be multiple independent computers, with strong separation among their several operating environments, sharing the total resources of the physical mainframe computer as decided by the system administrator.

Supercomputers might be considered a special class of mainframe. They share many architectural similarities, but where mainframes are designed for very high quantities of general processing, supercomputers are optimized for extremely complex central processing (which also happens to require the vast I/O capability of the mainframe architecture). Where a mainframe's several processors will balance the load of a very high number of general processes, a supercomputer's possibly massive number of processes may be custom designed to allow a large number of very highly parallelized copies of a particular application to communicate in real time, or a very small number of extremely complex scientific algorithms to leverage vast amounts of data at once.

E-mail Security

The Internet was first developed mainly for government agencies and universities to communicate and share information, but today businesses need it for productivity and profitability. Millions of individuals also depend upon it as their window to a larger world and as a quick and efficient communications tool.

E-mail has become an important and integrated part of people's lives. It is used to communicate with family and friends, business partners and customers, co-workers and management, and online merchants and government offices. Generally, the security, authenticity, and integrity of an e-mail message are not considered in day-to-day use. Users are more aware that attachments can carry viruses than the fact that an e-mail can be easily spoofed and that its contents can be changed while in transmission.

It is very easy to *spoof* e-mail messages, which means to alter the name in the From field. All an attacker needs to do is modify information within the Preferences section of his mail client and restart the application. As an example of a spoofed e-mail message, an attacker could change the name in the From field to the name of the network administrator and send an e-mail message to the CEO's secretary, telling her the IT department is having problems with some servers and needs her to change her network logon to "password." If she receives this e-mail and sees the From field has the network administrator's name in it, she will probably fulfill this request without thinking twice.

This type of activity is rampant today, and has become more of a social-engineering tactic. Another variant is referred to as *phishing*. This is the act of sending spoofed messages that pretend to originate from a source the user trusts and has a business relation with, such as a bank. In this scheme, the user is asked to click a link contained within the e-mail that will supposedly take them to their account login page so they can do account maintenance activities. Instead, the link takes the user to a web site that looks

Operators' Responsibilities

Mainframe operators have a long list of responsibilities: reassigning ports, mounting input and output volumes, overseeing and controlling the flow of the submitted jobs, renaming (or relabeling) resources, taking care of any IPLs, and buying donuts for the morning meetings.

If you see the term *operators* on the exam, it is dealing specifically with mainframe operators even if the term *mainframe* is not used in the question.

very similar to their bank's site but that is in fact owned by the attacker. The moment the user enters their credentials, the attacker has the credentials to the users' account information on the real site.

The solution to this and similar types of attacks is to require proper authentication to ensure the message actually came from the source indicated. Companies that regard security as one of their top priorities should implement an e-mail protection application that can digitally sign messages, like Pretty Good Privacy (PGP), or use a public key infrastructure (PKI). These companies may also consider using an encryption protocol to help fight network sniffing and the unauthorized interception of messages.

An e-mail message that travels from Arizona to Maine has many hops in between its source and destination. Several potential interception points exist where an attacker could intercept, view, modify, or delete the message during its journey, as shown in Figure 12-4.

If a user is going to use a security scheme to protect his messages from eavesdropping, modification, and forgery, he and the recipient must use the same encryption scheme. If public key cryptography is going to be used, both users must have a way to exchange encryption keys. This is true for PGP, digital signatures, and products that follow the S/MIME standard, which are discussed in detail in Chapter 8. If an administrator, or security proftessional, wants to ensure all messages are encrypted between two points and does not want to depend on users to properly encrypt their messages, she can implement a VPN (also discussed in Chapter 8).

How E-mail Works

I think e-mail is delivered by an e-mail fairy wearing a purple dress.
Response: Exactly.

A user has an e-mail client that is used to create, modify, address, send, receive, and forward messages. This e-mail client may provide other functionality, such as a personal address book and the ability to add attachments, set flags, recall messages, and store messages within different folders.

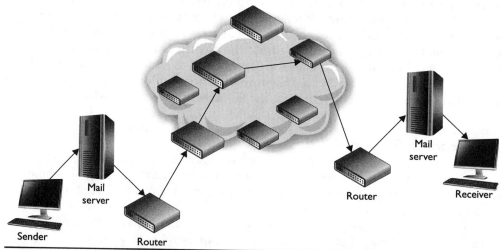

Figure 12-4 An e-mail message can be intercepted at several possible points.

A user's e-mail message is of no use unless it can actually be sent somewhere. This is where *Simple Mail Transfer Protocol (SMTP)* comes in. In some e-mail clients SMTP works as a message transfer agent, as shown in Figure 12-5, and moves the message from the user's computer to the mail server when the user clicks the Send button. SMTP also functions as a message transfer protocol between e-mail servers. Last, SMTP is a message-exchange addressing standard, and most people are used to seeing its familiar addressing scheme: something@somewhere.com.

Many times, a message needs to travel throughout the Internet and through different mail servers before it arrives at its destination mail server. SMTP is the protocol that carries this message, and it works on top of the Transmission Control Protocol (TCP). TCP is used as the transport protocol because it is a reliable protocol and provides sequencing and acknowledgments to ensure the e-mail message arrived successfully at its destination.

The user's e-mail client must be SMTP-compliant to be properly configured to use this protocol. The client provides an interface to the user so she can create and modify messages as needed, and then the client passes the message off to SMTP. So, to use the analogy of sending a letter via the post office, the e-mail client is the typewriter that a person uses to write the message, SMTP is the mail courier who picks up the mail and delivers it to the post office, and the post office is the mail server. The mail server has the responsibility of understanding where the message is heading and properly routing the message to that destination.

The mail server is often referred to as an SMTP server. The most common SMTP server software within the Unix world is Sendmail, which is actually an e-mail server application. This means that Unix uses Sendmail software to store, maintain, and route e-mail messages. Within the Microsoft world, Microsoft Exchange is mostly used, and in Novell, GroupWise is the common SMTP server. SMTP works closely with two mail server protocols, POP and IMAP, which are explained in the following sections.

POP

Post Office Protocol (POP) is an Internet mail server protocol that supports incoming and outgoing messages. A mail server that uses POP stores and forwards e-mail messages and works with SMTP to move messages between mail servers.

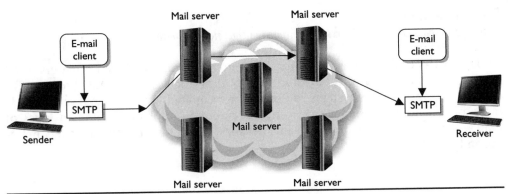

Figure 12-5 SMTP works as a transfer agent for e-mail messages.

A smaller company may have one POP server that holds all employee mailboxes, whereas larger companies may have several POP servers, one for each department within the organization. There are also Internet POP servers that enable people all over the world to exchange messages. This system is useful because the messages are held on the mail server until users are ready to download their messages, instead of trying to push messages right to a person's computer, which may be down or offline.

The e-mail server can implement different authentication schemes to ensure an individual is authorized to access a particular mailbox, but this is usually handled through usernames and passwords.

IMAP

Internet Message Access Protocol (IMAP) is also an Internet protocol that enables users to access mail on a mail server. IMAP provides the same types of functionality as POP, but has more capabilities and functionality. If a user is using POP, when he accesses his mail server to see if he has received any new messages, all messages are automatically downloaded to his computer. Once the messages are downloaded from the POP server, they are usually deleted from that server, depending upon the configuration. POP can cause frustration for mobile users because the messages are automatically pushed down to their computer or device and they may not have the necessary space to hold all the messages. This is especially true for mobile devices that can be used to access e-mail servers. This is also inconvenient for people checking their mail on other people's computers. If Christina checks her e-mail on Jessica's computer, all of Christina's new mail could be downloaded to Jessica's computer.

If a user uses IMAP instead of POP, she can download all the messages or leave them on the mail server within her remote message folder, referred to as a mailbox. The user can also manipulate the messages within this mailbox on the mail server as if the messages resided on her local computer. She can create or delete messages, search for specific messages, and set and clear flags. This gives the user much more freedom and keeps the messages in a central repository until the user specifically chooses to download all messages from the mail server.

IMAP is a store-and-forward mail server protocol that is considered POP's successor. IMAP also gives administrators more capabilities when it comes to administering and maintaining the users' messages.

E-mail Relaying

Could you please pass on this irritating message that no one wants?
Response: Sure.

E-mail has changed drastically from the purely mainframe days. In that era, mail used simple Systems Network Architecture (SNA) protocols and the ASCII format. Today, several types of mail systems run on different operating systems and offer a wide range of functionality. Sometimes companies need to implement different types of mail servers and services within the same network, which can become a bit overwhelming and a challenge to secure.

Most companies have their public mail servers in their DMZ and may have one or more mail servers within their LAN. The mail servers in the DMZ are in this protected space because they are directly connected to the Internet. These servers should be tightly locked down and their relaying mechanisms should be correctly configured. Mail servers use a *relay agent* to send a message from one mail server to another. This relay agent needs to be properly configured so a company's mail server is not used by another for spamming activity.

Spamming usually is illegal, so the people doing the spamming do not want the traffic to seem as though it originated from their equipment. They will find mail servers on the Internet or within company DMZs that have loosely configured relaying mechanisms and use these computers to send their spam. If relays are configured "wide open" on a mail server, the mail server can be used to receive *any* mail message and send it on to the intended recipients, as shown in Figure 12-6. This means that if a company does not properly configure its mail relaying, its server can be used to distribute advertisements for other companies, spam messages, and pornographic material. It is important that mail servers have proper antispam features enabled, which are actually antirelaying features. A company's mail server should only accept mail destined for its domain and should not forward messages to other mail servers and domains.

Many companies employ antivirus and content-filtering applications on their mail servers to try and stop the spread of malicious code and not allow unacceptable messages through the e-mail gateway. It is important to filter both incoming and outgoing messages. This helps ensure that inside employees are not spreading viruses or sending out messages that are against company policy.

Facsimile Security

Your covert strategic plans on how we are going to attack our enemy are sitting in a fax bin in the front office.

Faxing data is a very popular way of delivering information today and, like other types of communications channels, it must be incorporated into the security policy and program of companies.

Fax machines can present some security issues if they are being used to transmit sensitive or confidential information. The information is scanned into the device, transmitted over a phone line, and printed out on the destination fax machine. The received fax often just sits in a bin until the recipient walks over to retrieve it. If it contains confidential information, it might not be a good idea to have it just lying around for anyone to see it.

Some companies use *fax servers*, which are systems that manage incoming and outgoing faxed documents. When a fax is received by the fax server, the fax server properly routes it to the individual it is addressed to so it is kept in electronic form rather than being printed. Typically, the received fax is routed to the recipient's electronic mailbox.

The fax server lets many users transmit documents from their computers to the fax server, as illustrated in Figure 12-7, without having to pass the document through a fax

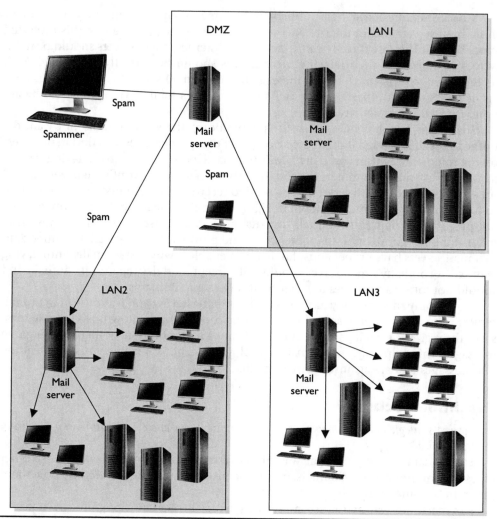

Figure 12-6 Mail servers can be used for spam if relay functionality is not properly configured.

device. This reduces the amount of sensitive documentation that needs to be properly destroyed and can save money on printing and thermal paper required by stand-alone fax machines.

A fax server usually has the capability to print the received faxes, but this can present the same security breaches as a stand-alone fax device. In environments that demand high security levels, the print feature should be disabled so sensitive documents can be stored and viewed by authorized individuals only and never printed.

Extensive logging and auditing are available for fax servers and should be implemented and monitored in companies that require this level of security. Because data travels to and from the fax server in cleartext form, some companies may choose to implement encryption for faxed materials. A company may implement a *fax encryptor*, a

Figure 12-7
A fax server can be used instead of stand-alone fax devices.

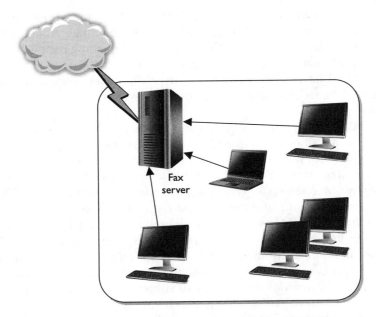

Fax server

bulk data-link encryption mechanism that encrypts all fax data that hits the network cable or telephone wire. A company would implement a fax encryptor if it did not want to depend on each individual user to encrypt documents that are faxed. Instead, by using a fax encryptor, the company is sure all data leaving that system are properly encrypted.

Hack and Attack Methods

Several types of attacks have been explained in the chapters throughout this book. This section brings together these attack methods, and others that have not been presented, to show how they are related, how they can be detected, and how they can be countered.

A majority of the tools used by hackers have dual capabilities in that they can be used for good or evil. An attacker could use tool ABC to find a vulnerability to exploit, and a security professional could use the same tool to identify a vulnerability so she could fix it. When this tool is used by black hats (attackers), it is referred to as *hacking*. When a white hat (security professional) uses this tool, it is considered *ethical hacking* or *penetration testing*.

The tools used to perform attacks on networks and systems have, over time, become so sophisticated that they offer even a moderately skilled individual (sometimes called a *script kiddie*) the ability to perform very damaging attacks. The tools are simple to use and often come with a GUI that walks the person through the steps of resource identification, network mapping, and the actual attack. The person no longer needs to understand protocol stacks, know what protocols' fields are used by different systems, understand how operating systems process program and assembly code, or know how to write program code at all. The hacker just needs to insert an IP range within a GUI tool and click Go. Many different types of tools are now used by the attacker community, some of which are even capable of generating virus and worm autocode and building specific exploits for a given operating system, platform, or application release level.

Hacking tools are easily and widely available to anyone who wants them. At one time, these types of tools were available only to a small group of highly skilled people, but today hundreds of web sites are devoted to telling people how to perform exploits and providing the tools for a small fee or for free. The ease of use of these tools, the increased interest in hacking, and the deep dependence that companies and people have upon technology have provided the ingredients to a recipe that can cause continuous damage.

Any security administrator who maintains a firewall, or any person who runs a personal firewall on a computer, knows how active the Internet is with probes and port scanners. These front-end protection devices are continually getting hit with packets requesting information. Some probes look for specific types of computers, such as Unix systems, web servers, or databases, because the attacker has specific types of attacks she wants to carry out, and these attacks target specific types of operating systems or applications. These probes could also be looking to plant Trojan horses or viruses in computers in the hope of causing destruction or compromising the systems so they can be used in future distributed denial-of-service (DDoS) attacks, as illustrated in Figure 12-8. These probes scan thousands of networks and computers, usually with no one target in mind. They just look for any and all vulnerabilities, and the attacker does not necessarily care where the vulnerable system happens to be located.

Sometimes the attacker has a specific target in mind and thus does not send out a wide-sweeping probe. When an attacker identifies her target, she will do network map-

Figure 12-8
Distributed denial-of-service attacks use other systems to amplify the attack's damage potential.

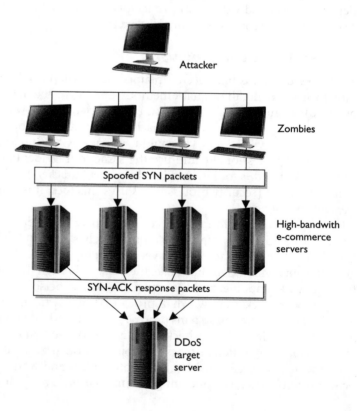

Attacker

Zombies

Spoofed SYN packets

High-bandwith e-commerce servers

SYN-ACK response packets

DDoS target server

ping and port scanning. Network-mapping tools send out seemingly benign packets to many different systems on a network. These systems respond to the packets, and the mapping tool interrogates the returned packets to find out what systems are up and running, the types of operating systems that responded, and possibly their place within the network. This might seem like a lot of information from just some packets being sent out, but these tools are highly calibrated to extract as much data from the returned packet as possible. Different operating systems vary in their protocol stacks, meaning they use different fields within protocol frames or populate those fields differently than other operating systems. So if the tool sent a message to two computers running different operating systems, they may respond with two slightly different answers. They may both respond with the same basic answer using the same protocol, but because the two operating systems use varied protocol stacks, one computer may use a certain value within its response and the other system may use a different value within its response, as shown in Figure 12-9. When the tool receives these two slightly different responses, it can determine what type of operating system just replied. The tool and the attacker then start to put together the topology of the victim's network.

The network-mapping tool may have a database that maps operating systems, applications, and versions to the type of responses and message fields they use. So if the networking tool received a reply from its ICMP ping sweep, which sends out ICMP packets to targets within a configured IP address range, and one reply has the ICMP "Don't fragment" bit enabled, the tool may determine that the target is a Unix host. Or if the tool sent out a TCP SYN packet and the response received was a FIN/ACK, the tool may determine that the target is a Windows NT system. This activity is referred to as *operating system fingerprinting*.

It is important to the attacker to know what systems are alive on the network. When the tool first sends out packets, it is looking to see what computers respond, which indicates that they are powered on and alive. Normally, when a computer sends an SYN packet, it is requesting to set up a conversation channel with the destination computer— the first step in the TCP handshaking procedure. However, hacking tools that use the SYN packet have no intention of setting up a real conversation channel, but instead

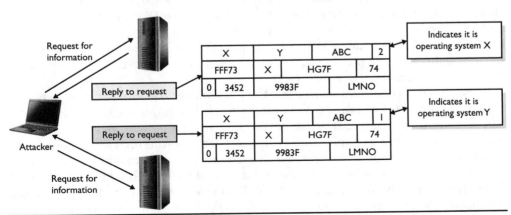

Figure 12-9 A tool can be used to determine the type of operating system with which an attacker is communicating.

hope to trick the target system into replying. The normal response to an SYN packet is SYN/ACK, but the administrator may have blocked this type of traffic at the firewall or router or disabled the port on the computer. The attacker may receive no response or receive a message saying "Port Unreachable." This response tells the network-mapping tool that the company's firewall allows this type of traffic to enter the network, but that specific port is closed on the target machine. These are all clues used by the attacker to learn more and more about an environment. This knowledge enables the attacker to figure out the most successful ways of attacking.

So, the first step for the attacker is to find out what systems are alive, attempt to find out what type of operating systems the targets are running, and start to build the network's topology. The next step for an attacker is to do *port scanning* on the target machines, which identifies open ports on a computer. Ports provide doors into the operating system for other computers, processes, protocols, and attackers. If an attacker can find out what ports are open, she can have a pretty good idea of what services are running on the systems. Knowing what services are available can further clarify the type of system the target is. For example, if a target computer responds to an SMTP packet sent to its port 25, the attacker could conclude that this computer may be an e-mail server. However, more work would need to be done to confirm this.

The attacker wants to know what operating systems, applications, and services are running so she knows what types of attacks to run. If she finds a Unix server running Apache, she would run totally different types of attacks on it than she would run for a Windows 2000 server running IIS. Each operating system, application, and service has its own vulnerabilities, and properly identifying these enables the attacker to be more successful in her attack.

Every computer system has 65,535 TCP and 65,535 UDP ports. The first 1023 are said to be well-known ports. This means that a specific port number under 1024 is usually mapped to a well-known and used protocol. For instance, port 80 is almost always mapped to the Hypertext Transfer Protocol (HTTP), port 21 is mapped to the File Transfer Protocol (FTP), and port 25 is mapped to SMTP. These ports can be reconfigured so port 21 is mapped to HTTP, let's say, but that is very uncommon.

A port-scanning utility is used to find out what ports are open on a system so the attacker knows what doors are available to her. This tool will send packets to each and every port on a system and listen for its response. If there is no response or a message indicating "Port Unreachable," this usually indicates the port and its corresponding service are disabled. If a predictable response comes from the port, the attacker knows the port is open and available for attack.

A port needs to be open and available for functionality. For example, most networks require the use of SMTP, port 25, for e-mail activity. The administrator needs to put a barrier between the potential attackers and this vulnerable port and its service. Of course, the first step is to implement a perimeter network with firewalls, proxy servers, and routers that only permit acceptable connections to the internal hosts. However, if an administrator or security professional wanted to add another layer of protection, on Unix-like systems, he could implement *TCP wrappers*. These software components (wrappers) monitor incoming network traffic to the host computer and control what can and cannot access the services mapped to specific ports. When a request comes to a computer at a specific port, the target operating system will check to see if this port is enabled. If it is enabled and the operating system sees that the corresponding service is wrapped, it knows to look at an access control list, which spells out who can access this service. If the person or computer attempting to access this service is allowed within the access control list, the operating system permits the connection to be made. If this person or computer is not allowed, the packet is dropped or a message is sent back to the initiator of the request, indicating that the request is refused.

At this point, the attacker has an idea of what systems are alive, what ports are open, and what services are listening and available for attack. Although the search for exploitable vulnerabilities is becoming more focused, there is still an incredible number of possible vulnerabilities one network can have. Sometimes attackers specialize in a few specific attacks that they know well enough to carry out manually, or have scripts that carry out specific attacks for them. But many attackers want a large range of possible attacks available to them, so they use *vulnerability scanning tools*.

Vulnerability scanning tools have a large database of vulnerabilities and the capability to exploit many of the vulnerabilities they identify. New vulnerabilities are found each week in operating systems, web servers, database software, and applications. It can be overwhelming to try to keep up-to-date on each of these and the proper steps to carry them out. The vulnerability scanners can do this for the security professional— and, unfortunately, for the attacker. These tools have an engine that can connect to the target machine and run through its database of vulnerabilities to see which apply to the target machine. Some tools can even go a step further and attempt the exploit to determine the actual degree of vulnerability.

As stated earlier, these tools are dual-purpose in nature. Administrators and security professionals should be using these types of tools on their environments to see what vulnerabilities are present and available to potential attackers. That way, when a vulnerability or weakness is uncovered, the security professional can fix it before an attacker finds it.

Browsing

I am looking for something, but I have no idea what it looks like.

Browsing is a general technique used by intruders to obtain information they are not authorized to access. This type of attack takes place when an attacker is looking for sensitive data but does not know the format of the data (word processing document, spreadsheet, database, piece of paper). Browsing can be accomplished by looking through another person's files kept on a server or workstation, rummaging through garbage looking for information that was carelessly thrown away, or reviewing information that has been saved on USB flash drives. A more advanced and sophisticated example of browsing is when an intruder accesses residual information on storage media. The original user may have deleted the files from a USB flash drive, but, as stated earlier, this only removes the pointers to the files within the file system on that disk. The talented intruder can access these data (residual information) and access information he is unauthorized to obtain.

Another type of browsing attack is called *shoulder surfing*, where an attacker looks over another's shoulder to see items on that person's monitor or what is being typed in at the keyboard.

Sniffers

A *network sniffer* is a tool that monitors traffic as it traverses a network. Administrators and network engineers often use sniffers to diagnose network problems. Sniffers are also referred to as *network analyzers* or *protocol analyzers*. When used as a diagnostic tool, a sniffer enables the administrator to see what type of traffic is being generated, in the hope of getting closer to the root of the network problem. When a sniffer is used as a tool by an attacker, the sniffer can capture usernames, passwords, and confidential information as they travel over the network.

The sniffer tool is usually a piece of software that runs on a computer with its NIC in promiscuous mode. NICs usually only pay attention to traffic addressed to them, but if they are in promiscuous mode, they see all traffic going past them on the network wire. Once a computer has been compromised by an attacker, the attacker will often install a sniffer on that system to look for interesting traffic. Some sniffers only look for passwords that are being transmitted and ignore the rest.

Sniffers have been very successful because a majority of LANs use Ethernet, which is a broadcast technology. Because such a great amount of data is continually broadcasted, it is easily available for an attacker who has planted a sniffer on a network segment. However, sniffers are becoming less successful because of the move to switched environments. Switched environments separate network segments by broadcast and collision domains. If the attacker is not within the broadcast and collision domain of the environment she is interested in sniffing, she will not receive the information she is looking for. This is because a switch is usually configured so the required source and destination ports on the switch carry the traffic, meaning the traffic is not blasted for everyone in the vicinity to hear. Switched traffic travels from point A to point B through the switch and does not spill over to every computer on the network, as it does in nonswitched networks. (Broadcast and collision domains are discussed in detail in Chapter 7.)

To combat sniffers within an environment, secure versions of services and protocols should be used whenever possible. Many services and protocols were developed to provide functionality, not security, but once it was figured out that security is also required in many environments, the protocols and services were improved upon to provide the same levels of functionality and security. Several protocols have a secure version. This means the regular protocol operates in a way that has vulnerabilities that can be exploited, and a more secure version has been developed to counter those vulnerabilities. One example is *Secure RPC (S-RPC)*, which uses Diffie-Hellman public key cryptography to determine the shared secret key for encryption with a symmetric algorithm. If S-RPC is used in an environment, a sniffer can capture this data, but not necessarily decrypt it.

Most protocols are vulnerable because they do not require strong authentication, if it is required at all. For example, the *r-utilities* used in Unix (rexec, rsh, rlogin, and rcp) are known to have several weaknesses. Authentication is usually provided through a .rhosts file that looks at IP addresses instead of individual usernames and passwords. These utilities should be disabled and replaced with one that requires stronger authentication, like Secure Shell (SSH).

Session Hijacking

Many attackers spoof their addresses, meaning that the address within the frame that is used to commit the attack has an IP address that is not theirs. This makes it much harder to track down the attacker, which is the attacker's purpose for spoofing in the first place. This also enables an attacker to hijack sessions between two users without being noticed.

If an attacker wanted to take over a session between two computers, she would need to put herself in the middle of their conversation without being detected. Two tools used for this are Juggernaut and the HUNT Project. These tools enable the attacker to spy on the TCP connection and then hijack it if the attacker decides that is what she wants to do.

If Kristy and David were communicating over a TCP session and the attacker wanted to bump David off and trick Kristy into thinking she is still communicating with David, the attacker would use a tool to spoof her address to be the same as David's and temporarily take David off the network with a type of DoS attack. Once this is in place, when Kristy sends a message to David, it actually goes to the attacker, who can then respond to Kristy. Kristy thinks she is getting a reply from David. The attacker may also choose to leave David on the network and intercept each of the users' messages, read them, and repackage them with headers that indicate no session hijacking took place, as shown in Figure 12-10.

If session hijacking is a concern on a network, the administrator can implement a protocol, such as IPSec or Kerberos, that requires mutual authentication between users or systems. Because the attacker will not have the necessary credentials to authenticate to a user, she cannot act as an imposter and hijack sessions.

Loki

A common covert channel in use today is the Loki attack. This attack uses the ICMP protocol for communications purposes. This protocol was not developed to be used in this manner; it is only supposed to send status and error messages. But someone developed a tool (Loki) that allows an attacker to write data right behind the ICMP header. This allows the attacker to communicate with another system through a covert channel. It is usually very successful because most firewalls are configured to allow ICMP traffic in and out of their environments. This channel is covert because it uses something for communication purposes that was not developed for this type of communication functionality. More information on this type of attack can be found at http://xforce.iss.net/xforce/xfdb/1452.

Password Cracking

Chapter 4 discussed access control and authentication methods in depth. Although there are various ways of authenticating a user, most of the time a static password is the method of choice for many companies. The main reason for this is that the computing society is familiar with using static passwords. It is how many systems and applications have their authentication processes coded, and it is an easier technique to maintain—and cheaper—than other options such as smart cards or biometrics.

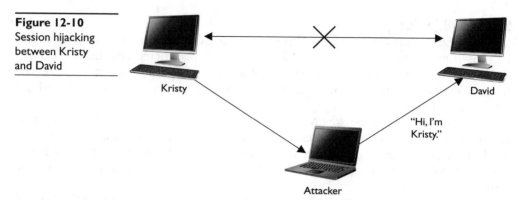

Figure 12-10
Session hijacking between Kristy and David

Kristy

David

"Hi, I'm Kristy."

Attacker

However, this static password method is easily cracked when a determined attacker has the right tools. John the Ripper is an example of a password-cracking tool that combines many password-cracking techniques into one tool. Once password data (typically encoded hashes) is captured, the attacker can initiate a dictionary attack using the John tool to try to reveal the captured password. The powerful tools Crack and L0phtcrack are also used to perform dictionary and brute force attacks on the captured password or password file.

A strong password policy is a major countermeasure to password-cracking efforts. The policy should dictate that passwords must be at least eight characters, with upper- and lowercase letters and two special characters (*.,$@). If the passwords are long, contain special characters, and are hard to guess, it will take cracking tools much longer to uncover them. The longer this process takes, the greater the chance of the attacker moving on to an easier victim. Software applications and add-ons are available to ensure that the password each user chooses meets the company's security policy.

Backdoors

Chapter 5 discussed backdoors and some of the potential damage that can be caused by them. It also looked at how backdoors are inserted into the code so a developer can access the software at a later time, bypassing the usual security authentication and authorization steps. Now we will look at how and why attackers install backdoors on victims' computers.

A *backdoor* is a program that is installed by an attacker to enable her to come back into the computer at a later date without having to supply login credentials or go through any type of authorization process. Access control is thwarted by the attacker because she can later gain access to the compromised computer. The backdoor program actually listens on specific ports for the attacker, and once the attacker accesses those ports, the backdoor program lets her come right in.

An attacker can compromise a computer and install the backdoor program or hide the code within a virus or Trojan horse that will install the backdoor when a predefined event takes place. Many times, these backdoors are installed so the attacker can later control the computer remotely to perform the tasks she is interested in. The tools used for backdoor remote-control actions are Back Orifice, NetBus, and SubSeven. A comprehensive list of backdoors and Trojans can be found at www.tlsecurity.org/tlfaq.htm.

Today, many antivirus software applications and IDSs look for signatures of these tools and scan for the known behavior patterns that they commit. Using a host-based IDS can be one of the best ways to detect a backdoor. Because the backdoor will be listening on specific ports, the host-based IDS can be configured to detect suspicious port activity. The administrator can also scan for known executables used by backdoor programs, view the startup files and Registry entries for suspicious executables, and run checksums on system files to see if any have been altered. These activities are not usually done manually, because of the time involved, but rather are done automatically through the use of antivirus and IDS software. But because attackers are smart and tricky, new tools are continually developed and old tools are morphed so that they will not be detected by these detection applications. And so the inevitable cat-and-mouse game continues between the hackers and the security community.

The following list contains a brief description of several attack types you should be familiar with:

- **Denial-of-service (DoS) attack** An attacker sends multiple service requests to the victim's computer until they eventually overwhelm the system, causing it to freeze, reboot, and ultimately not be able to carry out regular tasks.

- **Man-in-the-middle attack** An intruder injects herself into an ongoing dialog between two computers so she can intercept and read messages being passed back and forth. These attacks can be countered with digital signatures and mutual authentication techniques.

- **Mail bombing** This is an attack used to overwhelm mail servers and clients with unrequested e-mails. Using e-mail filtering and properly configuring e-mail relay functionality on mail servers can be used to protect against this type of DoS attack.

- **Wardialing** This is a brute force attack in which an attacker has a program that systematically dials a large bank of phone numbers with the goal of finding ones that belong to modems instead of telephones. These modems can provide easy access into an environment. The countermeasures are to not publicize these telephone numbers and to implement tight access control for modems and modem pools.

- **Ping of death** This is a type of DoS attack in which oversized ICMP packets are sent to the victim. Systems that are vulnerable to this type of attack do not know how to handle ICMP packets over a specific size and may freeze or reboot. Countermeasures are to patch the systems and implement ingress filtering to detect these types of packets.

- **Fake login screens** A fake login screen is created and installed on the victim's system. When the user attempts to log into the system, this fake screen is presented to the user, requesting he enter his credentials. When he does so, the screen captures the credentials and exits, showing the user the actual login screen for his system. Usually the user just thinks he mistyped his password and attempts to authenticate again without knowing anything malicious just took place. A host-based IDS can be used to detect this type of activity.

- **Teardrop** This attack sends malformed fragmented packets to a victim. The victim's system usually cannot reassemble the packets correctly and freezes as a result. Countermeasures to this attack are to patch the system and use ingress filtering to detect these packet types.

- **Traffic analysis** This is a method of uncovering information by watching traffic patterns on a network. For example, heavy traffic between the HR department and headquarters could indicate an upcoming layoff. Traffic padding can be used to counter this kind of attack, in which decoy traffic is sent out over the network to disguise patterns and make it more difficult to uncover them.

- **Slamming and cramming** Slamming is when a user's service provider has been changed without that user's consent. Cramming is adding on charges that are bogus in nature that the user did not request. Properly monitoring charges on bills is really the only countermeasure to these types of attacks.

This section only talked about some of the possible attacks. One of the most beneficial things a company, network administrator, network engineer, or security professional can do is to develop some good habits that deal with the previously mentioned items. Although it is great that an administrator installs a security patch after he reads about a dangerous attack that has recently become popular, it is more important that he continue to stay on top of all potential threats and vulnerabilities, scan his network regularly, and remain aware of some symptomatic effects of particular attacks, viruses, Trojan horses, and backdoors. It can be a tall order to follow, but these good habits, once developed, will keep a network healthy and the administrator's life less chaotic. One of the best ways to ensure you are properly protected is to investigate the matter yourself, instead of waiting for the hackers to find out for you. This is where vulnerability testing comes into play.

Vulnerability Testing

Vulnerability testing, whether manual, automated, or—preferably—a combination of both, requires staff and/or consultants with a deep security background and the highest level of trustworthiness. Even the best automated vulnerability scanning tool will produce output that can be misinterpreted as crying wolf (false positive) when there is only a small puppy in the room, or alert you to something that is indeed a vulnerability but that either does not matter to your environment or is adequately compensated elsewhere. There may also be two individual vulnerabilities that exist, which by themselves are not very important but when put together are critical. And of course, false negatives will also crop up, such as an obscure element of a single vulnerability that matters greatly to your environment, but that is not called out by the tool.

 CAUTION Before carrying out vulnerability testing, a written agreement from management is required! This protects the tester against prosecution for doing his job, and ensures there are no misunderstandings by providing in writing what the tester should—and should not—do.

The goals of the assessment are to

- Evaluate the true security posture of an environment (don't cry wolf, as discussed earlier).
- Identify as many vulnerabilities as possible, with honest evaluations and prioritizations of each.
- Test how systems react to certain circumstances and attacks, to learn not only what the known vulnerabilities are (such as this version of the database, that version of the operating system, or a user ID with no password set), but also how the unique elements of the environment might be abused (SQL injection attacks, buffer overflows, and process design flaws that facilitate social engineering).

Before the scope of the test is decided and agreed upon, the tester must explain the testing ramifications. Vulnerable systems could be knocked offline by some of the tests, and production could be negatively affected by the loads the tests place on the systems.

Management must understand that results from the test are just a "snapshot in time." As the environment changes, new vulnerabilities can arise. Management should also understand that various types of assessments are possible, each one able to expose different kinds of vulnerabilities in the environment, and each one limited in the completeness of results it can offer:

- *Personnel testing* includes reviewing employee tasks and thus identifying vulnerabilities in the standard practices and procedures that employees are instructed to follow, demonstrating social engineering attacks and the value of training users to detect and resist such attacks, and reviewing employee policies and procedures to ensure those security risks that cannot be reduced through physical and logical controls are met with the final control category: Administrative.
- *Physical testing* includes reviewing facility and perimeter protection mechanisms. For instance, do the doors actually close automatically, and does an alarm sound if a door is held open too long? Are the interior protection mechanisms of server rooms, wiring closets, sensitive systems, and assets appropriate? (For example, is the badge reader working, and does it really limit access to only authorized personnel?) Is Dumpster diving a threat? (In other words, is sensitive information being discarded without proper destruction?) And what of protection mechanisms for manmade, natural, or technical threats? Is there a fire suppression system? Does it work, and is it safe for the people and the equipment in the building? Are sensitive electronics kept above raised floors so they survive a minor flood? And so on.
- *System and network testing* are perhaps what most people think of when discussing information security vulnerability testing. For efficiency, an automated scanning product identifies known system vulnerabilities, and some may (if management has signed off on the performance impact and the risk of disruption) attempt to exploit vulnerabilities.

Typical Weaknesses

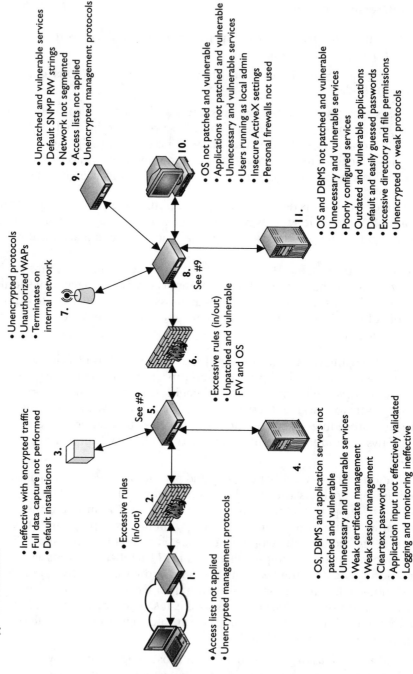

1.
- Access lists not applied
- Unencrypted management protocols

2.
- Excessive rules (in/out)

3.
- Ineffective with encrypted traffic
- Full data capture not performed
- Default installations

4.
- OS, DBMS and application servers not patched and vulnerable
- Unnecessary and vulnerable services
- Weak certificate management
- Weak session management
- Cleartext passwords
- Application input not effectively validated
- Logging and monitoring ineffective

5. See #9

6.
- Excessive rules (in/out)
- Unpatched and vulnerable FW and OS

7.
- Unencrypted protocols
- Unauthorized WAPs
- Terminates on internal network

8. See #9

9.
- Unpatched and vulnerable services
- Default SNMP RW strings
- Network not segmented
- Access lists not applied
- Unencrypted management protocols

10.
- OS not patched and vulnerable
- Applications not patched and vulnerable
- Unnecessary and vulnerable services
- Users running as local admin
- Insecure ActiveX settings
- Personal firewalls not used

11.
- OS and DBMS not patched and vulnerable
- Unnecessary and vulnerable services
- Poorly configured services
- Outdated and vulnerable applications
- Default and easily guessed passwords
- Excessive directory and file permissions
- Unencrypted or weak protocols

Because a security assessment is a point-in-time snapshot of the state of an environment, assessments should be performed regularly. Lower priority and better protected/less at-risk parts of the environment may be scanned once or twice a year. High-priority, more vulnerable targets such as e-commerce web server complexes and the middleware just behind them should be scanned nearly continuously.

To the degree automated tools are used, more than one tool—or a different tool on consecutive tests—should be used. No single tool knows or finds every known vulnerability. The vendors of different scanning tools update their tools' vulnerability database at different rates, and may add particular vulnerabilities in different orders. Always update the vulnerability database of each tool just before the tool is used. Similarly, from time to time different experts should run the test and/or interpret the results. No single expert always sees everything there is to be seen in the results.

Penetration Testing

Excuse me. Could you please attack me?
Response: I would love to!

Penetration testing is the process of simulating attacks on a network and its systems at the request of the owner, senior management. Penetration testing uses a set of procedures and tools designed to test and possibly bypass the security controls of a system. Its goal is to measure an organization's level of resistance to an attack and to uncover any weaknesses within the environment. Organizations need to determine the effectiveness of their security measures and not just trust the promises of the security vendors. Good computer security is based on reality, not on some lofty goals of how things are supposed to work.

A penetration test emulates the same methods attackers would use. Attackers can be clever, creative, and resourceful in their techniques, so penetration attacks should align with the newest hacking techniques along with strong foundational testing methods. The test should look at each and every computer in the environment, as shown in Figure 12-11, because an attacker will not necessarily scan one or two computers only and call it a day.

> ## Vulnerability Scanning Recap
> Vulnerability scanners provide the following capabilities:
>
> - The identification of active hosts on the network
> - The identification of active and vulnerable services (ports) on hosts
> - The identification of applications and banner grabbing
> - The identification of operating systems
> - The identification of vulnerabilities associated with discovered operating systems and applications
> - The identification of misconfigured settings
> - Test for compliance with host applications' usage/security policies
> - The establishment of a foundation for penetration testing

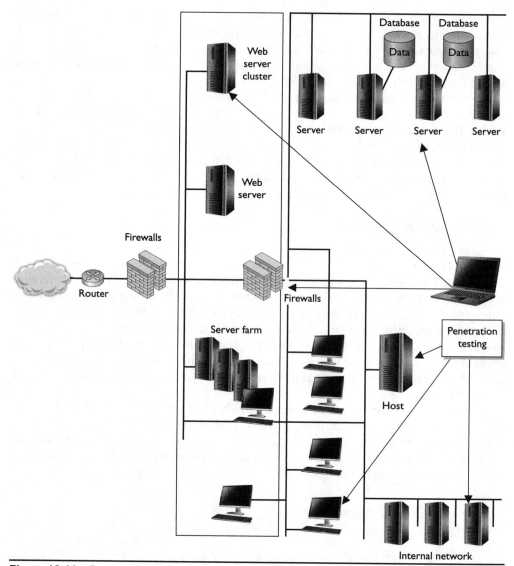

Figure 12-11 Penetration testing is used to prove an attacker can actually compromise systems.

The type of penetration test that should be used depends on the organization, its security objectives, and the management's goals. Some corporations perform periodic penetration tests on themselves using different types of tools, or they use scanning devices that continually examine the environment for new vulnerabilities in an automated fashion. Other corporations ask a third party to perform the vulnerability and penetration tests to provide a more objective view.

Penetration tests can evaluate web servers, DNS servers, router configurations, workstation vulnerabilities, access to sensitive information, remote dial-in access, open ports, and available services' properties that a real attacker might use to compromise the company's overall security. Some tests can be quite intrusive and disruptive. The timeframe for the tests should be agreed upon so productivity is not affected and personnel can bring systems back online if necessary.

The result of a penetration test is a report given to management that describes the vulnerabilities identified and the severity of those vulnerabilities, along with suggestions on how to deal with them properly. From there, it is up to management to determine how the vulnerabilities are actually dealt with and what countermeasures are implemented.

It is critical that senior management be aware of any risks involved in performing a penetration test before it gives the authorization for one. In rare instances, a system or application may be taken down inadvertently using the tools and techniques employed during the test. As expected, the goal of penetration testing is to identify vulnerabilities, estimate the true protection the security mechanisms within the environment are providing, and see how suspicious activity is reported—but accidents can and do happen.

Security professionals should obtain an authorization letter that includes the extent of the testing authorized, and this letter or memo should be available to members of the team during the testing activity. This type of letter is commonly referred to as a "Get Out of Jail Free Card." Contact information for key personnel should also be available, along with a call tree in the event something does not go as planned and a system must be recovered.

NOTE A "Get Out of Jail Free Card" is a document you can present to someone who thinks you are up to something malicious, when in fact you are carrying out an approved test. There have been many situations in which an individual (or a team) was carrying out a penetration test and was approached by a security guard or someone who thought this person was in the wrong place at the wrong time.

When performing a penetration test, the team goes through a five-step process:

1. **Discovery**   Footprinting and gathering information about the target
2. **Enumeration**   Performing port scans and resource identification methods
3. **Vulnerability mapping**   Identifying vulnerabilities in identified systems and resources
4. **Exploitation**   Attempting to gain unauthorized access by exploiting vulnerabilities
5. **Report to management**   Delivering to management documentation of test findings along with suggested countermeasures

The penetration testing team can have varying degrees of knowledge about the penetration target before the tests are actually carried out.

- **Zero knowledge**   The team does not have any knowledge of the target and must start from ground zero.
- **Partial knowledge**   The team has some information about the target.

• **Full knowledge**   The team has intimate knowledge of the target.

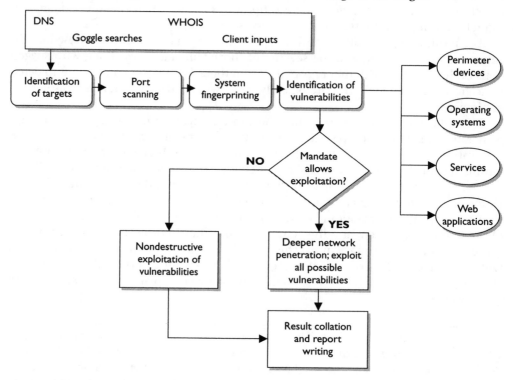

Security testing of an environment may take several forms, in the sense of the degree of knowledge the tester is permitted to have up front about the environment, and also the degree of knowledge the environment is permitted to have up front about the tester.

Tests should be conducted externally (from a remote location) or internally (meaning the tester is within the network). Both should be carried out to understand threats from either domain (internal and external).

Tests may be blind, double-blind, or targeted. A *blind test* is one in which the assessors only have publicly available data to work with. The network staff is aware that this type of test will take place.

A *double-blind test* (stealth assessment) is also a blind test to the assessor as mentioned previously, plus the security staff is not notified. This enables the test to evaluate the network's security level and the staff's responses, log monitoring, and escalation

Types of Tests

A vulnerability assessment identifies a wide range of vulnerabilities in the environment. This is commonly carried out through a scanning tool. By contrast, in a penetration test, the security professional exploits one or more vulnerabilities to prove to the customer (or your boss) that a hacker can actually gain access to company resources.

processes, and is a more realistic demonstration of the likely success or failure of an attack.

Targeted tests can involve external consultants and internal staff carrying out focused tests on specific areas of interest. For example, before a new application is rolled out, the team might test it for vulnerabilities before installing it into production. Another example is to focus specifically on systems that carry out e-commerce transactions and not the other daily activities of the company.

It is important that the team start off with only basic user-level access, to properly simulate different attacks. The team needs to utilize a variety of different tools and attack methods, and look at all possible vulnerabilities, because this is how actual attackers will function.

The following sections cover common activities carried out in a penetration test.

Wardialing

As touched on earlier, wardialing allows attackers and administrators to dial large blocks of phone numbers in search of available modems. Several free and commercial tools are available to dial all of the telephone numbers in a phone exchange (for example, all numbers from 212-555-0000 through 212-555-9999) and make note of those numbers answered by a modem. Wardialers can be configured to call only those specific exchanges and their subsets that are known to belong to a company. They can be smart, calling only at night when most telephones are not monitored, to reduce the likelihood of several people noticing the odd hang-up phone calls and thus raising the alarm. Wardialers can call in random order so nobody notices the phones are ringing at one desk after another after another, and thus raise an alarm. Wardialing is a mature science, and can be accomplished quickly with low-cost equipment. Wardialers can go so far as to fingerprint the hosts that answer, similar to a network vulnerability scanner, and attempt a limited amount of automated penetration testing, returning a ready-made compromise of the environment to the attacker. Finally, some PBXes (phone systems) or telephony diagnostic tools may be able to identify modem lines and report on them.

Testing Oneself

Some of the same tactics an attacker may use when wardialing may be useful to the system administrator, such as wardialing at night to reduce disruption to the business. Be aware, when performing wardialing proactively, that dialing at night may also miss some unauthorized modems that are attached to systems that are turned off by their users at the end of the day. Wardialers can be configured to avoid certain numbers or blocks of numbers, so the system administrator can avoid dialing numbers known to be voice-only, such as help desks. This can also be done on more advanced PBXes, with any number assigned to a digital voice device that is configured to not support a modem.

Any unauthorized modems identified by wardialing should be investigated and either brought into compliance or removed, and staff who installed the unauthorized modems retrained or disciplined.

Other Vulnerability Types

As noted earlier, vulnerability scans find the potential vulnerabilities. Actual penetration testing is required to identify those vulnerabilities that can actually be exploited in the environment and cause damage.

Commonly exploited vulnerabilities include the following:

- **Kernel flaws** These are problems that occur below the level of the user interface, deep inside the operating system. Any flaw in the kernel that can be reached by an attacker, if exploitable, gives the attacker the most powerful level of control over the system.
  - **Countermeasure** Ensure that security patches to operating systems—after sufficient testing—are promptly deployed in the environment to keep the window of vulnerability as small as possible.

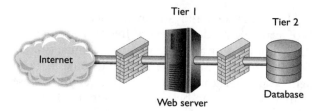

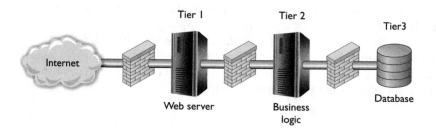

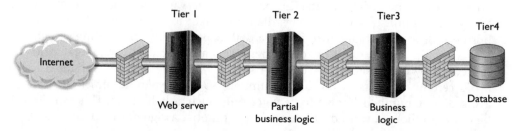

- **Buffer overflows** Poor programming practices, or sometimes bugs in libraries, allow more input than the program has allocated space to store it. This overwrites data or program memory after the end of the allocated buffer, and sometimes allows the attacker to inject program code and then cause the processor to execute it. This gives the attacker the same level of access as that held by the program that was attacked. If the program was run as an administrative user or by the system itself, this can mean complete access to the system.

- **Countermeasure**   Good programming practices and developer education, automated source code scanners, enhanced programming libraries, and strongly typed languages that disallow buffer overflows are all ways of reducing this extremely common vulnerability.

- **Symbolic links**   Though the attacker may be properly blocked from seeing or changing the content of sensitive system files and data, if a program follows a symbolic link (a stub file that redirects the access to another place) and the attacker can compromise the symbolic link, then the attacker may be able to gain unauthorized access. (Symbolic links are used in Unix and Linux type systems.) This may allow the attacker to damage important data and/or gain privileged access to the system. A historical example of this was to use a symbolic link to cause a program to delete a password database, or replace a line in the password database with characters that, in essence, created an unpassworded root-equivalent account.

  - **Countermeasure**   Programs and especially scripts must be written to ensure that the full path to the file cannot be circumvented.

- **File descriptor attacks**   File descriptors are numbers many operating systems use to represent open files in a process. Certain file descriptor numbers are universal, meaning the same thing to all programs. If a program makes unsafe use of a file descriptor, an attacker may be able to cause unexpected input to be provided to the program, or cause output to go to an unexpected place with the privileges of the executing program.

  - **Countermeasure**   Good programming practices and developer education, automated source code scanners, and application security testing are all ways of reducing this type of vulnerability.

- **Race conditions**   Race conditions exist when the design of a program puts it in a vulnerable condition before ensuring that those vulnerable conditions are mitigated. Examples include opening temporary files without first ensuring the files cannot be read, or written to, by unauthorized users or processes, and running in privileged mode or instantiating dynamic load library functions without first verifying that the dynamic load library path is secure. Either of these may allow an attacker to cause the program (with its elevated privileges) to read or write unexpected data, or perform unauthorized commands.

  - **Countermeasure**   Good programming practices and developer education, automated source code scanners, and application security testing are all ways of reducing this type of vulnerability.

- **File and directory permissions**   Many of the previously described attacks rely on inappropriate file or directory permissions—that is, an error in the access control of some part of the system, on which a more secure part of the system depends. Also, if a system administrator makes a mistake that results in decreasing the security of the permissions on a critical file, such as making a password database accessible to regular users, an attacker can take advantage of this to add an unauthorized user to the password database, or an untrusted directory to the dynamic load library search path.

- **Countermeasure**   File integrity checkers, which should also check expected file and directory permissions, can detect such problems in a timely fashion, hopefully before an attacker notices and exploits them.

Many, many types of vulnerabilities exist and we have covered some, but certainly not all, here in this book. The previous list includes only a few specific vulnerabilities you should be aware of for exam purposes.

Postmortem

Once the tests are over and the interpretation and prioritization are done, management will have in its hands a Booke of Doome showing many of the ways the company could be successfully attacked. This is the input to the next cycle in the remediation strategy. There exists only so much money, time, and personnel, and thus only so much of the total risk can be mitigated. Balancing the risks and risk appetite of the company, and the costs of possible mitigations and the value gained from each, management must direct the system and security administrators as to where to spend those limited resources. An oversight program is required to ensure that the mitigations work as expected, and that the estimated cost of each mitigation action is closely tracked by the actual cost of implementation. Any time the cost rises significantly, or the value is found to be far below what was expected, the process should be briefly paused and reevaluated. It may be that a risk-versus-cost option initially considered less desirable will now make more sense than continuing with the chosen path.

Finally, when all is well, and the mitigations are underway, everyone can breathe easier. Except maybe for the security engineer who has the task of monitoring vulnerability announcements and discussion mailing lists, as well as the early warning services offered by some vendors. To put it another way, the risk environment keeps changing. Between tests, monitoring may make the company aware of newly discovered vulnerabilities that would be found the next time the test is run, but which are too high risk to allow to wait that long. And so another smaller cycle of mitigation decisions and actions must be taken.

And then it is time to run the tests again. Table 12-3 provides an example of a testing schedule that each operations and security department should develop and carry out.

We have covered the assurance mechanisms in this chapter or earlier ones. These are methods used to make sure the operations department is carrying out its responsibilities correctly and securely.

Test Type	Frequency	Benefits
Network Scanning	Continuously to quarterly	- Enumerates the network structure and determines the set of active hosts and associated software - Identifies unauthorized hosts connected to a network - Identifies open ports - Identifies unauthorized services
Wardialing	Annually	- Detects unauthorized modems and prevents unauthorized access to a protected network
War Driving	Continuously to weekly	- Detects unauthorized wireless access points and prevents unauthorized access to a protected network
Virus Detectors	Weekly or as required	- Detects and deletes viruses before successful installation on the system
Log Reviews	Daily for critical systems	- Validates that the system is operating according to policy
Password Cracking	Continuously to same frequency as expiration policy	- Verifies the policy is effective in producing passwords that are more or less difficult to break - Verifies that users select passwords compliant with the organization's security policy
Vulnerability Scanning	Quarterly or bimonthly (more often for high risk systems), or whenever the vulnerability database is updated	- Enumerates the network structure and determines the set of active hosts and associated software - Identifies a target set of computers to focus vulnerability analysis - Identifies potential vulnerabilities on the target set - Validates operating systems and major applications are up-to-date with security patches and software versions
Penetration Testing	Annually	- Determines how vulnerable an organization's network is to penetration and the level of damage that can be incurred - Tests the IT staff's response to perceived security incidents and their knowledge and implementation of the organization's security policy and the system's security requirements
Integrity Checkers	Monthly and in case of a suspicious event	- Detects unauthorized file modifications

Table 12-3 Example Testing Schedules for Each Operations and Security Department

Summary

Operations security involves keeping up with implemented solutions, keeping track of changes, properly maintaining systems, continually enforcing necessary standards, and following through with security practices and tasks. It does not do much good for a company to develop a strong password policy if, after a few months, enforcement gets lax and users can use whatever passwords they want. It is similar to working out and staying physically fit. Just because someone lifts weights and jogs for a week does not mean he can spend the rest of the year eating jelly donuts and expect to stay physically fit. Security requires discipline day in and day out, sticking to a regime, and practicing due care.

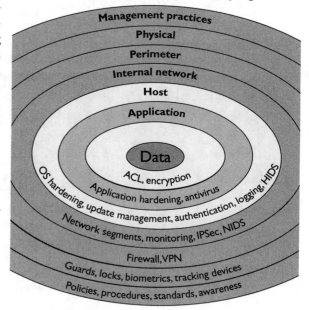

Quick Tips

- Facilities that house systems that process sensitive information should have physical access controls to limit access to authorized personnel only.
- Data should be classified, and the necessary technical controls should be put into place to protect its integrity, confidentiality, and availability.
- Hacker tools are becoming increasingly more sophisticated while requiring increasingly less knowledge by the attacker about how they work.
- Quality assurance involves the verification that supporting documentation requirements are met.
- Quality control ensures that an asset is operating within accepted standards.
- System and audit logs should be monitored and protected from unauthorized modification.
- Repetitive errors can indicate lack of training or issues resulting from a poorly designed system.
- Sensitive data should not be printed and left at stand-alone printers or fax devices.
- Users should have the necessary security level to access data and resources, but must also have a need to know.
- Clipping levels should be implemented to establish a baseline of user activity and acceptable errors.

- Separation of responsibilities and duties should be in place so that if fraud takes place, it requires collusion.

- Sensitive information should contain the correct markings and labels to indicate the corresponding sensitivity level.

- Contract and temporary staff members should have more restrictive controls put upon their accounts.

- Access to resources should be limited to authorized personnel, applications, and services and should be audited for compliance to stated policies.

- Change control and configuration management should be put in place so changes are approved, documented, tested, and properly implemented.

- Activities that involve change management include requesting a change, approving a change, documenting a change, testing a change, implementing a change, and reporting to management.

- Systems should not allow their bootup sequences to be altered in a way that could bypass operating system security mechanisms.

- Potential employees should have background investigations, references, experience, and education claims checked out.

- Proper fault-tolerant mechanisms should be put in place to counter equipment failure.

- Antivirus and IDS signatures should be updated on a continual basis.

- System, network, policy, and procedure changes should be documented and communicated.

- When media is reused, it should contain no residual data.

- Media holding sensitive data must be properly purged, which can be accomplished through zeroization, degaussing, or media destruction.

- Life-cycle assurance involves protecting a system from inception to development to operation to removal.

- The key aspects of operations security include resource protection, change control, hardware and software controls, trusted system recovery, separation of duties, and least privilege.

- Least privilege ensures that users, administrators, and others accessing a system have access only to the objects they absolutely require to complete their job.

- Vulnerability assessments should be done on a regular basis to identify new vulnerabilities.

- The operations department is responsible for any unusual or unexplained occurrences, unscheduled initial program loads, and deviations from standards.

- Standards need to be established that indicate the proper startup and shutdown sequence, error handling, and restoration procedures.

- A teardrop attack involves sending malformed fragmented packets to a vulnerable system.

- Improper mail relay configurations allow for mail servers to be used to forward spam messages.

- Phishing involves an attacker sending false messages to a victim in the hopes that the victim will provide personal information that can be used to steal their identity.

- A browsing attack occurs when an attacker looks for sensitive information without knowing what format it is in.

- A fax encryptor encrypts all fax data leaving a fax server.

- A system can fail in one of the following manners: system reboot, emergency system restart, and system cold start.

- The main goal of operations security is to protect resources.

- Operational threats include disclosure, theft, corruption, interruption, and destruction.

- Operations security involves balancing the necessary level of security with ease of use, compliance, and cost constraints.

Questions

Please remember that these questions are formatted and asked in a certain way for a reason. Keep in mind that the CISSP exam is asking questions at a conceptual level. Questions may not always have the perfect answer, and the candidate is advised against always looking for the perfect answer. Instead, the candidate should look for the best answer in the list.

1. Which of the following best describes operations security?

   A. Continual vigilance about hacker activity and possible vulnerabilities

   B. Enforcing access control and physical security

   C. Taking steps to make sure an environment, and the things within it, stay at a certain level of protection

   D. Doing strategy planning to develop a secure environment and then implementing it properly

2. Which of the following describes why operations security is important?

   A. An environment continually changes and has the potential of lowering its level of protection.

   B. It helps an environment be functionally sound and productive.

   C. It ensures there will be no unauthorized access to the facility or its resources.

   D. It continually raises a company's level of protection.

3. What is the difference between due care and due diligence?

  A. Due care is the continual effort of ensuring that the right thing takes place, and due diligence is the continual effort to stay compliant to regulations.

  B. Due care and due diligence are in contrast to the "prudent person" concept.

  C. They mean the same thing.

  D. Due diligence involves investigating the risks, while due care involves carrying out the necessary steps to mitigate these risks.

4. Why should employers make sure employees take their vacations?

  A. They have a legal obligation.

  B. It is part of due diligence.

  C. It is a way for fraud to be uncovered.

  D. To ensure the employee does not get burnt out.

5. Which of the following best describes separation of duties and job rotation?

  A. Separation of duties ensures that more than one employee knows how to perform the tasks of a position, and job rotation ensures that one person cannot perform a high-risk task alone.

  B. Separation of duties ensures that one person cannot perform a high-risk task alone, and job rotation can uncover fraud and ensure that more than one person knows the tasks of a position.

  C. They are the same thing, but with different titles.

  D. They are administrative controls that enforce access control and protect the company's resources.

6. If a programmer is restricted from updating and modifying production code, what is this an example of?

  A. Rotation of duties

  B. Due diligence

  C. Separation of duties

  D. Controlling input values

7. Why is it important to control and audit input and output values?

  A. Incorrect values can cause mistakes in data processing and be evidence of fraud.

  B. Incorrect values can be the fault of the programmer and do not comply with the due care clause.

  C. Incorrect values can be caused by brute force attacks.

  D. Incorrect values are not security issues.

8. What is the difference between least privilege and need to know?

    A. A user should have least privilege that restricts her need to know.

    B. A user should have a security clearance to access resources, a need to know about those resources, and least privilege to give her full control of all resources.

    C. A user should have a need to know to access particular resources, and least privilege should be implemented to ensure she only accesses the resources she has a need to know.

    D. They are two different terms for the same issue.

9. Which of the following would not require updated documentation?

    A. An antivirus signature update

    B. Reconfiguration of a server

    C. A change in security policy

    D. The installation of a patch to a production server

10. If sensitive data are stored on a CD-ROM and are no longer needed, which would be the proper way of disposing of the data?

    A. Degaussing

    B. Erasing

    C. Purging

    D. Physical destruction

11. If SSL is being used to encrypt messages that are transmitted over the network, what is a major concern of the security professional?

    A. The network segments that have systems that use different versions of SSL.

    B. The user may have encrypted the message with an application layer product that is incompatible with SSL.

    C. Network tapping and wiretapping.

    D. The networks that the message will travel that the company does not control.

12. What is the purpose of SMTP?

    A. To enable users to decrypt mail messages from a server

    B. To enable users to view and modify mail messages from a server

    C. To transmit mail messages from the client to the mail server

    D. To encrypt mail messages before being transmitted

13. If a company has been contacted because its mail server has been used to spread spam, what is most likely the problem?

    A. The internal mail server has been compromised by an internal hacker.

    B. The mail server in the DMZ has private and public resource records.

    C. The mail server has e-mail relaying misconfigured.

    D. The mail server has SMTP enabled.

14. Which of the following is not a reason fax servers are used in many companies?

    A. They save money by not needing individual fax devices and the constant use of fax paper.

    B. They provide a secure way of faxing instead of having faxed papers sitting in bins waiting to be picked up.

    C. Faxes can be routed to employees' electronic mailboxes.

    D. They increase the need for other communication security mechanisms.

15. If a company wants to protect fax data while it is in transmission, which of the following are valid mechanisms?

    A. PGP and MIME

    B. PEM and TSL

    C. Data link encryption or fax encryptor

    D. Data link encryption and MIME

16. What is the purpose of TCP wrappers?

    A. To monitor requests for certain ports and control access to sensitive files

    B. To monitor requests for certain services and control access to password files

    C. To monitor requests for certain services and control access to those services

    D. To monitor requests to system files and ensure they are not modified

17. How do network sniffers work?

    A. They probe systems on a network segment.

    B. They listen for ARP requests and ICMP packets.

    C. They require an extra NIC to be installed and configured.

    D. They put the NIC into promiscuous mode.

18. Which of the following is not an attack against operations?

    A. Brute force

    B. Denial-of-service

    C. Buffer overflow

    D. ICMP Sting

19. Why should user IDs be included in data captured by auditing procedures?

    A. They show what files were attacked.

    B. They establish individual accountability.

    C. They are needed to detect a denial-of-service attack.

    D. They activate corrective measures.

20. Which of the following controls requires separate entities, operating together, to complete a task?

   A. Least privilege

   B. Data hiding

   C. Dual control

   D. Administrative

21. Which of the following would not be considered an operations media control task?

   A. Compressing and decompressing storage materials

   B. Erasing data when its retention period is over

   C. Storing backup information in a protected area

   D. Controlling access to media and logging activities

22. How is the use of clipping levels a way to track violations?

   A. They set a baseline for normal user errors, and any violations that exceed that threshold should be recorded and reviewed to understand why they are happening.

   B. They enable the administrator to view all reduction levels that have been made to user codes, which have incurred violations.

   C. They disallow the administrator to customize the audit trail to record only those violations deemed security related.

   D. They enable the administrator to customize the audit trail to capture only access violations and denial-of-service attacks.

23. Tape library management is an example of operations security through which of the following?

   A. Archival retention

   B. The review of clipping levels

   C. Resource protection

   D. Change management

24. A device that generates coercive magnetic force for the purpose of reducing magnetic flux density to zero on media is called

   A. Magnetic saturation

   B. Magnetic field

   C. Physical destruction

   D. Degausser

25. Which of the following controls might force a person in operations into collusion with personnel assigned organizationally within a different function for the sole purpose of gaining access to data he is not authorized to access?

    A. Limiting the local access of operations personnel

    B. Enforcing auditing

    C. Enforcing job rotation

    D. Limiting control of management personnel

26. What does the following graphic represent and what is the technology's importance?

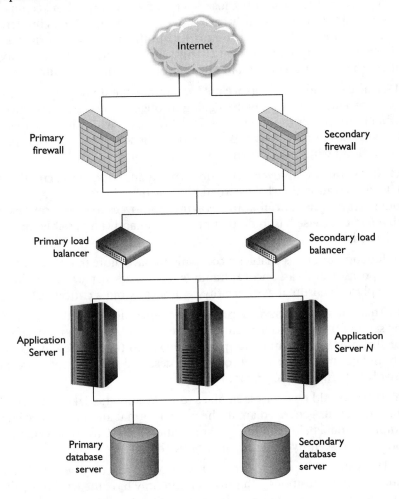

    A. Hierarchical storage management

    B. Storage access network

    C. Network redundancy

    D. Single point of failure

Answers

1. **C.** All of these are necessary security activities and procedures—they just don't all fall under the operations umbrella. Operations is about keeping production up and running in a healthy and secure manner. Operations is not usually the entity that carries out strategic planning. It works at an operational, day-to-day level, not at the higher strategic level.

2. **A.** This is the best answer because operations has the goal of keeping everything running smoothly each and every day. Operations implements new software and hardware and carries out the necessary security tasks passed down to it. As the environment changes and security is kept in the loop with these changes, there is a smaller likelihood of opening up vulnerabilities.

3. **D.** Due care and due diligence are legal terms that do not just pertain to security. Due diligence involves going through the necessary steps to know what a company's or individual's actual risks are, while due care involves carrying out responsible actions to reduce those risks. These concepts correspond with the "prudent person" concept.

4. **C.** Many times, employees who are carrying out fraudulent activities do not take the vacation they have earned because they do not want anyone to find out what they have been doing. Forcing employees to take vacations means that someone else has to do that person's job and can possibly uncover any misdeeds.

5. **B.** Rotation of duties enables a company to have more than one person trained in a position and can uncover fraudulent activities. Separation of duties is put into place to ensure that one entity cannot carry out a critical task alone.

6. **C.** This is just one of several examples of separation of duties. A system must be set up for proper code maintenance to take place when necessary, instead of allowing a programmer to make changes arbitrarily. These types of changes should go through a change control process and should have more entities involved than just one programmer.

7. **A.** There should be controls in place to make sure the data input into a system and the results generated are in the proper format and have expected values. Improper data being put into an application or system could cause bad output and security issues, such as buffer overflows.

8. **C.** Users should be able to access only the resources they need to fulfill the duties of their positions. They also should only have the level of permissions and rights for those resources that are required to carry out the exact operations they need for their jobs, and no more. This second concept is more granular than the first, but they have a symbiotic relationship.

9. **A.** Documentation is very important for data processing and networked environments. This task often gets pushed to the back burner or is totally ignored. If things are not properly documented, employees will forget

what actually took place with each device. If the environment needs to be rebuilt, for example, it may be done incorrectly if the procedure was poorly or improperly documented. When new changes need to be implemented, the current infrastructure may not be totally understood. Continually documenting when virus signatures are updated would be overkill. The other answers contain events that certainly require documentation.

10. **D.** One cannot properly erase data held on a CD-ROM. If the data are sensitive and you need to ensure no one has access to the same, the media should be physically destroyed.

11. **D.** This is not a great question, but could be something that you run into on the exam. Let's look at the answers. Different SSL versions are usually not a concern, because the two communicating systems will negotiate and agree upon the necessary version. There is no security violation issue here. SSL works at the transport layer; thus, it will not be affected by what the user does, as stated in answer B. SSL protects against network tapping and wiretapping. Answer D talks about the network segments the company does not own. You do not know at what point the other company will decrypt the SSL connection because you do not have control of that environment. Your data could be traveling unencrypted and unprotected on another network.

12. **C.** Simple Mail Transfer Protocol (SMTP) is the protocol used to allow clients to send e-mail messages to each other. It lets different mail servers exchange messages.

13. **C.** Spammers will identify the mail servers on the Internet that have relaying enabled and are "wide open," meaning the servers will forward any e-mail messages they receive. These servers can be put on a black list, which means other mail servers will not accept mail from them.

14. **D.** The other three answers provide reasons why fax servers would be used instead of individual fax machines: ease of use, they provide more protection, and their supplies may be cheaper.

15. **C.** This is the best answer for this question. The other components could provide different levels of protection, but a fax encryptor (which is a data link encryptor) provides a higher level of protection across the board because everything is encrypted. Even if a user does not choose to encrypt something, it will be encrypted anyway before it is sent out the fax server.

16. **C.** This is a technology that wraps the different services available on a system. What this means is that if a remote user makes a request to access a service, this product will intercept this request and determine whether it is valid and legal before allowing the interaction to take place.

17. **D.** A sniffer is a device or software component that puts the NIC in promiscuous mode, meaning the NIC will pick up all frames it "sees" instead of just the frames addressed to that individual computer. The sniffer then shows the output to the user. It can have capture and filtering capabilities.

18. **D.** The first three choices are attacks that can directly affect security operations. There is no such attack as an ICMP Sting.

19. **B.** For auditing purposes, the procedure should capture the user ID, time of event, type of event, and the source workstation. Capturing the user ID allows the company to hold individuals accountable for their actions.

20. **C.** Dual control requires two or more entities working together to complete a task. An example is key recovery. If a key must be recovered, and key recovery requires two or more people to authenticate to a system, the act of them coming together and carrying out these activities is known as dual control. This reduces the possibility of fraud.

21. **A.** The last three tasks fall under the job functions of an individual or department responsible for controlling access to media. Compressing and decompressing data does not.

22. **A.** Clipping levels are thresholds of acceptable user errors and suspicious activities. If the threshold is exceeded, it should be logged and the administrator should decide if malicious activities are taking place or if the user needs more training.

23. **C.** The reason to have tape library management is to have a centralized and standard way of protecting how media is stored, accessed, and destroyed.

24. **D.** A degausser is a device that generates a magnetic field (coercive magnetic force) that changes the orientation of the bits held on the media (reducing magnetic flux density to zero).

25. **A.** If operations personnel are limited in what they can access, they would need to collude with someone who actually has access to the resource. This question is not very clear, but it is very close to the way many CISSP exam questions are formatted.

26. **C.** Network redundancy is duplicated network equipment that can provide a backup in case of network failures. This technology protects the company from single points of failures.

Security Content Automation Protocol Overview

Provided by G2 Incorporated

Once software code is compiled, shrink-wrapped, and shipped to the far ends of the earth, there are only so many approaches to secure that software against exploitation. Although a seemingly simple problem to solve, for two decades the vast majority of all software vulnerabilities have been attributable to security setting misconfiguration.[1] Remediating security-affecting software flaws is a more complex problem. These echoes of software coding errors are compiled in the latest major version of your favorite software. In this instance, the world is left with patch management because it's the best defense against threats as varied as intellectual thrill seekers and the most nefarious forces on the face of the planet.

Background

Over the past few decades, the world has experienced an incredible change in the number and complexity of vulnerability management processes. In the 1990s, we had only subject matter experts to evaluate systems for the presence of vulnerabilities and for subsequent remediation. People who had this skill set could fetch premium consulting fees delivering their knowledge as vulnerability scanning, hardening, and remediation services. Since then, security software vendors have architected solutions that allow organizations of any size to own and operate a vulnerability scanning solution. In this same period, security setting configuration guides (a.k.a. hardening guides) became prevalent and repositories of software flaw information emerged. Vulnerability alerting, Computer Emergency Response Teams (CERT), and Security Operations Centers (SOC) all became common place. As these technologies and processes emerged and evolved, one thing became glaringly obvious. Why aren't these processes connected and interoperable? While we awaited an answer, lack of connection standards, reporting standards, and interoperability drove all sorts of really high-cost and high-risk

---

[1] SANS Top 20 Internet Security Attack Targets 2006 cites three of the top 20 were categorized as "configuration weaknesses." Many of the remaining 20 can be partially mitigated via proper configuration.

behaviors, such as creating solutions that would only last as long as your current vulnerability scanner version (a.k.a. point solution). There has to be a better way . . .

. . . and there is. Security Content Automation Protocol (SCAP, pronounced *es-cap*) is a format for expressing both security configuration and software flaw information (that is, vulnerability information). SCAP is both the input and the output of vulnerability management software and processes. Although some folks get confused by SCAP's six-ingredient recipe (more on that shortly), fundamentally it's just specialized eXtensible Markup Language (XML). In other words, it's structured text that's both human readable through your favorite web browser and machine readable by SCAP-validated software products. Standardization around the structure of SCAP XML is the key to product and process interoperability. It is the "protocol" in Security Content Automation Protocol.

SCAP—More Than Just a Protocol

However, SCAP is more than just an input and output format. SCAP is also centralized XML content. Because SCAP Content specifies *how* a computer should be evaluated to determine proper configuration or presence of a software flaw, centralized SCAP Content brings repeatability to vulnerability assessments. It eliminates differing assessment methods across security software vendors, thereby enabling a level of transparency that did not previously exist. SCAP Content is obtained in the form of reference data from the National Institute of Standards and Technology's (NIST) National Vulnerability Database (NVD, http://nvd.nist.gov). Historically, NVD has hosted information about software flaws. In recent years, the NVD web site has also become the home for relevant U.S. Federal security configurations. Per the U.S. Cyber Security Research and Development Act of 2002, NIST has organized these security configurations into the National Checklist Program (NCP). The NCP web site is now available through NVD, making http://nvd.nist.gov the singular web site for U.S. Federal SCAP Content. As indicated through NVD web statistics, this content is highly applicable for commercial usage and international governments as well.

The process for developing and publishing security configurations for the NCP is available in NIST Special Publication 800-70 Revision 1. Revision 1 is the Summer 2009 update to NIST Special Publication 800-70. Per that update, security configurations in NCP are now organized into tiers. While Tier 1 checklists can be prose and Tier 2 are non-SCAP automation content, Tiers 3 and 4 are SCAP Content. This restructure of NCP content harkens to SCAP as the preferred format of U.S. National security configurations. It also reveals a next step in the maturity of SCAP. Formal validation of SCAP Content is on the horizon. It remains to be seen how Content Validation will be implemented. However, third-party laboratory validation is likely, given the sheer volume of SCAP Content that needs to be (and will need to be) validated.

A Vulnerability Management Problem

So what does SCAP Content look like? In summary, it is composed of six different specifications. To think about the structure of SCAP, let's first examine a common vulnerability management problem.

Today, much of the software flaw and security misconfiguration information in our vulnerability management processes originates from proprietary products with proprietary data sources. Although this seems innocuous, it can actually cause a lot of difficult problems. For example, pretend you are an Information Security Officer (ISO) for a large organization. You require all business units in your organization to provide periodic vulnerability scan data to you. Further, you want to automate aggregation and analysis of vulnerability scan data for the entire organization, such that you can understand the vulnerability and make remediation decisions. However, all business units use different products to perform their vulnerability scans, and due to a variety of factors, not all business units can convert to a single vulnerability scanning product. To highlight the complexity of aggregating data, we compare the two different non-SCAP vulnerability scanning products from Business Unit A and Business Unit B in Exhibit A (see Table A-1). You, as the ISO for this organization, have your work cut out for you.

Vulnerability Scanner Function	Business Unit A (Non-SCAP Product A)	Business Unit B (Non-SCAP Product B)
Unique hardware, operating system, and/or application identifiers	Proprietary numeric ID, different from Product B	Proprietary numeric ID, different from Product A
Unique misconfiguration identifiers	Proprietary numeric ID, different from Product B	Proprietary numeric ID, different from Product A
Unique software flaw identifiers	Bugtraq ID	CAN ID
Software flaw severity scoring	Numeric (exact mathematics unknown)	Color-coded red/yellow/green/blue (exact color assignment method unknown)
API-level test procedures	Obscured and different from Product B	Obscured and different from Product A
Vulnerability descriptions	Different from Product B	Different from Product A
Exploit steps (for confirmation purposes)	Different from Product B	Different from Product A
Diagnosis instructions	Different from Product B	Different from Product A
Remediation suggestions	Different from Product B	Different from Product A
Mappings to security guidelines, standards, and policies	No guarantee the mappings have been vetted with relevant authorities	None

Table A-1   Exhibit A

In thinking about merging scan reports from these non-SCAP vulnerability scanners, you see that some issues are obvious. How can I aggregate scan data if vulnerable products are identified using two different systems of unique numeric identifiers? The same problem holds true for unique misconfiguration identifiers. Additionally, these two products use two entirely different software flaw severity scoring systems: one uses numbers and one uses color coding, and both are proprietary. Which do I trust more? How can I even determine trust if the mathematics for assigning a number or color are not revealed to me? Similarly, the products have differing and proprietary text for vulnerability descriptions, exploit steps, diagnosis instructions, and remediation suggestions (that is, decisioning material). Does one vendor provide better decisioning material than the other, or does the quality of the text vary on a case-by-case basis? What about mapping security configuration to related security guidelines, standards, and policies? Product B does not have mappings. Product A has mappings, but they are unreliable in that I cannot tell how well the mappings are vetted with the authorities behind those guidelines, standards, and policies.

The preceding scenario is an extremely common one across organizations worldwide. It has left the modern IT enterprise with limited ability to understand and address vulnerability. Organizations who have embarked on in-house solutions to aggregate vulnerability data across varying security products are now burdened with a significant and perpetual development cost.

A Vulnerability Management Solution—SCAP and SCAP Specifications

A comparable world with SCAP is depicted in Exhibit B (see Table A-2). As you can see, SCAP ensures a standardized system of identifiers, severity scoring, and prose. Further, any mappings to security guidelines, standards, and policies must be vetted in SCAP Content.[2]

Per Exhibit B, Common Configuration Enumeration (CCE) and Common Vulnerabilities and Exposures (CVE) provide unique identifiers and standardized descriptions for security configurations and software flaws. Common Platform Enumeration (CPE) provides uniform resource names (URN) and defines relationships between affected platforms, operating systems, and applications. Common Vulnerability Scoring System (CVSS) is a Forum for Incident Responders and Security Teams (FIRST) specification for expressing the severity of a vulnerability. Open Vulnerability and Assessment Language (OVAL) XML defines how to interact with a host to determine vulnerability. Finally, CCE, CVE, CPE, and CVSS are all related to each other by being embedded in eXtensible Common Checklist Data Format (XCCDF) XML. XCCDF also points to a separate OVAL XML file for information about interrogating the computer system.[3]

---

[2] More specifically, National Checklist Program Type IV security configurations require vetting with relevant authorities.

[3] The formulation of SCAP is detailed in NIST Special Publication 800-126.

Function	Business Unit A (SCAP Product A)	Business Unit B (SCAP Product B)
Unique hardware, operating system, and/or application identifiers	CPE	CPE
Unique misconfiguration identifiers	CCE	CCE
Unique software flaw identifiers	CVE	CVE
Software flaw severity scoring	CVSS	CVSS
API-level test procedures	Standardized and transparent	Standardized and transparent
Misconfiguration and software flaw descriptions	Uniform	Uniform
Exploit description and steps (for confirmation purposes)	Uniform	Uniform
Diagnosis instructions	Uniform	Uniform
Remediation suggestions	Uniform	Uniform
Mappings to security guidelines, standards, and policies	Vetted with relevant authorities	Vetted with relevant authorities

Table A-2   Exhibit B

Beyond its ability to determine software flaws and security misconfiguration, SCAP has significant potential to make technical compliance reporting a byproduct of vulnerability assessment. Leveraging a capability of the XCCDF schema, SCAP Content can contain mappings from individual security configurations to corresponding security documents in which those settings are prescribed. Whether hardening guide, security policy, or controls framework, a mapping is possible. To further enhance SCAP's value to U.S. Federal security policy compliance, NIST now hosts a CCE-to-FISMA (Federal Information System Management Act) Security Control data feed.[4] This means security software can resolve unique identifiers for security configurations as expressed in CCE to NIST Special Publication 800-53 Security Controls by reading the NIST-hosted data feed.

Exhibit C provides the features and benefits of SCAP specifications (see Table A-3). In summary, the enumerations of CPE, CVE, and CCE are the basis for vulnerability product interoperability. CVSS and the text prose of XCCDF provide uniform decisioning material. XCCDF and OVAL provide full transparency—absolutely nothing is hidden in SCAP. Finally, OVAL defines the manner in which vulnerability scanning products interact with the platform in question. As such, OVAL is the key to repeatability of security scan results across many different vulnerability scanning products.

---

[4] FISMA Security Controls are declared and explained in NIST Special Publication (SP) 800-53 Revision 3.

Specification	Features	Benefits
CPE	Unique uniform resource names (URN) Standardized URN text	Interoperability
CVE and CCE	Unique identifiers Standard prose description	Interoperability
CVSS	Standardized security score Customized via environmental factor	Uniform decisioning material
XCCDF	Links configuration to derivative documents Prose Not obscured	Uniform decisioning material Transparency
OVAL	Interacts at the API level	Repeatability Transparency

Table A-3   Exhibit C

One very important nuance of SCAP is it's contextual formulation, meaning the exact combination of the six SCAP specifications in SCAP Content may vary depending on your intent for the content. For instance, hardening guides can be expressed in SCAP Content. Subsequently, a product that has been validated as an "Authenticated Configuration Scanner" in the SCAP Validation Program could process the SCAP-expressed hardening guide to evaluate whether a computer was configured according to the guide. The SCAP Content in this example would consist of CPE and CCE embedded in XCCDF, which calls OVAL. In other words, only four SCAP specifications are actually needed to express a security configuration in SCAP Content. In contrast, a software flaw alert can be expressed in SCAP Content and processed by products validated as "Authenticated Vulnerability and Patch Scanner." The software flaw alert would be composed of five SCAP specifications: CPE, CVE, CVSS, XCCDF, and OVAL.

SCAP Product Validation Program

As you may have noted from the preceding examples, the SCAP Product Validation Program (SPVP) is very important to the responsible adoption of SCAP. At its heart, the SPVP is about ensuring consumers understand which products and to what extent products are proficient at processing and outputting SCAP. The SPVP tests products against SCAP capabilities, meaning the function the SCAP product performs.[5] This testing approach accounts for the contextual nature of SCAP content and architectural aspects of any given product. In the previous paragraph, we highlighted some basic examples of how SCAP Content can change given context. Products and testing thereof might differ based on that context. In other words, the test procedures within any given product validation might vary based on the function of the product. For instance, performing software flaw scanning as a privileged user might be performed on the computer itself (for example, through an agent-server architecture), whereas nonprivileged scanning might be performed from a network-attached remote computer. Regardless of architecture, SCAP must be processed correctly for the product in question to become validated.

---

[5] SPVP test requirements are declared and explained in NIST Interagency Report (IR) 7511 Revision 1.

The Future of Security Automation

NIST purposefully scoped SCAP as a format for expressing and reporting on software flaw and security configuration assessments. However, there is a larger vision for SCAP and security automation. On the immediate horizon, NIST is considering a number of additional specifications for inclusion in future versions of SCAP. The listing of emerging SCAP specifications and the change control process thereof is available at http:// scap.nist.gov. Additionally, NIST is developing a remediation capability, which will likely be included in SCAP sometime in the upcoming few years. SCAP analogs are also envisioned, and preliminary formulation has begun on an expression and reporting format for network security events (working title of Event Management Automation Protocol, EMAP). This analog would bring interoperability to network security components such as intrusion detection/prevention systems, SIM/SEM, firewalls, and more. Not only is there first-order value to both SCAP and its network event analog, but complimentary design will lead to second-order value. For instance, the likelihood of false positive for network-observed security events might be determined by comparing EMAP output from an intrusion detection system against SCAP output from the latest vulnerability assessment scan. Unique CVE identifiers in both EMAP and SCAP allow this correlation. More SCAP analogs are envisioned, with similar first- and second-order value.

Conclusion

The standardized and open approach of SCAP brings the worlds of vulnerability, asset, configuration, and compliance management together in a novel way, enabling repeatability, interoperability, and ultimately automation for vulnerability management technology and processes. The expansion of SCAP and research on SCAP analogs for information security represent taking a great idea and applying it to other use cases. Seeing these security use cases through completion will take several years. It also begs the question whether SCAP principles can be applied to Information Technology in general. Whether SCAP standardization plays out to that extent remains to be seen; however, the near-term benefit of SCAP itself looks incredibly promising for vulnerability management worldwide.

About the CD-ROM

The CD-ROM that comes with the CISSP All-in-One Exam Guide includes

- **Live cryptography video training** A QuickTime video/audio file with "live" video training on cryptography, presented by Shon Harris (see Figure B-1). This is a portion of a complete CISSP training product. For more information on the complete product, please see the ad that follows the index of this book. The QuickTime player must be installed on your computer to play this file. It is available from www.apple.com. See the following sections for more instructions.

- **Practice questions** Total Seminars' Total Tester Software, with more than 500 practice questions covering all ten CISSP domains. This testing engine features Practice and Final modes of testing.

The CD-ROM is set up with an autorun function. If your computer does not have autorun turned on, browse the CD-ROM and double-click the launcher.exe file to access the software menu page. From the software menu page, you can launch the installation wizard (to install the Total Tester) or run the video training QuickTime file.

Figure B-1   CISSP CBT cryptography demo

Running the QuickTime Cryptography Video Sample

Once you have started the launcher.exe file (either through autorun or by double-clicking the file on the CD-ROM), click the Play CISSP Video Training link to start the QuickTime file, a frame of which is shown in Figure B-2.

The following are the minimum system requirements for the cryptography video sample:

- Windows 98, 800 MHz Pentium II, 24X CD-ROM drive, 64MB RAM, 800×600 monitor, millions of colors, QuickTime 5, Microsoft Internet Explorer 5 or Netscape Navigator 4.5, and speakers or headphones

- Macintosh OS 9.2.1, 450 MHz G3, 24X CD-ROM drive, 64MB RAM, 800×600 monitor, millions of colors, QuickTime 5, Microsoft Internet Explorer 5 or Netscape Navigator 4.5, and speakers or headphones

The following are the recommended system requirements for the cryptography video sample:

- Windows 2000, 2 GHz Pentium IV, 48X CD-ROM drive, 128MB RAM, 1024×768 monitor, millions of colors, QuickTime 6, Microsoft Internet Explorer 5.5 or Netscape Navigator 4.7, and speakers or headphones

- Macintosh OS 10.1, 800 MHz G4, 48X CD-ROM drive, 128MB RAM, 1024×768 monitor, millions of colors, QuickTime 6, Microsoft Internet Explorer 5.5 or Netscape Navigator 4.7, and speakers or headphones

Figure B-2   CISSP computer-based training segment

Troubleshooting

This software runs inside of your Internet browser. You must have its preferences set for correct playback of QuickTime movies to view the video. The QuickTime installer (free download from www.apple.com/quicktime) may not change all of your file helpers properly.

After QuickTime is installed, if movies take a very long time to load or don't load at all, verify that your browser associates the file type .mov with the QuickTime plug-in. To verify this, do the following:

- If using Internet Explorer for Windows, go to Tools | Internet Options | Advanced | Multimedia or Control Panels | QuickTime.

- If using Internet Explorer for Macintosh, go to Preferences | Receiving Files | Helpers.

Installing Total Seminars' Test Software

Click the Install Test Software button on the wizard, and the installation will proceed automatically.

Once you've completed installation, you can open the test program by selecting Start | Programs | Total Seminars and clicking on the CISSP test suites. There is one suite for each domain of the CISSP exam. You can also start the program with the shortcut the installation places on your desktop.

Navigation

The program enables you to test in each of the ten domains in either Practice or Final mode. An Adaptive mode exam, which uses a large pool of questions, is also included. Begin by selecting a testing mode and specific test from the menu bar.

Practice Mode

In Practice mode, the test includes an assistance window. This gives you access to several features: Hint (helps you figure out the correct answer), Reference (where in the book to learn more), Check (is your selection correct?), and Explanation (a short note explaining the correct answer). This is a good way to study and review: answer each question, check to see if you answered correctly, review the explanation, and refer to the book for more detailed coverage. At the end of the test, you are graded by topic and can review missed questions.

Final Mode

Final mode enables you to test yourself without the ability to see the correct answers. This is a better way to see how well you understand the material. Upon completion, you receive a final grade by topic, and you can look over the questions you missed.

Minimum System Requirements for Total Seminars' Software

The software is easy to install on any Windows 98/NT/2000/XP/Vista computer and must be installed to access the Total Tester practice exams and the video sample. The Glossary and eBook are Adobe Acrobat files. If you don't have Adobe Acrobat Reader, it is available for installation on the CD.

Software requires Windows 98 or higher, Internet Explorer 5.0 or above, and 50MB of hard disk space for full installation.

Technical Support

For technical support of the Total Tester practice test application, please check www .totalsem.com. For other technical support issues or questions about the content of the Total Tester, please visit www.osborne.com or e-mail customer.service@mcgraw-hill .com. For customers outside the 50 United States, e-mail international_cs@mcgraw-hill.com.

A

access A subject's ability to view, modify, or communicate with an object. Access enables the flow of information between the subject and the object.

access control Mechanisms, controls, and methods of limiting access to resources to authorized subjects only.

access control list (ACL) A list of subjects that are authorized to access a particular object. Typically, the types of access are read, write, execute, append, modify, delete, and create.

access control mechanism Administrative, physical, or technical control that is designed to detect and prevent unauthorized access to a resource or environment.

accountability A security principle indicating that individuals must be identifiable and must be held responsible for their actions.

accredited A computer system or network that has received official authorization and approval to process sensitive data in a specific operational environment. There must be a security evaluation of the system's hardware, software, configurations, and controls by technical personnel.

add-on security Security protection mechanisms that are hardware or software retrofitted to a system to increase that system's protection level.

administrative controls Security mechanisms that are management's responsibility and referred to as "soft" controls. These controls include the development and publication of policies, standards, procedures, and guidelines; the screening of personnel; security-awareness training; the monitoring of system activity; and change control procedures.

AIC triad The three security principles: availability, integrity, and confidentiality.

annualized loss expectancy (ALE) A dollar amount that estimates the loss potential from a risk in a span of a year.

single loss expectancy (SLE) · annualized rate of occurrence (ARO) = ALE

annualized rate of occurrence (ARO) The value that represents the estimated possibility of a specific threat taking place within a one-year timeframe.

assurance A measurement of confidence in the level of protection that a specific security control delivers and the degree to which it enforces the security policy.

attack An attempt to bypass security controls in a system with the mission of using that system or compromising it. An attack is usually accomplished by exploiting a current vulnerability.

audit trail   A chronological set of logs and records used to provide evidence of a system's performance or activity that took place on the system. These logs and records can be used to attempt to reconstruct past events and track the activities that took place, and possibly detect and identify intruders.

authenticate   To verify the identity of a subject requesting the use of a system and/ or access to network resources. The steps to giving a subject access to an object should be identification, authentication, and authorization.

authorization   Granting access to an object after the subject has been properly identified and authenticated.

automated information system (AIS)   A computer system that is used to process and transmit data. It is a collection of hardware, software, and firmware that works together to accept, compute, communicate, store, process, transmit, and control data-processing functions.

availability   The reliability and accessibility of data and resources to authorized individuals in a timely manner.

B

back up   Copy and move data to a medium so that it may be restored if the original data is corrupted or destroyed. A full backup copies all the data from the system to the backup medium. An incremental backup copies only the files that have been modified since the previous backup. A differential backup backs up all files since the last full backup.

backdoor   An undocumented way of gaining access to a computer system. After a system is compromised, an attacker may load a program that listens on a port (back-door) so that the attacker can enter the system at any time. A backdoor is also referred to as a trapdoor.

baseline   The minimum level of security necessary to support and enforce a security policy.

Bell-LaPadula model   The model uses a formal state transition model that describes its access controls and how they should perform. When the system must transition from one state to another, the security of the system should never be lowered or compromised. See also multilevel security, simple security property, and star property (*-property).

Biba model   A formal state transition system of computer security policy that describes a set of access control rules designed to ensure data integrity.

biometrics   When used within computer security, identifies individuals by physiological characteristics, such as a fingerprint, hand geometry, or pattern in the iris.

browsing   Searching through storage media looking for specific information without necessarily knowing what format the information is in. A browsing attack is one in which the attacker looks around a computer system either to see what looks interesting or to find specific information.

brute force attack   An attack that continually tries different inputs to achieve a predefined goal, which can be used to obtain credentials for unauthorized access.

C

callback   A procedure for identifying a system that accessed an environment remotely. In a callback, the host system disconnects the caller and then dials the authorized telephone number of the remote terminal in order to reestablish the connection. Synonymous with dialback.

capability   A capability outlines the objects a subject can access and the operations the subject can carry out on the different objects. It indicates the access rights for a specific subject; many times, the capability is in the form of a ticket.

certification   The technical evaluation of the security components and their compliance for the purpose of accreditation. A certification process can use safeguard evaluation, risk analysis, verification, testing, and auditing techniques to assess the appropriateness of a specific system processing a certain level of information within a particular environment. The certification is the testing of the security component or system, and the accreditation is the approval from management of the security component or system.

challenge-response method   A method used to verify the identity of a subject by sending the subject an unpredictable or random value. If the subject responds with the expected value in return, the subject is authenticated.

ciphertext   Data that has been encrypted and is unreadable until it has been converted into plaintext.

Clark-Wilson model   An integrity model that addresses all three integrity goals: prevent unauthorized users from making modifications, prevent authorized users from making improper modifications, and maintain internal and external consistency through auditing.

classification   A systematic arrangement of objects into groups or categories according to a set of established criteria. Data and resources can be assigned a level of sensitivity as they are being created, amended, enhanced, stored, or transmitted. The classification level then determines the extent to which the resource needs to be controlled and secured, and is indicative of its value in terms of information assets.

cleartext   In data communications, cleartext is the form of a message or data which is transferred or stored without cryptographic protection.

collusion   Two or more people working together to carry out a fraudulent activity. More than one person would need to work together to cause some type of destruction or fraud; this drastically reduces its probability.

communications security   Controls in place to protect information as it is being transmitted, especially by telecommunications mechanisms.

compartment   A class of information that has need-to-know access controls beyond those normally provided for access to confidential, secret, or top-secret information. A compartment is the same thing as a category within a security label. Just because a subject has the proper classification, that does not mean it has a need to know. The category, or compartment, of the security label enforces the subject's need to know.

compartmented mode workstation (CMW)   A workstation that contains the necessary controls to be able to operate as a trusted computer. The system is trusted to keep data from different classification levels and categories in separate compartments and properly protected.

compensating controls   Controls that are alternative procedures designed to reduce the risk. They are used to "counterbalance" the effects of an internal control weakness.

compromise   A violation of the security policy of a system or an organization such that unauthorized disclosure or modification of sensitive information occurs.

computer fraud   Computer-related crimes involving deliberate misrepresentation, modification, or disclosure of data in order to compromise a system or obtain something of value.

confidentiality   A security principle that works to ensure that information is not disclosed to unauthorized subjects.

configuration management   The identification, control, accounting, and documentation of all changes that take place to system hardware, software, firmware, supporting documentation, and test results throughout the lifespan of the system.

confinement   Controlling information in a manner that prevents sensitive data from being leaked from a program to another program, subject, or object in an unauthorized manner.

contingency plan   A plan put in place before any potential emergencies, with the mission of dealing with possible future emergencies. It pertains to training personnel, performing backups, preparing critical facilities, and recovering from an emergency or disaster so that business operations can continue.

control zone   The space within a facility that is used to protect sensitive processing equipment. Controls are in place to protect equipment from physical or technical unauthorized entry or compromise. The zone can also be used to prevent electrical waves carrying sensitive data from leaving the area.

cost/benefit analysis   An assessment that is performed to ensure that the cost of a safeguard does not outweigh the benefit of the safeguard. Spending more to protect an asset than the asset is actually worth does not make good business sense. All possible safeguards must be evaluated to ensure that the most security-effective and cost-effective choice is made.

countermeasure A control, method, technique, or procedure that is put into place to prevent a threat agent from exploiting a vulnerability. A countermeasure is put into place to mitigate risk. Also called a safeguard or control.

covert channel A communications path that enables a process to transmit information in a way that violates the system's security policy.

covert storage channel A covert channel that involves writing to a storage location by one process and the direct or indirect reading of the storage location by another process. Covert storage channels typically involve a resource (for example, sectors on a disk) that is shared by two subjects at different security levels.

covert timing channel A covert channel in which one process modulates its system resource (for example, CPU cycles), which is interpreted by a second process as some type of communication.

cryptanalysis The practice of breaking cryptosystems and algorithms used in encryption and decryption processes.

cryptography The science of secret writing that enables storage and transmission of data in a form that is available only to the intended individuals.

cryptology The study of cryptography and cryptanalysis.

cryptosystem The hardware or software implementation of cryptography.

D

data classification Assignments to data that indicate the level of availability, integrity, and confidentiality that is required for each type of information.

data custodian An individual who is responsible for the maintenance and protection of the data. This role is usually filled by the IT department (usually the network administrator). The duties include performing regular backups of the data, implementing security mechanisms, periodically validating the integrity of the data, restoring data from backup media, and fulfilling the requirements specified in the company's security policy, standards, and guidelines that pertain to information security and data protection.

Data Encryption Standard (DES) Symmetric key encryption algorithm that was adopted by the government as a federal standard for protecting sensitive unclassified information. DES was later replaced with Advanced Encryption Standard (AES).

data remanence A measure of the magnetic flux density remaining after removal of the applied magnetic force, which is used to erase data. Refers to any data remaining on magnetic storage media.

database shadowing A mirroring technology used in databases, in which information is written to at least two hard drives for the purpose of redundancy.

declassification An administrative decision or procedure to remove or reduce the security classification information.

dedicated security mode The mode in which a system operates if all users have the clearance or authorization to access, and the need to know about, all data processed within the system. All users have been given formal access approval for all information on the system and have signed nondisclosure agreements pertaining to this information.

degauss Process that demagnetizes magnetic media so that a very low residue of magnetic induction is left on the media. Used to effectively erase data from media.

Delphi technique A group decision method used to ensure that each member of a group gives an honest and anonymous opinion pertaining to the company's risks.

denial of service (DoS) Any action, or series of actions, that prevents a system, or its resources, from functioning in accordance with its intended purpose.

dial-up The service whereby a computer terminal can use telephone lines, usually via a modem, to initiate and continue communication with another computer system.

dictionary attack A form of attack in which an attacker uses a large set of likely combinations to guess a secret, usually a password.

digital signature An electronic signature based upon cryptographic methods of originator authentication, computed by using a set of rules and a set of parameters such that the identity of the signer and the integrity of the data can be verified.

disaster recovery plan A plan developed to help a company recover from a disaster. It provides procedures for emergency response, extended backup operations, and post-disaster recovery when an organization suffers a loss of computer processing capability or resources and physical facilities.

discretionary access control (DAC) An access control model and policy that restricts access to objects based on the identity of the subjects and the groups to which those subjects belong. The data owner has the discretion of allowing or denying others access to the resources it owns.

domain The set of objects that a subject is allowed to access. Within this domain, all subjects and objects share a common security policy, procedures, and rules, and they are managed by the same management system.

due care Steps taken to show that a company has taken responsibility for the activities that occur within the corporation and has taken the necessary steps to help protect the company, its resources, and employees.

due diligence The process of systematically evaluating information to identify vulnerabilities, threats, and issues relating to an organization's overall risk.

E

electronic vaulting The transfer of backup data to an offsite location. This process is primarily a batch process of transmitting data through communications lines to a server at an alternative location.

emanations Electrical and electromagnetic signals emitted from electrical equipment that can transmit through the airwaves. These signals carry information that can be captured and deciphered, which can cause a security breach. These are also called emissions.

encryption The transformation of plaintext into unreadable ciphertext.

end-to-end encryption A technology that encrypts the data payload of a packet.

Evaluated Products List (EPL) A list of products that have been evaluated and assigned an assurance rating. The products could be evaluated using several different criteria: TCSEC, ITSEC, or Common Criteria.

exposure An instance of being exposed to losses from a threat. A weakness or vulnerability can cause an organization to be exposed to possible damages.

exposure factor The percentage of loss a realized threat could have on a certain asset.

F

failover A backup operation that automatically switches to a standby system if the primary system fails or is taken offline. It is an important fault-tolerant function that provides system availability.

fail-safe A functionality that ensures that when software or a system fails for any reason, it does not end up in a vulnerable state. After a failure, software might default to no access instead of allowing full control, which would be an example of a fail-safe measure.

firmware Software instructions that have been written into read-only memory (ROM) or a programmable ROM (PROM) chip.

formal security policy model A mathematical statement of a security policy. When an operating system is created, it can be built upon a predeveloped model that lays out how all activities will take place in each and every situation. This model can be expressed mathematically, which is then translated into a programming language.

formal verification Validating and testing of highly trusted systems. The tests are designed to show design verification, consistency between the formal specifications and the formal security policy model, implementation verification, consistency between the formal specifications, and the actual implementation of the product.

G

gateway A system or device that connects two unlike environments or systems. The gateway is usually required to translate between different types of applications or protocols.

guidelines Recommended actions and operational guides for users, IT staff, operations staff, and others when a specific standard does not apply.

H

handshaking procedure A dialog between two entities for the purpose of identifying and authenticating the entities to one another. The dialog can take place between two computers or two applications residing on different computers. It is an activity that usually takes place within a protocol.

honeypot A computer set up as a sacrificial lamb on the network in the hope that attackers will attack this system instead of actual production systems.

I

identification A subject provides some type of data to an authentication service. Identification is the first step in the authentication process.

information owner The person who has final corporate responsibility of data protection and would be the one held liable for any negligence when it comes to protecting the company's information assets. The person who holds this role—usually a senior executive within the management group of the company—is responsible for assigning a classification to the information and dictating how the information should be protected.

integrity A security principle that makes sure that information and systems are not modified maliciously or accidentally.

intrusion detection system (IDS) Software employed to monitor and detect possible attacks and behaviors that vary from the normal and expected activity. The IDS can be network based, which monitors network traffic, or host based, which monitors activities of a specific system and protects system files and control mechanisms.

isolation The containment of processes in a system in such a way that they are separated from one another to ensure integrity and confidentiality.

K

kernel The core of an operating system, a kernel manages the machine's hardware resources (including the processor and the memory), and provides and controls the way any other software component accesses these resources.

key A discrete data set that controls the operation of a cryptography algorithm. In encryption, a key specifies the particular transformation of plaintext into ciphertext, or vice versa during decryption. Keys are also used in other cryptographic algorithms, such as digital signature schemes and keyed-hash functions (also known as HMACs), which are often used for authentication and integrity.

keystroke monitoring A type of auditing that can review or record keystrokes entered by a user during an active session.

L

lattice-based access control model A mathematical model that allows a system to easily represent the different security levels and control access attempts based on those levels. Every pair of elements has a highest lower bound and a lowest upper bound of access rights. The classes stemmed from military designations.

least privilege The security principle that requires each subject to be granted the most restrictive set of privileges needed for the performance of authorized tasks. The application of this principle limits the damage that can result from accident, error, or unauthorized use.

life-cycle assurance Confidence that a trusted system is designed, developed, and maintained with formal designs and controls. This includes design specification and verification, implementation, testing, configuration management, and distribution.

link encryption A type of encryption technology that encrypts packets' headers, trailers, and the data payload. Each network communications node, or hop, must decrypt the packets to read its address and routing information and then re-encrypt the packets. This is different from **end-to-end encryption**.

logic bomb A malicious program that is triggered by a specific event or condition.

loss potential The potential losses that can be accrued if a threat agent actually exploits a vulnerability.

M

maintenance hook Instructions within a program's code that enable the developer or maintainer to enter the program without having to go through the usual access control and authentication processes. Maintenance hooks should be removed from the code before it is released to production; otherwise, they can cause serious security risks. Also called trapdoor or backdoor.

malware Malicious software. Code written to perform activities that circumvent the security policy of a system. Examples are viruses, malicious applets, Trojan horses, logical bombs, and worms.

mandatory access control (MAC) An access policy that restricts subjects' access to objects based on the security clearance of the subject and the classification of the object. The system enforces the security policy, and users cannot share their files with other users.

masquerading Impersonating another user, usually with the intention of gaining unauthorized access to a system.

message authentication code (MAC) In cryptography, a message authentication code (MAC) is a generated value used to authenticate a message. A MAC can be generated by HMAC or CBC-MAC methods. The MAC protects both a message's integrity (by ensuring that a different MAC will be produced if the message has changed) as well as its authenticity, because only someone who knows the secret key could have modified the message.

multilevel security A class of systems containing information with different classifications. Access decisions are based on the subject's security clearances, need to know, and formal approval.

N

need to know A security principle stating that users should have access only to the information and resources necessary to complete their tasks that fulfill their roles within an organization. Need to know is commonly used in access control criteria by operating systems and applications.

node A system that is connected to a network.

O

object A passive entity that contains or receives information. Access to an object potentially implies access to the information that it contains. Examples of objects include records, pages, memory segments, files, directories, directory trees, and programs.

object reuse Reassigning to a subject media that previously contained information. Object reuse is a security concern because if insufficient measures were taken to erase the information on the media, the information may be disclosed to unauthorized personnel.

one-time pad A method of encryption in which the plaintext is combined with a random "pad," which should be the same length as the plaintext. This encryption process uses a nonrepeating set of random bits that are combined bitwise (XOR) with the message to produce ciphertext. A one-time pad is a perfect encryption scheme, because it is unbreakable and each pad is used exactly once, but it is impractical because of all of the required overhead.

operational assurance A level of confidence of a trusted system's architecture and implementation that enforces the system's security policy. This can include system architecture, covert channel analysis, system integrity, and trusted recovery.

operational goals Daily goals to be accomplished to ensure the proper operation of an environment.

operator An individual who supports the operations of computer systems—usually a mainframe. The individual may monitor the execution of the system, control the flow of jobs, and develop and schedule batch jobs.

Orange Book The common name for the Trusted Computer Security Evaluation Criteria (TCSEC).

overt channel A path within a computer system or network that is designed for the authorized transfer of data.

P

password A sequence of characters used to prove one's identity. It is used during a logon process and should be highly protected.

penetration A successful attempt at circumventing security controls and gaining access to a system.

penetration testing Penetration testing is a method of evaluating the security of a computer system or network by simulating an attack that a malicious hacker would carry out. This is done so that vulnerabilities and weaknesses can be uncovered.

permissions The type of authorized interactions that a subject can have with an object. Examples include read, write, execute, add, modify, and delete.

personnel security The procedures that are established to ensure that all personnel who have access to sensitive information have the required authority as well as appropriate clearances. Procedures confirm a person's background and provide assurance of necessary trustworthiness.

physical controls Controls that pertain to controlling individual access into the facility and different departments, locking systems and removing unnecessary floppy or CD-ROM drives, protecting the perimeter of the facility, monitoring for intrusion, and checking environmental controls.

physical security Controls and procedures put into place to prevent intruders from physically accessing a system or facility. The controls enforce access control and authorized access.

piggyback Unauthorized access to a system by using another user's legitimate credentials.

plaintext In cryptography, the original readable text before it is encrypted.

playback attack Capturing data and resending the data at a later time in the hope of tricking the receiving system. This is usually carried out to obtain unauthorized access to specific resources.

privacy A security principle that protects an individual's information and employs controls to ensure that this information is not disseminated or accessed in an unauthorized manner.

procedure   Detailed step-by-step instructions to achieve a certain task, which are used by users, IT staff, operations staff, security members, and others.

protection ring   An architecture that provides hierarchies of privileged operation modes of a system, which gives certain access rights to processes that are authorized to operate in that mode. Supports the integrity and confidentiality requirements of multi-tasking operating systems and enables the operating system to protect itself from user programs and rogue processes.

protocol   A set of rules and formats that enables the standardized exchange of information between different systems.

pseudo-flaw   An apparent loophole deliberately implanted in an operating system or program as a trap for intruders.

public key encryption   A type of encryption that uses two mathematically related keys to encrypt and decrypt messages. The private key is known only to the owner, and the public key is available to anyone.

purge   The removal of sensitive data from a system, storage device, or peripheral device with storage capacity at the end of a processing period. This action is performed in such a way that there is assurance proportional to the sensitivity of the data that the data cannot be reconstructed.

Q

qualitative risk analysis   A risk analysis method that uses intuition and experience to judge an organization's exposure to risks. It uses scenarios and ratings systems. Compare to quantitative risk analysis.

quantitative risk analysis   A risk analysis method that attempts to use percentages in damage estimations and assigns real numbers to the costs of countermeasures for particular risks and the amount of damage that could result from the risk. Compare to qualitative risk analysis.

R

RADIUS (Remote Authentication Dial-in User Service)   A security service that authenticates and authorizes dial-up users and is a centralized access control mechanism.

read   An operation that results in the flow of information from an object to a subject and does not give the subject the ability to modify the object or the data within the object.

recovery planning   The advance planning and preparations that are necessary to minimize loss and to ensure the availability of the critical information systems of an organization after a disruption in service or a disaster.

reference monitor concept An access control concept that refers to an abstract machine that mediates all accesses to objects by subjects. The security kernel enforces the reference monitor concept.

reliability The assurance of a given system, or individual component, performing its mission adequately for a specified period of time under the expected operating conditions.

remote journaling A method of transmitting changes to data to an offsite facility. This takes place as parallel processing of transactions, meaning that changes to the data are saved locally and to an off-site facility. These activities take place in real time and provide redundancy and fault tolerance.

repudiation When the sender of a message denies sending the message. The countermeasure to this is to implement digital signatures.

residual risk The remaining risk after the security controls have been applied. The conceptual formulas that explain the difference between total and residual risk are

threats $\cdot$ vulnerability $\cdot$ asset value = total risk
(threats $\cdot$ vulnerability $\cdot$ asset value) $\cdot$ controls gap = residual risk

risk The likelihood of a threat agent taking advantage of a vulnerability and the resulting business impact. A risk is the loss potential, or probability, that a threat will exploit a vulnerability.

risk analysis A method of identifying risks and assessing the possible damage that could be caused in order to justify security safeguards.

risk management The process of identifying, assessing, and reducing the risk to an acceptable level and implementing the right mechanisms to maintain that level of risk.

role-based access control (RBAC) Type of model that provides access to resources based on the role the user holds within the company or the tasks that the user has been assigned.

S

safeguard A software configuration, hardware, or procedure that eliminates a vulnerability or reduces the risk of a threat agent from being able to exploit a vulnerability. Also called a countermeasure or control.

secure configuration management Implementing the set of appropriate procedures to control the life cycle of an application, document the necessary change control activities, and ensure that the changes will not violate the security policy.

security evaluation Assesses the degree of trust and assurance that can be placed in systems for the secure handling of sensitive information.

security kernel The hardware, firmware, and software elements of a trusted computing base (TCB) that implement the reference monitor concept. The kernel must mediate all access between subjects and objects, be protected from modification, and be verifiable as correct.

security label   An identifier that represents the security level of an object.

security perimeter   An imaginary boundary between the components within the trusted computing base (TCB) and mechanisms that do not fall within the TCB. It is the distinction between trusted and untrusted processes.

security policy   Documentation that describes senior management's directives toward the role that security plays within the organization. It provides a framework within which an organization establishes needed levels of information security to achieve the desired confidentiality, availability, and integrity goals. A policy is a statement of information values, protection responsibilities, and organization commitment managing risks.

security testing   Testing all security mechanisms and features within a system to determine the level of protection they provide. Security testing can include penetration testing, formal design and implementation verification, and functional testing.

sensitive information   Information that would cause a negative effect on the company if it were lost or compromised.

sensitivity label   A piece of information that represents the security level of an object. Sensitivity labels are used by the TCB as the basis for mandatory access control (MAC) decisions.

separation of duties   A security principle that splits up a critical task among two or more individuals to ensure that one person cannot complete a risky task by himself.

shoulder surfing   When a person looks over another person's shoulder and watches keystrokes or watches data as it appears on the screen in order to uncover information in an unauthorized manner.

simple security property   A Bell-LaPadula security model rule that stipulates that a subject cannot read data at a higher security level.

single loss expectancy (SLE)   A dollar amount that is assigned to a single event that represents the company's potential loss amount if a specific threat were to take place.

asset value · exposure factor = SLE

social engineering   The act of tricking another person into providing confidential information by posing as an individual who is authorized to receive that information.

spoofing   Presenting false information, usually within packets, to trick other systems and hide the origin of the message. This is usually done by hackers so that their identity cannot be successfully uncovered.

standards   Rules indicating how hardware and software should be implemented, used, and maintained. Standards provide a means to ensure that specific technologies, applications, parameters, and procedures are carried out in a uniform way across the organization. They are compulsory.

star property (*-property)   A Bell-LaPadula security model rule that stipulates that a subject cannot write data to an object at a lower security level.

strategic goals   Long-term goals that are broad, general statements of intent. Operational and tactical goals support strategic goals and all are a part of a planning horizon.

subject   An active entity, generally in the form of a person, process, or device, that causes information to flow among objects or that changes the system state.

supervisor state   One of several states in which an operating system may operate, and the only one in which privileged instructions may be executed by the CPU.

T

TACACS (Terminal Access Controller Access Control System)   A client/server authentication protocol that provides the same type of functionality as RADIUS and is used as a central access control mechanism mainly for remote users.

tactical goals   Midterm goals to accomplish. These may be milestones to accomplish within a project or specific projects to accomplish in a year. Strategic, tactical, and operational goals make up a planning horizon.

technical controls   These controls, also called logical access control mechanisms, work in software to provide confidentiality, integrity, or availability protection. Some examples are passwords, identification and authentication methods, security devices, auditing, and the configuration of the network.

Tempest   The study and control of spurious electronic signals emitted by electrical equipment. Tempest equipment is implemented to prevent intruders from picking up information through the airwaves with listening devices.

threat   Any potential danger that a vulnerability will be exploited by a threat agent.

top-down approach   An approach in which the initiation, support, and direction for a project come from top management and work their way down through middle management and then to staff members.

topology   The physical construction of how nodes are connected to form a network.

total risk   When a safeguard is not implemented, an organization is faced with the total risk of that particular vulnerability.

Trojan horse   A computer program that has an apparently or actually useful function, but that also contains additional hidden malicious capabilities to exploit a vulnerability and/or provide unauthorized access into a system.

trusted computer system   A system that has the necessary controls to ensure that the security policy will not be compromised and that can process a range of sensitive or classified information simultaneously.

trusted computing base (TCB)   All of the protection mechanisms within a computer system (software, hardware, and firmware) that are responsible for enforcing a security policy.

trusted path   A mechanism within the system that enables the user to communicate directly with the TCB. This mechanism can be activated only by the user or the TCB and not by an untrusted mechanism or process.

trusted recovery   A set of procedures that restores a system and its data in a trusted manner after the system has been disrupted or a system failure has occurred.

U

user   A person or process that is accessing a computer system.

user ID   A unique set of characters or code that is used to identify a specific user to a system.

V

validation   The act of performing tests and evaluations to test a system's security level to see if it complies with security specifications and requirements.

virus   A small application, or string of code, that infects applications. The main function of a virus is to reproduce, and it requires a host application to do this. It can damage data directly or degrade system performance.

vulnerability   The absence or weakness of a safeguard that could be exploited.

W

wardialing   An attack in which a long list of phone numbers is inserted into a wardialing program in the hope of finding a modem that can be exploited to gain unauthorized access.

work factor   The estimated time and effort required for an attacker to overcome a security control.

worm   An independent program that can reproduce by copying itself from one system to another. It may damage data directly or degrade system performance by tying up resources.

write   An operation that results in the flow of information from a subject to an object.

INDEX

Symbols and Numbers

*-property rule, Bell-LaPadula model, 336–339
100-VG-AnyLAN, 519
10Base-T, 518
10Base2 (ThinNet), 518, 523
10Base5 (ThickNet), 518, 523
1G wireless communication, 648
2.4GHz frequency range, 630, 632
2.5G wireless communication, 649
2G wireless communication, 648
3DES (Triple DES), 703, 710, 733
3G wireless communication, 646–649
50-ohm coaxial cable, 523
5GHz frequency range, 630–632
75-ohm coaxial cable, 523
802.11 wireless standard, 630, 632–633
802.11a wireless standard, 630–631
802.11b wireless standard, 630, 632
802.11e wireless standard, 631
802.11f wireless standard, 631
802.11g wireless standard, 631–632
802.11h wireless standard, 632
802.11i wireless standard, 632–638
802.11j wireless standard, 639
802.11n wireless standard, 639
802.15 wireless standard, 640
802.16 wireless standard, 640
802.1X wireless standard, 634–636, 639

A

AAA (Authentication, Authorization, and Accounting/Audit) architecture, 224–228
ABR (Available Bit Rate), ATM, 599
absolute addresses, memory mapping, 304–307
abstraction, 297–298, 981
academic software, 1068
acceptable use policy, software, 1065
acceptance, of risk, 101–102
acceptance testing, 963
access control administration, 221–229, 1054
access control lists. See ACLs (access control lists)
access control matrix model, 352
access control methods, 229–236
    administrative controls, 230–232
    layers, 230
    overview of, 229–230
    physical controls, 232–233
    technical controls, 233–236

access control models, 210–221
    access control matrix, 218–220
    constrained user interfaces, 218
    content-dependent access control, 220
    context-dependent access control, 220–221
    defined, 210
    discretionary access control, 210–211
    mandatory access control, 211–212
    role-based access control, 213–216
    sensitivity labels, 212–213
access controls
    accountability, 157–158, 242–245
    authentication. see authentication
    authorization. see authorization
    CISSP exam description, 5
    constrained user interfaces and, 218
    cryptography, 676
    current wireless structures, 639
    database management and, 929
    database views, 945
    designing enterprise security architecture, 378
    external boundary. see external boundary protection mechanisms
    to facility, 425, 447–454
    identity management. see identity management
    media, 1070, 1074
    monitoring using IDSs. see IDSs (intrusion detection systems)
    monitoring using IPSs, 106–108
    overview of, 153–154
    password management for. see passwords
    of personnel, 454–455
    polyinstantiation and, 945
    practices, 245–248
    rule-based, 216–217
    security principles, 154–156
    system hardening with, 1063–1065
    threats, 260–266
    types of, 236–241
    Web security issues, 1005–1007
access criteria, authorization, 194–198
access, defined, 153
access points (APs), 627–629, 631, 644–645
accessibility, Web security issues, 1006
account management, 172–173
accountability
    access control and, 160

automated workflow, 172
    defined, 158
    keystroke monitoring and, 244–245
    overview of, 242–243
    protecting audit data and logs, 245
    reviewing audit information, 244
    security administrator responsibilities, 1055
accreditation, 370–372, 962
ACID test, online transaction processing, 947–948
ACK (acknowledgement) packet, 504–505, 1033
ACLs (access control lists)
    dynamic packet filtering using, 562–563
    in layered approach, 40
    overview of, 219–220
    packet filtering using, 555
    remote access guidelines, 624
    routers using, 544–545
acoustical detection system, IDS, 466
acrylic glass windows, 423–424
active attacks, 761–762
Active Directory, 163
Active Email Content, 1016
active monitor, Token Ring, 520
Active Server Pages (ASP), 1004
ActiveX controls, mobile code, 1015–1016
ActiveX Data Objects (ADO), 936
activity support, CPTED, 414
ad hoc WLANs, 629
address buses, CPUs, 287–288
Address Resolution Protocol (ARP), 533–534, 537, 253
Adelphia Communications Corp., 120
administration
    executive succession planning, 808
    information security. see security administration
    operations security, 1051–1056
administrative controls, 230–232, 236–237, 240–241, 452–453
administrative interfaces threat, 1005
administrative/regulatory law, 860
ADO (ActiveX Data Objects), 936
ADSL (Asymmetrical DSL), 614
Advanced Encryption Standard (AES), 633, 704, 711, 746
advisory policy, 106
adware, 650–651
AES (Advanced Encryption Standard), 633, 704, 711, 746

PSTN (public-switched telephone network), 601, 603
PSW (program status word), CPUs, 287
psychological crime scene analysis (profiling), 890
PTZ (pan, tilt, or zoom), CCTV cameras, 464
public algorithms, vs. secret, 762
Public classification, private sector, 112–113
public key cryptography
    mitigating e-mail attacks, 1096
    public key infrastructure vs., 716, 733
        using asymmetric and symmetric algorithms, 696–699
public key infrastructure. See PKI (public key infrastructure)
public keys, cryptography, 189, 688–691
public-switched telephone network (PSTN), 601, 603
pulse-code modulation (PCM), 590
PVCs (permanent virtual circuits), 597, 604

Q

QL (query language), in database models, 937
QoS (Quality of Service)
    802.11e and, 631
    ATM and, 598–600
    benefits of IPv6, 508–510
qualitative risk analysis
    of assets, 79–80
    basing on opinion and scenarios, 86
    business continuity planning, 789
    overview of, 91–94
    quantitative vs., 94–95
quality assurance process, Web, 1002
Quality of Service. See QoS (Quality of Service)
quantitative risk analysis, 79–80, 86–91, 94–95
quantum cryptography, 748–750
query language (QL), in database models, 937

R

r-utilities, Unix, 1106
RA (registration authority), PKI, 737–738
race conditions, 383–384, 1119
    authorization and authentication, 157
RACE Integrity Primitives Evaluation (RICE), 728

RAD (rapid application development), 968
radio frequency interference (RFI), 431–432
RADIUS (Remote Authentication Dial-In User Service), 624, 222–228
RAID (redundant array of inexpensive disks), 1082–1086
Rainbow Series, 362–364, 367–369
rainbow tables, 185, 1089
raised floors, placing water detectors, 427
RAIT (redundant array of independent tapes), 1087
raking (lock picking), 453–454
RAM (random access memory)
    creating virtual memory, 308–309
    memory management and, 297–298
    overview of, 300–302
    video card, 322
random access memory. See RAM (random access memory)
rapid application development (RAD), 968
RARP (Reverse Address Resolution Protocol), 536–537
RAS (remote access server), 610–611, 624
rate-of-rise temperature sensor, 441
RATs (Remote Access Trojans), 1022
RBACs (role-based access controls), 213–217
RC4 algorithm, 633, 712, 733
RC5 and 6 algorithms, 712
read-only memory (ROM), 302–303
readers, card badge, 455
ready state, processes in, 291
Real-time Transport Protocol (RTP), 605, 607
realms, Kerberos, 201
rebar construction material, 420
receipt, 676
reciprocal agreements, business continuity plan, 801–802
reconstitution phase, disaster recovery, 819
recording systems, closed-circuit TVs, 461
recovery. See also backups
    access controls, 237
    best practices, 780
    business process, 796–797
    data, 809–815
    developing goals for, 821–823
    different types of recovery plans, 824
    facility, 797–801
    implementing, 823–824

incident response stage, 1090
operations security, 1060–1062
overview of, 794–796, 817–821
supply and technology, 803–808
testing and revising plan, 824–829
user environment, 808–809
Red Book, 363–364
redirect server, SIP, 605
redundant array of independent tapes (RAIT), 1087
redundant array of inexpensive disks (RAID), 1082–1086
redundant hardware, 1079
redundant sites, business continuity plan, 802–803
reference monitor, system architecture, 330–331
references, verifying when hiring, 131
referential integrity, 941
registers, CPU, 284–285, 299
registrar server, SIP, 605
registration authority (RA), PKI, 737–738
regression testing, 963
regulations
    board of director requirements, 118
    physical security, 414
    privacy and confidentiality laws, 28–29
    rights and permissions, 195
regulatory law, 860
regulatory policy, 106
relational database model, 931, 936–940
relative addresses, memory mapping, 304–305
relay agents, mail servers, 1099
relaying, e-mail, 1098–1099
reliable evidence, 901
religious law systems, 858
remote access
    authentication protocols, 621–623
    cable modems, 613–615
    dial-up and RAS, 610–611
    DSL, 613
    guidelines, 623
    IPSec, 617
    ISDN, 611–612
    L2TP, 620–621
    operations security and, 1066
    overview of, 610
    PAP vs. CHAP, 623
    PPP, 617–619
    PPTP, 619–620
    tunneling protocols for, 622
    VPN, 615–616
remote access server (RAS), 610–611, 624
Remote Access Trojans (RATs), 1022